POLITICS IN AMERICA

POLITICS IN AMERICA

SIXTH EDITION

BRIEF TEXAS EDITION

Thomas R. Dye
Emeritus McKenzie
Professor of Government
Florida State University

with L. Tucker Gibson, Jr.
Trinity University

and Clay Robison
Houston Chronicle

Upper Saddle River, New Jersey 07458

Library of Congress Cataloging in Publication Data

Dye, Thomas R.
Politics in America / Thomas R. Dye with L. Tucker Gibson, Jr. and Clay Robison—
Brief Texas ed.
p. cm.
ISBN 0–13–193001–X
1. United States—Politics and government.—Textbooks 2. Texas—Politics and government.—Textbooks
I. Gibson, L. Tucker. II. Robison, Clay. III. Title.

JK276.D926 2005d
320.473—dc22 2004025195

Editorial Director: Charlyce Jones Owen
Acquisitions Editor: Glenn Johnston
Editorial Assistant: Suzanne Remore
Marketing Manager: Kara Kindstrom
Marketing Assistant: Jennifer Lang
Managing Editor: Lisa Iarkowski
Production Liaison: Fran Russello
Permissions Supervisor: Lisa Black
Manufacturing Buyer: Sherry Lewis
Design Manager: Anne Nieglos
Interior Design: Susan Walrath
Cover Design: Susan Walrath
Cover Illustration/Photo: Gary Randall/Taxi/Getty Images, Inc. and Siede Preis/Photodisc Green/Getty Images, Inc.
Illustrator (Interior): Mirella Signoretto
Photo Researcher: David Tietz
Image Permission Coordinator: Debbie Hewitson
Composition/Full-Service Project Management:
Bruce Hobart/Pine Tree Composition
Printer/Binder: Courier Companies, Inc.

Credits and acknowledgments borrowed from other sources and reproduced, with permission, in this textbook appear on page PC-1.

Pearson Education LTD. London
Pearson Education Singapore, Pte. Ltd
Pearson Education, Canada, Ltd
Pearson Education–Japan
Pearson Education Australia PTY, Limited
Pearson Education North Asia Ltd
Pearson Educación de Mexico, S.A. de C.V.
Pearson Education Malaysia, Pte. Ltd
Pearson Education, Upper Saddle River, New Jersey
PEARSON Prentice Hall

10 9 8 7 6 5 4

ISBN 0-13-193001-X

Brief Contents

PREFACE *xv*
PREFACE TO THE TEXAS EDITION *xxi*
ABOUT THE AUTHORS *xxiii*

PART I Politics

CHAPTER 1 Politics: Who Gets What, When, and How 2
CHAPTER 2 Political Culture: Ideas in Conflict 24

PART II Constitution

CHAPTER 3 The Constitution: Limiting Governmental Power 52
CONSTITUTION OF THE UNITED STATES 85
CHAPTER 4 Federalism: Dividing Governmental Power 100

PART III Participants

CHAPTER 5 Participation, Campaigns, and Elections: Deciding Who Governs Thinking and Acting in Politics 130
CHAPTER 6 Mass Media: Setting the Political Agenda 170
CHAPTER 7 Political Parties and Interest Groups: Organizing Politics 200

PART IV Institutions

CHAPTER 8 Congress: Politics on Capitol Hill 240
CHAPTER 9 The President: White House Politics 294
CHAPTER 10 The Bureaucracy: Bureaucratic Politics 340
CHAPTER 11 Courts: Judicial Politics 380

PART V Outcomes

CHAPTER 12 Politics, Personal Liberty, and Civil Rights 416
CHAPTER 13 Politics, Economics, and Social Welfare Policy 462
CHAPTER 14 Politics and National Security 488

PART VI Texas Politics

CHAPTER 15 The Social and Economic Milieu of Texas Politics 512
CHAPTER 16 The Texas Constitution 536
CHAPTER 17 Interest Groups, Political Parties, and Elections in Texas 562
CHAPTER 18 The Texas Legislature 598
CHAPTER 19 The Texas Executive and Bureaucracy 636
CHAPTER 20 The Texas Judiciary 674
CHAPTER 21 Local Government in Texas: Cities, Towns, Counties, and Special Districts 710

Appendix

The Declaration of Independence A-1
The Federalist, No. 10, James Madison A-2
The Federalist, No. 51, James Madison A-5
Presidents and Vice Presidents A-8
Supreme Court Justices A-9
Presidential Elections and Voting A-11
Party Control of Congress A-15

Contents

PREFACE xv
PREFACE TO THE TEXAS EDITION xxi
ABOUT THE AUTHORS xxiii

PART I Politics

The study of politics is the study of influence and the influential . . . The influential are those who get the most of what there is to get. Those who get the most are elite; the rest are mass.

Harold Lasswell

1 POLITICS: WHO GETS WHAT, WHEN, AND HOW 2

Politics and Political Science 3
Politics and Government 4
WHAT DO YOU THINK? Can You Trust the Government? 6
The Purposes of Government 7
A CONFLICTING VIEW Sometimes It's Right to Disobey the Law 8
The Meaning of Democracy 9
WHAT DO YOU THINK? What Government Programs Do You Support? 10
COMPARED TO WHAT? Freedom and Democracy around the World 11
The Paradox of Democracy 13
Direct Versus Representative Democracy 15
Who Really Governs? 16
UP CLOSE Terrorism's Threat to Democracy 18
WHAT DO YOU THINK? Is the American Government "Of, By and For the People"? 20
Democracy in America 20
Summary Notes 21
Key Terms 21
Suggested Readings 22
Make It Real 23

2 POLITICAL CULTURE: IDEAS IN CONFLICT 24

Political Culture 25
Individual Liberty 26
Dilemmas of Equality 27
WHAT DO YOU THINK? Beliefs about Fairness 30
Inequality of Income and Wealth 30
COMPARED TO WHAT? Income and Inequality 31
Social Mobility 33
A CONFLICTING VIEW Success Is Determined by the Bell Curve 34
Race, Ethnicity, and Immigration 35
WHAT DO YOU THINK? Could You Pass the Citizenship Test? 39
Ideologies: Liberalism and Conservatism 40
ACROSS THE USA Liberalism and Conservatism 42
PEOPLE IN POLITICS Bill O'Reilly, "The No Spin Zone?" 43
PEOPLE IN POLITICS Barbara Boxer, Defending Liberalism in Congress 44
Dissent in the United States 45
WHAT DO YOU THINK? Are You a Liberal or a Conservative? 47
Summary Notes 50
Key Terms 51
Suggested Readings 51
Make It Real 51

PART II Constitution

The ascendancy of any elite depends upon the success of the practices it adopts. . . . The Constitution, written and unwritten, embodies the practices which are deemed most fundamental to the governmental and social order.

Harold Lasswell

3 THE CONSTITUTION: LIMITING GOVERNMENTAL POWER 52

Constitutional Government 53
The Constitutional Tradition 53
Troubles Confronting a New Nation 55
Consensus in Philadelphia 58

PEOPLE IN POLITICS
George Washington, Founder of a Nation 59

Conflict in Philadelphia 60
Resolving the Economic Issues 63

A CONFLICTING VIEW
An Economic Interpretation of the Constitution 64

Protecting National Security 65
The Structure of the Government 67

UP CLOSE
Why the Founders Created an Electoral College to Choose the President 69

Separation of Powers and Checks and Balances 69

A CONFLICTING VIEW
Let the People Vote on National Issues 70

Conflict over Ratification 73

PEOPLE IN POLITICS
James Madison and the Control of "Faction" 75

A Bill of Rights 75

COMPARED TO WHAT?
Canada's Parliamentary System 76

A CONFLICTING VIEW
Objections to the Constitution by an Anti-Federalist 77

Constitutional Change 79
Summary Notes 82
Key Terms 83
Suggested Readings 83
Make It Real 84
The Constitution of the United States 85

4 FEDERALISM: DIVIDING GOVERNMENTAL POWER 100

Indestructible Union, Indestructible States 101
Why Federalism? The Argument for a "Compound Republic" 103

COMPARED TO WHAT?
The European Union 104

WHAT DO YOU THINK?
Which Government Seems Closer to You? 107

A CONFLICTING VIEW
The Dark Side of Federalism 108

The Original Design of Federalism 109

A CONFLICTING VIEW
Don't Make Everything a Federal Crime! 112

The Evolution of American Federalism 112

UP CLOSE
Historical Markers in the Development of American Federalism 114

Federalism Revived? 118

WHAT DO YOU THINK?
Should Violence Against Women Be a Federal Crime? 120

Money and Power Flow to Washington 120

UP CLOSE
How Congress Set a National Drinking Age 121

A CONFLICTING VIEW
Liberals, Conservatives, and Federalism 123

Coercive Federalism: Preemptions and Mandates 125

UP CLOSE
Arnold: From Bodybuilder, to Superstar, to Governor 126

Summary Notes 128
Key Terms 128
Suggested Readings 129

PART III Participants

People strive for power—to get the most of what there is to get.
Harold Lasswell

5 PARTICIPATION, CAMPAIGNS, AND ELECTIONS: DECIDING WHO GOVERNS 130

Individual Participation in Politics 131
Voters and Nonvoters 131

COMPARED TO WHAT?
Voter Turnout in Western Democracies 134

Elections in a Democracy 134

UP CLOSE
How to Run for Office 136

The Advantages of Incumbency 138
Campaign Strategies 139

UP CLOSE
Dirty Politics 141

How Much Does It Cost to Get Elected? 143
Raising Campaign Cash 145
What Do Contributors Buy? 147
Regulating Campaign Finance 151
The Presidential Campaign: The Primary Race 152

The Presidential Campaign: The General Election Battle 156

UP CLOSE
Primaries 2004: Democrats Seek "Electability" 157

UP CLOSE
Bush v. Kerry 2004 158

UP CLOSE
The Presidential Debates 160

ACROSS THE USA
How the States Voted 162

The Voter Decides 163
Summary Notes 168
Key Terms 169
Suggested Readings 169
Make It Real 169

6 MASS MEDIA: SETTING THE POLITICAL AGENDA 170

The Power of the Media 171

UP CLOSE
The Generation Gap in News 173

Sources of Media Power 174

PEOPLE IN POLITICS
Stars of the Network News 176

The Business of the Media 178
The Politics of the News 180

WHAT DO YOU THINK?
Are the Media Biased? 183

A CONFLICTING VIEW
Fox News: "Fair and Balanced"? 184

Mediated Elections 184
Freedom versus Fairness 188
Libel and Slander 189

PEOPLE IN POLITICS
Larry King Live 190

Politics and the Internet 190

COMPARED TO WHAT?
America's TV Culture in Perspective 191

Media Effects: Shaping Political Life 193

UP CLOSE
The Media Age 194

Summary Notes 198
Key Terms 198
Suggested Readings 199

7 POLITICAL PARTIES AND INTEREST GROUPS: ORGANIZING POLITICS 200

The Power of Organization 201
Political Parties and Democratic Government 201

WHAT DO YOU THINK?
Which Party Does a Better Job? 206

Parties as Organizers of Elections 207
National Party Conventions 210

UP CLOSE
Democratic and Republican Platforms: Can You Tell the Difference? 212

Party Finances 213
Party Voters 214
Why the Two-Party System Persists 217

ACROSS THE USA
Democratic and Republican Party Strength in the States 218

Interest-Group Power 220
The Organized Interests in Washington 221

UP CLOSE
The Christian Coalition: Organizing the Faithful 224

The Washington Lobbyists 225
The Fine Art of Lobbying 227

UP CLOSE
AARP: The Nation's Most Powerful Interest Group 230

UP CLOSE
EMILY's List

UP CLOSE
Payback: Money and Medicare 223

Lobbying the Bureaucracy 233
Lobbying the Courts 236
Summary Notes 237
Key Terms 238
Suggested Readings 238
Make It Real 239

PART IV Institutions

Authority is the expected and legitimate possession of power.
Harold Lasswell

8 CONGRESS: POLITICS ON CAPITOL HILL 240

The Powers of Congress 241
Congressional Apportionment and Redistricting 246

ACROSS THE USA
Reapportionment, 2000 248

Getting to Capitol Hill 252

WHAT DO YOU THINK?
Why Do Voters Reelect Members of an Unpopular Congress? 256

Party Fortunes in Congress 257
Life in Congress 260

PEOPLE IN POLITICS
Hillary Rodham Clinton in the Senate 263

Home Style 265
Organizing Congress: Party and Leadership 266

PEOPLE IN POLITICS
Nancy Pelosi, Leading House Democrats 270

In Committee 271

PEOPLE IN POLITICS
"Ted" Kennedy: Keeping Liberalism Alive in the U.S. Senate 274

On the Floor 276
Decision Making in Congress 278

UP CLOSE
Polarization on Capitol Hill 281

UP CLOSE
Tips on Lobbying Congress 284

A CONFLICTING VIEW
Congress Can Act Responsibly on Occasion 286

PEOPLE IN POLITICS
Bill Frist, M.D., Leading the Senate 288

Congressional Ethics 289
Summary Notes 291
Key Terms 292
Suggested Readings 292
Make It Real 293

9 THE PRESIDENT: WHITE HOUSE POLITICS 294

Presidential Power 295

WHAT DO YOU THINK?
How Would You Rate the Presidents? 296

Constitutional Powers of the President 298

PEOPLE IN POLITICS
George Bush and the War on Terrorism 300

COMPARED TO WHAT?
Mexican President Vicente Fox 302

UP CLOSE
Sex, Lies, and Impeachment 304

UP CLOSE
Watergate and the Limits of Presidential Power 306

Political Resources of the President 308

WHAT DO YOU THINK?
Should We Judge Presidents on Private Character or Performance in Office? 311

Personality Versus Policy 312
Chief Executive 313

PEOPLE IN POLITICS
John Kerry, War Hero, Anti-War Leader 314

UP CLOSE
Contrasting Presidential Styles 316

Chief Legislator and Lobbyist 321
Global Leader 325
Commander-in-Chief 330

UP CLOSE
George Bush and "Operation Iraqi Freedom" 332

The Vice Presidential Waiting Game 334

PEOPLE IN POLITICS
Dick Cheney, Presidential Confidant 336

Summary Notes 337
Key Terms 338
Suggested Readings 338
Make It Real 339

10 THE BUREAUCRACY: BUREAUCRATIC POLITICS 340

Bureaucratic Power 341

WHAT DO YOU THINK?
How Would You Rate These Federal Agencies? 344

The Federal Bureaucracy 346

UP CLOSE
Why Government Grows, and Grows, and Grows 347

COMPARED TO WHAT?
The Size of Government in Other Nations 349

UP CLOSE
The Department of Homeland Security 352

PEOPLE IN POLITICS
Alan Greenspan, Managing the Nation's Economy 356

Bureaucracy and Democracy 357
Bureaucratic Politics 360
The Budgetary Process 362

The Politics of Budgeting 366
UP CLOSE
Bureaucratic Budget Strategies 367
WHAT DO YOU THINK?
How Much Money Does the Government Waste? 368
Regulatory Battles 368
A CONFLICTING VIEW
Bureaucratic Regulations Are Suffocating America 370
Regulating America 372
Congressional Constraints on the Bureaucracy 373
UP CLOSE
How to Use the Freedom of Information Act 374
Interest Groups and Bureaucratic Decision Making 376
Judicial Constraints on the Bureaucracy 376
Summary Notes 377
Key Terms 378
Suggested Readings 379
Make It Real 379

11 COURTS: JUDICIAL POLITICS 380
Judicial Power 381
PEOPLE IN POLITICS
John Marshall and Early Supreme Court Politics 383
UP CLOSE
William Jefferson Clinton Versus Paula Corbin Jones 385
Activism Versus Self-Restraint 386
PEOPLE IN POLITICS
Sandra Day O'Connor, Holding the Middle Ground 387
Structure and Jurisdiction of Federal Courts 389
ACROSS THE USA
Geographic Boundaries of Federal Courts 392
A CONFLICTING VIEW
America Is Drowning Itself in a Sea of Lawsuits 393
The Special Rules of Judicial Decision Making 394
The Politics of Selecting Judges 397
Who Is Selected? 400
UP CLOSE
The Confirmation of Clarence Thomas 401
UP CLOSE
Women and the Courts 402
Supreme Court Decision Making 403
Politics and the Supreme Court 405
UP CLOSE
Bush v. Gore, Majority and Dissenting Opinions 408
Bush v. Gore in the U.S. Supreme Court 409
Checking Court Power 410
WHAT DO YOU THINK?
Do You Have Confidence in the Supreme Court? 411
Summary Notes 414
Key Terms 415
Suggested Readings 415

PART V Outcomes

That political science concentrates upon the influential does not imply the neglect of the total distribution of values throughout the community. . . . The emphasis upon the probability that the few (elite) will get the most does not imply that the many (mass) do not profit from some political changes.

Harold Lasswell

12 POLITICS, PERSONAL LIBERTY, AND CIVIL RIGHTS 416
Power and Individual Liberty 417
Freedom of Religion 418
Freedom of Speech 424
Privacy, Abortion, and the Constitution 426
Obscenity and the Law 428
The Right to Bear Arms 429
Rights of Criminal Defendants 430
WHAT DO YOU THINK?
Are Persons Captured on the Battlefields of Afghanistan and Iraq Entitled to the
Protections of the U.S. Constitution? 432
A CONFLICTING VIEW
Terrorism Requires Restrictions on Civil Liberties 433
The Death Penalty 436
The Politics of Equality 438
Slavery, Segregation, and the Constitution 438
The Civil Rights Acts 442
PEOPLE IN POLITICS
Martin Luther King, Jr., "I Have a Dream" 444
Affirmative Action: Opportunity versus Results 445
A CONFLICTING VIEW
The Constitution Should Be Color-Blind 450
Hispanics in America 451
Hispanic Politics 453

Gender Equality and the Fourteenth Amendment 455
Gender Equality in the Economy 456
WHAT DO YOU THINK?
What Constitutes Sexual Harassment? 459
Summary Notes 460
Key Terms 461
Suggested Readings 461
Make It Real 461

13 POLITICS, ECONOMICS, AND SOCIAL WELFARE POLICY 462
Politics and Economics 463
The Performance of the American Economy 463
Economic Globalization 466
The Tax Burden 469
WHAT DO YOU THINK?
Does Globalization Help or Hurt America? 470
COMPARED TO WHAT?
Tax Burdens in Advanced Democracies 471
Tax Politics 473
Poverty in the United States 475
UP CLOSE
Who Are the Poor? 477
Social Welfare Policy 478
Politics and Welfare Reform 480
UP CLOSE
Is Welfare Reform Working? 481
Health Care in America 482
Summary Notes 486
Key Terms 486
Suggested Readings 487
Make It Real 487

14 POLITICS AND NATIONAL SECURITY 488
Power among Nations 489
The Legacy of the Cold War 491
Nuclear Threats 496
When to Use Military Force? 499
A CONFLICTING VIEW
We Should Defend Ourselves against a Ballistic Missile Attack 500
PEOPLE IN POLITICS
Colin Powell, An American Journey 502
The War on Terrorism 503
COMPARED TO WHAT?
World Opinion about America's War against Terrorism 507
Military Force Levels 507
Summary Notes 510
Key Terms 511
Suggested Readings 511
Make It Real 511

PART VI Texas Politics

15 THE SOCIAL AND ECONOMIC MILIEU OF TEXAS POLITICS 512
Decades of Change and Challenge 513
UP CLOSE
Perpetuating an Image: The Cowboy President and the "Killer Ds" 514
The Political Culture of Texas 515
Texas Myths 517
The People of Texas 518
Politics, Race, and Ethnicity 522
The Political Implications of Demographics 522
The Economy of Texas 526
Economic Regions of Texas 528
Transnational Regionalism 529
Summary Notes 534
Key Terms 535
Suggested Readings 535

16 THE TEXAS CONSTITUTION 536
The Constitutional Legacy 537
General Principles of the Texas Constitution 546
Weaknesses and Criticisms of the Constitution of 1876 548
UP CLOSE
Budget Restrictions 550
Constitutional Change and Adaptation 551
ACROSS THE USA
States Frequently Amend Their Constitutions 552
UP CLOSE
A Lot of Trouble for a Minor Office 553
UP CLOSE
Oops! How Did That Happen? 557

UP CLOSE
High Stakes Over Lawsuits 559

Constitutional Restraints and the Ability to Govern 559
Summary Notes 560
Key Terms 561
Suggested Readings 561

17 INTEREST GROUPS, POLITICAL PARTIES, AND ELECTIONS IN TEXAS 562

The Power of Interest Groups 563

WHAT DO YOU THINK?
Is It Summer School or Recess for Lawmakers? 564

Pluralism or Elitism? 565
Dominant Interest Groups in Texas 566

WHAT DO YOU THINK?
Do Texas Lobbyists Look Out for Your Interests? 567

UP CLOSE
The Religious Right and Republican Growth 571

The Development of a Two-Party System in Texas 572

UP CLOSE
La Raza Unida 578

Changing Patterns of Party Support and Identification 578

UP CLOSE
Where Have All the Yellow Dogs Gone? 581

The Party Organization 581
Parties and Government 584
Minorities and Political Participation 585
Political Gains by Minorities and Women 586
Elections in Texas 590
Campaign Finances 592

PEOPLE IN POLITICS
Bob Perry: Homebuilder and Big Contributor 594

Summary Notes 595
Key Terms 596
Suggested Readings 596

18 THE TEXAS LEGISLATURE 598

The Texas Legislature: A Time of Change 599
Legislative Functions 600
The Institutionalization of the Texas Legislature 601
The Organization and Composition of the Texas Legislature 601

WHAT DO YOU THINK?
How Much Is a Legislator Worth? 603

Representation and Redistricting 606

UP CLOSE
Redistricting: Partisans at War 608

Legislative Leadership 608
The Committee System 616
Rules and Procedures 619
The Emerging Party System 623
Other Legislative Caucuses 625

PEOPLE IN POLITICS
Gregory Luna and Irma Rangel, Champions of Education 626

Legislators and Their Constituents 626
Legislative Decision Making 627
The Development of Legislative Staff 629

UP CLOSE
Legislative Reputations: Not All the Same 630

Legislative Ethics and Reforms 631
Summary Notes 633
Key Terms 635
Suggested Readings 635

19 THE TEXAS EXECUTIVE AND BUREAUCRACY 636

A Fragmented Government 637
The Structure of the Plural Executive 638
The Governor 639

PEOPLE IN POLITICS
Governor Bill Clements, On-the-Job Training 642

PEOPLE IN POLITICS
Governor Ann Richards, Saleswoman 646

PEOPLE IN POLITICS
Governor Rick Perry, Claiming His Inheritance 650

ACROSS THE USA
Party Control of the Governor's Office, 2004 653

PEOPLE IN POLITICS
Governor George W. Bush, Consensus Builder 654

Other Offices of the Executive Branch 656

PEOPLE IN POLITICS
Dan Morales, a Spectacular Rise and Fall 658

Elected Boards and Commissions 660
The Texas Bureaucracy 661
The Growth of Government in Texas 662
Bureaucrats and Public Policy 664
Strategies for Controlling the Bureaucracy 666

UP CLOSE
What Can Happen to a Whistleblower? 667

Summary Notes 671
Key Terms 672
Suggested Readings 672

20 THE TEXAS JUDICIARY 674

The Power of the Courts in Texas 675
The State Courts in the Federal System 676
The Legal Framework of the Judicial System 676
The Structure of the Texas Court System 677

WHAT DO YOU THINK?
Justice Delayed, Justice Denied? 681

The Jury System 684

WHAT DO YOU THINK?
Is This Any Way to Round Up a Jury? 685

Judicial Procedures and Decision Making 686
Judicial Concerns and Controversies 687

PEOPLE IN POLITICS
Steve Mansfield, An Election Day Surprise 688

UP CLOSE
An Attack on Affirmative Action 695

Crime and Punishment 700

UP CLOSE
A Huge Injustice in Tulia 701

The Politics of Criminal Justice 703

UP CLOSE
Criminal Justice, An Expensive Headache 703

UP CLOSE
More Is Involved Than Technicalities 704

WHAT DO YOU THINK?
Can Justice Afford a Nap? 705

Increased Policy Role of the State Courts 705

UP CLOSE
The Constitution Is for Everybody 706

Summary Notes 708
Key Terms 709
Suggested Readings 709

21 LOCAL GOVERNMENT IN TEXAS: CITIES, TOWNS, COUNTIES, AND SPECIAL DISTRICTS 710

The Legacy of Local Government 711
Local Governments in the Texas Political System 712
Municipal Government in Texas 713

WHAT DO YOU THINK?
Is This Any Way to Change a City's Charter? 715

Forms of City Government in Texas 715

WHAT DO YOU THINK?
Why Different Forms of City Government? 716

PEOPLE IN POLITICS
Ron Kirk and Lee Brown, History-Making Mayors 721

UP CLOSE
The Job of the City Council Member 722

Municipal Election Systems 723

A CONFLICTING VIEW
The Debate over Electoral Systems 724

City Revenues and Expenditures 725
Urban Problems in Texas 726
County Government in Texas 728
Criticisms of County Government 734
Special Districts in Texas 735
Independent School Districts 737
Councils of Government 739
Solutions to the Problems of Local Government 741

WHAT DO YOU THINK?
Circle C Ranch: A Subdivision's Fight against Austin 742

UP CLOSE
Expensive Tax Breaks 744

Summary Notes 746
Key Terms 747
Suggested Readings 747

Appendix

The Declaration of Independence A-1
The Federalist, No. 10, James Madison A-2
The Federalist, No. 51, James Madison A-5
Presidents and Vice Presidents A-9
Supreme Court Justices A-9
Presidential Elections and Voting A-11
Party Control of Congress A-15
Glossary G-1
Notes N-1
Photo Credits PC-1
Index I-1

Preface

Politics is an activity by which people try to get more of whatever there is to get. It is not about the pursuit of liberty as much as it is about the struggle over the allocation of values in society. Simply put, it is about "who gets what, when, and how."

By using Lasswell's classic definition of politics as the unifying framework, *Politics in America, Sixth Edition,* strives to present a clear, concise, and stimulating introduction to the American political system. Politics consists of all of the activities—reasonable discussion, impassioned oratory, campaigning, balloting, fund raising, advertising, lobbying, demonstrating, rioting, street fighting, and waging war—by which conflict is carried on. Managing conflict is the principal function of the political system and power is the ultimate goal.

By examining the struggle for power—the participants, the stakes, the processes, and the institutional arenas—*Politics in America, Sixth Edition,* introduces students to the politics that is the basis for our democracy.

Why Politics in America?

Instructors teaching the Introductory American Government course find engaging their students to be the most difficult task facing them. *Politics in America, Sixth Edition,* is written to be lively and absorbing, reflecting the teaching philosophy that *stimulating students' interest in politics and public affairs is the most important goal of an introductory course.* Interesting examples and controversial debates spark students' interest and keep them connected to the material. The struggle for power in society is not a dull topic, and textbooks should not make it so.

Politics in America, Sixth Edition, strives for a balanced presentation, but "balanced" does not mean boring. It does not mean the avoidance of controversy. Liberal and conservative arguments are set forth clearly and forcefully. Race and gender are given particular attention, not because it is currently fashionable to do so, but because American politics has long been driven by these factors. As in previous editions, the trademark of this book continues to be its desire to pull students into the debate that is our political system.

Organization

Part I, "Politics," begins with Lasswell's classic definition of politics and proceeds to describe the nature and functions of government and the meaning of democracy. It poses the question. How democratic is the American political system? It describes the American political culture: its contradictions between liberty and conformity, political equality and economic inequality, equality of opportunity and inequality of results, the role of ideology—liberalism and conservatism, thus laying the groundwork for understanding the struggle over who gets what.

Part II, "Constitution," describes the politics of constitution making—deciding how to decide. It describes how the struggle over the U.S. Constitution reflected the distribution of power in the new nation. It focuses on the classic arguments of the Founders for limiting and dividing governmental power and the structural arrangements designed to accomplish this end.

Part III, "Participants," begins by examining individual participation in politics—the way people acquire and hold political opinions and act on them through voting and protest activity. It examines the influences of family, school, gender, race, and the role of media in shaping political opinion. It describes how organization concentrates power—to win public office in the case of party organizations, and to influence policy in the case of interest groups. It assesses the role of personal ambition in politics and the role of money.

Part IV, "Institutions," describes the various governmental arenas in which the struggle for power takes place—the Congress, the presidency, the bureaucracy, the courts. More important, it evaluates the power that comes with control of each of these institutions.

Part V, "Outcomes," deals with public policies—the result of the struggle over the allocation of values. It is especially concerned with the two fundamental values of American society—liberty and equality. Each is examined in separate chapters, as are economic policies, welfare policies, and national security policies.

Part VI, "Texas Politics," covers similar questions and issues as they relate to Texas government.

New to the Sixth Edition

Americans went to the polls in 2004 in numbers never seen before and percentages not seen in forty years. Perhaps it was a lesson learned in 2000 that a few hundred votes can change the Electoral College vote and determine the presidency. Perhaps it was the projected closeness of the race between Bush and Kerry, or concern over the continuing war in Iraq, or an increased turnout of religious people concerned with growing secularism in society. Perhaps all of these conditions combined to inspire Americans to renew their commitment to the political system.

The Sixth Edition of *Politics in America* describes the recent changes in the political landscape of the nation. It updates students on the war on terrorism and the restrictions on freedom that it has inspired. It describes and analyzes the presidential and congressional election of 2004: the campaign strategies of George W. Bush and John F. Kerry; the impact of the war in Iraq; campaign finance "reform" and how it was evaded during the campaign; popular images of Bush and Kerry and the issues considered most important by the voters; the Republican victory in the congressional elections and the growing polarization on Capitol Hill.

The Sixth Edition also assesses bias in the media and how it has been modified by newer cable network broadcasting and the Internet; it describes new leadership in Congress, including Senate Republican Leader Bill Frist, Sen. Hillary Clinton, and House Democratic Leader Nancy Pelosi; it describes charges of partisanship in the Supreme Court (especially in *Bush vs. Gore*) and controversial court decisions on cross burning, gay marriage, and the rights of enemy combatants captured on the battlefield.

As in previous editions, the Sixth Edition invites controversy and spirited discussion in the classroom. It raises "politically incorrect" issues—affirmative action and "diversity" in education; rising income inequality in America; how much campaign contributions affect congressional voting; amending the Constitution to ban gay marriages; when is the right to disobey the law; what is the appropriate justification for the use of military force; is the American government really "Of, by, and for the people."

New Features

- *What Do You Think?* "What Government Programs Do You Support?"
- *What Do You Think?* "Beliefs about Fairness"
- *People in Politics:* Bill O'Reilly, "The No Spin Zone?"
- *Up Close:* Why the Founders Created an Electoral College
- *People in Politics:* Arnold, from Bodybuilder to Superstar to Governor.
- *What Do You Think?* "Do Gender Stereotypes Affect Voting?"
- *Up Close:* "The Generation Gap in News"
- *A Conflicting View:* "Fox News, 'Fair and Balanced'?"
- *Up Close:* "The Brief History of Money in Politics"
- *Up Close:* "New Ways to Evade Campaign Reform Laws"
- *A Conflicting View:* "Payback, Money and Medicare"
- *Up Close:* "Polarization on Capitol Hill"
- *People in Politics* "Bill First M.D., Leading the Senate"
- *Up Close:* "Tips on Lobbying Congress"
- *Up Close:* "Contrasting Presidential Styles"
- *What Do You Think?* "How Would You Rate Federal Agencies?"
- *People in Politics:* "George Bush and 'Operator Iraqi Freedom' "
- *Up Close:* "How to Use the Freedom of Information Act"
- *Up Close:* "Women and the Courts"
- *What Do You Think?* "Do You Have Confidence in the Supreme Court?"
- *A Conflicting View.* "Terrorism Requires Restrictions on Civil Liberties"
- *Up Close.* "Why We Can Burn the Flag but Not a Cross"

The Sixth Edition provides a variety of new instructional aids, including running marginal Web site addresses on the topics under discussion.

Instructional Features

Interactive Chapter Opening Survey Each chapter opens with a brief poll called "Think about Politics" that alerts students to the crucial issues the chapter covers and the impact of those issues on their lives. This tool can be used to get students thinking about how and why politics is important to them as individuals and as members of a community.

Text and Features The body of each chapter is divided into text and features. The text provides the framework of understanding American politics. Each chapter begins with a brief discussion of power in relation to the subject matter of the chapter: for example, limiting governmental power (Chapter 3, "The Constitution"), dividing governmental power (Chapter 4, "Federalism"), and the power of the media (Chapter 6, "Mass Media"). By focusing the beginning of each chapter on questions of power, students can more easily set the chapter content in the context of Lasswell's definition of politics.

The features in each chapter provide timeliness, relevance, stimulation, and perspective. Each boxed feature in the Sixth Edition of *Politics in America* is designed to encourage students to voice their opinions and explore those of others. If the key to learning is active involvement, students should be encouraged to read and respond whenever possible.

- "**What Do You Think?**": These features pose controversial questions to students and provide national opinion survey data. They cover a wide range of interests designed to stimulate classroom discussion. Examples include: "Can You Trust the Government?" "Is American Government 'Of, By and For the People'?" "Are You a Liberal or a Conservative?" "Does Money Buy Influence in Washington?" "How Would You Rate the Presidents?" "Should We Judge Presidents on Private Character or Performance in Office?" "How Much Money Does the Government Waste?" "What Constitutes Sexual Harassment?"
- "**A Conflicting View**": These features challenge students to rethink conventional notions about American politics. They are designed to be controversial and to start students thinking about the push and pull that is politics. "Conflicting View" features include: "An Economic Interpretation of the Constitution," "Objections to the Constitution by an Anti-Federalist," "The War on Drugs Threatens Individual Liberty," "The Constitution Should Be Color-Blind."
- "**Compared to What?**": These features provide students with global context by comparing the United States with other nations. Discussions include "Freedom and Democracy around the World," as well as such topics as the size of government, tax burdens, voter turnout, political parties, television culture, health care, and the earnings gap between men and women.
- "**People in Politics**": These features are designed to personalize politics for students, to illustrate to them that the participants in the struggle for power are real people. They discuss where prominent people in politics went to school, how they got started in politics, how their careers developed, and how much power they came to possess. Both historical—John Locke and James Madison—and current figures, such as Arnold Schwarzeneggar, Ralph Nader, Colin Powell, and Ted Kennedy are discussed.
- "**Up Close**": These features illustrate the struggle over who gets what. They range over a wide variety of current political conflicts, such as "Sex, Lies, and Impeachment," "Abortion, the 'Hot Button' Issue," "Dirty Politics," "AARP: The Nation's Most Powerful Interest Group," "The Christian Coalition: Organizing the Faithful," "Is Welfare Reform Working?" A special feature, "How to Run for Office," provides practical advice on how to get into electoral politics.
- "**Across the USA**": These features provide maps that summarize important statistical and demographic information relevant to American politics.

Learning Aids Each chapter contains a running glossary in the margin to help students master important concepts, Web sites where students can obtain additional information direct from political sources, a chapter outline, a summary, and a list of annotated suggested readings, as well as marginal questions that relate to the chapter opening survey.

Technology Initiatives

With the development of new technologies, we have discovered more and more ways of helping students and instructors to further understand and analyze information. In this edition, we have made every effort to give both instructors and students a large array of multimedia tools to help with both the presentation and the learning of the material.

- **New! Make It Real** is a comprehensive Web site that contains dynamic simulations developed by Prentice Hall exclusively for American Government. In addition to simulations, Make It Real also contains activities on civic participation, interactive timelines and maps, quizzes, primary source documents, Census 2000 data, and exercises in visual literacy. Students will use information such as real election results, real demographics, maps and voting score cards. Self-study quizzes are available for the student to take to make sure they understand the concepts used in completing the simulations and other activities.

- **New and Improved Evaluating Online Resources for Political Science with Research Navigator™:** Our newest addition to the reliable Internet guide for political science, Prentice Hall's new Research Navigator™ keeps instructors and students abreast of the latest news and information and helps students create top quality research papers. From finding the right articles and journals, to citing sources, drafting and writing effective papers, and completing research assignments, Research Navigator simplifies and streamlines the entire process. It offers extensive help on the research process and three exclusive databases full of relevant and reliable source material including EBSCO's Content-Select Academic Journal Database, *The New York Times* Search-by-Subject Archive, and *"Best of the Web"* Link Library.

  A unique access code for Research Navigator™ is provided on the inside front cover of the booklet. The booklet contains an introduction to the Internet. Evaluating Online Resources for Political Science with Research Navigator is FREE when packaged with *Politics in America* and available for stand-alone sale. Take a tour on the web at http://www.researchnavigator.com
- **Improved Companion Website™** (www.prenhall.com/dye): Students can now take full advantage of the World Wide Web to enrich the study of American government through the *Politics in America* Website. Interactive Web exercises guide students to do research with a series of questions and links.
- **Evaluating Online Resources for Political Science with Research Navigator (ISBN 0-13-192288-2):** This timely supplement provides an introduction to the Internet and the numerous political sites on the World Wide Web. It describes e-mail, list servers, browsers, and how to document sources. It also includes Web addresses for the most current and useful political Web sites.

OneKey Instructors and students will find all of their resources—all in one place—all organized around the chapters of this text for maximum convenience and flexibility in OneKey, Prentice Hall's new and exclusive one-stop shop. Among the resources available for each chapter include all of the Make It Real simulations, chapter assessment with e-book PDF in feedback, flashcards, crossword puzzles, chapter opening questions, chapter outline/summary. For the instructor, OneKey also contains: Instructors Manual and Test Item File, powerpoints, image bank, audio of great speeches and video clips from campaigns and advertisements.

Supplements Available for the Instructor

- **New Instructor's Resource CD-ROM:** New from Prentice Hall, the Instructor's Resource CD-ROM allows you maximum flexibility as you prepare your lectures and manage your class. For presentation use, this CD contains a database featuring most of the art from the text, more than 30 video and audio segments of classical and contemporary political science footage, and several simulations from Make It Real. An easy to use interface (organized logically by chapter) allows you to customize your lectures with your own original material and the assets we've provided.
- **Instructor's Manual with Test Item File:** For each chapter, a summary, review of concepts, lecture suggestions and topic outlines, and additional resource materials—including a guide to media resources—are provided. An electronic version is also available on the Instructor's Resource CD-ROM.

  Thoroughly reviewed and revised to ensure test highest level of quality and accuracy, the test item file offers over 1,800 questions in multiple choice, true/false, and essay format with page references to the text.
- **Prentice Hall Test Manager:** A computerized test bank contains the items from the Test Item File. The program allows full editing of questions and the addition of instructor-generated items. Suitable for Windows and Macintosh versions.
- **American Government Transparencies, Series VI:** This set of over 100 four-color transparency acetates reproduces illustrations, charts, and maps from the text as well as from additional sources. An instructor's guide is also available.
- **Prentice Hall Custom Video: How a Bill Becomes a Law:** This 25-minute video chronicles an environmental law in Massachusetts—from its start as one citizen's concern to its passage in Washington, D.C. Students see step-by-step the process of how a bill becomes a law complete through narrative and graphics. Call your local Prentice Hall representative for details.
- **PowerPoint Gallery:** For each chapter, the PowerPoint Gallery provides electronic files for each figure and table in the text, along with pre-created PowerPoint slides ready for customization. With the use of this tool you may create a dynamic PowerPoint presentation or print your own customized 4-

color transparencies. (Available in the Faculty Resources section of the Companion Web Site™.)

- **Films for the Humanities and Social Sciences:** With a qualifying order of textbooks from Prentice Hall, you may select from a high quality library of political science videos from Films for the Humanities and Sciences. Please contact your local representative for a complete listing.

Supplements Available for the Student

- **Practice Tests:** Includes chapter outlines, study notes, a glossary, and practice tests designed to reinforce information in the text and help students develop a greater understanding of American government and politics.

Supplementary Books and Readings for American Government

Each of the following books features specialized topical coverage allowing you to tailor your American Government course to suit the needs of your region or your particular teaching style. Featuring contemporary issues or timely readings, any of the following books are available for a discount when bundled with *Politics in America.* Please visit our Online Catalog at www.prenhall.com/dye for additional details.

Government's Greatest Achievements: From Civil Rights to Homeland Security, 20th ed.
Paul C. Light, Brookings Institute
ISBN: 0-13-110192-7 © 2004

Issues in American Political Life: Money, Violence, and Biology, 4th ed.
Robert Thobaben, Wright State University
Donna Schlagheck, Wright State University
Charles Funderburk, Wright State University
ISBN: 0-13-0336726 © 2002

Choices: An American Government Reader—Custom Publishing
Gregory Scott, University of Central Oklahoma
Katherine Tate, University of California–Irvine
Ronald Weber, University of Wisconsin–Milwaukee
ISBN: 0-13-0219916 © 2002

Civil Rights and Liberties: Provocative Questions and Evolving Answers, 2nd ed.
Harold Sullivan, The City University of New York
ISBN: 0-13-1174355 © 2001

21 Debated: Issues in American Politics, 2nd ed.
Gregory Scott, University of Central Oklahoma
Loren Gatch, University of Central Oklahoma
ISBN: 0-13-1841785 © 2005

Government and Politics in the Lone Star State: Theory and Practice, 4th ed.
L. Tucker Gibson, Trinity University
Clay Robison, The Houston Chronicle
ISBN: 0-13-0340502 © 2002

Rethinking California: Politics and Policy in the Golden State
Matthew Cahn, California State University–Northridge
H. Eric Schockman, University of Southern California
David Shafie, Ohio University
ISBN: 0-13-0282677 © 2001

Strategies for Active Citizenship
Kateri M. Drexler
Gwen Garcelon
ISBN: 0-13-1172956 © 2005

Political Science: Evaluating Online Resources with Research Navigator, 2005
Melissa Payton
ISBN: 0-13-192288-2

The Political Science Student Writer's Manual, 4th ed.
Gregory M. Scott, University of Central Oklahoma
Stephen M. Garrison, University of Central Oklahoma
ISBN: 0-13-0404470 © 2002

Smoking and Politics: Policy Making and the Federal Bureaucracy, 5th ed.
A. Lee Fritschler, Dickinson College
James M. Hoefler, Dickinson College
ISBN: 0-13-4358015 © 1996

Real Politics in America series is another resource for contemporary instructional material. To bridge the gap between research and relevancy, we have launched a new series of supplemental books with the help of series editor Paul Herrnson of the University of Maryland. More descriptive than quantitative, more case study than data study, these books cut across all topics to bring students relevant details in current political science research. From exploring the growing phenomenon of direct democracy to who runs for the state legislature, these books show students that real political science is meaningful and exciting. Available for a discount when bundled with *Politics in America.* Please see your Prentice Hall representative or access www.prenhall.com for a complete listing of titles in the series.

Acknowledgments

Politics in America, Sixth Edition, reflects the influence of many splendid teachers, students, and colleagues who have helped me over the years. I am grateful for the early guidance of Frank Sorauf, my undergraduate student adviser at Pennsylvania State University, and James G. Coke, my Ph.D. dissertation director at the University of Pennsylvania. Georgia Parthemos at the University of Georgia and Malcolm Parsons at Florida State University gave me my first teaching posts. But my students over the years contributed most to my education—notably Susan MacManus, Kent Portney, Ed Benton, James Ammons, Aubrey Jewitt, and especially John Robey. Several of my colleagues gave advice on various parts of this book. Glen Parker (on Congress), Suzanne Parker (on public opinion), James Gwartney (on economics), Robert Lichter (on the mass media), Charles Barrioux (on Bureaucracy), and especially Harmon Zeigler, whose knowledge of politics is unbounded.

I would like to thank James Corey of High Point University for preparing the annotated Constitution and Chris Cardone for editorial management in the early stages of this Fifth Edition.

Finally, I would like to thank the many reviewers who evaluated the text and contributed invaluable advice:

Charles W. Chapman, University of Texas at Brownsville
John Pratt, Cedar Valley College
James Corey, High Point University
Christopher C. Lovett, Emporia State University
Kevin R. den Dulk, Grand Valley State University
Wayne Pryor, Brazosport College
James W. Lamare, Florida Atlantic University
Roger Marietta, Darton College
Paul Davis, Truckee Meadows Community College
Earl T. Sheridan, University of North Carolina

Thomas R. Dye

Preface to the Texas Edition

Texas government and politics have intrigued the authors for more than thirty years. Many outside of the state find our politics byzantine or outrageous, and Texans' "state patriotism" is often interpreted as quaint if not obnoxious. But underneath all of these images is a complex story of government and politics that links the state's history, diverse culture, and economics. In the chapters covering Texas, we attempt to tell this story.

Texas is often regarded as one of the more conservative states, and we think it is important that one understands why this is so. Moreover, it is important to understand the relationship of the state's political culture to public policy decisions, institutional arrangements, and contemporary party politics.

Texas is now the second largest state in terms of population and third in terms of its economy. While outsiders may have a rather singular view of Texans, Texans are extremely diverse as a people, and this diversity does much to shape our politics. From the high-tech sector of the economy to the traditional agricultural sector, economic change and development have been impressive over the past forty years. During much of the past decade, economic expansion in the state has outpaced the nation as a whole. Economic development supported by a rapidly expanding population has also contributed to this story of Texas politics.

As long-time political observers, we are often skeptical about what public leaders do or how they do it, but we are not cynical about the role and importance of politics and government. If we have developed insights into the process, we hope we are able to share them with you. More importantly, we hope that you develop a good understanding of our institutions and processes to enable you to shape and influence the manner in which they work. If you would like to share your views on what we have written, please feel free to contact us at lgibson@trinity.edu

Our thanks go to reviewers Wayne Pryor, Brazosport College, Laurie Robertstad, Navarro College; and Tracy Skopek, Stephen F. Austin State University.

Our special thanks go to the editorial staff at Prentice Hall.

L. Tucker Gibson, Jr.
Clay Robison

About the Authors

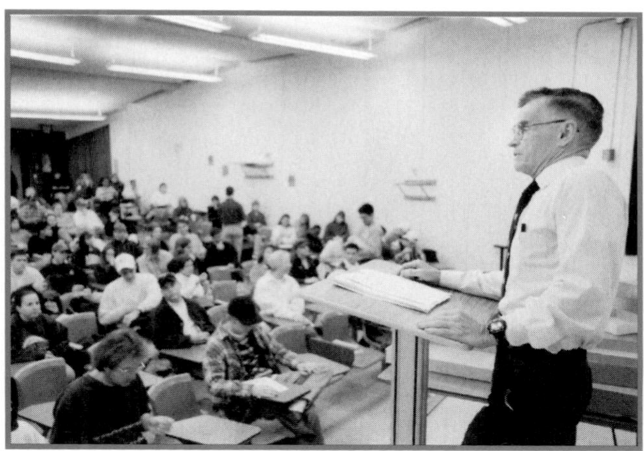

THOMAS R. DYE, Emeritus McKenzie Professor of Government at Florida State University regularly taught large introductory classes in American politics and was University Teacher of the Year in 1987. He received his B.A. and M.A. degrees from Pennsylvania State University and his Ph.D. degree from the University of Pennsylvania. He is the author of numerous books and articles on American government and public policy, including. *The Irony of Democracy, Politics in States and Communities, Understanding Public Policy, Who's Running America, American Politics in the Media Age, Power in Society, Politics, Economics, and the Public, and American Federalism: Competition Among Governments.* His books have been translated into many languages, including Russian and Chinese, and published abroad. He has served as president of the Southern Political Science Association, president of the Policy Studies Organization, and secretary of the American Political Science Association. He has taught at the University of Pennsylvania, the University of Wisconsin, and the University of Georgia, and served as a visiting scholar at Bar-Ilan University, Israel, the Brookings Institution in Washington, D.C., and elsewhere. He is a member of Phi Beta Kappa, Omicron Delta Kappa, and Phi Kappa Phi, and is listed in most major biographical directories. Additional information is available at www.thomasr.dye.com.

L. TUCKER GIBSON, JR., is chair and professor of political science at Trinity University, where he teaches introductory courses in American national and state government as well as courses on U.S. legislatures, political parties, and interest groups. He has served on the Civil Service Commission of the city of San Antonio, assisted local governments across central and south Texas in redistricting their government bodies, and conducted public opinion research for political candidates, businesses, and corporations. Gibson is the coauthor of *Government and Politics in the Lone Star State: Theory and Practice.*

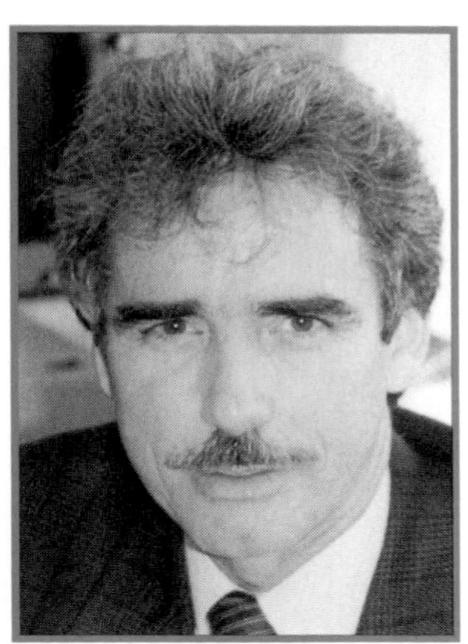

CLAY ROBISON has covered state government and politics in Texas for more than 30 years as a journalist, first for the *San Antonio Light*, and then, since 1982, for the *Houston Chronicle*. He is the *Houston Chronicle's* Austin bureau chief, and in addition to covering daily news events, he writes a weekly column that appears on the newspaper's Sunday editorial page. He has covered many of the personalities and events that are incorporated in the chapters on Texas government. Robison is the coauthor of *Government and Politics in the Lone Star State Theory and Practice.*

POLITICS IN AMERICA

CHAPTER 1

POLITICS: WHO GETS WHAT, WHEN, AND HOW

CHAPTER OUTLINE

Politics and Political Science
Politics and Government
The Purposes of Government
The Meaning of Democracy
The Paradox of Democracy
Direct Versus Representative Democracy
Who Really Governs?
Democracy in America

Politics and Political Science

Politics is deciding "who gets what, when, and how." It is an activity by which people try to get more of whatever there is to get—money, prestige, jobs, respect, sex, even power itself. Politics occurs in many different settings. We talk about office politics, student politics, union politics, church politics, and so forth. But political science usually limits its attention to *politics in government.*

Political science is the study of politics, or the study of who gets what, when, and how. The *who* are the participants in politics—voters, special-interest groups, political parties, television and the press, corporations and labor unions, lawyers and lobbyists, foundations and think tanks, and both elected and appointed government officials, including members of Congress, the president and vice president, judges, prosecutors, and bureaucrats. The *what* of politics are public policies—the decisions that governments make concerning social welfare, health care, education, national defense, law enforcement, the environment, taxation, and thousands of other issues that come before governments. The *when* and *how* are the political process—campaigns and elections, political reporting in the news media, television debates, fund raising, lobbying, decision making in the White House and executive agencies, and decision making in the courts.

Political science is generally concerned with three questions. *Who governs? For what ends? By what means?* Throughout this book, we are concerned with who participates in politics, how government decisions are made, who benefits most from those decisions, and who bears their greatest costs (see Figure 1.1).

Politics would be simple if everyone agreed on who should govern, who should get what, who should pay for it, and how and when it should be done. But conflict arises from disagreements over these questions, and sometimes the question of confidence in the government itself underlies the conflict (see *What Do You Think?* "Can You Trust the Government?"). Politics arises out of conflict, and it consists of all the activities—reasonable discussion, impassioned oratory, balloting, campaigning, lobbying, parading, rioting, street fighting, terrorism, and waging war—by which conflict is carried on.

THINK ABOUT POLITICS

1 Can you trust the government to do what is right most of the time?
Yes ● No ●

2 Should any group other than the government have the right to use force?
Yes ● No ●

3 Is violence ever justified as a means of bringing about political change?
Yes ● No ●

4 Is it ever right to disobey the law?
Yes ● No ●

5 Should important decisions in a democracy be submitted to voters rather than decided by Congress?
Yes ● No ●

6 Is the government run by a few big interests looking out for themselves?
Yes ● No ●

7 In a democracy should "majority rule" be able to limit the rights of members of an unpopular or dangerous minority?
Yes ● No ●

8 Is government trying to do too many things that should be left to individuals?
Yes ● No ●

9 Does the threat of terrorism on American soil justify increased government surveillance of its citizens?
Yes ● No ●

Who has power and how they use it are the basis of all these questions. Issues of power underlie everything we call politics and the study of political science.

FIGURE 1.1 Who Gets What, When, and How

Political science is the study of politics. The distinguished political scientist Harold Lassvell entitled his most popular book *Politics: Who Gets What, When and How.* The first topic of politics is "Who?" (that is, who are the participants in politics, both within and outside of government?), "When and how are political decisions made?" (that is, how do the institutions and processes of politics function?), and "What outcomes are produced?" (that is, what public policies are adopted?). Shown here are some of the topics of concern to political science.

Who Governs: Participants

Governmental	*Nongovernmental*
President and White House staff Executive Office of the President, including Office of Management and Budget Cabinet officers and executive agency heads Bureaucrats Congress members Congressional staff Supreme Court justices Federal appellate and district judges	Voters Campaign contributors Interest-group leaders and members Party leaders and party identifiers in the electorate Corporate and union leaders Media leaders, including press and television anchors and reporters Lawyers and lobbyists Think tanks and foundation personnel

When and How: Institutions and Processes

Institutions	*Processes*
Constitution Separation of powers Checks and balances Federalism Judicial review Amendment procedures Electoral system	Socialization and learning Opinion formation Party identification Voting Contributing Joining organizations Talking politics
Presidency Congress Senate House of Representatives Courts Supreme Court Appellate courts District courts	Running for office Campaigning Polling Fund raising Parading and demonstrating Nonviolent direct action Violence
Parties National committees Conventions State and local organizations Press and television	Agenda setting Lobbying Logrolling Deciding Budgeting Implementing and evaluating Adjudicating

What Outcomes: Public Policies

Civil liberties Civil rights Equality Criminal justice Welfare Social Security Health Education	Energy Environmental protection Economic development Economic stability Taxation Government spending and deficits National defense Foreign affairs

politics Deciding who gets what, when, and how.

political science The study of politics: who governs, for what ends, and by what means.

THINK AGAIN

Should any group other than the government have the right to use force?

government Organization extending to the whole society that can legitimately use force to carry out its decisions.

Politics and Government

What distinguishes governmental politics from politics in other institutions in society? After all, parents, teachers, unions, banks, corporations, and many other organizations make decisions about who gets what in society. The answer is that only **government** decisions can *extend to the whole society,* and only government can *legitimately use force.* Other institutions encompass only a part of society: for exam-

Conflict exists in all political activities as participants struggle over who gets what, when, and how. From the streets to the Congress to the White House, participants in the political process compete to further their goals and ambitions.

ple, students and faculty in a college, members of a church or union, employees or customers of a corporation. And individuals have a legal right to voluntarily withdraw from nongovernmental organizations. But governments make decisions affecting everyone, and no one can voluntarily withdraw from government's authority (without leaving the country, and thus becoming subject to some other government's authority). Some individuals and organizations—muggers, gangs, crime families—occasionally use physical force to get what they want. But only governments can use force legitimately—that is, people generally believe it is acceptable for the government to use force if necessary to uphold its laws, but they do not extend this right to other institutions or individuals.

Most people would say that they obey the law in order to avoid fines and stay out of prison. But if large numbers of people all decided to disobey the law at the same time, the government would not have enough police or jails to hold them all.

The government can rely on force only against relatively small numbers of offenders. Most of us, most of the time, obey laws out of habit—the habit of compliance. We have been taught to believe that law and order are necessary and that government is right to punish those who disobey its laws.

Government thus enjoys **legitimacy**, or rightfulness, in its use of force.[1] A democratic government has a special claim to legitimacy because it is based on the consent of its people, who participate in the selection of its leaders and the making of its laws. Those who disagree with a law have the option of working for its

American Political Science Association

Association of college and university teachers advises students how to study political science.
www.apsanet.org

THINK AGAIN

Is violence ever justified as a means of bringing about political change?

legitimacy Widespread acceptance of something as necessary, rightful, and legally binding.

WHAT DO YOU THINK?

Can You Trust the Government?

Americans are suspicious of big government. Many do not trust the government in Washington to "do what is right." Trust in government has varied over the years, as measured by polls asking, "How much of the time do you think you can trust the government in Washington to do what is right? Just about always? Most of the time? Some of the time? None of the time?" During the early years of the Johnson Administration (and even earlier, during the Kennedy and Eisenhower presidencies), public confidence in government was high. But in the late '60s and early '70s defeat and humiliation in Vietnam appeared to diminish public confidence. On the heels of the Vietnam experience came the Watergate scandal and President Richard Nixon's forced resignation in 1974—the first resignation of a president in U.S. history—causing public confidence in government to fall further.

Throughout the long years of decline in public confidence in government, television broadcast many negative images of government and public policy. Television producers seldom consider good news as "news" but instead focus on violence, scandal, corruption, and incompetence (see Chapter 6, "Mass Media: Setting the Political Agenda").

But public confidence in government can be restored, as it was in part during the Reagan presidency. Perhaps President Reagan's personal popularity was part of the reason that popular confidence in government rose.

Economic recessions erode public confidence in government. People expect the president and Congress to lead them out of "hard times." George Bush's Gulf War success raised public confidence only temporarily; the perceived failure of his administration to act decisively to restore the nation's economic health helped to send public confidence in government back down. Sustained growth in the economy during the 1990s under President Clinton improved public trust in government.

The terrorist attack of September 11, 2001, rallied Americans behind their government as no other event since the Japanese attack on Pearl Harbor in 1941. American flags sprouted from homes, businesses, and automobiles. Trust in government "to do the right thing" leaped to levels not seen since the 1960s. This dramatic rise in trust after "9/11" leveled off in 2002, but still remained higher than at any time in recent years.

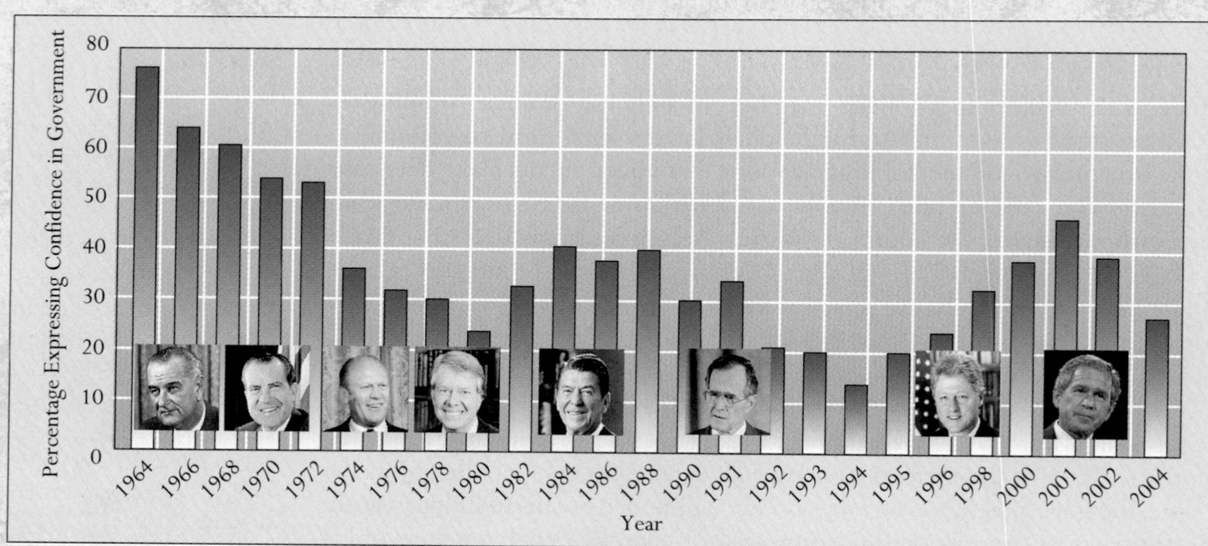

Public Confidence, That the Federal Government Can Be Trusted to "Do What is Right Most of the Time"

Source: 1992–2004 data from Gallup Opinion Polls (http://www.gallup.com/poll/topics/trust_gov.asd), Copyright © 1992–2004, The Gallup Organization, see also Arthur H. Miller, "Confidence in Government during the 1980's," *American Politics Quarterly* 19 (April 1991): 147–73. See also Marc J. Hetherington and Suzanne Globetti, "Political Trust and Racial Policy Preferences," *American Journal of Political Science* 46 (April, 2002): 253–275.

change by speaking out, petitioning, demonstrating, forming interest groups or parties, voting against unpopular leaders, or running for office themselves. Since people living in a democracy can effect change by "working within the system," they have a greater moral obligation to obey the law than people living under regimes in which they have no voice. However, there may be some occasions when "civil disobedience" even in a democracy may be morally justified (see *A Conflicting View:* "Sometimes It's Right to Disobey the Law").

THINK AGAIN

Is it ever right to disobey the law?

The Purposes of Government

All governments tax, penalize, punish, restrict, and regulate their people. Governments in the United States—the federal government in Washington, the 50 state governments, and the more than 86,000 local governments—take nearly 40 cents out of every dollar Americans earn. Each year, the Congress enacts about 500 laws; federal bureaucracies publish about 19,000 rules and regulations, the state legislatures enact about 25,000 laws; and cities, counties, school districts, and other local governments enact countless local ordinances. Each of these laws restricts our freedom in some way. Each dollar taken out of our wages or profits reduces our freedom to choose what to do with our money.

Why do people put up with governments? An answer to this question can be found in the words of the Preamble to the Constitution of the United States:

> We the people of the United States, in Order to form a more perfect Union, establish Justice, insure domestic Tranquility, provide for the common defense, promote the general Welfare, and secure the Blessings of Liberty to ourselves and our Posterity, do ordain and establish this Constitution for the United States of America.

WWW The King Center
Atlanta-based center commemorates the life and teachings of Martin Luther King, Jr.
www.theKingCenter.com

To Establish Justice and Insure Domestic Tranquility Government manages conflict and maintains order. We might think of government as a **social contract** among people who agree to allow themselves to be regulated and taxed in exchange for protection of their lives and property. No society can allow individuals or groups to settle their conflicts by street fighting, murder, kidnapping, rioting, bombing, or terrorism. Whenever government fails to control such violence, we describe it as "a breakdown in law and order." Without the protection of government, human lives and property are endangered, and only those skilled with fists and weapons have much of a chance of survival. The seventeenth-century English political philosopher Thomas Hobbes described life without government as "a war where every man is enemy to every man," where people live in "continual fear and danger of violent death."[2]

WWW Internet Encyclopedia of Philosophy
At this site, you can find a concise description of social contract theory along with a discussion of John Locke's writing.
www.utm.edu/research/iep/

To Provide for the Common Defense Many anthropologists link the origins of government to warfare—to the need of early communities to protect themselves from raids by outsiders and to organize raids against others. Since the Revolutionary War, the U.S. government has been responsible for the country's defense. During the long Cold War, when America confronted a nuclear-armed, expansionist-minded, communist-governed Soviet Union, the United States spent nearly half of the federal budget on national defense. With the end of the Cold War, defense spending fell to about 15 percent of the federal budget, but defense spending has begun to creep upward again as the nation confronts the new war on terrorism. National defense will always remain a primary responsibility of United States government.

WWW DefenseLink
Official site of the U.S. Department of Defense, with current news as well as links to Army, Navy, Air Force, Marine, and other defense agencies.
www.defenselink.gov

social contract Idea that government originates as an implied contract among individuals who agree to obey laws in exchange for protection of their rights.

A CONFLICTING VIEW

Sometimes It's Right to Disobey the Law

Civil disobedience is the nonviolent violation of laws that people believe to be unjust. Civil disobedience denies the *legitimacy,* or rightfulness, of a law and implies that a higher moral authority takes precedence over unjust laws. It is frequently a political tactic of minorities. (Majorities can more easily change laws through conventional political activity.)

Why resort to civil disobedience in a democracy? Why not work within the democratic system to change unjust laws? In 1963 a group of Alabama clergy posed these questions to Martin Luther King, Jr., and asked him to call off mass demonstrations in Birmingham, Alabama. King, who had been arrested in the demonstrations, replied in his now famous "Letter from Birmingham City Jail":

> One may well ask, "How can you advocate breaking some laws and obeying others?" The answer is found in the fact that there are unjust laws. I would be the first to advocate obeying just laws. One has not only a legal but a moral responsibility to obey just laws. Conversely, one has a moral responsibility to disobey unjust laws.

King argued that *nonviolent direct action* was a vital aspect of democratic politics. The political purpose of civil disobedience is to call attention or "to bear witness" to the existence of injustices. Only laws regarded as unjust are broken, and they are broken openly, without hatred or violence. Punishment is actively sought rather than avoided, since punishment will further emphasize the injustice of the laws.

The objective of nonviolent civil disobedience is to stir the conscience of an apathetic majority and to win support for measures that will eliminate the injustices. By accepting punishment for the violation of an unjust law, persons practicing civil disobedience demonstrate their sincerity. They hope to shame the majority and to make it ask itself how far it is willing to go to protect the status quo. Thus, according to King's teachings, civil disobedience is clearly differentiated from hatred and violence:

Dr. Martin Luther King, Jr., shown here marching in Mississippi with his wife, Coretta Scott King, and others, used civil disobedience to advance the rights of African Americans during the 1950s and 1960s. (Copyright Flip Schulke)

> One who breaks an unjust law must do it openly, lovingly (not hatefully as the white mothers did in New Orleans when they were seen on television screaming "nigger, nigger, nigger") and with a willingness to accept the penalty. I submit that an individual who breaks a law that conscience tells him is unjust, and willingly accepts the penalty by staying in jail to arouse the conscience of the community over its injustice, is in reality expressing the very highest respect for law.

In 1964 Martin Luther King, Jr., received the Nobel Peace Prize in recognition of his extraordinary contributions to the development of nonviolent methods of social change.

Source: Martin Luther King, Jr., "Letter from Birmingham City Jail," April 16, 1963.

public goods Goods and services that cannot readily be provided by markets, either because they are too expensive for a single individual to buy or because if one person bought them, everyone else would use them without paying.

To Promote the General Welfare Government promotes the general welfare in a number of ways. It provides **public goods**—goods and services that private markets cannot readily furnish either because they are too expensive for individuals to buy for themselves (for example, a national park, a highway, or a sewage disposal plant) or because if one person bought them, everyone else would "free-ride," or use them without paying (for example, clean air, police protection, or national defense).

Nevertheless, Americans acquire most of their goods and services on the **free market,** through voluntary exchange among individuals, firms, and corporations. The **gross domestic product (GDP)**—the dollar sum of all the goods and services produced in the United States in a year—amounts to more than $10 trillion. Government spending in the United States—federal, state, and local governments combined—amounts to about $3 trillion, or an amount equivalent to 30 percent of the gross domestic product.

Governments also regulate society. Free markets cannot function effectively if individuals and firms engage in fraud, deception, or unfair competition, or if contracts cannot be enforced. Moreover, many economic activities impose costs on persons who are not direct participants in these activities. Economists refer to such costs as **externalities.** A factory that produces air pollution or wastewater imposes external costs on community residents who would otherwise enjoy cleaner air or water. A junkyard that creates an eyesore makes life less pleasant for neighbors and passersby. Many government regulations are designed to reduce these external costs.

To promote general welfare, governments also use **income transfers** from taxpayers to people who are regarded as deserving. Government agencies and programs provide support and care for individuals who cannot supply these things for themselves through the private job market, for example, ill, elderly, and disabled people, and dependent children who cannot usually be expected to find productive employment. The largest income transfer programs are Social Security and Medicare, which are paid to the elderly regardless of their personal wealth. Other large transfer payments go to farmers, veterans, and the unemployed, as well as to a wide variety of businesses. As we shall see, the struggle of individuals and groups to obtain direct government payments is a major motivator of political activity (see What Do You Think? "What Government Programs Do You Support?").

To Secure the Blessings of Liberty All governments must maintain order, protect national security, provide public goods, regulate society, and care for those unable to fend for themselves. But *democratic* governments have a special added responsibility—to protect individual liberty by ensuring that all people are treated equally before the law. No one is above the law. The president must obey the Constitution and laws of the United States, and so must members of Congress, governors, judges, and the police. A democratic government must protect people's freedom to speak and write what they please, to practice their religion, to petition, to form groups and parties, to enjoy personal privacy, and to exercise their rights if accused of a crime.

The concentration of government power can be a threat to freedom. If a democratic government acquires great power in order to maintain order, protect national security, or provide many collective goods and services, it runs the risk of becoming too powerful for the preservation of freedom. The question is how to keep government from becoming so pervasive it threatens the individual liberty it was established to protect.

The Meaning of Democracy

Throughout the centuries, thinkers in many different cultures contributed to the development of democratic government. Early Greek philosophers contributed the word **democracy,** which means "rule by the many." But there is no single definition of *democracy,* nor is there a tightly organized system of democratic thought.

free market Free competition for voluntary exchange among individuals, firms, and corporations.

gross domestic product (GDP) The dollar sum of all the goods and services produced in a nation in a year.

externalities Costs imposed on people who are not direct participants in an activity.

income transfers Government transfers of income from taxpayers to persons regarded as deserving.

democracy Governing system in which the people govern themselves, from the Greek term meaning "rule by the many."

WHAT DO YOU THINK?

What Government Programs Do You Support?

Although many Americans lack confidence in their government in general, they support many specific programs of the government. In somewhat of a paradox, Americans often express distrust in the federal government, yet at the same time approve of many of the programs and activities of that government.

The Council on Excellence in Government, which conducted this poll, believes that the most highly regarded programs are those that serve (or potentially serve) all Americans, rather than target groups.

Support for Government Programs

Support a Great Deal	Percent
Social Security	69
The Armed Forces	64
Medicare	64
Enforcing workplace safety	63
Enforcing laws against discrimination	61
Programs for public schools	61
Enforcing food and drug safety	60
College student loans	56
Enforcing minimum wage laws	56
Enforcing environmental protection laws	55
Federal law enforcement, such as the FBI	45
Enforcing family and medical leave laws	40
NASA and the space program	34
Affirmative action programs	29
Welfare programs	24

Source: Council Excellence in Government nationwide survey, February, 1997. www.excelgov.org. Reprinted by permission of Council on Excellence in Government.

U.S. Information Agency
Official government site defining democracy, individual rights, and the culture of democracy
www.usinfo.state.gov/products/pubs/whatsdem

It is better, perhaps, to speak of democratic traditions than of a single democratic ideology.

Unfortunately, the looseness of the term *democracy* allows it to be perverted by *anti*democratic governments. Hardly a nation in the world exists that does not *claim* to be "democratic." Governments that outlaw political opposition, suppress dissent, discourage religion, and deny fundamental freedoms of speech and press still claim to be "democracies," "democratic republics," or "people's republics" (for example, the Democratic People's Republic of Korea is the official name of Communist North Korea). These governments defend their use of the term *democracy* by claiming that their policies reflect the true interests of their people. But they are unwilling to allow political freedoms or to hold free elections in order to find out whether their people really agree with their policies. In effect, they use the term as a political slogan rather than a true description of their government.[3]

democratic ideals Individual dignity, equality before the law, widespread participation in public decisions, and public decisions by majority rule, with one person having one vote.

The actual existence of **democratic ideals** varies considerably from country to country, regardless of their names (see *Compared to What?* "Freedom and Democracy around the World"). A meaningful definition of democracy must include the following ideals: recognition of the dignity of every individual; equal protection under the law for every individual; opportunity for everyone to participate in pub-

COMPARED TO WHAT?

Freedom and Democracy around the World

Worldwide progress toward freedom over the past half-century has been impressive. In 1950 there were 22 democracies accounting for 31 percent of the world population that were said to be "free." Another 21 nations with restricted democratic practices were labeled "partly free"; they accounted for an additional 11.9 percent of the world population. By 2000, democracy had spread to 120 "free" countries that constituted 58 percent of the world population; an additional 5 percent lived in nations labeled "partly free." In all, about 63 percent of the world population were living in democracies. Nonetheless, "not-free" authoritarian and totalitarian regimes governed more than one-third of the world's population.*

Worldwide progress toward freedom and democracy has been evident since 1989 notably as a result of the collapse of communism in Eastern Europe and the demise of the Soviet Union.

One way to assess the degree of democracy in a governmental system is to consider its record in ensuring political freedoms—enabling citizens to participate meaningfully in government—and individual liberties. A checklist for political freedoms might include whether the chief executive and national legislature are elected; whether elections are generally fair, with open campaigning and honest tabulation of votes; and whether multiple candidates and parties participate. A checklist for individual liberties might include whether the press and broadcasting are free and independent of the government; whether people are free to assemble, protest, and form opposition parties; whether religious institutions, labor unions, business organizations, and other groups are free and independent of the government; and whether individuals are free to own property, travel, and move their residence.

The Freedom House is a NewYork-based think tank that regularly surveys political conditions around the world (see map).

*Freedom House, *Democracy's Century* (New York: Freedom House, 2001).

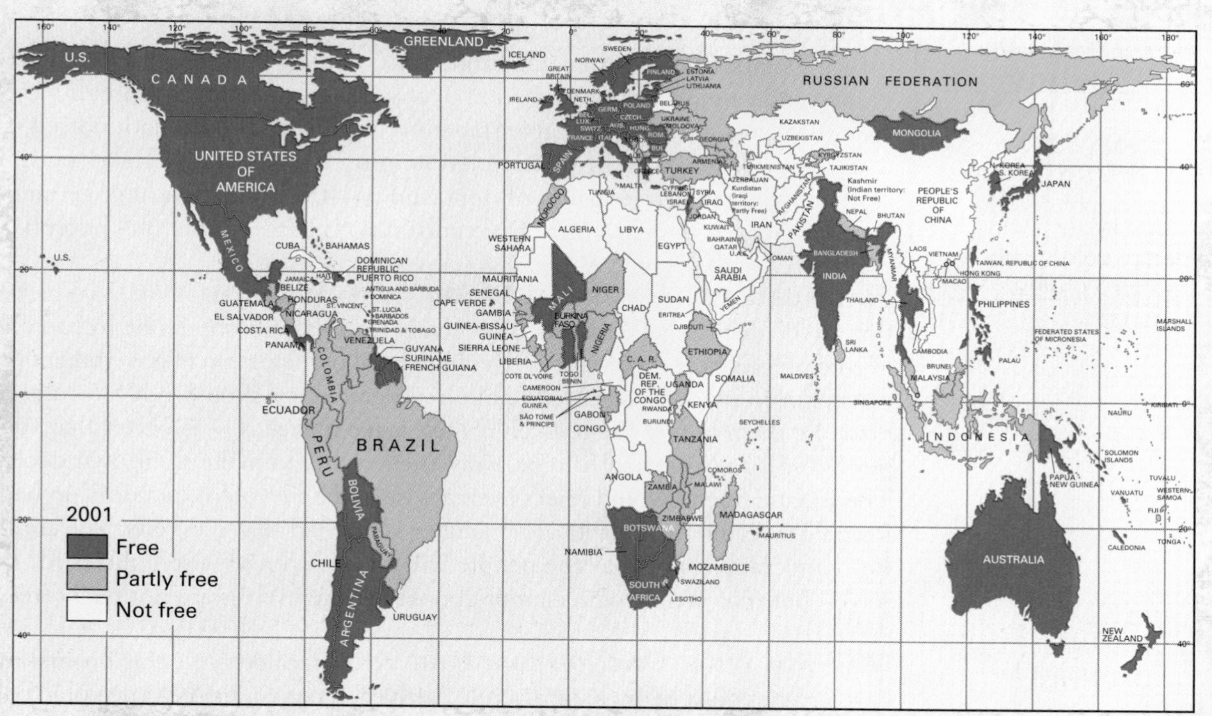

Source: Reprinted by permission of Freedom House, 2002.

lic decisions; and decision making by majority rule, with one person having one vote.

Individual Dignity The underlying value of democracy is the dignity of the individual. Human beings are entitled to life and liberty, personal property, and equal protection under the law. These liberties are *not* granted by governments; they belong to every person born into the world. The English political philosopher John Locke (1632–1704) argued that a higher "natural law" guaranteed liberty to every person and that this natural law was morally superior to all human laws and governments. Each individual possesses "certain inalienable Rights, among these are Life, Liberty, and Property."[4] When Thomas Jefferson wrote his eloquent defense of the American Revolution in the Declaration of Independence for the Continental Congress in Philadelphia in 1776, he borrowed heavily from Locke (perhaps even to the point of plagiarism):

> We hold these truths to be self-evident, that all Men are created equal, that they are endowed by their Creator with certain unalienable Rights, that among these are Life, Liberty and the Pursuit of Happiness—That to secure these Rights, Governments are instituted among Men, deriving their just powers from the Consent of the Governed, that whenever any Form of Government becomes destructive of these Ends, it is the Right of the People to alter or to abolish it.

Freedom House A think tank monitoring the ongoing evolution of global human rights and liberty; provides an annual world survey covering freedom's progress throughout the state system. ***www.freedomhouse.org/***

THINK AGAIN

Should important decisions in a democracy be submitted to voters rather than decided by Congress?

Individual dignity requires personal freedom. People who are directed by governments in every aspect of their lives, people who are "collectivized" and made into workers for the state, people who are enslaved—all are denied the personal dignity to which all human beings are entitled. Democratic governments try to minimize the role of government in the lives of citizens.

Equality True democracy requires equal protection of the law for every individual. Democratic governments cannot discriminate between blacks and whites, or men and women, or rich and poor, or any groups of people in applying the law. Not only must a democratic government refrain from discrimination itself, but it must also work to prevent discrimination in society generally. Today our notion of equality extends to equality of opportunity—the obligation of government to ensure that all Americans have an opportunity to develop their full potential.

Participation in Decision Making Democracy means individual participation in the decisions that affect individuals' lives. People should be free to choose for themselves how they want to live. Individual participation in government is necessary for individual dignity. People in a democracy should not have decisions made *for* them but *by* them. Even if they make mistakes, it is better that they be permitted to do so than to take away their rights to make their own decisions. The true democrat would reject even a wise and benevolent dictatorship because it would threaten the individual's character, self-reliance, and dignity. The argument for democracy is not that the people will always choose wise policies for themselves, but that people who cannot choose for themselves are not really free.

National Endowment for Democracy Private advocacy group for worldwide democracy and human rights. ***www.ned.org***

Majority Rule: One Person, One Vote Collective decision making in democracies must be by majority rule, with each person having one vote. That is, each person's vote must be equal to every other person's, regardless of status, money, or fame. Whenever any individual is denied political equality because of race, sex, or wealth, then the government is not truly democratic. Majorities are not always right. But majority *rule* means that all persons have an equal say in decisions affecting them. If people are truly equal, their votes must count equally, and a majority vote must decide the issue, even if the majority decides foolishly.

The Paradox of Democracy

What if a *majority* of the people decide to attack the rights of some unpopular individuals or minority groups? What if hate, prejudice, or racism infects a majority of people and they vote for leaders who promise to "get rid of the Jews" or "put blacks in their place" or "bash a few gays"? What if a majority of people vote to take away the property of wealthy people and distribute it among themselves.[5] Do we abide by the principle of majority rule and allow the majority to do what it wants? Or do we defend the principle of individual liberty and limit the majority's power? If we enshrine the principle of majority rule, we are placing all our confidence in the wisdom and righteousness of the majority of the people. Yet we know that democracy means more than majority rule, that it also means freedom and dignity for the individual. How do we resolve this **paradox of democracy**—the potential for conflict between majority rule and individual freedom?

THINK AGAIN

In a democracy should "majority rule" be able to limit the rights of members of an unpopular or dangerous minority?

THINK AGAIN

Is government trying to do too many things that should be left to individuals?

Limiting the Power of Majorities The Founders of the American nation were not sure that freedom would be safe in the hands of the majority. In *The Federalist Papers* in 1787, James Madison warned against a direct democracy: "Pure democracy . . . can admit of no cure for the mischiefs of faction. . . . There is nothing to check the inducements to sacrifice the weaker party, or an obnoxious individual."[6] So the Founders wrote a Constitution and adopted a Bill of Rights that limited the power of government over the individual, that placed some personal

paradox of democracy
Potential for conflict between individual freedom and majority rule.

The paradox of democracy balances the principle of majority rule against the principle of individual liberty. When the German people voted Adolf Hitler and the Nazi Party into power, did majority rule give the Nazis free rein to restrict the individual liberties of the people? Or did those who abhorred the trespasses of their government have the right to fight against its power?

Political sociologists have observed that the military in totalitarian societies has a distinct body language. Soldiers in Nazi Germany and, as seen here, communist North Korea used a "goose step" when on parade—a march in which the knee is unbent and the foot, encased in a heavy boot, is stamped on the ground, providing a powerful image of authority and force. In democratic societies, the goose step is not employed, indeed, it is regarded as somewhat ridiculous.

liberties beyond the reach of majorities. They established the principle of **limited government**—a government that is itself restrained by law. Under a limited government, even if a majority of voters wanted to, they could not prohibit communists or atheists or racists from speaking or writing. Nor could they ban certain religions, set aside the rights of criminal defendants to a fair trial, or prohibit people from moving or quitting their jobs. These rights belong to individuals, not to majorities or governments.

Totalitarianism: Unlimited Government Power No government can be truly democratic if it directs every aspect of its citizens' lives. Individuals must be free to shape their own lives, free from the dictates of governments or even majorities of their fellow citizens. Indeed, we call a government with *un*limited power over its citizens totalitarian. Under **totalitarianism**, the individual possesses no personal liberty. Totalitarian governments decide what people can say or write; what unions, churches, or parties they can join, if any; where people must live; what work they must do; what goods they can find in stores and what they will be allowed to buy and sell; whether citizens will be allowed to travel outside of their country; and so on. Under a totalitarian government, the total life of the individual is subject to government control.

Constitutional Government Constitutions, written or unwritten, are the principal means by which governmental powers are limited. Constitutions set forth the liberties of individuals and restrain governments from interfering with these liberties. Consider, for example, the opening words of the First Amendment to the U.S. Constitution: "Congress shall make no law respecting an establishment of religion, or prohibiting the free exercise thereof." This amendment places religious belief beyond the reach of the government. The government itself is restrained by law. It cannot, even by majority vote, interfere with the personal liberty to worship as one chooses. In addition, armed with the power of judicial review, the courts can declare unconstitutional laws passed by majority vote of Congress or state legislatures (see "Judicial Power" in Chapter 13).

Throughout this book we examine how well limited constitutional government succeeds in preserving individual liberty in the United States. We examine free

limited government Principle that government power over the individual is limited, that there are some personal liberties that even a majority cannot regulate, and that government itself is restrained by law.

totalitarianism Rule by an elite that exercises unlimited power over individuals in all aspects of life.

speech and press, the mass media, religious freedom, the freedom to protest and demonstrate, and the freedom to support political candidates and interest groups of all kinds. We examine how well the U.S. Constitution protects individuals from discrimination and inequality. And we examine how far government should go in protecting society without destroying individual liberty (see *Up Close:* "Terrorism's Threat to Democracy" on page 18).

Direct Versus Representative Democracy

In the Gettysburg Address, Abraham Lincoln spoke about "a government of the people, by the people, for the people," and his ringing phrase remains an American ideal. But can we take this phrase literally? More than 281 million Americans are spread over 4 million square miles. If we brought everyone together, standing shoulder to shoulder, they would occupy 66 square miles. One round of five-minute speeches by everyone would take over 2,500 years. "People could be born, grow old, and die while they waited for the assembly to make one decision."[7]

Direct democracy (also called pure or participatory democracy), where everyone actively participates in every decision, is rare. The closest approximation to direct democracy in American government may be the traditional New England town meeting, where all of the citizens come together face to face to decide about town affairs. But today most New England towns vest authority in a board of officials elected by the townspeople to make policy decisions between town meetings, and professional administrators are appointed to supervise the day-to-day town services. The town meeting is rapidly vanishing because citizens cannot spend so much of their time and energy in community decision making.

Representative democracy recognizes that it is impossible to expect millions of people to come together and decide every issue. Instead, representatives of the people are elected by the people to decide issues on behalf of the people. Elections must be open to competition so that the people can choose representatives who reflect their own views. And elections must take place in an environment of free speech and press, so that both candidates and voters can freely express their views. Finally, elections must be held periodically so that representatives can be thrown out of office if they no longer reflect the views of the majority of the people.

WWW **New Rules Project**
An organization advocating local government solutions and "direct democracy," including the New England town meeting.
www.newrules.org

direct democracy
Governing system in which every person participates actively in every public decision, rather than delegating decision making to representatives.

representative democracy
Governing system in which public decision making is delegated to representatives of the people chosen by popular vote in free, open, and periodic elections.

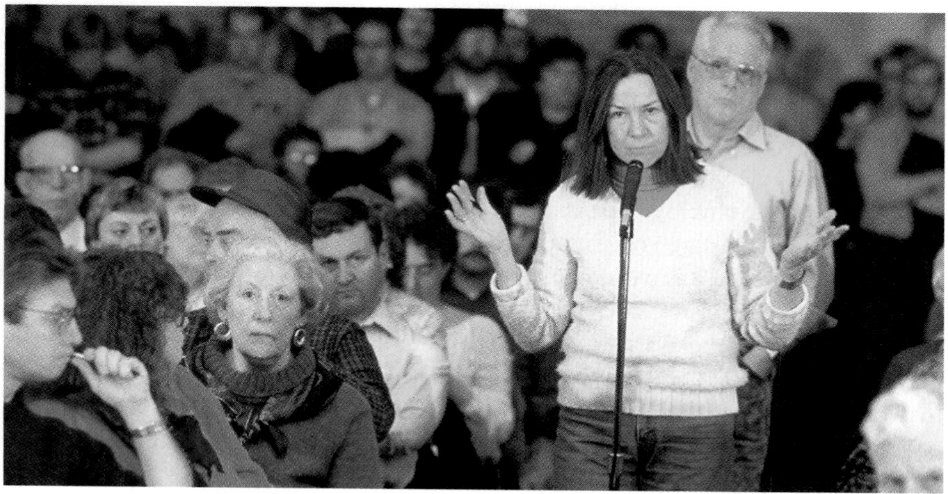

Direct democracy still lives in many New England towns, where citizens come together periodically to pass laws, elect officials, and make decisions about such matters as taxation and land use.

No government can claim to be a representative democracy, then, unless

1. Representatives are selected by vote of all the people.
2. Elections are open to competition.
3. Candidates and voters can freely express themselves.
4. Representatives are selected periodically.

So when we hear of "elections" in which only one party is permitted to run candidates, candidates are not free to express their views, or leaders are elected "for life," then we know that these governments are not really democracies, regardless of what they may call themselves.

Throughout this book, as we examine how well representative democracy works in the United States, we consider such issues as participation in elections—why some people vote and others do not—whether parties and candidates offer the voters real alternatives, whether modern political campaigning informs voters or only confuses them, and whether elected representatives are responsive to the wishes of voters. These are the kinds of issues that concern political science.

THINK AGAIN

Is the government run by a few big interests looking out for themselves?

Who Really Governs?

Democracy is an inspiring ideal. But is democratic government really possible? Is it possible for millions of people to govern themselves, with every voice having equal influence? Or will a small number of people inevitably acquire more power than others? To what extent is democracy attainable in *any* society, and how democratic is the American political system? That is, who really governs?

The Elitist Perspective "Government is always government by the few, whether in the name of the few, the one, or the many."[8] This quotation from political scientists Harold Lasswell and Daniel Lerner expresses the basic idea of **elitism.** All societies, including democracies, divide themselves into the few who have power and the many who do not. In every society, there is a division of labor. Only a few people are directly involved in governing a nation; most people are content to let others undertake the tasks of government. The *elite* are the few who have power; the *masses* are the many who do not. This theory holds that an elite is inevitable in any social organization. We cannot form a club, a church, a business, or a government without selecting some people to provide leadership. And leaders will always have a perspective on the organization different from that of its members.

In any large, complex society, then, whether or not it is a democracy, decisions are made by tiny minorities. Out of more than 281 million Americans, only a few thousand individuals at most participate directly in decisions about war and peace, wages and prices, employment and production, law and justice, taxes and benefits, health and welfare. Even the people themselves have doubts about the accuracy of Lincoln's words, "a government of, by and for the people." (See *What Do You Think?* "Is the American Government 'Of, By and For the People'?")

elitism Theory that all societies, even democracies, are divided into the few who govern and the many who do not.

Elitism does *not* mean that leaders always exploit or oppress members. On the contrary, elites may be very concerned for the welfare of the masses. Elite status may be open to ambitious, talented, or educated individuals from the masses or may be closed to all except the wealthy. Elites may be very responsive to public opinion, or they may ignore the usually apathetic and ill-informed masses. But whether elites are self-seeking or public spirited, open or closed, responsive or unresponsive, it is they and not the masses who actually make the decisions.

Contemporary elite theory argues that power in America is concentrated in a small *institutional* elite. Sociologist C. Wright Mills popularized the term *power elite* in arguing that leaders of corporations, the military establishment, and the national government come together at the top of a giant pyramid of power.[9] Other social scientists have found that more than half of the nation's total assets are concentrated in the 100 largest corporations and 50 largest banks; that the officers and directors of these corporations and banks interact frequently with leaders of government, the mass media, foundations, and universities, and that these leaders are drawn disproportionately from wealthy, educated, upper-class, white, male, Anglo-Saxon Protestant groups in American society.[10]

C. Wright Mills Web site devoted to Mills, with photos, books, and writings. *www.cwrightmills.org*

Most people do not regularly concern themselves with decision making in Washington. They are more concerned with their jobs, family, sports, and recreation than they are with politics. They are not well informed about tax laws, foreign policy, or even who represents them in Congress. Since the "masses" are largely apathetic and ill informed about policy questions, their views are likely to be influenced more by what they see and hear on television than by their own experience. Most communication flows downward from elites to masses. Elitism argues that the masses have at best only an indirect influence on the decisions of elites.

Opinion polls indicate that many Americans agree with the elitist contention that government is run by "a few big interests" (see Figure 1.2).

The Pluralist Perspective No one seriously argues that all Americans participate in *all* of the decisions that shape their lives; that majority preferences *always* prevail; that the values of life, liberty, and property are *never* sacrificed; or that every American enjoys equality of opportunity. Nevertheless, most American political scientists argue that the American system of government, which they describe as "pluralist," is the best possible approximation of the democratic ideal in a large, complex society. Pluralism is designed to make the theory of democracy "more realistic."[11]

pluralism Theory that democracy can be achieved through competition among multiple organized groups and that individuals can participate in politics through group memberships and elections.

Pluralism is the belief that democracy can be achieved in a large, complex society by competition, bargaining, and compromise among organized groups and

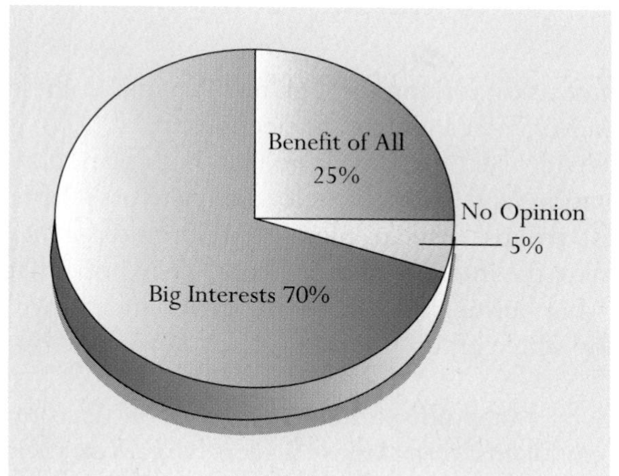

FIGURE 1.2 Public Opinion about Who Runs the Country

Would you say the government is pretty much run by a few big interests looking out for themselves or that it is run for the benefit of all the people?

Source: The Gallup Poll, July 6–9, 2000. Copyright © 1996–2004 by The Gallup Organization.

UP CLOSE

Terrorism's Threat to Democracy

The horrifying images of "9/11" will not be easily forgotten—America's tallest skyscrapers exploding in flames and crumbling to earth—images projected over and over again on the nation's television screens. Commercial airliners, loaded with fuel and passengers, flown at high speeds directly into the symbols of America's financial and military power—the World Trade Center in New York and the Pentagon in Washington. Within minutes, thousands of lives are lost on American soil—more than at any time since the Civil War. After September 11 America found itself in a new war, a war against worldwide networks of terrorists.

The Goal of Terrorism Terrorism is violence directed against innocent civilians to advance political goals. As barbaric as terrorism appears to civilized peoples, it is not without a rationale. Terrorists are not "crazies." Their first goal is to announce in the most dramatic fashion their own grievances, their commitment to violence, and their disregard for human life, often including their own. In its initial phase the success of a terrorist act is directly related to the publicity it receives. Terrorist groups jubilantly claim responsibility for their acts. The more horrendous, the more media coverage, the more damage, the more dead—all add to the success of the terrorists in attracting attention to themselves.

A prolonged campaign of terrorism is designed to inspire pervasive fear among people, to convince them that their government cannot protect them, and to undermine their confidence in their political system. If the government fails to suppress terrorism, people become ever more fearful, more willing to accept restrictions on liberties, and more open to the appeals of demagogues who promise to restore order to protect people at any cost. Or a weakened government may resort to "negotiations" with the leaders of terrorist groups, implicitly granting them legitimacy and providing them the opportunity to advance their goals.

America's Response But America's response to the terrorist attacks of September 11, 2001, was precisely the *opposite* of the intention of the terrorists. National pride, confidence in national leadership, and faith in human nature, all soared among the American people in the aftermath of the attack. Patriotism flourished. Flags flew from businesses, homes, and automobiles. The attack united the country in a way that no other event since the 1941 Japanese attack on Pearl Harbor had done. Trust in government rose to highs not seen since the 1960s. Popular support for military action was overwhelming.

Security vs. Liberty However, threats to national security have historically resulted in challenges to individual liberty. Abraham Lincoln suspended the *writ of habeas corpus* (the requirement that authorities bring defendants before a judge and show cause for their detention) during the Civil War. (Only after the war did the U.S. Supreme Court hold that he had no authority to suspend the writ.*)

*Ex parte Milligan (1866).

See Robert A. Pape, "The Strategic Logic of Suicide Terrorism," *American Political Science Review* 97 (August 2003): 343–361.

Democracy Net Democracy site of the League of Women Voters linking ZIP codes to your federal, state, and local representatives. ***www.dnet.org***

that individuals can participate in decision making through membership in these groups and by choosing among parties and candidates in elections.

Pluralists recognize that the individual acting alone is no match for giant government bureaucracies, big corporations and banks, the television networks, labor unions, or other powerful interest groups. Instead, pluralists rely on *competition* among these organizations to protect the interests of individuals. They hope that countervailing centers of power—big business, big labor, big government—will check one another and prevent any single group from abusing its power and oppressing individual Americans.

Individuals in a pluralist democracy may not participate directly in decision making, but they can join and support *interest groups* whose leaders bargain on their behalf in the political arena. People are more effective in organized groups—for

The horrifying images of "9/11" will not be easily forgotten—America's tallest skyscrapers exploding and crumbling to earth—images projected over and over again on the nation's television screens.

In February 1942, shortly after the Japanese attack on Pearl Harbor, President Franklin D. Roosevelt authorized the removal and internment of Japanese Americans living on the West Coast. The U.S. Supreme Court upheld this flagrant violation of the Constitution,[†] not until 1988 did the U.S. Congress vote reparations and make public apologies to the surviving victims.

New Restrictions on Americans The "9/11" terrorist attack on America inspired Congress and the president to enact and enforce greater restrictions on individual liberty than the nation had experienced since World War II. Congress passed the Patriot Act that, among other things, allows searches without notice to the suspect; grants "roving" wiretap warrants that allow government eavesdropping on any telephones used by suspects; allows the interception of e-mail; allows investigators to obtain information from creditcard companies, banks, libraries, and other businesses; authorizes the seizure of properties used to commit or facilitate terrorism; and allows the detention of noncitizens charged with terrorism. President George W. Bush created a new Department of Homeland Security reorganizing more than forty federal agencies that have a role in combating terrorism. All of these measures enjoyed widespread popular support.

Terrorism and Democracy Terrorism has brought mixed blessings to American democracy. It has succeeded in uniting Americans, inspiring patriotism, and increasing their trust in government. But it has also inspired a greater willingness to accept new restrictions on individual liberty. In the past, restrictions on individual liberty have been relaxed when the perceived crisis has subsided. How long will the "war on terrorism" last? Will Americans be asked to sacrifice additional liberties in this war? How far are Americans willing to go in sacrificing individual liberty to achieve national security?

[†]Korematsu p. U.S., 323 U.S. 214 (1944).

example, the Sierra Club for environmentalists, the American Civil Liberties Union (ACLU) for civil rights advocates, the National Association for the Advancement of Colored People (NAACP) and the Urban League for African Americans, the American Legion and Veterans of Foreign Wars for veterans, and the National Rifle Association (NRA) for opponents of gun control.

According to the pluralist view, the Democratic and Republican parties are really coalitions of groups: the national Democratic Party is a coalition of union members, big-city residents, blacks, Catholics, Jews, and, until recently, southerners; the national Republican Party is a coalition of business and professional people, suburbanites, farmers, and white Protestants. When voters choose candidates and parties, they are helping to determine which interest groups will enjoy a better reception in government.

The Terrorism Research Center

News and information on terrorist attacks around the world and list of terrorist organizations.

www.terrorism.com

WHAT DO YOU THINK?

Is the American Government "Of, By and For the People"?

Do you think of the government in Washington as OUR government or as THE government? If a democratic government is truly "of, by and for the people," we would expect that the people would think of it as their own. But national opinion polls indicate the majority of Americans do *not* believe that the government belongs to them:

Q. When you think and talk about government, do you tend to think of it more as THE government or as OUR government?

THE government	55%
OUR government	42
Not sure	3

Indeed, a majority do *not* believe that we have a government today that is "of, by and for the people."

Q. One goal that Americans have traditionally considered important is to have a government that is "of, by and for the people"—meaning that it involves people and represents them. In your opinion, do we have a government today that is "of, by and for the people"?

Yes	39%
No	54
Not sure	7

Source: Council on Excellence in Government, as reported in *The Polling Report*, June, 1999.

Pluralists contend that there are multiple leadership groups in society (hence the term *pluralism*). They contend that power is widely dispersed among these groups; that no one group, not even the wealthy upper class, dominates decision making; and that groups that are influential in one area of decision making are not necessarily the same groups that are influential in other areas of decision making. Different groups of leaders make decisions in different issue areas.

Pluralism recognizes that public policy does not always coincide with majority preferences. Instead, public policy is the "equilibrium" reached in the conflict among group interests. It is the balance of competing interest groups, and therefore, say the pluralists, it is a reasonable approximation of society's preferences.

Democracy in America

Is democracy alive and well in America today? Elitism raises serious questions about the possibility of achieving true democracy in any large, complex society. Pluralism is more comforting; it offers a way of reaffirming democratic values and providing some practical solutions to the problem of individual participation in a modern society.

There is no doubt about the strength of democratic ideals in American society. These ideals—individual dignity, equality, popular participation in government, and majority rule—are the standards by which we judge the performance of the American political system. But we are still faced with the task of describing the reality of American politics.

This book explores who gets what, when, and how in the American political system; who participates in politics; what policies are decided upon; and when and how these decisions are made. In so doing, it raises many controversial questions about the realities of democracy, elitism, and pluralism in American life. But this book does not supply the answers; as a responsible citizen, you have to provide your own answers. At the completion of your studies, you will have to decide for yourself whether the American political system is truly democratic. Your studies will help inform your judgment, but, in the end, you yourself must make that judgment. That is the burden of freedom.

SUMMARY NOTES

- Politics is deciding who gets what, when, and how. It occurs in many different settings, but political science focuses on politics in government.
- Political science focuses on three central questions:
  Who governs?
  For what ends?
  By what means?
- Government is distinguished from other social organizations in that it
  Extends to the whole society
  Can legitimately use force
- The purposes of government are to
  Maintain order in society
  Provide for national defense
  Provide "public goods"
  Regulate society
  Transfer income
  Protect individual liberty
- The ideals of democracy include
  Recognition of individual dignity and personal freedom
  Equality before the law
  Widespread participation in decision making
  Majority rule, with one person equaling one vote
- The principles of democracy pose a paradox: How can we resolve conflicts between our belief in majority rule and our belief in individual freedom?
- Limited government places individual liberty beyond the reach of majorities. Constitutions are the principal means of limiting government power.
- Direct democracy, in which everyone participates in every public decision, is very rare. Representative democracy means that public decisions are made by representatives elected by the people, in elections held periodically and open to competition, in which candidates and voters freely express themselves.
- Threats to national security have historically reduced the scope of individual liberty in our nation. The terrorist attack on America of September 11, 2001, inspired greater unity, patriotism, and trust in government among the people. But it also brought greater restrictions on individual liberty.
- Who really governs? The elitist perspective on American democracy focuses on the small number of leaders who actually decide national issues, compared to the mass of citizens who are apathetic and ill informed about politics. A pluralist perspective focuses on competition among organized groups in society, with individuals participating through group membership and voting for parties and candidates in elections.
- How democratic is American government today? Democratic ideals are widely shared in our society. But you must make your own informed judgment about the realities of American politics.

KEY TERMS

politics 4
political science 4
government 4
legitimacy 5
social contract 7
public goods 8
free market 9
gross domestic product (GDP) 9
externalities 9
income transfers 9
democracy 9

democratic ideals 10
paradox of democracy 13
limited government 14
totalitarianism 14
direct democracy 15
representative democracy 15
elitism 16
pluralism 17

SUGGESTED READINGS

Barker, Lucius J., Mack H. Jones, and Katherine Tate. *African-Americans and the American Political System*. Upper Saddle River, NJ.: Prentice Hall, 1999. A dynamic analysis of how African Americans fare within the prevailing theoretical, structural, and functioning patterns of the American political system.

Cronin, Thomas J. *Direct Democracy*. Cambridge, Mass.: Harvard University Press, 1989. A thoughtful discussion of direct versus representative democracy, as well as a review of initiative, referendum, and recall devices.

Dahl, Robert A. *Democracy and Its Critics*. New Haven, Conn.: Yale University Press, 1989. A defense of modern democracy from the pluralist perspective.

Dye, Thomas R., and Harmon Zeigler. *The Irony of Democracy*. 12th ed. New York: Wadsworth, 2003. An interpretation of American politics from the elitist perspective.

Fukuyama, Francis. *Trust*. New York: Free Press, 1995. Argues that the breakdown of trust in America—not only in the government but at a person-to-person level—is burdening the nation with formal rules and regulations, lengthy contracts, bureaucracy, lawyers, and lawsuits.

Lasswell, Harold. Politics: *Who Gets What, When, and How*. New York: McGraw-Hill, 1936. Classic description of the nature of politics and the study of political science by America's foremost political scientist of the twentieth century.

Mills, C. Wright. *The Power Elite*. New York: Oxford University Press, 1956. Classic Marxist critique of elitism in American society, setting forth the argument that "corporate chieftains," "military warlords," and a "political directorate" come together to form the nation's power elite.

Neiman, Max. *Defending Government: Why Big Government Works*. Upper Saddle River, N.J.: Prentice Hall, 2000. A spirited defense of how big government can improve lives of people.

Page, Benjamin I., and Robert Y. Shapiro. *The Rational Public*. Chicago: University of Chicago Press, 1992. An examination of fifty years of public opinion polls convinces these authors that American government is generally responsive to the views of the majority.

Putnam, Robert D. *Bowling Alone: The Collapse and Revival of the American Community*. New York: Simon & Schuster, 2001. An argument that Americans are increasingly disconnected from one another, harming the health of democracy.

MAKE IT REAL

THE MAP OF FREEDOM

Freedom and democracy are not absolutes, they can develop in stages. No country allows its citizens complete freedom and no country can completely eliminate it. The map in this simulation describes countries as free, partly free, or not free, based on the criteria of political rights (right to vote, free and fair elections, participation of minorities, etc.). You will be asked to finish the map by describing the countries as "free," "partly free," or "not free."

CHAPTER 2

POLITICAL CULTURE: IDEAS IN CONFLICT

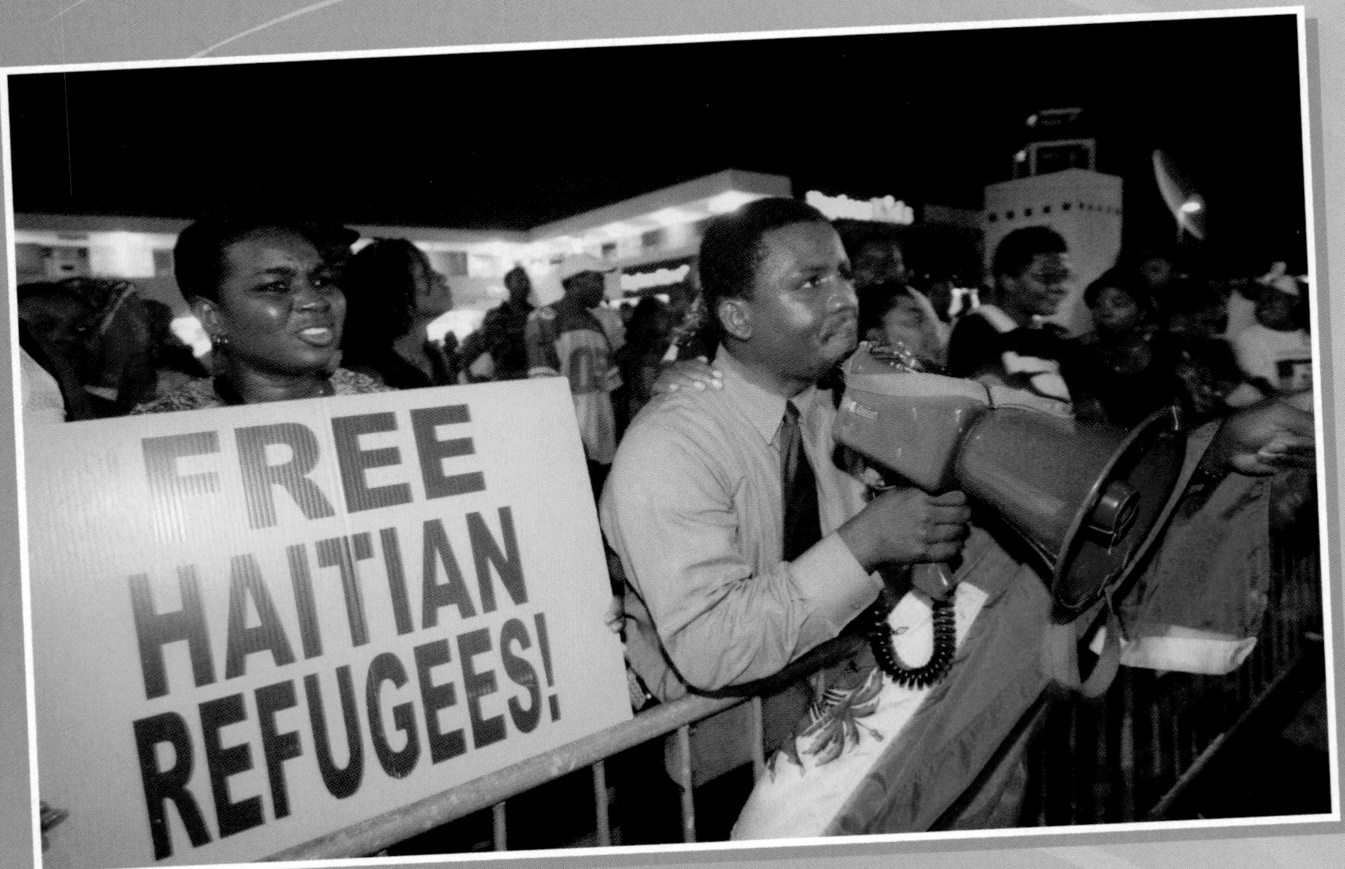

CHAPTER OUTLINE

Political Culture
Individual Liberty
Dilemmas of Equality
Inequality of Income and Wealth
Social Mobility
Race, Ethnicity, and Immigration
Ideologies: Liberalism and Conservatism
Dissent in the United States

THINK ABOUT POLITICS

1 Do you consider yourself politically conservative, moderate, or liberal?
Conservative ●
Moderate ●
Liberal ●

2 Are income differences in America widening?
Yes ● No ●

3 Is it the government's responsibility to reduce income differences between people?
Yes ● No ●

4 If incomes were made more equal, would people still be motivated to work hard?
Yes ● No ●

5 Do Americans today still have the opportunity to significantly improve their condition in life?
Yes ● No ●

6 Should the U.S. government curtail immigration to America?
Yes ● No ●

7 Should illegal immigrants be denied welfare benefits?
Yes ● No ●

8 Is American culture racist and sexist?
Yes ● No ●

Ask yourself if your answers to these questions are widely shared by most citizens of the United States. Your answers probably reflect not only your own beliefs and values but also those of the political culture to which you belong.

Political Culture

Ideas have power. We are all influenced by ideas—beliefs, values, symbols—more than we realize. Ideas provide us with rationalizations for ways of life, with guides for determining right and wrong, and with emotional impulses to action. Political institutions are shaped by ideas, and political leaders are constrained by them.

The term **political culture** refers to widely shared ideas about who should govern, for what ends, and by what means. **Values** are shared ideas about what is good and desirable. Values provide standards for judging what is right or wrong. **Beliefs** are shared ideas about what is true. Values and beliefs are often related. For example, if we believe that human beings are endowed by God with rights to life, liberty, and property, then we will value the protection of these rights. Thus beliefs can justify values.

Cultural descriptions are generalizations about the values and beliefs of many people in society, but these generalizations do not apply to everyone. Important variations in values and beliefs may exist within a society, these variations are frequently referred to as **subcultures** and may arise from such diverse bases as religion, racial or ethnic identity, or political group membership.

Contradictions between Values and Conditions Agreement over values in a political culture is no guarantee that there will not be contradictions between these values and actual conditions. People both in and out of politics frequently act contrary to their professed values. No doubt the most grievous contradiction between professed national beliefs and actual conditions in America is found in the long history of slavery, segregation, and racial discrimination. The contradiction between the words of the Declaration of Independence that "all men are created equal" and the practices of slavery and segregation became the "American dilemma."[1] But this contradiction does not mean that professed values are worthless; the very existence of the gap between values and behavior becomes a motivation for change. The history of the civil rights movement might be viewed as an effort to "bear witness" to the contradiction between the belief in equality and the existence of segregation and discrimination.[2] Whatever the obstacles to racial equality in America, these obstacles would be even greater if the nation's political culture did *not* include a professed belief in equality.

Inconsistent Applications A political culture does not mean that shared principles are always applied in every circumstance. For example, people may truly believe in the principle of "free speech for all, no matter what their views might be," and yet when asked whether racists should be allowed to speak on a college campus, many people will say no. Thus general agreement with abstract principles of freedom of speech, freedom of the press, and academic freedom does not always ensure their application to specific individuals or groups.[3] Americans are frequently willing to restrict the freedoms of particularly obnoxious groups. A generation ago it was alleged communists and atheists whose freedoms were questioned. Over time these groups have become less threatening, but today people are still willing to restrict the liberties of racists, pro-abortion or anti-abortion groups, "skinheads," and neo-Nazis, and people who resemble terrorists.

Conflict The idea of political culture does not mean an absence of conflict over values and beliefs. Indeed, much of politics involves conflict over very fundamental values. The American nation has experienced a bloody civil war, political assassinations, rioting and burning of cities, the forced resignation of a president, and other direct challenges to its political foundations. Indeed, much of this book deals with serious political conflict. Yet Americans do share many common ways of thinking about politics.

political culture Widely shared views about who should govern, for what ends, and by what means.

values Shared ideas about what is good and desirable.

beliefs Shared ideas about what is true.

subcultures Variations on the prevailing values and beliefs in a society.

Philosophy Pages History of Western philosophy and discussion of major democratic philosophers, including John Locke, Jean Jacques Rousseau, and Thomas Hobbes, among others. *www.philosophypages.com*

Individual Liberty

No political value has been more widely held in the United States than individual liberty. The very beginnings of our history as a nation were shaped by **classical liberalism**, which asserts the worth and dignity of the individual. This political philosophy emphasizes the rational ability of human beings to determine their own destinies, and it rejects ideas, practices, and institutions that submerge individuals into a larger whole and thus deprive them of their dignity. The only restriction on the individual is not to interfere with the liberties of others.

Political Liberty Classical liberalism grew out of the eighteenth-century Enlightenment, the Age of Reason in which great philosophers such as Voltaire, John Locke, Jean Jacques Rousseau, Adam Smith, and Thomas Jefferson affirmed their faith in reason, virtue, and common sense. Classical liberalism originated as an attack on the hereditary prerogatives and distinctions of a feudal society, the monarchy, the privileged aristocracy, and the state-established church.

Classical liberalism motivated America's Founders to declare their independence from England, to write the U.S. Constitution, and to establish the Republic. It rationalized their actions and provided ideological legitimacy for the new nation. The founders adopted the language of John Locke, who argued that a natural law, or moral principle, guaranteed every person "certain inalienable Rights," among them "Life, Liberty, and Property," and that human beings form a social contract with one another to establish a government to help protect their rights. Implicit in the social contract and the liberal notion of freedom is the belief that governmental activity and restrictions on the individual should be kept to a minimum.

classical liberalism Political philosophy asserting the worth and dignity of the individual and emphasizing the rational ability of human beings to determine their own destinies.

capitalism Economic system asserting the individual's right to own private property and to buy, sell, rent, and trade that property in a free market.

Economic Freedom Classical liberalism as a political idea is closely related to capitalism as an *economic* idea. **Capitalism** asserts the individual's right to own private property and to buy, sell, rent, and trade that property in a free market. The

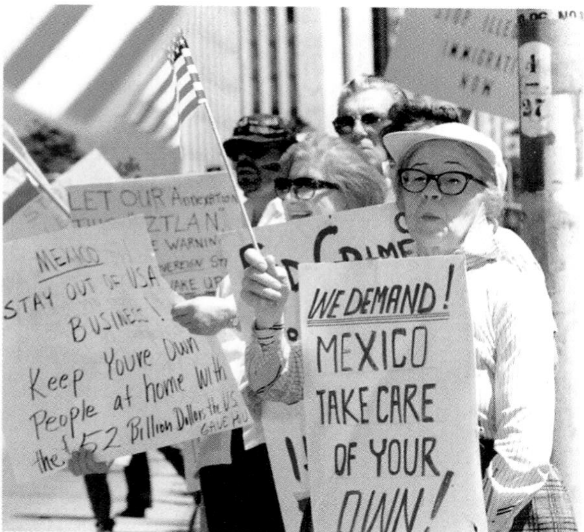

Proposition 187, a ballot initiative in California in 1994 denying state services to illegal immigrants, exposed a clash of cultures in Los Angeles.

economic version of freedom is the freedom to make contracts, to bargain for one's services, to move from job to job, to join labor unions, to start one's own business. Capitalism stresses individual rationality in economic matters—freedom of choice in working, producing, buying, and selling—and limited governmental intervention in economic affairs. Classical liberalism emphasizes individual rationality in voter choice—freedom of speech, press, and political activity—and limitations on governmental power over individual liberty. In classical liberal politics, individuals are free to speak out, to form political parties, and to vote as they please—to pursue their political interests as they think best. In classical liberal economics, individuals are free to find work, to start businesses, and to spend their money as they please—to pursue their economic interests as they think best. The role of government is restricted to protecting private property, enforcing contracts, and performing only those functions and services that cannot be performed by the private market.

The value of liberty in these political and economic spheres has been paramount throughout our history. Only equality competes with liberty as the most honored value in the American political culture.

 **Heritage Foundation**

This think tank site includes a ranking of over 150 nations on an "Index of Economic Freedom." The U.S. ranks sixth; Hong Kong ranks first.
www.heritage.org

Dilemmas of Equality

Since the bold assertion of the Declaration of Independence that "all men are created equal," Americans have generally believed that no person has greater worth than any other person. The principle of equal worth and dignity was a radical idea in 1776, when much of the world was dominated by hereditary monarchies, titled nobilities, and rigid caste and class systems. Belief in equality drove the expansion of voting rights in the early 1800s and ultimately destroyed the institution of slavery. Abraham Lincoln understood that equality was not so much a description of reality as an ideal to be aspired to: "a standard maxim for a free society which should be familiar to all, and revered by all; constantly looked to, constantly labored for, and even though never perfectly attained, constantly approximated and thereby augmenting the happiness and value of life to all people of all colors everywhere."[4] The millions who immigrated to the United States viewed this country as a land not only of opportunity but of *equal* opportunity, where everyone, regardless of birth, could rise in wealth and status based on hard work, natural talents, and perhaps good luck.

Today, most Americans agree that no one is intrinsically "better" than anyone else. This belief in equality, then, is fundamental to Americans, but a closer examination shows that throughout our history it has been tested, as beliefs and values so often are, by political realities.

Political Equality The nation's Founders shared the belief that the law should apply equally to all—that birth, status, or wealth do not justify differential application of the laws. But *legal equality* did not necessarily mean **political equality**, at least not in 1787, when the U.S. Constitution was written. The Constitution left the issue of voter qualifications to the states to decide for themselves. At that time, all states imposed either property or taxpayer qualifications for voting. Neither women nor slaves could vote anywhere. The expansion of voting rights to universal suffrage required many bitter battles over the course of two centuries. The long history of the struggle over voting rights illustrates the contradictions between values and practices (see the section "Securing the Right to Vote" in Chapter 5). Yet in the absence of the *value* of equality, voting rights might have remained restricted.

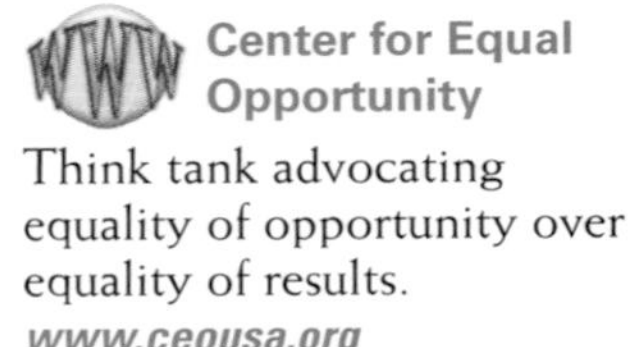

Center for Equal Opportunity
Think tank advocating equality of opportunity over equality of results.
www.ceousa.org

Equality of Opportunity The American ideal of equality extends to **equality of opportunity**—the elimination of artificial barriers to success in life. The term *equality of opportunity* refers to the ability to make of oneself what one can, to develop one's talents and abilities, and to be rewarded for one's work, initiative, and achievement. Equality of opportunity means that everyone comes to the same starting line in life, with the same chance of success, and that whatever differences develop over time do so as a result of abilities, talents, initiative, hard work, and perhaps good luck.

Americans do not generally resent the fact that physicians, engineers, airline pilots, and others who have spent time and energy acquiring particular skills make more money than those whose jobs require fewer skills and less training. Neither do most Americans resent the fact that people who risk their own time and money to build a business, bring new or better products to market, and create jobs for others make more money than their employees. Nor do many Americans begrudge multimillion-dollar incomes to sports figures, rock stars, and movie stars whose talents entertain the public. And few Americans object when someone wins a million-dollar lottery, as long as everyone who entered the lottery had an equal chance at winning. Americans are generally willing to have government act to ensure equality of opportunity—to ensure that everyone has an equal chance at getting an education, landing a job, and buying a home, and that no barriers of race, sex, religion, or ethnicity bar individual advancement. Differences arise over whether special efforts such as *affirmative action* should be undertaken to overcome the effects of past discriminatory barriers (see the section "Affirmative Action in the Courts" in Chapter 15). But the ideal of equality of opportunity is widely shared.

political equality Belief that the law should apply equally to all and that every person's vote counts equally.

equality of opportunity Elimination of artificial barriers to success in life and the opportunity for everyone to strive for success.

equality of results Equal sharing of income and material goods regardless of one's efforts in life.

Equality of Results **Equality of results** refers to the equal sharing of income and material rewards. Equality of results means that everyone starts *and finishes* the race together, regardless of ability, talent, initiative, or work. Those who argue on behalf of this notion of equality say that if individuals are truly equal, then everyone should enjoy generally equal conditions in life. According to this belief, we should appreciate an individual's skills, work, knowledge, and contributions to society without creating inequalities of wealth and income. Government should act to *transfer* wealth and income from the rich to the poor to increase the total happiness of all members of society.

But equality of results, or absolute equality, is *not* a widely shared value in the United States. This notion of equality was referred to as "leveling" by Thomas Jefferson and generally has been denounced by the nation's political leadership—and by most Americans—then and now:

> To take from one, because it is thought his own industry and that of his fathers has acquired too much, in order to spare to others who have not exercised equal industry and skill, is to violate arbitrarily . . . the guarantee to everyone the free exercise of his industry and the fruits acquired by it.[5]

Monticello Biography, letters, and a "Day in the Life" of Thomas Jefferson. *www.monticello.org*

The taking of private property from those who acquired it legitimately, for no other reason than to equalize wealth or income, is widely viewed as morally wrong. Moreover, many people believe that society generally would suffer if incomes were equalized. Absolute equality, in this view, would remove incentives for people to work, save, or produce. Everyone would slack off, production would decline, goods would be in short supply, and everyone would end up poorer than ever. So some inequality may be essential for the well-being of society.

Thus Americans believe strongly in equality of opportunity but not necessarily equality of results (see *What Do You Think?* "Beliefs About Fairness"). Americans seek fairness rather than equality of wealth and income.

Fairness Americans value "fairness" even though they do not always agree on what is fair. Most Americans support a "floor" on income and material well-being—a level that no one, regardless of his or her condition, should be permitted to fall below—even though they differ over how high that floor should be. Indeed, the belief in a floor is consistent with the belief in equality of opportunity; extreme poverty would deny people, especially children, the opportunity to compete in life.[6] But very few Americans want to place a "ceiling" on income or wealth. This unwillingness to limit top income extends to nearly all groups in the United States, the poor as well as the rich. Generally, Americans want people who cannot provide for themselves to be well cared for, especially children, the elderly, the ill, and the disabled. They are often willing to "soak the rich" when searching for new tax sources, believing that the rich can easily afford to bear the burdens of government. But, unlike citizens in other Western democracies, Americans generally do *not* believe that government should equalize incomes.

Equality in Politics *versus* Economics Americans make a clear distinction between the *private economic* sphere of life and the *public political* sphere.[7] In the private economic sphere, they value the principle of "earned deserts," meaning that individuals are entitled to what they achieve through hard work, skill, talent, risk, and even good luck. They are willing to tolerate inequalities of result in economics. Self-interested behavior in the marketplace is seen as appropriate and even beneficial, if properly constrained by rules that apply equally to everyone. But in the public political sphere, Americans value absolute equality—one person, one vote. They condemn disparities of power and influence among individuals. Self-interested behavior in politics is seen as corrupt.

WHAT DO YOU THINK?

Beliefs about Fairness

Americans believe that there is "plenty of opportunity" to get ahead and that the economic system of the United States is "basically fair." They do NOT believe that everyone's income should be made more equal. And they believe that "hard-working initiative" and "getting the right education or training" is the key to success in life. However, a substantial percentage of Americans acknowledge that "parents and family" and "connections" also play an important role in success.

Q. Some people say there's not much opportunity in America today—that the average person doesn't have much chance to really get ahead. Others say there's plenty of opportunity and anyone who work hard can go as far as they want. How you feel about this?

Plenty of opportunity	81%
Not much opportunity	17
Don't know	2

Q. Do you think the economic system in United States is basically fair, since all Americans have an equal opportunity to succeed, or basically unfair, since all Americans do not have an opportunity to succeed?

Basically fair	68%
Basically unfair	29
No opinion	3

Q. Do you believe that incomes should be more equal because everybody's contribution to society is equally important?

Yes	37%
No	61
No opinion	2

Q. I am going to read several reasons why some people get ahead and succeed in life and others do not. Please tell me how important it is as a reason for a person's success.

	Most or very important
Hard work and initiative	92%
Getting the right education or training	92
Parents and family	87
Willingness to take risks	69
Connections, knowing the right people	68
Ability or talent one is born with	60
Physical appearance, good looks	50
Good luck, in right place at right time	43
Money inherited from family	41
Gender (whether male or female)	33
Member of particular race/ethnic group	30

Source: James R. Kluegel and Eliot R. Smith, *Beliefs About Inequality* (New York: Aldine de Gruyter, 1986); Gallup Poll Special Report, "Have and Have-Nots: Perceptions of Fairness and Opportunity—1998," www.gallup.com

As long as the economic and political spheres of life are perceived as separate, then economic inequalities and political equalities can exist side by side in a society.

Inequality of Income and Wealth

THINK AGAIN

Are income differences in America widening?

Conflict in society is generated more often by inequalities among people than by hardship or deprivation. Material well-being and standards of living are usually expressed in aggregate measures for a whole society—for example, gross domestic product per capita, income per capita, average life expectancy, infant mortal-

COMPARED TO WHAT?

Income and Inequality

Capitalism has proven successful in creating wealth. The free market system has provided Americans with more purchasing power than any other people. ("Purchasing power parity" is a statistic used by international economists to adjust for the cost of living differences in measuring how much it costs to purchase a standard "basket" of goods and services.) However, relatively high incomes of average Americans exists side by side with relatively high inequality among Americans. The United States ranks well below many European countries in measures of income inequality. (The "Gini index" is a statistic used by economists to measure income equality/inequality.) But poverty and inequality exists side by side in most of the world's less-developed countries (not ranked below).

Rank by purchasing power	Rank by equality (Gini index)
1. **United States**	1. Denmark
2. Switzerland	2. Czech Republic
3. Norway	3. Japan
4. Belgium	4. Sweden
5. Denmark	5. Finland
6. Canada	6. Norway
7. Japan	7. Italy
8. Netherlands	8. Belgium
9. Ireland	9. Germany
10. Australia	10. Canada
11. Germany	11. South Korea
12. Finland	12. Poland
13. France	13. Spain
14. Sweden	14. Netherlands
15. United Kingdom	15. Taiwan
16. Italy	16. France
17. Taiwan	17. Greece
18. Israel	18. Switzerland
19. Spain	19. Portugal
20. South Korea	20. Israel
21. Portugal	21. Ireland
22. Greece	22. United Kingdom
23. Czech Republic	23. **United States**
24. Poland	24. Costa Rica
25. Mexico	25. Mexico

Source: Rank by purchasing power, *The Economist Pocket World in Figures*, 2003; rank by Gini index, Central Intelligence Agency, *The World Factbook*, 2003. Both sources rank many more nations.

ity rate. These measures of societal well-being are vitally important to a nation and its people, but *political* conflict is more likely to occur over the *distribution* of well-being *within* a society. Unequal distributions can generate conflict even in a very affluent society with high levels of income and a high standard of living (see *Compared to What?* "Income and Inequality").

Inequality of Income Let us examine inequality of income in the United States systematically. Figure 2.1 divides all American households into two groups—the lowest one-fifth in income and the highest one-fifth—and shows the shares (percentage) of total household income received by each of these groups over the

Global Policy Forum Information on many global issues. Click to "social and economic policy" and then to "inequality of wealth and income" for cross-national data. *www.globalpolicy.org*

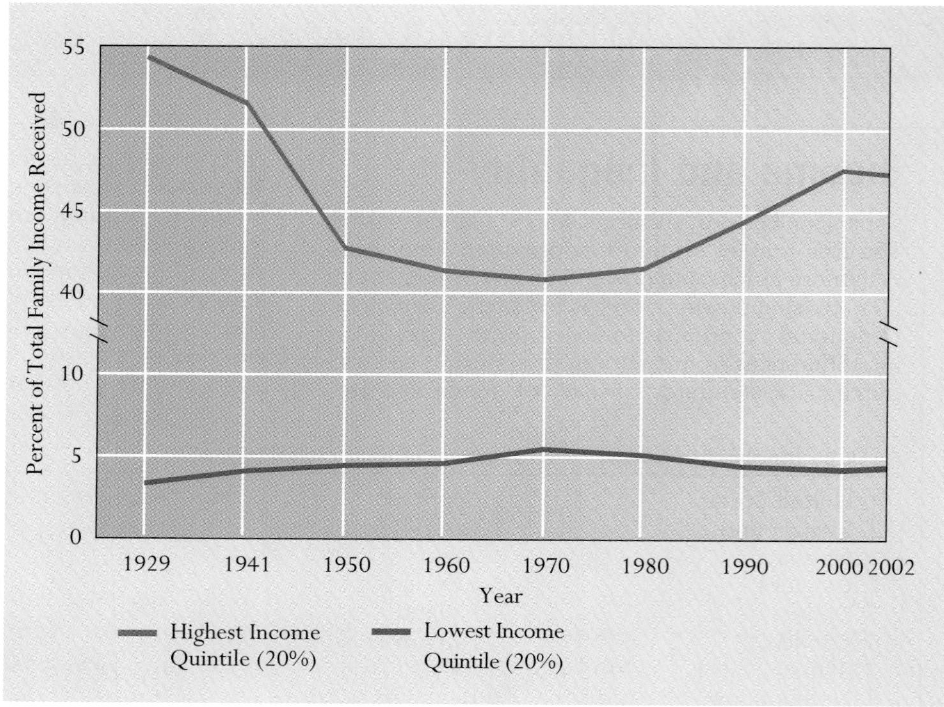

FIGURE 2.1 Shares of Total Household Income Received by Highest and Lowest Income Groups

years. (If perfect income equality existed, each fifth of American households would receive 20 percent of all personal income.) The poorest one-fifth received only 3.5 percent of all household income in 1929; today, this group does a little better, at 4.2 percent of household income. The highest one-fifth received 54.4 percent of all household income in 1929; today, its percentage stands at 46.2.

However, while income differences in the United States have declined over the long run, inequality has actually *increased* in recent years. The income of the poorest households declined from 5.4 to 4.3 percent of total income between 1970 and 2000; the income of the highest quintile rose from 40.9 to 47.4 percent of total income. This reversal of historical trends has generated both political rhetoric and serious scholarly inquiry about its causes.

Explaining Recent Increases in Income Inequality Recent increases in income inequality in the United States are a product of several social and economic trends: (1) the decline of the manufacturing sector of the economy (and the loss of many relatively high-paying blue-collar jobs) and the ascendancy of the communications, information, and service sectors of the economy (with a combination of high-paying and low-paying jobs); (2) the rise in the number of two-wage families, making single-wage, female-headed households relatively less affluent; (3) demographic trends, which include larger proportions of aged and larger proportions of female-headed families; and (4) global competition, which restrains wages in unskilled and semiskilled jobs while rewarding people in high-technology, high-productivity occupations.

Inequality of Wealth Inequalities of wealth in the United States are even greater than inequalities of income. *Wealth* is the total value of a family's assets—

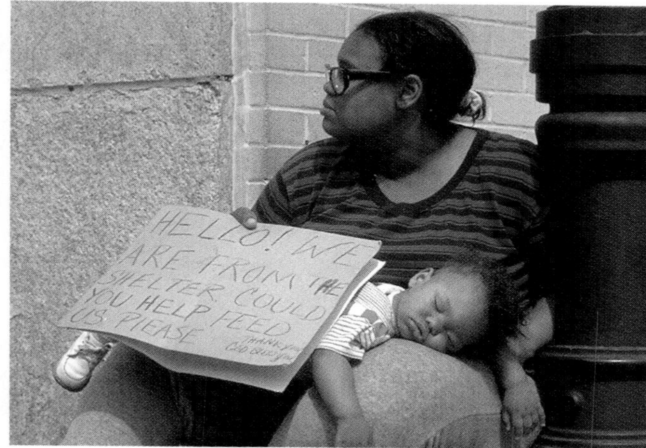

Income and wealth differences between the "haves" and the "have-nots" increased in America during the 1980s and the early 1990s.

bank accounts, stocks, bonds, mutual funds, business equity, houses, cars, and major appliances—minus outstanding debts, such as credit card balances, mortgages, and other loans. The top 1 percent of families in the United States owns over 40 percent of all family wealth. Inequality of wealth appeared to be diminishing until the mid-1970s, but in recent years it has surged sharply. Not surprisingly, age is the key determinant of family wealth; persons age fifty to sixty-five are by far the wealthiest, with persons over sixty-five close behind; young families generally have less than one-third of the assets of retirees.

Social Mobility

Political conflict over inequality might be greater in the United States if it were not for the prospect of **social mobility.** All societies are stratified, or layered, but societies differ greatly in the extent to which people move upward or downward in income and status over a lifetime or over generations. When there is social mobility, people have a good opportunity to get ahead if they study or work long and hard, save and invest wisely, or display initiative and enterprise in business affairs (however, see *A Conflicting View:* "Success Is Determined by the Bell Curve"). Fairly steep inequalities may be tolerated politically if people have a reasonable expectation of moving up over time, or at least of seeing their children do so.

How Much Mobility? The United States describes itself as the land of opportunity. The really important political question may be how much real opportunity exists for individual Americans to improve their conditions in life relative to others. The impression given by Figure 2.1 is one of a static distribution system, with families permanently placed in upper or lower fifths of income earners. But there is considerable evidence of both upward and downward movement by people among income groupings.[8] About a third of the families in the poorest one-fifth will move upward within a decade, and about a third of families in the richest one-fifth will fall out of this top category. However, there appears to have been some slowing of this mobility in recent years; one's chances of escaping the bottom have diminished somewhat. Thus the nation is currently experiencing not only an increase in inequality but also a slowing of social mobility.

social mobility Extent to which people move upward or downward in income and status over a lifetime or generations.

A CONFLICTING VIEW

Success Is Determined by the Bell Curve

Most Americans believe in social mobility—the idea that anyone who studies or works hard, saves and invests wisely, and makes good use of his or her talents, initiative, and enterprise can get ahead. But a controversial book, *The Bell Curve* by Richard J. Herrnstein and Charles Murray, sets forth the argument that general intelligence largely determines success in life. General intelligence, the authors contend, is distributed among the population in a bell-shaped curve, with most people clustered around the median, smaller numbers with higher intelligence (a "cognitive elite") at one end, and an unfortunate few trailing behind at the other end (see graph). Over time, say Herrnstein and Murray, intelligence is becoming ever more necessary for the performance of key jobs in the "information society." The result will be the continuing enhancement of the power and wealth of the cognitive elite and the further erosion of the lifestyle of the less intelligent.

Even more controversial than the authors' claim that general intelligence determines success is their contention that general intelligence is mostly (60 percent) genetic. Because intelligence is mostly inherited, programs to assist the underprivileged are useless or even counterproductive.

The cognitive elite, the authors predict, will continue to distance themselves from the masses in knowledge, skills, technical competence, income, and power while social problems will be concentrated among the "dullest." Indeed, they amass statistics showing that educational deficiencies, emotional problems, welfare reliance, early childbirth, and even criminal behavior are disproportionately concentrated in low-intelligence groups (see table).

But critics of *The Bell Curve* point out the lack of consensus on the role of genetics in intelligence. Indeed, recent research on infant development indicates that brain activity and the interconnections among brain cells are greatly affected by early human interaction. Infants in a stimulating environment—who are frequently coddled, spoken to, and sung to, for example—exhibit more brain activity than those with little environmental stimuli. Moreover, the implication of the bell curve thesis is that social classes and elitism are both natural and inevitable—and therefore that most efforts to ensure equality of opportunity are useless. Finally, a racial dimension Herrnstein and Murray add to their argument is unnecessary to their thesis. Although they claim that the differences between African Americans, whites, and Asians on IQ tests should not matter if every individual were judged separately on IQ, clearly their argument reinforces racial stereotypes.

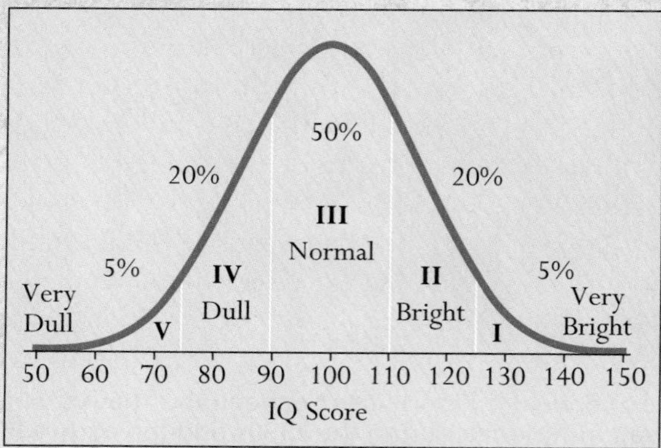

Population Distribution of IQ Scores

Source: Adapted with the permission of The Free Press, a division of Simon & Schuster Adult Publishing Group, from *The Bell Curve Intelligence and Class Structure in American Life* by Richard J. Herrnstein and Charles Murray. Copyright © 1994 by Richard J. Herrnstein and Charles Murray. All rights reserved.

	Cognitive Class	High School Dropout	Women on Welfare Assistance	Mean Age at First Childbearing	Convictions (young white males)
I	Very Bright	0%	0%	27.2 years	3%
II	Bright	0	2	25.6	7
III	Normal	6	8	23.4	15
IV	Dull	35	17	21.0	21
V	Very Dull	55	31	19.8	14

Source: Table adapted from various chapters in Herrnstein and Murray, *The Bell Curve* (1994).

Mobility, Class Conflict, and Class Consciousness Social mobility and the expectation of mobility, over a lifetime or over generations, may be the key to understanding why **class conflict**—conflict over wealth and power among social classes—is not as widespread or as intense in America as it is in many other nations. The *belief* in social mobility reduces the potential for class conflict because it diminishes **class consciousness**, the awareness of one's class position and the feeling of political solidarity with others in the same class in opposition to other classes. If class lines were impermeable and no one had any reasonable expectation of moving up or seeing his or her children move up, then class consciousness would rise and political conflict among classes would intensify.

Most Americans describe themselves as "middle class" rather than "rich" or "poor" or "lower class" or "upper class." There are no widely accepted income definitions of "middle class." The federal government officially defines a "poverty level" each year based on the annual cash income required to maintain a decent standard of living ($18,244 in 2002 for a family of four). Roughly 12 percent of the U.S. population lives with annual cash incomes below this poverty line. (For more discussion, see the section on "Poverty in the United States" in Chapter 17.) This is the only income group in which a majority of people describe themselves as poor.[9] Large majorities in every other income group identify themselves as middle class. So it is no surprise that presidents, politicians, and political parties regularly claim to be defenders of America's "middle class"!

Race, Ethnicity, and Immigration

America has always been an ethnically and racially pluralist society. All groups were expected to adopt the American political culture—including individual liberty, economic freedom, political equality, and equality of opportunity—and to learn American history and the English language. The nation's motto "E Pluribus Unum" (from many, one) is inscribed on its coins. Yet each of America's racial and ethnic groups brings its own traditions and values to the American political culture.

THINK AGAIN

Is American culture racist and sexist?

African Americans Historically African Americans constituted the nation's largest minority. Blacks composed about 20 percent of the population at the time the U.S. Constitution was written in 1787 (although as we shall see in Chapter 3 an enslaved African American was to be counted as only 3/5ths of a person in the original Constitution). Heavy European immigration in the late nineteenth century diluted the black population to roughly 12 percent of the nation's total. As late as 1900, most African Americans (90 percent) were still concentrated in the Southern states. But World Wars I and II provided job opportunities in large cities of the Northeast and Midwest. Blacks could not cast ballots in most Southern counties, but they could "vote with their feet." The migration of African Americans from the rural South to the urban North was one of the largest internal migrations in our history. Today only about half of the nation's African Americans live in the South—still more than in any other region but less of a concentration than earlier in American history. Today the nation's 36 million African Americans comprise 12.3 percent of the total population of the United States (see Figure 2.2). "African-American Politics in Historical Perspective" is discussed in Chapter 15, as well as the long struggle against slavery, segregation, and discrimination. This struggle has given African Americans a somewhat different perspective on American politics (see "Race and Opinion" in Chapter 5).

class conflict Conflict between upper and lower social classes over wealth and power.

class consciousness Awareness of one's class position and a feeling of political solidarity with others within the same class in opposition to other classes.

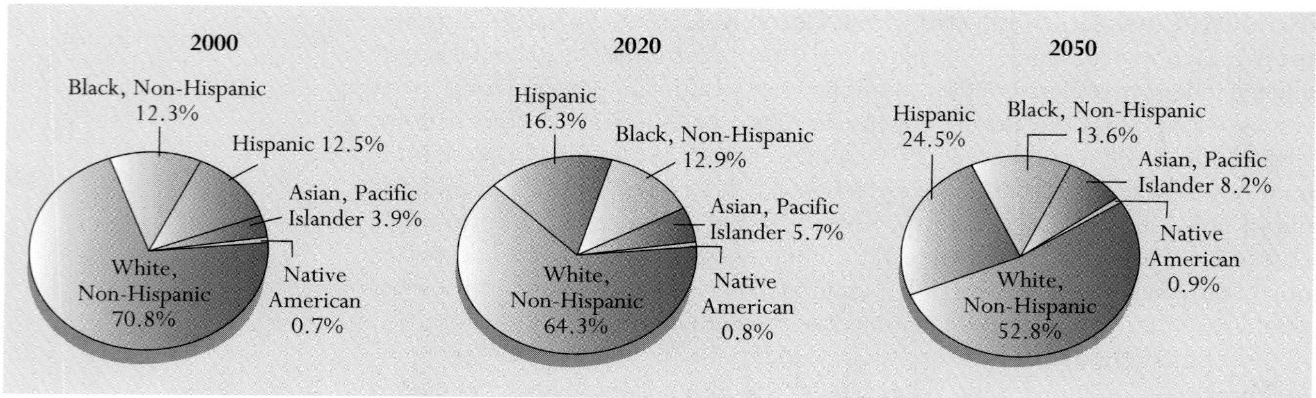

FIGURE 2.2 Racial and Ethnic Composition of the United States 2000, 2020, 2050

Source: U.S. Bureau of the Census (Middle Series).

Hispanic Americans Hispanics are now the nation's largest minority. The term *Hispanic* generally refers to persons of Spanish-speaking ancestry and culture; it includes Mexican Americans, Cuban Americans, and Puerto Ricans. Today there are an estimated 37 million Hispanics in the United States, or 12.5 percent of the total population. The largest subgroup is Mexican Americans, some of whom are descendants of citizens living in Mexican territory that was annexed to the United States in 1848, but most of whom have come to the United States in accelerating numbers in recent years. The largest Mexican American populations are found in Texas, Arizona, New Mexico, and California. The second-largest subgroup is Puerto Ricans, many of whom move back and forth from the island to the mainland, especially New York City. The third-largest subgroup is Cubans, most of whom have fled from Castro's Cuba. They live mainly in the Miami metropolitan area. The politics of each of these Hispanic groups differs somewhat (see "Hispanic Politics" in Chapter 15).

A Nation of Immigrants The United States is a nation of immigrants, from the first "boat people" (Pilgrims) to the latest Haitian refugees and Cuban *balseros* ("rafters"). Historically, most of the people who came to settle in this country did so because they believed their lives would be better here, and American political culture today has been greatly affected by the beliefs and values they brought with them. Americans are proud of their immigrant heritage and the freedom and opportunity the nation has extended to generations of "huddled masses yearning to be free"—words emblazoned on the Statue of Liberty in New York's harbor. Today about 8 percent of the U.S. population is foreign-born.

Immigration policy is a responsibility of the national government. It was not until 1882 that Congress passed the first legislation restricting entry into the United States of persons alleged to be "undesirable" and virtually all Asians. After World War I, Congress passed the comprehensive Immigration Act of 1921, which established maximum numbers of new immigrants each year and set a quota for immigrants for each foreign country at 3 percent of the number of that nation's foreign-born who were living in the United States in 1910, later reduced to 2 percent of the number living here in 1890. These restrictions reflected anti-immigration feelings that were generally directed at the large wave of Southern and

Immigration places responsibility on public schools to provide for the needs of children from different cultures. Here, Latino pupils assemble in Santa Ana, California.

Eastern European Catholic and Jewish immigrants (from Poland, Russia, Hungary, Italy, and Greece) entering the United States prior to World War I (see Figure 2.3). It was not until the Immigration and Naturalization Act of 1965 that national origin quotas were abolished, replaced by preference categories for close relatives of U.S. citizens, professionals, and skilled workers.

Immigration "reform" was the announced goal of Congress in the Immigration Reform and Control Act of 1986, also known as the Simpson-Mazzoli Act. It sought to control immigration by placing principal responsibility on employers; it set fines for knowingly hiring an illegal alien. However, it allowed employers to

The U.S. Coast Guard may intercept boats at sea and return their occupants to their country of origin. But once immigrants reach the U.S. shore, they are entitled to a hearing in any deportation proceedings.

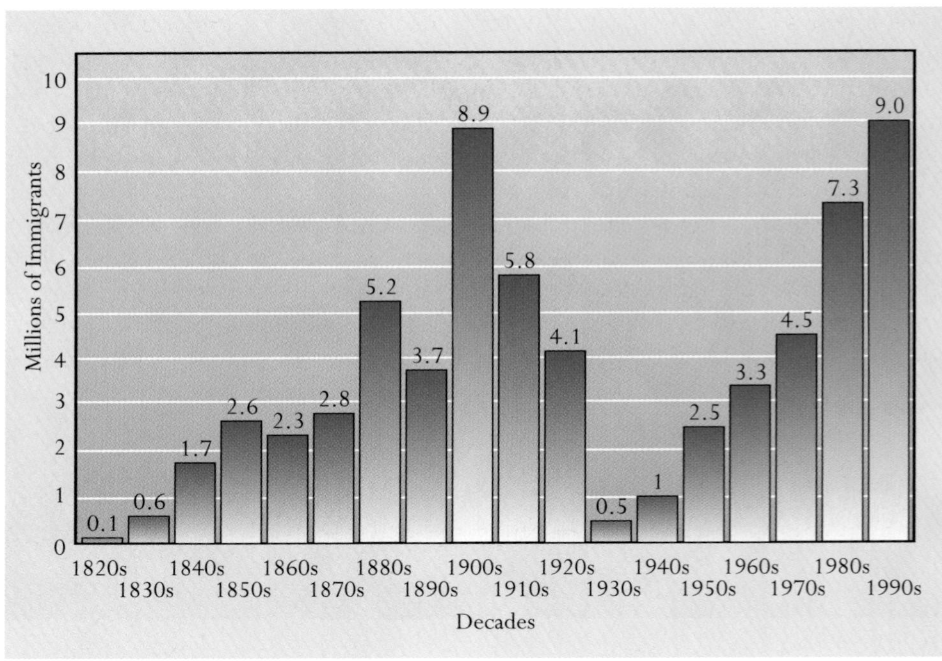

FIGURE 2.3 Legal Immigration to the United States by Decades

Source: Statistical Abstract of the United States, 2002, p. 10.

Center for Immigration Studies

Advocacy organization for strengthening enforcement of immigration law.
www.cis.org

accept many different forms of easily forged documentation and at the same time subjected them to penalties for discriminating against legal foreign-born residents. To win political support, the act granted amnesty to illegal aliens who had lived in the United States since 1982. But the act failed to reduce the flow of either legal or illegal immigrants.

Today, roughly a million people per year are admitted *legally* to the United States as "lawful permanent residents" (persons who have needed job skills or who have relatives who are U.S. citizens) or as "political refugees" (persons with "a well-founded fear of persecution" in their country of origin). In addition, each year more than 25 million people are awarded temporary visas to enter the United States for study, business, or pleasure.

Source: Steve Kelley © 2004.

Illegal Immigration The United States is a free and prosperous society with more than 5,000 miles of borders (2,000 with Mexico) and hundreds of international air- and seaports. In theory, a sovereign nation should be able to maintain secure borders, but in practice the United States has been unwilling and unable to do so. Estimates of illegal immigration vary widely, from the official U.S. Bureau of Immigration and Citizenship Services (formerly the Immigration and Naturalization Service, INS) estimate of 400,000 per year (about 45 percent of the legal immigration) to unofficial estimates ranging up to 3 million per year. The government estimates that about 4 million illegal immigrants currently reside in the United States; unofficial estimates range up to 10 million or more. Many illegal immigrants slip across U.S. borders or enter ports with false documentation; many more overstay tourist, worker, or student visas.[10]

As a free society, the United States is not prepared to undertake massive roundups and summary deportations of millions of illegal residents. The Fifth and Fourteenth Amendments to the U.S. Constitution require that every *person* (not just citizen) be afforded "due process of law." The government may turn back persons at the border or even hold them in detention camps. The Coast Guard may intercept boats at sea and return persons to their country of origin.[11] Aliens have no constitutional right to come to the United States. However, once in the United States, whether legally or illegally, every person is entitled to due process of law and equal protection of the laws. People are thus entitled to a fair hearing prior to any government attempt to deport them. Aliens are entitled to apply for asylum and present evidence at a hearing of their "well-founded fear of prosecution" if

WHAT DO YOU THINK?

Could You Pass the Citizenship Test?

To ensure that new citizens "understand" the history, principles, and form of government of the United States, the INS administers a citizenship test. Could you pass it today?

Answer correctly at least 18 of 30 questions to pass:

1. How many stars are there on our flag?
2. What do the stars on the flag mean?
3. What color are the stripes?
4. What do the stripes on the flag mean?
5. What is the date of Independence Day?
6. Independence from whom?
7. What do we call a change to the Constitution?
8. How many branches are there in our government?
9. How many full terms can a president serve?
10. Who nominates judges of the Supreme Court?
11. How many Supreme Court justices are there?
12. Who was the main writer of the Declaration of Independence?
13. What holiday was celebrated for the first time by American colonists?
14. Who wrote the Star-Spangled Banner?
15. What is the minimum voting age in the U.S.?
16. Who was president during the Civil War?
17. Which president is called the "Father of our Country"?
18. What is the 50th state of the Union?
19. What is the name of the ship that brought the Pilgrims to America?
20. Who has the power to declare war?
21. What were the 13 original states of the U.S. called?
22. In what year was the Constitution written?
23. What is the introduction to the Constitution called?
24. Which president was the first Commander-in-Chief of the U.S. Army and Navy?
25. In what month do we vote for the president?
26. How many times may a senator be re-elected?
27. Who signs bills into law?
28. Who elects the president of the U.S.?
29. How many states are there in the U.S.?
30. Who becomes president if both the president and V.P. die?

Answers: 1. 50; 2. One for each state in the Union, 3. Red and white, 4. They represent the 13 original states, 5. July 4, 6. England, 7. Amendments, 8. 3, 9. 2, 10. The president, 11. 9, 12. Thomas Jefferson, 13. Thanksgiving, 14. Francis Scott Key, 15. 18, 16. Abraham Lincoln; 17. George Washington, 18. Hawaii, 19. *The Mayflower,* 20. The Congress, 21. Colonies, 22. 1787, 23. The Preamble, 24. George Washington, 25. November, 26. There is no limit at the present time, 27. The president, 28. The Electoral College, 29. 50, 30. Speaker of the House of Representatives.

Source: Bureau of Citizenship and Immigration Services.

returned to their country. Experience has shown that the only way to reduce the flow of illegal immigration is to control it at the border, an expensive and difficult but not impossible task. Localized experiments in border enforcement have indicated that, with significant increases in personnel and technology, illegal immigration can be reduced by half or more.

Bureau of Citizenship and Immigration Services
Official site with information on immigration laws, citizenship requirements, etc. (previously INS). *www.immigration.gov*

Citizenship Persons born in the United States are U.S. citizens. People who have been lawfully admitted into the United States and granted permanent residence, and who have resided in the United States for at least five years and in their home state for the last six months, are eligible for naturalization as U.S. citizens. Federal district courts as well as offices of the INS may grant applications for citizenship. By law, the applicant must be over age eighteen, be able to read, write, and speak English, possess good moral character, and understand and demonstrate an attachment to the history, principles, and form of government of the United States (see *What Do You Think?* "Could You Pass the Citizenship Test?").

Ideologies: Liberalism and Conservatism

An **ideology** is a consistent and integrated system of ideas, values, and beliefs. A political ideology tells us who *should* get what, when, and how; that is, it tells us who *ought* to govern and what goals they *ought* to pursue. When we use ideological terms such as *liberalism* and *conservatism,* we imply reasonably integrated sets of values and beliefs. And when we pin ideological labels on people, we imply that those people are fairly consistent in the application of these values and beliefs in public affairs. In reality, neither political leaders nor citizens always display integrated or consistent opinions; many hold conservative views on some issues and liberal views on others.[12] Many Americans avoid ideological labeling, either by describing themselves as "moderate" or "middle-of-the-road" or by simply declining to place themselves on an ideological scale. But as Figure 2.4 shows, among those who choose an ideological label to describe their politics, conservatives consistently outnumber liberals. (See also *Across the USA:* "Liberalism and Conservatism" on page 42.)

THINK AGAIN
Do you consider yourself politically conservative, moderate, or liberal?

Despite inconsistencies in opinion and avoidance of labeling, ideology plays an important role in American politics. Political *elites*—elected and appointed officeholders; journalists, editors, and commentators; party officials and interest-group leaders; and others active in politics—are generally more consistent in their political views than nonelites and are more likely to use ideological terms in describing politics.[13]

American Conservative Union
Conservative news and views and rankings of Congress members on conservative index. *www.conservative.org*

ideology Consistent and integrated system of ideas, values, and beliefs.

conservatism Belief in the value of free markets, limited government, and individual self-reliance in economic affairs, combined with a belief in the value of tradition, law, and morality in social affairs.

Modern Conservatism: Individualism plus Traditional Values Modern **conservatism** combines a belief in free markets, limited government, and individual self-reliance in economic affairs with a belief in the value of tradition, law, and morality in social affairs. Conservatives wish to retain our historical commitments to individual freedom from governmental controls; reliance on individual initiative and effort for self-development; a free-enterprise economy with a minimum of governmental intervention; and rewards for initiative, skill, risk, and hard work. These views are consistent with the early classical liberalism of Locke, Jefferson, and the nation's Founders, discussed at the beginning of this chapter. The result is a confusion of ideological labels: modern conservatives claim to be the true inheritors of the (classical) liberal tradition.

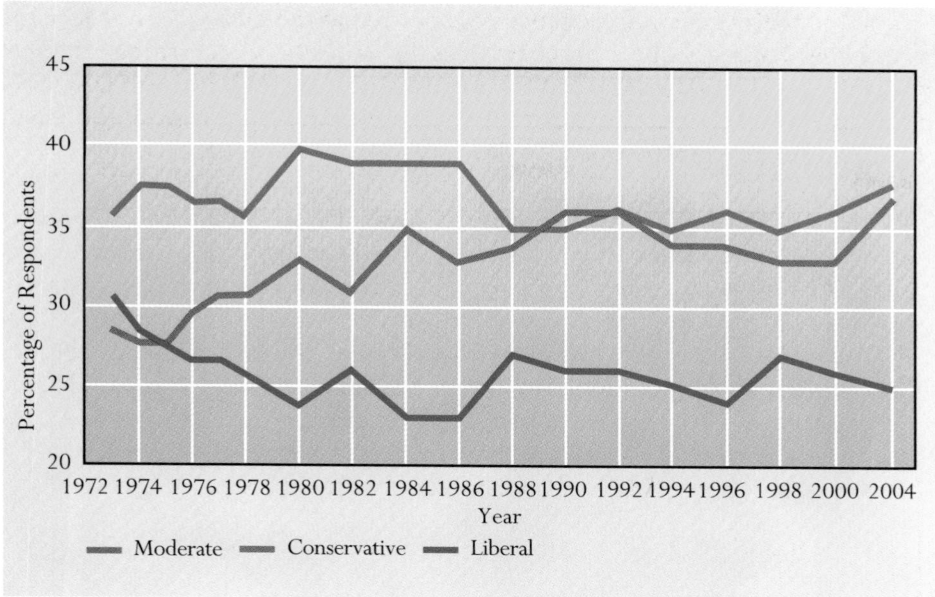

FIGURE 2.4 Americans: Liberal, Moderate, Conservative

Source: General Social Surveys, National Opinion Research Center, University of Chicago; Updated from *The American Enterprise,* January/February 2000, and Gallup, 2004.

Modern conservatism does indeed incorporate many classical liberal ideals, but it also has a distinct ideological tradition of its own. Conservatism is less optimistic about human nature. Traditionally, conservatives have recognized that human nature includes elements of irrationality, ignorance, hatred, and violence. Thus they have been more likely to place their faith in *law* and *traditional values* than in popular fads, trends, or emotions. To conservatives, the absence of law does not mean freedom but, rather, exposure to the tyranny of terrorism and violence. They believe that without the guidance of traditional values, people would soon come to grief through the unruliness of their passions, destroying both themselves and others. Conservatives argue that strong institutions—family, church, and community—are needed to control individuals' selfish and immoral impulses and to foster civilized ways of life.

It is important to note that conservatism in America incorporates different views of the role of government in economic versus social affairs. Conservatives generally prefer *limited noninterventionist government in economic affairs*—a government that relies on free markets to provide and distribute goods and services; minimizes its regulatory activity; limits social welfare programs to the "truly needy"; keeps taxes low; and rejects schemes to equalize income or wealth. On the other hand, conservatives would *strengthen government's power to regulate social conduct.* They support restrictions on abortion; endorse school prayer; favor a war on drugs and pornography; oppose the legitimizing of homosexuality; support the death penalty; and advocate tougher criminal penalties.

Young Americans for Freedom

The "YAF" archives site contains background on the conservative organization and conservative views on key issues of the day.
www.yaf.com

Americans for Democratic Action

The ADA is the nation's oldest liberal political action organization.
www.adaction.org

liberalism Belief in the value of strong government to provide economic security and protection for civil rights, combined with a belief in personal freedom from government intervention in social conduct.

Modern Liberalism: Governmental Power to "Do Good" Modern **liberalism** combines a belief in a strong government to provide economic security and protection for civil rights with a belief in freedom from government

ACROSS THE USA

Liberalism and Conservatism

States might be classified in terms of their voters' self-identification in opinion surveys as liberal, moderate, or conservative. The most conservative state is Utah (45 percent conservative, 37 percent moderate, 13 percent liberal), followed by Indiana (42 percent conservative, 39 percent moderate, 13 percent liberal). The most liberal states are Massachusetts (26 percent conservative, 42 percent moderate, 26 percent liberal), New York (29 percent conservative, 39 percent moderate, 26 percent liberal), and New Jersey (28 percent conservative, 40 percent moderate, 26 percent liberal).

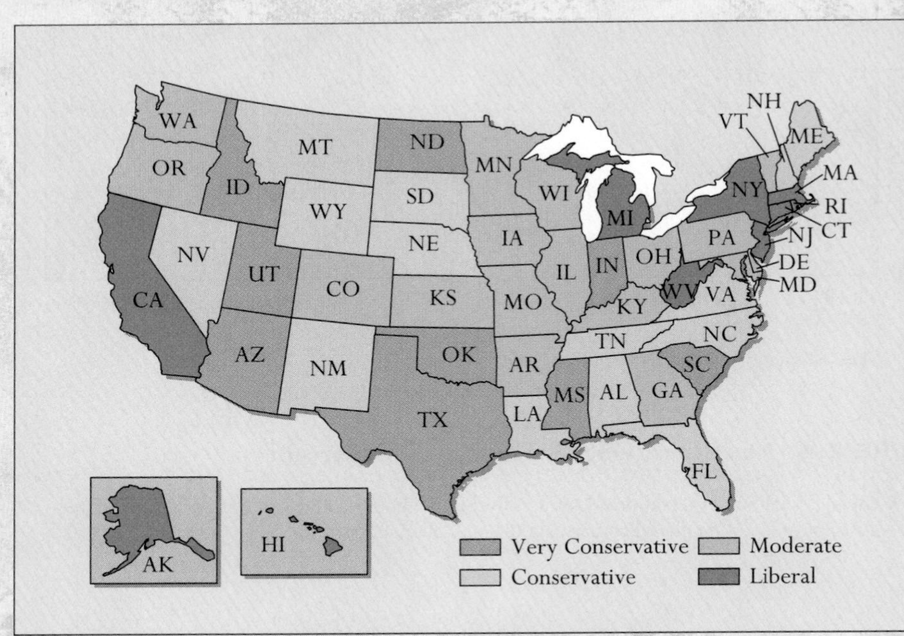

Source: Gerald C. Wright, Robert S. Erikson, and John P. McIver, "Public Opinion and Policy Liberalism in the American States," *American Journal of Political Science* 31 (November 1987): 980–1001. Reprinted by permission of the University of Wisconsin Press.

intervention in social conduct. Modern liberalism retains the classical liberalism commitment to individual dignity, but it emphasizes the importance of social and economic security for the whole population. In contrast to classical liberalism which looked at governmental power as a potential threat to personal freedom, modern liberalism looks on the power of government as a positive force for eliminating social and economic conditions that adversely affect people's lives and impede their self-development. The modern liberal approves of the use of governmental power to correct the perceived ills of society (see *People in Politics:* "Barbara Boxer, Defending Liberalism in Congress" on page 44).

Today's liberals believe that government can change people's lives by working to end racial and sexual discrimination, abolish poverty, eliminate slums, create jobs, uplift the poor, provide medical care for all, educate the masses, protect the environment, and instill humanitarian values in everyone. The prevailing impulse is to "do good," to perform public services, and to assist the least fortunate in society, particularly the poor and minorities. Modern liberalism is impatient with what it sees as the slow progress of individual initiative and private enterprise toward solving socioeconomic problems, so it seeks to use the power of the national government to find solutions to society's troubles.

WWW **Bill O'Reilly**
Popular Web site for conservative views as well as promotion of O'Reilly programs, books, editorials, etc. ***www.billoreilly.com***

PEOPLE IN POLITICS

Bill O'Reilly, "The No Spin Zone?"

Bill O'Reilly assures "fair and balanced" broadcast journalism to Fox News viewers. He describes his popular TV show as a "no spin zone" and refers to himself as an "independent." Yet O'Reilly has emerged as the nation's most popular voice of conservatism on television.

O'Reilly boasts of an Irish Catholic working-class upbringing in Long Island. He graduated from Catholic Marist College, briefly taught in a Miami high school, and earned a master's degree from Boston University in journalism. He bounced around the country as a reporter for various TV stations, and by 1986 he had become a top correspondent for ABC News. He eventually replaced David Frost as anchor of the TV tabloid *Inside Edition,* but left that job in 1995 to earn a master's degree from the John F. Kennedy School of Government at Harvard University.

The Fox News network recruited O'Reilly to create a new evening talk show, *The O'Reilly Factor.* The show quickly grew into the most watched program on cable news, out-distancing even *Larry King Live.*

O'Reilly mixes humor with bombast. He ferociously attacks liberals bold enough to come on his show as guests. He constantly interrupts guests, both liberal and conservative, to broadcast his own views. He is convinced that liberal "secularists" are waging war against religion and traditional moral values. His favorite targets include Hollywood liberals, Hillary Clinton, Jesse Jackson, and the American Civil Liberties Union. The occasional twinkle in his Irish eyes tempers his often venomous commentary.

Modern liberalism defines equality somewhat differently from the way classical liberalism does. Classical liberalism stresses the value of equality of opportunity. Individuals should be free to make the most of their talents and skills, but differences in wealth or power that are a product of differences in talent, initiative, risk taking, and skill are accepted as natural. In contrast, modern liberalism contends that individual dignity and equality of opportunity depend in some measure on *reduction of absolute inequality* in society. Modern liberals believe that true equality of opportunity cannot be achieved where significant numbers of people are suffering from hopelessness, hunger, treatable illness, or poverty. Thus modern liberalism supports government efforts to reduce inequalities in society.

Liberals also have different views of the role of government in economic versus social affairs. Liberals generally prefer an active, powerful government in economic affairs—a government that provides a broad range of public services; regulates business; protects civil rights; protects consumers and the environment; provides generous unemployment, welfare, and Social Security benefits; and reduces economic inequality. But many of these same liberals would limit the government's power to regulate social conduct. They oppose restrictions on abortion; oppose school prayer; favor "decriminalizing" marijuana use and "victimless" offenses like public intoxication and vagrancy; support gay rights and tolerance toward alternative lifestyles; oppose government restrictions on speech, press, and protest; oppose the death penalty; and strive to protect the rights of criminal defendants. Liberalism is the prevailing ideology among college professors (see Figure 2.5).

PEOPLE IN POLITICS

Barbara Boxer, Defending Liberalism in Congress

Perhaps no one has been more successful in defending liberal causes in Congress than California's outspoken U.S. senator, Barbara Boxer. Her political résumé boasts awards and honors from such organizations as Planned Parenthood (family planning, reproductive health, and abortion rights), the Sierra Club (environmental causes), Mobilization against AIDS, Anti-Defamation League (civil rights), and Public Citizen (consumer affairs).

A graduate of Brooklyn College with a B.A. in economics, Boxer worked briefly as a stockbroker before moving to San Francisco, where she became a journalist and later a campaign aide to a local congressional representative. Her political career is based in Marin County, a trendy, upper-class, liberal community north of San Francisco, where she first won elected office as a member of the County Board of Supervisors. She was elected to the U.S. House of Representatives from her Marin County district in 1982 and quickly won a reputation as one of the most liberal members of the House. Appointed to the House Armed Services Committee, she became a leading critic of defense spending and virtually every weapon requested by the military.

When her state's liberal Democratic senator, Alan Cranston, announced he would not seek reelection to the Senate in the wake of his censure in the Keating Five affair, Boxer sought the open seat. Her opponent, conservative Republican radio and TV commentator Bruce Herschensohn, hammered at Boxer's 143 overdrafts at the House bank, her frequent absenteeism, and her extensive use of congressional perks. But with the help of Clinton's 1992 landslide (47 to 32 percent) victory over George Bush in California, Boxer eked out a 48 to 46 percent victory over Herschensohn. Her victory, together with that of Dianne Feinstein, gave California a historical first—two women U.S. senators.

Boxer quickly emerged as a powerful force in the U.S. Senate on behalf of abortion rights. She led the Senate fight for a federal law protecting abortion clinics from obstruction by demonstrators. On the Environmental and Public Works Committee she helped block efforts to relax federal environmental regulations. She led the movement to oust Republican senator Bob Packwood from the Senate on charges of sexually harassing staff members. She helped lead the fight for the Family Medical Leave Act, passed in the early days of the Clinton administration, as well as the Freedom of Access to [Abortion] Clinics Act. She was reelected by a wide margin in 1998.

Youth and Ideology Young people are more likely to hold liberal views than their elders. Especially on social issues, young people, 18–24, are more likely to describe themselves as liberals (see Table 2.1). Older adults are more likely to describe themselves as conservatives on social as well as economic issues.

U.S. Senator Barbara Boxer

The official Web site of U.S. Senator Barbara Boxer of California contains biographical material, information about Boxer's committee assignments, and her stands on various political issues.

www.senate.gov/~boxer/

FIGURE 2.5 Ideology Among Professors

Source: American Enterprise, vol. 2, July/August 1991, http://www.TAEmag.com. Published by the American Enterprise Institute for Public Policy Research, Washington,DC..

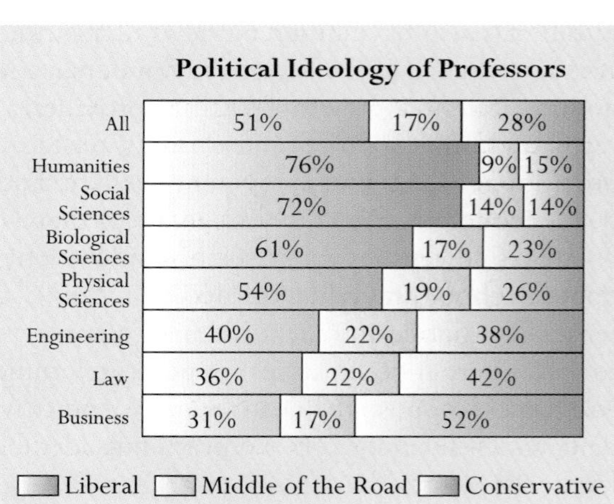

Political Ideology of Professors

	Liberal	Middle of the Road	Conservative
All	51%	17%	28%
Humanities	76%	9%	15%
Social Sciences	72%	14%	14%
Biological Sciences	61%	17%	23%
Physical Sciences	54%	19%	26%
Engineering	40%	22%	38%
Law	36%	22%	42%
Business	31%	17%	52%

TABLE 2.1 Ideology and Age

Thinking about social issues, would you say your views on social issues are conservative, moderate, or liberal?

Age	Conservative	Moderate	Liberal
18–24	27%	36%	36%
25–38	33	34	31
39 plus	40	38	19

Thinking about economic issues, would you say your views on economic issues are conservative, moderate, or liberal?

Age			
18–24	33%	40%	26%
25–38	39	39	20
39 plus	47	38	12

Source: Gallup Poll reported May 20, 2003. Copyright © 2003 by The Gallup Organization.

Dissent in the United States

Dissent from the principal elements of American political culture—individualism, free enterprise, democracy, and equality of opportunity—has arisen over the years from both the *left* and the *right*. The **left** generally refers to socialists and communists, but it is sometimes used to brand liberals. The **right** generally refers to fascists and extreme nationalists, although it is sometimes used to stamp conservatives. Despite their professed hostility toward each other, **radicals** on the left and right share many characteristics. Both are **extremist.** They reject democratic politics, compromise, and coalition building as immoral, and they assert the supremacy of the "people" over laws, institutions, and individual rights. Extremists view politics with hostility, although they may make cynical use of democratic politics as a short-term tactical means to their goals.

Conspiracy theories are popular among extremists. For example, the left sees a conspiracy among high government, corporate, and military chieftains to profit from war; the right sees a conspiracy among communists, intellectuals, the United Nations, and Wall Street bankers to subordinate the United States to a world government. The historian Richard Hofstadter has referred to this tendency as "the paranoid style of politics."[14] Both the left and right are intolerant of the opinions of others and are willing to disrupt and intimidate those with whom they disagree. Whether shouting down speakers or disrupting meetings or burning crosses and parading in hoods, the impulse to violence is often present in those who subscribe to radical politics.

left A reference to the liberal, progressive, and/or socialist side of the political spectrum.

right A reference to the conservative, traditional, anticommunist side of the political spectrum.

radicalism Advocacy of immediate and drastic changes in society, including the complete restructuring of institutions, values, and beliefs. Radicals may exist on either the extreme left or extreme right.

extremism Rejection of democratic politics and the assertion of the supremacy of the "people" over laws, institutions, and individual rights.

Antidemocratic Ideologies Dissent in the United States has historical roots in antidemocratic movements that originated primarily outside its borders. These movements have spanned the political spectrum from the far right to the far left.

At the far-right end of this spectrum lies **fascism,** an ideology that asserts the supremacy of the state or race over individuals. The goal of fascism is unity of people, nation, and leadership—in the words of Adolf Hitler: *"Ein Volk, Ein Reich, Ein Führer"* (One People, One Nation, One Leader). Every individual, every interest, and every class are to be submerged for the good of the nation. Against the rights of liberty or equality, fascism asserts the duties of service, devotion, and discipline. Its goal is to develop a superior type of human being, with qualities of bravery, courage, genius, and strength. The World War II defeat of the two leading fascist regimes in history—Adolf Hitler's Nazi Germany and Benito Mussolini's fascist Italy—did not extinguish fascist ideas. Elements of fascist thought are found today in extremist movements in both the United States and Europe.

fascism Political ideology in which the state and/or race is assumed to be supreme over individuals.

Marxism arose out of the turmoil of the Industrial Revolution as a protest against social evils and economic inequalities. Karl Marx (1818–83), its founder, was not an impoverished worker but rather an upper-middle-class intellectual unable to find an academic position. Benefiting from the financial support of his wealthy colleague Friedrich Engels (1820–95), Marx spent years writing *Das Kapital* (1867), a lengthy work describing the evils of capitalism, especially the oppression of factory workers (the proletariat) and the inevitability of revolution. The two men collaborated on a popular pamphlet entitled *The Communist Manifesto* (1848), which called for a workers' revolution: "Workers of the world, unite. You have nothing to lose but your chains."

Marxism The theories of Karl Marx, among them that capitalists oppress workers and that worldwide revolution and the emergence of a classless society are inevitable.

It fell to Vladimir Lenin (1870–1924) to implement Marx and Engels's revolutionary ideology in the Russian Revolution in 1917. According to **Leninism,** the key to a successful revolution is the organization of small, disciplined, hard-core groups of professional revolutionaries into a centralized totalitarian party. To explain why Marx's predictions about the ever-worsening conditions of the masses under capitalism proved untrue (workers' standards of living in Western democracies rose rapidly in the twentieth century), Lenin devised the theory of imperialism: advanced capitalist countries turned to war and colonialism, exploiting the Third World, in order to make their own workers relatively prosperous.

Leninism The theories of Vladimir Lenin, among them that advanced capitalist countries turned toward war and colonialism to make their own workers relatively prosperous.

Communism is the outgrowth of Marxist-Leninist ideas about the necessity of class warfare, the inevitability of a worldwide proletarian revolution, and the con-

communism System of government in which a single totalitarian party controls all means of production and distribution of goods and services.

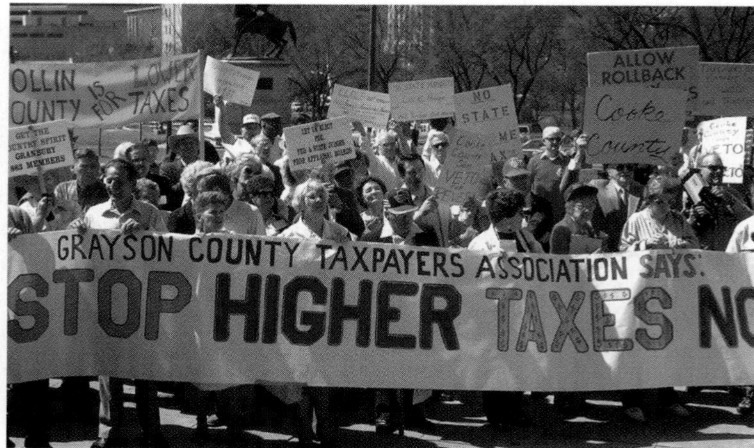

Liberals' concern about efforts to curtail social welfare programs reflects their support of strong government, whereas conservatives' demands for tax cuts reflect their preference for government that encourages self-reliance and individual initiative.

WHAT DO YOU THINK?

Are You a Liberal or a Conservative?

Not everyone consistently takes a liberal or a conservative position on every issue. But if you find that you agree with more positions under one of the following "liberal" or "conservative" lists, you are probably ready to label yourself ideologically.

	You are *Liberal* If You Agree That	**You Are *Conservative* If You Agree That**
Economic policy	Government should regulate business to protect the public interest. The rich should pay higher taxes to support public services for all. Government spending for social welfare is a good investment in people.	Free-market competition is better at protecting the public than government regulation. Taxes should be kept as low as possible. Government welfare programs destroy incentives to work.
Crime	Government should place primary emphasis on alleviating the social conditions (such as poverty and joblessness) that cause crime.	Government should place primary emphasis on providing more police and prisons and stop courts from coddling criminals.
Social policy	Government should protect the right of women to choose abortion and fund abortions for poor women. Government should pursue affirmative action programs on behalf of minorities and women in employment, education, and so on. Government should keep religious prayers and ceremonies out of schools and public places.	Government should restrict abortion and not use taxpayer money for abortions. Government should not grant preferences to anyone based on race or sex. Government should allow prayers and religious observances in schools and public places.
National security policy	Government should support "human rights" throughout the world. Military spending should be reduced now that the Cold War is over.	Government should pursue the "national interest" of the United States. Military spending must reflect a variety of new dangers in this post Cold-War period.
You generally describe yourself as	"caring" "compassionate" "progressive"	"responsible" "moderate" "sensible"
and you describe your political opponents as	"extremists" "right-wing radicals" "reactionaries"	"knee jerks" "bleeding hearts" "left-wing radicals"

centration of all power in the "vanguard of the proletariat"—the Communist Party. Communism justifies violence as a means to attain power by arguing that the bourgeoisie (the capitalistic middle class) will never voluntarily give up its control over "the means of production" (the economy). Democracy is only "window dressing" to disguise capitalist exploitation. The Communist Party justifies authoritarian single-party rule as the "dictatorship of the proletariat." In theory, after a period of rule by the Communist Party, all property will be owned by the government, and a "classless" society of true communism will emerge.

WWW **Socialist Party USA** News and views from America's Socialist party. ***http://sp-usa.org***

Socialism **Socialism** shares with communism a condemnation of capitalist profit making as exploitative of the working classes. Communists and socialists agree on the "evils" of industrial capitalism: the concentration of wealth, the insensitivity of the profit motive to human needs, the insecurities and suffering brought on by the business cycle, the conflict of class interests, and the tendency of capitalist nations to involve themselves in imperialist wars. However, socialists are committed to the democratic process as a means of replacing capitalism with collective ownership of economic enterprise. Socialists generally reject the notion of violent revolution as a way to replace capitalism and instead advocate peaceful, constitutional roads to bring about change. Moreover, many socialists are prepared to govern in a free society under democratic principles, including freedom of speech and press and the right to organize political parties and oppose government policy. Socialism is egalitarian, seeking to reduce or eliminate inequalities in the distribution of wealth. It attempts to achieve equality of results, rather than mere equality of opportunity.

The End of History? Much of the history of the twentieth century has been the struggle between democratic capitalism and totalitarian communism. Thus the collapse of communism in Eastern Europe and the Soviet Union, symbolized by the tearing down of the Berlin Wall in 1989, as well as the worldwide movement toward free markets and democracy at the end of the twentieth century, has been labeled the **end of history.**[15] Democratic revolutions were largely inspired by the realization that free-market capitalism provided much higher standards of living than communism. The economies of Eastern Europe were falling further and further behind the economies of the capitalist nations of the West. Similar comparative observations of the successful economies of the Asian capitalist "Four Tigers"—South Korea, Taiwan, Singapore, and Hong Kong—even inspired China's communist leadership to experiment with market reforms. Communism destroyed the individual's incentive to work, produce, innovate, save, and invest in the future. Under communism, production for government goals (principally a strong military) came first; production for individual needs came last. The result was long lines at stores, shoddy products, and frequent bribery of bureaucrats to obtain necessary consumer items. More important, perhaps, the concentration of both economic and political power in the hands of a central bureaucracy proved to be incompatible with democracy. Communism relies on central direction, force, and repression. Communist systems curtail individual freedom and prohibit the development of separate parties and interest groups outside of government.

Capitalism does not *ensure* democracy; some capitalist nations are authoritarian. But economic freedom inspires demands for political freedom. Thus market reforms, initiated by communist leaders to increase productivity, led to democracy movements, and those movements eventually dismantled the communist system in Eastern Europe and the old Soviet Union.

socialism System of government involving collective or government ownership of economic enterprise, with the goal being equality of results, not merely equality of opportunity.

end of history The collapse of communism and the worldwide movement toward free markets and political democracy.

Political extremists of the left and right often have more in common than they would like to admit. Although decidedly different in their political philosophies, both members of right-wing American neo-Nazi groups and members of left-wing communist groups reject democratic politics and assert the supremacy of the "people" over laws, institutions, and individual rights. Gregory Johnson (left) was the catalyst for the flag burning controversy that is still raging in Congress today. Buford O'Neal Furrow, Jr. (right), was arrested for opening fire on children in a Jewish day care center in California. Several children died in this attack.

Academic Radicalism Marxism survives on campuses today largely as an academic critique of the functioning of capitalism.[16] It provides some disaffected academics with ideas and language to attack everything that disturbs them about the United States—from poverty, racism, and environmental hazards to junk food, athletic scholarships, and obnoxious television advertising—conveniently blaming the "profit motive" for many of the ills of American society.

Contemporary radicals argue that the institutions of capitalism have conditioned people to be materialistic, competitive, and even violent. The individual has been transformed into a one-dimensional person in whom genuine humanistic values are repressed.[17] Profitability, rather than humanistic values, remains the primary criterion for decision making in the capitalist economy, and thus profitability is the reason for poverty and misery despite material abundance. Without capitalist institutions, life would be giving, cooperative, and compassionate. Only a *radical restructuring* of social and economic institutions will succeed in liberating people from these institutions to lead humanistic, cooperative lives.

National Association of Scholars
Association of college and university professors opposed to PC restrictions on campus.
www.nas.org

To American radicals, the problem of social change is truly monumental, because capitalist values and institutions are deeply rooted in this country. Since most people are not aware that they are oppressed and victimized, the first step toward social change is consciousness raising—that is, making people aware of their misery.

politically correct (PC) Repression of attitudes, speech, and writings that are deemed racist, sexist, homophohic (anti-homosexual), or otherwise "insensitive."

The agenda of academic radicalism has been labeled **politically correct** (PC) thinking. Politically correct thinking views American society as racist, sexist, and homophobic. Overt bigotry is not the real issue, but rather Western institutions, language, and culture, which systematically oppress and victimize women, people of color, gays, and others.

Academic radicalism "includes the assumption that Western values are inherently oppressive, that the chief purpose of education is political transformation, and that all standards are arbitrary.[18] In PC thinking, "everything is political." Therefore curriculum, courses, and lectures—even language and demeanor—are judged according to whether they are politically correct or not. Universities have always been centers for the critical examination of institutions, values, and culture, but PC thinking does not really tolerate open discussion or debate. Opposition is denounced as "insensitive," racist, sexist, or worse, and intimidation is not infrequent (see *Up Close:* "Political Correctness versus Free Speech on Campus" in Chapter 14).

SUMMARY NOTES

- Ideas are sources of power. They provide people with guides for determining right and wrong and with rationales for political action. Political institutions are shaped by the values and beliefs of the political culture, and political leaders are restrained in their exercise of power by these ideas.
- The American political culture is a set of widely shared values and beliefs about who should govern, for what ends, and by what means.
- Americans share many common ways of thinking about politics. Nevertheless, there are often contradictions between professed values and actual conditions, problems in applying abstract beliefs to concrete situations, and even occasional conflict over fundamental values.
- Individual liberty is a fundamental value in American life. The classical liberal tradition that inspired the nation's Founders included both political liberties and economic freedoms.
- Equality is another fundamental American value. The nation's Founders believed in equality before the law; yet political equality, in the form of universal voting rights, required nearly two centuries to bring about.
- Equality of opportunity is a widely shared value; most Americans are opposed to artificial barriers of race, sex, religion, or ethnicity barring individual advancement. But equality of results is not a widely shared value; most Americans support a "floor" on income and well-being for their fellow citizens but oppose placing a "ceiling" on income or wealth.
- Income inequality has increased in recent years primarily as a result of economic and demographic changes. Most Americans believe that opportunities for individual advancement are still available, and this belief diminishes the potential for class conflict.
- Liberal and conservative ideologies in American politics present somewhat different sets of values and beliefs, even though they share a common commitment to individual dignity and private property. Generally, liberals favor an active, powerful government to provide economic security and protection for civil rights but oppose government restrictions on social conduct. Generally, conservatives favor minimal government intervention in economic affairs and civil rights but support many government restrictions on social conduct.
- Many Americans who identify themselves as liberals or conservatives are not always consistent in applying their professed views. Populists are liberal on economic issues but conservative in their views on social issues. Libertarians are conservative on economic issues but liberal in their social views.
- Liberal and conservative ideas evolve over time in response to new challenges and changing conditions. Neoconservatives share the historical classical liberal concerns about the nation's social problems but no longer believe that solutions can be found in large-scale, costly bureaucratic government programs. Neo-liberals retain their faith in the power of government but focus their attention on efforts to promote economic growth as a prerequisite to solving social problems.
- The collapse of communism in Eastern Europe and the former Soviet Union and the worldwide movement toward free markets and democracy have undermined support for socialism throughout the world. Yet Marxism survives in academic circles as a critique of the functioning of capitalism.

KEY TERMS

political culture 25
values 25
beliefs 25
subcultures 25
classical liberalism 26
capitalism 26
political equality 28
equality of opportunity 28
equality of results 28
social mobility 33
class conflict 35
class consciousness 35
ideology 40
conservatism 40
liberalism 41
left 45
right 45
radicalism 45
extremism 45
fascism 46
Marxism 46
Leninism 46
communism 46
socialism 48
end of history 48
politically correct (PC) 49

SUGGESTED READINGS

Ebenstein, Alan, William Ebenstein, and Edwin Fogelman. *Today's Isms: Communism, Fascism, Capitalism, Socialism.* 11th ed. Upper Saddle River, N.J.: Prentice Hall, 2000. A concise description and history of the major isms.

Herrnstein, Richard J., and Charles Murray. *The Bell Curve: Intelligence and Class Structure in American Life.* New York: Free Press, 1994. A controversial argument that success in life is mainly a result of inherited intelligence and that a very bright "cognitive elite" will continue to distance themselves from the duller masses.

Huntington, Samuel P. *American Politics: The Promise of Disharmony.* Cambridge, Mass.: Harvard University Press, 1981. An examination of the gaps between the promise of the American ideals of liberty and equality and the performance of the American political system.

Ingersoll, David E., Richard K. Matthews, and Andrew Davidson. *The Philosophical Roots of Modern Ideology: Liberalism, Communism, Fascism, Islamism.* 3rd ed. Upper Saddle River, N.J.: Prentice Hall, 2001. Overview of political ideologies, including extensive quotes from original sources, from Locke, Jefferson, Madison, Marx, and Lenin to Gorbachev, Hitler, and Khomeini.

Ryscavage, Paul. *Income Inequality in America.* Armonk, N.Y.: M.E. Sharpe, 1999. A careful analysis of current trends toward income inequality in the United States.

Tocqueville, Alexis de. *Democracy in America* (1835). Chicago: University of Chicago Press. 2000. Classic early assessment of American political culture by French traveler.

Wolff, Edward N. *Top Heavy.* 2nd Ed. New York: News Press, 2002. A fact-filled report on the increasing inequality of wealth in America, together with a proposal to tax wealth as well as income.

Wray, J. Harry. *Sense and Non-Sense: American Culture and Politics.* Upper Saddle River, N.J.: Prentice Hall, 2001. Introduction to American political culture and the values that influence political life in the United States today.

MAKE IT REAL

POLITICAL SURVEY: WHAT DO YOU BELIEVE?

Political culture consists of widely shared beliefs, values, and norms concerning the relationship of citizens to government and to one another. However, just because they are widely shared does not mean they are universally shared. To what degree do you share beliefs with the general population? With your generation? With your classmates? In this simulation you will complete a questionnaire to see how your political beliefs compare with those of people around you.

CHAPTER 3

THE CONSTITUTION: LIMITING GOVERNMENTAL POWER

CHAPTER OUTLINE

- Constitutional Government
- The Constitutional Tradition
- Troubles Confronting a New Nation
- Consensus in Philadelphia
- Conflict in Philadelphia
- Resolving the Economic Issues
- Protecting National Security
- The Structure of the Government
- Separation of Powers and Checks and Balances
- Conflict over Ratification
- A Bill of Rights
- Constitutional Change

THINK ABOUT POLITICS

1 Was the original constitution of 1787 a truly democratic document?
Yes ● No ●

2 Should citizens be able to vote directly on national policies such as prayer in public schools or doctor-assisted suicides?
Yes ● No ●

3 Should a large state like California, with 32 million people, elect more U.S. senators than a small state like Wyoming, with only half a million people?
Yes ● No ●

4 Should federal laws always supersede state laws?
Yes ● No ●

5 In which do you have the most trust and confidence?
President ●
Congress ●
Supreme Court ●

6 Should the Constitution be amended to require congress to pass only balanced budgets?
Yes ● No ●

7 Should the Constitution be amended to guarantee that equal rights shall not be denied based on sex?
Yes ● No ●

In a democracy "of the people, by the people, and for the people," who really has the power to govern? Are strong national government and personal liberty compatible? Can majorities limit individual rights? America's Founders struggled with such questions, and in resolving them established the oldest existing constitutional government.

Constitutional Government

Constitutions govern government. **Constitutionalism**—a government of laws, not of people—means that those who exercise governmental power are restricted in their use of it by a higher law. If individual freedoms are to be placed beyond the reach of government and beyond the reach of majorities, then a constitution must truly limit the exercise of authority by government. It does so by setting forth individual liberties that the government—even with majority support—cannot violate.

A **constitution** legally establishes government authority. It sets up governmental bodies (such as the House of Representatives, the Senate, the presidency, and the Supreme Court in the United States). It grants them powers. It determines how their members are to be chosen. And it prescribes the rules by which they make decisions.

Constitutional decision making is deciding how to decide; that is, it is deciding on the rules for policy making. It is not policy making itself. Policies will be decided later, according to the rules set forth in the constitution.

A constitution cannot be changed by the ordinary acts of governmental bodies; change can come only through a process of general popular consent.[1] The U.S. Constitution, then, is superior to ordinary laws of Congress, orders of the president, decisions of the courts, acts of the state legislatures, and regulations of the bureaucracies. Indeed, the Constitution is "the supreme law of the land."

The Constitutional Tradition

Americans are strongly committed to the idea of a written constitution to establish government and limit its powers. In fact, the Constitutional Convention of 1787 had many important antecedents.

The Magna Carta, 1215 English lords, traditionally required to finance the king's wars, forced King John to sign the Magna Carta, a document guaranteeing their feudal rights and setting the precedent of a limited government and monarchy.

The Mayflower Compact, 1620 Puritan colonists, while still aboard the Mayflower, signed a compact establishing a "civil body politic . . . to enact just and equal laws . . . for the general good of the colony, unto which we promise all due submission and obedience." After the Puritans landed at Plymouth, in what is today Massachusetts, they formed a colony based on the Mayflower Compact, thus setting a precedent of a government established by contract with the governed.

National Constitution Center
Located in Philadelphia Independence Mall, this museum is devoted to explaining the U.S. Constitution.
www.constitutioncenter.org

The Colonial Charters, 1624–1732 The charters that authorized settlement of the colonies in America were granted by royal action. For some of the colonies, the British king granted official proprietary rights to an individual, as in Maryland (granted to Lord Baltimore), Pennsylvania (to William Penn), and Delaware (also to Penn). For other colonies, the king granted royal commissions to companies to establish governments, as in Virginia, Massachusetts, New Hampshire, New York, New Jersey, Georgia, and North and South Carolina. Royal charters were granted directly to the colonists themselves only in Connecticut and Rhode Island. These colonists drew up their charters and presented them to the king, setting a precedent in America for written contracts defining governmental power.

The "Charter Oak Affair" of 1685–88 began when King James II became displeased with his Connecticut subjects and issued an order for the repeal of the Connecticut Charter. In 1687 Sir Edmund Andros went to Hartford, dissolved the colonial government, and demanded that the charter be returned. But Captain John Wadsworth hid it in an oak tree. After the so-called Glorious Revolution in England in 1688, the charter was taken out and used again as the fundamental law of the colony. Subsequent British monarchs silently acquiesced in this restoration of rights, and the affair strengthened the notion of loyalty to the constitution rather than to the king.

The Declaration of Independence, 1776 The First Continental Congress, a convention of delegates from twelve of the thirteen original colonies, came together in 1774 to protest British interference in American affairs. But the Revolutionary War did not begin until April 19, 1775. The evening before, British regular troops marched out from Boston to seize arms stored by citizens in Lexington and Concord, Massachusetts. At dawn the next morning, the Minutemen—armed citizens organized for the protection of their towns—engaged the British regulars in brief battles, then harassed them all the way back to Boston. In June of that year, the Second Continental Congress appointed George Washington Commander-in-Chief of American forces and sent him to Boston to take command of the American militia surrounding the city. Still, popular support for the Revolution remained limited, and even many members of the Continental Congress hoped only to force changes—not to split off from Britain.

constitutionalism A government of laws, not people, operating on the principle that governmental power must be limited and government officials should be restrained in their exercise of power over individuals.

constitution The legal structure of a political system, establishing governmental bodies, granting their powers, determining how their members are selected, and prescribing the rules by which they make their decisions. Considered basic or fundamental, a constitution cannot be changed by ordinary acts of governmental bodies.

As this hope died, however, members of the Continental Congress came to view a formal Declaration of Independence as necessary to give legitimacy to their cause and establish the basis for a new nation. Accordingly, on July 2, 1776, the Continental Congress "Resolved, that these United Colonies are, and, of right, ought to be free and independent States." Thomas Jefferson had been commissioned to write a justification for the action, which he presented to the congress on July 4, 1776. In writing the Declaration of Independence, Jefferson lifted several phrases directly from the English political philosopher John Locke asserting the rights of individuals, the contract theory of government, and the right of revolution. The declaration was signed first by the president of the Continental Congress, John Hancock.

After numerous drafts by Thomas Jefferson, including such changes as the deletion of a clause condemning the slave trade that offended North Carolina and Georgia, the Declaration of Independence was accepted by the majority of the Continental Congress on July 4, 1776. The document then became "the unanimous declaration of the thirteen United States of America" on July 19, and was signed by all members of the Continental Congress on August 2. Shown in this painting are (left to right) Benjamin Franklin, Thomas Jefferson, Robert Livingston, John Adams, and Roger Sherman.

U.S. History The Independence Hall Association Web site with "Documents of Freedom" including Mayflower Compact, Declaration of Independence, Articles of Confederation, etc. *www.ushistory.org*

The Revolutionary War ended when British General Charles Cornwallis surrendered at Yorktown, Virginia, in October 1781. But even as the war was being waged, the new nation was creating the framework of its government.

The Articles of Confederation, 1781–1789 Although Richard Henry Lee, a Virginia delegate to the Continental Congress, first proposed that the newly independent states form a confederation on July 6, 1776, the Continental Congress did not approve the Articles of Confederation until November 15, 1777, and the last state to sign them, Maryland, did not do so until March 1, 1781. Under the Articles, Congress was a single house in which each state had two to seven members but only one vote. Congress itself created and appointed executives, judges, and military officers. It also had the power to make war and peace, conduct foreign affairs, and borrow and print money. But Congress could *not* collect taxes or enforce laws directly; it had to rely on the states to provide money and enforce its laws. The United States under the Articles was really a confederation of nations. Within this "firm league of friendship" (Article III of the Articles of Confederation), the national government was thought of as an alliance of independent states, not as a government "of the people."

Troubles Confronting a New Nation

Two centuries ago the United States was struggling to achieve nationhood. The new U.S. government achieved enormous successes under the Articles of Confederation: It won independence from Great Britain, the world's most powerful colonial nation at the time; it defeated vastly superior forces in a prolonged war for independence; it established a viable peace and won powerful allies (notably, France) in the international community; it created an effective army and navy, established a postal system, and laid the foundations for national unity. But despite these successes in war and diplomacy, the political arrangements under the Articles were unsatisfactory to many influential groups—notably, bankers and investors who held U.S. government bonds, plantation owners, real estate developers, and merchants and shippers.

Constitution Society
Web site includes comprehensive list of founding documents, essays, and commentaries on the Constitution.
www.constitution.org

Financial Difficulties Under the Articles of Confederation, Congress had no power to tax the people directly. Instead, Congress had to ask the states for money to pay its expenses, particularly the expenses of fighting the long and costly War of Independence with Great Britain. There was no way to force the states to make their payments to the national government. In fact, about 90 percent of the funds requisitioned by Congress from the states was never paid, so Congress had to borrow money from wealthy patriot investors to fight the war. Without the power to tax, however, Congress could not pay off these debts. Indeed, the value of U.S. governmental bonds fell to about 10 cents for every dollar's worth because few people believed the bonds would ever be paid off. Congress even stopped making interest payments on these bonds.

Commercial Obstacles Under the Articles of Confederation, states were free to tax the goods of other states. Without the power to regulate interstate commerce, the national government was unable to protect merchants from heavy tariffs imposed on shipments from state to state. Southern planters could not ship their agricultural products to northern cities without paying state-imposed tariffs, and northern merchants could not ship manufactured products from state to state without interference. Merchants, manufacturers, shippers, and planters all wanted to develop national markets and prevent the states from imposing tariffs or restrictions on interstate trade. States competed with one another by passing low tariffs on foreign goods (to encourage the shipment of goods through their own ports) and high tariffs against one another's goods (to protect their own markets). The result was a great deal of confusion and bad feeling—as well as a great deal of smuggling.

Currency Problems Under the Articles, the states themselves had the power to issue their own currency, regulate its value, and require that it be accepted in payment of debts. States had their own "legal tender" laws, which required creditors to accept state money if "tendered" in payment of debt. As a result, many forms of money were circulating: Virginia dollars, Rhode Island dollars, Pennsylvania dollars, and so on. Some states (Rhode Island, for example) printed a great deal of money, creating inflation in their currency and alienating banks and investors whose loans were being paid off in this cheap currency. If creditors refused payment in a particular state's currency, the debt could be abolished in that state. So finances throughout the states were very unstable, and banks and creditors were threatened by cheap paper money.

Civil Disorder In several states, debtors openly revolted against tax collectors and sheriffs attempting to repossess farms on behalf of creditors who held unpaid mortgages. The most serious rebellion broke out in the summer of 1786 in western Massachusetts, where a band of 2,000 insurgent farmers captured the courthouses in several counties and briefly held the city of Springfield. Led by Daniel Shays, a veteran of the Revolutionary War battle at Bunker Hill, the insurgent army posed a direct threat to investors, bankers, creditors, and tax collectors by burning deeds, mortgages, and tax records to wipe out proof of the farmers' debts.

Shays's Rebellion, as it was called, was finally put down by a small mercenary army, paid for by well-to-do citizens of Boston.

Reports of Shays's Rebellion filled the newspapers of the large eastern cities. George Washington, Alexander Hamilton, James Madison, and many other prominent Americans wrote their friends about it. The event galvanized property owners to support the creation of a strong central government capable of dealing with "radicalism." Only a strong central government, they wrote one another, could "insure domestic tranquility," guarantee "a republican form of government," and protect property "against domestic violence." It is no accident that all of these phrases appear in the Constitution of 1787.

The Road to the Constitutional Convention In the spring of 1785, some wealthy merchants from Virginia and Maryland met at Alexandria, Virginia, to try to resolve a conflict between the two states over commerce and navigation on the Potomac River and Chesapeake Bay. George Washington, the new nation's most prominent citizen, took a personal interest in the meeting. As a wealthy plantation owner and a land speculator who owned more than 30,000 acres of land upstream on the Potomac, Washington was keenly interested in commercial problems under the Articles of Confederation. He lent his great prestige to the Alexandria meeting by inviting the participants to his house at Mount Vernon. Out of this conference came the idea for a general economic conference for all of the states, to be held in Annapolis, Maryland, in September 1786.

The Annapolis Convention turned out to be a key stepping-stone to the Constitutional Convention of 1787. Instead of concentrating on commerce and navigation between the states, the delegates at Annapolis, including Alexander Hamilton and James Madison, called for a general constitutional convention to suggest remedies to what they saw as defects in the Articles of Confederation.

In an attempt to prevent the foreclosure of farms by creditors, Revolutionary War veteran Daniel Shays led an armed mass of citizens in a march on a western Massachusetts court-house. This uprising, which came to be known as Shays's Rebellion, exposed the Confederation's military weakness and increased support for a strong central government.

On February 21, 1787, the Congress called for a convention to meet in Philadelphia for the "sole and express purpose" of *revising* the Articles of Confederation and reporting to the Congress and the state legislatures "such alterations and provisions therein as shall, when agreed to in Congress and confirmed by the states, to render the federal Constitution adequate to the exigencies of government and the preservation of the union." Notice that Congress did not authorize the convention to write a new constitution or to call constitutional conventions in the states to ratify a new constitution. State legislatures sent delegates to Philadelphia expecting that their task would be limited to revising the Articles and that revisions would be sent back to Congress and state legislatures for their approval. But that is not what happened.

WWW George Washington Papers
The life of George Washington with images, maps, documents, and papers.
http://gwpapers.virgina.edu

The Nation's Founders The fifty-five delegates to the Constitutional Convention, which met in Philadelphia in the summer of 1787, quickly discarded the congressional mandate to merely "revise" the Articles of Confederation. The Virginia delegation, led by James Madison, arrived before a quorum of seven states had assembled and used the time to draw up an entirely new constitutional document. After the first formal session opened on May 25 and George Washington was elected president of the convention, the Virginia Plan became the basis of discussion. Thus, at the very beginning of the convention, the decision was made to scrap the Articles of Confederation altogether, write a new constitution, and form a new national government.[2]

The Founders were very confident of their powers and abilities. They had been selected by their state legislatures (only Rhode Island, dominated by small farmers, refused to send a delegation). When Thomas Jefferson, then serving in the critical post of ambassador to France (the nation's military ally in the Revolutionary War), first saw the list of delegates, he exclaimed, "It is really an assembly of demigods." Indeed, among the nation's notables, only Jefferson and John Adams (then serving as ambassador to England) were absent. The eventual success of the convention, and the ratification of the new Constitution, resulted in part from the enormous prestige, experience, and achievements of the delegates themselves.

WWW Our Documents
National Archives Web site with access to 100 "milestone documents" in American history.
www.ourdocuments.gov

Above all, the delegates at Philadelphia were cosmopolitan. They approached political, economic, and military issues from a "continental" point of view. Unlike most Americans in 1787, their loyalties extended beyond their states. They were truly nationalists.[3]

Consensus in Philadelphia

THINK AGAIN
Was the original constitution of 1787 a truly democratic document?

The Founders shared many ideas about government. We often focus our attention on *conflict* in the Convention of 1787 and the compromises reached by the participants, but the really important story of the Constitution is the *consensus* that was shared by these men of influence.

Liberty and Property The Founders had read John Locke and absorbed his idea that the purpose of government is to protect individual liberty and property. They believed in a natural law, superior to any human-made laws, that endowed each person with certain inalienable rights—the rights to life, liberty, and property. They believed that all people were equally entitled to these rights. Most of them, including slave owners George Washington and Thomas Jefferson, un-

PEOPLE IN POLITICS

George Washington, Founder of a Nation

From the time he took command of the American Revolutionary forces in 1775 until he gave his Farewell Address to the nation in 1796 and returned to his Mount Vernon plantation, George Washington (1732– 99) was, indeed, "First in war, first in peace, first in the hearts of his countrymen." His military success, combined with his diplomacy and practical political acumen, gave him overwhelming moral authority, which he used to inspire the Constitutional Convention, to secure the ratification of the Constitution, and then to guide the new nation through its first years.

Washington was raised on a Virginia plantation and inherited substantial landholdings, including his Mount Vernon plantation on the Potomac River. He began his career as a surveyor. His work took him deep into the wilderness of America's frontier. This experience later served him well when at age twenty-one, he was appointed an officer in the Virginia militia. In 1754 he led a small force toward the French Fort Duquesne, but after a brief battle at makeshift "Fort Necessity," he was obliged to retreat. In 1755 British Major General Edward Braddock asked the young militia officer to accompany his heavy regiments on a campaign to dislodge the French from Fort Duquesne. Braddock disregarded Washington's warnings about concealed ways of fighting in the New World; Braddock's parading redcoat forces were ambushed by the French and Indians near Pittsburgh, and the general was killed. Washington rallied what remained of the British forces and led them in a successful retreat back to Virginia.

Washington was viewed by Virginians as a hero, and at age twenty-two he was appointed by the Virginia Assembly "Colonel of the Virginia Regiment and Commander in Chief of all Virginia Forces." But regular British officers ridiculed the militia forces and asserted their authority over Washington. British General John Forbes occupied Fort Duquesne, renamed it Fort Pitt, and gave Washington's men the task of garrisoning it.

In 1759, having completed his service in the French and Indian Wars, Washington left his military post and returned to plantation life. He married a wealthy widow, Martha Custis, expanded his plantation holdings, and prospered in western land speculation.

The Virginia legislature elected Washington to attend the First Continental Congress in September 1774. Washington was the most celebrated veteran of the French and Indian Wars who was still young enough (forty-two) to lead military forces in a new struggle. John Adams of Massachusetts was anxious to unite the continent in the coming contest, and he persuaded the Second Continental Congress to give the Virginian command of the American revolutionary forces surrounding the British army in Boston in 1775.

Throughout the Revolutionary War Washington persevered by employing many of the tactics later defined as the principles of guerrilla warfare. By retreating deep into Pennsylvania's Valley Forge, Washington avoided defeat and saved his army. His bold Christmas night attack against Hessian troops at Trenton, New Jersey, encouraged French intervention on America's behalf. Slowly Washington was able to wear down the British resolve to fight. In the end, he succeeded in trapping a British army at Yorktown, Virginia. Assisted by a French naval blockade, he accepted the surrender of Lord Cornwallis and 8,000 of his men on October 19, 1781.

Perhaps Washington's greatest contribution to democratic government occurred in 1783 in Newburgh, New York, near West Point, where the veterans of his Continental Army were encamped. Despite their hardships and ultimate victory in the Revolutionary War, these soldiers remained unpaid by Congress. Indeed, Congress ignored a series of letters, known as the Newburgh Addresses, that threatened military force if Congress continued to deny benefits to the veterans. Washington was invited to Newburgh by officers who hoped he would agree to lead a military coup against the Congress. But when Washington mounted the platform he denounced the use of force and the "infamous propositions" contained in their earlier addresses to Congress. There is little doubt that he could have chosen to march on the Congress with his veteran army and install himself as military dictator. World history is filled with revolutionary army leaders who did so. But Washington chose to preserve representative government.

One of the few noncontroversial decisions of the Constitutional Convention in 1787 was the selection of George Washington to preside over the meetings. He took little part in the debates; however, his enormous prestige helped to hold the convention together and later to win support for the new Constitution.

derstood that the belief in personal liberty conflicted with the practice of slavery and found the inconsistency troubling.

Social Contract The Founders believed that government originated in an implied contract among people. People agreed to establish government, obey laws, and pay taxes in exchange for protection of their natural rights. This social contract gave government its legitimacy—a legitimacy that rested on the consent of the governed, not with gods or kings or force. If a government violated individual liberty, it broke the social contract and thus lost its legitimacy.

Representative Government Although most of the world's governments in 1787 were hereditary monarchies, the Founders believed the people should have a voice in choosing their own representatives in government. They opposed hereditary aristocracy and titled nobility. Instead, they sought to forge a republic. **Republicanism** meant government by representatives of the people. The Founders expected the masses to consent to be governed by their leaders—men of principle and property with ability, education, and a stake in the preservation of liberty. The Founders believed the people should have only a limited role in directly selecting their representatives: they should vote for members of the House of Representatives, but senators, the president, and members of the Supreme Court should be selected by others more qualified to judge their ability.

Limited Government The Founders believed unlimited power was corrupting and a concentration of power was dangerous. They believed in a written constitution that limited the scope of governmental power. They also believed in dividing power within government by creating separate bodies able to check and balance one another's powers.

Nationalism Most important, the Founders shared a belief in **nationalism**—a strong and independent national (federal) government with power to govern directly, rather than through state governments. They sought to establish a government that would be recognized around the world as representing "We the people of the United States." Not everyone in America shared this enthusiasm for a strong federal government; indeed, opposition forces, calling themselves Anti-Federalists, almost succeeded in defeating the new Constitution. But the leaders meeting in Philadelphia in the summer of 1787 were convinced of the need for a strong central government that would share power with the states.

republicanism Government by representatives of the people rather than directly by the people themselves.

nationalism Belief that shared cultural, historical, linguistic, and social characteristics of a people justify the creation of a government encompassing all of them; the resulting nation-state should be independent and legally equal to all other nation-states.

Conflict in Philadelphia

Consensus on basic principles of government was essential to the success of the Philadelphia convention. But conflict over the implementation of these principles not only tied up the convention for an entire summer but later threatened to prevent the states from ratifying, or voting to approve, the document the convention produced.

Representation Representation was the most controversial issue in Philadelphia. Following the election of George Washington as president of the convention, Governor Edmund Randolph of Virginia rose to present a draft of a new constitution. This Virginia Plan called for a legislature with two houses: a lower house chosen by the people of the states, with representation according to population;

TABLE 3.1 Constitutional Compromise

The Virginia Plan	The New Jersey Plan	The Connecticut Compromise The Constitution of 1787
Two-house legislature, with the lower house directly elected based on state population and the upper house elected by the lower.	One-house legislature, with equal state representation, regardless of population.	Two-house legislature, with the House directly elected based on state population and the Senate selected by the state legislatures; two senators per state, regardless of population.
Legislature with broad power, including veto power over laws passed by the state legislatures.	Legislature with the same power as under the Articles of Confederation, plus the power to levy some taxes and to regulate commerce.	Legislature with broad power, including the power to tax and to regulate commerce.
President and cabinet elected by the legislature.	Separate multiperson executive, elected by the legislature, removable by petition from a majority of the state governors.	President chosen by an Electoral College.
National judiciary elected by the legislature.	National judiciary appointed by the executive.	National judiciary appointed by the president and confirmed by the Senate.
"Council of Revision" with the power to veto laws of the legislature.	National Supremacy Clause similar to that found in Article VI of the 1787 Constitution.	National Supremacy Clause: the Constitution is "the supreme Law of the Land."

and an upper house to be chosen by the lower house (see Table 3.1). Congress was to have the broad power to "legislate in all cases to which the separate States are incompetent, or in which the harmony of the United States may be interrupted." Congress was to have the power to nullify state laws that it believed violated the Constitution, thus ensuring the national government's supremacy over the states. The Virginia Plan also proposed a *parliamentary* form of government, in which the legislature (Congress) chose the principal executive officers of the government as well as federal judges. Finally, the Virginia Plan included a curious "council of revision," with the power to veto acts of Congress.

Delegates from New Jersey and Delaware objected strongly to the great power given to the national government in the Virginia Plan, the larger representation it proposed for the more populous states, and the plan's failure to recognize the role of the states in the composition of the new government. After several weeks of debate, William Paterson of New Jersey submitted a counterproposal. The New Jersey Plan called for a single-chamber Congress in which each state, regardless of its population, had one vote, just as under the Articles of Confederation. But unlike the Articles, the New Jersey Plan proposed separate executive and judicial branches of government and the expansion of the powers of Congress to include levying taxes and regulating commerce. Moreover, the New Jersey Plan included a National Supremacy Clause, declaring that the Constitution and federal laws would supersede state constitutions and laws.

Debate over representation in Congress raged into July 1787. At one point, the convention actually voted for the Virginia Plan, 7 votes to 3, but without New York, New Jersey, and Delaware, the new nation would not have been viable.

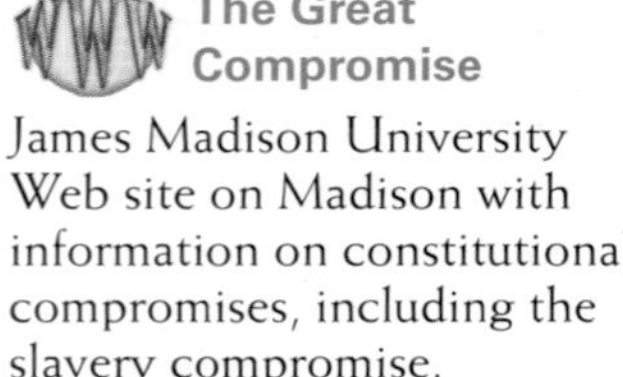

The Great Compromise

James Madison University Web site on Madison with information on constitutional compromises, including the slavery compromise.
www.jmu.edu/madison

Eventually, Roger Sherman of Connecticut came forward with a compromise. This Connecticut Compromise—sometimes called the Great Compromise—established two houses of Congress: in the upper house, the Senate, each state would have two members regardless of its size, in the lower body, the House of Representatives, each state would be represented according to population. Members of the House would be directly elected by the people; members of the Senate would be selected by their state legislatures. Legislation would have to pass both houses to be enacted. This compromise was approved by the convention on July 16.

Slavery Another conflict absorbing the attention of the delegates was slavery. In 1787 slavery was legal everywhere except in Massachusetts. Nevertheless, the delegates were too embarrassed to use the word *slave* or *slavery* in their debates or in the Constitution itself. Instead, they referred to "other persons" and "persons held to service or labour."

Delegates from the southern states, where slaves were a large proportion of the population, believed slaves should be counted in representation afforded the states, but not counted if taxes were to be levied on a population basis. Delegates from the northern states, with small slave populations, believed that "the people" counted for representation purposes should include only free persons. The Connecticut Plan included the now-infamous Three-fifths Compromise: three-fifths of the slaves of each state would be counted for purposes both of representation in the House of Representatives and for apportionment for direct taxes.

Slave owners also sought protection for their human "property" in the Constitution itself. They were particularly concerned about slaves running away to other states and claiming their freedom. So they succeeded in writing into the Constitution (Article IV, Section 2) a specific guarantee: "No person held to Service or Labour in one State . . . escaping into another, shall . . . be discharged from such Service or Labour, but shall be delivered up on Claim of the Party to whom such Service or Labour may be due."

Yet another compromise dealt with the slave trade. The capture, transportation, and "breaking in" of African slaves was considered a nasty business, even by southern planters. Many wealthy Maryland and Virginia plantations were already well supplied with slaves and thus could afford the luxury of conscience to call for an end to slave importation. But other planters from the less-developed southern states, particularly South Carolina and Georgia, wanted additional slave labor. The final compromise prohibited the slave trade—but not before the year 1808, thereby giving the planters twenty years to import all the slaves they needed before the slave trade ended.

Voter Qualifications Another important conflict centered on qualifications for voting and holding office in the new government. Most of the delegates believed that voters as well as officeholders should be men of property. (Only Benjamin Franklin went so far as to propose universal *male* suffrage.) But delegates argued over the specific wording of property qualifications, their views on the subject reflecting the source of their own wealth. Merchants, bankers, and manufacturers objected to making the ownership of a certain amount of land a qualification for officeholding. James Madison, a plantation owner himself, was forced to admit that "landed possessions were no certain evidence of real wealth. Many enjoyed them who were more in debt than they were worth."

After much debate, the convention approved a constitution without any expressed property qualifications for voting or holding office, except those that the states might impose themselves: "The Electors in each State shall have the

Although hotly debated, the issue of slaveholding was not resolved by the Founders in either the Declaration of Independence or the Constitution. As a result, the practice of buying and selling slaves—and the debate over this practice—continued for years to come, until political conflict exploded in the Civil War.

Qualifications requisite for Electors of the most numerous Branch of the State Legislature." At the time, every state had property qualifications for voting, and women were not permitted to vote or hold office. (The New Jersey Constitution of 1776 enfranchised women as well as men who owned property, but in 1787, a new state law limited the vote to "free white male citizens.")

Resolving the Economic Issues

The Founders were just as concerned with "who gets what, when, and how" as today's politicians are. Important economic interests were at stake in the Constitution. Historian Charles A. Beard pointed out that the delegates to the Constitutional Convention were men of wealth: planters, slaveholders, merchants, manufacturers, shippers, bankers and investors, and land speculators. Moreover, most of the delegates owned Revolutionary War bonds that were now worthless and would remain so unless the national government could obtain the tax revenues to pay them off[4] (see *A Conflicting View:* "An Economic Interpretation of the Constitution"). But it is certainly not true that the Founders acted only out of personal interest. Wealthy delegates were found on both sides of constitutional debates, arguing principles as well as economic interests.[5]

Levying Taxes A central purpose of the Constitution was to enable the national government to levy its own **taxes**, so that it could end its dependence on state contributions and achieve financial credibility. The very first power given to Congress in Article 1, Section 8, is the power to tax: "The Congress shall have Power to lay and collect Taxes, Duties, Imposts and Excises, to pay the Debts and provide for the common Defence and general Welfare."

The financial credit of the United States and the interests of Revolutionary War bondholders were guaranteed by Article VI in the Constitution, which specifically declared that the new government would be obligated to pay the debts of the old government. Indeed, the nation's first secretary of the treasury, Alexander

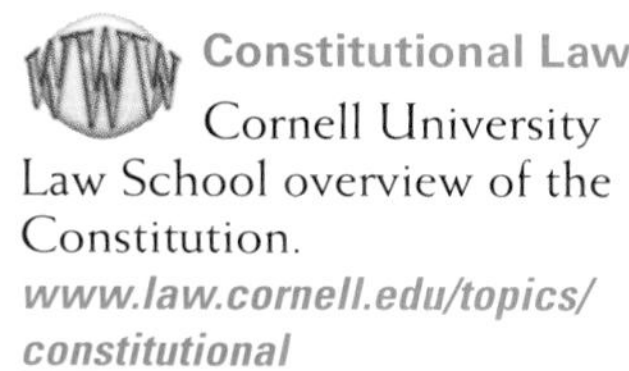

Constitutional Law Cornell University Law School overview of the Constitution. *www.law.cornell.edu/topics/constitutional*

taxes Compulsory payments to the government.

A CONFLICTING VIEW

An Economic Interpretation of the Constitution

Charles Beard, historian and political scientist, provided the most controversial historical interpretation of the origin of American national government in his landmark book. *An Economic Interpretation of the Constitution of the United States* (1913). Not all historians agree with Beard's economic interpretation, but all concede that it is a milestone in understanding the U.S. Constitution. Beard closely studied unpublished financial records of the U.S. Treasury Department and the personal letters and financial accounts of the fifty-five delegates to the Philadelphia convention. He concluded that they represented the following five economic interest groups, each of which benefited from specific provisions of the Constitution:

- ***Public security interests*** (persons holding U.S. bonds from the Revolutionary War: 37 of the 55 delegates). The taxing power was of great benefit to the holders of public securities, particularly when it was combined with the provision in Article VI that "all Debts contracted and Engagements entered into, before the Adoption of this Constitution, shall be as valid against the United States under this Constitution, as under the Confederation." That is, the national government would be obliged to pay off all those investors who held U.S. bonds, and the taxing power would give the national government the ability to do so on its own.
- ***Merchants and manufactures*** (persons engaged in shipping and trade: 11 of the 55 delegates). The Interstate Commerce Clause, which eliminated state control over commerce, and the provision in Article I, Section 9, which prohibited the states from taxing exports, created a free-trade area, or "common market," among the thirteen states.
- ***Bankers and investors*** (24 of 55 delegates). Congress was given the power to make bankruptcy laws, to coin money and regulate its value, to fix standards of weights and measures, to punish counterfeiting, to establish post offices and post roads, to pass copyright and patent laws to protect authors and inventors, and to punish piracies and felonies committed on the high seas. Each of these powers is a specific asset to bankers and investors as well as merchants, authors inventors, and shippers.
- ***Western land speculators*** (persons who purchased large tracts of land west of the Appalachian Mountains: 14 of the 55 delegates). If western settlers were to be protected from the Indians, and if the British were to be persuaded to give up their forts in Ohio and open the way to American westward expansion, the national government could not rely on state militias but must have an army of its own. Western land speculators welcomed the creation of a national army that would be employed primarily as an Indian-fighting force over the next century.
- ***Slave owners*** (15 of the 55 delegates). Protection against domestic insurrection also appealed to the southern slaveholders' deep-seated fear of a slave revolt. The Constitution permitted Congress to outlaw the *import of slaves* after the year 1808. But most southern planters were more interested in protecting their existing property and slaves than they were in extending the slave trade, and the Constitution provided an explicit advantage to slaveholders in Article IV, Section 2 (later revoked by the Thirteenth Amendment, which abolished slavery), by specifically requiring the forced return of slaves who might escape to free states.

Beard argued that the members of the Philadelphia convention who drafted the Constitution were, with a few exceptions, immediately, directly, and personally interested in, and derived economic advantages from, the establishment of the new system. But many historians disagree with Beard's emphasis on the economic motives of the Founders. The Constitution, they point out, was adopted in a society that was fundamentally democratic, and it was adopted by people who were primarily middle-class property owners, especially farmers, rather than owners of businesses. The Constitution was not just an economic document, although economic factors were certainly important. Since most of the people were middle class and owned private property, practically all Americans were interested in the protection of property.

Under the Articles of Confederation, each state issued its own currency. Differences in currency regulation from state to state led to financial uncertainty and inflation. By creating a national currency and putting the national government in charge of the money supply, the Founders hoped to restore stability and control inflation.

Hamilton, made repayment of the national debt the first priority of the Washington Administration.

The original Constitution placed most of the tax burden on consumers in the form of **tariffs** on goods imported into the United States. For more than a century, these tariffs provided the national government with its principal source of revenue. Tariffs were generally favored by American manufacturers, who wished to raise the price paid for foreign goods to make their home-produced goods more competitive. No taxes were permitted on *exports,* a protection for southern planters, who exported most of their tobacco and, later, cotton. Direct taxes on individuals were prohibited (Article 1, Section 2) except in proportion to *population.* This provision prevented the national government from levying direct taxes in proportion to income until the Sixteenth Amendment (income tax) was ratified in 1913.

The power to tax and spend was given to Congress, not to the president or executive agencies. Instead, the Constitution was very specific: "No Money shall be drawn from the Treasury, but in Consequence of Appropriations made by Law." This is the constitutional basis of Congress's "power of the purse."

Regulating Commerce The new Constitution gave Congress the power to "regulate Commerce with foreign Nations, and among the several States" (Article 1, Section 8), and it prohibited the states from imposing tariffs on goods shipped across state lines (Article 1, Section 10). This power created what we call today a **common market;** it protected merchants against state-imposed tariffs and stimulated trade among the states. States were also prohibited from "impairing the Obligation of Contracts"—that is, passing any laws that would allow debtors to avoid their obligations to banks and other lenders.

Protecting Money The Constitution also ensured that the new national government would control the money supply. Congress was given the power to coin money and regulate its value. More important, the states were prohibited from issuing their own paper money, thus protecting bankers and creditors from the repayment of debts in cheap state currencies. (No one wanted to be paid for goods or labor in Rhode Island's inflated dollars.) If only the national government could issue money, the Founders hoped, inflation could be minimized.

tariff Tax imposed on imported products (also called a customs duty).

common market Unified trade area in which all goods and services can be sold or exchanged free from customs or tariffs.

Protecting National Security

At the start of the Revolutionary War, the Continental Congress had given George Washington command of a small regular army—"Continentals"—paid for by Congress and also had authorized him to take command of state militia units. During the entire war, most of Washington's troops had been state militia. (The "militia" in those days was composed of every free adult male, each was expected to bring his own gun.) Washington himself had frequently decried the militia units as undisciplined, untrained, and unwilling to follow his orders. He wanted the new United States to have a *regular* army and navy, paid for by the Congress with its new taxing power, to back up the state militia units.

War and the Military Forces Congress was authorized to "declare War," to raise and support a regular army and navy, and to make rules regulating these forces. It was also authorized to call up the militia, as it had done in the Revolution, in order to "execute the Laws of the Union, suppress Insurrections and repel Invasions." When the militia are called into national service, they come under the rule of Congress and the command of the president.

The United States relied primarily on militia—citizen-soldiers organized in state units—until World War I. The regular U.S. Army, stationed in coastal and frontier forts, directed most of its actions against Native Americans. The major actions in America's nineteenth-century wars—the War of 1812 against the British, the Mexican War of 1846–48, the Civil War in 1861–65, and the Spanish-American War in 1898—were fought largely by citizen-soldiers from these state units.

Commander-in-Chief Following the precedent set in the Revolutionary War, the new president, who everyone expected to be George Washington, was made "Commander-in-Chief of the Army and Navy of the United States, and of the Militia of the several States, when called into the actual Service of the United States." Clearly, there is some overlap in responsibility for national defense: Congress has the power to declare war, but the president is Commander-in-Chief. During the next two centuries, the president would order U.S. forces into 200 or more military actions, but Congress would pass an official Declaration of War only five times. Conflict between the president and Congress over war-making powers continues to this day (see the section "Commander-in-Chief" in Chapter 11).

Foreign Affairs The national government also assumed full power over foreign affairs and prohibited the states from entering into any "Treaty, Alliance, or Con-

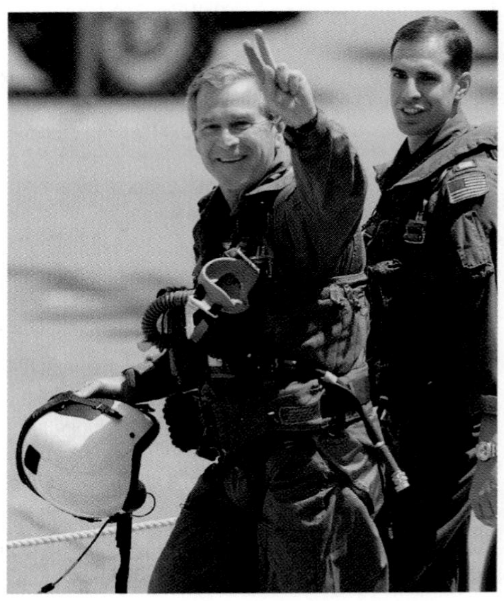

On May 1, 2003, President Bush landed on an aircraft carrier and declared "Mission Accomplished"—the end of major combat operations in Iraq. But guerrilla attacks on U.S. troops continued. By August more soldiers had died in the aftermath of the war than during the capture of Baghdad.

federation." The Constitution gave the president, not Congress, the power to "make Treaties" and "appoint Ambassadors." However, the Constitution stipulated that the president could do these things only "by and with the Advice and Consent of the Senate," indicating an unwillingness to allow the president to act autonomously in these matters. The Senate's power to "advise and consent" to treaties and appointments, together with the congressional power over appropriations, gives the Congress important influence in foreign affairs. Nevertheless, the president remains the dominant figure in this arena.

The Structure of the Government

The Constitution that emerged from the Philadelphia convention on September 17, 1787, founded a new government with a unique structure. That structure was designed to implement the Founders' beliefs in nationalism, limited government, republicanism, the social contract, and the protection of liberty and property. The Founders were realists; they did not have any romantic notions about the wisdom and virtue of "the people." James Madison wrote, "A dependence on the people is, no doubt, the primary control on the government, but experience has taught mankind the necessity of auxiliary precautions." The key structural arrangements in the Constitution—national supremacy, federalism, republicanism, separation of powers, checks and balances, and judicial review—all reflect the Founders' desire to create a strong national government while at the same time ensuring that it would not become a threat to liberty or property.

THINK AGAIN

Should a large state like California, with 32 million people, elect more U.S. senators than a small state like Wyoming, with only half a million people?

National Supremacy The heart of the Constitution is the National Supremacy Clause of Article VI:

> This Constitution, and the Laws of the United States which shall be made in Pursuance thereof, and all Treaties made, or which shall be made, under the Authority of the United States, shall be the supreme Law of the Land, and the Judges in every State shall be bound thereby, any Thing in the Constitution or Laws of any State to the Contrary notwithstanding.

This sentence ensures that the Constitution itself is the supreme law of the land and that laws passed by Congress supersede state laws. This National Supremacy Clause establishes the authority of the Constitution and the U.S. government.

Federalism The Constitution *divides power* between the nation and the states (see Chapter 4). It recognizes that both the national government and the state governments have independent legal authority over their own citizens: both can pass their own laws, levy their own taxes, and maintain their own courts. The states have an important role in the selection of national officeholders—in the apportionment of congressional seats and in the allocation of electoral votes for president. Most important, perhaps, both the Congress and three-quarters of the states must consent to changes in the Constitution itself.

Republicanism To the Founders, a *republican* government meant the delegation of powers by the people to a small number of gifted individuals "whose wisdom may best discern the true interest of their country, and whose patriotism and love of justice, will be least likely to sacrifice it to temporary or partial considerations."[6] The Founders believed that enlightened leaders of principle and property with ability, education, and a stake in the preservation of liberty could govern the people better than the people could govern themselves. So they gave the voters only a limited voice in the selection of government leaders.

TABLE 3.2 Decision-Making Bodies in the Constitution of 1787

House of Representatives	Senate	President	Supreme Court
Members alloted to each state "according to their respective numbers," but each state guaranteed at least one member.	"Two senators from each state" (regardless of the size of the state).	Single executive.	No size specified in the Constitution, but by tradition, nine.
Two-year term. No limits on number of terms that can be served.	Six-year term. No limits on number of terms that can be served.	Four-year term (later limited to two terms by the Twenty-second Amendment in 1951).	Life term.
Directly elected by "the People of the several States."	Selected by the state legislatures (later changed to direct election by the Seventeenth Amendment in 1913).	Selected by "Electors," appointed in each state "In such Manner as the Legislature thereof may direct" and equal to the total number of U.S. senators and House members to which the state is entitled in Congress.	Appointed by the president, "by and with the Advice and Consent of the Senate."

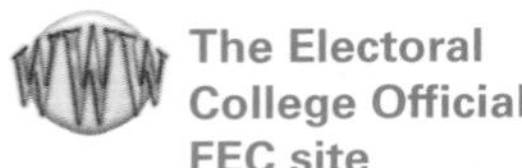

The Electoral College Official FEC site

Provides brief history of the electoral college and a description of how it works.
www.fec.gov/pages/ecmenu

The Constitution of 1787 created *four* decision-making bodies, each with separate numbers, terms of office, and selection processes (see Table 3.2). Note that in the *original* Constitution only one of these four bodies—the House of Representatives—was to be directly elected by the people. The other three were removed from direct popular control: state legislatures selected U.S. senators; "electors" (chosen at the discretion of the state legislatures) selected the president; the president appointed Supreme Court and other federal judges (see *Up Close:* "Why the Founders created an Electoral college to choose the president").

Democracy? The Founders believed that government rests ultimately on "the consent of the governed." But their notion of republicanism envisioned decision making by *representatives* of the people, not the people themselves (see *A Conflicting View:* "Let the People Vote on National Issues"). The U.S. Constitution does not provide for *direct* voting by the people on national questions, that is, unlike many state constitutions today, it does *not* provide for national **referenda.** Moreover, as noted earlier, only the House of Representatives (sometimes referred to even today as "the people's house") was to be elected directly by voters in the states.

referenda Proposed laws or constitutional amendments submitted to the voters for their direct approval or rejection, found in state constitutions but not in the U.S. Constitution.

These republican arrangements may appear "undemocratic" from our perspective today, but in 1787 the U.S. Constitution was more democratic than any other governing system in the world. Although other nations were governed by monarchs, emperors, chieftains, and hereditary aristocracies, the Founders recognized that government depended on the *consent of the governed.* Later democratic impulses in America greatly altered the original Constitution (see "Constitutional Change" later in this chapter) and reshaped it into a much more democratic document.

UP CLOSE

Why the Founders Created an Electoral College to Choose the President

In the 2000 presidential election, Democrat Al Gore received about 500,000 more votes nationwide than Republican George W. Bush. But Bush won the presidency with 271 "electoral votes" to Gore's 267. Why did the Founders decide to have "Electors" choose the president? Why not allow the people themselves to directly elect their president?

The Founders believed in "republicanism," not "democracy." They believed that the people should entrust governmental power to a small number of gifted individuals "whose wisdom may best discern the true interest of their country, and whose patriotism and love of justice will be least likely to sacrifice it to temporary or partial consideration."

At the Constitutional Convention of 1787 the Founders considered several systems for electing the president: direct election by the people, election by the Congress, election by the state legislatures, or election by citizens especially chosen to be "Electors."

Election by a direct popular vote had the least support in the Convention. Not only did the Founders distrust direct democracy, but they also worried that the 4 million people spread over 1,000 miles of Atlantic seaboard would have little knowledge or information about candidates from outside their own state, and that they would most likely vote for a "favorite son" from their own state. The result might be that no candidate would win a popular majority, or that the choice of the president would be decided by the largest most populous state, with little opportunity for candidates from smaller states to win the office.

The Founders also considered giving the Congress the power to choose the president. But the debates suggested that the Founders worried that this procedure would encourage unseemly political bargaining and corruption in the Congress itself. Moreover, it would upset the notion of separation of powers and checks and balances, the basic framework of the government that the Founders were creating.

Recognizing the pitfalls of both direct election of the president and election by Congress, the Founders turned to election of the president by the states. The first idea was to allow the state legislatures to select the president. But in the Constitution of 1787 the state legislatures were already charged with responsibility of electing U.S. Senators. So the Founders argued about whether to give additional power to state legislatures or to set up a separate system of presidential "Electors" in the states. Following much argument, the Founders finally decided on a compromise: Electors in each state, equal to the total number of House and Senate members from that state, would choose the president. However, *state legislatures* would decide how to choose Electors.

The Founders designed the Electoral College to ensure that the winning presidential candidate had support distributed across the nation—support in small states as well as large. (Small states are actually overrepresented in the Electoral College, owing to the fact that each state has two Electors based on their representation in the U.S. Senate regardless of their population.) Opponents of the Electoral College worry about the possibility of electing a president who receives fewer popular votes than his opponent, as occurred in the Bush-Gore election in 2000 (and the Harrison-Cleveland election of 1888). Indeed, if one candidate's popular support is heavily concentrated in a few states while the other candidate maintains a slim popular lead in enough states to win the needed majority of the Electoral College, this will be the outcome. But the Founders deliberately structured the Electoral College so that voters in a few populous states could not themselves determine the outcome. (See "Should We Scrap the Electoral College?" in Chapter 8.)

Separation of Powers and Checks and Balances

The Founders believed that unlimited power was corrupting and that the concentration of power was dangerous. James Madison wrote, "Ambition must be made to counteract ambition." The **separation of powers** within the national government—the creation of separate legislative, executive, and judicial branches in Articles I, II, and III of the Constitution—was designed to place internal controls on governmental power. Power is not only apportioned among three branches of government,

separation of powers Constitutional division of powers among the three branches of the national government—legislative, executive, and judicial.

A CONFLICTING VIEW

Let the People Vote on National Issues

"Direct democracy" means that the people themselves can initiate and decide policy questions by popular vote. The Founders were profoundly skeptical of this form of democracy. They had read about direct democracy in the ancient Greek citystate of Athens, and they believed the "follies" of direct democracy far outweighed any virtues it might possess. It was not until more than 100 years after the U.S. Constitution was written that widespread support developed in the American states for direct voter participation in policy making. Direct democracy developed in states and communities, and it is to be found today *only* in state and local government.

Why not extend our notion of democracy to include nationwide referenda voting on key public issues? Perhaps Congress should be authorized to place particularly controversial issues on a national ballot, Perhaps a petition signed by at least 1 million voters should also result in a question being placed on a national ballot.

Proponents of direct voting on national issues argue that national referenda would

- Enhance government responsiveness and accountability to the people.
- Stimulate national debate over policy questions.
- Increase voter interest and turnout on election day.
- Increase trust in government and diminish feelings of alienation from Washington.
- Give voters a direct role in policy making.

Opponents of direct democracy, from our nation's Founders to the present, argue that national referenda voting would

- Encourage majorities to sacrifice the rights of individuals and minorities.
- Lead to the adoption of unwise and unsound policies because voters are not sufficiently informed to cast intelligent ballots on many complex issues.
- Prevent consideration of alternative policies or modifications or amendments to the proposition set forth on the ballot. (In contrast, legislators devote a great deal of attention to writing, rewriting, and amending bills, as well as seeking out compromises among interests.)
- Enable special interests to mount expensive referendum campaigns; the outcomes of referenda would be heavily influenced by paid television advertising.

How would voters' decisions in national referenda differ from current government policies? A national poll on key policy issues produced the results shown here.

THINK AGAIN

In which do you have the most trust and confidence? President, Congress, Supreme Court

checks and balances
Constitutional provisions giving each branch of the national government certain checks over the actions of other branches.

but, perhaps more important, each branch is given important **checks and balances** over the actions of the others (see Figure 3.1 on page 72). According to Madison, "The constant aim is to divide and arrange the several offices in such a manner as that each may be a check on the other." No bill can become a law without the approval of both the House and the Senate. The president shares legislative power through the power to sign or to veto laws of Congress, although Congress may override a presidential veto with a two-thirds vote in each house. The president may also suggest legislation, "give to the Congress Information of the State of the Union, and recommend to their Consideration such Measures as he shall judge necessary and expedient." The president may also convene special sessions of Congress.

However, the president's power of appointment is shared by the Senate, which confirms cabinet and ambassadorial appointments. The president must also secure

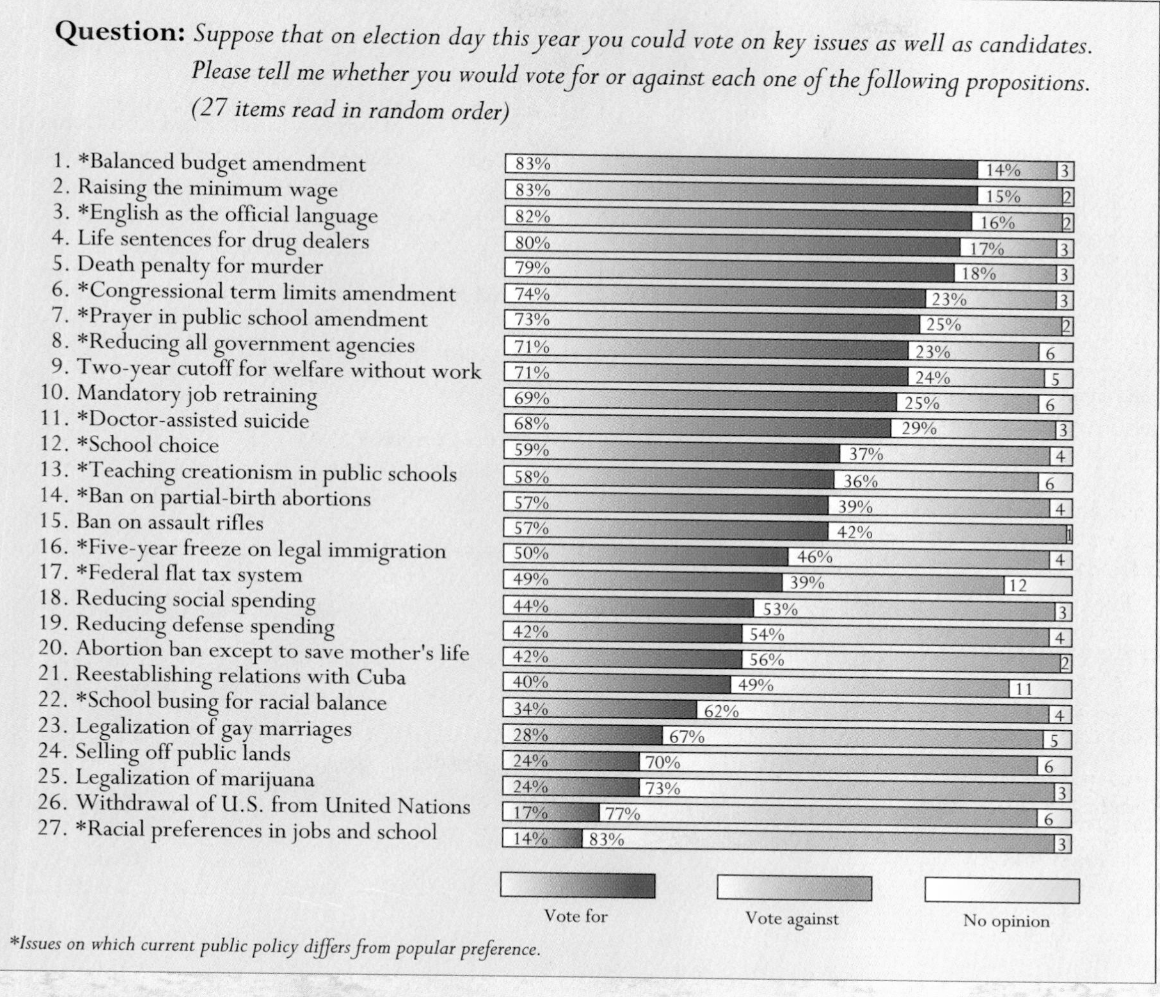

Source: *The Gallup Poll Monthly*, May 1996. Copyright © 1996 by The Gallup Organization.

the advice and consent of the Senate for any treaty. The president must execute the laws, but it is Congress that provides the money to do so. The president and the rest of the executive branch may not spend money that has not been appropriated by Congress. Congress must also authorize the creation of executive departments and agencies. Finally, Congress may impeach and remove the president from office for "Treason, Bribery, or other High Crimes and Misdemeanors."

Members of the Supreme Court are appointed by the president and confirmed by the Senate. Traditionally, this court has nine members, but Congress may determine the number of justices. More important, Congress must create lower federal district courts as well as courts of appeal. Congress must also determine the number of these judgeships and determine the jurisdiction of federal courts. But the most important check of all is the Supreme Court's power of judicial review.

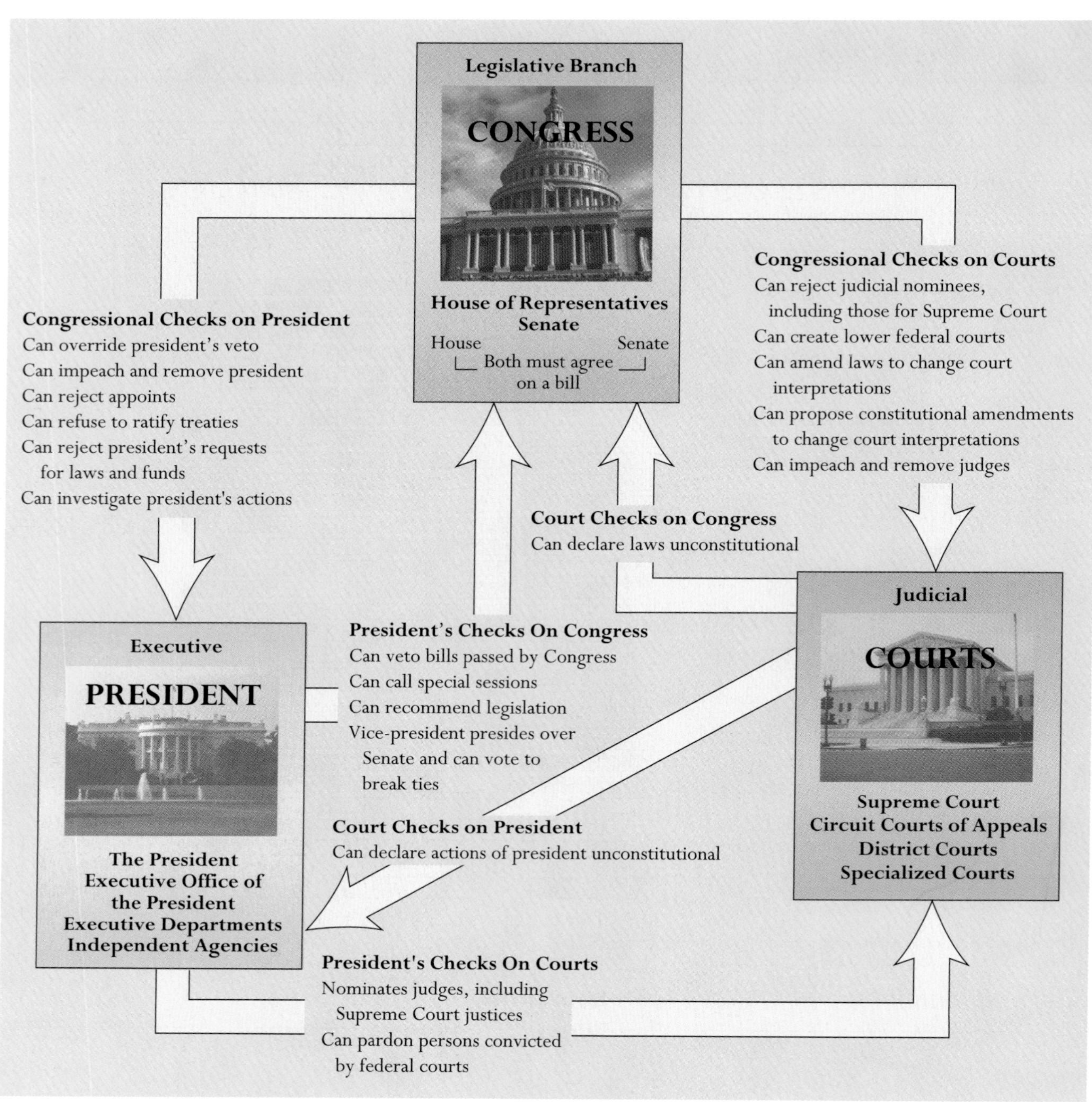

FIGURE 3.1 **Checks and Balances**

judicial review Power of the U.S. Supreme Court and federal judiciary to declare laws of Congress and the states and actions of the president unconstitutional and therefore legally invalid.

Judicial review, which is not specifically mentioned in the Constitution itself, is the power of the judiciary to overturn laws of Congress and the states and actions of the president that the courts believe violate the Constitution (see "Judicial Power" in Chapter 13). Judicial review, in short, ensures compliance with the Constitution.

Many Federalists, including Alexander Hamilton, believed the Constitution of 1787 clearly implied that the Supreme Court could invalidate any laws of Congress or presidential actions it believed to be unconstitutional. Hamilton wrote in 1787, "[Limited government] . . . can be preserved in no other way than through the

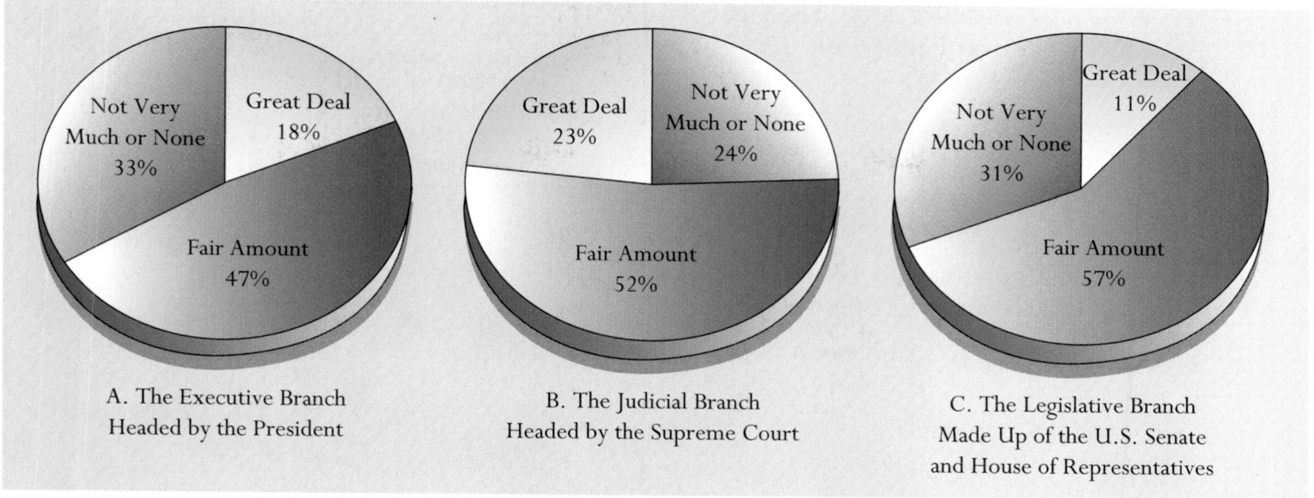

FIGURE 3.2 Trust and Confidence in the Three Branches of Government

As you know, the federal government is made up of three branches: an Executive branch, headed by the President, a Judicial branch, headed by the U.S. Supreme Court, and a Legislative branch, made up of the U.S. Senate and House of Representatives. How much trust and confidence do you have at this time in [A,B,C]—a great deal, a fair amount, not very much, or none at all? (Mechanism not shown.)

Source: Gallup Poll, July, 2000, as reported in *The Polling Report*, www.pollingreport.com. Copyright © 2000 by The Gallup Organization.

medium of courts of justice, whose duty it is to declare all acts contrary to the manifest tenor of the Constitution void."[7] But it was not until *Marbury v. Madison* in 1803 that Chief Justice John Marshall asserted a Supreme Court ruling that the Supreme Court possessed the power of judicial review over laws of Congress. (See *People in Politics:* "John Marshall and Early Supreme Court Politics" in Chapter 13.) Today the American people express more trust and confidence in the Supreme Court than in either the president or the Congress (see Figure 3.2).

Conflict over Ratification

Today the U.S. Constitution is a revered document, but in the winter of 1787–88, the Founders had real doubts about whether they could get it accepted as "the supreme Law of the Land." Indeed, the Constitution was ratified by only the narrowest of margins in the key states of Massachusetts, Virginia, and New York.

The Founders adopted a **ratification** procedure that was designed to enhance chances for acceptance of the Constitution. The ratification procedure written into the new Constitution was a complete departure from what was then supposed to be the law of the land, the Articles of Confederation, in two major ways. First, the Articles of Confederation required that amendments be approved by *all* of the states. But since Rhode Island was firmly in the hands of small farmers, the Founders knew that unanimous approval was unlikely. So they simply wrote into their new Constitution that approval required only nine of the states. Second, the Founders called for special ratifying conventions in the states rather than risk submitting the Constitution to the state legislatures. Because the Constitution placed many prohibitions on the powers of states, the Founders believed that special constitutional ratifying conventions would be more likely to approve the document than would state legislatures.

ratification Power of a legislature to approve or reject decisions made by other bodies. State legislators or state conventions must ratify constitutional amendments submitted by Congress. The U.S. Senate must ratify treaties made by the president.

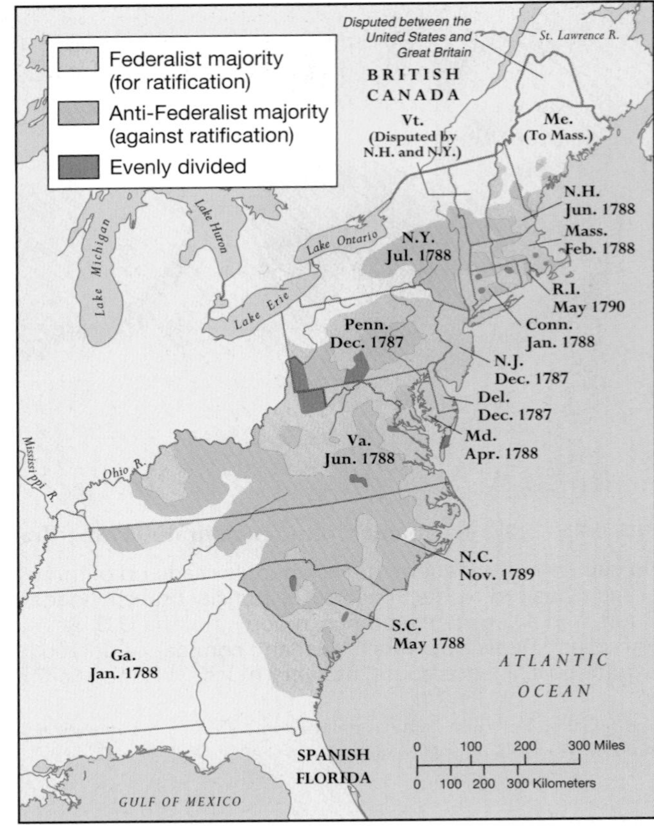

FIGURE 3.3 The Fight over Ratification

Source: Map from p. 118, retitled "The Fight Over Ratification," from Encyclopedia of American History by Richard B. Morris, editor and Jeffrey B. Morris, assistant editor. Copyright 1953, © 1961, 1965, 1970, 1976 by Harper & Row Publishers, Inc. Reprinted by permission of HarperCollins Publishers, Inc.

The Founders enjoyed some important tactical advantages over the opposition. First, the Constitutional Convention was held in secret; potential opponents did not know what was coming out of it. Second, the Founders called for ratifying conventions to be held as quickly as possible so that the opposition could not get itself organized. Many state conventions met during the winter months, so it was difficult for some rural opponents of the Constitution to get to their county seats in order to vote (see Figure 3.3 above).

The Founders also waged a very professional (for 1787–88) media campaign in support of the Constitution. James Madison, Alexander Hamilton, and John Jay issued a series of eighty-five press releases, signed simply "Publius," on behalf of the Constitution. Major newspapers ran these essays, which were later collected and published as *The Federalist Papers.* The essays provide an excellent description and explanation of the Constitution by three of its writers and even today serve as a principal reference for political scientists and judges faced with constitutional ambiguities (see *People in Politics:* "James Madison and the Control of 'Faction' "). Two of the most important *Federalist Papers* are reprinted in the Appendix to this textbook.

Nevertheless, opponents of the Constitution—the Anti-Federalists—almost succeeded in defeating the document in New York and Virginia. They charged that the new Constitution would create an "aristocratic tyranny" and pose a threat to the "spirit of republicanism." They argued that the new Senate would be an aristocratic upper house and the new president a ruling monarch. They complained that neither the Senate nor the president were directly elected by the people. They also argued that the new national government would trample state governments and deny the people of the states the opportunity to handle their own political and economic affairs. Virginia patriot Patrick Henry urged the defeat of the

PEOPLE IN POLITICS

James Madison and the Control of "Faction"

The most important contributions to American democracy by James Madison (1751–1836) were his work in helping to write the Constitution and his insightful and scholarly defense of it during the ratification struggle. Indeed, Madison is more highly regarded by political scientists and historians as a *political theorist* then as the fourth president of the United States.

Madison's family owned a large plantation in Virginia. He graduated from the College of New Jersey (now Princeton University) at eighteen and assumed a number of elected and appointed positions in Virginia's colonial government. In 1776 Madison drafted a new Virginia Constitution. While serving in Virginia's Revolutionary assembly, he met Thomas Jefferson; the two became lifetime political allies and friends. In 1787 Madison represented Virginia at the Constitutional Convention and took a leading role in its debates over the form of a new federal government.

Madison's political insights are revealed in *The Federalist Papers,* a series of eighty-five essays published in major newspapers in 1787–88, all signed simply "Publius." Alexander Hamilton and John Jay contributed some of them, but Madison wrote the two most important essays. Number 10, which explains the nature of political conflict (faction) and how it can be "controlled," and Number 51, which explains the system of separation of powers and checks and balances (both reprinted in the Appendix of this textbook). According to Madison, "controlling faction" was the principal task of government.

What creates faction? Madison believed that conflict is part of human nature. In all societies, we find "a zeal for different opinions concerning religion, concerning government, and many other points," as well as "an attachment to different leaders ambitiously contending for preeminence and power." Even when there are no serious differences among people, these "frivolous and fanciful distinctions" will inspire "unfriendly passions" and "violent conflicts."

Clearly, Madison believed conflict could arise over just about any matter. Yet "the most common and durable source of factions, has been the various and unequal distribution of property." That is, economic conflicts between rich and poor and between people with different kinds of wealth and sources of income are the most serious conflicts confronting society.

Madison argued that factions could best be controlled in a republican government extending over a large society with a "variety of parties and interests." He defended republicanism (representative democracy) over "pure democracy," which he believed "incompatible with personal security, or the rights of property." And he argued that protection against "factious combinations" can be achieved by including a great variety of competing interests in the political system so that no one interest will be able to "outnumber and oppress the rest." Modern pluralist political theory (see Chapter 1) claims Madison as a forerunner.

Constitution "to preserve the poor Commonwealth of Virginia." Finally, their most effective argument was that the new Constitution lacked a bill of rights to protect individual liberty from government abuse (see *A Conflicting View:* "Objections to the Constitution by an Anti-Federalist" on page 83).

A Bill of Rights

It may be hard to imagine today, but the original Constitution had no **Bill of Rights.** This was a particularly glaring deficiency because many of the new state constitutions proudly displayed these written guarantees of individual liberty.

Bill of Rights Written guarantees of basic individual liberties; the first ten amendments to the U.S. Constitution.

The Founders certainly believed in limited government and individual liberty, and they did write a few liberties into the body of the Constitution, including protection against ex post facto laws, a limited definition of treason, a guarantee of the writ of habeas corpus, and a guarantee of trial by jury (see Chapter 14).

COMPARED TO WHAT?

Canada's Parliamentary System

The United States and Canada are both democracies, but there are very important differences in the way Americans and Canadians govern themselves.

Canada is recognized as a constitutional monarchy rather than a republic. Officially the head of state for Canada is the Queen of England, who is represented in Canada by a Governor-General. The Governor-General, and occasionally the queen, undertake ceremonial roles in Canada. The Canadian government was initially established by the British North American Act of 1867, passed by the British Parliament.

Rather than a separation of powers between the legislative, executive, and judicial branches of government as in the United States, governmental powers in Canada are concentrated in the hands of the Prime Minister and his Cabinet. The Prime Minister is the leader of the majority party in the Canadian House of Commons. The PM names the Cabinet. The PM and the Cabinet are themselves members of the House of Commons. All legislation is initiated by the PM and the Cabinet for submission to the House of Commons. Passage is almost always assured because the PM's party controls the House of Commons. In the event of a defeat of a PM and the Cabinet, usually on a motion of censure or went of confidence, the PM and the Cabinet resign, and the Governor-General calls for new elections to the House of Commons. There is no specific "term" of office for the PM and Cabinet; they stay in office as long as they have the support of the House of Commons. However, by tradition, new elections are always held sometime within a five-year period. Occasionally, "by-elections" are held to replace Members of Parliament who have died or resigned.

The House of Commons currently includes 301 Members of Parliament (MPs). The Canadian Senate usually rubber-stamps legislation passed by the House of Commons, although occasionally it adds amendments or clarifications that are accepted by the House of Commons. The Senate is appointed by the Prime Minister, membership is generally considered an honor rather than a responsibility. Currently, five parties are represented in the House of Commons (see *Compared to What?* "Canada's Multiparty System" in Chapter 7). The Liberal Party currently holds a majority; its leader, Paul Martin, is the Prime Minister. The second-largest party in the House of Commons is officially known as the Opposition, and its leader the Leader of the Opposition.

Canadians view their parliamentary system as more responsible and responsive than the separate presidential and congressional branches of the U.S. government.

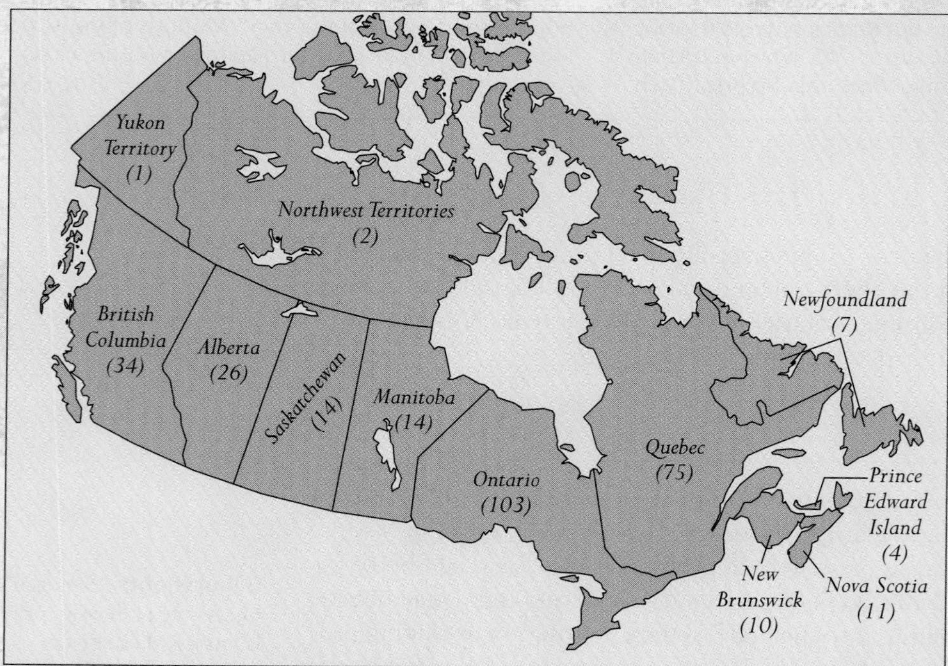

Parenthetical numbers indicate how many seats each province has in the House of Commons.

A CONFLICTING VIEW

Objections to the Constitution by an Anti-Federalist

Virginia's George Mason was a delegate to the Constitutional Convention of 1787, but he refused to sign the final document and became a leading opponent of the new Constitution. Mason was a wealthy plantation owner and a heavy speculator in western (Ohio) lands. He was a friend of George Washington's, but he considered most other political figures of his day to be "babblers" and he generally avoided public office. However, in 1776 he authored Virginia's Declaration of Rights, which was widely copied in other state constitutions and later became the basis for the Bill of Rights. Although an ardent supporter of states' rights, he attended the Constitutional Convention of 1787 and, according to James Madison's notes on the proceedings, was an influential force in shaping the new national government. His refusal to sign the Constitution and his subsequent leadership of the opposition to its ratification made him the recognized early leader of the Anti-Federalists.

Mason's first objection to the Constitution was that it included no Bill of Rights. But he also objected to the powers given to the Senate, which was not directly elected by the people in the original document; to the federal courts; and to the president. He was wary of the Necessary and Proper Clause, which granted Congress the power to "make all laws which shall be necessary and proper" for carrying out the enumerated powers—those specifically mentioned in the Constitution. Mason correctly predicted that this clause would be used to preempt the powers of the states.

In his "objections to the Constitution" Mason wrote,

> There is no declaration of rights; and the laws of the general government being paramount to the laws and constitutions of the several States, the declaration of rights in the separate States are no security.
>
> Senators are not the representatives of the people, or amenable to them.
>
> The judiciary of the United States is so constructed and extended as to absorb and destroy the judiciaries of the several States; thereby rendering law as tedious, intricate and expensive. . .
>
> Under their own construction of the general clause at the end of the enumerated powers, the Congress may . . . extend their power as far as they shall think proper; so that the State Legislatures have no security for the powers now presumed to remain to them; or the people for their rights.

Note that virtually all of Mason's objections to the original Constitution had to be remedied at a later date. The Bill of Rights was added as the first ten amendments. Eventually (1913) the Seventeenth Amendment provided for the direct election of U.S. senators. And Mason correctly predicted that the federal judiciary would eventually render the law "tedious, intricate, and expensive" and that the Necessary and Proper Clause, which he refers to as "the general clause at the end of the enumerated powers," would be used to expand congressional powers at the expense of the states.

The Federalists argued that there was really no need for a bill of rights because (1) the national government was one of **enumerated powers** only, meaning it could not exercise any power not expressly enumerated, or granted, in the Constitution; (2) the power to limit free speech or press, establish a religion, or otherwise restrain individual liberty was not among the enumerated powers; (3) therefore it was not necessary to specifically deny these powers to the new government. But the Anti-Federalists were unwilling to rest fundamental freedoms on a thin thread of logical inference from the notion of enumerated powers. They wanted specific written guarantees that the new national government would not interfere with the rights of individuals or the powers of the states. So Federalists at the New York, Massachusetts, and Virginia ratifying conventions promised to support the addition of a bill of rights to the Constitution in the very first Congress.

enumerated powers Powers specifically mentioned in the Constitution as belonging to the national government.

TABLE 3.3 The Bill of Rights

Guaranteeing Freedom of Expression

First Amendment prohibits the government from abridging freedom of speech, press, assembly, and petition.

Guaranteeing Religious Freedom

First Amendment prohibits the government from establishing a religion or interfering with the free exercise of religion.

Affirming the Right to Bear Arms and Protecting Citizens from Quartering Troops

Second Amendment guarantees the right to bear arms.

Third Amendment prohibits troops from occupying citizens' homes in peacetime.

Protecting the Rights of Accused Persons

Fourth Amendment protects against unreasonable searches and seizures.

Fifth Amendment requires an indictment by a grand jury for serious crimes; prohibits the government from trying a person twice for the same crime; prohibits the government from taking life, liberty, or property without due process of law; and prohibits the government from taking private property for public use without fair compensation to the owner.

Sixth Amendment guarantees a speedy and public jury trial, the right to confront witnesses in court, and the right to legal counsel for defense.

Seventh Amendment guarantees the right to a jury trial in civil cases.

Eighth Amendment prohibits the government from setting excessive bail or fines or inflicting cruel and unusual punishment.

Protecting the Rights of People and States

Ninth Amendment protects all other unspecified rights of the people.

Tenth Amendment reserves to the states or to the people those powers neither granted to the federal government nor prohibited to the states in the Constitution.

WWW **James Madison** The legacy of Madison organized by topic. *www.jmu.edu/madison*

A young member of the new House of Representatives, James Madison, rose in 1789 and presented a bill of rights that he had drawn up after reviewing more than 200 recommendations sent from the states. Interestingly, the new Congress was so busy debating new tax laws that Madison had a difficult time attracting attention to his bill. Eventually, in September 1789, Congress approved a Bill of Rights as ten **amendments**, or formal changes, to the Constitution and sent them to the states. (Congress actually passed twelve amendments. One was never ratified; another, dealing with pay raises for Congress, was not ratified by the necessary three-quarters of the states until 1992.) The states promptly ratified the first ten amendments to the Constitution (see Table 3.3 above), and these changes took effect in 1791.

The Bill of Rights was originally designed to limit the powers of the new *national* government. The Bill of Rights begins with the command "Congress shall make no law. . . ." It was not until after the Civil War that the Constitution was amended to also prohibit states from violating individual liberties. The Fourteenth Amendment, ratified in 1868, includes the command "No State shall. . . ." It prohibits the states from depriving any person of "life, liberty or property, without due process of law," or abridging "the privileges or immunities of citizens of the United States," or denying any person "equal protection of the laws." Today virtually all of the liberties guaranteed in the Constitution protect individuals not only from the national government but also from state governments.

amendment Formal change in a bill, law, or constitution.

Constitutional Change

The purpose of a constitution is to govern government—to place limits on governmental power. Thus government itself must not be able to alter or amend a constitution easily. Yet the U.S. Constitution has changed over time, sometimes by formal amendment and other times by judicial interpretation, presidential and congressional action, and general custom and practice.

THINK AGAIN

Should the Constitution be amended to guarantee that equal rights shall not be denied based on sex?

Amendments A constitutional amendment must first be proposed, and then it must be ratified. The Constitution allows two methods of *proposing* a constitutional amendment: (1) by passage in the House and the Senate with a two-thirds vote, or (2) by passage in a national convention called by Congress in response to petitions by two-thirds of the state legislatures. Congress then chooses the method of *ratification*, which can be either (1) by vote in the legislatures of three-fourths of the states, or (2) by vote in conventions called for that purpose in three-fourths of the states (see Figure 3.4 below).

Of the four possible combinations of proposal and ratification, the method involving proposal by a two-thirds vote of Congress and ratification by three-quarters of the legislatures has been used for all the amendments except one. Only for the Twenty-first Amendment's repeal of Prohibition did Congress call for state ratifying conventions (principally because Congress feared that southern Bible Belt state legislatures would vote against repeal). The method of proposal by national convention has never been used.

In addition to the Bill of Rights, most of the constitutional amendments ratified over the nation's 200 years have expanded our notion of democracy. Today the Constitution includes 27 amendments, which means that only 17 (out of more

The Anti-Federalist Papers

Essays by Anti-Federalists opposed to the ratification of the Constitution.
www.thisnation.com/library/antifederalist

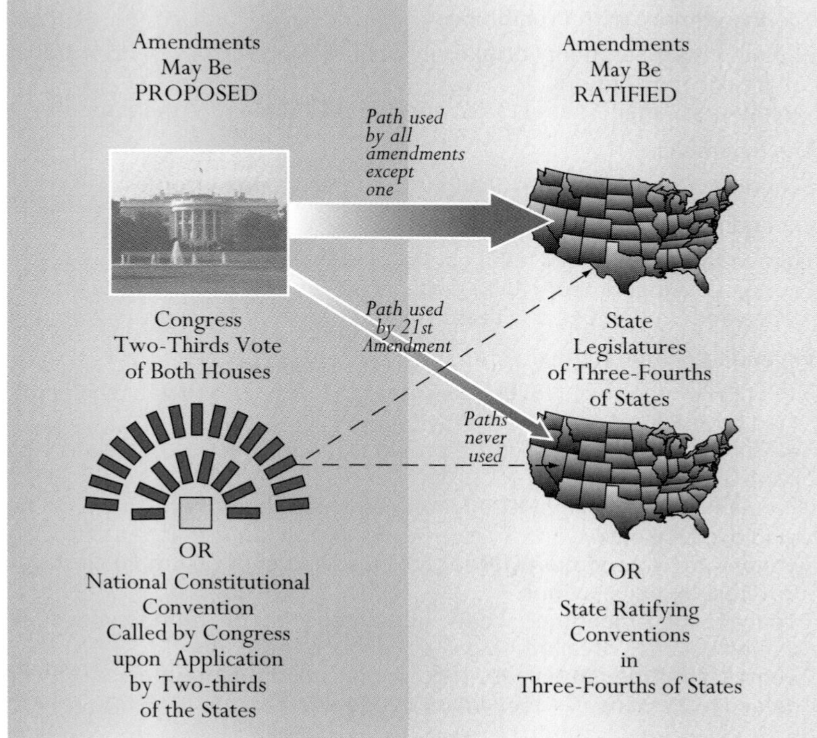

FIGURE 3.4
Constitutional Amendment Process

The Constitution set up two alternative routes for proposing amendments and two for ratifying them. One of the four possible combinations has actually been used for all except one (the Twenty-first) amendment. However, in our time there have been persistent calls for a constitutional convention to propose new amendments permitting school prayer, making abortion illegal, and requiring a balanced national budget.

than 10,000) proposed amendments have been ratified since the passage of the Bill of Rights. It is possible to classify the amendments that have been ratified into the broad categories of constitutional processes, Prohibition, income tax, individual liberty, and voting rights (see Table 3.4 below).

Equal Rights Amendment (ERA) Proposed amendment to the Constitution guaranteeing that equal rights under the law shall not be denied or abridged on account of sex. Passed by Congress in 1972, the amendment failed to win ratification by three of the necessary three-fourths of the states.

Amending the U.S. Constitution requires not only a two-thirds vote in both houses of Congress, reflecting *national* support, but also ratification by three-fourths of the states, reflecting widespread support within the states. The fate of the **Equal Rights Amendment,** popularly known as the ERA, illustrates the need for nationwide consensus in order to amend the Constitution. The Equal Rights Amendment is a simple statement to which the vast majority of Americans agree, according to public opinion polls: "Equality of rights under the law shall not be denied or abridged by the United States or any state on account of sex." Congress passed the ERA in 1972 with far more than the necessary two-thirds vote; both Republicans

TABLE 3.4 Amendments to the Constitution Since the Bill of Rights

Perfecting Constitutional Processes

Eleventh Amendment (1798) forbids federal lawsuits against a state by citizens of another state or nation

Twelfth Amendment (1804) provides separate ballots for president and vice president in the Electoral College to prevent confusion.

Twentieth Amendment (1933) determines the dates for the beginning of the terms of Congress (January 3) and the president (January 20).

Twenty-second Amendment (1951) limits the president to two terms.

Twenty-fifth Amendment (1967) provides for presidential disability.

Twenty-seventh Amendment (1992) prevents Congress from raising its own pay in a single session.

The Experiment with Prohibition

Eighteenth Amendment (1919) prohibits the manufacture, sale, or transportation of intoxicating liquors.

Twenty-first Amendment (1933) repeals the Eighteenth Amendment.

The Income Tax

Sixteenth Amendment (1913) allows Congress to tax incomes.

Expanding Liberty

Thirteenth Amendment (1865) abolishes slavery.

Fourteenth Amendment (1868) protects life, liberty, and property and the privileges and immunities of citizenship and provides equal protection of the law.

Expanding Voting Rights

Fifteenth Amendment (1870) guarantees that the right to vote shall not be denied because of race.

Seventeenth Amendment (1913) provides for the election of senators by the people of each state.

Nineteenth Amendment (1920) guarantees that the right to vote shall not be denied because of sex.

Twenty-third Amendment (1961) gives the District of Columbia electoral votes for presidential elections.

Twenty-fourth Amendment (1964) guarantees that the right to vote shall not be denied because of failure to pay a poll tax or other tax.

Twenty-sixth Amendment (1971) guarantees that the right to vote shall not be denied to persons eighteen years of age or older.

and Democrats supported the ERA, and it was endorsed by Presidents Nixon, Ford, and Carter as well as most other national political leaders and organizations. By 1978, thirty-five state legislatures had ratified the amendment—three states short of the necessary thirty-eight (three-quarters). (Five states subsequently voted to rescind, or cancel, their earlier ratification. However, because there is no language in the Constitution regarding rescission, there is some disagreement about the constitutionality of this action.) Promising that the "ERA won't go away," proponents of the amendment have continued to press their case. But to date Congress has not acted to resubmit the ERA to the states.

Judicial Interpretations Some of the greatest changes in the Constitution have come about not by formal amendment but by interpretations of the document by federal courts, notably to U.S. Supreme Court.

Indeed, through **judicial review,** the U.S. Supreme Court has come to play the central role in giving meaning to the Constitution. Judicial review is the power of federal courts, and ultimately the Supreme Court, to declare laws of Congress and actions of the president unconstitutional and therefore invalid. This power was first asserted by Chief Justice John Marshall in the case of *Marbury vs. Madison* in 1803 (see *People in Politics:* "John Marshall and Early Supreme Court Politics" in Chapter 13). It is now an important part of the system of checks and balances (see Figure 3.1). This power is itself an interpretation of the Constitution, because it is not specifically mentioned in the document.

Supreme Court interpretations of the Constitution have given specific meaning to many of our most important constitutional phrases. Among the most important examples of constitutional change through judicial interpretation are the important meanings given to the Fourteenth Amendment, particularly its provisions that "No State shall . . . deprive any person of life, liberty, or property, without due process of law; nor deny to any person within its jurisdiction the equal protection of the laws":

- Deciding that "equal protection of the laws" requires an end to segregation of the races (*Brown v. Board of Education of Topeka,* 1954, and subsequent decisions).
- Deciding that "liberty" includes a woman's right to choose an abortion, and that the term *person* does not include the unborn fetus (*Roe v. Wade,* 1973, and subsequent decisions).
- Deciding that "equal protection of the laws" requires that every person's vote should be weighed equally in apportionment and districting plans for the House of Representatives, state legislatures, city councils, and so on (*Baker v. Carr,* 1964, and subsequent decisions).

Presidential and Congressional Action Congress and the president have also undertaken to interpret the Constitution. Nearly every president, for example, has argued that the phrase "executive Power" in Article II includes more than the specific powers mentioned afterward. Thomas Jefferson purchased the Louisiana Territory from France in 1803 even though there is no constitutional authorization for the president, or even the national government, to acquire new territory. Presidents from George Washington to Richard Nixon have argued that Congress cannot force the executive branch to turn over documents it does not wish to disclose (see Chapter 11).

Congress by law has tried to restrict the president's power as Commander-in-Chief of the Armed Forces by requiring the president to notify Congress when U.S.

judicial review The power of federal courts to declare laws of Congress and actions of the president unconstitutional.

troops are sent to "situations where imminent involvement in hostilities is clearly indicated" and limiting their stay to sixty days unless Congress authorizes an extension. This War Powers Act (1973), passed by Congress over President Richard Nixon's veto in the immediate aftermath of the Vietnam War, has been ignored by every president to date (see Chapter 11). Yet it indicates that Congress has its own ideas about interpreting the Constitution.

Custom and Practice Finally, the Constitution changes over time as a result of generally accepted customs and practice. It is interesting to note, for example, that the Constitution never mentions political parties. (Many of the Founders disapproved of parties because they caused "faction" among the people.) But soon after Thomas Jefferson resigned as President Washington's first secretary of state (in part because he resented the influence of Secretary of the Treasury Alexander Hamilton), the Virginian attracted the support of Anti-Federalists, who believed the national government was too strong. When Washington retired from office, most Federalists supported John Adams as his successor. But many Anti-Federalists ran for posts as presidential electors, promising to be "Jefferson's men." Adams won the presidential election of 1796, but the Anti-Federalists organized themselves into a political party, the Democratic-Republicans, to oppose Adams in the election of 1800. The party secured pledges from candidates for presidential elector to cast their electoral vote for Jefferson if they won their post, then the party helped win support for its slate of electors. In this way the Electoral College was transformed from a deliberative body where leading citizens from each state came together to decide for themselves who should be president into a ceremonial body where pledged electors simply cast their presidential vote for the candidate who had carried their state in the presidential election. (For a full discussion of the current operation of the Electoral College, see *Up Close:* "Understanding the Electoral College" in Chapter 8.)

SUMMARY NOTES

- The true meaning of constitutionalism is the limitation of governmental power. Constitutions govern governments; they are designed to restrict those who exercise governmental power. Constitutions not only establish governmental bodies and prescribe the rules by which they make their decisions, but, more important, they also limit the powers of government.
- The American tradition of written constitutions extends back through the Articles of Confederation, the colonial charters, and the Mayflower Compact to the thirteenth-century English Magna Carta. The Second Continental Congress in 1776 adopted a written Declaration of Independence to justify the colonies' separation from Great Britain. All of these documents strengthened the idea of a written contract defining governmental power.
- The movement for a Constitutional Convention in 1787 was inspired by the new government's inability to levy taxes under the Articles of Confederation, its inability to fund the Revolutionary War debt, obstacles to interstate commerce, monetary problems, and civil disorders, including Shays's Rebellion.
- The nation's Founders—fifty-five delegates to the Constitutional Convention in Philadelphia in 1787—shared a broad consensus on liberty and property, the social contract, republicanism, limited government, and the need for a national government.
- The Founders compromised their differences over representation by creating two co-equal houses in the Congress: the House of Representatives, with members

apportioned to the states on the basis of population and directly elected by the people for two-year terms, and the Senate, with two members allotted to each state regardless of its population and originally selected by state legislatures for six-year terms.

- The infamous slavery provisions in the Constitution—counting each slave as three-fifths of a person for purposes of taxation and representation, guaranteeing the return of escaped slaves, and postponing the end of the slave trade for twenty years—were also compromises. Voter qualifications in national elections were left to the states to determine.
- The structure of the national government reflects the Founders' beliefs in national supremacy, federalism, republicanism, separation of powers, checks and balances, and judicial review.
- The original Constitution gave the people very little influence on their government: only members of the House of Representatives were directly elected; senators were elected by state legislatures; the president was elected indirectly by "electors" chosen in each state; and members of the Supreme Court and federal judiciary were appointed for life by the president and confirmed by the Senate. Over time, the national government became more democratic through the expansion of voting rights, the direct election of senators, the emergence of political parties, and the practice of voting for presidential electors pledged to cast their vote for the candidates of one party.
- The separation of powers and checks and balances written into the Constitution was designed, in Madison's words, "to divide and arrange the several offices in such a manner as that each may be a check on the other." Judicial review was not specifically described in the original Constitution, but the Supreme Court soon asserted its power to overturn laws of Congress and the states, as well as presidential actions, that the Court determined to be in conflict with the Constitution.
- Opposition to the new Constitution was strong. Anti-Federalists argued that it created a national government that was aristocratic, undemocratic, and a threat to the rights of the states and the people. Their concerns resulted in the Bill of Rights: ten amendments added to the original Constitution, all designed to limit the power of the national government and protect the rights of individuals and states.
- Over time, constitutional changes have come about as a result of formal amendments, judicial interpretations, presidential and congressional actions, and changes in custom and practice. The most common method of constitutional amendment has been proposal by two-thirds vote of both houses of Congress followed by ratification by three-fourths of the state legislatures.

KEY TERMS

constitutionalism 54
constitution 54
republicanism 60
nationalism 60
taxes 63
tariff 65
common market 65
referenda 68
separation of powers 69
checks and balances 70
judicial review 72
ratification 73
Bill of Rights 75
enumerated powers 77
amendment 78
Equal Rights Amendment (ERA) 80
judicial review 81

SUGGESTED READINGS

Beard, Charles. *An Economic Interpretation of the Constitution*. New York: Macmillan, 1913. A classic work setting forth the argument that economic self-interest inspired the Founders in writing the Constitution.

Finkelman, Paul. *Slavery and the Founders*. 2nd ed. Armark NY: M.E. Sharpe, 2000. A critical account of the Founders' attitudes toward slavery and the resulting 3/5th's compromise.

Frohren, Bruce. Ed. *The American Republic: Primary Sources.* Indianapolis: Liberty Fund Inc., 2002. Excellent collection of earliest American documents, from the Mayflower Compact to the Declaration of Independence.

Madison, James, Alexander Hamilton, and John Jay. *The Federalist Papers.* New York: Modern Library, 1937. These eighty-five collected essays, written in 1787–88 in support of ratification of the Constitution, remain the most important commentary on that document. Numbers 10 and 51 (reprinted in the Appendix) ought to be required reading for all students of American government.

McDonald, Forrest B. *Novus Ordo Seculorum.* Lawrence: University Press of Kansas, 1986. A description of the intellectual origins of the Constitution and the "new secular order" that it represented.

Peltason, J.W. and Sue Davis. *Understanding the Constitution.* 16th ed. New York: Harcourt Brace, 2004. Of the many books that explain the Constitution, this is one of the best. It contains explanations of the Declaration of Independence, the Articles of Confederation, and the Constitution. The book is written clearly and well suited for undergraduates.

Rossiter, Clinton L. 1787, *The Grand Convention.* New York: Macmillan, 1960. A very readable account of the people and events surrounding the Constitutional Convention in 1787, with many insights into the conflicts and compromises that took place there.

Storing, Herbert J. *What the Anti-Federalists Were For.* Chicago: University of Chicago Press, 1981. An examination of the arguments of the Anti-Federalists in opposition to the ratification of the Constitution.

MAKE IT REAL

THE CONSTITUTION: WHAT IF YOU WERE A FOUNDING FATHER?

The democratic principles that guide this nation are embodied in the Constitution, or are they? In this simulation, it is 1789 and you have been asked to make final revisions on the Constitution. You will be challenged to apply some of the principles, both modern and traditional, to the original Constitution. Decide whether or not to include these principles and see how your choices might affect the Constitution and American history.

The Constitution of the United States

The Preamble

We the People of the United States, in Order to form a more perfect Union, establish Justice, insure domestic Tranquility, provide for the common defense, promote the general Welfare, and secure the Blessings of Liberty to ourselves and our Posterity, do ordain and establish this Constitution for the United States of America.

"We, the people." Three simple words, yet of profound importance and contentious origin. Every government in the world at the time of the Constitutional Convention was some type of monarchy wherein sovereign power flowed from the top. The Founders of our new country rejected monarchy as a form of government and proposed instead a republic, which would draw its sovereignty from the people.

The Articles of Confederation that governed the U.S. from 1776 until 1789 started with: "We the under signed Delegates of the States." Early drafts of the new constitution started with: "We, the states . . ." But again, the Founders were not interested in another union of states but rather the creation of a new national government. Therefore, "We, the states" was changed to "We, the people." The remainder of the preamble describes the generic functions of government. These would apply to almost any type of government. Some have proven more critical than others. For example, "promote the general welfare" has been cited as the authority for social welfare programs of the federal government.

Article I—The Legislative Article

Legislative Power

The very first article in the Constitution established the legislative branch of the new national government. Why did the framers start with the legislative power instead of the executive branch? Under the Articles of Confederation, the legislature was the only functional instrument of government. Therefore, the framers truly believed it was the most important component of the new government.

Section 1 All legislative Powers herein granted shall be vested in a Congress of the United States, which shall consist of a Senate and House of Representatives.

Section 1 established a bicameral (two-chamber) legislature or an upper (Senate) and lower (House of Representatives) organization of the legislative branch.

House of Representatives: Composition; Qualifications; Apportionment; Impeachment Power

Section 2 Clause 1. The House of Representatives shall be composed of Members chosen every second Year by the People of the several States, and the Electors in each State shall have the Qualifications requisite for Electors of the most numerous Branch of the State Legislature.

This section sets the term of office for House members (2 years) and indicates that those voting for Congress will have the same qualifications as those voting for the state legislatures. Originally, states limited voters to white property owners. Some states even had religious disqualifications, such as Catholic or Jewish. Most property and religious qualifications for voting were removed by the 1840s, but race and gender restrictions remained.

Clause 2. No Person shall be a Representative who shall not have attained to the Age of twenty five Years, and been seven Years a Citizen of the United States, and who shall not, when elected, be an inhabitant of that State in which he shall be chosen.

This section sets forth the basic qualifications of a representative: at least 25 years of age, a U.S. citizen for at least 7 years, and a resident of a state. Note that the Constitution does not require a person to be a resident of the district he or she represents. At the time the Constitution was written, life expectancy was about 43 years of age. So a person 25 years old was middle aged. Considering today's life expectancy of about 78 years, the equivalent age of 25 would be about 45. The average age of a current representative is 53. Because of the specificity of the Constitution as to the qualifications for office, the U.S. Supreme Court ruled that term limits could not be imposed.

Clause 2 does not specify how many terms a Representative can serve in Congress. One provision of the Republican House *Contract with America* "The Citizens Legislature Act" called for term limits for legislators. This provision was not enacted. Subsequently some states passed legislation to limit the terms of their U.S. Representatives. Because of the specificity of the qualifications for office, the USSC ruled in *U.S. Term Limits, Inc. v. Thomton,* 514 U.S. 779 (1995) that term limits for U.S. legislators could not be imposed by any state but would require a constitution amendment.

Clause 3. Representatives and direct Taxes[1] shall be appointed among the several States which may be included within this Union, according to their respective Numbers, which shall be determined by adding to the whole Number of free Persons, including those bound to Service for a Term of Years, and excluding Indians not taxed, three fifths of all other Persons.[2] The actual Enumeration shall be made within three Years after the first Meeting of the Congress of the United States, and within every subsequent Term of ten Years in such Manner as they shall by Law direct. The Number of Representatives shall not exceed one for every thirty Thousand, but each State shall have at Least one Representative, and until such enumeration shall be made, the State of New Hampshire shall be entitled to chuse three, Massachusetts eight Rhode Island and Providence Plantations one, Connecticut five, New York six, New Jersey four, Pennsylvania eight, Delaware one, Maryland six, Virginia ten, North Carolina five, South Carolina five, and Georgia three.

This clause contains the Three-Fifths Compromise wherein American Indians and Blacks were only counted as 3/5 of a person for congressional representation purposes. This clause also addresses the question of congressional reapportionment every 10 years, which requires a census. Since the 1911 Reapportionment Act, the size of the House of Representatives has been set at 435. This is the designated size that is reapportioned every 10 years. Based on changes of population, some states gain and some states lose representatives. This clause also provides that every state, regardless of population, will have at least one (1) representative. Currently, seven states have only one representative.

Clause 4. When vacancies happen in the Representation from any State, the Executive Authority thereof shall issue Writs of Election to fill such Vacancies.

This clause provides a procedure for replacing a U.S. representative in the case of death, resignation, or expulsion from the House. Essentially, the governor of the representative's state will assign a successor. Generally, if less than half a term is left, the governor will appoint a successor. If more than half a term is remaining, most states require a special election to fill the vacancy.

Clause 5. The House of Representatives shall chuse their Speaker and other Officers, and shall have the sole Power of Impeachment.

Only one officer of the House is specified—the Speaker. All other officers are decided by the House.

[1]Modified by the 16th Amendment
[2]Replaced by Section 2, 14th Amendment

This clause also gives the House authority for impeachments (accusations) against officials of the executive and judicial branches.

Senate Composition: Qualifications, Impeachment Trials

*Section 3*Clause 1. The Senate of the United States shall be composed of two Senators from each State, *chosen by the Legislature thereof,*[3] for six Years and each Senator shall have one Vote.

This clause treats each state equally—all have two senators each. Originally, senators were chosen by state legislators, but since passage and ratification of the 17th Amendment, they are now elected by popular vote. This clause also establishes the term of a senator—6 years—three times that of a House member.

Clause 2. Immediately after they shall be assembled in Consequence of the first Election, they shall be divided as equally as may be into three Classes. The Seats of the Senators of the first Class shall be vacated at the Expiration of the second Year, of the second Class at the Expiration of the fourth Year, and of the third Class at the Expiration of the sixth Year, so that one third may be chosen every second Year *and if Vacancies happen by Resignation, or otherwise, during the Recess of the Legislature of any State, the Executive thereof may make temporary Appointments until the next Meeting of the Legislature which shall then fill such Vacancies.*[4]

To prevent a wholesale election of senators every six years, this clause provides that one-third of the Senate will be elected every two years. Senate vacancies are filled similar as the House—either appointment by the governor or a special election.

Clause 3. No person shall be a Senator who shall not have attained to the Age of thirty Years, and been nine Years a Citizen of the United States, and who shall not, when elected be an Inhabitant of that State for which be shall be chosen.

This clause sets forth the qualifications for U.S. senator: at least 30 years old, a U.S. citizen for at least nine years, and a citizen of a state. The equivalent age of 30 today would be 54 years old. The average age of a U.S. senator at present is 58.3 years.

Clause 4. The Vice President of the United States shall be President of the Senate but shall have no Vote, unless they be equally divided.

The only constitutional duty of the vice president is specified in this clause—president of the Senate. This official only has a vote if there is a tie vote in the Senate; then the vice president's vote breaks the tie.

Clause 5. The Senate shall chuse their other Officers, and also a President pro tempore, in the Absence of the Vice President, or when he shall exercise the Office of President of the United States

One official office in the U.S. Senate is specified—temporary president, who fills in during the vice president's absence (which is normally the case). All other Senate officers are designated and selected by the Senate.

[3]Repealed by the 17th Amendment
[4]Modified by the 17th Amendment

Clause 6. The Senate shall have the sole Power to try all Impeachments. When sitting for that Purpose, they shall be on Oath or Affirmation. When the President of the United States is tried, the Chief Justice shall preside. And no Person shall be convicted without the Concurrence of two thirds of the Members present.

Judgment in Cases of impeachment shall not extend further than to removal from Office, and disqualification to hold and enjoy any Office of honor. Trust or Profit under the United States, but the Party convicted shall nevertheless be liable and subject to Indictment, Trial, Judgment and Punishment according to Law.

The Senate acts as a trial court for impeached federal officials. If the accused is the president, the Chief Justice of the U.S. Supreme Court presides. Otherwise, the vice president normally presides. Conviction of the charges requires a 2/3 majority vote of those senators present at the time of the vote. Conviction results in the federal official's removal from office and disqualification to hold any other federal appointed office. Removal from office does not bar further prosecution under applicable criminal or civil laws, nor does it apparently bar one from elected office. A current representative, Alcee L. Hastings, was removed as a federal district judge. He subsequently ran for Congress and now represents Florida's 23rd Congressional District.

Congressional Elections: Times, Places, Manner

Section 4 The Times, Places and Manner of holding Elections for Senators and Representatives, shall be prescribed in each State by the Legislature thereof, but the Congress may at any time by Law make or alter such Regulations, except as to the Places of chusting Senators.

The Congress shall assemble at least once in every Year, *and such Meeting shall be on the first Monday in December, unless they shall by Law appoint a different Day.*[5]

The states determine the place and manner of electing representatives and senators, but Congress has the right to make or change these laws or regulations, except for the election sites. Congress is required to meet annually, and now, by law, annual meetings begin in January.

Powers and Duties of the Houses

Section 5 Clause 1. Each House shall be the Judge of the Elections, Returns and Qualifications of its own Members, and a Majority of each shall constitute a Quorum to do Business, but a smaller Number may adjourn from day to day, and may be authorized to compel the Attendance of absent Members, in such Manner, and under the Penalties as each House may provide.

This clause enables each legislative branch to essentially make its own rules. Normally, to take a vote, a quorum is necessary. But if no votes are scheduled, fewer than a quorum can convene a session.

Clause 2. Each House may determine the Rules of its Proceedings, punish its Members for disorderly Behaviour, and with the Concurrence of two thirds, expel a Member.

Essentially, each branch promulgates its own rules and punishes its own members. The ultimate punishment is expulsion of the member, which requires a 2/3 vote. Expulsion does not prevent the member from running again.

Clause 3. Each House shall keep a Journal of its Proceedings, and from time to time publish the same, excepting such Parrs as may in their Judgment require Secrecy, and the Yeas and Nays of the Members of either House on any question shall, at the Desire of one fifth of those Present, be entered on the Journal

An official record called the Congressional Record, House Journal, etc., is kept for all sessions. It is a daily account of House and Senate floor debates, votes, and members' remarks. However, a record is not printed if a proceeding is closed to the public for security reasons. Many votes are by voice vote, and if at least 1/5 of the members request, a recorded vote of Yeas and Nays will be conducted and recorded. This procedure permits analysis of congressional role-call votes.

Clause 4. Neither House, during the Session of Congress shall, without the Consent of the other, adjourn for more than three days, nor to any other Place than that in which the two Houses shall be sitting.

This clause prevents one branch from adjourning for a long period of time or to some other location without the consent of the other branch.

Rights of Members

Section 6 Clause I. The Senators and Representatives shall receive a Compensation for their Services, to be ascertained by Law, and paid out of the Treasury of the United States. They shall in all Cases, except Treason Felony and Breach of the Peace, be privileged from Arrest during then Attendance at the Session of their respective Houses, and in going to and returning from the same, and for any Speech or Debate in either House, they shall not be questioned in any other Place.

This section ensures that senators and congressional representatives will be paid a salary from the U.S. Treasury. This salary is determined by no other than the legislature. According to the Library of Congress legislative Web site THOMAS "The current salary for members of Congress is $145,100. A small number of leadership positions, like Speaker of the House, receive a somewhat higher salary." In addition, members of Congress receive many other benefits; free health care, fully funded retirement system, free gyms, 26 free round trips to their home state or district, etc. This section also provides immunity from arrest or prosecution for congressional actions on the floor or in travel to and from the Congress. For example, few members of Congress have ever been charged with drunk driving.

Clause 2. No Senator or Representative, shall, during the Time for which he was elected, be appointed to any civil Office under the Authority of the United States, which shall have been created, or the Emoluments whereof shall have been encreased during such time; and no Person holding any Office under the United States, shall be a Member of either House during his Continuance in Office.

This section prevents the U.S. from adopting a parliamentary democracy, since congressional members cannot hold executive offices and members of the executive branch cannot be members of Congress.

[5]Changed by the 20th Amendment

Legislative Powers: Bills and Resolutions

Section 7 Clause 1. All Bills for raising Revenue shall originate in the House of Representatives; but the Senate may propose or concur with Amendments as on other Bills.

This clause specifies one of the few powers specific to the U.S. House—revenue bills.

Clause 2. Every Bill which shall have passed the House of Representatives and the Senate, shall, before it becomes a Law, be presented to the President of the United States; If he approve be shall sign it, but if nor he shall return it, with his Objections to that House in which it shall have originated, who shall enter the Objections at large on their Journal, and proceed to reconsider it. If after such Reconsideration two thirds of that House shall agree to pass the Bill, it shall be sent, together with the Objections, to the other House, by which it shall likewise be reconsidered, and if approved by two thirds of that House, it shall become a Law. But in all such Cases the Votes of both Houses shall be determined by yeas and Nays, and the Names of the Persons voting for and against the Bill shall be entered on the Journal of each House respectively. If any Bill shall not be returned by the President within ten Days (Sundays excepted) after it shall have been presented to him, the Same shall be a Law, in like Manner as if he had signed it, unless the Congress by their Adjournment prevent its Return, in which Case it shall not be a Law.

The heart of the checks and balances system is contained in this clause. Both the House and Senate must pass a bill and present it to the president. If the president fails to act on the bill within 10 days (not including Sundays), the bill will automatically become law. If the president signs the bill, it becomes law. If the president vetoes the bill and sends it back to Congress, this body may override the veto by a 2/3 vote in each branch. This vote must be a recorded vote.

Clause 3. Every Order, Resolution, or Vote to which the Concurrence of the Senate and House of Representatives may be necessary (except on a question of Adjournment) shall be presented to the President of the United States; and before the Same shall take Effect, shall be approved by him, or being disapproved by him, shall be repassed by two thirds of the Senate and House of Representatives, according to the Rules and Limitations prescribed in the Case of a Bill.

This clause covers every other type of legislative action other than a bill. Essentially, the same procedures apply in most cases. There are a few exceptions. For example, a joint resolution proposing a new congressional amendment is not subject to presidential veto.

Powers of Congress

Section 8 Clause 1. The Congress shall have Power To lay and collect Taxes, Duties, Imposts and Excises, to pay the Debts and provide for the common Defence and general Welfare of the United States, but all Duties, Imposts and Excises shall be uniform throughout the United States.

To borrow Money on the credit of the United States;

To regulate Commerce with foreign Nations, and among the several States, and with the Indian Tribes;

To establish an uniform Rule of Naturalization, and uniform Laws on the subject of Bankruptcies throughout the United States;

To coin Money, regulate the Value thereof, and of foreign Coin, and fix the Standard of Weights and Measures;

To provide for the Punishment of counterfeiting the Securities and current Coin of the United States;

To establish Post Offices and post Roads;

To promote the Progress of Science and useful Arts, by securing for limited Times to Authors and Inventors the exclusive Right to their respective Writings and Discoveries;

To constitute Tribunals inferior to the supreme Court;

To define and punish Piracies and Felonies committed on the high Seas, and Offences against the Law of Nations;

To declare War, grant Letters of Marque and Reprisal, and make Rules concerning Captures on Land and Water;

To raise and support Armies, but no Appropriation of Money to that Use shall be for a longer Term than two Years;

To provide and maintain a Navy;

To make Rules for the Government and Regulation of the land and naval Forces;

To provide for calling for the Militia to execute the Laws of the Union, suppress Insurrections and repel Invasions;

To provide for organizing, arming, and disciplining, the Militia, and for governing such Part of them as may be employed in the Service of the United States, reserving to the States respectively, the Appointment of the Officers, and the Authority of training the Militia according to the discipline prescribed by Congress;

This *extensive* clause establishes what are known as the "expressed" or "specified" powers of Congress. In theory, this serves as a limit or brake on congressional power.

Clause 2. To exercise exclusive Legislation in all Cases whatsoever, over such District (not exceeding ten Miles square) as may, by Cession of particular States, and the Acceptance of Congress, become the Seat of the Government of the United States, and to exercise like Authority over all Places purchased by the Consent of the Legislature of the State in which the Same shall be, for the Erection of Forts, Magazines, Arsenals, dock Yards, and other needful Buildings—And

This clause establishes the seat of the federal government, which was first started in New York but eventually was moved to Washington, D.C., when both Maryland and Virginia ceded land to the new national government, which then established the District of Columbia.

Clause 3. To make all Laws which shall be necessary and proper for carrying into Execution the foregoing Powers, and all other Powers vested by this Constitution in the Government of the United States, or in any Department or Officer thereof.

This clause, known as the "Elastic Clause," provides the basis for the doctrine of "implied" congressional powers, which was first introduced in the U.S. Supreme Court case of *McCulloch v. Maryland,* 1819. This doctrine tremendously expanded the power of Congress to pass legislation and make regulations.

Powers Denied to Congress

Section 9. Clause 1. The Migration or Importation of such Persons as any of the States now existing shall think proper to admit, shall not be prohibited by the Congress prior to the Year one thousand eight hundred and eight, but a Tax or duty may be imposed on such Importation, not exceeding ten dollars for each Person.

This clause was part of the Three-Fifths Compromise. Essentially, the new Congress was prohibited from stopping the importation of slaves until 1808,

but it could impose a head tax, not to exceed ten dollars for each slave.

Clause 2. The Privilege of the Writ of Habeas Corpus shall not be suspended, unless when in Cases of Rebellion or Invasion the public Safety may require it.

Congress cannot suspend the writ of habeas corpus except in cases of rebellion or invasion. The writ of habeas corpus permits a judge to inquire about the legality of detention or deprivation of liberty of any citizen.

Clause 3. No Bill of Attainder or ex post facto Law shall be passed.

This provision prohibits Congress from passing either a bill of attainder (forfeiture of property in capital cases) or ex post facto laws (retroactive crimes after passage of legislation). Similar restrictions were enshrined in many state constitutions.

Clause 4. No Capitation, or other direct. Tax shall be laid, unless in Proportion to the Census or Enumeration herein before directed to be taken.[6]

This clause prevents Congress from passing an Income tax. Only with passage of the 16th Amendment in 1913 did Congress gain this power.

Clause 5. No Tax or Duty shall be laid on Articles exported from any State.

This section establishes free trade within the U.S. The federal government cannot tax state exports.

Clause 6. No Preference shall be given by any Regulation of Commerce or Revenue to the Ports of one State over those of another; nor shall Vessels bound to, or from one State, be obliged to enter, clear, or pay Duties in another.

This clause also applies to free trade within the U.S. The national government cannot show any preference to any state or maritime movements among the states.

Clause 7. No Money shall be drawn from the Treasury, but in Consequence of Appropriations made by Law, and a regular Statement and Account of the Receipts and Expenditures of all public Money shall be published from time to time.

This provision of the Constitution prevents any expenditure unless it has been specifically provided for in an appropriations bill. At the beginning of most fiscal years, Congress has not completed its work on the budget. Technically, the government cannot spend any money according to this provision and would have to shut down. So Congress normally passes a Continuing Resolution Authority providing temporary authority to continue to spend money until the final budget is approved and signed into law.

Clause 8. No Title of Nobility shall be granted by the United States. And no Person holding any Office of Profit or Trust under them, shall, without the Consent of Congress, accept of any present, Emolument, Office, or Title, of any kind whatever, from any King, Prince, or foreign State.

Feudalism would not be established in the new country. We would have no nobles. No federal official can even accept a title of nobility (even honorary) without permission of Congress.

Powers Denied to the States

This section sets out the prohibitions on state actions.

Section 10 Clause 1. No State shall enter into any Treaty. Alliance, or Confederation, grant Letters of Marque and Reprisal, coin Money, emit Bills of Credit, make any Thing but gold and silver Coin a Tender in Payment of Debts, pass any Bill of Attainder, ex post facto Law, or Law impairing the Obligation of Contracts of grant any Title of Nobility.

This particular clause is a laundry list of denied powers. Note that these restrictions cannot even be walved by Congress. States are not to engage in foreign relations, nor acts of war. A letter of Marque and Reprisal was used during these times to provide legal cover for privateers. The federal government's currency monopoly is established. The sanctity of contracts is specified. And similar state prohibitions are specified for bills of attainder, ex post facto, etc.

Clause 2. No State shall, without the Consent of the Congress, lay any Imposts or Duties on Imports or Exports, except what may be absolutely necessary for executing its inspection Laws: and the net Produce of all Duties and Imposts, laid by any State on Imports or Exports, shall be for the Use of the Treasury of the United States, and all such Laws shall be subject to the Revision and Controul of the Congress.

This section establishes the monopoly control of the national government in matters of both national and international trade. The only concession to states is health and safety inspections.

Clause 3. No State shall, without the Consent of Congress, lay any Duty of Tonnage, keep Troops, or Ships of War in time of Peace, enter into any Agreement or Compact with another State, or with a foreign Power, or engage in War, unless actually invaded, or in such imminent Danger as will not admit of delay.

This final section of the Legislative article establishes the war monopoly power of the national government. The only exception to state action is actual invasion or threat of imminent danger.

Article II—The Executive Article

This article establishes an entirely new concept in government—an elected executive power.

Nature and Scope of Presidential Power

Section 1 Clause 1. The executive Power shall be vested in a President of the United States of America. He shall hold his Office during the Term of four Years and, together with the Vice President, chosen for the same Term, be elected as follows

[6]Modified by the 16th Amendment.

This clause establishes the executive power in the office of the president of the United States of America. It also establishes a second office—vice president. A four-year term was established, but no limit on the number of terms. A limit was later established by the 22nd Amendment.

Clause 2. Each State shall appoint, in such Manner as the Legislature thereof may direct, a Number of Electors, equal to the whole Number of Senators and Representatives to which the State may be entitled in the Congress: but no Senator or Representative, or Person holding an Office of Trust or Profit under the United States, shall be appointed an Elector.

This paragraph essentially establishes the Electoral College to choose the president and vice president.

Clause 3. The Electors shall meet in their respective States, and vote by Ballot for two Persons, of whom one at least shall not be an Inhabitant of the same State with themselves. And they shall make a List of all the Persons voted for, and of the Number of Votes for each; which List they shall sign and certify, and transmit sealed to the Seat of the Government of the United States, directed to the President of the Senate. The President of the Senate shall, in the Presence of the Senate and House of Representatives, open all the Certificates, and the Votes shall then be counted. The Person having the greatest Number of Votes shall be the President, if such Number be a Majority of the whole Number of Electors appointed; and if there be more than one who have such Majority and have an equal Number of Votes, then the House of Representatives shall immediately chuse by Ballot one of them for President; and if no Person have a Majority, then from the five highest on the List the said House shall in like Manner chuse the President. But in chusing the President, the Votes shall be taken by States, the Representation from each State having one Vote, A quorum for this Purpose shall consist of a Member or Members from two thirds of the States, and a Majority of all the States shall be necessary to a Choice. In every Case, after the Choice of the President, the Person having the greatest Number of Votes of the Electors shall be the Vice President. But if there should remain two or more who have equal Votes, the Senate shall chuse from them by Ballot the Vice President.[7]

This paragraph has been superseded by the 12th Amendment. The original language did not require a separate vote for president and vice president. This resulted in a tied vote in the Electoral College in 1800 when both Thomas Jefferson and Aaron Burr received 73 electoral votes. The 12th Amendment requires a separate vote for each. Only one of the two can be from the state of the elector. This means that it is highly unlikely that the presidential and vice presidential candidates would be from the same state. This question arose in the 2000 election when Dick Cheney, who lived and worked in Texas, had to reestablish his residence in Montana.

The original language provided for a House election in the case of no majority vote or a tie vote among the top five candidates. The amendment lowered the number of candidates to the top three. The Senate is to select the vice president if a candidate does not have an electoral majority or in the case of a tie vote. The Senate considers only the top two candidates. The amendment also clarifies that the qualifications of the vice president are the same as those for president.

Clause 4. The Congress may determine the Time of chusing the Electors, and the Day on which they shall give their Votes; which Day shall be the same throughout the United States.

Congress is given the power to establish a uniform day and time for the state selection of electors.

Clause 5. No Person except a natural born Citizen, or a Citizen of the United States, at the time of the Adoption of this Constitution, shall be eligible to the Office of President; neither shall any Person be eligible to that Office who shall not have attained to the Age of thirty five Years, and been fourteen Years a Resident within the United States.

The qualifications for the offices of president and vice president are specified here—at least 35 years old, 14 years' resident in the U.S., and a natural-born citizen or citizen of the U.S. The 14th Amendment clarified who is a citizen of the U.S., a person born or naturalized in the U.S. and subject to its jurisdiction. But the term "natural-born citizen" is unclear and has never been further defined by the judicial branch. Does it mean born in the U.S. or born of U.S. citizens in the U.S. or somewhere else in the world? Unfortunately, there is no definitive answer.

Clause 6 In Case of the Removal of the President from Office, or of his Death, Resignation, or Inability to discharge the Powers and Duties of the said Office, the Same shall devolve on the Vice President, and the Congress may by Law provide for the Case of Removal, Death, Resignation, or Inability, both of the President and Vice President, declaring what Officer shall then act as president, and such Officer shall act accordingly, until the Disability be removed, or a President shall be elected.[8]

This clause has been modified by the 25th Amendment. Upon the death, resignation, or impeachment conviction of the president, the vice president becomes president. The new president nominates a new vice president, who assumes the office, if approved by a majority vote in both congressional branches. The president is also now able to notify the Congress of his inability to perform his office.

Clause 7. The President shall, at stated Times, receive for his Services, a Compensation which shall neither be encreased nor diminished during the Period of which he shall have been elected, and he shall not receive within that Period any other Emolument from the United States, or any of them.

This section covers the compensation of the president, which cannot be increased or decreased during his office. The current salary is $400,000/year.

Clause 8. Before he enter on the Execution of his Office, he shall take the following Oath or Affirmation—"I do solemnly swear (or affirm) that I will faithfully execute the Office of President of the United States, and will to the best of my Ability, preserve, protect and defend the Constitution of the United States."

[7]Changed by the 12th and 20th Amendments

[8]Modified by the 25th Amendment

This final clause in Section 1 is the oath of office administered to the new president.

Powers and Duties of the President

Section 2 Clause 1. The President shall be the Commander in Chief of the Army and Navy of the United States, and of the Militia of the several States, when called into the actual Service of the United States, he may require the Opinion, in writing, of the principal Officer in each of the executive Departments, upon any Subject relating to the Duties of their respective Offices, and he shall have the Power to grant Reprieves and Pardons for Offences against the United States, except in Cases of Impeachment.

This clause establishes the president as Commander-in-Chief of the U.S. armed forces. George Washington was the only U.S. president to actually lead U.S. armed forces during the Whiskey Rebellion. The second provision provides the basis for cabinet meetings that are used to acquire the opinions of executive department heads. The last provision provides an absolute pardon or reprieve power from the president. The provision was controversial, but legal, when former President Clinton pardoned fugitive Marc Rich.

Clause 2. He shall have Power, by and with the Advice and Consent of the Senate to make Treaties, provided two thirds of the Senators present concur, and he shall nominate, and by and with the Advice and Consent of the Senate, shall appoint Ambassadors, other public Ministers and Consuls, Judges of the supreme Court, and all other Officers of the United States, whose Appointments are not herein otherwise provided for, and which shall be established by Law but the Congress may by Law vest the Appointment of such inferior Officers, as they think proper in the President alone, in the Courts of Law, or in the Heads of Departments.

This clause covers two important presidential powers; treaty making and appointments. The president (via the State Department) can negotiate treaties with other nations, but these do not become official until ratified by a 2/3 vote of the U.S. Senate. The president is empowered to appoint judges, ambassadors, and other U.S. officials (cabinet officers, military officers, agency heads, etc.) subject to Senate approval. The Congress can and does delegate this approval to the president in the case of inferior officers. For example, junior military officer promotions are not submitted to the Senate, but senior officer promotions are.

Clause 3. The President shall have Power to fill up all Vacancies that may happen during the Recess of the Senate, by granting Commissions which shall expire at the End of their next Session.

This provision allows recess appointments of the officials listed in Clause 2 above. These commissions automatically expire unless approved by the Senate by the end of the next session. Presidents have used this provision to fill jobs when the nomination process is stalled. Some of these appointments have been very controversial. The regular nomination was stalled because the Senate did not want to confirm the nominee.

Section 3 He shall from time to time give to the Congress Information of the State of the Union, and recommend to their Consideration such Measures as he shall judge necessary and expedient, he may, on extraordinary Occasions convene both Houses, or either of them and in Case of Disagreement between them, with Respect to the Time of Adjournment, he may adjourn them to such Time as he shall think proper, he shall receive Ambassadors and other public Ministers, he shall take Care that the Laws be faithfully executed, and shall Commission all the Officers of the United States.

This section provides for the annual State of the Union address to a joint session of Congress and the American people. The president is also authorized to call special meetings of either the House or Senate. If there is disagreement between the House and Senate regarding adjournment, the president is empowered to adjourn them. This would be extremely rare. The president formally receives other nations' ambassadors. The next to last provision to faithfully execute laws provides the basis for the whole administrative apparatus of the presidency. All officers of the U.S. receive a formal commission from the president (most of these are signed with a signature machine).

Section 4 The President, Vice President and all civil Officers of the United States, shall be removed from Office on Impeachment for, and Conviction of, Treason, Bribery, or other high Crimes and Misdemeanors.

This section provides the constitutional authority for the impeachment and trial of the president, vice president, and all civil officers of the U.S. for treason, bribery, or other high crimes and misdemeanors (the exact meaning of this phrase is unclear and is often more political than judicial).

Article III—The Judicial Article

Judicial Power, Courts, Judges

Section 1 The judicial Power of the United States, shall be vested in one supreme Court, and in such inferior Courts as the Congress may from time to time ordain and establish. The Judges, both the supreme and inferior Courts, shall hold their Offices during good Behaviour, and shall, at stated Times, receive for their Services, a Compensation, which shall not be diminished during their Continuance in Office.

This section establishes the judicial branch in very general terms. It specifically provides only for the Supreme Court. Congress is given the responsibility to flesh out the court system. It initially did so in the Judiciary Act of 1789, when it established 13 district courts (one for each state), and 3 appellate courts. All federal judges hold their offices for life and can only be removed for breaches of good behavior—a very nebulous term. Federal judges have been removed for drunkenness, accepting bribes, and other misdemeanors. To date, no justice of the U.S. Supreme Court has ever been removed.

The salary of federal judges is set by congressional act, but can never be reduced. Although the American Bar Association and the Federal Bar Association consider federal judges' salaries inadequate, most Americans would probably disagree. Federal district judges earn $145,100/year, appellate judges

$153,900, and Supreme Court justices $178,300. The Chief Justice is paid $186,300. These are lifetime salaries, even upon retirement.

Jurisdiction

Section 2 The judicial Power shall extend to all Cases, in Law and Equity, arising under this Constitution, the Laws of the United States, and Treaties made, or which shall be made, under their Authority,—to all Cases affecting Ambassadors, other public Ministers and Consuls;—to all Cases of admiralty and maritime Jurisdiction;—to Controversies to which the United States shall be a Party;—to Controversies between two or more States; between a State and Citizens of another State;[9]—between Citizens of different States;—between Citizens of the same State claiming Lands under Grants of different States, and between a State, or the Citizens thereof, and foreign States, Citizens, or Subjects.

In all Cases affecting Ambassadors, other public Ministers and Consuls, and those in which a State shall be Party, the supreme Court shall have original Jurisdiction. In all the other Cases before mentioned, the supreme Court shall have appellate Jurisdiction, both as to Law and Fact, with such Exceptions, and under such Regulations as Congress shall make.

The Trial of all Crimes, except in Cases of Impeachment, shall be by Jury; and such Trial shall be held in the State where the said Crimes shall have been committed, but when not committed within any State, the Trial shall be at such Place or Places as the Congress may by Law have directed.

This section establishes the original and appellate jurisdiction of the U.S. Supreme Court. With the Congress of Vienna's 1815 establishment of "diplomatic immunity," the U.S. Supreme Court no longer hears cases involving ambassadors. Since 1925, the Supreme Court no longer hears every case on appeal but can select which cases it will accept, which is now only about 150 cases per year. This section also establishes the right of trial by jury for federal crimes.

Treason

Section 3 Treason against the United States, shall consist only in levying War against them, or in adhering to their Enemies, giving them Aid and Comfort. No Person shall be convicted of Treason unless on the Testimony of two Witnesses to the same overt Act, or on Confession in open Court.

The Congress shall have Power to declare the Punishment of Treason, but no Attainder of Treason shall work Corruption of Blood, or Forfeiture except during the Life of the Person attainted.

Treason is the only crime defined in the U.S. Constitution. Congress established the penalty of death for treason convictions. Note that two witnesses are required to convict anyone of treason. Even in cases of treasonable conduct, seizure of estates is prohibited.

Article IV—Interstate Relations

Full Faith and Credit Clause

Section 1 Full Faith and Credit shall be given in each State to the public Acts, Records, and judicial Proceedings of every other State. And the Congress may by general Laws prescribe the Manner in which such Acts, Records and Proceedings shall be proved, and the Effect thereof.

This section provides that the official acts, records of one state will be recognized and given credence by other states, e.g., marriages and divorces.

Privileges and Immunities, Interstate Extradition

Section 2 Clause 1. The Citizens of each State shall be entitled to all Privileges and Immunities of Citizens in the several States.

This clause requires states to treat citizens of other states equally. For example, when driving in another state, my driver's license is recognized. One area not so clear is that of charging higher state tuitions at educational institutions for out-of-state students.

Clause 2. A person charged in any State with Treason, Felony or other Crime, who shall flee from Justice, and be found in another State, shall on Demand of the executive Authority of the State from which he fled, be delivered up, to be removed to the State having Jurisdiction of the Crime.

Extradition is the name of this clause. A criminal fleeing to another state, if captured, can be returned to the state where the crime was committed. But this is not an absolute. A state's governor can refuse, for good reason, to extradite someone to another state.

Clause 3. No person held to Service or Labour in one State, under the Laws thereof, escaping into another, shall, in Consequence of any Law or Regulation therein, be discharged from such Service or Labour, but shall be delivered up on Claim of the Party to whom such Service or Labour may be due.[10]

This clause was included to cover runaway slaves. It has been made inoperable by the 13th Amendment, which abolished slavery.

Admission of States

Section 3 New States may be admitted by the Congress into this Union but no new State shall be formed or erected within the Jurisdiction of any other State, nor any State to be formed by the Junction of two or more States, or Parts of States, without the Consent of the Legislatures of the States concerned as well as of the Congress.

The Congress shall have Power to dispose of and make all needful Rules and Regulations respecting the Territory or other Property belonging to the United States, and nothing in this Constitution shall be so construed as to Prejudice any Claims of the United States, or of any particular State.

This section concerns the admission of new states to the Union. In theory, no state can be created from part of another state without permission of the state legislature. But West Virginia was formed from Virginia during the Civil War without the permission of Virginia, which was part of the Confederacy. With fifty states now part of the Union, this section has not been used for many decades. The only future use may be in the case of Puerto Rico or perhaps Washington, D.C.

Republican Form of Government

Section 4 The United States shall guarantee to every State in this Union a Republican Form of Government, and shall protect each

[9]Modified by the 11th Amendment

[10]Repealed by the 13th Amendment

of them against Invasion, and on Application of the Legislature, or of the Executive (when the Legislature cannot be convened) against domestic Violence.

This section commits the federal government to guarantee a republican form of government to each state and protect the state against foreign invasion or domestic insurrection.

Article V—the Amending Power

The Congress, whenever two thirds of both Houses shall deem it necessary, shall propose Amendments to this Constitution, or, on the Application of the Legislatures of two thirds of several States, shall call a Convention for proposing Amendments, which, in either Case, shall be valid to all Intents and Purposes, as Part of this Constitution, when ratified by the Legislatures of three fourths of the several States, or by Conventions in three fourths thereof, as the one or the other Mode of Ratification may be proposed by the Congress, Provided that no Amendment which may be made prior to the Year One thousand eight hundred and eight shall in any Manner affect the first and fourth Clauses in the Ninth Section of the first Article, and that no State, without its Consent, shall be deprived of its equal Suffrage in the Senate.

Amendment to the U.S. Constitution can be originated by a 2/3 vote in both the U.S. House and Senate or by 2/3 of the state legislatures asking for a convention to propose amendments. Proposed amendments, by either route, must be approved by 3/4 of state legislatures or by 3/4 of conventions convened in the states for purposes of ratification. Only one amendment has been ratified by the convention method—Amendment 21 to repeal the 18th Amendment establishing Prohibition.

Thousands of amendments have been proposed; few have been passed by 2/3 vote in each branch of Congress. The Equal Rights Amendment was one such case, but it was not ratified by 3/4 of state legislatures. There have only been 27 successful amendments to the U.S. Constitution.

Article VI—the Supremacy Act

Clause 1. All Debts contracted and Engagements entered into, before the Adoption of this Constitution, shall be as valid against the United States under the Constitution, as under the Confederation.

This clause made the new national government responsible for all debts incurred during the Revolutionary War. This was very important to banking and commercial Interests.

Clause 2. This Constitution, and the Laws of the United States which shall be made in Pursuance thereof, and all Treaties made, or which shall be made, under the Authority of the United States, shall be the supreme Law of the Land, and the Judges in every State shall be bound thereby any Thing in the Constitution or Laws of any State to the Contrary norwithstanding.

This is the National Supremacy Clause, which provides the basis for the supremacy of the national government.

Clause 3. The Senators and Representatives before mentioned, and the Members of the several State Legislatures, and all executive and judicial Officers, both of the United States and of the several States, shall be bound by Oath or Affirmation, to support this Constitution, but no religious Test shall ever be required as a Qualification to any Office or public Trust under the United States.

This clause requires essentially all federal and state officials to swear or affirm their allegiance to and support of the U.S. Constitution. Note that a religious test was prohibited for federal office. However, some states used religious tests for voting and office qualification until the 1830s.

Article VII—Ratification

The Ratification of the Conventions of nine States, shall be sufficient for the Establishment of this Constitution between the States so ratifying the Same.

Done in Convention by the Unanimous Consent of the States present the Seventeenth Day of September in the Year of our Lord one thousand seven hundred and Eighty seven and of the Independence of the United States of America the Twelfth. *In Witness whereof We have hereunto subscribed our Names.*

Amendments

Realizing the unanimous ratification of the 13 states of the new Constitution might never have occurred, the framers wisely specified that only 9 states would be needed for ratification. Even this proved to be a test of wills between Federalists and Anti-Federalists, leading to publication of the great political work *The Federalist Papers.*

The Bill of Rights

[The first ten amendments were ratified on December 15, 1791, and form what is known as the "Bill of Rights."]

The Bill of Rights applied initially only to the federal government and not to state or local governments. Beginning in 1925 in the case of *Gitlow v. New York,* the U.S. Supreme Court began to selectively incorporate the Bill of Rights, making its provisions applicable to state and local governments. There are only three exceptions, which will be discussed at the appropriate amendment.

Amendment 1—
Religion, Speech, Assembly, and Politics

Congress shall make no law respecting an establishment of religion, or prohibiting the free exercise thereof; or abridging the freedom of speech, or of the press; or the right of the people peaceably to assemble, and to petition the Government for a redress of grievances.

This is the godfather of all amendments in that it protects five fundamental freedoms: religion, speech, press, assembly, and petition. Note that the press is the only business that is specifically protected by the U.S. Constitution. Freedom of religion and speech are two of the most contentious issues and generate a multitude of Supreme Court cases.

Amendment 2—Militia and the Right to Bear Arms

A well-regulated Militia, being necessary to the security of a free State, the right of the people to keep and bear Arms, shall not be infringed.

This amendment is the favorite of the National Rifle Association. This amendment also has not been incorporated for state/local governments; that is, state and local governments are free to regulate arms within their respective jurisdictions. There is also controversy as to the meaning of this amendment. Some believe that it specifically refers to citizen militias, which were common at the time of the Constitution but now have been replaced by permanent armed forces. Therefore, is the amendment still applicable? Do private citizens need weapons for the security of a free state?

Amendment 3—Quartering of Soldiers

No Soldier shall, in time of peace be quartered in any house, without the consent of the Owner, nor in time of war, but in manner to be prescribed by law.

It was the practice of the British government to insist that colonists provide room or board to British troops. This amendment was designed to prohibit this practice. Today, military and naval bases provide the necessary quarters.

Amendment 4—Searches and Seizures

The right of the people to be secure in their persons, houses, papers, and effects, against unreasonable searches and seizures, shall not be violated, and no Warrants shall issue, but upon probable cause, supported by Oath or affirmation, and particularly describing the place to be searched, and the persons or things to be seized.

This is an extremely important amendment to prevent the abuse of state police powers. Essentially, unreasonable searches or seizures of homes, persons, or property cannot be undertaken without probable cause or a warrant that specifically describes the place to be searched, the person involved, and suspicious things to be seized.

Amendment 5—Grand Juries, Self-Incrimination, Double Jeopardy, Due Process, and Eminent Domain

No person shall be held to answer for a capital, or otherwise infamous crime, unless on a presentment or indictment of a Grand jury, except in cases arising in the land or naval forces, or in the Militia, when in actual service in time of War or public danger; nor shall any person be subject for the same offence to be twice put in jeopardy of life or limb, nor shall be compelled in any criminal case to be a witness against himself, nor be deprived of life, liberty, or property, without due process of law, nor shall private property be taken for public use, without just compensation.

Only a grand jury can indict a person for a federal crime. This provision does not apply to state/local governments. This amendment also covers double jeopardy, or being tried twice for the same crime in the same jurisdiction. Note that since the federal government and state governments are different jurisdictions, one could be tried in each jurisdiction for essentially the same crime. For example, it is a federal crime to kill a congressperson. It is also a state crime to murder anyone. Further, this amendment also covers the prohibition of self-incrimination. Pleading the 5th Amendment used to be common in Mafia cases, but recently was used by Enron witnesses. The deprivation of life, liberty, or property by any level of government is prohibited unless due process of law is applied. Finally, private property may not be taken under the doctrine of "eminent domain" unless the government provides just compensation.

Amendment 6—Criminal Court Procedures

In all criminal prosecutions, the accused shall enjoy the right to a speedy and public trial, by an impartial jury of the State and district wherein the crime shall have been committed, which district shall have been previously ascertained by law, and to be informed of the nature and cause of the accusation, to be confronted with the witnesses against him, to have compulsory process for obtaining witnesses in his favor, and to have the Assistance of Counsel for his defence.

This amendment requires public trials by jury for criminal prosecutions. Anyone accused of a crime is guaranteed the right to be informed of the charges; confront witnesses; to subpoena witnesses for their defense; and to have a lawyer for their defense. Currently, the government must provide a lawyer for a defendant unable to afford one.

Amendment 7—Trial by Jury in Common Law Cases

In Suits at common law, where the value in controversy shall exceed twenty dollars, the right of trial by jury shall be preserved, and no fact tried by a jury shall be otherwise re-examined in any Court of the United States, than according to the rules of the common law.

This amendment is practically without meaning in modern times. Statutory law has largely superseded common law. Federal civil law suits with a guaranteed jury are now restricted to cases that exceed $50,000. The Bill of Rights, which includes the right to trial by jury, applied orginally only to the national government. Beginning in 1925, the USSC began a selective process of incorporating provisions in the Bill of Rights and making them applicable to state/local governments as well. There are just a few provisions that have not been thus incorporated. Trial by jury is one. Some state/local governments have trials by judges, not by juries.

Amendment 8—Bail, Cruel and Unusual Punishment

Excessive bail shall not be required, nor excessive fines imposed, nor cruel and unusual punishments inflicted.

Capital punishment is covered by this amendment, which also prohibits excessive bail. But this is rela-

tive. Million-dollar bails are not uncommon in some cases. One federal judge offered voluntary castration for sex offenders in lieu of jail time. Higher courts held this to be a cruel or unusual punishment. But it is the death penalty that generates the most heated controversy. Court cases challenging the constitutionality of capital punishment cite this amendment's language prohibiting cruel and unusual punishment. For a period of 4 years, the USSC banned capital punishment. When states modified their statutes to provide a two part judicial process of guilt determination and punishment, the USSC allowed the reinstitution of capital punishment by the states.

Amendment 9—Rights Retained by the People

The enumeration in the Constitution of certain rights, shall not be construed to deny or disparage others retained by the people.

This amendment implies that there may be other rights of the people not specified by the previous amendments. Indeed, the Warren Court established the right to privacy even though it is not specifically mentioned in any previous amendment. Some would claim the persons have a right to adequate medical care and education.

Amendment 10—Reserved Powers of the States

The powers not delegated to the United States by the Constitution, nor prohibited by it to the States, are reserved to the States respectively, or to the people.

The 10th Amendment was seen as the reservoir of reserved powers for state governments. If the national government had been limited only to expressed powers in Article 1, Section 8, of the Constitution, this would have been the case. But the doctrine of implied national government powers, which was established by the U.S. Supreme Court in *McCulloch v. Maryland* in 1819, made the intent of this amendment almost meaningless. What reserved powers that were retained by the states were virtually removed by the U.S. Supreme Court's decision in the *Garcia v. San Antonio Metropolitan Transit Authority* case in 1985, which basically told state/local governments not to look to the courts to protect their residual rights but rather to their political representatives. In subsequent cases, the USSC has retreated somewhat from this position when the court found the federal government encroaching in state jurisdictional areas.

Amendment 11—Suits against the States

[Ratified February 7, 1795]

The Judicial power of the United States shall not be construed to extend to any suit in law or equity, commented or prosecuted against one of the United States by Citizens of another State, or by Citizens or Subjects of any Foreign State.

Article 3 of the U.S. Constitution originally allowed federal jurisdiction in cases of one state citizen against another state citizen or state. This amendment removes federal jurisdiction in this area. In essence, states may not be sued in federal court by citizens of another state or country.

Amendment 12—Election of the President

[Ratified June 15, 1804]

The Electors shall meet in their respective states, and vote by ballot for President and Vice-President, one of whom, at least, shall not be an inhabitant of the same state with themselves; they shall name in their ballots the person voted for as President, and in distinct ballots the person voted for as Vice-President, and they shall make distinct lists of all persons voted for as President, and of all persons voted for as Vice-President, and of the number of votes for each, which lists they shall sign and certify, and transmit sealed to the seat of the government of the United States, directed to the President of the Senate;—The President of the Senate shall, in presence of the Senate and House of Representatives, open all the certificates and the votes shall then be counted;—The person having the greatest number of votes for President, shall be the President, if such number be a majority of the whole number of Electors appointed; and if no person have such majority, then from the persons having the highest numbers not exceeding three on the list of those voted for as President, the House of Representatives shall choose immediately, by ballot, the President. But in choosing the President, the votes shall be taken by states, the representation from each state having one vote; a quorum for this purpose shall consist of a member or members from two-thirds of the states, and a majority of all states shall be necessary to a choice. And if the House of Representatives shall not choose a President whenever the right of choice shall devolve upon them, *before the fourth day of March next following*, then the Vice-President shall act as President, as in the case of the death or other constitutional disability of the President.[11] The person having the greatest number of votes as Vice-President, shall be the Vice-President, if such a number be a majority of the whole numbers of Electors appointed, and if no person have a majority, then from the two highest numbers on the list, the Senate shall choose the Vice-President, a quorum for the purpose shall consist of two-thirds of the whole number of Senators, and a majority of the whole number shall be necessary to a choice. But no person constitutionally ineligible to the office of President shall be eligible to that of Vice-President of the United States.

This was a necessary amendment to correct a flaw in the Constitution covering operations of the Electoral College. In the election of 1800, both Thomas Jefferson and Aaron Burr, of the same Democratic-Republican Party, received the same number of electoral votes, 73, for president. Article II of the original Constitution specified that each elector would cast two ballots. It did not specify for whom. This amendment clarifies that the electoral vote must be specific for president and vice president. The original Constitution provided that if no candidate received a majority of electoral votes, the House would decide from the candidates with the top five vote totals. This amendment reduces the candidate field to the top three vote totals. If the House delays in this selection past the fourth day of March, the elected vice president will act as president until the House selects the president. The original Constitution provided that the candidate with the second highest number of electoral votes would become vice president.

[11] Changed by the 20th Amendment

This amendment, which requires a separate vote tally for vice president, provides for selection by the U.S. Senate if no vice presidential candidate receives an electoral vote majority.

Amendment 13—Prohibition of Slavery

[Ratified December 6, 1865]

Section 1 Neither slavery nor involuntary servitude, except as a punishment for crime whereof the party shall have been duly convicted, shall exist within the United States, or any place subject to their jurisdiction.

Section 2 Congress shall have power to enforce this article by appropriate legislation.

This is the first of the three Civil War amendments. Slavery is prohibited under all circumstances. Involuntary servitude is also prohibited unless it is a punishment for a convicted crime.

Amendment 14—Citizenship, Due Process, and Equal Protection of the Laws

[Ratified July 9, 1868]

Section 1 All persons born or naturalized in the United States, and subject to the jurisdiction thereof, are citizens of the United States and of the State wherein they reside. No State shall make or enforce any law which shall abridge the privileges or immunities of citizens of the United States; nor shall any State deprive any person of life, liberty, or property, without due process of law; nor deny to any person within its jurisdiction the equal protection of the laws.

This section defines the meaning of U.S. citizenship and protection of these citizenship rights. It also establishes the Equal Protection Clause that each state must guarantee to its citizens. It extended the provisions of the 5th Amendment of due process and protection of life, liberty, and property and made these applicable to the states.

Section 2 Representatives shall be apportioned among the several States according to their respective numbers, counting the whole number of persons in each State, excluding Indians not taxed. But when the right to vote at any election for the choice of electors for President and Vice President of the United States, Representatives in Congress, the Executive and Judicial officers of a State, or the members of the Legislature thereof, is denied to any of the male inhabitants of such State, being twenty-one[12] years of age, and citizens of the United States, or in any way abridged, except for participation in rebellion, or other crime, the basis of representation therein shall be reduced in the proportion which the number of such male citizens shall bear to the whole number of male citizens twenty-one years of age in such State.

This section changes the Three-Fifths Clause of the original Constitution. Now all male citizens, 21 or older, will be used to calculate representation in the House of Representatives. If a state denies the right to vote to any male 21 or older, the number of denied citizens will be deducted from the overall state total to determine representation.

Section 3 No person shall be a Senator or Representative in Congress, or elector of President and Vice President, or bold any office, civil or military under the United States, or under any State, who, having previously taken an oath, as a member of Congress, or as an officer of the United States, or as a member of any State legislature, or as an executive or judicial officer of any State, to support the Constitution of the United States, shall have engaged in insurrection or rebellion against the same, or given aid or comfort to the enemies thereof. But Congress may by a vote of two-thirds of each House, remove such disability.

This section disqualifies from federal office or elector for president or vice president anyone who rebelled or participated in an insurrection against the Constitution. This was specifically directed against citizens of southern states. Congress by a 2/3 vote could override this provision.

Section 4 The validity of the public debt of the United States, authorized by law, including debts incurred for payment of pensions and bounties for services in suppressing insurrection or rebellion, shall nor be questioned. But neither the United States nor any State shall assume or pay any debt or obligation incurred in aid of insurrection or rebellion against the United States or any claim for the loss or emancipation of any slave, but all such debts, obligations and claims shall be held illegal and void.

Section 5 The Congress shall have power to enforce, by appropriate legislation, the provisions of this article.

Sections 4 and 5 cover the Civil War debts.

Amendment 15—The Right to Vote

[Ratified February 3, 1870]

Section 1 The right of citizens of the United States to vote shall not be demed or abridged by the United States or by any State on account of race, color, or previous condition of servitude.

Section 2 The Congress shall have power to enforce this article by appropriate legislation.

This final Civil War amendment state that voting rights could not be denied by any states on account of race, color, or previous servitude. Unfortunately, it did not mention gender. Accordingly, all male citizens 21 or over were guaranteed the right to vote by this amendment.

Amendment 16—Income Taxes

[Ratified February 3, 1913]

The Congress shall have power to lay and collect taxes on incomes, from whatever source derived, without apportionment among the several States, and without regard to any census or enumeration.

Article 1, Section 9, of the original Constitution prohibited Congress from enacting a direct tax (head tax) unless in proportion to a census. Congress in 1894 passed an income tax law, levying a 2 percent tax on incomes over $4,000. In 1895, the U.S. Supreme Court in a split decision (5–4) found that the income tax was a direct tax not apportioned among the states and was thus unconstitutional. Thus, Congress proposed an amendment allowing it to enact an income tax. Once this amendment was ratified, the flow of tax money to Washington increased tremendously.

[12]Changed by the 26th Amendment

Amendment 17—Direct Election of Senators

[Ratified April 8, 1913]

The Senate of the United States shall be composed of two Senators from each State, elected by the people thereof, for six years and each Senator shall have one vote. The electors in each State shall have the qualifications requisite for electors of the most numerous branch of the State legislatures.

When vacancies happen in the representation of any State in the Senate, the executive authority of such State shall issue writs of election to fill such vacancies: Provided, That the legislature of any State may empower the executive thereof to make temporary appointment until the people fill the vacancies by election as the legislature may direct.

This amendment shall not be so construed as to affect the election or term of any Senator chosen before it becomes valid as part of the Constitution.

Prior to this amendment, U.S. senators were selected by state legislatures. Now U.S. senators would be selected by popular vote in each state. Further, the governor of each state may fill vacancies, subject to state laws.

Amendment 18—Prohibition

[Ratified January 16, 1919, Repealed December 5, 1933 by Amendment 21]

Section 1 After one year from the ratification of this article the manufacture, sale, or transportation of intoxicating liquors within, the importation thereof into, or the exportation thereof from the United States and all territory subject to the jurisdiction thereof for beverage purposes is hereby prohibited.

Section 2 The Congress and the several States shall have concurrent power to enforce this article by appropriate legislation.

Section 3 This article shall be inoperative unless it shall have been ratified as an amendment to the Constitution by the legislatures of the several States, as provided in the Constitution, within seven years from the date of the submission hereof to the States by the Congress.[13]

This amendment was largely the work of the Women's Christian Temperance Union and essentially banned the manufacture, sale, or transportation of alcoholic beverages. Unintended consequences of this attempt to legislate morality were the brewing of "bathtub gin" and moonshine liquor, the involvement of the mob in importing liquor from Canada, and the "Untouchables" of Elliott Ness. Fortunately, this ill-fated social experiment was corrected by the 21st Amendment. This is also the first amendment where Congress fixed a period for ratification—7 years.

Amendment 19—For Women's Suffrage

[Ratified August 18, 1920]

The right of the citizens of the United States to vote shall not be denied or abridged by the United States or by any State on account of sex.

Congress shall have power, by appropriate legislation, to enforce the provision of this article.

[13]Repealed by the 21st Amendment

At long last, women achieved voting parity with men.

Amendment 20—The Lame Duck Amendment

[Ratified January 23, 1933]

Section 1 The terms of the President and Vice President shall end at noon on the 20th day of January, and the terms of the Senators and Representatives at noon on the 3d day of January, of the years in which such terms would have ended if this article had not been ratified, and the terms of their successors shall then begin.

Section 2 The Congress shall assemble at least once in every year, and such meeting shall begin at noon on the 3d day of January, unless they shall by law appoint a different day.

Section 3 If, at the time fixed for the beginning of the term of the President, the President elect shall have died, the Vice President elect shall become President. If a President shall not have been chosen before the time fixed for the beginning of his term, or if the President elect shall have failed to qualify, then the Vice President elect shall act as President until a President shall have qualified, and the Congress may by law provide for the case wherein neither a President elect nor a Vice President elect shall have qualified, declaring who shall then act as President, or the manner in which one who is to act shall be selected, and such person shall act accordingly until a President or Vice President shall have qualified.

Section 4 The Congress may by law provide for the case of the death of any of the persons from whom the House of Representatives may choose a President whenever the right of choice shall have developed upon them, and for the case of the death of any of the persons from whom the Senate may choose a Vice President whenever the right of choice shall have devolved upon them.

Section 5 Sections 1 and 2 shall take effect on the 15th day of October following the ratification of this article.

Section 6 This article shall be inoperative unless it shall have been ratified as an amendment to the Constitution by the legislatures of three-fourths of the several States within seven years from the date of its submission.

Called the Lame Duck amendment, this amendment fixes the dates for the end of presidential and legislative terms. A new president is elected in November, but the current president remains in office until January 20 of the following year. Thus, the term "lame duck." Legislative terms begin earlier, on January 3.

Amendment 21—Repeal of Prohibition

[Ratified December 5, 1933]

Section 1 The eighteenth article of amendment to the Constitution of the United States is hereby repealed.

Section 2 The transportation or importation into any State. Territory, or possession of the United States for delivery or use therein of intoxicating liquors, in violation of the laws thereof, is hereby prohibited.

Section 3 This article shall be inoperative unless it shall have been ratified as an amendment to the Constitution by conventions in the several States, as provided in the Constitution, within seven years from the date of the submission hereof to the States by the Congress.

This unusual amendment nullified the 18th Amendment. The end of Prohibition unless prohibited by state laws.

Amendment 22—Number of Presidential Terms

[Ratified February 27, 1951]

Section 1 No person shall be elected to the office of the President more than twice, and no person who has held the office of President, or acted as President, for more than two years of a term to which some other person was elected President shall be elected to the office of the President more than once. But this article shall not apply to any person holding the office of President when this article was proposed by the Congress, and shall not prevent any person who may be holding the office of President, or acting as President, during the term within which this article becomes operative from holding the office of President or acting as President during the remainder of such term.

Section 2 This article shall be inoperative unless it shall have been ratified as an amendment to the Constitution by the legislatures of three-fourths of the several states within seven years from the date of its submission to the states by the Congress.

This amendment could be called the Franklin D. Roosevelt amendment. It was FDR who broke the previous unwritten pattern of no more than two-term presidents. Democrat Roosevelt won an unprecedented four terms as president. When the Republicans took control of the Congress in 1948, they pushed through the 22nd Amendment, limiting the U.S. president to a lifetime of two full four-year terms of office.

Amendment 23—Presidential Electors for the District of Columbia

[Ratified March 29, 1961]

Section 1 The District constituting the seat of government of the United States shall appoint in such manner as the Congress may direct:

A number of electors of President and Vice President equal to the whole number of Senators and Representatives in Congress to which the District would be entitled if it were a state, but in no event more than the least populous state, they shall be in addition to those appointed by the states, but they shall be considered for the purposes of the election of President and Vice President, to be electors appointed by a state, and they shall meet in the District and perform such duties as provided by the twelfth article of amendment.

Section 2 The Congress shall have power to enforce this article by appropriate legislation

This amendment gave electoral votes to the citizens of Washington, D.C., which is not a state and thus not included in the original scheme of state electoral votes. Currently, Washington, D.C., has 3 electoral votes, bringing the total of presidential electoral votes to 538. Puerto Ricans are citizens of the U.S. but have no electoral votes.

Amendment 24—The Anti-Poll Tax Amendment

[Ratified January 23, 1964]

Section 1 The right of citizens of the United States to vote in any primary or other election for President or Vice President, for electors for President or Vice President or for Senator or Representative in Congress, shall not be denied or abridged by the United States or any state by reason of failure to pay any poll tax or other tax.

Section 2 The Congress shall have power to enforce this article by appropriate legislation.

The poll tax was a procedure used mostly in southern states to discourage poor white and black voters from registering to vote. Essentially, one would have to pay a tax to register to vote. The tax was not much—around $34/year. But for a poor white or black voter, this might not be disposable income. As part of the assault against disenfranchisement of voters, the poll tax was abolished. Literacy tests, another device to disqualify voters, were abolished by the Voting Rights Act of 1965.

Amendment 25—Presidential Disability, Vice Presidential Vacancies

[Ratified February 10, 1967]

Section 1 In case of the removal of the President from office or his death or resignation, the Vice President shall become President.

Section 2 Whenever there is a vacancy in the office of the Vice President, the President shall nominate a Vice President who shall take the office upon confirmation by a majority vote of both Houses of Congress.

Section 3 Whenever the President transmits to the President pro tempore of the Senate and the Speaker of the House of Representatives his written declaration that he is unable to discharge the powers and duties of his office, and until he transmits to them a written declaration to the contrary, such powers and duties shall be discharged by the Vice President as Acting President.

Section 4 Whenever the Vice President and a majority of either the principal officers of the executive departments or of such other body as Congress may by law provide, transmit to the President pro tempore of the Senate and the Speaker of the House of Representatives their written declaration that the President is unable to discharge the powers and duties of his office, the Vice President shall immediately assume the powers and duties of the office as Acting President.

Thereafter, when the President transmits to the President pro tempore of the Senate and the Speaker of the House of Representatives his written declaration that no inability exists, he shall resume the powers and duties of his office unless the Vice President and a majority of either the principal officers of the executive departments, or of such other body as Congress may by law provide, transmit within four days to the President pro tempore of the Senate and the Speaker of the House of Representatives their written declaration that the President is unable to discharge the powers and duties of his office. Thereupon Congress shall decide the issue, assembling within forty-eight hours for that purpose if not in session. If the Congress, within twenty-one days after receipt of the latter written declaration, or, if Congress is not in session, within twenty-one days after Congress is required to assemble, determines by two-thirds vote of both Houses that the President is unable to discharge the powers and duties of his office, the Vice President shall continue to discharge the same as Acting President otherwise the President shall resume the powers and duties of his office.

During the administration of President Woodrow Wilson, his final year in office, in 1919, was marked by serious illness. It is rumored that his wife acted as president. There was no constitutional provision to cover an incapacitating illness of a president. So this amendment provides a procedure for this eventuality. The president can inform congressional lead-

ers of his incapacitation and the vice president takes over. When he recovers, the president can so inform congressional leaders and he resumes office.

But the amendment also recognizes that the president may not be able or wish to indicate this debilitation; so the vice president and a majority of cabinet members can inform congressional leaders and the vice president takes over. When the president informs congressional leadership that he is back in form, he resumes the presidency unless the vice president and majority of the cabinet disagree. Then Congress must decide. The likelihood that this procedure will ever be used is relatively very small.

The most immediate importance of this amendment concerns the office of vice president. The original Constitution did not address the issue of a vacancy in this office. So the 25th Amendment established the procedure, just in time! This amendment was ratified in 1967. In 1973, the sitting vice president, Spiro Agnew, resigned his office. Under the provisions of this amendment, President Nixon nominated Gerald Ford as vice president. As a former member of the House, the Congress quickly approved him. But a year later, President Nixon also resigned. Now Vice President Ford became President Ford, and he in turn appointed Nelson Rockefeller as the new vice president. So, now for the first time in our history, we had both a president and vice president, neither of whom was elected by the Electoral College.

AMENDMENT 26—EIGHTEEN-YEAR-OLD VOTE

[Ratified July 1, 1971]

Section 1 The right of citizens of the United States, who are 18 years of age or older, to vote, shall not be denied or abridged by the United States or by any state on account of age.

Section 2 The Congress shall have power to enforce this article by appropriate legislation.

During the Vietnam War, 18 year olds were being drafted and sent out to possibly die in the service of their country. Yet they did not even have the right to vote. This incongruity led to the 22nd Amendment, which lowered the legal voting age from 21 to 18.

AMENDMENT 27—CONGRESSIONAL SALARIES

[Ratified May 7, 1992]

No law varying the compensation for the services of the Senators and Representatives shall take effect until an election of Representatives shall be intervened.

This is a "sleeper" amendment that was part of 12 amendments originally submitted by the first Congress to the states for ratification. The states only ratified 10 of the 12, which collectively became known as the Bill of Rights. But since Congress did not set a time limit for ratification, the other two amendments remained on the table. Much to the shock of the body politic, in 1992, 3/4 of the states ratified original amendment 12 of 12. This reflected the disgust of seeing Congress continuing to increase its salary and benefits. The amendment delays any increase of compensation for at least one election cycle.

Annotations by James Corey, High Point University.

CHAPTER 4

FEDERALISM: DIVIDING GOVERNMENTAL POWER

CHAPTER OUTLINE

Indestructible Union, Indestructible States

Why Federalism? The Argument for a "Compound Republic"

The Original Design of Federalism

The Evolution of American Federalism

Federalism Revived?

Money and Power Flow to Washington

Coercive Federalism: Preemptions and Mandates

THINK ABOUT POLITICS

1 Which level of government deals best with the problems it faces?
Federal ● State ● Local ●

2 In which level of government do you have the most confidence?
Federal ● State ● Local ●

3 Should the national government be able to prosecute a high school student for bringing a gun to school?
Yes ● No ●

4 Should welfare benefits be the same in all states?
Yes ● No ●

5 Should each state determine its own minimum age for drinking alcohol?
Yes ● No ●

6 Should each state determine its own maximum highway speed limit?
Yes ● No ●

7 When the federal government requires states to provide safe drinking water, clean air, or access for the handicapped, should it provide funds to carry out these mandates?
Yes ● No ●

What should be the relationship between the national government and the states? Questions like these lie at the heart of the issue of who gets what, when, and how. They affect employment, transportation, health, education, the very air we breathe. And when there has been disagreement, the nation has been plunged into conflict at best and the bloodiest war in its history at worst.

Indestructible Union, Indestructible States

In December 1860 South Carolina seceded from the Union and in April 1861 authorized its state militia to expel U.S. troops from Fort Sumter in Charleston harbor. Although there is no provision in the Constitution for states leaving the Union, eleven southern states—South Carolina, Mississippi, Florida, Alabama, Georgia, Louisiana, Texas, Virginia, Arkansas, Tennessee, and North Carolina, in that order—argued that the Union was a voluntary association and they were entitled to withdraw.[1] President Abraham Lincoln declared these states to be in armed rebellion and sent federal troops to crush the "rebels." The result was the nation's bloodiest war: more than 250,000 battle deaths and another 250,000 deaths from disease and privation, out of a total population of less than 30 million.

Following the Civil War, Chief Justice Salmon P. Chase confirmed what had been decided on the battlefield. "The Constitution in all its provisions looks to an indestructible union, composed of indestructible states."[2]

Federalism divides power between two separate authorities—the nation and the states—each of which enforces its own laws directly on its citizens. Both the nation and the states pass laws, impose taxes, spend money, and maintain their own courts. Neither the nation nor the states can dissolve the Union or amend the Constitution without the consent of the other. The Constitution itself is the only legal source of authority for both the states and the nation, the states do not get their power from the national government, and the national government does not get its power from the states. Both national and state governments derive their power directly from the people.

American federalism differs from a **unitary system** of government, in which formal authority rests with the national government, and whatever powers are exercised by states, provinces, or subdivisions are given to those governments by the national government. Most of the world's governments—including France and Britain—are unitary. Federalism also differs from a **confederation** of states, in which the national government relies on the states for its authority, not the people (see Figure 4.1). Under the Articles of Confederation of 1781, the United States was a confederation. The national government could not even levy taxes, it had to ask the states for revenue. Like the United States, a number of other countries were confederations before establishing federal systems, and today new types of

FIGURE 4.1 The Federal, Confederation, and Unitary Systems of Government

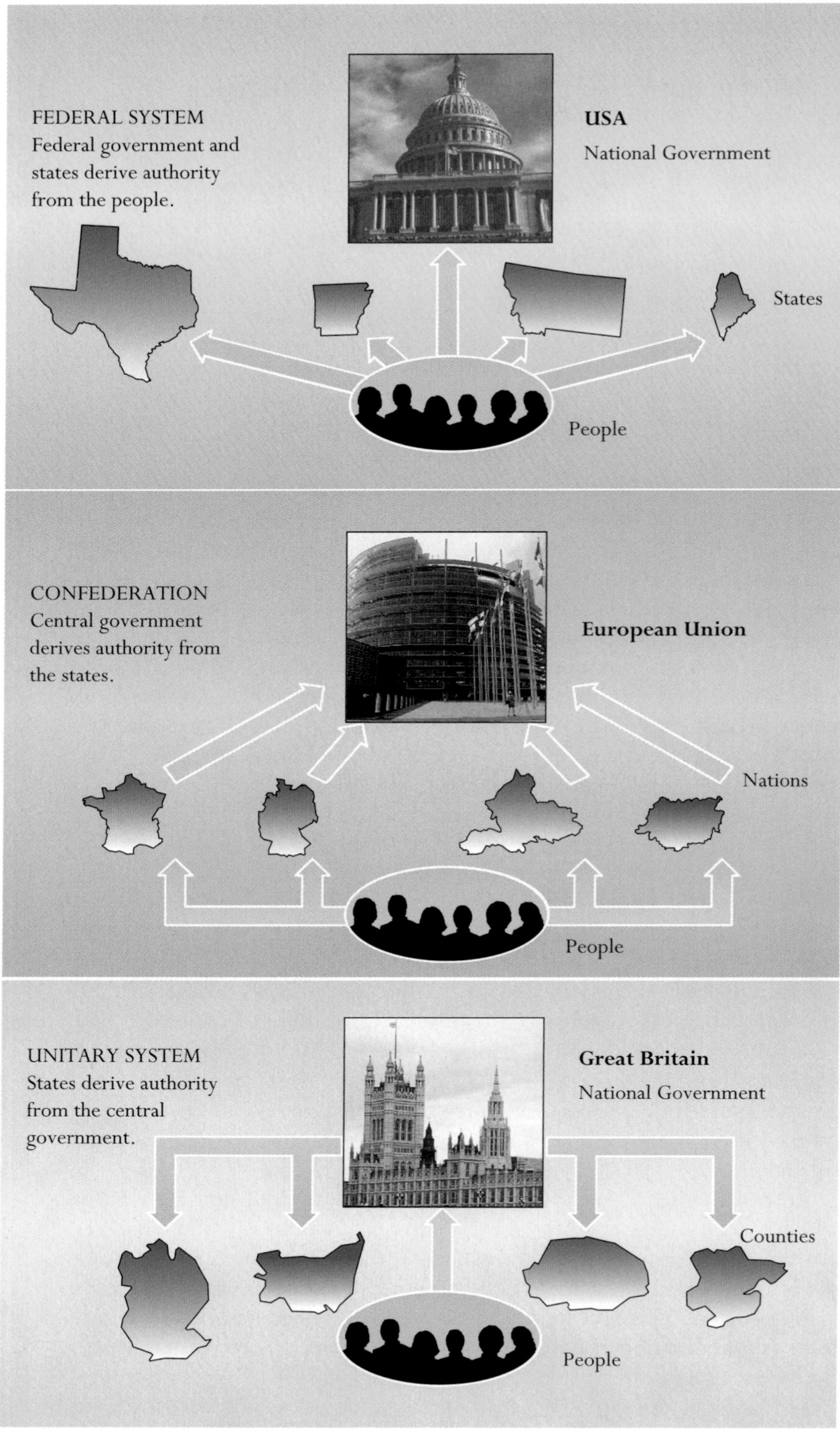

confederations with limited functions are being formed (see *Compared to What?* "The European Union").

People in the United States often think of the *federal government* when the word *government* comes up. In fact, today there are more than 87,000 American governments. These state and local governments are important in American life, for they provide such essential day-to-day services as schools, water, and police and fire departments (see Table 4.1). However, the U.S. Constitution, the supreme law of the land, recognizes the existence of only the national government and the states. Local governments have no guarantees of power—or even existence—under the U.S. Constitution. Whatever powers they have are given to them by their state governments. States can create or abolish local governments, grant or withhold their powers, or change their boundaries without their consent. Some local governments have powers guaranteed in *state* constitutions, and some are even given **home rule**—the power to pass laws affecting local affairs, so long as those laws do not conflict with state or federal laws. About 60,000 of these 87,000 governments have the power to levy taxes to support activities authorized by state law.

In short, the American federal system is large and complex, with three levels of government—national, state, and local—sharing power. Indeed, the numbers and complexity of governments in the United States make **intergovernmental relations**—all of the interactions among these governments and their officials—a major concern of political scientists and policy makers.

federalism A constitutional arrangement whereby power is divided between national and subnational governments, each of which enforces its own laws directly on its citizens and neither of which can alter the arrangement without the consent of the other.

unitary system Constitutional arrangement whereby authority rests with the national government, subnational governments have only those powers given to them by the national government.

confederation Constitutional arrangement whereby the national government is created by and relies on subnational governments for its authority.

home rule Power of local government to pass laws affecting local affairs, so long as those laws do not conflict with state or federal laws.

Why Federalism? The Argument for a "Compound Republic"

The nation's Founders believed that "republican principles" would help make government responsible to the people, but they also argued that "auxiliary precautions" were necessary to protect the liberties of minorities and individuals. They believed that majority rule in a democratic government made it particularly important to devise ways to protect minorities and individuals from "unjust" and "interested" *majorities*. They believed that federalism would better protect liberty, disperse power, and manage "faction" (conflict).

THINK AGAIN

Which level of government deals best with the problems it faces?

intergovernmental relations Network of political, financial, and administrative relationships between units of the federal government and those of state and local governments.

TABLE 4.1 How Many American Governments?

U.S. government	1
States	50
Counties	3,034
Municipalities	19,431
Townships	16,506
Special districts	35,356
School districts	13,522
All governments	**87,900**

Source: Statistical Abstract of the United States, 2002, p. 260.

COMPARED TO WHAT?

The European Union

The European Union incorporates features of both federalism and confederation. The EU includes fifteen member nations—Austria, Belgium, Denmark, Finland, France, Germany, Greece, Ireland, Italy, Luxembourg, the Netherlands, Portugal, Spain, Sweden, and the United Kingdom—and embraces 374 million people. It grew slowly from a European Economic Community established in 1957 (designed to reduce and eventually abolish all tariffs among member nations), through a European Community established in 1965 (designed to create a single market free of all barriers to the movement of goods, services, capital, and labor), to its much more unified European Union established in 1991. The objectives of the European Union are to

- Promote economic progress through a single market and a single currency.
- Assert the identity of the European Union in international affairs, through common foreign and security policies and actions in international crises.
- Promote the free movement of persons and products throughout member nations.
- Promote European citizenship, not to replace national citizenship but to complement it and confer civil and political rights on European citizens.

Council of the European Union

The Council is the EU's principal decision-making body. It is composed of the foreign ministers of the member nations. Each country takes the presidency for six months; the Council votes by majority, although each country's vote is weighted differently. Germany, France, Italy, and the United Kingdom each have ten votes; Spain has eight; Belgium, Greece, the Netherlands, and Portugal have five; Austria and Sweden have four; Ireland, Denmark, and Finland have three; and Luxembourg has two. The Council meets in Brussels.

European Parliament

Deputies of the European Parliament (626) are directly elected every five years by the European Union's 374 million citizens. The major political parties operating in each of the member nations nominate candidates. The Parliament oversees the EU budget and passes on proposals to the Council of Ministers and the Commission. The Parliament also passes on new applicants to the EU.

The Commission

The Commission of the EU supervises the implementation of EU treaties, implements EU policies, and manages EU funds. It is composed of 20 commissioners appointed by member governments. The five largest countries—France, Germany, Italy, Spain, and the United Kingdom—appoint two commissioners each; the remaining countries appoint one commissioner each.

The Court of Justice

A Court of Justice hears complaints about member governments' treaty violations and interprets EU treaties and legislation. Its fifteen justices are appointed by the member governments and serve six-year terms.

The "Euro"

Perhaps the most far-reaching accomplishment of the EU was the introduction of the "euro"—a single European currency for use in all member states. The euro was first introduced January 1, 1999, and officially replaced old national currencies—such as francs, marks, pesetas, and lira—on January 1, 2002. However, the United Kingdom, Sweden, and Denmark have refused to substitute the euro for their own currency.

European Union Online Official EU site

Describes the structure of the organization, its membership current issues, etc.
www.europa.eu.int

Protecting Liberty Constitutional guarantees of individual liberty do not enforce themselves. The Founders argued that to guarantee liberty, government should be structured to encourage "opposite and rival" centers of power *within* and *among* governments. So they settled on both *federalism*—dividing powers between the national and state governments—and *separation of powers*—the dispersal of power among branches within the national government.

> In the compound republic of America, the power surrendered by the people is first divided between two distinct governments, and then the portion allotted to each is sub-

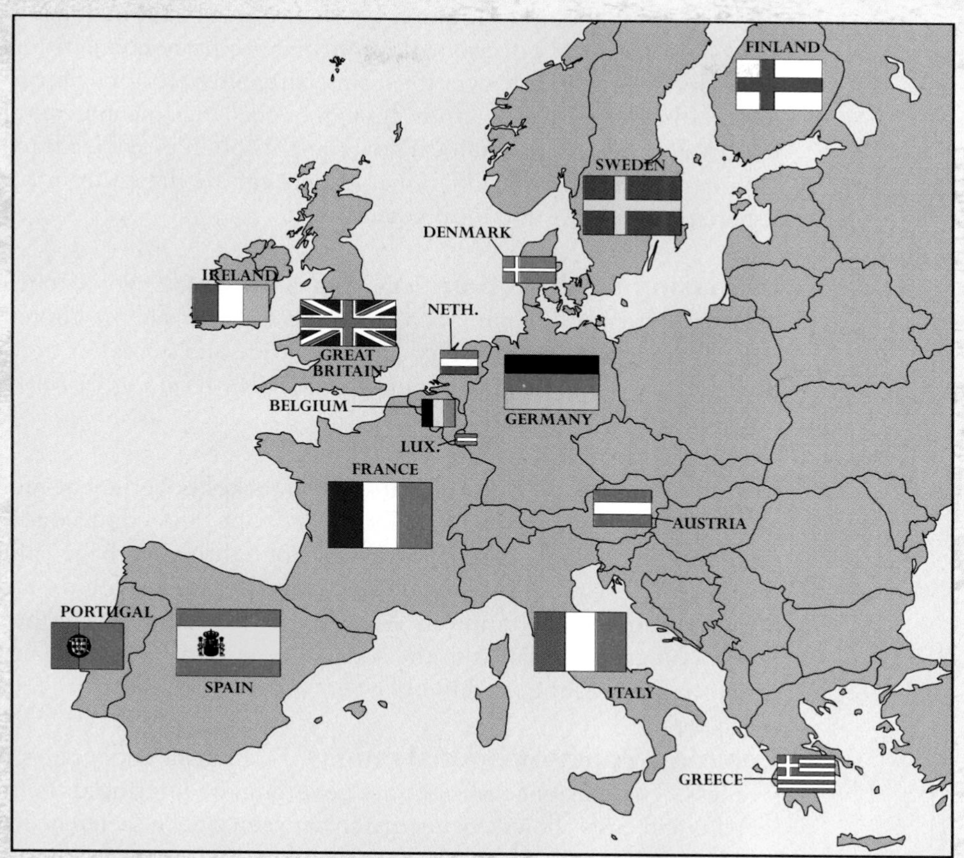

The future of the European Union remains under discussion. Will there be a common Bill of Rights guaranteeing Europeans individual liberties and protections against government? Will European governments create a common military? Will the European Union admit additional nations—Poland, the Czech Republic, or Hungary, for example? How will the voting strength of large nations and small nations be balanced? How much power will be allocated to the central European Union government relative to the powers of member nations? Note that these questions were the same as many of those discussed in the American Constitutional Convention of 1787 (see Chapter 3).

divided among distinct and separate departments. Hence a double security arises to the rights of the people. The different governments will control each other, at the same time that each will be controlled by itself.[3]

Thus the Founders deliberately tried to create competition within and among governmental units as a means of protecting liberty. Rather than rely on the "better motives" of leaders, the Founders sought to construct a system in which governments and government officials would be constrained by competition with other governments and other government officials: "Ambition must be made to counteract ambition."[4]

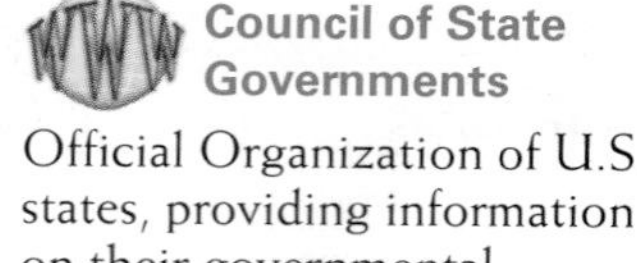

Council of State Governments

Official Organization of U.S. states, providing information on their governmental structures, officials, and current issues. ***www.csg.org***

Dispersing Power Federalism distributes power widely among different sets of leaders, national as well as state and local officeholders. The Founders believed that multiple leadership groups offered more protection against tyranny than a single set of all-powerful leaders. State and local government offices also provide a political base for the opposition party when it has lost a national election. In this way, state and local governments contribute to party competition in the United States by helping to tide over the losing party after electoral defeat at the national level so that it can remain strong enough to challenge incumbents at the next election. And finally, state and local governments often provide a training ground for national political leaders. National leaders can be drawn from a pool of leaders experienced in state and local government.

Increasing Participation Federalism allows more people to participate in the political system. With more than 87,000 governments in the United States—state, county, municipality, township, special district, and school district—nearly a million people hold some kind of public office (See *What Do You Think?* "Which Government Seems Closer to You?").

Improving Efficiency Federalism also makes government more manageable and efficient. Imagine the bureaucracy, red tape, and confusion if every governmental activity—police, schools, roads, fire fighting, garbage collection, sewage disposal, and so forth—in every local community in the nation were controlled by a centralized administration in Washington. Government can become arbitrary when a bureaucracy far from the scene directs local officials. Thus decentralization often softens the rigidity of law.

Ensuring Policy Responsiveness Federalism encourages policy responsiveness. The existence of multiple governments offering different packages of benefits and costs allows a better match between citizen preferences and public policy. Americans are very mobile. People and businesses can "vote with their feet" by relocating to those states and communities that most closely conform to their own policy preferences. This mobility not only facilitates a better match between citizen preferences and public policy but also encourages competition between states and communities to offer improved services at lower costs.[5]

Encouraging Policy Innovation The Founders hoped that federalism would encourage policy experimentation and innovation. Today federalism may seem like a "conservative" idea, but it was once the instrument of liberal reformers. Federal programs as diverse as the income tax, unemployment compensation, Social Security, wage and hour legislation, bank deposit insurance, and food stamps were all state programs before becoming national undertakings. Today much of the current "liberal" policy agenda—mandatory health insurance for workers, child-care programs, notification of plant closings, government support of industrial research and development—has been embraced by various states. The phrase **laboratories of democracies** is generally attributed to the great progressive jurist Supreme Court Justice Louis D. Brandeis, who used it in defense of state experimentation with new solutions to social and economic problems.[6]

laboratories of democracy
A reference to the ability of states to experiment and innovate in public policy.

Managing Conflict Federalism allows different peoples to come together in a nation without engendering irresolvable conflict. Conflicts between geographically separate groups in America are resolved by allowing each to pursue its own poli-

WHAT DO YOU THINK?

Which Government Seems Closer to You?

Americans seem to favor governments closer to home. Most surveys show that Americans have greater confidence in their local governments than in their state or federal government. Americans feel most "connected" to their local government and least "connected" to the federal government.

Sources: Responses on confidence from Gallup, September, 2003; responses on connectedness from Council for Excellence in Government, July, 1999.

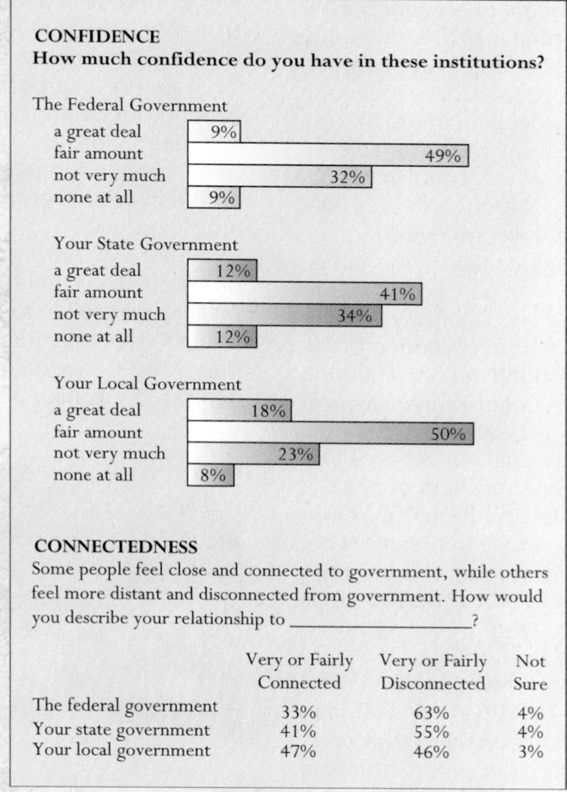

CONNECTEDNESS

Some people feel close and connected to government, while others feel more distant and disconnected from government. How would you describe your relationship to ______________?

	Very or Fairly Connected	Very or Fairly Disconnected	Not Sure
The federal government	33%	63%	4%
Your state government	41%	55%	4%
Your local government	47%	46%	3%

cies within its separate state or community instead of battling over a single national policy to be applied uniformly throughout the land.

Some Important Reservations Despite the strengths of federalism, it has its problems. First of all, federalism can obstruct action on national issues. Although decentralization may reduce conflict at the national level, it may do so at the price of "sweeping under the rug" very serious national injustices (see *A Conflicting View:* "The Dark Side of Federalism" on page 114). Federalism also permits local leaders and citizens to frustrate national policy, to sacrifice national interest to local interests. Decentralized government provides an opportunity for local NIMBYs (people who subscribe to the motto *"Not In My Back Yard"*) to obstruct airports, highways, waste disposal plants, public housing, drug rehabilitation centers, and many other projects that would be in the national interest.

A CONFLICTING VIEW

The Dark Side of Federalism

Segregationists once regularly used the argument of "states rights" to deny equal protection of the law to African Americans. Indeed, *states' rights* became a code word for opposition to federal civil rights laws. In 1963 Governor George Wallace invoked the states' rights argument when he stood in the doorway at the University of Alabama to prevent the execution of a federal court order that the university admit two African American students and integrate. Federal marshals were on hand to enforce the order, and Wallace only temporarily delayed them. Shortly after his dramatic stand in front of the television cameras, he retreated to his office. Later in his career, Wallace sought African American votes, declaring, "I was wrong. Those days are over."

Federalism in America remains tainted by its historical association with slavery, segregation, and discrimination. In the Virginia and Kentucky Resolutions of 1798, Thomas Jefferson and James Madison asserted the doctrine of "nullification," claiming that states could nullify unconstitutional laws of Congress. Although the original intent of this doctrine was to counter congressional attacks on a free press under the Alien and Sedition Acts of 1798, it was later revived to defend slavery. John C. Calhoun of South Carolina argued forcefully in the years before the Civil War that slavery was an issue for the states to decide and the Constitution gave Congress no power to interfere with slavery in the southern states or in the new western territories.

In the years immediately following the Civil War, the issues of slavery, racial inequality, and African American voting rights were *nationalized*. Nationalizing these issues meant removing them from the jurisdiction of the states and placing them in the hands of the national government. The Thirteenth, Fourteenth, and Fifteenth Amendments to the Constitution were enforced by federal troops in the southern states during the post–Civil War Reconstruction era. But after the Compromise of 1876 led to the withdrawal of federal troops from the southern states, legal and social segregation of African Americans became a "way of life" in the region. Segregation was *denationalized*, which reduced national conflict over race but exacted a high price from the nation's African American population. Segregationists asserted the states' rights argument so often in defense of racial discrimination that it became a code phrase for racism. Not until the 1950s and 1960s were questions of segregation and equality again made into national issues. The civil rights movement asserted the supremacy of national law and in 1954 won a landmark decision in the case of *Brown v. Board of Education of Topeka*, when the U.S. Supreme Court ruled that segregation enforced by state (or local) officials violated the Fourteenth Amendment's guarantee that no state could deny any person the equal protection of the law. Later the *national* Civil Rights Act of 1964 outlawed discrimination in private employment and businesses serving the public.

Only now that national constitutional and legal guarantees of equal protection of the law are in place is it possible to reassess the true worth of federalism. Having established that federalism will not mean racial inequality, Americans are now free to explore the values of decentralized government.

In an attempt to block the admission of two African American students to the University of Alabama in 1963, Governor George Wallace barred the door with his body in the face of U.S. federal marshals. The tactic did not succeed, and the two students were admitted.

Finally, federalism permits the benefits and costs of government to be spread unevenly across the nation. For example, some states spend more than twice as much on the education of each child in the public schools as other states do. Taxes in some states are more than twice as high per capita as they are in other states. Welfare benefits in some states are more than twice as high as in other states. Competition among states may keep welfare benefits low in states that want to discourage poor people from moving there. Thus federalism obstructs uniformity in policy.

delegated, or enumerated, powers Powers specifically mentioned in the Constitution as belonging to the national government.

THINK AGAIN

In which level of government do you have the most confidence?

The Original Design of Federalism

The U.S. Constitution *originally* defined American federalism in terms of (1) the powers expressly delegated to the national government plus the powers implied by those that are specifically granted, (2) the concurrent powers exercised by both states and the national government, (3) the powers reserved to the states, (4) the powers denied by the Constitution to both the national government and the states, and (5) the constitutional provisions giving the states a role in the composition of the national government (see Figure 4.2).

Necessary and Proper Clause Clause in Article I, Section 8, of the U.S. Constitution granting Congress the power to enact all laws that are "necessary and proper" for carrying out those responsibilities specifically delegated to it. Also referred to as the Implied Powers Clause.

Delegated Powers

The U.S. Constitution lists seventeen specific grants of power of Congress, in Article I, Section 8. These are usually referred to as the **delegated, or enumerated, powers.** They include authority over war and foreign affairs, authority over the economy ("interstate commerce"), control over the money supply, and the power to tax and spend "to pay the debts and provide for the common defence and general welfare." After these specific grants of power comes the power "to make all laws which shall be necessary and proper for carrying into execution the foregoing powers, and all other powers vested by this Constitution in the government of the United States or in any department or officer thereof." This statement is generally known as the **Necessary and Proper Clause,** and it is the principal source of the national government's **implied powers**—powers not specifically listed in the Constitution but inferred from those that are.

implied powers Powers not mentioned specifically in the Constitution as belonging to Congress but inferred as necessary and proper for carrying out the enumerated powers.

National Supremacy Clause Clause in Article VI of the U.S. Constitution declaring the constitution and laws of the national government "the supreme law of the land" superior to the constitutions and laws of the states.

National Supremacy

The delegated and implied powers, when coupled with the assertion of "national supremacy" (in Article VI), ensure a powerful national government. The **National Supremacy Clause** is very specific in asserting the supremacy of federal laws over state and local laws:

> This Constitution, and the laws of the United States which shall be made in pursuance thereof, and all treaties made, or which shall be made, under the authority of the United States, shall be the supreme law of the land, and the Judges in every state shall be bound thereby, any thing in the constitution or laws of any state to the contrary notwithstanding.

concurrent powers Powers exercised by both the national government and state governments in the American federal system.

reserved powers Powers not granted to the national government or specifically denied to the states in the Constitution that are recognized by the Tenth Amendment as belonging to the state governments. This guarantee, known as the Reserved Powers Clause, embodies the principle of American federalism.

Concurrent and Reserved Powers

Despite broad grants of power to the national government, the states retain considerable governing power. **Concurrent powers** are those recognized in the Constitution as belonging to *both* the national and state governments, including the power to tax and spend, make and enforce laws, and establish courts of justice. The Tenth Amendment reassured the states that "the powers not delegated to the United States . . . are reserved to the States respectively, or to the people." Through these **reserved powers,** the states

POWERS GRANTED BY THE CONSTITUTION

NATIONAL GOVERNMENT
Delegated Powers

Military Affairs and Defense
- Provide for the common defense (I-8).
- Declare war (I-8).
- Raise and support armies(I-8).
- Provide and maintain a navy (I-8).
- Define and punish piracies (I-8).
- Define and punish offenses against the law of nations (I-8).
- Provide for calling forth the militia to execute laws, suppress insurrections, and repel invasions (I-8).
- Provide for organizing, arming, and disciplining the militia (I-8).
- Declare the punishment of treason (III-3).

Economic Affairs
- Regulate commerce with foreign nations, among the several states, and with Indian tribes (I-8).
- Establish uniform laws on bankruptcy (I-8).
- Coin money and regulate its value (I-8).
- Fix standards of weights and measures (I-8).
- Provide for patents and copyrights (I-8).
- Establish post offices and post roads (I-8).

Governmental Organization
- Constitute tribunals inferior to the Supreme Court (I-8, III-1).
- Exercise exclusive legislative power over the seat of government and over certain military installations (I-8).
- Admit new states (IV-3).
- Dispose of and regulate territory or property of the United States (IV-3).

"Implied" Powers
- Make laws necessary and proper for carrying the expressed powers into execution (I-8).

NATIONAL AND STATE GOVERNMENTS
Concurrent Powers
- Levy taxes (I-8).
- Borrow money (I-8).
- Contract and pay debts (I-8).
- Charter banks and corporations (I-8).
- Make and enforce laws (I-8).
- Establish courts (I-8).
- Provide for the general welfare (I-8).

STATE GOVERNMENTS
Reserved to the States
- Regulate intrastate commerce.
- Conduct elections.
- Provide for public health, safety, and morals.
- Establish local government.
- Maintain the militia (National Guard).
- Ratify amendments to the federal Constitution (V).
- Determine voter qualifications (I-2).

"Reserved" Powers
- Powers not delegated to national government nor denied to the States by the Constitution (X).

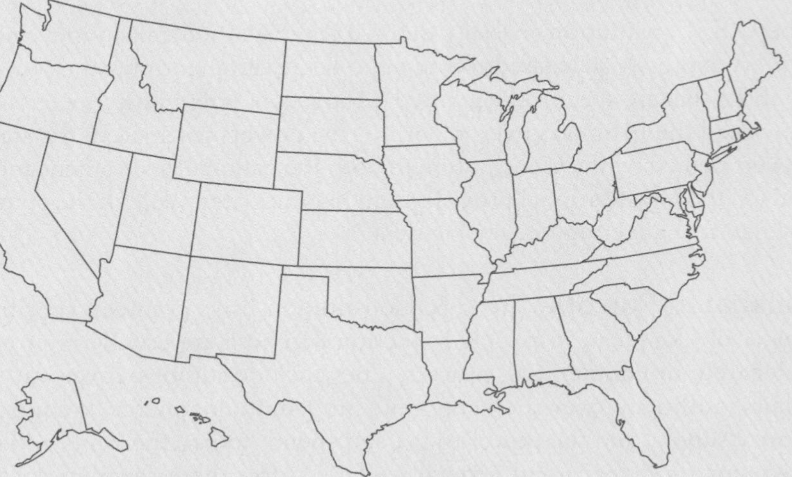

POWERS DENIED BY THE CONSTITUTION

NATIONAL GOVERNMENT
- Give preference to the ports of any state (I-9).
- Impose a tax or duty on articles exported from any state (I-9).
- Directly tax except by apportionment among the states on a population basis (I-9), now superseded as to income tax (Amendment XVI).
- Draw money from the Treasury except by appropriation (I-9).

NATIONAL AND STATE GOVERNMENTS
- Grant titles of nobility (I-9).
- Limit the suspension of habeas corpus (I-9).
- Issue bills of attainder (I-10).
- Make ex post facto laws (I-10).
- Establish a religion or prohibit the free exercise of religion (Amendment I).
- Abridge freedom of speech, press, assembly,or right of petition (Amendment I).
- Deny the right to bear arms protected (Amendment II).
- Restrict quartering of soldiers in private homes (Amendment III).
- Conduct unreasonable searches or seizures. (Amendment IV).
- Deny guarantees of fair trials (Amendment V, Amendment VI, and Amendment VII).
- Impose excessive bail or unusual punishments (Amendment VII).
- Take life, liberty, or property without due process (Amendment V).
- Permit slavery (Amendment XIII).
- Deny life, liberty, or property without due process of law (Amendment XIV).
- Deny voting because of race, color, previous servitude (Amendment XV), sex (Amendment XIX), or age if 18 or over (Amendment XXVI).
- Deny voting because of nonpayment of any tax (Amendment XXIV).

STATE GOVERNMENTS

Economic Affairs
- Use legal tender other than gold or silver coin (I-10).
- Issue separate state coinage (I-10).
- Impair the obligation of contracts (I-10).
- Emit bills of credit (I-10).
- Levy import or export duties, except reasonable inspection fees, without the consent of Congress (I-10).
- Abridge the privileges and immunities of national citizenship (Amendment XIV)
- Make any law that violates federal law (Amendment VI).
- Pay for rebellion against the United States or for emancipated slaves (Amendment XIV)

Foreign Affairs
- Enter into treaties, alliances, or confederations (I-10).
- Make compact with a foreign state, except by congressional consent (I-10).

Military Affairs
- Issue letters of marque and reprisal (I-10).
- Maintain standing military forces in peace without congressional consent (I-10).
- Engage in war, without congressional consent, except in imminent danger or when invaded (I-10).

FIGURE 4.2 Original Constitutional Distribution of Powers

Under the Constitution of 1787, certain powers were delegated to the national government, other powers were shared by the national and state governments, and still other powers were reserved for state governments alone. Similarly, certain powers were denied by the Constitution to the national government, other powers were denied to both the national and state governments, and still other powers were denied only to state governments. Later amendments especially protected individual liberties.

generally retain control over property and contract law, criminal law, marriage and divorce, and the provision of education, highways, and social welfare activities. (But for a discussion of increasing federal involvement in crime fighting, traditionally a "reserved" power of the states, see *A Conflicting View:* "Don't Make Everything a Federal Crime!") The states control the organization and powers of their own local governments. Finally, the states, like the federal government, retain the power to tax and spend for the general welfare.

"Look, the American people don't want to be bossed around by federal bureaucrats. They want to be bossed around by state bureaucrats."

Source: © 2002 Robert Mankoff from cartoonbank.com. All Rights Reserved.

Powers Denied to the States The Constitution denies the states some powers in order to safeguard national unity. States are specifically denied the power to coin money, enter into treaties with foreign nations, interfere with the "obligation of contracts," levy taxes on imports or exports, or engage in war.

Powers Denied to the Nation and the States The Constitution denies some powers to both national and state government—namely, the powers to abridge individual rights. The Bill of Rights originally applied only to the national government, but the Fourteenth Amendment, passed by Congress in 1866 and ratified by 1868, provided that the states must also adhere to fundamental guarantees of individual liberty.

State Role in National Government The states are basic units in the organizational scheme of the national government. The House of Representatives apportions members to the states by population, and state legislatures draw up the districts that elect representatives. Every state has at least one member in the House of Representatives, regardless of its population. Each state elects two U.S. senators, regardless of its population. The president is chosen by the electoral votes of the states, with each state having as many electoral votes as it has senators and representatives combined. Finally, three-fourths of the states must ratify amendments to the U.S. Constitution.

State Obligations to Each Other To promote national unity, the Constitution requires the states to recognize actions and decisions taken by other states. Article IV requires the states to give "Full Faith and Credit . . . to the public Acts, Records, and judiciary Proceedings of every other State." This provision ensures that contracts, property ownership, insurance, civil judgments, marriages and divorces, among other things, made in one state are recognized in all states.

Recently, controversy has arisen over recognition of gay and lesbian marriages or "civil unions." A strict reading of Article IV would suggest that if any state legalized same-sex marriages, all states would be obliged to recognize them. (In 1999 the Vermont Supreme Court prohibited discrimination against gay marriages.) Anticipating this issue, the Congress passed a Defense of Marriage Act in 1996 stating that "No State . . . shall be required to give effect to any public act, record, or judicial proceeding of any other State respecting a relationship between persons of the same sex that is treated as a marriage. . ." The Congress relied on language in the next sentence of Article IV: "the Congress may by general law prescribe the Manner in which such Acts, Records and Proceedings shall be proved, *and the Effect thereof*" (italics added). It is not altogether clear whether this constitutional language in the second sentence allows Congress to nullify the "Full Faith and Credit" clause in the first sentence. If Vermont or any other state persists in recognizing gay marriages, the issue may end up in the Supreme Court (see also "Privacy and the Constitution" in Chapter 14).

A CONFLICTING VIEW

Don't Make Everything a Federal Crime!

Political officeholders in Washington are continually pressured to make "a federal crime" out of virtually every offense in society. Neither Democrats nor Republicans, liberals nor conservatives, are willing to risk their political futures by telling their constituents that crime fighting is a state and local responsibility. So Washington lawmakers continue to add common offenses to the ever lengthening list of federal crimes.

Traditionally, federal crimes were limited to a relatively narrow range of offenses, including counterfeiting and currency violations; tax evasion, including alcohol, tobacco, and firearm taxes; fraud and embezzlement; robbery of federally insured banks; murder or assault of a federal official; and violations of customs and immigrations laws. While some federal criminal laws overlapped state laws, most criminal activity—murder, rape, robbery, assault, burglary, theft, auto theft, gambling, sex offenses, and so on—fell under state jurisdiction. Indeed, the *police power* was believed to be one of the "reserved" powers states referred to in the Tenth Amendment.

But over time Congress has made more and more offenses *federal* crimes. Today federal crimes range from drive-by shootings to obstructing sidewalks in front of abortion clinics. Any violent offense motivated by racial, religious, or ethnic animosity is a "hate crime" subject to federal investigation and prosecution. "Racketeering" and "conspiracy" (organizing and communicating with others about the intent to commit a crime) is a federal crime. The greatest impact of federal involvement in law enforcement is found in drug-related crime. Drug offenders may be tried in either federal or state courts, or both. Federal drug laws, including those prohibiting possession, carry heavier penalties than those of most states.

The effect of federalizing crime is to subject citizens to the possibility of being tried twice for the same crime—in federal court and in state court for an offense that violates both federal and state criminal codes. The U.S. Supreme Court has held that such multiple prosecution does *not* violate the Double Jeopardy Clause of the Fifth Amendment—"nor shall any person be subject for the same offense to be twice put in jeopardy of life or limb" (*Heath vs. Alabama,* 474 U.S. 82 (1985)). In the well-publicized Rodney King case, a California state jury acquitted police officers of beating King, but a federal court jury later convicted them of violating King's civil rights.

Another effect of federalizing crime is to further fragment an already fragmented law enforcement structure in the United States. The federal government's principal investigative agencies are the Federal Bureau of Investigation (FBI) and the Drug Enforcement Administration (DEA), both units of the Department of Justice; the Bureau of Alcohol, Tobacco, and Firearms (ATF) and the Internal Revenue Service (IRS) in the Treasury Department; and the Customs Bureau and Immigration and Naturalization Service (INS) in the Department of Homeland Security. Efforts to combine these law enforcement agencies have consistently foundered in bureaucratic battles. It is not uncommon at a major crime scene to see FBI, DEA, and ATF agents mingling with officers from state-level agencies, county sheriff's departments, and local police forces.

Yet, despite growing federalization of crime, state and local governments in America continue to bear the major burden of law enforcement. Over 10 million people are arrested and charged with offenses from misdemeanors to felonies in the United States today. But only about 50,000 people are prosecuted for crime by federal authorities in federal courts.

The Evolution of American Federalism

American federalism has evolved over 200 years from a state-centered division of power to a national-centered system of government. Although the original constitutional wordings have remained in place, power has flowed toward the national government since the earliest days of the Republic. American federalism has been forged in the fires of political conflicts between states and nation, conflicts that have usually been resolved in favor of the national government. (See *Up Close:* "Historical Markers in the Development of American Federalism."). Generalizing

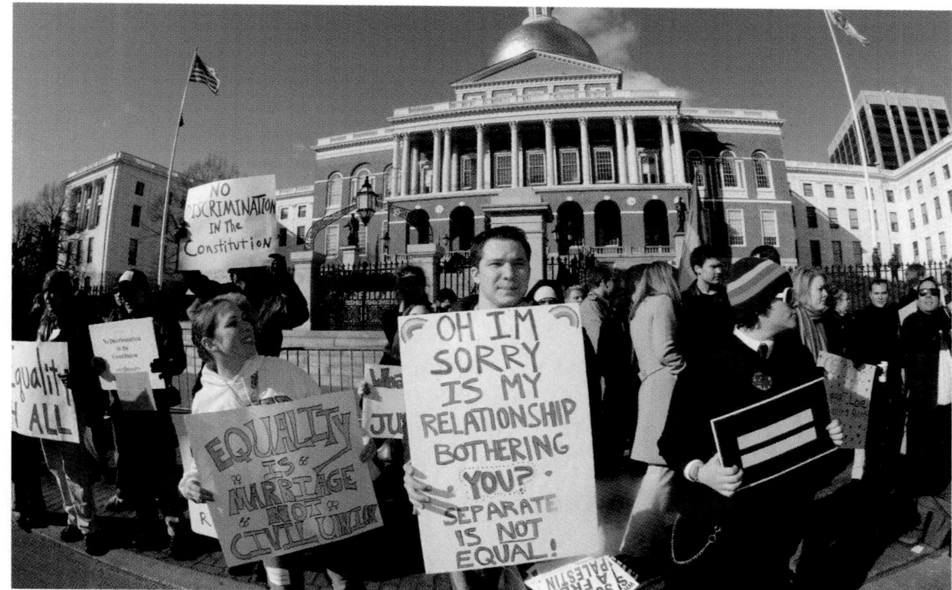

Battles over same-sex marriages are currently being fought in state capitals across the country. The Constitution requires every state to give "Full Faith and Credit" to the official acts of other states. But Congress' Defense of Marriage Act relieves states from recognizing same-sex marriages consummated in other states. The Supreme Court may end up deciding the issue.

about the evolution of American federalism is no easy task. But let us try to describe broadly some major periods in the evolution of federalism, then look at five specific historical developments that had far-reaching impact on that evolution.

State-Centered Federalism, 1787–1868 From the adoption of the Constitution of 1787 to the end of the Civil War, the states were the most important units in the American federal system. It is true that during this period the legal foundation for the expansion of national power was being laid, but people looked to the states for resolving most policy questions and providing most public services. Even the issue of slavery was decided by state governments. The supremacy of the national government was frequently questioned, first by the Anti-Federalists (including Thomas Jefferson) and later by John C. Calhoun and other defenders of slavery.

Dual Federalism, 1868–1913 The supremacy of the national government was decided on the battlefields of the Civil War. Yet for nearly a half-century after that conflict, the national government narrowly interpreted its delegated powers, and the states continued to decide most domestic policy issues. The resulting pattern has been described as **dual federalism.** Under this pattern, the states and the nation divided most governmental functions. The national government concentrated its attention on the "delegated" powers—national defense, foreign affairs, tariffs, interstate commerce, the coinage of money, standard weights and measures, post office and post roads, and the admission of new states. State governments decided the important domestic policy issues—education, welfare, health, and criminal justice. The separation of policy responsibilities was once compared to a layer cake, with local governments at the base, state governments in the middle, and the national government at the top.[7]

dual federalism Early concept of federalism in which national and state powers were clearly distinguished and functionally separate.

Cooperative Federalism, 1913–1964 The distinction between national and state responsibilities gradually eroded in the first half of the twentieth century. American federalism was transformed by the Industrial Revolution and the development of a national economy, by the federal income tax in 1913, which shifted financial resources to the national government, and by the challenges of two world

UP CLOSE

Historical Markers in the Development of American Federalism

Among the most important events in the development of American federalism: (1) the Supreme Court's decision in *McCulloch v. Maryland* in 1819 giving a broad interpretation of the Necessary and Proper Clause; (2) the victory of the national government in the Civil War 1861–65; (3) the establishment of a national system of civil rights based on the Fourteenth Amendment culminating in the Supreme Court's desegregation decision in *Brown v. Board of Education;* (4) the expansion of the national government's power under the Interstate Commerce Clause during the Great Depression of the 1930s; and (5) the growth of federal revenues after the passage of the Sixteenth (income tax) Amendment in 1913.

McCulloch v. Maryland and the Necessary and Proper Clause

Political conflict over the scope of national power is as old as the nation itself. In 1790 Secretary of the Treasury Alexander Hamilton proposed the establishment of a national bank. Congress acted on Hamilton's suggestion in 1791, establishing a national bank to serve as a depository for federal money and to aid the federal government in borrowing funds. Jeffersonians believed the national bank was a dangerous centralization of government. They objected that the power to establish the bank was nowhere to be found in the enumerated powers of Congress.

Hamilton replied that Congress could derive the power to establish a bank from grants of authority in the Constitution relating to money, in combination with the clause authorizing Congress "to make all laws which shall be necessary and proper for carrying into execution the foregoing powers."

The question finally reached the Supreme Court in 1819, when the State of Maryland levied a tax on the national bank and the bank refused to pay it. In the case of *McCulloch v. Maryland,* Chief Justice Marshall accepted the broader Hamiltonian version of the Necessary and Proper Clause: "Let the end be legitimate, let it be within the scope of the Constitution, and all means which are appropriate, which are plainly adopted to that end, which are not prohibited but consistent with the letter and the spirit of the Constitution, are constitutional."*

The *McCulloch* case firmly established the principle that the Necessary and Proper Clause gives Congress the right to choose its means in carrying out the enumerated powers of the national government. Because of this broad interpretation of the Necessary and Proper Clause, today Congress can devise programs, create agencies, and establish national laws on the basis of long chains of reasoning from the most meager phrases of the constitutional text.

Secession and Civil War

The Civil War was the greatest crisis of the American federal system. Did a state have the right to oppose national law to the point of secession, that is, withdrawing from the federal Union? The question of secession was decided on Civil War battlefields between 1861 and 1865. Yet the states' rights doctrine and political disputes over the character of American federalism did not disappear with General Robert E. Lee's surrender at Appomattox. In addition to establishing that states cannot secede from the federal union, the Civil War led to three constitutional amendments clearly aimed at limiting state power in the interests of individual freedom. The Thirteenth Amendment eliminated slavery in the states; the Fifteenth Amendment prevented states from denying the vote on the basis of race, color, or previous enslavement; and the Fourteenth Amendment declared,

> No State shall make or enforce any law which shall abridge the privileges or immunities of citizens of the United States; nor shall any state deprive any person of life, liberty, or property, without due process of law; nor deny to any person within its jurisdiction the equal protection of the laws.

During the post–Civil War Reconstruction era (1866–77), Congress passed several laws designed to enforce these amendments—laws guaranteeing the right to vote, providing remedies for the denial of rights by any person acting under "the color of law" (any public official), and prohibiting discrimination in public accommodation.† But after 1877, Congress gave up its efforts to reconstruct southern society, and the Supreme Court also failed to uphold these Reconstruction laws.

National Guarantees of Civil Rights

However, in the twentieth century, the Supreme Court began to build a national system of civil rights based on the Fourteenth Amendment. First, the Court held that the Fourteenth Amendment prevented states from interfering with free speech, free press, or religious practices. But it was not until 1954, in the desegregation decision in *Brown v. Board of Education of Topeka,* that the Court began to call for the full assertion of national authority on behalf of civil rights.[‡] When it decided that the Fourteenth Amendment prohibited the states from segregating the races in public schools, the Court was asserting national authority over longstanding practices in many of the states.

But in the years following *Brown,* some state officials tried to prevent the enforcement of a national law. Governor Orval Faubus called out the Arkansas National Guard to prevent a federal court from desegregating Little Rock Central High School in 1957. President Dwight D. Eisenhower responded by ordering the Arkansas National Guard removed and sent units of the U.S. Army to enforce national authority. This presidential action reinforced the principle of national supremacy in the American political system.

The Expansion of Interstate Commerce

The growth of national power under the Interstate Commerce Clause of the Constitution is another important development in the evolution of American federalism. For many years, the U.S. Supreme Court narrowly defined *interstate commerce* to mean only the movement of goods and services across state lines. Until the late 1930s, it insisted that agriculture, mining, manufacturing, and labor relations were outside the reach of the delegated powers of the national government. However, when confronted with the Great Depression of the 1930s and Franklin Roosevelt's threat to add enough members to the Supreme Court to win favorable rulings, the Court yielded. It redefined *interstate commerce* to include any activity that "substantially affects" the national economy.[§] Indeed, the Court frequently approved of congressional restrictions on economic activities that had only very indirect effects on interstate commerce.[||]

In a long bloody war to establish national supremacy, the North's ultimate victory served to prove once and for all that the federal union cannot be dissolved.

The Income Tax and Federal Grants

In the famous Northwest Ordinance of 1787, which provided for the governing of the territories west of the Appalachian Mountains, Congress made grants of land for the establishment of public schools. Then in the Morrill Land Grant Act of 1862, Congress provided grants of land to the states to promote higher education, especially agricultural and mechanical studies. Federal support for "A and M" or "land grant" universities continues today.

With the money provided to Washington by the passage of the Sixteenth (income tax) Amendment in 1913, Congress embarked on cash grants to the states. Among the earliest cash grant programs were the Federal Highway Act of 1916 and the Smith-Hughes Act of 1917 (vocational education). With federal money came federal direction. For example, states that wanted federal money for highways after 1916 had to accept uniform standards of construction and even a uniform road-numbering system (U.S. 1, U.S. 30, and so on). Shortly after these programs began, the U.S. Supreme Court considered the claim that these federal grants were unconstitutional intrusions into areas "reserved" for the states. But the Court upheld grants as a legitimate exercise of Congress's power to tax and spend for the general welfare.[¶]

---

[*] *McCulloch v. Maryland,* 4 Wheaten 316 (1819).

[†] Civil Rights Acts of 1866, 1872, and 1875.

[‡] *Brown v. Board of Education of Topeka, Kansas,* 347 U.S. 483 (1954).

[§] *National Labor Relations Board v. Jones & Laughlin Steel Corporation,* 301 U.S. 1 (1937).

[||] *Wickard v. Filburn,* 317 U.S. 128 (1938).

[¶] *Massachusetts v. Mellon, Framingham v. Mellon,* 262 U.S. 447 (1923).

wars and the Great Depression. In response to the Great Depression of the 1930s, state governors welcomed massive federal public works projects under President Franklin D. Roosevelt's New Deal program. In addition, the federal government intervened directly in economic affairs, labor relations, business practices, and agriculture. Through its grants of money, the national government cooperated with the states in public assistance, employment services, child welfare, public housing, urban renewal, highway building, and vocational education.

cooperative federalism
Model of federalism in which national, state, and local governments work together exercising common policy responsibilities.

The Close Up Foundation
A nonprofit, nonpartisan citizenship education organization with excellent historical materials about federalism's evolution and information about federalism issues. A related link on the Close Up site contains the complete text of the pro-states' rights 1798 Kentucky and Virginia Resolutions (authored by Jefferson).
www.closeup.org

This new pattern of federal-state relations was labeled **cooperative federalism.** Both the nation and the states exercised responsibilities for welfare, health, highways, education, and criminal justice. This merging of policy responsibilities was compared to a marble cake: "As the colors are mixed in a marble cake, so functions are mixed in the American federal system."[8] Yet even in this period of shared national-state responsibility, the national government emphasized cooperation in achieving common national and state goals. Congress generally acknowledged that it had no direct constitutional authority to regulate public health, safety, or welfare. Instead, it relied primarily on its powers to tax and spend for the general welfare, providing financial assistance to state and local governments to achieve shared goals. Congress did not usually legislate directly on local matters.

centralized federalism
Model of federalism in which the national government assumes primary responsibility for determining national goals in all major policy areas and directs state and local government activity through conditions attached to money grants.

Centralized Federalism, 1964–1980 Over the years, it became increasingly difficult to maintain the fiction that the national government was merely assisting the states to perform their domestic responsibilities. By the time President Lyndon B. Johnson launched the Great Society program in 1964, the federal government clearly had its own *national* goals. Virtually all problems confronting American society—from solid-waste disposal and water and air pollution to consumer safety, home insulation, noise abatement, and even "highway beautification"—were declared to be national problems. Congress legislated directly on any matter it chose, without regard to its *enumerated powers* and without pretending to render only financial assistance. The Supreme Court no longer concerned itself with the reserved powers of the states, and the Tenth Amendment lost most of its meaning. The pattern of national-state relations became **centralized federalism.** As for the cake analogies, one commentator observed, "The frosting had moved to the top, something like a pineapple upside-down cake."[9]

During the Great Depression of the 1930s, the massive public works projects sponsored by the federal government under President Franklin Roosevelt's New Deal reflected the emergence of cooperative federalism. Programs of the Work Progress Administration, like the one shown here, were responsible for the construction of buildings, bridges, highways, and airports throughout the country.

New Federalism, 1980–1985 **New federalism** was a phrase frequently applied to efforts to reverse the flow of power to Washington and to return responsibilities to states and communities. (The phrase originated in the administration of Richard M. Nixon, 1969–74, who used it to describe general revenue sharing—making federal grants to state and local governments with few strings attached.) New Federalism was popular early in the administration of President Ronald Reagan, who tried to reduce federal involvement in domestic programs and encourage states and cities to undertake greater policy responsibilities themselves. The result was that state and local governments were forced to rely more on their own sources of revenue and less on federal money. Still, centralizing tendencies in the American federal system continued. While the general public usually gave better marks to state and local governments than to the federal government, paradoxically that same public also favored greater federal involvement in policy areas traditionally thought to be state or local responsibilities (see Figure 4.3).

Representational Federalism, 1985–1995 Despite centralizing tendencies, it was still widely assumed prior to 1985 that the Congress could not directly legislate how state and local governments should go about performing their traditional functions. However, in its 1985 *Garcia v. San Antonio Metropolitan Transit Authority* decision, the U.S. Supreme Court appeared to remove all barriers to direct

new federalism Attempts to return power and responsibility to the states and reduce the role of the national government in domestic affairs.

Which level of government should run the following programs?

Program	Federal	State	Local
Service to immigrants	60%	15%	6%
Welfare	40%	38%	17%
Health care for the disabled, poor, and elderly	36%	28%	18%
Opportunity for minorities	35%	30%	28%
Air/water quality	35%	40%	22%
Public education	21%	47%	30%
Child care	16%	34%	29%
Employment and job training	15%	59%	24%
Law enforcement	15%	36%	45%

FIGURE 4.3 Public Views about Which Level of Government Should Run Various Programs

Source: Gallup/CNN/USA Today Poll, reported in *The Polling Report*, February 10, 1997. Copyright © 1996–2004 by The Gallup Organization.

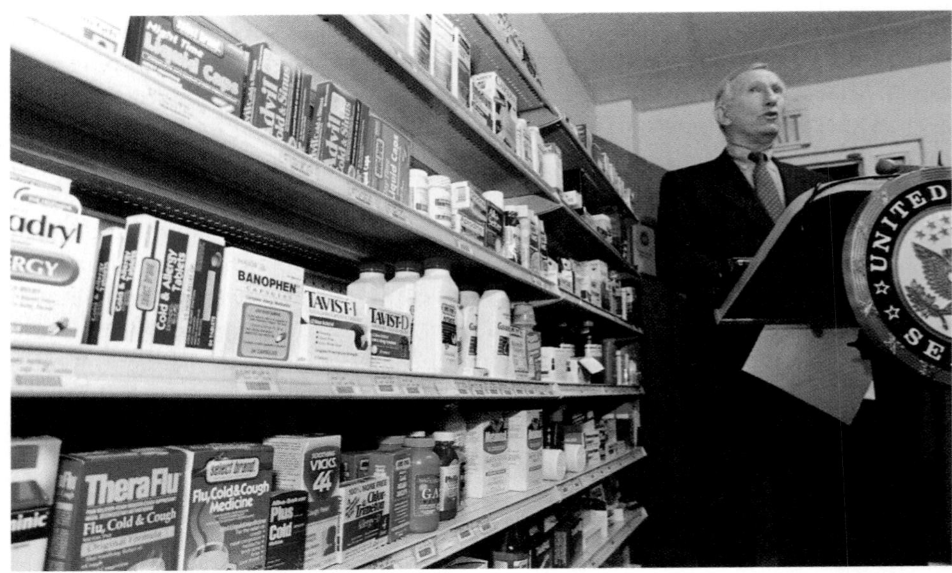

Medicare for the elderly was added to Social Security in 1965 as part of President Lyndon B. Johnson's Great Society program. Increasingly, health care has come to be viewed as a federal government responsibility. A Republic-controlled congress added prescription drug coverage in 2003, albeit with "gaps" that Democrats vowed to eliminate.

congressional legislation in matters traditionally reserved to the states. The case arose after Congress directly ordered state and local governments to pay minimum wages to their employees. The Court dismissed arguments that the nature of American federalism and the Reserved Powers Clause of the Tenth Amendment prevented Congress from directly legislating in state affairs. It said that the only protection for state powers was to be found in the states' role in electing U.S. senators, members of the U.S. House of Representatives, and the president. The Court's ruling asserts a concept known as **representational federalism**: Federalism is defined by the role of the states in electing members of Congress and the president, not by any constitutional division of powers. The United States is said to retain a federal system because its national officials are selected from subunits of government—the president through the allocation of Electoral College votes to the states and the Congress through the allocation of two Senate seats per state and the apportionment of representatives based on state population. Whatever protection exists for state power and independence must be found in the national political process, in the influence of state and district voters on their senators and representatives. In a strongly worded dissenting opinion in *Garcia*, Justice Lewis Powell argued that if federalism is to be retained, the Constitution—not Congress—should divide powers. "The states' role in our system of government is a matter of constitutional law, not legislative grace. . . . [This decision] today rejects almost 200 years of the understanding of the constitutional status of federalism."[10]

THINK AGAIN

Should the national government be able to prosecute a high school student for bringing a gun to school?

representational federalism Assertion that no constitutional division of powers exists between the nation and the states but the states retain their constitutional role merely by selecting the president and members of Congress.

Federalism Revived?

In recent years federalism has experienced a modest revival. The U.S. Supreme Court today appears to be somewhat more respectful of the powers of states and somewhat less willing to see these powers trampled upon by the national government.[11]

In 1995 the U.S. Supreme Court issued its first opinion in more than sixty years that recognized a limit on Congress's power over interstate commerce and reaffirmed the Founders' notion of a national government with only the powers enumerated in the Constitution.[12] The Court found that the federal Gun-Free School

Zones Act was unconstitutional because it exceeded Congress's powers under the Interstate Commerce Clause. When a student, Alfonso Lopez, was apprehended at his Texas high school carrying a .38 caliber hand-gun, federal agents charged him with violating the *federal* Gun-Free School Zones Act of 1990.

National Conference of State Legislatures

This conference site provides information on 50 state legislatures and the issues they confront. *www.ncsl.org*

The U.S. government argued that the act was a constitutional exercise of its interstate commerce power, because "violent crime reduces the willingness of individuals to travel to areas within the country that are perceived to be unsafe." But after reviewing virtually all of the key commerce clause cases in its history, the Court determined that an activity must *substantially affect* interstate commerce in order to be regulated by Congress. Chief Justice William H. Rehnquist, writing for the majority in a 5 to 4 decision in *U.S. vs. Lopez,* even cited James Madison with approval: "The powers delegated by the proposed Constitution to the federal government are few and defined. Those which are to remain in the state governments are numerous and indefinite" (*Federalist,* No. 45).

In another victory for federalism, the U.S. Supreme Court ruled in 1996 in *Seminole Tribe v. Florida* that the Eleventh Amendment shields states from lawsuits by private parties that seek to force states to comply with federal laws enacted under the commerce power.[13] And in 1999 in *Alden v. Maine,* the Supreme Court held that states were also shielded in their own courts from lawsuits in which private parties seek to enforce federal mandates. In an opinion that surveyed the history of American federalism, Justice Kennedy wrote: "Congress has vast power but not all power. . . . When Congress legislates in matters affecting the states it may not treat these sovereign entities as mere prefectures or corporations."[14]

In defense of federalism, the Supreme Court invalidated a provision of a very popular law of Congress—the Brady Handgun Violence Protection Act. The Court decided in 1997 that the law's command to local law enforcement officers to conduct background checks on gun purchasers violated "the very principle of separate

Former presidential Press Secretary James Brady was permanently disabled in the assassination attempt on President Reagan in 1981. Brady and his wife led the effort to pass the Brady Act, which, among other things, ordered state and local officials to conduct background checks on gun purchasers. The Supreme Court held that portion of the act to be an unconstitutional violation of the principle of federalism.

WHAT DO YOU THINK?

Should Violence Against Women Be a Federal Crime?

When a student at VPI (Virginia Polytechnic Institute) was raped, she argued that the attack violated the federal Violence against Women Act of 1994, a popular bill that passed overwhelmingly in Congress and was signed by President Bill Clinton. The act allowed victims of "gender motivated violence," including rape, to sue their attackers for monetary damages in *federal* court. The U.S. government defended its constitutional authority to involve itself in crimes against women by citing the Interstate Commerce Clause, arguing that crimes against women interfered with interstate commerce, the power over which is given to the national government in Article I of the Constitution.

But in 2000 the U.S. Supreme Court said, "If accepted, this reasoning would allow Congress to regulate any crime whose nationwide, aggregated impact has substantial effects on employment, production, transit, or consumption. Moreover, such reasoning will not limit Congress to regulating violence, but may be applied equally as well to family law and other areas of state regulation since the aggregate effect of marriage, divorce, and childrearing on the national economy is undoubtedly significant." The Court reasoned that "the Constitution requires a distinction between what is truly national and what is truly local, and there is no better example of the police power, which the Founders undeniably left reposed in the States and denied the central government." In Justice Scalia's opinion, allowing Congress to claim that violence against women interfered with interstate commerce would open the door to federalizing all crime because all crime affects interstate commerce.

Source: U.S. v. Morrison, May 15, 2000.

state sovereignty." The Court affirmed that the federal government "may neither issue directives requiring the states to address particular problems, nor command the states' officers, or those of their political subdivisions, to administer or enforce the federal regulatory program" (*Printz v. U.S.*, 521 U.S. 890 (1997).[15] And the Court held that in the Violence against Women Act, Congress also invaded the reserved police power of the states[16] (see *What Do You Think?* "Should Violence Against Women Be a Federal Crime?").

The Supreme Court's apparent revival of federalism has been greeted with cautious optimism. However, all of the recent Supreme Court rulings reaffirming federalism have come in narrow 5 to 4 decisions. The closeness of these votes, together with these decisions' contrast to more than a half-century of case law in support of national power, provide no guarantee that in the future the Supreme Court will continue to move in the direction of strengthening federalism.

Money and Power Flow to Washington

THINK AGAIN

When the federal government requires states to provide safe drinking water, clean air, or access for the handicapped, should it provide funds to carry out these mandates?

Over the years, power in the federal system has flowed to Washington because tax money has flowed to Washington. With its financial resources, the federal government has been able to offer assistance to state and local governments and thereby involve itself in just about every governmental function performed by these governments. Today the federal government is no longer one of *enumerated* or *delegated* powers. No activities are really *reserved* to the states. Through its power to tax and spend for the *general welfare*, the national government is now deeply involved in welfare, education, transportation, police protection, housing, hospitals, urban development, and other activities that were once the exclusive domain of state and local government (see *Up Close*: "How Congress Set a National Drinking Age").

UP CLOSE

How Congress Set a National Drinking Age

Traditionally the *reserved* powers of the states included protection of the health, safety, and well-being of their citizens. The *enumerated* powers of Congress in the Constitution did not include regulating the sale and consumption of alcoholic beverages. Every state determined its own minimum age for drinking.

When the Twenty-sixth Amendment to the Constitution was passed in 1971, guaranteeing eighteen-year-olds the right to vote, most states lowered their minimum drinking age to eighteen. But by the early 1980s, some states had raised their minimums back to twenty-one in response to reports of teenage drinking and driving. Indeed, the National Transportation Safety Board reported that teenagers were statistically more likely to be involved in alcohol-related deaths than nonteenagers. The National Student Association, restaurant owners, and the beverage industry claimed that the selection of *all* teenagers for restriction was age discrimination. Whatever the merits of the argument, the issue was widely considered to be a *state* concern.

But the minimum drinking age became a national issue as a result of emotional appeals by groups such as Mothers Against Drunk Driving (MADD). Tragic stories told at televised committee hearings by grieving relatives of dead teenagers swept away federalism arguments. A few Congress members tried to argue that a national drinking age infringed on the powers of the state in a matter traditionally under state control. However, the new law did not directly mandate a national drinking age. Instead, it ordered the withholding of 10 percent of all federal highway funds from any state that failed to raise its minimum drinking age to twenty-one. States retained the rights to ignore the national minimum and give up a portion of their highway funds. (Congress used this same approach in 1974 in establishing a national 55-mile-per-hour speed limit.) Opponents of this device labeled it federal blackmail and a federal intrusion into state responsibilities. For some state officials, then, the issue was not teen drinking but rather the preemption of state authority.

Proponents of the legislation cited the *national* interest in setting a uniform minimum drinking age. They argued that protecting the lives of young people outweighed the states' interest in preserving their authority. Moreover, teens were crossing state lines to drink in states with lower drinking ages. New York, for example, with a minimum drinking age of nineteen, was attracting teenagers from Pennsylvania and New Jersey, where the drinking age was twenty-one. Reports of "bloody borders" were used to justify national action to establish a uniform drinking age. Although the Reagan White House had pledged to return responsibility to the states, it did not wish to offend the nation's mothers on such an emotional issue. Despite initial reservations, President Ronald Reagan supported the bill and signed it into law in 1984.

From a purely constitutional perspective, Congress simply exercised its power to spend money for the general welfare; it did not *directly* legislate in an area *reserved* to the states. Technically, states remain free to set their own minimum drinking age. Despite heated arguments in many state legislatures, all of the states adopted the twenty-one-year-old minimum national drinking age by 1990.

Appeals by groups such as Mothers Against Drunk Driving (MADD) helped overcome concerns that legislation effectively setting a national drinking age would infringe on state authority.

Grants-in-aid Today grant-in-aid programs are the single most important source of federal influence over state and local activity. A **grant-in-aid** is defined as "payment of funds by one level of government (national or state) to be expended by another level (state or local) for a specified purpose, usually on a matching-funds basis (the federal government puts up only as much as the state or locality) and in accordance with prescribed standards of requirements."[17] No state or local government is *required* to accept grants-in-aid. Participation in grant-in-aid programs is voluntary. So in theory, if conditions attached to the grant money are too oppressive, state and local governments can simply decline to participate and pass up these funds.

About one-quarter of all state and local government revenues currently come from federal grants. Federal grants are available in nearly every major category of state and local government activity. Over 500 separate grant programs are administered by various federal agencies. So numerous and diverse are these grants that state and local officials often lack information about their availability, purpose, and requirements. "Grantmanship"—knowing where and how to obtain federal grants—is highly valued in state and local governments. Federal grants can be obtained to preserve historic buildings, develop minority-owned businesses, aid foreign refugees, drain abandoned mines, control riots, and subsidize school milk programs, and so on. However, welfare (including cash benefits and food stamps) and health (including Medicaid for the poor) account for two-thirds of federal aid money (see Figure 4.4).

Thus many of the special projects and ongoing programs carried out today by state and local governments are funded by grants from the federal government. These funds have generally been dispersed as either categorical grants or block grants.

grants-in-aid Payments of funds from the national government to state or local governments or from a state government to local governments for specific purposes.

- *Categorical Grant:* A grant for a specific, narrow project. The project must be approved by a federal administrative agency. About 90 percent of federal aid money is distributed in the form of categorical grants. Categorical grants can be distributed on a project basis or a formula basis. Grants made on a project basis are distributed by federal administrative agencies to state or local governments that compete for project funds in their applications. Federal agencies have a great deal of discretion in selecting specific projects for support, and

FIGURE 4.4 Purposes of Federal Grants to State and Local Governments

Over one-fifth of all state and local government revenues are derived from federal grants. Federal grants-in-aid to state and local governments are especially vital in the areas of health and welfare.

Source: Budget of United States Government, 2004.

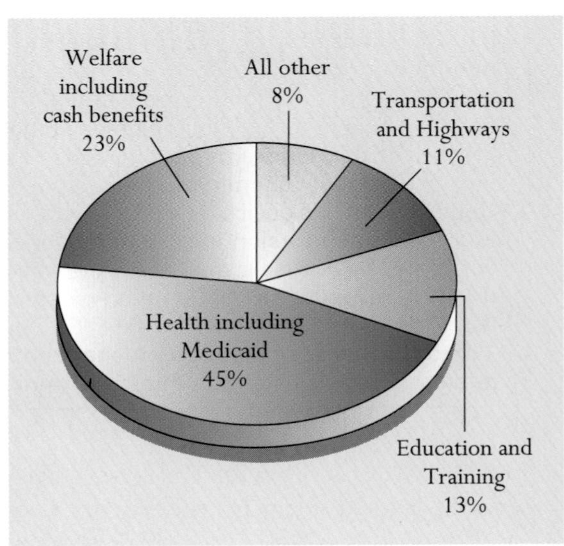

A CONFLICTING VIEW

Liberals, Conservatives, and Federalism

From the earliest days of the Republic, American leaders and scholars have argued over federalism. Political interests that constitute a majority at the national level and control the national government generally praise the virtue of national supremacy. Political interests that do not control the national government but exercise controlling influence in one or more states generally see great merit in preserving the powers of the states.

In recent years, political conflict over federalism—over the division between national versus state and local responsibilities and finances—has tended to follow traditional "liberal" and "conservative" political cleavages. Generally, liberals seek to enhance the power of the *national* government because they believe people's lives can be changed—and bettered—by the exercise of national governmental power. The government in Washington has more power and resources than do state and local governments, which many liberals regard as too slow, cumbersome, weak, and unresponsive. Thus liberalism and centralization are closely related in American politics. The liberal argument for national authority can be summarized as follows:

- There is insufficient concern about social problems by state and local governments. The federal government must take the lead in civil rights, equal employment opportunities, care for the poor and aged, the provision of adequate medical care for all Americans, and the elimination of urban poverty and blight.
- It is difficult to achieve change when reform-minded citizens must deal with 50 state governments and more than 85,000 local governments. Change is more likely to be accomplished by a strong central government.
- State and local governments contribute to inequality in society by setting different levels of services in education, welfare, health, and other public functions. A strong national government can ensure uniformity of standards throughout the nation.
- A strong national government can unify the nation behind principles and ideals of social justice and economic progress. Extreme decentralization may favor local or regional "special" interests at the expense of the general "public" interest.

In contrast, conservatives generally seek to return power to *state and local* governments. Conservatives are skeptical about the "good" that government can do and believe that adding to the power of the national government is not an effective way of resolving society's problems. On the contrary, they argue that "government is the problem, not the solution." Excessive government regulation, burdensome taxation, and inflationary government spending combine to restrict individual freedom, penalize work and savings, and destroy incentives for economic growth. Government should be kept small, controllable, and close to the people. The conservative argument for state and local autonomy can be summarized as follows:

- Grass-roots government promotes a sense of self-responsibility and self-reliance.
- State and local governments can better adapt public programs to local needs and conditions.
- State and local governments promote participation in politics and civic responsibility by allowing more people to become involved in public questions.
- Competition between states and cities can result in improved public programs and services.
- The existence of multiple state and local governments encourages experimentation and innovation in public policy, from which the whole nation may gain.

There is no way to settle the argument over federalism once and for all. Debates about federalism are part of the fabric of American politics.

they can exercise direct control over the projects. Most categorical grants are distributed to state or local governments according to a fixed formula set by Congress. Medicaid and Food Stamps (see Chapter 17) are the largest categorical grant programs.

- *Block Grant:* A grant for a general governmental function, such as health, social services, law enforcement, education, or community development. State and local governments have fairly wide discretion in deciding how to spend federal block grant money within a functional area. For example, cities receiving "community development" block grants can decide for themselves about specific neighborhood development projects, housing projects, community facilities, and so on. All block grants are distributed on a formula basis set by Congress. Federal administrative agencies may require reports and adherence to rules and guidelines, but they do not choose which specific projects to fund. Only about 10 percent of federal grant-in-aid money is distributed in the form of block grants.

"Devolution" Controversy over federalism—what level of government should do what and who should pay for it—is as old as the nation itself (see *A Conflicting View*: "Liberals, Conservatives, and Federalism"). Beginning in 1995, with a new Republican majority in both houses of Congress and Republicans holding a majority of state governorships, debates over federalism were renewed. The new phrase was **devolution**—the passing down of responsibilities from the national government to the states.

Welfare reform turned out to be the key to devolution. Bill Clinton once promised "to end welfare as we know it," but it was a Republican Congress in 1996 that did so. After President Clinton had twice vetoed welfare reform bills, he and Congress finally agreed to merge welfare reform with devolution. A new Temporary Assistance to Needy Families program (see Chapter 17) replaced direct federal cash aid welfare "entitlements." The new program:

- Establishes block grants with lump-sum allocations to the states for cash welfare payments.
- Grants the states broad flexibility in determining eligibility and benefit levels for persons receiving such aid.
- Limits the use of federally aided cash grants for most recipients to two continuing years and five years over their lifetime.
- Allows states to deny additional cash payments for children born to women already receiving welfare assistance and allowing states to deny cash payments to parents under eighteen who do not live with an adult and attend school.

Since Franklin D. Roosevelt's New Deal, with its federal guarantee of cash Aid to Families with Dependent Children (AFDC), low-income mothers and children had enjoyed a federal "entitlement" to welfare payments. But welfare reform, with its devolution of responsibility to the states, ended this 60-year-old federal entitlement. Note, however, that Congress continues to place "strings" on the use of federal welfare funds, including a two-year limit on continuing payments to beneficiaries in a five-year lifetime limit.

WWW **Urban Institute** Washington think tank offers viewpoints on federalism and issues confronting state/local government. ***www.urban.org***

Political Obstacles to Devolution and Federalism Politicians in Washington are fond of the rhetoric of federalism. They know that Americans generally prefer governments closer to home. Yet at the same time they confront strong political pressures to "DO SOMETHING!" about virtually every problem that confronts individuals, families, or communities, whether or not doing so may overstep the enumerated powers of the national government. Politicians gain very little by telling their constituents that a particular problem—violence in the schools, domestic abuse, physician-assisted suicide, and so on—is not a federal responsibility and should be dealt with at the state or local level of government.

devolution Passing down of responsibilities from the national government to the states.

Moreover, neither presidents nor members of Congress are inclined to restrain their own power. Both liberals and conservatives in Washington are motivated to tie their own strings to federal grant-in-aid money, issue their own federal mandates, and otherwise "correct" what they perceive to be errors or inadequacies of state policies.

Coercive Federalism: Preemptions and Mandates

Traditionally, Congress avoided issuing direct orders to state and local governments. Instead, it sought to influence them by offering grants of money with federal rules, regulations, or "guidelines" attached. In theory at least, states and communities were free to forgo the money and ignore the strings attached to it. But increasingly Congress has undertaken direct regulation of areas traditionally reserved to the states and restricted state authority to regulate these areas. And it has issued direct orders to state and local governments to perform various services and comply with federal law in the performance of these services.

Federal Preemptions The supremacy of federal laws over those of the states, spelled out in the National Supremacy Clause of the Constitution, permits Congress to decide whether or not there is **preemption** of state laws in a particular field by federal law. In **total preemption,** the federal government assumes all regulatory powers in a particular field—for example, copyrights, bankruptcy, railroads, and airlines. No state regulations in a totally preempted field are permitted. **Partial preemption** stipulates that a state law on the same subject is valid as long as it does not conflict with the federal law in the same area. For example, the Occupational Safety and Health Act of 1970 specifically permits state regulation of any occupational safety or health issue on which the federal Occupational Safety and Health Administration (OSHA) has *not* developed a standard; but once OSHA enacts a standard, all state standards are nullified. A specific form of partial preemption called **standard partial preemption** permits states to regulate activities in a field already regulated by the federal government, as long as state regulatory standards are at least as stringent as those of the federal government. Usually states must submit their regulations to the responsible federal agency for approval; the federal agency may revoke a state's regulating power if that state fails to enforce the approved standards. For example, the federal Environmental Protection Agency (EPA) permits state environmental regulations that meet or exceed EPA standards.

preemption Total or partial federal assumption of power in a particular field, restricting the authority of the states.

total preemption Federal government's assumption of all regulatory powers in a particular field.

partial preemption Federal government's assumption of some regulatory powers in a particular field, with the stipulation that a state law on the same subject as a federal law is valid if it does not conflict with the federal law in the same area.

standard partial preemption Form of partial preemption in which the states are permitted to regulate activities already regulated by the federal government if the state regulatory standards are at least as stringent as the federal government's.

Federal Mandates Federal **mandates** are direct orders to state and local governments to perform a particular activity or service or to comply with federal laws in the performance of their functions. Federal mandates occur in a wide variety of areas, from civil rights to minimum-wage regulations. Their range is reflected in some recent examples of federal mandates to state and local governments:

- *Age Discrimination Act, 1986:* Outlaws mandatory retirement ages for public as well as private employees, including police, fire fighters, and state college and university faculty.
- *Asbestos Hazard Emergency Act, 1986:* Orders school districts to inspect for asbestos hazards and remove asbestos from school buildings when necessary.
- *Safe Drinking Water Act, 1986:* Establishes national requirements for municipal water supplies; regulates municipal waste treatment plants.

mandates Direct federal orders to state and local governments requiring them to perform a service or to obey federal laws in the performance of their functions.

UP CLOSE

Arnold: From Bodybuilder, to Superstar, to Governor

Arnold's message to California Governor Grey Davis was "Hasta la vista, baby!" In 2003 Davis became only the second governor in history to be recalled by the voters. Arnold himself had never held political office. He had risen from an impoverished immigrant who barely spoke English, to champion bodybuilder, to world-famous movie star, to Kennedy family in-law, to governor of America's largest state.

Eighteen states include recall provisions in their constitutions: petitions signed by a specified number of voters (12 percent in California) force an incumbent official to face the voters and risk being ousted before the end of their terms. Petition drives for a California governor's recall had failed on thirty-one previous occasions; even Governor Ronald Reagan faced three recall attempts. The recall grew out of the Progressive Movement of the early twentieth century, which advanced elements of direct democracy, including the initiative and referendum, in American politics. But the initiative, referendum, and recall exist only at the state level; America's Founders were extremely skeptical of direct democracy (see Chapter 1, "Direct versus Representative Democracy" and Chapter 3, "The Structure of the Government").

So what did Grey Davis do to deserve ouster only one year after his reelection to a second term? Unlike impeachment, a successful recall does not require specific charges of malfeasance or criminal conduct in office. Voters can recall an officeholder for any reason, or for no reason. But Davis was particularly inept: he failed to act decisively during California's electricity blackouts of 2000 and 2001, which resulted in higher utility bills; he engaged in reckless spending despite an economic downturn and consequently drowned the state in red ink; and perhaps most enraging to voters, he tripled the car tax, raising license fees from about $70 to $210 for the average passenger car.

Arnold's father had been a local police chief in Austria and a Nazi Party member prior to World War II. Arnold donated hundreds of thousands of dollars to the Simon Wiesenthal Center, a Jewish human rights organization, and asked the Center to investigate his father's activities.

The Center found no evidence that his father had committed any war crimes. Arnold spent his teenage years developing his body in the hope of one day becoming Mr. Universe. At age 20 he fulfilled his dream, and then came to America to pursue his second goal, to become a movie actor. His 1982 *Conan the Barbarian* became a cult classic; in 1984 he starred in *The Terminator* and later made two sequels.

Arnold revealed an interest in politics by becoming involved with the Special Olympics and serving on President George H. W. Bush's Council on Physical Fitness. In 2002 he sponsored a California ini-

- *Clean Air Act, 1990:* Bans municipal incinerators and requires auto emission inspections in certain urban areas.
- *Americans with Disabilities Act, 1990:* Requires all state and local government buildings to promote handicapped access.
- *National Voter Registration Act, 1993:* Requires states to register voters at driver's license, welfare, and unemployment compensation offices.
- *No Child Left Behind Act, 2001:* Requires states and their school districts to test public school pupils.

State and local governments frequently complain that the costs imposed on them by complying with such federal mandates are seldom reimbursed by Washington.

unfunded mandates
Mandates that impose costs on state and local governments (and private industry) without reimbursement from the federal government.

"Unfunded" Mandates Federal mandates often impose heavy costs on states and communities. When no federal monies are provided to cover these costs, the mandates are said to be **unfunded mandates**. Governors, mayors, and other state and local officials have often urged Congress to stop imposing unfunded mandates on states and communities. Private industries have long voiced the

tiative to spend more money for before- and after-school programs. He offered very few specifics in his campaign for governor: "I am a man of the people"; "We have tough choices ahead"; "For the people to win, politics as usual must lose." When the liberal *Los Angeles Times* charged Arnold with "groping" women on movie sets, Arnold's wife, television personality Maria Shriver, daughter of Robert Kennedy, came to his defense. His poll numbers actually went up following the charges. Davis lost the recall vote 54 to 46 percent. Arnold won 48 percent of the vote in the 135-candidate race. As a moderate Rebublican, he won easily over the Democratic Lieutenant Governor and a conservative Republican state senator, among many others. But in a Democratic state, with a Democratic-controlled legislature, can *The Terminator* end California's financial problems?

same complaint. Regulations and mandates allow Congress to address problems while pushing the costs of doing so onto others.

Homeland Security The Constitution gives the federal government the responsibility for national defense. The terrorist attack on the World Trade Center in New York and the Pentagon in Washington, September 11, 2001, began what President George W. Bush described as a long and difficult to "war on terrorism." Washington reorganized itself, creating a new Department of Homeland Security (see Chapter 12), and allocated billions of dollars for homeland defenses. But the "first responders" to any terrorist attack are state and local police, fire, medical, and other emergency agencies. States, counties, and cities now face unprecedented and permanent responsibilities in homeland security, even including dealing with the results of nuclear, biological, and chemical attacks. Governors, mayors, city and county officials, and especially police, fire, and emergency officers, have urged the Congress to provide more federal funding and resources to state and local agencies for homeland security. Congress has responded with billions of dollars in additional aid, but states and communities claim that assistance for their "first responders" is inadequate.

SUMMARY NOTES

- The struggle for power between the national government and the states over two centuries has shaped American federalism today.
- Federalism is the division of power between two separate authorities, the nation and the state, each of which enforces its own laws directly on its citizens and neither of which can change the division of power without the consent of the other.
- American federalism was designed by the Founders as an additional protection for individual liberty by providing for the division and dispersal of power among multiple units of government.
- Federalism has also been defended as a means of increasing opportunities to hold public office, improving governmental efficiency, ensuring policy responsiveness, encouraging policy innovation, and managing conflict.
- However, federalism can also obstruct and frustrate national action. Narrow state interests can sometimes prevail over national interests or the interests of minorities within states. Segregation was long protected by theories of states' rights. Federalism also results in uneven levels of public services through the nation.
- Power has flowed to the national government over time, as the original state-centered division of power has evolved into a national-centered system of government. Among the most important historical influences on this shift in power toward Washington have been the Supreme Court's broad interpretation of national power, the national government's victory over the secessionist states in the Civil War, the establishment of a national system of civil rights based on the Fourteenth Amendment, the growth of a national economy governed by Congress under its interstate commerce power, and the national government's accumulation of power through its greater financial resources.
- Federal grants to state and local governments have greatly expanded the national government's powers in areas previously regarded as *reserved* to the states.
- Federal grants are available for most state and local government activities, but health and welfare account for about two-thirds of these grants.
- Although Congress has generally refrained from directly legislating in areas traditionally *reserved* to the states, federal power in local affairs has grown as a result of federal rules, regulations, and guidelines established as conditions for the receipt of federal funds.
- The Supreme Court in its *Garcia* decision in 1985 removed all constitutional barriers to direct congressional legislation in matters traditionally reserved to the states. Establishing the principle of representational federalism, the Court said that states could defend their own interests through their representation in the national government.
- Representational federalism focuses on the role of the states in electing national officials—the president through the allocation of Electoral College votes to the states, the Senate through the allocation of two seats for each state, and the House through the appointment of representatives based on the state's population.
- Recent efforts at the "devolution" of federal responsibilities for welfare resulted in an end to federal individual "entitlements" to cash welfare payments and their replacement with block grants for cash aid to the states. But Congress continues to place "strings" on the use of federal welfare grants to the states.

KEY TERMS

federalism 103
unitary system 103
confederation 103
home rule 103
intergovernmental relations 103
laboratories of democracy 106
delegated, or enumerated, powers 109
Necessary and Proper Clause 109
implied powers 109
National Supremacy Clause 109
concurrent powers 109
reserved powers 109
dual federalism 113
cooperative federalism 116
centralized federalism 116
new federalism 117
representational federalism 118
grant-in-aid 122
devolution 124
preemption 125
total preemption 125
partial preemption 125
standard partial preemption 125
mandates 125
unfunded mandates 126

SUGGESTED READINGS

Beer, Samuel H. *To Make a Nation: The Rediscovery of American Federalism.* Cambridge, Mass.: Harvard University Press, 1993. A historical account of the development of both federalism and nationalism in American political philosophy.

Dye, Thomas R. *American Federalism: Competition among Governments.* Lexington, Mass.: Lexington Books, 1990. A theory of "competitive federalism" arguing that rivalries among governments improve public services while lowering taxes, restrain the growth of government, promote innovation and experimentation in public policies, inspire greater responsiveness to the preferences of citizen-taxpayers, and encourage economic growth.

Elazar, Daniel J. *The American Partnership.* Chicago: University of Chicago Press, 1962. Classic study of the historical evolution of federalism, stressing the nation-state sharing of policy concerns and financing, from the early days of the Republic, and the politics behind the gradual growth of national power.

Greve, Michael S. *Real Federalism.* Washington, D.C.: AEI Press, 1999. Why real "competitive" federalism matters and how it can be achieved in the current political environments.

Nagel, Robert F. *The Implosion of Federalism.* NewYork: Oxford University Press, 2001. America's political institutions are collapsing into the center, reducing the opportunity for competition and participation.

Ostrum, Vincent. *The Meaning of American Federalism.* San Francisco: ICS Press, 1991. A theoretical examination of federalism, setting forth the conditions for a self-governing society and arguing that multiple, overlapping units of government, with various checks on one another's power, provide a viable democratic system of conflict resolution.

O'Toole, Laurence J., ed. *American Intergovernmental Relations.* 3rd ed. Washington, D.C.: CQ Press, 1999. A collection of readings, both classic and contemporary, describing the theory, history, and current problems of intergovernmental relations in America.

Peterson, Paul E. *The Price of Federalism.* Washington, D.C.: Brookings Institution, 1995. Historical, theoretical, and empirical perspectives merged into a new, timely model of federalism that would allocate social welfare functions to the national government and education and economic development to states and communities.

Van Horn, Carl E. *The State of the States.* 3rd ed. Washington, D.C.: CQ Press, 1996. An assessment of the challenges facing state governments as a result of the devolution revolution.

CHAPTER 5

PARTICIPATION, CAMPAIGNS, AND ELECTIONS: DECIDING WHO GOVERNS

CHAPTER OUTLINE

Individual Participation in Politics
Voters and Nonvoters
Elections in a Democracy
The Advantages of Incumbency
Campaign Strategies
How Much Does It Cost to Get Elected?
Raising Campaign Cash
What Do Contributors "Buy"?
Regulating Campaign Finance
The Presidential Campaign: The Primary Race
The Presidential Campaign: The General Election Battle
The Voter Decides

THINK ABOUT POLITICS

1 Is our government really legitimate when only about half the people vote in presidential elections?
Yes ● No ●

2 Should people vote on the basis of a candidate's personal character rather than his or her policy positions?
Yes ● No ●

3 Would you vote for a candidate who used negative ads to discredit an opponent?
Yes ● No ●

4 Do political campaign contributions have too much influence on elections and government policy?
Yes ● No ●

5 Are high campaign costs discouraging good people from becoming candidates?
Yes ● No ●

What real power do you have in a democracy? By casting ballots, citizens in a democracy have the power to determine who will represent them, who will make up the government under which they live. You, then, are an integral part of the democratic process every time you vote in an election.

Individual Participation in Politics

Democracies provide a variety of ways for individuals to participate in politics. People may run for, and win, public office; take part in marches, demonstrations, and protests; make financial contributions to political candidates or causes; attend political meetings, speeches, and rallies; write letters to public officials or to newspapers; wear a political button or place a bumper sticker on their car; belong to organizations that support or oppose particular candidates or take stands on public issues; attempt to influence friends while discussing candidates or issues; and vote in elections. Individuals may also participate in politics passively, by simply following political issues and campaigns in the media, acquiring knowledge, forming opinions about public affairs, and expressing their views to others. These forms of political participation can be ranked according to their order of frequency (see Figure 5.1). Only a little more than half of the voting-age population vote in presidential elections, and far fewer vote in congressional and state and local elections (see Figure 5.2).

Voters and Nonvoters

Who votes and who doesn't? The perceived benefits and costs of voting apparently do not fall evenly across all social groups. Nonvoting would generate less concern if voters were a representative cross section of nonvoters. But voters differ from nonvoters in politically important ways.

Voters are better educated than nonvoters. Education appears to be the most important determinant of voter turnout (see Figure 5.3). It may be that schooling promotes an interest in politics, instills the ethic of citizen participation, or gives people a better awareness of public affairs and an understanding of the role of elections in a democracy. Education is associated with a sense of confidence and political *efficacy*, the feeling that one can indeed have a personal impact on public affairs.

FIGURE 5.1 Political Participation

Only a small percentage of the American people are actively engaged in the political process, yet they receive most of the media attention. Less than 1 percent of the population runs for office at any level of government, and only about half of all voting-age Americans bother to go to the polls even in a presidential election.

Source: National Election Studies Cumulative File. See also M. Margaret Conway, *Political Participation in the United States,* 3rd ed. (Washington, D.C.: CQ Press, 2000).

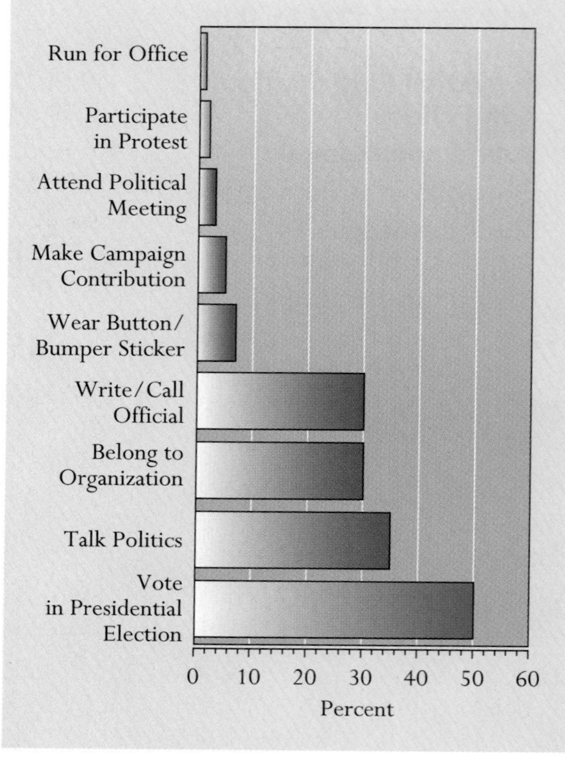

Age is another factor affecting voter participation. Perhaps because young people have more distractions, more demands on their time in school, work, or new family responsibilities, nonvoting is greatest among eighteen- to twenty-four-year-olds. In contrast, older Americans are politically influential in part because candidates know they turn out at the polls.

High-income people are more likely to vote than are low-income people. Most of this difference stems from the fact that high-income people are more likely to be well educated and older. But poor people may also feel alienated from the political system—they may lack a sense of political efficacy; they may feel they have little control over their own lives, let alone over public affairs. Or poor people may simply be so absorbed in the problems of life that they have little time or energy to spend on registering and voting.[1]

Income and education differences between participants and nonparticipants are even greater when other forms of political participation are considered. Higher-income, better-educated people are much more likely to be among those who make campaign contributions, who write or call their elected representatives, and who join and work in active political organizations.[2]

Historically, race was a major determinant of nonvoting. Black voter turnout, especially in the South, was markedly lower than white voter turnout. African Americans continue today to have a slightly lower overall voter turnout than whites, but most of the remaining difference is attributable to differences between blacks and whites in educational and income levels. Blacks and whites at the same educational and income levels register and vote with the same frequency. Indeed, in cities where African Americans are well organized politically, black voter turnout may exceed white voter turnout.[3]

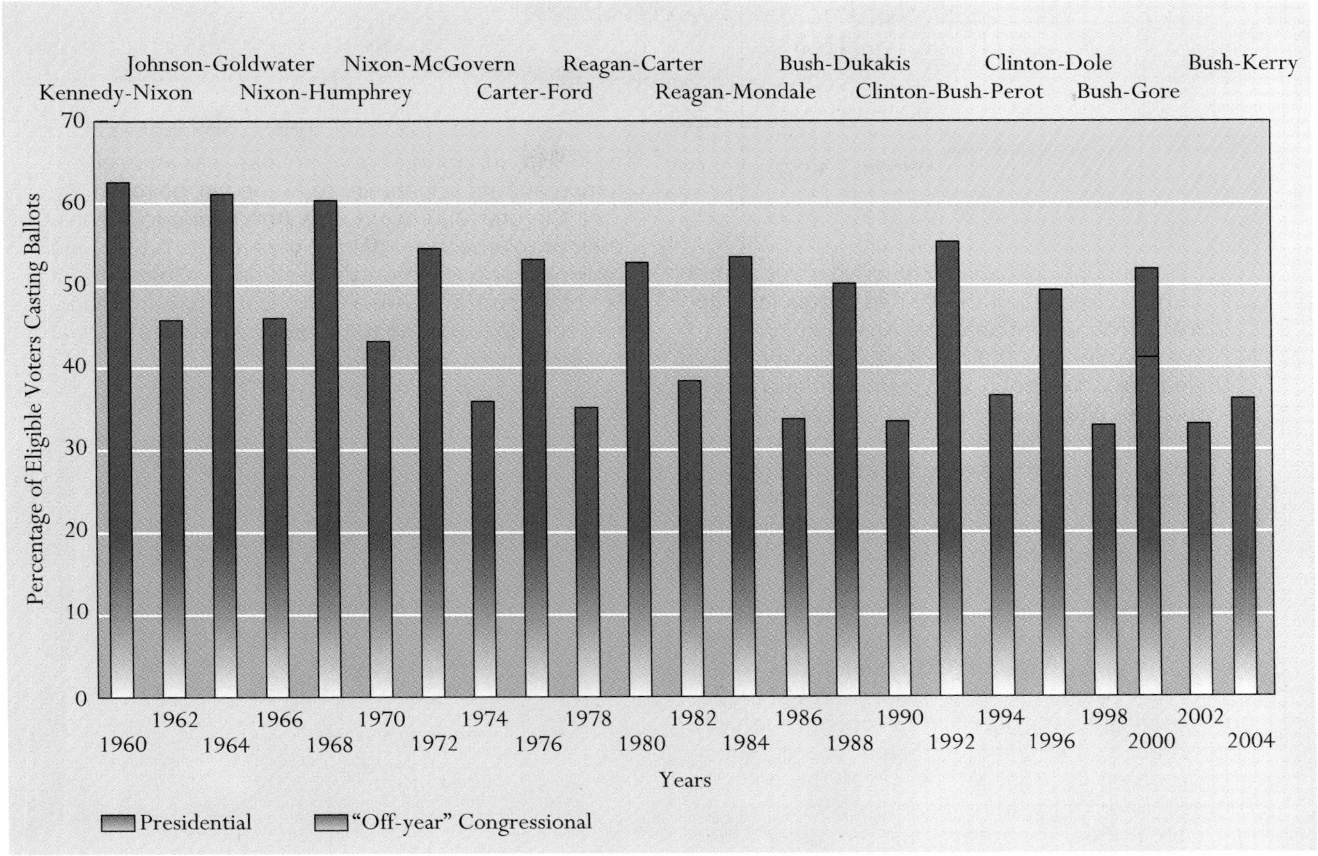

FIGURE 5.2 Voter Turnout in Presidential and Congressional Elections

Voter turnout is always higher in years with a presidential election. However, voter turnout has generally declined since 1960, even in presidential election years. The exception came in 1992, when intense interest in the contest between George Bush and Bill Clinton—spiced by the entry of independent Ross Perot—led to a higher-than-normal turnout. In 1996 fewer than half of voting-age Americans bothered to cast ballots. However, in 2004 voter turnout rose to levels not seen since the 1960's.

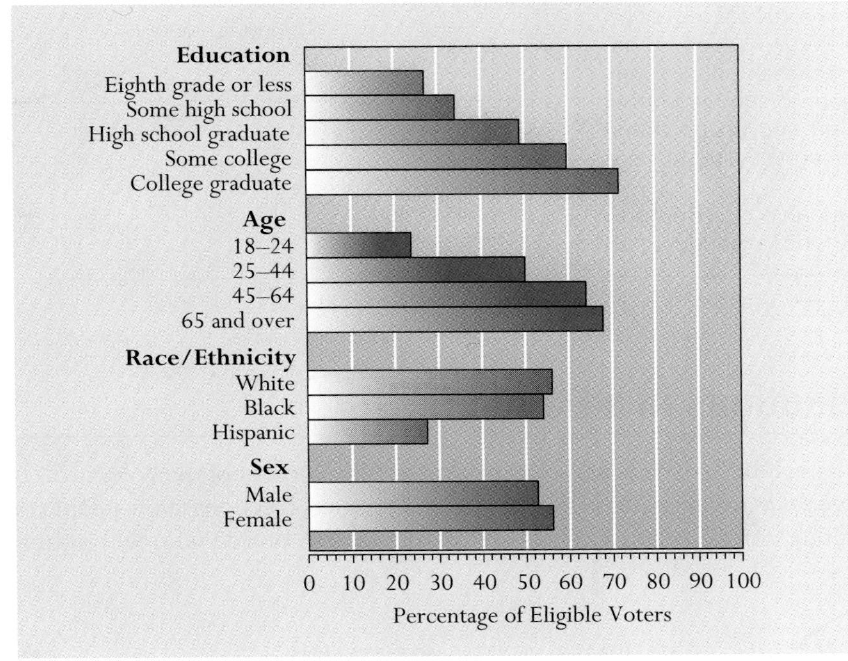

FIGURE 5.3 Voter Turnout by Social Groups

Although there is virtually no gender gap in who goes to the polls, voter turnout increases with education, age, and income. Major efforts to "get out the vote" in the African American community have raised voter turnout to nearly that of whites, but turnout among Hispanics continues to lag.

Source: U.S. Bureau of the Census, *Statistical Abstract of the United States, 2001*. Data for 2000 presidential election.

COMPARED TO WHAT?

Voter Turnout in Western Democracies

Other Western democracies regularly report higher voter turnout rates than the United States (see figure). Yet in an apparent paradox, Americans seem to be more supportive of their political institutions, less alienated from their political system, and even more patriotic than citizens of Western European nations. Why, then, are voter turnouts in the United States so much lower than in these other democracies?

The answer to this question lies primarily in the legal and institutional differences between the United States and the other democracies. First of all, in Austria, Australia, Belgium, and Italy, voting is *mandatory.* Penalties and the level of enforcement vary within and across these countries. Moreover, registration laws in the United States make voting more difficult than in other countries. In Western Europe, all citizens are required to register with the government and obtain identification cards. These cards are then used for admission to the polls. In contrast, voter registration is entirely voluntary in the United States, and voters must reregister if they change residences. Nearly 50 percent of the U.S. population changes residence at least once in a five-year period, thus necessitating reregistration.

Parties in the United States are more loosely organized, less disciplined, and less able to mobilize voters than are European parties. Moreover, many elections in the United States, notably elections for Congress, are not very competitive. The United States organizes congressional elections by district with winner-take-all rules, whereas many European parliaments are selected by proportional representation, with seats allocated to parties based on national vote totals. Proportional representation means every vote counts toward seats in the legislative body. Thus greater competition and proportional representation may encourage higher voter turnout in European democracies.

But cultural differences may also contribute to differences in turnout. The American political culture, with its tradition of individualism and self-reliance and its reluctance to empower government (see Chapter 2), encourages Americans to resolve their problems through their own efforts rather than looking to government for solutions. Government is not as central to Americans as it is to Europeans, and therefore getting to the polls on election day is not seen as so important.

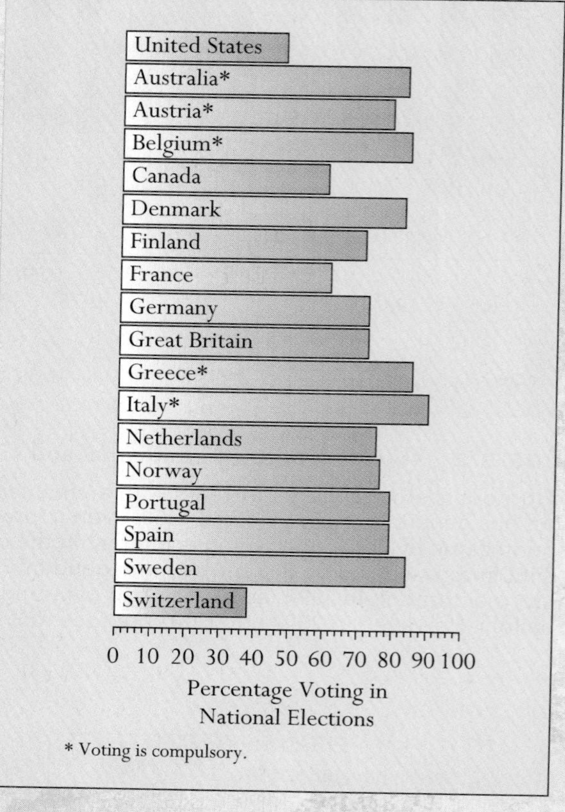

Average Turnout 1991–2000

Source: Center for Voting and Democracy, 2002, www.fairvote.org.

Elections in a Democracy

Democratic government is government by "the consent of the governed." Elections give practical meaning to this notion of "consent." Elections allow people to choose among competing candidates and parties and to decide who will occupy public office. Elections give people the opportunity to pass judgment on current officeholders, either by reelecting them (granting continued consent) or by throwing them out of office (withdrawing consent).

In a representative democracy, elections function primarily to choose personnel to occupy public office—to decide "who governs." But elections also have an indirect influence on public policy, allowing voters to influence policy directions by choosing between candidates or parties with different policy priorities. Thus elections indirectly influence "who gets what"—that is, the outcomes of the political process.

Elections as Mandates? However, it is difficult to argue that elections serve as "policy mandates"—that is, that elections allow voters to direct the course of public policy. Frequently, election winners claim a **mandate**—overwhelming support from the people—for their policies and programs. But for elections to serve as policy mandates, four conditions have to be met:

1. Competing candidates have to offer clear policy alternatives.
2. The voters have to cast their ballots on the basis of these policy alternatives alone.
3. The election results have to clearly indicate the voters' policy preferences.
4. Elected officials have to be bound by their campaign promises.[4]

As we shall see, *none* of these conditions is fully met in American elections. Often candidates do not differ much on policy questions or they deliberately obscure their policy positions to avoid offending groups of voters. Voters themselves frequently pay little attention to policy issues in elections but rather vote along traditional party lines or group affiliations, or on the basis of the candidate's character, personality, or media image.

Moreover, even in elections in which issues seem to dominate the campaign, the outcome may not clearly reflect policy preferences. Candidates take stands on a variety of issues. It is never certain on which issues the voters agreed with the winner and on which issues they disagreed yet voted for the candidate anyway.

Finally, candidates often fail to abide by their campaign promises once they are elected. Some simply ignore their promises, assuming voters have forgotten about the campaign. Others point to changes in circumstances or conditions as a justification for abandoning a campaign pledge.

THINK AGAIN

Should elected officials be bound by their campaign promises?

Retrospective Voting Voters can influence future policy directions through **retrospective voting**—votes cast on the basis of the performance of incumbents, by either reelecting them or throwing them out of office.[5] Voters may not know what politicians will do in the future, but they can evaluate how well politicians performed in the past. When incumbent officeholders are defeated, it is reasonable to assume that voters did not like their performance and that newly elected officials should change policy course if they do not want to meet a similar fate in the next election. But it is not always clear what the defeated incumbents did in office that led to their ouster by the voters. Nor, indeed, can incumbents who won reelection assume that all of their policies are approved of by a majority of voters. Nevertheless, retrospective voting provides an overall judgment of how voters evaluate performance in office.

mandate Perception of popular support for a program or policy based on the margin of electoral victory won by a candidate who proposed it during a campaign.

retrospective voting Voting for or against a candidate or party on the basis of past performance in office.

UP CLOSE

How to Run for Office

Many rewards come with elected office—the opportunity to help shape public policy, public attention and name recognition, and many business, professional, and social contacts. But there are many drawbacks as well—the absence of privacy, a microscopic review of one's past, constant calls, meetings, interviews and handshaking, and perhaps most onerous of all, the continual need to solicit campaign funds.

Before You Run—Getting Involved

Get involved in various organizations in your community:

- Neighborhood associations.
- Chambers of commerce, business associations.
- Churches and synagogues (become an usher, if possible, for visibility).
- Political groups (Democratic or Republican clubs, League of Women Voters, and so on).
- Parent-Teacher Associations (PTAs).
- Service clubs (Rotary, Kiwanis, Civitan, Toastmasters).
- Recreation organizations (Little League, flag football, soccer leagues, running and walking clubs, for example, as participant, coach, or umpire).

Deciding to Run—Know What You're Doing

In deciding to run, and choosing the office for which you wish to run, you should become thoroughly familiar with the issues, duties, and responsibilities.

- Attend council or commission meetings, state legislative sessions, and/or committee hearings.
- Become familiar with current issues and officeholders, and obtain a copy of and read the budget.
- Learn the demographics of your district (racial, ethnic, and age composition; occupational mix; average income; neighborhood differences). If you do not fit the prevailing racial, ethnic, or age composition, think about moving to another district.
- Memorize a brief (preferably less than seven seconds) answer to the question, "Why are you running?"

Getting in the Race

Contact your county elections department to obtain the following:

- Qualifying forms and information.
- Campaign financing forms and regulations.
- District and street maps for your district.
- Recent election results in your district.
- Election-law book or pamphlet.
- Voter registration lists (usually sold as lists, or labels, or tapes).
- Contact your party's county chairperson for advice; convince the party's leaders that you can win. Ask for a list of their regular campaign contributors.

Raising Money

The easiest way to finance a campaign is to be rich enough to provide your own funds. Failing that, you must:

- Establish a campaign fund, according to the laws of your state.
- Find a treasurer/campaign-finance chairperson who knows many wealthy, politically involved people.
- Invite wealthy, politically involved people to small coffees, cocktail parties, dinners; give a brief campaign speech and then have your finance chairperson solicit contributions.
- Follow up fund-raising events and meetings with personal phone calls.
- Be prepared to continue fund-raising activities throughout your campaign; file accurate financial disclosure statements as required by state law.

Getting Organized

Professional campaign managers and management firms almost always outperform volunteers. If you cannot afford professional management, you must rely on yourself or trusted friends to perform the following:

- Draw up a budget based on reasonable expectations of campaign funding.
- Interview and select a professional campaign-management firm, or appoint a trusted campaign manager.
- Ask trusted friends from various clubs, activities, neighborhoods, churches, and so on, to meet and serve as a campaign committee. If your district is racially or ethnically diverse, make sure all groups are represented on your committee.
- Decide on a campaign theme; research issues important to your community; develop brief, well-articulated positions on these issues.
- Open a campaign headquarters with desks and telephones. Buy a cell phone; use call forwarding; stay in contact. Use your garage if you can't afford an office.

- Arrange to meet with newspaper editors, editorial boards, TV station executives, and political reporters. Be prepared for tough questions.
- Hire a media consultant or advertising agency, or appoint a volunteer media director who knows television, radio, and newspaper advertising.
- Arrange a press conference to announce your candidacy. Notify all media well in advance. Arrange for overflow crowd of supporters to cheer and applaud.
- Produce eyecatching, inspirational 15- or 30-second television and radio ads that present a favorable image of you and stress your campaign theme.
- Prepare and print attractive campaign brochures, signs, and bumper stickers.
- Hire a local survey-research firm to conduct telephone surveys of voters in your district, asking what they think are the most important issues, how they stand on them, whether they recognize your name and your theme, and how they plan to vote. Be prepared to change your theme and your position on issues if surveys show strong opposition to your views.

On the Campaign Trail

Campaigns themselves may be primarily *media centered* or primarily *door-to-door* ("retail") or some combination of both.

- Buy media time as early as possible from television and radio stations; insist on prime-time slots before, during, and after popular shows.
- Buy newspaper ads; insist on their placement in popular, well-read sections of the paper.
- Attend every community gathering possible, just to be seen, even if you do not give a speech. Keep all speeches short. Focus on one or two issues that your polls show are important to voters.
- Recruit paid or unpaid volunteers to hand out literature door-to-door. Record names and addresses of voters who say they support you.
- Canvass door-to-door with a brief (seven-second) self-introduction and statement of your reasons for running. Use registration lists to identify members of your own party, and try to address them by name. Also canvass offices, factories, coffee shops, shopping malls—anywhere you find a crowd.
- Organize a phone bank, either professional or volunteer. Prepare *brief* introduction and phone statements. Record names of people who say they support you.
- Know your opponent: Research his or her past affiliations, indiscretions if any, previous voting record, and public positions on issues.
- Be prepared to "define" your opponent in negative terms. Negative advertising works. But be fair: Base your comments on your opponent's public record. Emphasize his or her positions that clearly deviate from your district voters' known preferences.

Primary versus General Elections

Remember that you will usually have to campaign in two elections—your party's primary and the general election.

- Before the primary, identify potential opposition in your own party, try to dissuade them from running.
- Allocate your budget first to win the primary election. If you lose the primary, you won't need any funds for the general election.
- In general elections, you must broaden your appeal without distancing your own party supporters. Deemphasize your party affiliation unless your district regularly elects members of your party. In a close district or a district that regularly votes for the opposition party, stress your independence and your commitment to the *district's* interests.

On Election Day

Turning out your voters is the key to success. Election day is the busiest day of the campaign for you and your staff.

- Use your phone bank to place as many calls as possible to party members in your district (especially those who have indicated in previous calls and visits that they support you). Remind them to vote; make sure your phone workers can tell each voter where to go to cast his or her vote.
- Solicit volunteers to drive people to the polls.
- Assign workers to as many polling places as possible. Most state laws require that they stay a specified distance from the voting booths. But they should be in evidence with your signs and literature to buttonhole voters before they go into the booths.
- Show up at city or county election office on election night with prepared victory statement thanking supporters and pledging your service to the district. (Also draft a courteous concession statement pledging your support to the winner, in case you lose.)
- Attend victory party with your supporters; meet many "new" friends.

The Advantages of Incumbency

In theory, elections offer voters the opportunity to "throw the rascals out." But in practice, voters seldom do so. **Incumbents,** people already holding public office, have a strong advantage when they seek reelection. The reelection rates of incumbents for *all* elective offices—city council, mayor, state legislature, governor, and especially Congress—are very high. Since 1950, more than 90 percent of all members of the House of Representatives who have sought reelection have been successful. The success rate of U.S. Senate incumbents is not as great, but it is still impressive; since 1950, more than 70 percent of senators seeking reelection have been successful.

Why do incumbents win so often? This is a particularly vexing question, inasmuch as so many people are distrustful of government and hold politicians in low esteem. Congress itself is the focal point of public disapproval and even ridicule. Yet people seem to distinguish between Congress as an institution—which they distrust—and their own members of Congress—whom they reelect. The result is something of a contradiction: popular members of Congress serving in an unpopular Congress (see *What Do You Think?*: "Why Do Voters Reelect Members of an Unpopular Congress?" in Chapter 8). Three major advantages tend to enhance incumbents' chances of winning: name recognition, campaign contributions, and the resources of office.

Name Recognition One reason for incumbents' success is that they begin the campaign with greater **name recognition** than their challengers, simply because they are the incumbent and their name has become familiar to their constituents over the previous years. Much of the daily work of all elected officials, especially members of Congress, is really public relations. Name recognition is a strategic advantage at the ballot box, especially if voters have little knowledge of policy positions or voting records. Voters tend to cast ballots for recognizable names over unknowns. Cynics have concluded that there is no such thing as bad publicity, only publicity. Even in cases of well-publicized scandals, incumbent members of Congress have won reelection; presumably voters preferred "the devil they knew" to the one they did not.

incumbent Candidate currently in office seeking reelection.

name recognition Public awareness of a political candidate—whether they know his or her name.

challengers In politics, a reference to people running against incumbent officeholders.

Campaign Contributions Incumbents have a strong advantage in raising campaign funds, simply because individuals and groups seeking access to those already in office are inspired to make contributions (see Table 5.1). **Challengers**

TABLE 5.1 Incumbent Advantage in Fund Raising

Senate	**2002**	**2004**
Average Incumbent Raised	$5,803,639	$7,212,068
Average Challenger Raised	1,013,314	869,688
House		
Average Incumbent Raised	898,382	982,941
Average Challenger Raised	197,608	171,551

Source: Center for Responsive Politics; figures for 2002 and 2004 congressional elections.

have no immediate favors to offer; they must convince a potential contributor that they will win office and also that they are devoted to the interests of their financial backers.[6]

Contributing individuals and interest groups show a strong preference for incumbents over challengers. They do not wish to offend incumbent officeholders by contributing to their challengers; doing so risks both immediate retribution and future "freezing out" in the likely event of the challengers' defeat. Thus only when an incumbent has been especially hostile to an organization's interest or in rare cases where an incumbent seems especially vulnerable will an interest group support a challenger. Yet challengers need even larger campaign war chests than incumbents to be successful. Challengers must overcome the greater name recognition of incumbents, their many office resources, and their records of constituency service. Thus even if incumbents and challengers had equal campaign treasuries, incumbents would enjoy the advantage.

Campaigns and Elections

The Web site for "Campaigns and Elections," a magazine directed toward candidates, campaign managers, political TV advertisers, political consultants, and lobbyists. *www.campaignline.com*

Resources of Office Successful politicians use their offices to keep their names and faces before the public in various ways—public appearances, interviews, speeches, and press releases. Congressional incumbents make full use of the **franking privilege** (free use of the U.S. mails) to send self-promotional newsletters to tens of thousands of households in their district at taxpayers' expense. They travel on weekends to their district virtually year-round, using tax-funded travel allowances, to make local appearances, speeches, and contacts.

Members of Congress have large staffs working every day over many years with the principal objective of ensuring the reelection of their members. Indeed, Congress is structured as an "incumbent-protection society" organized and staffed to help guarantee the reelection of its members (see "Home Style" in Chapter 8). Service to constituents occupies the energies of congressional office staffs both in Washington and in local district offices established for this purpose. Casework wins voters one at a time: tracing lost Social Security checks, ferreting out which federal loans voters qualify for and helping them with their applications, and performing countless other personal favors. These individual "retail-level" favors are supplemented by larger scale projects that experienced members of Congress can bring to their district or state (roads, dams, post offices, buildings, schools, grants, contracts), as well as undesirable projects (landfills, waste disposal sites, halfway houses) that they can keep out of their district. The longer incumbents have occupied the office, the more favors they have performed and the larger their networks of grateful voters.

Campaign Strategies

Campaigning is largely a media activity, especially in presidential and congressional campaigns. Media campaigns are highly professionalized, relying on public relations and advertising specialists, professional fund raisers, media consultants, and pollsters. Campaign management involves techniques that strongly resemble those employed in marketing commercial products. Professional media campaign management includes developing a **campaign strategy**: compiling computerized mailing lists and invitations for fund-raising events; selecting a campaign theme and coming up with a desirable candidate image; monitoring the progress of the campaign with continual polling of the voters; producing television tapes for commercials, newspaper advertisements, signs, bumper stickers, and radio spots;

franking privilege Free use of the U.S. mails granted to members of Congress to promote communication with constituents.

campaign strategy Plan for a political campaign, usually including a theme, an attempt to define the opponent or the issues, and an effort to coordinate images and messages in news broadcasts and paid advertising.

An early leader in the Democratic polls, Vermont Governor Howard Dean appeared overly excitable after the Iowa caucus.

selecting clothing and hairstyles for the candidate; writing speeches and scheduling appearances; and even planning the victory party.

Selecting a Theme Finding the right theme or "message" for a campaign is essential; this effort is not greatly different from that of launching an advertising campaign for a new detergent. A successful theme or "message" is one that characterizes the candidate or the electoral choice confronting the voters. A campaign theme need not be controversial; indeed, it need not even focus on a specific issue. It might be as simple as "a leader you can trust"—an attempt to "package" the candidate as competent and trustworthy.

Most media campaigns focus on candidates' personal qualities rather than on their stands on policy issues. Professional campaigns are based on the assumption that a candidate's "image" is the most important factor affecting voter choice. This image is largely devoid of issues, except in very general terms: for example, "tough on crime," "stands up to the special interests," "fights for the taxpayer," or "cares about you."

Negative Campaigning: "Defining" the Opponent A media campaign also seeks to "define" the opponent in negative terms. The original negative TV ad is generally identified as the 1964 "Daisy Girl" commercial, aired by the Lyndon B. Johnson presidential campaign (see *Up Close:* "Dirty Politics"). Negative ads can serve a purpose in exposing the record of an opponent. But **negative campaigning** risks an opponent's counterattack charges of "mudslinging," "dirty tricks," and "sleaze."

THINK AGAIN

Would you vote for a candidate who used negative ads to discredit an opponent?

Research into the opponent's public and personal background ("oppo research") provides the data for negative campaigning. Previous speeches and writings can be mined for embarrassing or mean-spirited statements. The voting record of the opponent can be scrutinized for unpopular policy positions. Any evils that occurred during an opponent's term of office can be attributed to him or her, either directly ("She knew and conspired in it") or indirectly ("He should have known and done something about it"). Personal scandals or embarrassments can be developed as evidence of "character." If campaign managers fear that highly personal attacks on an opponent will backfire, they may choose to leak the information to reporters and try to avoid attribution of the story to themselves or their candidate.

Negative advertising is often blamed on television's dominant role in political campaigns. "The high cost of television means now that you have to go for the jugular."[7] A political consultant summarized the current rules of political engagement as follows:

1. Advertise early if you have the money. . . .
2. Go negative early, often, and right through election day, if necessary.
3. Appeal to the heart and gut, rather than to the head.
4. Define your opponent to the voters before he or she can define him/herself or you.
5. If attacked, hit back even harder.
6. It's easier to give voters a negative impression of your opponent than it is to improve their image of you.[8]

negative campaigning Speeches, commercials, or advertising attacking a political opponent during a campaign.

Does negative campaigning really work? Professional campaign managers and consultants are convinced that negative ads are effective—more effective than positive ads. Regarding ads praising one's own qualities, they say "save them for your tombstone."

UP CLOSE

Dirty Politics

Political campaigning frequently turns ugly with negative advertising that is vicious and personal. It is widely believed that television's focus on personal character and private lives—rather than on policy positions and governmental experience—encourages negative campaigning. But vicious personal attacks in political campaigns began long before television. They are nearly as old as the nation itself.

"If Jefferson is elected," proclaimed Yale's president in 1800, "the Bible will be burned and we will see our wives and daughters the victims of legal prostitution." In 1864 *Harper's Weekly* decried the "mudslinging" of the day, lamenting that President Abraham Lincoln was regularly referred to by his opponent as a "filthy storyteller, despot, liar, thief, braggart, buffoon, monster, ignoramus Abe, robber, swindler, tyrant, fiend, butcher, and pirate."

Television's first memorable attack advertisement was the "Daisy Girl" commercial broadcast by Lyndon Johnson's presidential campaign in 1964 against his Republican opponent, Barry Goldwater. Although never mentioning Goldwater by name, the purpose of the ad was to "define" him as a warmonger who would plunge the world into a nuclear holocaust. The ad opens with a small, innocent girl standing in an open field plucking petals from a daisy and counting, "1, 2, 3 . . ." When she reaches 9, an ominous adult male voice begins a countdown: "10, 9, 8 . . ." as the camera closes in on the child's face. At "zero," a mushroom cloud appears, reflected in her eyes, and envelops the screen. Lyndon Johnson's voice is heard: "These are the stakes."

The infamous Willie Horton ad, broadcast by an independent organization supporting Republican George Bush in 1988, portrayed Democrat Michael Dukakis as weak on crime prevention. It featured a close-up mug shot of a very threatening convicted murderer, Willie Horton, with a voice proclaiming, "Dukakis not only opposes the death penalty, he allowed first-degree murderers to have weekend passes from prison. One was Willie Horton who murdered a boy in a robbery, stabbing him nineteen times. Despite a life sentence, Horton received ten weekend passes from prison." A final photo shows Dukakis, with a voice-over announcing, "Weekend prison passes, Dukakis weak on crime."

"Attack ads" have multiplied in recent elections at all levels of government. John Kerry had volunteered for Vietnam following his graduation from Yale. In four months as commander of a small "swift boat" he won a Silver Star, a Bronze Star, and three Purple Hearts. But an independent group, Swift Boat Veterans for the Truth, challenged the legitimacy of Kerry's medals in a series of TV ads. Later, the Swift Boat group redirected their attacks toward Kerry's post Vietnam behavior as a leader in the Vietnam Veterans against the War. These ads showed a young Kerry at a congressional hearing accusing his fellow veterans of terrible atrocities, "murdering civilians, cutting off heads, and burning villages." These ads corresponded to a slight drop in Kerry's poll numbers.

But Bush's service in the Texas National Guard during the Vietnam War was also a target of attack. Bush joined the Guard with the possible help of family friends, but he won his wings as a fighter pilot and was honorably discharged after five years. The Texas Guard was never called active-duty and Bush never saw combat. But a CBS News report by Dan Rather, based on forged documents, asserted that Bush failed to meet all of his Guard responsibilities. Later CBS News recanted the charge. The affair may have helped Bush somewhat, by convincing viewers that Dan Rather and others at CBS were biased against him.

What are the effects of negative advertising? First of all, it works more often than not. Controlled experiments indicate that targets of attack ads are rated less positively by people who have watched these ads. But another effect of negative advertising is to make voters more cynical about politics and government in general. There is conflicting evidence about whether or not negative campaigning by opposing candidates reduces voter turnout.

What, if anything, can be done? Government regulation of political speech directly contravenes the First Amendment. American democracy has survived negative campaigning for a long time.

Source: Kathleen Hall Jamieson, *Dirty Politics: Deception, Distraction, and Democracy* (New York: Oxford University Press, 1992); also Stephen Ansolabehere et al., "Does Attack Advertising Demobilize the Electorate?" *American Political Science Review* 88 (December 1994): 829–38; Kim Fridkin Kahn and Patrick J. Kenney, "Do Negative Campaigns Mobilize or Suppress Turnout?" *American Political Science Review* 93 (December, 1999): 877–89.

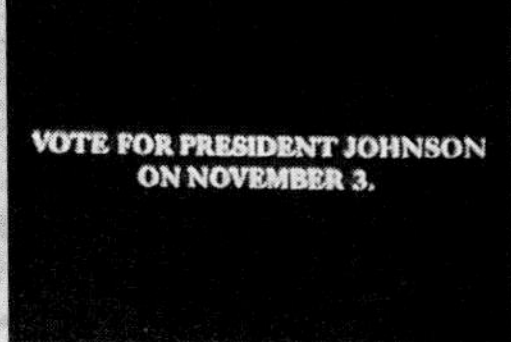

Frames from Lyndon Johnson's 1964 "Daisy Girl" commercial.

Using Focus Groups and Polling Focus group techniques can help in selecting campaign themes and identifying negative characteristics in opponents. A **focus group** is a small group of people brought together to view videotapes, listen to specific campaign appeals, and respond to particular topics and issues. Media professionals then develop a campaign strategy around "hot-button" issues—issues that generate strong responses by focus groups—and avoid themes or issues that fail to elicit much interest.

The results of focus group work can then be tested in wider polling. Polling is a central feature of professional campaigning. Serious candidates for national and statewide offices almost always employ their own private polling firms, distinct from the national survey organizations that supply the media with survey data. Initial polling is generally designed to determine candidates' name recognition—the extent to which the voters recognize the candidates—and whatever positive and negative images are already associated with their names.

Campaign polling is highly professionalized, with telephone banks, trained interviewers, and computer-assisted-telephone-interviewing (CATI) software that records and tabulates responses instantly and sends the results to campaign managers. In well-financed campaigns, polling is continual throughout the campaign, so that managers can assess progress on a daily basis. Polls chart the candidate's progress and, perhaps more important, help assess the effectiveness of specific campaign themes. If the candidate appears to be gaining support, the campaign stays on course. But if the candidate appears to be falling in the polls, the campaign manager comes under intense pressure to change themes and strategies. As election day nears, the pressure increases on the trailing candidate to "go negative"—to launch even more scathing attacks on the opponent.

Incumbent versus Challenger Strategies Campaign strategies vary by the offices being sought, the nature of the times, and the imagination and inventiveness of the candidates' managers. But incumbency is perhaps the most important factor affecting the choice of a strategy. The challenger must attack the record of the incumbent; deplore current conditions in the city, state, or nation; and stress the need for change. Challengers are usually freer to take the offensive; incumbents must defend their record in office and either boast of accomplishments during their term or blame the opposition for blocking them. Challengers frequently opt for the "outsider" strategy, capitalizing on distrust and cynicism toward government.

News Management News management is the key to the media campaign. News coverage of the candidates is more credible in the eyes of viewers than paid advertisements. The campaign is planned to get the maximum favorable "free" exposure on the evening news. Each day a candidate must do something interesting and "newsworthy," that is, likely to be reported as news. Pictures are as important as words. Candidates must provide good **photo ops** for the media—opportunities where they can be photographed in settings or backgrounds that emphasize their themes. For example, if the theme is patriotism, then the candidate appears with war veterans, at a military base, or at a flag factory. If the theme is education, the candidate appears at a school; if crime control, then with police officers; if environmentalism, then in a wilderness area; if the economy, then at a closed factory or unemployment line or soup kitchen for the homeless.

Themes must be stated in concise and catchy **sound bites** that will register in the viewers' minds. Candidates now understand that the news media will select

focus group In a political context, a small number of people brought together in a comfortable setting to discuss and respond to themes and issues, allowing campaign managers to develop and analyze strategies.

photo ops Staged opportunities for the media to photograph the candidate in a favorable setting.

sound bites Concise and catchy phrases that attract media coverage.

only a few seconds of an entire day of speech making for broadcast. The average length of a network news sound bite has shrunk from forty-five to seven seconds over the last thirty years. Thus extended or serious discussion of issues during a campaign is sacrificed to the need for one-liners on the nightly news. Indeed, if a campaign theme cannot fit on a bumper sticker, it is too complex.

Consequently, each day's campaigning is a series of photo ops and sound bites, all prepared with the evening news in mind. Between events, candidates must scramble to various fund-raising events—dinners, parties, personal meetings with large contributors. Thus candidates balance their time between "getting out the message" and finding ways to pay for getting it out.

Paid Advertising Television "spot" ads must be prepared prior to and during the campaign. They involve employing expensive television advertising and production firms well in advance of the campaign and keeping them busy revising and producing new ads throughout the campaign to respond to changing issues or opponents' attacks. Commercial advertising is the most expensive aspect of the campaign. Heavy costs are incurred in the production of the ads and in the purchase of broadcast time. The Federal Communications Commission (FCC) does not permit television networks or stations to charge more than standard commercial rates for political ads, but these rates are already high. Networks and stations are required to offer the same rates and times to all candidates, but if one candidate's campaign treasury is weak or exhausted, an opponent can saturate broadcast airtime.

Free Airtime All candidates seek free airtime on news and talk shows, but the need to gain free exposure is much greater for underfunded candidates. They must go to extremes in devising media events, and they must encourage and participate in free televised debates. The debate format is particularly well suited for candidates who cannot match their opponents in paid commercial advertising. Thus well-funded and poorly funded candidates may jockey over the number and times of public debates.

How Much Does It Cost to Get Elected?

Getting elected to public office has never been more expensive. The professionalization of campaigning and the heavy costs of television advertising drive up the costs of running for office. Campaign costs are rising with each election cycle (see Figure 5.4). In the presidential election year 2004, campaign spending by *all* presidential and congressional candidates, the Democratic and Republican parties, and independent political organizations is estimated to have topped *$4 billion*.

THINK AGAIN

Are high campaign costs discouraging good people from becoming candidates?

Congressional Costs The typical winning campaign for a seat in the House of Representatives costs nearly $900,000 (see Table 5.2). House members seeking to retain their seats must raise this amount *every two years*. The typical winning campaign for a U.S. Senate seat costs $5 to $7 million. But Senate campaign costs vary a great deal from state to state; Senate seats in the larger states may cost $20 million or $40 million or more.

The upward spiral in congressional campaign spending continued through 2004 with over $1 *billion* spent by all House and Senate candidates. New York's

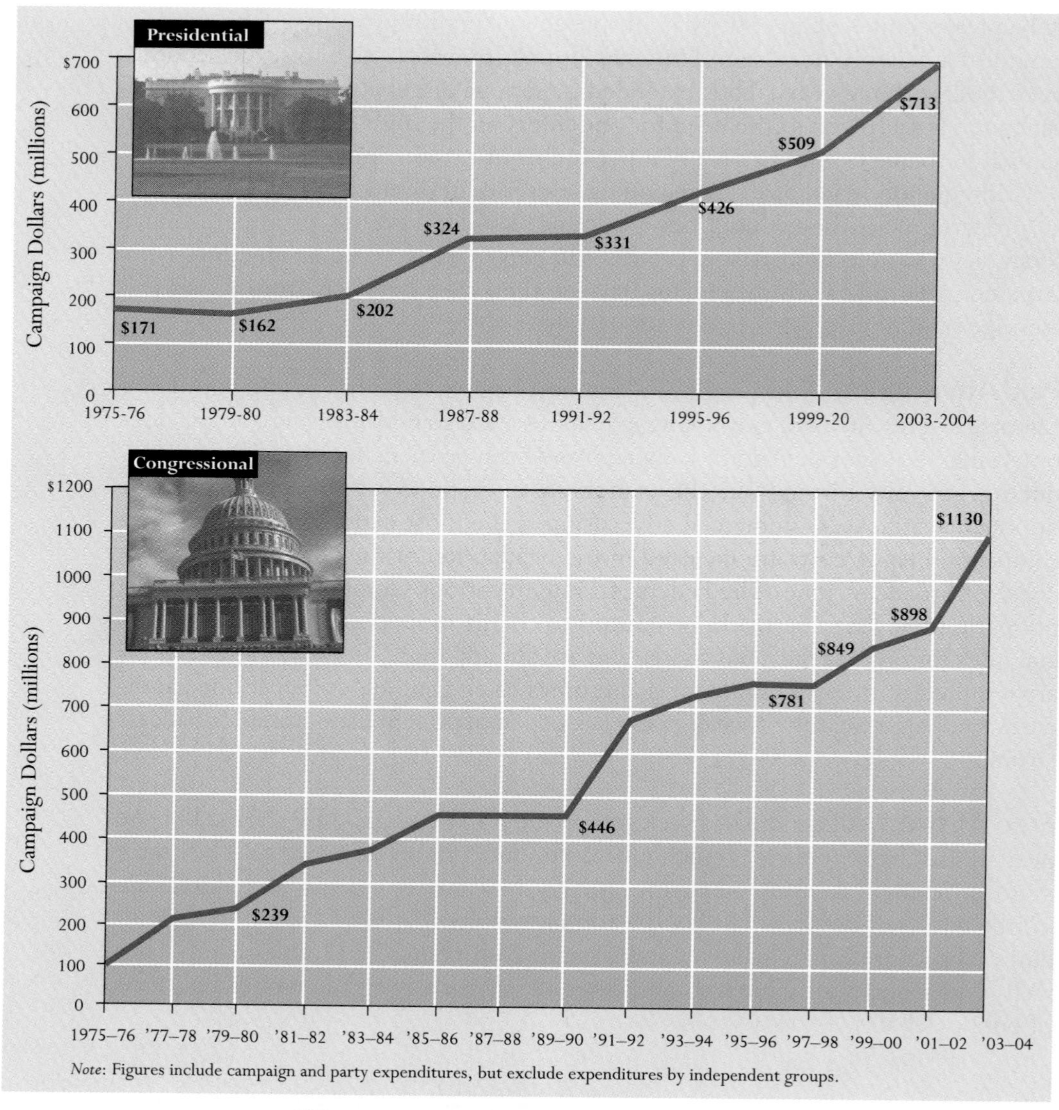

FIGURE 5.4 The Growing Costs of Campaigns

Source: Center for Responsive Politics.

high-profile Senate race in 2002 between Democrat Hillary Clinton and Republican Rick Lazio attracted a combined $85 million in contributions from across the nation. A new individual spending record was set by multimillionaire Democrat Jon Corzine in his successful bid for a U.S. Senate seat from New Jersey in 2002; Corzine spent about $63 million of his *own* money.

Spending for House seats also varies a great deal from one race to another. (The spending record for a House seat is held by former Speaker Republican Newt Gingrich of Georgia, who spent more than $7.5 million awaiting reelection in 1998.) In nearly two-thirds of all House districts, one candidate (almost always the incumbent) outspends his or her opponent by a factor of ten to one or more. Only about 16 percent of House campaigns are financially competitive; that is, neither candidate spends more than twice as much as his or her opponent. In the remaining 84 percent of House campaigns one candidate spends more than twice as much as his or her opponent.[9]

TABLE 8.2 The Cost of Getting Elected to Congress

Senate	
Average Democratic Incumbent	$8,582,559
Average Democratic Challenger	$772,381
Average Republican Incumbent	$5,750,211
Average Republican Challenger	$1,126,857
Most Expensive Campaign	Tom Daschle (D, SD) $17.4 million (lost)
House of Representatives	
Average Democratic Incumbent	$918,481
Average Democratic Challenger	$174,694
Average Republican Incumbent	$1,041,327
Average Republican Challenger	$192,960
Most Expensive Campaign	Martin Frost (D,TX), $3.9 million (lost)

Source: Center for Responsive Politics.

Raising Campaign Cash

Center for Responsive Politics
The site of an organization devoted to the study of campaign finance laws, the role of money in elections, PACs, "soft money," and special-interest groups.
www.opensecrets.org

Fund raising to meet the high costs of campaigning is the most important hurdle for any candidate for public office. Campaign funds come from a wide range of sources—small donors, big donors, interest group PACs of every stripe, labor unions, even taxpayers. In some cases, candidates pay their own way (or most of it). More typically, however, candidates for high public office—particularly incumbents—have become adept at running their campaigns using other people's money, not their own.

Public Money Presidential campaigns can be partly funded with taxpayer money through an income tax checkoff system. Each year taxpayers are urged to check the box on their tax forms which authorize $3 of their tax payment to go to the Federal Elections Commission for distribution to presidential candidates' campaigns, as well as to political party conventions. However, taxpayers are becoming less and less willing to allow their tax monies to go into political campaigning (even though the $3 checkoff does not add to the taxpayers' total taxes). Only about 11 percent of taxpayers currently check the box. The Presidential Election Campaign Fund has been in jeopardy of not having enough money to make its promised payments to the candidates and parties.

Presidential candidates may opt out of taxpayer financed funding if they choose to do so. This allows them to spend as much money as they wish, but they receive no public money. Nonetheless, all presidential candidates, and all candidates for Congress, must abide by federal campaign finance laws (see below).

Small Donations Millions of Americans participate in campaign financing, either by giving directly to candidates or the parties or by giving to political action committees, which then distribute their funds to candidates. For members of Congress, small donors typically make up less than 20 percent of their campaign funds. The proportion is higher for presidential candidates. Under federal law, donations

Candidates seek to appear "in touch" with ordinary voters. John Kerry made many efforts to overcome his image as too serious, too aloof, too senatorial, during the campaign.

under $200 need not be itemized, so contributors' names and addresses are recorded only by the candidates and parties, not passed along to the Federal Election Commission as part of the public record.

Large Individual Donors "Fat cats" are the preferred donors. These are the donors whose names are on the candidates' Rolodexes. They are the ones in attendance when the president, the Speaker of the House, or other top political dignitaries travel around the country doing fund raisers. They are also the ones who are wined, dined, prodded, and cajoled in a seemingly ceaseless effort by the parties and the candidates to raise funds for the next election.

In its 2002 campaign finance reform legislation, Congress raised the maximum individual contribution to federal candidates to $2,000 (up from $1,000 in the 2000 election). Fat cats are expected to give the maximum, and indeed even more. They can do so by giving their maximum $2,000 once in the primary election and a second time in the general election. And their spouses can do the same. And, of course, they can also give to the parties and to independent political organizations committed to helping their preferred candidates.

Candidate Self-Financing Candidates for federal office also pump millions into their own campaigns. There are no federal restrictions on the amount of money individuals can spend on their own campaign.[10] Leading the field in the last two presidential races was publishing magnate Steve Forbes, whose unsuccessful bids for the Republican nomination for president were largely funded with millions from his personal fortune. Senate and House candidates frequently put $50,000 to $100,000 or more of their own money into their campaigns, through either outright gifts or personal loans. (Candidates who loan themselves the money to run are able to pay themselves back later from outside contributions.)

Issue Ads **Issue ads** are produced independently by interest groups. Issue ads advocate policy positions rather than explicitly advising voters cast their ballots for or against particular candidates. But most of these ads leave little doubt about which candidate is being supported or targeted. Beginning in 2002, money spent for issue ads must be reported to the Federal Elections Commission. However, there are no dollar limits on the size of contributions to these groups (often referred to as 527s from the section of the Internal Revenue Code under which they operate).

What Do Contributors "Buy"?

What does money buy in politics? A cynic might say that money can buy anything—for example, special appropriations for public works directly benefiting the contributor, special tax breaks, special federal regulations. Public opinion views big-money contributions as a major problem in the American political system. Scandals involving the direct (quid pro quo) purchase of special favors, privileges, exemptions, and treatments have been common enough in the past, and they are likely to continue in the future. But campaign contributions are rarely made in the form of a direct trade-off for a favorable vote. Such an arrangement risks exposure as bribery and may be prosecuted under the law. Campaign contributions are more likely to be made without any *explicit* quid pro quo but rather with a general understanding that the contributor has confidence in the candidate's good judgment on issues directly affecting the contributor. The contributor expects the candidate to be smart enough to figure out how to vote in order to keep the contributions coming in the future.

THINK AGAIN

Do political campaign contributions have too much influence on elections and govenment policy?

The Big-Money Contributors Big-money contributors—businesses, unions, professional associations—pump millions into presidential and congressional elections. Figure 5.5 lists the top fifty contributors to candidates and parties since 1989. Note that union contributions are heavily weighted toward Democrats, as are the contributions of the Association of Trial Lawyers. Businesses and business

issue ads Ads that advocate policy positions rather than explicitly supporting or opposing particular candidates.

BOTTOM LINERS

Eric & Bill

11/23

"Ultimately, I want to get into political fund raising . . . I'm just here to make some contacts."

Source: © Tribune Media Services, Inc. All Rights Reserved. Reprinted with permission.

Rank	Contributor	Total Contributions	% Dem.	% Rep.	Rank	Contributor	Total Contributions	% Dem.	% Rep.
1.	American Federation of State/County/Municipal Employees	$34,944,356	98%	1%	25.	National Rifle Assn	$14,345,042	13%	86%
					26.	AFL-CIO	$14,143,542	88%	11%
					27.	American Bankers Assn	$13,753,323	39%	60%
2.	National Assn of Realtors	$24,159,780	50%	49%	28.	Time Warner	$13,408,561	70%	28%
3.	National Education Assn	$23,382,034	86%	13%	29.	SBC Communications	$13,032,502	34%	65%
4.	Assn of Trial Lawyers of America	$23, 310,366	89%	10%	30.	Verizon Communications	$12,617,393	38%	61%
					31.	BellSouth Corp	$12,427,578	43%	56%
5.	Communications Workers of America	$21,968,716	98%	1%	32.	Microsoft Corp	$12,327,062	58%	41%
					33.	National Beer Wholesalers Assn	$12,207,798	30%	69%
6.	Service Employees International Union	$21,865,215	88%	11%	34.	EMILY's List	$11,777,389	100%	0%
7.	Intl Brotherhood of Electrical Workers	$21,522,812	96%	3%	35.	Sheet Metal Workers Union	$11,687,901	97%	2%
8.	Carpenters &Joiners Union	$20,995,637	68%	31%	36.	Ernst & Young	$11,672,581	31%	67%
					37.	Lockheed Martin	$11,486,880	39%	60%
9.	Teamsters Union	$20,838,115	85%	13%	38.	JP Morgan Chase & Co	$11,455,069	49%	50%
10.	American Medical Assn	$20,632,636	28%	71%	39.	RJR Nabisco/ RJ Reynolds Tobacco	$10,959,872	11%	88%
11.	Altria Group (Philip Morris)	$20,567,067	41%	57%					
12.	FedEx Corp	$20,500,993	33%	66%	40.	American Dental Assn	$10,898,735	43%	56%
13.	Laborers Union	$20,497,632	86%	13%	41.	Morgan Stanley	$10,850,938	34%	65%
14.	United Auto Workers	$19,832,550	98%	0%	42.	Blue Cross/Blue Shield	$10,757,914	42%	57%
15.	AT&T	$19,484,567	47%	52%	43.	American Hospital Assn	$10,748,440	44%	55%
16.	American Federation of Teachers	$19,291,514	99%	0%	44.	National Assn of Insurance & Financial Advisors	$10,629,255	37%	62%
17.	Goldman Sachs	$18,607,643	50%	49%					
18.	Machinists & Aerospace Workers Union	$18,429,464	98%	0%	45.	General Electric	$10,596,818	46%	53%
					46.	American Institute of CPAs	$10,381,169	37%	62%
19.	United Food & Commercial Workers Union	$18,318,526	98%	1%	47.	Union Pacific Corp	$10,131,658	22%	77%
					48.	Credit Union National Assn	$10,110,853	43%	56%
20.	Citigroup Inc	$17,080,206	48%	50%					
21.	United Parcel Service	$16,859,844	29%	70%	49.	Deloitte Touche Tohmatsu	$10,108,211	28%	71%
22.	National Auto Dealers Assn	$16,474,442	29%	70%	50.	United Steelworkers of America	$10,089,196	97%	2%
23.	National Assn of Home Builders	$14,930,228	38%	61%					
24.	National Assn of Letter Carriers	$14,608,734	71%	27%					

FIGURE 5.5 The Big-Money Contributors

Source: Center for Responsive Politics, *The Big Picture* (Washington, D.C., 2001). Reprinted by permission of the Center for Responsive Politics.

associations tend to split their contributions between the parties, but Republicans usually get the largest share.

Buying Access to Policy Makers Large contributors expect to be able to call or visit and present their views directly to "their" officeholders. At the presidential level, major contributors who cannot get a meeting with the president expect to meet at least with high-level White House staff or cabinet officials. At the congressional level, major contributors usually expect to meet or speak directly with their representative or senator. Members of Congress boast of responding to letters, calls, or visits by any constituent, but contributors can expect a more immediate and direct response than noncontributors can. Lobbyists for contributing organizations routinely expect and receive a hearing from members of Congress.

Celebrity entertainers are a major source of campaign funding for Democratic candidates. They attract crowds to hear the candidates and open their wallets.

Political Action Committees **Political action committees** (PACs) are the most reliable source of money for reelection campaigns in Congress. Corporations and unions are not allowed to contribute directly to campaigns from corporate or union funds, but they may form PACs to seek contributions from managers and stockholders and their families, or union workers and their families. PACs are organized not only by corporations and unions but also by trade and professional associations, environmental groups, and liberal and conservative ideological groups. The wealthiest PACs are based in Washington, D.C. (see Table 7.7 in Chapter 7). PACs are very cautious; their job is to get a maximum return on their contributions, winning influence and goodwill with as many lawmakers as possible in Washington. There's no return on their investment if their recipients lose at the polls, therefore most PACs—particularly business PACs—give most of their dollars to incumbents seeking reelection.

Buying Government Assistance Many individual large contributors do business with government agencies. They expect any representative or senator they have supported to intervene on their behalf with these agencies, sometimes acting to cut red tape, ensure fairness, and expedite their cases, and other times pressuring the agencies for a favorable decision. Officials in the White House or the cabinet may also be expected to intervene on behalf of major contributors. There is little question raised when the intervention merely expedites consideration of a contributor's case, but pressure to bend rules or regulations to get favorable decisions raises ethical problems for officeholders (see "Congressional Ethics" in Chapter 8).

Individual Contributors Those who contribute to presidential and/or congressional campaign funds do so for a variety of reasons. Some contributors are ideologically motivated. They make their contributions based on their perception of the ideological position of the candidate (or perhaps their perception of the candidate's opponent). They may make contributions to congressional candidates across the country who share their policy views. Liberal and conservative networks of contributors can be contacted through specialized mailing lists—for

political action committee (PAC) Organization created by a corporation, union, or other interest group to collect and distribute campaign funds to candidates.

example, liberals through television producer Norman Lear's People for the American Way. Feminists have been effective in soliciting individual contributions across the country and funneling them very early in a campaign to women candidates through EMILY's list. Ideological contributors may only get the satisfaction of knowing that they are financially backing their cause in the political process. Some contributors simply enjoy the opportunity to be near and to be seen with high-ranking politicians. Politicians pose for photos with contributors, who later frame the photos and hang them in their office to impress their friends, associates, and customers. About 7 to 10 percent of the population claims in national surveys to have contributed to candidates running for public office. Contributors are disproportionately high-income, older people with strong partisan views (see Figure 5.6).

Fund-Raising Chores Fund raising occupies more of a candidate's time than any other campaign activity. Candidates must personally contact as many individual contributors as possible. They work late into the evening on the telephone with potential contributors. Fund-raising dinners, cocktail parties, barbecues, fish frys, and so on, are scheduled nearly every day of a campaign. The candidate is expected to appear personally to "press the flesh" of big contributors. Movie and rock stars and other assorted celebrities may also be asked to appear at fund-raising affairs to generate attendance. Dinners may run to $2,000 a plate in presidential affairs, although often less in Senate or House campaigns. Tickets may be "bundled" to well-heeled individual contributors or sold in blocks to organiza-

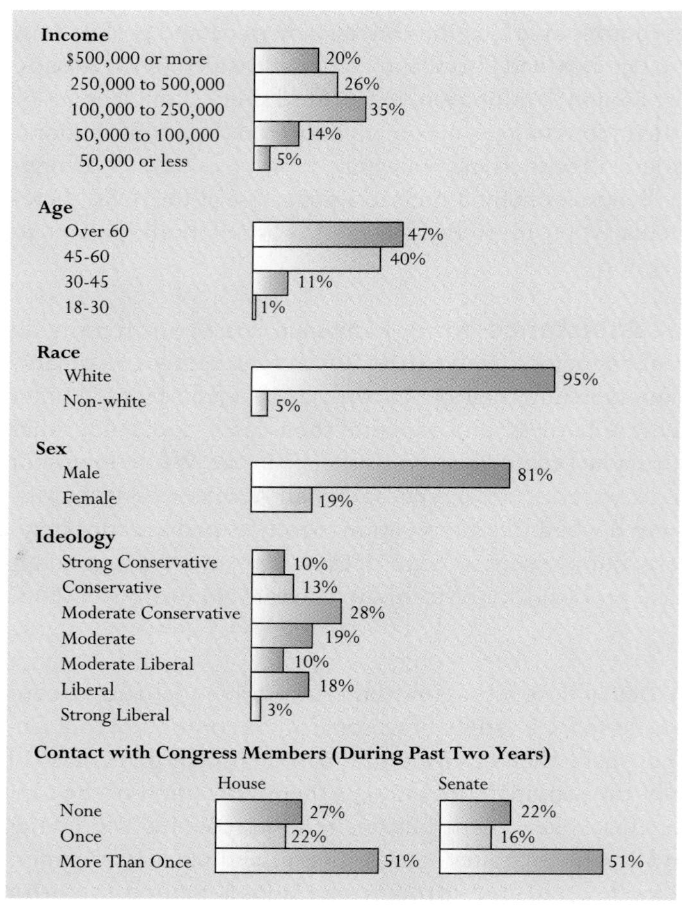

FIGURE 5.6
Characteristics of Individual Political Contributors

Contributors to political campaigns generally have been older, and have higher incomes than most Americans. Whites and males contribute more than blacks and females, and conservatives contribute more than liberals.

Source: John Green, Paul Herrnson, Lynda Powell, Clyde Wilcox, "Individual Congressional Campaign Contributions," press release, June 9, 1998, Center for Responsive Politics.

Democratic presidential hopefuls line up for a debate prior to the New Hampshire primary, won by Massachusetts Senator John Kerry (third from right). Others are Missouri's Dick Gephardt, New York's Al Sharpton, Ohio's Dennis Kucinich, Connecticut's Joe Lieberman, North Carolina's John Edwards, Illinois' Carol Moseley-Braun, and Vermont's Howard Dean.

tions. Fund-raising techniques are limited only by the imagination of the campaign manager.

Regulating Campaign Finance

The **Federal Election Commission (FEC)**, is responsible for enforcing limits on individual and organizational contributions to all federal elections, administering the public funding of presidential campaigns, and requiring full disclosure of all campaign financial activity in presidential and congressional elections. Enforcement of these federal election and campaign finance laws lies in the hands of the six-member FEC. Appointed by the president to serve staggered six-year terms, commission members are traditionally split 3 to 3 between Republicans and Democrats.

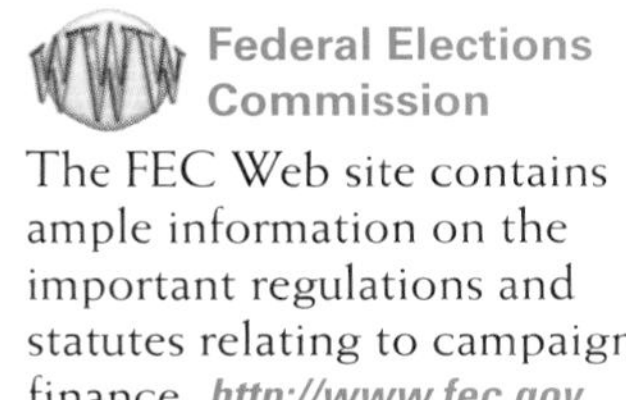

Federal Elections Commission

The FEC Web site contains ample information on the important regulations and statutes relating to campaign finance. *http://www.fec.gov*

Limits on Contributions The FEC now limits direct individual contributions to a candidate's campaign to $2,000 per election and organizational contributions to $5,000 per election. But there are many ways in which individuals and organizations can legally surmount these limits. Contributors may give a candidate $2,000 for each member of their family in a primary election and then another $2,000 per member in the general election. Organizations may generate much more than the $5,000 limit by bundling (combining) $2,000 additional contributions from individual members. (Soft-money contributions—unregulated amounts given to the national parties officially for "party building" but actually used in support of candidates—were banned in 2002.) Independent organizations can spend whatever they wish in order to promote their political views, so long as these organizations do so "without cooperation or consultation with the candidate of his or her campaign." Finally, as noted, individuals may spend as much of their own money on their own campaigns as they wish.[11]

Federal Funding of Presidential Elections Federal funding, financed by the $3 checkoff box on individual income tax returns, is available to presidential candidates in primary and general elections, as well as to major-party nominating conventions. Candidates seeking the nomination in presidential primary elections

Federal Election Commission (FEC) Agency charged with enforcing federal election laws and disbursing public presidential campaign funds.

can qualify for federal funds by raising $5,000 from private contributions no greater than $250 each in each of twenty states. In the general election, Democratic and Republican nominees are funded equally at levels determined by the FEC. In order to receive federal funding, presidential candidates must agree to FEC limits on their campaign spending in both primary and general elections.

Federal funding pays about one-third of the primary campaign costs of presidential candidates and all the *official* presidential campaign organization costs in the general election. The parties also receive federal funds for their nominating conventions.

Campaign Finance Reform Unregulated soft money contributions to the parties grew rapidly during the 1990s. These contributions represented a giant black hole in the original Federal Election Campaign Act of 1974. Contributions made directly to a candidate's campaign—hard money contributions—were limited (originally to $1,000). But individuals, organizations, corporations, and unions could contribute as much as they wanted to the Democratic and Republican national parties. These contributions were supposed to be for party building, voter registration, getting out the vote, etc., but in fact went into candidate campaigning.

In the 2000 Republican presidential primaries, U.S. Senator John McCain made campaign finance reform his principal issue. He surprised the Republican Party leaders by defeating George W. Bush in the New Hampshire primary that year. Bush and both Democratic and Republican leaders decided to jump on the campaign finance reform bandwagon, although with little real enthusiasm. In 2002 a somewhat reluctant Congress finally passed the Bipartisan Campaign Finance Reform Act (see Table 5.3).

Among other things, this act eliminates soft money contributions to the parties; increases the individual contribution limit to candidates' campaigns from $1,000 to $2,000; prohibits independent groups from coordinating their campaign spending with candidates or parties; does not allow independent groups to mention the name of a candidate in their issue ads; and bans independent groups from broadcasting their views in the final days of a campaign.

But contributions to nonprofit independent groups remain unregulated. Big money contributors who can no longer provide large amounts of cash to candidates or to parties can establish nonprofit independent groups (known as "527s," referring to their Internal Revenue Service code) to accept big contributions to enable them to produce and broadcast campaign advertisements.

The act was challenged as a violation of First Amendment free speech rights, but upheld by the U.S. Supreme Court in *McConnell vs. Federal Elections Commission,* December 10, 2003.

The Presidential Campaign: The Primary Race

The phrase *presidential fever* refers to the burning political ambition required to seek the presidency. The grueling presidential campaign is a test of strength, character, endurance, and determination. It is physically exhausting and mentally and emotionally draining. Every aspect of the candidates' lives—and the lives of their families—is subject to microscopic inspection by the news media. Most of this coverage is critical, and much of it is unfair. Yet candidates are expected to handle it all with grace and humor, from the earliest testing of the waters through a full-fledged campaign.

TABLE 5.3 Campaign Finance Rules, 2004

General

All federal election contributions and expenditures must be reported to the Federal Election Commission, which may investigate and prosecute violators.
All contributions over $200 must be reported, with name, address, and occupation of contributor.
No foreign contributions can be made.
There are no restrictions on how much individuals may spend on their own campaigns (*Buckley vs Valeo*)
No large contributions (Soft Money) may be made to the national parties; party contributions by individuals and committees are limited.

Presidential Primaries

Federal matching funds are available for money raised by candidates from individual donors giving $250 dollars or less. To be eligible, the primary candidate must raise $5,000 in each of twenty states in contributions of $250 or less.

Presidential Elections

The federal government pays all campaign costs of major party candidates and contributes to the costs of party conventions. The federal government will also pay part of the costs of minor party candidates who win between 5 and 25 percent of the vote.

Limits on Contributions

Donor	Candidate	PAC	National Party	State/Local	Special
Individual	$2,000	$5,000	$25,000	$10,000	Biennial total: $95,000
National party	5,000	5,000	—	—	—
State/local party	5,000	5,000	—	—	—
PAC (multi-candidate)	5,000	5,000	1,500	5,000	—
PAC (single-candidate)	2,000	5,000	25,000	10,000	—

Millionaire Amendment

If a candidate spends more of his own money beyond specified thresholds (e.g., $350,000 for House candidates), contribution limits for his or her opponent are tripled.

Independent Group Expenditures

Independent individuals or groups airing TV or radio ads must not coordinate with candidates or parties in order to avoid contribution limits.

Election Communications

Independent individuals or groups may not broadcast TV or radio ads referring to a candidate 60 days prior to a general election or 30 days prior to the primary election.

Note: This table summarizes the Bipartisan Campaign Finance Reform Act of 2002.

Media Mentions Politicians with presidential ambitions may begin by promoting presidential *mentions* by media columnists and commentators. The media help to identify "presidential timber" years in advance of a presidential race simply by drawing up lists of potential candidates, commenting on their qualifications, and speculating about their intentions. Mentions are likely to come to prominent governors or senators who start making speeches outside of their state, who grab the media spotlight on a national issue, or who simply let it be known to the media "off the record" that they are considering a presidential race. Visiting New Hampshire and giving speeches there is viewed as "testing the waters" and a signal of presidential ambitions.

The Decision to Run The decision to run for president involves complex personal and political calculations. Ambition to occupy the world's most powerful office must be weighed against the staggering costs—emotional as well as financial—of a presidential campaign.

Serious planning, organizing, and fund raising must begin at least two years before the general election. A staff must be assembled—campaign managers and strategists, fund raisers, media experts, pollsters, issues advisers and speech writers, lawyers and accountants—and supporters must be identified in key states throughout the nation. Paid and volunteer workers must be assembled (see Figure 5.7). Leaders among important interest groups must be contacted. A general campaign strategy must be developed, an organization put in place, and several millions of dollars in campaign contributions pledged in advance of the race. Often the decision to run hinges on whether initial pledges of campaign contributions appear adequate. The serious candidate must be able to anticipate contributions of $25 million or more for primary elections. Most of this work must be accomplished in the pre-primary season—the months after Labor Day of the year preceding the election, and before the first primary election.

A Strategy for the Primaries The road to the White House consists of two separate races: the primary elections and caucuses leading to the Democratic and Republican party nominations, and the general election. Each of these races requires a separate strategy. The primary race requires an appeal to party activists and the more ideologically motivated primary voters in key states. The general election requires an appeal to the less partisan, less attentive, more ideologically moderate

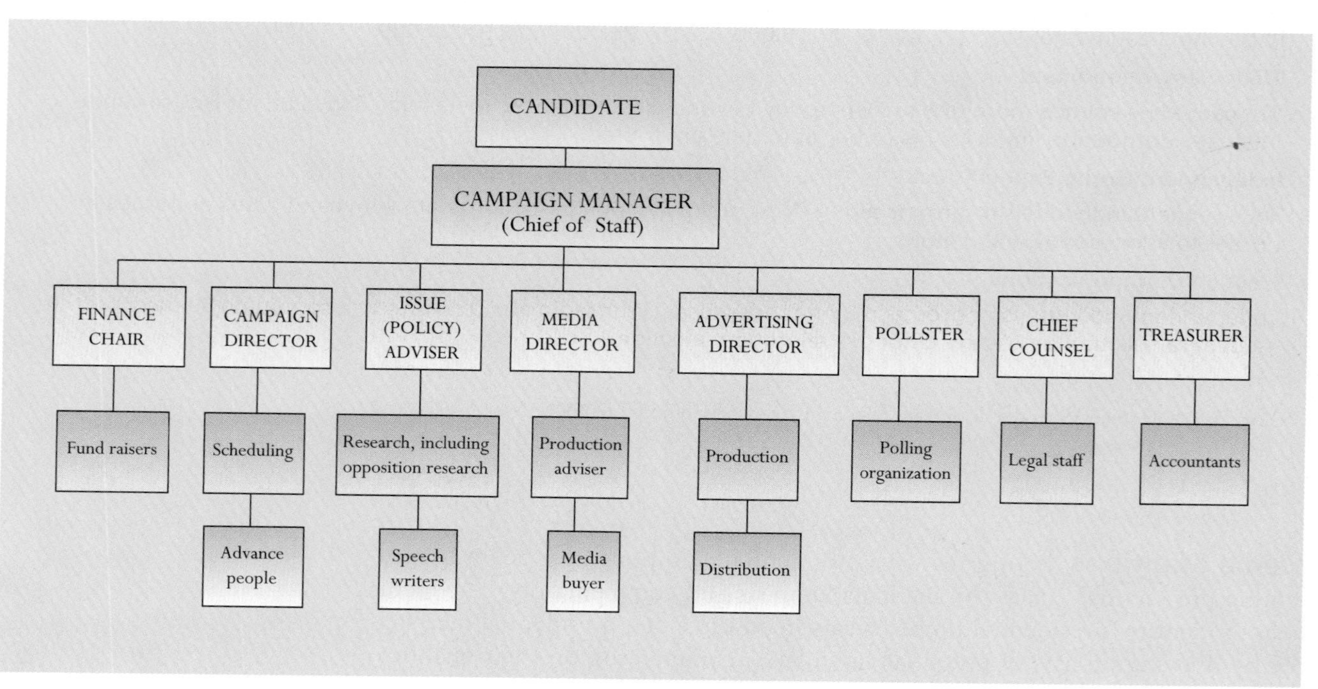

FIGURE 5.7 Typical Campaign Organization

Campaign organizations vary, but most assign someone to perform these tasks: funding, scheduling appearances, speech writing, media production and buying, polling, advertising, legal compliance, and check writing, even if, in local campaigns, all these tasks must be performed by the candidate or his or her family members.

general election voters. Thus the campaign strategy developed to win the nomination must give way after the national conventions to a strategy to win the November general election.

Primary Campaigns Primary campaigns come in different varieties. An incumbent president with no serious competition from within his own party can safely glide through his party's primaries, saving campaign money for the general election. In contrast, the party out of the White House typically goes through a rough-and-tumble primary (and pre-primary) season, with multiple presidential aspirants. And when no incumbent president is running for reelection, both parties experience heavy party infighting among multiple presidential hopefuls.

Candidates strive during the pre-primary season to win media attention, to climb the poll ratings, and raise campaign funds. Early front runners must beware of stumbles and gaffs; they must be prepared for close scrutiny by the media; and they must expect to be the targets of their competitors. Not infrequently, early front runners lose their momentum even before the first primary elections.[12]

Primary voters are heavily weighted toward party activists, who are more ideologically motivated than the more moderate voters in general elections. Democratic primary voters are more liberal, and Republican primary voters are more conservative, than the voters in the November general election. Democratic primary voters include large numbers of the party's core constituents—union members, public employees, minorities, environmentalists, and feminists.

Presidential candidates must try to appeal not only to the ideological predispositions of their party's primary voters, but also convince them of their "electability"—the likelihood that they can win the party's nomination and more importantly go on to win the presidential election. Often primary voters are torn between voting for their favorite candidate based on his or her ideological and issue positions, or voting for the most electable candidate.

The New Hampshire Primary The primary season begins in the winter snows of New Hampshire, traditionally the first state to hold a presidential primary election. New Hampshire is far more important *strategically* to a presidential campaign than it is in delegate strength. As a small state, New Hampshire supplies fewer than 1 percent of the delegates at the Democratic and Republican conventions. But the New Hampshire primary looms very large in media coverage and hence in overall campaign strategy. Although the popular Democratic Iowa party caucuses are held even earlier, New Hampshire is the nation's first primary, and the media begin speculating about its outcome and reporting early state-poll results months in advance.

The New Hampshire primary inspires **retail politics**—direct candidate contact with the voters. Presidential aspirants begin visiting New Hampshire in the year preceding the primary elections, speaking at town hall meetings, visiting with small groups, standing outside of supermarkets, walking through restaurants, greeting workers at factories and offices, and so on. These personal contacts bypass the media's filtering and interpreting of the candidate's personality and message. Retail politics is largely confined to New Hampshire, a small state and a year of pre-primary time to reach voters personally. And there is some evidence that voters who actually meet candidates come away with a more favorable view of them.[13]

New Hampshire provides the initial *momentum* for the presidential candidates. "Momentum" is more than just a media catchword. The Democratic and Republican winners in New Hampshire have demonstrated their voter appeal, their

retail politics Direct candidate contact with individual voters.

"electability." Favorable New Hampshire results inspire more financial contributions and thus the resources needed to carry the fight into the next group of primary elections. Unfavorable New Hampshire results tend to dry up contributions; weaker candidates may be forced into an early withdrawal.

The Front-End Strategy A **front-end strategy** places heavy emphasis on the results from New Hampshire and other early primary states. This strategy involves spending all or most of the candidate's available resources—time, energy, and money—on the early primary states, in the hopes that early victories will provide the momentum, in media attention and financial contributions, to continue the race.

The "expectations" game is played with a vengeance in the early primaries. Media polls and commentators set the candidates' expected vote percentages, and the candidates and their spokespersons try to deflate these expectations. On election night, the candidates' **spin doctors** sally forth among the crowds of television and newspaper reporters to give a favorable interpretation of the outcome. The candidates themselves appear at campaign headquarters (and, they hope, on national television) to give the same favorable spin to the election results. But the media itself—particularly the television network anchors and reporters and commentators—interpret the results for the American people, determining the early favorites in the presidential horse race.

Front Loading Presidential nominees are now selected by early March. State legislators in a number of states expressed their frustration over the media attention given to tiny New Hampshire by moving up the dates of their presidential primary elections. (The New Hampshire Legislature responded by officially setting its primary date one week earlier than any other state's primary.) In 2004 many big states, including California, Connecticut, Georgia, Massachusetts, Minnesota, New York, and Ohio, held their primary on March 2; Florida and Texas held theirs on March 7; and Michigan held its primary on February 7. (See *Up Close:* "Primaries 2004: Democrats Seek 'Electability.'"

This **front loading** of presidential primaries appears to favor the candidate who peaks in the polls in the first six weeks of the primary season.[14]

Convention Showplace Once a presidential candidate has enough votes to assure nomination, this uncrowned winner must prepare for the party's convention. Organizing and orchestrating convention forces, dominating the platform and rules writing, enjoying the nominating speeches and the traditional roll call of the state delegations, mugging for the television camera when the nominating vote goes over the top, submitting the vice presidential nominee's name for convention approval, and preparing and delivering a rousing acceptance speech to begin the fall campaign are just a few of the many tasks awaiting the winner—and the winner's campaign team.

front-end strategy Presidential political campaign strategy in which a candidate focuses on winning early primaries to build momentum.

spin doctor Practitioner of the art of spin control, or manipulation of media reporting to favor one's own candidate.

front loading The scheduling of presidential primary elections early in the year.

The Presidential Campaign: The General Election Battle

Buoyed by the conventions—and often by postconvention bounces in the polls—the new nominees must now face the general electorate.

UP CLOSE

Primaries 2004: Democrats Seek "Electability"

The Democrats lost their two most popular presidential candidates even before the "pre-primary," when former Vice President Al Gore and New York Senator Hillary Clinton both announced that they would not seek their party's nomination. Both had led in Democratic opinion polls before their announcements. Their decisions to forego the race brought a small army of Democratic candidates into the race.

The pre-primary season began in earnest in August, 2003. Initially, Connecticut Senator Joe Lieberman led in name recognition, but soon fell to fourth or fifth place as a battle progressed. Massachusetts Senator John Kerry and Missouri Congressman Dick Gephardt were getting double digit numbers in the polls. Former NATO Commander General Wesley Clark also appeared to be a serious contender; he was rumored to be the choice of Bill and Hillary Clinton.

The Dean Bubble By early November the media began to focus on a little-known Vermont governor, Howard Dean. Dean separated himself from the other candidates with his heated opposition to the war in Iraq and his vitriolic attacks on President Bush. The media was entranced with his lurid anti-Bush rhetoric and his passionate "Hate Bush" followers. Dean was also successful in exploiting the Internet to tap into his most zealous followers, amassing $50 million in campaign funds—the largest war chest of any Democratic candidate. But could money and passion win votes in the early primaries?

Iowa and New Hampshire Grass-roots Democrats in the Iowa caucuses and the New Hampshire primary appeared unfazed by Dean's intensity and the media attention given him. Many admired his "raw meat" attacks on Bush, but more seemed committed to finding an electable Democrat. John Kerry's relatively low key yet well-organized work in Iowa and New Hampshire paid off. He surprised the pundits, commentators, and pollsters with come-from-behind victories in both states. Dean was stunned. He reacted with a high-volume shouting speech which appeared to confirm the voters' notion that he was too emotional and perhaps unstable for the presidency.

Front-Loaded Victories Kerry's Iowa and New Hampshire victories gave him much-needed momentum for a series of Democratic primaries that had been moved up into February. By March 2, Kerry had effectively won the Democratic nomination. (He lost only to Clark in Oklahoma and Edwards in South Carolina.) His Democratic poll numbers skyrocketed. One by one his competitors dropped out. North Carolina Senator John Edwards ended up a distant second in the primary voting. Although Kerry's liberal voting record matched that of his mentor, Ted Kennedy, he appeared moderate in contrast to Dean. And perhaps the youthful looking Edwards did not appear to have the experience necessary to win what Democrats expected to be a hard-fought election. Kerry's Vietnam War heroism set him apart from the other candidates and reassured voters that he would be a capable Commander-in-Chief. (He had voted for the war in Iraq, but later criticized its execution.)

A Long Campaign The front loading of the primary season in 2004 produced a Democratic challenger to President Bush a full eight months before the general election in November. Kerry's victories reported in the media catapulted the Massachusetts Senator to near-even standing with Bush. Indeed, the Bush camp decided to begin running television campaign advertisements in early March. The stage was set for a long and brutal general election campaign.

General Election Strategies Strategies in the general election are as varied as the imaginations of campaign advisers, media consultants, pollsters, and the candidates themselves. As noted earlier, campaign strategies are affected by the nature of the times and the state of the economy; by the incumbent or challenger status of the candidate; by the issues, conditions, scandals, or events currently being spotlighted by the media; and by the dynamics of the campaign itself as the candidates attack and defend themselves.

UP CLOSE

Bush v. Kerry

John F. Kerry wrapped up the Democratic nomination in the early spring, and his poll numbers quickly matched those of President Bush. Despite one of the most liberal voting records in Congress, Kerry appeared to be a "moderate" in contrast to his boisterous primary opponent, Vermont Governor Howard Dean (See *Up Close:* "Primaries 2004" in Chapter 7). At the Democratic National Convention Kerry took the stage with a snappy military salute, "I'm John Kerry and I'm reporting for duty!" The early intent was to use his war hero's status to demonstrate his ability to be Commander-in-Chief in time of war. It was a risky strategic decision because President Bush was perceived in all of the polls as a "strong leader" in the war on terrorism. But events thirty-five years ago seemed irrelevant in 2004. Kerry got very little "bounce" from the Democratic Convention.

George Bush had little choice but to make the war on terrorism his major theme. Bush's advisors believed it was to their candidate's advantage to make terrorism the "chief concern" of Americans, rather than the economy. They believed that in wartime most voters wanted a "strong leader," "decisive," and a "man of his word"—qualities in whom the polls indicated Bush was strongest. Kerry was to be cast as a "waffler"—first voting to authorize military force against Iraq and then later voting against a bill to finance operations there. Kerry supported continuing U.S.military efforts in Iraq, but he attacked Bush's decision to invade Iraq without the support of other United Nations members. He referred to Iraq as "the wrong war, the wrong place, the wrong time," and accused Bush of a "colossal error of judgment" in shifting anti-terrorist efforts to catch Osama bin Laden in Afghanistan to the attack on Iraq.

Bush maintained a slim lead in the polls throughout the spring and summer, a lead that he was to lose briefly after the first presidential debate in October. Kerry's carefully-crafted image in the debate seemed to reassure many Americans that he too would make a strong Commander-in-Chief. He claimed that Bush had "misled" the American people about the existence of weapons of mass destruction in Iraq, that he failed to "exhaust the remedies of the United Nations," and that he, Kerry, would not commit American troops to battle without satisfying "the global test." Bush jumped on the phrase "the global test" to claim that Kerry would place America's security in the hands of the United Nations: "I'll never turn over America's national security needs to leaders of other countries." Kerry was judged by the polls as the winner of the debates. But Bush had found a theme—that Kerry was indecisive, that he flip-flopped, and that he would hesitate to act when confronted with threats to national security. Within a week, Bush regained his slim lead in the polls.

As election day neared, the rhetoric became more bitter. Bush had "lied" about the reasons for the war in Iraq, rather than simply being misinformed by the intelligence community about the existence of weapons of mass destruction in Saddam's hands. It was charged that Bush secretly intended to bring back the draft and that he would cut social security benefits for the elderly. Kerry was "unfit for command": early in his career he had accused his fellow veterans of committing atrocities in Vietnam. The terrorists were hoping for a Kerry victory. The nation would not be "safe" if Kerry won.

Bush succeeded in making Iraq part of the war on terrorism: "We will fight the terrorists abroad, rather than fight them at home." Kerry could never fully take advantage of the controversial war: he had voted for it in the first place. He said he would call upon our allies in the United Nations to help in Iraq, but it seemed unlikely to many Americans that UN members who opposed the war would want to assist the U.S.

Contrary to expectations, Americans went to the polls in record numbers. And while Iraq and terrorism ranked high among their concerns, they cited "moral values"as the most important issue in the election. Bush's folksy image and his moral values seemed to match their own. He was "honest and trustworthy," he "took a clear stand," he was "decisive" and "better at handling the war on terrorism." He not only won a majority of the popular vote (51 to 48%), but also helped to increase the Republican majorities in the House and Senate.

Presidential election campaigns must focus on the **Electoral College**. The president is not elected by the national popular vote total but rather by a majority of the *electoral* votes of the states. Electoral votes are won by plurality, winner-take-all popular voting in each of the states. Thus a narrow plurality win in a state delivers *all* of that state's electoral votes. Big-state victories, even by very narrow margins, can deliver big electoral prizes. The biggest prizes are California with 54 electoral votes, New York with 33, and Texas with 32. With a total of 538 electoral votes at stake, *the winner must garner victories in states that total a minimum of 270 electoral votes.*

Targeting the Swing States In focusing on the most populous states, with their large electoral votes, candidates must decide which of these states are "winnable," then direct their time, energy, and money to these **swing states**. Candidates cannot afford to spend too much effort in states that already seem to be solidly in their column, although they must avoid the perception that they are ignoring these strong bases of support. Neither can candidates waste much effort on states that already appear to be solidly in their opponent's column. So the swing states receive most of the candidates' time, attention, and television advertising money.

The Presidential Debates The nationally televised presidential debates are the central feature of the general election campaign. These debates attract more viewers than any other campaign event. Moreover, they enable a candidate to reach undecided voters and the opponent's supporters, as well as the candidate's own partisans. Even people who usually pay little attention to politics may be drawn in by the drama of the confrontation (see *Up Close:* "The Presidential Debates" on page 160).

The debates allow viewers an opportunity to see and hear candidates together and to compare their responses to questions as they stand side by side. The debates give audiences a better view of the candidates than they can get from thirty-second commercial ads or seven-second news sound bites. Viewers can at least judge how the candidates react under pressure.

However, the debates emphasize candidate image over substantive policy issues. Candidates must appear presidential. They must appear confident, compassionate, concerned, and good humored. They must not appear uncertain or unsure of themselves, or aloof or out of touch with viewers, or easily upset by hostile questions. They must avoid verbal slips or gaffes or even unpolished or awkward gestures. They must remember that the debates are not really debates so much as joint press conferences in which the candidates respond to questions with rehearsed mini-speeches and practiced sound bites.

The Electoral College Vote In recent presidential elections, the Democratic candidates (Clinton in 1992 and 1996 and Gore in 2000) have won the north-eastern states, including New York; the upper midwestern states, including Michigan and Illinois; and, perhaps most importantly, the West Coast, including California (see *Across the USA:* "How the States Voted" on page 162). Republican presidential candidates (Bush in 1992, Dole in 1996, and Bush in 2000 and 2004) have shown greater strength in the Great Plains and Rocky Mountain states and in the south-eastern states (forming a Republican "L" on the Electoral College map). If these patterns continue in presidential elections, Democrats can depend on two of the four largest Electoral College vote states in 2004, California (55) and New York (31), while Republicans can feel comfortable in the other two, Texas (34)

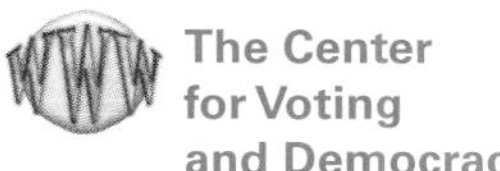

The Center for Voting and Democracy
A site with material on possible changes in the Electoral College. *www.fairvote.org*

Electoral College The 538 presidential electors apportioned among the states according to their congressional representation (plus 3 for the District of Columbia) whose votes officially elect the president and vice president of the United States.

swing states States that are not considered to be firmly in the Democratic or Republican column.

UP CLOSE

The Presidential Debates

Presidential debates attract more viewers than any other campaign activity. Most campaign activities—speeches, rallies, motorcades—reach only supporters. Such activities may inspire supporters to go to the polls, contribute money, and even work to get others to vote their way. But televised debates reach undecided voters as well as supporters, and they allow candidates to be seen by supporters of their opponent. Even if issues are not really discussed in depth, people see how presidential candidates react as human beings under pressure.

Kennedy-Nixon

Televised presidential debates began in 1960 when John F. Kennedy and Richard M. Nixon confronted each other on a bare stage before an America watching on black-and-white TV sets. Nixon was the vice president in the popular presidential administration of Dwight Eisenhower; he was also an accomplished college debate-team member. He prepared for the debates as if they were college debates, memorizing facts and arguments. But he failed to realize that image triumphs over substance on television. By contrast, Kennedy was handsome, cool, confident; whatever doubts the American people may have had regarding his youth and inexperience were dispelled by his polished manner. Radio listeners tended to think that Nixon won, and debate coaches scored him the winner. But television viewers preferred the glamorous young Kennedy. The polls shifted in Kennedy's direction after the debate, and he won in a very close general election.

Carter-Ford

President Lyndon Johnson avoided debating in 1964, and Nixon, having learned his lesson, declined to debate in 1968 and 1972. Thus televised presidential debates did not resume until 1976, when incumbent president Gerald Ford, perceiving he was behind in the polls, agreed to debate challenger Jimmy Carter. Ford made a series of verbal slips. Carter was widely perceived as having won the debate, and he went on to victory in the general election.

Reagan-Carter and Reagan-Mondale

It was Ronald Reagan who demonstrated the true power of television. Reagan had lived his life in front of a camera. It was the principal tool of both of his trades—actor and politician. In 1980 incumbent president Jimmy Carter talked rapidly and seriously about programs, figures, and budgets. But Reagan was master of the stage; he was relaxed, confident, joking. He appeared to treat the president of the United States as an overly aggressive, impulsive younger man, regrettably given to exaggeration. When it was all over, it was clear to most viewers that Carter had been bested by a true professional in media skills.

However, in the first of two televised debates with Walter Mondale in 1984, Reagan's skills of a lifetime seemed to desert him. He stumbled over statistics and groped for words. Reagan's poor performance raised the only issue that might conceivably defeat him—his age. The president had looked and sounded *old.* But in the second debate, Reagan laid the perfect trap for his questioners. When asked about his age and capacity to lead the nation, he responded with a serious deadpan expression to a hushed audience and waiting America: "I want you to know that I will not make age an issue in this campaign. I am not going to exploit for political purposes [pause] my opponent's youth and inexperience." The studio audience broke into uncontrolled laughter. Even Mondale had to laugh. With a classic one-liner, Reagan buried the age issue and won not only the debate but also the election.

Bush-Dukakis

In 1988 Michael Dukakis ensured his defeat with a cold, detached performance in the presidential debates, beginning with the very first question. When CNN anchor Bernard Shaw asked, "Governor, if Kitty Dukakis were raped and murdered, would you favor an irrevocable death penalty for the killer?" The question demanded an emotional reply. Instead, Dukakis responded with an impersonal recitation of his stock position on law enforcement. Bush seized the opportunity to establish a more personal relationship with the viewers. Voters responded to Bush, electing him.

Clinton-Bush-Perot

The three-way presidential debates of 1992 drew the largest television audiences in the history of presidential debates. In the first debate, Ross Perot's Texas twang and downhome folksy style stole the show. Chided by his opponents for having no governmental experience, he shot back, "Well, they have a point. I don't have any experience in running up a $4 trillion dollar debt." But it was Bill Clinton's smooth performance in the second debate, with its talk-show format, that seemed to wrap up the election. Ahead in the polls, Clinton appeared at ease walking about the stage and responding to audience questions with sympathy and sincerity. By contrast, George Bush appeared stiff and formal, and somewhat ill at case with the "unpresidential" format.

Clinton-Dole

A desperate Bob Dole, running 20 points behind, faced a newly "presidential" Bill Clinton in their two 1996 debates. (Perot's poor standing in the polls led to his exclusion.) Dole tried to counter his image as a grumpy old man in the first encounter; his humor actually won more laughs from the audience than Clinton. Dole injected more barbs in the second debate, complaining of "ethical problems in the White House." But Clinton remained cool and comfortable, ignoring the challenger and focusing on the nation's economic health. Viewers, most of whom were already in Clinton's court, judged him the winner of both debates.

Bush-Gore

Separate formats were agreed upon for three debates—the traditional podium, a conference table, and a town hall setting. Gore was assertive, almost to the point of rudeness, but both candidates focused on policy differences rather than on personal attacks. Viewers gave Gore the edge in these debates but they found Bush more likable. Bush appeared to benefit more in the post-debate polls.

Bush-Kerry

Kerry prepared well for the three debates. He appeared tall, earnest, confident, well-informed, and "presidential." He spoke forcefully, avoiding the qualifying clauses and lengthy sentences that had plagued his speeches in the past. Bush appeared uncomfortable, scowling at Kerry's answers, often repeating himself, and failing to "connect" with his audiences. Polls showed Kerry winning each debate.

ACROSS THE USA

How the States Voted

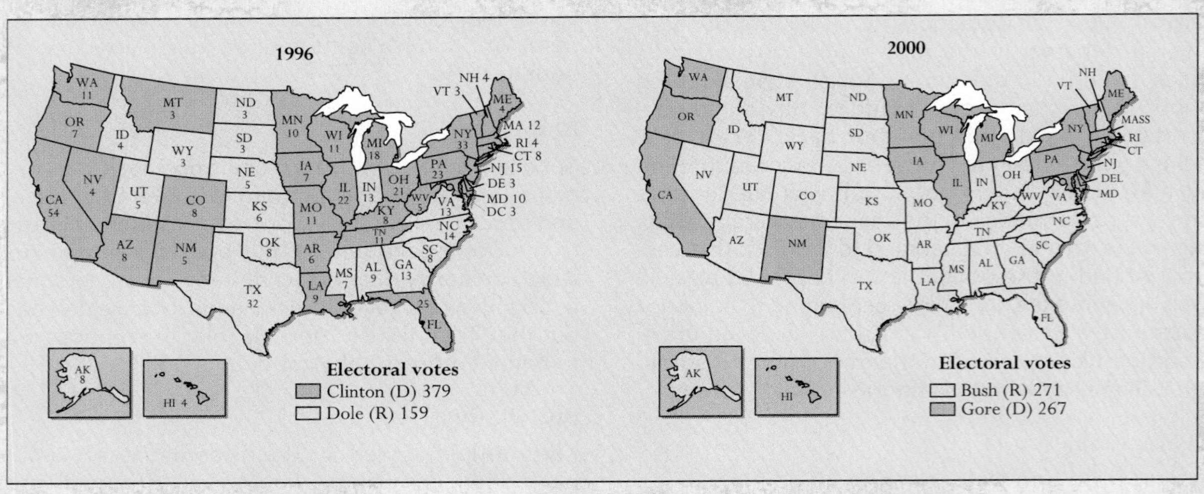

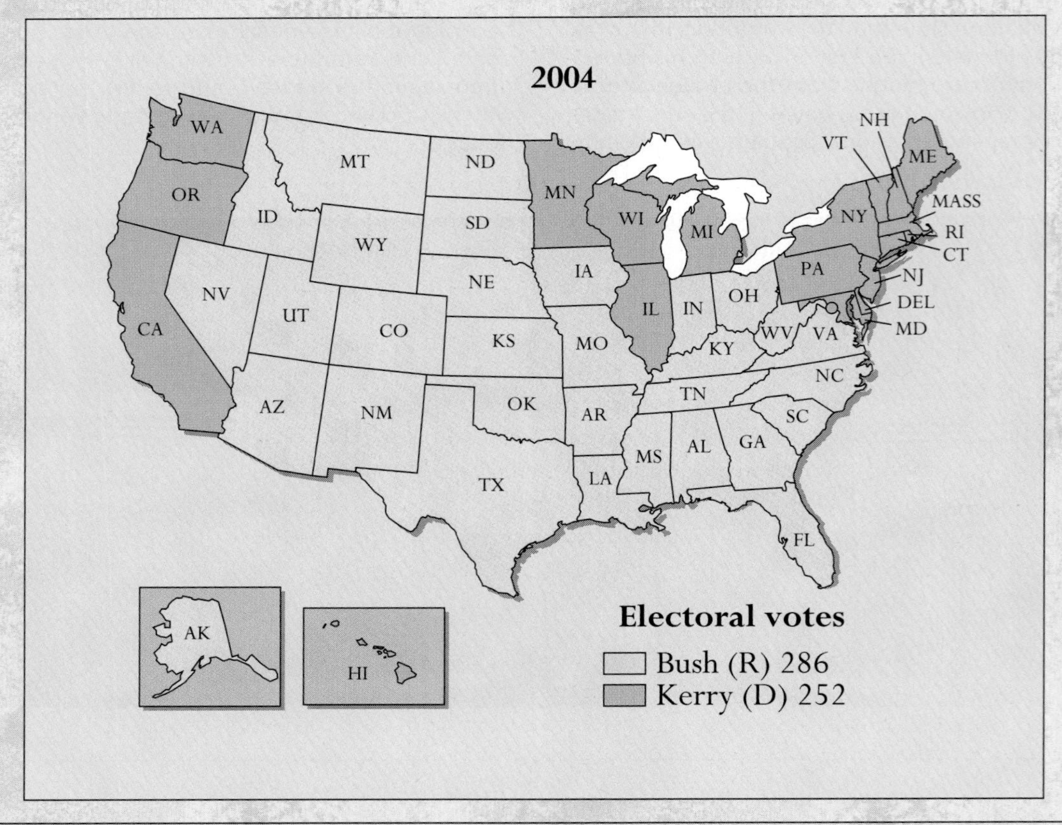

and Florida (27). The Electoral College battleground may be states such as Ohio, Pennsylvania, and Missouri—"swing states" that have cast their votes alternatively for Democratic and Republican candidates in recent presidential elections.

The Voter Decides

Understanding the reasons behind the voters' choice at the ballot box is a central concern of candidates, campaign strategists, commentators, and political scientists. Perhaps no other area of politics has been investigated so thoroughly as voting behavior. Survey data on voter choice have been collected for presidential elections for the past half century.[15] We know that voters cast ballots for and against candidates for a variety of reasons—party affiliation, group interests, characteristics and images of the candidates themselves, the economy, and policy issues. But forecasting election outcomes remains a risky business.

Party Affiliation Although many people claim to vote for "the person, not the party," party identification remains a powerful influence in voter choice. Party ties among voters have weakened over time, with increasing proportions of voters labeling themselves as independents or only weak Democrats or Republicans, and more voters opting to split their tickets or cross party lines than did so a generation ago (see Chapter 7). Nevertheless, party identification remains one of the most important influences on voter choice. Party affiliation is more important in congressional than in presidential elections, but even in presidential elections the tendency to see the candidate of one's own party as "the best person" is very strong.

Consider the three presidential elections (see Figure 5.8 on page 164). Self-identified Republicans voted overwhelmingly for Bush in 1992, for Dole in 1996, and for George W. Bush in 2000 and 2004. Self-identified Democrats voted overwhelmingly for Clinton in 1992 and 1996, for Gore in 2000, and for Kerry in 2004.

Because Republican identifiers are outnumbered in the electorate by Democratic identifiers, Republican presidential candidates, and many Republican congressional candidates as well, *must* appeal to independent and Democratic crossover voters.

Group Voting We already know that various social and economic groups give disproportionate support to the Democratic and Republican parties (see Chapter 7). So it comes as no surprise that recent Democratic presidential candidates have received disproportionate support from African Americans, Catholics, Jews, less-educated, and union workers; Republican presidential candidates have fared better among whites, Protestants, and better-educated voters (see Figure 5.9 on page 165). That is, these groups have given a larger percentage of their vote to the Democratic or Republican candidates than the candidate received from the total electorate.

Race and Gender Gaps Among the more interesting group voting patterns is the serious *gender gap* affecting recent Republican candidates. Although Reagan won the women's vote in both 1980 and 1984, his vote percentages among men were considerably higher than among women. George H.W. Bush lost the women's vote in both 1988 and 1992. In 1996 the gender gap widened, with a 54 percent of women voting for Clinton as opposed to only 38 percent for Dole, and continued in 2000 with women giving Gore 54 percent of the vote as opposed to George W. Bush's 43 percent. Again in 2004 women gave Democrat John F. Kerry 54 percent of their vote. African Americans have long constituted the most loyal group of Democratic voters, regularly giving the Democratic presidential

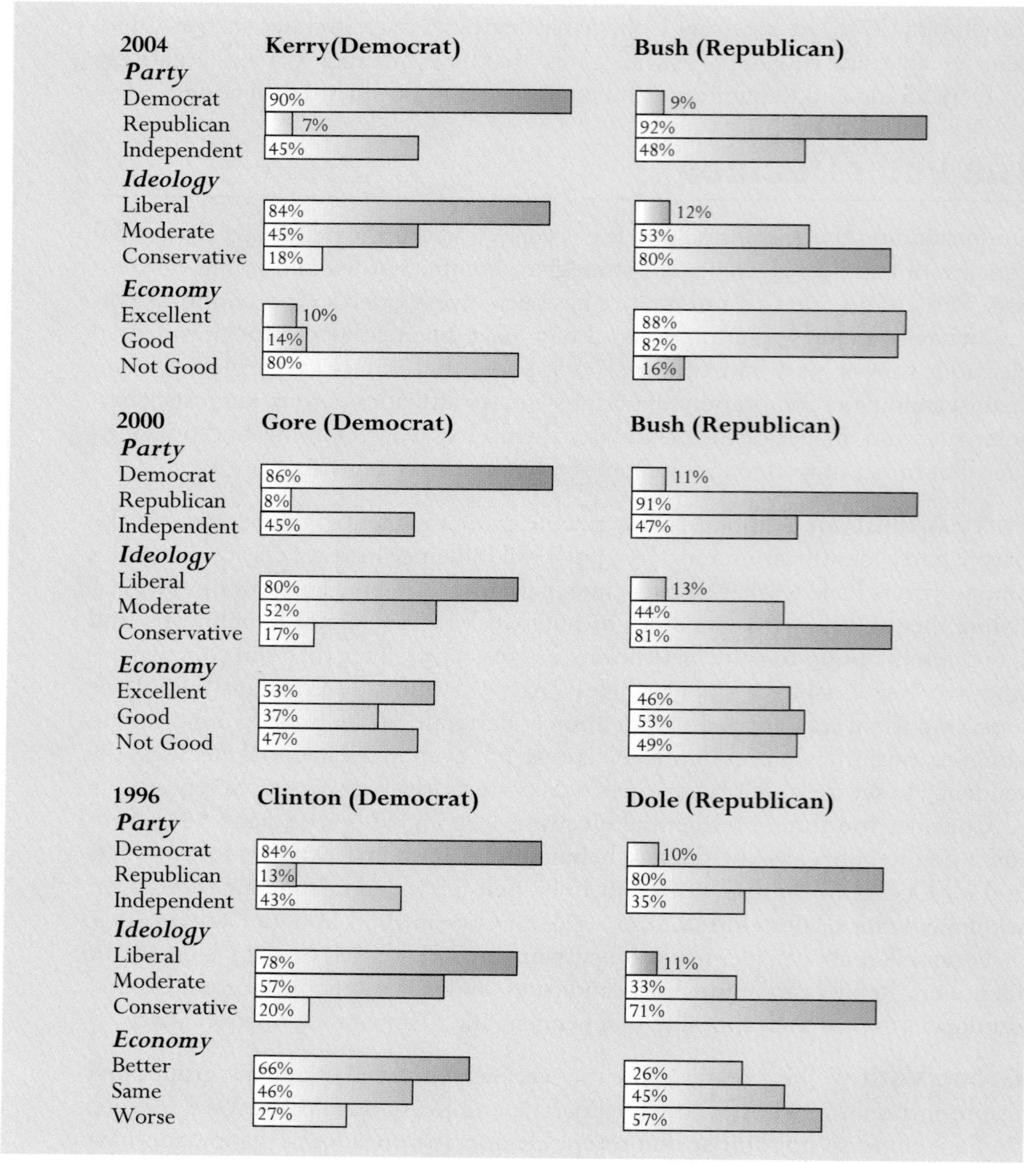

2004	Kerry (Democrat)	Bush (Republican)
Party		
Democrat	90%	9%
Republican	7%	92%
Independent	45%	48%
Ideology		
Liberal	84%	12%
Moderate	45%	53%
Conservative	18%	80%
Economy		
Excellent	10%	88%
Good	14%	82%
Not Good	80%	16%

2000	Gore (Democrat)	Bush (Republican)
Party		
Democrat	86%	11%
Republican	8%	91%
Independent	45%	47%
Ideology		
Liberal	80%	13%
Moderate	52%	44%
Conservative	17%	81%
Economy		
Excellent	53%	46%
Good	37%	53%
Not Good	47%	49%

1996	Clinton (Democrat)	Dole (Republican)
Party		
Democrat	84%	10%
Republican	13%	80%
Independent	43%	35%
Ideology		
Liberal	78%	11%
Moderate	57%	33%
Conservative	20%	71%
Economy		
Better	66%	26%
Same	46%	45%
Worse	27%	57%

FIGURE 5.8 Party, Ideology, and Nature of the Times in Presidential Voting

Those who identify themselves as members of a major political party are highly likely to vote for the presidential candidates of their party. Likewise, those who identify themselves as liberals are more likely than average to vote for Democrats, and those who identify themselves as conservatives are more likely to vote for Republicans in presidential elections. In addition, voters who see the economic picture as better are more likely to vote for the incumbent; those who are concerned about the nation's economy are more likely to vote against the incumbent.

Source: Election exit polls, Voter News Service.

nominee up to 90 percent or more of their vote. The overall Hispanic vote is Democratic, although a significant portion of Hispanics, notably Cuban Americans in Florida, vote Republican.

Candidate Image In an age of direct communication between candidates and voters via television, the image of candidates and their ability to relate to audiences have emerged

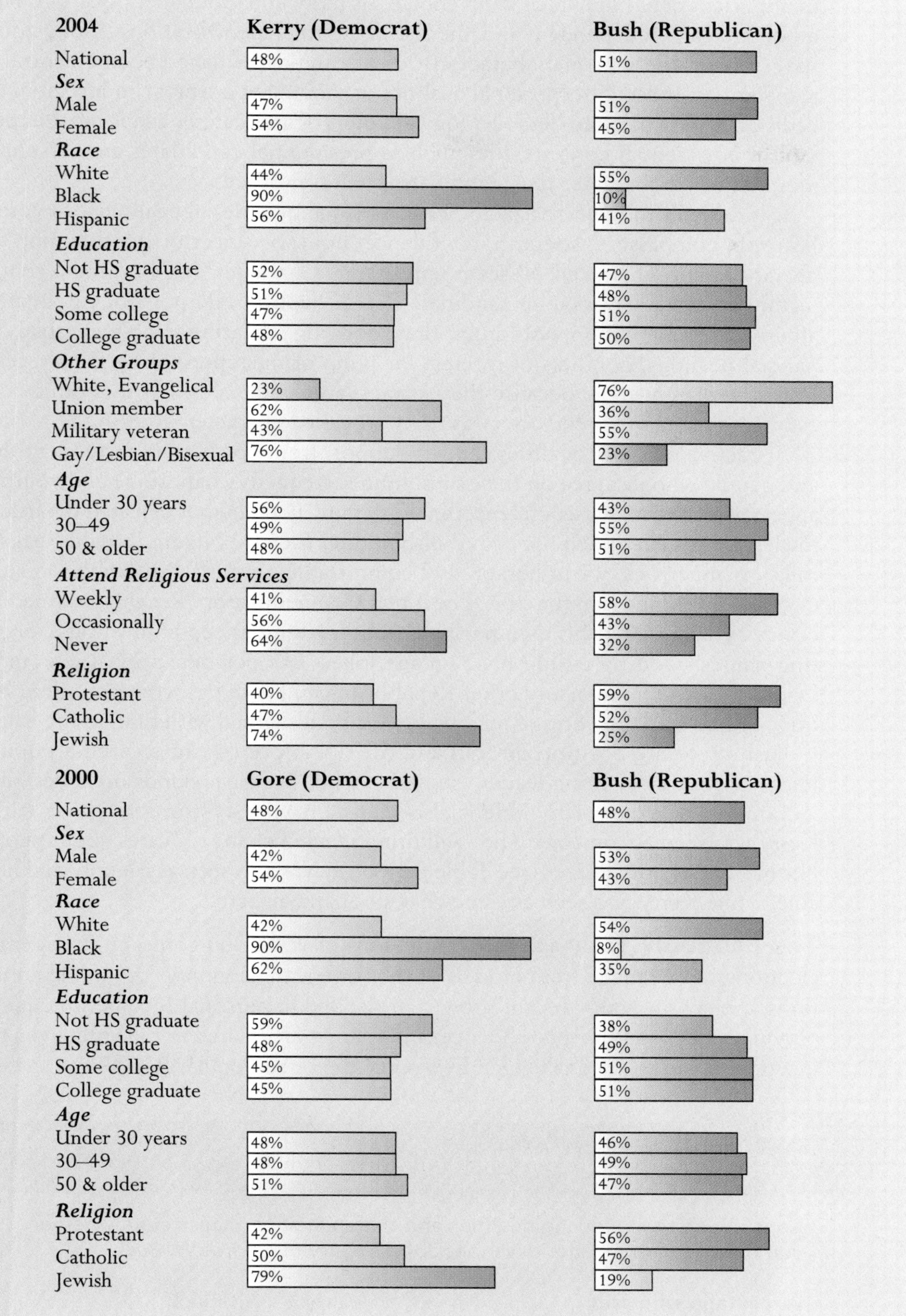

FIGURE 5.9 Group Voting in Presidential Elections

Democratic presidential candidates regularly do better among African American, Hispanic, lower-income, less-educated voters. The gender gap—men tending to vote Republican and women Democratic—first emerged in the Reagan years. Increasingly, white religious voters are casting their ballots for Republican candidates.

Source: Election exit polls, Voter News Service, National Election Pool.

as important determinants of voter choice. As party and group identifications have moderated and independent and middle-of-the-road identifications among voters have grown, the personal characteristics of candidates have become central to many voters. Indeed, the personal qualities of candidates are most important in the decision of less partisan, less ideological voters. Candidate image is most important in presidential contests, inasmuch as presidential candidates are personally more visible to the voter than candidates for lesser offices.[16]

THINK AGAIN

Should people vote on the basis of a candidate's personal character rather than his or her policy positions?

It is difficult to identify exactly what personal qualities appeal most to voters. Warmth, compassion, strength, confidence, honesty, sincerity, good humor, appearance, and "character" all seem important. "Character" has become a central feature of media coverage of candidates (see Chapter 6). Reports of extramarital affairs, experimentation with drugs, draft dodging, cheating in college, shady financial dealings, conflicts of interest, or lying or misrepresenting facts receive heavy media coverage because they attract large audiences. But it is difficult to estimate how many voters are swayed by so-called character issues.

Attractive personal qualities can win support from opposition-party identifiers and people who disagree on the issues. John F. Kennedy's handsome and youthful appearance, charm, self-confidence, and disarming good humor defeated the heavy-jowled, shifty-eyed, defensive, and ill-humored Richard Nixon. Ronald Reagan's folksy mannerisms, warm humor, and comfortable rapport with television audiences justly earned him the title "The Great Communicator." Reagan disarmed his critics by laughing at his own personal flubs—falling asleep at meetings, forgetting names—and by telling his own age jokes. His personal appeal won more Democratic voters than any other Republican candidate has won in modern history, and he won the votes of many people who disagreed with him on the issues.

Bush's resolute position on Iraq and the war on terrorism created a popular image of him as "a strong leader," someone who "has clear stands on issues," and is "honest and trustworthy." He is also seen as having a "strong religious faith." Kerry was seen as someone who "will bring needed change," "cares about people like me, and is "intelligent" (see Table 8.5). Bush was also seen as friendly and likeable, while Kerry was seen as somewhat aloof and austere.

The Economy Fairly accurate predictions of voting outcomes in presidential elections can be made from models of the American economy. Economic conditions at election time—recent growth or decline in personal income, the unemployment rate, consumer confidence, and so on—are related to the vote given the incumbent versus the challenger. Ever since the once-popular Republican incum-

TABLE 5.4 Images of Bush and Kerry, 2004

Considering the following qualities and characteristics, please state whether you think each one better describes John F. Kerry or George W. Bush.

Percentage who said:		Kerry	Bush
25%	Will bring needed change	95%	4%
17%	Has clear stand on issues	23%	75%
16%	Strong leader	14%	85%
11%	Honest, trustworthy	28%	70%
10%	Cares about people like me	76%	23%
8%	Intelligent	91%	7%
7%	Strong religious faith	9%	90%

bent Herbert Hoover was trounced by Franklin Roosevelt as the Great Depression of the 1930s deepened, politicians have understood that voters hold the incumbent party responsible for hard economic times.

Perhaps no other lesson has been as well learned by politicians: hard economic times hurt incumbents and favor challengers. The economy may not be the only important factor in presidential voting, but it is certainly a factor of great importance.[17] Some evidence indicates that it is not voters' *own* personal economic well-being that affects their vote but rather voter perception of *general* economic conditions. People who perceive the economy as getting worse are likely to vote against the incumbent party, whereas people who think the economy is getting better support the incumbent.[18] Thus voters who thought the economy was getting *worse* in 1992 supported challenger Bill Clinton over incumbent president George Bush. But the reverse was true in 1996; more people thought the economy was better, and the people who thought so voted heavily for incumbent Bill Clinton. In 2000, Gore won the votes of those who thought the economy was "excellent," but economic voting did not seem to be as influential as in previous presidential races. The economy was cited as "most important" by about one-fifth of the voters in 2004 and Kerry won the vast majority of these voters.

Issue Voting Casting one's vote exclusively on the basis of the policy positions of the candidates is rare. Most voters are unaware of the specific positions taken by candidates on the issues. Indeed, voters often believe that their preferred candidate agrees with them on the issues, even when this is not the case. In other words, voters project their own policy views onto their favorite candidate more often than they decide to vote for a candidate because of his or her position on the issues.

However, when asked specifically about issues, voters are willing, to name those they care most about (see Table 5.5). Voters do not always make their choices based on a candidate's stated policy positions, but voters *do* strongly favor candidates whose policy views they assume match their own. Only when a key issue takes center stage do voters really become aware of what the candidates actually propose to do. In the 1992, 1996, and 2000 elections, the economy was the issue that voters cared about most. In all three elections, Clinton and Gore won the votes of the people most concerned about the economy (see Table 5.5). .

To the surprise of many commentators, "moral values" was cited as the most important issue by voters leaving the polls in 2004. Bush won over three-

TABLE 5.5 Issues the Voters Cared about in 2004

Presidential Vote of Those Who Listed Issue as "Most Important"

Rank	Percentage who said:		Who they voted for: Kerry	Bush
1	21%	Moral values	19%	78%
2	20%	Economy/jobs	82%	16%
3	18%	Terrorism	15%	85%
4	15%	Iraq	76%	23%
5	8%	Health care	79%	20%
6	5%	Taxes	47%	53%
7	4%	Education	75%	24%

quarters of these voters. Faith and family appeared to underlie concern with moral values. Bush had never disguised his religious faith. Bans on same-sex marriage were on referenda ballots in eleven states and may have helped inspire a heavy turnout for Bush.

Bush had tried to portray the war in Iraq as part of a broader war on terrorism. But while Bush won the votes of people concerned with terrorism, Kerry won the votes of those concerned with the war in Iraq. Voters opposed to the war in Iraq went heavily for Kerry, while supporters of the war voted heavily for Bush.

SUMMARY NOTES

- Public opinion commands the attention of elected public officials in a democracy, yet many Americans are poorly informed and unconcerned about politics; their opinions on public issues are often changeable and inconsistent. Only a few highly salient issues generate strong and stable opinions.
- Ideology also shapes opinion, especially among politically interested and active people who employ fairly consistent liberal or conservative ideas in forming their opinions on specific issues.
- Race and gender also influence public opinion. Blacks and whites differ over the extent of discrimination in the United States, as well as over its causes and remedies. Men and women tend to differ over issues involving the use of force. In recent years, women have tended to give greater support to the Democratic Party than men have.
- Individuals can exercise power in a democratic political system in a variety of ways. They can run for public office, take part in demonstrations and protests, make financial contributions to candidates, attend political events, write letters to newspapers or public officials, belong to political organizations, vote in elections, or simply hold and express opinions on public issues.
- About half of the voting-age population fails to vote even in presidential elections. Voter turnout has steadily declined in recent decades. Voter registration is a major obstacle to voting. Turnout is affected by competition as well as by feelings of political alienation and distrust of government. Young people have the poorest record of voter turnout of any age group.
- Although winning candidates often claim a mandate for their policy proposals, in reality few campaigns present clear policy alternatives to the voters, few voters cast their ballots on the basis of policy considerations, and the policy preferences of the electorate can seldom be determined from election outcomes.
- Nevertheless, voters can influence future policy directions through retrospective judgments about the performance of incumbents, returning them to office or turning them out. Most retrospective voting appears to center on the economy.
- Incumbents begin campaigns with many advantages: name recognition, financial support, goodwill from services they perform for constituents, large-scale public projects they bring to their districts, and the other resources of office.
- Campaigning for office is largely a media activity, dominated by professional advertising specialists, fund raisers, media consultants, and pollsters.
- The professionalization of campaigning and the heavy costs of a media campaign drive up the costs of running for office. These huge costs make candidates heavily dependent on financial support from individuals and organizations. Fund raising occupies more of a candidate's time than any other campaign activity.
- Campaign contributions are made by politically active individuals and organizations, including political action committees. Many contributions are made in order to gain access to policy makers and assistance with government business. Some contributors are ideologically motivated; others merely seek to rub shoulders with powerful people.
- Presidential primary election strategies emphasize appeals to party activists and core supporters, including the more ideologically motivated primary voters.
- In the general election campaign, presidential candidates usually seek to broaden their appeal to moderate, centrist voters while holding on to their core supporters. Campaigns must focus on states where the candidate has the best chance of gaining the 270 electoral votes needed to win.
- Voter choice is influenced by party identification, group membership, perceived image of the candidates, economic conditions, and, to a lesser extent, ideology and issue preferences.

KEY TERMS

mandate 135
retrospective voting 135
incumbent 138
name recognition 138
challengers 138
franking privilege 139
campaign strategy 139
negative campaigning 140
focus group 142
photo ops 142
sound bites 142
issue ads 147
political action committee (PAC) 149
Federal Election Commission (FEC) 151
retail politics 155
front-end strategy 156
spin doctor 156
front loading 156
Electoral College 159
swing states 159

SUGGESTED READINGS

Conway, M. Margaret. *Political Participation in the United States.* 3rd ed. Washington, D.C.: CQ Press, 2000. A comprehensive summary of who participates in politics and why.

Conway, M. Margaret, Gertrude A. Stevernagel, and David Ahern. *Women and Political Participation.* Washington, D.C.: CQ Press, 1998. An examination of cultural change and women's participation in politics, including treatment of the gender gap in political attitudes and the impact of women's membership in the political elite.

Erikson, Robert S., and Kent L. Tedin. *American Public Opinion.* 6th ed. Longman, 2002. A comprehensive review of the forces influencing public opinion and an assessment of the influence of public opinion in American politics.

Flanigan, William H., and Nancy H. Zingale. *Political Behavior of the American Electorate.* 11th ed. Washington, D.C.: CQ Press, 2002. A brief but comprehensive summary of the extensive research literature on the effects of party identification, opinion, ideology, the media, and candidate image on voter choice and election outcomes.

Iyengar, Shanto, and Stephen Ansolabehere. *Going Negative: How Political Advertisements Shrink and Polarize the Electorate.* New York: Free Press, 1996. The real problem with negative political ads is not that they sway voters to support one candidate over another, but that they reinforce the belief that all are dishonest and cynical.

Walton, Hanes, and Robert C. Smith. *African American Politics and the African American Quest for Universal Freedom.* New York: Pearson Longman, 2002. A comprehensive American government textbook emphasizing the diversity of African American opinions and behavior.

MAKE IT REAL

ELECTION IN ACTION: 2004 PRESIDENTIAL ELECTION

No presidential election in recent history illustrated not only the importance of every vote but the importance of a candidate's campaign tactics in accumulating votes and more importantly how those votes translate into Electoral College votes. And although the Electoral College's continued existence has been hotly disputed, it still forms the backbone strategy of anyone who is seriously considering a run at the Presidency. Also playing a huge role in determining the outcome of the 2000 presidential campaign were the continued importance of raising money (lots of it) and the influence of third party candidates on the race. In this simulation you will become the presidential campaign manager of either the Republicans or the Democrats for the 2004 race. But watch out—you need to raise enough money and skillfully position your candidate on the issues to fend off potential third party candidates to win the White House.

CHAPTER 6

MASS MEDIA: SETTING THE POLITICAL AGENDA

CHAPTER OUTLINE

The Power of the Media
Sources of Media Power
The Business of the Media
The Politics of the News
Mediated Elections
Freedom versus Fairness
Libel and Slander
Politics and the Internet
Media Effects: Shaping Political Life

The Power of the Media

Politics—the struggle over who gets what, when, and how—is largely carried out in the **mass media.** The arenas of political conflict are the various media of mass communication—television, newspapers, magazines, radio, books, recordings, motion pictures, and the Internet. What we know about politics comes to us largely through these media. Unless we ourselves are admitted to the White House Oval Office or the committee rooms of Congress or dinner parties at foreign embassies, or unless we ourselves attend political rallies and demonstrations or travel to distant battlefields, we must rely on the mass media to tell us about politics. Furthermore, few of us ever have the opportunity to personally evaluate the character of presidential candidates or cabinet members or members of Congress, or to learn their views on public issues by talking with them face to face. Instead, we must learn about people as well as events from the mass media.

Great power derives from the control of information. *Who knows what* helps to determine *who gets what.* The media not only provide an arena for politics; they are themselves players in that arena. The media not only report on the struggles for power in society; they are themselves participants in those struggles. The media have long been referred to as America's "fourth branch" of government—and for good reason.[1]

The Power of Television Television is the most powerful medium of communication. It is the first true *mass* communication medium. Virtually every home in the United States has a television set, and the average home has the set turned on for about seven hours a day. Television is regularly chosen over other news media by Americans as the most common news source.

Americans turn to *local* TV news broadcasts as their most regular source of news. Daily newspapers are read by less than half of the adult public (see Figure 6.1). The national network evening news shows (*NBC Nightly News, ABC World News Tonight, CBS Evening News*) have lost viewership in recent years. But viewership of cable CNN, Fox News Cable, CNBC, and MSNBC is rising. Television weekly news magazines, notably CBS's *60 Minutes* and ABC's 20/20 have also become major sources of news for many Americans.

A growing number of Americans, especially young people, are turning to online news sources (see *Up Close* "The Generation Gap in News").

During a national crisis—for example, the terrorist attack of 9/11—Americans become even more dependent on television for their news. When asked "Where would you go first," for information during a crisis, 66 percent of Americans said they would turn on their TV sets. CNN was mentioned most often.[2]

THINK ABOUT POLITICS

1 Are media professionals—news reporters, editors, anchors—the true voice of the people in public affairs?
Yes ● No ●

2 Do the media mirror what is really news, rather than deciding themselves what's important and then making it news?
Yes ● No ●

3 Is television your most important source of news?
Yes ● No ●

4 Should the media report on all aspects of the private lives of public officials?
Yes ● No ●

5 Do the media report equally fairly on Democratic and Republican candidates for office?
Yes ● No ●

6 Should the media be legally required to be fair and accurate in reporting political news?
Yes ● No ●

7 Are you more alienated than attracted by the media's coverage of politics?
Yes ● No ●

8 Is your choice of candidates in elections affected by their advertising?
Yes ● No ●

Ask yourself how much of your knowledge about politics in America comes from television and newspapers and the radio. What you know about politics and how you participate are, in fact, largely determined by the power of the media to decide what they want you to know.

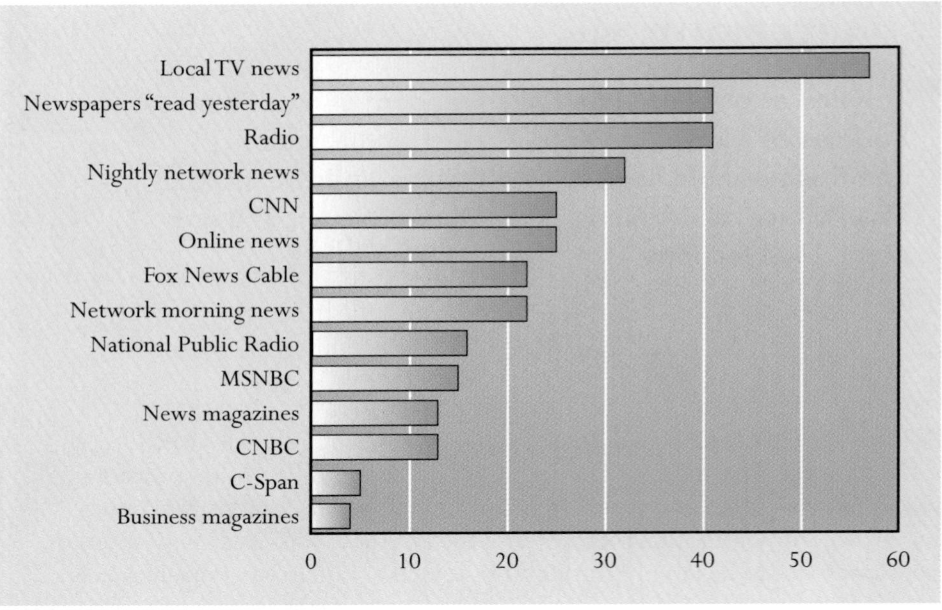

FIGURE 6.1 Where Americans Get Their News

Source: Adapted from the Pew Research Center for the People and the Press, "Public News Habits," www.people-press.org/ (June 9, 2002).

Note: More than one answer accepted in survey, so the sum adds up to well over 100%.

mass media All means of communication with the general public, including television, newspapers, magazines, radio, books, recordings, motion pictures, and the Internet.

Believability Television is also rated by Americans as the most *believable* medium of communication. Compared to television news, print sources are generally seen as less believable, with one exception, the *Wall Street Journal.* CNN is rated highest among all news sources (see Table 6.1). Not many people rate the tabloids as very believable.

Newspapers and Magazines Less than one-half of the adult population reads one or another of the nation's 1,500 daily newspapers. But the nation's prestige newspapers—the *New York Times, Washington Post,* and *Wall Street Journal*—are regularly read by government officials, corporate chiefs, interest-group leaders, and

TABLE 6.1 Believing in the Media

Believe all or most of what you see and hear (percent)

Wall Street Journal	41%	*Time*	29%
CNN	39%	Your daily paper	25%
60 Minutes	34%	*New York Times*	24%
C-Span	33%	*Newsweek*	24%
Local TV news	33%	*USA Today*	23%
ABC News	30%	AOL News	13%
CBS News	29%	*People*	10%
NBC News	29%	*National Enquirer*	4%

Source: Pew Research Center for the People and the Press. http://www.people-press.org. Reprinted by permission of Pew Research Center for the People & The Press.

UP CLOSE

The Generation Gap in News

Young people are far less likely to spend time watching the news than than older people. Indeed, people 65 and older or nearly twice as likely as those under 30 to watch television news. And older people are more than twice as likely to read a newspaper.

However, young people are more likely than older people to hear radio news, perhaps because radio news periodically interrupts music programming. And young people are the principal consumers of online news. Yet overall, young people are exposed to far less news than seniors.

The News Generation Gap

	18–29	30–49	50–64	65+
Watch TV news	40	52	62	73
Local TV	28	41	49	52
Network evening news	17	25	38	46
Cable TV news	16	23	30	35
Morning TV news	11	16	21	27
Read newspaper	26	37	52	59
Listen to radio news	34	49	42	29
News magazines	12	13	15	13
Online news	31	30	24	7
No news (yesterday)	33	19	15	12

Source: Pew Research Center for People and the Press. http://www.people-press.org. Reprinted by permission of Pew Research Center for the People & The Press.

other media people. Stories appearing in these newspapers are generally picked up by daily papers around the country, and these stories almost always appear on national network television.

The leading weekly newsmagazines—*Time, Newsweek,* and *U.S. News & World Report*—reach a smaller but more politically attentive audience than do newspapers. Magazines of political commentary—for example, the *Nation* (liberal), *New Republic* (liberal), *National Review* (conservative), *American Spectator* (conservative), *Weekly Standard* (conservative), *Public Interest* (neo-conservative), and *Washington Monthly* (neo-liberal)—reach very small but politically active audiences.

Television's Emotional Communication The power of television derives not only from its large audiences but also from its ability to communicate emotions as well as information. Television's power is found in its visuals—angry faces in a rioting mob, police beating an African American motorist, wounded soldiers being unloaded from a helicopter—scenes that convey an emotional message. Gripping pictures can inflame public opinion, inspire a clamor for action, and even pressure the government into hasty action. (This "CNN effect" has been cited as a cause of the disastrous American intervention in Somalia in 1992; visuals of starving children forced the Bush administration to airlift relief supplies and later to send troops to monitor distribution. The effort failed, and American lives were lost.)

Moreover, television focuses on the faces of individuals as well as on their words, portraying honesty or deception, humility or arrogance, compassion or

WWW **Network Television** All major networks now maintain news sites on the Web.
www.cbsnews.com
www.abcnews.com
www.cnn.com
www.msnbc.com
www.foxnews.com

indifference, humor or meanness, and a host of other personal characteristics. Skillful politicians understand that *what* one says may not be as importants as *how* one says it. Image triumphs over substance on television.[3]

Influence on Decision Makers The media's impact on political decision makers is vastly more significant than their impact on ordinary viewers. Media stories often relate more directly to the immediate concerns of politicians and government officials. They are more attentive to these stories; they are often asked to respond or comment upon news stories. They correctly perceive that media coverage of particular events and issues sets the agenda for public discussion. Even media stories that have relatively little widespread public interest can create a buzz "inside the Beltway," that is, within Washington circles.

Pew Research Center for People and the Press

Information, including opinion polls, on the media.
http://www.people-press.org

The Myth of the Mirror Media people themselves often deny that they exercise great power. They sometimes claim that they only "mirror" reality. They like to think of themselves as unbiased reporters who simply narrate happenings and transmit videotaped portrayals of people and events as they really are. But whether or not the editors, reporters, producers, or anchors acknowledge their own power, it is clear that they do more than passively mirror reality.

Sources of Media Power

THINK AGAIN

Do the media mirror what is really news, rather than deciding themselves what's important and then making it news?

Government and the media are natural adversaries. (Thomas Jefferson once wrote that he would prefer newspapers without government to a government without newspapers. But after serving as president, he wrote that people who never read newspapers are better informed than those who do, because ignorance is closer to the truth than the falsehoods spread by newspapers.) Public officials have long been frustrated by the media. But the U.S. Constitution's First Amendment guar-

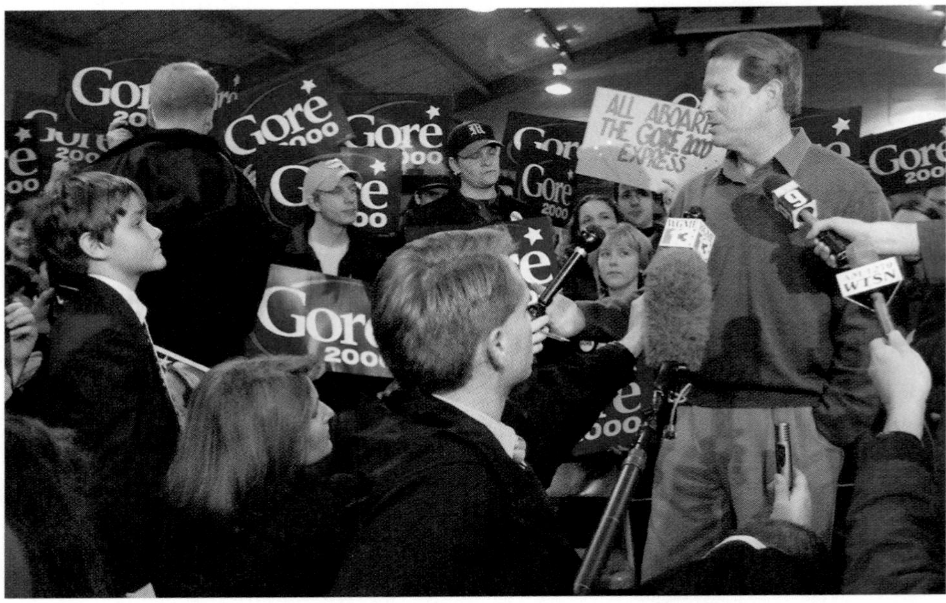

Politicians have a love-hate relationship with the media. They crave the recognition and celebrity that the media can confer on them, but they also fear attack from the media.

antee of a free press anticipates this conflict between government and the media. It prohibits government from resolving this conflict by silencing its critics.

Media professionals—television and newspaper reporters, editors, anchors, and producers—are not neutral observers of American politics but rather are active participants. They not only report events but also discover events to report, assign them political meaning, and predict their consequences (see *People in Politics:* "Stars of the Network News: Rather, Jennings, and Brokaw"). They seek to challenge government officials, debate political candidates, and define the problems of society. They see their profession as a "sacred trust" and themselves as the true voice of the people in public affairs.

Newsmaking Deciding what is "news" and who is "newsworthy"—**newsmaking**—is the most important source of media power. It is only through the media that the general public comes to know about events, personalities, and issues. Media attention makes topics public, creates issues, and elevates personalities from obscurity to celebrity. Each day, editors, producers, and reporters must select from millions of events, topics, and people those that will be videotaped, written about, and talked about. The media can never be a "picture of the world" because the whole world cannot be squeezed into the picture. The media must decide what is and is not "news."

Newspaper Web Sites

Virtually all major daily newspapers have Web sites that summarize each day's stories. For national news the most frequently consulted sites are *USA Today, Wall Street Journal, New York Times, Washington Post.*
www.usatoday.com
www.nytimes.com
www.washingtonpost.com
www.wallstreetjournal.com

Decisions about what will be news both influence popular discussion and cue public officials about topics they must turn their attention to. Politicians cannot respond to reporters' questions by saying, "I don't know," or 'That's not important," or "No comment." Media attention to a topic *requires* public officials to respond to it. Moreover, the media decide how important an issue or person or event is by their allocation of time and space. Topics given early placement on the newscast and several minutes of airtime or that receive front-page newspaper coverage with headlines and pictures are believed to be important by viewers and readers.

Politicians have a love-hate relationship with the media. They need media attention to promote themselves, their message, and their programs. They crave the exposure, the name recognition, and the celebrity status that the media can confer. At the same time, they fear attack by the media. They know the media are active players in the political game, not just passive spectators. The media seek sensational stories of sin, sexuality, corruption, and scandal in government to attract viewers and readers, and thus the media pose a constant danger to politicians. Politicians understand the power of the media to make or break their careers.

Agenda Setting **Agenda setting** is the power to decide what will be decided. It is the power to define society's "problems," to create political issues, and to set forth alternative solutions. Deciding which issues will be addressed by government may be even more important than deciding how the issues will be resolved. The distinguished political scientist E. E. Schattschneider once wrote, "He who determines what politics is about runs the country."[4]

The real power of the media lies in their ability to set the political agenda for the nation. This power grows out of their ability to decide what is news. Media coverage determines what both citizens and public officials regard as "crises" or "problems" or "issues" to be resolved. Conditions ignored by the media seldom get on the agenda of political leaders. Media attention forces public officials to speak on the topic, take positions, and respond to questions. Media inattention allows problems to be ignored by government. "TV is the Great Legitimator. TV confers reality. Nothing happens in America, practically everyone seems to agree, until it happens on television."[5]

newsmaking Deciding what events, topics, presentations, and issues will be given coverage in the news.

agenda setting Deciding what will be decided, defining the problems and issues to be addressed by decision makers.

PEOPLE IN POLITICS

Stars of the Network News

From left to right: Network news anchors Tom Brokaw, Dan Rather, and Peter Jennings.

Television news strives for credibility. Anchors are chosen not only for their personal appearance but also for the credibility they can lend to the news. The recognized all-time champion of credibility was CBS's Walter Cronkite, who for many years was "the most trusted man in America," according to all of the national polls.

Each night about 28 million Americans watch one of three men: Dan Rather, Peter Jennings, or Brian Williams (who replaced 20-year veteran anchor Tom Brokaw in 2004). No other individuals—not presidents, movie stars, or popes—have had such extensive contact with so many people. These network celebrities are recognized and heard by more people than anyone else on the planet. The networks demand that an anchor be the network's premier journalist, principal showman, top editor, star, symbol of news excellence, and single most important living logo.

Anchors, then, are both celebrities and newspeople. They are chosen for their mass appeal, but they must also bring journalistic expertise to their jobs. The anchors help select from thousands of hours of videotapes and hundreds of separate stories that will be squeezed into the twenty-two minutes of nightly network news (eight minutes are reserved for commercials). Each minute represents approximately 160 spoken words; the total number of words on the entire newscast is less than found on a single newspaper page. These inherent restrictions of the medium give great power to the anchors and their executive producers through their selection of what Americans will see and hear about the world each night.

All three network anchors are middle-aged, Anglo-Saxon, male Protestants. All share liberal and reformist social values and political beliefs.

Dan Rather, who deliberately projects an image of emotional intensity, has created both strong attachments and heated animosities among his audiences. He is most despised by conservatives because of his undisguised and passionate liberal views. Rather worked his way up through the ranks of CBS News following graduation from Sam Houston State College. He was a reporter and news director for the CBS affiliate station in Houston, then chief of the CBS London Bureau, and later Vietnam correspondent. He came to national prominence in 1966 as a CBS White House correspondent and took over the anchor position from Walter Cronkite in 1981.

The Canadian born Peter Jennings projects an image of thoughtful, urbane sophistication. He is widely traveled (his father was a journalist), but his formal education ended in the tenth grade. ABC's *World News Tonight with Peter Jennings* devotes slightly more time to international news than do its rival news shows.

The first change in anchors in two decades occurred when Brian Williams replaced the retiring Tom Brokaw at *NBC Nightly News* in 2004. Williams attended George Washington University and Catholic University, both in Washington, before becoming a White House intern under President Jimmy Carter. He served as a lobbyist for the American Association of Broadcasters before becoming a news reporter at stations in Philadelphia and Washington. He won the coveted NBC job as Chief White House News Correspondent in 1994 and became a regular face on NBC broadcasts.

The ratings race among the anchors is very close. Indeed, the closeness of those ratings may be driving the shows toward even more sensational themes, violent confrontations, and dramatic hype.

Political issues do not just "happen." The media are crucial to their development. Organized interest groups, professional public relations firms, government bureaucracies, political candidates, and elected officials all try to solicit the assistance of the media in shaping the political agenda. Creating an issue, publicizing it, dramatizing it, turning it into a "crisis," getting people to talk about it, and ultimately forcing government to do something about it are the tactics of agenda setting. The participation of the mass media is vital to their success.[6]

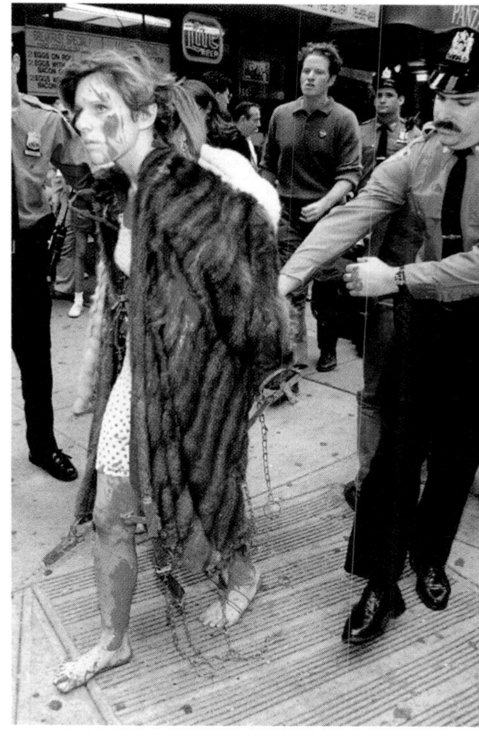

Groups hoping for free media coverage of their cause can improve their chances by framing their protests in dramatic form. Here, members of an animal-rights group attract the press by getting arrested during a protest against the fur industry, in which they painted themselves with red paint and wore leghold traps.

Interpreting The media not only decide what will be news; they also interpret the news for us. Editors, reporters, and anchors provide each story with an *angle*, an interpretation that places the story in a context and speculates about its meaning and consequences. The interpretation tells us what to think about the news.

News is presented in "stories." Reporters do not report facts; they tell stories. The story structure gives meaning to various pieces of information. Some common angles or themes of news stories are these:

- *Good guys versus bad guys:* for example, corrupt officials, foreign dictators, corporate polluters, and other assorted villains versus honest citizens, exploited workers, endangered children, or other innocents.
- *Little guys versus big guys:* for example, big corporations, the military, or insensitive bureaucracies versus consumers, taxpayers, poor people, or the elderly.
- *Appearance versus reality:* for example, the public statements of government officials or corporate executives versus whatever contradicting facts hardworking investigative reporters can find.

News is also "pictures." A story without visuals is not likely to be selected as television news in the first place. The use of visuals reinforces the angle. A close-up shot can reveal hostility, insincerity, or anxiety on the face of villains or can show fear, concern, sincerity, or compassion on the face of innocents. To emphasize elements of a story, an editor can stop the action, use slow motion, zoom the lens, add graphics, cut back and forth between antagonists, cut away for audience reaction, and so on. Videotaped interviews can be spliced to make the interviewees appear knowledgeable, informed, and sincere or, alternatively, ignorant, insensitive, and mean-spirited. The media jealously guard the right to edit interviews themselves, rejecting virtually all attempts by interviewees to review and edit their own interviews.

Socializing The media have power to socialize audiences to the political culture. News, entertainment, and advertising all contribute to **socialization**—to the learning of political values. Socialization through television and motion pictures begins in early childhood and continues throughout life. Most of the political information people learn comes to them through television—specific facts as well as general values. Election coverage, for example, shows "how democracy works," encourages political participation, and legitimizes the winner's control of government. Advertising shows Americans desirable middle-class standards of living even while it encourages people to buy automobiles, detergent, and beer, and entertainment programming socializes them to "acceptable" ways of life. Political values such as racial tolerance, sexual equality, and support for law enforcement are reinforced in movies, situation comedies, and police shows. Realistic "docudramas" seize on specific political themes, from abortion, to homosexuality, to drug use, to child abuse, to AIDS. Entertainment news programming such as the highly popular *60 Minutes* is now regular prime-time fare.

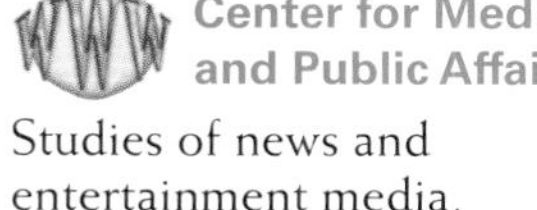

Center for Media and Public Affairs
Studies of news and entertainment media, including election coverage.
www.cmpa.com

socialization The learning of a culture and its values.

Persuading The media, in both paid advertising and news and entertainment programming, engage in direct efforts to change our attitudes; opinions, and behavior. Newspaper editorials have traditionally been employed for direct persuasion. A great deal of the political commentary on television news and interview programs is aimed at persuading people to adopt the views of the commentators. Even many entertainment programs and movies are intended to promote specific political viewpoints. But most direct persuasion efforts come to us through paid advertising.

Corporations may use their advertising dollars not only to promote sales of their product but also to convey the message that they are good citizens—sensitive to the environment, concerned with worker and consumer safety, devoted to providing more and better jobs, goods, and services to America.

Political campaigning is now largely a media battle, with paid political advertisements as the weapons. Candidates rely on professional campaign-management firms, with their pollsters, public relations specialists, advertising-production people, and media consultants, to carry on the fight (see Chapter 8).

Governments and political leaders must rely on persuasion through the mass media to carry out their programs. Presidents can take their message directly to people in televised speeches, news conferences, and the yearly State of the Union message. Presidents by custom are accorded television time whenever they request it. In this way, they can go over the heads of Congress and even the media executives and reporters themselves to communicate directly with the people.

In short, persuasion is central to politics, and the media are the key to persuasion.

The Business of the Media

National Association of Broadcasters

News and views of the media industry from their trade association.
www.nab.org

The business of the media is to gather mass audiences to sell to advertisers. Economic interest drives all media to try to attract and hold the largest numbers of readers and viewers in order to sell time and space to advertisers. Over one-quarter of all prime-time television (8–11 P.M.) is devoted to commercial advertising. Americans get more than one minute of commercials for every three minutes of news and entertainment. Television networks and commercial stations charge advertisers on the basis of audience estimates made by rating services. One rating service, A. C. Nielsen, places electronic boxes in a national sample of television homes and calculates the proportion of these homes that watch a program (the rating), as well as the proportion of homes with their television sets turned on that watch a particular program (the share). Newspapers' and magazines' advertising revenue is based primarily on circulation figures (see Table 6.2).

Soft Fluff versus Hard Programming Lightweight entertainment—"soft fluff"—prevails over serious programming in virtually all media, but particularly on television. Critics of the "boob tube" abound in intellectual circles, but the mass public clearly prefers fluffy entertainment programming. Political scientist Doris Graber writes:

> Although "lightweight" programming draws the wrath of many people, particularly intellectual elites, one can argue that their disdain constitutes intellectual snobbery. Who is to say that the mass public's tastes are inferior to those of elites? . . .Proof is plentiful that the mass public does indeed prefer light entertainment to more serious programs.[7]

And it is the mass public that advertisers want to reach. Channels devoted to highbrow culture, including public television stations, languish with low ratings.

TABLE 6.2 The Largest Circulation U.S. Newspapers and Magazines

Daily Newspapers		Magazines	
Rank Newspaper	**Circulation**	**Rank Magazine**	**Circulation**
1. *USA Today* (Arlington, Va.)	2,136,068	1. *AARP Modern Maturity*	17,360,979
2. *Wall Street Journal* (New York, N.Y.)	1,800,607	2. *Reader's Digest*	12,078,469
3. *Times* (New York, N.Y.)	1,113,000	3. *TV Guide*	9,067,124
4. *Times* (Los Angeles)	925,135	4. *Better Homes and Gardens*	7,605,204
5. *Post* (Washington, DC)	746,724	5. *National Geographic*	6,774,138
6. *Daily News* (New York, N.Y.)	715,070	6. *Good Housekeeping*	4,699,736
7. *Tribune* (Chicago)	679,327	7. *Family Circle*	4,634,069
8. *Post* (New York, N.Y.)	590,061	8. *Woman's Day*	4,205,049
9. *Newsday* (Long Island, N.Y.)	578,809	9. *TIME*	4,111,927
10. *Chronicle* (Houston)	552,052	10. *Ladies' Home Journal*	4,101,347

Source: Editor and Publisher International Yearbook 2003. Copyright © 2003 VNU Business Media, Inc. Used with permission.

News as TV Entertainment Increasingly news is being presented as television entertainment. In recent years there has been a dramatic increase in the number of entertainment-oriented, quasi-news programming, sometimes referred to as the "soft news media."[8] Soft news comes mainly in two formats: talk shows, both daytime and nighttime; and tabloid news programs (see Table 6.3). Even late-night entertainment programs—Jay Leno, David Letterman, Conan O'Brien—include comedy monologues that occasionally refer to political events or issues.

Soft news is no major source of information for people who are not interested in politics or public affairs. It is true, of course, that most soft news programming favors celebrity gossip, murder trials, sex scandals, disasters, and other human interest stories. But on some high-profile news issues these programs provide an otherwise inattentive public with what little information it absorbs.

TABLE 6.3 TV Soft News Programming

Network news magazines

Dateline NBC
20/20
Primetime Live
48 Hours
60 Minutes

Late-night TV talk shows

Jay Leno
David Letterman
Conan O'Brien
Politically Incorrect

Daytime TV talk shows

Oprah Winfrey
Rosie O'Donnell
Regis and Kelly
Geraldo Rivera
Phil Donahue

Network TV soft news

Extra
Entertainment Tonight
Inside Edition
A Current Affair
Access Hollywood

Cable TV soft news

E! Network
Black Entertainment Television
Comedy Central's *Daily Show*
MTV News

"Bad news" is far more likely to be seen on television than "good news." The 1999 shooting at Columbine High School in Colorado was one of the most widely covered news stories of the year.

60 Minutes attracts more viewers than any other soft news program. *Dateline* and 20/20 are not far behind. (Arguably these programs are oriented toward a somewhat more sophisticated audience than talk shows or tabloid news programs.) These programs, as well as *Entertainment Tonight* and Oprah Winfrey attract more viewers than any of the nightly network newscasts.

Politicians themselves have come to understand the importance of soft news programming in reaching segments of the public that seldom watch news programs, speeches or debates, or campaign advertising. Presidential candidates welcome invitations to appear with Oprah, or Leno, or Letterman, and try to reformulate their messages in a light, comedic style that fits the program.

The Media Conglomerates Mega-mergers in recent years have created corporate empires that spread across multiple media—television, film, newspapers, music, and the Internet. Conglomerate media corporations combined television broadcasting and cable programming, movie production and distribution, magazine and book publication, music recording, Internet access, and even sports and recreation. The seven multinational corporations listed in Table 6.4 currently dominate world media and cultural interests.

The Politics of the News

The politics of the news media are shaped by (1) their *economic interest,* (2) their *professional environment,* and (3) their *ideological leanings.*

Sensationalism The economic interest of the media—the need to capture and hold audience attention—creates a bias toward "hype" in the selection of news, its presentation, and its interpretation. To attract viewers and readers, the media bias the news toward violence, conflict, scandal, corruption, sex, scares of various sorts, and the personal lives of politicians and celebrities. News is selected primarily for its emotional impact on audiences, its social, economic, or political significance is secondary to the need to capture attention.

News must "touch" audiences personally, arouse emotions, and hold the interest of people with short attention spans. Scare stories—street crime, drug use, AIDS, nuclear power plant accidents, global warming, and a host of health alarms—make "good" news, for they cause viewers to fear for their personal safety. The sex lives of politicians, once by custom off limits to the press, are now public "affairs." Scandal and corruption among politicians, as well as selfishness and greed among business executives, are regular media themes.[9]

Negativism The media are biased toward bad news. Bad news attracts larger audiences than good news. Television news displays a pervasive bias toward the negative in American life—in government, business, the military, politics, education, and everywhere else. Bad-news stories on television vastly outnumber good-news stories.

Good news gets little attention. For example, television news watchers are not likely to know that illegal drug use is declining in the United States, that both the air and water are measurably cleaner today than in past decades, that the nuclear power industry has the best safety record of any major industry in the United States, and that the aged in America are wealthier and enjoy higher incomes than the nonaged. Television has generally failed to report these stories or, even worse, has implied that the opposite is true. Good news—stories about improved health

TABLE 6.4 The Media Empires

AOL-Time Warner

Television: HBO, TNT, TBS, CNN, CNNSI, CNNFN, Cinemax, Time Warner Cable
Motion Pictures: Warner Brothers, New Line Cinema, Castle Rock, Looney Tunes
Magazines: Time, People, Sports Illustrated, Fortune, plus twenty-eight other specialty magazines
Books: Warner Books, Little, Brown Publishing, Book-of-the-Month Club
Music: Warner Brothers Records, Atlantic Records, Elektra
Sports and Entertainment: Atlanta Braves, Atlanta Hawks, World Championship Wrestling
Internet: AOL, Netscape, CompuServe

Walt Disney

Television: ABC-TV, plus ten stations; ESPN, ESPN-2, Disney Channel, A&E, EI, Life-time
Motion Pictures: Walt Disney Pictures, Miramax, Touchstone
Music: Walt Disney Records, Mammoth
Sports and Recreation: Disney theme parks in Florida, California, France, Japan; cruise line; Anaheim, Mighty Ducks

Viacom

Television: CBS, plus thirty-four TV stations: MTV, TNN, Nickelodeon, Showtime, VH1, Nick-At-Nite
Motion Pictures: Paramount Pictures, Spelling, Viacom
Books: Simon & Schuster, Scribner, Free Press
Music: Famous Music Publishing
Sports and Recreation: Blockbuster Video, SportsLine, plus five Paramount parks

NewsCorp (Fox)

Television: Fox Network plus fifteen TV stations; Fox News, Fox Sports, Fox Family Channel, National Geographic Channel
Motion Pictures: 20th Century Fox, Searchlight
Books: HarperCollins
Magazines: TV Guide
Music: Mushroom Records
Sports and Recreation: Los Angeles Dodgers

Seagram

Television: USA Network
Motion Pictures: Universal Pictures
Music: MCA, Geffen, Def Jam, Motown
Sports and Recreation: Universal Studios theme parks in California and Florida

Sony

Television: Game Show Network
Motion Pictures: Columbia Pictures, Sony Pictures, Tri Star
Music: Columbia Records, Epic Records, Nashville Records
Sports and Recreation: Sony Theaters

General Electric

Television: NBC Network plus thirteen TV stations; CNBC, MSNBC

Source: Thomas R. Dye, *Who's Running America? The Bush Restoration,* 6th ed. (Upper Saddle River, N.J.: Prentice Hall, 2002).

statistics, longer life spans, better safety records, higher educational levels, for example—seldom provides the dramatic element needed to capture audience attention. The result is an overwhelming bad-news bias, especially on television.[10]

muckraking Journalistic exposés of corruption, wrongdoing, or mismanagement in government, business, and other institutions of society.

Muckraking The professional environment of reporters and editors predisposes them toward an activist style of journalism once dubbed **muckraking**. Reporters today view themselves as "watchdogs" of the public trust. They see themselves in noble terms—enemies of corruption, crusaders for justice, defenders of the disadvantaged. "The watchdog function, once considered remedial and subsidiary. . .[is now] paramount: the primary duty of the journalists is to focus attention on problems and deficits, failures and threats."[11] Their professional models are the crusading "investigative reporters" who expose wrongdoing in government, business, the military, and every other institution in society—except the media.

Many reporters go beyond the watchdog role and view themselves as adversaries of government. They see it as their job to expose politicians by unmasking their disguises, debunking their claims, and piercing their rhetoric. In short, until proven otherwise, political figures of any party or persuasion are presumed to be opponents. Even on entertainment shows, politicians are usually depicted as corrupt, hypocritical, and self-seeking, and business executives as crooked, greedy, and insensitive. Reporters are particularly proud of their work when it results in official investigations.

The "Feeding Frenzy" Occasionally, muckraking episodes grow into "**feeding frenzies**"—intense coverage of a scandal or event that blocks out most other news. Political scientist Larry Sabato describes the feeding frenzy: "In such situations a development is almost inevitably magnified and overscrutinized, the crush of cameras, microphones, and people, combined with the pressure of instant deadlines and live broadcasts, hype events and make it difficult to keep them in perspective. When a frenzy begins to gather, the intensity grows exponentially. . .. Television news time is virtually turned over to the subject of the frenzy."[12] Increasingly stiff competition among the media for attention and the need for round-the-clock cable news to fill long hours contribute to feeding frenzies.

Liberalism in the Newsroom The activist role that the media have taken upon themselves means that the personal values of reporters, editors, producers, and anchors are a very important element of American politics. The political values of the media are decidedly liberal and reformist. Political scientist Doris A. Graber writes about the politics of the media: "Economic and social liberalism prevails, especially in the most prominent media organizations. So does a preference for an internationalist foreign policy, caution about military intervention, and some suspicion about the ethics of established large institutions, particularly big business and big government."[13] Most Americans agree that media news coverage is biased and the bias is in a liberal direction (see *What Do You Think?* "Are the Media Biased?").

People for the American Way
Web site founded by Hollywood "liberals" to combat "right-wing" influence.
www.pfaw.org

Liberalism in Hollywood With a few exceptions, Hollywood producers, directors, writers, studio executives, and actors are decidedly liberal in their political views, especially when compared with the general public. Of the Hollywood elite, more than 60 percent describe themselves as liberal and only 14 percent as conservative,[14] whereas in the general public, self-described conservatives outnumber liberals by a significant margin. Hollywood leaders are five times more likely to be Democrats than Republicans, and Hollywood is a major source of Democratic Party campaign funds. On both economic and social issues, the Hollywood elite is significantly more liberal than the nation's general public or college-educated public.[15] (However, see *A Conflicting View*, "Fox News 'Fair and Balanced'?").

"feeding frenzy" Intense media coverage of a scandal or event that blocks out most other news.

The question remains, however, how much political influence Hollywood exercises over its audiences. Many television shows and motion pictures have little political content, they are designed almost exclusively to entertain, to gather the

WHAT DO YOU THINK?

Are the Media Biased?

Are the media biased, and if so in what direction—liberal or conservative? Arguments over media bias have grown in intensity as the media have come to play a central role in American politics.

Nearly three out of four Americans (74 percent) see "a fair amount" or "a great deal" of media bias in news coverage (see table below). And of those who see a bias, over twice as many see a liberal bias rather than a conservative bias. Indeed, even liberals see a liberal bias in the news; it is not a perception limited to conservatives, although they are more likely to see it. The liberal bias is much more likely to be seen by college graduates than by people who did not finish high school. It is also more likely to be seen by political activists than by those who engage in little or no political activity. However, African Americans are likely to see a conservative bias in the news, in contrast to the liberal bias perceived more often by whites.

Political bias is not Americans' only complaint about the national news media. Indeed, the most common complaint is that the media "ignore people's privacy" (80 percent). And majorities also complain about "one-sided coverage" (63 percent), "too negative" (61 percent), and "too much influence" (58 percent)—and they believe the media "abuse freedom of the press" (52 percent).

At the same time, Americans have high expectations of the role of the media in society: they expect the media to protect them from "abuse of power" by government, to hold public officials accountable, and to point out and help solve the problems of society.

Perceptions of Media Bias

	How Much Bias? "A Great Deal" or "Fair Amount" (%)	Direction of Bias: Liberal (%)	Direction of Bias: Conservative (%)
All	74	43	19
Race			
White	75	46	15
Black	64	24	40
Education			
Less than high school	56	29	33
High school graduate	75	42	19
College graduate	81	57	19
Ideology			
Liberal	70	41	22
Moderate	70	30	16
Conservative	81	57	19
Political Activism			
High	82	54	14
Low	76	42	22
None	65	34	22

Source: Data from *Media Monitor,* May/June 1997, Center for Media and Public Affairs, Washington, D.C. Reprinted by permission.

largest audiences for advertisers, and to sell theater tickets. Even shows or movies with political themes or pronounced political biases may not influence audiences as much as Hollywood would wish.

Conservatism on Talk Radio Talk radio is the one medium where conservatism prevails. The single most listened-to talk radio show is the *Rush Limbaugh*

A CONFLICTING VIEW

Fox News: "Fair and Balanced"?

For many years conservatives complained about the liberal tilt of television news. But despite their ample financial resources, conservative investors failed to create their own network or purchase an existing one. It was an Australian billionaire, Rupert Murdoch, who eventually came to the rescue of American conservatives.

Murdoch's global media empire, News Corp, includes Fox Network, Fox News Cable, 20th Century Fox, the *New York Post, The Times* and *The Sun* of London, HarperCollins Publishing, thirty-five local TV stations, and the Los Angeles Dodgers. He began his career by injecting glitz and vulgarity into previously dull Australian newspapers he inherited. The formula worked worldwide: the *New York Post* became a noisy tabloid after Murdoch took over (most memorable headline: "HEADLESS BODY FOUND IN TOPLESS BAR"), and Fox TV entertainment airs even more vulgar shows than the mainstream networks.

Murdoch himself is not particularly conservative in his politics, but he recognized an unfilled market for conservative views on American television. In 1996 he founded Fox News and hired Roger Ailes (former TV ad producer for Richard Nixon, Ronald Reagan, and George Bush) to head up the new network. Ailes quickly signed Bill O'Reilly (see *People in Politics* in Chapter 2) for an hourlong nightly conservative talk show. Brit Hume, one of the few prominent TV reporters considered to be a conservative, was made managing editor.

Fox proclaims "fair and balanced" news—"We report, you decide." The implication is that mainstream media has a liberal bias and that Fox is rectifying it with its own fair and balanced reporting. According to Fox, if its reporting appears conservative, it is only because the country has become so accustomed to left-leaning media that a truly balanced network just seems conservative.

Regular news reporting on Fox is not much different than other networks, except that Fox may cover some stories ignored by the mainstream media, e.g. political correctness to run amok on college campuses, ridiculous environmental regulations, hypocrisy among Hollywood liberals, etc. But it is the talk and commentary shows that outrage liberals and warm the hearts of conservatives. Liberals bold enough to appear on Fox are badgered mercilessly, while conservative guests are tossed softball questions.

The bottom line, financially as well as politically, is that Fox News is now the most watched cable news network, even surpassing CNN. Whatever its flaws, Fox News had added diversity of views to American television.

WWW **Accuracy in Media** A self-described watchdog organization critical of liberal bias in the media.
www.aim.org

Show, whose host regularly bashes "limousine liberals," "femi-Nazis," "environmental wackos," and "croissant people."[16] Talk radio might be portrayed as "call-in democracy." Callers respond almost immediately to reported news events. Call-in shows are the first to sense the public mood. Callers are not necessarily representative of the general public. Rather they are usually the most intense and outraged of citizens. But their complaints are early warning signs for wary politicians.

Mediated Elections

Political campaigning is largely a media activity, and the media, especially television, shape the nation's electoral politics.

The Media and Candidate-Voter Linkage The media are the principal link between candidates and the voters. At one time, political party organizations performed this function, with city, ward, and precinct workers knocking on doors, distributing campaign literature, organizing rallies and candidate appearances, and getting out the vote on election day. But television has largely replaced party organizations and personal contact as the means by which candidates communicate with voters. Candidates come directly into the living room via television—on the nightly news, in broadcast debates and interviews, and in paid advertising (see Table 6.5).

Media campaigning requires candidates to possess great skill in communications. Candidates must be able to project a favorable media *image*. The image is a composite of the candidate's words, mannerisms, appearance, personality, warmth, friendliness, humor, and ease in front of a camera. Policy positions have less to do with image than the candidate's ability to project personal qualities—leadership, compassion, strength, and character.

Television places an especially important emphasis on personal communication skills. Print media—newspapers and magazines—communicate only what is said. But *television communicates not only what is said but also how it is said.* For example, newspaper reports of Ronald Reagan's commonplace speeches and time-worn slogans failed to capture his true audience appeal, the folksy, warm, comfortable, reassuring manner, the humor and humility, and the likable personality that made Reagan "the Great Communicator." Reagan prevailed over hostile reporters, editors, and commentators because he was able to effectively communicate directly to mass audiences.

Conservative talk-show host Rush Limbaugh became the symbol for the talk-radio phenomenon of the 1990s. In addition to his daily three-hour radio broadcast, Limbaugh also had a nightly syndicated television show.

The Media and Candidate Selection The media strongly influence the early selection of candidates. Media coverage creates **name recognition**, an essential quality for any candidate. Early media "mentions" of senators, governors, and other political figures as possible presidential contenders help to sort out the field even before the election year begins. Conversely, media inattention can condemn aspiring politicians to obscurity.

TABLE 6.5 Sources of Political Campaign News in Presidential Election Years

Over time network news (ABC, CBS, NBC) has been declining as a major source of campaign news, while cable news (CNN, MSNBC, Fox) has been gaining. The Internet has also gained ground as a source of campaign news, yet it was cited by only 11 percent of Americans as their source of "most news."

News Sources	1992	1996	2000
Television	82%	72%	70%
Cable	29	21	36
Network	55	36	22
Local	29	23	21
Newspapers	57	60	39
Radio	12	19	15
Internet	—	3	11
Magazines	9	11	4

Note: Respondents were asked, "How did you get most of your news about the presidential election campaign? From television, from newspapers, from radio, from magazines or from the Internet?" Television users were then asked, "Did you get most of your news about the presidential campaign from network TV news, from local TV news, or from cable news networks such as CNN or MSNBC?" Respondents could name two sources.

Source: Pew Research Center for the People and the Press data from a telephone survey of 1,113 voters, November 10–12, 2000, http://www.people-press.org/post00que.htm.

Name recognition Public awareness of a candidate—whether they even know his or her name.

Serious presidential campaigns now begin at least six months before the New Hampshire primary (or almost a year and a half before the November presidential election). This early time period, "the invisible primary," is increasingly critical for campaigns.[17] Candidates must position themselves relative to competitors in their own party—build their name recognition, raise poll numbers, and build a campaign war chest. Inasmuch as campaign contributions are just beginning to come in, candidates have relatively little money to spend on paid advertising. They are forced to focus their efforts on attracting media attention by staging media events and issuing press releases. But from the media's perspective, campaign news is neither timely nor immediately relevant. Candidates must try to win media coverage by catering to the conflict and horse race stories preferred by the media. Press releases and speeches focused on issues are most likely to be ignored.

The media sort out the serious candidates early in a race. They even assign front-runner status, which may be either a blessing or a curse, depending on subsequent media coverage. In presidential primaries, the media play the *expectations game,* setting vote margins that the front-runner must meet in order to maintain *momentum.* If the front-runner does not win by a large enough margin, the media may declare the runner-up the "real" winner. This sorting out of candidates by the media influences not only voters, but—more important—financial contributors. The media-designated favorite is more likely to receive campaign contributions; financial backers do not like to waste money on losers. And as contributions roll in, the favorite can buy more television advertising, adding momentum to the campaign.

In presidential elections, the media sorting process places great emphasis on the early primary states, particularly New Hampshire, whose primary in early February is customarily the first contest in a presidential election year. Less than 1 percent of convention delegates are chosen by this small state, but media coverage is intense, and the winner quickly becomes the media-designated front-runner.[18]

Drudge Report Controversial site that links to stories not always carried by mainstream media. Links to all major media outlets. ***www.drudgereport.com***

The Media as Kingmakers In the early months of campaign, media coverage of candidates and their standing in public opinion polls tend to move together. Candidates who receive heavy media coverage usually do well in the polls. Good poll ratings create more media coverage. Good poll ratings and increased media coverage inspire campaign contributions, which then allow candidates to buy television advertising to further increase their poll numbers. Media-sponsored public opinion polls play an important role in kingmaking. The CBS/*New York Times* poll, the NBC/Associated Press poll, the ABC/*Washington Post* poll, and the CNN/*USA Today* poll are widely reported, they become the benchmarks for voters, telling them who the winners and losers are.

The name of the game for candidates early in the race is *exposure.* Even appearances on entertainment shows, once considered "unpresidential," are now highly valued by political candidates. They vie to appear on *Larry King Live* and on late-night talk shows hosted by Jay Leno, David Letterman, and Conan O'Brien.

In spite of the growing importance of the Internet, most people continue to get campaign and election news from television.

Media Effects on the Campaign Political candidates are aware of the importance of the media to their success. Their campaign managers must be "media-savvy" and they must hire media consultants early in the campaign. Candidates are advised to arrange daily newsworthy events to keep their name and image in the news. Television producers, reporters, and editors do not like to receive position papers on substantive issues or to present "talking heads"—shots only of the faces of speakers. Rather they prefer attention-getting, action-oriented, emotion-laden videotape. Candidates and their managers know this and so they attract media attention and resort to *media events*—staged activities designed to polish the image of the candidate. Candidates arrange to appear at police conventions, at schools, at hazardous waste sites, on aircraft carriers, at flag factories, and so on in order to project an image on television of their concern for crime, education, the environment, national defense, patriotism, and the like. (See also "Campaign Strategies" in Chapter 8.)

The Media and the Horse Race The media give election campaigns **horse-race coverage**: reporting on who is ahead or behind, what the candidates' strategies are, how much money they are spending, and, above all, what their current standing in the polls is. Such stories account for more than half of all television news coverage of an election. Additional stories are centered on *campaign* issues—controversies that arise on the campaign trail itself, including verbal blunders by the candidate—and *character* issues, such as the sex life of the candidate. In contrast, *policy* issues typically account for only about one-third of the television news stories in a presidential election campaign.[19]

The Bad News Bias The media's bad-news bias is evident in election campaigns as well as in general news reporting. Negative stories about all presidential candidates usually outnumber positive stories. The media generally see their function in political campaigns as reporting on the weaknesses, blunders, and vulnerabilities of the candidates. It might be argued that exposing the flaws of the candidates is an important function in a democracy. But the media's negative reporting about candidates and generally skeptical attitude toward their campaign speeches, promises, and advertisements may contribute to political alienation and cynicism among voters.

The media focus intense scrutiny on the personal lives of candidates—their marriages, sex lives, drug or alcohol use, personal finances, past friendships, military service, club memberships, and other potential sources of embarrassment. Virtually any past error in judgment or behavior by a candidate is given heavy coverage. But the media defend their attention to personal scandal on the ground that they are reporting on the "character issue." They argue that voters must have information on candidates' character as well as on their policy positions.

The Shrinking Sound Bite Reporters and newsroom anchors dominate television broadcasting. They report roughly three-quarters of all campaign news themselves. The candidates are allocated less than 15 percent of the time devoted to campaign news stories. (Other sources—pundits, commentators, voters, etc.—account for the remaining airtime.) The candidates themselves have very little direct contact with audiences in network news. The average **sound bite**—time allowed the candidates to speak on their own behalf—has shrunk to less than eight seconds!

The Media and Political Bias The media are very sensitive to charges of bias toward candidates or parties. Media people are overwhelmingly liberal and Democratic but generally try to deflect charges of political bias during an election campaign by giving almost equal coverage to both Democratic and Republican candidates. Moreover, the media report negatively on both Republicans and Democrats, although some scholars count more negative stories about Republican candidates.

horse-race coverage Media coverage of electoral campaigns that concentrates on who is ahead and who is behind, and neglects the issues at stake.

sound bite Words actually spoken by candidates themselves on news broadcasts.

The media are generally more critical of front-runners than of underdogs during a campaign. A horse race loses audience interest if one horse gets too far ahead, so the media tend to favor the underdog. "Frontrunners and incumbents consistently experienced the least balanced, least favorable news coverage."[20] During the presidential primary season, media attacks on an early favorite may result in gains for the underdog, who then becomes the new object of attack.

Freedom versus Fairness

THINK AGAIN

Should the media be legally required to be fair and accurate in reporting political news?

Complaints about the fairness of media are as old as the printing press. Most early newspapers in the United States were allied with political parties, they were not expected to be fair in their coverage. It was only in the early 1900s that many large newspapers broke their ties with parties and proclaimed themselves independent. And it was not until the 1920s and 1930s that the norms of journalistic professionalism and accuracy gained widespread acceptance.

The Constitution protects the *freedom* of the press; it was not intended to guarantee *fairness*. The First Amendment's guarantee of freedom of the press was originally designed to protect the press from government attempts to silence criticism. Over the years, the U.S. Supreme Court has greatly expanded the meaning of the free-press guarantee.

No Prior Restraint The Supreme Court has interpreted freedom of the press to mean that government may place no **prior restraint** on speech or publication (that is, before it is said or published). Originally, this doctrine was designed to prevent the government from closing down or seizing newspapers. Today, the doctrine prevents the government from censoring any news items. In the famous case of the Pentagon Papers, the *New York Times* and *Washington Post* undertook to publish secret information stolen from the files of the State Department and Defense Department regarding U.S. policy in Vietnam while the war was still going on. No one disputed the fact that stealing the secret material was illegal. What was at issue was the ability of the government to prevent the publication of stolen documents in order to protect national security. The Supreme Court rejected the national security argument and reaffirmed that the government may place no prior restraint on publication.[21] If the government wishes to keep military secrets, it must not let them fall into the hands of the American press.

Press versus Electronic Media In the early days of radio, broadcast channels were limited, and anyone with a radio transmitter could broadcast on any frequency. As a result, interference was a common frustration of early broadcasters. The industry petitioned the federal government to regulate and license the assignment and use of broadcast frequencies.

Federal Communication Commission

The FCC's official Web site with announcements and consumer information. *www.fcc.gov.*

The Federal Communications Commission (FCC) was established in 1934 to allocate broadcast frequencies and to license stations for "the public interest, convenience and necessity." The act clearly instructed the FCC: "Nothing in this Act shall be understood or construed to give the Commission the power of censorship." However, the FCC views a broadcast license and exclusive right to use a particular frequency as a *public trust.* Thus broadcasters, unlike newspapers and magazines, are licensed by a government agency and supposed to operate in the *public interest.*

prior restraint Power of government to prevent publication or to require approval before publication, generally prohibited by the First Amendment.

The Ownership Controversy Until recently the FCC did not permit a single firm or individual to own both a leading TV station and a leading newspaper in the same city. This FCC rule was defended as necessary to ensure diversity and competition in the news. But early in 2003 the FCC proposed to drop this rule as "no longer in the public interest." The FCC's new argument was that the old rule failed to recognize the explosion of media channels—hundreds of cable TV channels, satellite television, and the Internet. The major media corporations (see Table 6.2), not surprisingly, strongly supported dropping the ownership rule, as did the Bush administration. (The Chairman of the FCC, Michael Powell, is the son of Secretary of State Colin Powell.) But liberal interest groups, including Ralph Nader who founded Common Cause, rallied against the change, arguing that big corporations would eventually squeeze out independent stations and monopolize the news. But the FCC, by a 3–2 vote of the commissioners, dropped the ownership rule. It is likely that this action will encourage the continuing concentration of media ownership.

The Equal-Time Requirement The FCC requires radio and television stations that provide airtime to a political candidate to offer competing candidates the same amount of airtime at the same price. Stations are not required to give free time to candidates, but if stations choose to give free time to one candidate, they must do so for the candidate's opponents. But this **equal-time rule** does *not* apply to newscasts, news specials, or even long documentaries, nor does it apply to talk shows like *Larry King Live* (see *People in Politics:* "Larry King Live"). Nor does it apply to presidential press conferences or presidential addresses to the nation, although the networks now generally offer free time for a "Democratic response" to a Republican president, and vice versa. A biased news presentation does not require the network or station to grant equal time to opponents of its views. And it is important to note that newspapers, unlike radio and television, have never been required to provide equal time to opposing views (see *Compared to What?* "America's TV Culture in Perspective").

equal-time rule Federal Communications Commission (FCC) requirement that broadcasters who sell time to any political candidate must make equal time available to opposing candidates at the same price.

Libel and Slander

Communications that wrongly damage an individual are known in law as **libel** (when written) and **slander** (when spoken). The injured party must prove in court that the communication caused actual damage and was either false or defamatory. A damaging falsehood or words or phrases that are defamatory (such as "Joe Jones is a rotten son of a bitch") are libelous and are not protected by the First Amendment from lawsuits seeking compensation.

THINK AGAIN

Should the media report on all aspects of the private lives of public officials?

libel Writings that are false and malicious and are intended to damage an individual.

slander Oral statements that are false and malicious and are intended to damage an individual.

Public Officials Over the years, the media have sought to narrow the protection afforded public officials against libel and slander. In 1964 the U.S. Supreme Court ruled in the case of *New York Times v. Sullivan* that public officials did not have a right to recover damages for false statements unless they are made with "malicious intent."[22] The **Sullivan rule** requires public officials not only to show that the media published or broadcast false and damaging statements but also to prove they did so knowing that their statements were false and damaging or that they did so with "reckless disregard" for the truth or falsehood of their statements. The effect of the Sullivan rule is to free the media to say virtually anything about public officials. Indeed, the media have sought to expand the definition of "public officials" to "public figures"—that is, to include anyone they choose as the subject of a story.

Sullivan rule Court guideline that false and malicious statements regarding public officials are protected by the First Amendment unless it can be proven they were known to be false at the time they were made or were made with "reckless disregard" for their truth or falsehood.

"Absence of Malice" The First Amendment protects the right of the media to be biased, unfair, negative, sensational, and even offensive. Indeed, even *damaging*

PEOPLE IN POLITICS

Larry King Live

Who turned presidential politics into talk-show entertainment? A strong argument can be made that Larry King was personally responsible for changing the nature of presidential campaigning. It was Larry King who nudged frequent talk-show guest Ross Perot into the presidential arena. And it was Larry King who demonstrated to the candidates that the talk-show format was a good way to reach out to the American people.

Larry King's supremacy in talk-show politics came late in life, after a half-century of hustling and hard knocks, no college education, bouts of gambling followed by bankruptcy, and multiple marriages. King has written five books about himself, describing his rise from Brooklyn neighborhoods; his friendships with Jackie Gleason, Frank Sinatra, and other celebrities; and his hardscrabble life. As he tells it, he hung around a New York radio station for five years before taking a bus to Miami to try his luck first as a disk jockey and later as a sports announcer. After a decade in Miami, he had his own TV interview show, a talk show on radio, and a newspaper column, and he was color commentator for the Miami Dolphins. He lived the fast life, running up huge debts and dealing in shady financial transactions. He was arrested in 1971 on grand larceny charges; they were dropped only because the statute of limitations had expired. He lost his TV and radio shows and his newspaper column. He ended up in Shreveport, Louisiana, doing play by play for the World Football League. In 1975 he was bankrupt but back in Miami doing radio. In 1978 he moved to Washington to launch his Mutual Network radio talk show. As radio talk shows gained popularity, so did King. When CNN started twenty-four-hour broadcasting in 1982, the network turned to King to do an evening interview show, *Larry King Live.* At first, the show merely filled the space between the evening and the late news. A decade later, the show was making news itself.

King's success is directly attributable to his accommodating style. He actually listens to his guests; he lets them speak for themselves; he unashamedly plugs their books, records, and movies. He does *not* attack his guests; he does not assume the adversarial, abrasive style preferred by reporters like Sam Donaldson, Dan Rather, and Mike Wallace, or interviewers like Bill O'Reilly. An old-fashioned liberal himself, King appears comfortable interviewing politicians of every stripe. He lets guests talk about themselves. He tosses "softball" questions: "If I were to interview the president about an alleged sexual affair, I wouldn't ask if he'd had one, I'd ask him, 'How does it feel to read these things about yourself?' "

With his emphasis on feelings, emotions, and motives rather than on facts, it is little wonder that King's style attracts politicians . . . or that *Larry King Live* is the highest rated show on CNN.

Source: Adapted from "A King Who Can Listen." *Time,* 10/5/92; © 1992 Time, Inc., reprinted by permission.

falsehoods may be printed or broadcast as long as the media can show that the story was not deliberately fabricated by them with malicious intent, that is, if the media can show an "absence of malice."

Shielding Sources The media argue that the First Amendment allows them to refuse to reveal the names of their sources, even when this information is required in criminal investigations and trials. Thus far, the U.S. Supreme Court has not given blanket protection to reporters to withhold information from court proceedings. However, a number of states have passed *shield laws* protecting reporters from being forced to reveal their sources.

Politics and the Internet

The development of any new media of communications invariably affects political life. Just as, first, radio and, later, television reshaped politics in America, today the Internet is having its own unique impact on public affairs. The Internet pro-

COMPARED TO WHAT?

America's TV Culture in Perspective

America is a TV culture. Americans rely more on television for news and entertainment than people in other advanced industrial nations do. Perhaps more important, Americans have greater confidence in the media than other peoples do. Consider, for example, the question "Would you say you have a great deal of confidence, only some confidence, hardly any confidence, or no confidence at all in the media—press, radio, and television?" When this question was asked of a national sample of Americans, 69 percent responded that they had a great deal or at least some confidence in the media. But majorities in four other countries—France, Great Britain, Germany, and Spain—said they had little or no confidence in the media (see "confidence in the media" figure).

How much do the media influence key decisions in society? A majority of people in both the United States and these same European nations believe the media exert a large influence on public opinion. Americans appear to be closer to unanimity on this point (88 percent) than are Europeans. When people are asked how much influence the media exerts on particular governing institutions—the executive, the legislature, and the judiciary—Americans are much more likely to perceive strong media influence than are Europeans (see "media influence" figure).

Source: Adapted from Lawrence Parisot, "Attitudes about the Media: A Five Country Study," Public Opinion 43 (January/February 1988): 18, 60.

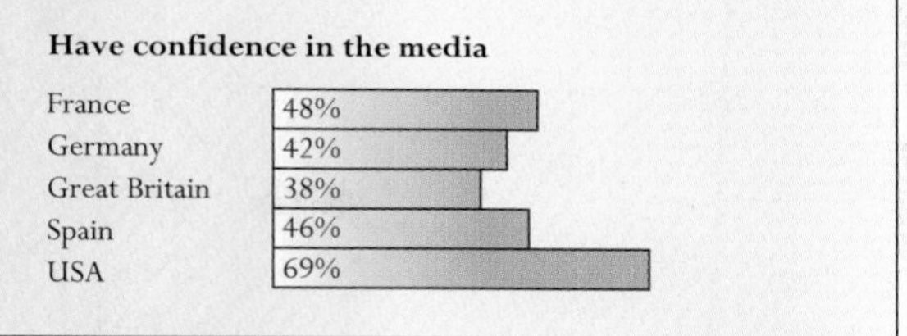

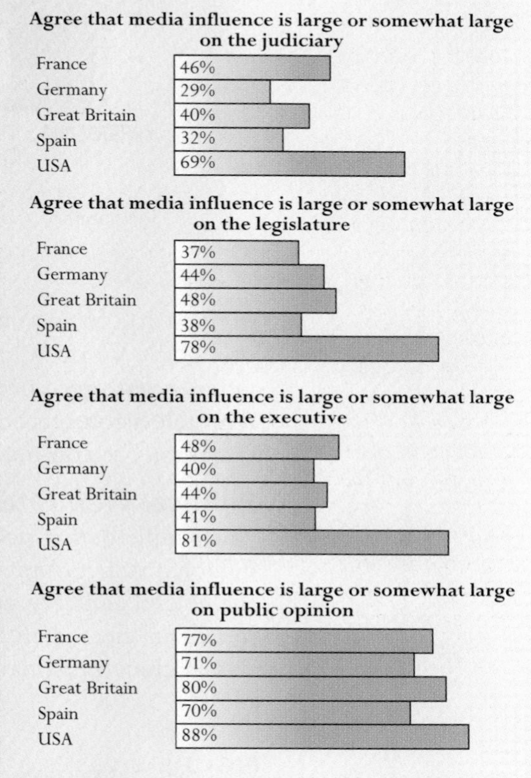

vides a channel for *interactive mass participation* in politics. It is unruly and chaotic by design. It offers the promise of abundant and diverse information in the opportunity for increased political participation. It empowers anyone who can design a Web site to spread their views, whether their views are profound and public-spirited or hateful and obscene.

Chaotic by Design During the Cold War, the RAND Corporation, a technological research think tank, proposed the Internet as a communications network that might survive a nuclear attack. It was deliberately designed to operate without any central authority or organization. Should any part of the system be destroyed, messages would still find their way to their destinations. The later development of the World Wide Web language allowed any connected computer

(© 1997 Jim Borgman, Cincinnati Enquirer. Reprinted with permission of King Feature Syndicate.)

in the world to communicate with any other connected computer. And introduction of the World Wide Web in 1992 also meant that users no longer needed computer expertise to communicate. By 1995 Americans were buying more computers than television sets and sending more e-mail than "snail mail." Since then, Internet usage has continued to mushroom (see Figure 6.2).

Political Web Sites Abound The Internet is awash in political Web sites. The simple query "politics" on a standard search program can return well over a million matches. Almost all federal agencies, including the White House, Congress, the federal judiciary, and executive departments and agencies, maintain Web sites. Individual elected officeholders, including all members of Congress, maintain sites that include personal biographies, committee assignments, legislative accom-

FIGURE 6.2
Growth of Internet Users

Source: Statistical Abstract of the United States, 2004.

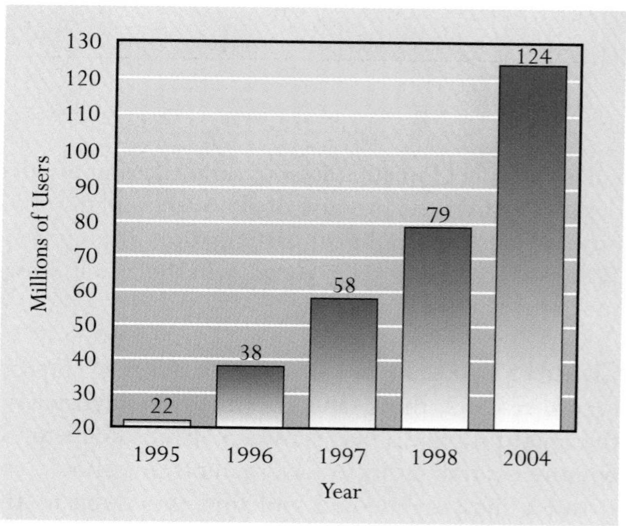

plishments, issue statements, and press releases. The home pages of the Democratic and Republican parties offer political news, issue positions, opportunities to become active in party affairs, and invitations to send them money. No serious candidate for major public office lacks a Web site; these campaign sites usually include flattering biographies, press releases, and, of course, invitations to contribute financially to the candidates' campaigns. All major interest groups maintain Web sites—business, trade, and professional groups; labor unions; ideological and issue groups; women's, religious, environmental, and civil rights groups. Indeed, this virtual tidal wave of politics on the Internet may turn out to offer too much information in too fragmented a fashion, thereby simply adding to apathy and indifference.

Internet Uncensored The Internet allows unrestricted freedom of expression, from scientific discourses on particle physics and information on the latest developments in medical science, to invitations to join in paramilitary "militia" and offers to exchange pornographic photos and messages. Commercial sex sites outnumber any other category on the Web.

Annenberg Public Policy Center

The Annenberg Center of the University of Pennsylvania conducts research on political use of the media, including the Internet.

www.appcpenn.org

Congress unsuccessfully attempted to outlaw "indecent" and "patently offensive" material on the Internet and its Communications Decency Act of 1996. But the U.S. Supreme Court gave the Internet First Amendment protection in 1997 in *Reno v. American Civil Liberties Union.*[23] The Court recognized the Internet as an important form of popular expression protected by the Constitution. Congress had sought to make it a federal crime to send or display "indecent" material to persons under 18 years of age (material describing or displaying sexual activities or organs in "patently offensive" fashion). But the Supreme Court reiterated its view that government may not limit the adult population to "only what is fit for children." The Court decision places the burden of filtering Internet messages on parents. Filtering software can be installed on home computers, but a First Amendment issue arises when it is installed on computers in public libraries.

The Privacy Problem While the Internet facilitates the exercise of the right of free expression, it poses a problem for the right of privacy. Government and private industry have been collecting information on individuals for many years, from driving records to credit reports. But the Internet offers a vastly expanded and easily accessible source of data on individuals, including their earnings, purchases, hobbies, medical condition, reading habits, and more. Surfing the Internet may seem anonymous but it is not. Web sites can easily track visitors and may even send out "cookies"—files quietly stored in visitors' computers that continue to provide identification and information. Encryption (coding) programs are available, but the Federal Bureau of Investigation demands "recovery keys" from manufacturers in order to maintain surveillance.

Media Effects: Shaping Political Life

What effects do the media have on public opinion and political behavior? Let us consider media effects on (1) information and agenda setting, (2) values and opinions, and (3) behavior. These categories of effects are ranked by the degree of influence the media are likely to have over us. The strongest effects of the media are on our information levels and societal concerns. The media also influence values and opinions, but the strength of media effects in these areas is diluted by many

THINK AGAIN

Is your choice of candidates in elections affected by their advertising?

UP CLOSE

The Media Age

The print media—newspapers, magazines, and books—have played a major role in American politics since colonial times. But today the electronic media—radio, television, and cable television—dominate in political communication.

Radio was widely introduced into American homes in the 1920s and 1930s, allowing President Franklin D. Roosevelt to become the first "media president," directly communicating with the American people through radio "fireside chats." After World War II, the popularity of television spread quickly; between 1950 and 1960, the percentage of homes with TV sets grew from 9 to 87.

Some notable political media innovations over the years:

- **1952:** The first paid commercial TV ad in a presidential campaign appeared, on behalf of Dwight D. Eisenhower. The black-and-white ad began with a voice-over—"Eisenhower answers the nation!"—followed by citizens asking favorable questions and Eisenhower responding, and ending with a musical jingle: "I like Ike." Although crude by current standards, it nevertheless set a precedent in media campaigning.
- **1952:** The "Checkers speech" by Eisenhower's running mate, Richard M. Nixon, represented the first direct television appeal to the people over the heads of party leaders. Nixon was about to be dumped from the Republican ticket for hiding secret slush-fund money from campaign contributors. He went on national television with an emotional appeal, claiming that the only personal item he ever took from a campaign contributor was his daughters' little dog, Checkers. Thousands of viewers called and wired in sympathy. Ike kept Nixon on the ticket.
- **1960:** The first televised debate between presidential candidates featured a youthful, handsome John F. Kennedy against a shifty-eyed Richard M. Nixon with a pronounced "five o'clock shadow." Nixon doggedly scored debater points, but JFK presented a cool and confident image and spoke directly to the viewers. The debate swung the popular tide toward Kennedy, who won in a very tight contest. Nixon attributed his defeat to his failure to shave before the broadcast.
- **1964:** The first "negative" TV ad was the "Daisy Girl" commercial sponsored by the Lyndon Johnson campaign against Republican conservative Barry Goldwater. It implied that Goldwater would start a nuclear war. It showed a little girl picking petals off a daisy while an ominous voice counted down "10-9-8-7 . . ." to a nuclear explosion, followed by a statement that Lyndon Johnson could be trusted to keep the peace.
- **1976:** President Gerald Ford was the first incumbent president to agree to a televised debate. (No televised presidential debates were held in the Nixon-Humphrey race in 1968 or in the Nixon-McGovern race in 1972. Apparently Nixon had learned his lesson.) Ford stumbled badly, and Jimmy Carter went on to victory.
- **1982:** CNN (Cable News Network), introduced by the maverick media mogul Ted Turner, began twenty-four-hour broadcasting.
- **1991:** The Persian Gulf War was the first war to be fought live on television. (Although film and videotape reports of the Vietnam War had been important molders of public opinion in America, the technology of that era did not allow live reporting.) In the Gulf War, the Iraqi government permitted CNN to continue live broadcasts from Baghdad, including spectacular coverage of the first night's air raids on the city.
- **1992:** In the presidential election, television talk shows became a major focus of the campaign. Wealthy independent candidate Ross Perot actually conducted an all-media campaign, rejecting

other influences. Finally, it is most difficult to establish the independent effect of the media on behavior.

Information and Agenda-Setting Effects The media strongly influence what we know about our world and how we think and talk about it. Years ago, foreign-policy expert Bernard Cohen, in the first book to assess the effects of the media on foreign policy, put it this way: "The mass media may not be successful

The first televised presidential election debates were in 1960 between Senator John F. Kennedy and Vice President Richard Nixon. Nixon came armed with statistics, but his dour demeanor, "five o'clock shadow," and stiff presentation fared poorly in contrast to Kennedy's open, relaxed, confident air.

in-person appearances in favor of such media techniques as half-hour "infomercials."

- **1994–95:** The arrest and trial of celebrity O.J. Simpson on murder charges so dominated the national news that more television time was devoted to the O.J. story than to the actions of the president and Congress.
- **1996:** The presidential election was given less television time and newspaper space than previous elections. Clinton's large lead throughout the campaign, public boredom with Whitewater and other scandals, and Dole's lackluster performance frustrated reporters in search of drama. Network TV news gave Clinton twice as much positive coverage as Dole.
- **1997–98:** Sex scandals involving Bill Clinton dominated the news and talk shows, but public opinion polls gave the president the highest approval ratings of his two terms in office.
- **2000:** On election night, the networks prematurely called the presidential election, first for Gore and then for Bush, causing confusion among the public and embarrassment for the networks. A "Florida feeding frenzy" ensued over the next month as television blanketed every phase of that state's recount, from local election officials staring at punch-card ballots to state and U.S. Supreme Court arguments.
- **2001:** Dramatic television coverage of commercial aircraft crashing into the World Trade Center and videotape of the collapse of the twin giant buildings shocked Americans and inspired the "War on Terrorism."
- **2003:** Reporters were "embedded" with American troops in the Iraqi War, providing ground-level narratives and video of combat.

in telling people what to think, but the media are stunningly successful in telling their audience what to think about."[24] (see *Up Close:* "The Media Age").

However, **information overload** diminishes the influence of the media in determining what we think about. So many communications are directed at us that we cannot possibly process them all. A person's ability to recall a media report depends on repeated exposure to it and reinforcement through personal experience. For example, an individual who has a brother in a trouble spot in the Middle East

information overload
Situation in which individuals are subjected to so many communications that they cannot make sense of them.

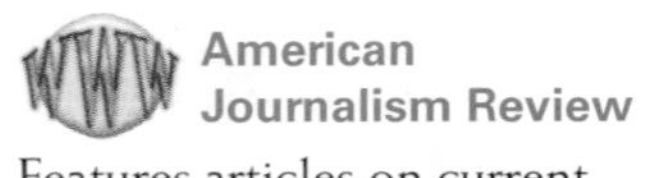

American Journalism Review

Features articles on current topics in print and television reporting, together with links to newspapers, television networks and stations, radio stations, media companies, etc. *www.ajr.org*

is more likely to be aware of reports from that area of the world. But too many voices with too many messages cause most viewers to block out a great deal of information.

Information overload may be especially heavy in political news. Television tells most viewers more about politics than they really want to know. Political scientist Austin Ranney writes, "The fact is that for most Americans politics is still far from being the most interesting and important thing in life. To them, politics is usually confusing, boring, repetitious, and above all irrelevant to the things that really matter in their lives."[25]

Effects on Values and Opinions The media often tell us how we *should* feel about news events or issues, especially those about which we have no prior feelings or experiences. The media can reinforce values and attitudes we already hold. However, the media seldom *change* our preexisting values or opinions. Media influence over values and opinions is reduced by **selective perception,** mentally screening out information or opinions we disagree with. People tend to see and hear only what they want to see and hear. For example, television news concentration on scandal, abuse, and corruption in government has not always produced the liberal, reformist values among viewers that media people expected. On the contrary, the focus of network executives on governmental scandals—Watergate, the Iran-Contra scandal, the sexual antics of politicians, congressional check kiting, and so on—has produced feelings of general political distrust and cynicism toward government and the political system. These feelings have been labeled **television malaise,** a combination of social distrust, political cynicism, feelings of powerlessness, and disaffection from parties and politics that seems to stem from television's emphasis on the negative aspects of American life.

selective perception Mentally screening out information or opinions with which one disagrees.

television malaise Generalized feelings of distrust, cynicism, and powerlessness stemming from television's emphasis on the negative aspects of American life.

The media do not *intend* to create television malaise; they are performing their self-declared watchdog role. They expect their stories to encourage liberal reform of our political institutions. But the result is often alienation rather than reform.

Direct Effects on Public Opinion Can the media change public opinion, and if so, how? For many years, political scientists claimed that the media had

Late night television is now a popular campaign forum. Young people rely heavily on the Jay Leno, David Letterman, and Conan O'Brien shows for their political news.

only minimal effects on public opinions and behavior. This early view was based largely on the fact that newspaper editorial endorsements seldom affected people's votes. But serious research on the effects of television tells a different story.

In an extensive study of eighty policy issues over fifteen years, political scientists examined public opinion polls on various policy issues at a first point in time, then media content over a following interval of time, and finally public opinion on these same issues at the end of the interval. The purpose was to learn if media content—messages scored by their relevance to the issue, their salience in the broadcast, their pro/con direction, the credibility of the news source, and quality of the reporting—changed public opinion. Most people's opinions remained constant over time (opinion at the first time period is the best predictor of opinion at the second time period). However, when opinion did change, it changed in the direction supported by the media. "News variables alone account for nearly half the variance in opinion change." Other findings include the following:

- Anchors, reporters, and commentators have the greatest impact on opinion change. Television newscasters have high credibility and trust with the general public. Their opinions are crucial in shaping mass opinion.
- Independent experts interviewed by the media have a substantial impact on opinion, but not as great as newscasters themselves.
- A popular president can also shift public opinion somewhat. Unpopular presidents do not have much success as opinion movers, however.
- Interest groups on the whole have a slightly negative effect on public opinion. "In many instances they seem actually to have antagonized the public and created a genuine adverse effect"; such cases include Vietnam War protesters, nuclear freeze advocates, and other demonstrators and protesters, even peaceful ones.[26]

THINK AGAIN

Are media professionals—news reporters, editors, anchors—the true voice of the people in public affairs?

Effects on Behavior Many studies have focused on the effects of the media on behavior: studies of the effects of TV violence, studies of the effects of television on children, and studies of the effects of obscenity and pornography.[27] Although it is difficult to generalize from these studies, television appears more likely to reinforce behavioral tendencies than to change them. For example, televised violence may trigger violent behavior in children who are already predisposed to such behavior, but televised violence has little behavioral effect on average children.[28] Nevertheless, we know that television advertising sells products. And we know that political candidates spend millions to persuade audiences to go out and vote for them on election day. Both manufacturers and politicians create name recognition, employ product differentiation, try to associate with audiences, and use repetition to communicate their messages. These tactics are designed to affect our behavior both in the marketplace and in the election booth.

Political ads are more successful in motivating a candidate's supporters to go to the polls than they are in changing opponents into supporters. It is unlikely that voters who dislike a candidate will be persuaded by political advertising to change their votes. But many potential voters are undecided, and the support of many others is dubbed "soft." Going to the polls on election day requires effort—people have errands to do, it may be raining, they may be tired. Television advertising is more effective with the marginal voters.

SUMMARY NOTES

- The mass media in America not only report on the struggle for power, they are participants themselves in that struggle.
- It is only through the media that the general public comes to know about political events, personalities, and issues. Newsmaking—deciding what is or is not "news"—is a major source of media power. Media coverage not only influences popular discussion but also forces public officials to respond.
- Media power also derives from the media's ability to set the agenda for public decision making—to determine what citizens and public officials will regard as "crises," "problems," or "issues" to be resolved by government.
- The media also exercise power in their interpretation of the news. News is presented in story form, pictures, words, sources, and story selection all contribute to interpretation.
- The media play a major role in socializing people to the political culture. Socialization occurs in news, entertainment, and advertising.
- The politics of the media are shaped by their economic interest in attracting readers and viewers. This interest largely accounts for the sensational and negative aspects of news reporting.
- The professional environment of newspeople encourages an activist, watchdog role in politics. The politics of most newspeople are liberal and Democratic.
- Political campaigning is largely a media activity. The media have replaced the parties as the principal linkage between candidates and voters. But the media tend to report the campaign as a horse race, at the expense of issue coverage, and to focus more on candidates' character than on their voting records or issue positions.
- The First Amendment guarantee of freedom of press protects the media from government efforts to silence or censor them and allows the media to be "unfair" when they choose to be. The Federal Communications Commission exercises some modest controls over the electronic media, since the rights to exclusive use of broadcast frequencies is a *public trust.*
- Public officials are afforded very little protection by libel and slander laws. The Supreme Court's Sullivan rule allows even damaging falsehoods to be written and broadcast as long as newspeople themselves do not deliberately fabricate lies with "malicious intent" or "reckless disregard."
- Media effects on political life can be observed in (1) information and agenda setting, (2) values and opinions, and (3) behavior—in that order of influence. The media strongly influence what we know about politics and what we talk about. The media are less effective in changing existing opinions, values, and beliefs than they are in creating new ones. Nevertheless, the media can change many people's opinions, based on the credibility of news anchors and reporters. Direct media effects on behavior are limited. Political ads are more important in motivating supporters to go to the polls, and in swinging undecided or "soft" voters, than in changing the minds of committed voters.

KEY TERMS

mass media 172
newsmaking 175
agenda setting 175
socialization 177
muckraking 181
"feeding frenzy" 182
name recognition 185
horse-race coverage 187
sound bite 187
prior restraint 188
equal-time rule 189
libel 189
slander 189
Sullivan rule 189
information overload 195
selective perception 196
television malaise 196

SUGGESTED READINGS

Alterman, Eric. *What Liberal Media?* New York: Simon & Schuster, 2003. A contrarian argument that the media does *not* have a liberal bias but rather bends over backward to include conservative views.

Ansolabehere, Stephen, Roy Behr, and Shanto Iyengar. *The Media Game: American Politics in the Television Age.* New York: Macmillan, 1993. A comprehensive text assessing the changes in the political system brought about by the rise of television since the 1950s.

Fallows, James. *Breaking the News: How the Media Undermine American Democracy.* New York: Pantheon, 1996. An argument that today's arrogant, cynical, and scandal-minded news reporting is turning readers and viewers away and undermining support for democracy.

Goldberg, Bernard *Bias: A CBS Insider Exposes How the Media Distort the News.* New York: Perennial, 2003. The title says it all.

Graber, Doris A. *Mass Media and American Politics.* 6th ed. Washington, D.C.: CQ Press, 2002. A wide-ranging description of media effects on campaigns, parties, and elections, as well as on social values and public policies.

Lichter, Robert S., Stanley Rothman, and Linda S. Lichter. *The Media Elite.* Bethesda, Md.: Adler and Adler, 1986. A thorough study of the social and political values of top leaders in the mass media, based on extensive interviews of key people in the most influential media outlets.

Patterson, Thomas E. *Out of Order.* New York: Random House, 1994. The antipolitical bias of the media poisons national election campaigns; policy questions are ignored in favor of the personal characteristics of candidates, their campaign strategies, and their standing in the horse race.

Prindle, David F. *Risky Business.* Boulder, Colo.: Westview Press, 1993. An examination of the politics of Hollywood, its liberalism, activism, self-indulgence, and celebrity egotism.

Sabato, Larry J. *Feeding Frenzy: How Attack Journalism Has Transformed American Politics.* New York: Free Press, 1992. A strong argument that the media prefer "to employ titillation rather than scrutiny" and as a result produce "trivialization rather than enlightenment."

CHAPTER 7

POLITICAL PARTIES AND INTEREST GROUPS: ORGANIZING POLITICS

CHAPTER OUTLINE

The Power of Organization
Political Parties and Democratic Government
Parties as Organizers of Elections
National Party Conventions
Party Finances
Party Voters
Why the Two-Party System Persists
Interest-Group Power
The Organized Interests in Washington
The Washington Lobbyists
The Fine Art of Lobbying
Lobbying the Bureaucracy
Lobbying the Courts

The Power of Organization

In the struggle for power, organization grants advantage. Italian political scientist Gaetano Mosca once put it succinctly: "A hundred men acting uniformly in concert, with a common understanding, will triumph over a thousand men who are not in accord and can therefore be dealt with one by one."[1] Thus politics centers on organization—on organizing people to win office and to influence public policy.

Parties and interest groups function as intermediaries between individuals and government. They organize individuals to give them power in selecting government officials—who governs—and in determining public policy—for what ends. Generally, **political parties** are more concerned with winning public office in elections than with influencing policy, whereas **interest groups** are more directly concerned with public policy and involve themselves with elections only to advance their policy interests (see Figure 7.1). In other words, parties and interest groups have an informal division of functions, with parties focusing on personnel and interest groups focusing on policy. Yet both organize individuals for more effective political action.

Political Parties and Democratic Government

"Political parties created democracy, and modern democracy is unthinkable save in terms of the parties."[2] Traditionally, political scientists have praised parties as indispensable to democratic government. They have argued that parties are essential for organizing popular majorities to exercise control over government. The development of political parties in all the democracies of the world testifies to the underlying importance of parties to democratic government. But political parties in the United States have lost their preeminent position as instruments of democracy. Other structures and organizations in society—interest groups, the mass media, independent campaign organizations, primary elections, social welfare agencies—now perform many of the functions traditionally regarded as prerogatives of

THINK ABOUT POLITICS

1 Generally speaking, how would you identify yourself: as a Republican, Democrat, Independent, or something else?
Republican ● Democrat ●
Independent ● Other ●

2 Which major party does a better job of protecting the Social Security system?
Republican ● Democrat ●

3 Which major party does a better job of handling foreign affairs?
Republican ● Democrat ●

4 Should elected officials be bound by their party's platform?
Yes ● No ●

5 Do special-interest groups in America obstruct the majority of citizens' wishes on public policy?
Yes ● No ●

6 Should interest groups be prohibited from making large campaign contributions in their effort to influence public policy?
Yes ● No ●

7 If a lobbyist makes a campaign contribution to a Congress member, hoping to gain support for a bill, is this a form of bribery?
Yes ● No ●

How much power do political parties really have to determine who gets what in America? What role do interest groups play in politics? Their organization, their money, and their influence in Washington raise the possibility that interest groups, rather than individuals, may in fact hold the real power in politics.

FIGURE 7.1 Political Organizations as Intermediaries

All political organizations function as intermediaries between individuals and government. Parties are concerned primarily with winning elected office, interest groups are concerned with influencing policy.

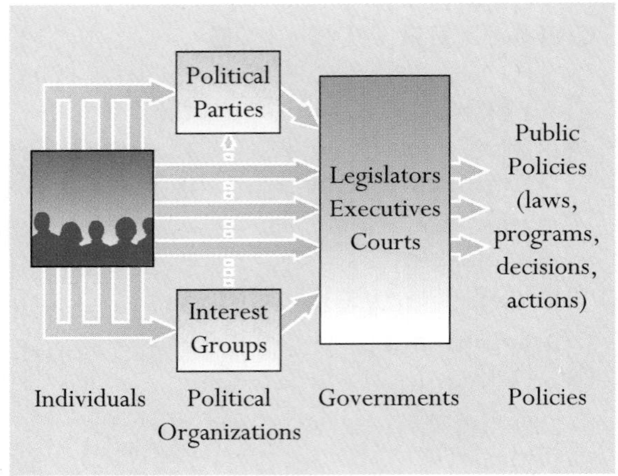

THINK AGAIN

Should elected officials be bound by their party's platform?

political parties. Nevertheless, the Democratic and Republican parties remain important organizing structures for politics in the United States (see Figure 7.2).

"Responsible" Parties in Theory In theory, political parties function in a democracy to organize majorities around broad principles of government in order to win public office and enact these principles into law. A "responsible" party should:

- Adopt a platform setting forth its principles and policy positions.
- Recruit candidates for public office who agree with the party's platform.
- Inform and educate the public about the platform.
- Organize and direct campaigns based on platform principles.
- Organize the legislature to ensure party control in policy making.
- Hold its elected officials responsible for enacting the party's platform.

If responsible, disciplined, policy-oriented parties competed for majority support, *if* they offered clear policy alternatives to the voters, and *if* the voters cast their ballots on the basis of these policy options, *then* the winning party would have a "policy mandate" from the people to guide the course of government. In that way, the democratic ideal of government by majority rule would be implemented.

political parties
Organizations that seek to achieve power by winning public office.

interest groups
Organizations that seek to influence government policy.

responsible party model
System in which competitive parties adopt a platform of principles, recruiting candidates and directing campaigns based on the platform, and holding their elected officials responsible for enacting it.

Winning Wins over Principle However, the **responsible party model** never accurately described the American party system. The major American parties have been loose coalitions of individuals and groups seeking to attract sufficient votes to gain control of government. *Winning has generally been more important than any principles or policies.* America's major parties must appeal to tens of millions of voters in every section of the nation and from all walks of life. If a major party is to acquire a majority capable of controlling the U.S. government, it cannot limit its appeal by relying on a single unifying principle. Instead, it must form coalitions of voters from as many sectors of the population as it can. Major American parties therefore usually do not emphasize particular principles or ideologies so much as try to find a common ground of agreement among many different people. This emphasis does not mean no policy differences exist between the American parties. On the contrary, each party tends to appeal to a distinctive coalition of interests, and therefore each party expresses somewhat distinctive policy views (see *What Do You Think?:* "Which Party Does a Better Job?").

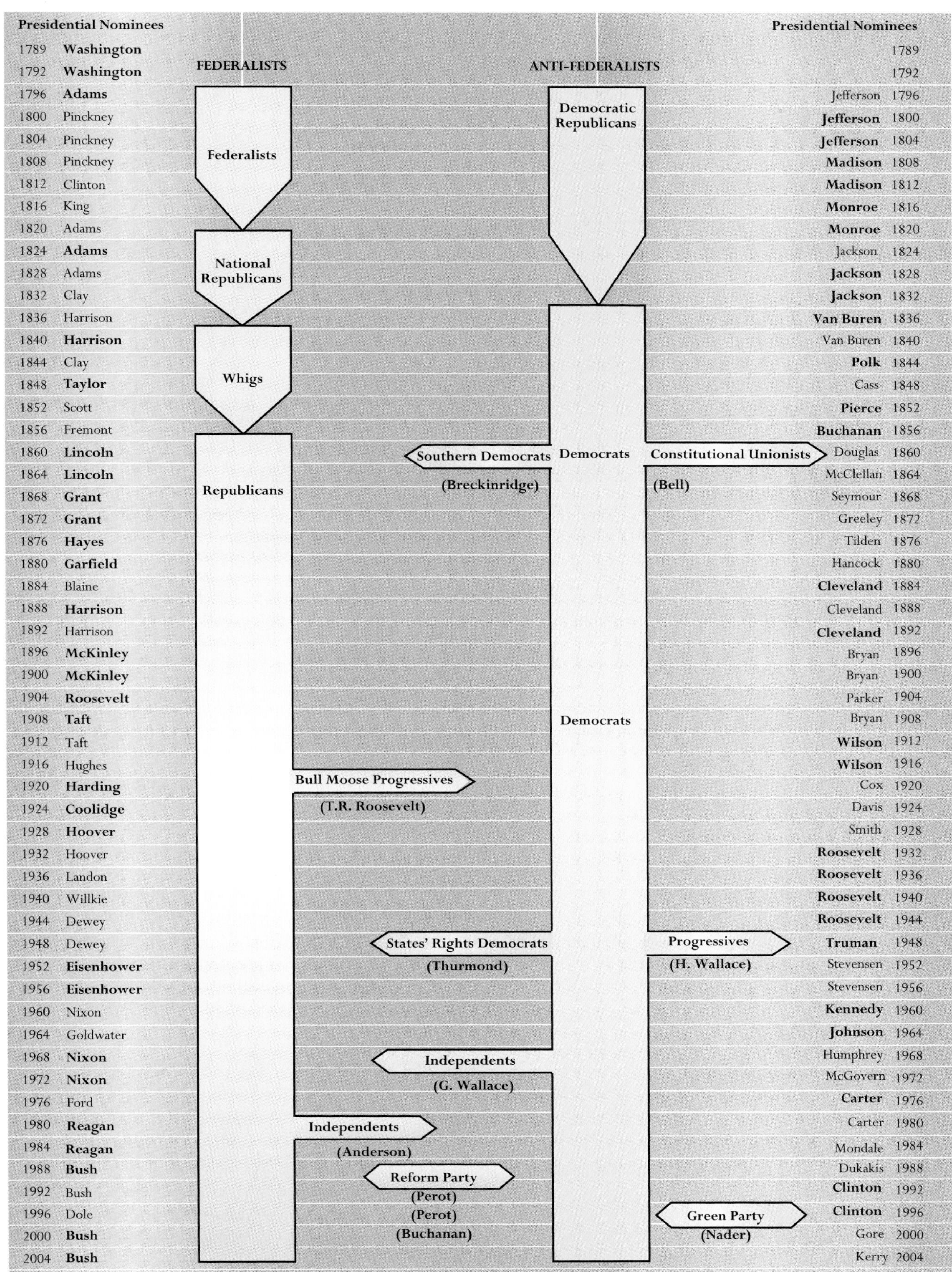

FIGURE 7.2 Change and Continuity in the American Party System

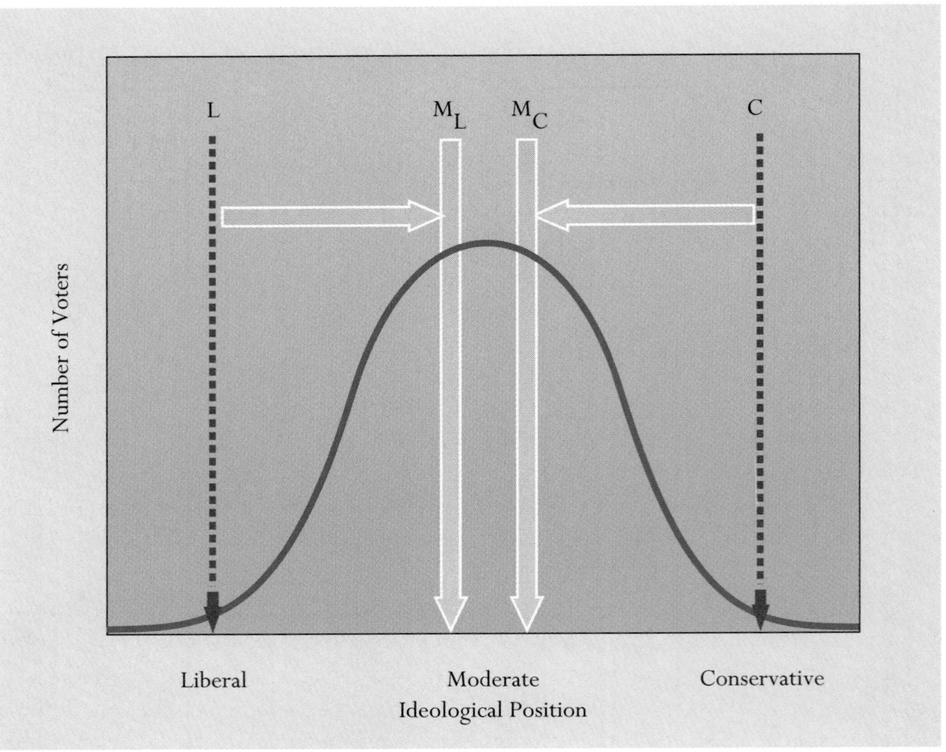

FIGURE 7.3 Winning versus Principle

Why don't we have a party system based on principles, with a liberal party and a conservative party, each offering the voters a real ideological choice? Let's assume that voters generally choose the party closest to their own ideological position. If the liberal party (L) took a strong ideological position to the left of most voters, the conservative party (C) would move toward the center, winning more moderate votes, even while retaining its conservative supporters, who would still prefer it to the more liberal opposition party. Likewise, if the conservative party took a strong ideological position to the right of most voters, the liberal party would move to the center and win. So both parties must abandon strong ideological positions and move to the center, becoming moderate in the fight for support of moderate voters.

Democratic Party One of the main parties in American politics; it traces its origins to Thomas Jefferson's Democratic-Republican Party, acquiring its current name under Andrew Jackson in 1828.

Republican Party One of the two main parties in American politics; it traces its origins to the antislavery and nationalist forces that united in the 1850s and nominated Abraham Lincoln for president in 1860.

GOP "Grand Old Party"—popular label for the Republican Party.

In their efforts to win, major American political parties strive to attract the support of the large numbers of people near the center of public opinion. Generally more votes are at the center of the ideological spectrum—the middle-of-the-road—than on the extreme liberal or conservative ends. Thus *no real incentive exists for vote-maximizing parties to take strong policy positions in opposition to each other.* As the Democratic and Republican policy positions approach the center, the parties seem to echo each other, and critics attack them as Tweedledee and Tweedledum (see Figure 7.3).

Party and Ideology Despite incentives for the parties to move to the center of the political spectrum, the Republican and Democratic parties are perceived by the public as ideologically separate. The electorate tends to perceive the Republican Party as conservative and the Democratic Party as liberal.

Indeed, polls suggest that Republican voters described themselves as conservatives far more often than as liberals. And Democratic voters are more likely to identify themselves as liberals than as conservatives, although many like to think of themselves as moderates (see Table 7.1).

TABLE 7.1 Party and Ideology among Voters

	Democratic Voters	Republican Voters
Liberal	34%	11%
Moderate	46	38
Conservative	16	49

Source: As reported in the *New York Times*, August 14, 2000.

This relationship between ideological self-identification and party self-identification is relatively stable over time. It suggests that the parties are not altogether empty jars. Later we will observe that Democratic and Republican party activists (notably, delegates to the party conventions) are even more ideologically separate than Democratic and Republican Party voters.

Democratic and Republican party activists have become more ideologically separate in recent years. And voters have become increasingly aware of this **party polarization.** Indeed many voters are now prepared to say that the Democratic Party is more liberal and the Republican Party is more conservative on a variety of high-profile issues, including government services and spending, government provision of health insurance, and government help to African Americans.[3]

WWW **Democratic Party** Web site of the Democratic National Committee (DNC), with news, press releases, policy positions, etc. *www.democrat.org*

WWW **Republican Party** Web site of the Republican National Committee (RNC), with GOP news, press releases, policy positions, etc. *www.rnc.org*

The Erosion of Traditional Party Functions Parties play only a limited role in campaign organization and finance. Campaigns are generally directed by professional campaign management firms or by the candidates' personal organizations, not by parties. Party organizations have largely been displaced in campaign activity by advertising firms, media consultants, pollsters, and others hired by the candidates themselves (see Chapter 5).

Most political candidates today are self-recruited. American political parties also play only a limited role in recruiting candidates for elected office. People initiate their own candidacies, first contacting friends and financial supporters. Often in state and local races, candidates contact party officials only as a courtesy, if at all.

The major American political parties cannot really control who their **nominee**—the party's entry in a general election race—will be. Rather, party **nominations** for most elected offices are won in *primary elections.* In a **primary election,** registered voters select who will be their party's nominee in the general election. Party leaders may endorse a candidate in a primary election and may even work to try to ensure the victory of their favorite, but the voters in that party's primary select the nominee.

Candidates usually communicate directly with voters through the mass media. Television has replaced the party organization as the principal medium of communication between candidates and voters. Candidates no longer rely much on party workers to carry their message from door to door. Instead, candidates can come directly into the voters' living room via television.

Even if the American parties wanted to take stronger policy positions and to enact them into law, they would not have the means to do so. *American political parties have no way to bind their elected officials to the party platform or even to their campaign promises.* Parties have no strong disciplinary sanctions to use against members of Congress who vote against the party's policy position. The parties cannot deny

party polarization The tendency of the Democratic Party to take more liberal positions in the Republican Party to take more conservative positions on key issues.

nominee Political party's entry in a general election race.

nomination Political party's selection of its candidate for a public office.

primary elections Elections to choose party nominees for public office; may be open or closed.

WHAT DO YOU THINK?

Which Party Does a Better Job?

What do Americans think of the Democratic and Republican parties? Generally speaking, the Democratic Party has been able to maintain an image of "the party of the common people," and the Republican Party has long been saddled with an image of "favoring the rich."

But when it comes to popular perceptions of each party's ability to deal with problems confronting the nation, the Democratic and Republican parties appear evenly matched. The Republican Party is trusted to "do a better job" in handling foreign affairs and maintaining a strong national defense. It also enjoys a reputation of being better at "holding down taxes."

The Democratic Party enjoys its greatest advantage on "compassion issues" like helping poor, elderly, and homeless people. And the Democrats have long enjoyed the support of the high-voter-turnout over-sixty-five age group because it is trusted to do a better job "protecting the Social Security system."

Source: Various polls reported in *The Polling Report,* November 22, 1999, September 10, 2001, January 28, 2002, August 11, 2003.

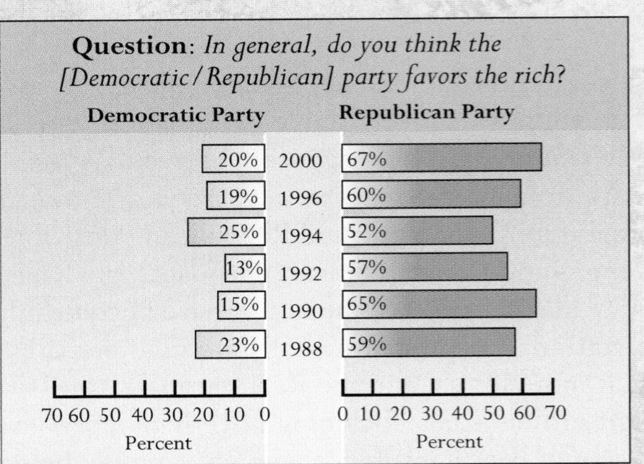

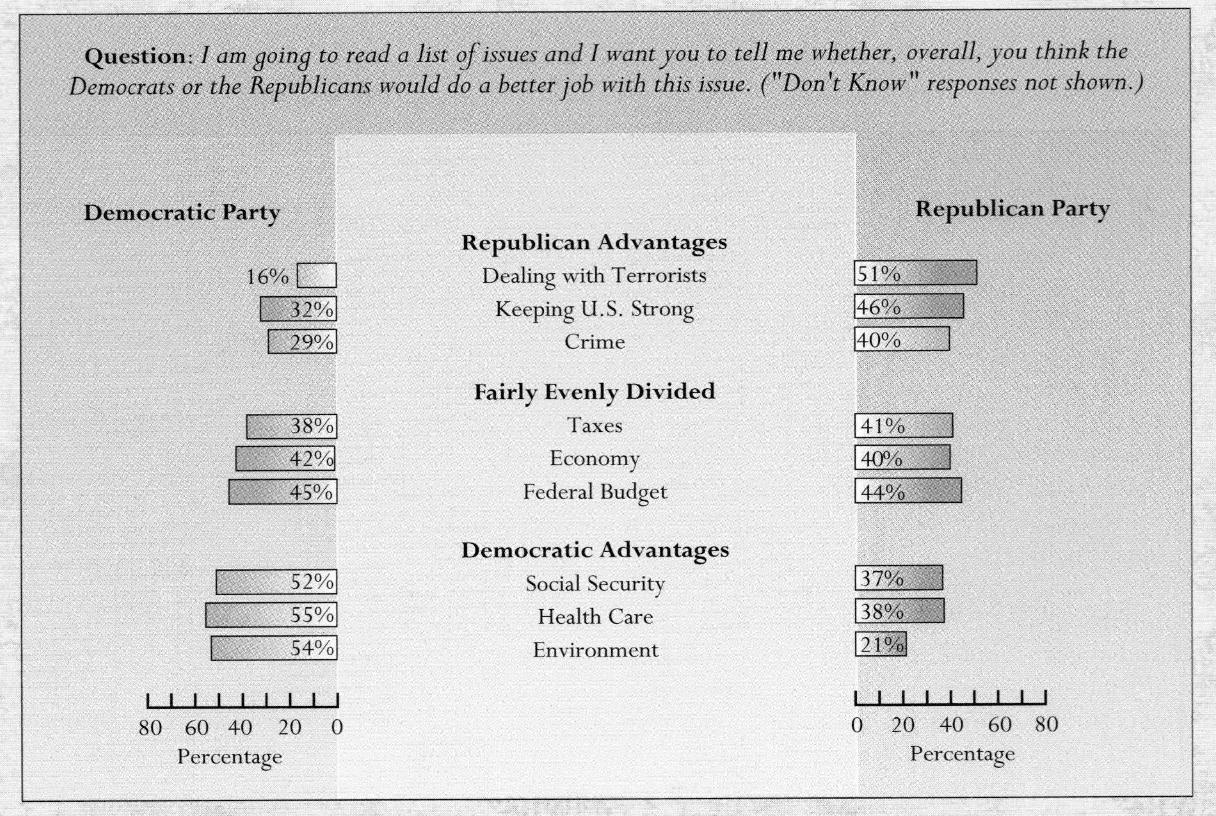

them renomination. At most, the party's leadership in Congress can threaten the status, privileges, and pet bills of disloyal members (see Chapter 8). Party cohesion, where it exists, is more a product of like-mindedness than of party discipline.

American political parties no longer perform social welfare functions—trading off social services, patronage jobs, or petty favors in exchange for votes. Traditional party organizations, or **machines**, especially in large cities, once helped immigrants get settled in, found **patronage** jobs in government for party workers, and occasionally provided aid to impoverished but loyal party voters. But *government bureaucracies have replaced the political parties as providers of social services.* Government employment agencies, welfare agencies, civil service systems, and other bureaucracies now provide the social services once undertaken by political machines in search of votes.

Divided Party Government Finally, to further confound the responsible party model, Americans seem to prefer **divided party government**—where one party controls the executive branch while the other party controls one or both houses of the legislative branch. Over the last forty years, American presidents have been more likely to face a Congress in which the opposition party controls one or both houses than to enjoy their own party's full control of Congress.[4] (Divided party government in the states—where one party controls the governorship and the opposition party controls one or both houses of the state legislature—is also increasing over time).[5] Divided party control of government makes it difficult for either party to fully enact its platform.

It is noteworthy that American public opinion seems to prefer divided party government over unified party control: *"Do you think it is better when one party controls both the presidency and the Congress, better when control is split between the Democrats and Republicans, or doesn't it matter?"*: Better one party—23.8%; Better control split—52.4%; Doesn't matter—23.8%.[6]

Parties as Organizers of Elections

Despite the erosion of many of their functions, America's political parties survive as the principal institutions for organizing elections. Party nominations organize electoral choice by narrowing the field of aspiring office seekers to the Democratic and Republican candidates in most cases. Very few independents or third-party candidates are elected to high political office in the United States. **Nonpartisan elections**—elections in which there are no party nominations and all candidates run without an official party label—are common only in local elections, for city council, county commission, school board, judgeships, and so on. Only Nebraska has nonpartisan elections for its unicameral (one-house) state legislature. Party conventions are still held in many states in every presidential year, but these conventions seldom have the power to determine the parties' nominees for public office.

Party Conventions Historically, party nominations were made by caucus or convention. The **caucus** was the earliest nominating process; party leaders (party chairs, elected officials, and "bosses") would simply meet several months before the election and decide on the party's nominee themselves. The early presidents—Thomas Jefferson, James Madison, James Monroe, and John Quincy Adams—were nominated by caucuses of Congress members. Complaints about the exclusion of people from this process led to nominations by convention—large meetings of

machine Tightly disciplined party organization, headed by a boss, that relies on material rewards—including patronage jobs—to control politics.

patronage Appointment to public office based on party loyalty.

divided party government One party controls the executive branch while the other party controls one or both houses of the legislative branch.

nonpartisan elections Elections in which candidates do not officially indicate their party affiliation; often used for city, county, school board, and judicial elections.

caucus Nominating process in which party leaders select the party's nominee.

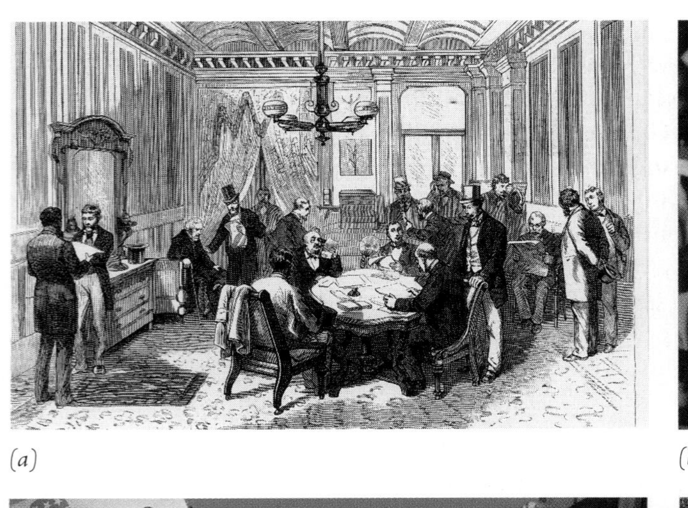

(a)

(b)

(c)

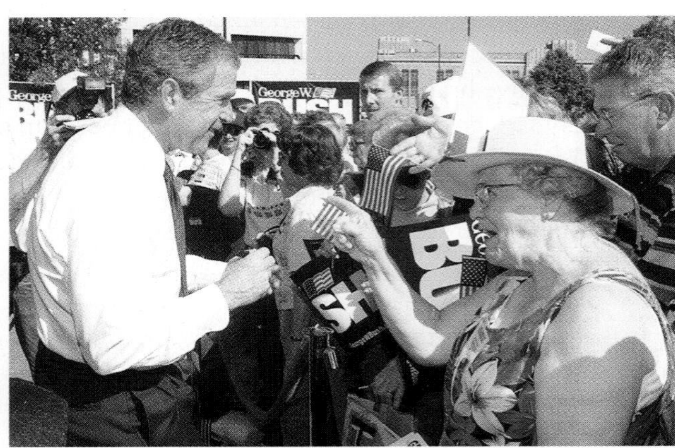

(d)

Political parties as organizers of elections. (a) The Executive Committee of the Republican National Convention in Chicago in 1880. Conventions emerged as the main way for parties to select candidates in the nineteenth century. (b) Al Gore celebrates after winning the nation's first Republican primary in New Hampshire. Today, party candidates are determined by primary elections rather than by convention. (c) Parties also seek to attract voters through registration drives. (d) George W. Bush campaigning on his way to the Republican National Convention in Philadelphia. Parties provide the organizational structure for political campaigns.

delegates sent by local party organizations—starting in 1832. Andrew Jackson was the first president to be nominated by convention. The convention was considered more democratic than the caucus.

For nearly a century, party conventions were held at all levels of government—local, state, and national. City or county conventions included delegates from local **wards** and **precincts**, who nominated candidates for city or county office, for the state legislature, or even for the House of Representatives when a congressional district fell within the city or country. State conventions included delegates from counties, and they nominated governors, U.S. senators, and other statewide officers. State parties chose delegates to the Republican and Democratic national conventions every four years to nominate a president.

ward Division of a city for electoral or administrative purposes or as a unit for organizing political parties.

precinct Subdivision of a city, county, or ward for election purposes.

Party Primaries Today, primary elections have largely replaced conventions as the means of selecting the Democratic and Republican nominees for public office.[7] Primary elections, introduced as part of the progressive reform movement of the early twentieth century, allow the party's *voters* to choose the party's nominee directly. The primary election was designed to bypass the power of party organizations and party leaders and to further democratize the nomination process. It generally succeeded in doing so, but it also had the effect of seriously weakening political parties, since candidates seeking a party nomination need only appeal to party *voters*—not *leaders*—for support in the primary election.[8]

Types of Primaries There are some differences among the American states in how they conduct their primary elections.[9] **Closed primaries** allow only voters who have previously registered as Democrats or Republicans (or in some states voters who choose to register as Democrats or Republicans on primary election day) can cast a ballot in their chosen party's primary. Closed primaries tend to discourage people from officially registering as independents, even if they think of themselves as independent, because persons registered as independents cannot cast a ballot in either party's primary.

Open primaries allow voters to choose on election day which party primary they wish to participate in. Anyone, regardless of prior party affiliation, may choose to vote in either party's primary election. Voters simply request the ballot of one party or the other. Open primaries provide opportunities for voters to cross over party lines and vote in the primary of the party they usually do not support. Opponents of open primaries have argued that these types of primary elections allow for **raiding**—organized efforts by one party to get its members to cross over to the opposition party's primary and defeat an attractive candidate and thereby improve the raiding party's chances of winning the general election. But there is little evidence to show that large numbers of voters connive in such a fashion.

Louisiana is unique in its nonpartisan primary elections. All candidates, regardless of their party affiliation, run in the same primary election. If a candidate gets over 50 percent of the vote, he or she wins the office, without appearing on the general election ballot. If no one receives over 50 percent of the primary election votes, then the top two vote-getters, regardless of party, face each other in the general election.

closed primaries Primary elections in which voters must declare (or have previously declared) their party affiliation and can cast a ballot only in their own party's primary election.

open primaries Primary elections in which a voter may cast a ballot in either party's primary election.

raiding Organized efforts by one party to get its members to cross over in a primary and defeat an attractive candidate in the opposition party's primary.

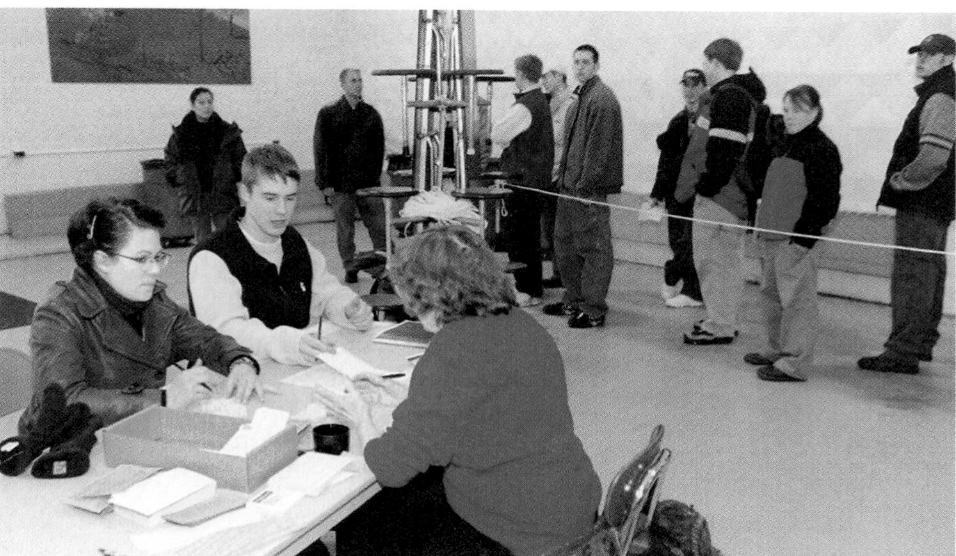

Voter turn-out among 18 to 21 year olds is lower than any other age group. Here, University of New Hampshire students register to vote in the 2000 election.

Some states hold a **runoff primary** when no candidate receives a majority or a designated percentage of the vote in the party's first primary election. A runoff primary is limited to the two highest vote-getters in the first primary. Runoff elections are more common in the southern United States. In most states, only a plurality of votes is needed to win a primary election.

General Elections Several months after the primaries and conventions, the **general election** (usually held in November, on the first Tuesday after the first Monday for presidential and most state elections) determines who will occupy elective office. Winners of the Democratic and Republican primary elections must face each other—and any independent or third-party candidates—in the general election. Voters in the general election may choose any candidate, regardless of how they voted earlier in their party's primary or whether they voted in the primary at all.

Independent and minor-party candidates can get on the general election ballot, although the process is usually very difficult. Most states require independent candidates to file a petition with the signatures of several thousand registered voters. The number of signatures varies from state to state and office to office, but it may range up to 5 or 10 percent of *all* registered voters, a very large number that, in a big state especially, presents a difficult obstacle. The same petition requirements usually apply to minor parties, although some states automatically carry a minor party's nominee on the general election ballot if that party's candidate or candidates received a certain percentage (for example, 10 percent) of the vote in the previous general election.

runoff primary Additional primary held between the top two vote-getters in a primary where no candidate has received a majority of the vote.

general election Election to choose among candidates nominated by parties and/or independent candidates who gained access to the ballot by petition.

convention Nominating process in which delegates from local party organizations select the party's nominees.

presidential primaries Primary elections in the states in which voters in each party can choose a presidential candidate for its party's nomination. Outcomes help determine the distribution of pledged delegates to each party's national nominating convention.

National Party Conventions

The Democratic and Republican parties are showcased every four years at the national party **convention.** The official purpose of these four-day fun-filled events is the nomination of the presidential candidates and their vice presidential running mates. Yet the presidential choices have usually already been made in the parties' **presidential primaries** and caucuses earlier in the year. By midsummer convention time, delegates pledged to cast their convention vote for one or another of the presidential candidates have already been selected. Not since 1952, when the Democrats took three convention ballots to select Adlai Stevenson as their presidential candidate, has convention voting gone beyond the first ballot.[10] The possibility exists that in some future presidential race no candidate will win a majority of delegates in the primaries and caucuses, and the result will be a *brokered* convention in which delegates will exercise independent power to select the party nominee. But this event is unlikely.

The Democratic and Republican national conventions are really televised party rallies, designed to showcase the presidential nominee, confirm the nominee's choice for a running mate, and inspire television viewers to support the party and its candidates in the forthcoming general election. Indeed, the national party conventions are largely media events, carefully staged to present an attractive image of the party and its nominees. Party luminaries jockey for key time slots at the podium, and the party prepares slick videotaped commercials touting its nominee for prime-time presentation.

Convention Delegates Over time, the spread of presidential primary elections has taken the suspense out of the national party conventions. As late as 1968, fewer than half of the delegates were selected in primary elections. But today, the selection of more than 80 percent of pledged delegates by the party's primary voters has greatly diminished the role of party officials in presidential selection.

Both parties award **delegates** to each state in rough proportion to the number of party voters in the state. Convention delegates are generally party activists, ideologically motivated and strongly committed to their presidential candidates. Democratic delegates are much more *liberal* than Democratic voters, and Republican delegates are more *conservative* than Republican voters (see Figure 7.4). There is a slight tendency for Democratic and Republican delegates to differ in social backgrounds; usually more African Americans, women, public employees, and union members are found among Democratic delegates than among Republican delegates.

Party Platforms National conventions also write party **platforms,** setting out the party's goals and policy positions. Because a party's platform is not binding on its nominees, platform *planks* are largely symbolic, although they often provide heated arguments and provide distinct differences between the parties to present to voters (see *Up Close:* "Democratic and Republican Platforms: Can You Tell the Difference?").

Selecting a Running Mate The convention *always* accepts the presidential candidate's recommendation for a running mate. No formal rules require the convention to do so, but it would be politically unacceptable for the convention to override the first important decision of the party's presidential nominee. Convention delegates set aside any personal reservations they may have and unanimously endorse the presidential nominee's choice. (For a discussion of various strategies in selecting a running mate, see "The Vice Presidential Waiting Game" in Chapter 9.)

Campaign Kickoff The final evening of the national conventions is really the kickoff for the general election campaign. The presidential nominee's acceptance speech tries to set the tone for the fall campaign. Party celebrities, including

delegates Accredited voting members of a party's national presidential nominating convention.

platform Statement of principles adopted by a political party at its national convention (specific portions of the platform are known as planks); a platform is not binding on the party's candidates.

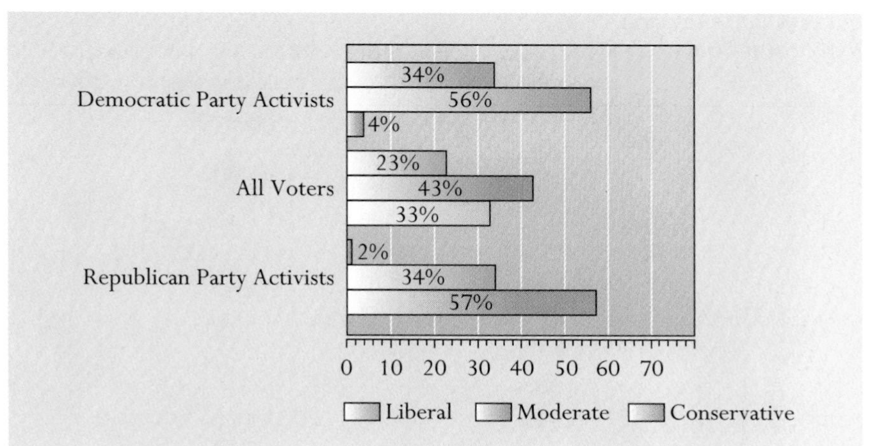

FIGURE 7.4 Ideologies of Voters versus Party Activists

Democratic and Republican party activists (convention delegates in 2000) are far more likely to hold divergent liberal and conservative views than voters generally.

Source: As reported in *New York Times,* August 14, 2000.

UP CLOSE

Democratic and Republican Platforms: Can You Tell the Difference?

Iraq

A "We cannot allow a failed state in Iraq that inevitably would become a haven for terrorists and a destabilizing force in the Middle East."

B ". . . today there are more than 50 million newly freed people in the nation of Afghanistan and Iraq—America is safer."

Taxes

A "We will roll back the tax cuts for those making more than $200,000."

B "Tax reform is necessary to achieve tax simplicity, efficiency, fairness, and predictability. . . . In particular we must: Make the tax relief of 2001 and 2003 permanent."

Foreign Policy

A "They rush to force before exhausting diplomacy. They bully rather than persuade. They act alone when they could assemble a team."

B "We are defending the peace by taking the fight to the enemy. We are confronting terrorists overseas so that we do not have to confront them here at home."

Health-care

A "We will offer individuals and businesses tax credits to make quality, reliable health coverage more affordable."

B "Enact Health Savings Accounts which allow individuals to save and pay for their health-care tax free."

Social Security

A "We are absolutely committed to preserving Social Security."

B "Social Security needs to be strengthened and enhanced for our children and grandchildren . . . Each of today's workers should be free to direct a portion of their payroll taxes to personal investments for their retirement."

Other

A "Their energy policy is simple: government by big oil, of big oil, and for big oil."

B "We will curb the burden of frivolous lawsuits . . . One of their nominees made his fortune as a trial lawyer . . . They offer no hope for reform of this badly broken system."

A "We will raise the minimum wage to $7.00."

B "We strongly support the policy that prevents taxpayers dollars from being used to encourage the future destruction of human embryos."

A "We will create new jobs and protect existing ones by ending tax breaks for companies that ship jobs overseas."

B "We support legislation requiring a supermajority vote in both houses of Congress to raise taxes."

Source: Excerpts from Democratic [A] and Republican [B] party platforms, 2004.

defeated presidential candidates, join hands at the podium as a symbol of party unity. Presidential and vice presidential candidates, spouses, and families assemble under balloons and streamers, amid the happy noise and hoopla, to signal the start of the general election campaign. . . .TV coverage helps provide the parties with small postconvention "bumps" in the polls.[11]

Party Finances

Parties as well as candidates raise hundreds of millions of dollars in every election year. (In Chapter 6 we examined campaign financing by candidates themselves.) At the national level, contributions to the parties go to the Democratic and Republican National Committees, and to the Democratic and Republican House and Senatorial Committees (see Table 7.2).

The Partisan Tilt of Campaign Contributions. The Republican Party has generally been able to raise and spend more money in each election cycle than the Democratic Party, but the dollar differences have narrowed over the years. Perhaps more interesting are the differences in sources of support for each party. Broken down by sector (as in Table 7.3), the Democratic Party relies more heavily on lawyers and law firms, on the TV, movie and music industries (Hollywood), teachers and public sector employee unions, and industrial and building trade unions. Business interests divide their contributions, but they tilt toward the Republican Party, notably the health care industry, insurance, manufacturing, oil and gas, automotive, and general and special contractors.

TABLE 7.2 Party Finances (m$)

	2004	2002	2000
Totals			
Democratic Party	$618	$463	$520
Republican Party	744	691	715
National Committees			
Dem. National Committee	299	162	260
Rep. National Committee	330	284	379
House Party Committees			
Dem. Cong. Camp. Com.	76	103	105
Nat'l Rep. Cong. Com.	156	211	145
Senate Party Committees			
Dem. Senatorial Campaign Com.	76	143	104
Nat'l Rep. Senatorial Campaign Com.	69	125	96

Source: Federal Elections Commission.

TABLE 7.3 Contributors to the Republican and Democratic Parties by Sector

Democratic Party	Republican Party
1. Lawyers/law firms	1. Real estate
2. Securities/investment	2. Health professionals
3. Real estate	3. Securities/investment
4. TV/movies/music	4. Lawyers/law firms
5. Business services	5. Insurance
6. Health professionals	6. Manufacturing/distributing
7. Education	7. Oil and gas
8. Lobbyists	8. Business services
9. Computers/Internet	9. General contractors
10. Insurance	10. Automotive
11. Public sector unions	11. Computers/Internet
12. Commercial banks	12. Commercial banks
13. Industrial unions	13. Special trade contractors
14. Building trade unions	14. Retail sales
15. Liberal/ideological	15. Food and beverage

Source: Center for Responsive Politics. Candidate committees, miscellaneous, and "retired" are excluded from this table.

Party Voters

The Polling Report Up-to-date polling information from a variety of polls on Democratic and Republican party preferences. *www.pollingreport.com*

Traditionally, the Democratic Party has been able to claim to be the majority party in the United States (see Figure 7.5). In opinion polls, those who "identify" with the Democratic Party generally outnumber those who "identify" with the Republican Party. (**Party identification** is determined by response to the question, "Generally speaking, how would you identify yourself: as a Republican, Democrat, independent, or something else?") But the Democratic Party advantage among the voters eroded over time, partly as a result of a gradual increase in the number of people who call themselves independents.

party identification Self-described identification with a political party, usually in response to the question, "Generally speaking, how would you identify yourself: as a Republican, Democrat, independent, or something else?"

dealignment Declining attractiveness of the parties to the voters, a reluctance to identify strongly with a party, and a decrease in reliance on party affiliation in voter choice.

Dealignment **Dealignment** describes the decline in attractiveness of the political parties to the voters, the growing reluctance of people to identify themselves with either party, and a decrease in reliance on a candidate's party affiliation in voter choice. Dealignment is evident not only in the growing numbers of self-described independents but also in the declining numbers of those who identify themselves as "strong" Democrats or Republicans. In short, the electorate is less partisan than it once was.

Party Loyalty in Voting Despite the decline in partisan identification in the electorate, it is important to note that *party identification is a strong influence in voter choice in elections.* Most voters cast their ballot for the candidate of their party. This is true in presidential elections (see Figure 7.6) and even more true in congressional and state elections. Those who identify themselves as Democrats are somewhat more likely to vote for a Republican presidential candidate than those who identify themselves as Republicans are to vote for a Democratic presidential candidate. Republican Ronald Reagan was able to win more than one-quarter of

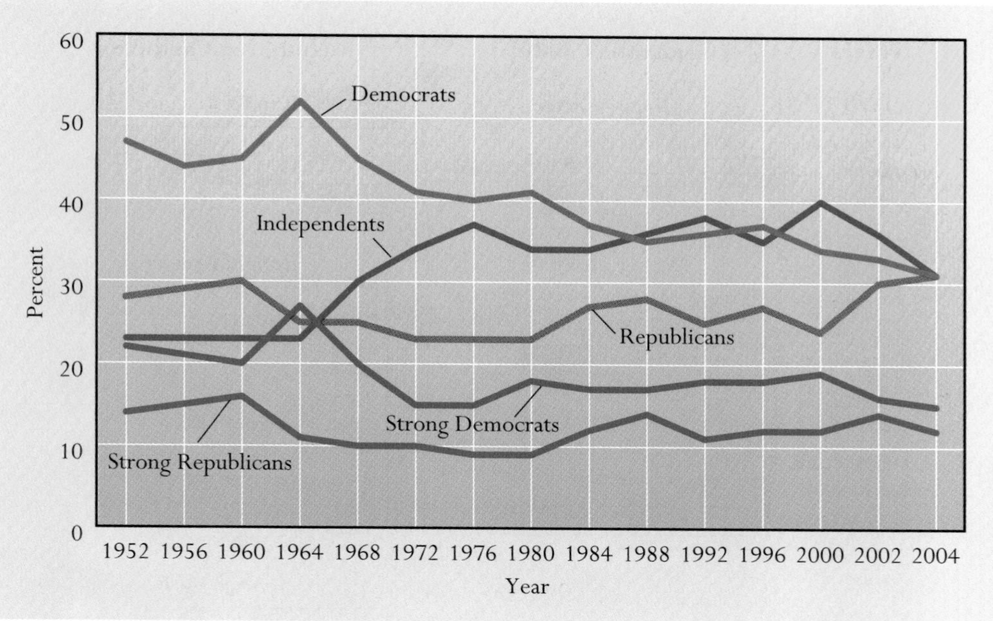

FIGURE 7.5 Party Identification in the Electorate

For many years, the Democratic Party enjoyed a substantial lead in party identification among voters. This Democratic lead eroded in the late 1960s as more people began to identify themselves as independents. Independent identification suggests that many voters have become disillusioned with both parties. Relatively few people consider themselves "strong" Democrats or Republicans.

Source: Data from *National Election Studies,* University of Michigan.

self-identified Democrats in 1980 and 1984, earning these crossover voters the label "Reagan Democrats."[12]

Realignment? Although Democratic Party loyalty has eroded over the last thirty years, it is not clear whether or not this erosion is a classic party **realignment.**[13] Most scholars agree that party realignments occurred in the presidential elections of 1824 (Jackson, Democrats), 1860 (Lincoln, Republicans), 1896 (Bryan, Democrats), and 1932 (Roosevelt, Democrats). This historical sequence gave rise to a theory that realigning elections occur every thirty-six years. According to this theory, the election of 1968 should have been a realigning one. It is true that Richard Nixon's 1968 victory marked the beginning of a 24-year Republican era in presidential election victories that was broken only by Jimmy Carter in 1976. But there was relatively little shifting of the party loyalties of major social groups, and the Democratic Party remained the dominant party in the electorate and in Congress.

realignment Long-term shift in social-group support for various political parties that creates new coalitions in each party.

The Democratic Party still receives *disproportionate* support from Catholics, Jews, African Americans, less educated and lower income groups, blue-collar workers, union members, and big-city residents. The Republican Party still receives *disproportionate* support from Protestants, whites, more educated and higher income groups, white-collar workers, nonunion workers, and suburban and small-town

FIGURE 7.6
Republican, Democratic, and Independent Voters in Presidential Elections

As the percentages here indicate, in recent years registered Democrats have been more likely to "cross over" and vote for a Republican candidate for president than registered Republicans have been to vote for the Democratic presidential candidate.

Source: New York Times.

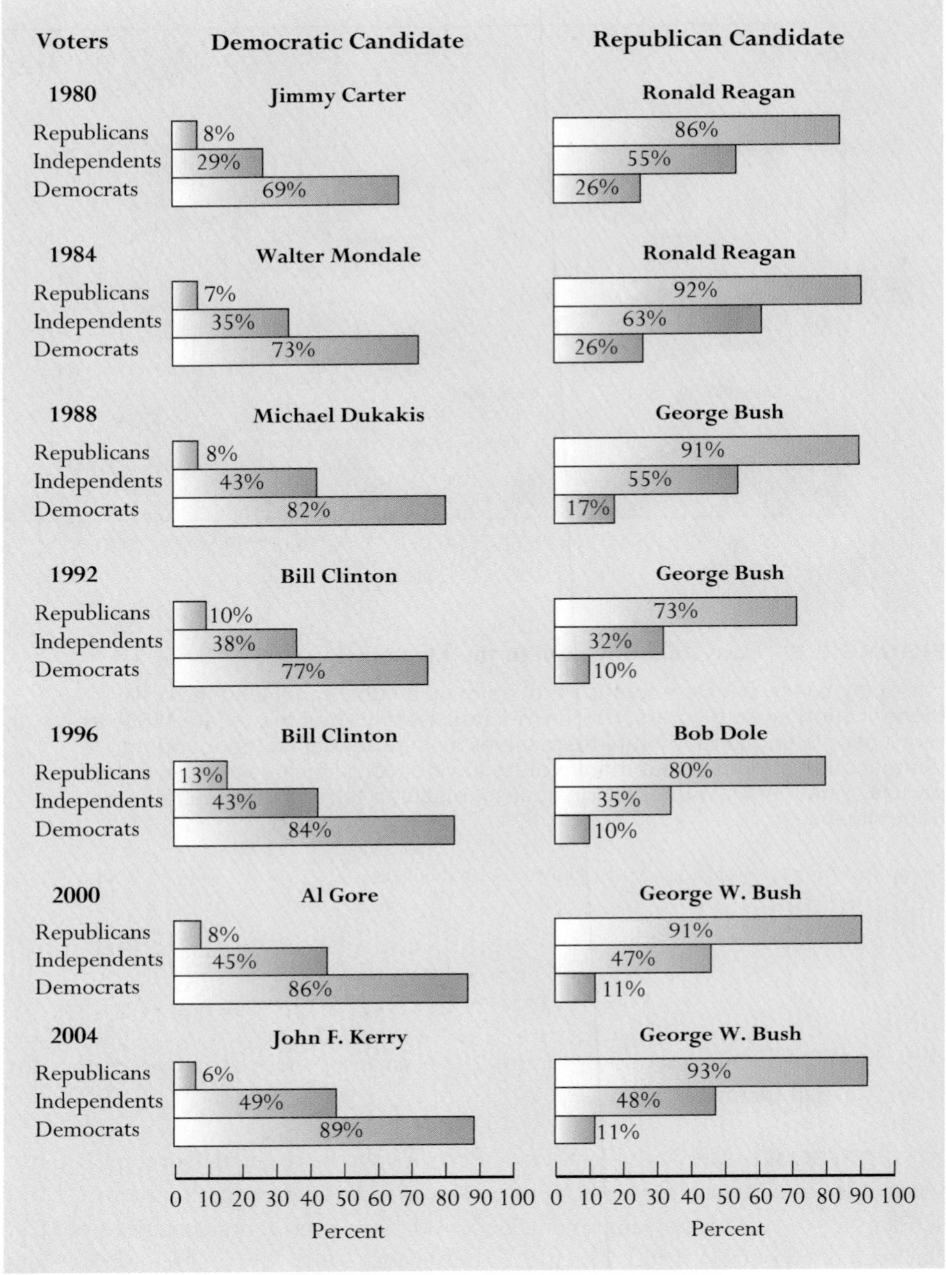

dwellers. Disproportionate support does not mean these groups *always* give a majority of their votes to the indicated party, but only that they give that party a larger percentage of their votes than the party receives from the general electorate. This pattern of social-group voting and party identification has remained relatively stable over the years, even though the GOP has made some gains among many of the traditionally Democratic groups (see Figure 7.7). The only major *shift* in social-group support has occurred among southern whites. This group has shifted from heavily Democratic in party identification to a substantial Republican preference. Thus it is questionable whether a true party realignment has occurred[14] (see *Across the USA*: "Democratic and Republican Party Strength in the States").

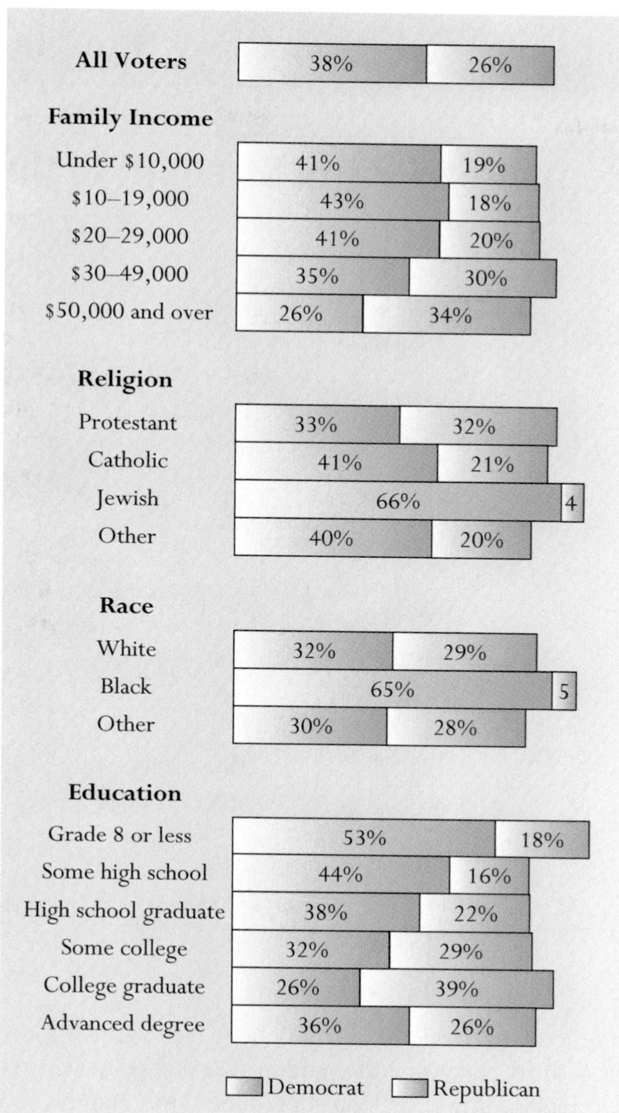

FIGURE 7.7 Social-Group Support for the Democratic and Republican Parties

The Democratic Party draws disproportionate support from low-income, less educated, Catholic, Jewish, and African American voters. The Republican Party relies more heavily on support from high-income, college-educated, white Protestant voters.

Source: Data from *National Election Studies,* University of Michigan.

Why the Two-Party System Persists

The two-party system is deeply ingrained in American politics. Although third parties have often made appearances in presidential elections, no third-party candidate has ever won the Oval Office. (Lincoln's new Republican Party in 1860 might be counted as an exception, but it quickly became a major party.) Very few third-party candidates have won seats in Congress. Many other democracies have multiple-party systems, so the question arises as to why the United States has had a two-party system throughout its history.[15]

Third Party Prospects In recent years, polls have reported that a majority of Americans favor the idea of a third party. But support for the *general* idea of a third party has never been matched by voter support for *specific* third-party or

ACROSS THE USA

Democratic and Republican Party Strength in the States

The Democratic and Republican parties compete in every state. But sectionalism is evident in the "Republican L"—the strength of the Republican party in the Mountain and Southern states. The Democratic Party is becoming bicoastal—strong in the North East and the Pacific Coast. Of the four largest states, California and New York lean Democratic, while Texas and Florida lean Republican.

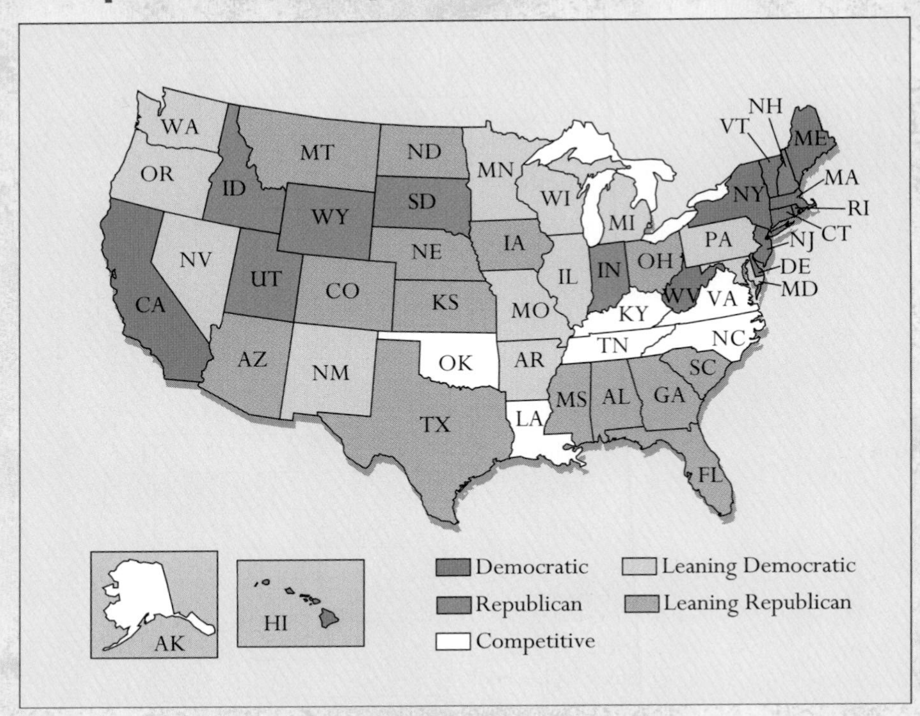

independent presidential candidates (see Table 7.4). Moreover, it is very difficult for a third party or independent candidate to win electoral votes (see *Up Close:* "Understanding the Electoral College" in Chapter 5). Only Theodore Roosevelt, Robert M. La Follette, and George C. Wallace managed to win any electoral votes in the past century. The Reform Party, founded by billionaire Ross Perot in 1992, was the latest serious attempt to create a nationwide third party.

Cultural Consensus One explanation of the nation's two-party system focuses on the broad consensus supporting the American political culture (see Chapter 2). The values of democracy, capitalism, free enterprise, individual liberty, religious freedom, and equality of opportunity are so widely shared that no party challenging these values has ever won much of a following. There is little support in the American political culture for avowedly fascist, communist, authoritarian, or other antidemocratic parties. Moreover, the American political culture includes a strong belief in the separation of church and state. Political parties with religious affiliations, common in European democracies, are absent from American politics. Socialist parties have frequently appeared on the scene under various labels—the Socialist Party, the Socialist Labor Party, and the Socialist Workers Party. But the largest popular vote ever garnered by a socialist candidate in a presidential election was the 6 percent won by Eugene V. Debs in 1912. In contrast, socialist parties have frequently won control of European governments.

TABLE 7.4 Twentieth-Century Third-Party Presidential Votes

Third-Party Presidential Candidates	Popular Vote (percentage)	Electoral Votes (number)
Theodore Roosevelt (1912), Progressive (Bull Moose) Party	27.4%	88
Robert M. La Follette (1924), Progressive Party	16.6	13
George C. Wallace (1968), American Independent Party	13.5	46
John Anderson (1980), Independent	6.6	0
Ross Perot (1992), Independent	18.9	0
Ross Perot (1996), Reform Party	8.5	0
Ralph Nader (2000), Green Party	2.7	0
Ralph Nader (2004) Independent	0.4	0

On broad policy issues, most Americans cluster near the center. This general consensus tends to discourage multiple parties. There does not appear to be sufficient room for them to stake out a position on the ideological spectrum that would detach voters from the two major parties.

This cultural explanation blends with the influence of historical precedents. The American two-party system has gained acceptance through custom. The nation's first party system developed from two coalitions, Federalists and Anti-Federalists, and this dual pattern has been reinforced over two centuries.

Winner-Take-All Electoral System Yet another explanation of the American two-party system focuses on the electoral system itself. Winners in presidential and congressional elections, as well as in state gubernatorial and legislative elections, are usually determined by a plurality, winner-take-all vote. Even in elections that require a majority of more than 50 percent to win—which may involve a runoff election—only one party's candidate wins in the end. Because of the winner-take-all nature of U.S. elections, parties and candidates have an overriding incentive to broaden their appeal to a plurality or majority of voters. Losers come away empty-handed. There is not much incentive in such a system for a party to form to represent the views of 5 or 10 percent of the electorate.

Americans are so accustomed to winner-take-all elections that they seldom consider alternatives. In some countries, legislative bodies are elected by **proportional representation,** whereby all voters cast a single ballot for the party of their choice and legislative seats are then apportioned to the parties in proportion to their total vote in the electorate. Minority parties are assured of legislative seats, perhaps with as little as 10 or 15 percent of the vote. If no party wins 50 percent of the votes and seats, the parties try to form a coalition of parties to establish control of the government. In these nations, party coalition building to form a governing majority occurs *after* the election rather than *before* the election, as it does in winner-take-all elections systems.

proportional representation Electoral system that allocates seats in a legislature based on the proportion of votes each party receives in a national election.

Legal Access to the Ballot Another factor in the American two-party system may be electoral system barriers to third parties. The Democratic and Republican nominees are automatically included on all general election ballots, but third-party and independent candidates face difficult obstacles in getting their names listed. In presidential elections, a third-party candidate must meet the varied requirements of fifty separate states to appear on their ballots along with the Democratic and Republican nominees. These requirements often include filing petitions signed by up to 5 or 10 percent of registered voters. In addition, states require third parties to win 5 or 10 percent of the vote in the last election in order to retain their position on the ballot in subsequent elections. But just doing so required a considerable expenditure of effort and money that the major parties were able to avoid.

Interest-Group Power

THINK AGAIN

Do special-interest groups in America obstruct the majority of citizens' wishes on public policy?

Organization is a means to power—to determining who gets what in society. The First Amendment to the Constitution recognizes "the right of the people peaceably to assemble, and to petition the government for a redress of grievances." Americans thus enjoy a fundamental right to organize themselves to influence government.

Electoral versus Interest-Group Systems The *electoral system* is organized to represent geographically defined constituencies—states and congressional districts in Congress. The *interest-group system* is organized to represent economic, professional, ideological, religious, racial, gender, and issue constituencies. In other words, the interest-group system supplements the electoral system by providing people with another avenue of participation. Individuals may participate in politics by supporting candidates and parties in elections, and also by joining interest groups, organizations that pressure government to advance their interests.[16]

Interest-group activity provides more direct representation of policy preferences than electoral politics. At best, individual voters can influence government policy only indirectly through elections (see Chapter 5). Elected politicians try to represent many different—and even occasionally conflicting—interests. But interest groups provide concentrated and direct representation of policy views in government.

Checking Majoritarianism The interest-group system gives voice to special interests, whereas parties and the electoral system cater to the majority interest. Indeed, interest groups are often defended as a check on **majoritarianism,** the tendency of democratic governments to allow the faint preferences of a majority to prevail over the intense feelings of minorities. However, the interest-group system is frequently attacked because it obstructs the majority from implementing its preferences in public policy.

majoritarianism Tendency of democratic governments to allow the faint preferences of the majority to prevail over the intense feelings of minorities.

Concentrating Benefits While Dispersing Costs Interest groups seek special benefits, subsidies, privileges, and protections from the government. The costs of these *concentrated* benefits are usually *dispersed* to all taxpayers, none of whom individually bears enough added cost to merit spending time, energy, or money to organize a group to oppose the benefit. Thus the interest-group system concentrates benefits to the few and disperses costs to the many. The system favors small, well-organized, homogeneous interests that seek the expansion of government activity at the expense of larger but less well-organized citizen-taxpayers. Over long periods of time, the cumulative activities of many special-interest groups, each seeking concentrated benefits to themselves and dispersed costs to others, result in what has been termed **organizational sclerosis**, a society so encrusted with subsidies, benefits, regulations, protections, and special treatments for organized groups that work, productivity, and investment are discouraged and everyone's standard of living is lowered.

The Organized Interests in Washington

There are more than 1 million nonprofit organizations in the United States, several thousand of which are officially registered in Washington as lobbyists.[17] Trade and professional associations and corporations are the most common lobbies in Washington, but unions, public-interest groups, farm groups, environmental groups, ideological groups, religious and civil rights organizations, women's groups, veterans and defense-related groups, groups organized around a single issue (for example, Mothers Against Drunk Driving), and even organizations representing state and local governments also recognize that they need to be "where the action is." Among this huge assortment of organizations, many of which are very influential in their highly specialized field, there are a number of well-known organized interests. Even a partial list of organized interest groups (see Table 7.5) demonstrates the breadth and complexities of interest-group life in American politics.

Business and Trade Organizations Traditionally, economic organizations have dominated interest-group politics in Washington. There is ample evidence that economic interests continue to play a major role in national policy making, despite the rapid growth over the last several decades of consumer and environmental organizations. Certainly in terms of the sheer number of organizations with offices and representatives in Washington, business and professional groups and occupational and trade associations predominate. More than half of the organizations with offices in Washington are business or **trade associations**, and all together these organizations account for about 75 percent of all of the reported lobbying expenditures.[18]

Professional Associations Professional associations rival business and trade organizations in lobbying influence. The American Bar Association (ABA), the American Medical Association (AMA), and the National Education Association (NEA) are three of the most influential groups in Washington. For example, the American Bar Association, which includes virtually all of the nation's practicing attorneys, and its more specialized offspring, the American Association of Trial Lawyers, have successfully resisted efforts to reform the nation's tort laws (see *A Conflicting View:* "America Drowning in a Sea of Lawsuits," Chapter 11).

Organized Labor Labor organizations have declined in membership over the past several decades. The percentage of the nonagricultural work force belonging to unions has declined from about 37 percent in the 1950s to about 13 percent today. Nevertheless, labor unions remain a major political influence in Congress and the Democratic Party. The AFL-CIO is a federation of sixty-eight separate unions with more than 13 million members. The AFL-CIO has long maintained a large and capable lobbying staff in Washington, and it provides both financial contributions

organizational sclerosis Society encrusted with so many special benefits to interest groups that everyone's standard of living is lowered.

trade associations Interest groups composed of businesses in specific industries.

TABLE 7.5 Major Organized Interest Groups, by Type

Type	Groups
Business	Business Roundtable; National Association of Manufacturers; National Federation of Independent Businesses; National Small Business Association; U.S. Chamber of Commerce
Trade	American Bankers Association; American Gas Association; American Iron and Steel Institute; American Petroleum Institute; American Truckers Association; Automobile Dealers Association; Home Builders Association; Motion Picture Association of America; National Association of Broadcasters; National Association of Real Estate Boards
Professional	American Bar Association; American Medical Association; Association of Trial Lawyers; National Education Association
Union	AFL-CIO; American Federation of State, County, and Municipal Employees; American Federation of Teachers; International Brotherhood of Teamsters; International Ladies' Garment Workers Union; National Association of Letter Carriers; United Auto Workers; United Postal Workers; United Steel Workers
Agricultural	American Farm Bureau Federation; National Cattlemen's Association; National Farmers Union; National Grange; National Milk Producers Federation; Tobacco Institute
Women	League of Women Voters; National Organization for Women
Public Interest	Common Cause; Consumer Federation of America; Public Citizen; Public Interest Research Groups
Ideological	American Conservative Union; Americans for Constitutional Action (conservative); Americans for Democratic Action (liberal); People for the American Way (liberal)
Single Issue	Mothers Against Drunk Driving; National Abortion Rights Action League; National Rifle Association; National Right to Life Committee; Planned Parenthood Federation of America; National Taxpayers Union
Environmental	Environmental Defense Fund; Greenpeace; National Wildlife Federation; National Resources Defense Council; Nature Conservancy; Sierra Club; Wilderness Society
Religious	American Israel Public Affairs Committee; Anti-Defamation League of B'nai B'rith; Christian Coalition; National Council of Churches; U.S. Catholic Conference
Civil Rights	American Civil Liberties Union; American Indian Movement; Mexican-American Legal Defense and Education Fund; National Association for the Advancement of Colored People; National Urban League; Rainbow Coalition; Southern Christian Leadership Conference
Age Related	American Association of Retired Persons; Children's Defense Fund
Veterans	American Legion; Veterans of Foreign Wars; Vietnam Veterans of America
Defense	Air Force Association; American Security Council; Army Association; Navy Association
Government	National Association of Counties; National Conference of State Legislators; National Governors Association; National League of Cities; U.S. Conference of Mayors

and campaign services (registration, get-out-the-vote, information, endorsements) for members of Congress it favors. Many of the larger individual unions also maintain offices in Washington and offer campaign contributions and services.

Today union influence is greatest among government employees, including teachers. About 38 percent of all public sector employees are unionized. The American Federation of State, County, and Municipal Employees (AFSCME), the

National Education Association (NEA), the American Federation of Teachers (AFT), and the Teamsters Union (which recruits public employees in sanitation and transportation) are among the few unions growing in membership.

AFL-CIO
Home page of labor confederation; includes information on wages, unemployment, strikes, as well as news and press releases on union affairs. *www.alfcio.org*

Women's Organizations Women's organizations date back to the antislavery societies in pre-Civil War America. The first generation of feminists—Lucretia Mott, Elizabeth Cady Stanton, Lucy Stone, and Susan B. Anthony—learned to organize, hold public meetings, and conduct petition campaigns as abolitionists. After the Civil War, women were successful in changing many state laws that abridged the rights of married women and otherwise treated them as "chattel" (property) of their husbands. Women were also prominent in the Anti-Saloon League, which succeeded in outlawing prostitution and gambling in every state except Nevada and provided a major source of support for the Eighteenth Amendment (Prohibition). In the early twentieth century, the feminist movement concentrated on obtaining the vote (suffrage) for women. Today the League of Women Voters—a broad-based organization that provides information to voters—backs registration and get-out-the-vote drives and generally supports measures seeking to ensure honesty and integrity in government.

American Farm Bureau
The American Farm Bureau site reveals that the largest farm organization in America represents more than 5 million families in the 50 states and Puerto Rico. *www.fb.com*

Interest in feminist politics revived in the wake of the civil rights movement of the 1960s. New organizations sprang up to compete with the conventional activities of the League of Women Voters by taking a more activist stance toward women's issues. The largest of these organizations is the National Organization for Women (NOW), founded in 1966.

Christian Coalition
Organization "defending our godly heritage" by giving "people of faith a voice in government." *www.cc.org*

Religious Groups Churches and religious groups have a long history of involvement in American politics—from the pre-Civil War antislavery crusades, to the prohibition effort in the early twentieth century, to the civil rights movement of the 1960s. The leadership for the historic Civil Rights Act of 1964 came from the Reverend Martin Luther King, Jr., and his Southern Christian Leadership Conference. Today religious groups span the political spectrum, from liberal organizations such as the National Council of Churches and Anti-Defamation League of B'nai B'rith, to conservative and fundamentalist organizations, such as the Christian Coalition, often referred to as the "religious right" (see *Up Close:* "The Christian Coalition: Organizing the Faithful").

The American Israel Public Affairs Committee is regularly ranked as one of Washington's most powerful lobbies. It is actually a foreign policy lobby rather than a religious lobby, although its support is concentrated in the American Jewish community. It lobbies on behalf of Israel's interests, including continuing substantial foreign aid.

public-interest groups
Interest groups that claim to represent broad classes of people or the public as a whole.

Public-Interest Groups **Public-interest groups** claim to represent broad classes of people—consumers, voters, reformers, or the public as a whole. Groups with lofty-sounding names, such as Common Cause, Public Citizen, and the Consumer Federation of America, perceive themselves as balancing the narrow, "selfish" interests of business organizations, trade associations, unions, and other "special" interests. Public-interest groups generally lobby for greater government regulation of consumer products, public safety, campaign finance, and so on. Their reform agenda, as well as their call for a larger regulatory role for government, makes them frequent allies of liberal ideological groups, civil rights organizations, and environmental groups.[19]

Many public-interest groups were initially formed in the 1970s by "entrepreneurs" who saw an untapped "market" for the representation of these interests.

Public Citizen
Organization, founded by Ralph Nader, devotes its site to "protecting health, safety and democracy" as well as lobbying for "strong citizen and consumer protection laws." *www.publiccitizen.com*

UP CLOSE

The Christian Coalition: Organizing the Faithful

Christian fundamentalists, whose religious beliefs are based on a literal reading of the Bible, have become a significant political force in the United States through effective organization. Perhaps the most influential Christian fundamentalist organization today is the Christian Coalition, with nearly 2 million active members throughout the country.

Fundamentalist Christians are opposed to abortion, pornography, and homosexuality; they favor the recognition of religion in public life, including prayer in schools; and they despair at the decline of traditional family values in American culture, including motion pictures and television broadcasting. Historically, fundamentalist Protestant churches avoided politics as profane and concentrated evangelical efforts on saving individual souls. Their few ventures into worldly politics—notably the prohibition movement in the early twentieth century—ended in defeat. Their strength tended to be in the southern, rural, and poorer regions of the country. They were widely ridiculed in the national media.

In the 1960s, television evangelism emerged as a religious force in the United States. The Reverend Pat Robertson founded the Christian Broadcasting Network (CBN) and later purchased the Family Channel. But efforts by social conservatives to build a "moral majority" for political action largely failed, as did Robertson's presidential candidacy in 1988. Televangelists, including Jerry Falwell and Tammy Fay Baker, suffered popular disdain following some well-publicized scandals.

Although officially nonpartisan, the Coalition became an important force in Republican politics; religious fundamentalists may constitute as much as one-third of the party's voter support. The Christian Coalition does not officially endorse candidates, but its voter guides clearly indicate which candidates reflect the coalition's position on major issues. The distribution of millions of these guides, mostly in churches on the weekend before the Tuesday election, was credited with helping Republicans capture control of Congress in 1994. The political influence of the Christian Coalition in Republican politics, and the "religious right" generally, ensures that most GOP candidates for public office publicly express support for a "pro-family" agenda. This agenda includes a constitutional amendment allowing prayer in public schools; vouchers for parents to send their children to private, religious schools; banning late-term abortions as well as banning the use of taxpayer funds to pay for abortions; restrictions on pornography on cable television and the Internet; and opposition to human embryo research and human cloning.

Among the most influential public-interest groups are Common Cause, a self-styled "citizens' lobby," and the sprawling network of organizations created by consumer advocate Ralph Nader. Common Cause tends to focus on election-law reform, public financing of elections, and limitations on political contributions. The Nader organization began as a consumer protection group focusing on auto safety but soon spread to encompass a wide variety of causes.

Single-Issue Groups Like public-interest groups, **single-issue groups** appeal to principle and belief. But as their name implies, single-issue groups concentrate their attention on a single cause. They attract the support of individuals with a strong commitment to that cause. Among the most vocal single-issue groups in recent years have been the organizations on both sides of the abortion issue. The National Abortion Rights Action League (NARAL) describes itself as "pro-choice" and opposes any restrictions on a woman's right to obtain an abortion. The National Right-to-Life Committee describes itself as "pro-life" and opposes abortion for any reason other than to preserve the life of the mother. Other prominent single-issue groups include the National Rifle Association (opposed to gun control) and Mothers Against Drunk Driving (MADD).

single-issue groups Organizations formed to support or oppose government action on a specific issue.

Ideological Groups **Ideological organizations** pursue liberal or conservative agendas, often with great passion and considerable financial resources derived from true-believing contributors. The ideological groups rely heavily on computerized mailings to solicit funds from persons identified as holding liberal or conservative views. The oldest of the established ideological groups is the liberal Americans for Democratic Action (ADA), well known for its annual liberalism ratings of members of the Congress according to their support for or rejection of programs of concern. The American Conservative Union (ACU) also rates members of Congress each year.

National Rifle Association

The National Rifle Association site is devoted to opposing gun control legislation as well as employing the Second Amendment in it anti-gun control argument.
www.nra.org

Government Lobbies The federal government's grant-in-aid programs to state and local governments (see Chapter 4) have spawned a host of lobbying efforts by these governments in Washington, D.C. Thus state- and local-government taxpayers foot the bill to lobby Washington to transfer federal taxpayers' revenues to states and communities. The National Governors Association occupies a beautiful marble building, the Hall of the States, in Washington, along with representatives of the separate states and many major cities. The National League of Cities and the National Association of Counties also maintain large Washington offices, as does the U.S. Conference of Mayors. The National Conference of State Legislators sends its lobbyists to Washington from its Denver headquarters. These groups pursue a wide policy agenda and often confront internal disputes. But they are united in their support for increased federal transfers of tax revenues to states and cities.

The Washington Lobbyists

Washington is a labyrinth of interest representatives—lawyers and law firms; independent consultants; public and governmental relations firms; business, professional, and trade associations; and advocates of special causes. It is estimated that more than 15,000 people in Washington fit the definition of **lobbyist**, a person working to influence government policies and actions. This figure suggests at least twenty-eight lobbyists for every member of Congress. Roughly $1.5 *billion* are spent on direct lobbying activities *each year;*[20] this figure does *not* include political campaign contributions. The top spenders for direct lobbying are listed in Table 7.6.

Who Are the Lobbyists? Lobbyists in Washington share a common goal—to influence the making and enforcing of laws—and common tactics to achieve this goal. Many lobbyists are the employees of interest-group organizations who devote all of their efforts to their sponsors.

Other lobbyists are located in independent law, consulting, or public relations firms that take on clients for fees. Independent lobbyists, especially law firms, are often secretive about whom they represent, especially when they represent foreign governments. Lobbyists frequently prefer to label their activities as "government relations," "public affairs," "regulatory liaison," "legislative counseling," or merely "representation."

In reality, many independent lawyers and lobbyists in Washington are "fixers" who offer to influence government policies for a price. Many are former government officials—former Congress members, cabinet secretaries, White House aides, and the like—who "know their way around." Their personal connections help to "open doors" to allow their paying clients to "just get a chance to talk" with top officials.

ideological organizations Interest groups that pursue ideologically based (liberal or conservative) agendas.

lobbyist Person working to influence government policies and actions.

TABLE 7.6 Top Lobbying Spenders

Rank	Organization	Annual Spending
1	Chamber of Commerce of the U.S.	$18,760,000
2	American Medical Assn.	$18,180,000
3	Philip Morris	$14,820,000
4	American Hospital Assn.	$12,480,000
5	Exxon Mobil Corp.	$11,695,800
6	Edison Electric Institute	$11,580,000
7	Blue Cross/Blue Shield	$11,162,354
8	SBC Communications	$9,500,000
9	Schering-Plough Corp.	$9,231,000
10	AT &T	$8,560,000
11	Ford Motor Co.	$8,360,000
12	General Electric	$8,318,024
13	Business Roundtable	$8,300,000
14	Boeing Co.	$8,200,000
15	Sprint Corp.	$7,951,711
16	United Services Automobile Assn. Group	$7,470,000
17	Natl. Cmte. to Preserve Social Security	$7,220,000
18	General Motors	$7,017,874
19	Abbott Laboratories	$6,789,000
20	National Assn. of Realtors	$6,760,000

Source: Reprinted by permission of the Center for Responsive Politics, *Influence, Inc.* 2002. There is considerable change from year to year in the list, depending on the nature of the legislation before Congress.

Some lobbying organizations rely heavily on their campaign contributions to achieve lobbying power; others rely on large memberships, and still others on politically active members who concentrate their attention on a narrow range of issues.

Washington's army of lobbyists includes many former members of Congress. Lobbying is a favorite occupation of former members; they can command much higher salaries as lobbyists than they did as Congress members. Lobbying firms are pleased to have people who know the lawmaking process from the inside and who can easily "schmooze" with their former colleagues.

Most Powerful Lobby Groups. A survey of more than 2,000 Washington "insiders" by *Fortune* magazine asking them to rank the most powerful lobbyists in the Capitol suggests that lobbying clout is a combination of money spent lobbying, money contributed to political campaigns, the size of the interest group, the intensity of the membership on behalf of their cause, and the narrowness of the cause. The American Association of Retired Persons, with its 36 million members, is regularly ranked among the nation's most powerful lobby groups. Other large groups rated as powerful were the AFL-CIO and the National Federation of Independent Business, but so also was the relatively small American Israel Public Affairs Committee. The Association of Trial Lawyers, the National Rifle Association, and the Christian Coalition were also rated highly, probably because of the intensity of their members' commitment.

The Fine Art of Lobbying

Any activity directed at a government decision maker with the hope of influencing decisions is a form of **lobbying.** (The term arose from the practice of waiting in the lobbies of legislative chambers to meet and persuade legislators.) For organized interests, lobbying is continuous—in congressional committees, in congressional staff offices, at the White House, at executive agencies, at Washington cocktail parties. If a group loses a round in Congress, it continues the fight in the agency in charge of executing the policy, or it challenges the policy in the courts. The following year it resumes the struggle in Congress: it fights to repeal the offending legislation, to weaken amendments, or to reduce the agency's budget enough to cripple enforcement efforts.

lobbying Activities directed at government officials with the hope of influencing their decisions.

Lobbying techniques are as varied as the imagination of interest-group leaders, but such activities generally fall into seven categories: (1) public relations; (2) access; (3) information; (4) grass-roots mobilization; (5) protests and demonstrations; (6) coalition building; and (7) campaign support. In the real world of Washington power struggles, all these techniques may be applied simultaneously or innovative techniques may be discovered and applied at any time (see Figure 7.8).

American League of Lobbyists

Lobbyists have their own Web site, one devoted to "ethical conduct" in the lobbying process and the "advancement of the lobbying profession." *www.alldc.org*

Public Relations Many interest groups actually spend more of their time, energy, and resources on **public relations**—developing and maintaining a favorable climate of opinion in the nation—than on direct lobbying of Congress. The mass media—television, magazines, newspapers—are saturated with expensive ads by

public relations Building and maintaining goodwill with the general public.

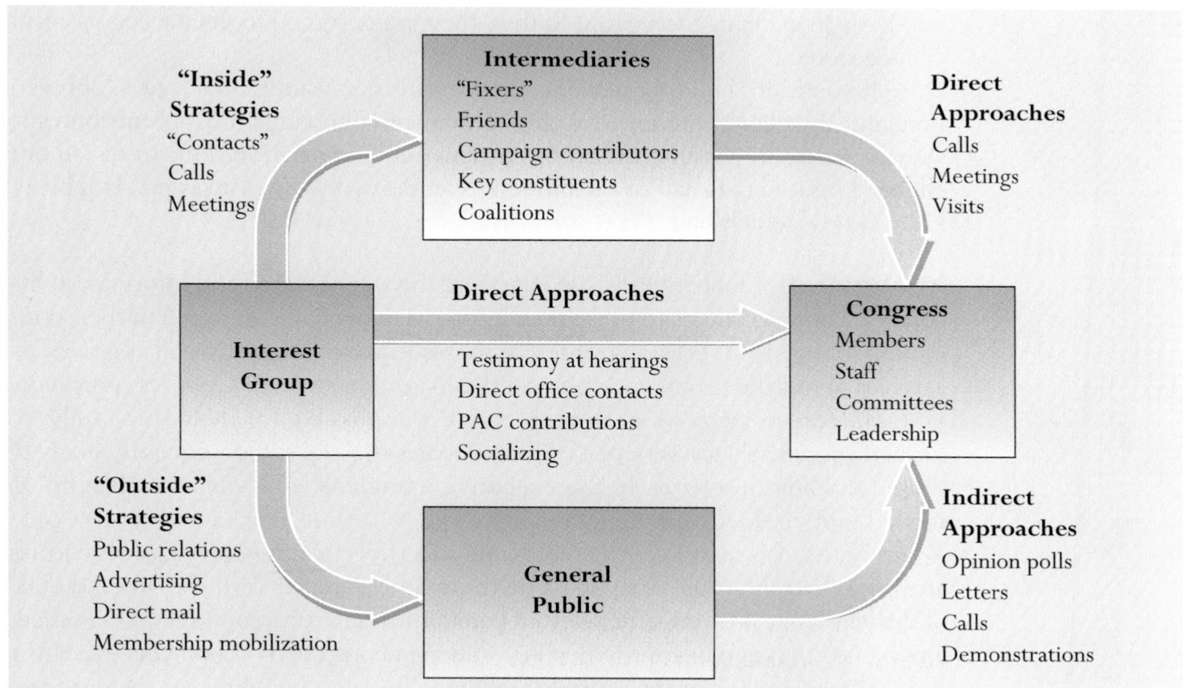

FIGURE 7.8 A Guide to the Fine Art of Lobbying

Interest groups seek to influence public policy both directly through lobbying and campaign contributions (inside strategy) and indirectly through public relations efforts to mold public opinion (outside strategy).

oil companies, auto companies, chemical manufacturers, trade associations, teachers' unions, and many other groups, all seeking to create a favorable image for themselves with the general public. These ads are designed to go well beyond promoting the sale of particular products; they portray these organizations as patriotic citizens, protectors of the environment, providers of jobs, defenders of family values, and supporters of the American way of life. Generally, business interests have an advantage in the area of public relations because public relations and sales and marketing activities are synonymous. But paid advertising is less credible than news stories and media commentary. Hence interest groups generate a daily flood of press releases, media events, interviews, reports, and studies for the media. Media news stories appear to favor liberal public interest groups.

Access "Opening doors" is a major business in Washington. To influence decision makers, organized interests must first acquire **access** to them. Individuals who have personal contacts in Congress, the White House, or the bureaucracy (or who say they do) sell their services at high prices. Washington law firms, public relations agencies, and consultants—often former insiders—all offer their connections, along with their advice, to their clients. The personal prestige of the lobbyist, together with the group's perceived political influence, helps open doors in Washington.

Washington socializing is often an exercise in access—rubbing elbows with powerful people. Well-heeled lobbyists regularly pay hundreds, even thousands, of dollars per plate at fund-raising dinners for members of Congress. Lobbyists regularly provide dinners, drinks, travel, vacations, and other amenities to members of Congress, their families, and congressional staff, as well as to White House and other executive officials. These favors are rarely provided on a direct quid pro quo basis in exchange for votes. Rather, they are designed to gain access—"just a chance to talk."

"Schmoozing," building personal relationships, consumes much of a lobbyist's time and the client's money. It is difficult to know how much this contributes to actual success in passing, defeating, or amending legislation. But, to quote one client: "I figured that half of the money I spend on lobbying is wasted. Trouble is, I don't know which half."[21]

Information Once lobbyists gain access, their knowledge and information become valuable resources to those they lobby. Members of Congress and their staffs look to lobbyists for *technical expertise* on the issue under debate as well as *political information* about the group's position on the issue. Members of Congress must vote on hundreds of questions each year, and it is impossible for them to be fully informed about the wide variety of bills and issues they face. Consequently many of them (and administrators in the executive branch as well) come to depend on trusted lobbyists.

Lobbyists also spend considerable time and effort keeping informed about bills affecting their interests. They must be thoroughly familiar with the "ins and outs" of the legislative process—the relevant committees and subcommittees, their schedules of meetings and hearings, their key staff members, the best moments to act, the precise language for proposed bills and amendments, the witnesses for hearings, and the political strengths and weaknesses of the legislators themselves. In their campaign to win congressional and bureaucratic support for their programs, lobbyists engage in many different types of activities. Nearly all testify at congressional hearings and make direct contact with government officials on issues that

access Meeting and talking with decision makers, a prerequisite to direct persuasion.

affect them. In addition, lobbyists provide the technical reports and analyses used by congressional staffs in their legislative research. Engaging in protest demonstrations is a less common activity, in part because it involves a high risk of alienating some members of Congress.

Experienced lobbyists develop a reputation for accurate information. Most successful lobbyists do not supply faulty information; their success depends on maintaining the trust and confidence of decision makers. A reputation for honesty is as important as a reputation for influence.

Grass-Roots Mobilization Many organized interests lobby Congress from both the *outside* and the *inside*. From the outside, organizations seek to mobilize **grass-roots lobbying** of members of Congress by their constituents. Lobbyists frequently encourage letters and calls from "the folks back home." Larger organized interests often have local chapters throughout the nation and can mobilize these local affiliates to apply pressure when necessary. Lobbyists encourage influential local people to visit the office of a member of Congress personally or to make a personal phone call on behalf of the group's position. And, naturally, members are urged to vote for or against certain candidates, based on their policy stances (see *Up Close*: "AARP: The Nation's Most Powerful Interest Group").

WWW **AARP** The AARP site covers issues and provides information relevant to the concerns of citizens who are 50 years of age or older. *www.aarp.org*

Experienced lawmakers recognize attempts by lobby groups to orchestrate "spontaneous" grass-roots outpourings of cards and letters. Pressure mail is often identical in wording and content. Nevertheless, members of Congress dare not ignore a flood of letters and telegrams from home, for the mail shows that constituents are aware of the issue and care enough to sign their names.

Another grass-roots tactic is to mobilize the press in the home district of a member of Congress. Lobbyists may provide news, analyses, and editorials to local newspapers and then clip favorable articles to send to lawmakers. Lobby groups may also buy advertisements in hometown newspapers.

Protests and Demonstrations Interest groups occasionally employ protests and demonstrations to attract media attention to their concerns and thereby apply pressure on officials to take action. For these actions to succeed in getting issues on the agenda of decision makers in Congress, in the White House, and in executive agencies, participation by the media, especially television, is essential. The media carry the message of the protest or demonstration both to the general public and directly to government officials (see "Protest as Political Participation" in Chapter 5).

Coalition Building Interest groups frequently seek to build **coalitions** with other groups in order to increase their power. Coalitions tend to form among groups with parallel interests: for example, the National Organization for Women, the League of Women Voters, and the National Abortion Rights Action League on women's issues. Coalitions usually form temporarily around a single piece of legislation in a major effort to secure or prevent its passage.

grass-roots lobbying Attempts to influence government decision making by inspiring constituents to contact their representatives.

Campaign Support Perhaps the real key to success in lobbying is the campaign contribution. Interest-group contributions not only help lobbyists gain access and a favorable hearing but also help elect people friendly to the group's goals. As the costs of campaigning increase, legislators must depend more heavily on the contributions of organized interests.

coalition A joining together of interest groups to achieve a common goal.

UP CLOSE

AARP: The Nation's Most Powerful Interest Group

The American Association of Retired Persons (AARP) is the nation's largest and most powerful interest group, with more than 36 million members. The AARP's principal interests are the Social Security and Medicare system programs, the nation's largest and most expensive entitlements.

Like many other interest groups, the AARP has grown in membership not only by appealing to the political interests of retired people but also by offering a wide array of material benefits. For a $12.50 annual fee, members are offered a variety of services, including discounted rates on home, auto, life, and health insurance; discounted mail-order drugs; tax advisory services; discounted rates on hotels, rental cars, and so on; a newsletter, *The AARP Bulletin;* a semi-monthly magazine, *Modern Maturity;* and for babyboomers now reaching their 50s, a new magazine, *My Generation.*

The political power of senior citizens is so great that prospects for limiting current or even future increases in government benefits for the elderly are slim. Social Security is said to be the "third rail of American politics—touch it and you're dead."

Critics of the AARP argue that its lobbyists in Washington do not fairly represent the views of the nation's senior citizens, that few of its members know what its lobbying arm does at the nation's capital. Indeed, in the struggle over prescription drug coverage under Medicare in 2003, the AARP leadership was accused of favoring its own interest in selling private insurance over the interests of its members in receiving government-paid insurance. AARP keeps its dues low, and consequently its membership high, through its business ties with insurance companies, its magazine advertising revenue, and commercial royalties revenues for endorsing products and services.

Source: Reprinted, with permission, from the April 1997 issue of *Reason* Magazine. Copyright 2000 by the Reason Foundation, 3415 S. Sepulveda Blvd., Suite 400, Los Angeles, CA. 90034. www.reason.com.

Distributing PAC Money Because **political action committee** (PAC) contributions are in larger lumps than individual contributions, PAC contributions often attract more attention from members of Congress. The PACs listed in Table 7.7 gave millions of dollars to finance the campaigns of their potential allies in 2000.

Most PACs use their campaign contributions to acquire access and influence with decision makers. Corporate, trade, and professional PAC contributions go overwhelmingly to incumbents, regardless of party. Leaders of these PACs know that incumbents are rarely defeated, and they do not wish to antagonize even unsympathetic members of Congress by backing challengers. However, ideological and issue-oriented PACs are more likely to allocate funds according to the candidates' policy positions and voting records. Labor PACs give almost all of their contributions to Democrats. Ideological and issue-oriented PACs give money to challengers as well as incumbents; in recent years, these groups collectively favored Democrats as women's, environmental, abortion rights, and elderly groups proliferated. (See *Up Close:* "EMILY's List.")

political action committees (PACs) Organizations that solicit and receive campaign contributions from corporations, unions, trade associations, and ideological and issue-oriented groups, and their members, then distribute these funds to political candidates.

TABLE 7.7 The Big Money PACs in 2000

Nearly 4,000 PACs made contributions to presidential and congressional candidates in 1999-2000. The 25 largest contributors are listed.

Rank/Organization	Total	Democrats	Republicans
1 National Assn. of Realtors	$3,423,441	41%	59%
2 Assn. of Trial Lawyers of America	$2,661,000	86%	13%
3 American Fedn. of St./Cnty./Munic. Employees	$2,590,074	95%	5%
4 Teamsters Union	$2,565,495	93%	7%
5 National Auto Dealers Assn.	$2,498,700	32%	68%
6 Intl. Brotherhood of Electrical Workers	$2,470,125	96%	4%
7 Laborers Union	$2,255,900	90%	9%
8 Machinists/Aerospace Workers Union	$2,188,138	99%	1%
9 United Auto Workers	$2,155,050	99%	1%
10 American Medical Assn.	$2,028,354	48%	52%
11 Service Employees International Union	$1,871,774	89%	11%
12 National Beer Wholesalers Assn.	$1,871,500	21%	79%
13 Carpenters & Joiners Union	$1,869,920	84%	15%
14 National Assn. of Home Builders	$1,824,599	36%	64%
15 United Parcel Service	$1,755,065	35%	65%
16 United Food & Commercial Workers Union	$1,743,652	97%	2%
17 National Education Assn.	$1,717,125	95%	5%
18 Verizon Communications	$1,677,617	33%	67%
19 American Bankers Assn.	$1,657,615	35%	64%
20 American Federation of Teachers	$1,599,555	98%	2%
21 National Rifle Assn.	$1,583,574	15%	84%
22 Marine Engineers Union	$1,578,432	58%	42%
23 SBC Communications	$1,561,738	42%	58%
24 National Assn. of Letter Carriers	$1,552,350	84%	16%
25 Credit Union National Assn.	$1,526,584	49%	51%

Source: Reprinted by permission of the Center for Responsive Politics.

UP CLOSE

EMILY's List

Fund raising is the greatest obstacle to mounting a successful campaign against an incumbent. And the most difficult problem facing challengers is raising money *early* in the campaign, when they have little name recognition and little or no standing in the polls.

EMILY's List is a politically adroit and effective effort to support liberal Democratic women candidates by infusing *early money* into their campaigns. EMILY stands for Early Money is Like Yeast, because "it makes the dough rise." Early contributions provide the initial credibility that a candidate, especially a challenger, needs in order to solicit additional funds from individuals and organizations. EMILY is a fund-raising network of thousands of contributors, each of whom pays $100 to join and pledges to give at least $100 to two women from a list of candidates prepared by EMILY's leaders. Most of the contributors are professional women who appreciate EMILY's screening of pro-choice, liberal women candidates around the country.

EMILY's List was begun in 1985 by a wealthy heir to a founder of IBM, Ellen Malcolm. Women challengers for congressional races traditionally faced frustration in fund raising. Incumbent male officeholders enjoyed a huge fund-raising advantage because contributors expected them to win and therefore opened their wallets to gain access and goodwill. EMILY's List has helped to overcome defeatism among both women candidates and contributors.

Senator Barbara Milkulski, Democrat of Maryland and an early beneficiary of EMILY's List, at a news conference.

EMILY's List Political network for pro-choice Democratic women that raises early money for women candidates.
www.emilyslist.org

The pattern of contributing to congressional incumbents resulted in a shift of contributions from Democrats to Republicans when the GOP took control of both houses of Congress after the 1994 election. PAC money is less important in the Senate than in the House. PAC contributions account for about 35 percent of House campaign contributions; they only account for about 20 percent of Senate campaign contributions. Actually PACs contribute more *dollars* to the average senator than to the average House member. But because Senate campaigns cost so much more than House campaigns, PAC contributions are *proportionally* less. Senators must rely more on individual contributions than House members do.

Instead of bribery, organized interests contribute to an incumbent member of Congress over a long period of time and leave it to the lawmaker to figure out how to retain their support. Only when a legislator consistently works against an organized interest will it consider contributing to that lawmaker's opponent in an election.

Payback Representatives of organized interest groups say that their PAC contributions are designed to buy access—"a chance to talk"—with members of Congress, their staffs, and executives in the administration (see "What Do Contributors

UP CLOSE

Payback: Money and Medicare

After years of struggle, Congress finally passed a prescription drug benefit for Medicare recipients in 2003. The bill was one of the most heavily lobbied pieces of legislation in the Congress in many years. The House and Senate passed very different measures, and the conference committee required months of behind-the-scenes negotiations before sending the bill to both chambers for final passage.

The principal beneficiaries of the bill were supposed to be the nation's senior citizens. And indeed the AARP was heavily involved in every stage of the bill's progress. But the biggest campaign contributors, and arguably the biggest beneficiaries of the final bill, were the drug manufacturers, the health maintenance organizations (HMOs), and the insurance industry.

The House passed the final bill by a close vote of 220–215. An analysis of congressional voting on the bill shows that lawmakers who voted to approve the legislation received average of roughly twice as much in campaign contributions from the drug companies, HMOs, and insurance companies, as those who voted against the bill.

Republicans controlled the House as well as the Senate, and Republicans were generally more favorable toward the positions taken by these industries. So is no surprise that Republican Congress members on average received much larger contributions from these industries than Democrats, even Democrats who supported the industries' positions.

PAC Contributions and the Prescription Drug Vote in the House

	Average Contributions 1990–2003	
	Supporters	**Opponents**
Drug manufacturers	27,618	11,308
HMOs	11,582	6,630
Health insurers	19,510	10,128

Buy?" in Chapter 5). Both interest groups and government officials usually deny that campaign contributions can "buy" support.

Nevertheless, the pattern of campaign contributions by major industries corresponds closely with the pattern of congressional voting on many key issues. Congress members who receive the largest PAC contributions from an industry group tend to vote in favor that group's position. Congress members who oppose the industry's position generally receive far less (see *Up Close:* "Payback: Money and Medicare").

Lobbying the Bureaucracy

Lobbying does not cease after a law is passed. Rather, interest groups try to influence the implementation of the law. Interest groups know that bureaucrats exercise considerable discretion in policy implementation (see "Bureaucratic Power" in Chapter 10). Thus many interests spend as much or more time and energy trying to influence executive agencies than Congress.

Lobbying the bureaucracy involves various types of activities, including monitoring regulatory agencies for notices of new rules and regulatory changes, providing reports, testimony, and evidence in administrative hearings; submitting contract and grant applications and lobbying for their acceptance; and monitoring the performance of executive agencies on behalf of group members.

Groups may try to influence the creation of a new agency to carry out the law or influence the assignment of implementation to an existing "friendly" agency. They may try to influence the selection of personnel to head the implementing agency. They may lobby the agency to devote more money and personnel to enforcement of the law (or less, depending on a group's preference). They may argue for strict rules and regulations—or loose interpretations of the law—by the implementing agencies. Lobbyists frequently appear at administrative hearings to offer information. They often undertake to sponsor test cases of administrative regulations on behalf of affected members. In short, lobbying extends throughout the government.

Iron Triangles In general, interest groups strive to maintain close working relationships with the departments and agencies that serve their members or regulate their industries. Conversely, bureaucracies seek to nourish relationships with powerful "client" groups that are capable of pressuring Congress to expand their authority and increase their budgets. Both bureaucracies and interest groups seek close working relationships with the congressional committees that exercise jurisdictions over their policy function. Finally, members of Congress seek the political and financial support of powerful interest groups, and members also seek to influence bureaucrats to favor supportive interest groups.

The mutual interests of congressional committee members, organized groups, and bureaucratic agencies come together to form what has been labeled the "iron triangles" of American government. **Iron triangles** refer to stable relationships among interest groups, congressional committees, and administrative agencies functioning in the same policy area. Each of the three sides of these triangles depends on the support of the other two; their cooperation serves their own interests (see Figure 7.9).

iron triangles Mutually supportive relationships among interest groups, government agencies, and legislative committees with jurisdiction over a specific policy area.

In an iron triangle, bureaucracies, interest groups, and congressional committees "scratch each other's back." Bureaucrats get political support from interest

FIGURE 7.9 Iron Triangles

The iron triangle approach provides a convenient way to look at the interrelationship among interest groups, executive agencies, and congressional committees. As this example shows, veterans' interest groups work closely with both the Department of Veterans Affairs (executive agency) and the House Veterans Affairs Committee.

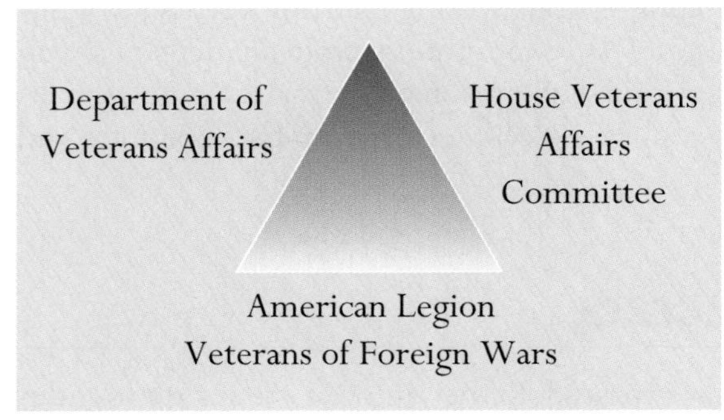

groups in their requests for expanded power and authority and increased budgetary allocations. Interest groups get favorable treatment of their members by the bureaucracy. Congressional committee members get political and financial support from interest groups, as well as favorable treatment for their constituents and contributors who are served or regulated by the bureaucracy.

Policy Networks Generally, we think of American government in terms of the separate branches—Congress, the president and the bureaucracy, and the courts—with interest groups portrayed as external to government itself. But it is also possible to envision government as a series of **policy networks**—interactions in a common policy area among interest-group leaders and lobbyists, members of Congress and their staff personnel, executive agency officials, lawyers and consultants, foundation and think tank people, and even reporters and journalists assigned to the field. Policy networks develop among people who share some knowledge and interest in a policy field—for example, weapons procurement, housing, environment, transportation, or energy—and who regularly interact with each other in the policy arena. Policy networks may include people who differ strongly with each other as well as people who share similar views. What they have in common is their policy expertise and regular interaction. They can participate in negotiations and reach compromises as well as try to outwit and outmaneuver each other.

Revolving Doors It is not uncommon in Washington for people in a policy network to switch jobs, moving from a post in the government to a job in the private sector, or vice versa, or moving to different posts within the government. In one example, an individual might move from a job in a corporation (Pillsbury or General Mills) to the staff of an interest group (American Farm Bureau Federation), and then to the executive agency charged with implementing policy in the field (U.S. Department of Agriculture) or to the staff of a House or Senate committee with jurisdiction over the field (House Agricultural Committee or Senate Agriculture, Nutrition, and Forestry Committee). The common currency of moves within a network is both policy expertise and contacts within the field.

The term **revolving doors** is often used to criticize people who move from a government post (where they acquired experience, knowledge, and personal contacts) to a job in the private sector as a consultant, lobbyist, or salesperson. Defense contractors may recruit high-ranking military officers or Defense Department officials to help sell weapons to their former employers. Trade associations may recruit congressional staffers, White House staffers, or high-ranking agency heads as lobbyists, or these people may leave government service to start their own lobbying firms. Attorneys from the Justice Department, the Internal Revenue Service, and federal regulatory agencies may be recruited by Washington law firms to represent clients in dealings with their former employers.

Former members of Congress are considered the most viable commodity a lobby firm can offer their clients. The Center for Responsive Politics reports that 125 to 150 former Congress members are lobbyists, many of them among the highest paid in the profession. When asked, lobbyists themselves, especially former members of Congress, acknowledge that their success depends mostly on "schmoozing" with their former colleagues.[22]

policy networks Interaction in a common policy area among lobbyists, elected officials, staff personnel, bureaucrats, journalists, and private-sector experts.

revolving doors The movement of individuals from government positions to jobs in the private sector, using the experience, knowledge, and contacts they acquired in government employment.

Lobbying Ethics Concern about revolving doors centers not only on individuals cashing in on their knowledge, experience, and contacts obtained through government employment, but also on the possibility that some government officials will be tempted to tilt their decisions in favor of corporations, law firms, or interest groups that promise these officials well-paid jobs after they leave government employment.

The Ethics in Government Act limits postgovernment employment in an effort to reduce the potential for corruption. Former members of Congress are not permitted to lobby Congress for one year after leaving that body. Former employees of executive agencies are not permitted to lobby their agency for one year after leaving government service, and they are not permitted to lobby their agency for two years on any matter over which they had any responsibility while employed by the government.

Experienced lobbyists also avoid offering a campaign contribution in exchange for a specific vote.[23] Crude "vote buying" (bribery) is illegal and risks repulsing politicians who refuse bribes. **Bribery,** when it occurs, is probably limited to very narrow and specific actions—payments to intervene in a particular case before an administrative agency; payments to insert a very specific break in a tax bill or a specific exemption in a trade bill; payments to obtain a specific contract with the government. Bribery on major issues is very unlikely; there is too much publicity and too many participants for bribery to be effective (but see *Up Close:* "The Cash Constituents of Congress" in Chapter 8).

Lobbying the Courts

Interest groups play an important role in influencing federal courts. Many of the key cases brought to the federal courts are initiated by interest groups. Indeed, **litigation** is becoming a favored instrument of interest-group politics. Groups that oppose a new law or an agency's action often challenge it in court as unconstitutional or as violating the law. Interest groups bring issues to the courts by (1) supplying the attorneys for individuals who are parties to a case; (2) bringing suits to the courts on behalf of classes of citizens; or (3) filing companion **amicus curiae** (literally "friend of the court") arguments in cases in which they are interested.

The nation's most powerful interest groups all have legal divisions specializing in these techniques. The American Civil Liberties Union is one of the most active federal court litigants on behalf of criminal defendants (see *Up Close:* "Politics and the ACLU" in Chapter 12). The early civil rights strategy of the National Association for the Advancement of Colored People (NAACP) was directed by its Legal Defense and Education Fund under the leadership of Thurgood Marshall (see *People in Politics:* "Thurgood Marshall" in Chapter 12). The NAACP chose to sponsor a suit by Linda Brown against the Board of Education in her hometown—Topeka, Kansas—in order to win the historic 1954 desegregation decision. The National Abortion Rights Action League (NARAL) is active in sponsoring legal challenges to abortion restrictions. The Environmental Defense Fund and the Natural Resources Defense Council specialize in environmental litigation.

The special rules of judicial decision making preclude direct lobbying of judges by interest groups (see "The Special Rules of Judicial Decision Making" in Chapter 11). Directly contacting federal judges about a case, letter writing, telephoning, and demonstrating outside of federal courtrooms are all considered inappropriate

bribery Giving or offering anything of value in an effort to influence government officials in the performance of their duties.

litigation Legal dispute brought before a court.

amicus curiae Person or group other than the defendant or the plaintiff or the prosecution that submits an argument in a case for the court's consideration.

conduct. They inspire more resentment than support among federal judges. However, interest groups have been very active in direct lobbying of Congress over judicial appointments. Key interest groups supporting abortion rights—the National Abortion Rights Action League, People for the American Way, the National Organization for Women, and so on—have played a central role in confirmation battles (see *Up Close:* "The Confirmation of Clarence Thomas" in Chapter 11).

SUMMARY NOTES

- Organization grants advantage in the struggle for power. Political parties organize individuals and groups to exercise power in democracies by winning elected office. Interest groups are organizations that seek to influence government policy directly.
- In theory, political parties are "responsible" organizations that adopt a principled platform, recruit candidates who support the platform, educate the public about it, direct an issue-oriented campaign, and then organize the legislature and ensure that their candidates enact the party's platform.
- But in the American two-party system, winning office by appealing to the large numbers of people at the center of the political spectrum becomes more important than promoting strong policy positions. American parties cannot bind elected officials to campaign promises anyway.
- American parties have lost many of their traditional functions over time. Party nominations are won by individual candidates in primary elections rather than through selection by party leaders. Most political candidates are self-selected; they organize their own campaigns. Television has replaced the party as the principal means of educating the public. And government bureaucracies, not party machines, provide social services.
- Party nominations are won in primary elections as earlier caucus and convention methods of nomination have largely disappeared. Party primary elections in the various states may be open or closed and may or may not require runoff primaries. The nominees selected in each party's primary election then battle each other in the general election.
- The parties battle in three major arenas. The *party-in-the-electorate* refers to party identification among voters. The *party-in-the-government* refers to party identification and organization among elected officials. The *party organization* refers to party offices at the local, state, and national levels.
- Since presidential nominations are now generally decided in primary elections—with pledged delegates selected before the opening of the national conventions and with party platforms largely symbolic and wholly unenforceable on the candidates—the conventions have become largely media events designed to kick off the general election campaign.
- *Dealignment* refers to a decline in the attractiveness of the parties to the voters, a growing reluctance of people to identify strongly with either party, and greater voter willingness to cross party lines. Despite dealignment, party identification remains a strong influence in voter choice.
- The interest-group system supplements the electoral system as a form of representation. The electoral system is designed to respond to broad, majority preferences in geographically defined constituencies. The interest-group system represents narrower, minority interests in economic, professional, ideological, religious, racial, gender, and issue constituencies.
- Washington lobbying groups represent a wide array of organized interests. But business, trade, and professional associations outnumber labor union, women's, public-interest, single-issue, and ideological groups.
- Lobbying activities include advertising and public relations, obtaining access to government officials, providing them with technical and political information, mobilizing constituents, building coalitions, organizing demonstrations, and providing campaign support. Bribery is illegal, and most lobbyists avoid exacting specific vote promises in exchange for campaign contributions.
- Organized political action committees (PACs) proliferated following the 1974 "reform" of campaign finance laws. Most PAC money goes to incumbents; interest-group leaders know that incumbents are rarely defeated.
- The mutual interests of organized groups, congressional committees, and bureaucratic agencies sometimes come

together to form "iron triangles" of mutual support and cooperation in specific policy areas. In many policy areas, loose "policy networks" emerge among people who share an interest and expertise—although not necessarily opinions—about a policy and are in regular contact with each other.

- The "revolving door" problem emerges when individuals use the knowledge, experience, and contacts obtained through government employment to secure high-paying jobs with corporations, law firms, lobbying and consulting firms, and interest groups doing business with their old agencies.
- Interest groups influence the nation's courts not only by providing financial and legal support for issues of concern to them but also by lobbying Congress over judicial appointments.

KEY TERMS

political parties 202
interest groups 202
responsible party model 202
Democratic Party 204
Republican Party 204
GOP 204
party polarization 205
nominee 205
nomination 205
primary elections 205
machine 207
patronage 207
divided party government 207
nonpartisan elections 207
caucus 207
ward 208
precinct 208
closed primaries 209
open primaries 209
raiding 209
runoff primary 210
general election 210
convention 210
presidential primaries 210
delegates 211
platform 211
party identification 214
dealignment 214
realignment 215
proportional representation 219
majoritarianism 220
organizational sclerosis 221
trade associations 221
public-interest groups 223
single-issue groups 224
ideological organizations 225
lobbyist 225
lobbying 226
public relations 226
access 228
grass-roots lobbying 229
coalition 229
political action committees (PACs) 231
iron triangles 234
policy networks 235
revolving doors 235
bribery 236
litigation 236
amicus curiae 236

SUGGESTED READINGS

BECK, PAUL, and MARJORIE HERSHEY. *Party Politics in America.* 10th ed. New York: Longman, 2003. An authoritative text on the American party system—party organizations, the parties-in-government, and the parties-in-the-electorate.

BERRY, JEFFREY M. *The New Liberalism: The Rising Power of Citizen Groups.* Washington, D.C.: Brookings Institution Press, 1999. A description of the increasing number and activities of liberal interest groups in Washington and their success in defeating both business and conservative groups.

CIGLER, ALLAN J., and BURDETT A. LOOMIS, eds. *Interest Group Politics.* 6th ed. Washington, D.C.: CQ Press, 2002. A collection of essays examining interest-group politics.

DOWNS, ANTHONY. *An Economic Theory of Democracy.* New York: Harper & Row, 1957. The classic work describing rational choice winning strategies for political parties and explaining why there is no incentive for vote-maximizing parties in a two-party system to adopt widely separate policy positions.

GOLDSTEIN, KENNETH M. *Interest Groups, Lobbying and Participation in America.* New York: Cambridge University Press, 2003. When and why people join interest groups, how they are recruited, and how groups try to influence legislation.

HERNSON PAUL S., RONALD G. SHAIKO, and CLYDE WILCOX. *The Interest Group Connection: Electioneering, Lobbying and Poli-*

cymaking. Boston: Chatham House, 2003. Interest group activities in the electoral, legislative, judicial, and policy-making processes.

KEEFE, WILLIAM J. *Parties, Politics, and Public Policy in America*. 9th ed. Washington, D.C.: CQ Press, 2003. A comprehensive survey of American political parties, from the nominating process to campaign finance and the changing affiliations of voters.

LOWI, THEODORE J. *The End of Liberalism*. New York: Norton, 1969. The classic critique of "interest-group liberalism," describing how special interests contribute to the growth of government and the development of "clientism."

MAKE IT REAL

THE GREAT AMERICAN DIVIDE

Following the 1932 election, the New Deal Democrats—a new coalition of union households, immigrant workers, and people hurt by the Great Depression—established a voting base which dominated the Congress until Newt Gingrich led the Republican Revolution in 1994. Now, as memories of the New Deal fade and the agenda of American politics shifts, the alignments of the 1930s and 1940s hold less and less relevance. The Democrats will need to create a new voting base if it hopes to return to power. In this simulation, you will study the factors that led to the 1932 election and then try to decide where the Democrats had their support in the 2000 election.

THE POLITICAL HORIZON

Every four years, during the presidential election season, the parties write their platforms, which delineate their principles and policy position and proposals. While these platforms are not binding on individual candidates, they are a good indicator of what that party considers important. This simulation contains two parts; in the first part you can explore which party holds views closest to your own. In the second part you can test your knowledge of the issue positions espoused by the various parties.

CHAPTER 8

CONGRESS: POLITICS ON CAPITOL HILL

CHAPTER OUTLINE

- The Powers of Congress
- Congressional Apportionment and Redistricting
- Getting to Capitol Hill
- Party Fortunes in Congress
- Life in Congress
- Home Style
- Organizing Congress: Party and Leadership
- In Committee
- On the Floor
- Decision Making in Congress
- Customs and Norms
- Congressional Ethics

THINK ABOUT POLITICS

1 Should members of Congress be limited in the number of terms they can serve?
Yes ● No ●

2 Should congressional districts be drawn to ensure that minorities win seats in Congress in rough proportion to their populations in the states?
Yes ● No ●

3 Do Congress members spend too much time in their home districts seeking re-election?
Yes ● No ●

4 Is the nation better served when president and the majority in Congress are from the same party?
Yes ● No ●

5 Is it ethical for Congress members to pay special attention to requests for assistance by people who make large campaign contributions?
Yes ● No ●

6 Are there too many lawyers in Congress?
Yes ● No ●

7 Are members of Congress obliged to vote the way their constituents wish, even if they personally disagree?
Yes ● No ●

Who are the members of Congress? How did they get there, and how do they manage to stay there? How did Congress—the official institution for deciding who gets what in America—get its powers, and how does it use them?

The Powers of Congress

James Madison argued that the control of "faction" was "the principal task of modern legislation."[1] He meant that in enacting laws, legislators were really balancing interests, finding compromises, and resolving conflicts. Public policies—laws, regulations, and budgets—represent temporary balances of power among conflicting interests. As the relative power of these interests changes over time, new laws, amendments, and increases or decreases in funding will be enacted, reflecting new balances of power.

Constitutional Powers The Constitution gives very broad powers to Congress. "All legislative Powers herein granted shall be vested in a Congress of the United States, which shall consist of a Senate and House of Representatives." The nation's Founders envisioned Congress as the first and most powerful branch of government. They equated national powers with the powers of Congress and gave Congress the most clearly specified role in national government.

Article I empowers Congress to levy taxes, borrow and spend money, regulate interstate commerce, establish a national money supply, establish a post office, declare war, raise and support an army and navy, establish a court system, and pass all laws "necessary and proper" to implement these powers. Congress may also propose amendments to the Constitution or (with a two-thirds vote of both the House and the Senate) admit new states. In the event that no presidential candidate receives a majority of votes in the Electoral College, the House of Representatives selects the president. The Senate has two additional powers, it is called on for advice and consent to treaties, and it confirms presidential nominations to executive and judicial posts. The House has the power to impeach, and the Senate to try any officer of the U.S. government, including the president. Each **congressional session** convenes on January 3 following congressional elections in November of even-numbered years.

Institutional Conflict Over two centuries, the separate branches of the national government—the Congress, the presidency and the executive branch, and the Supreme Court and federal Judiciary—have struggled for power and preeminence in governing. This struggle for power among the separate institutions is precisely what the Founders envisioned. In writing the Constitution, they sought to create "opposite and rival interests" among the separate branches of the national government. "The constant aim," explained Madison, "is to divide and arrange the several offices in such a manner as that each may be a check on the other."[2] (see Appendix, *Federalist Papers,* No. 51). From time to time, first the Congress, then the presidency, and occasionally the Supreme Court have appeared to become the most powerful branch of government.

"The President Initiates, Congress Deliberates" Throughout much of the twentieth century, Congress ceded leadership in national policy making to the president and the executive branch. Congress largely responded to the policy initiatives and spending requests originating from the president, executive agencies, and interest groups. Congress did not merely ratify or "rubber-stamp" these initiatives and requests; it played an independent role in the policy-making process. But this role was essentially a deliberative one, in which Congress accepted, modified, amended, or rejected the policies and budget requests initiated by others.

U.S. House of Representatives
Official Web site of the House, with schedule of floor and committee actions, legislative information, and links to every Representative's Web site and every committee Web site.
www.house.gov

It is easier for the Congress to obstruct the policy initiatives of the president than it is to assume policy leadership itself. Congress can defeat presidential policy proposals, deny presidential budget requests, delay or reject presidential appointments, investigate executive agencies, hold committee hearings to spotlight improprieties, and generally immobilize the executive branch. It can investigate and question nominees for the Supreme Court and the federal judiciary; it can legislate changes in the jurisdiction of the federal courts; and it can try to reverse court decisions by amending laws or the Constitution itself. The Congress can even threaten to impeach the president or federal judges. But these are largely reactive, obstructionist actions, usually accompanied by a great deal of oratory.

Dividing Congressional Power: House and Senate Congress must not only share national power with the executive and judicial branches of government; it must share power within itself. The framers of the Constitution took the advice of the nation's eldest diplomat, Benjamin Franklin: "It is not enough that your legislature should be numerous; it should also be divided. . . . One division should watch over and control the other, supply its wants, correct its blunders, and cross its designs, should they be criminal or erroneous."[3] Accordingly, the U.S. Congress is **bicameral**—composed of two houses (see Figure 8.1).

congressional session Each Congress elected in November of even-numbered years meets the following January 3 and remains in session for two years. Since the first Congress to meet under the Constitution in 1789, Congresses have been numbered by session (for example, 107th Congress 2001–2003, 108th Congress 2003–2005, 109th Congress 2005–2007).

bicameral Any legislative body that consists of two separate chambers or houses; in the United States, the Senate represents 50 statewide voter constituencies, and the House of Representatives represents voters in 435 separate districts.

No law can be passed and no money can be spent unless both the House of Representatives and the Senate pass identical laws. Yet the House and the Senate have very different constituencies and terms. The House consists of 435 voting members, elected from districts within each state apportioned on the basis of equal population. (The average congressional district since the 1990 census has a population of 571,700; the House also includes nonvoting delegates from Puerto Rico, the District of Columbia, Guam, the Virgin Islands, and American Samoa.) All House members face election every two years. The Senate consists of 100 members serving six-year terms, elected by statewide constituencies. Senate terms are staggered so that one-third of senators are elected every two years (see Table 8.1).

The House of Representatives, with its two-year terms, was designed to be more responsive to the popular mood. Representatives are fond of referring to their chamber as "the people's House," and the Constitution requires that all revenue-raising bills originate in the House. The Senate was designed to be a smaller, more deliberative body, with its members serving six-year terms. Indeed, the Senate is the more prestigious body. House members frequently give up their seats to run for the Senate; the reverse has seldom occurred. Moreover, the Senate exercises

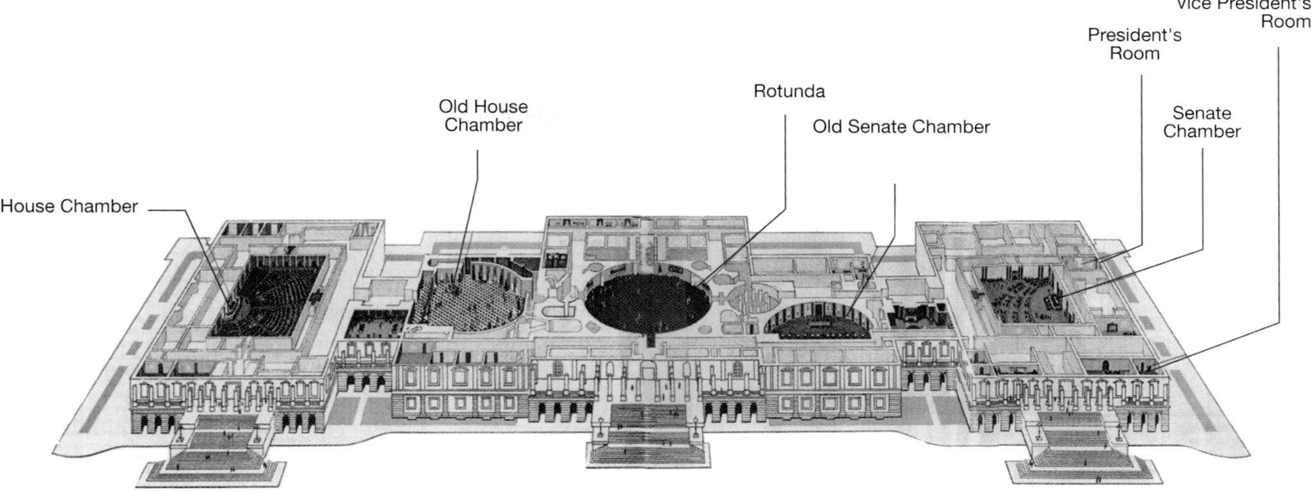

FIGURE 8.1 Corridors of Power in Congress

The architecture and floor plan of the Capitol Building in Washington reflect the bicameral division of Congress, with one wing for the House of Representatives and one for the Senate.

certain powers not given to the House: the power to ratify treaties and the power to confirm federal judges, ambassadors, cabinet members, and other high executive officials.

U.S. Senate Official Senate Web site, with floor and committee schedules, Senate news, and links to each Senator's Web site. *www.senate.gov*

Domestic versus Foreign and Defense Policy Congress is more powerful in domestic than in foreign and military affairs. It is freer to reject presidential initiatives in domestic policy areas such as welfare, health, education, the environment, and taxation. But Congress usually follows presidential leadership in foreign and defense policy even though constitutionally the president and Congress share power in these arenas. The president is "Commander-in-Chief" of the armed forces, but only Congress can "declare war." The president appoints and receives ambassadors and "makes treaties," but the Senate must confirm appointments and provide "advice and consent" to treaties. Historically presidents have led the nation in matters of war and peace. Presidents have sent U.S. troops beyond the borders of the United States in military actions on more than two hundred occasions. In contrast, Congress has formally declared war only five times: the War of 1812, the Mexican War in 1846, the Spanish-American War in 1898, World War I in 1917, and World War II in 1941. Congress did not declare war in the Korean War (1950–53), the Vietnam War (1965–73), the Persian Gulf War (1991), or the wars in Afghanistan (2002) or Iraq (2003).

The Vietnam experience inspired Congress to try to reassert its powers over war and peace. Military embarrassment, prolonged and indecisive fighting, and accumulating casualties—all vividly displayed on national television—encouraged Congress to challenge presidential war-making power. The War Powers Act of 1973, passed over the veto of President Richard Nixon, who was weakened by the Watergate scandal, sought to curtail the president's power to commit U.S. military forces to combat (see "Commander-in-Chief" in Chapter 9). But this act has not proven effective, and both Republican and Democratic presidents have continued to exercise war-making powers.

TABLE 8.1 Comparing the House and Senate

	House of Representatives	Senate
Terms	Two years	Six years
Members	435	100
Elections	All every two years	One-third every two years
Constituencies	Congressional districts	States
Unique powers	Originate tax bills Bring impeachment charges	Advise and consent to (ratify) treaties by two-thirds vote Confirm appointments Try impeachment charges
Debate on bills	Limited by Rules Committee	Unlimited, except by unanimous consent or vote of cloture (three-fifths)
Member prestige	Modest; smaller personal staffs, fewer committee assignments	High: larger personal staffs, more committee assignments, always addressed as "Senator"
Leadership	Hierarchical, with speaker, majority and minority leaders and whips and committees, especially Rules, concentrating power	Less hierarchical, with each senator exercising more influence on leadership, committees, and floor votes
Committees	Twenty standing and select committees Each member on about five committees Difficult to bypass	Twenty standing and select committees Each member on about seven committees Easier to bypass

The Power of the Purse Congress's real power in both domestic and foreign (defense) policy centers on its **power of the purse**—its power over federal taxing and spending. Only Congress can "lay and collect Taxes, Duties, Imposts and Excises" (Article I, Section 8), and only Congress can authorize spending: "No Money shall be drawn from the Treasury, but in Consequence of Appropriations made by Law" (Article I, Section 9).

Congress jealously guards these powers. Presidents initiate taxing and spending policies by sending their budgets to the Congress each year (see "The Bureaucracy and the Budgetary Process" in Chapter 10 for details). But Congress has the last word on taxing and spending. The most important bills that Congress considers each year are usually the budget resolutions setting ceilings on various categories of expenditures and the later appropriations bills authorizing specific expenditures. It is often in these appropriations bills that Congress exercises its greatest influence over national policy. Thus, for example, the Congress's involvement in foreign affairs centers on its annual consideration of appropriations for foreign aid, its involvement in military affairs centers on its annual deliberations over the defense appropriations bill, and so on.

power of the purse Congress's exclusive, constitutional power to authorize expenditures by all agencies of the federal government.

oversight Congressional monitoring of the activities of executive branch agencies to determine if the laws are being faithfully executed.

Oversight of the Bureaucracy Congressional **oversight** of the federal bureaucracy is a continuing process by which Congress reviews the activities of the executive branch. The *formal* rationale of oversight is to determine whether the purposes of laws passed by Congress are being achieved by executive agencies and whether appropriations established by Congress are being spent as intended. Often the *real* purpose is to influence executive branch decisions, secure favorable treatment for friends and constituents, embarrass presidential appointees, undercut political support for particular programs or agencies, lay the political groundwork for budgetary increases or decreases for an agency, or simply enhance the power of congressional committees and subcommittees and those who chair them.

Oversight is carried out primarily through congressional committees and subcommittees. Individual senators and representatives can engage in a form of oversight simply by writing or calling executive agencies, but committees and their staffs carry on the bulk of oversight activity. Because committees and subcommittees specialize in particular areas of policy making, each tends to focus its oversight activities on particular executive departments and agencies. Oversight is particularly intense during budget hearings. Subcommittees of both the House and the Senate Appropriations Committees are especially interested in how money is being spent by the agencies they oversee.

John Ashcroft, former U.S. Senator from Missouri, during his confirmation hearings to become Bush's Attorney General. Ashcroft would later lead the fight for the controversial Patriot Act as part of the war on terror.

Senate Advice and Consent and Confirmation of Presidential Appointments The Constitution provides that the President must obtain the **advice and consent** of the Senate for treaties "provided that two-thirds of the Senators present concur." In fact, the Senate has seldom provided "advice" to the president regarding treaties prior to their submission to the Senate for "consent." The president enjoys a high degree of autonomy over U.S. foreign policy (see "Global Leader" in Chapter 9). The process of treaty ratification begins when a president submits an already negotiated treaty to the Senate. Once submitted, treaties are automatically referred to the Senate Foreign Relations Committee. That Committee cannot make changes in the treaty itself; it can either reject the treaty or forward it to the full Senate. The Senate itself cannot make changes in the formal treaty but must accept or reject it. Ratification requires a two-thirds vote. The Senate can, however, express its reservations to a treaty and/or instruct the president how the treaty is to be interpreted.[4]

The Senate also exercises a special power over the president and the executive branch of government through its constitutional responsibility for approving presidential appointments of key executive officers, including Cabinet members, ambassadors, and other high officials (see "Congressional Constraints on the Bureaucracy" in Chapter 10). And the Senate exercises a special power over the judicial branch through its constitutional responsibility to ratify presidential appointments to the federal judiciary including the Supreme Court (see "The Politics of Selecting Judges" in Chapter 11). Confirmation of appointments requires only a simple majority vote of the Senate.

confirmation The constitutionally required consent of the Senate to appointments of high-level executive officials by the president and appointments of federal judges.

advice and consent The constitutional power of the U.S. Senate to reject or ratify (by a two-thirds vote) treaties made by the president.

Agenda Setting and Media Attention **Congressional hearings** and investigations often involve agenda setting—bringing issues to the public's attention and placing them on the national agenda. For agenda-setting purposes, congressional committees or subcommittees need the assistance of the media. Televised hearings and investigations are perhaps the most effective means by which Congress can attract attention to issues as well as to itself and its members.

Hearings and investigations are similar in some ways, but hearings are usually held on a specific bill in order to build a record of both technical information (what is the problem and how legislation might be crafted to resolve it) and political information (who favors and who opposes various legislative options). In contrast, investigations are held on alleged misdeeds or scandals. Although the U.S. Supreme Court has held that there must be some "legislative purpose" behind a **congressional investigation,** that phrase has been interpreted very broadly indeed.[5]

The *formal* rationale for congressional investigations is that Congress is seeking information to assist in its lawmaking function. But from the earliest Congress to the present, the investigating powers of Congress have often been used for

congressional hearings Congressional committee sessions in which members listen to witnesses who provide information and opinions on matters of interest to the committee, including pending legislation.

congressional investigation Congressional committee hearings on alleged misdeeds or scandals.

political purposes: to rally popular support for policies or programs favored by Congress; to attack the president, other high officials in the administration, or presidential policies or programs; to focus media attention and public debate on particular issues; or simply to win media coverage and popular recognition for members of Congress. Congressional investigators have the legal power to subpoena witnesses (force them to appear), administer oaths, compel testimony, and initiate criminal charges for contempt (refusing to cooperate) and perjury (lying). These powers can be exercised by Congress's regular committees and subcommittees and by committees appointed especially to conduct a particular investigation.

Congress cannot impose criminal punishments as a result of its investigations. But the information uncovered in a congressional investigation can be turned over to the U.S. Department of Justice, which may proceed with its own criminal investigation and perhaps indictment and trial of alleged wrongdoers in federal courts.

Congressional investigations have long been used as an opportunity for Congress to expose wrongdoing on the part of executive branch officials. The first congressional investigation (1792) examined why General Arthur St. Clair had been defeated by the Indians in Ohio; the Crédit Mobilier investigations (1872–73) revealed scandals in the Grant Administration; the Select Committee on Campaign Practices, known universally as the "Watergate Committee," exposed the activities of President Richard Nixon's inner circle that led to impeachment charges and Nixon's forced resignation; a House and Senate Joint Select Committee conducted the Iran-Contra investigation in the Reagan Administration; the Senate Special Whitewater Committee investigated matters related to Bill and Hillary Clinton's real estate investments in Arkansas.

Impeachment and Removal Potentially Congress's most formidable power is that of impeaching and removing from office the president, other officers of the United States, and federal judges, including Supreme Court justices. Congress can do so only for "Treason, Bribery or other High Crimes and Misdemeanors." The House of Representatives has the sole authority to bring charges of impeachment by a simple majority vote. Impeachment is analogous to a criminal indictment; it does not remove an officer but merely subjects him or her to trial by the Senate. Only the Senate, following a trial, can remove the federal official from office, and then only by a two-thirds vote.

Bill Clinton is the second president in the nation's history to be impeached by the U.S. House of Representatives. (Andrew Johnson was the first in 1867; after a one-month trial in the Senate, the "guilty" vote fell one short of two-thirds needed for removal. President Richard Nixon resigned just prior to an impending impeachment vote in 1974.) The 1998 House impeachment vote split along partisan lines, with Republicans voting "yes" and Democrats voting "no." Two Articles of Impeachment were passed, one for perjury before a grand jury and one for obstruction of justice. In the subsequent Senate trial, only 45 senators (less than a majority and far less than the needed two-thirds) voted to convict President Clinton on the first charge, and only 50 voted to convict on the second (see *Up Close:* "Sex, Lies, and Impeachment" in Chapter 9).

THINK AGAIN

Should congressional districts be drawn to ensure that minorities win seats in Congress in rough proportion to their populations in the states?

Congressional Apportionment and Redistricting

The Constitution states that "Representatives . . . shall be apportioned among the several states . . . according to their respective Numbers." It orders an "actual enumeration" (census) every ten years. And it provides that every state shall have at least one representative, in addition to two senators, regardless of population. But the Constitution is silent on the size of the House of Representatives. Congress itself determines its own size; for more than a century, it allowed itself to grow to accommodate new states and population growth. In 1910 it fixed the membership of the House at 435.

The effect of doing so has been to expand the population of House districts over the years. Following the 2000 census, House districts have populations of about 650,000. It is sometimes argued that such large House constituencies prevent meaningful communication between citizens and their representatives. (The Framers originally envisioned House districts of no more than 30,000 people.) But expanding the size of the House would complicate its work, reduce the influence of individual members, require more procedural controls, and probably strengthen the power of party leaders.

Apportionment **Apportionment** refers to the allocation of House seats to the states after each ten-year census. The Constitution does not specify a mathematical method of apportionment; Congress adopted a complex "method of equal proportion" in 1929, which so far has withstood court challenges (see *Across the USA*: "Reapportionment, 2000," which shows the current apportionment, together with the states that gained and lost seats after the 2000 census).

Malapportionment Historically, State legislatures were notorious for their **malapportionment**—congressional (and state legislative) districts with grossly unequal numbers of people. Some congressional districts had twice the average number of people per district, and others had only half as many. In a district twice the size of the average district, the value of an individual's vote was heavily diluted. In a district half the size of the average, the value of an individual's vote was greatly magnified.

Enter the Supreme Court Prior to 1962, the Supreme Court refused to intervene in apportionment, holding that this question belonged to the state legislatures and that the federal courts should avoid this "political thicket." So the Supreme Court's decision in the landmark case *Baker v. Carr* (1962) came as a surprise. The Court ruled that inequalities in voters' influence resulting from different-size districts violated the Equal Protection Clause of the Fourteenth Amendment. The case dealt with a complaint about Tennessee's state legislative districts, but the Court soon extended its holding to congressional districts as well.[6] The conception of political equality from the Declaration of Independence to Lincoln's Gettysburg Address, to the Fourteenth, Fifteenth, Seventeenth, and Nineteenth Amendments, can mean only one thing—one person, one vote."[7]

The shift in the Supreme Court's policy raised a new question: How equal must districts be in order to guarantee voters "equal protection of the law"? The courts have ruled that only official U.S. Bureau of the Census figures may be used: estimated changes since the last census may *not* be used. In recent years, the courts have insisted on nearly exact mathematical equality in congressional districts in a state.

"Enumeration" The U.S. Constitution is very specific in its wording: It calls for an "actual Enumeration" (Article I, Section 2) of the population in each ten-year census. However, the U.S. Bureau of the Census has considered the use of samples and estimates to correct what it perceives to be "undercounts." Undercounting is said to occur when certain populations are difficult to identify and count on an individual basis, populations such as recent non-English-speaking immigrants or

apportionment The allocation of legislative seats to jurisdictions based on population. Seats in the U.S. House of Representatives are apportioned to the states on the basis of their population after every ten-year census.

malapportionment Unequal numbers of people in legislative districts resulting in inequality of voter representation.

ACROSS THE USA

Reapportionment, 2000

Since 1910, the number of seats in the House of Representatives has remained constant at 435. Each ten-year census requires a reapportionment of seats among states based on their populations. States with rapid population growth such as Arizona. Texas, Georgia, and Florida gain seats (each of the states gained two seats following the 2000 census). States with slow population growth lose seats (New York and Pennsylvania both lost two seats). The newly apportioned House convened in January 2003.

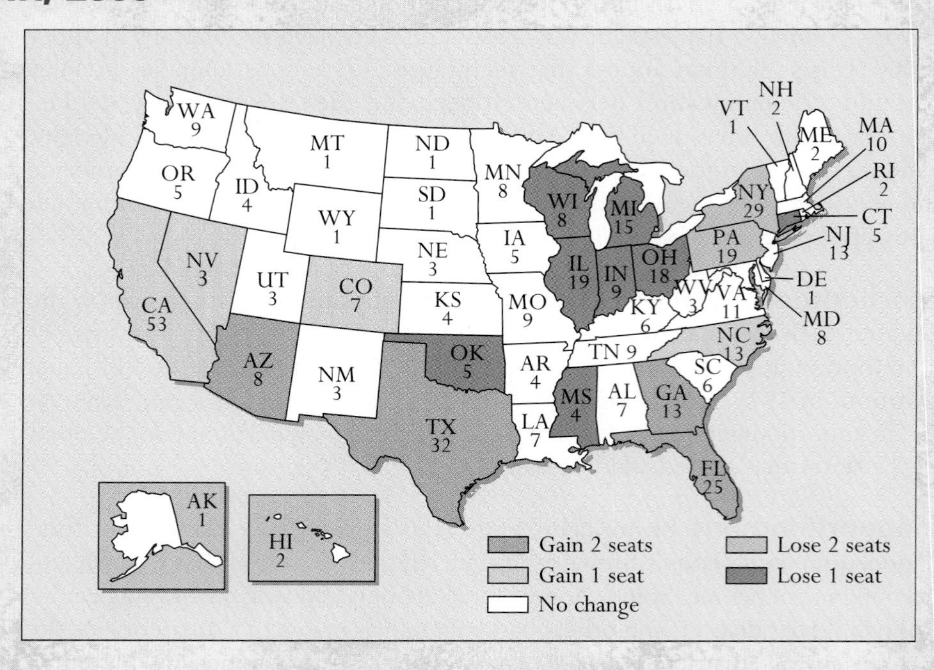

residents of neighborhoods likely to mistake government census takers for law enforcement officers or other unwelcome government officials. Political leaders (usually Democrats) of states and cities with large immigrant and minority populations have favored the substitution of samples and estimates for actual head counts. However, the U.S. Supreme Court held in 1999 that the Census Act of 1976 prohibits sampling for purposes of apportioning House members among the states.[8] Congress may use sampling for determining the allocation of grant-in-aid funds if it wishes.

Redistricting **Redistricting** refers to the drawing of boundary lines of congressional districts following the census. After each census, some states gain and others lose seats, depending on whether their populations have grown faster or slower than the nation's population. In addition, population shifts within a state may force districting changes. Congressional district boundaries are drawn by state legislatures in each state, a state's redistricting act must pass both houses of the state legislature and win the governor's signature (or be passed over a gubernatorial veto). The U.S. Justice Department and the federal judiciary are also deeply involved in redistricting issues, particularly questions of whether or not redistricting disadvantages African Americans or other minorities.

redistricting Drawing of legislative district boundary lines following each ten-year census.

gerrymandering Drawing district boundary lines for political advantage.

Gerrymandering **Gerrymandering** is the drawing of district lines for political advantage (see Figure 8.2). The population of districts may be equal, yet the dis-

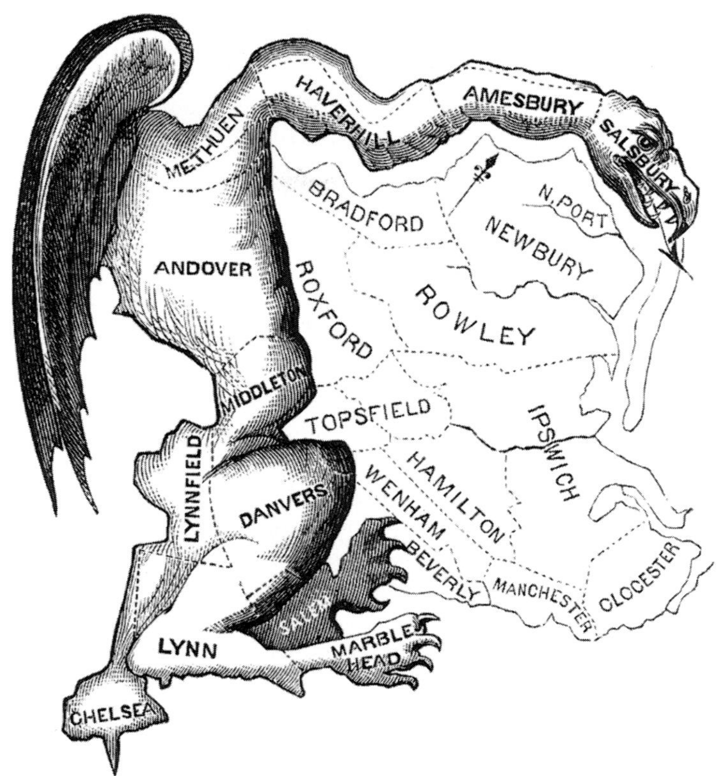

FIGURE 8.2 The Original Gerrymander

The term *gerrymander* immortalizes Governor Elbridge Gerry (1744–1814) of Massachusetts, who in 1811 redistricted the state legislature to favor Democrats over Federalists. A district north of Boston was designed to concentrate, and thus "waste," Federalist votes. This political cartoon from the *Boston Gazette,* March 26, 1812, depicted the new district lines as a salamander, dubbing the process the "gerrymander."

trict boundaries are drawn in such a fashion as to grant advantage or disadvantage to specific groups of voters. Gerrymandering has long been used by parties in control of the state legislatures to maximize their seats in Congress and state legislatures.

Gerrymandering, with the aid of sophisticated computer-mapping programs and data on past voting records of precincts, is a highly technical task. But consider a simple example where a city is entitled to three representatives and the eastern third of the city is Republican but the western two-thirds is Democratic (see Figure 8.3). If the Republicans could draw the district lines, they might draw them along a north-south direction to allow their party to win in one of the three districts. In contrast, if Democrats could draw the district lines, they might draw them along an east-west direction to allow their party to win all three districts by diluting the Republican vote. Such dividing up and diluting of a strong minority to deny it the power to elect a representative is called **splintering.** Often gerrymandering is not as neat as our example; district lines may twist and turn, creating grotesque patterns in order to achieve the desired effects. Another gerrymandering strategy—**packing**—is the heavy concentration of one party's voters in a single district in order to "waste" their votes and allow modest majorities of the party doing the redistricting to win in other districts.

splintering Redistricting in which a strong minority is divided up and diluted to prevent it from electing a representative.

packing Redistricting in which partisan voters are concentrated in a single district, "wasting" their majority vote and allowing the opposition to win by modest majorities in other districts.

Partisan Gerrymandering Generally, partisan gerrymandering does not violate federal court standards for "equal protection" under the Fourteenth Amendment. There is no constitutional obligation to allocate seats "to the contending parties in proportion to what their anticipated statewide vote will be."[9] However, the federal courts may intervene in political gerrymandering if it "consistently degrades a voter's or a group of voters' influence on the political process as a whole."[10]

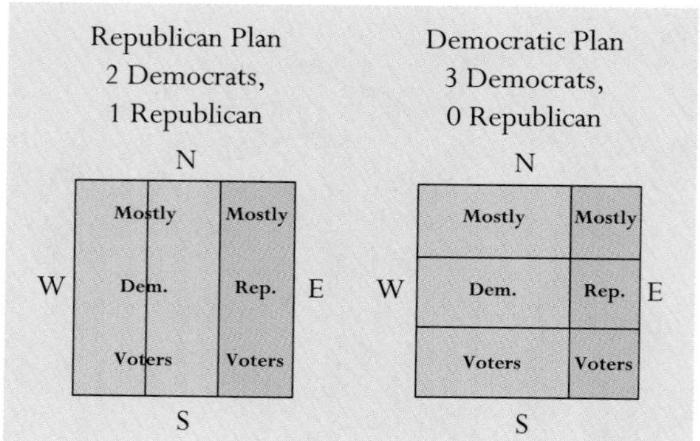

FIGURE 8.3
Gerrymandering in Action
Depending on how an area is divided into districts, the result may benefit one party or the other. In this example, dividing the area so one district has virtually all the Republicans gives that party a victory in that district while ceding the other two districts to the Democrats. In contrast, Democrats benefit when Republican voters are divided among the three districts so that their votes are splintered.

These vague standards set forth by the U.S. Supreme Court open the door to judicial intervention in particularly grievous cases of partisan gerrymandering.

Re-redistricting The redrawing of congressional districts usually occurs after each ten-year census. However, several states have been embroiled in a second round of redistricting, notably Texas. (If one party dominated a state legislature during the first redistricting after the census, and drew district lines in a partisan fashion, there is then a strong temptation for the opposition party to undertake a second round of partisan redistricting if it subsequently wins control of the state legislature.) It is theoretically possible that redistricting could be undertaken every time a state legislature changes party control. If this becomes a common practice in the states, partisan wrangling over redistricting may tie up state legislatures for years.

Incumbent Gerrymandering Yet another problem confronting state legislatures in redistricting is the preservation of incumbent Congress members, that is, **incumbent gerrymandering.** Incumbents generally have sufficient political clout with their state parties to inspire efforts in the legislature to protect their districts.

Incumbent gerrymandering means drawing district lines in such a way so as to ensure that districts of incumbents include enough supporters of their party to provide a high probability of their reelection. But often ensuring incumbents' security and maximizing the party's total number of seats are conflicting goals. It is not always possible to redraw district lines in such a way as to protect incumbents and at the same time ensure the largest number of party seats in a state. Incumbents themselves want the largest number of their party's voters packed in their district. But this tactic may result in losses for their party in other districts that have been robbed of party voters. Redistricting almost always confronts incumbents with new voters—voters that were previously in a different incumbent's district. As a result, incumbents usually have a somewhat more difficult reelection campaign following redistricting than in other elections.[11]

Racial Gerrymandering Racial gerrymandering to disadvantage African Americans and other minorities violates both the Equal Protection Clause of the Fourteenth Amendment and the Voting Rights Act of 1965. The Voting Rights Act specifies that redistricting in states with a history of voter discrimination or low voter participation must be "cleared" in advance with the U.S. Justice Department. The act extends special protection not only to African American voters but also to Hispanic, Native American, Alaska Native, and Asian voters.

incumbent gerrymandering
Drawing legislative district boundaries to advantage incumbent legislators.

In 1982 Congress strengthened the Voting Rights Act by outlawing any electoral arrangement that has the effect of weakening minority voting power. This *effects test* replaced the earlier *intent test*, under which redistricting was outlawed only if boundaries were intentionally drawn to dilute minority political influence. In *Thornburg v. Gingles* (1986), the Supreme Court interpreted the effects test to require state legislatures to redistrict their states in a way that maximizes minority representation in Congress and the state legislatures.[12] The effect of this ruling was to require **affirmative racial gerrymandering**—the creation of predominately African American and minority districts (labeled "majority-minority" districts) whenever possible. Following the 1990 census, redistricting in legislatures in states with large minority populations was closely scrutinized by the U.S. Justice Department and the federal courts. The result was a dramatic increase in African American and Hispanic representation in Congress (see Figure 8.7 later in this chapter).

However, the Supreme Court later expressed constitutional doubts about bizarre-shaped districts based *solely* on racial composition. In a controversial 5 to 4 decision in *Shaw v. Reno* (1993), Justice Sandra Day O'Connor wrote, "Racial gerrymandering, even for remedial purposes, may balkanize us into competing racial factions. . . . A reapportionment plan that includes in one district individuals who have little in common with one another but the color of their skin bears an uncomfortable resemblance to political apartheid"[13] (see Figure 8.4). Later the Court held that the use of race as the "predominant factor" in dividing district lines in unconstitutional: "When the state assigns voters on the basis of race, it engages in the offensive and demeaning assumption that voters of a particular race, because of their race, think alike, share the same political interests and will prefer the same candidates at the polls."[14] But the Court has stopped short of saying that *all* race-conscious districting is unconstitutional.

Partisanship Interacts with Race Racial gerrymandering appears to help Republican congressional candidates. If African American voters are concentrated in heavily black districts, the effect is to "bleach" surrounding districts of Democratic-leaning black voters and thus improve the chances for Republican victories.

affirmative racial gerrymandering Drawing district boundary lines to maximize minority representation.

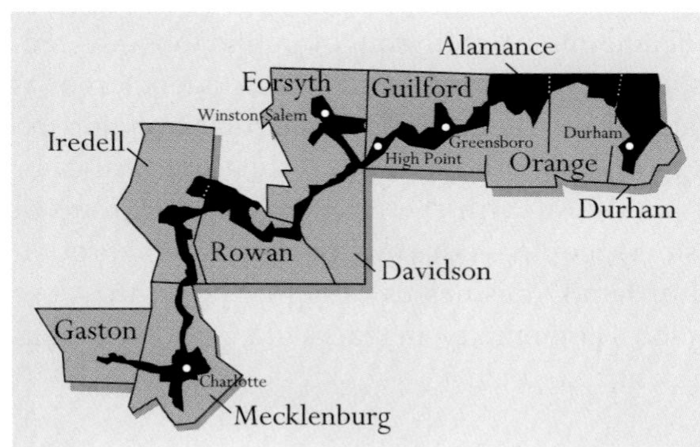

FIGURE 8.4 Affirmative Racial Gerrymandering

North Carolina's Twelfth Congressional District was drawn up to be a "majority-minority" district by combining African American communities over a wide region of the state. The U.S. Supreme Court in *Shaw v. Reno* (1993) ordered a court review of this district to determine whether it incorporated any common interest other than race. The North Carolina legislature redrew the district in 1997, lowering its black population from 57 to 46 percent, yet keeping its lengthy connection of black voters from Charlotte to Greensboro.

Republican Party congressional gains in the South during the 1990s may be partly attributed to racial gerrymandering.[15] In what has been described as a "paradox of representation," the creation of majority-minority districts brought more minority members to Congress, but it also led to a more conservative House of Representatives, as Republicans gained seats previously held by white liberal Democrats.[16]

Republican led efforts to "pack" black (Democratic) voters into relatively few districts suffered a setback in 2003 when the U.S. Supreme Court recognized that doing so might diminish the power of African-American voters overall. The Court approved of a plan that "unpacked" some heavily concentrated majority-minority districts in Georgia. The Court reasoned that the result would be to create additional black "influence" districts where African-American voters would not be in a majority but would be a large influential voting bloc.[17]

Getting to Capitol Hill

Members of Congress are independent political entrepreneurs—selling themselves, their services, and their personal policy views to the voters in 435 House districts and 50 states across the country. They initiate their own candidacies, raise most of their campaign funds from individual contributors, put together personal campaign organizations, and get themselves elected with relatively little help from their party. Their reelection campaigns depend on their ability to raise funds from individuals and interest groups and on the services and other benefits they provide to their constituents.

THINK AGAIN

Are there too many lawyers in Congress?

Roll Call This online magazine covers a variety of current topics about Congress but is especially strong on stories dealing with running for Congress and/or campaign financing. *www.rollcall.com*

Who Runs for Congress? Members of Congress come from a wide variety of backgrounds, ranging from acting and professional sports to medicine and the ministry. However, exceptionally high percentages of senators and representatives have prior experience in at least one of three fields—law, business, or public service (see Table 8.2). Members of Congress are increasingly career politicians, people who decided early in life to devote themselves to running for and occupying public office.[18] The many lawyers, by and large, are *not* practicing attorneys. Rather, the typical lawyer-legislator is a political activist with a law degree. These are people who graduated from law school and immediately sought public jobs—as federal or state prosecuting attorneys, as attorneys for federal or state agencies, or as staff assistants in congressional, state, or city offices. They used their early job experiences to make political contacts and learn how to organize a political campaign, find financial contributors, and deal with the media. Another group of Congress members are former businesspeople—not employees of large corporations, but people whose personal or family businesses brought them into close contact with government and their local community, in real estate, insurance, franchise dealerships, community banks, and so forth.

Competition for Seats Careerism in Congress is aided by the electoral advantages enjoyed by incumbents over challengers. Greater name recognition, advantages in raising campaign funds, and the resources of congressional offices all combine to limit competition for seats in Congress and to reelect the vast majority of incumbents (see "The Advantages of Incumbency" in Chapter 8). The result is an incumbent reelection percentage for House members that usually exceeds 90 percent. The average reelection rate for U.S. senators is more than 80 percent (see Figure 8.5).

TABLE 8.2 Backgrounds of Congress Members

	House			Senate			Congress
	D	R	Total	D	R	Total	Total
Occupation							
Actor/entertainer		2	2				2
Aeronautics		2	2	1		1	3
Agriculture	8	18	26		5	5	31
Artistic/Creative		1	2*				2*
Business/Banking	56	109	165	9	16	25	190
Clergy	1	1	2				2
Education	50	37	88*	7	5	12	100*
Engineering	1	7	8		1	1	9
Health Care	4	1	5				5
Homemaker/Domestic	2	2	4				4
Journalism	3	7	11*	1	5	6	17*
Labor	5	2	7		2	2	9
Law	86	75	161	29	30	60	221†
Law Enforcement	6	3	9				9
Medicine	5	11	16		3	3	19
Military		3	3		1	1	4
Professional Sports		1	1		1	1	2
Public Service/Politics	77	68	145	17	13	30	175
Real Estate	3	27	30	2	1	3	33
Secretarial/Clerical		2	2				2
Technical/Trade	1	3	4				4
Miscellaneous	1	3	4				4
Religion							
African Methodist Episcopal	3		3				3
Baptist	33	33	66	1	5	6	72
Christian Church	4		4				4
Christian Reformed Church		2	2				2
Christian Scientist		5	5				5
Eastern Orthodox		2	2	1	1	2	4
Episcopalian	10	24	34	3	7	10	44
Jewish	24	1	26*	9	2	11	37*
Lutheran	9	10	19	3	1	4	23
Methodist	16	34	50	7	5	12	62
Mormon	3	9	12	1	4	5	17
Pentecostal		4	4				4
Presbyterian	11	26	37	3	10	13	50
Roman Catholic	71	53	124	14	11	25	149
Seventh-Day Adventist	1	1	2				2
Unitarian	1	1	2	1		1	3
United Church of Christ/ Congregationalist		2	2	3	2	6†	8†
Unspecified, Protestant	12	22	34	2	2	4	38
Unspecified, other	7		7		1	1	8

*Includes Independent Bernard Sanders of Vermont.

†Includes Independent James M. Jeffords of Vermont.

Source: Congressional Quarterly Weekly Report, January 25, 2003, for 108th Congress, 2003–2005.

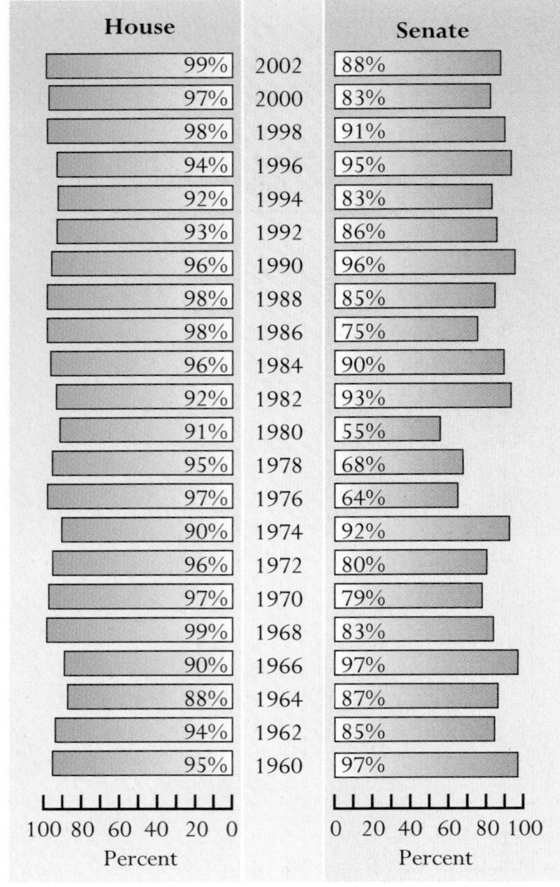

FIGURE 8.5 Incumbent Advantage

Despite periodic movements to "throw the bums out," voters in most districts and states routinely reelect their members of Congress. In recent decades, more than 90 percent of representatives and 80 percent of senators who have sought reelection have been returned to Congress by votes in their districts or states.

Aspirants for congressional careers are well advised to wait for open seats. **Open seats** in the House of Representatives are created when incumbents retire or vacate the seat to run for higher office. These opportunities occur on average in about 10 percent of House seats in each election. But every ten years reapportionment creates many new opportunities to win election to Congress. Reapportionment creates new seats in states gaining population, just as it forces out some incumbents in states losing population. Redistricting also threatens incumbents with new constituencies, where they have less name recognition, no history of casework, and perhaps no common racial or ethnic identification. Thus forced retirements and electoral defeats are more common in the first election following each ten-year reapportionment and redistricting of Congress.

Winning Big Not only do incumbent Congress members usually win, they usually win big. Over 70 percent of House members win by margins of 60 percent or more or run unopposed. (In recent years, 10 to 18 percent of House members have had no opposition in the general election.) Senate races are somewhat more competitive. Senate challengers are usually people who have political experience and name recognition as members of the House, governors, or other high state officials. Even so, most Senate incumbents seeking reelection are victorious over their challengers.

open seat Seat in a legislature for which no incumbent is running for reelection.

safe seat Legislative district in which the incumbent regularly wins by a large margin of the vote.

Most members of Congress, then, sit comfortably in **safe seats**—that is, they regularly win reelection by a large margin of the vote (see Table 8.3).

TABLE 8.3 Winning Big: House and Senate Elections Won by 60 Percent or More of the Vote

	House	Senate
1984	78.9%	65.5%
1986	84.5	50.0
1988	87.3	37.5
1990	79.5	66.7
1992	65.0	46.4
1994	63.0	48.0
1996	68.0	30.0
1998	77.2	65.5
2000	81.1	69.0
2002	84.7	57.1
2004	79.7	52.9

Source: Harold Stanley and Richard G. Niemi, *Vital Statistics on American Politics* 2002–2004. Washington, D.C.: CQ Press, 2004; plus calculations by author.

Turnover Despite a high rate of reelection of incumbents in Congress, about 15 percent of members arrive new to their jobs each session. **Turnover** occurs more frequently as a result of retirement, resignation (sometimes to run for higher office), or reapportionment (and the loss of an incumbent's seat) that it does as a result of an incumbent's defeat in a bid for reelection. Roughly 10 percent of Congress members voluntarily leave office when their term expires.[19]

Congressional Term Limits? Public distrust of government helped to fuel a movement in the states to limit congressional terms. Several states attempted to limit their state's House members to four two-year terms and their senators to two six-year terms. Proponents of congressional term limits argued that career politicians become isolated from the lives and concerns of average citizens, that they acquire an "inside the Beltway" (the circle of highways that surrounds Washington) mentality. They also argued that term limits would increase competition, creating "open-seat" races on a regular basis and encouraging more people to seek public office.

THINK AGAIN

Should members of Congress be limited in the number of terms they can serve?

Opponents of congressional term limits argued that they infringe on the voters' freedom of choice. If voters are upset with the performance of their Congress members, they can limit their terms by not reelecting them. But if voters wish to keep popular and experienced legislators in office, they should be permitted to do so. Opponents also argued that inexperienced Congress members would be forced to rely more on the policy information supplied them by bureaucrats, lobbyists, and staff people—thus weakening the institution of Congress.

But the U.S. Supreme Court ruled in 1995 that the states themselves cannot limit the terms of their members of Congress. "If the qualifications set forth in the text of the Constitution are to be changed, that text must be amended."[20] In a controversial 5 to 4 decision, the Court held that the Founders intended age, citizenship, and residency to be the *only* qualifications for members of Congress.

It is not likely that the necessary two-thirds of both houses of Congress will ever vote for a constitutional amendment to limit their own stay in office. Thus, the Supreme Court's decision effectively killed the movement for congressional term limits.

turnover Replacement of members of Congress by retirement or resignation, by reapportionment, or (more rarely) by electoral defeat, usually expressed as a percentage of members newly elected.

WHAT DO YOU THINK?

Why Do Voters Reelect Members of an Unpopular Congress?

Congress is the least popular branch of government. Public approval of Congress is well below that of the presidency and the Supreme Court. What accounts for this lack of popularity? The belief that members of Congress "spend more time thinking about their own political futures than they do in passing legislation" may contribute to this sentiment.

But public distrust of Congress may also arise from a misunderstanding of democratic government. "People do not wish to see uncertainty, conflicting options, long debate, competing interests, confusion and compromised imperfect solutions. . . . They often see a patently unrealistic form of democracy."*

But in an apparent paradox, most voters *approve of their own* representative (see figure below), even while Congress itself is the object of popular distrust and ridicule. A majority of voters believe that their own representatives "deserve reelection."

This apparent contradiction is explained in part by differing expectations: Americans expect Congress to deal with national issues, but they expect their own representatives to deal with local concerns and even personal problems. Members of Congress understand this concern and consequently devote a great deal of their time to constituent service. Indeed, many members of Congress try to dissociate themselves from Congress, attacking Congress in their own campaigns and contributing to negative images of the institution. Finally, the national news media are highly critical of Congress, but local news media frequently portray local members of Congress in a more favorable light.

Q. "Do you approve of the way the U.S. Congress is handling its job?"

Q. "Do you approve or disapprove of the way the representative from your own congressional district is handling his or her job?"

*John R. Hibbing and Elizabeth Theiss-Morse, *Congress as Public Enemy* (Cambridge: Cambridge University Press, 1995), p. 147. Also cited by Roger H. Davidson and Walter J. Oleszak, *Congress and Its Members* 9th ed. (Washington, D.C.: CQ Press, 2004), p. 487.

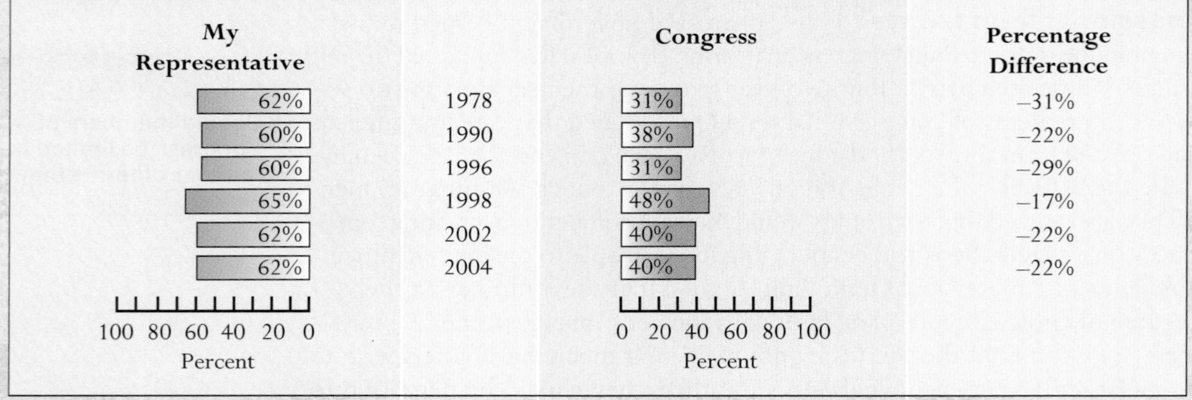

My Representative	Year	Congress	Percentage Difference
62%	1978	31%	–31%
60%	1990	38%	–22%
60%	1996	31%	–29%
65%	1998	48%	–17%
62%	2002	40%	–22%
62%	2004	40%	–22%

Percentage of Those Expressing Approval of Their Representatives and Congress

Source: Data from surveys by the Gallup Organization, as reported in www.thepollingreport.com

The Congressional Electorate Congressional elections generally fail to arouse much interest among voters. Indeed, only about 60 percent of the general public can name one U.S. senator from their state, and only about 40 percent can name both of their U.S. senators. Members of the House of Representatives fare no better: less than half of the general public can name their representative. But even constituents who know the names of their congressional delegation seldom know anything about the policy positions of these elected officials or about their votes on specific issues. Turnout in congressional *general elections* averages only about 35 percent in off-year (nonpresidential) elections. Turnout in congressional *primary elections* seldom exceeds 15 to 20 percent of persons eligible to vote. This lack of public attentiveness to congressional elections gives a great advantage to candidates with high name recognition, generally the incumbents (see *What Do You Think?* Why Do Voters Reelect Members of an Unpopular Congress).

Independence of Congressional Voting Congressional voting is largely independent of presidential voting. The same voters who elected Republican presidents in 1968, 1972, 1980, 1984, and 1988 simultaneously elected Democratic majorities to the House of Representatives. And while reelecting Democratic President Bill Clinton in 1996, voters simultaneously reelected Republican majorities in the House and Senate. In 2000, Republicans maintained a razor-thin margin in the House, despite Gore's popular vote victory. Only in 2004 did voters elect a Republican president and add to Republican majorities in the House and Senate. It is unlikely that voters deliberately seek to impose *divided party government* on the nation. Rather, they cast their presidential and congressional votes on the basis of differing expectations of presidents versus members of Congress.[21]

Congressional Campaign Financing Raising the $900,000 it can take to win a House seat or the $5 to $10 million for a successful Senate campaign is a major job in and of itself (see "How Much Does It Cost to Get Elected?" in Chapter 8). Even incumbents who face little or no competition still work hard at fund raising, "banking" contributions against some future challenger. Large campaign chests, assembled well in advance of an election, can also be used to frighten off would-be challengers. Campaign funds can be used to build a strong personal organization back home, finance picnics and other festivities for constituents, expand the margin of victory, and develop a reputation for invincibility that may someday protect against an unknown challenger.[22]

Does money buy elections? In about 90 percent of all congressional races, the candidate who spends the most money wins. However, because most winning candidates are incumbents, the money probably reflects the expected political outcome rather than shapes it. But even in open-seat races, the candidate who spends the most money usually wins.

Party Fortunes in Congress

For forty years (1954–94) Democrats enjoyed an advantage in congressional races; in fact, the Democratic Party was said to have a "permanent majority" in the House of Representatives (see Figure 8.6). The Republican victory in the congressional election of 1994 was widely described as a political "earthquake." It gave the GOP control of the House for the first time in four decades, as well as control of the Senate. Republicans have remained in control of the House, and the Senate (except for a brief period in 2001–2002) through the 2004 elections.

The Historic Democratic Party Dominance of Congress The historic Democratic dominance of Congress was attributed to several factors. First, over those four decades more voters identified themselves with the Democratic Party than with the Republican Party (see Chapter 7). Party identification plays a significant role in congressional voting; it is estimated that 75 percent of those who

FIGURE 8.6 Party Control of the House and Senate

Except for two very brief periods, Democrats continuously controlled both the House of Representatives and the Senate for more than forty years. The Democratic Party's "permanent" control of Congress was ended in 1994, when Republicans won majorities in both houses. Republicans retained control of Congress despite President Clinton's victory in 1996, and retained control by a slim margin in the House in 1998, 2000, and 2002. President George W. Bush's reelection victory in 2004 increased Republican margins in both the House and Senate.

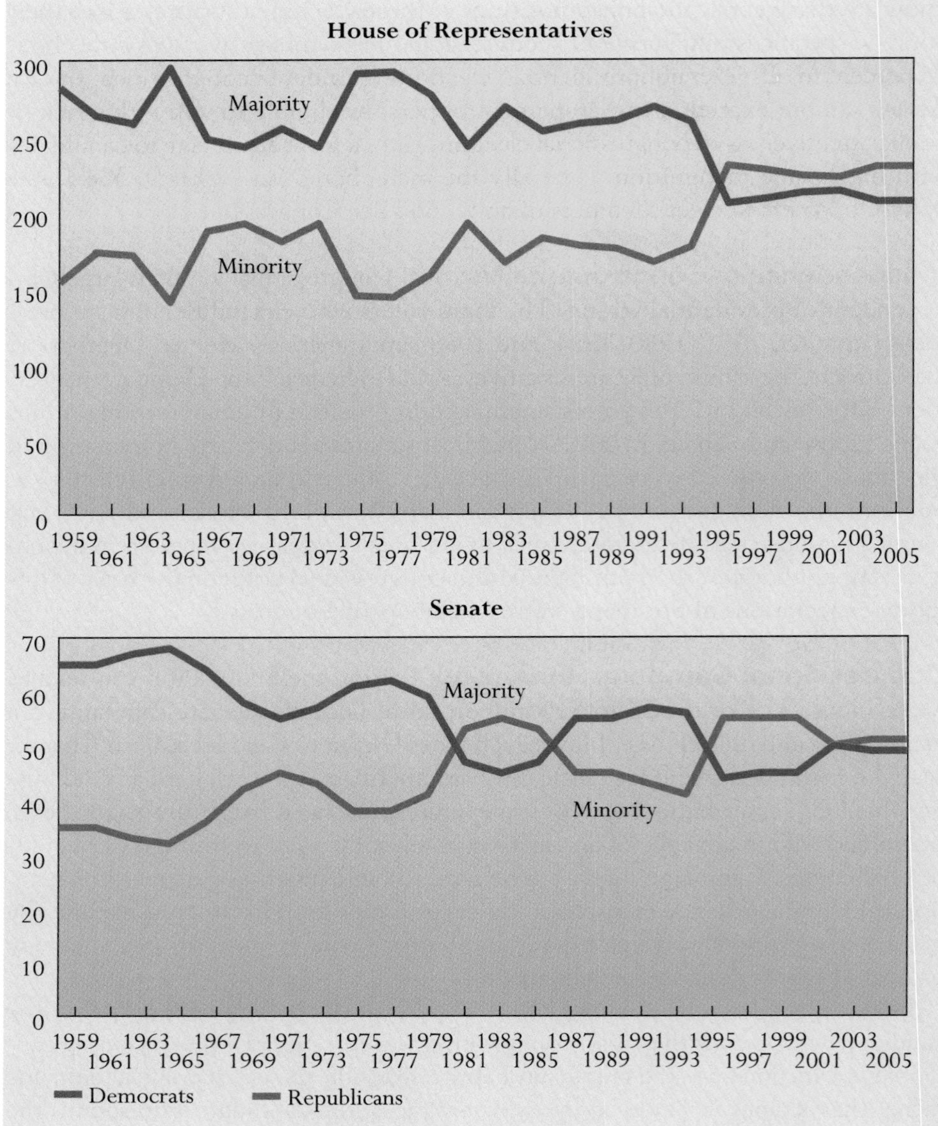

identify themselves with a party cast their vote for the congressional candidate of their party.[23] Second, the Democratic advantage was buttressed by the fact that many voters considered local rather than national conditions when casting congressional votes. Voters may have wanted to curtail overall federal spending in Washington (a traditional Republican promise), but they wanted a member of Congress who would "bring home the bacon." Although both Republican and Democratic congressional candidates usually promised to bring money and jobs to their districts, Democratic candidates appeared more creditable on such promises because their party generally supported large domestic-spending programs. Finally, Democratic congressional candidates over those years enjoyed the many advantages of incumbency. It was thought that only death or retirement would dislodge many of them from their seats.

The Republican "Revolution"? The sweeping Republican victory in 1994—especially the party's capturing control of the House of Representatives—surprised many analysts.[24] Just two years after a Democratic president won election and

Democrats won substantial majorities in both houses of Congress, the GOP gained its most complete victory in many years. How did it happen?

First of all, the Republican congressional candidates, under the leadership of Newt Gingrich, largely succeeded in *nationalizing* the midterm congressional election. That is, Republican candidates sought to exploit the voters' general skepticism about government and disenchantment with its performance. Voters were often unfamiliar with specific Republican promises, but they correctly sensed that the Republicans favored "less government."

The GOP's capture of control of both houses of Congress in 1994 for the first time in forty years raised conservatives' hopes of a "revolution" in public policy. The new Republican House Speaker, Newt Gingrich, was the acknowledged leader of the revolution, with Republican Senate Majority Leader Bob Dole in tow. But soon the revolution began to fizzle out. Two key Republican campaign promises failed to pass the Congress: the House failed to muster the necessary two-thirds majority for a constitutional amendment to impose congressional term limits, and the Senate failed to do so on behalf of a balanced budget amendment.

But worse was yet to come for the Republicans. Congress passed several budget resolutions aimed at balancing the federal budget in seven years, only to see them vetoed. Clinton positioned himself as the defender of popular programs—Medicare, Medicaid, education, and the environment—consistently referring to congressional efforts to reduce the rate of growth in these programs as "cuts." The failure of Congress and the president to agree on appropriations temporarily shut down the federal government in 1995. To the surprise of the Republican leadership, opinion polls reported that Americans blamed the GOP Congress for the gridlock. Clinton's approval ratings rose, and Newt Gingrich was portrayed as a mean-spirited "extremist."

Newt Gingrich (R-Ga.) led the Republican Party to victory in the House of Representatives in 1994 after forty years of Democratic control of that body.

The Democratic Revival Republicans succeeded in maintaining their control of Congress despite Clinton's reelection in 1996. But Democrats gained House seats in both the 1996 and 1998 congressional elections. Although the GOP retained a slim majority in the House of Representatives, the 1998 midterm election stunned Republicans. They had expected to benefit from Clinton's acknowledged sexual misconduct and the House impeachment investigation. But voters generally sided with Clinton. Democrats were encouraged because historically the party controlling the White House had *lost* seats in midterm elections.

Congress Divided The congressional elections of 2000 reflected the close partisan division of the nation. Republicans barely held on to their majority in the House of Representatives. The election produced a historic 50–50 tie in the Senate. Formal control of the Senate should have rested with Republicans, owing to the tie-breaking vote of Republican Vice President Dick Cheney. But in a precedent-shattering midsession shift of power, Democrats took control of the Senate in 2001, when Republican Senator Jim Jeffords from Vermont abandoned his party, declared himself an Independent, but gave his vote to the Democrats in the Senate. Other senators had defected from their party in the past, but no previous switch ever produced a change in party control. The new 51–49 Democratic majority took control of all Senate committees as well as the floor of that body.

Breaking with the Midterm Election Tradition Traditionally, the party that had won the White House in the previous presidential election *lost* seats in the following midterm congressional election. (Indeed, since Abraham Lincoln was president, the party holding the presidency lost House seats in every midterm election except three—1902, 1934, and 1998.) It was theorized that presidential popularity tended to wane after two years in office, and that voters usually sought to check presidential power in the following midterm election. It was also believed that even popular presidents had little impact on midterm congressional elections; these elections were thought to be decided by the popularity of individual candidates and local district issues.

But in 2002 President George W. Bush designated himself as "Campaigner-in-Chief," traveling about the country raising campaign money and lending his popularity to Republican House and Senate candidates. His continuing high approval rating throughout the year following the "9/11" terrorist attack on America made him a highly welcomed campaigner in districts and states across the nation. In his campaign stops, Bush talked about the war on terrorism and his need for "allies" in the Congress. Democratic candidates for Congress tried to shift the voters' focus to the weak economy. And indeed, most voters told pollsters that the economy was a more important issue than the war on terrorism and that Bush himself was not a major factor in determining their vote. Nonetheless, President Bush appeared to influence just enough voters in key districts and states to reverse the historic pattern of presidential midterm congressional losses. The GOP won back control of the U.S. Senate and strengthened their majority in the House of Representatives. Again in 2004 President Bush appeared to help GOP congressional candidates across the country. Republicans increased their control of the Senate from 51 to 55. They picked up several seats of retiring older-generation Southern Democrats. And they even succeeded in defeating the Democratic Senate Minority Leader, Tom Daschle of South Dakota. Nevertheless, Democrats retained sufficient strengths in the Senate (where a 3/5th "cloture" vote—60—is required to end a filibuster) to obstruct legislation and judicial nominations which they oppose. Senate Republican Majority Leader Bill Frist has threatened to revise the rules of the Senate regarding cloture votes, especially on judicial nominations. (He argues that the Constitution requires only a majority vote to "consent" for presidential nominations.) But support for the filibuster rule is strong. Supreme Court nominations are likely to generate heated controversy.The election also made the Senate slightly more "diverse": African-American Barack Obama was elected from Illinois, and Hispanic Mel Martinez was elected from Florida. In the House, Republicans also increased their margin of control. President Bush was quick to claim that winning the White House, the Senate, and the House of Representatives meant that the American People supported his "agenda."

Life in Congress

"All politics is local," declared former House Speaker Thomas P. "Tip" O'Neill, himself once the master of both Boston ward politics and the U.S. House of Representatives. Attention to the local constituency is the key to survival and success in congressional politics. If Congress often fails to deal responsibly with national problems, the explanation lies in part with the design of the institution. House members must devote primary attention to their districts and Senate members to their states. Only *after* their constituencies are served can they turn their attention to national policy making.

The "Representativeness" of Congress The Constitution requires only that members of the House of Representatives be (1) residents of the state they represent (they need not live in their congressional district, although virtually all do so); (2) U.S. citizens for at least seven years; and (3) at least twenty-five years old. Senators must also be residents of the state they represent, but they must be at least thirty years old and U.S. citizens for at least nine years.

- *African Americans* African Americans were first elected to Congress following the Civil War—seven black representatives and one black senator served in 1875. But with the end of Reconstruction, black membership in Congress fell to a single seat in the House from 1891 to 1955. Following the Civil Rights Act of 1964 and the Voting Rights Act of 1965, black membership in Congress rose steadily. Redistricting following the 1990 census resulted in many new "majority-minority" congressional districts. After the 1992 elections, black membership in the House rose dramatically (see Figure 8.7), with most elected from predominantly African American districts.[25] As a result, although African Americans today make up a little more than 12 percent of the U.S. population, they make up less than 9 percent of the House membership. African American, Carol Mosely Brown of Illinois served in the Senate from 1993 to 1999, and Barack Obama won a Senate seat in the same state in 2004.
- *Hispanics* Hispanics now comprise the nation's largest minority, with slightly more than 12 percent of the U.S. population. But Hispanic representation in the Congress lags considerably behind their population growth. Currently only about 5 percent of House members are Hispanic, and no Hispanics serve in the U.S. Senate. The Voting Rights Act of 1965 protects "language minorities" as well as racial and ethnic minorities. Prior to the 1990 census and the creation of many court-ordered "majority-minority" congressional districts, very few Hispanics served in the Congress. But with the creation of new Hispanic majority districts, Hispanic representation began to increase in the House of Representatives. Most Hispanic House members come from California, Florida, and Texas. In the 108th Congress, 23 Hispanics served in the House; 19 were Democrats, and 4 (all from Florida) were Republicans.
- *Women* Women have made impressive gains in both the House and the Senate in the last decade. The "year of the woman" election in 1992 brought a significant increase in the number of women in the House of Representatives. Since then

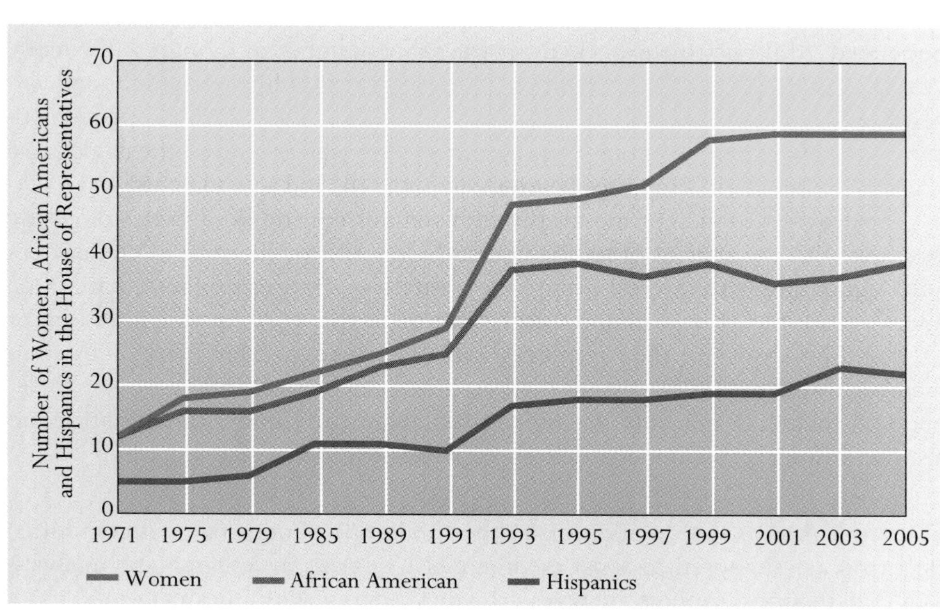

FIGURE 8.7 Women, African Americans, and Hispanics in the House of Representatives

Although the House of Representatives is still far short of "looking like America," in recent years the number of African Americans, Hispanics, and female members has risen noticeably. Particularly impressive advances were made in the 1992 elections, following court-ordered creation of "majority–minority" districts.

women's representation in the House continued upward, 59 women serve in the House in 108th Congress (2003–2005), divided between 38 Democrats and 21 Republicans. In the Senate, 14 women serve. California is represented by two Democratic women, Dianne Feinstein and Barbara Boxer. They are joined by seven other Democratic women Senators, including former First Lady Hillary Rodham Clinton. (See *People in Politics:* "Hillary Rodham Clinton in the Senate.") Five Republican women serve in the Senate: Elizabeth Dole from North Carolina, Kay Hutchinson from Texas, Olympia Snowe and Susan Collins from Maine, and Lisa Murkowski from Alaska. Although this is the largest delegation of women ever to serve together in the U.S. Senate, it is still only 14 percent of that body.

The number of women in Congress has grown as result of many factors, including strides that women have made in the workplace and other societal institutions. Yet stereotypes about women as politicians remain. Generally, voters view women as better able to handle "feminine" issues, such as health care, child care and education, but less able to handle "masculine" issues, including the economy and war. In the past, some women candidates tried to counter these stereotypes by emphasizing their toughness, especially on crime. But new evidence suggests that women candidates can use female stereotypes to their advantage by focusing the campaign on gender-owned issues—health, welfare, education, and other compassion issues.[26]

Congressional Staff Congress is composed of a great deal more than 535 elected senators and representatives. Congressional staff and other support personnel now total some 25,000 people. Each representative has a staff of twenty or more people, usually headed by a chief of staff or administrative assistant and including legislative assistants, communications specialists, constituent-service personnel, office managers, secretaries, and aides of various sorts. Senators frequently have staffs of thirty to fifty or more people. All representatives and senators are provided with offices both in Washington and in their home districts and states. In addition, representatives receive more than $500,000 apiece for office expenses, travel, and staff; and senators receive $2 million or more, depending on the size of their state's population. Overall, Congress spends more than $2 *billion* on itself each year.

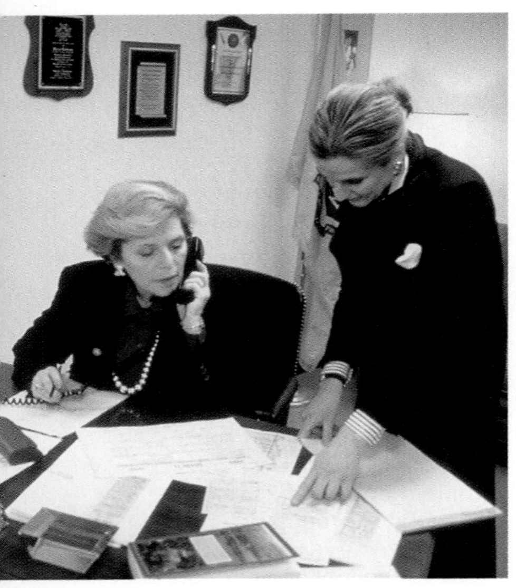

Congresswoman Marge Roukema of New Jersey meets with a staff member at her offices in Washington, D.C. Congressional staff play a key role in the legislative process.

Congressional staff people exercise great influence over legislation. Many experienced "Hill rats" have worked for the same member of Congress for many years. They become very familiar with "their" member's political strengths and vulnerabilities and handle much of the member's contacts with interest groups and constituents. Staff people, more than members themselves, move the legislative process—scheduling committee hearings, writing bills and amendments, and tracking the progress of such proposals through committees and floor proceedings. By working with the staff of other members of Congress or the staff of committees and negotiating with interest-group representatives, congressional staff are often able to work out policy compromises, determine the wording of legislation, or even outline "deals" for their member's vote (all subject to later approval by their member). With multiple demands on their time, members of Congress come to depend on their staff not only for information about the content of legislation but also for political recommendations about what position to take regarding it.

Support Agencies In addition to the thousands of personal and committee staff who are supposed to assist members of Congress in research and analysis, four congressional support agencies provide Congress with information:

PEOPLE IN POLITICS

Hillary Rodham Clinton in the Senate

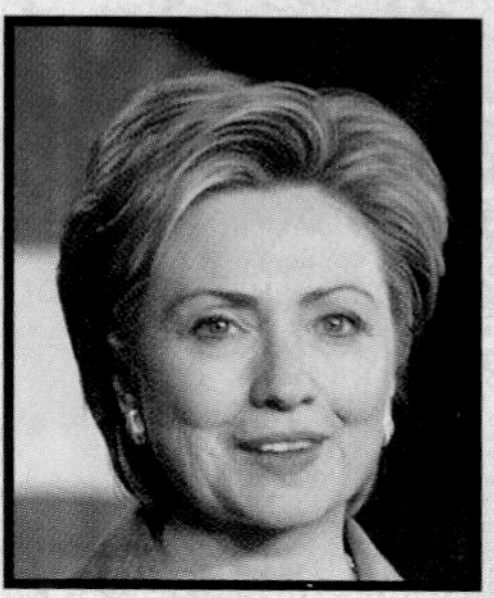

Hillary Rodham Clinton is the first First Lady ever elected to the Congress and the first woman senator from New York. Her celebrity attracts the media wherever she goes, sometimes causing resentment among her ninety-nine other Senate colleagues, all of whom think of themselves as stars in their own right. Her initial efforts in the Senate have been directed toward establishing herself as a serious, knowledgeable, and effective legislator. And she tries particularly hard to identify herself with the interests of her adopted state, New York.

Hillary Rodham grew up in suburban Chicago, the daughter of wealthy parents who sent her to the private, prestigious Wellesley College. A 1969 honors graduate with a counterculture image—hornrimmed glasses, long, straggling hair, no makeup—she was chosen by her classmates to give a commencement speech—a rambling statement about "more immediate, ecstatic, and penetrating modes of living."

At Yale Law School Hillary met a long-haired, bearded Rhodes scholar from Arkansas, Bill Clinton, who was just as politically ambitious as she was. Both Hillary and Bill received their law degrees in 1973. Bill returned to Arkansas to build a career in state politics, and Hillary went to Washington as an attorney—first for a liberal lobbying group, the Children's Defense Fund, and later on the staff of the House Judiciary Committee seeking to impeach President Richard Nixon. But Rodham and other Yale grads traveled to Arkansas to help Clinton run, unsuccessfully, for Congress in 1974. Hillary decided to stay with Bill in Little Rock: they married before his next campaign, a successful run for state attorney general in 1976. Hillary remained Hillary Rodham, even as her husband went on to the governorship in 1978.

Her husband's 1980 defeat for reelection as governor was blamed on his liberal leanings; therefore, in his 1982 comeback Bill repackaged himself as a moderate and centrist. Hillary cooperated by becoming Mrs. Bill Clinton, shedding her horn-rims for contacts, blonding her hair, and echoing her husband's more moderate line. These tactics helped propel them back into the governor's mansion. Hillary soon became a full partner in Little Rock's Rose law firm, regularly earning more than $200,000 a year (while Bill earned only $35,000 as Arkansas governor). She won national recognition as one of the "100 most influential lawyers in the United States," according to the *American National Law Journal*. She chaired the American Bar Association's Commission on Women and the Profession.

Hillary's steadfast support of Bill during the White House sex scandals and subsequent impeachment by the House of Representatives in all likelihood saved his presidency. Her approval ratings in public opinion polls skyrocketed during the affair. Whatever she thought in private, she never chastised her husband in public and blamed much of the scandal on "a vast right-wing conspiracy."

Her Senate race attracted national media attention as well as campaign contributions from supporters throughout the nation. When New York City's Mayor Rudolph Giuliani announced that he would *not* run for the Senate, Hillary was relieved to confront a little-known opponent, Congressman Rick Lazio. New York voters were unimpressed with charges that Hillary was not a true New Yorker. She studied New York problems diligently, and overwhelmed Lazio in the campaign. Over $85 million were spent by the candidates, making the campaign the most expensive congressional campaign in history.

Senator Clinton has developed a reputation as an advocate for children and families. Her early work with the Children's Defense Fund and Marian Wright Edelman (see *People in Politics:* "Marian Wright Edelman, Lobbying for the Poor" in Chapter 9) was carried forward in her book *It Takes a Village* in 1997. She was prominently mentioned in all of the early 2004 presidential polls, but she declined to run.

- The Library of Congress and its Congressional Research Service (CRS) are the oldest congressional support agencies. Members of Congress can turn to the Library of Congress for references and information. The CRS responds to direct requests of members for factual information on virtually any topic. It tracks major bills in Congress and produces summaries of each bill introduced. This information is available on computer terminals in members' offices.

- The General Accounting Office (GAO) has broad authority to oversee the operations and finances of executive agencies, to evaluate their programs, and to report its findings to Congress. Established as an arm of Congress in 1921, the GAO largely confined itself to financial auditing and management studies in its early years but expanded to more than five thousand employees in the 1970s and undertook a broad agenda of policy research and evaluation. Most GAO studies and reports are requested by members of Congress and congressional committees, but the GAO also undertakes some studies on its own initiative.

WWW Congressional Budget Office
The Web site of the CBO is an excellent source of data on federal finances, economic projections, and the budgetary process.
www.cbo.gov

- The Congressional Budget Office (CBO) was created by the Congressional Budget and Impoundment Act of 1974 to strengthen Congress's role in the budgeting process. It was designed as a congressional counterweight to the president's Office of Management and Budget (see Chapter 14). The CBO supplies the House and Senate budget committees with its own budgetary analyses and economic forecasts, sometimes challenging those found in the president's annual budget.
- The Government Printing Office (GPO), created in 1860 as the publisher of the *Congressional Record,* now distributes over 20,000 different government publications in U.S. government bookstores throughout the nation.

Note that the CBO was created at a time when Congress was growing in power relative to a presidency weakened by Vietnam and Watergate. In these same years, Congress encouraged the GAO to undertake a more active and critical role relative to executive agencies. Thus, the growth of congressional staff and supporting agencies is tied to the struggle for power between the legislative and executive branches.

Workload Members of Congress claim to work twelve- to fifteen-hour days: two to three hours in committee and subcommittee meetings; two to three hours on the floor of the chamber; three to four hours meeting with constituents, interest groups, other members, and staff in their offices; and two to three hours attending conferences, events, and meetings in Washington.[27] Members of Congress may introduce anywhere from ten to fifty bills in a single session of Congress. Most bills are introduced merely to exhibit the member's commitment to a particular group or issue. Cosigning a popular bill is a common practice; particularly popular bills may have 100 or 200 cosigners in the House of Representatives. Although thousands of bills are introduced, only 400 to 800 are passed in a session.

Members of Congress resent the notion that they are overpaid, underworked, pampered, self-seeking, corrupt, and ineffective. They respond to the bell calling them to the floor for a recorded vote 900 to 1,000 times a session. Each representative is a member of at least two standing committees and four subcommittees, and each senator may be a member of four committees and many more subcommittees. Thousands of committee and subcommittee meetings are scheduled each session.

Pay and Perks Taxpayers can relate directly to what members of Congress spend on themselves, even while millions—and even billions—of dollars spent on government programs remain relatively incomprehensible. Taxpayers thus were enraged when Congress, in a late-night session in 1991, raised its own pay from $89,500 to $129,000. Congress claimed the pay raise was a "reform," since it was coupled with a stipulation that members of Congress would no longer be allowed to accept honoraria from interest groups for their speeches and appearances, thus supposedly reducing members' dependence on outside income. Many angry taxpayers saw only a 44 percent pay raise, in the midst of a national recession, for a Congress that was doing little to remedy the nation's problems. By 2004, automatic cost-of-living increases, also enacted by Congress, had raised members' pay to $154,700.

As the pay-raise debate raged in Washington, several states resurrected a constitutional amendment originally proposed by James Madison. Although passed by the Congress in 1789, it had never been ratified by the necessary three-quarters of the states. The 203-year-old amendment, requiring a House election to intervene before a congressional pay raise can take effect, was added as the Twenty-seventh Amendment when ratified by four states (for a total of thirty-nine) in 1992.

Home Style

Members of Congress spend as much time politically cultivating their districts and states as they do legislating. **Home style** refers to the activities of senators and representatives in promoting their images among constituents and personally attending to constituents' problems and interests.[28] These activities include members' allocations of their personnel and staff resources to constituent services; members' personal appearances in the home district or state to demonstrate personal attention; and members' efforts to explain their Washington activities to the voters back home.

THINK AGAIN

Do Congress members spend too much time in their home districts seeking re-election?

Casework **Casework** is really a form of "retail" politics. Members of Congress can win votes one at a time by helping constituents on a personal level. Casework can involve everything from tracing lost Social Security checks and Medicare claims to providing information about federal programs, solving problems with the Internal Revenue Service, and assisting with federal job applications. Over time, grateful voters accumulate, giving incumbents an advantage at election time. Congressional staff do much of the actual casework, but letters go out over the signature of the member of Congress. Senators and representatives blame the growth of government for increasing casework, but it is also clear that members solicit casework, frequently reminding constituents to bring their problems to their member of Congress.

The downside to extensive casework is that it may detract from Congress members' ability to deal effectively with national issues. Former U.S. Senator and vice president Walter Mondale observed:

> Constituent service can . . . be a bottomless pit. The danger is that a member of Congress will end up as little more than an ombudsman between citizens and government agencies. As important as this work is, it takes precious time away from Congress's central responsibilities as both a deliberative and a lawmaking body.[29]

Pork Barrel **Pork barreling** describes the efforts of senators and representatives to "bring home the bacon"—to bring federally funded projects, grants, and contracts that primarily benefit a single district or state to their home constituencies. Opportunities for pork barreling have never been greater: roads, dams, parks, and post offices are now overshadowed by redevelopment grants to city governments, research grants to universities, weapons contracts to local plants, "demonstration" projects of all kinds, and myriad other "goodies" tucked inside each year's annual appropriations bills. Members of Congress understand the importance of supporting each other's pork barrel projects, cooperating in the "incumbent-

home style Activities of Congress members specifically directed at their home constituencies.

casework Services performed by legislators or their staff on behalf of individual constituents.

pork barreling Legislation designed to make government benefits, including jobs and projects used as political patronage, flow to a particular district or state.

protection society." Even though pork barreling adds to the public's negative image of Congress as an institution, individual members gain local popularity for the benefits they bring to home districts and states.

Pressing the Flesh Senators and representatives spend a great deal of time in their home states and districts. Although congressional sessions last virtually all year, members of Congress find ways to spend more than a hundred days per year at home[30] It is important to be seen at home—giving speeches and attending dinners, fund-raising events, civic occasions, and so on. To accommodate this aspect of home style, Congress usually follows a Tuesday-to-Thursday schedule of legislative business, allowing members to spend longer weekends in their home districts. Congress also enjoys long recesses during the late summer and over holidays.

Puffing Images To promote their images back home, members make generous use of their **franking privilege** (free mailing) to send their constituents newsletters, questionnaires, biographical material, and information about federal programs. Newsletters "puff" the accomplishments of the members; questionnaires are designed more to flatter voters than to assess opinions; and informational brochures tout federal services members claim credit for providing and defending. Congress's penchant for self-promotion has also kept pace with the media and electronic ages. Congress now provides its members with television studios and support for making videotapes to send to local stations in home districts, and all members maintain Web sites on the Internet designed to puff their images.

Hill Styles and Home Styles Members of Congress spend their lives "moving between two contexts, Washington and home, and between two activities, governing and campaigning."[31] They must regularly ask themselves how much time they should spend at home with their constituents versus how much time they should spend on lawmaking assignments in Washington. It is no surprise that freshman legislators spend more time in their districts; indeed, very few first-termers move their families to Washington. Long-term incumbents spend more time in Washington, but all Congress members spend more time at home in an election year.

Congressional Quarterly (CQ)

The *Congressional Quarterly Weekly Report* provides the most comprehensive coverage of events in Congress, including key issues, House and Senate roll call votes, backgrounds of members, and political and election information. The CQ Press is a major publisher of books on politics and government. ***www.cq.com***

Much of the time spent at home—with small groups of constituents, among contributors, in public speeches, and appearances on radio and television—is devoted to explaining issues in justifying the member's vote on them. "Often members defend their own voting record by belittling Congress—portraying themselves as knights errant battling sinister forces and feckless colleagues."[32]

Members of Congress have even been known to change lifestyles between home and Washington. "The legendary Speaker Mr. Sam Rayburn represented his East Texas district for nearly 50 years (1913–61) as a plain dirt farmer. Once back in his hometown of Bonham, his drawl thickened; his tailored suits were exchanged for khakis, an old shirt and a slouch hat; and he traveled in a well-dented pickup truck, not the Speaker's limousine he used while in the Capitol."[33]

Organizing Congress: Party and Leadership

Congress is composed of people who think of themselves as leaders, not followers. They got elected without much help from their party. Yet they realize that their chances of attaining their personal goals—getting reelected and influencing policy—are enhanced if they cooperate with each other.

franking privilege Free mail service afforded members of Congress.

Party Organizations in Congress The Democratic and Republican party organizations within the House of Representatives and the Senate are the principal bases for organizing Congress (see Figure 8.8). The leadership of each house of Congress, although nominally elected by the entire chamber, is actually chosen by secret ballot of the members of each party at a "conference" or caucus (see Table 8.4).

The parties and their leaders do not choose congressional candidates, nor can they deny them renomination; all members of Congress are responsible for their own primary and general election success. But party leadership in each chamber can help incumbents achieve their reelection goals. Each party in the House and Senate sponsors a campaign committee that channels some campaign funding to party members seeking reelection, although these Republican and Democratic congressional and senatorial campaign committees contribute less money than either PACs or individuals to the candidates.[34] Rather, good relations between members and their party's leadership are more important in the quest for power and influence in Washington.

Occasionally, congressional party leaders are urged to exercise more discipline over their members, to ensure that they support the party's position on key votes. Theoretically, party leaders in the House and Senate could do so by denying disloyal members appointment to preferred committees, by regularly burying their favorite bills, by cutting their pork barrel projects from the budget, or by denying them party campaign funds. But except in very extreme cases, party leaders have been reluctant to employ these punishments. Members of Congress cherish their independence. They respect each other's need to get reelected. A member's vote lost today may be won next week if the member is not alienated by disciplinary action.

Majority status confers great power on the party that controls the House and the Senate. The majority party chooses the leadership in each body, selects the chairs of every committee, and ensures that every committee has a majority of

TABLE 8.4 Leadership in Congress

	Senate
President Pro Tempore	An honorary post, usually the senior member of the majority party
Majority Leader	Top Senate post, elected by majority party members
Majority Whip	Second-ranking post in the majority party
Minority Leader	Leader of the minority opposition party
Minority Whip	Second-ranking post in the minority party
	House
Speaker	Powerful presiding officer, elected with the votes of the majority party
Majority Leader	Officially the leader of the majority party but second in power to the Speaker
Majority Whip	Third-ranking leader of the majority party
Minority Leader	Top post in the minority party
Minority Whip	Second-ranking post in the minority party

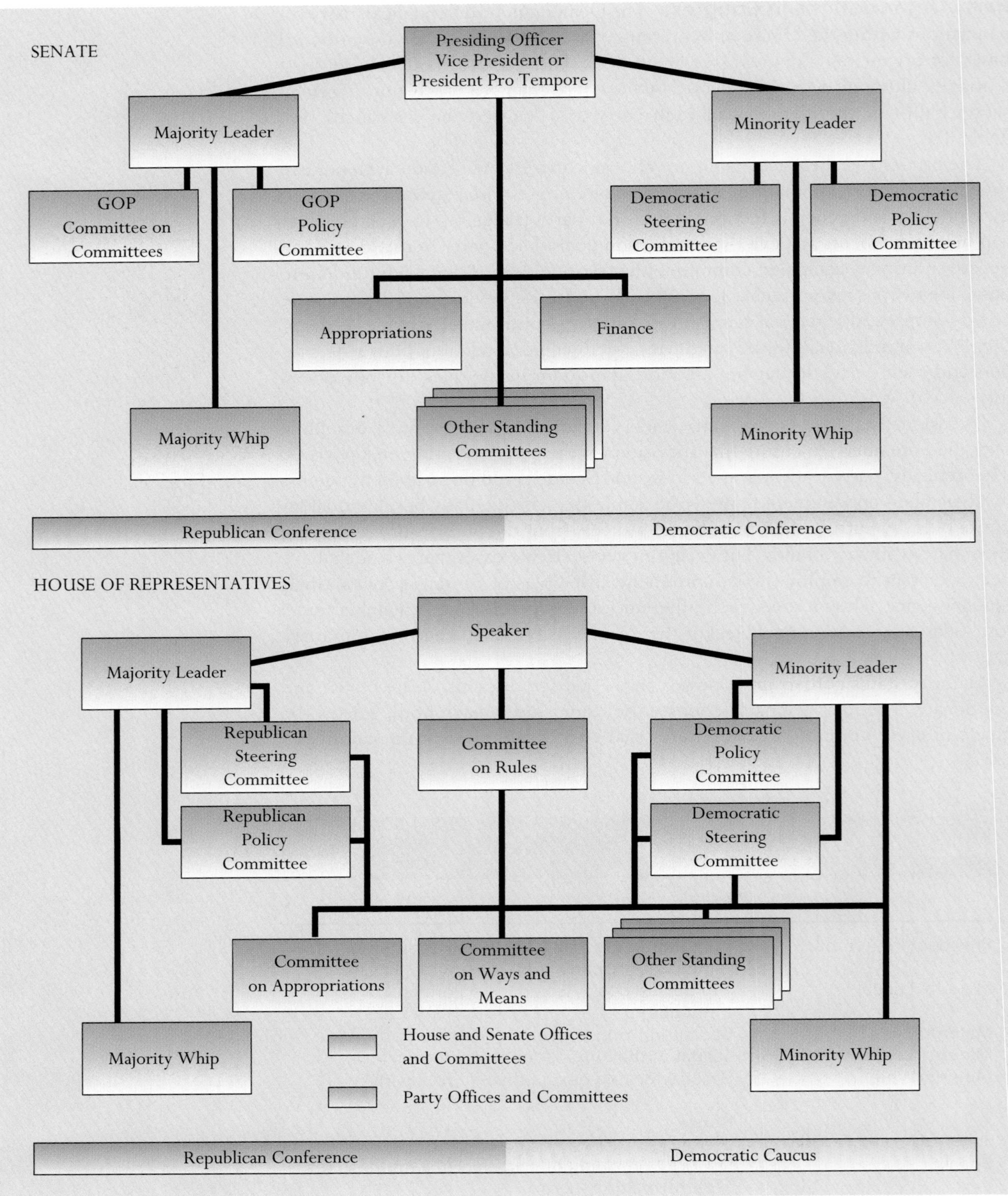

FIGURE 8.8 The Organization of Congress

Aside from naming the Speaker of the House as head of that body's operations and the vice president as overseer of Senate deliberations, the Constitution is silent on the organization of Congress. Political parties have filled this gap: both majority and minority parties have their own leadership, which governs the appointment of members to the various committees, where much of the work of Congress actually takes place.

members from the majority party. In other words, if Republicans are in the majority in either the House or the Senate or both, Republicans will occupy all leadership positions, chair every committee, and constitute a majority of the members of every committee, and, of course, the Democrats enjoy the same advantages when they capture a majority of either body. Majority-party members in each house even take in more campaign contributions than minority members.[35]

Republican Speaker of the House Dennis Hastert leads the Republican majority.

In the House: "Mr. Speaker" In the House of Representatives, the key leadership figure is the **Speaker of the House**, who serves as both presiding officer of the chamber and leader of the majority party. In the House, the Speaker has many powers. The Speaker decides who shall be recognized to speak on the floor and rules on points of order (with advice from the parliamentarian), including whether a motion or amendment is germane (relevant) to the business at hand. The Speaker decides to which committees new bills will be assigned and can schedule or delay votes on a bill. The Speaker appoints members of select, special, and conference committees and names majority-party members to the Rules Committee. And the Speaker controls both patronage jobs and office space in the Capitol. Although the norm of fairness requires the Speaker to apply the rules of the House consistently, the Speaker is elected by the majority party and is expected to favor that party.

Over the years, different Speakers have displayed different leadership styles. Republican Speaker Newt Gingrich was an ideological leader with a dramatic and aggressive agenda—a "Contract with America"—who contributed to partisan rancor in the House. In contrast, Republican Speaker Dennis Hastert has been a pragmatic leader who deals with his colleagues in an accommodating fashion.[36]

House Leaders and Whips The Speaker's principal assistant is the **majority leader.** The majority leader formulates the party's legislative program in consultation with other party leaders and steers the program through the House. The majority leader also must persuade committee leaders to support the aims of party leaders in acting on legislation before their committees. Finally, the majority leader arranges the legislative schedule with the cooperation of key party members.

The minority party in the House selects a **minority leader** whose duties correspond to those of the majority leader, except that the minority leader has no authority over the scheduling of legislation. The minority leader's principal duty has been to organize the forces of the minority party to counter the legislative program of the majority and to pass the minority party's bills. It is also the minority leader's duty to consult ranking minority members of House committees and to encourage them to adopt party positions and to follow the lead of the president if the minority party controls the White House (see *People in Politics:* "Nancy Pelosi, Leading House Democrats.")

In both parties, **whips** assist leaders in keeping track of the whereabouts of party members and in pressuring them to vote the party line. Whips are also responsible for ensuring the attendance of party members at important roll calls and for canvassing their colleagues on their likely support for or opposition to party-formulated legislation. Finally, whips are involved regularly in the formation of party policy and the scheduling of legislation.

In the Senate: "Mr. President" The Constitution declares the vice president of the United States to be the presiding officer of the Senate. But vice presidents seldom exercise this senatorial responsibility, largely because the presiding officer of the Senate has very little power. Having only 100 members, the Senate usually

Speaker of the House Presiding officer of the House of Representatives.

majority leader In the House, the majority-party leader and second in command to the Speaker; in the Senate, the leader of the majority party.

minority leader In both the House and Senate, the leader of the opposition party.

whips In both the House and Senate, the principal assistants to the party leaders and next in command to those leaders.

PEOPLE IN POLITICS

Nancy Pelosi, Leading House Democrats

Nancy Pelosi is the first woman in the history of the U.S. Congress to lead a major party. In 2001 her Democratic colleagues elected her Minority Leader, the highest-ranking leadership position among Democratic members. Pelosi has represented her San Francisco district since her first election to the Congress in 1986.

Congresswoman Pelosi comes from a highly political family. Her father, Thomas D'Alesandro, served five terms in Congress and later 12 years as mayor of Baltimore. Pelosi's brother also served as mayor of Baltimore. Young Nancy grew up in Washington and graduated from that city's Trinity College in 1962. She served as a congressional intern to her Maryland senator. She married Paul Pelosi, moved to his hometown of San Francisco, and raised five children. Prior to her election to Congress, she served on the National Democratic Committee.

In her years in Congress, Pelosi built a solid liberal reputation, serving on the powerful Appropriations Committee. She won the post as Democratic whip in 2001 in a close election against a more moderate Democrat. But Pelosi's real strength within the Democratic Party has long been her fund-raising ability. Her San Francisco district is the home of some of the party's wealthiest individual donors, and Democrats across the nation rely heavily upon money from California. Pelosi created her own leadership PAC and handed out over $1 million to her Democratic colleagues in 2000. She spends relatively little (about $400,000) on her own reelection races in her heavily Democratic district.

In 2002, Pelosi was reelected with an astonishing 80 percent of the vote in her California district. She topped that with 85 percent of the vote in 2004.

does not restrict debate and has fewer scheduling constraints than the House. The only significant power of the vice president is the right to cast a deciding vote in the event of a tie on a Senate roll call. In the usual absence of the vice president, the Senate is presided over by a *president pro tempore.* This honorific position is traditionally granted by the majority party to one of its senior stalwarts. The job of presiding over the Senate is so boring that neither the vice president nor the president pro tempore is found very often in the chamber. Junior senators are often asked to assume the chore. Nevertheless, speeches on the Senate floor begin with the salutation "Mr. President," referring to the president of the Senate, *not* the president of the United States.

Senate Majority and Minority Leaders Senate leadership is actually in the hands of the Senate majority leader, but the Senate majority leader is not as powerful in that body as the Speaker is in the House. With fewer members, all of whom perceive themselves as powerful leaders, the Senate is less hierarchically organized than the House. The Senate majority leader's principal power is scheduling the business of the Senate and recognizing the first speaker in floor debate. To be effective in policy making, the majority leader must be skilled in interpersonal persuasion and communication. Moreover, in the media age, the Senate majority leader must also be a national spokesperson for the party, along with the Speaker of the House. Republican Senate Leader Bill Frist and Republican Speaker of the House Dennis Hastert are their party's leading congressional spokesmen. The minority-party leader in the Senate represents the opposition in negotiations with the majority leader over Senate business. With the majority leader, the minority-party leader tends to dominate floor debate in the Senate.

TABLE 8.5 Top Congressional Leadership PACs, 2002

Name	Sponsor
Americans for a Republican Majority	Tom DeLay (R-Tex.)
HillPAC	Hillary Clinton (D-N.Y.)
Dedicated Americans	Tom Daschle (D-S.D.)
Responsible Opportunity PAC	Joseph Lieberman (D-Conn.)
StraightTalk America	John McCain (R-Ariz.)
New American Optimists	John Edwards (D-N.C.)
Keep Our Majority PAC	Dennis Hastert (R-Ill.)
Republican Majority Fund	Don Nickles (R-Okla.)
PAC to the Future	Nancy Pelosi (D-Ca.)
Majority Leaders Fund	Dick Army (R-Tex.)
Committee for a Democratic Majority	Ted Kennedy (D-Mass.)
Effective Government PAC	Richard Gephardt (D-Missouri)

Source: Center for Responsive Politics.

Career Paths within Congress Movement up the party hierarchy in each house is the most common way of achieving a leadership position. The traditional succession pattern in the House is from whip to majority leader to Speaker. In the Senate, Republicans and Democrats frequently resort to election contests in choosing their party leaders, yet both parties have increasingly adopted a two-step succession route from whip to leader.[37]

Leadership PACs House and Senate leaders, and members who aspire to become leaders, often ingratiate themselves to their colleagues by distributing campaign funds to them. In recent years, *leadership PACs* have proliferated on Capitol Hill. Table 8.5 lists the top leadership PACs by the size of their total contributions in the 2000 congressional elections.

In Committee

Much of the real work of Congress is done in committee. The floor of Congress is often deserted, C-SPAN focuses on the podium, not the empty chamber. Members dash to the floor when the bell rings throughout the Capitol signaling a roll-call vote. Otherwise they are found in their offices or in the committee rooms, where the real work of Congress is done.

WWW **Library of Congress** The Thomas system allows the tracing of bills from their introduction, through the committee system, floor schedule vote, etc. *http://thomas.loc.gov*

Standing Committees The committee system provides for a division of labor in the Congress, assigning responsibility for work and allowing members to develop some expertise. The committee system is as old as the Congress itself: the very first Congress regularly assigned the task of wording bills to selected members who were believed to have a particular expertise. Soon a system of **standing committees**—permanent committees that specialize in a particular area of legislation—emerged. House committees have forty to sixty or more members and Senate committees fifteen to twenty-five members each. The proportions of Democrats and Republicans on each committee reflect the proportions of Democrats and Republicans in the House and Senate as a whole. Thus the majority party has a

standing committee Permanent committee of the House or Senate that deals with matters within a specified subject area.

majority of members on every committee; and every committee is chaired by a member of the majority party. The minority membership on each committee is led by the **ranking minority member,** the minority-party committee member with the most seniority.

The principal function of standing committees is the screening and drafting of legislation. With 8,000 to 10,000 or more bills introduced each session, the screening function is essential. The standing committees are the gatekeepers of Congress; less than 10 percent of the legislation introduced will pass the Congress. With rare exceptions, bills are not submitted to a vote by the full membership of the House or Senate without prior approval by the majority of a standing committee. Moreover, committees do not merely sort through bills assigned to them to find what they like. Rather, committees—or more often their subcommittees—draft (write) legislation themselves. Committees may amend, rewrite, or write their own bills. Committees are "little legislatures" within their own policy jurisdictions. Each committee guards its own policy jurisdiction jealously; jurisdictional squabbles between committees are common.

The Pecking Order of Committees The most powerful standing committees, and, therefore, the most sought-after committee assignments, are the Appropriations Committees in the House and the Senate. These committees hold the federal purse strings, arguably Congress's most important power. These committees are closely followed in influence and desirability by the Ways and Means Committee in the House and the Senate Finance Committee; these committees must pass on all tax matters, as well as Social Security and Medicare financing. In the House, the Rules Committee is especially powerful, owing to its control over floor consideration of every bill submitted to the full House. The Senate Judiciary Committee is especially influential because of its influence over all presidential nominees to the federal judiciary, including Supreme Court justices. Perhaps the least desirable committee assignments are those on the Senate Ethics Committee and the House Standards of Official Conduct Committee; these ethics panels are obliged to sit in judgment of their own colleagues.

Decentralization and Subcommittees Congressional **subcommittees** within each standing committee further decentralize the legislative process. At present, the House has about 90 subcommittees and the Senate about 70 subcommittees, each of which functions independently of its full committee (see Table 8.6). Subcommittees have fixed jurisdictions (for example, the House International Relations Committee has subcommittees on Africa, Asia and the Pacific, International Economic Policy, International Operations and Human Rights, and the Western Hemisphere); they meet and schedule their own hearings; and they have their own staffs and budgets. However, bills recommended by a subcommittee still require full standing-committee endorsement before being reported to the floor of the House or Senate. Full committees usually, but not always, ratify the decisions of their subcommittees.

Subcommittees decentralize power in Congress. Interest groups no longer concentrate their attention on a few senior standing-committee chairs and party leaders. Rather, they concentrate on those subcommittees dealing most directly with their concerns. Likewise, executive agencies must respond to subcommittees with policy oversight. Both lobbyists and bureaucrats must seek out "their" subcommittee and try to win the support of the chair and perhaps the ranking minority member. (For example, agents of the postal workers' union, the U.S. Postal Service,

ranking minority member The minority-party committee member with the most seniority.

subcommittees Specialized committees within standing committees; subcommittee recommendations must be approved by the full standing committee before submission to the floor.

TABLE 8.6 Committees in Congress

Senate	
Agriculture, Nutrition, and Forestry	Governmental Affairs
Appropriations	Indian Affairs
Armed Services	Judiciary
Banking, Housing, and Urban Affairs	Health, Education, Labor and Pensions
Budget	Rules and Administration
Commerce, Science, and Transportation	Small Business and Entrepreneurship
Energy and Natural Resources	Select Aging
Environment and Public Works	Select Ethics
Finance	Select Intelligence
Foreign Relations	Veterans Affairs

House	
Agriculture	Resources
Appropriations	Rules
Armed Forces	Science
Budget	Small Business
Energy and Commerce	Standards of Official Conduct
Education and the Workforce	Transportation and Infrastructure
Financial Services	Veterans Affairs
Government Reform	Ways and Means
House Administration	Select Intelligence
International Relations	Select Homeland Security
Judiciary	

Joint Committees
Joint Economic Committee
Joint Taxation
Joint Committee on Printing
Joint Committee on the Library

and private competitors such as FedEx and United Parcel Service all converge on the Post Office and Civil Service Subcommittee of the Senate Governmental Affairs Committee.) The result has been hundreds of policy networks, each featuring subcommittee members and staff, lobbyists with an interest in the subcommittee's field, and bureaucrats in the executive branch charged with implementing congressional policy in that field.

Chairing a committee or subcommittee gives members of Congress the opportunity to exercise power, attract media attention, and thus improve their chances of reelection. Often committees have become "fiefdoms" over which their chairs exercise complete control and jealously guard their power. This situation allows a very small number of House and Senate members to block legislation. Many decisions are not really made by the whole Congress. Rather, they are made by subcommittee members with a special interest in the policy under consideration. Although the committee system may satisfy the desire of members to gain power, prestige, and reelection opportunities, it weakens responsible government in the Congress as a whole.

PEOPLE IN POLITICS

"Ted" Kennedy: Keeping Liberalism Alive in the U.S. Senate

To the American public, Massachusetts Senator, Edward M. "Ted" Kennedy is largely a symbol of his family's legendary triumphs and tragedies. But in the U.S. Senate, Kennedy has established himself over the years as the recognized leader of liberal Democrats and a highly effective legislator.

Ted Kennedy's father, Joseph P. Kennedy, was a wealthy banker and stock market manipulator who provided key financial backing for the 1932 presidential campaign of Franklin D. Roosevelt. FDR later appointed "Old Joe" as ambassador to England. The senior Kennedy fathered nine children, including Joseph P. Jr., who was killed in World War II; President John F. Kennedy, who was assassinated in 1963; Senator Robert F. Kennedy, who was assassinated in 1968; and youngest, Edward M. "Ted" Kennedy.

Although born to great wealth (he received his first communion from the Pope), Ted Kennedy acquired the sense of competition fostered in the large Kennedy household. In 1951, suspended from Harvard for cheating on an examination, he joined the Army and served two years in Germany. He was later readmitted to Harvard where he graduated in 1956. Rejected by Harvard Law School, he enrolled instead in the University of Virginia Law School and completed his law degree in 1959. When he was just 30 years old, the minimum age for a U.S. senator, he announced his candidacy for the Massachusetts Senate seat formerly held by his brother, who was then president. His 1962 election to the U.S. Senate reflected the esteem that Massachusetts voters have always held for his family.

Kennedy performed better in the Senate than many had expected. He worked hard learning about national health problems and problems of the elderly. In 1969 he was elected Senate Democratic whip by his colleagues. But his personal life was marred by accident, tragedy, and scandal. He nearly died in a 1964 plane crash in which he suffered a broken back. He was frequently the object of romantic gossip in Washington, In 1969, a young women died when the car Kennedy was driving plunged off a narrow bridge on Chappaquiddick Island after a late-night party. Missing for

Committee Membership Given the power of the committee system, it is not surprising that members of Congress have a very keen interest in their committee assignments. Members strive for assignments that will give them influence in Congress, allow them to exercise power in Washington, and ultimately improve their chances for reelection. For example, a member from a big city may seek a seat on Banking, Housing, and Urban Affairs, a member from a farm district may seek a seat on Agriculture, and a member from a district with a large military base may seek a seat on National Security or Veterans Affairs. Everyone seeks a seat on Appropriations, because both the House and the Senate Appropriations committees have subcommittees in each area of federal spending.[38]

Party leadership in both the House and the Senate largely determines committee assignments. These assignments are given to new Democratic House members by the Democratic Steering and Policy Committee; new Democratic senators receive their assignments from the Senate Democratic Steering Committee. New Republican members receive their committee assignments from the Republican Committee on Committees in both houses. The leadership generally tries to honor new members' requests and improve their chances for reelection, but because incumbent members of committees are seldom removed, openings on powerful committees are infrequent.

ten hours after the accident, Kennedy later made a dramatic national television appearance claiming that the tragedy had been an accident that he had been too confused to report until the next day. He pled guilty to the minor charge of leaving the scene of the accident. Senate Democrats removed Kennedy from his position as majority party whip.

Kennedy deliberately avoided Democratic presidential battles in both 1972 and 1976, believing that the public's memory of Chappaquiddick was still too fresh. However, in late 1979, with President Jimmy Carter standing in a near all-time low for presidents in opinion polls, Kennedy announced his presidential candidacy. But shortly thereafter, Soviet troops invaded neighboring Afghanistan. Support for the president was equated with support for America, and Carter benefited from this "rally round the flag" effect. Carter defeated Kennedy in the Democratic primaries, but Kennedy polished his own charismatic image with a dramatic inspiring speech at the 1980 Democratic national convention.

Kennedy avoided subsequent presidential races, citing family affairs as his reason. And indeed, family problems continued to plague him. He was divorced from his first wife, Joan, and stories were published in women's magazines portraying her as a victim of his heavy drinking and "womanizing." At the same time, he felt responsible for the many "third-generation" offspring of his deceased brother Robert, as well as his own children. One nephew died a drug-related death in a Miami motel in 1984, and another was found not guilty of rape charges in a nationally televised trial in 1992. That same year Kennedy married an accomplished Washington attorney and undertook to change his personal lifestyle. He delivered a moving eulogy on national television at the funeral of his nephew John F. Kennedy, Jr. after a plane crash in 1999 that killed JFK Jr., his wife, and sister-in-law.

As the ranking Democrat on the Senate Health, Education, and Labor Committee, Kennedy has undertaken the lead in a variety of important legislative issues. He helped pass the Family Leave Act of 1993, the Kennedy-Kasselbaum Act of 1996 that mandated health insurance "portability" (see Chapter 17), and increases in the minimum wage. While conservatives have frequently targeted Kennedy for his liberal politics, he has proven adept at working with Republicans in the Senate to win compromises in legislation. In 2000 he was elected to his seventh full term as U.S. senator from Massachusetts.

"50 Ways to Do the Job of Congress," *Congressional Quarterly*, October 30, 1999.

Seniority Committee chairs are elected in the majority-party caucus. But the **seniority system** governs most movement into committee leadership positions. The seniority system ranks all committee members in each party according to the length of time they have served on the committee. If the majority-party chair exits the Congress or leaves the committee, that position is filled by the next *ranking majority-party member.* New members of a committee are initially added to the bottom of the ranking of their party; they climb the seniority ranking by remaining on the committee and accruing years of seniority. Members who stay in Congress but "hop" committees are usually placed at the bottom of their new committee's list.

The seniority system has a long tradition in the Congress. The advantage is that it tends to reduce conflict among members, who otherwise would be constantly engaged in running for committee posts. It also increases the stability of policy direction in committees over time. Critics of the system note, though, that the seniority system grants greater power to members from "safe" districts—districts that offer little electoral challenge to the incumbent. (Historically in the Democratic Party, these districts were in the conservative South, and opposition to the seniority system developed among liberal northern Democrats. But in recent years, many liberal Democrats gained seniority and the seniority system again became entrenched (see *People in Politics:* "'Ted' Kennedy, Keeping Liberalism Alive in the

seniority system Custom whereby the member of Congress who has served the longest on the majority side of a committee becomes its chair and the member who has served the longest on the minority side becomes its ranking member.

Senator Joe Biden (left), of the Senate Foreign Relations Committee, speaks to reporters after meeting with President Bush about the arms treaty with Russia.

U.S. Senate"). The seniority rule for selecting committee chairs has been violated on only a few notable occasions.

Committee Hearings The decision of a congressional committee to hold public hearings on a bill or topic is an important one. It signals congressional interest in a particular policy matter and sets the agenda for congressional policy making. Ignoring an issue by refusing to hold hearings on it usually condemns it to oblivion. Public hearings allow interest groups and government bureaucrats to present formal arguments to Congress. Testimony comes mostly from government officials, lobbyists, and occasional experts recommended by interest groups or committee staff members. Hearings are usually organized by the staff under the direction of the chair. Staff members contact favored lobbyists and bureaucrats and schedule their appearances. Committee hearings are regularly listed in the *Washington Post* and are open to the public. Indeed, the purpose of many hearings is not really to inform members of Congress but instead to rally public support behind an issue or a bill. The media are the real target audience of many public hearings, with committee members jockeying in front of the cameras for a "sound bite" on the evening news.

Markup Once hearings are completed the committee's staff is usually assigned the task of writing a report and **drafting a bill.** The staff's bill generally reflects the chair's policy views. But the staff draft is subject to committee **markup,** a line-by-line consideration of the wording of the bill. Markup sessions are frequently closed to the public in order to expedite work. Lobbyists are forced to stand in the hallways, buttonholing members as they go into and out of committee rooms.

It is in markup that the detailed work of lawmaking takes place. Markup sessions require patience and skill in negotiation. Committee or subcommittee chairs may try to develop consensus on various parts of the bill, either within the whole committee or within the committee's majority. In marking up a bill, members of a subcommittee must always remember that the bill must pass both in the full committee and on the floor of the chamber. Although they have considerable freedom in writing their own policy preferences into law, especially on the details of the legislation, they must give some consideration to the views of these larger bodies. Consultations with party leadership are not infrequent.

Most bills die in committee. Some are voted down, but most are simply ignored. Bills introduced simply to reassure constituents or interest groups that a representative is committed to "doing something" for them generally die quietly. But House members who really want action on a bill can be frustrated by committee inaction. The only way to force a floor vote on a bill opposed by a committee is to get a majority (218) of House members to sign a **discharge petition.** Out of hundreds of discharge petition efforts, only a few dozen have succeeded. The Senate also can forcibly "discharge" a bill from committee by simple majority vote; but because senators can attach any amendment to any bill they wish, there is generally no need to go this route.

drafting a bill Actual writing of a bill in legal language.

markup Line-by-line revision of a bill in committee by editing each phrase and word.

discharge petition Petition signed by at least 218 House members to force a vote on a bill within a committee that opposes it.

On the Floor

A favorable "report" by a standing committee of the House or Senate places a bill on the "calendar." The word *calendar* is misleading, because bills on the calendar are not considered in chronological order, and many die on the calendar without ever reaching the floor.

House Rules Committee Even after a bill has been approved by a standing committee, getting it to the floor of the House of Representatives for a vote by the full membership requires favorable action by the Rules Committee. The Rules Committee acts as a powerful "traffic cop" for the House. In order to reach the floor, a bill must receive a rule from the Rules Committee. The Rules Committee can kill a bill simply by refusing to give it a rule. A **rule** determines when the bill will be considered by the House and how long the debate on the bill will last. More important, a rule determines whether amendments from the floor will be permitted and, if so, how many. A **closed rule** forbids House members from offering any amendments and speeds up consideration of the bill in the form submitted by the standing committee. A **restricted rule** allows certain specified amendments to be considered. An **open rule** permits unlimited amendments. Most key bills are brought to the floor of the House with fairly restrictive rules. In recent sessions, about three-quarters of all bills reaching the floor were restricted, and an additional 10 to 15 percent were fully closed. Only a few bills were open.

Senate Floor Traditions The Senate has no rules committee but relies instead on a **unanimous consent agreement** negotiated between the majority and minority leader to govern consideration of a bill. The unanimous consent agreement generally specifies when the bill will be debated, what amendments will be considered, and when the final vote will be taken. But as the name implies, a single senator can object to a unanimous consent agreement and thus hold up Senate consideration of a bill. Senators do not usually do so, because they know that a reputation for obstructionism will imperil their own favorite bills at a later date. Once accepted, a unanimous consent agreement is binding on the Senate and cannot be changed without another unanimous consent agreement. To get unanimous consent, Senate leaders must consult with all interested senators. Unanimous consent agreements have become more common in recent years as they have become more specific in their provisions.

The Senate cherishes its tradition of unrestricted floor debate. Senators may speak as long as they wish or even try to **filibuster** a bill to death by talking nonstop and tying up the Senate for so long that the leadership is forced to drop the bill in order to go on to other work. Senate rules also allow senators to place a "hold" on a bill, indicating their unwillingness to grant unanimous consent to its consideration. Debate may be ended only if *sixty* or more senators vote for **cloture,** a process of petition and voting that limits the debate. A cloture vote requires a petition signed by sixteen senators, two days must elapse between the petition's introduction and the cloture vote. If cloture passes, then each senator is limited to one hour of debate on the bill. But getting the necessary sixty votes for cloture is difficult. Recently Democrats, although a minority in the Senate, have defeated cloture motions in order to derail President Bush's nominees for federal judgeships (see Chapter 11).

Senate floor procedures also permit unlimited amendments to be offered, even those that are not "germane" to the bill. A **rider** is an amendment to a bill that is not germane to the bill's purposes.

These Senate traditions of unlimited debate and unrestricted floor amendments give individual senators considerably more power over legislation than individual representatives enjoy.

Floor Voting The key floor votes are usually on *amendments* to bills rather than on their final passage. Indeed, "killer amendments" are deliberately designed to

rule Stipulation attached to a bill in the House of Representatives that governs its consideration on the floor, including when and for how long it can be debated and how many (if any) amendments may be appended to it.

closed rule Rule that forbids adding any amendments to a bill under consideration by the House.

restricted rule Rule that allows specified amendments to be added to a bill under consideration by the House.

open rule Rule that permits unlimited amendments to a bill under consideration by the House.

unanimous consent agreement Negotiated by the majority and minority leaders of the Senate, it specifies when a bill will be taken up on the floor, what amendments will be considered, and when a vote will be taken.

filibuster Delaying tactic by a senator or group of senators, using the Senate's unlimited debate rule to prevent a vote on a bill.

cloture Vote to end debate—that is, to end a filibuster—which requires a three-fifths vote of the entire membership of the Senate.

rider Amendment to a bill that is not germane to the bill's purposes.

defeat the original purpose of the bill. Other amendments may water down the bill so much that it will have little policy impact. Thus the true policy preferences of senators or representatives may be reflected more in their votes on amendments than their vote on final passage. Members may later claim to have supported legislation on the basis of their vote on final passage, even though they earlier voted for amendments designed to defeat the bill's purposes.

Members may also obscure their voting records by calling for a voice vote—simply shouting "aye" or "nay"—and avoiding recording of their individual votes. In contrast, a **roll-call vote** involves the casting of individual votes, which are reported in the *Congressional Record* and are available to the media and the general public. Electronic voting machines in the House allow members to insert their cards and record their votes automatically. The Senate, truer to tradition, uses no electronic counters.

Conference Committees The Constitution requires that both houses of Congress pass a bill with identical wording. However, many major bills pass each house in different forms, not only with different wording but sometimes with wholly different provisions. Occasionally the House or the Senate will resolve these differences by reconsidering the matter and passing the other chamber's version of the bill. But about 15 percent of the time, serious differences arise and bills are assigned to **conference committees** to reach agreement on a single version for resubmission to both houses. Conference committees are temporary, with members appointed by the leadership in each house, usually from among the senior members of the committees that approved the bills.

Conference committees can be very powerful. Their final bill is usually (although not always) passed in both houses and sent to the president for approval. In resolving differences between the House and the Senate versions, the conference committee makes many final policy decisions. Although conference committees have considerable leeway in striking compromises, they focus on points of disagreement and usually do not change provisions already approved by both houses. Figure 8.9 on facing page summarizes the lawmaking process.

roll-call vote Vote of the full House or Senate on which all members' individual votes are recorded and made public.

conference committee Meeting between representatives of the House and Senate to reconcile differences over provisions of a bill passed by both houses.

party vote Majority of Democrats voting in opposition to a majority of Republicans.

party unity Percentage of Democrats and Republicans who stick with their party on party votes.

Decision Making in Congress

How do senators and representatives decide about how they will vote on legislation? From an almost limitless number of considerations that go into congressional decision making, a few factors recur across a range of voting decisions: party loyalty, presidential support or opposition, constituency concerns, interest-group pressures, and the personal values and ideologies of members themselves.

Party Voting Party appears to be the most significant influence on congressional voting. **Party votes** are roll-call votes on which a majority of voting Democrats oppose a majority of voting Republicans. Traditionally, party votes occurred on roughly *half* of all roll-call votes in Congress. Partisanship in Congress, as reflected in the percentage of party votes, rose during the 1990s but may be moderating somewhat today (see Figure 8.10 on page 356).

Party unity is measured by the percentage of Democrats and Republicans who stick by their party on party votes. Both Democratic and Republican Party unity has remained at fairly constant levels (75–85 percent) in both the House and the Senate over the past twenty years.

Bill Introduction

Subcommittee Hearings

Committee Action

Floor Action

Conference Action

Presidential Decision

HOUSE	SENATE
Bill is introduced and assigned to a committee, which refers it to the appropriate subcommittee.	Bill is introduced and assigned to a committee, which refers it to the appropriate subcommittee.
Subcommittee Subcommittee holds hearings and "marks up" the bill. If the bill is approved in some form, it goes to the full committee.	**Subcommittee** Subcommittee holds hearings, debates provisions and "marks up" the bill. If a bill is approved, it goes to the full committee.
Committee Full committee considers the bill. If the bill is approved in some form, it is "reported" to the full House and placed on the House calendar.	**Committee** Full committee considers the bill. If the bill is approved in some form, it is "reported" to the full Senate and placed on the Senate calendar.
Rules Committee Rules Committee issues a rule to govern debate on the floor. Sends it to the full House.	**Leadership** Majority and minority leaders negotiate "unanimous consent" agreements scheduling full Senate debate and vote on the bill.
Full House Full House debates the bill and may amend it. If the bill passes and it is in a form different from the Senate version, it must go to a conference committee.	**Full Senate** Full Senate debates the bill. Senate may amend it. If the bill passes and is in a form different from the House version, it must go to a conference committee.

Conference Committee

Conference committee of senators and representatives meets to reconcile differences between bills. When agreement is reached, a compromise bill is sent back to both the House and the Senate.

President

President signs or vetoes the bill. Congress can override a veto by a two-thirds majority vote in both the House and Senate.

FIGURE 8.9 How a Bill Becomes a Law

This diagram depicts the major hurdles a successful bill must overcome in order to be enacted into law. Few bills introduced travel this full path; less than 10 percent of bills introduced are passed by Congress and sent to the president for approval or veto. Bills fail at every step along the path, but most die in committees and subcommittees, usually from inaction rather than from being voted down.

FIGURE 8.10 Party Voting in Congress

Partisanship varies over time in Congress. For many years, between 30 and 40 percent of votes in the House and Senate were party votes—votes on which a majority of Democrats were in opposition to a majority of Republicans—but during the 1990s the percentage rose, indicating an increasingly partisan environment in Congress.

Note: Data indicate the percentage of all recorded votes on which a majority of voting Democrats opposed a majority of voting Republicans.

Source: Based on data from *Congressional Quarterly Weekly Report,* January 12, 2002, p. 136.

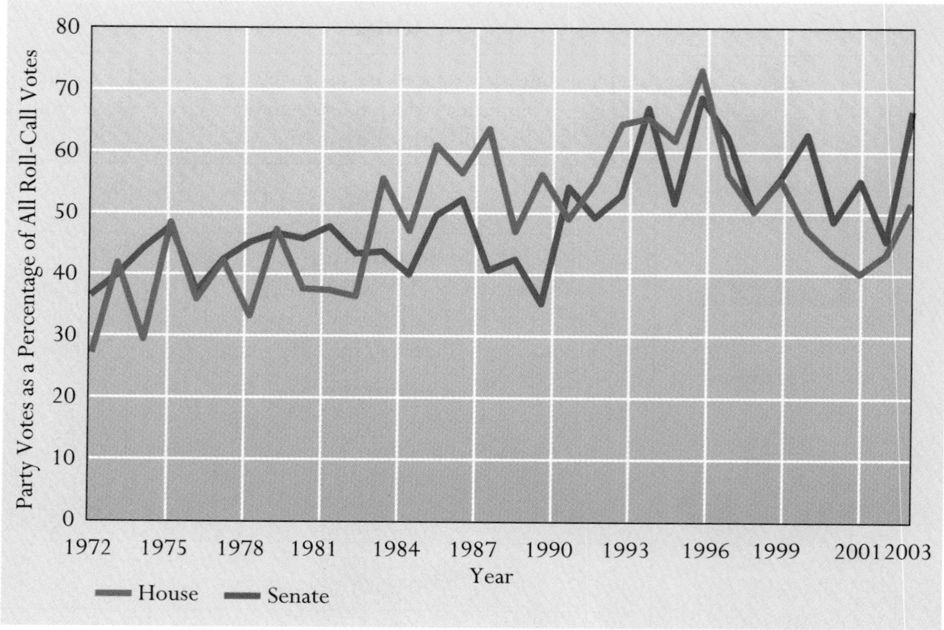

Sources of Partisanship Why do Democrats and Republicans in Congress vote along party lines? First of all, the Democratic Party has become more liberal and the Republican Party has become more conservative over the years (see *Up Close:* "Polarization on Capitol Hill"). Conservative Democrats, once very common in southern politics, are rapidly disappearing. At the same time, the ranks of liberal Republicans, mostly from the Northeast, have thinned. Second, the decline in voter turnout, especially in primary elections, has added to the importance of well-organized and ideologically motivated groups. A reputation as a "moderate" is not much help in a low-voter-turnout primary election. In these elections Republicans must be more concerned with pleasing conservative activists (e.g., the Christian Coalition, National Right-to-Life Committee, National Rifle Association, etc.), and Democrats must be more concerned with pleasing liberal groups (National Education Association, American Federation of State, County, and Municipal Employees, EMILY's List, etc.). And third, the rising costs of campaigning make members ever more dependent upon the financial support of these interests.

Conflict between the parties occurs frequently on domestic social and economic issues—welfare, housing and urban affairs, health, business regulation, taxing, and spending. On civil rights issues, voting often follows party lines on amendments and other preliminary matters but then swings to **bipartisan** voting on a final bill. This pattern suggests that the parties tend to agree on the general goals of civil rights legislation but not on the means. Traditionally, bipartisanship was the goal of both presidents and congressional leaders on foreign and defense policy issues. Since the Vietnam War, however, Democrats in the House have been more critical of U.S. military involvements (and defense spending in general) than have Republicans.

bipartisan Agreement by members of both the Democratic and the Republican parties.

divided party government One party controls the presidency while the other party controls one or both houses of Congress.

Presidential Support or Opposition Presidential influence in congressional voting is closely tied to party. Presidents almost always receive their greatest support from members of their own party (see Figure 8.11). Indeed, the policy gridlock associated with **divided party government**—in past decades, a Republican

UP CLOSE

Polarization on Capitol Hill

The Democratic and Republican parties in Congress are further apart ideologically than ever before. The Republicans are more uniformly conservative, and the Democrats more liberal, than in previous decades. "The proportion of political moderates—conservative Democrats or liberal Republicans—hovered at about 30 percent in the 1960s and 1970s. . . . Fewer than one in ten of today's lawmakers fall into this centrist category."* Conservative Southern Democrats once represented a third of their party's members, and a "conservative coalition" of Republicans and Southern Democrats was once a strong force in the Senate. Indeed, in the early 1980s President Ronald Reagan won the support of many moderate-to-conservative Democrats for his tax cutting measures. But today conservative Democrats account for less than ten percent of their party's membership in Congress; with the retirement of several Southern Democratic senators in 2004, conservative Democrats have practically disappeared from the Senate. And even rarer breed—liberal Republicans—are also nearing extinction.

Partisanship and ideology are closely connected in this polarization on Capitol Hill. The result is more conflict, less bipartisan cooperation, and more acrimony in the halls of Congress.

The most common explanation for this polarization is the realignment of Southern voters from the Democratic to the Republican party. Southern conservatives moved almost en bloc into the Republican Party in the 1980s. As conservatives in the Republican Party gained strength, liberal Republicans, mostly from the Northeast, lost ground. Geographically, the Republican Party became centered in the Mountain states and the South, while the Democratic Party held the Northeast and West Coast. Finally, more polarizing issues—abortion, term limits, budget balancing—and a more aggressive leadership style, notably speaker Newt Gingrich in the 1990s, also contributed to party polarization.†

*Roger H. Davidson and Usltard Oleszek *Congress and Its Members.* 9th ed. Washington, D.C.: CQ Press, 2004, p. 276.

†Jason M. Roberts and Steven S. Smith, "Procedure Contexts Party Strategy and Conditional Party Voting in the U.S. House of Representatives, 1971–2000." *American Journal of Political Science* 47 (April 2003): pp 305–317.

president and a Democratic-controlled Congress, but beginning in 1995 a Democratic president and a Republican-controlled Congress—arises directly from the tendency of the opposition party to obstruct the president's policy proposals.

The decentralization of power in the congressional committee system also limits the president's ability to influence voting. The president cannot simply negotiate with the leadership of the House and Senate but instead must deal with scores of committee and subcommittee chairs and ranking members. To win the support of so many members of Congress, presidents often music agree to insert pork into presidential bills, promise patronage jobs, or offer presidential assistance in campaign fund raising.

If negotiations break down, presidents can "go over the heads" of Congress, using the media to appeal directly to the people to support presidential programs and force Congress to act. The president has better access to the media than Congress has. But such threats and appeals can only be effective when (1) the president himself is popular with the public; and (2) the issue is one about which constituents can be made to feel intensely.

Finally, presidents can threaten to veto legislation. This threat, expressed or implied, confronts congressional leaders, committee chairs, and sponsors of a bill with several options. They must decide whether to (1) modify the bill to overcome the president's objections; (2) try to get two-thirds of both houses to commit to overriding the threatened veto; or (3) pass the bill and dare the president

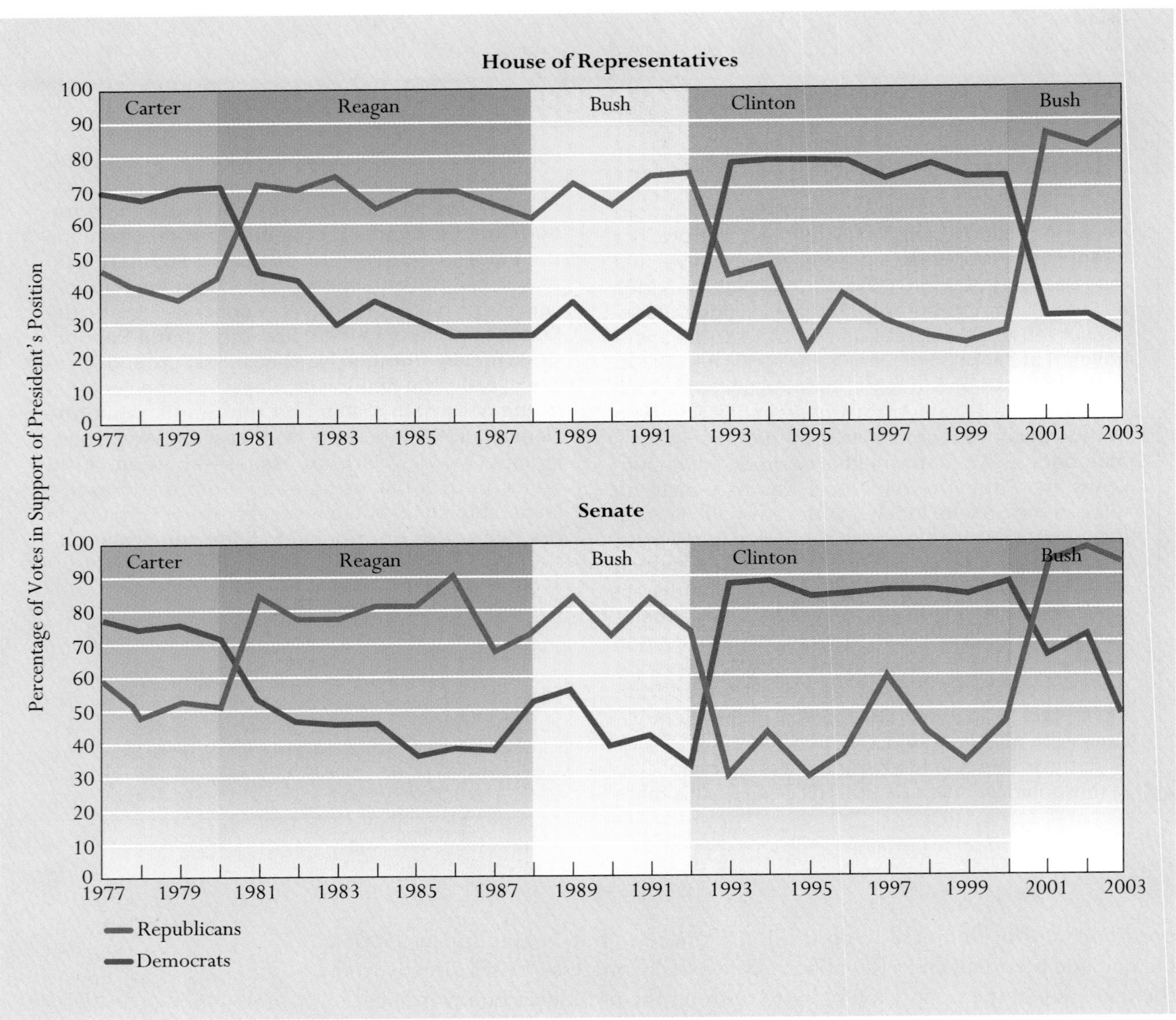

FIGURE 8.11 Congressional Voting in Support of the President

Presidents always receive more support in Congress from members of their own party. Democratic Presidents Jimmy Carter and Bill Clinton could count on winning large majorities of Democratic members' votes, Republican Presidents Ronald Reagan and George Bush won large majorities of GOP members' votes Percentages indicate congressional votes supporting the president on votes on which the president took a position.

Source: Norman J. Ornstein, Thomas E. Mann, and Michael J. Malbin, Vital Statistics on Congress 1999–2000 (Washington, D.C.: CQ Press, 2000), pp. 254–55; and Congressional Quarterly Weekly Report, December 11, 1999, p. 2987, January 12, 2002, p. 136; December 14, 2003, p. 3275 January 3, 2004.

to veto it, then make a political issue out of the president's opposition. Historically, less than 5 percent of vetoes have been overridden by the Congress. Unless the president is politically very weak (as Richard Nixon was during the Watergate scandal), Congress cannot count on overriding a veto. If members of Congress truly want to address an important problem and not just define a political issue, they must negotiate with the White House to write a bill the president will sign.

Constituency Influence **Constituency** influence in congressional voting is most apparent on issues that attract media attention and discussion and generate intense feelings among the general public. If many voters in the home state or district know about an issue and have intense feelings about it, members of Congress are likely to defer to their constituents' feeling, regardless of the position of their party's leadership or even their own personal feelings. Members of Congress from *safe seats* seem to be just as attuned to the interests of their constituents as members from competitive seats (see *Up Close:* "Tips on Lobbying Congress").

Constituency influence is particularly important on economic issues. Members from districts heavily dependent on a particular industry are routinely found protecting and advancing the interests of that industry. This kind of constituency representation is not unlike pork-barrel politics.

Constituencies may also exercise a subtle influence by conditioning the personal views of members. Many members were born, were raised, and continue to live in the towns they represent; over a lifetime they have absorbed and internalized the views of their communities. Moreover, some members of Congress feel an obligation to represent their constituents' opinions even when they personally disagree.

Members of Congress have considerable latitude in voting against their constituents' opinions if they choose to do so. Constituents, as noted earlier, lack information about most policy issues and the voting records of their senators and representatives. Even when constituents know about an issue and feel strongly about it, members can afford to cast a "wrong" vote from time to time. A long record of home-style politics—casework, pork barreling, visits, public appearances, and so on—can isolate members of Congress from the wrath generated by their voting records. Only a long string of "wrong" votes on issues important to constituents is likely to jeopardize an incumbent.

THINK AGAIN

Are members of Congress obliged to vote the way their constituents wish, even if they personally disagree?

Interest-Group Influence Inside the Washington Beltway, the influence of interest groups, lobbyists, and fund raisers on members of Congress is well understood. This influence is seldom talked about back home or on the campaign trail, except perhaps by challengers. Lobbyists have their greatest effects on the *details* of public policy. Congressional decisions made in committee rooms, at markup sessions, and around conference tables can mean billions of dollars to industries and tens of millions to individual companies. Pressures from competing interest groups can be intense as lobbyists buttonhole lawmakers and try to win legislative amendments that can make or break business fortunes. One of the most potent tools in the lobbyist's arsenal is money. The prohibitive cost of modern campaigning has dictated that dollars are crucial to electoral victory, and virtually all members of Congress spend more time than they would like courting it, raising it, and stockpiling it for the next election.

Voters may be wrong when they think that all members of Congress are crooks, but they are not far off the mark when they worry that their own representatives may be listening to two competing sets of constituents—the real constituents back home in the district and the "cash constituents" who come calling in Washington.[39]

THINK AGAIN

Is it ethical for Congress members to pay special attention to requests for assistance by people who make large campaign contributions?

Personal Values It was the eighteenth-century English political philosopher Edmund Burke, himself a member of Parliament, who told his constituents; "You choose a member indeed; but when you have chosen him, he is not a member of Bristol, but he is a member of *Parliament*." Burke defended the classic notion of

constituency The votes in a legislator's home district.

UP CLOSE

Tips on Lobbying Congress

YourCongress.com has some good suggestions about how to lobby Congress.

1. Keep it short and to the point. (Good lobbyists tell exactly what they want and why, in the least amount of words.)
2. Say thank you. (So few people say anything positive to members of Congress or their staff. If you know that they've done something good, say thank you. They'll remember it.)
3. Get to know the staff. (Good lobbyists don't complain when they don't get to meet the member of Congress. The staff does most of the work anyway, and has a knack for making requests disappear if given a reason to do so.)
4. Tell the whole story. (Good lobbyists don't patronize. They acknowledge when something is difficult and are up front about the opposition.)
5. Timing is everything. (Good lobbyists know the process of Congress, mention the proper deadlines, and don't ask for requests at the last minute.)
6. Always one page, and always written up in advance. (Good lobbyists have already written a draft of what they want before they ask for it, and are always happy to leave it or send it over.)
7. Capitol Hill is the last place to burn bridges. (Good lobbyists don't go ballistic when they are told no. They regroup and wait for another chance. D.C. is a very small place, and being a jerk will only mean you quickly get a reputation for being a jerk.)

representatives as **trustees** who feel obligated to use their own best judgment about what is good for the nation as a whole. In this theory, representatives are not obligated to vote the views of their constituents. This notion contrasts with the idea of representatives as **delegates** who feel obligated to vote according to the views of "the folks back home" regardless of their own personal viewpoint. Most legislators *claim* to be trustees, perhaps because of the halo effect generated by the independence implied in the term.

Democratic political philosophers have pondered the merits of trustee versus delegate representation over the centuries, but the question only rarely arises in actual congressional deliberations. In many cases, members' own personal views and those of their constituents are virtually identical. Moreover, members may overestimate the knowledge and issue-oriented tendencies of voters, since those most likely to communicate directly with their members of Congress are among the most knowledgeable and issue-oriented people in the district. Even when legislators perceive conflicts between their own views and those of their constituents, most attempt to find a compromise between these competing demands rather than choose one role or another exclusively. The political independence of members of Congress—their independence from party, combined with the ignorance of their constituents about most policy issues—allows members to give great weight to their own personal ideologies in voting.

trustees Legislators who feel obligated to use their own best judgment in decision making.

delegates Legislators who feel obligated to present the views of their home constituents.

Customs and Norms

Over time, institutions develop customs and norms of behavior to assist in their functioning. These are not merely quaint and curious folkways; they promote the purposes of the institution. Congressional customs and norms are designed to help members work together, to reduce interpersonal conflict, to facilitate bargining and promote compromise, and in general to make life in Congress a little more pleasant.

Civility Traditionally members of Congress understood that uncivil behavior—expressions of anger, personal attacks on character, ugly confrontations, flaming rhetoric—undermined the lawmaking function. Indeed, civility was encouraged by the longstanding custom of members of Congress referring to each other in elaborately courteous terms: "my distinguished colleague from Ohio," "the honorable representative from Pennsylvania," and the like. By custom, even bitter partisan enemies in Congress were expected to avoid harsh personal attacks on each other. The purpose of this custom was to try to maintain an atmosphere in which people who hold very different opinions can nevertheless function with some degree of decorum. Unfortunately, many of these customs and norms of behavior are breaking down. Individual ambition and the drive for power and celebrity have led to a decline in courtesy, cooperation, and respect for traditional norms. One result is that it has become increasingly difficult for Congress to reach agreement on policy issues. Another result is that life in Congress is increasingly tedious, conflict-filled, and unpleasant (see *A Conflicting View:* "Congress Can Act Responsibly on Occasion").

The Demise of the Apprenticeship Norm Not too many years ago, "the first rule"[40] of congressional behavior was that new members were expected to be seen but not heard on the floor, to be studious in their committee work, and to be cooperative with party leaders. But the institutional norm of apprenticeship was swept aside in the 1970s as increasingly ambitious and independent senators and representatives arrived on Capitol Hill. Today new members of Congress feel free to grab the spotlight on the floor, in committee, and in front of television cameras. "The evidence is clear, unequivocal, and overwhelming: the [apprenticeship] norm is simply gone."[41] Nevertheless, experienced members are more active and influential in shaping legislation than are new members.[42]

Specialization and Deference The committee system encourages members of Congress to specialize in particular policy areas. Even the most independent and ambitious members can perceive the advantage of developing power and expertise in an area especially relevant to their constituents. Traditionally, members who developed a special expertise and accumulated years of service on a standing committee were deferred to in floor proceedings. These specialists were "cue givers" for party members when bills or amendments were being voted on. Members are still likely to defer to specialized committee members when the issues are technical or complicated, or when the issue is outside of their own area of policy specialization, but deference is increasingly rare on major public issues.

Bargaining Bargaining is central to the legislative process. Little could be achieved if individual members were unwilling to bargain with each other for votes both in committees and on the floor. A willingness to bargain is a longstanding functional norm of Congress.

Members of Congress are not expected to violate their consciences in the bargaining process. On the contrary, members respect one another's issues of conscience and receive respect in return. On most issues, however, members can and do bargain their support. "Horse trading" is very common in committee work. Members may bargain in their own personal interest, in the interests of constituents or groups, or even in the interests of their committee with members of other committees. Because most bargaining occurs in a committee setting, it is seldom a matter of public record. The success and reputation of committee chairs largely depend on their ability to work out bargains and compromises.

A CONFLICTING VIEW

Congress Can Act Responsibly on Occasion

Congress is not always mired in partisanship, squabbling, and gridlock. On occasion it acts responsibly in the national interest. Indeed, consider the following congressional landmarks in U.S. history:

Louisiana Purchase (1803) President Thomas Jefferson offered to purchase from France nearly 830,000 square miles between the Mississippi and the Rockies for $15 million—about three cents an acre. There is no constitutional provision authorizing the federal government to buy foreign territory, but the Senate, accepting Jefferson's broad interpretation of the Constitution, approved the purchase. The House appropriated the money to consummate the deal. On December 29, 1803, the United States took possession of North America's heartland, doubling the nation's size with territory that would comprise thirteen states.

Homestead Act (1862) This Civil War–era legislation allowed any family head or adult male to claim 160 acres of prairie land for a $10 registration fee and a promise to live there continuously for five years. It opened up the midwestern United States for immediate settlement. The act drew thousands of English, Irish, Germans, Swedes, Danes, Norwegians, and Czechs to the United States, pushing settlement farther west.

Social Security Act (1935) The act was designed to secure "the men, women, and children of the nation against certain hazards and vicissitudes of life," explained President Franklin Roosevelt. The act's best-known measure is the social insurance system that provides monthly checks to the elderly.

National Labor Relations Act (1935) By declaring workers had a right to join unions and bargain collectively with employers for pay raises and improved working conditions, the act spurred the growth of the nation's major industrial unions. Labor's Magna Carta also provided workers with the legal weapons to improve plant conditions and protect themselves from employer harassment.

G.I. Bill of Rights (1944) The G.I. Bill of Rights, known officially as the Serviceman's Readjustment Act of 1944, offered to pay tuition for college or trade education to ex–World War II servicemen. It also mandated that they receive up to $500 a year for tuition, books, and supplies. Nearly 8 million veterans took advantage of this first G.I. Bill and American higher education expanded rapidly as a result. Veterans also made use of the bill's guaranteed mortgages and low interest rates to buy new homes in the suburbs, inspiring a development boom.

Truman Doctrine (1947) and NATO (1949) The Truman Doctrine initiated U.S. resistance to expansion of the Soviet Union into Western Europe following World War II, and the NATO treaty has provided the framework for European security for half a century. Truman declared to a joint session of Congress, "I believe that it must be the policy of the United States to support free people who are resisting attempted subjugation by armed minorities or by outside pressures."

Federal Highway Act (1956) President Dwight D. Eisenhower was right when he said, "More than any single action by the government since the end of the war, this one would change the face of America." The most expensive public-works project in U.S. history, the highway act built the 41,000 mile nationwide interstate highway system.

Civil Rights Act of 1964 Only Congress could end racial segregation in privately owned businesses and facilities. It did so by an overwhelming vote of both houses in the Civil Rights Act of 1964. Injustices endure, but the end of segregated restaurants, theaters, and drinking fountains provided new opportunities for African Americans and helped change white attitudes. In addition, Title VII of the act prohibits gender discrimination and serves as the legal bulwark for the women's rights.

Voting Rights Act of 1965 President Lyndon B. Johnson signed this act in the same room in the Capitol where Abraham Lincoln had penned the Emancipation Proclamation. This legislation guaranteed all Americans the most fundamental of all rights—the right to vote. Between the 1964 and 1968 presidential elections, black voter registration increased 50 percent across the nation, even in the reluctant southern states, giving African Americans newfound political clout.

Medicare and Medicaid (1965) Congress amended the Social Security Act of 1935 to provide for national health insurance for the aged (Medicare) and for the poor (Medicaid). In 2003 (28 years later) Congress added prescription drug coverage to Medicare.

Bargaining can assume different forms. Explicit trade-offs such as "If you vote for my bill, I'll vote for yours" are the simplest form of bargaining, but implicit understandings may be more common. Members may help other members in anticipation of receiving reciprocal help at some future unspecified time. Moreover, representatives who refuse to cooperate on a regular basis may find little support for their own bills. Mutual "back scratching" allows members to develop a reservoir of IOUs for the future. Building credit is good business for most members, one can never tell when one will need help in the future.

Bargaining requires a certain kind of integrity. Members of Congress must stick to their agreements. They must not consistently ask too high a price for their cooperation. They must recognize and return favors. They must not renege on promises. They must be trustworthy.

Conference-committee bargaining is essential if legislation acceptable to both houses is to be written. Indeed, it is expected that conferees from each house will bargain and compromise their differences. "Every House-Senate conference is expected to proceed via the methods of 'give and take,' 'trading back and forth,' 'pulling and hauling,' 'horse-trading and compromise,' 'splitting the difference,' etc."[43]

Reciprocity The norm of *reciprocity*—favors rendered should be repaid in kind—supports the bargaining process. Reciprocity may mean simply supporting a bill that is important to a colleague. But it may also extend to committees and subcommittees. In order to minimize intercommittee disputes over legislation, jurisdiction, or appropriations, "committees negotiate treaties of reciprocity ranging from 'I will stay out of your specialty if you will stay out of mine,' to 'I'll support your bill if you will support mine.' "[44]

The norm of reciprocity facilitates compromise and agreement and getting the work of Congress accomplished. Members who were willing to accept "half a loaf" traditionally accomplished more than those who insisted on a "whole loaf." But the norm of reciprocity may have weakened in recent years.

Logrolling Perhaps the most celebrated and reviled form of reciprocity, **logrolling** is mutual agreement to support projects that primarily benefit individual members of Congress and their constituencies. Logrolling is closely associated with pork-barrel legislation. Yet it can occur in virtually any kind of legislation. Even interest-group lobbyists may logroll with each other, promising to support each other's legislative agendas.

Leader-Follower Relations Because leaders have few means of disciplining members, they must rely heavily on their bargaining skills to solicit cooperation and get the work of Congress accomplished. Party leaders can appeal to members' concerns for their party image among the voters. Individual majority members want to keep their party in the majority—if for no other reason than to retain their committee and subcommittee chairs. Individual minority members would like their party to win control of their house in order to assume the power and privileges of committee and subcommittee chairs. Party leaders must appeal to more than partisanship to win cooperation, however.

To secure cooperation, leaders can grant—or withhold—some tangible benefits. A member of the House needs the Speaker's support to get recognition, to have a bill called up, to get a bill scheduled, to see to it that a bill gets assigned to a preferred committee, to get a good committee assignment, and to help a bill get out of the Rules Committee, for example.

logrolling Bargaining for agreement among legislators to support each other's favorite bills, especially projects that primarily benefit individual members and their constituents.

PEOPLE IN POLITICS

Bill Frist, M.D., Leading the Senate

At Senator Strom Thurmond's 100th birthday party, then Republican Majority Leader Trent Lott noted that the aged Thurmond had been the segregationist "Dixiecrat" candidate for president in 1948 and that Lott's state of Mississippi had voted for him. Then Lott went on: "If the rest of the country had followed our lead, we wouldn't have had all these problems over the years." This off-the-cuff remark was immediately denounced as racist and a political fire storm swept Washington. Lott apologized, but it was too late. President Bush declared, "Recent comments by Senator Lott do not reflect the spirit of our country." Lott was forced to resign as Majority Leader of the Senate.

Bill Frist, a highly respected heart surgeon first elected to the Senate in 1994, was viewed by his Republican colleagues as the remedy for the party's embarrassment. Born and raised in Nashville, Frist graduated from Princeton and went on to Harvard Medical School. (His father was the founder of the hospital chain, H.C.A.) Later at Vanderbilt University Medical Center, Frist performed over 150 heart and lung transplants and wrote more than a hundred medical research articles and several books.

Frist was a big winner in his first try at politics—defeating the three-term incumbent Tennessee Senator Jim Sasser. Frist spent nearly $10 million of his own money on his campaign. Upon arriving in Washington, he quickly won the respect of his Republican colleagues for his expertise on health-care issues. And he proved to be immensely popular with Tennessee voters, winning reelection in 2000 with 66 percent of the vote, the largest margin of victory in a statewide election in Tennessee history.

In December, 2002, Senate Republicans turned to Frist to provide respectability to the Majority Leader post. (Frist had served fewer years in the Senate than any Majority Leader in history.) Frist influenced his friend, President George Bush, to initiate a heavily-funded worldwide effort to fight AIDS. And Frist won a difficult fight to add a prescription drug benefit to Medicare, an issue that had plagued the Congress for years. Assuming that Frist continues to be popular and successful in his job, he is likely to emerge as a presidential candidate in 2008.

Party leaders may also seek to gain support from their followers by doing favors that ease their lives in Washington, advance their legislative careers, and help them with their reelection. Favors from party leaders oblige members to respond to leaders' requests at a later time. Members themselves like to build up a reservoir of good feeling and friendship with the leadership, knowing that eventually they will need some favors from the leadership (see *People in Politics:* Bill Frist, M.D., Leading the Senate).

Gridlock Congress is often criticized for legislative **gridlock**—the failure to enact laws, including appropriations acts, that are widely perceived to have merit. Indeed, much of the popular frustration with Congress relates to gridlock arising from policy and budgetary stalemates. Research has suggested that the following factors contribute to congressional gridlock:[45]

- Divided party control of the presidency and Congress
- Divided party control of the House and Senate
- Greater ideological polarization (liberal versus conservative) of the parties
- In the Senate, the willingness of members to filibuster against a bill, requiring 60 votes to overcome the opposition

gridlock The failure to enact laws that are widely perceived to have merit because of partisan or ideological bickering.

In contrast, the factors that appear to lessen gridlock and encourage significant legislative accomplishment include:

- Unified party control of the presidency, House, and Senate
- Larger numbers of moderates among Democrats and Republicans in Congress (as opposed to larger numbers of strong liberals and strong conservatives)
- Overwhelming public support for new legislation

Note that the constitutional structure of American government—separation of powers and checks and balances, as well as bicameralism—plays a major role in gridlock, as does the American two-party system. Overcoming gridlock requires a willingness of members of both parties in both houses of Congress, as well as the White House, to bargain and compromise over legislation. And it requires strong public opinion in support of congressional action.

Congressional Ethics

Although critics might consider the phrase *congressional ethics* to be an oxymoron, the moral climate of Congress today is probably better than in earlier eras of American history. Nevertheless, Congress as an institution has suffered from well-publicized scandals that continue to prompt calls for reform.

Ethics Rules Congress has an interest in maintaining the integrity of the institution itself and the trust of the people. Thus Congress has established its own rules of ethics. These rules include the following:

- *Financial disclosure:* All members must file personal financial statements each year.
- *Honoraria:* Members cannot accept fees for speeches or personal appearances.
- *Campaign funds:* Surplus campaign funds cannot be put to personal use. (A loophole allowed members elected before 1980 to keep such funds if they left office before January 1, 1993. A record number of House members resigned in 1992; many of them kept substantial amounts of campaign money.)
- *Gifts:* Members may not accept gifts worth more than $200 for representatives and $300 for senators (with annual increases in these amounts for inflation).
- *Free travel:* Members may not accept free travel from private corporations or individuals for more than four days of domestic travel and seven days of international travel per year. (Taxpayer-paid "junkets" to investigate problems at home or abroad or attend international meetings are not prohibited.)
- *Lobbying:* Former members may not lobby Congress for at least one year after retirement.

But these limited rules have not gone very far in restoring popular trust in Congress.

Gray Areas: Services and Contributions Congress members are expected to perform services for their political contributors. However, a direct *quid pro quo*—receiving a financial contribution specifically for the performance of official duty—is illegal. Few Congress members would be so foolish as to openly state a price to a potential contributor for a specific service, and most contributors know not to state a dollar amount that would be forthcoming if the member performed a particular service for them. But what if the contribution and the service occur close together? A Senate Ethics Committee once found that a close relationship between a service and a contribution to be an "impermissible pattern of conduct [that] violated established norms of behavior in the Senate . . . [and] was improper and repugnant."[46] But the Ethics Committee offered little in the way of a future guidance in handling services for campaign contributors.

Expulsion The Constitution gives Congress the power to discipline its own members. "Each House may . . . punish its Members for disorderly Behaviour, and, with the Concurrence of two thirds, expel a Member." But the Constitution fails to define *disorderly behavior.*

It seems reasonable to believe that criminal conduct falls within the constitutional definition of disorderly behavior. Bribery is a criminal act: it is illegal to solicit or receive anything of value in return for the performance of a government duty. During its notorious Abscam investigation in 1980, the Federal Bureau of Investigation set up a sting operation in which agents posing as wealthy Arabs offered bribe money to members of Congress while secretly videotaping the transactions. Six representatives and one senator were convicted. But criminal conviction does not automatically result in expulsion from Congress. In the Abscam case, only one defendant, Representative Michael Ozzie Myers (D-Pa.), was expelled, becoming the first member to be expelled since the Civil War. (Two other House members and the senator resigned rather than face expulsion, and the other three representatives were defeated for reelection. Perhaps the most interesting result of the Abscam investigation: only one member of Congress approached by the FBI, Democratic Senator Larry Presler of South Dakota, turned down the bribe.) The powerful chair of the House Ways and Means Committee, Democrat Dan Rostenkowski (Ill.), was indicted by a federal grand jury in 1994 for misuse of congressional office funds; he refused to resign from Congress, but his Chicago constituents voted him out of office. Democratic Representative Mel Reynolds (Ill.) resigned in 1995, following his criminal conviction on charges of sexual misconduct. (A special election to fill his vacated seat was won by Jesse Jackson, Jr., son of the popular preacher, commentator, and former Democratic presidential contender.) Republican Senator Robert Packwood (Oreg.) resigned in 1995 in order to avoid official expulsion following a Senate Ethics Committee report charging him with numerous counts of sexual harassment of female staff.

Censure A lesser punishment in the Congress than expulsion is official **censure.** Censured members are obliged to "stand in the well" and listen to the charges read against them. It is supposed to be a humiliating experience and fatal to one's political career. In 1983 two members of Congress were censured for sexual misconduct with teenage congressional pages. Both were obliged to "stand in the well." In 2002 New Jersey Democratic Senator Robert Torricelli was "severely admonished" by the Senate Ethics Committee for "at least the appearance of impropriety" for improperly accepting gifts and campaign contributions. Torricelli abruptly dropped out of his reelection race.

Lesser forms of censure included a public reprimand or admonition by the Ethics Committee expressing disapproval of the Congress member's behavior. And the Ethics Committee may also order a member to repay funds improperly received.

censure Public reprimand for wrongdoing, given to a member standing in the chamber before Congress.

SUMMARY NOTES

- The Constitution places all of the delegated powers of the national government in the Congress. The Founders expected Congress to be the principal institution for resolving national conflicts, balancing interests, and deciding who gets what. Today, Congress is a central battleground in the struggle over national policy. Congress generally does not initiate but responds to policy initiatives and budget requests originating from the president, the bureaucracy, and interest groups. Over time, the president and the executive branch, together with the Supreme Court and federal judiciary, have come to dominate national policy making.
- The Congress represents local and state interests in policy making. The Senate's constituencies are the 50 states, and the House's constituencies are 435 separate districts. Both houses of Congress, but especially the House of Representatives, wield power in domestic and foreign affairs primarily through the "power of the purse."
- Congressional powers include oversight and investigation. These powers are exercised primarily through committees. Although Congress claims these powers are a necessary part of lawmaking, their real purpose is usually to influence agency decision making, to build political support for increases or decreases in agency funding, to lay the political foundation for new programs and policies, and to capture media attention and enhance the power of members of Congress.
- Congress is gradually becoming more "representative" of the general population in terms of race and gender. Redistricting, under federal court interpretations of the Voting Rights Act, has increased African American and Hispanic representation in Congress. And women have significantly increased their presence in Congress in recent years. Nevertheless, women and minorities do not occupy seats in Congress proportional to their share of the general population.
- Members of Congress are independent political entrepreneurs. They initiate their own candidacies, raise their own campaign funds, and get themselves elected with very little help from their party. Members of Congress are largely career politicians who skillfully use the advantages of incumbency to stay in office. Incumbents outspend challengers by large margins. Interest-group political action committees and individual contributors strongly favor incumbents. Congressional elections are seldom focused on great national issues but rather on local issues and personalities and the ability of candidates to "bring home the bacon" from Washington and serve their constituents.
- Congress as an institution is not very popular with the American people. Scandals, pay raises, perks, and privileges reported in the media have hurt the image of the institution. Nevertheless, individual members of Congress remain popular with their districts' voters.
- Members of Congress spend as much time on "home-style" activities—promoting their images back home and attending to constituents' problems—as they do legislating. Casework wins votes one at a time, gradually accumulating political support back home, and members often support each other's "pork-barrel" projects.
- Despite the independence of members, the Democratic and Republican party structures in the House and Senate remain the principal bases for organizing Congress. Party leaders in the House and Senate generally control the flow of business in each house, assigning bills to committees, scheduling or delaying votes, and appointing members to committees. But leaders must bargain for votes; they have few formal disciplinary powers. They cannot deny renomination to recalcitrant members.
- The real legislative work of Congress is done in committees. Standing committees screen and draft legislation; with rare exceptions, bills do not reach the floor without approval by a majority of a standing committee. The committee and subcommittee system decentralizes power in Congress. The system satisfies the desires of members to gain power, prestige, and electoral advantage, but it weakens responsible government in the Congress as a whole. All congressional committees are chaired by members of the majority party. Seniority is still the major determinant of power in Congress.
- In order to become law, a bill must win committee approval and withstand debate in both houses of Congress. The rules attached to a bill's passage in the House can significantly help or hurt its chances. Bills passed with differences in the two houses must be reworked in a conference committee composed of members of both houses and then passed in identical form in both.
- In deciding how to vote on legislation, Congress members are influenced by party loyalty, presidential support or opposition, constituency concerns, interest-group pressures, and their own personal values and ideology. Party majorities oppose each other on roughly half of all roll-call votes in Congress. Presidents receive the greatest support in Congress from members of their own party.
- The customs and norms of Congress help reduce interpersonal conflict, facilitate bargaining and compromise, and make life more pleasant on Capitol Hill. They

include the recognition of special competencies of members, a willingness to bargain and compromise, mutual "back scratching" and logrolling, reciprocity, and deference toward the leadership. But traditional customs and norms have weakened over time as more members have pursued independent political agendas. And partisanship and incivility in Congress have risen in recent years.

- Congress establishes its own rules of ethics. The Constitution empowers each house to expel its own members for "disorderly conduct" by a two-thirds vote, but expulsion has seldom occurred. Some members have resigned to avoid expulsion; others have been officially censured yet remained in Congress.

KEY TERMS

congressional session 242
bicameral 242
power of the purse 244
oversight 244
confirmation 245
advice and consent 245
congressional hearings 245
congressional investigation 245
apportionment 247
malapportionment 247
redistricting 248
gerrymandering 248
splintering 249
packing 249
incumbent gerrymandering 250
affirmative racial gerrymandering 251
open seat 254
safe seat 254
turnover 255
home style 265
casework 265
pork barreling 265
franking privilege 266
Speaker of the House 269
majority leader 269
minority leader 269
whips 269
standing committee 271
ranking minority member 272
subcommittee 272
seniority system 275
drafting a bill 276
markup 276
discharge petition 276
rule 277
closed rule 277
restricted rule 277
open rule 277
unanimous consent agreement 277
filibuster 277
cloture 277
rider 277
roll-call vote 278
conference committee 278
party vote 278
party unity 278
bipartisan 280
divided party government 280
constituency 283
trustees 284
delegates 284
logrolling 287
gridlock 288
censure 290

SUGGESTED READINGS

Bond, Jon R., and Richard Fleisher, eds. *Polarized Politics: Congress and the President in a Partisan Era.* Washington, D.C.: CQ Press, 2000. Essay on the rise of partisanship in Washington and its effect on congressional-presidential relations.

Congressional Quarterly. *How Congress Works.* 3rd ed. Washington, D.C.: CQ Press, 1998. A description and explanation of the rules and procedures that govern the House and the Senate.

Davidson, Robert H., and Walter J. Oleszek. *Congress and Its Members.* 9th ed. Washington, D.C.: CQ Press, 2004. Authoritative text on Congress covering the recruitment of members, elections, House styles and Hill styles, leadership, decision making, and relations with interest groups, presidency, and courts. Emphasizes tension between lawmaking responsibilities and desire to be reelected.

Fenno, Richard F. *Home Style.* Boston: Little, Brown, 1978. The classic description of how attention to constituency by members of Congress enhances their reelection prospects. Home-style activities, including casework, pork barreling, travel and appearances back home, newsletters, and surveys, are described in detail.

Herrnson, Paul S. *Playing Hardball: Campaigning for the* U.S. *Congress.* Upper Saddle River, N.J.: Prentice Hall, 2001. Congressional candidates' strategies, targeting, fund raising, and getting out the vote.

Herrson, Paul S. *Congressional Elections: Campaigning at Home and in Washington.* 4th ed. Washington, D.C.: CQ Press. Interviews with candidates, campaign aides, and political consultants to paint a comprehensive portrait of congressional campaigns.

Jones, Charles O. *Separate but Equal Branches: Congress and the Presidency.* 2nd ed. Washington, D.C.: CQ Press, 1999.

Presidential–congressional relations under Johnson, Nixon, Ford, Carter, Reagan, Bush, and Clinton.

Kaptur, Marcy. *Women of Congress.* Washington, D.C.: CQ Press, 1996. An account of the progress of women toward longer tenure, greater seniority, and more influential committee appointments and how women in Congress still differ from men on these factors.

Oleszek, Walter J. *Congressional Procedures and Policy Processes.* 6th ed. Washington, D.C.: CQ Press, 2003. The definitive work on congressional rules, procedures and traditions and their effect on the course and content of legislation.

Ornstein, Norman J., Thomas E. Mann, and Michael J. Malbin. *Vital Statistics on Congress.* Washington, D.C.: CQ Press, 2004. Published biennially. Excellent source of data on members of Congress, congressional elections, campaign finance, committees and staff, workload, and voting alignments.

Sinclair, Barbara. *Unorthodox Lawmaking.* 2nd ed. Washington, D.C.: CQ Press, 2000. A description of the various detours and shortcuts a major bill is likely to take in Congress, including five case studies.

Stathis, Stephen W. *Landmark Legislation 1774–2002.* Washington, D.C.: CQ Press, 2003. A summary of major congressional legislation over 225 years, in a single volume.

MAKE IT REAL

RUNNING FOR CONGRESS

You are a Republican or Democratic Party leader and the hottest campaign manager in American politics. You can have your pick of candidates you will work for in the upcoming congressional elections, but your help is most needed in Missouri. You will have to guide your candidate through the general election. You research the district and help your candidate raise money and create a strong media-based campaign. Good luck!

CHAPTER 9

THE PRESIDENT: WHITE HOUSE POLITICS

CHAPTER OUTLINE

- Presidential Power
- Constitutional Powers of the President
- Political Resources of the President
- Personality Versus Policy
- Chief Executive
- Chief Legislator and Lobbyist
- Global Leader
- Commander-in-Chief
- The Vice Presidential Waiting Game

THINK ABOUT POLITICS

1 Do you approve of the way the president is handling his job?
Yes • No •

2 Should presidents have the power to take actions not specifically authorized by law or the Constitution that they believe necessary for the nation's well-being?
Yes • No •

3 Should the American people consider private moral conduct in evaluating presidential performance?
Yes • No •

4 Should Congress rally to support a president's decision to send U.S. troops into action even if it disagrees with the decision?
Yes • No •

5 Should Congress have the authority to call home U.S. troops sent by the president to engage in military actions overseas?
Yes • No •

6 Should Congress impeach and remove a president whose policy decisions damage the nation?
Yes • No •

7 Is presidential performance more related to character and personality than to policy positions?
Yes • No •

8 Do you think the situation in Iraq was worth going to war?
Yes No

How much power does the president of the United States really have—over policies, over legislation, over the budget, over how this country is viewed by other nations, even over how it views itself?

Presidential Power

Americans look to their president for "Greatness." The presidency embodies the popular "great man" view of history and public affairs—attributing progress in the world to the actions of particular individuals. Great presidents are those associated with great events: George Washington with the founding of the nation, Abraham Lincoln with the preservation of the Union, Franklin D. Roosevelt with the nation's emergence from economic depression and victory in World War II (see *What Do You Think?* "How Would You Rate the Presidents?"). People tend to believe that the president is responsible for "peace and prosperity" as well as for "change." They expect their president to present a "vision" of America's future and to symbolize the nation.

The Symbolic President The president personifies American government for most people. People expect the president to act decisively and effectively to deal with national problems. They expect the president to be "compassionate"—to show concern for problems confronting individual citizens.[1] The president, while playing these roles, is the focus of public attention and the nation's leading celebrity. Presidents receive more media coverage than any other person in the nation, for everything from their policy statements to their favorite foods to their dogs and cats.

Managing Crises In times of crisis, the American people look to their president to take action, to provide reassurance, and to protect the nation and its people. It is the president, not the Congress or the courts, who is expected to speak on behalf of the American people in times of national triumph and tragedy.[2] The president gives expression to the nation's pride in victory. The nation's heroes are welcomed and its championship sports teams are feted in the White House Rose Garden.

The president also gives expression to the nation's sadness in tragedy and strives to help the nation go forward. How presidents respond to crises often defines their place in history. Franklin D. Roosevelt raised public morale during the Great Depression of the 1930s by reassuring Americans that "the only thing we have to fear is fear itself." Later he led the nation into war following the Japanese attack on Pearl Harbor, December 7, 1941, "a day which will live in infamy." When the *Challenger* spaceship disintegrated before the eyes of millions of television viewers in 1986, Ronald Reagan gave voice to the nation's feelings about the disaster: "I want to say something to the school children of America who were watching the live

How Would You Rate the Presidents?

From time to time, historians have been polled to rate U.S. presidents (see table). The survey ratings given the presidents have been remarkably consistent. Abraham Lincoln, George Washington, and Franklin Roosevelt are universally recognized as the greatest American presidents. It is more difficult for historians to rate recent presidents; the views of historians are influenced by their own (generally liberal and reformist) political views. Richard Nixon once commented, "History will treat me fairly. Historians probably won't."

Historians may tend to rank activist presidents who led the nation through war or economic crisis higher than passive presidents who guided the nation in peace and prosperity. Initially Dwight Eisenhower, who presided in the relatively calm 1950s, was ranked low by historians. But later, after comparing his performance with those who came after him, his steadiness and avoidance of war raised his ranking dramatically.

Arthur M. Schlesinger (1948)

Great
1. Lincoln
2. Washington
3. F. Roosevelt
4. Wilson
5. Jefferson
6. Jackson

Near Great
7. T. Roosevelt
8. Cleveland
9. J. Adams
10. Polk

Average
11. J. Q. Adams
12. Monroe
13. Hayes
14. Madison
15. Van Buren
16. Taft
17. Arthur
18. McKinley
19. A. Johnson
20. Hoover
21. B. Harrison

Below Average
22. Tyler
23. Coolidge
24. Fillmore
25. Taylor
26. Buchanan
27. Pierce

Failure
28. Grant
29. Harding

Arthur M. Schlesinger, Jr. (1962)

Great
1. Lincoln
2. Washington
3. F. Roosevelt
4. Wilson
5. Jefferson

Near Great
6. Jackson
7. T. Roosevelt
8. Polk
   Truman (tie)
10. J. Adams
11. Cleveland

Average
12. Madison
13. J. Q. Adams
14. Hayes
15. McKinley
16. Taft
17. Van Buren
18. Monroe
19. Hoover
20. B. Harrison
21. Arthur
    Eisenhower (tie)
23. A. Johnson

Below Average
24. Taylor
25. Tyler
26. Fillmore
27. Coolidge
28. Pierce
29. Buchanan

Failure
30. Grant
31. Harding

Robert Murray (1982)

Presidential Rank
1. Lincoln
2. F. Roosevelt
3. Washington
4. Jefferson
5. T. Roosevelt
6. Wilson
7. Jackson
8. Truman
9. J. Adams
10. L. Johnson
11. Eisenhower
12. Polk
13. Kennedy
14. Madison
15. Monroe
16. J. Q. Adams
17. Cleveland
18. McKinley
19. Taft
20. Van Buren
21. Hoover
22. Hayes
23. Arthur
24. Ford
25. Carter
26. B. Harrison
27. Taylor
28. Tyler
29. Fillmore
30. Coolidge
31. Pierce
32. A. Johnson
33. Buchanan
34. Nixon
35. Grant
36. Harding

Arthur M. Schlesinger, Jr. (1996)

Great
1. Lincoln
2. Washington
3. F. Roosevelt

Near Great
4. Jefferson
5. Jackson
6. T. Roosevelt
7. Wilson
8. Truman
9. Polk

High Average
10. Eisenhower
11. J. Adams
12. Kennedy
13. Cleveland
14. L. Johnson
15. Monroe
16. McKinley

Average
17. Madison
18. J. Q. Adams
19. B. Harrison
20. Clinton
21. Van Buren
22. Taft
23. Hayes
24. Bush
25. Reagan
26. Arthur
27. Carter
28. Ford

Below Average
29. Taylor
30. Coolidge
31. Fillmore
32. Tyler

Failure
33. Pierce
34. Grant
35. Hoover
36. Nixon
37. A. Johnson
38. Buchanan
39. Harding

W. J. Ridings, S. B. McIver (1997)

Overall Ranking
1. Lincoln
2. F. Roosevelt
3. Washington
4. Jefferson
5. T. Roosevelt
6. Wilson
7. Truman
8. Jackson
9. Eisenhower
10. Madison
11. Polk
12. L. Johnson
13. Monroe
14. J. Adams
15. Kennedy
16. Cleveland
17. McKinley
18. J. Q. Adams
19. Carter
20. Taft
21. Van Buren
22. Bush
23. Clinton
24. Hoover
25. Hayes
26. Reagan
27. Ford
28. Arthur
29. Taylor
30. Garfield
31. B. Harrison
32. Nixon
33. Coolidge
34. Tyler
35. W. Harrison
36. Fillmore
37. Pierce
38. Grant
39. A. Johnson
40. Buchanan
41. Harding

Note: These ratings result from surveys of scholars ranging in number from 55 to 950.

Sources: Arthur Murphy, "Evaluating the Presidents of the United States," *Presidential Studies Quarterly* 14 (1984): 117–26; Arthur M. Schlesinger, Jr., "Rating the Presidents: Washington to Clinton," *Political Science Quarterly* 112 (1997): 179–90; William J. Ridings and Stuart B. McIver, *Rating the Presidents* (Secaucus, N.J.: Citadel Press, 1997).

The president and first lady personify government for many Americans. They become national celebrities and the focus of media attention.

coverage of the shuttle's takeoff. I know it is hard to understand, but sometimes painful things like this happen. The future doesn't belong to the faint-hearted. It belongs to the brave." And the terrorist attack on America, September 11, 2001, transformed President George W. Bush in the eyes of the nation:

> Tonight we are a country awakened to danger and called to defend freedom. Our grief has turned to anger, and anger to resolution. Whether we bring our enemies to justice, or bring justice to our enemies, justice will be done.[3]

The White House This official White House site provides up-to-date information or news about the current president's policies, speeches, appointments, proclamations, and cabinet members. *www.whitehouse.gov*

Providing Policy Leadership The president is expected to set policy priorities for the nation. Most policy initiatives originate in the White House and various departments and agencies of the executive branch, then are forwarded to Congress with the president's approval. Presidential programs are submitted to Congress in the form of messages, including the president's annual State of the Union Address, and in the Budget of the United States Government, which the president presents each year to Congress.

As a political leader, the president is expected to mobilize political support for policy proposals. It is not enough for the president to send policy proposals to Congress. The president must rally public opinion, lobby members of Congress, and win legislative battles. To avoid being perceived as weak or ineffective, presidents must get as much of their legislative programs through Congress as possible. The president is responsible for "getting things done" in the policy arena.

Managing the Economy The American people hold the president responsible for maintaining a healthy economy. Presidents are blamed for economic downturns, whether or not governmental policies had anything to do with market conditions. The president is expected to "Do Something!" in the face of high unemployment, declining personal income, high mortgage rates, rising inflation, or even a stock market crash. Herbert Hoover in 1932, Gerald Ford in 1976, Jimmy Carter in 1980, and George Bush in 1992—all incumbent presidents defeated for reelection during recessions—learned the hard way that the general public holds the president responsible for hard economic times. Presidents must have an economic "game plan" to stimulate the economy—tax incentives to spur investments, spending proposals to create jobs, plans to lower interest rates (see Chapter 16).

Managing the Government As the chief executive of a mammoth federal bureaucracy with 2.8 million civilian employees, the president is responsible for implementing policy, that is, for achieving policy goals. Policy making does not end when a law is passed. Policy implementation involves issuing orders, creating organizations, recruiting and assigning personnel, disbursing funds, overseeing work, and evaluating results. It is true that the president cannot perform all of these tasks personally. But the ultimate responsibility for implementation—in the words of the Constitution, "to take Care that the Laws be faithfully executed"—rests with the president.

The Global President Nations strive to speak with a single voice in international affairs; for the United States, the global voice is that of the president. As Commander-in-Chief of the armed forces of the United States, the president is a powerful voice in foreign affairs. Efforts by Congress to speak on behalf of the nation in foreign affairs and to limit the war-making power of the president have been generally unsuccessful. It is the president who orders American troops into combat (see *People in Politics:* "George Bush, and the War on Terrorism").

Constitutional Powers of the President

Popular expectations of presidential leadership far exceed the formal constitutional powers granted to the president. Compared with the Congress, the president has only modest constitutional powers (see Table 9.1). Nevertheless, presidents have pointed to a variety of clauses in Article II to support their rights to do everything from doubling the land area of the nation (Thomas Jefferson) to routing out terrorists from Afghanistan and invading Iraq (George W. Bush).

Who May Be President? To become president, the Constitution specifies that a person must be a natural-born citizen at least thirty-five years of age and a resident of the United States for fourteen years.

Initially, the Constitution put no limit on how many terms a president could serve. George Washington set a precedent for a two-term maximum that endured until Franklin Roosevelt's decision to run for a third term in 1940 (and a fourth term in 1944). In reaction to Roosevelt's lengthy tenure, in 1947 Congress proposed the Twenty-second Amendment (ratified in 1951), which officially restricts the president to two terms (or one full term if a vice president must complete more than two years of the previous president's term). (See *Compared to What?* "Mexican President Vicente Fox.")

Biographical facts and key events in the life of all U.S. presidents.
www.americanpresidents.org

Presidential Succession Until the adoption of the Twenty-fifth Amendment in 1967, the Constitution had said little about presidential succession, other than designating the vice president as successor to the president "in Case of the Removal, . . . Death, Resignation, or Inability" and giving Congress the power to decide "what Officer shall then act as President" if both the president and vice president are removed. The Constitution was silent on how to cope with serious presidential illnesses. It contained no provision for replacing a vice president. The incapacitation issue was more than theoretical: James A. Garfield lingered months

TABLE 9.1 The Constitutional Powers of the President

Chief Administrator

Implement policy: "take Care that the Laws be faithfully executed" (Article II, Section 3)
Supervise executive branch of government
Appoint and remove executive officials (Article II, Section 2)
Prepare executive budget for submission to Congress (by law of Congress)

Chief Legislator

Initiate policy: "give to the Congress Information of the State of the Union, and recommend to their Consideration such Measures as he shall judge necessary and expedient" (Article II, Section 3)
Veto legislation passed by Congress, subject to override by a two-thirds vote in both houses
Convene special session of Congress "on extraordinary Occasions" (Article II, Section 3)

Chief Diplomat

Make treaties "with the Advice and Consent of the Senate" (Article II, Section 2)
Exercise the power of diplomatic recognition: "receive Ambassadors" (Article II, Section 3)
Make executive agreements (by custom and international law)

Commander-in-Chief

Command U.S. armed forces: "The president shall be Commander-in-Chief of the Army and Navy" (Article II, Section 2)
Appoint military officers

Chief of State

"The executive Power shall be vested in a President" (Article II, Section 1)
Grant reprieves and pardons (Article II, Section 2)
Represent the nation as chief of state
Appoint federal court and Supreme Court judges (Article II, Section 2)

after being shot in 1881; Woodrow Wilson was an invalid during his last years in office (1919–20); Dwight Eisenhower suffered major heart attacks in office; and Ronald Reagan was in serious condition following an assassination attempt in 1981.

The Twenty-fifth Amendment stipulates that when the vice president and a majority of the cabinet notify the Speaker of the House and the president pro tempore of the Senate in writing that the president "is unable to discharge the powers and duties of his office," then the vice president becomes *acting* president. To resume the powers of office, the president must then notify Congress in writing that "no inability exists." If the vice president and a majority of cabinet officers do not agree that the president is capable of resuming office, then the Congress "shall decide the issue" within twenty-one days. A two-thirds vote of both houses is required to replace the president with the vice president.

The disability provisions of the amendment have never been used, but the succession provisions have been. The Twenty-fifth Amendment provides for the selection of a new vice president by presidential nomination and confirmation by a majority vote of both houses of Congress. When Vice President Spiro Agnew resigned in the face of bribery charges in 1973, President Richard Nixon nominated the Republican leader of the House, Gerald Ford, as vice president; and when Nixon resigned in 1974, Ford assumed the presidency and made Nelson Rockefeller, governor of New York, his vice president. Thus Gerald Ford's two-year tenure in the White House marked the only time in history when the man serving as president had not been elected to either the presidency or the vice presidency. (If the offices of president and vice president are both vacated, then Congress by law has specified the next in line for the presidency as the Speaker

PEOPLE IN POLITICS

George Bush and the War on Terrorism

In times of crises for the nation, presidents matter. What they say, and what they do, create indelible images that determine how their presidencies are viewed by history. George W. Bush's place in history will likely be measured by his ability to inspire and mobilize the American public for the war on terrorism.

An Unpromising Start

George W. Bush was born into his family's tradition of wealth, privilege, and public service. (Bush's grandfather, investment banker Prescott Bush, was a U.S. senator from Connecticut and chairman of the Yale Corporation, the university's governing board.)

He grew up in Midland, Texas, where his father had established himself in the oil business before going into politics—first as a Houston congressman, then Republican National Chairman, director of the CIA, ambassador to China, and finally vice president and president of the United States. George W. followed in his father's footsteps to Yale University but he was not the scholar-athlete that his father had been. Rather, he was a friendly, likable, heavy-drinking president of his fraternity. Upon graduation in 1968, he joined the Texas Air National Guard, completed flight school, but never faced combat in Vietnam. He earned an MBA degree from the Harvard Business School and returned to Midland to enter the oil business himself. Later in his career he would acknowledge his "youthful indiscretions," including a drunk driving arrest in 1976.

Although his famous name attracted investors in a series of oil companies he managed, virtually all of them lost money. Even a deal with the government of oil-rich Bahrain, negotiated while his father was president, failed to bail out Bush's Harken Energy Company. But Bush was able to sell off his oil interests and reinvest the money in the Texas Rangers baseball team; he eventually sold his interest in the Rangers in a deal that netted him a substantial profit.

Texas Governor

George W. Bush had never held public office before running for governor of Texas in 1994. But he had gained valuable political experience serving as an unofficial adviser to his father during his presidential campaigns. He went up against the sharp-tongued incumbent Democratic Governor Ann Richards, who ridiculed him as the "shrub" (little Bush). Bush heavily outspent Richards and won 54 percent of the vote, to become Texas's second Republican governor in modern times.

George W.'s political style fit comfortably with the Texas "good old boys" in both parties. Although the Texas legislature was controlled by Democrats, Bush won most of his early legislative battles. Bush's style was to meet frequently and privately with his Democratic opponents and to remain on friendly personal terms with them. He easily won reelection as governor in 1998.

Running for President

Bush denies that his father ever tried to influence his decision to run for president, but many of his father's friends and political associates did, believing that only he could reclaim the White House for the GOP. They compared "Dubya" to Ronald Reagan—amiable, charming, and good-humored, even if a little vague on the details of public policy. His mother's 10,000-name Christmas card list of closest family friends helped in building a bankroll of more than $100 million before the campaign even began. And the GOP establishment stuck with him when he was challenged in the early primary elections by maverick Arizona Republican Senator and Vietnam war hero John McCain.

His Father's Friends

While "Dubya's" father remained in the background, the president's White House and cabinet appointments indicated his reliance on experienced people to run the government. People who served in the Reagan and earlier Bush administrations surround George W. Bush. Bush chose Richard Cheney as his vice president, even though Cheney, as a former small state (Wyoming) congressman, brought no significant electoral votes to the ticket. But Cheney had won the confidence of the Bushes as secretary of defense during the Gulf War. Bush also brought the former chairman of the Joint Chiefs of Staff, Colin Powell, into his administration as secretary of state. President Gerald Ford's secretary of defense, Donald Rumsfeld, was reappointed to his old job. National Security Adviser Condoleeza Rice brought a reputation for brilliance and independence to her position. It was clear that "Dubya" was not afraid of being overshadowed by "heavyweights" in his administration.

"9/11"

The terrorist attack on America, September 11, 2001, dramatically changed the political landscape in Washington and the nation. The attack became the defining moment in the presidency of George W. Bush. He grew in presidential stature, respect, and decisiveness. His public appearances and statements reassured the American people. He promptly declared a "War on Terrorism" against both the terrorist organizations themselves and in the nations that harbor and support them.

Military action in Afghanistan followed quickly. Bush showed no hesitation, no indecision, no willingness to negotiate with terrorists. His public approval ratings skyrocketed: 90 percent of Americans approved of the way he was handling his job, a figure that even exceeded his father's approval ratings during the Gulf War. The rapid collapse of the hated Taliban government in Afghanistan seems to confirm the wisdom of Bush's actions.

Good Versus Evil

George Bush convinced the American people that the war on terrorism is "a monumental struggle of good versus evil." In his 2002 State of the Union message he specifically identified an "axis of evil"—Iraq, Iran, and North Korea. While many in the media scoffed at Bush's portrayal of the war on terrorism as a struggle between good and evil, most Americans heralded what they saw as Bush's "moral clarity" and the firmness of his convictions. He tried to define the enemy as the terrorists and not Islam itself. "The face of terror is not the true faith of Islam." Bush failed to win the support of the United Nations to oust Saddam Hussein from power in Iraq, but he succeeded in getting Congress to pass the joint resolution granting him authority to launch a preemptive military strike against Iraq. The early military phase of the war in Iraq went well; U.S. forces captured Baghdad in a mere 21 days, with precious few casualties. But remnants of Saddam's forces together with terrorists and other hard-line organizations began a guerrilla war against American and other coalition forces. Confronted with a prolonged struggle, costly lives and money, critics at home and abroad questioned American purposes in Iraq. Bush's high approval ratings began a slow decline. Throughout most of 2004, polls showed Bush running neck and neck with John Kerry in the presidential race. Kerry won the debates, but Bush remained "better at handling the war on terrorism." Election day brought the highest turnout in almost thirty years, and exit polls reported that "moral values" were the single most important concern of voters. These voters seemed to appreciate Bush's commitment to faith and family. He won a comfortable 51 percent of the popular vote.

After the September 11 terrorist attacks, U.S. troops moved quickly into Afghanistan to eliminate the Taliban.

COMPARED TO WHAT?

Mexican President Vicente Fox

For the first time in nearly a century, Mexico's long-dominant PRI party (Partido Revolucionario institucional) lost a presidential election in 2000. The winner was a tall, charismatic, business-politician, Vicente Fox, leader of the PAN party (Partido Acción Nacional).

Mexico's president is elected by nationwide popular vote for a six-year term. The president cannot succeed himself. He must deal with a bicameral National Congress composed of a Senate (Cámera de Senatores) and a Chamber of Deputies (Cámera de Diputados). Mexico has a tradition of a strong presidency. The Mexican Revolution of 1911, ending the dictatorship of Porfirio Díaz, was followed for several years by fighting among contending forces, including those of Emiliano Zapata and Pancho Villa. (U.S. Army forces pursued Villa throughout northern Mexico for many months.) A new Mexican Constitution of 1917 established the current structure of government. The PRI laid claim to the popular revolutionary tradition, and Mexico was essentially a one-party system until the 1980s. But splits occurred within the PRI, and gradually a new party, the PAN, began to win local and state elections. The PAN promoted free enterprise and economic development and attacked the alleged corruption in the PRI. In 1997, for the first time the PRI lost its majority in the Chamber of Deputies.

In the July 2000 presidential elections three viable candidates competed for the job: Francisco Labastida of the PRI, Cuauhtemoc Cárdenas (who had earlier split with the PRI), and Vicente Fox of the PAN. The results: Fox—43 percent, Labastida—37 percent, Cárdenas—17 percent.

Fox studied business administration at the Ibero-American University (in Mexico City) and management at the Harvard University Business School. He worked his way up through the ranks of Coca-Cola de México to the position of president for Latin America. He was elected to the Chamber of Deputies in 1988, failed in his first run for governor of the state of Guanajuato in 1991, but then won that governorship overwhelmingly in 1995. He developed a friendship with a fellow governor across the border, George W. Bush.

Fox and Bush agree that the solution to many of Mexico's problems is economic development. Both are strong supporters of the North American Free Trade Agreement (NAFTA) and both have sought to normalize immigration and border problems along the 2,000-mile Mexican-American frontier. The terrorist "9/11" attack on America set back progress on immigration reform, and recession in the United States did little to help Mexico's economy. Fox's popularity in Mexico has slipped somewhat, but he has until 2006 to restore confidence in his policies and his party.

of the House of Representatives, followed by the president pro tempore of the Senate, then the cabinet officers, beginning with the secretary of state.)

Impeachment The Constitution grants Congress the power of **impeachment** over the president, vice president, and "all civil Officers of the United States" (Article II, Section 4). Technically, impeachment is a charge similar to a criminal indictment brought against an official. The power to bring charges of impeachment is given to the House of Representatives. The power to try all impeachments is given to the Senate, and "no Person shall be convicted without the Concurrence of two thirds of the Members present" (Article I, Section 3). Impeachment by the House and conviction by the Senate only remove an official from office; a subsequent criminal trial is required to inflict any other punishment.

impeachment Equivalent of a criminal charge against an elected official; removal of the impeached official from office depends on the outcome of a trial.

The Constitution specifies that impeachment and conviction can only be for "Treason, Bribery, or other High Crimes and Misdemeanors." These words indicate that Congress is not to impeach presidents, federal judges, or any other officials simply because Congress disagrees with their decisions or policies. Indeed, the phrase implies that only serious criminal offenses, not political conflicts, can result in impeachment. Nevertheless, politics was at the root of the impeachment of President Andrew Johnson in 1867. Johnson was a southern Democrat who had remained loyal to the Union. Lincoln had chosen him as vice president in 1864 as a gesture of national unity. A Republican House impeached him on a party-line vote, but after a month-long trial in the Senate, the "guilty" vote fell one short of the two-thirds needed for removal.[4] And partisan politics in the House impeachment and later Senate trial of Bill Clinton (see *Up Close:* "Sex, Lies, and Impeachment").

Presidential Pardons The Constitution grants the president the power to "grant Reprieves and Pardons." This power derives from the ancient right to appeal to the king to reverse errors of law or justice committed by the court system. It is absolute: the president may grant pardons to anyone for any reason. The most celebrated use of the presidential pardon was President Ford's blanket pardon of former President Nixon "for all offenses against the United States which he, Richard Nixon, has committed or may have committed or taken part in." Ford defended the pardon as necessary to end "the bitter controversy and divisive national debate," but his actions may have helped cause his defeat in the 1976 election.

THINK AGAIN

Should presidents have the power to take actions not specifically authorized by law or the Constitution that they believe necessary for the nation's well-being?

Executive Power The Constitution declares that the "executive Power" shall be vested in the president, but it is unclear whether this statement grants the president any powers that are not specified later in the Constitution or given to the president by acts of Congress. In other words, does the grant of "executive Power" give presidents constitutional authority to act as they deem necessary *beyond* the actions specified elsewhere in the Constitution or specified in laws passed by Congress?

Center for the Study of the Presidency

Studies of the presidency and publication of the scholarly journal *Presidential Studies Quarterly*.
www.thepresidency.org

Contrasting views on this question have been offered over two centuries. President William Howard Taft provided the classic narrow interpretation of executive power:

> The true view of the executive function is, as I conceive it, that the president can exercise no power which cannot be fairly and reasonably traced to some specific grant of power or justly implied and included within such express grant as proper and necessary to its exercise. Such specific grants must be either in the federal constitution or in the pursuance thereof. There is no undefined residuum of power which can be exercised which seems to him to be in the public interest.[5]

Theodore Roosevelt, Taft's bitter opponent in a three-way race for the presidency in 1912, expressed the opposite view:

> I decline to adopt the view that what was imperatively necessary for the nation could not be done by the president unless he could find some specific authorization to do it. My belief was that it was not only his right but his duty to do anything that the needs of the nation demanded, unless such action was forbidden by the Constitution or by the laws.[6]

Although the constitutional question has never been fully resolved, history has generally sided with those presidents who have taken an expansive view of their powers. John F. Kennedy expressed the modern view of the constitutional presidency:

> The Constitution is a very wise document. It permits the president to assume just about as much power as he is capable of handling. . . . I believe that the president should use whatever power is necessary to do the job unless it is expressly forbidden by the Constitution.[7]

UP CLOSE

Sex, Lies, and Impeachment

Bill Clinton is the second president in the nation's history (following Andrew Johnson in 1867) to be impeached by the U.S. House of Representatives. (President Richard Nixon resigned just prior to an impeachment vote in 1974.)

Clinton's impeachment followed a report to the House by Independent Counsel Kenneth Starr in 1998 that accused the president of perjury, obstruction of justice, witness tampering, and "abuse of power." The Starr Report describes in graphic and lurid detail Clinton's sexual relationship with young White House intern Monica Lewinsky.

Does engaging in extramartial sex and lying about it meet the Constitution's standard for impeachment? "Treason, Bribery, or other High Crimes and Misdemeanors"? Perjury—knowingly giving false testimony in a sworn legal proceeding—is a criminal offense. But does the Constitution envision more serious misconduct? According to Alexander Hamilton in the Federalist, No. 65, impeachment should deal with "the abuse or violation of some public trust." Is Clinton's acknowledged "inappropriate behavior" a private affair or a violation of the public trust?

How are such questions decided? Despite pious rhetoric in Congress about the "search for truth," "impartial investigation," and "unbiased constitutional judgment," the impeachment process, whatever the merits of the charges against a president, is *political,* not judicial.

The House vote to impeach Clinton on December 19, 1998 (228 to 205) was largely along partisan lines, with all but five Republicans voting "yes" and all but five Democrats voting "no." And the vote in Clinton's Senate "trial" on February 12, 1999, was equally partisan. Even on the strongest charge—that Clinton had tried to obstruct justice—the Senate failed to find the president guilty. Removing Clinton failed to win even a majority of Senate votes, far less than the required two-thirds. All forty-five Democrats were joined by five Republicans to create a 50–50 tie vote that left Clinton tarnished but still in office.

Most Americans believed the president had a sexual affair in the White House and subsequently lied about it, however, they also *approved* of the way Clinton was performing his job as president. Indeed, the public appeared to rally around the president following the allegations of sexual misconduct.

Various explanations have been offered for this apparent paradox—a public that believed the president had an affair in the White House and lied about it, yet gave the president the highest approval ratings of his career. Many Americans believe that private sexual conduct is irrelevant to the performance of public duties. Private morality is viewed as a personal affair about which Americans should be nonjudgmental. Some people said, "If it's okay with Hillary, why should we worry?" Haven't we had adulterous presidents before, from Thomas Jefferson to John F. Kennedy, presidents who were ranked high in history? And many Americans believe that "they all do it."

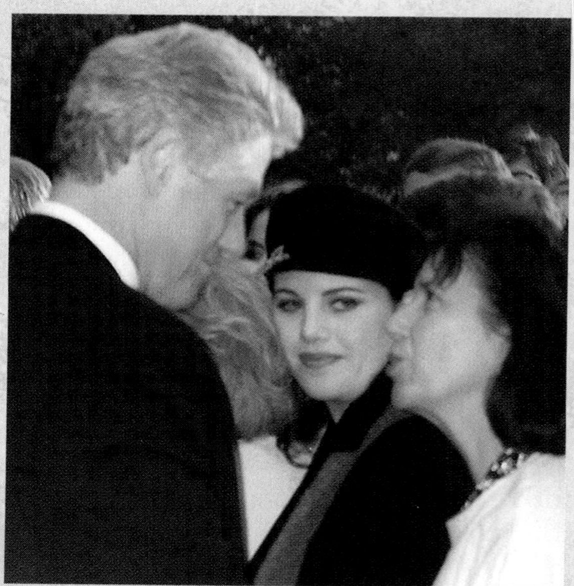

President Clinton greets well-wishers, including Monica Lewinsky, at a Democratic Party event in January 1996. Clinton's acknowledged "inappropriate behavior" and his efforts to conceal his relationship with Lewinsky were the subjects of the impeachment investigation opened against him by the House in 1998.

Others argue, nonetheless, that private character counts in presidential performance, indeed, that it is a prerequisite for public trust. The president, in this view, performs a symbolic role that requires dignity, honesty, and respect. A president publicly embarrassed by sexual scandal, diminished by jokes, and laughed at by late-night television audiences cannot perform this role. The acceptance of a president's adulterous behavior, according to one commentator, lowers society's standards of behavior. "The president's legacy . . . will be a further vulgarization and demoralization of society."*

* Gertrude Himmelfarb, "Private Lives, Public Morality," *New York Times,* February 9, 1998.

Some Historical Examples U.S. history is filled with examples of presidents acting independently, beyond specific constitutional powers or laws of Congress. Among the most notable:

- George Washington issued a Proclamation of Neutrality during the war between France and Britain following the French Revolution, thereby establishing the president's power to make foreign policy.
- Thomas Jefferson, who prior to becoming president argued for a narrow interpretation of presidential powers, purchased the Louisiana Territory despite the fact that the Constitution contains no provision for the acquisition of territory, let alone authorizing presidential action to do so.
- Andrew Jackson ordered the removal of federal funds from the national bank and removed his secretary of the treasury from office, establishing the president's power to *remove* executive officials, a power not specifically mentioned in the Constitution.
- Abraham Lincoln, asking, "Was it possible to lose the nation yet preserve the Constitution?" established the precedent of vigorous presidential action in national emergencies: He blockaded southern ports, declared martial law in parts of the country, and issued the Emancipation Proclamation—all without constitutional or congressional authority.
- Franklin D. Roosevelt, battling the Great Depression during the 1930s, ordered the nation's banks to close temporarily. Following the Japanese attack on Pearl Harbor in 1941, he ordered the incarceration without trial of many thousands of Americans of Japanese ancestry living on the West Coast.

Checking Presidential Power President Harry Truman believed that "the president has the right to keep the country from going to hell," and he was willing to use means beyond those specified in the Constitution or authorized by Congress. In 1952, while U.S. troops were fighting in Korea, steelworkers at home were threatening to strike. Rather than cross organized labor by forbidding the strike under the terms of the Taft-Hartley Act of 1947 (which he had opposed), Truman chose to seize the steel mills by executive order and continue their operations under U.S. government control. The U.S. Supreme Court ordered the steel mills returned to their owners, however, acknowledging that the president may have inherent powers to act in a national emergency but arguing that Congress had provided a legal remedy, however distasteful to the president. Thus the president can indeed act to keep the country from "going to hell" but if Congress has already acted to do so, the president must abide by the law.[8]

THINK AGAIN
Should Congress have the authority to call home U.S. troops sent by the president to engage in military actions overseas?

The most dramatic illustration of the checking of presidential power was the forced resignation of Richard M. Nixon in 1974 (for details, see *Up Close*: "Watergate and the Limits of Presidential Power"). Nixon's conduct inspired the intense hostility of the nation's media, particularly the prestigious *Washington Post*. His high public approval ratings following the Vietnam peace agreement plummeted. A Democratic-controlled Senate created a special committee to investigate **Watergate** that produced damaging revelations almost daily. Congressional Republicans began to desert the embattled president. The Supreme Court ordered him to turn over White House audiotapes to a special investigator, tapes that implicated Nixon in cash payments to the men who had burglarized the Democratic National Committee offices during his 1972 reelection campaign. Facing the enmity of the media, the loss of public approval, opposition from his own party in the Congress, and

Watergate The scandal that led to the forced resignation of President Richard M. Nixon. Adding "gate" as a suffix to any alleged corruption in government suggests an analogy to the Watergate scandal.

UP CLOSE

Watergate and the Limits of Presidential Power

Richard Nixon was the only president ever to resign the office. He did so to escape certain impeachment by the House of Representatives and a certain guilty verdict in trial by the Senate. Yet Nixon's first term as president included a number of historic successes. He negotiated the first ever strategic nuclear arms limitation treaty, SALT I, with the Soviet Union. He changed the global balance of power in favor of the Western democracies by opening relations with the People's Republic of China and dividing the communist world. In his second term, he withdrew U.S. troops from Vietnam, negotiated a peace agreement, and ended one of America's longest and bloodiest wars. But his remarkable record is forever tarnished by his failure to understand the limits of presidential power.

On the night of June 17, 1972, five men with burglary tools and wiretapping devices were arrested in the offices of the Democratic National Committee in the Watergate Building in Washington. Also arrested were E. Howard Hunt, Jr., G. Gordon Liddy, and James W. McCord, Jr., all employed by the Committee to Reelect the President (CREEP). All pleaded guilty and were convicted, but U.S. District Court Judge John J. Sirica believed that the defendants were shielding whoever had ordered and paid for the operation.

Although there is no evidence that Nixon himself ordered or had prior knowledge of the break-in, he discussed with his chief of staff, H. R. Haldeman, and White House advisers John Ehrlichman and John Dean the advisability of payoffs to buy the defendants' silence. Nixon hoped his landslide electoral victory in November 1972 would put the matter to rest.

But a series of sensational revelations in the *Washington Post* kept the story alive. Using an inside source known only as Deep Throat, Bob Woodward and Carl Bernstein, investigative reporters for the *Post,* alleged that key members of Nixon's reelection committee, including its chairman, former Attorney General John Mitchell, and White House staff were actively involved in the break-in and, more important, in the subsequent attempts at a cover-up.

In February 1973 the U.S. Senate formed a Special Select Committee on Campaign Activities—the "Watergate Committee"—to delve into Watergate and related activities. The committee's nationally televised hearings enthralled millions of viewers with lurid stories of "the White House horrors." John Dean broke with the White House and testified before the committee that he had earlier warned Nixon the cover-up was "a cancer growing on the presidency." Then, in a dramatic revelation, the committee—and the nation—learned that President Nixon maintained a secret tape-recording system in the Oval Office. Hoping that the tapes would prove or disprove charges of Nixon's involvement in the cover-up, the committee issued a subpoena to the White House. Nixon refused to comply, arguing that the constitutional separation of powers gave the president an "executive privilege" to withhold his private conversations from Congress. However, the U.S. Supreme Court, voting 8 to 0 in *United States v. Richard M. Nixon* ordered Nixon to turn over the tapes.

Despite the rambling nature of the tapes, committee members interpreted them as confirming Nixon's involvement in the payoffs and cover-up. Informed by congressional leaders of his own party that impeachment by a majority of the House and removal from office by two-thirds of the Senate were assured, on August 9, 1974, Richard Nixon resigned his office.

On September 8, 1974, new President Gerald R. Ford pardoned former President Nixon "for all offenses against the United States which he, Richard Nixon, has committed or may have committed or taken part in" during his presidency. Upon his death in 1994, Nixon was eulogized for his foreign policy successes.

---

the failure of his constitutional claim of "executive privilege" in the Supreme Court, Nixon became the only president of the United States ever to resign that office.

executive privilege Right of a president to withhold from other branches of government confidential communications within the executive branch; although posited by presidents, it has been upheld by the Supreme Court only in limited situations.

Executive Privilege Over the years, presidents and scholars have argued that the Constitution's establishment of a separate executive branch of government entitles the president to **executive privilege**—the right to keep confidential communications from other branches of government. Public exposure of internal executive communications would inhibit the president's ability to obtain candid advice from subordinates and would obstruct the president's ability to conduct negotiations with foreign governments or to command military operations.

But Congress has never recognized executive privilege. It has frequently tried to compel the testimony of executive officials at congressional hearings. Presidents have regularly refused to appear themselves at congressional hearings and have frequently refused to allow other executive officials to appear or divulge specific information, citing executive privilege. The federal courts have generally refrained from intervening in this dispute between the executive and legislative branches. However, the Supreme Court has ruled that the president is not immune from court orders when illegal acts are under investigation. In *United States v. Nixon* (1974), the U.S. Supreme Court acknowledged that although the president might legitimately claim executive privilege where military or diplomatic matters are involved, such a privilege cannot be invoked in a criminal investigation. The Court ordered President Nixon to surrender tape recordings of White House conversations between the president and his advisors during the Watergate scandal.[9]

Presidential Impoundment The Constitution states that "no Money shall be drawn from the Treasury, but in Consequence of appropriations made by Law" (Article I, Section 9). Clearly the president cannot spend money *not* appropriated by Congress. But the Constitution is silent on whether the president must spend all of the money appropriated by Congress for various purposes. Presidents from Thomas Jefferson onward frequently refused to spend money appropriated by Congress, an action referred to as **impoundment.** But taking advantage of a presidency weakened by the Watergate scandal, the Congress in 1974 passed the Budget and Impoundment Control Act, which requires the president to spend all appropriated funds. The act does provide, however, that presidents may send Congress a list of specific **deferrals**—items on which they wish to postpone spending—and **rescissions**—items they wish to cancel altogether. Congress by *resolution* (which cannot be vetoed by the president) may restore the deferrals and force the president to spend the money. Both houses of Congress must approve a rescission; otherwise the government must spend the money.

Responsibility to the Courts The president is not "above the law"; that is, his conduct is not immune from judicial scrutiny. The president's official conduct must be lawful; federal courts may reverse presidential actions found to be unconstitutional or violative of laws of Congress. And presidents are not immune from criminal prosecution, they cannot ignore demands to provide information in criminal cases. However, the Supreme Court has held that the president has "absolute immunity" from civil suits "arising out of the execution of official duties."[10] In other words, the president cannot be sued for damages caused by actions or decisions that are within his constitutional or legal authority.

But can the president be sued for *private* conduct beyond the scope of his official duties? In 1994 Paula Corbin Jones sued William Jefferson Clinton in federal district court in Arkansas, alleging that he made "abhorrent" sexual advances toward her in Little Rock in 1991 while he was governor and she was a state employee. Clinton's defense lawyers argued that the president should be immune from civil actions, especially those arising from events alleged to occur before he assumed office. They argued that the president's constitutional responsibilities are so important and demanding that he must devote his undivided time and attention to them. He cannot be distracted by civil suits; otherwise a large volume of politically motivated frivolous litigation might undermine his ability to function effectively in office.

impoundment Refusal by a president to spend monies appropriated by Congress; outlawed except with congressional consent by the Budget and Impoundment Control Act of 1974.

deferrals Items on which a president wishes to postpone spending.

rescissions Items on which a president wishes to cancel spending.

However, in 1997 the U.S. Supreme Court rejected the notion of presidential immunity from civil claims arising from actions outside of the president's official duties. Although advising lower courts to give "utmost deference to Presidential responsibilities" in handling the case, the Court held that "the doctrine of separation of powers does not require federal courts to stay all private actions against the president until he leaves office."[11] Clinton was obliged to settle the case with a financial payment to Jones.

The Constitution's Congressional Tilt The Constitution, reflecting the Founders' view of the preeminence of the legislative branch, gives the last word to the Congress in disputes with the president:

- The Congress can override the president's veto of legislation if it can muster a two-thirds vote in both houses.
- The Congress can impeach and remove the president from office.
- Only the Congress can appropriate money.
- Major presidential appointments require Senate confirmation.
- The president is obliged by the Constitution to "take Care that the Laws be faithfully executed"—that is, the *laws of Congress*—regardless of any personal feelings about these laws.

Thus, Congress is *constitutionally* positioned to dominate American government. But it is the president who *politically* dominates the nation's public affairs.

Political Resources of the President

The real sources of presidential power are not found in the Constitution. The president's power is the *power to persuade.* As Harry Truman put it, "I sit here all day trying to persuade people to do things they ought to have sense enough to do without my persuading them. . . . That's all the powers of the president amount to."[12]

The president's political resources are potentially very great. The nation looks to the president for leadership, for direction, for reassurance. The president is the focus of public and media attention. The president has the capacity to mobilize public opinion, to communicate directly with the American people, and to employ the symbols of office to advance policy initiatives in both foreign and domestic affairs.

The Reputation for Power A reputation for power is itself a source of power. Presidents must strive to maintain the image of power in order to be effective. A president perceived as powerful can exercise great influence abroad with foreign governments and at home with the Congress, interest groups, and the executive bureaucracy. A president perceived as weak, unsteady, bumbling, or error prone will soon become unpopular and ineffective.

THINK AGAIN

Is presidential performance more related to character and personality than to policy positions?

Presidential Popularity Presidential popularity with the American people is a political resource. Popular presidents cannot always transfer their popularity into foreign policy successes or legislative victories, but popular presidents usually have more success than unpopular presidents.

Presidential popularity is regularly tracked in national opinion polls. For more than forty years, national surveys have asked the American public: "Do you approve or disapprove of the way _____ is handling his job as president?" (see Figures 9.1 and 9.2). Analyses of variations over time in these poll results suggest some generalizations about presidential popularity (see Figure 9.1).[13]

Presidential popularity is usually high at the beginning of a president's term of office, but this period can be very brief. The American public's high expectations for a new president can turn sour within a few months. A president's popularity will vary a great deal during a term in office, with sharp peaks and steep valleys in the ratings. But the general trend is downward.[14] Presidents usually recover some popularity at the end of their first term as they campaign for reelection.

Presidential popularity rises during crises. People "rally 'round the president" when the nation is confronted with an international threat or the president initiates a military action.[15] President George Bush, for example, registered the all-time high in presidential ratings during the Persian Gulf War. Likewise, the invasion of Grenada in 1983 and Panama in 1989 rallied support to the president. And the "9/11" terrorist attack on America rallied the American people behind George W. Bush (see Figure 9.2). But prolonged warfare and stalemate erode popular support. In both the Korean and the Vietnam wars, initial public approval of the president and support for the war eroded over time as military operations stalemated and casualties mounted.[16]

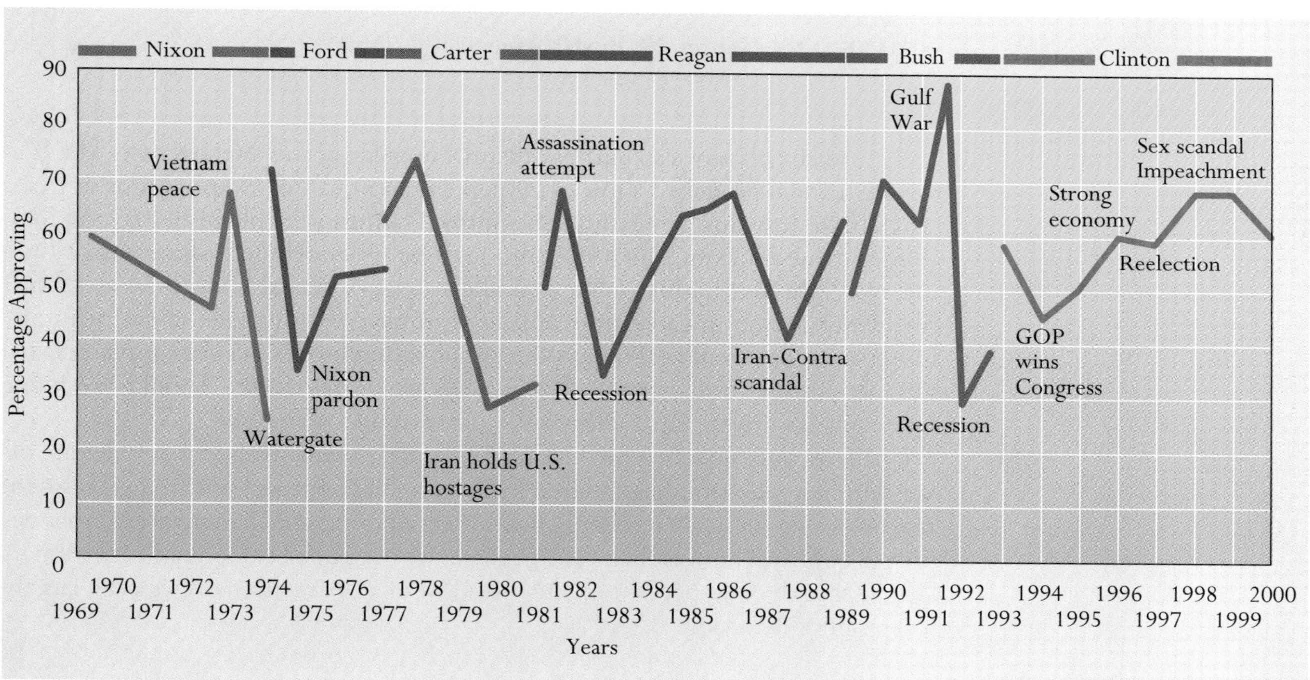

FIGURE 9.1 Presidential Popularity over Time

Americans expect a great deal from their presidents and are quick to give these leaders the credit—and the blame—for major events in the nation's life. In general; public approval (as measured by response to the question "Do you approve or disapprove of the way _____ is handling the job of president?") is highest at the beginning of a new president's term in office and declines from that point. Major military confrontations generally raise presidential ratings initially but can (as in the case of Lyndon Johnson) cause dramatic decline if the conflict drags on. In addition, public approval of the president is closely linked to the nation's economic health. When the economy is in recession, Americans tend to take a negative view of the president.

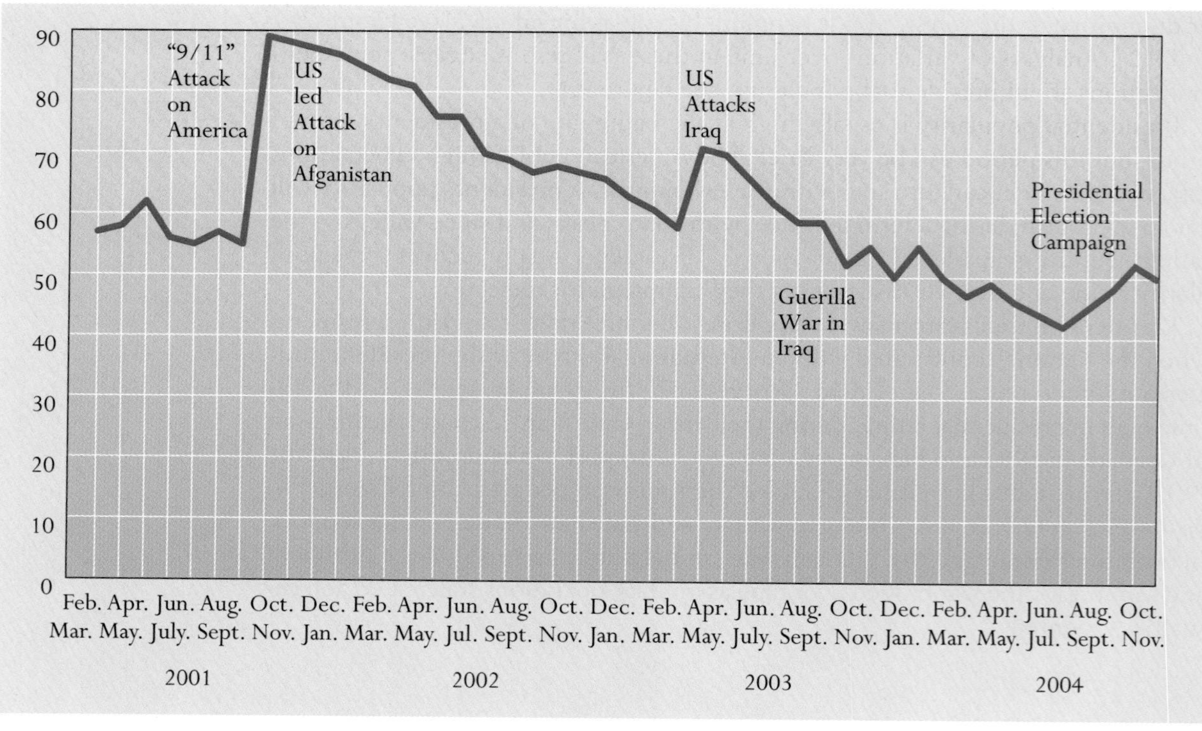

FIGURE 9.2 **George W. Bush's Approval Ratings**

Major scandals *may* also hurt presidential popularity and effectiveness. The Watergate scandal produced a low of 22 percent approval for Nixon just prior to his resignation. Reagan's generally high approval ratings were blemished by the Iran-Contra scandal hearings in 1987, although he ultimately left office with a high approval rate. But highly publicized allegations of sexual improprieties against President Clinton in early 1998 appeared to have the opposite effect; Clinton's approval ratings went *up*. Perhaps the public differentiates between private sexual conduct and performance in office. (see *What Do You Think?* "Should We Judge Presidents on Private Character or Performance in Office?").

Finally, economic recessions erode presidential popularity. Every president in office during a recession has suffered loss of popular approval, including President Reagan during the 1982 recession. But no president suffered a more precipitous decline in approval ratings than George Bush, whose popularity plummeted from its Gulf War high of 89 percent in 1991 to a low of 37 percent in only a year, largely as a result of recession.

Access to the Media The president dominates the news more than any other single person. All major television networks, newspapers, and newsmagazines have reporters (usually their most experienced and skilled people) covering the "White House beat." The presidential press secretary briefs these reporters daily, but the president also may appear in person in the White House press room at any time. Presidents regularly use this media access to advance their programs and priorities.[17]

White House press corps Reporters from both print and broadcast media assigned to regularly cover the president.

The **White House press corps** is an elite group of reporters assigned to cover the president. It includes the prestige press—the *New York Times, Washington Post, Wall Street Journal, Time, Newsweek, U.S. New and World Report,* as well as the television networks—ABC, CBS, NBC, CNN, FOX, and even the foreign press. Indeed, more

WHAT DO YOU THINK?

Should We Judge Presidents on Private Character or Performance in Office?

In evaluating presidents, should we consider their private moral conduct or should we focus on how they perform their public duties? Can private morality be divorced from public trust? The sex scandals surrounding Bill Clinton, not only those alleged to have occurred before he was elected president but also those alleged to have occurred in the Oval Office itself, brought these questions forcefully to the American people.

When allegations first emerged in January 1998 that Clinton had had an affair with a twenty-one-year-old intern working at the White House, President Clinton himself emphatically denied the allegations, saying, "I did not have sexual relations with that woman, Ms. Lewinsky!"

Most Americans (62 percent) believed the president had a sexual affair in the White House and subsequently lied abut it, however, they also approved of the way Clinton was performing his job as president. Indeed, the public appeared to rally around the president following the allegations of sexual misconduct. Clinton's job rating, already a healthy 60 percent at the beginning of 1998, experienced a "Lewinsky bounce" following lurid news stories of the affair. Indeed, many people blamed the independent counsel Kenneth Starr for investigating the private life of the president. And many people blamed the news media for focusing so much attention on the affair.

Various explanations have been offered for this apparent paradox—a public that believed the president had an affair in the White House and lied about it, yet gave the president the highest approval ratings of his career. Many Americans believe that private sexual conduct is irrelevant to the performance of public duties. Private morality is viewed as a personal affair about which Americans should be nonjudgmental. Some people said, "If it's okay with Hillary, why should we worry?" Haven't we had adulterous presidents before, from Thomas Jefferson to John F. Kennedy, presidents who were ranked high in history? And many Americans believe that "they all do it."

Others argue, nonetheless, that private character counts in presidential performance, indeed, that it is a prerequisite for public trust. The president, in this view, performs a symbolic role that requires dignity, honesty, and respect. A president publicly embarrassed by sexual scandal, diminished by jokes, and laughed at by late-night television audiences cannot perform this role. The acceptance of a president's adulterous behavior, according to one commentator, lowers society's standards of behavior. "The president's legacy . . . will be a further vulgarization and demoralization of society."*

*Gertrude Himmelfarb, "Private Lives, Public Morality," *New York Times*, February 9, 1998. Poll results reported in *The Polling Report*, February 9, 1998. See also George C. Edwards and Stephen J. Wayne, *Presidential Leadership*. 6th ed (Belmont, Calif.: Wadsworth, 2003). "How Important is Character?," p. 263.

than 1,800 journalists have White House press credentials. However, fortunately not all show up at once (there are only 48 seats in the White House briefing room, and attendance at press conferences is usually less than 300). The great majority of daily newspapers have no Washington correspondents, but instead rely on national news services such as the Associated Press.

Formal press conferences are a double-edged sword for the president. They *can* help mobilize popular support for presidential programs. Presidents often try to focus attention on particular issues, and they generally open press conferences with a policy statement on these issues. But reporters' questions and subsequent reporting often refocus the press conference in other directions. Often the lead media story emerging from a press conference has nothing to do with the president's purpose in holding the conference. The president cannot control questions or limit the subject matter of press conferences.

Presidents may also use direct television addresses from the White House. (President Reagan made heavy use of national prime time television appeals to mobi-

President George W. Bush answers questions during a press conference. These meetings with the press can be a double-edged sword. They give the president an opportunity to present his point of view to the public, but they also allow the press to raise issues a president might rather avoid.

lize support for his programs; he was exceptionally successful in generating telephone calls, wires, and letters to Congress in support of his programs.) President George Bush has used direct addresses to try to mobilize support the war on terrorism, including military actions in Afghanistan and Iraq.

Personality Versus Policy

A president with an engaging personality—warmth, charm, and good humor—can add to his political power. And, of course, a president who seems distant, uncaring, or humorless can erode his political resources. (Richard Nixon's seeming mean-spiritedness contributed to the collapse of his approval ratings during the Watergate scandal; Jimmy Carter's often cold and distant appearance failed to inspire much popular support for his programs; and George H. W. Bush appeared to be uncaring about the economic circumstances of ordinary Americans.) The public evaluates presidents as much on style as on policy substance.[18] (Perhaps no other president in recent times enjoyed such personal popularity while pursuing relatively unpopular policies as Ronald Reagan.) If the public thinks the president understands and cares about their problems, they may be willing to continue to approve of the job he is doing despite policy setbacks. In other words, the public evaluates the president by how much they like him as a person. (President Bill Clinton's likability kept his public approval ratings high during the sex scandal and impeachment effort.) Yet, as we have seen, public approval ratings of presidents can rise or fall based on wars and crises, scandals, and economic prosperity or recession, even while their personal style remains unaltered.

George Bush graduated from Yale two years ahead of John Kerry. Both were inducted into the prestigious leadership society, Scull and Bones, yet each displayed a distinctly different personality even in college. Bush was a hard-drinking fraternity man, a "regular guy." Kerry was hard-working, serious, austere, and eager to please his mentors (see *People in Politics* "John Kerry, War Hero and Anti-War Leader").

Bush's presidential campaigns, both against Al Gore in 2000 and John Kerry in 2004, rested largely on his personal appeal to voters—his perceived trustworthiness, warmth, good humor, and general "likeability." With a strong economy, budget surpluses, relative peace, and a popular president to follow, Al Gore should have won the 2000 presidential election. But compared to Bush, Gore seemed stiff, wooden, artificial, and out of touch with common people. Bush mangled his sentences (and even joked about it) and offered fewer details about public policy issues.

Bush never hid his religious faith. He admitted to giving up drinking and carousing and finding religion earlier in his life. Kerry seemed to be embarrassed by his Catholic faith and its stand on abortion, same-sex marriage, and stem-cell research. He also seemed conflicted about the war in Iraq: he had initially voted to give the president power to use military force, yet later he would talk of "the wrong war, in the wrong place, at the wrong time." He was a thoughtful, sensitive, and careful thinker; his position on issues was often qualified and nuanced. In the presidential debates Kerry appeared presidential, strong-voiced, articulate, and well-informed on the issues. He won the debates but failed to shed his image as aloof, austere, and lacking in strong commitment to issues that mattered. Bush was able to characterize him as a "waffler" and a "flip-flopper." Bush, despite all his flaws, was seen as strong, uncomplicated, and "willing to take a stand."

Party Leadership Presidents are leaders of their party, but this role is hardly a source of great strength. It is true that presidents select the national party chair, control the national committee and its Washington staff, and largely direct the national party convention. Incumbent presidents can use this power to help defeat challengers *within* their own parties. President Ford used this power to help defeat challenger Ronald Reagan in 1976; President Carter used it to help defeat challenger Ted Kennedy in 1980; and President Bush used it against challenger Pat Buchanan in 1992. But the role of party leader is of limited value to a president because the parties have few direct controls over their members (see Chapter 7).

Nevertheless, presidents enjoy much stronger support in Congress from members of their own party than from members of the opposition party (see "Decision Making in Congress" in Chapter 8). Some of the president's party support in Congress is a product of shared ideological values and policy positions. But Republican Congress members do have some stake in the success of a Republican president, as do Democratic members in the success of a Democratic president. Popular presidents may produce those few extra votes that make the difference for party candidates in close congressional districts.

Chief Executive

The president is the chief executive of the nation's largest bureaucracy: 2.8 million civilian employees, 60 independent agencies, 15 departments, and the large Executive Office of the President. The formal organizational chart of the federal government places the president at the head of this giant structure (see Figure 8.1, "The Federal Bureaucracy," in Chapter 8). But the president cannot command this bureaucracy in the fashion of a military officer or a corporation president. When Harry Truman was preparing to turn over the White House to Dwight Eisenhower, he predicted that the general of the army would not understand the presidency: "He'll sit here and say 'Do this! Do that!' and nothing will happen. Poor Ike—it won't be a bit like the army. He'll find it very frustrating." Truman vastly underestimated the political skills of the former general, but the crusty Missourian clearly understood the frustrations confronting the nation's chief executive. The president does not command the executive branch of government but rather stands at its center—persuading, bargaining, negotiating, and compromising to achieve goals (see *Up Close* Contrasting Presidential Styles).

The Constitutional Executive The Constitution is vague about the president's authority over the executive branch. It vests executive power in the presi-

PEOPLE IN POLITICS

John Kerry, War Hero, Anti-War Leader

John Kerry was born into Boston's privileged elite. His father, Richard, was a Yale University and Harvard law school graduate who married into the internationally wealthy Forbes family. He served in various diplomatic posts in Europe while his son, John Forbes Kerry, attended boarding schools in France and Switzerland. Eventually, John returned to the United States to attend the private prestigious preparatory school St. Paul's in Concord, New Hampshire. He dated Janet Auchincloss, half-sister of Jackie Kennedy and was a frequent guest of the Kennedys. John F. Kennedy became his idol; young Kerry exulted in the fact that they shared initials.

At Yale, John Kerry played varsity soccer and was inducted into the prestigious leadership honorary Skull and Bones (only two years after George W. Bush). After graduation from Yale in 1966, Kerry sought to follow in his idol's footsteps by serving in the Navy. The war was still supported by most Americans. Kerry already envisioned a political career. Like JFK he volunteered for duty with small PT-like "swift boats" so that he could achieve a command as a relatively low ranking officer. But he soon found that swift boat duty was extremely dangerous, patrolling close inshore in Vietnam's Mekong Delta.

War Hero Kerry distinguished himself as an aggressive and courageous commander. He was directly engaged in many firefights, suffering three minor wounds for which he received Purple Hearts. When his boat was ambushed on the Mekong River, instead of fleeing, he beached the boat and personally led his sailors on an attack that destroyed an enemy machine gun position. He was awarded a Silver Star for his actions. Later he risked his own life to pull a Green Beret from the water while under enemy fire. He was awarded a Bronze Star for this action.

Anti-War Hero Like many Vietnam veterans, Kerry was shocked by anti-war protests upon his return to the United States. In 1970 he married Julia Thorne, the wealthy heiress, and immediately sought to run for Congress as a war hero. But with anti-war sentiment strong in Massachusetts, he failed even to win the Democratic nomination. He retreated to the Thorne's 200-acre estate on Long Island to replan his political career. His personal reservations about the wisdom of the Vietnam War began to involve him in the anti-Vietnam War movement. When he was approached by billionaire Edgar Bronfman, owner of Seagrams, and offered business support to create an anti-war organization, the Vietnam Veterans Against the War (VVAW), he accepted. In April, 1971, representing the VVAW, he appeared before the Senate Foreign Relations Committee dressed in green fatigues wearing his medals and angrily testified against the war. He became an overnight celebrity appearing on "60 Minutes" and other popular shows. But when he tried to run again for Congress in 1972 as an anti-war candidate, he again suffered defeat. Disappointed again, he decided to enter the Boston College of Law. Upon graduation in 1976 he became a prosecuting attorney for Middlesex County. He took up private practice in 1979.

Rapid Political Rise Kerry never really lost his ambition for high political office. When the Massachusetts lieutenant governorship post opened up in 1982, Kerry entered a crowded Democratic field. Arguments over the Vietnam war had faded, so Kerry's new rallying cry was opposition to Reagan's military buildup. He won a narrow victory to join the Democratic ticket with Michael Dukakis as the gu-

dency and grants the president authority to appoint principal officers of the government "by and with the Advice and Consent of the Senate." Under the Constitution, the president may also "require the Opinion, in writing, of the principal Officer in each of the executive Departments, upon any Subject relating to the Duties of their respective Offices." This awkward phrase presumably gives the president the power to oversee operations of the executive departments. Finally, and perhaps most important, the president is instructed to "take Care that the Laws be faithfully executed."

At the same time, Congress has substantial authority over the executive branch. Through its lawmaking abilities, Congress can establish or abolish executive departments and regulate their operations. Congress's "power of the purse" allows it to determine the budget of each department each year and thus to limit or broaden bernatorial nominee. In Democratic Massachusetts, they won easily.

When illness forced the popular Massachusetts Senator Paul Tsongas to leave office in 1984, Kerry again jumped into the Democratic primary for the open seat. He adopted the nuclear freeze movement as his campaign theme and brought thousands of liberal Democrats to his cause. He won the Democratic nomination by a paper thin margin and went on to represent Massachusetts in the U.S. Senate.

Senate Career Kerry's Senate career can at best be described as lackluster. He never sponsored any significant legislation and he was never selected for any significant leadership position by his fellow Democrats. His voting reflected that of his Massachusetts Senate colleague Ted Kennedy. Both regularly compiled the Senate's most liberal voting record. Kerry served on the Senate Foreign Relations Committee, the same committee before which he had testified as a young anti-war protester years earlier.

After years of separation, Kerry and his wife divorced in 1988. The divorce from the wealthy heiress left Kerry short of cash. He began accepting large campaign contributions from interest groups, and over time won the unwanted recognition as the largest recipient of interest group money in the Senate. In 1995 Kerry married Teresa Heinz, the widow of Pennsylvania Senator John Heinz who had died in a plane crash. Teresa Heinz inherited the bulk of the Heinz ketchup fortune, and is listed as one of the richest women in the country.

Kerry faced his first real reelection battle in 1996 when challenged by Massachusetts Governor William Weld, one of the few Republicans ever to win that state's governorship in modern times. Kerry spent heavily in the race, and with Clinton's sweep of the state, he managed a narrow reelection victory. Kerry was now ready to set his sights on higher office.

Running for President. Kerry was one of ten Democratic candidates to announce their intentions to seek their party's nomination in 2004. But in early debates Kerry stood out as taller, stronger-voiced, and more articulate. Only Vermont Governor Howard Dean appeared to offer a real challenge to Kerry. Dean vigorously opposed the war in Iraq; Kerry had voted for it. Dean appealed to many hardcore "hate Bush" Democratic activists. But Democratic primary voters chose Kerry as more "electable" than the boisterous Dean.

The political landscape seemed to favor Kerry. Polls reported that most Americans thought the country was going in the wrong direction; Bush's approval rating was barely 50 percent; the economy had not yet recovered as many jobs as it had when Bush entered office; Iraq was in chaos, American troops were dying every day, and there appeared to be no end to the conflict.

But Kerry failed to convince most Americans that he could do any better in resolving the war in Iraq than Bush. His contradictory comments on the war allowed Bush to label him a "waffler"; his position that the United States should have waited for approval from the United Nations before going into Iraq allowed Bush to characterize him as someone who would turn over America's national security to the U.N. Kerry won the debates, yet Bush was still perceived as a stronger leader for the war on terrorism.

The largest voter turnout in recent history rejected Kerry. Kerry won the voters that cited the economy, Iraq, health care, and education as most important to them. But most important to the largest number of voters was "moral values" and Bush won 79 percent of these voters. Kerry had focused on the issues but Bush had won the voters on a simple message of faith and family.

or even "micromanage" the activities of these departments. Moreover, Congress can pressure executive agencies by conducting investigations, calling administrators to task in public hearings, and directly contacting agencies with members' own complaints or those of their constituents.

Executive Orders Presidents frequently use **executive orders** to implement their policies. Executive orders may direct specific federal agencies to carry out the president's wishes, or they may direct all federal agencies to pursue the president's preferred course of action. In any case, they must be based on either a president's constitutional powers or on powers delegated to the president by laws of Congress. Presidents regularly issue 50 to 100 executive orders each year, but some stand out. In 1942 President Franklin D. Roosevelt issued Executive Order 9066 for the

executive order Formal regulation governing executive branch operations issued by the president.

UP CLOSE

Contrasting Presidential Styles

Every president brings to the White House his own personal administrative style. Some presidents work almost constantly, putting in 12–14 hour days (Carter, Clinton). Others pursue a more leisurely schedule, leaving the Oval Office at 5 or 6 PM and spending weekends at the presidential retreat at Camp David or their home (Eisenhower, Reagan, Bush). Some presidents delegate a great deal of responsibility to Cabinet members and White House aides (Eisenhower, Reagan, Bush). Others closely monitor what is happening in executive departments and agencies (Johnson, Carter, Clinton). Some pursue a great many policy initiatives (Clinton), while others focus on a few key priorities (Reagan, Bush). Some are well informed about the specifics of public policy (Carter, Clinton), while others care more about overall goals and directions of their administration (Reagan, Bush). Some operate informally, communicating frequently with staff, Cabinet members, and others (Clinton). Other presidents function in a more business-like fashion, communicating mostly through their chief-of-staff (Eisenhower, Reagan). Below are the differences between the Bush and Clinton administrative styles as seen by two prominent political scientists:

Differences Between the Bush and Clinton Presidencies

George W. Bush	Bill Clinton
Disciplined White House	Less disciplined White House
Scripted presidency	Unscripted presidency
Strict focus on few key priorities	Wide-ranging policy focus
More reliance on vice president	Less reliance on vice president
Punctuality required for meetings with clear starting and ending times	Meetings start late and seldom end on time
Little use of the bully pulpit	More use of the bully pulpit
Direct public communicator	Skillful public communicator
Frequent reliance on experts to provide policy overviews	Well informed on policy issues
Somewhat more attentive to Congress and its members	Less attentive to Congress and its members
Large responsibilities delegated to aides	Close supervisory role maintained over all top aides
Preference for executive summaries	Enamored of thick briefing books
Regular working days observed insofar as practicable	A "24/7" president

Source: Roger H. Davidson and Walter J. Oleszak, *Congress and Its Members*. 9th ed. (Washington, D.C.: CQ Press, 2004), p. 302.

internment of Japanese Americans during World War II. In 1948 President Harry Truman issued Executive Order 9981 to desegregate the U.S. armed forces. In 1965 President Lyndon Johnson issued Executive Order 11246 to require that private firms with federal contracts institute affirmative action programs. A president can even declare a national emergency by executive order, a step that authorizes a broad range of unilateral actions.

Executive orders have legal force when they are based on the president's constitutional or statutory authority. And presidents typically take an expansive view of their own authority. (President George Washington issued an executive order declaring American neutrality in the war between France and England in 1793, while the Constitution gave the power to "declare war" to Congress, Washington assumed the authority to declare neutrality.) Federal courts have generally upheld presidential executive orders. However, the Supreme Court overturned an order by President Harry Truman in 1951 during the Korean War seizing the nation's steel mills.[19] Research on the frequency of executive orders suggests that: Democratic presidents issue more orders than Republican presidents; presidents may issue executive orders to circumvent Congress but only when they believe that Congress will not overturn their orders; and presidents issue more executive orders when they are running for reelection.[20]

Appointments Presidential power over the executive branch derives in part from the president's authority to appoint and remove top officials. Presidents can shape policy by careful attention to top appointments—cabinet secretaries, assistant secretaries, agency heads, and White House staff. The key is to select people who share the president's policy views and who have the personal qualifications to do an effective job. However, in cabinet appointments political considerations weigh heavily: unifying various elements of the party; appealing for interest-group support; rewarding political loyalty; providing a temporary haven for unsuccessful party candidates; achieving a balance of racial, ethnic, and gender representation.[21] The appointment power gives the president only limited control over the executive branch of government. Of the executive branch's 2.8 million civilian employees, the president actually appoints only about 3,000. The vast majority of federal executive branch employees are civil servants—recruited, paid, and protected under civil service laws—and are not easily removed or punished by the president. Cabinet secretaries and heads of independent regulatory agencies require congressional confirmation, but presidents can choose their own White House staff without the approval of Congress.

Presidents have only limited power to remove the heads of independent regulatory agencies. By law, Congress sets the terms of these officials. Federal Communications Commission members are appointed for five years; Securities and Exchange Commission members for five years; and Federal Reserve Board members, responsible for the nation's money supply, enjoy the longest term of any executive officials—fourteen years. Congress's responsibility for term length for regulatory agencies is supposed to insulate those agencies, in particular their quasijudicial responsibilities, from "political" influence.

Even having a presidential appointee at the helm of a department does not always guarantee the president control over that department. Many political appointees are stymied by the career bureaucrats in departments and agencies who have the knowledge, skills, and experience to function with little or no supervision from their nominal political chiefs. Rather than carrying out the president's policies, some appointees "go native": they yield to the career bureaucrats, adopt the prevailing customs and values of their agencies, and seek the support of the bureaucrats, interest groups, and congressional committees that determine the agencies' future. Republican presidents have an especially difficult task controlling the bureaucracy because the majority of career bureaucrats are Democrats.[22]

Budget Presidential authority also derives from the president's role in the budgetary process. The Constitution makes no mention of the president with regard to expenditures; rather, it grants the power of the purse to Congress. Indeed, for nearly 150 years, executive departments submitted their budget requests directly to the Congress without first submitting them to the president. But with the passage of the Budget and Accounting Act in 1921, Congress established the Office of Management and Budget (originally named the Bureau of the Budget) to assist the president in preparing an annual Budget of the United States Government for presentation to the Congress. The president's budget is simply a set of recommendations to the Congress. Congress must pass appropriations acts before the president or any executive department or agency may spend money. Congress can and frequently does alter the president's budget recommendations (see "The Politics of Budgeting" in Chapter 10).

WWW **Cabinet**
The White House site provides the names of the current president's cabinet as well as those individuals with "cabinet-rank" status.
www.whitehouse.gov/government/cabinet.html

The Cabinet The **cabinet** is not mentioned in the U.S. Constitution; it has no formal powers. It consists of the secretaries of the executive departments and others the president may designate, including the vice president, the ambassador to the United Nations, the director of the Central Intelligence Agency, and the Special Trade Representative. According to custom, cabinet officials are ranked by the date their departments were created (see Table 9.2). Thus the secretary of state is the senior cabinet officer, followed by the secretary of the treasury. They sit next to the president at cabinet meetings; heads of the newest departments sit at the far ends of the table.

cabinet The heads (secretaries) of the executive departments together with other top officials accorded cabinet rank by the president; only occasionally does it meet as a body to advise and support the president.

The cabinet rarely functions as a decision-making body. Cabinet officers in the United States are powerful because they head giant administrative organizations. The secretary of state, the secretary of defense, the secretary of the treasury, the attorney general, and, to a lesser extent, the other departmental secretaries are all people of power and prestige. But seldom does a strong president hold a cabinet meeting to decide important policy questions. More frequently, presidents know what they want and hold cabinet meetings only to help promote their views.

The Constitution requires that "Officers of the United States" be confirmed by the Senate. In the past, the Senate rarely rejected a presidential cabinet nomina-

TABLE 9.2 The Cabinet Departments

Department	Created
State	1789
Treasury	1789
Defense*	1947
Justice	1789
Interior	1849
Agriculture†	1889
Commerce	1913
Labor	1913
Health and Human Services‡	1953
Housing and Urban Development	1965
Transportation	1966
Energy	1977
Education	1979
Veterans' Affairs	1989
Homeland Security	2002

* Formerly the War and Navy Departments, created in 1789 and 1798, respectively.

†Agriculture Department created in 1862, made part of cabinet in 1889.

‡Originally Health, Education, and Welfare; reorganized in 1979, with the creation of a separate Department of Education.

President George W. Bush meets with his cabinet and advisers at Camp David on September 15, 2001.

tion; the traditional view was that presidents were entitled to pick their own people and even make their own mistakes. In recent years, however, the confirmation process has become more partisan and divisive, with the Senate conducting lengthy investigations and holding public hearings on presidential cabinet nominees. In 1989 the Senate rejected President Bush's nomination of John Tower as secretary of defense in a partisan battle featuring charges that the former Texas senator was a heavy drinker. In 1993 President Clinton was obliged to withdraw the nomination of Zoe Baird as attorney general following Senate hearings featuring the charge that she had employed an illegal alien as a babysitter and had failed to pay the woman's Social Security taxes. The intense public scrutiny and potential for partisan attacks, together with financial disclosure and conflict-of-interest laws, may be discouraging some well-qualified people from accepting cabinet posts.

The National Security Council The **National Security Council** (NSC) is really an "inner cabinet" created by law in 1947 to advise the president and coordinate foreign, defense, and intelligence activities. The president is chair, and the vice president, secretary of state, and secretary of defense are participating members. The chair of the Joint Chiefs of Staff and the director of the Central Intelligence Agency serve as advisers to the NSC, which is headed by the special assistant to the president for national security affairs. The purposes of the council are to advise and coordinate policy; but in the Iran-Contra scandal in 1987, a staff member of the NSC, Lt. Col. Oliver North, undertook to *implement* security policy by directly channeling funds and arms to Nicaraguan "contras" fighting a communist-dominated government. Various investigative committees strongly recommended that the NSC staff confine itself to an advisory role.

National Security Council

Site provides brief history of NSC plus new releases dealing with national security

www.whitehouse.gov/nsc

White House Staff Today, presidents exercise their powers chiefly through the White House staff.[23] This staff includes the president's closest aides and advisers. Over the years, the White House staff has grown from Roosevelt's small "brain trust" of a dozen advisers to several hundred people, many with impressive titles, such as assistant to the president, deputy assistant to the president, special assistant to the president, and counsel to the president.

Senior White House staff members are trusted political advisers, often personal friends and long-time associates of the president. Some enjoy office space in the White House itself and daily contact with the president (see Figure 9.3). Appointed without Senate confirmation, they are loyal to the president alone, not to departments, agencies, or interest groups. Their many tasks include the following:

National Security Council (NSC) "Inner cabinet" that advises the president and coordinates foreign, defense, and intelligence activities.

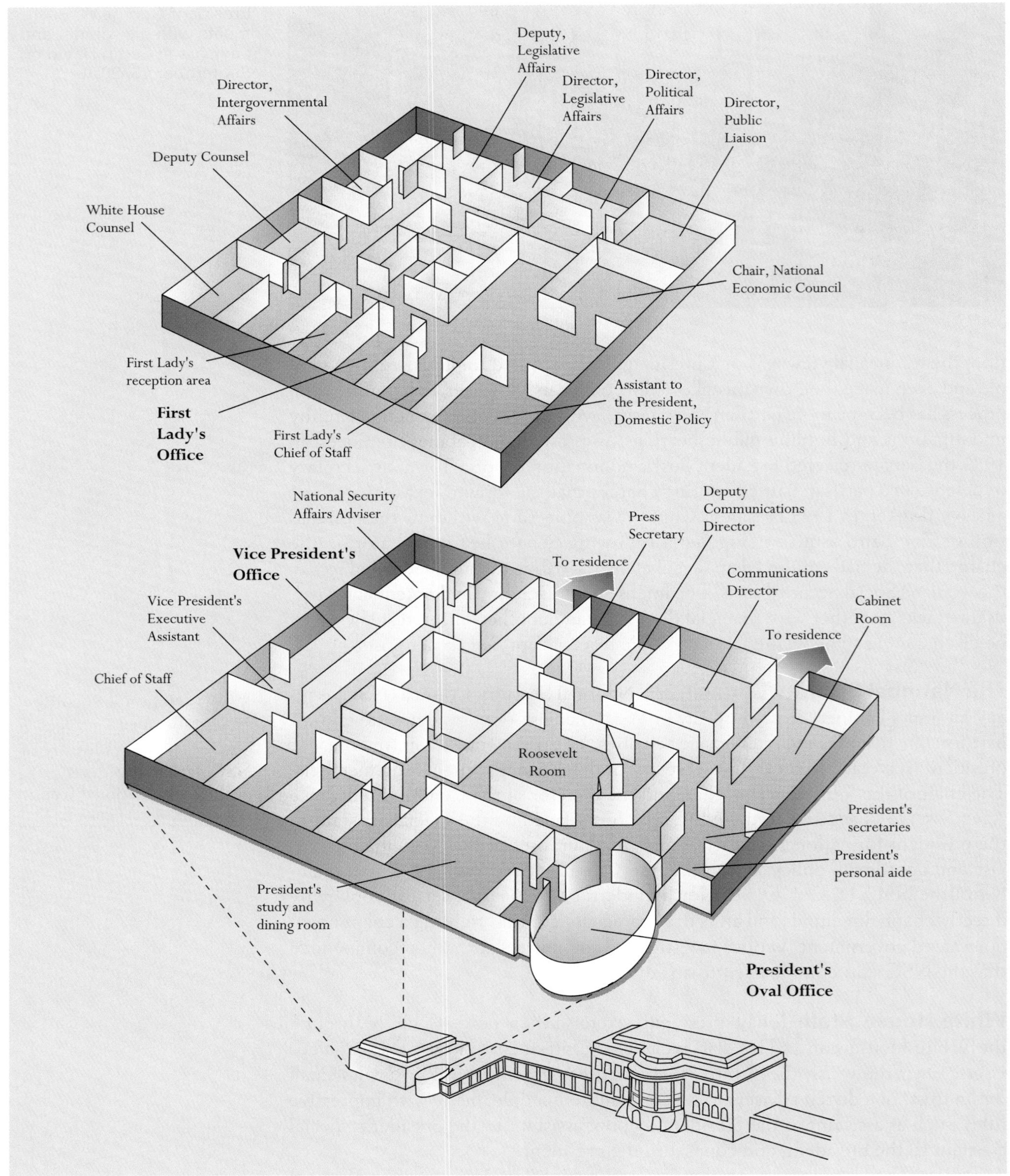

FIGURE 9.3 The White House Corridors of Power

Presidents allocate office space in the White House according to their own desires. An office located close to the president's is considered an indication of the power of the occupant. This diagram shows the office assignments during the Clinton Administration.

- Providing the president with sound advice on everything from national security to congressional affairs, policy development, and electoral politics.
- Monitoring the operations of executive departments and agencies and evaluating the performance of key executive officials.
- Setting the president's schedule, determining whom the president will see and call, where and when the president will travel, and where and to whom the president will make personal appearances and speeches.
- Above all, the staff must protect their boss, steering the president away from scandal, political blunders, and errors of judgment.

The senior White House staff normally includes a chief of staff, the national security adviser, a press secretary, the counsel to the president (an attorney), a director of personnel (patronage appointments), and assistants for political affairs, legislative liaison, management, and domestic policy. Staff organization depends on each president's personal taste. Some presidents have organized their staffs hierarchically, concentrating power in the chief of staff. Others have maintained direct contact with several staff members.

Chief Legislator and Lobbyist

The president has the principal responsibility for the initiation of national policy. Indeed, about 80 percent of the bills considered by Congress originate in the executive branch. Presidents have a strong incentive to fulfill this responsibility: the American people hold them responsible for anything that happens in the nation during their term of office, whether or not they have the authority or capacity to do anything about it.

Policy Initiation The Founders understood that the president would be involved in policy initiation. The Constitution requires the president to "give to the Congress Information of the State of the Union," to "recommend to their Consideration such Measures as he shall judge necessary and expedient" (Article II, Section 3). "On extraordinary Occasions" the president may call a recessed Congress into special session. Each year the principal policy statement of the president comes in the State of the Union message to Congress. It is followed by the president's Budget of the United States Government, which sets forth the president's programs with price tags attached. Many other policy proposals are developed by executive departments and agencies, transmitted to the White House for the president's approval or "clearance," and then sent to Congress.

Congress may not accept all or even most of the president's proposals. Indeed, from time to time it may even try to develop its own legislative agenda in competition with the president's. But the president's legislative initiatives usually set the agenda of congressional decision making. As one experienced Washington lobbyist put it, "Obviously when the president sends up a bill, it takes first place in the queue. All other bills take second place."[24]

White House Lobbying Presidents do not simply send their bills to Congress and then await the outcome. The president is also expected to be the chief lobbyist on behalf of the administration's bills as they make their way through the legislative labyrinth. The White House staff includes "legislative liaison" people—lobbyists for the president's programs. They organize the president's legislative proposals, track them through committee and floor proceedings, arrange committee appearances by executive department and agency representatives, count votes, and advise the president on when and how to "cut deals" and "twist arms."

Presidents are not without resources in lobbying Congress. They may exchange many favors, large and small, for the support of individual members. They can help direct "pork" to a member's district, promise White House support for a member's pet project, and assist in resolving a member's problems with the bureaucracy. Presidents also may issue or withhold invitations to the White House for prestigious ceremonies, dinners with visiting heads of state, and other glittering social occasions—an effective resource because most members of Congress value the prestige associated with close White House "connections."

The president may choose to "twist arms" individually—by telephoning and meeting with wavering members of Congress. Arm twisting is generally reserved for the president's most important legislative battles. There is seldom time for a president to contact individual members of Congress personally about many bills in various stages of the legislative process—in subcommittee, full committee, floor consideration, conference committee, and final passage—in both the House and the Senate. Instead, the president must rely on White House staff for most legislative contacts and use personal appeals sparingly.

The Honeymoon The **honeymoon period** at the very start of a president's term offers the best opportunity to get the new administration's legislative proposals enacted into law. Presidential influence in Congress is generally highest at this time both because the president's personal popularity is typically at its height and because the president can claim the recent election results as a popular mandate for key programs. Sophisticated members of Congress know that votes cast for a presidential candidate are not necessarily votes cast for that candidate's policy position (see "The Voter Decides" in Chapter 8). But election results signal members of Congress, in a language they understand well, that the president is politically popular and that they must give the administration's programs careful consideration. President Lyndon Johnson succeeded in getting the bulk of his Great Society program enacted in the year following his landslide victory in 1964. Ronald Reagan pushed through the largest tax cut in American history in the year following his convincing electoral victory over incumbent president Jimmy Carter in 1980. Bill Clinton was most successful with the Congress during his first year in office, in 1993, even winning approval for a major tax increase as part of a deficit-reduction package. And George W. Bush succeeded in getting a tax cut through Congress in his first six months in office. Both Democrat Clinton and Republican Bush benefited from having their party control the Congress during their first months in office.

Presidential "Box Scores" How successful are presidents in getting their legislation through Congress? *Congressional Quarterly* regularly compiles "box scores" of presidential success in Congress—percentages of presidential victories on congressional votes on which the president took a clear-cut position. The measure does not distinguish between bills that were important to the president and bills that may have been less significant. But viewed over time (see Figure 9.4), the presidential box scores provide interesting insights into the factors affecting the president's legislative success.

The most important determinant of presidential success in Congress is party control. Presidents are far more successful when they face a Congress controlled

honeymoon period Early months of a president's term in which his popularity with the public and influence with the Congress are generally high.

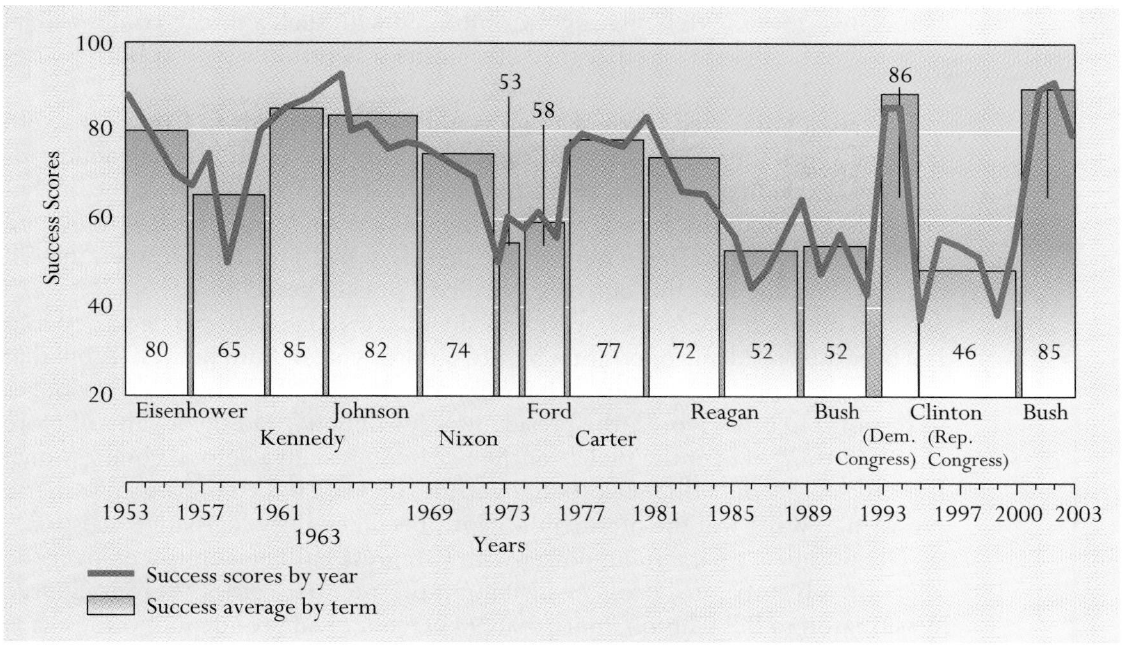

FIGURE 9.4 Presidential Success Scores in Congress

Presidential "box scores"—the percentage of times that a bill endorsed by the president is enacted by Congress—are closely linked to the strength of the president's party in Congress. For example, both Dwight D. Eisenhower and Ronald Reagan benefited from having a Republican majority in the Senate in their first terms and suffered when Democrats gained control of the Senate in their second terms. Democratic control of both houses of Congress resulted in significantly higher box scores for Democratic presidents John Kennedy, Lyndon Johnson, and Jimmy Carter than for Republicans Richard Nixon, Gerald Ford, and George Bush. Clinton was very successful in his first two years, when the Democrats controlled Congress, but when the Republicans won control following the 1994 midterm election, Clinton's box score plummeted.

by their own party. Democratic presidents John F. Kennedy and Lyndon Johnson enjoyed the support of Democratic-controlled Congresses and posted average success scores over 80 percent. Jimmy Carter was hardly a popular president, but he enjoyed the support of a Democratic Congress and an average of 76.8 percent presidential support. Republican presidents Richard Nixon and Gerald Ford fared poorly with Democratic-controlled Congresses. Republican president Ronald Reagan was very successful in his first term when he faced a Democratic House and a Republican Senate, but after Democrats took over both houses of Congress, Reagan's success rate plummeted. During the Reagan and Bush presidencies, divided party control of government (Republicans in the White House and Democrats controlling one or both houses of Congress) was said to produce **gridlock**, the political inability of the government to act decisively on the nation's problems. President Bill Clinton's achievements when Democrats controlled the Congress (1993–94), contrasted with his dismal record in dealing with Republican-controlled Congresses (1995–99), provide a vivid illustration of the importance of party in determining a president's legislative success.

gridlock Political stalemate between the executive and legislative branches arising when one branch is controlled by one major political party and the other branch by the other party.

veto Rejection of a legislative act by the executive branch; in the U.S. federal government, overriding of a veto requires a two-thirds majority in both houses of Congress.

The Veto Power The **veto** is the president's most powerful weapon in dealing with Congress. The veto is especially important to a president facing a Congress controlled by the opposition party. Even the *threat* of a veto enhances the president's bargaining power with Congress.[25] Confronted with such a threat, congressional leaders must calculate whether they can muster a two-thirds vote of both houses to override the veto.

To veto a bill passed by the Congress, the president sends to Congress a veto message specifying reasons for not signing it. If the president takes no action for ten days (excluding Sundays) after a bill has been passed by Congress, the bill becomes law without the president's signature. However, if Congress has adjourned within ten days of passing a bill and the president has not signed it, then the bill does not become law; this outcome is called a **pocket veto.**

A bill returned to Congress with a presidential veto message can be passed into law over the president's opposition by a two-thirds vote of both houses. (A bill that has received a pocket veto cannot be overridden because the Congress is no longer in session.) In other words, the president needs only to hold the loyalty of more than one-third of *either* the House or the Senate to sustain a veto. If congressional leaders cannot count on the votes to **override,** they are forced to bargain with the president. "What will the president accept?" becomes a key legislative question.

The president's bargaining power with Congress has been enhanced over the years by a history of success in sustaining presidential vetoes.[26] From George Washington to Bill Clinton, more than 96 percent of all presidential vetoes have been sustained (see Table 9.3). For example, although Bush was unable to achieve much success in getting his own legislative proposals enacted by a Democratic Congress, he was extraordinarily successful in saying no. Of Bush's many vetoes, only one (regulation of cable TV) was overridden by Congress. Clinton did not veto any bills when Democrats controlled Congress, but he began a series of vetoes in his struggle with the Republican Congress elected in 1994. He was able to sustain almost all of his vetoes because Republicans did not have two-thirds of the seats in both houses and most Democratic Congress members stuck with their president.

pocket veto Effective veto of a bill when Congress adjourns within ten days of passing it and the president fails to sign it.

override Voting in Congress to enact legislation vetoed by the president; requires a two-thirds vote in both the House and Senate.

TABLE 9.3 Presidential Vetoes

President	Total Vetoes*	Vetoes Overridden	Percentage of Vetoes Sustained
F. Roosevelt	633	9	99%
Truman	250	12	95
Eisenhower	181	2	99
Kennedy	21	0	100
L. Johnson	30	0	100
Nixon	43	5	90
Ford	66	12	85
Carter	31	2	94
Reagan	78	8	91
Bush	46	1	98
Clinton	37	2	95
Bush	0	0	—

*Regular vetoes plus pocket vetoes.

Source: Harold W. Stanley and Richard G. Niemi, *Vital Statistics on American Politics, 1999–2000* (Washington, D.C.: CQ Press, 2000), p. 256. Updated by author.

Line-Item Veto Power Denied For many years, presidents, both Democratic and Republican, petitioned Congress to give them the **line-item veto,** the ability to veto some provisions of a bill while accepting other provisions. The lack of presidential line-item veto power was especially frustrating when dealing with appropriations bills because the president could not veto specific pork-barrel provisions from major spending bills for defense, education, housing, welfare, and so on. Finally, in 1996 Congress granted the president authority to "cancel" spending items in any appropriation act and any limited tax benefit. Such cancellation would take effect immediately unless blocked by a special "disapproval bill" passed by Congress. The president could veto the disapproval bill, and a two-thirds vote of both houses would be required to override the veto.

However, opponents of the line-item veto successfully challenged its constitutionality, arguing that it transfers legislative power—granted by the Constitution only to Congress—to the president. The U.S. Supreme Court agreed: "There is no provision in the Constitution that authorizes the president to enact or amend or repeal statutes." The line-item veto, the Court said, "authorizes the president himself to elect to repeal laws, for his own policy reasons" and therefore violates the law-making procedures set forth in Article I of the Constitution.[27]

Global Leader

The president of the United States is the leader of the world's largest and most powerful democracy. During the Cold War, the president of the United States was seen as the leader of the "free world." The threat of Soviet expansionism, the huge military forces of the Warsaw Pact, and Soviet-backed guerrilla wars around the world all added to the global role of the American president as the defender of democratic values. In today's post—Cold War world, Western Europe and Japan are formidable economic competitors and no longer routinely defer to American political leadership. But if a new stable world order based on democracy and self-determination is to emerge, the president of the United States must provide the necessary leadership.

Global leadership is based on a president's powers of persuasion. Presidents are more persuasive when the American economy is strong, when American military forces are perceived as ready and capable, and when the president is seen as having the support of the American people and Congress. America's allies as well as its enemies perceive the president as the controlling force over U.S. foreign and military policy. Only occasionally do they seek to bypass the president and appeal to the Congress or to American public opinion.

Presidents sometimes prefer their global role to the much more contentious infighting of domestic politics. Abroad, presidents are treated with great dignity as head of the world's most powerful state. In contrast, at home presidents must confront hostile and insulting reporters, backbiting bureaucrats, demanding interest groups, and contentious members of Congress.

Foreign Policy As the nation's chief diplomat, the president has the principal responsibility for formulating U.S. foreign policy. The president's constitutional powers in foreign affairs are relatively modest. Presidents have the power to make treaties with foreign nations "with the Advice and Consent of the Senate." Presidents may negotiate with nations separately or through international organizations such as the North Atlantic Treaty Organization (NATO) or the United Nations, where the president determines the U.S. position in that body's

line-item veto Power of the chief executive to reject some portions of a bill without rejecting all of it.

State Department Official site includes news, travel warnings, international issues, and background notes on countries of the world. *www.state.gov*

deliberations. The Constitution also empowers the president to "appoint Ambassadors, other public Ministers, and Consuls" and to "receive Ambassadors." This power of **diplomatic recognition** permits a president to grant legitimacy to or withhold it from ruling groups around the world (to declare or refuse to declare them "rightful"). Despite controversy, President Franklin Roosevelt officially recognized the communist regime in Russia in 1933, Richard Nixon recognized the communist government of the People's Republic of China in 1972, and Carter recognized the communist Sandinistas' regime in Nicaragua in 1979. To date, all presidents have withheld diplomatic recognition of Fidel Castro's government in Cuba.

Presidents have expanded on these modest constitutional powers to dominate American foreign policy making. In part, they have done so as a product of their role as Commander-in-Chief. Military force is the ultimate diplomatic language. During wartime, or when war is threatened, military and foreign policy become inseparable. The president must decide on the use of force and, equally important, when and under what conditions to order a cease-fire or an end to hostilities.

Presidents have also come to dominate foreign policy as a product of the customary international recognition of the head of state as the legitimate voice of a government. Although nations may also watch the words and actions of the American Congress, the president's statements are generally taken to represent the official position of the U.S. government.

Treaties Treaties the president makes "by and with the Advice and Consent of the Senate" are legally binding upon the United States. The Constitution specifies that "all Treaties made . . . under the Authority of the United States, shall be the supreme Law of the Land, and the Judges in every State shall be bound thereby" (Article VI). Thus treaty provisions are directly enforceable in federal courts.

Although presidents may or may not listen to "advice" from the Senate on foreign policy, no formal treaty is valid unless "two-thirds of the Senators present concur" to its ratification. Although the Senate has ratified the vast majority of treaties, presidents must be sensitive to Senate concerns. The Senate defeat of the Versailles Treaty in 1920, which formally ended World War I and established the League of Nations, prompted Presidents Roosevelt and Truman to include prominent Democratic and Republican members of the Senate Foreign Relations Committee in the delegation that drafted the United Nations Charter in 1945 and the NATO Treaty in 1949.

diplomatic recognition Power of the president to grant "legitimacy" to or withhold it from a government of another nation (to declare or refuse to declare it "rightful").

President Clinton was sharply reminded of the need to develop bipartisan support for treaties in the Senate in 1999 when that body rejected the Comprehensive Test Ban Treaty. This treaty would have prohibited all signatory nations from conducting any tests of nuclear weapons. Most Western European nations had already signed and ratified the nuclear test ban, but North Korea, Iraq, Iran, India, and Pakistan, among other nations, had rejected it. China and Russia appeared to be waiting for the United States to act first. The president argued that the United States should take moral leadership in worldwide nonproliferation of nuclear weapons. His opponents in the Senate argued that too many rogue nations would ignore the treaty and continue their own nuclear testing. Despite the Senate's rejection of the treaty, Clinton continued by executive order his own moratorium on nuclear testing by the United States (see Chapter 14).

Treaties in Force Complete list of all treaties of the U.S. in force as of January 1, 2000. *www.state.gov/www/global/legalaffairs*

executive agreement Agreement with another nation signed by the president of the United States but less formal (and hence potentially less binding) than a treaty because it does not require Senate confirmation.

Executive Agreements Over the years, presidents have come to rely heavily on **executive agreements** with other governments rather than formal treaties. An executive agreement signed by the president of the United States has much the

President Bush, acting as the United States' "Chief Diplomat," with British Prime Minister Tony Blair as they begin two days of talks dominated by the rise of violence in the Middle East.

same effect in international relations as a treaty. However, an executive agreement does not require Senate ratification. Presidents have asserted that their constitutional power to execute the laws, command the armed services, and determine foreign policy gives them the authority to make agreements with other nations and heads of state without obtaining approval of the U.S. Senate. However, unlike treaties, executive agreements do not supersede laws of the United States or of the states with which they conflict, but they are otherwise binding on the United States.

The use of executive agreements in important foreign policy matters was developed by President Franklin Roosevelt. Prior to his administration, executive agreements had been limited to minor matters. But in 1940, Roosevelt agreed to trade fifty American destroyers to England in exchange for naval bases in Newfoundland and the Caribbean. Roosevelt was intent on helping the British in their struggle against Nazi Germany, but before the Japanese attack on Pearl Harbor in 1941, isolationist sentiment in the Senate was too strong to win a two-thirds ratifying vote for such an agreement. Toward the end of World War II, Roosevelt at the Yalta Conference and Truman at the Potsdam Conference negotiated secret executive agreements dividing the occupation of Germany between the Western Allies and the Soviet Union.

Congress has sometimes objected to executive agreements as usurping its own powers. In the Case Act of 1972, Congress required the president to inform Congress of all executive agreements within sixty days, but the act does not limit the president's power to make agreements. It is easier for Congress to renege on executive agreements than on treaties that the Senate has ratified. In 1973 President Nixon signed an executive agreement with South Vietnamese President Nguyen Van Thieu pledging that the United States would "respond with full force" if North Vietnam violated the Paris Peace Agreement that ended American participation in the Vietnam War. But when North Vietnam reinvaded the south in 1975, Congress rejected President Gerald Ford's pleas for renewed military aid to the South Vietnamese government, and Ford knew that it had become politically impossible for the United States to respond with force.

Intelligence The president is responsible for the intelligence activities of the United States. Presidents have undertaken intelligence activities since the founding of the nation. During the Revolutionary War, General George Washington nurtured small groups of patriots living behind British lines who supplied him with information on Redcoat troop movements.[28] Today, the director of central intelligence (DCI) is appointed by the president (subject to Senate confirmation) and reports directly to the president.

The DCI coordinates the activities of the "intelligence community" (see Figure 9.5). Some elements of the intelligence community—the Central Intelligence Agency, the Defense Intelligence Agency, the National Security Agency, the Na-

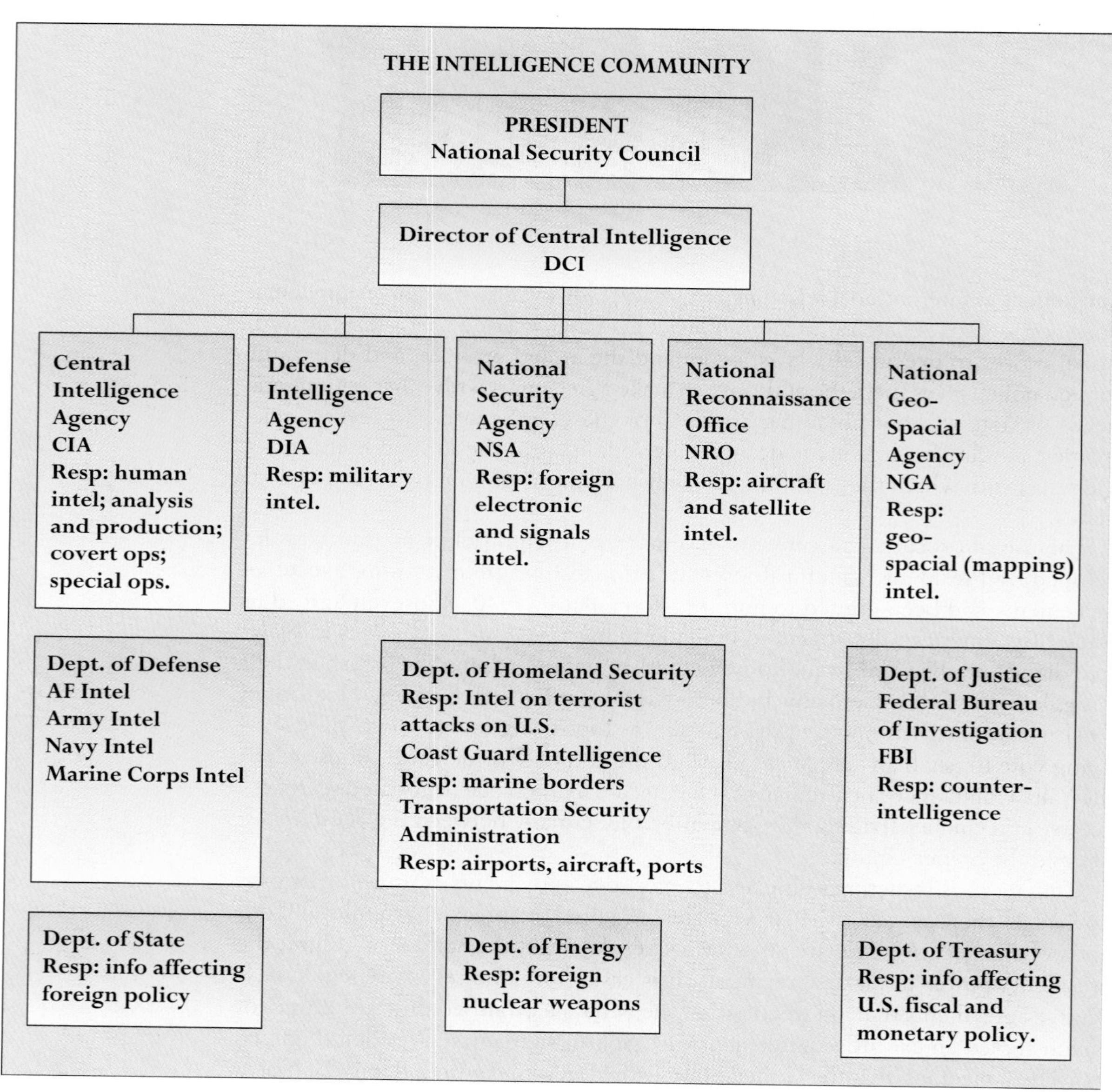

FIGURE 9.5 The Intelligence Community

Note: The CIA, DIA, NSA, NRO, and NGA are concerned exclusively with intelligence. The Departments of Defense, Homeland Security, Justice, State, Energy, and Treasury are concerned primarily with other missions, but do have intelligence responsibilities.

tional Reconnaissance Office, and the National Geo-Spacial Agency—deal exclusively with intelligence collection, analysis and distribution. Other elements of the intelligence community are located in the Department of Defense, Department of Homeland Security, Federal Bureau of Investigation, Department of State, Department of Energy, and the Department of Treasury. The DCI has no direct supervision over any of these agencies other than the Central Intelligence Agency. Indeed, the fragmentation of the intelligence community may be its principal weakness.[29]

Central Intelligence Agency

The CIA site provides information about the agency's mission, organization, values, press releases, and congressional testimony along with employment possibilities.
www.CIA.gov

The Central Intelligence Agency The CIA is directly supervised by the DCI. It provides intelligence on national security to the president, the National Security Council, and other top Washington decision makers. The CIA is responsible for (1) assembly, analysis, and dissemination of intelligence information from all agencies in the intelligence community; (2) collection of human intelligence from abroad; (3) with specific "presidential findings," the conduct of **covert actions,** including paramilitary special operations.

Covert actions refer to activities in support of the national interest of United States that would be ineffective if their sponsorship were made public. For example, one of the largest covert actions ever undertaken by the United States was the support, for nearly ten years, of the Afghan rebels fighting Soviet occupation of their country during the Afghanistan war (1978–88). Public acknowledgment of such aid would have assisted the Soviet-backed regime in Afghanistan to claim that the rebels were not true patriots but rather "puppets" of the United States. The rebels themselves did not wish to acknowledge U.S. aid publicly, even though they knew it was essential to the success of their cause. Hence Presidents Carter and Reagan aided the Afghan rebels through covert action.

covert action Secret intelligence activity outside U.S. borders undertaken with specific authorization by the president, acknowledgment of U.S. sponsorship would defeat or compromise its purpose.

Covert action is, by definition, secret. And secrecy spawns elaborate conspiracy theories and flamboyant tales of intrigue and deception. In fact, most covert actions consist of routine transfers of economic aid and military equipment to pro-U.S. forces that do not wish to acknowledge such aid publicly. Although most covert actions would have widespread support among the American public if they

Although still part of the "Big Three," along with Prime Minister Winston Churchill of Great Britain (right) and Marshal Josef Stalin of the Soviet Union (left), it was a gravely ill President Franklin Roosevelt (middle) who traveled to Yalta, a port on Russia's Crimean peninsula, and negotiated secret executive agreements dividing Germany among the Allies in 1945. Germany remained divided until 1989, when protesters tore down the Berlin Wall and the Soviet Union under Mikhail Gorbachev acquiesced in the unification of Germany under a democratic government.

were done openly, secrecy opens the possibility that a president will undertake to do by covert action what would be opposed by Congress and the American people if they knew about it.

In the atmosphere of suspicion and distrust engendered by the Watergate scandal, Congress passed intelligence oversight legislation in 1974 requiring a written "presidential finding" for any covert action and requiring that members of the House and Senate Intelligence Committees be informed of all covert actions. The president does not have to obtain congressional approval for covert actions; but Congress can halt such actions if it chooses to do so.

Commander-in-Chief

Global power derives primarily from the president's role as Commander-in-Chief of the armed forces of the United States. Presidential command over the armed forces is not merely symbolic; presidents may issue direct military orders to troops in the field. As president, Washington personally led troops to end the Whiskey Rebellion in 1794; Abraham Lincoln issued direct orders to his generals in the Civil War; Lyndon Johnson personally chose bombing targets in Vietnam; and George Bush personally ordered the Gulf War cease-fire after 100 hours of ground fighting. All presidents, whether they are experienced in world affairs or not, soon learn after taking office that their influence throughout the world is heavily dependent upon the command of capable military forces.

War-making Power Constitutionally, war-making power is divided between the Congress and the president. Article I, Section 8, says, "The Congress shall have Power . . . to . . . provide for the common Defence . . . to declare War . . . to raise and support Armies . . . to provide and maintain a Navy . . . to make Rules for the Government and Regulation of the land and naval forces." However, Article II, Section 2, says, "The President shall be Commander-in-Chief of the Army and Navy of the United States." In defending the newly written Constitution, the *Federalist Papers* construed the president's war powers narrowly, implying that the war-making power of the president was little more than the power to defend against imminent invasion when Congress was not in session.

DefenseLink Official site of U.S. Department of Defense, with news and links to Army, Navy, Air Force, and Marine Corps Web sites and other defense agencies and commands. *www.defenselink.gov*

In reality, however, presidents have exercised their powers as Commander-in-Chief to order U.S. forces into military action overseas on many occasions—from John Adams's ordering of U.S. naval forces to attack French ships (1789–99) to Harry Truman's decision to intervene in the Korean War (1951–53) to Lyndon Johnson's and Richard Nixon's conduct of the Vietnam War (1965–73), to George Bush's Operation Desert Storm (1991), to Bill Clinton's interventions in Bosnia and Kosovo (1998–99), to George W.'s military actions in Afghanistan (2001) and Iraq (2003). The Supreme Court has consistently refused to hear cases involving the war powers of the president and Congress.[30]

Thus, although Congress retains the formal power to "declare war," in modern times wars are seldom "declared." Instead, they begin with direct military actions, and the president, as Commander-in-Chief of the armed forces, determines what those actions will be. Historically, Congress accepted the fact that only the president has the information-gathering facilities and the ability to act with the speed and secrecy required for military decisions during the periods of crisis. Not until the Vietnam War was there serious congressional debate over whether the president has the power to commit the nation to war.

War Powers Act In the early days of the Vietnam War, the liberal leadership of the nation strongly supported Democratic President Lyndon Johnson's power to commit the nation to war. By 1969, however, many congressional leaders had withdrawn their support of the war. With a new Republican president, Richard Nixon, and a Democratic Congress, congressional attacks on presidential policy became much more partisan.

Antiwar members of Congress made several attempts to end the war by cutting off money for U.S. military activity in Southeast Asia. Such legislation only passed after President Nixon announced a peace agreement in 1973, however. It is important to note that Congress has *never* voted to cut off funds to support American armies while they were in the field.

Congress also passed the **War Powers Act,** designed to restrict presidential war-making powers, in 1973. (President Nixon vetoed the bill, but the Watergate affair undermined his support in Congress, which overrode his veto.) The act has four major provisions:

1. In the absence of a congressional declaration of war, the president can commit armed forces to hostilities or to "situations where imminent involvement in hostilities is clearly indicated by the circumstances" *only*:
   - To repel an armed attack on the United States or to forestall the "direct and imminent threat of such an attack."
   - To repel an armed attack against U.S. armed forces outside the United States or to forestall the threat of such attack.
   - To protect and evacuate U.S. citizens and nationals in another country if their lives are threatened.To
2. The president must report promptly to Congress the commitment of forces for such purposes.
3. Involvement of U.S. forces must be no longer than sixty days unless Congress authorizes their continued use by specific legislation.
4. Congress can end a presidential commitment by resolution, an action that does not require the president's signature.

THINK AGAIN

Should Congress have the authority to call home U.S. troops sent by the president to engage in military actions overseas?

Presidential Noncompliance The War Powers Act raises constitutional questions. A Commander-in-Chief clearly can order U.S. forces to go anywhere. Presumably, Congress cannot constitutionally command troops, yet that is what the act attempts to do by specifying that troops must come home if Congress orders them to do so or if Congress simply fails to endorse the president's decision to commit them. No president—Democrat or Republican—can allow Congress to usurp this presidential authority. Thus, since the passage of the War Powers Act, presidents have continued to undertake military actions on their own initiative (see Table 14.1 in Chapter 14).

The War Powers Act is not only constitutionally questionable but also politically weak. The president almost always enjoys great popular support in the initial stages of an international conflict. At this point, members of Congress are likely to be swept along and to endorse the president's action rather than invoking the War Powers Act and appearing unsupportive of U.S. troops. Only if the fighting goes badly, becomes protracted, or fails to produce decisive results is the War Powers Act likely to be invoked by Congress. Thus the War Powers Act

War Powers Act Bill passed in 1973 to limit presidential war-making powers; it restricts when, why, and for how long a president can commit U.S. forces and requires notification of and, in many cases, approval by Congress.

UP CLOSE

George Bush and "Operation Iraqi Freedom"

At the end of the Gulf War in 1991, the Iraqi regime of Saddam Hussein agreed to destroy all of its chemical and biological weapons and end his efforts to acquire nuclear weapons. United Nations inspectors were to verify Iraqi compliance with these conditions. But Saddam refused to cooperate. U.N. inspectors were hindered and harassed, and finally in 1998 they were ordered out of the country. Over a twelve-year period Iraq violated at least a dozen U.N. resolutions. Following a U.S. military buildup in the region in late 2002, Saddam allowed U.N. inspectors to return but continued to obstruct their work.

President Bush did not believe that the Constitution required him to obtain congressional authorization to use military force against Iraq. But he believed that a congressional resolution would put added political pressure on the United Nations Security Council to authorize military force, and that such a Security Council resolution would compel Saddam to allow open inspections for the presence of weapons of mass destruction. In October 2002 Congress passed a resolution authorizing the president "to use the Armed Forces of the United States as he determines to be necessary and appropriate in order to (1) defend the national security of the United States against the continuing threat posed by Iraq; and (2) enforce all relevant United Nations Security Council resolutions regarding Iraq." The resolution passed overwhelmingly in both the House and Senate.

At different times President Bush stated the purposes of "Operation Iraqi Freedom" as (1) the elimination of Iraq's weapons of mass destruction, (2) a "regime change" in Iraq to end the threat that Saddam posed for his neighbors and to free the Iraqi people from his oppressive rule, and (3) to ensure that Saddam would not harbor or assist terrorist organizations. But President Bush and Secretary of State Colin Powell failed to secure U.N. Security Council approval for military action. Among the permanent members of the Security Council, only the British, with the strong support of Prime Minister Tony Blair, were prepared to offer significant military support for the war against Saddam. Public opinion in America supported military action, but public opinion in Europe opposed it. France and Germany led the diplomatic opposition; Turkey refused to let U.S. troops use its territory to attack Iraq.

On March 19, 2003, after giving Saddam a forty-eight hour warning to leave Iraq, United States and Great Britain launched airstrikes designed to eliminate Saddam in his top command. Baghdad was captured in just 21 days, with precious few Allied casualties.

But Bush's critics at home and abroad complained of the president's "unilateralism"—his willingness to go it alone, without the support of United Nations. Bush's actions clearly alienated our traditional allies—France and Germany—and were strongly opposed by Russia and China and most of the Muslim world. Bush's critics also charged that he misled the Congress and the American people about the existence of weapons of mass destruction in Iraq and the immediacy of any threat to United States. While most Americans believed that Saddam was allied with Al Qaeda, no real evidence of such an alliance emerged.

remains largely a symbolic reminder to presidents that if things go badly, the Congress will desert them.

Politically, it is often important for the president to show the world, and especially enemies of the United States, that he has congressional support for going to war. For this reason, presidents have asked Congress for resolutions in support of using military means to achieve specific goals. President George H. W. Bush asked for and received (by a close vote) a resolution of support to use military force to oust Iraqi forces from Kuwait in 1991. President George W. Bush won strong support for a congressional resolution in 2002 to allow him to use military force to make Saddam Hussein comply with U.N. resolutions. Both presidents claimed that they had the constitutional authority as Commander-in-Chief to use military force even without such resolutions. But politically such resolutions strengthen the president when he chooses to use military force. (See *Up Close,* "George Bush and 'Operation Iraqi Freedom'.")

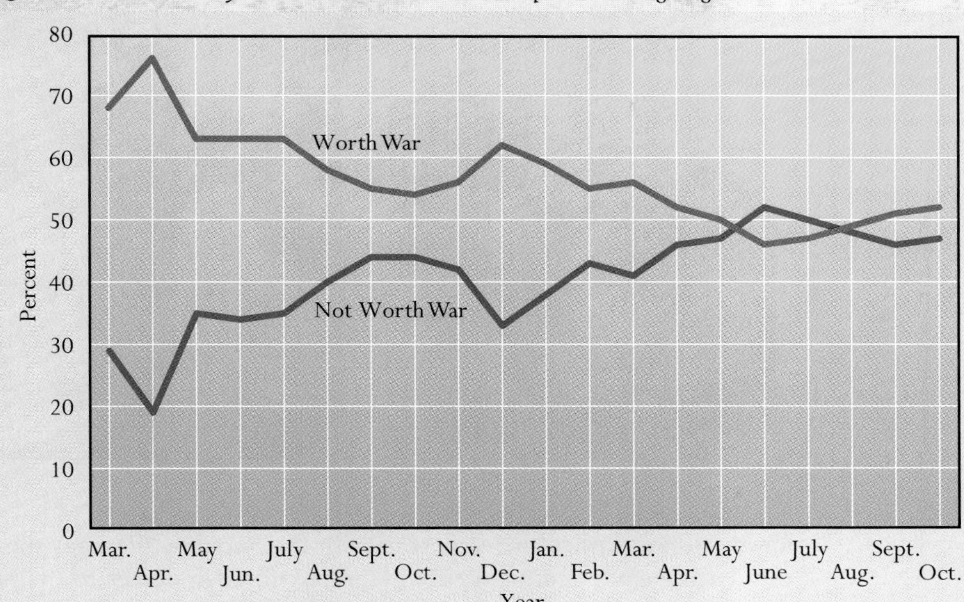

Support for the War in Iraq

Finally, critics charge that Bush had "no plan" for the reconstruction of Iraq after the fall of Saddam. Continuing attacks on American troops in Iraq resulted in a continuing stream of casualties. But the capture of Saddam Hussein in December 2003 was widely hailed throughout the world. Evidence of his oppressive rule was found in mass graves and torture chambers. Few people regretted the "regime change" in Baghdad. Overall, the American people initially supported going to war in Iraq (see figure above). But support fell with the prolonged guerilla war that followed U.S. occupation of that country. By the summer of 2004 a majority of Americans thought Iraq was not worth going to war over. The presidential campaign raised support for the war slightly, but Americans were fairly evenly divided.

Presidential Use of Military Force in Domestic Affairs Democracies are generally reluctant to use military force in domestic affairs. Yet the president has the constitutional authority to "take Care that the Laws be faithfully executed" and, as Commander-in-Chief of the armed forces, can send them across the nation as well as across the globe. The Constitution appears to limit presidential use of military forces in domestic affairs to protecting states "against domestic Violence" and only "on Application of the [state] Legislature or the [state] Executive (when the Legislature cannot be convened)" (Article IV, Section 4). Although this provision would seem to require states themselves to request federal troops before they can be sent to quell domestic violence, historically presidents have not waited for state requests to send troops when federal laws, federal court orders, or federal constitutional guarantees are being violated.

Relying on their constitutional duty to "faithfully execute" federal laws and their command over the nation's armed forces, presidents have used military force in do-

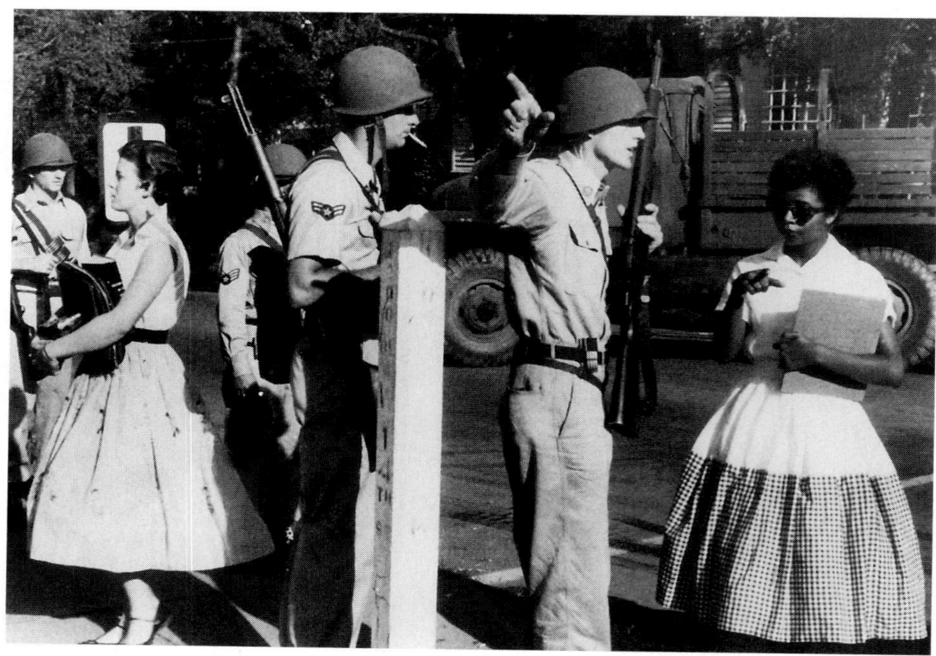

Despite a Supreme Court ruling that segregation in education was illegal, many southern states continued to try to keep their schoolhouse doors closed to black students. Here Elizabeth Eckford, a fifteen-year-old resident of Little Rock, Arkansas, is denied entry to Central High School by a member of the National Guard under the orders of Governor Orval Faubus. Not until President Dwight Eisenhower sent the 101st Airborne Division to Little Rock were the high court's desegregation orders enforced.

mestic disputes since the earliest days of the Republic. Perhaps the most significant example of a president's use of military force in domestic affairs was Dwight Eisenhower's 1957 dispatch of U.S. troops to Little Rock, Arkansas, to enforce a federal court's desegregation order. In this case, the president acted directly *against* the expressed wishes of the state's governor, Orval Faubus, who had posted state units of the National Guard at the entrance of Central High School to prevent the admission of black students who had been ordered by the federal court. Eisenhower officially called Arkansas's National Guard units into federal service, took personal command of them, and then ordered them to leave the high school. Ike then replaced the Guard units with U.S. federal troops under orders to enforce desegregation. Eisenhower's action marked a turning point in the struggle over school desegregation. The Supreme Court's historic desegregation decision in *Brown v. Board of Education of Topeka* might have been rendered meaningless had not the president chosen to use military force to secure compliance.

The Vice Presidential Waiting Game

Historically, the principal responsibility of the vice president is to be prepared to assume the responsibilities of the president. Eight vice presidents have become president following the death of their predecessor. But vice presidents have not always been well prepared: Harry Truman, who succeeded Franklin Roosevelt while World War II still raged, had never even been informed about the secret atomic bomb project.

Political Selection Process The political process surrounding the initial choice of vice presidential candidates does not necessarily produce the persons best qualified to occupy the White House. It is, indeed, a "crap shoot"[31]; if it produces a person well qualified to be president, it is only by luck. Candidates may *claim* that they select running mates who are highly qualified to take over as president, but this claim is seldom true.

Traditionally, vice presidential candidates have been chosen to give political "balance" to the ticket, to attract voters who might otherwise desert the party or stay home. Democratic presidential candidates sought to give ideological and geographical balance to the ticket. Northern liberal presidential candidates (Adlai Stevenson, John Kennedy) selected southern conservatives (John Sparkman, Estes Kefauver, Lyndon Johnson) as their running mates. Walter Mondale selected New York Congresswoman Geraldine Ferraro in a bold move to exploit the gender gap. Liberal Massachusetts Governor Michael Dukakis returned to the earlier Democratic tradition, choosing to run with conservative Texas Senator Lloyd Bentsen. Bill Clinton sought a different kind of balance: Al Gore's military service in Vietnam and his unimpeachable family life helped offset reservations about Clinton's avoidance of the draft and his past marital troubles. Massachusetts Senator John Kerry was viewed as serious, sober, and reserved; so the choice of the cheerful, enthusiastic, and outgoing North Carolinian John Edwards seemed to balance the ticket in both image and geography.

Republican presidential candidates sought to accommodate either the conservative or moderate wing of their party in their vice presidential selections. Moderate Eisenhower chose conservative Nixon. Conservative Barry Goldwater's selection of William Miller, an unknown conservative member of the House, ensured his loss of moderate support in 1964. In 1980 conservative Reagan first asked his moderate predecessor, Gerald Ford, to join him on the ticket before turning to his moderate primary opponent George Bush, who in 1988 tapped conservative Senator Dan Quayle. In 1996 Bob Dole gambled big in choosing the popular and charismatic— but opinionated and unpredictable—Jack Kemp as his running mate. Far behind in the polls, Dole could not afford a "safe" choice. He needed the former star quarterback of the Buffalo Bills to add excitement to the ticket, even at the risk of seeing Kemp call plays not approved by the coach.

Running behind in the polls prior to the 2000 Democratic convention, Al Gore believed he needed a dramatic choice of a running mate to stir interest in his campaign. Connecticut Senator Joe Lieberman would make history as the first Jew to run on a major party national ticket. Moreover, his moderate voting record balanced Gore's appeal to liberals.

Bush's dream running mate, General Colin Powell, turned down the offer. So Bush turned to Dick Cheney, secretary of defense in his father's administration during the Gulf War. It was hoped that Cheney would add *gravitas* (experience and wisdom) to the ticket. And Cheney's conservative voting record, as a former Congressman from Wyoming, helped reassure conservatives in the Republican Party that Bush was not overlooking them. Cheney's public approval ratings dropped as the Iraq war lengthened. Bush was urged to replace him with the popular former New York City Mayor Rudolph Giuliani. But Bush remained loyal to his family's old adviser.

Vice Presidential Roles Presidents determine what role their vice presidents will play in their administration. Constitutionally, the only role given the vice president is to preside over the Senate and to vote in case of a tie in that body. Presiding over the Senate is so tiresome that vice presidents perform it only on rare ceremonial occasions, but they have occasionally cast important tie-breaking votes. If the president chooses not to give the vice president much responsibility, the vice presidency becomes what its first occupant, John Adams, described as "the most insignificant office that ever the invention of man contrived or his imagination conceived." One of Franklin Roosevelt's three vice presidents, the salty Texan

PEOPLE IN POLITICS

Dick Cheney, Presidential Confidant

For many weeks after the "9/11" attack on America, Vice President Dick Cheney remained out of sight "in a secure undisclosed location." A direct attack on the White House was viewed as a distinct possibility, and Cheney's absence from Washington was designed to ensure "continuity of government."

Yet during the crisis—indeed, throughout George W. Bush's presidency—Dick Cheney has been his chief's closest adviser—a prime minister, a *consigliore,* pal, tutor, and big brother to the president. Reportedly, Cheney and Bush confer several times a day, and Cheney's recommendations are seldom ignored. Cheney exercises more influence in the White House than perhaps any previous vice president.

Why does Bush place so much trust in his vice president? Cheney served as secretary of defense for Bush's father, and also served in the Nixon and Ford administrations. He also served as a Republican Congress member from Wyoming and a leader of the conservatives in the House of Representatives. But perhaps his most valued characteristic as vice president is his absence of political ambition. Unlike any other recent vice president. Cheney has no plans to run for president, no personal agenda other than to give his best advice to his president. This elevates the level of trust between the two men.

Dick Cheney has experienced four heart attacks and quadruple bypass heart surgery, and wears a surgically implanted heart pacemaker. Yet he follows a very demanding schedule, including lengthy trips to the Middle East and elsewhere in the world.

Cheney was reported to be a strong supporter of the Iraq invasion, and his public approval ratings tumbled as the war lengthened. But he remained Bush's closest advisor.

John Nance Garner, put it more pithily, saying that the job "ain't worth a bucket of warm spit" (reporters of that era may have substituted "spit" for Garner's actual wording).

The political functions of vice presidents are more significant than their governmental functions. Vice presidents are obliged to support their president and the administration's policies. But sometimes a president will use the vice president to launch strongly partisan political attacks on opponents while the president remains "above" the political squabbles and hence more "presidential." Richard Nixon served as a partisan "attack dog" for Eisenhower, then gave Spiro Agnew this task in his own administration. George Bush was a much more reserved vice president, but Dan Quayle renewed the tradition of the vice president as political "hit man." The attack role allows the vice president also to help cement political support for the president among highly partisan ideologues. Vice presidents are also useful in campaign fund raising. Large contributors expect a personal touch; the president cannot be everywhere at once, so the vice president is frequently a guest at political fund-raising events. Presidents also have traditionally sent their vice presidents to attend funerals of world leaders and placed them at the head of governmental commissions.

Vice presidents themselves strive to play a more significant policy-making role, often as senior presidential adviser and confidant. Recent presidents have encouraged the development of the vice presidency along these lines. Walter Mondale, the first modern vice president to perform this function, had an office in the White House next to the president's, had access to all important meetings and policy decisions, and was invited to lunch privately each week with President Carter. Vice President Al Gore was routinely stationed behind President Clinton during major policy pronouncements. Clinton reportedly gave great weight to Gore's views on the environment, on cost savings in government, and on information technology. Gore also spoke out aggressively in defense of Clinton's policies. Thus the senior advisory role is becoming institutionalized over time (see *People in Politics*: "Dick Cheney, Presidential Confidant").

The Waiting Game Politically ambitious vice presidents are obliged to play a torturous waiting game. They can use their time in office to build a network of contacts that can later be tapped for campaign contributions, workers, and support in their own race for the presidency, should they decide to run. But winning the presidency following retirement of their former boss requires a delicate balance. They must show loyalty to the president in order to win the president's endorsement and also to help ensure that the administration in which they participated is judged a success by voters. At the same time, vice presidents must demonstrate that they have independent leadership qualities and a policy agenda of their own to offer voters. This dilemma becomes more acute as their boss's term nears its end.

Historically, only a few sitting vice presidents have won election to the White House: John Adams (1797), Thomas Jefferson (1801), Martin Van Buren (1837), and George Bush (1988). In addition, four vice presidents won election in their own right after entering the Oval Office as a result of their predecessors' death: Theodore Roosevelt (1901), Calvin Coolidge (1923), Harry Truman (1945), and Lyndon Johnson (1963). Only one nonsitting former vice president has been elected president: Richard Nixon (1968, after losing to Kennedy in 1960). Thus, out of the forty-seven men who served the nation as vice president through 2000, only nine were ever elected to higher office.

SUMMARY NOTES

- The American presidency is potentially the most powerful office in the world. As head of state, the president symbolizes national unity and speaks on behalf of the American people to the world. And as Commander-in-Chief of the armed forces, the president has a powerful voice in national and international affairs. The president also symbolizes government for the American people, reassuring them in times of hardship and crises.
- As head of the government, the president is expected to set forth policy priorities for the nation, to manage the economy, to mobilize political support for the administration's programs in Congress, to manage the giant federal bureaucracy, and to recruit people for policy-making positions in both the executive and judicial branches of government.
- Popular expectations of presidential leadership far exceed the formal constitutional powers of the president: chief administrator, chief legislator, chief diplomat, Commander-in-Chief, and chief of state. The vague reference in the Constitution to "executive Power" has been used by presidents to justify actions beyond those specified elsewhere in the Constitution or in laws of Congress.
- It is the president's vast political resources that provide the true power base of the presidency. These include the president's reputation for power, personal popularity with the public, access to the media, and party leadership position.
- Presidential popularity and power are usually highest at the beginning of the term of office. Presidents are more likely to be successful in Congress during this honeymoon period. Presidents' popularity also rises during crises, especially during international threats and military actions. But prolonged indecision and stalemate erode popular support, as do scandals and economic recessions.
- As chief executive, the president oversees the huge federal bureaucracy. Presidential control of the executive branch is exercised through executive orders, appointments and removals, and budgetary recommendations to Congress. But

the president's control of the executive branch is heavily circumscribed by Congress, which establishes executive departments and agencies, regulates their activities by law, and determines their budgets each year.

- Presidents are expected not only to initiate programs and policies but also to shepherd them through Congress. Presidential success scores in Congress indicate that presidents are more successful early in their term of office. Presidents who face a Congress controlled by the opposition party are far less successful in winning approval for their programs than presidents whose party holds a majority.
- The veto is the president's most powerful weapon in dealing with Congress. The president needs to hold the loyalty of only one more than one-third of either the House or the Senate to sustain a veto. Few vetoes are overridden. The threat of a veto enables the president to bargain in Congress for more acceptable legislation.
- During the long years of the Cold War, the president of the United States was the leader of the "free world." In the post—Cold War world, the president is still the leader of the world's most powerful democracy and is expected to exercise global leadership on behalf of a stable world order.
- Presidents have come to dominate foreign policy through treaty making, executive agreements, control of intelligence activities, and international recognition of their role as head of state. Above all, presidents have used their power as Commander-in-Chief of the armed forces to decide when to make war and when to seek peace.
- The global power of presidents derives primarily from this presidential role as Commander-in-Chief. Constitutionally, war-making power is divided between Congress and the president, but historically, it has been the president who has ordered U.S. military forces into action. In the War Powers Act, Congress tried to reassert its war-making power after the Vietnam War, but the act has failed to restrain presidents. Presidents have also used the armed forces in domestic affairs to "take Care that the Laws be faithfully executed."
- The principal responsibility of the vice president is to be prepared to assume the responsibilities of the president. However, the selection of the vice president is dominated more by political concerns than by consideration of presidential qualifications. Aside from officially presiding over the U.S. Senate, vice presidents perform whatever roles are assigned them by the president.

KEY TERMS

impeachment 302
Watergate 305
executive privilege 306
impoundment 307
deferrals 307
rescissions 307
White House press corps 310
executive order 315
cabinet 318
National Security Council (NSC) 319
honeymoon period 322
gridlock 323
veto 323
pocket veto 324
override 324
line-item veto 325
diplomatic recognition 326
executive agreement 326
covert action 329
War Powers Act 331

SUGGESTED READINGS

Barber, James David. *The Presidential Character; Predicting Performance in the White House.* 4th ed. Upper Saddle River, N.J.: Prentice Hall, 1992. Barber's original thesis that a president's performance in office is largely a function of active/passive and positive/negative character; includes classifications of twentieth-century presidents through Reagan.

Brace, Paul, and Barbara Hinckley. *Follow the Leader.* New York: Basic Books, 1992. The most marked increases in public approval of the president come on the heels of international crises, especially when the president responds with bold and decisive action.

Brody, Richard A. *Assessing Presidents: The Media, Elite Opinion, and Public Support.* Stanford, Calif.: Stanford University Press, 1991. Develops the thesis that media and elite interpretations of presidential actions shape public evaluations of the president; includes analysis of the president's "honeymoon," "rally round the president" events, and the rise and fall of public approval ratings.

DiClerico, Robert E. *The American President.* 5th ed. Upper Saddle River, N.J.: Prentice Hall, 2000. Comprehensive text on the presidency, focusing on selection, power, accountability, decision making, personality, and leadership.

Edwards, George C. and Stephen J. Wayne. *Presidential Leadership.* 6th ed. Belmont, Calif.: Wadsworth, 2003. Comprehensive text covering nomination and election of the president, relations with the public, the media, the bureaucracy, Congress and the courts.

Lowi, Theodore. *The Personal President.* Ithaca, N.Y.: Cornell University Press, 1987. An examination of the presidency from the perspective of the public and its reliance on the president for reassurance in crises.

Milkus, Stanley, and Michael Nelson. *The American Presidency: Origins and Development, 1776–2002* 4th ed. Washington, D.C.: CQ Press, 2003. A comprehensive history of the presidency which argues that the institution is best understood by examining its development over time, describes the significant presidential actions in the early days of the Republic that shaped the office, as well as the modern era in which the president has replaced Congress and the political parties as the leading instrument of popular rule.

Neustadt, Richard E. *Presidential Power.* New York: Wiley, 1960. The classic argument that the president's power is the power to persuade, that the formal constitutional powers of the presidency provide only a framework for the president's use of persuasion, public prestige, reputation for power, and other personal attributes to exercise real power.

Pika, Joseph A., John Maltese, and Norman C. Thomas. *The Politics of the Presidency.* 6th ed. Washington, D.C.: CQ Press, 2003. An overview of the institution of the presidency.

Schultz, Jeffrey D. *Presidential Scandals.* Washington, D.C.: CQ Press, 1999. An historical survey of scandals in presidential administrations, from George Washington to Bill Clinton.

Van Tassel, Emily Field, and Paul Finkelman. *Impeachable Offenses.* Washington, D.C.: CQ Press, 1999. A documentary history of impeachment from 1787 to the present.

MAKE IT REAL

WHO'S GOT THE POWER?

Although presidents share with Congress the responsibility for making foreign policy, in practice a president has the primary responsibility to shape foreign policy. Presidents can bargain, negotiate, persuade, apply economic pressures, threaten, or even use armed force. In addition, the agencies that carry out foreign policy report directly or indirectly to the president. However, Congress can block the president's foreign policy and undermine the chief executive's decisions. In this simulation, as the president of the United States, you are expected to provide strong leadership in foreign policy matters. This will entail choosing policies and responding to international events. You will make decisions regarding three policies and respond to one international crisis. Your success or failure depends on which issues you choose to address and how well you can gain the support of the U.S. Senate.

PRESIDENTIAL GREATNESS: HOW DO WE JUDGE THEM?

Most Americans judge contemporary presidents against the standard of the Mount Rushmore presidents. We want presidents who can summon us to live up to our shared ideals about liberty and freedom and who will pay close attention to our immediate needs. In sum, we use varying and sometimes unfair standards when we judge presidents. The opinions of historians differ from what the general public believes. They rate presidents as outstanding, great, or near great on the basis of whether they brought about desirable changes and acted wisely to guide the nation through turbulent times. But why should historians have all the fun? In this simulation, we ask you to rate the last nine presidents—from Dwight D. Eisenhower to William J. Clinton. Do some research first, to refresh your memory, then see how your opinions rate against some of the most respected presidential historians of our time.

CHAPTER 10

THE BUREAUCRACY: BUREAUCRATIC POLITICS

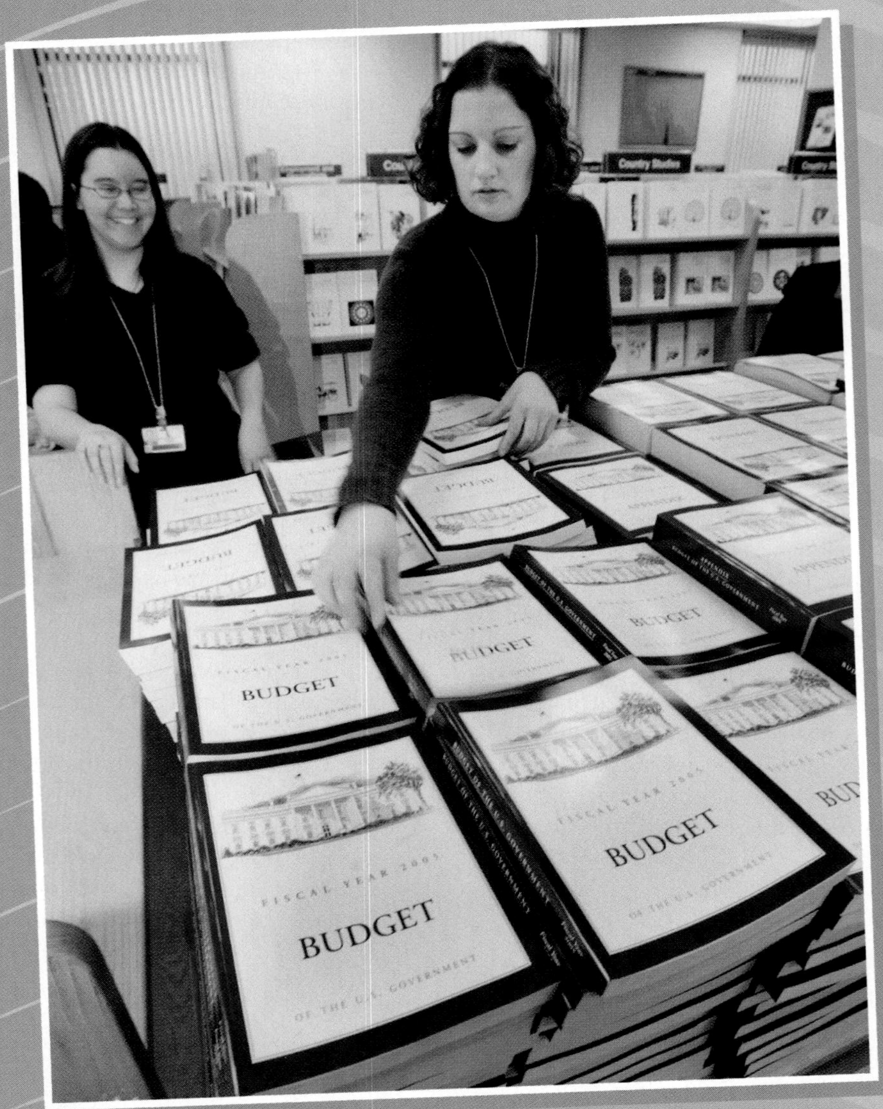

CHAPTER OUTLINE

Bureaucratic Power
The Federal Bureaucracy
Bureaucracy and Democracy
Bureaucratic Politics
The Budgetary Process
The Politics of Budgeting
Regulatory Battles
Regulating America
Congressional Constraints on the Bureaucracy
Interest Groups and Bureaucratic Decision Making
Judicial Constraints on the Bureaucracy

THINK ABOUT POLITICS

1 Do bureaucrats in Washington have too much power?
Yes ● No ●

2 Should the federal bureaucracy be managed by nonpartisan professionals rather than people politically loyal to the president?
Yes ● No ●

3 Should the federal bureaucracy at all levels reflect the gender and minority ratios of the total civilian work force?
Yes ● No ●

4 Do you believe the bureaucrats in Washington waste a lot of the money we pay in taxes?
Yes ● No ●

5 Do you believe the federal government is spending more money but delivering less service?
Yes ● No ●

6 Do you believe that the overall costs of federal regulatory activity are justified by the benefits?
Yes ● No ●

7 Do you believe bureaucratic regulations of all kinds are hurting America's competitiveness in the global economy?
Yes ● No ●

Power in Washington is not only exercised by the president, Congress, and courts, but also by 2.8 million federal bureaucrats—neither elected nor accountable to ordinary citizens—who determine in large measure who gets what in America.

Bureaucratic Power

Political conflict does not end after a law has been passed by Congress and signed by the president. The arena for conflict merely shifts from Capitol Hill and the White House to the **bureaucracy**—to the myriad departments, agencies, and bureaus of the federal executive branch that implement the law. Despite the popular impression that policy is decided by the president and Congress and merely implemented by the federal bureaucracy, in fact policy is also made by the bureaucracy. Indeed, it is often remarked that "implementation is the continuation of policy making by other means." The Washington bureaucracy is a major base of power in the American system of government—independent of Congress, the president, the courts, and the people. Indeed, controlling the bureaucracy has become a major challenge of democratic government.

The Nature of Bureaucracy "Bureaucracy" has become a negative term equated with red tape,[1] paper shuffling, duplication of effort, waste and inefficiency, impersonality, senseless regulations, and unresponsiveness to the needs of "real" people. But bureaucracy is really a form of social organization found not only in governments but also in corporations, armies, schools, and many other societal institutions. The German sociologist Max Weber described bureaucracy as a "rational" way for society to organize itself that has the following characteristics: a **chain of command** (hierarchical structure of authority in which command flows downward); a **division of labor** (work divided among many specialized workers in an effort to improve productivity); and **impersonality** (all persons within the bureaucracy treated on "merit" principles, and all "clients" served by the bureaucracy treated equally according to rules; all activities undertaken according to rules; records maintained to assure rules are followed).[2] Thus, according to Weber's definition, General Motors and IBM, the U.S. Marine Corps, the U.S. Department of Education, and all other institutions organized according to these principles are "bureaucracies."

The Growth of Bureaucratic Power Bureaucratic power has grown with advances in technology and increases in the size and complexity of society. There is a variety of explanation for this growth of power.

First Gov
Official Web portal to all federal departments and agencies, information on government benefits, agency links, etc. *www.firstgov.gov*

1. *Needed Expertise and Technological Advances* Congress and the president do not have the time, energy, or expertise to handle the details of policy making. A related explanation is that the increasing complexity and sophistication of technology require technical experts ("technocrats") to actually carry out the intent of Congress and the president. Neither the president nor the 535 members of Congress can look after the myriad details involved in environmental protection, occupational safety, air traffic control, or thousands of other responsibilities of government. So the president and Congress create bureaucracies, appropriate money for them, and authorize them to draw up detailed rules, regulations, and "guidelines" that actually govern the nation. Bureaucratic agencies receive only vague and general directions from the president and Congress. Actual governance is in the hands of the Environmental Protection Agency, the Occupational Safety and Health Administration, the Federal Aviation Administration, and hundreds of similar agencies (see Figure 10.1).
2. *Symbolic Politics* But there are also political explanations for the growth of bureaucratic power. Congress and the president often deliberately pass vague and ambiguous laws. These laws allow elected officials to show symbolically their concerns for environmental protection, occupational safety, and so on, yet avoid the controversies surrounding actual application of those lofty principles. Bureaucracies must then give practical meaning to these symbolic measures by developing specific rules and regulations. If the rules and regulations prove unpopular, Congress and the president can blame the bureaucrats and pretend that these unpopular decisions are a product of an "ungovernable" Washington bureaucracy (see *What Do You Think?* "How Would You Rate These Federal Agencies?")
3. *Bureaucratic Explanation* There is also a bureaucratic explanation of the growth in the size and influence of government agencies. Bureaucracy has become its own source of power. Bureaucrats have a personal stake in expanding the size of their own agencies and budgets and adding to their own regulatory authority. They can mobilize their "client" groups (interest groups that directly benefit from the agency's programs, such as environmental groups on behalf of the Environmental Protection Agency, farm groups for the Department of Agriculture, the National Education Association for the Department of Education) in support of larger budgets and expanded authority.
4. *Popular Demands* Finally, it has been argued that "big government" is really an expression of democratic sentiments. People want to use the power of government to improve their lives—to regulate and develop the economy, to guarantee civil rights, to develop their communities, and so on. Conservative opponents of the government are really expressing their disdain for popular demands.[3]

THINK AGAIN

Do bureaucrats in Washington have too much power?

bureaucracy Departments, agencies, bureaus, and offices that perform the functions of government.

chain of command Hierarchical structure of authority in which command flows downward; typical of a bureaucracy.

division of labor Division of work among many specialized workers in a bureaucracy.

impersonality Treatment of all persons within a bureaucracy on the basis of "merit" and of all "clients" served by the bureaucracy equally according to rules.

implementation Development by the federal bureaucracy of procedures and activities to carry out policies legislated by Congress; it includes regulation as well as adjudication.

Bureaucratic Power: Implementation Bureaucracies are not *constitutionally* empowered to decide policy questions. But they do so, nevertheless, as they perform their tasks of implementation, regulation, and adjudication.

Implementation is the development of procedures and activities to carry out policies legislated by Congress. It may involve creating new agencies or bureaus or assigning new responsibilities to old agencies. It often requires bureaucracies to translate laws into operational rules and regulations and usually to allocate resources—money, personnel, offices, supplies—to the new function. All of these

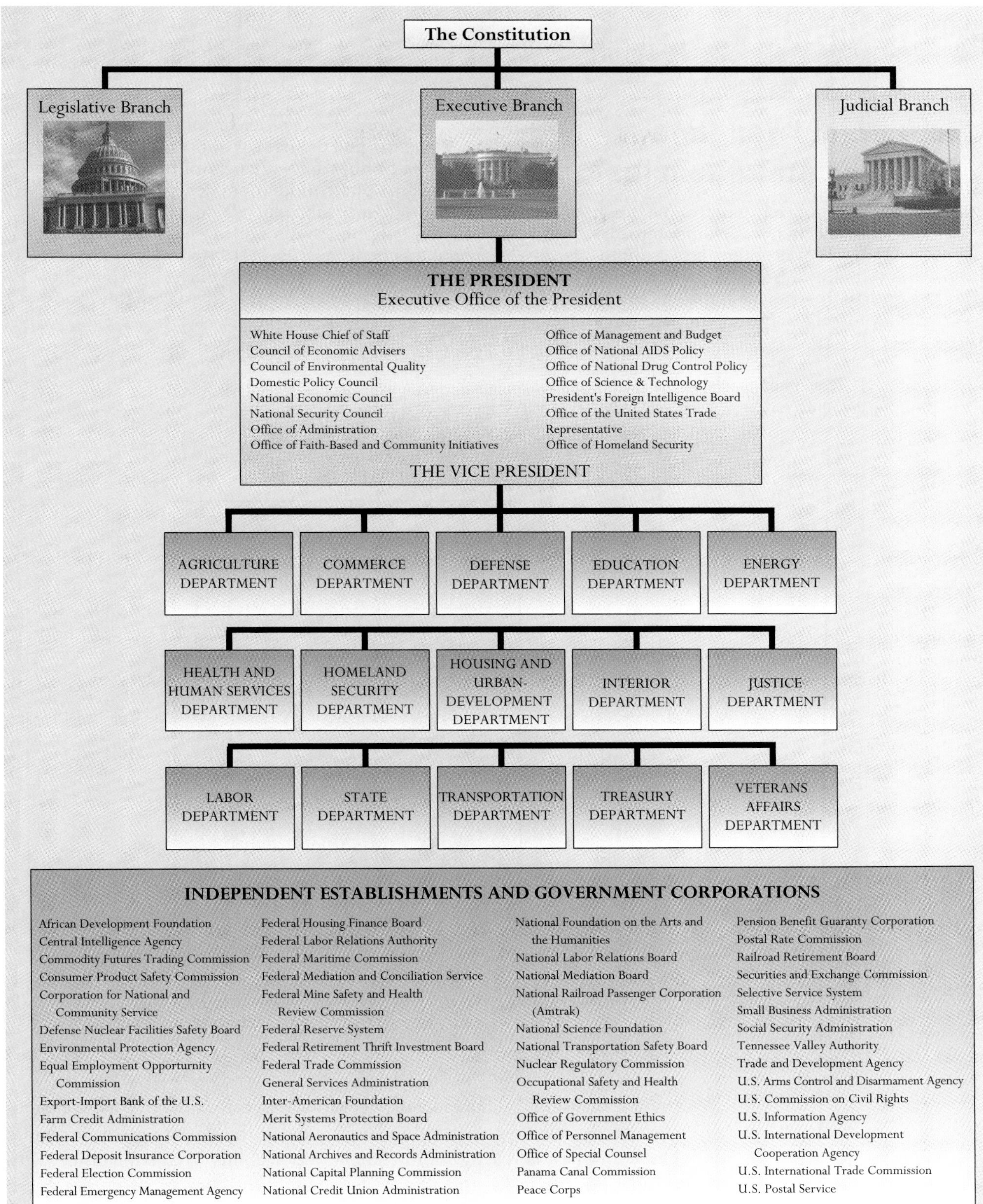

FIGURE 10.1 The Federal Bureaucracy

Although the president has constitutional authority over the operation of the executive branch, Congress creates departments and agencies and appropriates their funds, and Senate approval is needed for presidential appointees to head departments. The new Department of Homeland Security will be the 15th department in the executive branch.

WHAT DO YOU THINK?

How Would You Rate These Federal Agencies?

Many federal agencies have come under close scrutiny following the devastating terrorist attacks of 9/11, deadly anthrax letters, and economic recession, the threat of a SARS epidemic, and a space shuttle explosion. A poll near the end of 2003 asked Americans to rate some of the key government agencies charged with protecting the American public. While the poll did not ask about all government agencies, it does give a sense of how the public views some of the more prominent of them.

Overall, Americans rate individual agencies fairly highly. Even though the opinion polls regularly report that Americans believe "the federal government in Washington" has "too much power" (60 percent), individual agencies are given reasonably good marks.

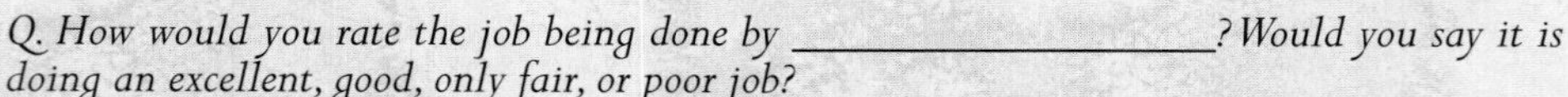

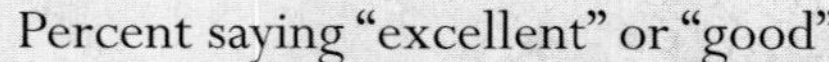

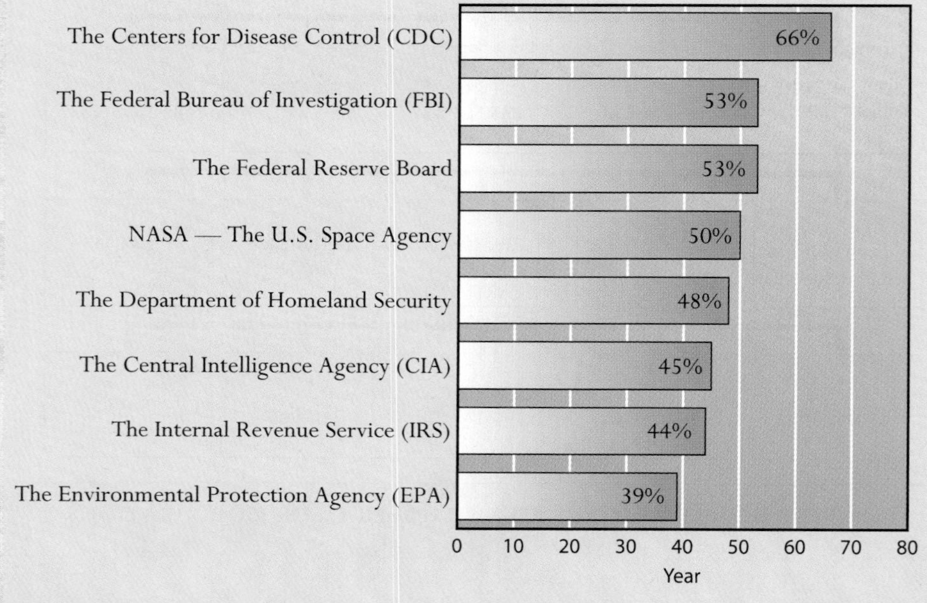

Source: Gallup poll, September 30, 2003. Copyright © 1996–2004 by The Gallup Organization.

tasks involve decisions by bureaucrats, decisions that drive how the law will actually affect society. In some cases, bureaucrats delay the development of regulations based on a new law, assign enforcement responsibility to existing offices with other higher priority tasks, and allocate few people with limited resources to the task. In other cases, bureaucrats act forcefully in making new regulations, insist on strict enforcement, assign responsibilities to newly created aggressive offices with no other assignments, and allocate a great deal of staff time and agency resources to the task. Interested groups have a strong stake in these decisions, and they actively seek to influence the bureaucracy.

Bureaucratic Power: Regulation **Regulation** involves the development of formal rules for implementing legislation. The federal bureaucracy publishes about 60,000 pages of rules in the *Federal Register* each year. The Environmental Protection Agency (EPA) is especially active in developing regulations governing the handling of virtually every substance in the air, water, or ground. The rule-making process for federal agencies is prescribed by an Administrative Procedures Act, first passed in 1946 and amended many times. Generally, agencies must:

1. Announce in the *Federal Register* that a new regulation is being considered.
2. Hold hearings to allow interested groups to present evidence and arguments regarding the proposed regulation.
3. Conduct research on the proposed regulation's economic and environmental impacts.
4. Solicit "public comments" (usually the arguments of interest groups).
5. Consult with higher officials, including the Office of Management and Budget.
6. Publish the new regulation in the *Federal Register.*

American Society for Public Administration
Organization of scholars and practitioners in public administration. Site includes information on careers, job listings, etc. *www.apsanet.org*

Regulatory battles are important because formal regulations that appear in the *Federal Register* have the effect of law. Congress can amend or repeal a regulation only by passing new legislation and obtaining the president's signature. Controversial bureaucratic regulations often remain in place because Congress is slow to act, because key committee members block corrective legislation, or because the president refuses to sign bills overturning the regulation.

Bureaucratic Power: Adjudication **Adjudication** involves bureaucratic decisions about individual cases. Rule making resembles the legislative process, and adjudication resembles the judicial process. In adjudication, bureaucrats decide whether a person or firm is failing to comply with laws or regulations and, if so, what penalties or corrective actions are to be applied. Regulatory agencies and commissions—for example, the National Labor Relations Board, the Federal Communications Commission, the Equal Employment Opportunity Commission, the Federal Trade Commission, the Securities and Exchange Commission—are heavily engaged in adjudication. Their elaborate procedures and body of previous decisions closely resemble the court system. Losers may appeal to the federal courts, but the record of agency success in the federal courts discourages many appeals.

Bureaucratic Power: Administrative Discretion Much of the work of bureaucrats is administrative routine—issuing Social Security checks, printing forms, delivering the mail. Routines are repetitive tasks performed according to established rules and procedures. Yet bureaucrats almost always have some discretion in performing even the most routine tasks. Discretion is greatest when cases do not exactly fit established rules, or when more than one rule might be applied to the same case, resulting in different outcomes. The Internal Revenue Service administers the hundreds of thousands of rules developed to implement the U.S. Tax Code, but each IRS auditing agent has wide discretion in deciding which rules to apply to a taxpayer's income, deductions, business expenses, and so on. Indeed, identical tax information submitted to different IRS offices almost always results in different estimates of tax liability. But even in more routine tasks, from processing Medicare applications to forwarding mail, individual bureaucrats can be friendly and helpful or hostile and obstructive.[4]

regulation Development by the federal bureaucracy of formal rules for implementing legislation.

adjudication Decision making by the federal bureaucracy as to whether or not an individual or organization has complied with or violated government laws and/or regulation.

An Internal Revenue Service processing center. The IRS administers the nation's complex tax code, leaving wide discretion to its agents to determine how to apply the rules to individual taxpayers.

Bureaucratic Power and Budget Maximization Bureaucrats generally believe strongly in the value of their programs and the importance of their tasks. Senior military officers and civilian officials of the Department of Defense believe in the importance of a strong national defense, and top officials in the Social Security Administration are committed to maintaining the integrity of the retirement system and serving the nation's senior citizens. Beyond these public-spirited motives, bureaucrats, like everyone else, seek higher pay, greater job security, and added power and prestige for themselves.

These public and private motives converge to inspire bureaucrats to seek to expand the powers, functions, and budgets of their departments and agencies. Rarely do bureaucrats request a reduction in authority, the elimination of a program, or a decrease in their agency's budget. Rather, over time, **budget maximization**—expanding the agency's budget, staff, and authority as much as possible—becomes a driving force in government bureaucracies. This is especially true of discretionary funds. **Discretionary funds** are those that bureaucrats have flexibility in deciding how to spend, rather than money committed by law to specific purposes.[5] Thus, bureaucracies continually strive to add new functions, acquire more authority and responsibility, and increase their budgets and personnel. Bureaucratic expansion is just one of the reasons that government grows over time (see *Up Close:* "Why Government Grows, and Grows, and Grows").

budget maximization Bureaucrats' tendencies to expand their agencies' budgets, staff, and authority.

discretionary funds Budgeted funds not earmarked for specific purposes but available to be spent in accordance with the best judgment of a bureaucrat.

The Federal Bureaucracy

The federal bureaucracy—officially the executive branch of the U.S. government—consists of about 2.7 million civilian employees (plus 1.4 million persons in the armed forces) organized into 15 cabinet departments, more than 60 independent agencies, and a large Executive Office of the President (see Figure 10.2). The expenditures of *all* governments in the United States—the federal government, the 50 state governments, and some 86,000 local governments—now amount

UP CLOSE

Why Government Grows, and Grows, and Grows

What accounts for the growth of government activity? Many theories offer explanations. The theories listed below are not mutually exclusive; indeed, probably all of the forces they identify contribute to government growth.

Societal Demands: Wagner's Law

In the nineteenth century, economist Adolf Wagner proposed a "law of increasing state activity"—the notion that government activity increased faster than economic output in all developing societies.* He attributed this growth to a variety of factors, including increasing demands in a developed society for social services such as education, welfare, and public health.

Wars and Crises

Another theory is based on the fact that during periods of social upheaval, especially war or economic turnoil, people willingly accept higher-than-normal levels of taxation. During these periods, then, government grows. But after the stressful period is over, government size does not return to its previous levels. Instead, governments substitute new expenditures for those accepted during the crisis. Thus expenditures increase during crisis periods but never return to the precrisis levels after the crisis passes.

Fiscal "Illusion"

This explanation assumes that government officials can increase revenues, and then expenditures, by altering tax-collecting devices so that voters do not realize how much money government is actually taking from them. The federal income tax grew very rapidly *after* the introduction of federal tax "withholding" in 1943. Since that time, wage earners have not received all of the money they earn and have come to perceive the missing portion as "belonging" to the federal government. This illusion is also aided by government-mandated withholding of Social Security taxes.

Bureaucratic Expansionism

Bureaucrats and legislators have a personal interest in expanding government budgets. Bureaucrats want to increase the amount of money they can spend and the number of employees under their supervision. Legislators want to increase the resources over which they have jurisdiction and to enhance the government benefits bestowed on their constituents.

Interest-Group Pressures

This explanation assumes that interest groups want to increase the size of government programs that benefit their own members. Benefits are visible and concentrated. Costs are invisible in many cases or are of less significance to those who will clearly benefit. As each interest group is motivated to act on behalf of its own members, largely ignoring the associated costs, government grows.

Politicians Seeking Votes

Politicians in competitive elections frequently promise their constituents visible and exaggerated benefits while hiding or minimizing the costs to other voters. When these promises become policies, government grows.

Cumulative Unintended Consequences

The current size of the government is the result of previous efforts to solve earlier problems. Once established, bureaucracies and programs live on, even when their original tasks no longer need doing. Over the years, the effects of all these decisions accumulate beyond what anyone originally intended.

Incrementalism

Governments expand because decision making is incremental. Presidents and members of Congress focus on a narrow range of new policy proposals and *increases* or *decreases* in the budget. Old programs are never reviewed as a whole every year. The value of existing programs is seldom reconsidered.

*Adolf Wagner's major work is *Grundlegung der Politischen Okonomie* (Leipzig, 1883). This work is discussed at length in Alan T. Peacock and Jack Wiseman, *The Growth of Public Expenditures in the United Kingdom* (Princeton, N.J.: Princeton University Press, 1961).

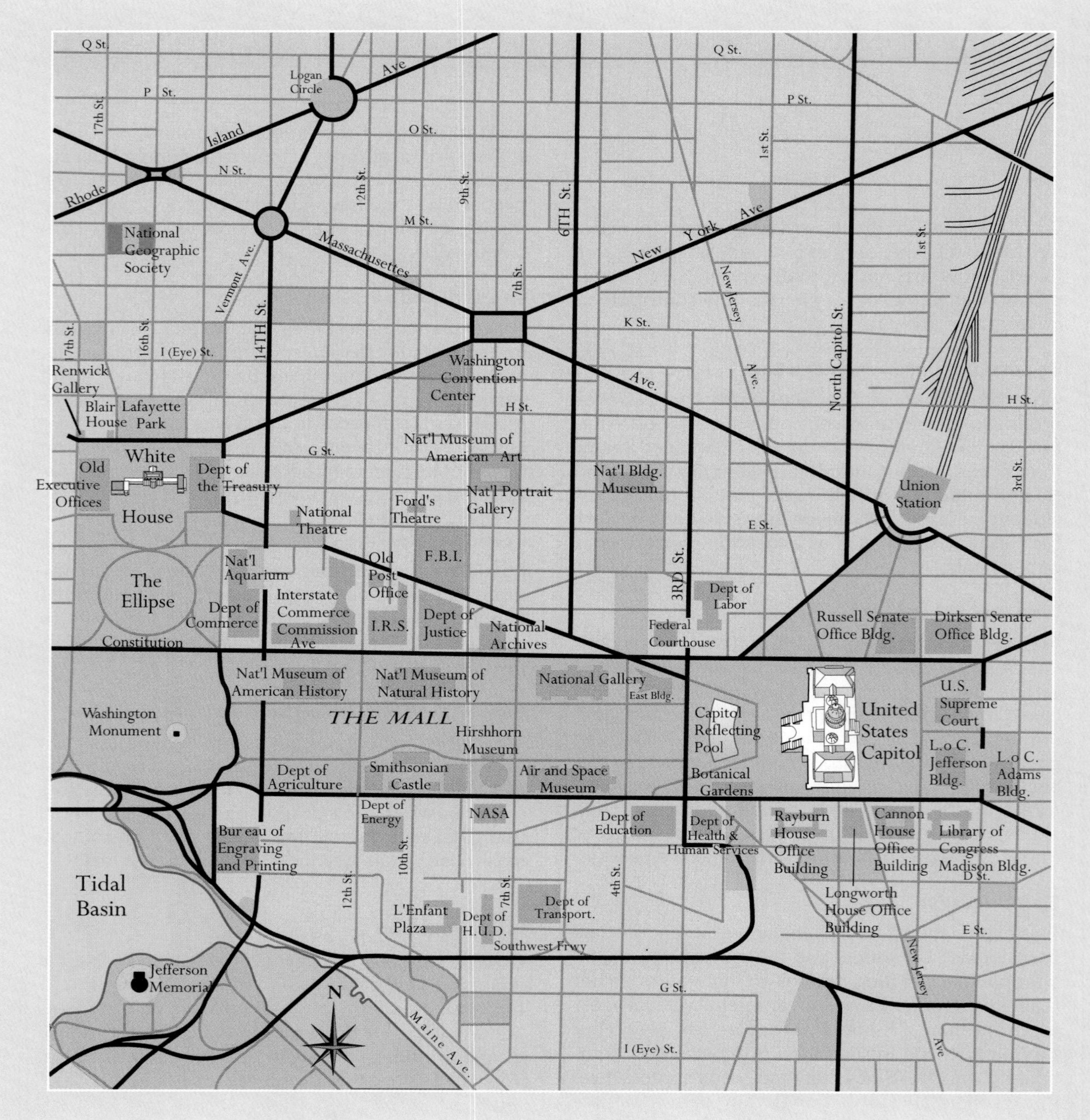

FIGURE 10.2 Corridors of Power in the Bureaucracy

This map shows the Capitol, the White House, and the major departments of the federal bureaucracy in Washington, D.C.

to more than $3.0 *trillion* (roughly 30 percent of the U.S. gross domestic product, or GDP of $10.4 *trillion*). About two-thirds of this—about $2.2 *trillion* a year (about 20 percent of GDP)—is spent by the *federal* government. Government spending in the United States remains relatively modest compared to that of many nations (see *Compared to What?* "The Size of Government in Other Nations" on the facing page).

COMPARED TO WHAT?

The Size of Government in Other Nations

How does the size of the public sector in the United States compare with the size of the public sector in other economically advanced, democratic countries? There is a great deal of variation in the size of government across countries. Government spending accounts for nearly two-thirds of the total output in Sweden. Government spending exceeds one-half of the total output of Denmark, Netherlands, Finland, Germany, Italy, Austria, Belgium, and France. The high level of government spending in these countries primarily reflects greater public-sector involvement in the provision of housing, health care, retirement insurance, and aid to the unemployed. The sizes of the public sectors in Australia, Japan, and Switzerland are only slightly higher than that of United States.

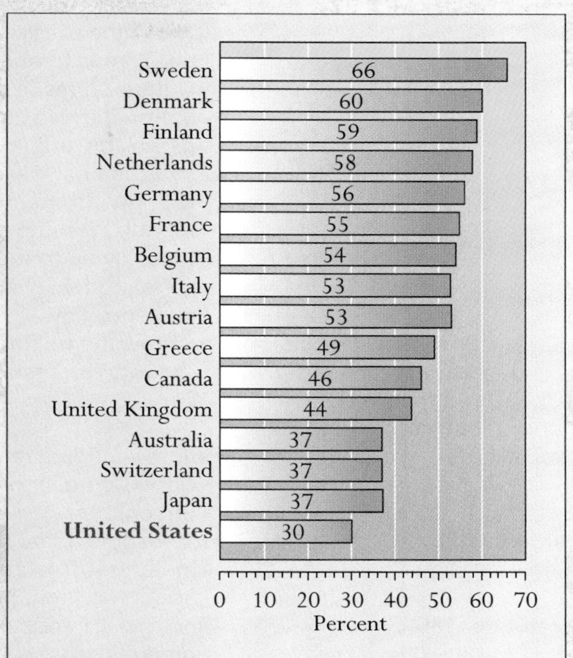

Governmental Percentage of Gross Domestic Product

Source: Joint Economic Committee of Congress, "The Size and Function of Government" (Washington, D.C.: 1998). United States updated to 2002.

Cabinet Departments Cabinet departments employ about 60 percent of all federal workers (see Table 10.1). Each department is headed by a secretary (with the exception of the Justice Department, which is headed by the attorney general) who is appointed by the president and must be confirmed by the Senate. Each department is hierarchically organized; each has its own organization chart. Although organizational patterns differ among departments, the chart for the Department of Health and Human Services shown in Figure 10.3 is typical.

Cabinet status confers great legitimacy on a governmental function and prestige on the secretary, thus strengthening that individual's voice in the government. Therefore the elevation of an executive department to cabinet level often reflects political considerations as much as or more than national needs. Strong pressures from "client" interest groups (groups principally served by the department), as well as presidential and congressional desires to pose as defenders and promoters of particular interests, account for the establishment of all of the newer departments. President Woodrow Wilson appealed to the labor movement in 1913 when he separated out a Department of Labor from the earlier business-dominated Department of Commerce and Labor. In 1965 President Lyndon Johnson created the Department of Housing and Urban Development to demonstrate his concern for urban problems. Seeking support from teachers and educational administrators,

WWW Fed World Run by the U.S. Commerce Department, this site contains information about federal/state–local agency links, government jobs, IRS forms, Supreme Court decisions, and the vast array of governmental services. *www.fedworld.gov*

TABLE 10.1 Cabinet Departments and Functions

Department and Date Created	Function
State (1789)	Advises the president on the formation and execution of foreign policy; negotiates treaties and agreements with foreign nations; represents the United States in the United Nations and in the more than fifty major international organizations and maintains U.S. embassies abroad; issues U.S. passports and, in foreign countries, visas to the United States.
Treasury (1789)	Serves as financial agent for the U.S. government; issues all payments of the U.S. government according to law; manages the debt of the U.S. government by issuing and recovering bonds and paying their interest; collects taxes owed to the U.S. government; collects taxes and enforces laws on alcohol, tobacco, and firearms and on customs duties; manufactures coins and currency.
Defense (1947: formerly the War Department, created in 1789, and the Navy Department, created in 1798)	Provides the military forces needed to deter war and protect the national security interest; includes the Departments of the Army, Navy, and Air Force.
Justice (1789)	Enforces all federal laws, including consumer protection, antitrust, civil rights, drug, and immigration and naturalization; maintains federal prisons.
Interior (1849)	Has responsibility for public lands and natural resources, for American Indian reservations, and for people who live in island territories under U.S. administration; preserves national parks and historical sites.
Agriculture (1889)	Works to improve and maintain farm income and to develop and expand markets abroad for agricultural products; safeguards standards of quality in the food supply through inspection and grading services; administers rural development, credit, and conservation programs; administers food stamp program.
Commerce (1913)	Encourages the nation's international trade, economic growth, and technological advancement; conducts the census; provides social and economic statistics and analyses for business and government; maintains the merchant marine; grants patents and registers trademarks.
Labor (1913)	Oversees working conditions; administers federal labor laws; protects workers' pension rights; sponsors job training programs; keeps track of changes in employment, price, and other national economic indicators.
Health and Human Services (1953 as Health, Education, and Welfare; reorganized with Education as a separate department in 1979)	Administers to social welfare programs for the elderly, children, and youths; protects the health of the nation against impure and unsafe foods, drugs, and cosmetics; operates the Centers for Disease Control; funds the Medicare and Medicaid programs.
Housing and Urban Development (1965)	Is responsible for programs concerned with housing needs, fair housing opportunities, and the improvement and development of the nation's communities; administers mortgage insurance programs, rental subsidy programs, and neighborhood rehabilitation and preservation programs.
Transportation (1966)	Is responsible for the nation's highway planning, development, and construction; also urban mass transit, railroads, aviation, and the safety of waterways, ports, highways, and oil and gas pipelines.
Energy (1977)	Is responsible for the research, development, and demonstration of energy technology; marketing of federal electric power; energy conservation; the nuclear weapons program; regulation of energy production and use; and collection and analysis of energy data.
Education (1979)	Administers and coordinates most federal assistance to education.
Veterans Affairs (1989)	Operates programs to benefit veterans and members of their families.
Homeland Security (2002)	Prevent terrorist attacks within the United States, reduce the vulnerability of the nation to terrorism, and minimize the damage and assist in recovery from terrorist attacks.

Source: The United States Government Manual 2002/03 (Washington, D.C.: Government Printing Office, 2003).

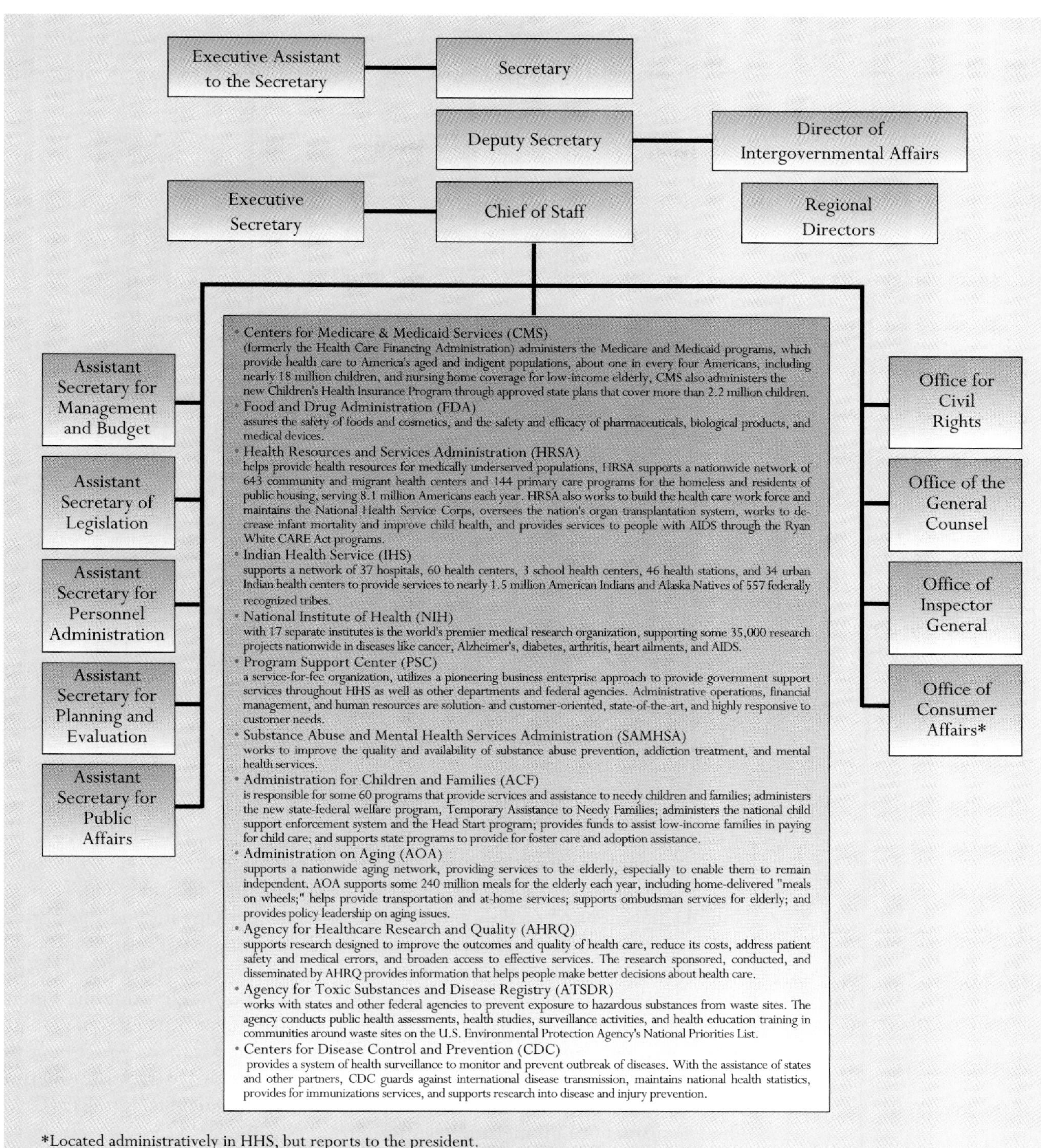

FIGURE 10.3 Department of Health and Human Services

The internal structures of various cabinet-level departments differ somewhat in specifics, but this chart of the Department of Health and Human Services (HHS) is typical of most. It includes secretary, deputy secretary, assistant secretaries, and multiple "administrations" (subdepartments), agencies, offices, and services. The Social Security Administration became an independent agency in 1995.

UP CLOSE

The Department of Homeland Security

Presidents often create new bureaucratic organizations to symbolize their commitment to a policy direction. On October 8, 2001, less than one month after the "9/11" terrorist attack on America, President George W. Bush issued an executive order establishing the Office of Homeland Security and naming

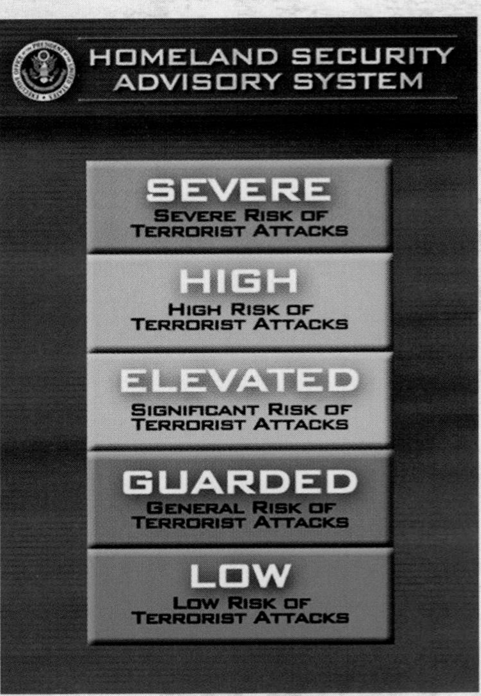

Director Tom Ridge speaks to the newly created Department of Homeland Security.

President Jimmy Carter created a separate Department of Education in 1979 and changed the name of the former Department of Health, Education, and Welfare to the Department of Health and Human Services (perhaps finding the phrase "human services" more politically acceptable than "welfare"). President Ronald Reagan tried, and failed, to "streamline" government by abolishing the Department of Education. But Reagan himself added a cabinet post, elevating the Veterans Administration to the Department of Veterans Affairs in an attempt to ingratiate himself with veterans. President George W. Bush created a new Department of Homeland Security in 2002 in response to the "9/11" terrorist attack on America and the threat of future attacks directly on the soil of the United States (see *Up Close:* "The Department of Homeland Security").

Cabinet Department Functions The relative power and prestige of each cabinet-level department is a product not only of its size and budget but also of the importance of its function. By custom, the "pecking order" of departments—and therefore the prestige ranking of their secretaries—is determined by their years of origin. Thus the Departments of State, Treasury, Defense (War), and Justice, created by the First Congress in 1789, head the protocol list of departments. Overall, the duties of the fifteen cabinet-level departments of the executive branch

Pennsylvania's popular governor Tom Ridge as its director with "cabinet-level" status. The announced mission of the new office: "to develop a comprehensive national strategy to strengthen protection against terrorist threats or attacks on the United States . . . and to coordinate the executive branch's efforts to detect, prepare for, prevent, protect against, respond to, and recover from terrorist attacks within the United States."

But Ridge was given very little direct authority to carry out these monumental tasks. Working out of a small White House office, Ridge is expected to coordinate the counterterrorism activities of 46 separate bureaucracies, including the Federal Bureau of Investigation, the Central Intelligence Agency, the Department of Defense, the State Department, the Immigration and Naturalization Service, the Federal Aviation Administration, the Department of Transportation, and the Federal Emergency Management Administration, as well as many state and local government agencies. The authority to "coordinate" did *not* give Ridge or his office direct control over any government department or agency.

In 2002, in response to growing concerns that he had not done enough to reassure the American public of the federal government's commitment to protect them from terrorism, President George W. Bush proposed a new Department of Homeland Security. Its mission is to prevent terrorist attacks within the United States, to reduce vulnerability of the United States to terrorism, and to minimize damage and assist recovery when and if terrorist attacks occur within the country.

The new department does more than just "coordinate" other federal agencies. In a major reorganization, the Department of Homeland Security has been given direct responsibility over agencies concerned with border protection, transportation security, and emergency preparedness, including the U.S. Border Patrol, the U.S. Customs Service, the Immigration and Naturalization Service, the U.S. Coast Guard, the Secret Service, the Federal Emergency Management Agency, and a newly created Transportation Security Administration.

But the Department of Homeland Security does *not* have authority over the Federal Bureau of Investigation in the Justice Department or the independent Central Intelligence Agency. So questions remain as to whether these two law enforcement and intelligence organizations can coordinate information among themselves and with the new Department of Homeland Security.

cover an enormous range—everything from providing mortgage insurance to overseeing the armed forces of the United States (see Table 10.1).

Cabinet Appointments The Constitution requires that "Officers of the United States" be confirmed by the Senate. In the past, the Senate rarely rejected a presidential cabinet nomination; the traditional view was that presidents were entitled to pick their own people and even make their own mistakes. In recent years, however, the confirmation process has become more partisan and divisive, with the Senate conducting lengthy investigations and holding public hearings on presidential cabinet nominees. In 1989 the Senate rejected President Bush's nomination of John Tower as secretary of defense in a partisan battle featuring charges that the former Texas senator was a heavy drinker. The intense public scrutiny and potential for partisan attacks, together with financial disclosure and conflict-of-interest laws, may be discouraging some well-qualified people from accepting cabinet posts.

Independent Regulatory Commissions Independent regulatory commissions differ from cabinet departments in their function, organization, and accountability to the president. Their function is to *regulate* a sector of

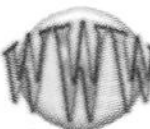

Internal Revenue Service

The tax-collecting IRS is potentially the most powerful of all government agencies with financial records on every tax-paying American. ***www.irs.gov***

Food and Drug Administration

The Food and Drug Administration site is a reflection of the agency's mission "to promote and protect the public health by helping safe and effective products reach the market in a timely way." ***www.fda.gov***

society—transportation, communications, banking, labor relations, and so on (see Table 10.2). These commissions are empowered by Congress both to make and to enforce rules, and they thus function in a quasi-judicial fashion. To symbolize their impartiality, many of these organizations are headed by *commissions,* usually with five to ten members, rather than by a single secretary. Major policy decisions are made by majority vote of the commission. Finally, these agencies are more independent of the president than are cabinet departments. Their governing commissions are appointed by the president and confirmed by the Senate in the same fashion as cabinet secretaries, but their terms are fixed; they cannot be removed by the president.[6] These provisions are designed to insulate regulators from direct partisan or presidential pressures in their decision making.

A few powerful regulatory agencies remain inside cabinet departments. The most notable are the Food and Drug Administration (FDA), which remains in the Department of Health and Human Services and has broad authority to prevent the sale of drugs not deemed by the agency to be both "safe" and "effective"; the Occupational Health and Safety Administration (OSHA) in the Department of Labor, with authority to make rules governing any workplace in America; and the most powerful government agency of all, the Internal Revenue Service in the Treasury Department, with its broad authority to interpret the tax code, maintain records on every American, and investigate and punish alleged violations of the tax code.

Independent Agencies Congress has created a number of independent agencies outside of any cabinet department. Like cabinet departments, these agencies are hierarchically organized with a single head—usually called an "administrator"—who is appointed by the president and confirmed by the Senate. Administrators have no fixed terms of office and can be dismissed by the president; thus they are independent only insofar as they report directly to the president rather than through a cabinet secretary. Politically, this independence ensures that their interests and budgets will not be compromised by other concerns, as may occur in agencies located within departments. (For more on their operations, see "Regulatory Battles" later in this chapter.)

Cleaning up an oil spill on a California beach. The Environmental Protection Agency is perhaps the most powerful independent agency in the bureaucracy.

One of the most powerful independent agencies is the Environmental Protection Agency (EPA), which is responsible for implementing federal legislation dealing with clean air, safe drinking water, solid waste disposal, pesticides, radiation, and toxic substances. EPA establishes and enforces comprehensive and complex standards for thousands of substances in the environment. It enjoys the political support of influential environmental interest groups, including the Environmental Defense Fund, Friends of the Earth, National Audubon Society, National Wildlife Federation, Natural Resources Defense Council, Sierra Club, and the Wilderness Society.

The Federal Reserve System is the most independent of all federal government agencies. The function of the "Fed" is to regulate the supply of money and thereby avoid both inflation and recession (see Chapter 13). The Federal Reserve System is independent of either the president or Congress. Its seven-member Board of Governors is appointed for *14-year terms.* Members are appointed by the president, with the consent of the Senate, but they may not be removed from the board except for "cause." No member has ever been removed since the creation of the board in 1913. The chairman of the board serves only a four-year term, but the chairman's term overlaps that of president, so that new presidents cannot immediately name

TABLE 10.2 Major Regulatory Bureaucracies

Commission	Date Created	Primary Functions
Federal Communications Commission (FCC)	1934	Regulates interstate and foreign communications by radio, television, wire, and cable.
Food and Drug Administration (FDA)	1930	Sets standards of safety and efficacy for foods, drugs, and medical devices.
Federal Home Loan Bank	1932	Regulates savings and loan associations that specialize in making home mortgage loans.
Federal Maritime Commission	1961	Regulates the waterborne foreign and domestic offshore commerce of the United States.
Federal Reserve Board (FRB)	1913	Regulates the nation's money supply by making monetary policy, which influences the lending and investing activities of commercial banks and the cost and availability of money and credit.
Federal Trade Commission (FTC)	1914	Regulates business to prohibit unfair methods of competition and unfair or deceptive acts or practices.
National Labor Relations Board (NLRB)	1935	Protects employees' rights to organize; prevents unfair labor practices.
Securities and Exchange Commission (SEC)	1934	Regulates the securities and financial markets (such as the stock market).
Occupational Safety and Health Administration (OSHA)	1970	Issues workplace regulations; investigates, cites, and penalizes for noncompliance.
Consumer Product Safety Commission (CPSC)	1972	Protects the public against product-related deaths, illnesses, and injuries.
Commodity Futures Trading Commission	1974	Regulates trading on the futures exchanges as well as the activities of commodity exchange members, public brokerage houses, commodity salespersons, trading advisers, and pool operators.
Nuclear Regulatory Commission (NRC)	1974	Regulates and licenses the users of nuclear energy.
Federal Energy Regulatory Commission (formerly Federal Power Commission)	1977	Regulates the transportation and sale of natural gas, the transmission and sale of electricity, the licensing of hydroelectric power projects, and the transportation of oil by pipeline.
Equal Employment Opportunity Commission (EEOC)	1964	Investigates and rules on charges of racial, gender, and age discrimination by employers and unions, in all aspects of employment.
Environmental Protection Agency (EPA)	1970	Issues and enforces pollution control standards regarding air, water, solid waste, pesticides, radiation, and toxic substances.

Source: The United States Government Manual 2001/02 (Washington, D.C.: Government Printing Office, 2002).

their own chair (see *People and Politics:* "Alan Greenspan, Managing the Nation's Economy").

Occupational Safety and Health Administration

This site covers news and information directly related to OSHA's mission "to ensure safe and healthful workplaces in America." ***www.osha.gov***

Government Corporations Government corporations are created by Congress to undertake independent commercial enterprises. They resemble private corporations in that they typically charge for their services. Like private corporations, too, they are usually governed by a chief executive officer and a board of directors, and they can buy and sell property and incur debts.

PEOPLE IN POLITICS

Alan Greenspan, Managing the Nation's Economy

The Federal Reserve System regulates the nation's monetary policy and credit conditions, supervises and regulates all banking activity, and provides various services to banks. Federal Reserve Banks are banks' banks. There are 12 Federal Reserve Banks serving the nation's nearly 8,000 commercial banks. The "Fed" requires all banks to maintain a reserve in deposits with a Federal Reserve Bank. The Fed also makes loans to banks, allowing them to add to their reserve and therefore allowing them to make more loans to customers. But the Fed charges banks an interest rate on these loans, called the "discount rate." By raising the discount rate, the Fed forces banks to raise their own interest rates and thereby contract the nation's money supply; lowering the discount rate encourages banks to expand the money supply. Interest rates generally—on loans to businesses, mortgages, car loans, and so on—rise and fall with rises and falls in the Fed's discount rate. Lowering rates encourages economic expansion; raising rates dampens inflation. These decisions by the Fed, referred to as monetary policy (see Chapter 16), have a vital impact on the economy.

Economist Alan Greenspan is the chairman of the Board of Governors of the Federal Reserve System. He was appointed in 1987 by President Ronald Reagan.

Born in New York City, Alan Greenspan studied music at the prestigious Julliard School and enjoyed a brief but successful career as a professional saxophone player in a big swing band before returning to the classroom at New York University. He received an M.A. in economics in 1950 under the tutelage of Arthur F. Burns, who served as chair of the Federal Reserve from 1970 to 1978. After graduation, Greenspan formed his own economic consulting company, Townsend-Greenspan, which provided economic forecasts for some of America's largest corporations. In his spare time, Greenspan completed his Ph.D. at New York University.

Greenspan began his public service in the Nixon Administration, serving on commissions and task forces, including the Commission on an All-Volunteer Armed Force. In 1974 President Nixon appointed Greenspan to chair the Council of Economic Advisers, a position Greenspan continued to hold under President Gerald Ford. When the Carter Administration came to Washington in 1977, Republican Greenspan returned to running his private company.

As Fed chairman under four presidents—Reagan, Bush, Clinton, and Bush — Greenspan has often acted independently and disagreed with the administration over the money supply. Yet his management of the Fed has been widely praised by both Democrats and Republicans. He has earned credibility with his fellow economists by avoiding the Washington political game. He is credited for his quick reaction to the stock market crash on October 19, 1987, when he ensured that Federal Reserve Banks would have enough cash on hand to prevent panic following the record drop in stock prices.

Greenspan successfully fought inflationary trends during the nation's economic expansion in the 1990s by raising interest rates. When recession threatened in 2001, he led the Fed in bringing down interest rates to an all-time low, preventing a deep recession. When Greenspan testifies before Congress, as he frequently does, stock traders closely monitor every word, and stock prices usually react to his mood. Arguably, the Fed chairman has more power over the nation's economy than any other single individual, including the president.

Federal Reserve System

This Federal Reserve System site covers general information about "Fed" operations, including monetary policy, reserve bank services, international banking, and supervisory and regulatory functions.
www.federalreserve.gov

Presumably, government corporations perform a service that the private enterprise system has been unable to carry out adequately. The first government corporation was the Tennessee Valley Authority, created by President Franklin Roosevelt during the Depression to build dams and sell electricity at inexpensive rates to impoverished citizens in the mid-South. In 1970 Congress created Amtrak to restore railroad passenger service to the United States. The U.S. Post Office had originally been created as a cabinet-level department, but in 1971 it became the U.S. Postal Service, a government corporation with a mandate from Congress to break even.

Contractors and Consultants How has the federal government grown enormously in power and size, yet kept its number of employees at roughly the same level in recent years? The answer is found in the spectacular growth of private firms that live off federal contracting and consulting fees. Nearly one-fifth of all federal government spending flows through private contractors: for supplies, equipment, services, leases, and research and development. An army of scientists, economists, education specialists, management consultants, transportation experts, social scientists, and others are scattered across the country in universities, think tanks, consulting firms, and laboratories. Many are concentrated in the "beltway bandit" firms surrounding Washington, D.C.

The federal grant and contracting system is enormously complex; an estimated 150,000 federal contracting offices in nearly 500 agencies oversee thousands of outside contractors and consultants[7] Although advertised bidding is sometimes required by law, most contracts and grants are awarded without competition through negotiation with favored firms or "sole source contracts" with organizations believed by bureaucrats to be uniquely qualified. Even when federal agencies issue public requests for proposals (RFPs), often a favored contractor has been alerted and advised by bureaucrats within the agency about how to win the award.

WWW **Amtrak** The Amtrak Web site provides valuable information about trip planning, reservations, train schedules, and respective train fares. *www.amtrak.com*

Bureaucracy and Democracy

Traditionally, conflict over government employment centered on the question of partisanship versus competence. Should the federal bureaucracy be staffed by people politically loyal to the president, the president's party, or key members of Congress? Or should it be staffed by nonpartisan people selected on the basis of merit and protected from "political" influence?

The Spoils System Historically, government employment was allocated by the **spoils system**—selecting employees on the basis of party loyalty, electoral support, and political influence. Or, as Senator William Marcy said in 1832, "They see nothing wrong in the rule that to the victors belong the spoils of the enemy."[8] The spoils system is most closely associated with President Andrew Jackson, who viewed it as a popular reform of the earlier tendency to appoint officials on the basis of kinship and class standing. Jackson sought to bring into government many of the common people who had supported him. Later in the nineteenth century, the bartering and sale of government jobs became so scandalous and time-consuming that presidents complained bitterly about the task. When President James Garfield was shot and killed in 1881 by a disgruntled job seeker, the stage was set for reform.

THINK AGAIN

Should the federal bureaucracy be managed by nonpartisan professionals rather than people politically loyal to the president?

The Merit System The **merit system**—government employment based on competence, neutrality, and protection from partisanship—was introduced in the Pendleton Act of 1883. The act created the Civil Service Commission to establish a system for selecting government personnel based on merit, as determined by competitive examinations. In the beginning, "civil service" coverage included only about 10 percent of total federal employees. Over the years, however, more and more positions were placed under civil service, primarily at the behest of presidents who sought to "freeze in" their political appointees. By 1978 more than 90 percent of federal employees were covered by civil service or other merit systems.

The civil service system established a uniform General Schedule (GS) of job grades from GS 1 (lowest) to GS 15 (highest), with an Executive Schedule added

spoils system Selection of employees for government agencies on the basis of party loyalty, electoral support, and political influence.

merit system Selection of employees for government agencies on the basis of competence, with no consideration of an individual's political stance and/or power.

USA JOBS This site is the official source for federal employment information. *www.usajobs.opm.gov*

later for top managers and pay ranges based on an individual's time in the grade. Each grade has specific educational requirements and examinations. College graduates generally begin at GS 5 or above; GS 9 through GS 12 are technical and supervisory positions; and GS 13, 14, and 15 are midlevel management and highly specialized positions. The Executive Schedule (the "supergrades") are reserved for positions of greatest responsibility. (In 2004 annual pay ranged from roughly \$25,000 to \$42,000 for Grades 5–8, up to \$62,000 to \$112,000 for Grades 13–15, and \$175,000 for some Executive Schedule positions.) When a position in a federal agency opens up, the agency is supposed to receive the names of the three people earning the highest examination scores for that position grade. The agency is supposed to hire one of the three, with the other two remaining at the top of the register for the next opening. But agencies often set highly specialized job qualifications that relatively few applicants possess, and special preferences abound in federal employment regulations.

About two-thirds of all federal civilian jobs come under the General Schedule system, with its written examinations and/or training, experience, and educational requirements. Most of the other one-third of federal civilian employees are part of the "excepted services"; they are employed by various agencies that have their own separate merit systems, such as the Federal Bureau of Investigation, the Central Intelligence Agency, the U.S. Postal Service, and the State Department Foreign Service. The military also has its own system of recruitment, promotion, and pay.

During the administration of Andrew Jackson, the spoils system was perhaps more overt than at any other time in the history of the U.S. federal government. Jackson claimed he was trying to involve more of the "common folk" in the government, but his selection of advisers on the basis of personal friendship rather than qualifications sometimes caused him difficulties.

Political Involvement Congress passed the Hatch Act in 1939, a law that prohibited federal employees from engaging in partisan political activity, including running for public office, soliciting campaign funds, or campaigning for or against a party or candidate. It also protected federal merit system employees from dismissal for partisan reasons. But over the years many federal employees came to believe that the Hatch Act infringed on their rights as citizens. In 1993, a Democratic-controlled Congress repealed major portions of the Hatch Act, allowing civil servants to hold party positions and involve themselves in political fund raising and campaigning. They still may not be candidates for public office in partisan elections, or solicit contributions from subordinate employees or people who do business with—or have cases before—their agencies.

The Problem of Responsiveness The civil service system, like most "reforms," eventually created problems at least as troubling as those in the system it replaced. First of all, there is the problem of a *lack of responsiveness* to presidential direction. Civil servants, secure in their protected jobs, can be less than cooperative toward their presidentially appointed department or agency heads. They can slow or obstruct policy changes with which they personally disagree. Each bureau and agency develops its own "culture," usually in strong support of the governmental function or client group served by the organization. Changing the culture of an agency is extremely difficult, especially when a presidential administration is committed to reducing its resources, functions, or services. Bureaucrats' powers of policy obstruction are formidable: they can help mobilize interest-group support against the president's policy; they can "leak" damaging information to sympathizers in Congress or the media to undermine the president's policy; they can delay and/or "sabotage" policies with which they disagree.

The Problem of Productivity Perhaps the most troublesome problem in the federal bureaucracy has involved *productivity*—notably the inability to improve job performance because of the difficulties in rewarding or punishing civil servants.

"Merit" salary rewards have generally proven ineffective in rewarding the performance of federal employees. More than 99 percent of federal workers regularly receive annual "merit" pay increases. Moreover, over time, federal employees have secured higher grade classifications and hence higher pay for most of the job positions in the General Schedule. This "inflation" in GS grades, combined with regular increases in salary and benefits, has resulted in many federal employees enjoying higher pay and benefits than employees in the private sector performing similar jobs.

At the same time, very poor performance often goes largely unpunished. Once hired and retained through a brief probationary period, a federal civil servant cannot be dismissed except for "cause." Severe obstacles to firing a civil servant result in a rate of dismissal of about one-tenth of 1 percent of all federal employees (see Table 10.3). It is doubtful that only such a tiny fraction are performing unsatisfactorily. A federal executive confronting a poorly performing or nonperforming employee must be prepared to spend more than a year in extended proceedings to secure a dismissal. Often costly substitute strategies are devised to work around or inspire the resignation of unsatisfactory federal employees—assigning them meaningless or boring tasks, denying them promotions, transferring them to distant or undesirable locations, removing secretaries or other supporting resources, and the like.

Civil Service Reform Presidents routinely try to remedy some of the problems in the system. The Civil Service Reform Act of 1978, initiated by President Jimmy Carter, replaced the Civil Service Commission with the Office of Personnel Management (OPM) and made OPM responsible for recruiting, examining, training, and promoting federal employees. Unlike the Civil Service Commission, OPM is headed by a single director responsible to the president. The act also sought to (1) streamline procedures through which individuals could be disciplined for poor performance; (2) establish merit pay for middle-level managers; and (3) create a Senior Executive Service (SES) composed of about 8,000 top people designated for higher Executive Schedule grades and salaries who also might be given salary bonuses, transferred among agencies, or demoted, based on performance.

But like many reforms, this act failed to resolve the major problems—the responsiveness and productivity of the bureaucracy. No senior executives were fired,

TABLE 10.3 Firing a Bureaucrat: What Is Required to Dismiss a Federal Employee

- Written notice at least thirty days in advance of a hearing to determine incompetence or misconduct.
- A statement of cause, indicating specific dates, places, and actions cited as incompetent or improper.
- The right to a hearing and decision by an impartial official, with the burden of proof falling on the agency that wishes to fire the employee.
- The right to have an attorney and to present witnesses in the employee's favor at the hearing.
- The right to appeal any adverse action to the Merit Systems Protection Board.
- The right to appeal any adverse action by the board to the U.S. Court of Appeals.
- The right to remain on the job and be paid until all appeals are exhausted.

TABLE 10.4 Women and Minorities in the Federal Bureaucracy

	Percentage Female	Percentage White, Non-Hispanic	Percentage African American	Percentage Hispanic
Overall	48.7%	74.7%	18.2%	7.0%
By pay grade				
Lowest GS 1–4	74.8	55.5	29.7	9.8
GS 5–8	53.5	65.5	27.0	8.6
GS 9–12	32.9	77.1	15.8	7.1
GS 13–15	17.0	85.6	10.1	4.3
Executive	9.1	87.5	7.5	3.0
U.S. population (2000)	50.9	75.2	12.3	12.5

Table excludes American Indians, Alaska Natives, and Asian and Pacific Islanders.

Source: Statistical Abstract of the United States, 2001, p. 320.

demoted, or involuntarily transferred. The bonus program proved difficult to implement: there are few recognized standards for judging meritorious work in the public service, and bonuses often reflect favoritism as much as merit.[9] Because the act creates a separate Merit Systems Protection Board to hear appeals by federal employees from dismissals, suspensions, and demotions, rates of dismissal for all grades have not changed substantially from earlier days.

THINK AGAIN

Should the federal bureaucracy at all levels reflect the gender and minority ratios of the total civilian work force?

Bureaucracy and Representation In addition to the questions of responsiveness and productivity, there is also the question of the representativeness of the federal bureaucracy. Today, the federal bureaucracy *as a whole* reflects fairly well the gender and minority ratios of the U.S. population. Nearly half of the total civilian work force is female, 18.2 percent is black, and 7.0 is Hispanic. However, a close look at *top* bureaucratic positions reveals a somewhat different picture. As Table 10.4 shows, only 9.1 percent of federal "executive" positions (levels GS 16–18) are filled by women, only 7.5 percent by blacks, and only 3.0 percent by Hispanics. Thus the federal bureaucracy, like other institutions in American society, is *un*representative of the general population in its top executive positions.

Bureaucratic Politics

To whom is the federal bureaucracy really accountable? The president, Congress, or itself? Article II, Section 2, of the Constitution places the president at the head of the executive branch of government, with the power to "appoint Ambassadors, other public Ministers and Consuls, Judges of the Supreme Court, and all other Officers of the United States . . . which shall be established by Law." Appointment of these officials requires "the Advice and Consent of the Senate"—that is, a majority vote in the Senate. The Constitution also states that "the Congress may by Law vest the Appointment of such inferior Officers, as they think proper, in the President alone." If the bureaucracy is to be made accountable to the president, we would expect the president to directly appoint *policy-making* executive officers. But it is difficult to determine exactly how many positions are truly "policy making."

Presidential "Plums" The president retains direct control over about 3,000 federal jobs. Some 700 of these jobs are considered policy-making positions. They include presidential appointments authorized by law—cabinet and subcabinet officers, judges, U.S. marshals, U.S. attorneys, ambassadors, and members of various boards and commissions. The president also appoints a large number of "Schedule C" jobs throughout the bureaucracy, described as "confidential or policy-determining" in character. Each new administration goes through many months of high-powered lobbying and scrambling to fill these posts. Applicants with congressional sponsors, friends in the White House, or a record of loyal campaign work for the president compete for these "plums." Political loyalty must be weighed against administrative competence.

Rooms at the Top The federal bureaucracy has "thickened" at the top, even as total federal employment has declined. Over time, departments and agencies have added layers of administrators, variously titled "deputy secretary," "undersecretary," "assistant secretary," "deputy assistant secretary," and so on. Cabinet departments have become top-heavy with administrators, and the same multiplication of layers of executive management has occurred in independent agencies as well.[10]

Whistle-Blowers The question of bureaucratic responsiveness is complicated by the struggle between the president and Congress to control the bureaucracy. Congress expects federal agencies and employees to respond fully and promptly to its inquiries and to report candidly on policies, procedures, and expenditures. **Whistle-blowers** are federal employees (or employees of a firm supplying the government) who report government waste, mismanagement, or fraud to the media or to congressional committees or who "go public" with their policy disputes with their superiors. Congress generally encourages whistle-blowing as a means of getting information and controlling the bureaucracy, but the president and agency heads whose policies are under attack are often less kindly disposed toward whistle-blowers. In 1989 Congress passed the Whistleblower Protection Act, which established an independent agency to guarantee whistle-blowers protection against unjust dismissal, transfer, or demotion.

Center for Public Integrity

Reform organization committed to "exposing" corruption, mismanagement, and waste in government.
www.publicintegrity.org

Agency Cultures Over time, every bureaucracy tends to develop its own "culture"—beliefs about the values of the organization's programs and goals and close associations with the agency's client groups and political supporters. Many government agencies are dominated by people who have been in government service most of their lives, and most of these people have worked in the same functional field most of their lives. They believe their work is important, and they resist efforts by either the president or Congress to reduce the activities, size, or budget of their agency. Career bureaucrats tend to support enlargement of the public sector—to enhance education, welfare, housing, environmental and consumer protection, and so on. Bureaucrats not only share a belief in the need for government expansion but also stand to benefit directly from increased authority, staffing, and funding as government takes on new and enlarged responsibilities.

whistle-blower Employee of the federal government or of a firm supplying the government who reports waste, mismanagement, and/or fraud by a government agency or contractor.

Friends and Neighbors Bureaucracies maintain their own cultures in part by staffing themselves. Informal practices in recruitment often circumvent civil service procedures. Very few people ever get hired by taking a federal civil service examination administered by OPM and then sitting and waiting to be called for an interview by an agency. Most bureaucratic hiring actually comes about through "networks" of personal friends and professional associates. People inside an agency contact their friends and associates when a position first becomes vacant; they then send their friends to OPM to formally qualify for the job. Thus inside candidates learn about an opening well before it appears on any list of vacant positions and can tailor their applications to the job description. Agencies may even send a "name request" to OPM, ensuring that the preselected person will appear on the list of qualified people. In this way, individuals sometimes move through many jobs within a specific policy network—for example, within environmental protection, within transportation, or within social welfare—shifting between the federal bureaucracy, state or local government, and private firms or interest groups in the same field. Network recruiting generally ensures that the people entering a bureaucracy will share the same values and attitudes of the people already there.

"Reinventing" Government Reformers lament "the bankruptcy of bureaucracy"—the waste, inefficiency, impersonality, and unresponsiveness of large government organizations. They decry "the routine tendency to protect turf, to resist change, to build empires, to enlarge one's sphere of control, to protect projects and programs regardless of whether or not they are any longer needed."[11] Many bureaucratic reform efforts have foundered, from Hoover Commission studies in the Truman and Eisenhower years to the Grace Commission work in the Reagan Administration. Clinton assigned a "reinventing government" task to Vice President Al Gore. Gore produced a report designed to put the "customer" (U.S. citizen) first, to "empower" government employees to get results, to cut red tape, to introduce competition and a market orientation wherever possible, and to decentralize government decision making.[12] The most impressive result was the overall decline in federal employment during the Clinton Administration, from 3.1 million to 2.7 million civilian employees.

Presidential Initiative Presidents can create some new agencies by executive order. Often Congress gives presidents the authority to reorganize agencies by legislation. But presidents have also acted on their own to create new agencies. Indeed, one study concludes that presidents have created about 40 percent of all new agencies[13]—perhaps the most famous was President Kennedy's Peace Corps. Of course, Congress has the last word, inasmuch as the continuation of a presidentially created agency requires funding and Congress controls the purse strings. It can end an agency's existence by cutting off its funds.

The Budgetary Process

THINK AGAIN

Do you believe the bureaucrats in Washington waste a lot of the money we pay in taxes?

The federal government's annual budget battles are the heart of political process. Budget battles decide who gets what and who pays the cost of government. The budget is the single most important policy statement of any government.

The president is responsible for submitting the annual *Budget of the United States Government*—with estimates of revenues and recommendations for expenditures—for consideration, amendment, and approval by the Congress. But the president's budget reflects the outcome of earlier bureaucratic battles over who gets what. Despite highly publicized wrangling between the president and Congress each year—and occasional declarations that the president's budget is "DOA" (dead on arrival)—final congressional appropriations rarely deviate by more than 2 or 3 percent from the original presidential budget. Thus the president and the Office of Management and Budget in the Executive Office of the President have real budgetary power.

The Office of Management and Budget The Office of Management and Budget (OMB) has the key responsibility for budget preparation. In addition to this major task, OMB has related responsibilities for improving the organization and management of the executive agencies, for coordinating the extensive statistical services of the federal government, and for analyzing and reviewing proposed legislation.

Office of Management and Budget

The OMB site includes all budget documents and information on regulatory oversight. *www.omb.gov*

Preparation of the budget begins when OMB, after preliminary consultations with the executive agencies and in accord with presidential policy, develops targets or ceilings within which the agencies are encouraged to build their requests (see Figure 10.4). Budget materials and instructions then go to the agencies, with the request that the forms be completed and returned to OMB. This request is followed by about three months of arduous work by agency budget officers, department heads, and the "grass-roots" bureaucracy in Washington, D.C., and out in the field. Budget officials at the bureau and departmental levels check requests from the smaller units, compare them with previous years' estimates, hold conferences, and make adjustments. The heads of agencies are expected to submit their completed requests to OMB by July or August. Although these requests usually remain within target levels, occasionally they include some "overceiling" items (requests above the suggested ceilings). With the requests of the spending agencies at hand, OMB begins its own budget review, including hearings at which top agency officials support their requests as convincingly as possible. Frequently OMB must say "no," that is, reduce agency requests. On rare occasions, dissatisfied agencies may ask the budget director to take their cases to the president.

The President's Budget In December, the president and the OMB director devote much time to the key document, *The Budget of the United States Government*, which by now is approaching its final stages of assembly. Each budget is named for the **fiscal year** in which it *ends*. The federal fiscal year begins on October 1 and ends the following September 30. (Thus *The Budget of the United States Government Fiscal Year* 2006 begins October 1, 2005, and ends September 30, 2006.) Although the completed document includes a revenue plan with general estimates for taxes and other income, it is primarily an expenditure budget. (Revenue and tax policy staff work centers in the Treasury Department, not in the Office of Management and Budget.) In late January, the president presents Congress with *The Budget of the United States Government* for the fiscal year beginning October 1. After the budget is in legislative hands, the president may recommend further alterations as needs dictate.

House and Senate Budget Committees The Constitution gives Congress the authority to decide how the government should spend its money: "No money shall be drawn from the Treasury, but in Consequence of Appropriations made by Law" (Article 1, Section 9). The president's budget is sent initially to the House and Senate Budget Committees, which rely on their own bureaucracy, the Congressional Budget Office (CBO), to review the president's budget. Based on the CBO's assessment, these committees draft a first **budget resolution** (due May 15) setting forth target goals to guide congressional committees regarding specific appropriations and revenue measures. If proposed spending exceeds the targets in the budget resolution, the resolution comes back to the floor in a reconciliation measure. A second budget resolution (due September 15) sets

fiscal year Yearly government accounting period, not necessarily the same as the calendar year. The federal government's fiscal year begins October 1 and ends September 30.

budget resolution Congressional bill setting forth target budget figures for appropriations to various government departments and agencies.

	WHO	WHAT	WHEN
 **Presidential budget making**	President and OMB	OMB presents long-range forecasts for revenues and expenditures to the president. President and OMB develop general guidelines for all federal agencies. Agencies are sent guidelines and forms for their budget requests.	January February March
	Executive agencies	Agencies prepare and submit budget requests to OMB.	April May June July
	OMB and agencies	OMB reviews agency requests and holds hearings with agency officials.	August September October
	OMB and president	OMB presents revised budget to president. President and OMB write budget message for Congress.	November December January
	President	President presents budget for the next fiscal year to Congress.	February
 **Congressional budget process**	CBO and congressional committees	CBO reviews taxing and spending proposals and reports to House and Senate budget committees.	February-April
	Congress; House and Senate budget committees	Committees present first concurrent resolution, which sets overall total for budget outlays in major categories. Full House and Senate vote on resolution. Committees are instructed to stay within Budget Committee's resolution.	May June
	Congress; House and Senate appropriations committees and budget committees	Appropriations committees and subcommittees draw up detailed appropriations bills and submit them to budget committees for second concurrent resolution. The full House and Senate vote on "reconciliations" and second (firm) concurrent resolution.	July August September
	Congress and president	House and Senate pass various appropriations bills (nine to sixteen bills, by major functional category, such as "defense"). Each is sent to president for signature. (If successfully vetoed, a bill is revised and resubmitted to the president.)	September October
 **Executive budget implementation**	Congress and president	Fiscal year for all federal agencies begins October 1. If no appropriations bill for an agency has been passed by Congress and signed by the president, Congress must pass and the president sign a continuing resolution to allow the agency to spend at last year's level until a new appropriations bill is passed. If no continuing resolution is passed, the agency must officially cease spending government funds and must officially shut down.	After October 1

FIGURE 10.4 The Budget Process

Development, presentation, and approval of the federal budget for any fiscal year takes almost two full years. The executive branch spends more than a year on the process before Congress even begins its review and revision of the president's proposals. The problems of implementing the budgeted programs then fall to the federal bureaucracy.

binding budget figures for committees and subcommittees considering appropriations. In practice, however, these two budget resolutions are often folded into a single measure because Congress does not want to argue the same issues twice.

Congressional Appropriations Committees Congressional approval of each year's spending is usually divided into thirteen separate appropriations bills (acts), each covering separate broad categories of spending (for example, defense, labor, human services and education, commerce, justice). These appropriations bills are drawn up by the House and Senate Appropriations Committees and their specialized subcommittees, which function as overseers of agencies included in their appropriations bills. Committee work in the House of Representatives is usually more thorough than it is in the Senate; the committee in the Senate tends to be a "court of appeal" for agencies opposed to House action. Each committee, moreover, has about ten largely independent subcommittees, each reviewing the requests of a particular agency or a group of related functions. Specific appropriations bills are taken up by the subcommittees in hearings. Departmental officers answer questions on the conduct of their programs and defend their requests for the next fiscal year; lobbyists and other witnesses testify. Although committees and subcommittees have broad discretion in allocating funds to the agencies they monitor, they must stay within overall totals set forth in the second budget resolution adopted by Congress.

Appropriations Acts In examining the interactions between Congress and the federal bureaucracy over spending, it is important to distinguish between appropriations and authorization. An **authorization** is an act of Congress that establishes a government program and defines the amount of money it may spend. Authorizations may be for one or several years. However, an authorization does not actually provide the money that has been authorized; only an **appropriations act** can do that. In fact, appropriations acts, which are usually for a single fiscal year, are almost always *less* than authorizations; deciding how much less is the real function of the Appropriations Committees and subcommittees. (By its own rules, Congress cannot appropriate money for programs it has not already authorized.) Appropriations acts include both obligational authority and outlays.

Obligational authority permits a government agency to enter into contracts that will require the government to make payments beyond the fiscal years in question. **Outlays** must be spent in the fiscal year for which they are appropriated.

Continuing Resolutions and "Shutdowns" All appropriations acts *should* be passed by both houses and signed by the president into law before October 1, the date of the start of the fiscal year. However, it is rare for Congress to meet this deadline, so the government usually finds itself beginning a new fiscal year without a budget. Constitutionally, any U.S. government agency for which Congress does not pass an appropriations act may not draw money from the Treasury and thus is obliged to shut down. To get around this problem, Congress usually adopts a **continuing resolution** that authorizes government agencies to keep spending money for a specified period at the same level as in the previous fiscal year.

A continuing resolution is supposed to grant additional time for Congress to pass, and the president to sign, appropriations acts. But occasionally this process has broken down in the heat of political combat over the budget: the time period specified in a continuing resolution has expired without agreement on appropriations acts or even on a new continuing resolution. Shutdowns occurred during the bitter battle between President Bill Clinton and the Republican-controlled

authorization Act of Congress that establishes a government program and defines the amount of money it may spend.

appropriations act Congressional bill that provides money for programs authorized by Congress.

obligational authority Feature of some appropriations acts by which an agency is empowered to enter into contracts that will require the government to make payments beyond the fiscal year in question.

outlays Actual dollar amounts to be spent by the federal government in a fiscal year.

continuing resolution Congressional bill that authorizes government agencies to keep spending money for a specified period at the same level as in the previous fiscal year; passed when Congress is unable to enact final appropriations measures by October 1.

The 2005 Budget of the United States government shows total outlays of $2.4 trillion, with a deficit of nearly $365 billion. The deficit is in part a product of increased spending for defense and home security.

Congress over the Fiscal Year 1996 budget. In theory, the absence of either appropriations acts or a continuing resolution should cause the entire federal government to "shut down," that is, to cease all operations and expenditures for lack of funds. But in practice, such shutdowns have been only partial, affecting only "nonessential" government employees and causing relatively little disruption.

The Politics of Budgeting

Budgeting is very political. Being a good "bureaucratic politician" involves (1) cultivating a good base of support for requests among the public at large and among people served by the agency; (2) developing interest, enthusiasm, and support for one's program among top political figures and congressional leaders; (3) winning favorable coverage of agency activities in the media; and (4) following strategies that exploit opportunities.[14] (see *Up Close:* "Bureaucratic Budget Strategies").

Budgeting Is "Incremental" The most important factor determining the size and content of the budget each year is last year's budget. Decision makers generally use last year's expenditures as a *base;* active consideration of budget proposals generally focuses on new items and requested increases over last year's base. The budget of an agency is almost never reviewed as a whole. Agencies are seldom required to defend or explain budget requests that do *not* exceed current appropriations; but requested increases *do* require explanation and are most subject to reduction by OMB or Congress.

The result of **incremental budgeting** is that many programs, services, and expenditures continue long after there is any real justification for them. When new needs, services, and functions arise, they do not displace older ones but rather are *added* to the budget. Budget decisions are made incrementally because policy makers do not have the time, energy, or information to review every dollar of every budget request every year. Nor do policy makers wish to refight every political battle over existing programs every year. So they generally accept last year's base spending level as legitimate and focus attention on proposed increases for each program.

Reformers have proposed "sunset" laws requiring bureaucrats to justify their programs every five to seven years or else the programs go out of existence, as well as **zero-based budgeting** that would force agencies to justify every penny requested—not just requested increases. In theory, sunset laws and zero-based budgeting would regularly prune unnecessary government programs, agencies, and expenditures and thus limit the growth of government and waste in government (see *What Do You Think?* "How Much Money Does the Government Waste?"). But in reality, sunset laws and zero-based budgeting require so much effort in justifying already accepted programs that executive agencies and legislative committees grow tired of the effort and return to incrementalism.

incremental budgeting Method of budgeting that focuses on requested increases in funding for existing programs, accepting as legitimate their previous year's expenditures.

zero-based budgeting Method of budgeting that demands justification for the entire budget request of an agency, not just its requested increase in funding.

The "incremental" nature of budgetary politics helps reduce political conflicts and maintain stability in governmental programs. As bruising as budgetary battles are today, they would be much worse if the president or Congress undertook to review the value of *all* existing expenditures and programs each year. Comprehensive budgetary review would "overload the system" with political conflict by refighting every policy battle every year.

Budgeting Is Nonprogrammatic Budgeting is *nonprogrammatic* in that an agency budget typically lists expenditures under ambiguous phrases: "personnel ser-

UP CLOSE

Bureaucratic Budget Strategies

How do bureaucrats go about "maximizing" their resources? Some of the most common budgetary strategies of bureaucrats are listed here. Remember that most bureaucrats believe strongly in the importance of their tasks; they pursue these strategies not only to increase their own power and prestige but also to better serve their client groups and the entire nation.

- ***Spend it all:*** Spend all of your current appropriation. Failure to use up an appropriation indicates the full amount was unnecessary in the first place, which in turn implies that your budget should be cut next year.
- ***Ask for more:*** Never request a sum less than your current appropriation. It is easier to find ways to spend up to current appropriation levels than it is to explain why you want a reduction. Besides, a reduction indicates your program is not growing, an embarrassing admission to most government administrators. Requesting an increase, at least enough to cover "inflation," demonstrates the continued importance of your program.
- ***Put vital programs in the "base":*** Put top priority programs into the basic budget—that is, that part of the budget within current appropriation levels. The Office of Management and Budget (OMB) and legislative committees seldom challenge programs that appear to be part of existing operations.
- ***Make new programs appear "incremental":*** Requested increases should appear to be small and should appear to grow out of existing operations. Any appearance of a fundamental change in a budget should be avoided.
- ***Give them something to cut:*** Give the OMB and legislative committees something to cut. Normally it is desirable to submit requests for substantial increases in existing programs and many requests for new programs, in order to give higher political authorities something to cut. This approach enables authorities to "save" the public untold millions of dollars and justify their claim of promoting "economy" in government. Giving them something to cut also diverts attention from the basic budget with its vital programs.
- ***Make cuts hurt:*** If your agency is faced with a real budget cut—that is, a reduction from last year's appropriation—announce pending cuts in vital and popular programs in order to stir up opposition to the cut. For example, the National Park Service might announce the impending closing of the Washington Monument. Never acknowledge that cuts might be accommodated by your agency without reducing basic services.

vices," "contractual services," "travel," "supplies," "equipment." It is difficult to tell from such a listing exactly what programs the agency is spending its money on. Such a budget obscures policy decisions by hiding programs behind meaningless phrases. Even if these categories are broken down into line items (for example, under "personnel services," the line-item budget might say, "John Doaks, Assistant Administrator, $85,000"), it is still next to impossible to identify the costs of various programs.

For many years, reformers have called for budgeting by programs. **Program budgeting** would require agencies to present budgetary requests in terms of the end products they will produce or at least to allocate each expense to a specific program. However, bureaucrats are often unenthusiastic about program budgeting; it certainly adds to the time and energy devoted to budgeting, and many agencies are reluctant to describe precisely what it is they do and how much it really costs to do it. Moreover, some political functions are best served by *non*program budgeting. Agreement comes more easily when the items in dispute can be treated in dollars instead of programmatic differences. Congressional Appropriations Committees can focus on increases or decreases in overall dollar amounts for agencies

program budgeting Identifying items in a budget according to the functions and programs they are to be spent on.

WHAT DO YOU THINK?

How Much Money Does the Government Waste?

Bureaucracy is often associated in the public's mind with waste and inefficiency. But it is very difficult to determine objectively how much money government really wastes. People disagree on the value of various government programs. What is "waste" to one person may be a vital governmental function to another. But even those who believe a government program is necessary may still believe some of the money going to that program is wasted by the bureaucracy.

Indeed, over the last twenty years, nearly two-thirds of Americans have described the government as wasting "a lot" of money rather than "some" or "not very much" (see graph). Americans believe that there is more waste in domestic spending than in military spending.

Is public opinion correct in estimating that "a lot" of money is wasted? The General Accounting Office is an arm of Congress with broad authority to audit the operations and finances of federal agencies. GAO audits have frequently found fraud and mismanagement amounting to 10 percent or more of the spending of many agencies it has reviewed, which suggests that *$200 billion* of the overall federal budget of $2.1 trillion may be wasted.* Citizens' commissions studying the federal bureaucracy place an even higher figure on waste. The Grace Commission estimated waste at more than 20 percent of federal spending.†

*General Accounting Office, *Federal Evaluation Issues* (Washington, D.C., 1989).

† *President's Private Sector Survey on Cost Control* (Grace Commission Report) (Washington, D.C.: Government Printing Office, 1984).

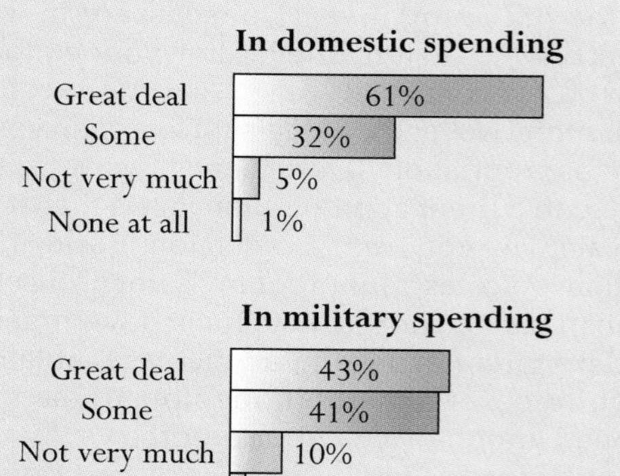

Source: Copyright © 2001, *The Washington Post*, Reprinted with permission.

rather than battle over even more contentious questions of which individual programs are worthy of support.

THINK AGAIN

Do you believe that the overall costs of federal regulatory activity are justified by the benefits?

THINK AGAIN

Do you believe bureaucratic regulations of all kinds are hurting America's competitiveness in the global economy?

Regulatory Battles

Bureaucracies regulate virtually every aspect of American life. Interest rates on loans are heavily influenced by the Federal Reserve Board. The National Labor Relations Board protects unions and prohibits "unfair labor practices." Safety in automobiles and buses is the responsibility of the National Transportation Safety Board. The Federal Deposit Insurance Corporation insures bank accounts. The Federal Trade Commission orders cigarette manufacturers to place a health warning on each pack. The Equal Employment Opportunity Commission investigates complaints about racial and sexual discrimination in jobs. The Consumer Product Safety Commission requires that toys be large enough that they cannot be swallowed by children. The Federal Communications Commission bans tobacco advertisements on television. The Environmental Protection Agency requires automobile companies to limit exhaust emissions. The Occupational Safety and Health Administration requires construction firms to place portable toilets at work sites. The Food and Drug Administration decides what drugs your doctor can prescribe. The list goes on and on. Indeed, it is difficult to find an activity in public or private life that is not regulated by the federal government (see *A Conflicting View:* "Bureaucratic Regulations Are Suffocating America").

Federal regulatory bureaucracies are legislators, investigators, prosecutors, judges, and juries—all wrapped into one. They issue thousands of pages of rules and regulations each year, they investigate thousands of complaints and conduct thousands of inspections; they require businesses to submit hundreds of thousands of forms each year; they hold hearings, determine "compliance" and "noncompliance," issue corrective orders, and levy fines and penalties. Most economists agree that regulation adds to the cost of living, is an obstacle to innovation and productivity, and hinders economic competition. Most regulatory commissions are independent; they are not under an executive department, and their members are appointed for long terms by a president who has little control over their activities.

Traditional Agencies: Capture Theory The **capture theory of regulation** describes how some regulated industries come to benefit from government regulation and how some regulatory commissions come to represent the industries they are supposed to regulate rather than representing "the people." Historically, regulatory commissions have acted against only the most wayward members of an industry. By attacking those businesses that gave the industry bad publicity, the commissions actually helped improve the public's opinion of the industry as a whole. Regulatory commissions provided symbolic reassurance to the public that the behavior of the industry was proper. Among the traditional regulatory agencies that have been accused of becoming too close to their regulated industry are the Federal Communications Commission (FCC, the communications industry, including the television networks), the Securities and Exchange Commission (SEC, the securities industry and stock exchanges), the Federal Reserve Board (FRB, the banking industry), and National Labor Relations Board (NLRB, unions).

Commission members often come from the industry they are supposed to regulate, and after a few years in government, the "regulators" return to high-paying jobs in the industry, creating the *revolving door problem* described in Chapter 9. In addition, many regulatory commissions attract young attorneys fresh from law school to their staffs. Industry siphons off the "best and the brightest" of these, offering them much higher paying jobs as defenders against government regulation. Over the years, then, some industries have come to support their regulatory bureaucracies. Industries have often strongly opposed proposals to reduce government controls. Proposals to deregulate railroads, interstate trucking, and airlines have met with substantial opposition from both the regulatory bureaucracies and the regulated industries, working together.

The Newer Regulators: The Activists In recent decades, Congress created several new "activist" regulatory agencies in response to the civil rights movement, the environmental movement, and the consumer protection movement. Unlike traditional regulatory agencies, the activist agencies do not regulate only a single industry; rather, they extend their jurisdiction to all industries. The Equal Employment Opportunity Commission (EEOC), the Environmental Protection Agency (EPA), and the Occupational Safety and Health Administration (OSHA) pose serious challenges to the business community. Many businesspeople argue that

capture theory of regulation
Theory describing how some regulated industries come to benefit from government regulation and how some regulatory commissions come to represent the industries they are supposed to regulate rather than representing "the people."

A CONFLICTING VIEW

Bureaucratic Regulations Are Suffocating America

Today, bureaucratic regulations of all kinds—environmental controls, workplace safety rules, municipal building codes, government contracting guidelines—have become so numerous, detailed, and complex that they are stifling initiative, curtailing economic growth, wasting billions of dollars, and breeding popular contempt for law and government.

Consider, for example, the Environmental Protection Agency's rules and regulations, now *seventeen volumes* of fine print. Under one set of rules, before any land on which "toxic" waste was once used can be reused by anyone for any purpose, it must be cleaned to near perfect purity. The dirt must be made cleaner than soil that has never been used for anything. The result is that most new businesses choose to locate on virgin land rather than incur the enormous expense of cleaning dirt, and a great deal of land previously used by industry sits vacant while new land is developed.

These and similar examples of "the death of common sense" in bureaucratic regulations are set forth by critic Philip K. Howard, who argues, "We have constructed a system of regulatory law that basically outlaws common sense."* The result is that we direct our energy and wealth into defensive measures, designed not to improve our lives but to avoid tripping over senseless rules. People come to see government as their adversary and government regulations as obstacles in their lives.

The explosive growth in federal regulations in the last two decades has added heavy costs to the American economy. The costs of regulations do not appear in the federal budget: rather, they are paid for by businesses, employees, and consumers. Indeed, politicians prefer a regulatory approach to the environment, health, and safety precisely because it forces costs on the private sector—costs that are largely invisible to voters and taxpayers. Yet as the costs of regulation multiply for American businesses, the prices of their products rise in world markets.

How large is the regulatory bill? Proponents of a regulatory activity usually object to estimating its cost. Politicians who wish to develop an image as protectors of the environment, of consumers, of the disabled, and so on, do not want to call attention to the costs of their legislation. Only recently has the Office of Management and Budget (OMB) even attempted to estimate the costs of federal regulatory activity. Overall, regulatory activity costs Americans between $300 billion (OMB estimate) and $700 billion a year (estimate by Center for the Study of American Business), an amount equal to over one-third of the total federal budget. If the $700 billion estimate is correct, it means that each of America's 100 million households pays about $7,000 per year in the hidden costs of regulation. Paperwork requirements consume more than 5 billion hours of people's time, mostly to comply with the administration by the Internal Revenue Service of the tax laws. However, the costs of environmental controls, including the Environmental Protection Agency's enforcement of clean air and water and hazardous waste disposal regulations, are the fastest growing regulatory costs.

The real question is whether the *benefits* of this regulatory activity—for example, cleaner air and water, safer disposal of toxic wastes, safer consumer products, fewer workplace injuries, fewer highway deaths, protections against discrimination, improved access for disabled, and so on—are greater or less than the costs. But assessing the value of benefits is extraordinarily difficult. Many people object on ethical grounds to economic estimates of the value of a human life saved.

Regulation also places a heavy burden on innovations and productivity. The costs and delays in winning permission for a new product tend to discourage invention and to drive up prices. For example, new drugs are difficult to introduce in the United States because the Food and Drug Administration (FDA) typically requires up to ten years of testing. Western European nations are many years ahead in their number of life-saving drugs available; they speak of the "drug lag" in the United States. Critics charge that if aspirin were proposed for marketing today, it would not be approved by the FDA. Recently activists have succeeded in speeding up FDA approval of drugs to treat AIDS, but the agency has continued to delay the introduction of drugs to treat other diseases.

*Philip K. Howard. *The Death of Common Sense: How Law Is Suffocating America* (New York: Random House, 1995), pp. 10–11.

EEOC rules designed to prevent racial and sexual discrimination in employment and promotion (affirmative action guidelines) ignore the problems of their industry or their labor market and overlook the costs of training or the availability of qualified minorities. Likewise, many of OSHA's thousands of safety regulations appear costly and ridiculous to people in industry. The complaint about EPA is that it seldom considers the cost of its rulings to business or the consumer. Industry representatives contend that EPA should weigh the costs of its regulations against the benefits to the environment.

The deregulation of the airline industry contributed to the development of the hub-and-spoke system currently used by most airlines to reduce their costs. Here American Airlines aircraft congregate at the airline's hub in Dallas/Fort Worth. Although deregulation has caused fares to decrease on heavily competitive routes, critics charge that it has contributed to higher rates on non-competitive routes.

Deregulation The demand to deregulate American life was politically very popular during President Ronald Reagan's administration in the 1980s. But **deregulation** made only limited progress in curtailing the power of the regulatory bureaucracies. Arguments for deregulation centered on the heavy costs of compliance with regulations, the burdens these costs imposed on innovation and productivity, and the adverse impact of regulatory activity on the global competitiveness of American industry. In 1978 Jimmy Carter succeeded in getting Congress to deregulate the airline industry. Against objections by the industry itself, which *wanted* continued regulation, the Civil Aeronautics Board was stripped of its powers to allocate airline routes to various carriers and to set rates. At the end of 1984, the board went out of existence, the first major regulatory agency ever to be abolished. With the airlines free to choose where to fly and what to charge, competition on heavily traveled routes (such as from New York to Los Angeles) reduced fares dramatically while prices rose on less traveled routes served by a single airline. Overall the cost of airline travel declined by 25 to 30 percent.[15] Competition caused airline profits to decline and financially weak airlines to declare bankruptcy. Also, during the 1980s the Interstate Commerce Commission (ICC), the first regulatory commission ever established by the federal government, dating from 1887, was stripped of most of its power to set railroad and trucking rates. The ICC itself was finally abolished in 1995. Prices to consumers of railroad and trucking services declined dramatically.

Reregulation Deregulation threatens to diminish politicians' power and to eliminate bureaucrats' jobs. It forces industries to become competitive and diminishes the role of interest group lobbyists. So in the absence of strong popular support for deregulation, pressures to continue and expand regulatory activity will always be strong in Washington.

Airline deregulation brought about a huge increase in airline travel. The airlines doubled their seating capacity and made more efficient use of their aircraft through the development of "hub-and-spoke" networks. Air safety continued to improve; fatalities per millions of miles flown declined; and by taking travelers away from far more dangerous highway travel, overall transportation safety was enhanced. But these favorable outcomes were overshadowed by complaints about congestion at major airports and increased flight delays, especially at peak hours. The major airports are publicly owned, and governments have been very slow in responding to increased air traffic. Congestion and delays are widely publicized, and politicians respond to complaints by calling for reregulation of airline travel.

The political incentives to create new regulatory agencies, grant additional powers to existing agencies, and add to the accumulation of federal regulations are great. Politicians want to be seen "doing something" about any well-publicized problem in America. When the media reports accidents, health scares, environmental dangers, etc., politicians are interviewed for their response, and most feel

deregulation Lifting of government rules and bureaucratic supervision from business and professional activity.

obliged to call for new laws and regulations, with little regard to their likely costs or effectiveness.

Regulating America

Code of Federal Regulations
All 50 titles of federal regulations can be found at the Cornell Law School site.
www.cfr.law.cornell.edu

Federal regulatory agencies continually add more rules to American life. Roughly 4,000 new rules, all with the force of law, are issued by regulatory agencies each year. The Environmental Protection Agency (EPA) leads in making new rules, closely followed by the Internal Revenue Service (IRS) and the Federal Communications Commission (FCC).

Over 50 federal agencies have rule-making power. These agencies must publish proposed rules in the *Federal Register* and allow time for interested groups to "comment" on them. "Major rules," those estimated to cost Americans at least $100 or more per year in compliance, are sent to the Office of Management and Budget before being finalized. In the five-year period 1996–2001, the General Accounting Office of Congress reported that 21,653 *new* final rules were issued. Some 335 of these new rules were listed as "major rules."[16]

Multiplying Regulations Inasmuch as proposed new regulations must be published in the *Federal Register,* the size of this publication is often used as an indicator of overall federal regulatory activity. In 1970, the *Federal Register* included roughly 20,000 pages; by 1980 it had expanded to over 73,000 pages. Only during the presidency of Ronald Reagan, who promised to reduce federal regulatory activity, did the size of the *Federal Register* decline somewhat (see Figure 10.5). But by 2000 it was again over 80,000 pages.

The accumulated regulations of federal government are published in the Code of Federal Regulations. The Code includes all regulations currently in effect. The Code has now expanded to over 144,000 pages in 205 volumes.

The Costs of Regulation Regulatory activity incurs costs for American businesses, employers, and consumers—costs which do not appear in federal budget.

FIGURE 10.5
Regulating America

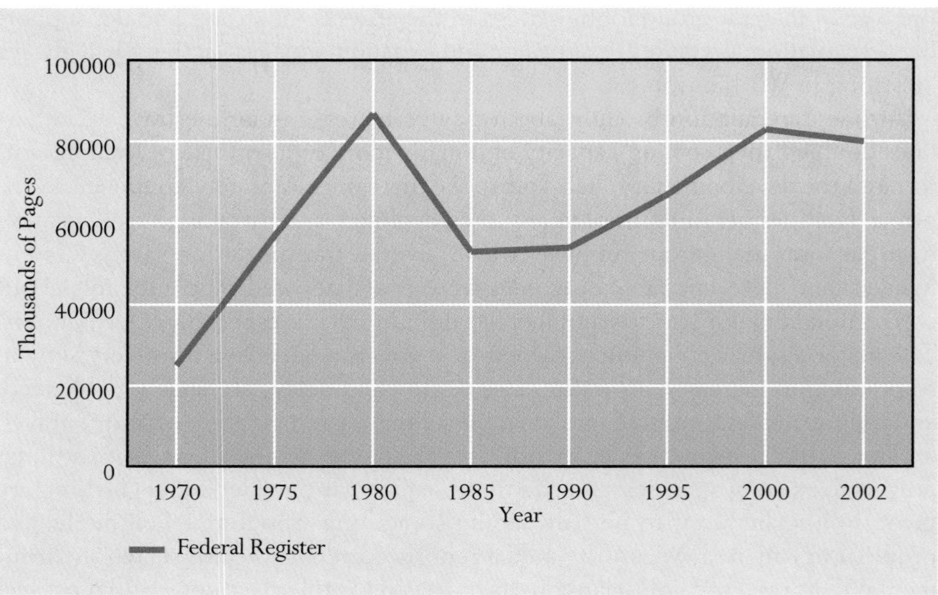

(The official budgets of all federal regulatory agencies combined add up to "only" about $15 billion.) Indeed, it is precisely because these costs do not appear in the federal budget that politicians prefer a regulatory approach to many of the nation's problems. Regulation shifts costs from the government itself onto the private sector, costs that are largely invisible to voters and taxpayers. Even when agencies themselves are supposed to calculate the costs of their regulations, their calculations vary in quality and almost always underestimate the true costs. One independent estimate of the total costs of federal regulation sets the figure at $700 *billion*, or about 7 percent of the nation's Gross Domestic Product.[17]

Regulations impose costs on Americans in a variety of ways. First of all, there are the direct costs of compliance. Direct costs include everything from adding pollution control devices and making businesses accessible to the disabled, to the overhead costs of paperwork, attorney and accounting fees, and staff time needed to negotiate the federal regulatory maze. Secondly, there are indirect economic costs—costs incurred by devoting resources to compliance that otherwise would be used to increase productivity. This lost economic output may amount to *$1 trillion* per year.[18] All of these costs, which typically are imposed on businesses, are ultimately passed onto American consumers in the form of higher prices.

Congressional Constraints on the Bureaucracy

Bureaucracies are unelected hierarchical organizations, yet they must function within democratic government. To wed bureaucracy to democracy, ways must be found to ensure that bureaucracy is responsible to the people. Controlling the bureaucracy is a central concern of democratic government. The federal bureaucracy is responsible to all three branches of government—the president, the Congress, and the courts. Although the president is the nominal head of the executive agencies, Congress—through its power to create or eliminate and fund or fail to fund these agencies—exerts its full share of control. Most of the structure of the executive branch of government (see Figure 10.1) is determined by laws of Congress. Congress has the constitutional power to create or abolish executive departments and independent agencies, or to transfer their functions, as it wishes. Congress can by law expand or contract the discretionary authority of bureaucrats. It can grant broad authority to agencies in vaguely written language, thereby adding to the power of bureaucracies, which can then determine themselves how to define and implement their own authority. In contrast, narrow and detailed laws place constraints on the bureaucracy.

In addition to specific constraints on particular agencies, Congress has placed a number of general constraints on the entire federal bureaucracy. Among the more important laws governing bureaucratic behavior are these:

- *Administrative Procedures Act (1946)*: Requires that agencies considering a new rule or policy give public notice in the *Federal Register*, solicit comments, and hold public hearings before adopting the new measures.
- *Freedom of Information Act (1966)*: Requires agencies to allow citizens (and the media) to inspect all public records, with some exceptions for intelligence, current criminal investigations, and personnel actions (see *Up Close*: "How to Use the Freedom of Information Act").
- *Privacy Act (1974)*: Requires agencies to keep confidential the personal records of individuals, notably their Social Security files and income tax records.

The Director of the Office of Management and Budget is one of the most influential bureaucrats in Washington. Yet he is seldom seen on national television. Here, President Bush's OMB Director Jushua B. Bolten testifies before a congressional committee.

UP CLOSE

How to Use the Freedom of Information Act

The Freedom of Information Act (FOIA) of 1966 requires agencies of the federal government to provide any member of the public records of the agencies. As amended by the Privacy Act of 1974, individuals can obtain personal records held by government agencies and are given the right to correct information that is inaccurate. The FOIA does not apply to Congress, the federal courts, state and local government agencies (unless a state has similar law), military plans and weapons, law enforcement investigations, records of financial institutions, or records which would invade the privacy of others. An agency must respond within ten days to an FOIA request, but it may charge fees for the costs of searching for the documents and duplicating them.

A good request must "reasonably describe" the records that are being sought; it must be specific enough that an agency employee will be able to locate the records within a reasonable amount of time. A good FOIA request letter includes:

Attention: Freedom of Information/Privacy Request
Name and Address of Agency

This is a request under the Freedom of Information Act, 5 U.S.C. Sec.552

I request a copy of the following documents be provided for me.

____

____

I am aware that if my request is denied I am entitled to know the grounds for this denial and make an administrative appeal.

I am willing to pay fees for this request up to a maximum of $___. If you estimate that fees will succeed this limit, please inform me first.

Thank you for your prompt attention.

Signature

Address

Senate Confirmation of Appointments The U.S. Senate's power to confirm presidential appointments gives it some added influence over the bureaucracy.[19] It is true that once nominated and confirmed, cabinet secretaries and regulatory commission members can defy the Congress; only the president can remove them from office. Senators usually try to impress their own views on presidential appointees seeking confirmation, however. Senate committees holding confirmation hearings often subject appointees to lengthy lectures on how the members believe their departments or agencies should be run. In extreme cases, when presidential appointees do not sufficiently reflect the views of Senate leaders, their confirmation can be held up indefinitely or, in very rare cases, defeated in a floor vote on confirmation.

Congressional Oversight Congressional oversight of the federal bureaucracy is a continuing activity.[20] Congress justifies its oversight activities on the ground that its lawmaking powers require it to determine whether the purposes of the laws it passed are being carried out. Congress has a legitimate interest in communicating legislative *intent* to bureaucrats charged with the responsibility for implementing laws of Congress. But often oversight activities are undertaken to influence bureaucratic decision making. Members of Congress may seek to secure favorable treatment for friends and constituents, try to lay the political groundwork for increases or decreases in agency appropriations, or simply strive to enhance their own power or the power of their committees or subcommittees over the bureaucracy.

Oversight is lodged primarily in congressional committees and subcommittees (see "In Committee" in Chapter 8) whose jurisdictions generally parallel those of executive departments and agencies. However, all too frequently, agencies are required to respond to multiple committee inquiries in both the House and the Senate.

Congressional Appropriations The congressional power to grant or to withhold the budget requests of bureaucracies and the president is perhaps Congress's most potent weapon in controlling the bureaucracy. Spending authorizations for executive agencies are determined by standing committees with jurisdiction in various policy areas, such as armed services, judiciary, education, and labor (see Table 8.4 in Chapter 8), and appropriations are determined by the House and Senate Appropriations Committees and, more specifically, their subcommittees with particular jurisdictions. These committees and subcommittees exercise great power over executive agencies. The Defense Department, for example, must seek *authorizations* for new weapons systems from the House and Senate Armed Services Committees and *appropriations* to actually purchase these weapons from the House and Senate Appropriations Committees, especially their Defense Appropriations subcommittees.

Lobbying Washington can take many forms. Although most professional lobbyists operate quietly within the balls of the nation's capital, groups of private citizens often take to the streets to get their message across. Demonstrations may capture the attention of the media and thus may force bureaucrats and politicians at least to consider a group's cause, but the attention span of both media and Washington power brokers can be extremely short. Here people protest in front of the White House against President Clinton's decision to back NATO air attacks on Serbia.

Congressional Investigation Congressional investigations offer yet another tool for congressional oversight of the bureaucracy. Historically, congressional investigations have focused on scandal and wrongdoing in the executive branch (see "Oversight of the Bureaucracy" in Chapter 8). Occasionally, investigations even produce corrective legislation, although they more frequently produce changes in agency personnel, procedures, or policies. Investigations are more likely to follow media reports of waste, fraud, or scandal than to uncover previously unknown problems. In other words, investigations perform a political function for Congress—assuring voters that the Congress is taking action against bureaucratic abuses. Studies of routine bureaucratic performance are likely to be undertaken by the General Accounting Office (GAO), an arm of Congress and frequent critic of executive agencies. GAO may undertake studies of the operations of executive agencies on its own initiative but more often responds to requests for studies by specific members of Congress.

Casework Perhaps the most frequent congressional oversight activities are calls, letters, and visits to the agencies by individual members of Congress seeking to influence particular actions on behalf of themselves or their constituents. A great deal of congressional **casework** involves intervening with executive agencies on behalf of constituents[21] (see Chapter 8). Executive departments and agencies generally try to deal with congressional requests and inquiries as favorably and rapidly as the law allows. Pressure from a congressional office will lead bureaucrats to speed up an application, correct an error, send information, review a case, or reinterpret a regulation to favor a client with congressional contacts. But bureaucrats become very uncomfortable when asked to violate established regulations on behalf of a favored person or firm. The line between serving constituents and unethical or illegal attempts to influence government agencies is sometimes very difficult to discern.

casework Services performed by legislators and their staffs on behalf of individual constituents.

Interest Groups and Bureaucratic Decision Making

Interest groups understand that great power is lodged in the bureaucracy. Indeed, interest groups exercise an even closer oversight of bureaucracy than do the president, Congress, and courts, largely because their interests are directly affected by day-to-day bureaucratic decisions. Interest groups focus their attention on the particular departments and agencies that serve or regulate their own members or that function in their chosen policy field. For example, the American Farm Bureau Federation monitors the actions of the Department of Agriculture; environmental lobbies—such as the National Wildlife Federation, the Sierra Club, and the Environmental Defense Fund—watch over the Environmental Protection Agency as well as the National Park Service; the American Legion, Veterans of Foreign Wars, and Vietnam Veterans "oversee" the Department of Veterans Affairs. Thus, specific groups come to have a proprietary interest in "their" specific departments and agencies. Departments and agencies understand that their "client" groups have a continuing interest in their activities.

Many bureaucracies owe their very existence to strong interest groups that successfully lobbied Congress to create them. The Environmental Protection Agency owes its existence to the environmental groups, just as the Equal Employment Opportunity Commission owes its existence to civil rights groups. Thus, many bureaucracies nourish interest groups' support to aid in expanding their authority and increasing their budgets.

Interest groups can lobby bureaucracies directly by responding to notices of proposed regulations, testifying at public hearings, and providing information and commentary. Or interest groups can lobby Congress either in support of bureaucratic activity or to reverse a bureaucratic decision. Interest groups may also seek to "build fires" under bureaucrats by holding press conferences, undertaking advertising campaigns, and soliciting media support for agency actions. Or interest groups may even seek to influence bureaucracies through appeals to the federal courts.

Judicial Constraints on the Bureaucracy

Judicial oversight is another source of restraint on the bureaucracy. Bureaucratic decisions are subject to review by the federal courts. Federal courts can even issue *injunctions* (orders) to an executive agency *before* it issues or enforces a regulation or undertakes a particular action. Thus, the judiciary poses a check on bureaucratic power.

Judicial Standards for Bureaucratic Behavior Historically, the courts have stepped in when agency actions have violated laws passed by Congress, when agencies have exceeded the authority granted them under the laws, when the agency actions have been adjudged "arbitrary and unreasonable," and when agencies have failed in their legal duties under the law. The courts have also restrained the bureaucracy on procedural grounds—ensuring proper notice, fair hearings, rights of appeal, and so on. In short, appeal to the courts must cite failures of agencies to abide by substantive or procedural laws.

Judicial oversight tends to focus on (1) whether or not agencies are acting beyond the authority granted them by Congress; and (2) whether or not they are abiding by rules of procedural fairness. It is important to realize that the courts do not usually involve themselves in the *policy* decisions of bureaucracies. If policy decisions are made in accordance with the legal authority granted agencies by Congress, and if they are made with procedural fairness, the courts generally do not intervene.

Bureaucrats' Success in Court Bureaucracies have been very successful in defending their actions in federal courts.[22] individual citizens and interest groups seeking to restrain or reverse the actions or decisions of executive agencies have been largely *unsuccessful*. What accounts for this success? Bureaucracies have established elaborate administrative processes to protect their decisions from challenge on procedural grounds. Regulatory agencies have armies of attorneys, paid for out of tax monies, who specialize in these narrow fields of law. It is very expensive for individual citizens to challenge agency actions. Corporations and interest groups must weigh the costs of litigation against the costs of compliance before undertaking a legal challenge of the bureaucracy. Excessive delays in court proceedings, sometimes extending to several years, add to the time and expense of challenging bureaucratic decisions.

SUMMARY NOTES

- The Washington bureaucracy—the departments, agencies, and bureaus of the executive branch of the federal government—is a major base of power in American government. Political conflict does not end when a law is passed by Congress and signed by the president. The arena merely shifts to the bureaucracy.
- Bureaucratic power has grown with increases in the size of government, advances in technology, and the greater complexity of modern society. Congress and the president do not have the time, resources, or expertise to decide the details of policy across the wide range of social and economic activity in the nation. Bureaucracies must draw up the detailed rules and regulations that actually govern the nation. Often laws are passed for their symbolic value; bureaucrats must give practical meaning to these laws. And the bureaucracy itself is now sufficiently powerful to get laws passed adding to its authority, size, and budget.
- Policy implementation is the development of procedures and activities and the allocation of money, personnel, and other resources to carry out the tasks mandated by law. Implementation includes regulation—the making of detailed rules based on the law—as well as adjudication—the application of laws and regulations to specific cases. Bureaucratic power increases with increases in administrative discretion.
- Bureaucracies usually seek to expand their own powers, functions, and budgets. Most bureaucrats believe strongly in the value of their own programs and the importance of their tasks. And bureaucrats, like everyone else, seek added power, pay, and prestige. Bureaucratic expansion contributes to the growth of government.
- The federal bureaucracy consists of 2.8 million civilian employees in 14 cabinet departments and more than 60 independent agencies, as well as a large Executive Office of the President. Federal employment is not growing, but federal spending, especially for Social Security, Medicare, and Medicaid, is growing rapidly.
- Today federal spending amounts to about 20 percent of GDP, and federal, state, and local government spending combined amounts to about 30 percent of GDP.
- Historically, political conflict over government employment centered on the question of partisanship versus competence. Over time, the "merit system" replaced the "spoils system" in federal employment, but the civil service system raised problems of responsiveness and productivity in the bureaucracy. Civil service reform efforts have not really resolved these problems.
- The president's control of the bureaucracy rests principally on the powers to appoint and remove policy-making officials, to recommend increases and decreases in

agency budgets, and to recommend changes in agency structure and function.

- But the bureaucracy has developed various means to insulate itself from presidential influence. Bureaucrats have many ways to delay and obstruct policy decisions with which they disagree. Whistle-blowers may inform Congress or the media of waste, mismanagement, or fraud. A network of friends and professional associates among bureaucrats, congressional staffs, and client groups helps create a "culture" within each agency and department. The bureaucratic culture is highly resistant to change.
- Women and minorities are represented in overall federal employment in proportion to their percentages of the U.S. population. However, women and minorities are not proportionately represented in the higher levels of the bureaucracy.
- Budget battles over who gets what begin in the bureaucracy as departments and agencies send their budget requests forward to the president's Office of Management and Budget. OMB usually reduces agency requests in line with the president's priorities. The president submits spending recommendations to Congress early each year in *The Budget of the United States Government.* Congress is supposed to pass its appropriations acts prior to the beginning of the fiscal year, October 1, but frequently falls behind schedule.
- Budgeting is incremental, in that last year's agency expenditures are usually accepted as a base and attention is focused on proposed increases. Incrementalism saves time and effort and reduces political conflict by not requiring agencies to justify every dollar spent, only proposed increases each year. Nonprogrammatic budgeting also helps reduce conflict over the value of particular programs. The result, however, is that many established programs continue long after the need for them has disappeared.
- Bureaucracies regulate virtually every aspect of our lives. The costs of regulation are borne primarily by business and consumers; they do not appear in the federal budget. In part for this reason, a regulatory approach to national problems appeals to elected officials who seek to obscure the costs of government activity. It is difficult to calculate the true costs and benefits of much regulatory activity. After a brief period of deregulation in the 1980s, regulation has regained popular favor.
- Congress can exercise control over the bureaucracy in a variety of ways: by creating, abolishing, or reorganizing departments and agencies; by altering their authority and functions; by requiring bureaucrats to testify before congressional committees; by undertaking investigations and studies through the General Accounting Office; by intervening directly on behalf of constituents; by instructing presidential nominees in Senate confirmation hearings and occasionally delaying or defeating nominations; and especially by withholding or threatening to withhold agency appropriations or by writing very specific provisions into appropriations acts.
- Interest groups also influence bureaucratic decision making directly by testifying at public hearings and providing information and commentary, and indirectly by contacting the media, lobbying Congress, and initiating lawsuits.
- Judicial control of the bureaucracy is usually limited to determining whether agencies have exceeded the authority granted them by law or have abided by the rules of procedural fairness. Federal bureaucracies have a strong record of success in defending themselves in court.

KEY TERMS

bureaucracy 342
chain of command 342
division of labor 342
impersonality 342
implementation 342
regulation 345
adjudication 345
budget maximization 346
discretionary funds 346
spoils system 357
merit system 357
whistle-blower 361
fiscal year 363
budget resolution 363
authorization 365
appropriations act 365
obligational authority 365
outlays 365
continuing resolution 365
incremental budgeting 366
zero-based budgeting 366
program budgeting 367
capture theory of regulation 369
deregulation 371
casework 375

SUGGESTED READINGS

Gore, Al. *Creating a Government That Works Better and Costs Less.* Washington, D.C.: Government Printing Office, 1993. Specific recommendations for "reinventing" government by making citizens "customers," introducing competition, cutting red tape, and privatizing government services.

Henry, Nicholas. *Public Administration and Public Affairs.* 9th ed. Upper Saddle River, N. J.: Prentice Hall, 2003. Authoritative introductory textbook on public organizations (bureaucracies), public management, and policy implementation.

Howard, Philip K. *The Death of Common Sense: How Law Is Suffocating America.* New York: Random House, 1995. Outrageous stories of bureaucratic senselessness coupled with a plea to allow bureaucrats flexibility in achieving the purposes of laws and holding them accountable for outcomes.

Maxwell, Bruce. *CQ's Insider's Guide to Finding a Job in Washington.* Washington, D.C.: CQ Press, 2000. How to locate job vacancies, make contacts, "market" oneself, and build a career in the Washington bureaucracy.

Neiman, Max. *Defending Government: Why Big Government Works.* Upper Saddle River, N. J.: Prentice Hall, 2000. A spirited defense of big government as a product of people's desire to improve their lives.

Osborne, David, and Ted Gaebler. *Reinventing Government.* New York: Addison-Wesley, 1992. The respected manual of the "reinventing government" movement with recommendations to overcome the routine tendencies of bureaucracies and inject "the entrepreneurial spirit" in them.

Radin, Beryl. *The Accountable Juggler: The Art of Leadership in a Federal Agency.* Washington, D.C.: CQ Press, 2002. A close-up look at managers in the Department of Health and Human Services, how they juggle competing accountability demands.

Schick, Allen. *The Federal Budget: Politics, Policy, Process.* Rev. ed. Washington, D.C.: Brookings Institution, 2000. A comprehensive explanation of the federal budgetary process.

Shafvitz, Jay M. and E.W. Russell. *Introducing Public Administration.* 3rd ed. New York: Pearson Longman, 2002. Comprehensive introductory textbook in public administration.

Wilson, James Q. *Bureaucracy: What Government Agencies Do and Why They Do It.* New York: Basic Books, 1989. In the author's words, "an effort to depict the essential features of bureaucratic life in the government agencies of the United States." Examining what really motivates middle-level public servants, Wilson argues that congressional attempts to "micromanage" government activities hamper the ability of bureaucrats to do their jobs.

MAKE IT REAL

BUREAUCRACY: A PLACE WHERE IDEALS MEET REALITY

Congratulations on your appointment as Deputy Director of the Census Bureau! With the change in administration you will help to rebuild a bureaucracy that was shaken up during the transition from the previous administration. One of your responsibilities is to shield the Director from the routine problems that arise in any bureaucratic organization. As bureaucratic problems arrive on your desk you must make the decisions that will establish you as a seasoned administrator.

CHAPTER 11

COURTS: JUDICIAL POLITICS

CHAPTER OUTLINE

- **Judicial Power**
- **Activism Versus Self-Restraint**
- **Structure and Jurisdiction of Federal Courts**
- **The Special Rules of Judicial Decision Making**
- **The Politics of Selecting Judges**
- **Who Is Selected?**
- **Supreme Court Decision Making**
- **Politics and the Supreme Court**
- ***Bush v. Gore* in the U.S. Supreme Court**
- **Checking Court Power**

Judicial Power

"There is hardly a political question in the United States which does not sooner or later turn into a judicial one."[1] This observation by French diplomat and traveler Alexis de Tocqueville, although made in 1835, is even more accurate today. It is the Supreme Court and the federal judiciary, rather than the president or Congress, that has taken the lead in deciding many of the most heated issues of American politics. It has undertaken to:

- Eliminate racial segregation and decide about affirmative action.
- Ensure separation of church and state and decide about prayer in public schools.
- Determine the personal liberties of women and decide about abortion.
- Define the limits of free speech and free press and decide about obscenity, censorship, and pornography.
- Ensure equality of representation and require legislative districts to be equal in population.
- Define the rights of criminal defendants, prevent unlawful searches, limit the questioning of suspects, and prevent physical or mental intimidation of suspects.
- Protect private homosexual acts between consenting adults from criminal prosecution.
- Decide the life-or-death issue of capital punishment.

Courts are "political" institutions. Like Congress, the president, and the bureaucracy courts decide who gets what in American society. Judges do not merely "apply" the law to specific cases. Years ago, former Supreme Court Justice Felix Frankfurter explained why this mechanistic theory of judicial objectivity fails to describe court decision making.

> The meaning of "due process" and the content of terms like "liberty" are not revealed by the Constitution. It is the Justices who make the meaning. They read into the neutral language of the Constitution their own economic and social views. . . . Let us face the fact that five Justices of the Supreme Court are the molders of policy rather than the impersonal vehicles of revealed truth.[2]

THINK ABOUT POLITICS

1 Have the federal courts grown too powerful?
Yes ● No ●

2 Is it really democratic to allow federal court judges, who are appointed, not elected, and who serve for life, to overturn laws of an elected Congress and president?
Yes ● No ●

3 Should the Constitution be interpreted in terms of the original intentions of the Founders rather than the morality of society today?
Yes ● No ●

4 Are the costs of lawsuits in America becoming too burdensome on the economy?
Yes ● No ●

5 Should presidents appoint only judges who agree with their judicial philosophy?
Yes ● No ●

6 Should the Senate confirm Supreme Court appointees who oppose abortion?
Yes ● No ●

7 Should the Supreme Court overturn the law of Congress that prohibits federal funding of abortions for poor women?
Yes ● No ●

8 Is there a need to appoint special prosecutors to investigate presidents and other high officials?
Yes ● No ●

Do the Supreme Court and the federal judiciary in fact have the real power to shape public policies in the United States?

THINK AGAIN

Have the federal courts grown too powerful?

Constitutional Power of the Courts The Constitution grants "the judicial Power of the United States" to the Supreme Court and other "inferior Courts" that Congress may establish. The Constitution guarantees that the Supreme Court and federal judiciary will be politically independent: judges are appointed, not elected, and hold their appointments for life (barring commission of any impeachable offenses). It also guarantees that their salaries will not be reduced during their time in office. The Constitution goes on to list the kinds of cases and controversies that the federal courts may decide. Federal judicial power extends to any case arising under the Constitution and federal laws and treaties, to cases in which officials of the federal government or of foreign governments are a party, and to cases between states or between citizens of different states.

Interpreting the Constitution: Judicial Review The Constitution is the "supreme Law of the Land" (Article VI). Judicial power is the power to decide cases and controversies and, in doing so, to decide what the Constitution and laws of Congress really mean. This authority—together with the guaranteed independence of judges—places great power in the Supreme Court and the federal judiciary. Indeed, because the Constitution takes precedence over laws of Congress as well as state constitutions and laws, it is the Supreme Court that ultimately decides whether Congress, the president, the states, and their local governments have acted constitutionally.

The power of **judicial review** is the power to invalidate laws of Congress or of the states that conflict with the U.S. Constitution. Judicial review is not specifically mentioned in the Constitution but has long been inferred from it. Even before the states had approved the Constitution, Alexander Hamilton wrote in 1787 that "limited government . . . can be preserved in practice no other way than through the medium of courts of justice, whose duty it is to declare all acts contrary to the manifest tenor of the Constitution void."[3] But it was the historic decision of *Marbury v. Madison* (1803)[4] that officially established judicial review as the most important judicial check on congressional power (see *People in Politics:* "John Marshall and Early Supreme Court Politics"). Writing for the majority, Chief Justice Marshall constructed a classic statement in judicial reasoning as he proceeded step by step to infer judicial review from the Constitution's Supremacy (Article VI) and Judicial Power (Article III, Section 1) clauses:

- The Constitution is the supreme law of the land, binding on all branches of government: legislative, executive, and judicial.
- The Constitution deliberately establishes a government with limited powers.
- Consequently, "an act of the legislature repugnant to the Constitution is void." If this were not true, the government would be unchecked and the Constitution would be an absurdity.
- Under the judicial power, "It is emphatically the province and duty of each of the judicial departments to say what the law is."
- "So if a law be in opposition to the Constitution . . . the court must determine which of these conflicting rules governs the case. This is the very essence of judicial duty."
- "If, then, the courts are to regard the Constitution, and the Constitution is superior to any ordinary act of the legislature, the Constitution, and not such ordinary act, must govern the case to which they both apply."

judicial review Power of the courts, especially the Supreme Court, to declare laws of Congress, laws of the states, and actions of the president unconstitutional and invalid.

PEOPLE IN POLITICS

John Marshall and Early Supreme Court Politics

John Marshall was a dedicated Federalist. A prominent Virginia lawyer, he was elected a delegate to Virginia's Constitution-ratifying convention, where he was instrumental in winning his state's approval of the document in 1788. Later Marshall served as secretary of state in the administration of John Adams, where he came into conflict with Adams's vice president, Thomas Jefferson.

In the election of 1800, Jefferson's Democratic-Republicans crushed Adams's Federalist Party. But Adams, taking advantage of the fact that his term of office would not expire until the following March,* sought to pack the federal judiciary with Federalists. The lame duck Federalist majority in the Senate confirmed the appointments, and John Marshall was sworn in as Chief Justice of the Supreme Court on February 4, 1801. Many of these "midnight appointments" came at the very last hours of Adams's term of office.

At that time, a specified task of the secretary of state was to deliver judicial commissions to new judges. When Marshall left his position as secretary of state to become Chief Justice, several of these commissions were still undelivered. Jefferson and the Democratic-Republicans were enraged over this last-minute Federalist chicanery, so when Jefferson assumed office in March, he ordered his new secretary of state, James Madison, not to deliver the remaining commissions. William Marbury, one of the disappointed Federalist appointees, brought a lawsuit to the Supreme Court, asking it to issue a writ of mandamus ("we command") to James Madison, ordering him to do his duty and deliver the valid commission.

The Judiciary Act of 1789, which established the federal court system, had included a provision granting original jurisdiction to the Supreme Court to issue writs of mandamus. The case, therefore, came directly to new Chief Justice John Marshall, who had failed to deliver the commission in the first place. (Today, we expect justices who are personally involved in a case to "recuse" themselves—that is, not to participate in that case, allowing the other justices to make the decision—but Marshall's actions were typical of his time.)

John Marshall realized that if he issued a direct order to Madison to deliver the commission, Madison would probably ignore it. The Court had no way to enforce such an order, and Madison had the support of President Jefferson. Issuing the writ would create a constitutional crisis in which the Supreme Court would most likely lose power. But if the Court failed to pronounce Madison's actions unlawful, it would lose legitimacy.

Marshall resolved his political dilemma with a brilliant judicial ploy. Writing for the majority in *Marbury v. Madison,* he announced that Madison was wrong to withhold the commission but that the Supreme Court could not issue a writ of mandamus because Section 13 of the Judiciary Act of 1789, which gave the Court *original* jurisdiction in the case, was unconstitutional. Giving the Supreme Court *original* jurisdiction conflicted with Article III, Section 2, of the Constitution, which gives the Supreme Court original jurisdiction only in cases affecting "Ambassadors, other public Ministers and Consuls, and those in which a State shall be a Party." "In all other Cases," the Constitution states that the Court shall have appellate jurisdiction. Thus Section 13 of the Judiciary Act was unconstitutional.

By declaring part of an act of Congress unconstitutional, Marshall accomplished multiple political objectives. He avoided a showdown with the executive branch that would undoubtedly have weakened the Court. He left Jefferson and Madison with no Court order to disobey. At the same time, Marshall forced Jefferson and the Democratic-Republicans to acknowledge the Supreme Court's power of judicial review—the power to declare an act of Congress unconstitutional. (To do otherwise would have meant acknowledging Marbury's claim.) Thus Marshall sacrificed Marbury's commission to a greater political goal, enhancing the Supreme Court's power.

* Not until the adoption of the Twentieth Amendment in 1933 was the president's inauguration moved up to January.

- Hence, if a law is repugnant to the Constitution, the judges are duty bound to declare that law void in order to uphold the supremacy of the Constitution.

Arguments over Judicial Review The power of the federal courts to invalidate *state* laws and constitutions that conflict with federal laws or the federal Constitution is easily defended. Article VI states that the Constitution and federal laws and treaties are the supreme law of the land, "any Thing in the Constitution or Laws of any State to the Contrary notwithstanding." Indeed, the Constitution specifically obligates state judges to be "bound" by the Constitution and federal laws and to give these documents precedence over state constitutions and laws in rendering decisions. Federal court power over state decisions is probably essential to maintaining national unity: fifty different state interpretations of the meaning of the Constitution or of the laws and treaties of Congress would create unimaginable confusion. Thus the power of federal judicial review over state constitutions, laws, and court decisions is seldom questioned.

Today, the power of federal courts to invalidate laws of Congress and actions of the president is also widely accepted. No serious challenge to the power of judicial review has emerged in American politics. But we still might ask: Why should an appointed court's interpretation of the Constitution prevail over the views of an elected Congress and an elected president? Members of Congress and presidents swear to uphold the Constitution, and we can assume they do not pass laws they believe to be unconstitutional. Because both houses of Congress and the president must approve laws, why should federal courts be allowed to set aside these decisions? Is not judicial review, especially by unelected justices appointed for life, undemocratic?

Judicial Review of Laws of Congress Judicial review is potentially the most powerful weapon in the hands of the Supreme Court. It enables the Court to assert its power over the Congress, the president, and the states and to substitute its own judgment for that of other branches of the federal government and the states. However, the Supreme Court has been fairly restrained in its use of judicial review to void acts of Congress. Prior to the Civil War, the Supreme Court invalidated very few laws of any kind. Since that time, however, the general trend has been for the U.S. Supreme Court to strike down more *state* laws as unconstitutional. In contrast, the Court has been relatively restrained in its rejection of *federal* laws; over two centuries the Court has struck down fewer than 150 of the more than 60,000 laws passed by Congress.

Nevertheless, some of the laws overturned by the Supreme Court have been very important. In *Buckley v. Valeo* (1976)[5] the Court struck down provisions of the Federal Election Campaign Act that had limited the amount individuals could spend to finance their own campaigns or express their own independent political views. In *United States v. Morrison* (2000), the Supreme Court struck down Congress's Violence Against Women Act[6] as an unconstitutional expansion of the interstate commerce power and an invasion of powers reserved to the states (see *Up Close:* "Is Violence Against Women a Federal Crime?" in Chapter 4). Overall, however, the Supreme Court's use of judicial review against the Congress has been restrained.

Judicial Review of Presidential Actions The Supreme Court has only rarely challenged presidential power. The Court has overturned presidential policies both on the grounds that they conflicted with laws of Congress and on the grounds that they conflicted with the Constitution. In *Ex parte Milligan* (1866)[7] for example, the Court held (somewhat belatedly) that President Abraham Lincoln could not suspend the writ of habeas corpus in rebellious states during the Civil

UP CLOSE

William Jefferson Clinton Versus Paula Corbin Jones

The president is not "above the law"; that is, his conduct is not immune from judicial scrutiny. The president's official conduct must be lawful; federal courts may reverse presidential actions found to be unconstitutional or violative of laws of Congress. And presidents are not immune from criminal prosecution; they cannot ignore demands to provide information in criminal cases.* However, the Supreme Court has held that the president has "absolute immunity" from civil suits "arising out of the execution of official duties."† In other words, the president cannot be sued for damages caused by actions or decisions that are within his constitutional or legal authority.

But can the president be sued for *private* conduct beyond the scope of his official duties? In 1994 Paula Corbin Jones sued William Jefferson Clinton in federal district court in Arkansas, alleging that he made "abhorrent" sexual advances toward her in Little Rock in 1991 while he was governor and she was a state employee.

The president's lead attorney, Robert Bennett (brother of conservative commentator and former Reagan cabinet official William Bennett), stated that Clinton "has no recollection of ever meeting this woman" and "did not engage in any inappropriate or sexual conduct with this woman." But the president's defense team also argued that the president should be immune from civil actions, especially those arising from events alleged to occur *before* he assumed office. They argued that the president's constitutional responsibilities are so important and demanding that he must devote his undivided time and attention to them. He cannot be distracted by civil suits; otherwise a large volume of politically motivated frivolous litigation might undermine his ability to function effectively in office. At the very least, the president's attorney argued, the president should be given "temporary immunity" by postponing the case until after he leaves office.

However, in 1997 the U.S. Supreme Court rejected the notion of presidential immunity (as well as temporary immunity) from civil claims arising from actions outside of the president's official duties. Although advising lower courts to give "utmost deference to Presidential responsibilities" in handling the case, the Court held that "the doctrine of separation of powers does not require federal courts to stay all private actions against the president until he leaves office."‡

Subsequently, after reviewing the case, federal district judge Susan Wright dismissed Jones's charges as insufficient to prove sexual assault or harassment.§ Clinton later settled the case with a financial payment to Jones, but with no admission or apology. The settlement ended Jones's appeals and avoided possible reopening of the case.

*United States v. Nixon (1974).

†Nixon v. Fitzgerald (1982).

‡Clinton v. Jones, May 27, 1997.

§Jones v. Clinton, April 1, 1998.

War. In *Youngstown Sheet and Tube Co. v. Sawyer,* in 1952,[8] it declared President Harry Truman's seizure of the nation's steel mills during the Korean War to be illegal. In 1974 it ordered President Richard Nixon to turn over taped White House conversations to the special Watergate prosecutor, leading to Nixon's forced resignation.[9] And in 1997 the Court held that President Bill Clinton was obliged to respond to a civil suit even while serving in the White House.[10] (See *Up Close:* "William Jefferson Clinton Versus Paula Corbin Jones.")

Judicial Review of State Laws The Supreme Court has used its power of judicial review far more frequently to invalidate state laws. Some of these decisions had impact far beyond the individual states on trial. For example, the historic 1954 decision in *Brown v. Board of Education of Topeka,* declaring segregation of the races in public schools to be unconstitutional, struck down the laws of twenty-one states[11] (see Chapter 10). The 1973 *Roe v. Wade* decision, establishing the constitutional right to abortion, struck down anti-abortion laws in more than forty states.[12] In 2003 the Court again struck down the laws of more than forty states by holding that private homosexual acts by consenting adults were protected by the constitution.[13]

Interpreting Federal Laws The power of the Supreme Court and the federal judiciary does not rest on judicial review alone. The courts also make policy in their interpretation of **statutory laws**—the laws of Congress. Frequently, Congress decides that an issue is too contentious to resolve. Members of Congress cannot themselves agree on specific language, so they write, sometimes deliberately, vague, symbolic language into the law—words and phrases like "fairness," "equitableness," "good faith," "good cause," and "reasonableness"—effectively shifting policy making to the courts by giving courts the power to read meaning into these terms.

Activism Versus Self-Restraint

THINK AGAIN

Is it really democratic to allow federal court judges, who are appointed, not elected, and who serve for life, to overturn laws of an elected Congress and president?

Supreme Court Justice Felix Frankfurter once wrote: "The only check upon our own exercise of power is our own sense of self-restraint. For the removal of unwise laws from the statute books, appeal lies not to the courts but to the ballot and to the processes of democratic government."[14]

Judicial Self-Restraint The idea behind **judicial self-restraint** is that judges should not read their own philosophies into the Constitution and should avoid direct confrontations with Congress, the president, and the states whenever possible. The argument for judicial self-restraint is that federal judges are not elected by the people and therefore should not substitute their own views for the views of elected representatives. The courts should defer to the judgments of the other branches of government unless there is a clear violation of constitutional principle. The benefit of the doubt should be given to actions taken by elected officials. Courts should only impose remedies that are narrowly tailored to correct specific legal wrongs. As Justice Sandra Day O'Connor (see *People in Politics:* "Sandra Day O'Connor, Holding the Middle Ground") argued in her Senate confirmation hearings, "The courts should interpret the laws, not make them. . . . I do not believe it is a function of the Court to step in because times have changed or social mores have changed."[15]

Wisdom versus Constitutionality A law may be unwise, unjust, or even stupid and yet still be constitutional. One should not equate the wisdom of a law with its constitutionality, and the Court should decide only the constitutionality and not the wisdom of a law. Justice Oliver Wendell Holmes once lectured a younger colleague, sixty-one-year-old Justice Harlan Stone, on this point:

> Young man, about 75 years ago I learned that I was not God. And so, when the people . . . want to do something I can't find anything in the Constitution expressly forbidding them to do, I say, whether I like it or not, "Goddamn it, let 'em do it."[16]

However, the actual role of the Supreme Court in the nation's power struggles suggests that the Court indeed often equates wisdom with constitutionality. People frequently cite broad phrases in the Fifth and Fourteenth Amendments establishing constitutional standards of "due process of law" and "equal protection of the laws" when attacking laws they believe are unfair or unjust. Most Americans have come to believe that unwise laws must be unconstitutional. If so, then the courts must be the final arbiters of fairness and justice.

statutory laws Laws made by act of Congress or the state legislatures, as opposed to constitutional law.

judicial self-restraint Self-imposed limitation on judicial power by judges deferring to the policy judgments of elected branches of government.

Original Intent Should the Constitution be interpreted in terms of the intentions of the Founders or according to the morality of society today? Most jurists

PEOPLE IN POLITICS

Sandra Day O'Connor, Holding the Middle Ground

For nearly two hundred years, the U.S. Supreme Court was America's most exclusive all-male club. After 101 male justices, Sandra Day O'Connor was named to the Supreme Court by President Ronald Reagan in 1981. On the high court, O'Connor has succeeded in molding a moderate bloc of votes that holds the balance of power on the Supreme Court between liberal and conservative blocs. More important, perhaps, O'Connor has taken the lead in shaping Court policy on women's issues, including the most controversial issue of all—abortion.

Sandra Day grew up on her family's large Arizona ranch, graduated from Stanford with honors, and went on to Stanford Law School, where she finished near the top of her class (along with now Chief Justice of the Supreme Court William Rehnquist, who was first in the class). After graduation, she married John Jay O'Connor, a Phoenix attorney, and had three sons. She entered Arizona politics about the time her youngest son entered school. In 1969 she was appointed to fill a vacancy in the Arizona state senate and was later elected twice to that body, where she rose to become majority leader in 1973. She left the Arizona legislature in 1975 to become a Phoenix trial judge and in 1979 was appointed by a Democratic governor to the Arizona Court of Appeals, an intermediate court that does not hear major constitutional issues.

O'Connor had some business experience: she was formerly a director of the First National Bank of Arizona and Blue Cross/Blue Shield of Arizona. But until her appointment to the U.S. Supreme Court, she was an obscure state court judge. Her service as a Republican leader in the Arizona state senate qualified her as a moderately conservative party loyalist. However, it appears that her professional and political friendships had more to do with bringing her to President Ronald Reagan's attention than her record as a jurist. She had known both Justice Rehnquist and former Chief Justice Warren Burger for many years, and Barry Goldwater, Arizona's senior U.S. senator and Republican warhorse, had been her mentor in Arizona Republican politics. When Reagan's political advisers told him during the presidential campaign that he was not doing well among women voters (he opposed the Equal Rights Amendment), he responded by pledging to appoint a woman to the Supreme Court. Reagan's fulfillment of his campaign pledge was a politically popular decision. Feminist groups felt forced to support the appointment, even though O'Connor's record in Arizona was moderately conservative.

In her early Court deliberations, Justice O'Connor generally reflected the moderate conservatism of recent Republican appointees, but on gender questions she took an independent role from the beginning. Over time, her independent course has made her a swing vote on many key policy issues, from affirmative action to abortion. Indeed, her leadership of the Court on the abortion issue has preserved the constitutional right to abortion.

agree the Constitution is a living document, that it must be interpreted by each generation in the light of current conditions, and to do otherwise would soon render the document obsolete. But in interpreting the document, whose values should prevail—the values of the judges or the values of the Founders? The doctrine of **original intent** takes the values of the Founders as expressed in the text of the Constitution and attempts to apply these values to current conditions. Defenders of original intent argue that the words in the document must be given their historical meaning and that meaning must restrain the courts as well as the legislative and executive branches of government. That is, the Supreme Court should not set aside laws made by elected representatives unless they conflict with the original intent of the Founders. Judges who set aside laws that do not accord with their personal views of today's moral standards are simply substituting their own morality for that of elected bodies. Such decisions lack democratic legitimacy because there is no reason why judges' moral views should prevail over those of elected representatives.

original intent Judicial philosophy under which judges attempt to apply the values of the Founders to current issues.

Judicial Activism However, the doctrine of original intent carries little weight with proponents of judicial activism. The idea behind **judicial activism** is that the Constitution is a living document whose strength lies in its flexibility, and judges should shape constitutional meaning to fit the needs of contemporary society. The argument for judicial activism is that viewing the Constitution as a broad and flexible document saves the nation from having to pass dozens of new constitutional amendments to accommodate changes in society. Instead, the courts need to give contemporary interpretations to constitutional phrases, particularly general phrases such as "due process of law" (Fifth Amendment), "equal protection of the laws" (Fourteenth Amendment), "establishment of religion" (First Amendment), and "cruel and unusual punishment" (Eighth Amendment). Courts have the responsibility to review the actions of other branches of government vigorously, to strike down unconstitutional acts, and to impose far-reaching remedies for legal wrongs whenever necessary.[17]

Stare Decisis Conflicts between judicial activism and judicial self-restraint are underscored by questions of whether to let past decisions stand or to find constitutional support for overturning them. The principle of **stare decisis**, which means the issue has already been decided in earlier cases, is a fundamental notion in law. Reliance on **precedent** gives stability to the law; if every decision were new law, then no one would know what the law is from day to day. Yet the Supreme Court has discarded precedent in many of its most important decisions: *Brown v. Board of Education* (1954), which struck down laws segregating the races; *Baker v. Carr* (1962), which guaranteed equal representation in legislatures; *Roe v. Wade* (1973), which made abortion a constitutional right; and many other classic cases. Former Justice William O. Douglas, a defender of judicial activism, justified disregard of precedent as follows:

> The decisions of yesterday or of the last century are only the starting points. . . . A judge looking at a constitutional decision may have compulsions to revere the past history and accept what was once written. But he remembers above all else that it is the Constitution which he swore to support and defend, not the gloss which his predecessors may have put on it. So he comes to formulate his own laws, rejecting some earlier ones as false and embracing others. He cannot do otherwise unless he lets men long dead and unaware of the problems of the age in which he lives do his thinking for him.[18]

Rules of Restraint Even an activist Supreme Court adheres to some general rules of judicial self-restraint, however, including the following:

- The Court will pass on the constitutionality of legislation only in an actual case; it will not advise the president or Congress on constitutional questions.
- The Court will not anticipate a question on constitutional law; it does not decide hypothetical cases.
- The Court will not formulate a rule of constitutional law broader than that required by the precise facts to which it must be applied.
- The Court will not decide on a constitutional question if some other ground exists on which it may dispose of the case.
- The Court will not decide on the validity of a law if the complainants fail to show that they have been injured by the law.
- When doubt exists about the constitutionality of a law, the Court will try to interpret the law so as to give it a constitutional meaning and avoid the necessity of declaring it unconstitutional.

judicial activism Making of new law through judicial interpretations of the Constitution.

stare decisis Judicial precept that the issue has already been decided in earlier cases and the earlier decision need only be applied in the specific case before the bench; the rule in most cases, it comes from the Latin for "the decision stands."

precedent Legal principle that previous decisions should determine the outcome of current cases; the basis for stability in law.

- Complainants must have exhausted all remedies available in lower federal courts or state courts before the Supreme Court will accept review.
- The Court will invalidate a law only when a constitutional issue is crucial to the case and is substantial, not trivial.
- Occasionally the Court defers to Congress and the president, classifies an issue as a political question, and refuses to decide it. The Court has generally stayed out of foreign and military policy areas.
- If the Court holds a law unconstitutional, it will confine its decision to the particular section of the law that is unconstitutional, the rest of the statute stays intact.

Structure and Jurisdiction of Federal Courts

The federal court system consists of three levels of courts—the Supreme Court, the Courts of Appeals, and the district courts—together with various special courts (see Figure 11.1). Only the Supreme Court is established by the Constitution, although the number of justices is determined by Congress. Article III authorizes Congress to establish such "inferior Courts" as it deems appropriate. Congress has designed a hierarchical system with a U.S. Court of Appeals divided into 12 regional circuit courts, a federal circuit, and 94 district courts in the 50 states and one each in Puerto Rico and the District of Columbia. Table 11.1 describes their **jurisdiction** and distinguishes between **original jurisdiction**—where cases are begun, argued, and initially decided—and **appellate jurisdiction**—where cases begun in lower courts are argued and decided on **appeal.**

The Supreme Court is the "court of last resort" in the United States, but it hears only a very small number of cases each year. In a handful of cases, the Supreme Court has original jurisdiction; these concern primarily disputes between states (or states and residents of other states), disputes between a state and the federal government, and disputes involving foreign dignitaries. However, most Supreme Court cases are appellate decisions involving cases from state supreme courts or cases tried first in a U.S. district court.

District Courts **District courts** are the original jurisdiction trial courts of the federal system. Each state has at least one district court, and larger states have more (New York, for example, has four). There are about eight hundred federal district judges, each appointed for life by the president and confirmed by the Senate. The president also appoints a U.S. marshall for each district to carry out orders of the court and maintain order in the courtroom. District courts hear criminal cases prosecuted by the Department of Justice as well as civil cases. As trial courts, the district courts make use of both **grand juries** (called to hear evidence and, if warranted, to indict a defendant by bringing formal criminal charges) and **petit (regular) juries** (which determine guilt or innocence). District courts may hear more than 250,000 cases in a year, including 70,000 criminal cases.

Courts of Appeals Federal **circuit courts** (see *Across the USA*: "Geographic Boundaries of Federal Courts") are appellate courts. They do not hold trials or accept new evidence but consider only the records of the trial courts and oral or written arguments (**briefs**) submitted by attorneys. Federal law guarantees everyone the right to appeal, so the Court of Appeals has little discretion in this regard. Appellate judges themselves estimate that more than 80 percent of all appeals are frivolous—that is, without any real basis. There are more than a hundred circuit

jurisdiction Power of a court to hear a case in question.

original jurisdiction Refers to a particular court's power to serve as the place where a given case is initially argued and decided.

appellate jurisdiction Particular court's power to review a decision or action of a lower court.

appeal In general, requests that a higher court review cases decided at a lower level. In the Supreme Court, certain cases are designated as appeals under federal law; formally, these must be heard by the Court.

WWW **U.S. Courts**

The goal of this site is "to function as a clearinghouse for information from and about the Judicial Branch of the U.S. government." The site covers the U.S. Supreme Court, U.S. Courts of Appeals, U.S. District Courts, and U.S. Bankruptcy courts.
www.uscourts.gov

district courts Original jurisdiction trial courts of the federal system.

grand juries Juries called to hear evidence and decide whether defendants should be indicted and tried.

petit (regular) juries Juries called to determine guilt or innocence.

circuit courts The twelve appellate courts that make up the middle level of the federal court system.

briefs Documents submitted by an attorney to a court, setting out the facts of the case and the legal arguments in support of the party represented by the attorney.

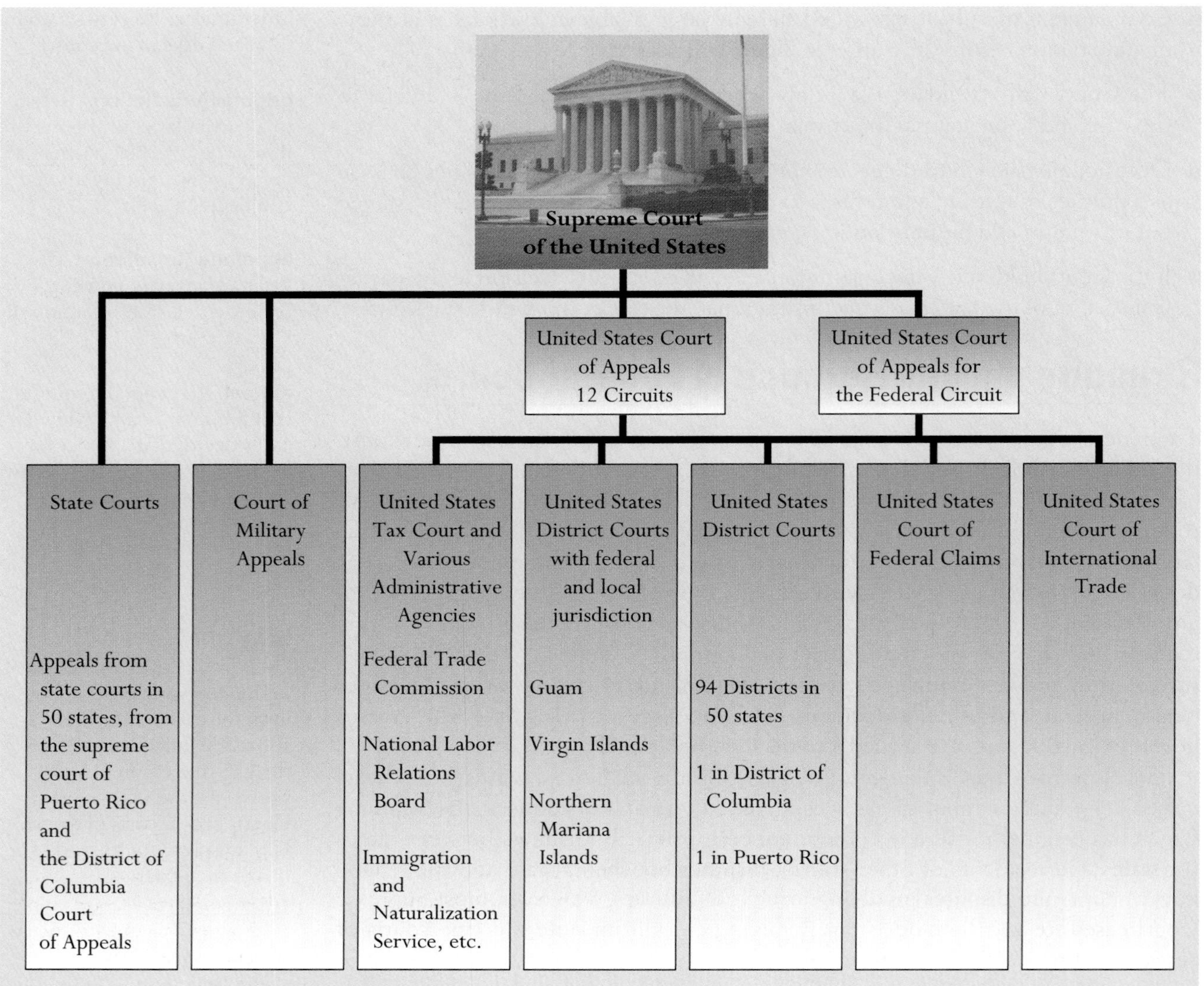

FIGURE 11.1 Structure of Federal Courts

The federal court system of the United States is divided into three levels: the courts of original jurisdiction (state courts, military courts, tax courts, district courts, claims courts, and international trade courts), U.S. Courts of Appeals (which hear appeals from all lower courts except state and military panels), and the U.S. Supreme Court, which can hear appeals from all sources.

judges, each appointed for life by the president subject to confirmation by the Senate. Normally, these judges serve together on a panel to hear appeals. More than 90 percent of the cases decided by the Court of Appeals end at this level. Further appeal to the Supreme Court is not automatic; it must be approved by the Supreme Court itself. Because the Supreme Court hears very few cases, in most cases the decision of the circuit court becomes law.

Supreme Court The Supreme Court of the United States is the final interpreter of all matters involving the Constitution and federal laws and treaties, whether the case began in a federal district court or in a state court. Appeals to the U.S. Supreme Court may come from a state court of last resort (usually a state's supreme court) or from lower federal courts. The Supreme Court determines

TABLE 11.1 Jurisdiction of Federal Courts

Supreme Court of the United States	United States Courts of Appeals	United States District Courts
Appellate jurisdiction (cases begin in a lower court); hears appeals, at its own discretion, from: 1. Lower federal courts 2. Highest state courts Original jurisdiction (cases begin in the Supreme Court) over cases involving: 1. Two or more states 2. The United States and a state 3. Foreign ambassadors and other diplomats 4. A state and a citizen of a different state (if begun by the state)	No original jurisdiction; hear only appeals from: 1. Federal district courts 2. U.S. regulatory commissions 3. Certain other federal courts	Original jurisdiction over cases involving: 1. Federal crimes 2. Civil suits under the federal law 3. Civil suits between citizens of states where the amount exceeds $50,000 4. Admiralty and maritime cases 5. Bankruptcy cases 6. Review of actions of certain federal administrative agencies 7. Other matters assigned to them by Congress

whether to accept an appeal and consider a case. It may do so when there is a "substantial federal question" presented in a case or when there are "special and important reasons," or it may reject a case—with or without explaining why.

In the early days of the Republic, the size of the Supreme Court fluctuated, but since 1869 the membership has remained at nine: the Chief Justice and eight associate justices. The Supreme Court is in session each year from October through June, hearing oral arguments, accepting written briefs, conferring, and rendering opinions.

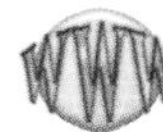

Supreme Court Cases

This Cornell Law School's Legal Information Institute site contains up-to-date information about important legal decisions rendered by federal and state courts along with an exhaustive online law library available to researchers.
www.law.cornell.edu

Appeals from State Courts Each of the fifty states maintains its own courts. The federal courts are not necessarily superior to those courts; state and federal courts operate independently. State courts have original jurisdiction in most criminal and civil cases. Because the U.S. Supreme Court has appellate jurisdiction over state supreme courts as well as over lower federal courts, the Supreme Court oversees the nation's entire judicial system, but the great bulk of cases begin and end in the state court systems. The federal courts do not interfere once a case has been started in a state court except in very rare circumstances. And Congress has stipulated that legal disputes between citizens of different states must involve $50,000 or more to be heard in federal courts. Moreover, parties to cases in state courts must "exhaust their remedies"—that is, appeal their case all the way through the state court system—before the federal courts will hear an appeal. Appeals from state supreme courts go directly to the U.S. Supreme Court and not to a federal district or circuit court. Such appeals are usually made on the grounds that a federal question is involved in the case—that is, a question has arisen regarding the application of the Constitution or a federal law.

The U.S. Supreme Court

Official site provides recent decisions, case dockets, oral arguments, public information, etc.
www.supremecourtus.gov

Federal Cases Some 10 million civil and criminal cases are begun in the nation's courts each year (see *A Conflicting View:* "America Is Drowning Itself in a Sea of Lawsuits" on page 393). Fewer than 300,000 (3 percent) of the cases are begun in the federal courts. About 8,000 are appealed to the Supreme Court each year, but

ACROSS THE USA

Geographic Boundaries of Federal Courts

For administrative convenience, the U.S. District Courts are organized into twelve circuits (regions), plus the Federal Circuit (Washington, D.C.). Within each region, circuit court judges form panels to hear appeals from district courts. U.S. Circuit Courts of Appeals are numbered. U.S. District Courts are named for geographic regions of the states (East, West, North, South, Middle), for example, U.S. District Court for Northern California.

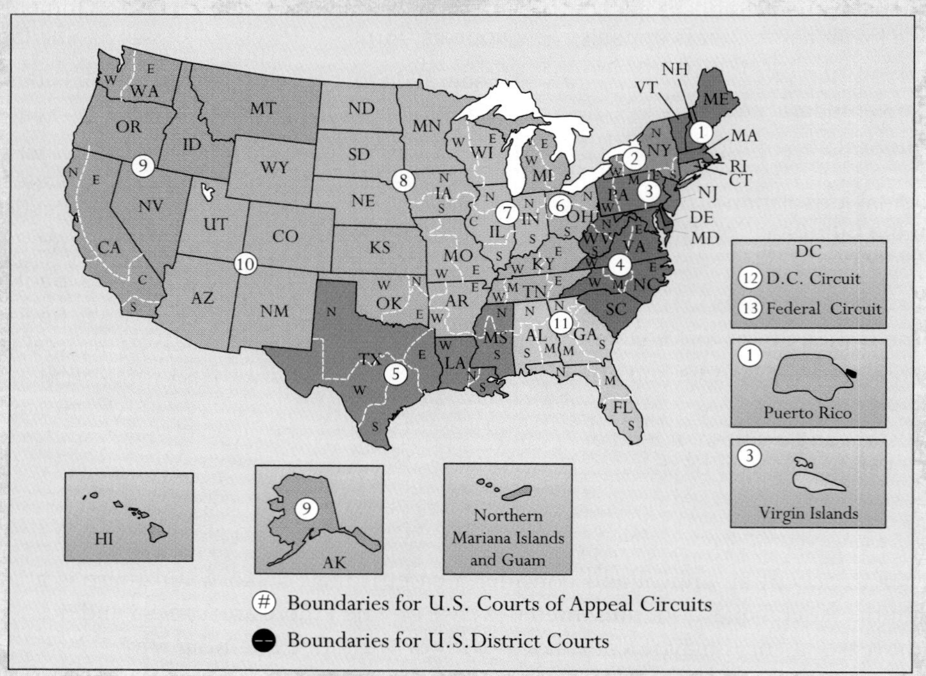

FIGURE 11.2
Caseloads in Federal Courts

Increasing caseloads in the federal courts have placed a heavy burden on prosecutors and judges. Although the increase in civil suits in the federal courts is the result of more plaintiffs insisting on taking their cases to the federal level both originally and on appeal, the increase in criminal cases is the result of Congress's decision to make more crimes—especially drug-related crimes—federal offenses and to pursue such criminals more vigorously.

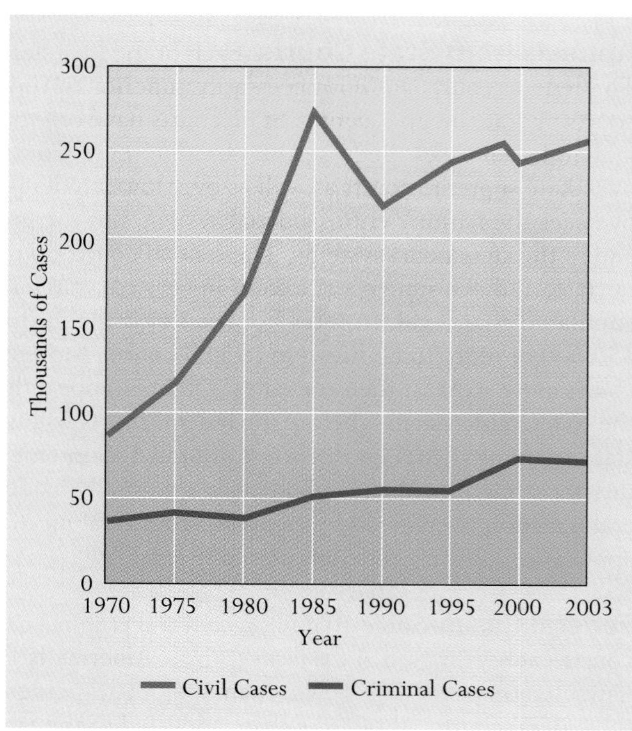

A CONFLICTING **VIEW**

America Is Drowning Itself in a Sea of Lawsuits

America is threatening to drown itself in a sea of lawsuits. Civil suits in the nation's courts exceed *10 million* per year. There are more than 805,000 lawyers in the United States (compared to about 650,000 physicians). These lawyers are in business, and their business is litigation. Generating business means generating lawsuits. And just as businesses search for new products, lawyers search for new legal principles on which to bring lawsuits. They seek to expand legal liability for civil actions—that is, to expand the definition of civil wrongdoings, or torts.

Unquestionably, the threat of lawsuits is an important safeguard for society, compelling individuals, corporations, and government agencies to behave responsibly toward others. Because victims require compensation for *actual* damages incurred by the wrongdoing of others, liability laws protect all of us.

But we need to consider the social costs of frivolous lawsuits, especially those brought without any merit but initiated in the hope that individuals or firms will offer a settlement just to avoid the expenses of defending themselves. Legal expenses and excessive jury awards leveled against corporations increase insurance premiums for businesses and service providers. The Insurance Information Institute estimates that the overall costs of civil litigation in America is many times more than that of other industrial nations, perhaps amounting to over 2 percent of our nation's GDP. For example, the risk of lawsuits forces physicians to practice "defensive medicine," ordering expensive tests, multiple consultations with specialists, and expensive procedures, not because they are adjudged medically necessary, but rather to protect themselves from the possibility of a lawsuit.

Insurance premiums have risen sharply for physicians seeking malpractice insurance, as have premiums for recreation facilities, nurseries and day-care centers, motels, and restaurants.

Product Liability

The threat of lawsuits discourages new products from entering the marketplace. Virtually any accident involving a commercial product can inspire a product liability suit. An individual who gets cut opening a can of peas can sue the canning company. A woman who spills hot coffee on herself while driving sues the fast-food restaurant for making the coffee too hot. Hotels pay damages to persons raped in their rooms.

Third-Party Suits

Defendants in civil cases are not necessarily the parties directly responsible for damages to the plaintiff. Instead, wealthier third parties, who may indirectly contribute to an accident, are favorite targets of lawsuits. For example, if a drunk driver injures a pedestrian but the driver has only limited insurance and small personal wealth, a shrewd attorney will sue the bar that sold the driver the drinks instead of the driver.

"Pain and Suffering" Awards

High jury awards in liability cases, sometimes running into tens of millions of dollars, cover much more than the doctor bills, lost wages, and cost of future care for injured parties. Most large damage awards are for *pain and suffering.* Pain and suffering awards are *added* compensation for the victim, beyond actual costs for medical care and lost wages.

"Joint and Severable" Liability

A legal rule known as *joint and severable liability* allows a plaintiff to collect the entire award from any party that contributed in any way to an accident if other defendants cannot pay. If, for example, a drunk driver crosses a median strip and crashes into another car, leaving its driver crippled, the victim may sue the city for not placing a guard railing in the median strip. The rule encourages trial lawyers to sue the party "with the deepest pockets," that is, the wealthiest party rather than the party most responsible for the accident.

Reform Politics

Reforming the nation's liability laws presents major challenges to the political system. The reform movement can count on support from some normally powerful interest groups—insurance companies, manufacturers, drug companies, hospitals, and physicians. But legal reform is an anathema to the legal profession itself, notably the powerful Association of Trial Lawyers. And lawyers compose the single largest occupational background of Congress members—indeed, of politicians generally.

only about 125 of them are openly argued and decided by signed opinions. The Constitution "reserves" general police powers to the states. That is, civil disputes and most crimes—murder, robbery, assault, and rape—are normally state offenses rather than federal crimes and thus are tried in state and local courts.

Law Info Web site offering legal documents, legal help guides, attorney references, etc. *www.lawinfo.com*

Federal court caseloads have risen in recent years (see Figure 11.2), in part because more civil disputes are being brought to federal courts. In addition, the U.S. Justice Department is prosecuting more criminal cases as federal law enforcement agencies—such as the Federal Bureau of Investigation (FBI), Drug Enforcement Administration (DEA), Internal Revenue Service (IRS), and Bureau of Alcohol, Tobacco and Firearms (ATF)—have stepped up their investigations. Most of this recent increase is attributable to enforcement of federal drug laws.

Traditionally, federal crimes were offenses directed against the U.S. government, its property, or its employees or were offenses involving the crossing of state lines. Over the years, however, Congress has greatly expanded the list of federal crimes so that federal and state criminal court jurisdictions often overlap, as they do, for example, in most drug violations.

The Special Rules of Judicial Decision Making

Courts are political institutions that resolve conflict and decide about public policy. But unlike Congress, the presidency, and the bureaucracy, the courts employ highly specialized rules in going about their work.

Cases and Controversies Courts do not initiate policy but rather wait until a case or controversy is brought to them for resolution. A case must involve two disputing parties, one of which must have incurred some real damage as a result of the action or inaction of the other. They do *not* issue policy declarations or decide hypothetical cases. Rather, the courts wait until disputing parties bring a case to them that requires them to interpret the meaning of a law or determine its constitutionality in order to resolve the case. Only then do courts render opinions.

The vast majority of cases do *not* involve important policy issues. Courts determine the guilt or innocence of criminal defendants. Courts enforce contracts and award damages to victims of negligence in **civil cases.** And courts render these decisions on the basis of established law. Only occasionally do courts make significant policy decisions.

civil cases Noncriminal court proceedings in which a plaintiff sues a defendant for damages in payment for harm inflicted.

Adversarial Proceedings Underlying judicial decision making is the assumption that the best way to decide an issue is to allow two disputing parties to present arguments on each side. Judges in the United States do not investigate cases, question witnesses, or develop arguments themselves (as they do in some European countries). This **adversarial system** depends on quality of argument on each side, which means it often depends on the capabilities of attorneys. There is no guarantee that the adversarial process will produce the best policy outcomes.

adversarial system Method of decision making in which an impartial judge or jury or decision maker hears arguments and reviews evidence presented by opposite sides.

Standing To bring an issue into court as a case, individuals or firms or interest groups must have **standing**; that is, they must be directly harmed by a law or action. People cannot "go to court" simply because they do not like what the government is doing. Merely being taxpayers does not entitle people to claim that they are damaged by government actions.[19] Individuals or firms automatically have standing when they are prosecuted by the government for violation of laws or regulations. Thus one way to gain standing in order to challenge the legality of a

standing Requirement that the party who files a lawsuit have a legal stake in the outcome.

regulation or the constitutionality of a law is to violate the regulation or law and invite the government to prosecute.

To sue the government, plaintiffs must show they have suffered financial damages, loss of property, or physical or emotional harm as a direct result of the government's action. (The party initiating a suit and claiming damages is the **plaintiff**; the party against whom a suit is brought is the **defendant**.) The ancient legal doctrine of **sovereign immunity** means that one cannot sue the government without the government's consent. But by law, the U.S. government allows itself to be sued in a wide variety of contract and negligence cases. A citizen can also personally sue to force government officials to carry out acts that they are required by law to perform or for acting contrary to law. The government does not allow suits for damages as a result of military actions.

plaintiffs Parties initiating suits and claiming damages. In criminal cases, the state acts as plaintiff on behalf of an injured society and requests fines and/or imprisonment as damages. In civil suits, the plaintiff is the injured party and seeks monetary damages.

defendants Parties against whom a criminal or civil suit is brought.

sovereign immunity Legal doctrine that individuals can sue the government only with the government's consent.

Class Action Suits **Class action suits** are cases brought into court by individuals on behalf not only of themselves but also of all other persons "similarly situated." That is, the party bringing the case is acting on behalf of a "class" of people who have suffered the same damages from the same actions of the defendant. One of the most famous and far-reaching class action suits was *Brown v. Board of Education of Topeka* (1954). The plaintiff, Linda Brown of Topeka, Kansas, sued her local board of education on behalf of herself and all other black pupils who were forced to attend segregated schools, charging that such schools violated the Equal Protection Clause of the Fourteenth Amendment. When she won the case, the Court's ruling affected not only Linda Brown and the segregated public schools in Topeka but also all other black pupils similarly situated across the nation (see Chapter 10).

Class action suits have grown in popularity. These suits have enabled attorneys and interest groups to bring multimillion-dollar suits against corporations and governments for damages to large numbers of people, even when none of them has

class action suits Cases initiated by parties acting on behalf of themselves and all others similarly situated.

THINK AGAIN

Are the costs of lawsuits in America becoming too burdensome on the economy?

Justices of the Supreme Court. Front row, from the left: Antonin Scalia, John Paul Stevens, Chief Justice William Rehnquist, Sandra Day O'Connor, and Anthony Kennedy. Back row, from the left: Ruth Bader Ginsburg, David Souter, Clarence Thomas, and Stephen Breyer.

individually suffered sufficient harm to merit bringing a case to court. For example, an individual overcharged by an electric utility would not want to incur the expense of suing for the return of a few dollars. But if attorneys sue the utility on behalf of a large number of customers similarly overcharged, the result may be a multimillion-dollar settlement from which the attorneys can deduct their hefty fees.

Legal Fees Going to court requires financial resources. Criminal defendants are guaranteed an attorney, without charge if they are poor, by the Sixth Amendment's guarantee of "Assistance of Counsel" (see Chapter 10).[20] However, persons who wish to bring a *civil* suit against governments or corporations must still arrange for the payment of legal fees. The most common arrangement is the **contingency fee,** in which plaintiffs agree to pay expenses and share one-third or more of the money damages with their lawyers if the case is won. If the case is lost, neither plaintiffs nor their lawyers receive anything for their labors. Lawyers do not usually participate in such arrangements unless the prospects for winning the case are good and the promised monetary reward is substantial. Civil suits against the government have increased since Congress enacted a law requiring governments to pay the attorneys' fees of citizens who successfully bring suit against public officials for violation of their constitutional rights.

Remedies and Relief Judicial power has vastly expanded through court determination of **remedies and relief.** These are the orders of a court following a decision that are designed to correct a wrong. In most cases, judges simply fine or sentence criminal defendants to jail or order losing defendants in civil suits to pay monetary damages to the winning plaintiffs. In recent years, however, federal district court judges have issued sweeping orders to governments to correct constitutional violations. For example, a federal district judge took over operation of the Boston public schools for more than ten years to remedy *de facto* (an existing, although not necessarily deliberate, pattern of) racial segregation. A federal district judge ordered the city of Yonkers, New York, to build public housing in white neighborhoods. A federal district judge took over the operation of the Alabama prison system to ensure proper prisoner treatment. A federal district judge ordered the Kansas City, Missouri, school board to increase taxes to pay for his desegregation plan.[21]

Independent Counsels? The Ethics in Government Act of 1978 (passed in the wake of the Watergate scandal) granted federal courts the power, upon request of the attorney general, to appoint an **independent counsel**, or "**special prosecutor,**" to investigate and prosecute violations of federal law by the president and other high officials. This act was challenged in the U.S. Supreme Court as a transferral of executive power ("to take care that the laws be faithfully executed"—Article II) to the judicial branch of government in violation of the separation of powers in the U.S. Constitution. But the Court upheld the law, noting that the attorney general, an executive branch official appointed by the president, had to request the judiciary to appoint the independent counsel.[22]

Whatever the original intent of the act, special prosecutors were often accused of *bringing politics into* the criminal justice system. Indeed, special prosecutor Kenneth Starr's dogged pursuit of Bill and Hillary Clinton (in "Whitewater" real estate deals and later the Monica Lewinsky sex scandal) was deemed a "witch hunt" by friends of the president. The First Lady linked Starr to "a vast right-wing conspiracy" trying to reverse the outcome of two presidential elections.

contingency fees Fees paid to attorneys to represent the plaintiff in a civil suit and receive in compensation an agreed-upon percentage of damages awarded (if any).

remedies and reliefs Orders of a court to correct a wrong, including a violation of the Constitution.

independent counsel ("special prosecutor") A prosecutor appointed by a federal court to pursue charges against a president or other high official. This position was allowed to lapse by Congress in 1999 after many controversial investigations by these prosecutors.

Class action suits initiated by attorneys or interest groups on behalf of large numbers of people are increasingly popular. Here an attorney announces a suit against the nation's tobacco companies on behalf of flight attendants previously subjected to smoke.

Congress allowed the independent counsel law to lapse in 1999. Democrats, infuriated by Starr's investigations, joined Republicans, who had earlier complained when Reagan and Bush administration officials were the targets of prosecution, in killing the act. Getting rid of the law, said its opponents, will help to "decriminalize" politics in Washington.

The Politics of Selecting Judges

The Constitution specifies that all federal judges, including justices of the Supreme Court, shall be appointed by the president and confirmed by a majority vote of the Senate. Judicial recruitment is a political process: presidents almost always appoint members of their own party to the federal courts. More than 80 percent of federal judges have held some political office prior to their appointment to the court. More important, political philosophy now plays a major role in the selection of judges. Thus the appointment of federal judges has increasingly become an arena for conflict between presidents and their political opponents in the Senate.

The Politics of Presidential Selection Presidents have a strong motivation to select judges who share their political philosophy. Judicial appointments are made for life. The Constitution stipulates that federal judges "shall hold their Offices during good Behaviour." Although a rather vague phrase, it has come to mean a virtually guaranteed life term. A president cannot remove a judge for any reason, and Congress cannot impeach judges just because it dislikes their decisions.

This independence of the judiciary has often frustrated presidents and Congresses. Presidents who have appointed people they thought were liberals or conservatives to the Supreme Court have sometimes been surprised by the decisions of their appointees. An estimated one-quarter of the justices of the Supreme Court have deviated from the political expectations of the presidents who appointed them.[23]

THINK AGAIN

Should presidents appoint only judges who agree with their judicial philosophy?

It is important to recognize that presidents' use of political criteria in selecting judges has a democratic influence on the courts. Presidents can campaign on the pledge to make the courts more liberal or conservative through their appointive powers, and voters are free to cast their ballots on the basis of this pledge.

Political Litmus Test Traditionally, presidents and senators have tried to discern where a Supreme Court candidate fits on the continuum of liberal activism versus conservative self-restraint. Democratic presidents and senators usually prefer liberal judges who express an activist philosophy. Republican presidents usually prefer conservative judges who express a philosophy of judicial self-restraint. Until very recently, both the president and the Senate denied using any political "litmus test" in judicial recruitment. A **litmus test** generally refers to recruitment based on a nominee's stand on a single issue. Since the Supreme Court ruling on *Roe v. Wade* (1973), however, the single issue of abortion has come to dominate the politics of judicial recruitment. President Clinton was forthright in his pledge to nominate only justices who specifically support the *Roe v. Wade* decision. Republican presidents have denied using a litmus test, but they have insisted that nominees generally support a philosophy of judicial self-restraint.

The Politics of Senate Confirmation All presidential nominations for the federal judiciary, including the Supreme Court, are sent to the Senate for confirmation. The Senate refers them to its powerful Judiciary Committee, which holds hearings, votes on the nomination, and then reports to the full Senate, where floor debate may precede the final confirmation vote.

The Senate's involvement in federal district judgeships traditionally centered on the practice of **senatorial courtesy.** If senators from the president's party from the same state for which an appointment was being considered disapproved of a nominee, their Senate colleagues would defeat the nomination. But if the president and senators from that party agreed on the nomination, the full Senate, even if controlled by the opposition, customarily confirmed the nomination. During the Reagan-Bush years, however, partisan divisions between these Republican presidents and Senate Democrats eroded the tradition of senatorial courtesy.

Supreme Court nominations have always received close political scrutiny in the Senate. Over the last two centuries, the Senate has rejected or refused to confirm about 20 percent of presidential nominees to the high court, but only five nominees in this century (see Table 11.2). In the past, most senators believed that presidents deserved to appoint their own judges; the opposition party would get its own opportunity to appoint judges when it won the presidency. Only if the Senate found some personal disqualification in a nominee's background (for example, financial scandal, evidence of racial or religious bias, judicial incompetence) would a nominee likely be rejected. But publicity and partisanship over confirmation of Supreme Court nominees have increased markedly in recent years.[24]

litmus test In political terms, a person's stand on a key issue that determines whether he or she will be appointed to public office or supported in electoral campaigns.

senatorial courtesy Custom of the U.S. Senate with regard to presidential nominations to the judiciary to defer to the judgment of senators from the president's party from the same state as the nominee.

The Bork Battle The U.S. Senate's rejection of President Ronald Reagan's nomination of Judge Robert H. Bork in 1987 set a new precedent in Senate confirmation of Supreme Court nominees. The Senate rejected Bork because of his views, not because he lacked judicial qualifications. Bork had a reputation for "conservative activism"—a desire better to reflect the "original intent" of the Constitution's framers by rolling back some of the Supreme Court's broad interpretations of privacy rights, free speech, and equal protection of the law. Perhaps most controversial were his views on *Roe v. Wade*; he had labeled the Court's striking down of state laws prohibiting abortion as "wholly unjustifiable judicial usurpation of state legislative authority."

Unlike previous nominees, Bork was subjected by the Senate Judiciary Committee to extensive case-by-case questioning in nationally televised confirmation hearings, during which the bearded, scholarly Bork presented a poor TV image. The Democrat-controlled U.S. Senate rejected his nomination. Victory in the Bork battle encouraged liberal interest groups to closely scrutinize the personal lives

TABLE 11.2 Senate Confirmation Votes on Supreme Court Nominations since 1950

Nominee	President	Year	Vote
Earl Warren	Eisenhower	1954	NRV*
John Marshall Harlan	Eisenhower	1955	71–11
William J. Brennan	Eisenhower	1957	NRV
Charles Whittaker	Eisenhower	1957	NRV
Potter Stewart	Eisenhower	1959	70–17
Byron White	Kennedy	1962	NRV
Arthur Goldberg	Kennedy	1962	NRV
Abe Fortas	Johnson	1965	NRV
Thurgood Marshall	Johnson	1967	69–11
Abe Fortas†	Johnson	1968	Withdrawn‡
Homer Thornberry	Johnson	1968	No action
Warren Burger	Nixon	1969	74–3
Clement Haynsworth	Nixon	1969	Defeated 45–55
G. Harrold Carswell	Nixon	1970	Defeated 45–51
Harry Blackmun	Nixon	1970	94–0
Lewis Powell	Nixon	1971	89–1
William Rehnquist	Nixon	1971	68–26
John Paul Stevens	Nixon	1975	98–0
Sandra Day O'Connor	Reagan	1981	99–0
William Rehnquist†	Reagan	1986	65–33
Antonin Scalia	Reagan	1986	98–0
Robert Bork	Reagan	1987	Defeated 42–58
Douglas Ginsburg	Reagan	1987	Withdrawn
Anthony Kennedy	Reagan	1988	97–0
David Souter	Bush	1990	90–9
Clarence Thomas	Bush	1991	52–48
Ruth Bader Ginsburg	Clinton	1993	96–3
Stephen G. Breyer	Clinton	1994	87–9

* No recorded vote.

† Elevation to Chief Justice.

‡ Nomination withdrawn after Senate vote failed to end filibuster against nomination; vote was 45 to 43 to end filibuster, and two-thirds majority was required.

Source: Congressional Quarterly, *The Supreme Court: Justice and the Law* (Washington, D.C.: Congressional Quarterly, 1983), p. 179; updated by the author.

and political views of subsequent nominees. Indeed, the Bork battle set the stage for an even more controversial political struggle—the confirmation of Justice Clarence Thomas (see *Up Close:* "The Confirmation of Clarence Thomas").

Filibustering Court Nominees The Constitution requires only a majority vote of the Senate to "advise and consent" to a presidential nominee for a federal court judgeship, including a seat on the Supreme Court. However recent partisan battles over nominees have centered on the Senate's filibuster rule and the 60 votes required for cloture to end a filibuster (see "Senate Floor Traditions" in Chapter 8). The Democrats in the Senate control more than 40 votes, so they can deny the majority the ability to end debate: This means they can deny the vote on a federal court nominee indefinitely and thereby effectively kill the nomination. The president cannot force an up-or-down vote on a court nominee.[25]

President George W. Bush has suffered several key defeats of judicial nominees for seats on the U.S. Court of Appeals by failing to get 60 votes to end filibusters over their nominations. All of his nominations were qualified from a judicial point of view, but all were considered conservatives by leading Democrats in the Senate. And Democrats wished to warn President Bush that a nomination of a conservative to the Supreme Court would bring about the same stalemate and failure at confirmation.

Republican Majority Leader Bill Frist has threatened to try to end the filibuster rule for judicial nominations. He argues that the Constitution itself specifies a "majority vote of the Senate", not a 3/5ths (60) vote for confirmation. But Senators of both parties are reluctant to give up the filibuster rule.

Who Is Selected?

What background and experiences are brought to the Supreme Court? Despite often holding very different views on the laws, the Constitution, and their interpretation, the justices of the U.S. Supreme Court tend to share a common background of education at the nation's most prestigious law schools and prior judicial experience.

Find Law for Students

Law school information for schools A–Z, state bar information, job listings, law school rankings, etc.
http://stu.findlaw.com

Law Degrees There is no constitutional requirement that Supreme Court justices be attorneys, but every person who has ever served on the High Court has been trained in law. Moreover, a majority of the justices have attended one or another of the nation's most prestigious law schools—Harvard, Yale, and Stanford (see Table 11.3).

Judicial Experience Historically, about half of all Supreme Court justices have been federal or state court judges. Many justices have served some time as U.S. attorneys in the Department of Justice early in their legal careers. Relatively few have held elected political office; among today's justices, only Sandra Day O'Connor ever won an election (to the Arizona state legislature), but one chief justice—William Howard Taft—previously held the nation's highest elected post, the presidency.

Age Most justices have been in their fifties when appointed to the Court. Presumably this is the age at which people acquire the necessary prominence and experience to bring themselves to the attention of the White House and Justice Department as potential candidates. At the same time, presidents seek to make a lasting imprint on the Court, and candidates in their fifties can be expected to serve on the Court for many more years than older candidates with the same credentials.

Race and Gender No African American had ever served on the Supreme Court until President Lyndon Johnson's appointment of Thurgood Marshall in 1967. A Howard University Law School graduate, Marshall had served as counsel for the National Association for the Advancement of Colored People Legal Defense Fund and had personally argued the historic *Brown v. Board of Education* case before the Supreme Court in 1954. He served as solicitor general of the United States under President Lyndon Johnson before his elevation to the high court. Upon Marshall's retirement in 1991, President George Bush sought to retain minority representation on the Supreme Court, yet at the same time to reinforce conservative judicial views, with his selection of Clarence Thomas.

No woman had served on the Supreme Court prior to the appointment of Sandra Day O'Connor by President Ronald Reagan in 1981. O'Connor was Reagan's first Supreme Court appointment. Although a relatively unknown Arizona state court judge, she had the powerful support of Arizona Republican Senator Barry

UP CLOSE

The Confirmation of Clarence Thomas

Television coverage of Senate confirmation hearings on Clarence Thomas's appointment to the Supreme Court in 1991 captivated a national audience. The conflict raised just about every "hot-button" issue in American politics, from abortion rights and affirmative action to sexual harassment.

Born to a teenage mother who earned $10 a week as a maid, Clarence Thomas and his brother lived in a dirt-floor shack in Pin Point, Georgia, where they were raised by strict, hardworking grandparents who taught young Clarence the value of education and sacrificed to send him to a Catholic school. He excelled academically and went on to mostly white Immaculate Conception Seminary College in Missouri to study for the Catholic priesthood. But when he overheard a fellow seminarian express satisfaction at the assassination of Dr. Martin Luther King, Jr., Thomas left the seminary in anger and enrolled at Holy Cross College, where he helped found the college's Black Student Union, and went on to graduate with honors and to win admission to Yale Law School.

Upon graduating from Yale, Thomas took a job as assistant attorney general in Missouri and later became a congressional aide to Republican Missouri Senator John Danforth. In 1981 he accepted the post as head of the Office of Civil Rights in the Department of Education. In 1982 he was named chair of the Equal Employment Opportunity Commission (EEOC), where he successfully eliminated much of that agency's financial mismanagement and aggressively pursued individual cases of discrimination. But at the same time, he spoke out against racial "quotas." In 1989 President Bush nominated him to the U.S. Court of Appeals, and he was easily confirmed by the Senate.

In tapping Thomas for the Supreme Court, the White House reasoned that the liberal groups who had blocked the earlier nomination of conservative Robert Bork would be reluctant to launch personal attacks on an African American. With the opposition fractured, the White House saw an opportunity to push a strong conservative nominee through the Democrat-dominated Senate Judiciary Committee and win confirmation by the full Senate.

But behind the scenes, liberal interest groups, including the National Abortion Rights Action League, People for the American Way, and the National Organization for Women, were searching for evidence to discredit Thomas. A University of Oklahoma law professor, Anita Hill, a former legal assistant to Thomas both at the Department of Education and later at the Equal Employment Opportunity Commission, charged, in a nationally televised press conference, that Thomas had sexually harassed her in both jobs. Thomas himself flatly denied the charges.

Democrats on the committee treated Hill with great deference, asking her to talk about her feelings and provide even more explicit details of Thomas's alleged misconduct. Given an opportunity to rebut Hill's charges, Thomas did so very emphatically: "This is a circus. It's a national disgrace. And from my standpoint as a black American, as far as I'm concerned, it is a high-tech lynching for uppity blacks who in any way deign to think for themselves."

In the end, there was no way to determine who was telling the truth, and "truth" in Washington is, at any rate, often determined by opinion polls. A majority of blacks as well as whites, and a majority of women as well as men, sided with the nominee.* In a fitting finale to the bitter and sleazy conflict, the final Senate confirmation vote was 52 to 48, the closest vote in the history of such confirmations. The best that can be said about the affair was that it placed the issue of sexual harassment on the national agenda.

Gallup Opinion Reports, October 15, 1991, p. 209.

TABLE 11.3 The Supreme Court

Justice	Age at Appointment	President Who Appointed	Law School	Position at Time of Appointment	Years as a Judge before Appointment
William H. Rehnquist					
Original appointment	47	Nixon (1971)	Stanford	Assistant Attorney	0
Chief Justice	61	Reagan (1986)		General	15
John Paul Stevens	50	Ford (1976)	Northwestern	U.S. Court of Appeals	5
Sandra Day O'Connor	51	Reagan (1981)	Stanford	State Court	6
Antonin Scalia	50	Reagan (1988)	Harvard	U.S. Court of Appeals	4
Anthony M. Kennedy	51	Reagan (1988)	Harvard	U.S. Court of Appeals	12
David H. Souter	50	Bush (1990)	Harvard	State Supreme Court	13
Clarence Thomas	43	Bush (1991)	Yale	U.S. Court of Appeals	2
Ruth Bader Ginsburg	60	Clinton (1993)	Columbia	U.S. Court of Appeals	13
Stephen G. Breyer	56	Clinton (1994)	Harvard	U.S. Court of Appeals	14

UP CLOSE

Women and the Courts

When Myra Bradwell applied for an attorney's license in Illinois in 1869, the state refused her application. Ms. Bradwell appealed to the U.S. Supreme Court which denied her claim, adding that:

> The paramount destiny and mission of women are to fulfill the noble and benign offices of wife and mother. This is the law of the Creator, *Bradwell vs. Illinois* 83 U.S. 130 (1873).

But states gradually began to accept women as lawyers. President Franklin D. Roosevelt appointed Florence Allen to the U.S. Court of Appeals in 1934, the first woman ever appointed to a federal court of general jurisdiction. Yet Harvard did not admit women to their law school prior to 1950 and continued to restrict women's applications until the 1960s.

Today women constitute about half of all law school admissions in the country. However, after graduation women are less likely to enter private practice than men and disproportionately tend to become government lawyers.* It is reported that fewer than 20 percent of senior partners in law firms are women.

Women judges are increasingly taking their seats on state and federal court benches. As of 2000, women made up about 15 percent of federal judges on both district courts and courts of appeal. And two women, Sandra Day O'Connor, first appointed by President Ronald Reagan in 1981, and Ruth Bader Ginsburg, first appointed by President Bill Clinton in 1993, currently serve on the U.S. Supreme Court.

* See Barbara Palmer "'To Do Justly': The Integration of Women into the American Judiciary," *P.S. Political Science and Politics* (June 2001): 235–38.

Goldwater and Stanford classmate Justice William Rehnquist. The second woman to serve on the High Court, Ruth Bader Ginsburg, had served as an attorney for the American Civil Liberties Union while teaching at Columbia Law School and had argued and won several important gender discrimination cases. President Jimmy Carter appointed her in 1980 to the U.S. Court of Appeals; President Bill Clinton elevated her to the Supreme Court in 1993 (see *Up Close:* "Women and the Court).

Supreme Court Decision Making

The Supreme Court sets its own agenda: it decides what it wants to decide. Of the more than 8,000 requests for hearing that come to its docket each year, the Court issues opinions on only about 150 cases. Another 150 or so cases are decided *summarily* (without opinion) by a Court order either affirming or reversing the lower court decision. The Supreme Court refuses to rule at all on the vast majority of cases that are submitted to it. Thus the rhetorical threat to "take this all the way to the Supreme Court" is usually an empty one. It is important, however, to realize that a refusal to rule also creates law by allowing the decision of the lower court to stand. That is why the U.S. Circuit Courts of Appeals are powerful bodies.

Setting the Agenda: Granting Certiorari Most cases reach the Supreme Court when a party in a case appeals to the Court to issue a **writ of certiorari** (literally to "make more certain"), a decision by the Court to require a lower federal or state court to turn over its records on a case.[26] To "grant certiorari"—that is, to decide to hear arguments in a case and render a decision—the Supreme Court relies on its **rule of four**: four justices must agree to do so. Deciding which cases to hear takes up a great deal of the Court's time.

What criteria does the Supreme Court use in choosing its policy agenda—that is, in choosing the cases it wishes to decide? The Court rarely explains why it accepts or rejects cases, but there are some general patterns. First, the Court accepts cases involving issues that the justices are interested in. The justices are clearly interested in the area of First Amendment freedoms—speech, press, and religion. Members of the Court are also interested in civil rights issues under the Equal Protection Clause of the Fourteenth Amendment and the civil rights laws and in overseeing the criminal justice system and defining the Due Process Clauses of the Fifth and Fourteenth Amendments.

In addition, the Court seems to feel an obligation to accept cases involving questions that have been decided differently by different circuit courts of appeals. The Supreme Court generally tries to see to it that "the law" does not differ from one circuit to another. Likewise, the Supreme Court usually acts when lower courts have made decisions clearly at odds with Supreme Court interpretations in order to maintain control of the federal judiciary. Finally, the Supreme Court is more likely to accept a case in which the U.S. government is a party and requests a review, especially when an issue appears to be one of overriding importance to the government. In fact, the U.S. government is a party in almost half of the cases decided by the Supreme Court.

Hearing Arguments Once the Supreme Court places a case on its decision calendar, attorneys for both sides submit written briefs on the issues. The Supreme Court may also allow interest groups to submit **amicus curiae** (literally, "friend of the court") briefs. This process allows interest groups direct access to the Supreme

writ of certiorari Writ issued by the Supreme Court, at its discretion, to order a lower court to prepare the record of a case and send it to the Supreme Court for review. Most cases come to the Court as petitions for writs of certiorari.

rule of four At least four justices must agree to hear an appeal (writ of certiorari) from a lower court in order to get a case before the Supreme Court.

amicus curiae Literally, "friend of the court"; a person, private group or institution, or government agency that is not a party to a case but participates in the case (usually through submission of a brief) at the invitation of the court or on its own initiative.

Court. In the affirmative action case of *University of California Regents v. Bakke* (1978)[27] the Court accepted 59 amicus curiae briefs representing more than 100 interest groups. The U.S. government frequently submits amicus curiae arguments in cases in which it is not a party. The **solicitor general** of the United States is responsible for presenting the government's arguments both in cases in which the government is a party and in cases in which the government is merely an amicus curiae.

Oral arguments before the Supreme Court are a time-honored ritual of American government. They take place in the marble "temple"—the Supreme Court building across the street from the U.S. Capitol in Washington, D.C. (see Figure 11.3). The justices, clad in their black robes, sit behind a high "bench" and peer down at the attorneys presenting their arguments. Arguing a case before the Supreme Court is said to be an intimidating experience. Each side is usually limited to either a half-hour or an hour of argument, but justices frequently interrupt with their own pointed questioning. Court watchers sometimes try to predict the Court's decision from the tenor of the questioning. Oral argument is the most public phase of Supreme Court decision making, but no one really knows whether these arguments ever change the justices' minds.

In Conference The actual decisions are made in private conferences among the justices. These conferences usually take place on Wednesdays and Fridays and cover the cases argued orally during the same week. The Chief Justice (currently William Rehnquist) presides, and only justices (no law clerks) are present. It is customary for the Chief Justice to speak first on the issues, followed by each associate justice in order of seniority. A majority must decide which party wins or loses and whether a lower court's decision is to be affirmed or reversed.

solicitor general Attorney in the Department of Justice who represents the U.S. government before the Supreme Court and any other courts.

majority opinion Opinion in a case that is subscribed to by a majority of the judges who participated in the decision.

Writing Opinions The *written* opinion determines the actual outcome of the case (votes in conference are not binding). When the decision is unanimous, the Chief Justice traditionally writes the opinion. In the case of a split decision, the Chief Justice may take on the task of writing the **majority opinion** or assign it to another

FIGURE 11.3
Corridors of Power in the Supreme Court

This cutaway shows the location of the principal offices and chambers of the Supreme Court building.

THE SUPREME COURT

1. Courtyards
2. Solicitor General's Office
3. Lawyers' Lounge
4. Marshall's Office
5. Main Hall
6. Courtroom
7. Conference and Reception Rooms

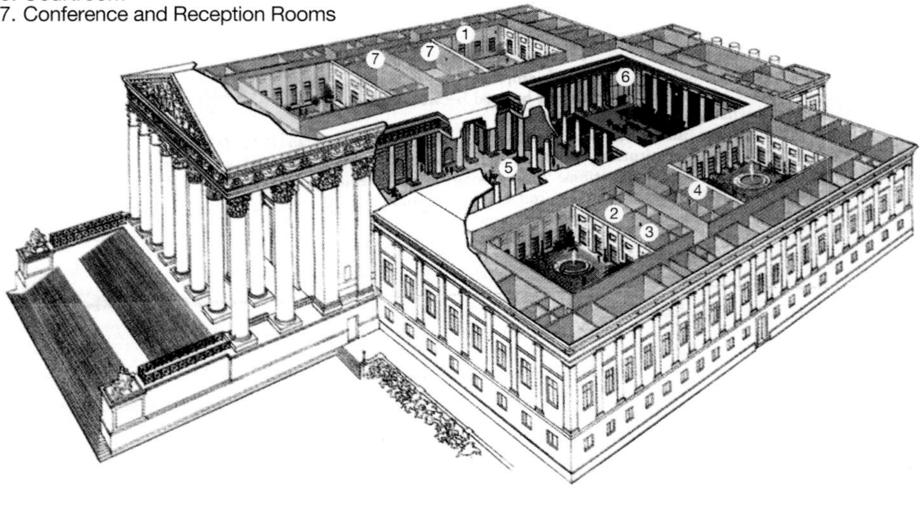

justice in the majority. If the Chief Justice is in the minority, the senior justice in the majority makes the assignment. Writing the opinion of the Court is the central task in Supreme Court policy making. Broadly written opinions may effect sweeping policy changes; narrowly written opinions may decide a particular case but have very little policy impact. The reasons cited for the decision become binding law, to be applied by lower courts in future cases. Yet despite the crucial role of opinion writing in Court policy making, most opinions are actually written by law clerks who are only recent graduates of the nation's prestigious law schools. The justices themselves read, edit, correct, and sometimes rewrite drafts prepared by clerks, but clerks may have a strong influence over the position taken by justices on the issues.

American Bar Association

ABA news and views; information for law students.
www.abanet.org

In addition, the views of the legal profession itself—as reflected by the American Bar Association (ABA) as well as the numerous law reviews published by law schools—influence the Court in subtle yet important ways. Often new interpretations of laws or the Constitution first appear in prestigious law journals, then are borrowed by Supreme Court clerks preparing drafts of opinions by justices, and finally become law when incorporated into majority opinions.

A draft of the opinion is circulated among members of the majority. Any majority member who disagrees with the reasoning in the opinion, and thus disagrees with the policy that is proposed, may either negotiate changes in the opinion with others in the majority or write a concurring opinion. A **concurring opinion** agrees with the decision about which party wins the case but sets forth a different reason for the decision, proposing, in fact, a different policy position.

Justices in the minority often agree to present a **dissenting opinion.** The dissenting opinion sets forth the views of justices who disagree with both the decision and the majority reasoning. Dissenting opinions do not have the force of law. They are written both to express opposition to the majority view and to appeal to a future Court to someday modify or reverse the position of the majority. Occasionally, the Court is unable to agree on a clear policy position on particularly vexing questions. If the majority is strongly divided over the reasoning behind their decision and as many as four justices dissent altogether from the decision, lower courts will lack clear guidance and future cases will be decided on a case-by-case basis, depending on multiple factors occurring in each case (see, for example, "Affirmative Action in the Courts" in Chapter 10). The absence of a clear opinion of the Court, supported by a unified majority of the justices, invites additional cases, keeping the issue on the Court's agenda until such time (if any) as the Court establishes a clear policy on the issue.

Politics and the Supreme Court

The political views of Supreme Court justices have an important influence on Court decisions. Justices are swayed primarily by their own ideological views; but public opinion, the president's position, and the arguments of interest groups all contribute to the outcome of cases.

Liberal and Conservative Voting Blocs Although liberal and conservative voting blocs on the Court are visible over time, on any given case particular justices may deviate from their perceived ideological position. Many cases do not present a liberal-conservative dimension. Each case presents a separate set of facts, and even justices who share a general philosophy may perceive the central facts of a case differently. Moreover, the liberal-versus-conservative dimension sometimes clashes with the activist-versus-self-restraint dimension. Although we

concurring opinion
Opinion by a member of a court that agrees with the result reached by the court in the case but disagrees with or departs from the court's rationale for the decision.

dissenting opinion
Opinion by a member of a court that disagrees with the result reached by the court in the case.

generally think of liberals as favoring activism and conservatives self-restraint, occasionally those who favor self-restraint are obliged to approve of legislation that violates their personal conservative beliefs because opposing it would substitute their judgment for that of elected officials. So ideological blocs are not always good predictors of voting outcomes on the Court.

Over time, the composition of the Supreme Court has changed, as has the power of its various liberal and conservative voting blocs (see Table 11.4). The liberal bloc, headed by Chief Justice Earl Warren, dominated Court decision making from the mid-1950s through the end of the 1960s. The liberal bloc gradually weakened following President Richard Nixon's appointment of Warren Burger as Chief Justice in 1969, but not all of Nixon's appointees joined the conservative bloc; Justice Harry Blackmun and Justice Lewis Powell frequently joined in voting with the liberal bloc. Among Nixon's appointees, only William Rehnquist has consistently adopted conservative positions. President Gerald Ford's only appointee to the Court, John Paul Stevens, began as a moderate and drifted to the liberal bloc. As a result, the Burger Court, although generally not as activist as the Warren Court, still did not reverse any earlier liberal holdings.

President Ronald Reagan, who had campaigned on a pledge to restrain the liberal activism of the Court, tried to appoint conservatives. His first appointee, Sandra Day O'Connor, turned out to be less conservative than expected, especially on women's issues and abortion rights. When Chief Justice Burger retired in 1986, Reagan seized on the opportunity to strengthen the conservative bloc by elevating Rehnquist to Chief Justice. Reagan also appointed Antonin Scalia, another strong conservative, to the Court. Reagan added Anthony Kennedy to the Court in 1988, hoping to give Rehnquist and the conservative bloc the opportunity to form a majority. Had President Reagan succeeded in getting the powerful conservative voice of Robert Bork on the Court, it is possible that many earlier liberal decisions, including *Roe v. Wade,* would have been reversed. But the Senate rejected Bork, David Souter, the man ultimately confirmed, compiled a moderate record.

Liberals worried that the appointment of conservative Clarence Thomas as a replacement for the liberal Thurgood Marshall would give the conservative bloc a

TABLE 11.4 Liberal and Conservative Voting Blocs on the Supreme Court

	Warren Court	The Burger Court	The Rehnquist Court
	1968	1975	2004
Liberal	Earl Warren Hugo Black William O. Douglas Thurgood Marshall William J. Brennan Abe Fortas	William O. Douglas Thurgood Marshall William J. Brennan	John Paul Stevens Ruth Bader Ginsburg Stephen G. Breyer
Moderate	Potter Stewart Byron White	Potter Stewart Byron White Lewis Powell Harry Blackmun	Anthony Kennedy Sandra Day O'Connor David Souter
Conservative	John Marshall Harlan	Warren Burger William Rehnquist	William Rehnquist Antonin Scalia Clarence Thomas

commanding voice in Supreme Court policy making. But no solid conservative majority emerged. Justices Rehnquist, Scalia, and Thomas are considered the core of the conservative bloc, but they must win over at least two of the more moderate justices in order to form a majority in a case. President Bill Clinton's appointees, Ruth Bader Ginsburg and Stephen G. Breyer, have consistently supported liberal views on the Supreme Court. On key questions, the moderate bloc has the deciding vote.

While the moderate bloc currently holds the balance of power on the Court, the Court as a whole has moved in a conservative direction since the high watermark of judicial liberalism during the era of Chief Justice Earl Warren (1953–68). Liberalism on the Court—as measured by pro-individual rights decisions against the government in civil liberties cases, pro-defendant decisions in criminal cases, and pro-women and minorities in civil rights cases—has declined significantly since the 1960s (see Table 11.5).

Public Opinion "By all arguable evidence of the modern Supreme Court, Court appears to reflect public opinion about as accurately as other policy makers."[28] And indeed, on the liberal-conservative dimension, it can be argued that Supreme Court decisions have generally followed shifts in American public opinion. However, the Court appears to lag behind public opinion. It is doubtful that the justices read opinion polls; their jobs do not depend on public approval ratings. Rather, it is more likely that the justices, whose nomination and confirmation depended on an elected president and Senate, generally share the views of those who put them on the bench. Thus, public opinion affects the Court only indirectly, through the nomination and confirmation process.

Presidential Influence Even after a president's initial appointment of a Justice to the High Court, a president may exercise some influence over judicial decision making. The Office of the U.S. Solicitor General is charged with the responsibility of presenting the government's (the president's) views in cases not only to which the U.S. government is a party, but also in cases in which the president and the Attorney General have a strong interest and present their arguments in amicus curiae briefs. The Solicitor General's Office, in both Democratic and Republican presidential administrations, has compiled an enviable record in Supreme Court cases. When representing federal agencies that are parties to cases, the Solicitor General has won two-thirds of their cases before the Supreme Court over

TABLE 11.5 Liberalism in the Supreme Court

	Percent Liberal Decisions		
Type of Case	**Warren Court**	**Burger Court**	**Rehnquist Court**
Civil Liberties	67.7	43.6	42.8
Civil Rights	76.3	51.8	55.3
Criminal Procedures	59.4	34.2	33.2
First Amendment	69.0	48.6	48.5

Note: First Amendment includes all First Amendment guarantees plus due process and privacy; Criminal Procedures includes rights of persons accused of crime except due process; Civil Rights includes non-First Amendment cases pertaining to race, sex, age, and other individual characteristics. Civil Liberties combines all three of these types of cases.

Source: Derived from Lee Epstein et al., *The Supreme Court Compendium*, 3rd ed. (Washington, D.C.: CQ Press, 2002).

UP CLOSE

Bush v. Gore, Majority and Dissenting Opinions

From the Majority Opinion

With respect to the equal protection question, we find a violation of the Equal Protection Clause. . . .

Much of the controversy seems to revolve around ballot cards designed to be perforated by a stylus but which, either through error or deliberate omission, have not been perforated with sufficient precision for a machine to count them.

In some cases a piece of the card—a chad—is hanging, say by two corners. In other cases there is no separation at all, just an indentation. The Florida Supreme Court has ordered that the intent of the voter be discerned from such ballots. . . .

The recount mechanisms implemented in response to the decisions of the Florida Supreme Court do not satisfy the minimum requirement for non-arbitrary treatment of voters necessary to secure the fundamental right (of equal protection). Florida's basic command for the count of legally cast votes is to consider the "intent of the voter." . . . This is unobjectionable as an abstract proposition and a starting principle. The problem inheres in the absence of specific standards to ensure its equal application.

From Justices Rehnquist, Scalia, and Thomas Concurring with the Majority

Moreover, the [Florida] court's interpretation of "legal vote," and hence its decision to order a contest-period recount, plainly departed from the legislative scheme. Florida statutory law cannot reasonably be thought to require the counting of improperly marked ballots. Each Florida precinct before election day provides instructions on how properly to cast a vote; each polling place on election day contains a working model of the voting machine it uses; and each voting booth contains a sample ballot. In precincts using punch-card ballots, voters are instructed to punch out the ballot cleanly:

Kweisi Mfume resigned from a Maryland congressional seat that he had held for ten years in order to assume the leadership of the NAACP, the nation's oldest and largest civil rights organization.

the years. And in cases where the Solicitor General has offered an amicus curiae brief, it has won about three-quarters of its cases. In contrast, the states have won fewer than half of the cases before the Supreme Court in which a state has been a party.

Interest-Group Influence Interest groups have become a major presence in Supreme Court cases. First of all, interest groups (for example, Planned Parenthood, National Association for the Advancement of Colored People, American Civil Liberties Union) sponsor many cases themselves. They find persons they believe to be directly damaged by a public policy, initiate litigation on their behalf, and provide the attorneys and money to pursue these cases all the way to the Supreme Court. Secondly, it is now a rare case that comes to the Court without multiple amicus curiae briefs filed by interest groups.

How influential are interest groups in Supreme Court decisions? Certainly interest groups have a significant influence in bringing issues before the Supreme Court through their sponsorship of cases. It is unlikely that the Court would have acted when it did on many key issues from racial segregation in 1954 (*Brown v. Board of Education* sponsored by the NAACP) to abortion in 1992 (*Planned Parenthood v. Casey* sponsored by Planned Parenthood) in the absence of interest-group activity. And interest-group amicus curiae briefs are now mentioned (cited) in about two-thirds of the written decisions of the Court. However, these briefs may not have much *independent* effect on decisions, that is, they may not have convinced the justices to decide a case one way or another. Several studies have found that interest-group briefs have had very little effect on Supreme Court decisions.[29]

"AFTER VOTING, CHECK YOUR BALLOT CARD TO BE SURE YOUR VOTING SELECTIONS ARE CLEARLY AND CLEANLY PUNCHED AND THERE ARE NO CHIPS LEFT HANGING ON THE BACK OF THE CARD."

From Dissenting Opinions, Justice Stevens

It is confidence in the men and women who administer the judicial system that is the true backbone of the rule of law. Time will one day heal the wound to that confidence that will be inflicted by today's decision. One thing, however, is certain. Although we may never know with complete certainty the identity of the winner of this year's presidential election, the identity of the loser is perfectly clear. It is the nation's confidence in the judge as an impartial guardian of the rule of law.

Source: Bush v. Gore.

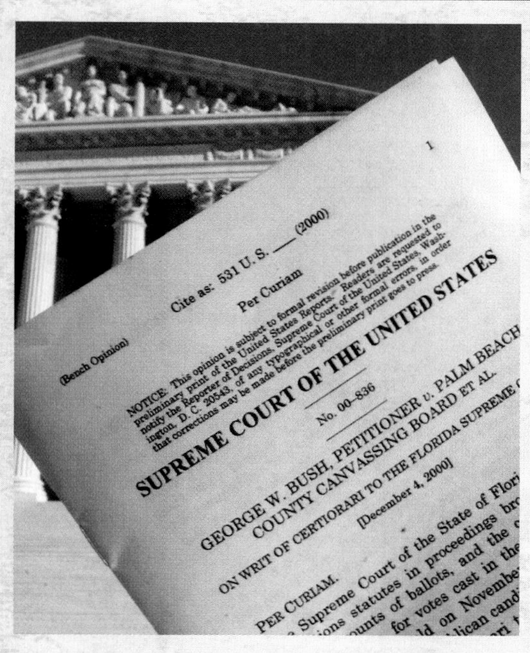

Bush v. Gore in the U.S. Supreme Court

The presidential election of 2000 was unique in American history in that the outcome was decided by the Supreme Court of the United States. The Supreme Court's decision on December 12, 2000, in *Bush v. Gore,* rested on constitutional issues, but the 5–4 decision of the justices raised the question of the High Court's political partisanship.[30]

"Too Close to Call" On the morning after Election Day, it became clear that the outcome of the presidential election depended on Florida's twenty-five electoral votes. Florida's Secretary of State (separately elected Republican Katherine Harris) initially reported a margin of 1,784 for Bush out of over 6 million votes cast in the state. But because Florida law provides for a recount when the margin of victory is less than one-half of 1 percent, the recount of machine votes was conducted as well as a count of absentee ballots. Bush's lead was reduced to a slim 930 votes. The Florida Secretary of State declined to accept any recount returns from the counties after November 14, the date set by Florida law as the final date for submission of returns to the Secretary.

Judicial Maneuvering But immediately after Election Day armies of lawyers descended on Florida's capital city, Tallahassee. The stakes were high—the presidency of the United States. Gore's legal team was headed by former Secretary of State Warren Christopher, and the Bush team by former Secretary of State James Baker (although neither argued directly before the courts). The Gore team demanded *manual* recounts of the ballots in the state's three largest (and most

Southeastern Legal Foundation

Public interest law firm advocating limited government, individual freedom, and the free enterprise system. *www.southeasternlegal.org*

Southern Poverty Law Center

Civil rights law firm opposing death penalty, hate groups, display of religion in public places, etc. *www.splcenter.org*

Democratic) counties—Miami-Dade, Broward (Fort Lauderdale), and Palm Beach. The case was first argued before a Leon County (Tallahassee) trial judge, who dismissed Gore's petition. But the case was quickly appealed to the Florida Supreme Court (with its seven justices, all appointed by Democratic governors). That Court set aside the state's legal deadline for recounts, and county canvassing boards began a tedious hand count of punch card ballots.

The Bush legal team appealed directly to the U.S. Supreme Court arguing, first of all, that the U.S. Constitution gives the power to appoint presidential electors "in such Manner as the *Legislature* thereof may direct" (Article II, Section 1), and that the Florida Supreme Court overreached its authority when it set aside legislative-enacted provisions of the election laws of the state, including the deadline for recounts. They also argued that hand counts in counties were late, unreliable, subjective, and open to partisan bias. The U.S. Supreme Court responded initially by ordering a halt to the recounts and remanding (sending back) the case to the Florida Supreme Court for clarification as to the grounds on which it had been decided.

The Florida Supreme Court was apparently not intimidated by the U.S. Supreme Court's implied judgment that it had erred in its decision. It ordered a manual recount of all legal votes in the state, especially undercounts (where ballots failed to register a vote for president). It specified that "the intent of the voter" should be the criterion for deciding how to count a ballot. The Florida Supreme Court decision, *Gore v. Harris*,[31] was immediately appealed to the U.S. Supreme Court.

By now more than a month had passed with the nation not knowing who would be its next president. It became clear that Al Gore had won the nationwide popular vote. But most Americans acknowledged that the popular vote was of secondary importance to the Constitution of the United States in its provisions for choosing the president by state electoral votes. (Indeed, nationwide polls indicated that 73 percent of Americans said they would accept the U.S. Supreme Court's decision as "the legitimate outcome no matter which candidate it favors."[32]) Only the U.S. Supreme Court seemed to possess sufficient legitimacy to resolve the first contested presidential election in over a century.

A Divided Supreme Court The Supreme Court held that "the use of standardless manual recounts violates the Equal Protection and Due Process Clauses [of the U.S. Constitution] . . . The judgment of the Supreme Court of Florida is reversed." (See *Up Close: "Bush v. Gore,* Majority and Dissenting Opinions.")

The narrow 5–4 decision appeared to follow partisan lines, with Justices O'Connor, Kennedy, Rehnquist, Scalia, and Thomas voting in the majority to allow Florida's Secretary of State to certify that state's electoral votes for Bush. Justices Souter, Stevens, Ginsburg, and Breyer dissented, arguing that the U.S. Supreme Court should not interfere with the Florida Supreme Court's order for a manual recount. Indeed, Justice Stevens implied that the Supreme Court's decision would undermine "the nation's confidence in the judge as an impartial guardian of the rule of law."

Checking Court Power

Many people are concerned about the extent to which we now rely on a nonelected judiciary to decide key policy issues rather than depending on a democratically elected president or Congress.

Legitimacy as a Restraint in the Judiciary Court authority derives from legitimacy rather than force. By that we mean that the courts depend on their au-

WHAT DO YOU THINK?

Do You Have Confidence in the Supreme Court?

The Supreme Court has issued many controversial rulings throughout its history, yet public confidence in the Court has remained fairly high. While many Americans disagree with specific Supreme Court decisions, they remain supportive of the Court itself. For example, in *Bush vs. Gore* many opponents of the decision claimed that the Court reached its decision based on "politics" and "partisanship." Yet most Americans accepted the decision as the final word on the election. The Supreme Court's institutional legitimacy appeared to be sufficient to persuade people to go along with the decision, even if they strongly disagreed with it. In short, Americans appear to distinguish between the Court's specific decisions and the legitimacy of the Court as a political institution.

However, the willingness of Americans to trust the Supreme Court has become more closely tied to party preferences than in the past. In recent years Republicans have been much more confident of the Supreme Court than Democrats. Perhaps this disparity is a result of the Court's decision in *Bush vs. Gore.* Partisanship, together with such highly contentious issues as abortion, the death penalty, and affirmative-action, will likely lead to huge battles in Washington over the replacement of any retiring justices.

Question: Now I am going to read you a list of institutions in American society. Please tell me how much confidence you, yourself, have in each one—a great deal, quite a lot, some, or very little? . . . The U.S. Supreme Court.

Source: Copyright © 2003 by The Gallup Organization.

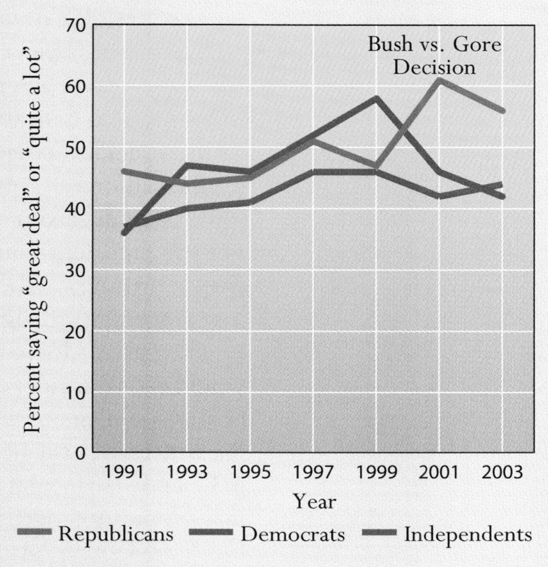

thority being seen as rightful, on people perceiving an obligation to abide by court decisions whether they agree with them or not. The courts have no significant force at their direct command. Federal marshals, who carry out the orders of federal courts, number only a few thousand. Courts must rely primarily on the executive branch for enforcement of their decisions.

Today most Americans believe that Supreme Court decisions are authoritative statements about the Constitution and that people have an obligation to obey these decisions whether they agree with them or not.[33] Thus public opinion constrains other public officials—from the president, to governors, to school superintendents, to law enforcement officials—to obey Supreme Court decisions. Their constituents do not hold them personally responsible for unpopular actions ordered by the Supreme Court or federal judges. On the contrary, their constituents generally expect them to comply with court decisions (see *What Do You Think?:* "Do You Have Confidence in the Supreme Court?")

Compliance with Court Policy Federal and state court judges must apply Supreme Court policies when ruling on cases in their own courts. Occasionally lower courts express their disagreement with the Supreme Court in an opinion, even when they feel obliged to carry out the High Court's policy. At times, lower federal and state courts try to give a narrow interpretation to a Supreme Court decision with which they disagree. But judges who seek to defy the Supreme Court face the ultimate sanction of reversal on appeal by the losing party. Professional pride usually inspires judges to avoid reversals of their judgments by higher courts even though a long record of reversals is not grounds for impeachment or removal of a federal judge.

Public officials who defy Supreme Court rulings risk lawsuits and court orders mandating compliance. Persons injured by noncompliance are likely to file suit against noncomplying officials, as are interest groups that monitor official compliance with the policies they support. These suits are expensive, time consuming, and potentially embarrassing to government officials and agencies. Once a court order is issued, continued defiance can result in fines and penalties for contempt of court.

The president of the United States is subject to federal court orders. Historically, this notion has been challenged: early presidents believed they were separate and at least co-equal to the courts and that their own determination about the legality or constitutionality of their own acts could not be overturned by the courts. President Andrew Jackson could—and did—say: "John Marshall has made his decision. Now let him enforce it," expressing the view that the president was not obliged to enforce court decisions he disagreed with.[34] But in the course of 200 years, the courts—not the president—have gained in legitimacy as the final authority on the law and the Constitution. Today a president who openly defied the Supreme Court would lose any claims to legitimacy and would risk impeachment by Congress.

The case of Richard Nixon illustrates the weakness of a modern president who would even consider defying the Supreme Court. When Nixon sought to invoke executive privilege to withhold damaging tapes of White House conversations in the Watergate investigation (see *Up Close:* "Watergate and the Limits of Presidential Power" in Chapter 9), federal district judge John Sirica rejected his claim and ordered that the tapes be turned over to the special prosecutor in the case. In arguments before the Supreme Court, Nixon's lawyers contended that the president would not have to comply with a Supreme Court decision to turn over the tapes. Yet when the Court ruled unanimously against him, Nixon felt bound to comply and released tapes that were very damaging to his cause. But Nixon understood that refusal to abide by a Supreme Court decision would most assuredly have resulted in impeachment. Under the circumstances, compliance was the better of two unattractive choices.

Presidential Influence on Court Policy The president and Congress can exercise some restraint over court power through the checks and balances built into the Constitution. Using the office's powers of appointment, presidents have effectively modified the direction of Supreme Court policy and influenced lower federal courts as well. Certainly presidents must await the death or retirement of Supreme Court justices and federal judges, and presidents are constrained by the need to secure Senate confirmation of their appointees. However, over time presidential influence on the courts can be significant. During their combined twelve years in the White House, Ronald Reagan and George Bush were able to fill 70 percent of federal district and appellate court judgeships and six of nine Supreme Court positions with their own appointees. As noted earlier, however, their appointees did not always reflect these presidents' philosophy of judicial self-restraint in rendering decisions. Nevertheless, the federal courts tilted in a somewhat more conservative direction. President Bill Clinton's appointments generally strengthened liberal, activist impulses throughout the federal judiciary.

Congressional Checks on the Judiciary The Constitution gives Congress control over the structure and jurisdiction of federal district and appellate courts, but congressional use of this control has been restrained. Only the Supreme Court is established by the Constitution; Article III gives Congress the power to "ordain and establish" "inferior" courts. In theory, Congress could try to limit court jurisdiction to hear cases that Congress did not wish it to decide. Congress has used this power to lighten the federal courts' workload; for example, Congress has limited the jurisdiction of federal courts in cases between citizens of different states by requiring that the dispute involve more than $50,000. But Congress has never used this power to change court policy—for example, by removing federal court jurisdiction over school prayer cases or desegregation cases. Indeed federal courts would probably declare unconstitutional any congressional attempt to limit their power to interpret the Constitution by limiting jurisdiction.

Likewise, although Congress could, in theory, expand membership on the Supreme Court, the custom of a nine-member Supreme Court is now so deeply ingrained in American government that "court packing" is politically unthinkable. Franklin Roosevelt's unsuccessful 1937 attempt to expand the Supreme Court was the last serious assault on its membership. However, President Jimmy Carter succeeded in getting Congress to add a large number of federal district judgeships, and he used these new posts to appoint more women and minorities to the federal judiciary.

A more common congressional constraint on the Supreme Court is amending statutory laws to reverse federal court interpretations of these laws that Congress believes are in error. Thus when the Supreme Court decided that civil rights laws did not mandate a cutoff of all federal funds to a college upon evidence of discrimination in a single program but only the funds for that program.[35] Congress amended its own laws to require the more sweeping remedy. Although members of Congress frequently berate the Court for what they see as misreading of the laws, all Congress needs to do to reverse a Court interpretation of those laws is to pass amendments to them.

Constitutional amendment is the only means by which the Congress and the states can reverse a Supreme Court interpretation of the Constitution itself. After the Civil War, the Thirteenth Amendment abolishing slavery reversed the Supreme Court's *Dred Scott* decision (1857) that slavery was constitutionally protected. The Sixteenth Amendment (1913) gave Congress the power to impose an income tax, thus reversing the Supreme Court's earlier decision in *Pollock v. Farmer's Loan*[36] holding income taxes unconstitutional (1895). But recent attempts to reverse Supreme Court interpretations of the Constitution by passing constitutional amendments on the issues of prayer in public schools, busing, and abortion have all failed to win congressional approval. The barriers to a constitutional amendment are formidable: a two-thirds vote of both houses of Congress and ratification by three-quarters of the states. Thus, for all practical purposes, the Constitution is what the Supreme Court says it is.

Congress can impeach federal court judges, but only for "cause" (committing crimes), not for their decisions. Although impeachment is frequently cited as a constitutional check on the judiciary, it has no real influence over judicial policy making. Only five federal court judges have ever been impeached by the House, convicted by the Senate, and removed from office, although two others were impeached and another nine resigned to avoid impeachment. In 1989 Federal District Court Judge Alcee Hastings became the first sitting judge in more than fifty years to be impeached, tried, and found guilty by the Congress. He was convicted by the Senate of perjury and conspiracy to obtain a $150,000 bribe; but a federal district court judge later ruled that he should have been tried by the full Senate, not a special committee of the Senate. Hastings declared the ruling a vindication; in 1992 he won a congressional seat in Florida, becoming the first person ever to become a member of the House after being impeached by that same body. Even criminal convictions do not ensure removal from office, although judges have resigned under fire.

SUMMARY NOTES

- Great power is lodged in the Supreme Court of the United States and the federal judiciary. These courts have undertaken to resolve many of the most divisive conflicts in American society. The judicial power is the power to decide cases and controversies, and in so doing to decide the meaning of the Constitution and laws of Congress.
- The power of judicial review is the power to invalidate laws of Congress or of the states that the federal courts believe conflict with the U.S. Constitution. This power is not specifically mentioned in the Constitution but was derived by Chief Justice John Marshall from the Supremacy Clause and the meaning of judicial power in Article III.
- The Supreme Court has been fairly restrained in its use of judicial review with regard to laws of Congress and actions of presidents; it has more frequently overturned state laws. The federal courts also exercise great power in the interpretation of the laws of Congress, especially when statutory language is vague.
- Arguments over judicial power are reflected in the conflicting philosophies of judicial activism and judicial self-restraint. Advocates of judicial restraint argue that judges must not substitute their own views for those of elected representatives and the remedy for unwise laws lies in the legislature, not the courts. Advocates of judicial activism argue that the courts must view the Constitution as a living document and its meaning must fit the needs of a changing society.
- The federal judiciary consists of three levels of courts—the Supreme Court, the U.S. Courts of Appeals, and the U.S. District Courts. The district courts are trial courts that hear both civil and criminal cases. The courts of appeals are appellate courts and do not hold trials but consider only the record of trial courts and the arguments (briefs) of attorneys. More than 90 percent of federal cases end in appeals courts. The Supreme Court can hear appeals from state high courts as well as lower federal courts. The Supreme Court hears only about 200 cases a year.
- Courts function under general rules of restraint that do not bind the president or Congress. The Supreme Court does not decide hypothetical cases or render advisory opinions. The principle of stare decisis, or reliance on precedent, is not set aside lightly.
- The selection of Supreme Court justices and federal judges is based more on political considerations than legal qualifications. Presidents almost always appoint judges from their own party, and presidents increasingly have sought judges who share their ideological views. However, because of the independence of judges once they are appointed, presidents have sometimes been disappointed in the decisions of their appointees. In addition, Senate approval of nominees has become increasingly politicized, with problems most evident when different parties control the White House and the Senate.
- The Supreme Court sets its own agenda for policy making, usually by granting or withholding certiorari. Generally four justices must agree to grant certiorari for a case to be decided by the Supreme Court. The Supreme Court has been especially active in policy making in interpreting the meaning of the Fourteenth Amendment's guarantee of "equal protection of the laws," as well as of the civil rights and voting rights acts of Congress. It has also been active in defining the meaning of freedom of press, speech, and religion in the First Amendment and "due process of law" in the Fifth Amendment. The federal courts are active in overseeing government regulatory activity. But federal courts have generally left the areas of national security and international relations to the president and Congress. In addition, the Court tends to accept cases involving questions decided differently by different courts of appeal, cases in which lower courts have challenged Supreme Court interpretations, and cases in which the U.S. government is a party and it requests review.
- Liberal and conservative blocs on the Supreme Court can be discerned over time. Generally, liberals have been judicial activists and conservatives have been restraintists. Today a moderate bloc appears to hold the balance of power.
- The Supreme Court risked its reputation for political impartiality when it intervened in the 2000 presidential election, and issued a decision that in effect gave Florida's

25 electoral votes to George W. Bush and by so doing won him a majority in the Electoral College.

- Court power derives primarily from legitimacy rather than force. Most Americans believe that Supreme Court decisions are authoritative statements about the Constitution and people have an obligation to obey these decisions whether they agree with them or not. Although early presidents thought of themselves as constitutional coequals with the Supreme Court and not necessarily bound by Court decisions, today it would be politically unthinkable for a president to ignore a court order.
- There are very few checks on Supreme Court power. Presidents may try to influence Court policy through judicial nominations, but once judges are confirmed by the Senate they can pursue their own impulses. Congress has never used its power to limit the jurisdiction of federal courts in order to influence judicial decisions.
- Only by amending the Constitution can Congress and the states reverse a Supreme Court interpretation of its meaning. Congress can impeach federal judges only for committing crimes, not for their decisions.

KEY TERMS

judicial review 382
statutory laws 386
judicial self-restraint 386
original intent 387
judicial activism 388
stare decisis 388
precedent 388
jurisdiction 389
original jurisdiction 389
appellate jurisdiction 389
appeal 389
district courts 389
grand juries 389
petit (regular) juries 389
circuit courts 389
briefs 389
civil cases 394
adversarial system 394
standing 394
plaintiffs 395
defendants 395
sovereign immunity 395
class action suits 395
contingency fees 396
remedies and reliefs 396
independent counsel ("special prosecutor") 396
litmus test 398
senatorial courtesy 398
writ of certiorari 403
rule of four 403
amicus curiae 403
solicitor general 404
majority opinion 404
concurring opinion 405
dissenting opinion 405

SUGGESTED READINGS

Baum, Lawrence. *The Supreme Court.* 8th ed. Washington, D.C.: CQ Press, 2003. Readable introduction to the Supreme Court as a political institution, covering the selection and confirmation of judges, the nature of the issues decided by courts, the process of judicial decision making, and the impact of Supreme Court decisions.

Bork, Robert H. *Coercing Virtue.* Washington DC: AEI Press, 2003. An argument that judges, rather than legislators, are making and repealing law and deciding cases with partisan and ideological subjectivity.

Carp, Robert A., and Ronald Stidham. *The Federal Courts.* 4th ed. Washington, D.C.: CQ Press, 2001. Overview of the federal judicial system, arguing that federal judges and Supreme Court justices function as part of the political system and engage in policy making that influences all our lives.

Epstein, Lee, and Thomas G. Walker. *Constitutional Law for a Changing America: Institutional Power and Constraints.* 4th ed. Washington, D.C.: CQ Press, 2001. Commentary and selected excerpts from cases dealing with the structure and powers of government.

Johnson, Charles, and Danette Buickman. *Independent Counsel: The Law and the Investigations.* Washington, D.C.: CQ Press, 2001. A comprehensive history of the independent counsel law and the investigations conducted under it since 1978, from Watergate to Whitewater.

Neubauer, David W. and Stephen S. Weinhold. *Judicial Politics: Law, Courts, and Politics in the United States.* Belmont, Calif.: Wadsworth, 2004. Introduction to the judicial process with controversial cases in each chapters.

U.S. Supreme Court decisions are available at most public and university libraries as well as at law libraries in volumes of *United States Reports.* Court opinions are cited by the names of the parties, for example, *Brown v. Board of Education of Topeka,* followed by a reference number such as 347 U.S. 483 (1954). The first number in the citation (347) is the volume number; "U.S." refers to *United States Reports;* the subsequent number is the page on which the decision begins; the year the case was decided is in parentheses.

CHAPTER 12

POLITICS, PERSONAL LIBERTY, AND CIVIL RIGHTS

CHAPTER OUTLINE

- Power and Individual Liberty
- Freedom of Religion
- Freedom of Speech
- Privacy, Abortion, and the Constitution
- Obscenity and the Law
- The Right to Bear Arms
- Rights of Criminal Defendants
- The Death Penalty
- The Politics of Equality
- Slavery, Segregation, and the Constitution
- The Civil Rights Acts
- Affirmative Action: Opportunity versus Results
- Hispanics in America
- Hispanic Politics
- Gender Equality and the Fourteenth Amendment
- Gender Equality in the Economy

THINK ABOUT POLITICS

1 Do you think the government has become so large and powerful that it poses a threat to the rights and freedoms of ordinary citizens?
Yes ● No ●

2 Do you believe that using tax funds to pay tuition at church-affiliated schools violates the separation of church and state?
Yes ● No ●

3 Is the death penalty a "cruel and unusual" punishment?
Yes ● No ●

4 Should persons captured on a foreign battlefield in the war on terrorism be entitled to constitutional protections?
Yes ● No ●

5 Does the U.S. Constitution require the government to be color blind with respect to different races in all its laws and actions?
Yes ● No ●

6 Do you generally favor affirmative action programs for women and minorities?
Yes ● No ●

7 Do dirty jokes and foul language at work constitute sexual harassment?
Yes ● No ●

Government power defends your most basic rights to life, liberty, and the pursuit of happiness while at the same time ensuring that all other Americans have the same rights. The Founders guaranteed individual liberty in the earliest days of our nation through the first ten amendments to the Constitution—our Bill of Rights.

Equality has long been the central issue of American politics. What do we mean by equality? And what if anything, should government do to achieve it?

Power and Individual Liberty

To the authors of the Declaration of Independence, individual liberty was inherent in the human condition. It was not derived from governments or even from constitutions. Rather, governments and constitutions existed to make individual liberty more secure:

> We hold these truths to be self-evident, that all men are created equal, that they are endowed by their Creator with certain unalienable Rights, that among these are Life, Liberty and the pursuit of Happiness. That to secure these rights, Governments are instituted among Men, deriving their just powers from the consent of the governed.

The authors of the Bill of Rights (the first ten amendments to the Constitution) did *not* believe that they were creating individual rights, but rather that they were recognizing and guaranteeing rights that belonged to individuals by virtue of their humanity.

Authority and Liberty To avoid the brutal life of a lawless society, where the weak are at the mercy of the strong, people form governments and endow them with powers to secure peace and self-preservation. People voluntarily relinquish some of their individual freedom to establish a government that is capable of protecting them from their neighbors as well as from foreign aggressors. This government must be strong enough to maintain its own existence or it cannot defend the rights of its citizens.

But what happens when a government becomes too strong and infringes on the liberties of its citizens? How much liberty must individuals surrender to secure an orderly society? This is the classic dilemma of free government: people must create laws and governments to protect their freedom, but the laws and governments themselves restrict freedom.

Democracy and Personal Liberty When democracy is defined only as a *decision-making process*—widespread popular participation and rule by majority—it offers little protection for individual liberty. Democracy must also be defined to include *substantive values*—a recognition of the dignity of all individuals and their equality under law. Otherwise, some people, particularly "the weaker party, or an obnoxious individual" would be vulnerable to deprivations of life, liberty, or property simply by decisions of majorities (see "The Paradox of Democracy" in Chapter 1). Indeed, the "great object" of the Constitution, according to James Madison, was to preserve popular government yet at the same time to protect individuals from "unjust" majorities.[1]

First Amendment Center
Vanderbilt University center provides sources of information on First Amendment issues.
www.firstamendmentcenter.org

The purpose of the Constitution—and especially its Bill of Rights, passed by the First Congress in September 1789—is to limit governmental power over the individual, that is, to place personal liberty beyond the reach of government (see Table 12.1). Each individual's rights to life, liberty, and property, due process of law, and equal protection of the law are not subject to majority vote. Or, as Supreme Court Justice Robert Jackson once declared, "One's right to life, liberty, and property, to free speech, a free press, freedom of worship and assembly, and other fundamental rights may not be submitted to vote: they depend on the outcome of no elections."[2]

Freedom of Religion

Americans are a very religious people. Belief in God and church attendance are more widespread in the United States than in any other advanced industrialized nation. Although many early American colonists came to the new land to escape religious persecution, they frequently established their own government-supported churches and imposed their own religious beliefs on others. Puritanism was the official faith of colonial Massachusetts, and Virginia officially established the Church of England. Only two colonies (Maryland and Rhode Island) provided for full religious freedom. In part to lesson the potential for conflict among the states, the framers of the Bill of Rights sought to prevent the new national government from establishing an official religion or interfering with religious exercises. The very first words of the First Amendment set forth two separate prohibitions on government: "Congress shall make no law respecting an *establishment of religion,* or prohibiting the *free exercise* thereof." These two restrictions on government power—the Free Exercise Clause and the No Establishment Clause—guarantee separate religious freedoms.

Free Exercise Clause Clause in the First Amendment to the Constitution that prohibits government from restricting religious beliefs and practices

Free Exercise of Religion The **Free Exercise Clause** prohibits government from restricting religious beliefs or practices. Although the wording of the First Amendment appears absolute ("Congress shall make no law . . ."), the U.S. Supreme Court has never interpreted the phrase to protect any conduct carried on in the name of religion. In the first major decision involving this clause, the Court ruled in 1879 that polygamy could be outlawed by Congress in Utah Territory even though some Mormons argued that it was part of their religious faith. The Court distinguished between belief and behavior, saying that "Congress was deprived of all legislative power over mere opinion [by the First Amendment], but was left free to reach actions which were in violation of social duties."[3] The Court also

TABLE 12.1 Constitutionally Protected Rights

The Bill of Rights

The first ten amendments to the Constitution of the United States, passed by the First Congress of the United States in September 1789 and ratified by the states in December 1791.

Amendments	Protections
First Amendment: Religion, Speech, Press, Assembly, Petition	
Congress shall make no law respecting an establishment of religion, or prohibiting the free exercise thereof, or abridging the freedom of speech, or of the press; or the right of the people peaceably to assemble, and to petition the Government for a redress of grievances.	Prohibits government establishment of religion. Protects the free exercise of religion. Protects freedom of speech. Protects freedom of the press. Protects freedom of assembly. Protects the right to petition government "for a redress of grievances."
Second Amendment: Right to Bear Arms	
A well regulated Militia, being necessary to the security of a free State, the right of the people to keep and bear Arms, shall not be infringed.	Protects the right of people to bear arms and states to maintain militia (National Guard) units.
Third Amendment: Quartering of Soldiers	
No Soldier shall, in time of peace, be quartered in any house, without the consent of the Owner, nor in time of war, but in a manner to be prescribed by law.	Prohibits forcible quartering of soldiers in private homes in peacetime, or in war without congressional authorization.
Fourth Amendment: Searches and Seizures	
The right of the people to be secure in their persons, houses, papers, and effects, against unreasonable searches and seizures, shall not be violated, and no Warrants shall issue, but upon probable cause, supported by Oath or affirmation, and particularly describing the place to be searched, and the persons or things to be seized.	Protects against "unreasonable searches and seizures." Requires warrants for searches of homes and other places where there is a reasonable expectation of privacy. Judges may issue search warrants only with "probable cause," and such warrants must be specific regarding the place to be searched and the things to be seized.
Fifth Amendment: Grand Juries, Double Jeopardy, Self-Incrimination, Due Process, Protection against Government Takings of Property	
No person shall be held to answer for a capital, or otherwise infamous crime, unless on a presentment or indictment of a Grand jury, except in cases arising in the land or naval forces, or in the Militia, when in actual service in time of war or public danger; nor shall any person be subject for the same offence to be twice put in jeopardy of life or limb, nor shall he be compelled in any criminal case to be a witness against himself, nor be deprived of life, liberty, or property, without due process of law; nor shall private property be taken for public use, without just compensation.	Requires that, before trial for a serious crime, a person (except military personnel) must be indicted by a grand jury. Prohibits double jeopardy (trial for the same offense a second time after being found innocent). Prohibits the government from forcing any person in a criminal case to be a witness against himself or herself. Prohibits the government from taking life, liberty, or property "without due process of law." Prohibits government from taking private property without paying "just compensation."

(continued)

TABLE 12.1 Constitutionally Protected Rights (continued)

Amendments	Protections
Sixth Amendment: Fair Trial	
In all criminal prosecutions, the accused shall enjoy the right to a speedy and public trial, by an impartial jury of the State and district wherein the crime shall have been committed, which district shall have been previously ascertained by law, and to be informed of the nature and cause of the accusation; to be confronted with the witnesses against him; to have compulsory process for obtaining witnesses in his favor, and to have the Assistance of Counsel for his defense.	Requires that the accused in a criminal case be given a speedy and public trial, and thus prohibits prolonged incarceration without trial or secret trials. Requires that trials be by jury and take place in the district where the crime was committed. Requires that the accused be informed of the charges, have the right to confront witnesses, have the right to force supporting witnesses to testify, and have the assistance of counsel.
Seventh Amendment: Trial by Jury in Civil Cases	
In Suits at common law, where the value in controversy shall exceed twenty dollars, the right of trial by jury shall be preserved, and no fact tried by a jury, shall be otherwise reexamined in any Court of the United States, than according to the rules of the common law.	Requires a jury trial in civil cases involving more than $20. Limits the degree to which factual questions decided by a jury may be reviewed by another court.
Eighth Amendment: Bail, Fines and Punishment	
Excessive bail shall not be required, nor excessive fines imposed, nor cruel and unusual punishments inflicted.	Prohibits excessive bail. Prohibits excessive fines. Prohibits cruel and unusual punishment.
Ninth Amendment: Unspecified Rights Retained by People	
The enumeration in the Constitution, of certain rights, shall not be construed to deny or disparage others retained by the people.	Protection of unspecified rights (including privacy) that are not listed in the Constitution. The Constitution shall not be interpreted to be a complete list of rights retained by the people.
Tenth Amendment: Rights Reserved to the States	
The powers not delegated to the United States by the Constitution, nor prohibited by it to the States, are reserved to the States respectively, or to the people.	States retain powers that are not granted by the Constitution to the national government or prohibited by it to the states.
Rights in the Text of the Constitution	
Several rights were written into the text of the Constitution in 1787 and thus precede in time the adoption of the Bill of Rights.	
Article 1 Section 9: Habeas Corpus, Bills of Attainder, and Ex Post Facto Laws	
The privilege of the Writ of Habeas Corpus shall not be suspended, unless when in Cases of Rebellion or Invasion the public Safety may require it. No Bill of Attainder or ex post facto Law shall be passed.	Habeas corpus prevents imprisonment without a judge's determination that a person is being lawfully detained. Prohibition of bills of attainder prevents Congress (and states) from deciding people guilty of a crime and imposing punishment without trial. Prohibition of ex post facto laws prevents Congress (and states) from declaring acts to be criminal that were committed before the passage of a law making them so.

(continued)

TABLE 12.1 Constitutionally Protected Rights (continued)

Thirteenth and Fourteenth Amendments

The Bill of Rights begins with the words "Congress shall make no law . . ." indicating that it initially applied only to the *federal* government. Although states had their own constitutions that guarantee many of the same rights, for more than a century the Bill of Rights did not apply to state and local governments. Following the Civil War, the Thirteenth, Fourteenth, and Fifteenth (voting rights) Amendments were passed, restricting *state* governments and their local subdivisions. But not until many years later did the U.S. Supreme Court, in a long series of decisions, apply the Bill of Rights against the states.

Thirteenth Amendment	
Neither slavery nor involuntary servitude, except as a punishment for crime whereof the party shall have been duly convicted, shall exist within the United States, or any place subject to their jurisdiction.	Prohibits slavery or involuntary servitude except for punishment by law; applies to both governments and private citizens.
Fourteenth Amendment	
All persons born or naturalized in the United States, and subject to the jurisdiction thereof, are citizens of the United States and of the State wherein they reside. No State shall make or enforce any law which shall abridge the privileges or immunities of citizens of the United States; nor shall any State deprive any person of life, liberty, or property, without due process of law; nor deny to any person within its jurisdiction the equal protection of the laws.	Protects "privileges and immunities of citizenship." Prevents deprivation of life, liberty, or property "without due process of law"; this phrase incorporates virtually all of the rights specified in the Bill of Rights. Prevents denial of "equal protection of the laws" for all persons.

employed the Free Exercise Clause to strike down as unconstitutional an attempt by a state to prohibit private religious schools and force all children to attend public schools.[4] This decision protects the entire structure of private religious schools in the nation.

What Constitutes "Establishment"? It has proven difficult for the Supreme Court to reconcile this wall-of-separation interpretation of the First Amendment with the fact that religion plays an important role in the life of most Americans. Public meetings, including sessions of the Congress, often begin with prayers;[5] coins are inscribed with the words "In God We Trust"; and the armed forces provide chaplains for U.S. soldiers.

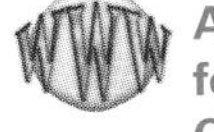

Americans United for Separation of Church and State
Organization advocating elimination of religious activity from public life.
www.au.org

The Supreme Court has set forth a three-part **Lemon test** for determining whether a particular state law constitutes "establishment" of religion and thus violates the First Amendment. To be constitutional, a law affecting religious activity:

1. Must have a secular purpose.
2. As its primary effect, must neither advance nor inhibit religion.
3. Must not foster "an excessive government entanglement with religion."[6]

Lemon test To be constitutional, a law must have a secular purpose; its primary effect must neither advance nor inhibit religion; and it must not foster excessive government entanglement with religion.

Using this three-part test, the Supreme Court held that it was unconstitutional for a state to pay the costs of teachers' salaries or instructional materials in parochial schools. The justices argued that this practice would require excessive government controls and surveillance to ensure that funds were used only for secular instruction and thus involved "excessive entanglement between government and religion."

A Menorah lighting ceremony celebrating Chanukah on public property near the White House. The Supreme Court is divided over whether such public displays violate the No Establishment Clause of the First Amendment.

Although the Supreme Court ruled in 1962 (*Engle v. Vitale*) that even voluntary prayer in public schools was an unconstitutional violation of the separation of church and state under the First Amendment, the question of prayer in the schools remains a heated one. Indeed, recent court rulings regarding nondenominational prayers at graduation ceremonies and sporting events have, if anything, further confused the issue.

However, the Court has upheld the use of tax funds to provide students attending church-related schools with nonreligious textbooks, lunches, transportation, sign-language interpreting, and special education teachers. And the Court has upheld a state's granting of tax credits to parents whose children attend private schools, including religious schools.[7] The Court has also upheld government grants of money to church-related colleges and universities for secular purposes.[8] The Court has ruled that if public buildings are open to use for secular organizations, they must also be opened to use by religious organizations.[9] And the Court has held that a state institution (the University of Virginia) not only can but must grant student activity fees to religious organizations on the same basis as it grants these fees to secular organizations.[10]

The Supreme Court has upheld tax exemptions for churches on the grounds that "the role of religious organizations as charitable associations, in furthering the secular objectives of the state, has become a fundamental concept in our society."[11] It held that schools must allow after-school meetings on school property by religious groups if such a privilege is extended to nonreligious groups.[12] Deductions on federal income tax returns for church contributions are also constitutional. The Supreme Court allows states to close stores on Sundays and otherwise set aside that day, as long as there is a secular purpose—such as "rest, repose, recreation and tranquility"—in doing so.[13]

But the Court has not always acted to "accommodate" religion. In a controversial case, the Court held that a Christmas nativity scene sitting alone on public property was an official "endorsement" of Christian belief and therefore violated the No Establishment Clause. However, if the Christian display was accompanied by a Menorah, a traditional Christmas tree, Santa Claus and reindeer, it would simply be "taking note of the season" and not an unconstitutional endorsement of religion.[14] And in another case, the Supreme Court held that a Louisiana law requiring the teaching of "creationism" along with evolution in the public schools was an unconstitutional establishment of a religious belief.[15]

Prayer in the School The Supreme Court's most controversial interpretation of the No Establishment Clause involved the question of prayer and Bible-reading ceremonies conducted by public schools. The practice of opening the school day with prayer and Bible-reading ceremonies was once widespread in American public schools. To avoid the denominational aspects of these ceremonies, New York State's Board of Regents substituted the following nondenominational prayer, which it required to be said aloud in each class in the presence of a teacher at the beginning of each school day: "Almighty God, we acknowledge our dependence upon Thee, and we beg Thy blessings upon us, our parents, our teachers, and our country." New York argued that this brief prayer did not violate the No Establishment Clause, because the prayer was denominationally neutral and because student participation in the prayer was voluntary. However, in *Engle v. Vitale* (1962), the Supreme Court stated that "the constitutional prohibition against laws respecting an establishment of a religion must at least mean in this country it is no part of the business of government to compose official prayers for any group of the American people to recite as part of a religious program carried on by government." The Court pointed out that making prayer voluntary did not free it from the prohibitions of the No Establishment Clause, and that clause prevented the *establishment* of a religious ceremony by a government agency regardless of whether the ceremony was voluntary.[16]

Anti-Defamation League

Organization opposing anti-Semitism and securing justice for the Jewish people.
www.adl.org

Christian Coalition

Organization dedicated to "take America back" from the "judicial tyranny" that would remove religion from public life.
www.cc.org

One year later, in the case of *Abington Township v. Schempp*, the Court considered the constitutionality of Bible-reading ceremonies in the public schools. Here again, even though the children were not required to participate, the Court found that Bible reading as an opening exercise in the schools was a religious ceremony. The justices went to some trouble in the majority opinion to point out that they were not "throwing the Bible out of the schools." They specifically stated that the *study* of the Bible or of religion, when presented objectively and as part of a secular program of education, did not violate the First Amendment; but religious *ceremonies* involving Bible reading or prayer established by a state or school did.[17]

"Voluntary" Prayer State efforts to encourage "voluntary prayer" in public schools have also been struck down by the Supreme Court as unconstitutional. When the state of Alabama authorized a period of silence for "meditation or voluntary prayer" in public schools, the Court ruled that this action was an "establishment of religion." The Court said the law had no secular purpose, that it conveyed "a message of state endorsement and promotion of prayer," and that its real intent was to encourage prayer in public schools.[18] In a stinging dissenting opinion, Justice William Rehnquist noted that the Supreme Court itself opened its session with a prayer and that both houses of Congress opened every session with prayers led by official chaplains paid by the government. In 1992 the Court held that invocations and benedictions at public high school graduation ceremonies were an unconstitutional establishment of religion.[19] And in 2000 the Court ruled that student-led "invocations" at football games were unconstitutional. A Texas school district that allowed students to use its public address system at football games "to solemnize the event" was violating the No Establishment Clause. "The Constitution demands that schools not force on students the difficult choice between whether to attend these games or to risk facing a personally offensive religious ritual.[20]

Freedom of Speech

Although the First Amendment is absolute in its wording ("Congress shall pass no law . . . abridging the freedom of speech"), the Supreme Court has never been willing to interpret this statement as a protection of *all* speech. What kinds of speech does the First Amendment protect from government control, and what kinds of speech may be constitutionally prohibited?

Clear and Present Danger Doctrine The classic example of speech that can be prohibited was given by Justice Oliver Wendell Holmes in 1919: "The most stringent protection of free speech would not protect a man in falsely shouting 'fire' in a theater and causing a panic."[21] Although Holmes recognized that the government may prevent speech that creates a serious and immediate danger to society, he objected to government attempts to stifle critics of its policies, such as the Espionage Act of 1917 and the Sedition Act of 1918. The Sedition Act prohibited, among other things, speech that was meant to discourage the sale of war bonds; "disloyal" speech about the government, the Constitution, the military forces, or the flag of the United States; and speech that urged the curtailment of war production. In the case of *Gitlow v. New York,* the majority supported the right of the government to curtail any speech that "tended to subvert or imperil the government," but Holmes dissented, arguing that "every idea is an incitement. It offers itself for belief and if believed it is acted on unless some other belief outweighs it."[22] Unless the expression of an idea created a *serious and immediate danger,* Holmes argued that it should be tolerated and combated or defeated only by the expression of better ideas. This standard for determining the limits of free expression became known as the **clear and present danger doctrine**. Government should not curtail speech merely because it *might tend* to cause a future danger: "The question in every case is whether the words used are used in such circumstances and are of such a nature as to create a clear and present danger that they will bring about the substantive evils that Congress has a right to prevent."[23] Holmes's dissent inspired a long struggle in the courts to strengthen constitutional protections for speech and press.

Although Holmes was the first to use the phrase "clear and present danger," it was Justice Louis D. Brandeis who later developed the doctrine into a valuable constitutional principle that the Supreme Court gradually came to adopt. Brandeis explained that the doctrine involved two elements: (1) the clearness or seriousness of the expression; and (2) the immediacy of the danger flowing from the speech. With regard to immediacy he wrote,

> No danger flowing from speech can be deemed clear and present, unless the incidence of the evil apprehended is so imminent that it may befall before there is opportunity for full discussion. If there be time to expose through discussion the falsehood and fallacies, to avert the evil by the processes of education, the remedy to be applied is more speech, not enforced silence.

And with regard to seriousness he wrote,

> Moreover, even imminent danger cannot justify resort to prohibition [of speech] . . . unless the evil apprehended is relatively serious. Prohibition of free speech and assembly is a measure so stringent that it would be inappropriate as the means for averting a relatively trivial harm to society. . . . There must be the probability of serious injury to the State.[24]

clear and present danger doctrine Standard used by the courts to determine whether speech may be restricted; only speech that creates a serious and immediate danger to society may be restricted.

Preferred Position Doctrine Over the years, the Supreme Court has given the First Amendment freedom of speech, press, and assembly a special **preferred position** in constitutional law. These freedoms are especially important to the preservation of democracy. If speech, press, or assembly are prohibited by government, the people have no way to correct the government through democratic processes. Thus the burden of proof rests on the *government* to justify any restrictions on speech, writing, or assembly.[25] In other words, any speech or writing is presumed constitutional unless the government proves that a serious and immediate danger would ensue if the speech were allowed.

Symbolic Speech The First Amendment's guarantees of speech, press, and assembly are broadly interpreted to mean **freedom of expression**. Political expression encompasses more than just words. For example, when Mary Beth Tinker and her brothers were suspended for wearing black armbands to high school to protest the Vietnam War, they argued that the wearing of armbands constituted **symbolic speech** protected by the First Amendment. The Supreme Court agreed, noting that the school did not prohibit all wearing of symbols but instead singled out this particular expression for disciplinary action.[26]

The Supreme Court continues to wrestle with the question of what kinds of conduct are symbolic speech protected by the First Amendment and what kinds of conduct are outside of this protection. Symbolic speech, like speech itself, cannot be banned just because it offends people. "If there is only one bedrock principle underlying the First Amendment, it is that the Government may not prohibit the expression of an idea simply because society finds the idea itself offensive or disagreeable."[27]

For example, flag desecration is a physical act, but it also has symbolic meaning—for example, hatred of the United States or opposition to government policies. In the case of *Texas v. Johnson* (1989), a majority of Supreme Court justices argued that "burning of the flag was conduct sufficiently imbued with elements of communication to implicate the First Amendment." They declared that when speech and conduct are combined in the same expressive act, the government must show that it has "a sufficiently important interest in regulating the non-speech element to justify incident limitations on First Amendment freedoms." In this case, "preserving the flag as a symbol of nationhood and national unity" was not deemed sufficiently important to justify limiting Johnson's freedom of expression. However, in 2003 the Court upheld a Virginia statute that prohibited the burning of a cross "with the intent of intimidating any person or group" and asserting that "any such burning . . . shall be prima facie evidence of an intent to intimidate." The Supreme Court cited the long history of cross burnings as a pool of intimidation and threats of impending violence. "As the history of cross burning in this country shows, that act is often intimidating, intended to create a pervasive fear in victims that they are a target of violence." Therefore, "the First Amendment permits Virginia to outlaw cross burnings done with the intent to intimidate because burning a cross is a particularly virulent form of intimidation."[28]

Campus Speech Many colleges and universities have undertaken to ban speech that is considered racist, sexist, homophobic, or otherwise "insensitive" to the feelings of women and minorities. Varieties of "speech codes," "hate codes," and sexual harassment regulations that prohibit verbal expressions raise serious constitutional questions, especially at state-supported colleges and universities. The First Amendment does not exclude insulting or offensive racist or sexist words

preferred position Refers to the tendency of the courts to give preference to the First Amendment rights to speech, press, and assembly when faced with conflicts.

freedom of expression Collectively, the First Amendment rights to free speech, press, and assembly.

symbolic speech Actions other than speech itself but protected by the First Amendment because they constitute political expression.

or comments from its protection. Many of these college and university regulations would not withstand a judicial challenge if students or faculty undertook to oppose them in federal court.

Libel and Slander Libel and slander have never been protected by the First Amendment against subsequent punishment (see "Libel and Slander" in Chapter 6). Once a communication is determined to be libelous or slanderous, it is outside of the protection of the First Amendment. The courts have traditionally defined "libel" as a "damaging falsehood." However, if plaintiffs are public officials they must prove that the statements made about them are not only false and damaging but also "made with actual malice"—that is, with knowledge that they are false or with "reckless disregard" of the truth—in order to prove libel.[29]

Privacy, Abortion, and the Constitution

A right of "privacy" is not expressly provided for anywhere in the Constitution. But does the word *liberty* in the First and Fourteenth Amendments include a constitutional right to privacy?

Finding a Right to Privacy The U.S. Supreme Court found a right of privacy in the Constitution when it struck down a Connecticut law prohibiting the use of contraceptives in 1965. Estelle Griswold had opened a birth control clinic on behalf of the Planned Parenthood League of that state and was distributing contraceptives in violation of the state statute prohibiting their use. She challenged the constitutionality of the statute, even though there is no direct reference to birth control in the Bill of Rights. The Supreme Court upheld Griswold's challenge, finding a right of privacy, according to Justice William O. Douglas, in the "penumbras formed by the emanations from" the First, Third, Fourth, Fifth, Ninth, and Fourteenth Amendments. "Various guarantees create a zone of privacy. . . . Would we allow the police to search the sacred precincts of marital bedrooms for telltale signs of the use of contraceptives? The very idea is repulsive to the notion of privacy surrounding the marriage relationship." In concurrent opinions, other justices found the right of privacy in the Ninth Amendment: "The enumeration in the Constitution of certain rights, shall not be construed to deny or disparage others retained by the people."[30]

WWW **Pro-Choice America** Formerly the National Abortion Rights Action League (NARAL), with information on current legislation and court cases. ***www.prochoiceamerica.org***

Roe v. Wade The fact that *Griswold* dealt with reproduction gave encouragement to groups advocating abortion rights. In 1969 Norma McCorvey sought an abortion in Texas, but was refused by doctors who cited a state law prohibiting abortion except to save a woman's life. McCorvey challenged the Texas law in federal courts on a variety of constitutional grounds, including the right to privacy. McCorvey became "Jane Roe," and the case became one of the most controversial in the Supreme Court's history.[31]

The Supreme Court ruled that the constitutional right of privacy as well as the Fourteenth Amendment's guarantee of "liberty" included a woman's decision to bear or not to bear a child. The Court held that the word "person" in the Constitution did *not* include the unborn child; therefore, the Fifth and Fourteenth Amendments' guarantee of "life, liberty, or property" did not protect the "life" of the fetus. The Court also ruled that a state's power to protect the health and safety of the mother could not justify any restriction on abortion in the first three months of pregnancy. Between the third and sixth months of pregnancy, a state could set standards for abortion procedures in order to protect the health of women, but a state could not prohibit abortions. Only in the final three months could a state prohibit or regulate abortion to protect the unborn.

Rather than end the political controversy over abortion, *Roe v. Wade* set off a conflagration. Congress defeated efforts to pass a constitutional amendment restricting abortion or declaring that life begins at conception. However, when Congress banned the use of federal funds under Medicaid (medical care for the poor) for abortions except to protect the life of a woman, the Supreme Court upheld the ban, holding that there was no constitutional obligation for governments to pay for abortions.[32]

Reaffirming *Roe v. Wade* Abortion has become such a polarizing issue that "pro-choice" and "pro-life" groups are generally unwilling to search out a middle ground. Yet the current Supreme Court appears to have chosen a policy of affirming a woman's right to abortion while upholding modest restrictions, as evidenced by the Court's ruling in *Planned Parenthood of Pennsylvania v. Casey* (1992).[33]

National Right to Life
Leading anti-abortion organization with information on current legislation and court cases.
www.nrlc.org

In this case, the Supreme Court considered a series of restrictions on abortion enacted by Pennsylvania: that physicians must inform women of risks and alternatives; that women must wait twenty-four hours after requesting an abortion before having one; and that the parents of minors must be notified. It struck down a requirement that spouses be notified.

Justice Sandra Day O'Connor took the lead in forming a moderate, swing bloc on the Court. Her majority opinion strongly reaffirmed the fundamental right of abortion, both on the basis of the Fourteenth Amendment and on the principle of stare decisis. But the majority also upheld states' rights to protect any fetus that reached the point of "viability." The Court went on to establish a new standard for constitutionally evaluating restrictions: they must not impose an "undue burden" on women seeking abortion or place "substantial obstacles" in her path. All of Pennsylvania's restrictions met this standard and were upheld except spousal notification.

"Partial Birth Abortion" A number of states have attempted to outlaw an abortion procedure known as "intact dilation and evacuation" or "partial birth" abortion. This procedure, which is used in less than one percent of all abortions, involves partial delivery of the fetus feet-first, then vacuuming out the brain and crushing the skull to ease complete removal. In a surprise 5 to 4 decision, with Justice O'Connor supporting the majority, the Supreme Court declared a Nebraska law prohibiting the procedure to be an unconstitutional "undue burden" on a woman's right to an abortion. The Nebraska law failed to make an exception in its prohibition of the procedure "for the preservation of the health of the mother."[34]

Sexual Conduct "Liberty gives substantial protection to adult persons in deciding how to conduct their lives in matters pertaining to sex." This Supreme Court ruling in *Lawrence v. Texas* (2003) struck down a state law against homosexual sodomy. The ruling overturned an earlier case in which the Court held that the Constitution granted no "fundamental right to homosexuals to engage in acts of consensual sodomy."[35] Rather, the Supreme Court decided that "The liberty protected by the Constitution allows homosexual persons the right to choose to enter upon relationships in the confines of their homes and their own private lives and still retain their dignity as free persons."[36]

Gay Marriage The Supreme Court has not yet spoken out on gay marriages—marriages between persons of the same sex. Several state courts, including the Supreme Court of Massachusetts, have held that the Equal Protection Clause of the 14th Amendment entitles gay couples to marry, that to deny them marriage rights while recognizing heterosexual marriages amounts to discrimination. The issue is complicated by the constitutional provision that requires all states to give "Full Faith and Credit" to judicial proceedings of other states (see "State Obligations to Each Other" in Chapter 4). This provision implies that gay marriages in any state must be recognized in all states. Congress passed a Defense of Marriage Act in 1996 declaring that no state need recognized a gay marriage. But Congress failed to pass a constitutional amendment banning same-sex marriage.

Obscenity and the Law

Obscene materials of all kinds—words, publications, photos, videotapes, films—are not protected by the First Amendment. Most states ban the publication, sale, or possession of obscene material, and Congress bans its shipment in the mails. Because obscene material is not protected by the First Amendment, it can be banned without even an attempt to prove that it results in antisocial conduct. In other words, it is not necessary to show that obscene material would result in a clear and present danger to society, the test used to decide the legitimacy of *speech*. In order to ban obscene materials, the government need only prove that they are *obscene*.

Defining "obscenity" has confounded legislatures and the courts for years, however. State and federal laws often define pornography and obscenity in such terms as "lewd," "lascivious," "filthy," "indecent," "disgusting"—all equally as vague as "obscene." "Pornography" is simply a synonym for "obscenity." *Soft-core pornography* usually denotes nakedness and sexually suggestive poses; it is less likely to confront legal barriers. *Hard-core pornography* usually denotes explicit sexual activity. After many fruitless efforts by the Supreme Court to come up with a workable definition of "pornography" or "obscenity," a frustrated Justice Potter Stewart wrote in 1974, "I shall not today attempt further to define [hard-core pornography]. . . . But *I know it when I see it.*"[37]

WWW **Internet Freedom** Organization opposed to all forms of censorship and content regulation on the Internet. *www.netfreedom.org*

Porn on the Internet New technologies continue to challenge courts in the application of First Amendment principles. Currently the Internet, the global computer communication network, allows users to gain access to information worldwide. Thousands of electronic bulletin boards give computer users access to everything from bomb-making instructions and sex conversations to obscene photos and even child pornography. Many commercial access services ban obscene messages and exclude bulletin boards with sexually offensive commentary. Software programs that screen out pornography Web sites are readily available to consumers. But can *government* try to ban such material from the Internet without violating First Amendment freedoms?

Congress tried unsuccessfully to ban "indecent" and "patently offensive" communications from the Internet in its Communications Decency Act of 1996. Proponents of the law cited the need to protect children from pornography. But in 1997 the Supreme Court held the act unconstitutional: "Notwithstanding the legitimacy and importance of the Congressional goal of protecting children from harmful materials, we agree that the statute abridges freedom of speech protected by the First Amendment." Government cannot limit Internet messages "to only what is fit for children." The Supreme Court agreed with the assertion that "as the most participatory form of mass speech yet developed [the Internet] deserves the highest protection from government intrusion."[38]

Child Pornography The U.S. Supreme Court struck a hard blow against child pornography in 1982—the "dissemination of material depicting children engaged in sexual conduct regardless of whether the material is obscene." Such material includes any visual depiction of children performing sexual acts or lewdly exhibiting their genitals. The Court reasoned that films or photographs of sexual exploitation and abuse of children were "intrinsically related" to criminal activity; such material was evidence that crime has been committed. Thus the test for *child* pornography was much stricter than the standards set for obscene material. It is not necessary to show that the sexual depiction of children is "obscene" in order to ban such material; it is only necessary to show that children were used in the production of the material.

The Right to Bear Arms

The Second Amendment to the U.S. Constitution states: "A well regulated Militia, being necessary to the security of a free State, the right of the people to keep and bear Arms, shall not be infringed."

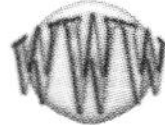

Right to Keep and Bear Arms
Organizations advocating self-defense rights with information on legislation, court cases, etc. ***www.rkba.org***

Bearing Arms What is meant by the right of the people "to keep and bear arms"? One view is that the Second Amendment confers on Americans an *individual* constitutional right, like the First Amendment freedom of speech or press. The history surrounding the adoption of the Second Amendment reveals the concern of colonists with attempts by despotic government to confiscate the arms of citizens and render them helpless to resist tyranny. James Madison wrote in the *Federalist Papers,* No. 46 that "the advantage of being armed which the Americans possess over the people of almost every other nation, forms a barrier against the enterprise of [tyrannical] ambition."[39] The Second Amendment was adopted with little controversy; most state constitutions at the time, like Pennsylvania's, declared that "the people have a right to bear arms for the defense of themselves and the state." Early American political rhetoric was filled with praise for an armed citizenry able to protect its freedoms by force if necessary.

THINK AGAIN

Do law-abiding citizens have a constitutional right to carry a handgun for self-protection?

State Militias But many constitutional scholars argue that the Second Amendment protects only the *collective* right of the states to form militias—that is, their right to maintain National Guard units. They focus on the qualifying phrase "a well-regulated Militia, being necessary to the security of a free State." The Second Amendment merely prevents Congress from denying the states the right to organize their own military units. If the Founders had wished to create an individual right to bear arms, they would not have inserted the phrase about a "well-regulated militia." (Opponents of this view argue that the original definition of a militia

Brady Campaign
The nation's leading gun control organization, with facts, legislation, and a "report card" on each state. ***www.bradycampaign.org***

The violent conclusion of the attempt by the Bureau of Alcohol, Tobacco and Firearms to enforce federal gun laws against the Branch Davidians in Waco, Texas. Members of citizen militia groups regard the ATF as a threat to their freedom to bear arms.

Bureau of Alcohol, Tobacco, and Firearms

Federal agency responsible for regulation of alcohol, tobacco, firearms, and explosives; site includes publications on gun crimes.
www.atf.gov

included all free males over eighteen.) Interpreted in this fashion, the Second Amendment does *not* protect private groups who form themselves into militias, nor does it guarantee citizens the right to own guns.

Citizen "Militias" In recent years, self-styled citizen "militias" have cropped up across the nation. They are armed groups who more or less regularly get together dressed in camouflage to engage in military tactics and training. They generally view federal government agencies, and often the United Nations, as potential threats to their freedom. They view themselves as modern-day descendants of the American patriot militias who fought in the Revolutionary War. Indeed, the Militia Act of 1792 *required* "every free white male citizen of the respective states, resident therein, who is or shall be of the age of 18 years and under the age of 45 years" to be enrolled in the militia and equipped with "a good musket," a bayonet, and "24 rounds of ammunition." This law was not changed until 1912, when National Guard units replaced state militia.

Citizen militia groups frequently come into conflict with federal firearms regulations. Enforcement of these regulations is the responsibility of the Bureau of Alcohol, Tobacco and Firearms. It was the ATF's violent efforts to enforce federal gun laws that led to the deaths of more than seventy people at the Branch Davidian compound in Waco, Texas, in 1993.

THINK AGAIN

Do you believe that the seizure of property believed by police to be used in drug trafficking, without a judicial hearing or trial, violates civil liberty?

Rights of Criminal Defendants

While society needs the protection of the police, it is equally important to protect society from the police. Arbitrary searches and arrests, imprisonment without trial, forced confessions, beatings and torture, secret trials, tainted witnesses, excessive punishments, and other human rights violations are all too common throughout the world. The U.S. Constitution limits the powers of the police and protects the rights of the accused (see Table 12.2).

TABLE 12.2 Individual Rights in the Criminal Justice Process

Rights	Process
Fourth Amendment: Protection against unreasonable searches and seizures Warranted searches for sworn "probable cause." Exceptions: consent searches, safety searches, car searches, and searches incident to a valid arrest.	**Investigation by law-enforcement officers** Expectation that police act lawfully.
Fifth Amendment: Protection against self-incrimination Miranda rules **Habeas corpus** Police holding a person in custody must bring that person before a judge with cause to believe that a crime was committed and the prisoner committed it.	**Arrest** Arrests based on warrants issued by judges and magistrates. Arrests based on crimes committed in the presence of law enforcement officials. Arrests for "probable cause."
Eighth Amendment: No excessive bail Defendant considered innocent until proven guilty; release on bail and amount of bail depends on seriousness of crime, trustworthiness of defendant, and safety of community.	**Hearing and bail** Preliminary hearing in which prosecutor presents testimony that a crime was committed and probable cause for charging the accused.
Fifth Amendment: Grand jury (federal) Federal prosecutors (but not necessarily state prosecutors) must convince a grand jury that a reasonable basis exists to believe the defendant committed a crime and he or she should be brought to trial.	**Indictment** Prosecutor, or a grand jury in federal cases, issues formal document naming the accused and specifying the charges.
Sixth Amendment: Right to counsel Begins in investigation stage, when officials become "accusatory"; extends throughout criminal justice process. Free counsel for indigent defendants.	**Arraignment** Judge reads indictment to the accused and ensures that the accused understands charges and rights and has counsel. Judge asks defendant to choose a plea: Guilty, *nolo contendere* (no contest), or not guilty. If defendant pleads guilty or no contest, a trial is not necessary and defendant proceeds to sentencing.
Sixth Amendment: Right to a speedy and public trial Impartial jury. Right to confront witnesses. Right to compel favorable witnesses to testify. **Fourth Amendment: Exclusionary rule** Illegally obtained evidence cannot be used against defendant.	**Trial** Impartial judge presides as prosecuting and defense attorneys present witnesses and evidence relevant to guilt or innocence of defendant and make arguments to the jury. Jury deliberates in secret and issues a verdict.
Eighth Amendment: Protection against cruel and unusual punishments	**Sentencing** If the defendant is found not guilty, the process ends. Defendants who plead guilty or no contest and defendants found guilty by jury are sentenced by fine, imprisonment, or both by the judge. Sentences imposed must be commensurate to the crimes committed.
Fifth Amendment: Protection against double jeopardy Government cannot try a defendant again for the same offense.	**Appeal** Defendants found guilty may appeal to higher courts for reversal of verdict or a new trial based on errors made anywhere in the process.

WHAT DO YOU THINK?

Are Persons Captured on the Battlefields of Afghanistan and Iraq Entitled to the Protections of the U.S. Constitution?

The United States has held 6,000 or more "enemy combatants" captured on the battlefields of Afghanistan and Iraq for several years. Many are held at the U.S. base in Guantanamo Bay, Cuba.

Prisoners of war have never been entitled to constitutional protection. Prisoners of war are uniformed members of the military forces of a nation. (The U.S. held tens of thousands of German and Japanese prisoners of war during World War II. They are entitled only to "humane treatment" under the Geneva Accords. They are not released until the war is ended.

"Detainees" from the war on terrorism are not officially prisoners of war, inasmuch as they are not uniformed soldiers of any nation. The U.S. has pledged humane treatment even though it is not clear that these detainees are protected by the Geneva Accords. They are not citizens of the United States and they are not held on U.S. soil. As military detainees, they are not given lawyers or access to courts or in most cases even identified by name. The U.S. military decides whether or not, or if, they will face a military tribunal or be released to their home countries. They fall in a "legal black hole."

But in a controversial decision in 2004 the Supreme Court held that enemy combatants captured on the battlefield and "imprisoned in territory over which the United States exercises an exclusive jurisdiction and control" are entitled to constitutional rights including habeas corpus—the right to bring their case to U.S. courts. "The fact that petitioners are being held in military custody is immaterial."* The Court reasoned that by agreement with Cuba, the U.S. exercises complete jurisdiction over its Guantanamo Base where detainees were being held. The Court was vague about whether enemy combatants held elsewhere in the world were entitled to constitutional protections.

Rasul v. Bush June 28, 2004.

The Guarantee of the Writ of Habeas Corpus One of the oldest and most *revered* rights in English common law is the right to obtain a **writ of habeas corpus**, which is a court order directing public officials who are holding a person in custody to bring the prisoner into court and explain the reasons for confinement. If a judge finds that the prisoner is being unlawfully detained, or finds insufficient evidence that a crime has been committed or that the prisoner could have committed it, the judge must order the prisoner's release. Thus the writ of habeas corpus is a means to test the legality of any imprisonment (see *What Do You Think?*: "Are Persons Captured on the Battlefields of Afghanistan and Iraq Entitled to Protections of the U.S. Constitution?").

writ of habeas corpus
Court order directing public officials who are holding a person in custody to bring the prisoner into court and explain the reasons for confinement; the right to habeas corpus is protected by Article I of the Constitution.

The writ of habeas corpus was considered so fundamental to the framers of the Constitution that they included it in the original text of Article I: "The privilege of the Writ of Habeas Corpus shall not be suspended, unless when in Cases of Rebellion or Invasion the public Safety may require it." Despite the qualifying phrase, the Supreme Court has never sanctioned suspension of the writ of habeas corpus even during wartime. President Abraham Lincoln suspended the writ of habeas corpus in several areas during the Civil War, but in the case of *Ex parte Milligan* (1866), the Supreme Court ruled that the president had acted unconstitutionally.[40] (With the war over, however, the Court's decision had no practical effect.)

ex post facto law
Retroactive criminal law that works against the accused; forbidden under Article I of the Constitution.

The Prohibition of Bills of Attainder and Ex Post Facto Laws Like the guarantee of habeas corpus, protection against bills of attainder and ex post facto laws was considered so fundamental to individual liberty that it was included in the

A CONFLICTING VIEW

Terrorism Requires Restrictions on Civil Liberties

The terrorist attack on America of September 11, 2001 was the most horrific violence committed against innocent American citizens in recent times. It created a new examination of Americans' commitment to personal freedoms and their willingness to trade these freedoms for the safety and security of society. All of the polls taken shortly after the attack indicated that Americans were prepared to accept many new restrictions on their freedom—more surveillance of their papers and communications, more searches of their belongings, roundups of suspected immigrants, and even prolonged detention without recourse to the courts. As time passed, however, fewer Americans expressed a willingness to sacrifice basic civil liberties to prevent additional acts of terrorism.

Following the attack, Congress moved swiftly to enact the "Patriot" Act, officially the Uniting and Strengthening America Act by Providing Appropriate Tools Required to Intercept and Obstruct Terrorism of 2001. President Bush and Attorney General John Ashcroft successfully lobbied Congress to increase the federal government's powers of searches, seizures, surveillance, and detention of suspects. The concerns of civil libertarians were largely swept aside. The Act was passed nearly unanimously in the Senate (98–1) and overwhelmingly in the House (357–66), with the support of both Democrats and Republicans.

Among the key provisions of the Patriot Act:

- *Roving wiretaps:* Allows wiretaps of any telephones that suspects might use instead of requiring separate warrants for each line.
- *Internet tracking:* Allows law enforcement authorities to track Internet communications, that is, to "surf the Web" without obtaining warrants.
- *Business Records:* Allows investigators to obtain information from credit cards, bank records, consumer purchases, libraries, schools and colleges, etc.
- *Foreign Intelligence Surveillance Court:* A special Foreign Intelligence Surveillance Court may issue search warrants on an investigator's assertion that the information sought is relevant to a terrorist investigation. No showing of "probable cause" is required. The warrant is not made public, in order to avoid "tipping off" the subject.
- *Property Seizure:* Authorizes the seizure of the property of suspected terrorists. Persons whose property is seized bear the burden of proof that the property was not used for terrorist purposes in order to secure the return of their property.
- *Detention:* Allows the detention of suspected terrorists for lengthy periods without judicial recourse.
- *Aliens Reporting and Detention:* Authorizes the Immigration and Naturalization Service to require reporting by aliens of selected nations and indefinite detention of illegal aliens suspected of terrorist connections.
- *Prohibits Harboring of Terrorists:* Creates a new federal crime: knowingly harboring persons who have committed, or are about to commit, a terrorist act.

What factors affect Americans' willingness to trade off restrictions on civil liberties in order to provide for safety and security from terrorism? Political science research suggests that the greater people's sense of threat, the greater their support for restrictions on civil liberties. The lower people's trust in government, the less willing they are to trade off civil liberties for security. Liberals are less willing to trade off civil liberties than moderates or conservatives. Overall it seems clear that Americans' commitment to civil liberties is highly contingent on their concerns about threats to national or personal security.

*Darren W. Davis and Brian D. Silver, "Civil Liberties vs. Security: Public Opinion in the Context of the Terrorist Attacks on America," *American Journal of Political Science* 48 (January 2004): 28–46.

original text of the Constitution. A **bill of attainder** is a legislative act inflicting punishment without judicial trial. An **ex post facto law** is a retroactive criminal law that works against the accused—for example, a law that makes an act criminal after the act is committed or a law that increases the punishment for a crime and applies it retroactively. Both the federal government and the states are prevented from passing such laws.

bill of attainder Legislative act inflicting punishment without judicial trial; forbidden under Article I of the Constitution.

The fact that relatively few cases of bills of attainder or ex post facto laws have come to the federal courts does not diminish the importance of these protections. Rather, it testifies to the widespread appreciation of their importance in a free society.

Unreasonable Searches and Seizures Individuals are protected by the Fourth Amendment from "unreasonable searches and seizures" of their private "persons, houses, papers, and effects." The Fourth Amendment lays out specific rules for searches and seizures of evidence: "No warrants shall issue, but upon probable cause, supported by Oath or affirmation, and particularly describing the place to be searched, and the persons or things to be seized." Judges cannot issue a **search warrant** just to let police see *if* an individual has committed a crime; there must be "probable cause" for such issuance. The indiscriminate searching of whole neighborhoods or groups of people is unconstitutional and is prevented by the Fourth Amendment's requirement that the place to be searched must be specifically described in the warrant. The requirement that the things to be seized must be described in the warrant is meant to prevent "fishing expeditions" into an individual's home and personal effects on the possibility that some evidence of unknown illegal activity might crop up. The only exception is if police, in the course of a valid search for a specified item, find other items whose very possession is a crime—for example, illicit drugs.

But the courts also permit police to undertake various other "reasonable" searches *without* a warrant: searches in connection with a valid arrest; searches to protect the safety of police officers; searches to obtain evidence in the immediate vicinity and in the suspect's control; searches to preserve evidence in danger of being immediately destroyed; and searches with the consent of a suspect. Indeed, most police searches today take place without warrant under one or another of these conditions. (See also *A Conflicting View:* "Terrorism Requires Restrictions on Civil Liberties.")

Arrests The Supreme Court permits *arrests without warrants* (1) when a crime is committed in the presence of an officer; and (2) when an arrest is supported by "probable cause" to believe that a crime has been committed by the person apprehended.[41] However, the Court has held that police may not enter a home to arrest its occupant without either a warrant for the arrest or the consent of the owner.[42]

Self-Incrimination and the Right to Counsel Freedom from self-incrimination had its origin in English common law; it was originally designed to prevent persons from being tortured into confessions of guilt. It is also a logical extension of the notion that individuals should not be forced to contribute to their own prosecution, that the burden of proof rests on the state. The Fifth Amendment protects people from both physical and psychological coercion.[43] It protects not only accused persons at their own trial but also witnesses testifying in trials of other persons, civil suits, congressional hearings, and so on. Thus "taking the Fifth" has become a standard phrase in our culture: "I refuse to answer that question on the grounds that it might tend to incriminate me." The protection also means that judges, prosecutors, and juries cannot use the refusal of people to take the stand at their own trial as evidence of guilt. Indeed, a judge or attorney is not even permitted to imply this to a jury, and a judge is obligated to instruct a jury not to infer guilt from a defendant's refusal to testify.

search warrant Court order permitting law-enforcement officials to search a location in order to seize evidence of a crime; issued only for a specified location, in connection with a specific investigation, and on submission of proof that "probable cause" exists to warrant such a search.

The Supreme Court the under Chief Justice Earl Warren greatly strengthened procedural protections for defendants in criminal cases in a series of rulings in the 1960s:

- *Mapp v. Ohio* (1961): Illegally obtained evidence of and confessions may not be used against the defendant in criminal trials. This exclusionary rule is one of the more controversial procedural rights that the Supreme Court has extended to criminal defendants. A the rule provides enforcement for the Fourth Amendment guarantee against unreasonable searches and seizures, as well as the Fifth Amendment guarantee against self-incrimination and the guarantee of counsel.[44,45]
- *Gideon v. Wainwright* (1963): Equal protection under the Fourteenth Amendment requires that free legal counsel be appointed for all indigent defendants in all criminal cases.[46]
- *Escobedo v. Illinois* (1964): Suspects are entitled to confer with counsel as soon as police investigation focuses on them or once "the process shifts from investigatory to accusatory."[47]
- *Miranda v. Arizona* (1966): Before questioning suspects, provide a **Miranda warning** police must informing them of their constitutional rights, including the right to counsel (appointed at no cost to the suspect if necessary) and the right to remain silent. Although suspects may knowingly waive these rights, the police cannot question anyone who at any point asks for a lawyer or declines "in any manner" to be questioned. If the police commit an error in these procedures, the accused goes free, regardless of the evidence of guilt.[48]

The Exclusionary Rule Illegally obtained evidence and confessions may not be used in criminal trials. If police find evidence of a crime in an illegal search or if they elicit statements from suspects without informing them of their rights to remain silent or to have counsel, the evidence or statements produced are not admissible in a trial. This **exclusionary rule** is one of the more controversial procedural rights that the Supreme Court has extended to criminal defendants. The rule is also unique to the United States: in Great Britain evidence obtained illegally may be used against the accused, although the accused may bring charges against the police for damages.

The rule provides *enforcement* for the Fourth Amendment guarantee against unreasonable searches and seizures, as well as the Fifth Amendment guarantee against compulsory self-incrimination and the guarantee of counsel. Initially applied only in federal cases, in *Mapp v. Ohio* (1961) the Supreme Court extended the exclusionary rule to all criminal cases in the United States.[49] A *good faith exception* is made "when law enforcement officers have acted in objective good faith or their transgressions have been minor."[50] And police are *not* prohibited from tricking a suspect into giving them incriminating evidence.[51] But the exclusionary rule is frequently attacked for the high price it extracts from society—the release of guilty criminals. Why punish society because of the misconduct of police? Why not punish police directly, perhaps with disciplinary measures imposed by courts that discover errors, instead of letting guilty persons go free?

Miranda warning Requirement that persons arrested be informed of their rights immediately after arrest.

exclusionary rule Rule of law that evidence found in an illegal search or resulting from an illegally obtained confession may not be admitted at trial.

Fair Trial The original text of the Constitution guaranteed jury trials in criminal cases, and the Sixth Amendment went on to correct weaknesses the framers saw in the English justice system at that time—closed proceedings, trials in absentia (where the defendant is not present), secret witnesses, long delays between arrest and trial, biased juries, and the absence of defense counsel. Specifically, the Sixth Amendment guarantees the following:

- The right to a speedy and public trial. ("Speedy" refers to the time between arrest and trial, not the time between the crime itself and trial,[52] but the Supreme Court has declined to set a specific time limit that defines speedy.[53])
- An impartial jury chosen from the state or district where the crime was committed.
- The right to confront (cross-examine) witnesses against the accused.
- The right of the accused to compel (subpoena) favorable witnesses to appear.
- The right of the accused to be represented by counsel.

Plea Bargaining Few criminal cases actually go to trial. More than 90 percent of criminal cases are plea bargained.[54] In **plea bargaining**, the defendant agrees to plead guilty and waives the right to a jury trial in exchange for concessions made by the prosecutor, perhaps the dropping of more serious charges against the defendant or a pledge to seek a reduced sentence or fine. Some critics of plea bargaining view it as another form of leniency in the criminal justice system that reduces its deterrent effects. Other critics view plea bargaining as a violation of the Constitution's protection against self-incrimination and guarantee of a fair jury trial. Prosecutors, they say, threaten defendants with serious charges and stiff penalties in order to force a guilty plea. Still other critics see plea bargaining as an "under-the-table" process that undermines respect for the criminal justice system.

Yet it is vital to the nation's court system that most defendants plead guilty. The court system would quickly break down from overload if any substantial proportion of defendants insisted on jury trials.

Double Jeopardy The Constitution appears to bar multiple prosecutions for the same offense: "Nor shall any person be subject for the same offense to be twice put in jeopardy of life or limb" (Fifth Amendment). But very early the Supreme Court held that this clause does not protect an individual from being tried a second time if jurors are deadlocked and cannot reach a verdict in the first trial (a "hung" jury).[55] Moreover, the Supreme Court has held that federal and state governments may separately try a person for the same offense if it violates both federal and state laws.[56]

THINK AGAIN

Is the death penalty a "cruel and unusual" punishment?

The Death Penalty

Perhaps the most heated debate in criminal justice policy today concerns capital punishment. Opponents of the death penalty argue that it violates the prohibition against "cruel and unusual punishments" in the Eighth Amendment to the Constitution. They also argue that the death penalty is applied unequally. A large proportion of those executed have been poor, uneducated, and nonwhite. In contrast, many Americans feel that justice demands strong retribution for heinous crimes—a life for a life. A mere jail sentence for a multiple murderer or rapist-murderer seems unjust compared with the damage inflicted on society and the victims. In

plea bargaining Practice of allowing defendants to plead guilty to lesser crimes than those with which they were originally charged in return for reduced sentences.

many cases, a life sentence means less than ten years in prison under the current early-release and parole policies in many states. Convicted murderers have been set free, and some have killed again.

Prohibition against Unfair Application Prior to 1971, the death penalty was officially sanctioned by about half of the states. Federal law also retained the death penalty. However, no one had actually suffered the death penalty since 1967 because of numerous legal tangles and direct challenges to the constitutionality of capital punishment.

In *Furman v. Georgia* (1972), the Supreme Court ruled that capital punishment, as then imposed, violated the Eighth and Fourteenth Amendment prohibitions against cruel and unusual punishment and due process of law. The justices' reasoning in the case was very complex. Only Justices William J. Brennan and Thurgood Marshall declared that capital punishment itself is cruel and unusual. The other justices in the majority felt that death sentences had been applied unfairly; some individuals received the death penalty for crimes for which many others received much lighter sentences. These justices left open the possibility that capital punishment would be constitutional if it was specified for certain kinds of crime and applied uniformly.[57]

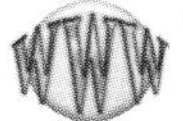

The National Coalition to Abolish the Death Penalty

This site provides information about public policies, institutions, and individuals that collectively work toward the "unconditional rejection of capital punishment." *www.ncadp.org*

After this decision, a majority of states rewrote their death penalty laws to try to ensure fairness and uniformity of application. Generally, these laws mandate the death penalty for murders committed during rape, robbery, hijacking, or kidnapping; murder of prison guards; murder with torture; and multiple murders. They call for two trials to be held—one to determine guilt or innocence and another to determine the penalty. At the second trial, evidence of "aggravating" and "mitigating" factors must be presented; if there are aggravating factors but no mitigating factors, the death penalty is mandatory.

Death Penalty Reinstated The revised death penalty laws were upheld in a series of cases that came before the Supreme Court in 1976. The Court concluded that "the punishment of death does *not* invariably violate the Constitution." The majority decision noted that the framers of the Bill of Rights had accepted death as a common penalty for crime. Although acknowledging that the Constitution and its amendments must be interpreted in a dynamic fashion, reflecting changing moral values, the Court's majority noted that most state legislatures have been willing to reenact the death penalty and hundreds of juries have been willing to impose that penalty. Thus "a large proportion of American society continues to regard it as an appropriate and necessary criminal sanction." Moreover, the Court held that the social purposes of retribution and deterrence justify the use of the death penalty; this ultimate sanction is "an expression of society's moral outrage at particularly offensive conduct."[58]

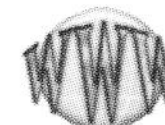

Bureau of Justice Statistics

Federal statistics on jails, prisons, probation, and capital punishment. Click on Capital Punishment for numbers of executions and persons under sentence of death. *www.ojp.usdoj.gov/bjs*

The Court reaffirmed that *Furman v. Georgia* struck down the death penalty only where it was invoked in "an arbitrary and capricious manner." A majority of the justices upheld the death penalty in states where the trial is a two-part proceeding, provided that during the second part the jury is given relevant information and standards for deciding whether to impose the death penalty. The Court approved the consideration of "aggravating and mitigating circumstances." Later the Court held that the jury, not a judge acting alone, must find aggravating circumstances in order to impose the death sentence.[59] The Court also called for automatic review of all death sentences by state supreme courts to ensure that none is imposed under

Do retribution and deterrence justify the use of the death penalty? Perhaps the most heated debate in criminal justice policy today concerns capital punishment.

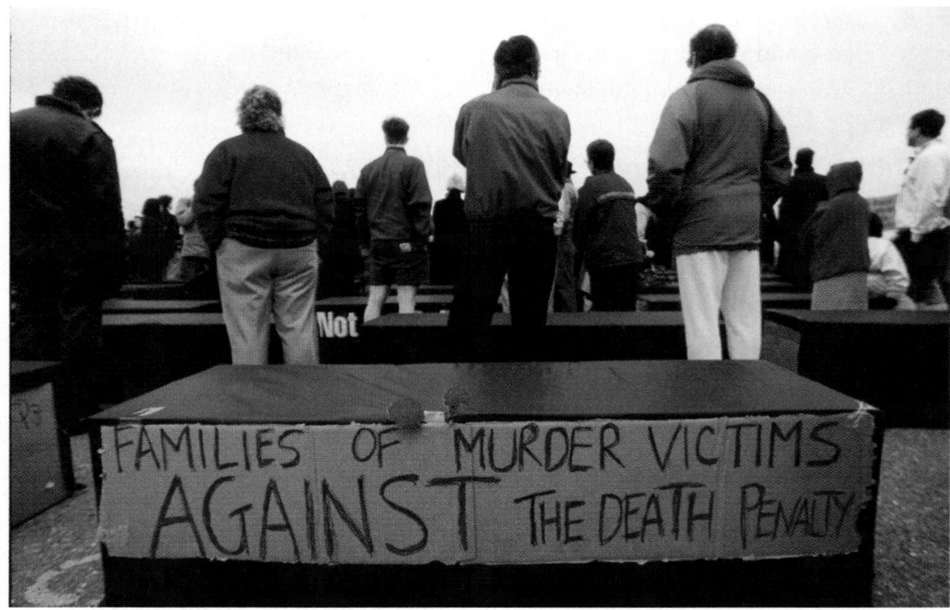

the influence of passion or prejudice, that aggravating factors are supported by the evidence, and that the sentence is not disproportionate to the crime. However, the court disapproved of state laws making the death penalty mandatory in all first-degree murder cases, holding that such laws were "unduly harsh and unworkably rigid." And the Court has held that executions of the mentally retarded are "cruel and unusual punishments" prohibited by the Eighth Amendment.[60]

The Politics of Equality

Equality has been the central issue of American politics throughout the history of the nation. It is the issue that sparked the nation's only civil war, and it continues today to be the nation's most vexing political concern.

Conflict begins over the very definition of "equality" (see "Dilemmas of Equality" in Chapter 2). Although Americans agree in the abstract that everyone is equal, they disagree over what they mean by "equality." Traditionally, equality meant "equality of *opportunity*": an equal opportunity to develop individual talents and abilities and to be rewarded for work, initiative, merit, and achievement. Over time, the issue of equality has shifted to "equality of *results*": an equal sharing of income and material rewards. With this shift in definition has come political conflict over the question of what, if anything, government should do to narrow the gaps between rich and poor, men and women, blacks and whites, and all other groups in society.

The nation's long struggle over equality has produced a number of constitutional and legal milestones in civil rights. These are summarized in Table 12.3. Much of the politics of civil rights centers on the development and interpretation of these guarantees of equality.

THINK AGAIN

Does the U.S. Constitution require the government to be color blind with respect to different races in all its laws and actions?

Slavery, Segregation, and the Constitution

In penning the Declaration of Independence in 1776, Thomas Jefferson affirmed that "All men are created equal." Yet from 1619, when the first slaves were brought to Jamestown, Virginia, until 1865, when the Thirteenth Amendment to the

TABLE 12.3 Guarantees of Civil Rights

Thirteenth Amendment (1865)

Neither slavery nor involuntary servitude, except as a punishment for crime whereof the party shall have been duly convicted, shall exist within the United States, or any place subject to their jurisdiction.

Fourteenth Amendment (1868)

No State shall make or enforce any law which shall abridge the privileges or immunities of citizens of the United States; nor shall any State deprive any person of life, liberty, or property, without due process of law; nor deny to any person within its jurisdiction the equal protection of the laws.

Fifteenth Amendment (1870)

The rights of the citizens of the United States to vote shall not be denied or abridged by the United States or by any State on account of race, color, or previous condition of servitude.

Nineteenth Amendment (1920)

The right of the citizens of the United States to vote shall not be denied or abridged by the United States or by any State on account of sex.

Civil Rights Acts of 1866, 1871, and 1875

Acts passed by the Reconstruction Congress following the Civil War. The Civil Rights Act of 1866 guaranteed newly freed persons the right to purchase, lease, and use real property. The Civil Rights Act of 1875 outlawed segregation in privately owned businesses and facilities, but in the Civil Rights Cases (1883), the Supreme Court declared the act an unconstitutional expansion of federal power, ruling that the Fourteenth Amendment limits only "State" actions. Other provisions of these acts were generally ignored for many decades. But the Civil Rights Act of 1871 has been revived in recent decades; the act makes it a federal crime for any person acting under the authority of state law to deprive another of rights protected by the Constitution.

Civil Rights Act of 1957

The first civil rights law passed by Congress since Reconstruction. It empowers the U.S. Justice Department to enforce voting rights, established the Civil Rights Division in the Justice Department, and created the Civil Rights Commission to study and report on civil rights in the United States.

Civil Rights Act of 1964

A comprehensive enactment designed to erase racial discrimination in both public and private sectors of American life. Major titles of the act: I. outlaws arbitrary discrimination in voter registration and expedites voting rights suits; II. bars discrimination in public accommodations, such as hotels and restaurants, that have a substantial relation to interstate commerce; III. and IV. authorize the national government to bring suits to desegregate public facilities and schools; V. extends the life and expands the power of the Civil Rights Commission; VI. provides for withholding federal funds from programs administered in a discriminatory manner; VII. establishes the right to equality in employment opportunities.

Civil Rights Act of 1968

Prohibits discrimination in the advertising, financing sale, or rental of housing, based on race, religion, or national origin and, as of 1974, sex. A major amendment to the act in 1988 extended coverage to the handicapped and to families with children.

Voting Rights Act

Enacted by Congress in 1965 and renewed and expanded in 1970, 1975, and 1982, this law has sought to eliminate restrictions on voting that have been used to discriminate against blacks and other minority groups. Amendments in 1975 (1) required bilingual ballots in all states; (2) required approval by the Justice Department or a federal court of any election law changes in states covered by the act; (3) extended legal protection of voting rights to Hispanic Americans, Asian Americans, and Native Americans. The 1982 act provides that *intent* to discriminate need not be proven if the *results* demonstrate otherwise. Although the 1982 extension does not require racial quotas for city councils, school boards, or state legislatures, a judge may under the law redraw voting districts to give minorities maximum representation.

Constitution outlawed the practice, slavery was a way of life in the United States. Africans were captured, enslaved, transported to America, bought and sold, and used as personal property.

Slavery and the Constitution The Constitution of 1787 recognized and protected slavery in the United States. Article I stipulated that slaves were to be counted as three-fifths of a person for purposes of representation and taxation; it also prohibited any federal restriction on the importation of slaves until 1808. Article IV even guaranteed the return of escaped slaves to their owners. The Founders were aware that the practice of slavery contradicted their professed belief in "equality," and this contradiction caused them some embarrassment. Thus they avoided the word "slave" in favor of the euphemism "person held to Service or Labour" in writing the Constitution.

Supreme Court Chief Justice Roger Taney, ruling in the notorious case of *Dred Scott v. Sandford* in 1857, reflected the racism that prevailed in early America:

> They had for more than a century before been regarded as beings of an inferior order, and altogether unfit to associate with the white race, either in social or political relations; and so far inferior, that they had no rights which the white man was bound to respect; and that the negro might justly and lawfully be reduced to slavery for his benefit.[61]

Emancipation and the Fourteenth Amendment The Civil War was the nation's bloodiest war. (Combined deaths of Union and Confederate forces matched the nation's losses in World War II, even though the nation's population in 1860 was only 31 million compared to 140 million during World War II.) Very few families during the Civil War did not experience a direct loss from that conflict. As casualties mounted, northern Republicans joined abolitionists in calling for emancipating, or freeing, the slaves simply to punish the Rebels. They knew that much of the South's power depended on slave labor. Lincoln also knew that if he proclaimed the war was being fought to free the slaves, military intervention by the British on behalf of the South was less likely. Accordingly, on September 22, 1862, Lincoln issued his **Emancipation Proclamation.** Claiming his right as Commander-in-Chief of the army and navy, he declared that, as of January 1, 1863, "all persons held as slaves within any State, or designated part of a State, the people whereof shall then be in rebellion against the United States, shall be then, thenceforward, and forever free." The Emancipation Proclamation did not come about as a result of demands by the people. It was a political and military action by the president intended to help preserve the Union.

The Emancipation Proclamation freed slaves in the seceding states, and the Thirteenth Amendment in 1865 abolished slavery everywhere in the nation. But freedom did not mean civil rights. The post–Civil War Republican Congress attempted to "reconstruct" southern society. The Fourteenth Amendment, ratified in 1868, made "equal protection of the laws" a command for every state to obey. The Fifteenth Amendment, passed in 1869 and ratified in 1870, prohibited federal and state governments from abridging the right to vote "on account of race, color, or previous condition of servitude." In addition, Congress passed a series of civil rights laws in the 1860s and 1970s guaranteeing the newly freed slaves protection in the exercise of their constitutional rights.

Emancipation Proclamation Lincoln's 1862 Civil War declaration that all slaves residing in rebel states were free. It did not abolish all slavery; that would be done by the Thirteenth Amendment in 1865.

The Imposition of Segregation But political support for these policies soon began to erode. In the Compromise of 1877, the national government agreed to end military occupation of the South, give up its efforts to rearrange southern society, and lend tacit approval to white supremacy in that region. In return, the southern states pledged their support to the Union, accepted national supremacy, and agreed to permit the Republican presidential candidate, Rutherford B. Hayes, to assume the presidency, although the Democratic candidate, Samuel Tilden, had received more popular votes in the disputed election of 1876.

Segregation became the social instrument by which African Americans were "kept in their place"—that is, denied social, economic, educational, and political equality. In many states, **Jim Crow** followed them throughout life: birth in segregated hospital wards, education in segregated schools, residence in segregated housing, employment in segregated jobs, eating in segregated restaurants, and burial in segregated graveyards. Segregation was enforced by a variety of public and private sanctions, from lynch mobs to country club admission committees. But government was the principal instrument of segregation in both the southern and the border states of the nation.

Early Court Approval of Segregation Segregation was imposed despite the Fourteenth Amendment's guarantee of "equal protection of the laws." In the 1896 case of *Plessy v. Ferguson,* the Supreme Court upheld state laws requiring segregation.[62] Although segregation laws involved state action, the Court held that segregation of the races did not violate the Equal Protection Clause of the Fourteenth Amendment so long as people in each race received equal treatment. Schools and other public facilities that were **separate but equal** were constitutional, the Court ruled. The effect of this decision was to give constitutional approval to segregation; the decision was not reversed until 1954.

The NAACP and the Legal Battle The National Association for the Advancement of Colored People (NAACP) and its Legal Defense and Education Fund led the fight to abolish lawful segregation. As chief legal counsel to the fund, Thurgood Marshall, later to become the first African American to sit on the U.S. Supreme Court, began a long legal campaign to ensure equal protection of the law for African Americans. Initially, the NAACP's strategy focused on achieving the "equal" portion of the separate-but-equal doctrine. Segregated facilities, including public schools, were seldom "equal," even with respect to physical conditions, teachers' salaries and qualifications, curricula, and other tangible factors. In other words, southern states failed to live up even to the segregationist doctrine of separate but equal. In a series of cases, Marshall and other NAACP lawyers convinced the Supreme Court to act when segregated facilities were clearly unequal.[63]

NAACP Legal Defense Fund
Founded in 1940 by Thurgood Marshall to provide legal assistance to poor African Americans. Originally affiliated with the NAACP; now a separate organization.
www.naacpldf.org

Jim Crow Second-class-citizen status conferred on blacks by southern segregation laws; derived from a nineteenth-century song-and-dance act (usually performed by a white man in blackface) that stereotyped blacks.

separate but equal Ruling of the Supreme Court in the case of *Plessy v. Ferguson* (1896) to the effect that segregated facilities were legal as long as the facilities were equal.

But Marshall's goal was to prove that segregation *itself* was inherently unequal whether or not facilities were equal in all tangible respects. In other words, Marshall sought a reversal of *Plessy v. Ferguson* and a ruling that separation of the races was unconstitutional. In 1952 Marshall led a team of NAACP lawyers in a suit to admit Linda Brown to the white public schools of Topeka, Kansas, one of the few segregated school systems where white and black schools were equal with respect to buildings, curricula, teachers' salaries, and other tangible factors. In choosing the *Brown* suit, the NAACP sought to prevent the Court from simply ordering the admission of black pupils because tangible facilities were not equal and to force the Court to review the doctrine of segregation itself.

Brown v. Board of Education of Topeka On May 17, 1954, the Court rendered its historic decision in the case of *Brown v. Board of Education of Topeka:*

> . . . Whatever may have been the extent of psychological knowledge of the time of *Plessy v. Ferguson,* this finding is amply supported by modern authority. Any language in *Plessy v. Ferguson* contrary to this source is rejected. . . . We conclude that in the field of public education the doctrine of "separate but equal" has no place. Separate educational facilities are inherently unequal.[64]

Enforcing Desegregation The *Brown* ruling struck down the laws of twenty-one states as well as congressional laws segregating the schools of the District of Columbia.[65] Such a far-reaching exercise of judicial power was bound to meet with difficulties in enforcement, and the Supreme Court was careful not to risk its own authority. It did not order immediate national desegregation but rather required state and local authorities, under the supervision of federal district courts, to proceed with "all deliberate speed" in desegregation.[66] For more than fifteen years, state and school districts in the South waged a campaign of resistance to desegregation. Delays in implementing school desegregation continued until 1969, when the Supreme Court rejected a request by Mississippi officials for further delay, declaring that all school districts were obligated to end their dual school systems "at once" and "now and hereafter" to operate only integrated schools.[67] The Court was careful to note, however, that racial imbalance in schools is not itself grounds for ordering these remedies unless it is also shown that some present or past governmental action contributed to the imbalance.[68]

De Facto Segregation However, in the absence of any past or present governmental actions contributing to racial imbalance, states and school districts are not required by the Fourteenth Amendment to integrate their schools. For example, where central-city schools are predominantly black and suburban schools are predominantly white owing to residential patterns, cross-district busing is not required unless some official action brought about these racial imbalances. Thus in 1974 the Supreme Court threw out a lower federal court order for massive busing of students between Detroit and fifty-two suburban school districts.[69] Although Detroit city schools were 70 percent black and the suburban schools almost all white, none of the area school districts segregated students within their own boundaries. This important decision means that largely black central cities surrounded by largely white suburbs will remain segregated in practice because there are not enough white students living within the city boundaries to achieve integration.

De facto segregation is more common in the northern metropolitan areas than in the South. The states with the largest percentages of African American students attending schools that have 90 to 100 percent minority enrollments are Illinois (62 percent), Michigan (60 percent), New York (57 percent), and New Jersey (54 percent). The persistence of de facto segregation, together with a renewed interest in the quality of education, has caused many civil rights organizations to focus their attention on improving the quality of schools in urban areas rather than trying to desegregate these schools.

The Civil Rights Acts

de facto segregation Racial imbalances not directly caused by official actions but rather by residential patterns.

The early goal of the civil rights movement was to eliminate discrimination and segregation practiced by *governments,* particularly states and school districts. When the civil rights movement turned to *private* discrimination—discrimination practiced by private owners of restaurants, hotels, motels, and stores; private employers, landlords, and real estate agents; and others who were not government officials—it had to take its fight to the Congress. The Constitution does not govern the activities of private individuals. Only Congress at the national level could outlaw discrimination in the private sector. Yet prior to 1964, Congress had been content to let the courts struggle with the question of civil rights. New political tactics and organizations were required to put the issue of equality on the agenda of Congress.

Martin Luther King, Jr., and Nonviolent Direct Action Leadership in the struggle to eliminate discrimination and segregation from private life was provided by a young African American minister, Martin Luther King, Jr. (see *People in Politics:* "Martin Luther King, Jr., 'I Have a Dream' "). Under King, the civil rights movement developed and refined political techniques for use by American minorities, including **nonviolent direct action**. Nonviolent direct action is a form of protest that involves breaking "unjust" laws in an open, "loving," nonviolent fashion. The purpose of nonviolent direct action is to call attention—to "bear witness"—to the existence of injustice. In the words of Martin Luther King, Jr., such civil disobedience "seeks to dramatize the issue so that it can no longer be ignored"[70] (see also *A Conflicting View:* "Sometimes It's Right to Disobey the Law" in Chapter 1).

King formed the Southern Christian Leadership Conference (SCLC) in 1957 to develop and direct the growing nonviolent direct action movement. During the next few years, the SCLC overshadowed the older NAACP in leading the fight against segregation. Where the NAACP had developed its strategy of court litigation to combat discrimination by *governments,* now the SCLC developed nonviolent direct action tactics to build widespread popular support and to pressure Congress to outlaw discrimination by *private businesses.*

The King Center Biography of M. L. K., Jr., together with news and information from Atlanta King Center. *http://thekingcenter.com*

The year 1963 was perhaps the most important for nonviolent direct action. The SCLC focused its efforts in Birmingham, Alabama, where King led thousands of marchers in a series of orderly and peaceful demonstrations. When police attacked the marchers with fire hoses, dogs, and cattle prods—in full view of national television cameras—millions of viewers around the country came of understand the injustices of segregation. The Birmingham action set off demonstrations in many parts of the country. The theme remained one of nonviolence, and it was usually whites rather than blacks who resorted to violence in these demonstrations. Responsible black leaders remained in control of the movement and won widespread support from the white community.

The culmination of King's nonviolent philosophy was a huge yet orderly march on Washington, D.C., held on August 28, 1963. More than 200,000 blacks and whites participated in the march, which was endorsed by many civic leaders, religious groups, and political figures. The march ended at the Lincoln Memorial, where Martin Luther King, Jr., delivered his most eloquent appeal, entitled "I Have a Dream." Congress passed the Civil Rights Act of 1964 by better than a two-thirds favorable vote in both houses; it won the overwhelming support of both Republican and Democratic members of Congress.

nonviolent direct action Strategy used by civil rights leaders such as Martin Luther King, Jr., in which protesters break "unjust" laws openly but in a "loving" fashion in order to bring the injustices of such laws to public attention.

The Civil Rights Act of 1964 Signed into law on July 4, 1964, the Civil Rights Act of 1964 ranks with the Emancipation Proclamation, the Fourteenth Amendment, and the *Brown* case as one of the most important steps toward full equality for African Americans. Among its most important provisions are the following:

Title II: It is unlawful to discriminate or segregate persons on the grounds of race, color, religion, or national origin in any public accommodation, including hotels, motels,

U.S. Department of Justice, Civil Rights Division Responsible for enforcement of U.S. civil rights laws. Site includes information on cases. *www.usdoj.gov/crt*

PEOPLE IN POLITICS

Martin Luther King, Jr., "I Have a Dream"

If a man hasn't discovered something he will die for, he isn't fit to live.*

For Martin Luther King, Jr. (1929–1968), civil rights was something to die for, and before he died for the cause, he would shatter a century of southern segregation and set a new domestic agenda for the nation's leaders. King's contributions to the development of nonviolent direct action won him international acclaim and the Nobel Peace Prize.

King's father was the pastor of one of the South's largest and most influential African American congregations, the Ebenezer Baptist Church in Atlanta, Georgia. Young Martin was educated at Morehouse College in Atlanta and received a Ph.D. in religious studies at Boston University. Shortly after beginning his career as a Baptist minister in Montgomery, Alabama, in 1955, a black woman, Rosa Parks, refused to give up her seat to whites on a Montgomery bus, setting in motion a year-long bus boycott in that city. Only twenty-six years old, King was thrust into national prominence as the leader of that boycott, which ended in the elimination of segregation on the city's buses. In 1957 King founded the Southern Christian Leadership Conference (SCLC) to provide encouragement and leadership to the growing nonviolent protest movement against segregation.

Perhaps the most dramatic application of nonviolent direct action occurred in Birmingham, Alabama, in the spring of 1963. Thousands of African Americans, ranging from schoolchildren to senior citizens, marched in protest. Although the demonstrators conducted themselves in a nonviolent fashion, police and firefighters attacked the demonstrators with fire hoses, cattle prods, and police dogs, all in clear view of national television cameras. Thousands of demonstrators were dragged off to jail, including King. (It was at this time that King wrote his "Letter from Birmingham Jail," explaining and defending nonviolent direct action.) Pictures of police brutality flashed throughout the nation and the world, touching the consciences of many white Americans.

King was also the driving force behind the most massive application of nonviolent direct action in U.S. history: the great "March on Washington" in August 1963, during which more than 200,000 black and white marchers converged on the nation's capital. The march ended at the Lincoln Memorial, where King delivered his most eloquent appeal, entitled "I Have a Dream."

> I still have a dream. It is a dream deeply rooted in the American dream. I have a dream that one day this nation will rise up and live out the true meaning of its creed: "We hold these truths to be self-evident, that all men are created equal."†

It was in the wake of the March on Washington that President John F. Kennedy sent to the Congress a strong civil rights bill that would be passed after his death—the Civil Rights Act of 1964. That same year, King received the Nobel Peace Prize.

White racial violence in the early 1960s, including murders and bombings of black and white civil rights workers, shocked and disgusted many whites in both the North and the South. In 1963 Medgar Evers, the NAACP's state chair for Mississippi, was shot to death by a sniper as he entered his Jackson home. That same year, a bomb killed four young black girls attending Sunday school in Birmingham. On the evening of April 3, 1968, King spoke to a crowd in Memphis, Tennessee, in eerily prophetic terms. "I just want to do God's will. And He's allowed me to go to the mountain. And I've looked over, and I've seen the promised land. I may not get there with you. But I want you to know tonight, that we, as a people will get to the promised land. So I'm happy tonight. I'm not worried about anything. I'm not fearing any man." On the night of April 4, 1968, the world's leading exponent of nonviolence was killed by an assassin's bullet.‡

*Martin Luther King, Jr., speech, June 23, 1963, Detroit, Michigan.

†Martin Luther King, Jr., "I Have a Dream" speech, August 28, 1963, at the Lincoln Memorial, Washington, D.C., printed in David J. Garrow, *Bearing the Cross: Martin Luther King, Jr., and the Southern Christian Leadership Conference* (New York: Vintage Books, 1988), pp. 283–84.

‡Martin Luther King, Jr., speech, April 3, 1968, Memphis, Tennessee, ibid., p. 621.

In the civil rights march of 1963 more than 200,000 people marched peacefully on Washington, D.C., to end segregation. It was here that Martin Luther King, Jr., delivered his famous "I Have a Dream" speech.

restaurants, movies; theaters, sports arenas, entertainment houses, and other places that offer to serve the public. This prohibition extends to all business establishments whose operations affect interstate commerce or whose discriminatory practices are supported by state action.

Title VI: Each federal department and agency is to take action to end discrimination in all programs or activities receiving federal financial assistance in any form. This action may include termination of financial assistance to persistently discriminatory agencies.

Title VII: It is unlawful for any employer or labor union to discriminate against any individual in any fashion in employment because of the individual's race, color, religion, sex, or national origin. The Equal Employment Opportunity Commission is established to enforce this provision by investigation, conference, conciliation, persuasion, and, if need be, civil action in federal court.

Affirmative Action: Opportunity versus Results

Although the gains of the civil rights movement were immensely important, these gains were primarily in *opportunity* rather than in *results.* The civil rights movement of the 1960s did not bring about major changes in the conditions under which most African Americans lived in the United States. Racial politics today center around the *actual* inequalities between blacks and whites in incomes, jobs, housing, health, education, and other conditions of life.

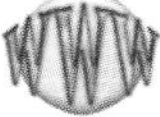

U.S. Commission on Civil Rights

National clearinghouse on information regarding discrimination because of race, color, religion, sex, age, disability, or national origin. Publishes reports, findings and recommendations.
www.usccr.gov

Continuing Inequalities The issue of inequality today is often posed as differences in the "life chances" of blacks and whites. Figures can reveal only the bare outline of an African American's "life chances" in this society (see Table 12.4). The average income of a black family is 62 percent of the average white family's income. Over 20 percent of all black families live below the recognized poverty line,

TABLE 12.4 Minority Life Chances

	Median Income of Families				
	1970	1975	1980	1985	2002
White	$10,236	$14,268	$21,904	$29,152	$46,900
Black	6,279	8,779	12,674	16,786	29,026
Hispanic	(NA)	9,551	14,716	19,027	33,103

	Percentage of Persons below Poverty Level			
	1975	1980	1985	2002
White	9.7%	10.2%	11.4%	10.3%
Black	31.3	32.5	31.3	24.1
Hispanic	26.9	25.7	29.0	21.8

	Unemployment Rate		
	1980	1985	2003
White	6.3%	6.2%	4.9%
Black	14.3	15.1	9.9
Hispanic	10.1	10.5	6.5

	Education: Percentage of Persons over Twenty-Five Completing High School				
	1960	1970	1980	1990	2000
White	43%	55%	69%	79%	85%
Black	20	31	51	66	79
Hispanic	(NA)	32	44	51	57

	Education: Percentage of Persons over Twenty-Five Completing College				
	1960	1970	1980	1990	2000
White	8%	11%	17%	22%	26%
Black	3	4	8	11	17
Hispanic	(NA)	4	8	9	11

Source: Statistical Abstract of the United States, various issues; U.S. Census Bureau, Income in the United States 2002 Washington: Government Printing Office, 2004.

affirmative action Any program, whether enacted by a government or by a private organization, whose goal is to overcome the results of past unequal treatment of minorities and/or women by giving members of these groups preferential treatment in admissions, hiring, promotions, or other aspects of life.

whereas less than 10 percent of white families do so. The black unemployment rate is more than twice as high as the white unemployment rate. Blacks are less likely to hold prestigious executive jobs in professional, managerial, clerical, or sales work. They do not hold many skilled craft jobs in industry but are concentrated in operative, service, and laboring positions. The civil rights movement opened up new opportunities for African Americans. But equality of *opportunity* is not the same as equality of *results*.

Policy Choices What public policies should be pursued to achieve equality in America? Is it sufficient that government eliminate discrimination, guarantee equality of opportunity, and apply color-blind standards to both blacks and whites? Or should government take **affirmative action** to overcome the results of past un-

TABLE 12.5 White and Minority Income by Educational Attainment

	Annual Mean Income				
	White	Black	Hispanic	Black/White Ratio	Hispanic/White Ratio
Graduate Degree	$52,475	$40,610	$46,556	77%	89%
Bachelor's Degree	41,439	32,062	33,465	77	81
High School Degree	23,618	18,930	19,558	80	83
No High School Degree	16,596	13,185	15,069	79	91

Source: U.S. Bureau of the Census, 2000. Data for 1998.

equal treatment of blacks—preferential or compensatory treatment to assist black applications for university admissions and scholarships, job hiring and promotion, and other opportunities for advancement in life?

The constitutional question posed by affirmative action programs is whether or not they discriminate against whites in violation of the Equal Protection Clause of the Fourteenth Amendment. A related question is whether or not affirmative action programs discriminate against whites in violation of the Civil Rights Act of 1964, which prohibits discrimination "on account of race," not just discrimination against blacks. Clearly, these are questions for the Supreme Court to resolve.

The Bakke Case In the absence of a history of racial discrimination, the Supreme Court has been willing to scrutinize affirmative action programs to ensure that they do not directly discriminate against whites. In *University of California Regents v. Bakke* (1978), the Supreme Court struck down a special admissions program for minorities at a state medical school on the grounds that it excluded a white applicant because of his race and violated his rights under the Equal Protection Clause.[71] Allan Bakke applied to the University of California Davis Medical School two consecutive years and was rejected; in both years, black applicants with significantly lower grade point averages and medical aptitude test scores were accepted through a special admissions program that reserved sixteen minority places in a class of one hundred.[72] The University of California did not deny that its admissions decisions were based on race. Instead, it argued that its racial classification was "benign," that is, designed to assist minorities.

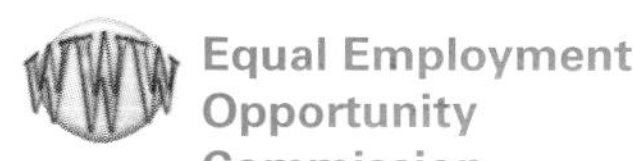

Equal Employment Opportunity Commission

Federal EEOC site with information on what constitutes discrimination by age, disability, race, ethnicity, religion, gender; how to file a charge; and guidance for employers *www.eeoc.gov*

The Supreme Court held that these objectives were legitimate and that race and ethnic origin *may* be considered in reviewing applications to a state school without violating the Fourteenth Amendment's Equal Protection Clause. However, the Court also held that a separate admissions program for minorities with a specific quota of openings which were unavailable to white applicants *did* violate the Equal Protection Clause. The Court ordered the university to admit Bakke to its medical school and to eliminate the special admissions program. It recommended that California consider an admissions program developed at Harvard, which considered disadvantaged racial or ethnic background as a "plus" in an overall evaluation of an application but did not set numerical quotas or exclude any person from competing for all positions.

Bakke case U.S. Supreme Court case challenging affirmative action.

Affirmative Action as a Remedy for Past Discrimination The Supreme Court has continued to approve of affirmative action programs where there is evidence of past discriminatory practices. In *United Steelworkers of America v. Weber* (1979), the Supreme Court approved a plan developed by a private employer and a union to reserve 50 percent of higher paying, skilled jobs for minorities. The Court held that "employers and unions in the private sector [are] free to take such race-conscious steps to eliminate manifest racial imbalances in traditionally segregated job categories. We hold that Title VII does not prohibit such . . . affirmative action plans." According to the Court, it would be "ironic indeed" if the Civil Rights Act were used to prohibit voluntary private race-conscious efforts to overcome the past effects of discrimination.[73] In *United States v. Paradise* (1987), the Court upheld a rigid 50 percent black quota system for promotions in the Alabama Department of Safety, which had excluded blacks from the ranks of state troopers prior to 1972 and had not promoted any blacks higher than corporal prior to 1984. In a 5 to 4 decision, the majority stressed the long history of discrimination in the agency as a reason for upholding the quota system. Whatever burdens imposed on innocent parties were outweighed by the need to correct the effects of past discrimination.[74]

Cases Questioning Affirmative Action However, the Supreme Court has continued to express concern about whites who are directly and adversely affected by government action solely because of their race. In *Firefighters Local Union 1784 v. Stotts* (1984), the Court ruled that a city could not lay off white fire fighters in favor of black fire fighters with less seniority.[75] In *City of Richmond v. Crosen Co.* (1989), the Supreme Court held that a minority **set-aside program** in Richmond, Virginia, which mandated that 30 percent of all city construction contracts must go to "blacks, Spanish-speaking, Orientals, Indians, Eskimos, or Aleuts," violated the Equal Protection Clause of the Fourteenth Amendment.[76]

Moreover, the Court has held that racial classifications in law must be subject to "strict scrutiny." This means that race-based actions by government—any disparate treatment of the races by federal, state, or local public agencies—must be found necessary to remedy past proven discrimination, or to further clearly identified, legitimate and "compelling" government interests. Moreover, race-based actions must be "narrowly tailored" and "least restrictive" so as to minimize adverse effects on rights of other individuals. In striking down a federal construction contract set-aside program for small businesses owned by racial minorities; the Court expressed skepticism about governmental racial classifications: "There is simply no way of determining what classifications are 'benign' and 'remedial' and what classifications are in fact motivated by illegitimate notions of racial inferiority or simple racial politics."[77]

Affirmative Action and "Diversity" in Higher Education Most colleges and universities in United States—public as well as private—identify "diversity," the term that refers to racial and ethnic representation in the student body and faculty as an institutional goal.

University administrators argue that students benefit when they interact with others from different cultural heritages. "Students must be engaged with diverse peers if we expect learning and development to occur," and the existence of a racially and ethnically diverse student body is "a necessary condition" for such engagement. There is some evidence that students admitted under policies designed to increase diversity do well in their post-college careers. And there are claims that racial and ethnic diversity on the campus improve students' "self-evaluation," "social-historical thinking," and "intellectual engagement."

set-aside program Program in which a specified number or percentage of contracts must go to designated minorities.

But despite numerous efforts to develop scientific evidence that racial or ethnic diversity on the campus improves learning, no definitive conclusions have emerged. Educational research on this topic is clouded by political and ideological conflict. There is no evidence that racial diversity does in fact promote the expression of ideas on the campus, or change perspectives or viewpoints of students.

Diversity and Affirmative Action Even if diversity provides educational benefits, the question arises as to how to achieve it. Diversity is closely linked to affirmative action programs on campuses throughout the nation. When affirmative action programs are designed as special efforts to recruit and encourage qualified minority students to attend college, they enjoy widespread public support. But when affirmative action programs include preferences for minority applicants over equally or better qualified nonminorities, public support falters and constitutional questions arise.

Diversity as a Constitutional Question The U.S. Supreme Court has held that the Equal Protection Clause of the Fourteenth Amendment requires that racial classifications be subject to "strict scrutiny." This means that race-based actions by governments—any disparate treatment of the racial or ethnic group by federal, state, or local public agencies, including colleges and universities—must be found necessary to advance a "compelling government interest" and must be "narrowly tailored" to further that interest.

The U.S. Supreme Court held in 2003 that diversity may be a compelling government interest because it "promotes cross-racial understanding, helps to break down racial stereotypes, and enables [students] to better understand persons of different races." This opinion was written by Justice Sandra Day O'Connor in a case involving the University of Michigan Law School's affirmative action program. In a 5–4 decision, O'Connor, writing for the majority, said the Constitution "does not prohibit the law school's narrowly tailored use of race in admissions decisions to further a compelling interests in obtaining the educational benefits that flow from a diverse student body."[78]

However, in a case involving the University of Michigan's affirmative action program for undergraduate admissions, the Supreme Court held that the admissions policy was "not narrowly tailored to achieve respondents' asserted interest in diversity" and therefore violated the Equal Protection Clause of the Fourteenth Amendment. The Court again recognized that diversity may be a compelling interest, but rejected and affirmative action plan that made race the decisive factor for even minimally qualified minority applicants. Yet the Supreme Court restated its support for limited affirmative action programs that use race as a "plus" factor the position the court has held since the *Bakke* case in 1978.[79]

Race-neutral Approaches to Diversity There is a variety of ways in which diversity can be achieved without using racial preferences in the admission of students. The U.S. Department of Education recommends (1) preferences based on socioeconomic status; (2) recruitment outreach efforts targeted at students from traditionally low-performing schools; and (3) the admission plans for students to finish at the top of their high school classes without regard to SAT or ACT scores.[80] California, Texas, and Florida currently give preference to students to stand at or near the top of their class in each of the states high schools. All three states officially abandoned racial preferences. Yet currently all three states enroll roughly the same numbers of minorities in their colleges and universities that they did before abandoning racial preferences.

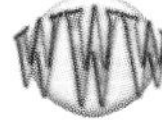

Fire: Foundation for Equal Rights in Education

Advocacy organization defending individual rights on campus and opposing racial preferences.
www.thefire.org

A CONFLICTING VIEW

The Constitution Should Be Color-Blind

In 1896 a single voice spoke out against *all* racial classifications—Supreme Court Justice John Harlan opposing segregation: "Our Constitution is color-blind and neither knows nor tolerates classes among the citizens." He was *dissenting* from the Supreme Court's majority opinion in the infamous case of *Plessy v. Ferguson,* which approved the segregationist doctrine of "separate but equal." Unfortunately, the ideal of a color-blind society remains almost as elusive today as it was more than a hundred years ago.

Martin Luther King, Jr., had a dream that "our children will one day live in a nation where they will not be judged by the color of their skin but by the content of their character." Can that dream be made a reality?

Over time, the civil rights movement shifted its focus from *individual rights* to *group benefits.* Affirmative action programs classify people by group membership, thereby challenging a belief widely held in the United States—that people be judged on individual attributes like character and achievement, rather than on race or gender. Racial and gender preferences are currently encountered in hiring and promotion practices in private and public employment and in college in university admissions, scholarships, and faculty recruitment.

Affirmative action programs divide Americans into two classes—those who enjoy legally mandated preferential treatment and those who do not. Majority support for civil rights laws is weakening under growing resentment among those who are denied preferential treatment.

Some early supporters of affirmative action have come to view race-conscious programs as no longer necessary. They argue that disadvantages in society today are based more on class than on race. If preferences are to be granted at all, in their view, they should be based on economic disadvantage, not race.

Misgivings also have been expressed by a few African American scholars about the unfair stigmatizing of the supposed beneficiaries of affirmative action—a resulting negative stereotyping of blacks as unable to advance on merit alone. Race-conscious government policies, they argue, have done more harm than good. African American economist Glenn Loury claims that proponents of affirmative action have an inferiority complex: "When blacks say we have to have affirmative action, please don't take it away from us, it's almost like saying, you're right, we can't compete on merit. But I know that we can compete." Conservative columnist William Bennett says that "toxic" race relations, aggravated by affirmative action, have led to damaging forms of new segregation: "Affirmative action has not brought us what we want—a color-blind society. It has brought us an extremely color-conscious society. In our universities we have separate dorms, separate social centers. What's next—water fountains? That's not good and everybody knows it."

Many argue that affirmative action has caused the civil rights movement to lose widespread public support and instead become contentious and divisive. In fact, civil rights has become such a hot topic that most elected officials now prefer to avoid it. As one anonymous member of Congress put it, "The problem is political correctness—you can't talk openly."

Source: Quotations reported in *Newsweek,* February 13, 1996.

The Absence of a Clear Constitutional Principle The Supreme Court's decisions on affirmative action have not yet established a clear and coherent interpretation of the Constitution. No clear rule of law or constitutional principle tells us exactly what is permissible and what is prohibited in the way of racially conscious laws and practices. Nevertheless, over time some general tendencies in Supreme Court policy can be identified. Affirmative action programs are *more likely to be found constitutional* when:

- They are adopted in response to a past proven history of discrimination.
- They do not absolutely bar whites or ban them from competing or participating.

- They serve a clearly identified, legitimate, and "compelling governmental interest."
- They are "narrowly tailored" to achieve the government's compelling interest and represent the "least restrictive" means of doing so.

It is important to note that the Supreme Court has never adopted the color-blind doctrine, first espoused by Justice Harlan in his *dissent* from *Plessy v. Ferguson,* that "Our Constitution is color-blind, and neither knows nor tolerates classes among the citizens." If the Equal Protection Clause required the laws of the United States and the states to be truly color-blind, then no racial guidelines, goals, or quotas would be tolerated. Occasionally this view has been expressed in recent minority dissents (*see A Conflicting View:* "The Constitution Should Be Color-Blind").

Hispanics in America

Hispanics—a term the U.S. Census Bureau uses to refer to Mexican Americans, Puerto Ricans, Cubans, and others of Spanish-speaking ancestry and culture—are now the nation's largest minority (see Table 12.6). The largest Hispanic subgroup is Mexican Americans. Some are descendants of citizens who lived in the Mexican territory annexed to the United States in 1848, but most have come to the United States in accelerating numbers in recent years. The largest Mexican American populations are found in Texas, Arizona, New Mexico, and California. Puerto Ricans constitute the second largest Hispanic subgroup. Many still retain ties to the commonwealth and move back and forth from Puerto Rico to New York. Cubans make up the third largest subgroup; most have fled from Fidel Castro's Cuba and live mainly in the Miami metropolitan area. Each of these Hispanic groups has encountered a different experience in American life. Indeed, some evidence indicates that these groups identify themselves separately, rather than as Hispanics.[81]

If all Hispanics are grouped together for statistical comparisons, their median family income level is well below that of whites (see Table 12.4). Hispanic poverty and unemployment rates are also higher than those of whites. The percentage of Hispanics completing high school and college education is well below that of both whites and blacks, suggesting language or other cultural obstacles in education. Yet within these overall racial comparisons, there are wide disparities among subgroups as well as among individuals.

TABLE 12.6 Minorities in America, 2000

	Number	Percentage of Population
African Americans	34,658,000	12.3
Hispanic Americans	35,306,000	12.5
Asian or Pacific Islander Americans	10,643,000	3.7
Native Americans, Eskimos, Aleuts	2,476,000	0.9
Total Population	281,422,000	100.0*

* In the 2000 census, for the first time, some people were recognized as "two or more races" (2.4%).

Source: Census of Population, 2000.

Advocacy and litigation on behalf of Latinos, with information on cases dealing with immigration rights.
www.maldef.org

Mexican Americans The Mexican American population in the southwestern United States is growing very rapidly; it doubled in size between 1980 and 1990. For many years, agricultural business encouraged immigration of Mexican farm laborers willing to endure harsh conditions for low pay. Many others came to the United States as *indocumentados*—undocumented, or illegal, aliens. In the Immigration Reform Act of 1986 Congress offered amnesty to all undocumented workers who had entered the United States prior to 1982.

Economic conditions in Mexico and elsewhere in Central America continue to fuel immigration, legal and illegal, to the United States. But with lower educational levels, average incomes of Mexican American families in the United States are lower and the poverty rate is higher than the general population. Although Mexican Americans have served as governors of Arizona and New Mexico and have won election to the U.S. Congress, their political power does not yet match their population percentages. Mexican American voter turnout is lower than other ethnic groups, perhaps because many are resident aliens or illegal immigrants not eligible to vote, or perhaps because of cultural factors that discourage political participation.[82]

Puerto Ricans Residents of Puerto Rico are American citizens because Puerto Rico is a commonwealth of the United States. Puerto Rico's commonwealth government resembles that of a state, with a constitution and elected governor and legislature, but the island has no voting members of the U.S. Congress and no electoral votes for president. As citizens, Puerto Ricans can move anywhere in the United States; many have immigrated to New York City.

Median family income in Puerto Rico is higher than anywhere else in the Caribbean but only half that of the poorest state in the United States. Puerto Ricans have not fared as well economically as other Hispanic groups within the United States: Puerto Ricans have lower median family incomes and higher poverty percentages, in part perhaps because of lower work force participation. One explanation centers on the history of access to federal welfare programs on the island and the resulting social dependency it fostered among some Puerto Rican families.[83]

Puerto Ricans have long debated whether to remain a commonwealth of the United States, apply for statehood, or seek complete independence from the United States. As citizens of a commonwealth, Puerto Ricans pay no U.S. income tax (although their local taxes are substantial) while receiving all the benefits that U.S. citizens are entitled to—Social Security, welfare assistance, food stamps, Medicaid, Medicare, and so forth. If Puerto Rico chose to become a state, its voters could participate in presidential and congressional elections, but its taxpayers would not enjoy the same favorable cost-benefit ratio they enjoy under commonwealth status. Some Puerto Ricans also fear that statehood would dilute the island's cultural identity and force English on them as the national language.

As a state, Puerto Rico would have two U.S. senators and perhaps six U.S. representatives. The island's majority party, the Popular Democratic Party, is closely identified with the Democratic Party, so most of these new members would likely be Democrats. But the island's New Progressive Party, identified with the Republican Party, supports statehood, and many GOP leaders believe their party should appeal to Hispanic voters. If Puerto Ricans were to choose independence, a new constitution for the Republic of Puerto Rico would be drawn up by the islanders themselves.

Only Congress can admit a new state, but Congress is unlikely to act without the full support of Puerto Ricans themselves. Several nonbinding referenda votes have been held in Puerto Rico over the years, the most recent in 1998. Opinion today appears to be closely divided, with commonwealth status edging out statehood by a small margin; independence has never received more than one percent of the vote.

Cuban Americans Many Cuban Americans, especially those in the early waves of refugees from Castro's revolution in 1959, were skilled professionals and businesspeople, and they rapidly set about building Miami into a thriving economy. Although Cuban Americans are the smallest of the Hispanic subgroups, today they are better educated and enjoy higher incomes than the others. They are well organized politically, and they have succeeded in electing Cuban Americans to local office in Florida and to the U.S. Congress.

Hispanic Politics

Mexican Americans constitute the largest portion, nearly three-quarters, of the nation's Hispanic population. Most reside in the southwestern United States—California, Texas, Arizona, New Mexico, and Colorado. Puerto Ricans in New York, and Cubans and other Central and South Americans in Florida, constitute only about one-quarter of the Hispanic population. Thus, generalizations about Hispanic politics are heavily influenced by Mexican Americans.

La Raza National Council of La Raza
Issue positions, programs, news, dedicated to improving life experiences of Hispanic Americans. *www.nclr.org*

Organizing for Political Activity For many decades American agriculture encouraged Mexican American immigration, both legal and illegal, to labor in fields as *braceros.* Most of these migrant farm workers lived and worked under very difficult conditions; they were paid less than minimum wages for backbreaking labor. Farm workers were not covered by the federal National Labor Relations Act and therefore not protected in the right to organize labor unions. But civil rights activity among Hispanics, especially among farm workers, grew during the 1960s under the leadership of Cesar Chavez and his United Farm Workers union. Chavez organized a national boycott of grapes from California vineyards that refused to recognize the union or improve conditions. *La Raza,* as the movement was called, finally ended in a union contract with the growers and later a California law protecting the right of farm workers to organize unions and bargain collectively with their employers. More importantly, the movement galvanized Mexican Americans throughout the Southwest to engage in political activity.[84]

However, inasmuch as many Mexican American immigrants were noncitizens, and many were *indocumentados* (undocumented residents of the United States), the voting strength of Mexican Americans never matched their numbers in the population. The Immigration Reform and Control Act of 1986 granted amnesty to illegal aliens living in the United States in 1982. But the same act also imposed penalties on employers who hired illegal aliens. The effect of these threatened penalties on many employers was to make them wary of hiring Hispanics, especially as permanent employees. At the same time, industries in need of cheap labor—agriculture, health and hospitals, restaurants, clothing manufacturers, etc.—continued to encourage legal and illegal immigration to fill minimum and even subminimum wage level jobs with few if any benefits.

Hispanic Political Power Most Hispanics today believe that they confront less prejudice and discrimination than their parents. Nonetheless, in 1994 California voters approved a referendum, Proposition 187, that would have barred welfare and other benefits to persons living in the state illegally. Most Hispanics opposed the measure, believing that it was motivated by prejudice. A federal court later declared major portions of Proposition 187 unconstitutional. And the U.S. Supreme Court has held that a state may not bar the children of illegal immigrants from attending public schools.[85]

Mexican American voter turnout remains weak. Various explanations have been advanced for the lower voter participation of Mexican Americans. Language barriers may still discourage some voters, even though ballots in many states are now available in Spanish language. Illegal immigrants, of course, cannot vote. Lower education and income levels are also associated with lower voter turnout. Nonetheless, Hispanic voting is on the increase throughout the nation and both Democratic and Republican candidates are increasingly aware of the importance of the Hispanic vote.

Overall, most Hispanics identify with the Democratic Party (see Table 12.7). Mexican Americans in the southwestern states and Puerto Ricans in New York have traditionally supported Democratic candidates, while the strong anticommunist heritage among Cuban Americans has fostered a Republican voting tradition in Florida. Hispanics are generally conservative on social issues (opposing abortion, opposing racial preferences, favoring government vouchers to pay parochial school tuitions) but liberal on economic issues (favoring government provision of health insurance for all, favoring a larger federal government with many services).

TABLE 12.7 Hispanic Politics

	Total	Mexican	Puerto Rican	Cuban	Other
"In politics today do you consider yourself a Republican, a Democrat, an Independent, or something else?"					
Democrat	37%	33%	52%	29%	39%
Republican	16	15	17	34	12
Independent	33	37	17	27	35
"Do you think abortion should be legal in all cases, illegal in most cases, or illegal in all cases?"					
Legal	40	36	60	49	32
Illegal	58	61	39	49	66
"Do you think the government should provide health insurance for Americans without insurance, or is this something the government should not do?"					
Should	83	83	84	87	86
Should not	14	14	15	11	11
"Should colleges sometimes take a student's racial and ethnic background into consideration when they decide which students to admit, or should they select students without considering their racial or ethnic backgrounds?"					
Consider	22	21	17	17	21
Don't consider	75	76	78	82	76
"Do you favor or oppose offering government financial aid or 'vouchers' to pay parents some of the cost of sending their children to private and parochial schools?"					
Favor	40	40	46	49	37
Oppose	18	16	12	22	23

Source: Copyright © *Public Perspective,* a publication of the Roper Center for Public Opinion Research, University of CT, Storrs. Reprinted by permission.

Gender Equality and the Fourteenth Amendment

The historical context of the Fourteenth Amendment implies its intent to guarantee equality for newly freed slaves, but the wording of its Equal Protection Clause applies to "any person." Thus the text of the Fourteenth Amendment could be interpreted to bar any gender differences in the law, in the fashion of the once proposed yet never ratified Equal Rights Amendment. But the Supreme Court has not interpreted the Equal Protection Clause to give the same level of protection to gender equality as to racial equality. Indeed, in 1873 the Supreme Court specifically rejected arguments that this clause applied to women. The Court once upheld a state law banning women from practicing law, arguing that "the natural and proper timidity and delicacy which belongs to the female sex evidently unfits it for many of the occupations of civil life. . . . The paramount destiny and mission of women are to fulfill the noble and benign offices of wife and mother. This is the law of the Creator."[86]

THINK AGAIN

Should gender equality receive the same level of legal protection as racial equality?

Early Feminist Politics The earliest active feminist organizations grew out of the pre–Civil War antislavery movement. There the first generation of feminists—including Lucretia Mott, Elizabeth Cady Stanton, Lucy Stone, and Susan B. Anthony—learned to organize, hold public meetings, and conduct petition campaigns. After the Civil War, women were successful in changing many state laws that abridged the property rights of married women and otherwise treated them as "chattel" (property) of their husbands. By the early 1900s activists were also successful in winning some protections for women in the workplace, including state laws limiting women's hours of work, working conditions, and physical demands. At the time, these laws were regarded as "progressive."

The most successful feminist efforts of the 1800s centered on protection of women in families. The perceived threats to women's well-being were their husbands' drinking, gambling, and consorting with prostitutes. Women led the Anti-Saloon League, succeeded in outlawing gambling and prostitution in every state except Nevada, and provided the major source of moral support for the Eighteenth Amendment (Prohibition).

In the early twentieth century, the feminist movement concentrated on women's suffrage—the drive to guarantee women the right to vote. The early suffragists employed mass demonstrations, parades, picketing, and occasional disruption and civil disobedience—tactics similar to those of the civil rights movement of the 1960s. The culmination of their efforts was the 1920 passage of the Nineteenth Amendment to the Constitution: "The right of citizens of the United States to vote shall not be denied or abridged by the United States or by any State on account of sex." The suffrage movement spawned the League of Women Voters; in addition to women's right to vote, the League has sought protection of women in industry, child welfare laws, and honest election practices.

Judicial Scrutiny of Gender Classifications In the 1970s, the Supreme Court became responsive to arguments that sex discrimination might violate the Equal Protection Clause of the Fourteenth Amendment. In *Reed v. Reed* (1971), it ruled that sexual classifications in the law "must be reasonable and not arbitrary, and must rest on some ground of difference having fair and substantial relation to . . . important governmental objectives."[87] This is a much more relaxed level of scrutiny than the Supreme Court gives to racial classification in the law. Since then, the Court has also made these rulings:

- A state can no longer set different ages for men and women to become legal adults [88] or purchase, alcoholic beverages.[89]

National Organization of Women (NOW)
Advocacy organization for feminist activists working to protect abortion rights, end discrimination against women, and "eradicate racism, sexism, and homophobia." ***www.now.org***

- Women cannot be barred from police or fire-fighting jobs by arbitrary height and weight requirements.[90]
- Insurance and retirement plans for women must pay the same monthly benefits (even though women on the average live longer).[91]
- Schools must pay coaches in girls' sports the same as coaches in boys' sports.[92]

Continuing Gender Differences The Supreme Court continues to wrestle with the question of whether some gender differences can be recognized in law. The question is most evident in laws dealing with sexual activity and reproduction. The Court has upheld statutory rape laws that make it a crime for an adult male to have sexual intercourse with a female under the age of eighteen, regardless of her consent. "We need not to be medical doctors to discern that young men and young women are not similarly situated with respect to the problems and the risks of sexual intercourse. Only women may become pregnant, and they suffer disproportionately the profound physical, emotional and psychological consequences of sexual activity."[93]

Women's participation in military service, particularly combat, raises even more controversial questions regarding permissible gender classifications. The Supreme Court appears to have bowed out of this particular controversy. In upholding Congress's draft registration law for men only, the Court ruled that "the constitutional power of Congress to raise and support armies and to make all laws necessary and proper to that end is broad and sweeping."[94] Congress and the Defense Department are responsible for determining assignments for women in the military. Women have won assignments to air and naval combat units but remain excluded from combat infantry, armor, artillery, special forces, and submarine duty.

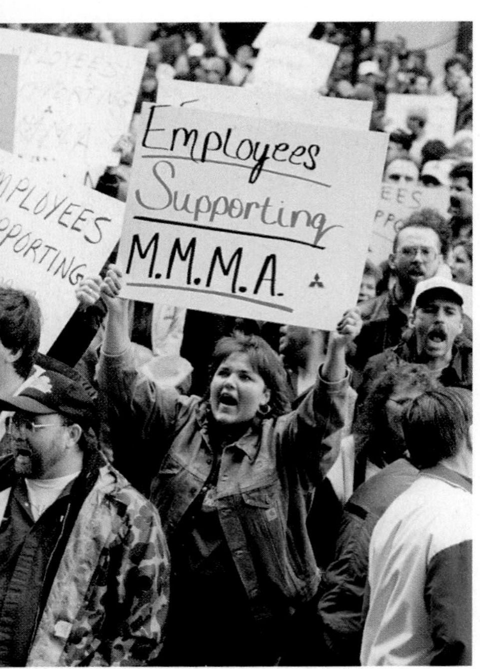

Employees of the Mitsubishi automobile plant in Normal, Illinois, demonstrated outside the offices of the Equal Employment Opportunity Commission in Chicago in April 1996, in support of the company after it became the target of a sexual harassment investigation. The company provided transportation to the demonstration and paid the workers for the day.

Aims of the Equal Rights Amendment The proposed Equal Rights Amendment to the U.S. Constitution, passed by Congress in 1972 but never ratified by the states, was worded very broadly: "Equality of rights under the law shall not be denied or abridged by the United States or any State on account of sex." Had it been ratified by the necessary thirty-eight states, it would have eliminated most, if not all, gender differences in the law. Without ERA, many important guarantees of equality for women rest on laws of Congress rather than on the Constitution.

Gender Equality in the Economy

As cultural views of women's roles in society have changed and economic pressures on family budgets have increased, women's participation in the labor force has risen. The gap between women's and men's participation in the nation's work force is closing over time.[95] With the movement of women into the work force, feminist political activity has shifted toward economic concerns—gender equality in education, employment, pay, promotion, and credit.

Gender Equality in Civil Rights Laws Title VII of the Civil Rights Act of 1964 prevents sexual (as well as racial) discrimination in hiring, pay, and promotions. The Equal Employment Opportunity Commission, the federal agency charged with eliminating discrimination in employment, has established guidelines barring stereotyped classifications of "men's jobs" and "women's jobs." The courts have repeatedly struck down state laws and employer practices that differentiate between men and women in hours, pay, retirement age, and so forth.

The Federal Equal Credit Opportunity Act of 1974 prohibits sex discrimination in credit transactions. Federal law prevents banks, credit unions, savings and loan associations, retail stores, and credit card companies from denying credit because of sex or marital status. However, these businesses may still deny credit for a poor or nonexistent credit rating, and some women who have always maintained accounts in their husband's name may still face credit problems if they apply in their own name.

Title IX of the Education Act Amendment of 1972 deals with sex discrimination in education. This federal law bars discrimination in admissions, housing, rules, financial aid, faculty and staff recruitment and pay, and—most troublesome of all—athletics. The latter problem has proven very difficult because men's football and basketball programs have traditionally brought in the money to finance all other sports, and men's football and basketball have received the largest share of school athletic budgets.

Feminist.Com Web site promoting women's business development, with information and advice. *www.feminist.com*

The Earnings Gap Despite protections under federal laws, women continue to earn substantially less than men do. Today women, on average, earn about 76 percent of what men do (see Figure 12.1). This earnings gap has been closing very slowly: In 1985 women earned an average 68 percent of men's earnings. The earnings gap is not primarily a product of **direct discrimination**; women in the same job with the same skills, qualifications, experience, and work record are not generally paid less than men. Such direct discrimination has been illegal since the Civil Rights Act of 1964. Rather, the earnings gap is primarily a product of a division in the labor market between traditionally male and female jobs, with lower salaries paid in traditionally female occupations.

direct discrimination Now illegal practice of differential pay for men versus women even when those individuals have equal qualifications and perform the same job.

The Dual Labor Market and "Comparable Worth" The existence of a "dual" labor market, with male-dominated "blue-collar" jobs distinguishable from female-dominated "pink-collar" jobs, continues to be a major obstacle to economic equality

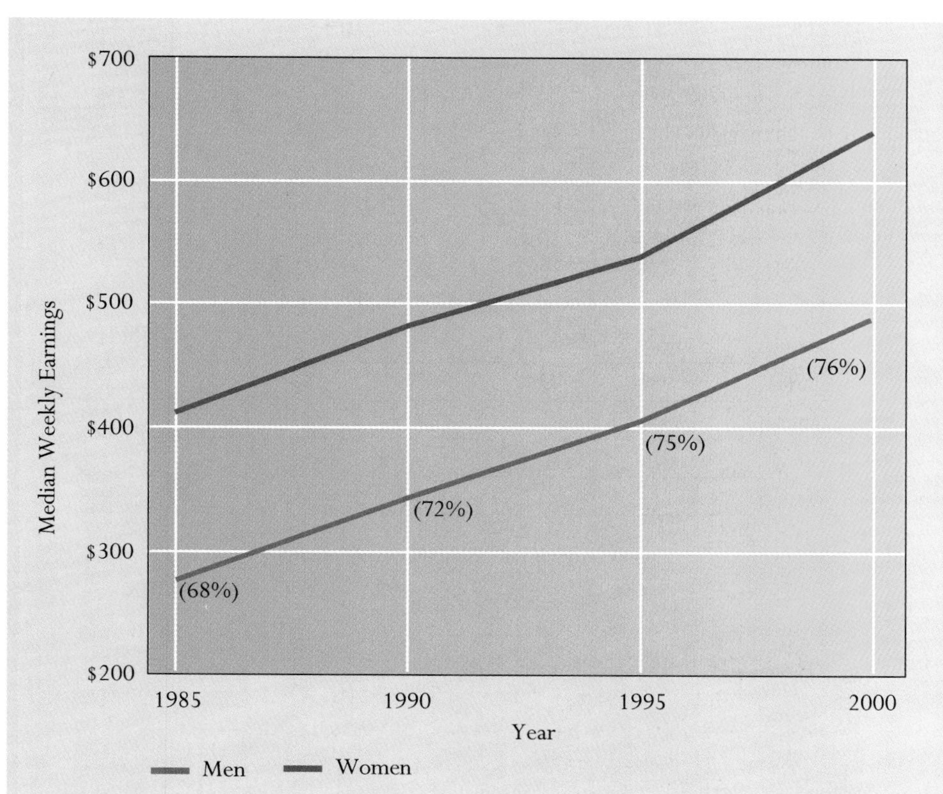

FIGURE 12.1 The Earnings Gap: Median Weekly Earnings of Men and Women

The continuing "earnings gap" between men and women reflects a division in the labor market between traditionally male higher paying occupations and traditionally female lower paying positions.

Note: Figures in parentheses indicate the ratio of women's to men's median weekly earnings.

Source: Statistical Abstract of the United States, 2001, p. 403.

between men and women. These occupational differences result from cultural stereotyping, social conditioning, and training and education—all of which narrow the choices available to women. Although significant progress has been made in reducing occupational sex segregation (see Figure 12.2), many observers nevertheless doubt that sexually differentiated occupations will be eliminated in the foreseeable future.

The "Glass Ceiling" The barriers to women's advancement to top positions in the corporate and financial worlds are often very subtle, giving rise to the phrase **glass ceiling**. In explaining "why women aren't getting to the top," one observer argues that "at senior management levels competence is assumed. What you're looking for is someone who fits, someone who gets along, someone you trust. Now that's subtle stuff. How does a group of men feel that a woman is going to fit? I think it's very hard." Or, as a woman bank executive says, "The men just don't feel comfortable."[96]

There are many other explanations for the glass ceiling, all controversial: Women choose staff assignments rather than fast-track, operating-head assignments. Women are cautions and unaggressive in corporate politics. Women have lower expectations about peak earnings and positions, and these expectations become self-fulfilling. Women bear children, and even during relatively short maternity absences they fall behind their male counterparts. Women are less likely to want to change locations than men, and immobile executives are worth less to a corporation than mobile ones. Women executives in sensitive positions come under even more pressure than men in similar posts. Women executives believe they get much more scrutiny than men and must work harder to succeed. And at all levels, increasing attention has been paid to sexual harassment (see *What Do You Think?*: "What

glass ceiling "Invisible" barriers to women rising to the highest positions in corporations and the professions.

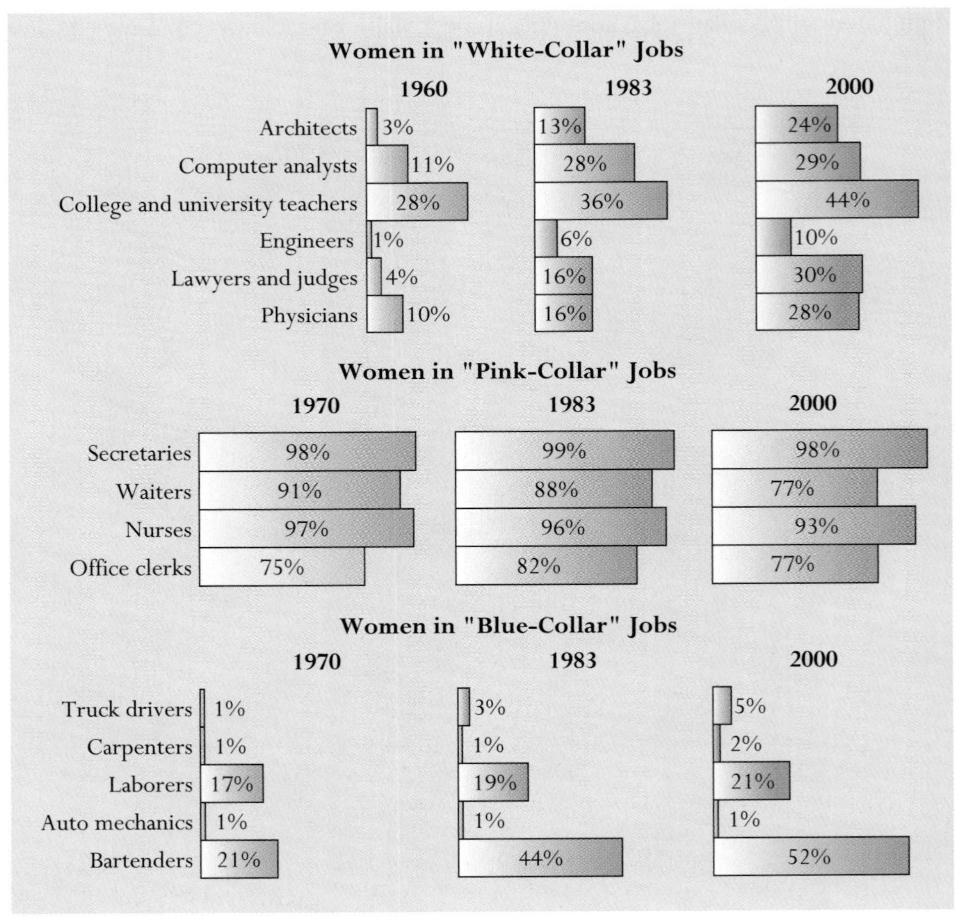

FIGURE 12.2 Gender Differentiation in the Labor Market

Most of the earnings gap between men and women in the U.S. labor force today is the result of the different job positions held by the two sexes. Although women are increasingly entering "white-collar" occupations long dominated by men, they continue to be disproportionately concentrated in "pink-collar" service positions. "Blue-collar" jobs have been the most resistant to change, remaining a male bastion, although women bartenders now outnumber men.

Source: Statistical Abstract of the United States, 2001, pp. 380–82.

WHAT DO YOU THINK?

What Constitutes Sexual Harassment?

Various surveys report that up to one-third of female workers say they have experienced sexual harassment on the job.[*] But it is not always clear exactly what kind of behavior constitutes "sexual harassment."

The U.S. Supreme Court has provided some guidance in the development of sexual harassment definitions and prohibitions. Title VII of the Civil Rights Act of 1964 makes it "an unlawful employment practice to discriminate against any individual with respect to his [sic] compensation, terms, conditions or privileges of employment because of such individual's race, color, religion, sex, or national origin." In the employment context, the U.S. Supreme Court has approved the following definition of sexual harassment:

> Unwelcome sexual advances, requests for sexual favors, and other verbal or physical conduct of a sexual nature constitute sexual harassment when (1) submission to such conduct is made either explicitly or implicitly a term or condition of an individual's employment; (2) submission to or rejection of such conduct by an individual is used as the basis for employment decisions affecting such individual; or (3) such conduct has the purpose or effect of unreasonably interfering with an individual's work performance or creating an intimidating, hostile, or offensive working environment.[†]

There are no great difficulties in defining sexual harassment when jobs or promotions are conditioned on the granting of sexual favors. But several problems arise in defining a "hostile working environment." This phrase may include offensive utterances, sexual innuendoes, dirty jokes, the display of pornographic material, and unwanted proposals for dates. First, it would appear to include speech and hence raise First Amendment questions regarding how far speech may be curtailed by law in the workplace. Second, the definition depends more on the subjective feelings of the individual employee about what is "offensive" and "unwanted" than on an objective standard of behavior easily understood by all. Justice Sandra Day O'Connor wrestled with the definition of a "hostile work environment" in *Harris v. Forklift* in 1993. She held that a plaintiff need not show that the utterances caused psychological injury but that a "reasonable person," not just the plaintiff, must perceive the work environment to be hostile or abusive. Presumably a single incident would not constitute harassment; rather, courts should consider "the frequency of the discriminatory conduct," "its severity," and whether it "unreasonably interferes with an employee's work performance."[‡]

What behaviors does a "reasonable person" believe to be sexual harassment? Some polls indicate that women are somewhat more likely to perceive sexual harassment in various behaviors than men (see figure). But neither women nor men are likely to perceive it to include repeated requests for a date, the telling of dirty jokes, or comments on attractiveness—even though these behaviors often inspire formal complaints.

Many university policies go well beyond both Supreme Court rulings and opinion polls in defining what constitutes sexual harassment, including the following: "remarks about a person's clothing" "suggestive or insulting sounds," and "leering at or ogling of a person's body."

---

[*] *Washington Post National Weekly Edition*, March 7, 1993.

[†] *Meritor Savings Bank v. Vinson*, 477 U.S. 57 (1986).

[‡] *Harris v. Forklift Systems*, 126 L. Ed. 2d 295 (1993).

Question: *Here is a list of some different situations. We're interested in knowing whether you think they are forms of sexual harassment—not just inappropriate or in bad taste, but sexual harassment.*

Definitely is sexual harassment...

	Men	Women
If a male boss makes it clear to a female employee that she must go to bed with him for a promotion	91%	92%
If a male boss asks very direct questions of a female employee about her personal sexual practices and preferences	59%	68%
If a female boss asks very direct questions of a male employee about his personal sexual practices and preferences	47%	57%
If a man once in a while asks a female employee of his to go out on dates, even though she has said no in the past	15%	21%
If a man once in a while tells dirty jokes in the presence of female employees	15%	16%
If a male boss tells a female employee that she looks very attractive today	3%	5%

Source: Roper Organization as reported in American Enterprise. September/October 1993, p. 93.

Constitutes Sexual Harassment?"). Finally, it is important to note that affirmative action efforts by governments—notably the EEOC—are directed primarily at entry-level positions rather than senior management posts.

SUMMARY NOTES

- Laws and government are required to protect individual liberty. Yet laws and governments themselves restrict liberty. To resolve this dilemma, constitutions seek to limit governmental power over the individual. In the U.S. Constitution, the Bill of Rights is designed to place certain liberties beyond the reach of government.
- Freedom of religion encompasses two separate restrictions on government: government must not establish religion or prohibit its free exercise. Although the wording of the First Amendment is absolute ("Congress shall make no law . . .") the Supreme Court has allowed some restrictions on religious practices that threaten health, safety, or welfare.
- The Supreme Court's efforts to maintain "a wall of separation" between church and state have proven difficult and controversial. The Court's banning of prayer and religious ceremony in public schools more than thirty years ago remains politically unpopular today.
- The Supreme Court has never adopted the absolutist position that all speech is protected by the First Amendment. The Court's clear and present danger doctrine and its preferred position doctrine recognize the importance of free expression in a democracy, yet the Court has permitted some restrictions on expression, especially in times of perceived national crisis.
- The Supreme Court has placed obscenity outside of the protection of the First Amendment, but it has encountered considerable difficulty in defining "obscenity."
- The Constitution includes a number of important procedural guarantees in the criminal justice system: the writ of habeas corpus; prohibitions against bills of attainder and ex post facto laws; protection against unreasonable searches and seizures; protection against self-incrimination; guarantee of legal counsel; protection against excessive bail; guarantee of a fair public and speedy trial by an impartial jury; the right to confront witnesses and to compel favorable witnesses to testify; and protection against cruel or unusual punishment.
- The Supreme Court has ruled that the death penalty is not a "cruel and unusual punishment," but the Court has insisted on fairness and uniformity of application.
- The original Constitution of 1787 recognized and protected slavery. Not until after the Civil War did the Thirteenth Amendment (1865) abolish slavery. But the Fourteenth Amendment's guarantee of "equal protection of the laws" and the Fifteenth Amendment's guarantee of voting rights were largely ignored in southern states after the federal government's Reconstruction efforts ended. Segregation was held constitutional by the U.S. Supreme Court in its "separate but equal" decision in *Plessy v. Ferguson* in 1896.
- The NAACP led the long legal battle in the federal courts to have segregation declared unconstitutional as a violation of the Equal Protection Clause of the Fourteenth Amendment. Under the leadership of Thurgood Marshall, a major victory was achieved in the case of *Brown v. Board of Education of Topeka* in 1954.
- Martin Luther King, Jr.'s, campaign of nonviolent direct action helped bring remaining racial injustices to the attention of Congress. Key legislation includes the Civil Rights Act of 1964, which bans discrimination in public accommodations, government-funded programs, and private employment.
- Generally the Supreme Court is likely to approve of affirmative action programs when these programs have been adopted in response to a past proven history of discrimination, when they are narrowly tailored so as not to adversely affect the rights of individuals, when they do not absolutely bar whites from participating, and when they serve clearly identified, compelling, and legitimate government objectives.
- Economic conditions in Mexico and other Spanish-speaking nations of the Western Hemisphere continue to fuel large-scale immigration, both legal and illegal, into the United States. But the political power of Mexican Americans, the nation's largest Hispanic group, does not yet match their population percentage. Their voter turnout remains lower than that of other ethnic groups in the United States.
- Gender discrimination in employment has been illegal since the passage of the Civil Rights Act of 1964. Nevertheless, differences in average earnings of men and women persist, although these differences have narrowed somewhat over time. The earnings gap appears to be mainly a product of lower pay in occupations traditionally dominated by women and higher pay in traditionally male occupations.

KEY TERMS

Free Exercise Clause 418
Lemon test 421
clear and present danger doctrine 424
preferred position 425
freedom of expression 425
symbolic speech 425
writ of habeas corpus 432
ex post facto law 432
bill of attainder 433
search warrant 434
Miranda warning 435
exclusionary rule 435
plea bargaining 436
Emancipation Proclamation 440
Jim Crow 441
separate but equal 441
de facto segregation 442
nonviolent direct action 443
affirmative action 446
Bakke case 447
set-aside program 448
direct discrimination 457
glass ceiling 458

SUGGESTED READINGS

Barker, Lucius J., and Mack H. Jones. *African Americans and the American Political System.* 4th ed. Upper Saddle River, N.J.: Prentice Hall, 1999. Comprehensive analysis of African American politics, examining access to the judicial arena, the interest-group process, political parties, Congress, and the White House.

Bowen, William G., and Derek Curtis Bok. *The Shape of the River.* Princeton, N.J.: Princeton University Press, 1999. An argument by two university presidents that preferential treatment of minorities in admissions to prestigious universities has led to the subsequent success in life by the beneficiaries of the preferences.

Conway, M. Margaret, Gertrude A. Steurnagel, and David W. Ahern. *Women and Political Participation.* Washington, D.C.: CQ Press, 1997. A wide-ranging review of changes in American political culture brought about by women's increasing political clout. Continuing gender differences in representation are explored.

Epstein, Lee, and Thomas G. Walker. *Constitutional Law for a Changing America: Rights, Liberties and Justice.* 5th ed. Washington, D.C.: CQ Press, 2003. An authoritative text on civil liberties and the rights of the criminally accused. It describes the political context of Supreme Court decisions and provides key excerpts from the most important decisions.

Etzioni, Amitai. *The Limits of Privacy.* New York: Basic Books, 1999. A "communitarian" argument that Americans' focus on individual rights, including the right of privacy, should be balanced against the legitimate needs of the community.

Garrow, David. *Liberty and Sexuality: The Right to Privacy and the Making of Roe v. Wade.* New York: Macmillan, 1994. Historical account of the background and development of the right to sexual privacy.

Hentoff, Nat. *Free Speech for Me—But Not for Thee.* New York: HarperCollins, 1992. Account of how both the right and the left in America try to suppress the opinions of those who disagree with them.

Sullivan, Harold J. *Civil Rights and Liberties: Provocative Questions and Evolving Answers.* Upper Saddle River, N.J.: Prentice Hall, 2001. Contemporary issues in civil liberties discussed in a question-and-answer format.

MAKE IT REAL

CIVIL LIBERTIES: THE GREAT BALANCING ACT

In this simulation you are the Mayor of the City. You will have to make decisions and policies for a number of situations dealing with civil liberties. The City has been in an uproar over political events lately. When political conflict occurs, you are expected to keep public order and at the same time respect the civil liberties of the people involved. The toughest part about being the Mayor of the City is that the City newspaper has little to write about other than your latest actions, especially the mistakes. Good luck trying to control conflict while guarding everyone's rights.

TRAVEL THE CIVIL RIGHTS TIMELINE Using this timeline of significant events in the civil rights struggle, you will access a wealth of information and multimedia to further explain the struggle. In addition the timeline will highlight all major events (good and bad), speeches, conflicts that are part of the civil rights story including constitutional disputes on slavery, abolition, women's suffrage, Jim Crow laws, and major sociological changes, to name a few.

CHAPTER 13

POLITICS, ECONOMICS, AND SOCIAL WELFARE POLICY

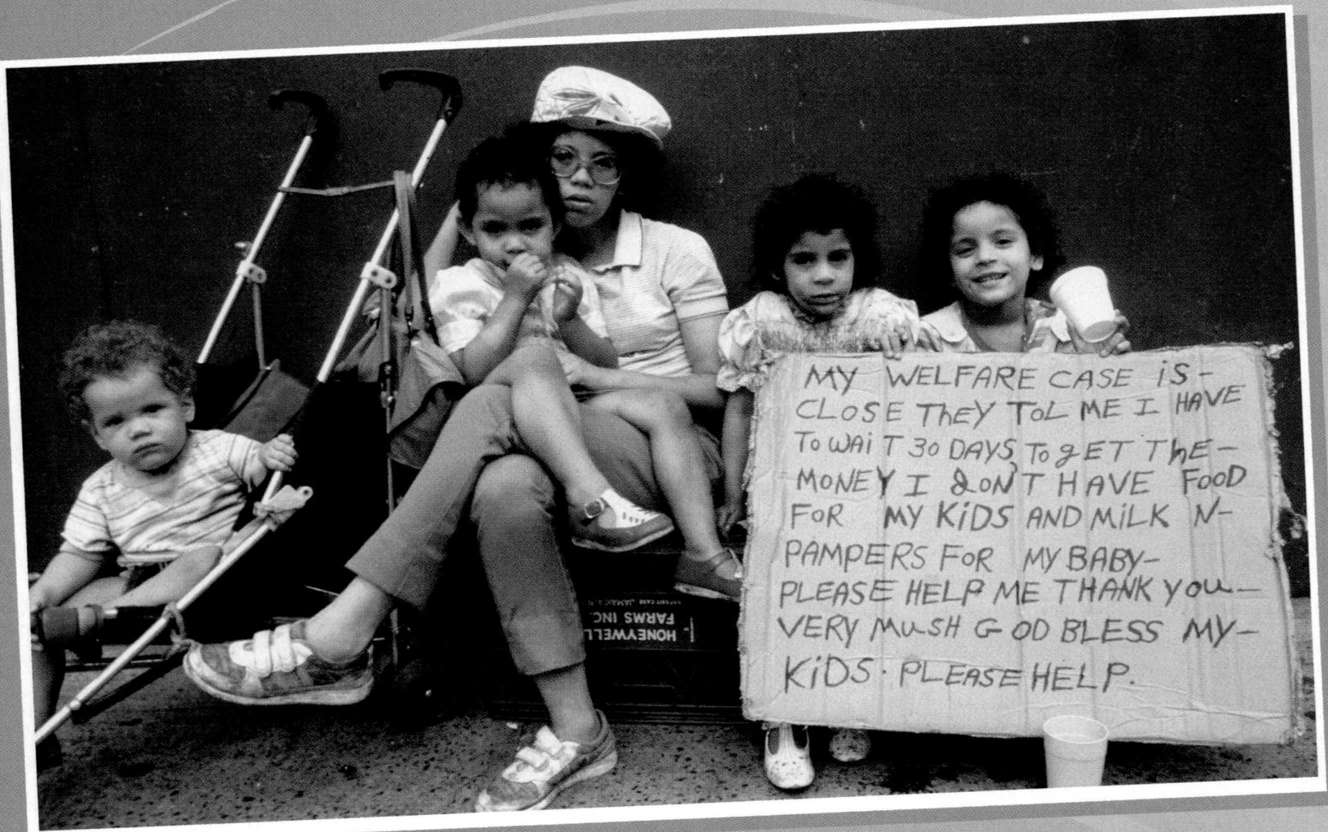

CHAPTER OUTLINE

- Politics and Economics
- The Performance of the American Economy
- Economic Globalization
- The Tax Burden
- Tax Politics
- Poverty in the United States
- Social Welfare Policy
- Politics and Welfare Reform
- Health Care in America

THINK ABOUT POLITICS

1 Do you believe government efforts to manage the economy usually make things better or worse?
Better ● Worse ●

2 Do you think the trend toward a global economy is a good thing or a bad thing for the United States?
Good thing ● Bad thing ●

3 Which is more important, holding down the size of government or providing needed services?
Holding down the size of government ● Providing needed services ●

4 Do you think government welfare programs perpetuate poverty?
Yes ● No ●

5 Should all retirees receive Social Security benefits regardless of their personal wealth or income?
Yes ● No ●

6 Should there be a time limit on how long a person can receive welfare payments?
Yes ● No ●

7 Should government provide health care insurance for all Americans?
Yes ● No ●

What should government do to encourage economic growth and keep unemployment and inflation low? How is globalization affecting the American economy? Are tax rates too low or too high? Is the government doing enough to assist the aged and poor? And what should be the government's role in health care?

Politics and Economics

Earlier, we observed that one of America's foremost political scientists, Harold Lasswell, defined "politics" as "who gets what, when, and how." One of America's foremost economists, Paul Samuelson, defined "economics" as "deciding what shall be produced, how, and for whom."[1] The similarity between these definitions is based on the fact that both the political system and the economic system provide society with means for deciding about the production and distribution of goods and services. The political system involves *collective* decisions—choices made by communities, states, or nations—and relies on government coercion through laws, regulations, taxes, and so on to implement them. A **free-market economic system** involves *individual* decisions—choices made by millions of consumers and thousands of firms—and relies on *voluntary exchange* through buying, selling, borrowing, contracting, and trading to implement them. Both politics and markets function to transform popular demands into goods and services, to allocate costs, and to distribute goods and services.

The Performance of the American Economy

Underlying the power of nations and the well-being of their citizens is the strength of their economy—their total productive capacity. The United States produces about *$12 trillion* worth of goods and services in a single year for its 281 million people—more than $40,000 worth of output for every person.

Economic Growth **Gross domestic product** (GDP) is a widely used measure of the performance of the economy.[2] GDP is a nation's total production of goods and services for a single year valued in terms of market prices. It is the sum of all the goods and services that people have been willing to pay for, from wheat production to bake sales, from machine tools to maid service, from aircraft manufacturing to bus rides, from automobiles to chewing gum. GDP counts only final purchases of goods and services (that is, it ignores the purchase of steel by car makers until it is sold as a car)

FIGURE 13.1 Economic Growth

The tendency for periods of economic growth to alternate with periods of contraction has led to the concept of the business cycle—the idea that at least some fluctuation is normal, even healthy, helping to keep the economy growing in the long run by keeping prices from getting too high. In recent decades, government intervention in the economy appears to have succeeded in reducing, although not in altogether eliminating, the depths of recessions to which the nation was formerly prone.

Source: Data from Council of Economic Advisers, Economic Indicators, August 2004.

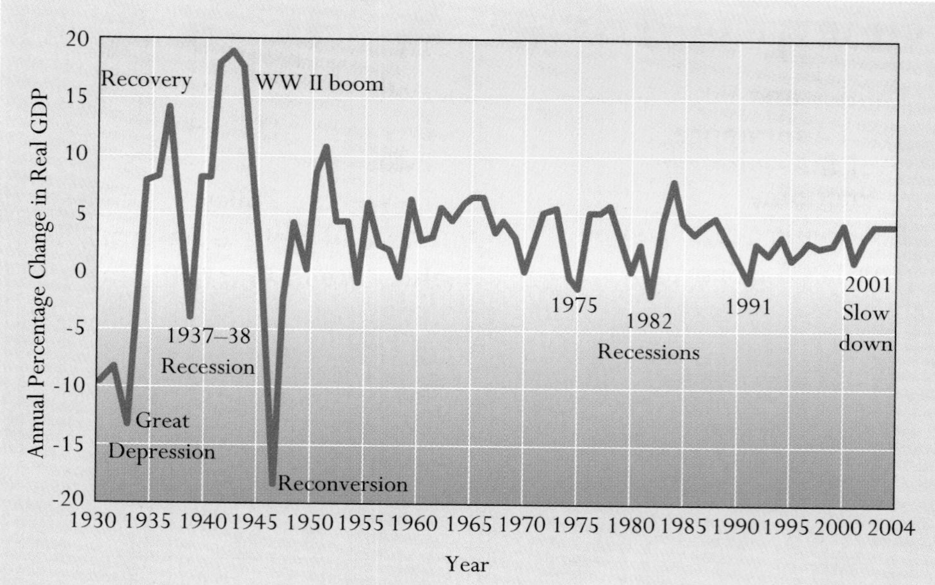

Bureau of Economic Analysis
Source of official economic statistics, listed A–Z.
www.bea.gov

free-market economic system Economic system in which individual choices by consumers and firms determine what shall be produced, how much, and for whom; this economic system relies on voluntary exchanges of buying and selling.

gross domestic product (GDP) Measure of economic performance in terms of the nation's total production of goods and services for a single year, valued in terms of market prices.

unemployment rate Percentage of the civilian labor force who are not working but who are looking for work or waiting to return to or to begin a job.

to avoid double counting in the production process. GDP also excludes financial transactions (such as the sale of bonds and stocks) and income transfers (such as Social Security, welfare, and pension payments) that do not add to the production of goods and services. Although GDP is expressed in current dollar prices, it is often recalculated in constant dollar terms to reflect real values over time, adjusting for the effect of inflation. GDP estimates are prepared each quarter by the U.S. Department of Commerce; these figures are widely reported and closely watched by the business and financial community.

Growth in real (constant dollar) GDP measures the performance of the overall economy. Economic recessions and recoveries are measured as fluctuations or swings in the growth of GDP. For example, a recession is usually defined as negative GDP growth in two or more consecutive quarters. Historical data reveal that periods of economic growth have traditionally been followed by periods of contraction, giving rise to the notion of *economic cycles*. Prior to 1950, economic cycles in the United States produced extreme ups and downs, with double-digit swings in real GDP. In recent decades, however, economic fluctuations have been more moderate. The United States still experiences economic cycles, but many economists believe that countercyclical government fiscal and monetary policy has succeeded in achieving greater stability (see Figure 13.1).

Unemployment From a political standpoint, the **unemployment rate** may be the most important measure of the economy's performance. The unemployment rate is the percentage of the civilian labor force who are looking for work or waiting to return to or begin a job. Unemployment is different from not working; people who have retired or who attend school and people who do not work because of sickness, disability, or unwillingness are not considered part of the labor force and so are not counted as unemployed. People who are so discouraged about finding a job that they have quit looking for work are also not counted in the official unemployment rate. The unemployed do include people who have been terminated from their last job or temporarily laid off from work, as well as people who voluntarily quit and those who have recently entered or reentered the labor force and are now seeking employment.

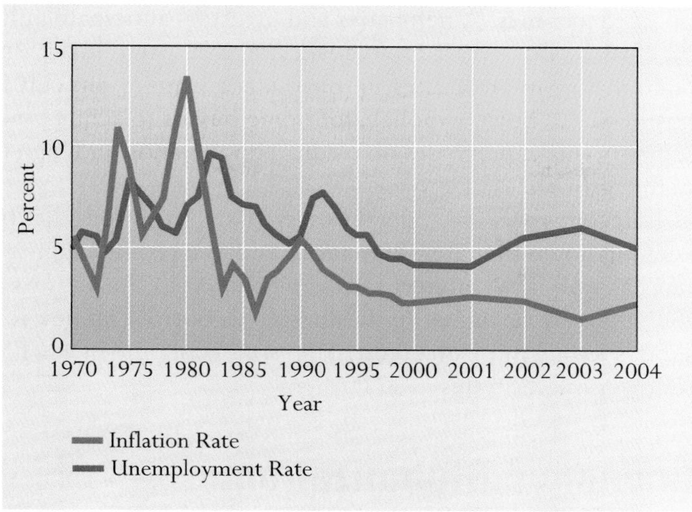

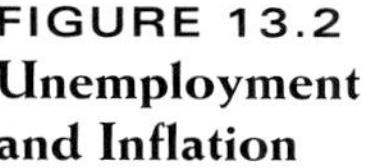

FIGURE 13.2
Unemployment and Inflation

Economic growth during the 1980s lowered both the inflation and unemployment rates, freeing the nation from the stagflation (combined inflation and high unemployment) that had characterized much of the 1970s. Unemployment rose during the recession 1990–91 and again in 2002–2003. Inflation has remained relatively low in recent years.

Source: Data from Council of Economic Advisers, 2004.

The unemployment rate is measured each month by the U.S. Department of Labor. It does so by contacting a random sample of more than 50,000 households in many locations throughout the country. Trained interviewers ask a variety of questions to determine how many (if any) members of the household are either working or have a job but did not work at it because of sickness, vacation, strike, or personal reasons (employed); or whether they have no job but are available for work and actively seeking a job (unemployed). The unemployment rate fluctuates with the business cycle, reflecting recessions and recoveries (see Figure 13.2). Generally, unemployment lags behind GDP growth, going down only after the recovery has begun. Following years of economic growth in the 1990s, the nation's unemployment rate fell to near record lows, below 5 percent. The economic slowdown of 2001–2002 pushed up unemployment above 5 percent again.

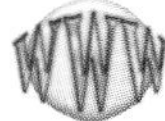

Bureau of Labor Statistics

The U.S. Department of Labor's Bureau of Labor Statistics site contains monthly information about the nation's employment rate plus a wealth of supporting data. *www.bls.gov*

Inflation Inflation erodes the value of the dollar because higher prices mean that the same dollars can now purchase fewer goods and services. Thus inflation erodes the value of savings, reduces the incentive to save, and hurts people who are living

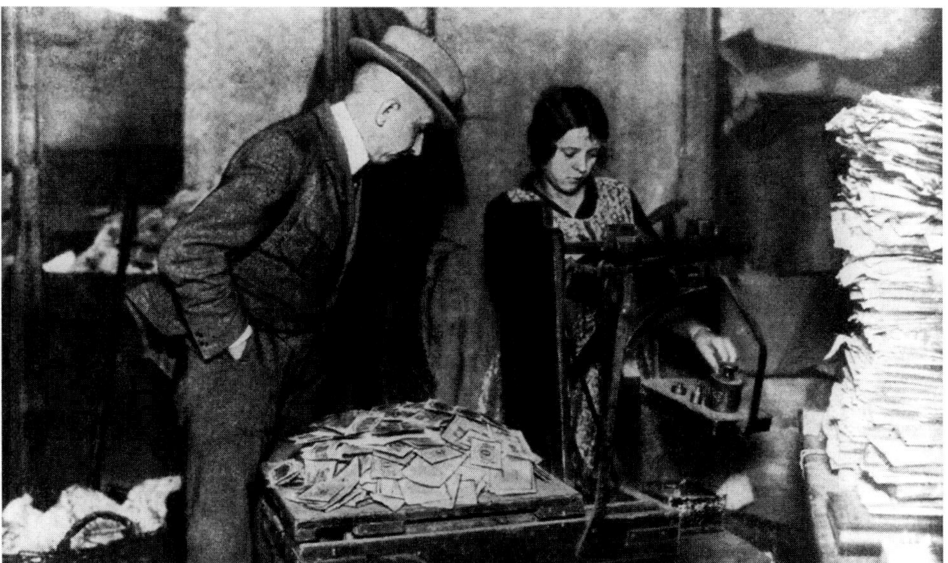

Just how bad can inflation get? Between the two world wars, inflation in Germany reached such levels that the nation's currency was often weighed, rather than counted, in order to speed transactions.

on fixed incomes. When banks and investors anticipate inflation, they raise interest rates on loans in order to cover the anticipated lower value of repayment dollars. Higher interest rates, in turn, make it more difficult for new or expanding businesses to borrow money, for home buyers to acquire mortgages, and for consumers to make purchases on credit. Thus inflation and high interest rates slow economic growth.

In recent years the Federal Reserve Bank ("the Fed") has been very successful in keeping down the rate of inflation, and as a result, keeping down overall interest rates as well. Low interest rates contributed to the nation's booming economy in the 1990s by encouraging businesses to borrow money for expansion and consumers to buy more on credit. The "soft" economy in 2001–2002 inspired the Fed to lower interest rates even farther.

Economic Globalization

The American economy is a major force in the global economy. International trade—the buying and selling of goods and services between individuals and firms located in different countries—has expanded rapidly in recent decades. Today, almost one-quarter of the world's total output is sold in a country other than the one in which it was produced. The United States exports about 11 percent of the value of its gross domestic product (GDP) and imports about 12 percent. As late as 1970, exports and imports were only about 3 percent of GDP (see Figure 13.3).

Historic Protectionism Historically, American business supported high tariffs—taxes on foreign imports. Prior to World War II, U.S. tariffs on imported goods averaged 30 to 50 percent in various decades. This eliminated most foreign competition from U.S. markets. American firms could raise prices to levels just below the price of imported goods with their high tariffs attached. Not only did this improve the profit margins of American manufacturers, but it also allowed them to be less efficient than foreign producers and yet survive and prosper under the protection of tariffs. The pressure to cut wages and downsize work forces was less than it would be if U.S. firms had to face foreign competition directly. Amer-

FIGURE 13.3 U.S. World Trade

Source: U.S. Bureau of Economic Analysis, December, 2003.

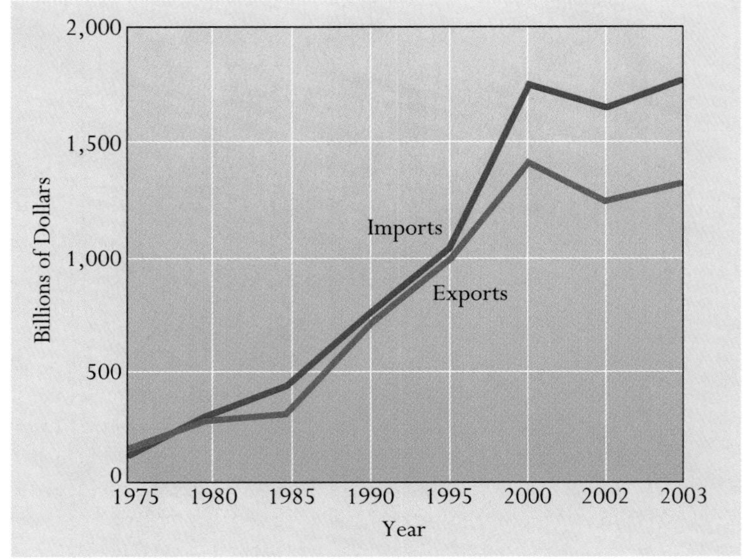

ican consumers, of course, paid higher prices than they otherwise would if foreign goods could come into the country without tariffs. The policy of high tariffs and quotas—limits on the number of units of specific goods imported into the country—was referred to as **protectionism**.

Free Trade But after World War II, the American economy became the most powerful in the world, and American businesses sought to expand their markets overseas. In order to lower trade barriers in other countries, the United States reduced or eliminated almost all of its own tariffs and import quotas. In effect, the United States became an open market. "Free trade" became a byword of American business, and "protectionism" became a derogatory term.

The argument for **free trade** is that it lowers the price of goods and improves the standard of living in nations that choose to trade with each other. Trade shifts resources (investment capital, jobs, technology, raw materials, etc.) in each nation toward what each does best. If one nation is much better producing aircraft and another better at producing clothing, then each nation will benefit more from trading than from trying to produce both airplanes and clothing. The efficiencies achieved by trading are said to directly benefit consumers by making available cheaper imported goods. Export industries also benefit when world markets are opened to their products. It is also argued that the pressure from competition from foreign-made goods in the American marketplace forces our own industries to become more efficient—cutting their costs and improving the quality of their goods. Finally, trade expands the menu of goods and services available to trading countries. American consumers gain access to everything from exotic foods and foreign-language movies to Porsches, BMWs, and Jaguars.

Uneven Benefits of Globalization While the U.S. economy has performed very well in recent years, the benefits of that performance have been unevenly distributed. A global economy inspires worldwide competition not only among corporations and businesses but also among workers. America's best educated and most highly skilled workers compete well in the global economy. U.S. export industries have thrived on international trade expansion, adding jobs to the American economy and raising the incomes of their executives, professionals, and skilled high-tech workers. But the global economy offers a huge supply of unskilled and semiskilled workers at very low wages. Increased trade, especially with less developed economies such as Mexico, China, and India, with their huge numbers of low-wage workers, creates competition with America's unskilled and semiskilled workers. It is difficult to maintain the wage levels of American jobs, especially in labor-intensive industries, in the face of competition from low-wage countries. And U.S. corporations can move their manufacturing plants to low-wage countries, for example to northern Mexico, where the transportation costs of moving these products back into the United States are minimal. Harvard economist Richard B. Freeman summarizes the problem:

> An economic disaster has befallen low-skilled Americans, especially young men, Researchers using several data sources—including household survey data from the Current Population Survey, other household surveys, and establishment surveys—have documented that wage inequality and skill-differentials in earnings and employment increased sharply in the United States from the mid-1970s through the 1980s and into the 1990s. The drop in the relative position of the less skilled shows up in a number of ways: greater earnings differentials between those with more and less education; greater earnings differentials between older and younger workers; greater differentials between

protectionism A policy of high tariffs and quotas on imports to protect domestic industries.

free trade A policy of reducing or eliminating tariffs and quotas on imports to stimulate international trade.

high-skilled and low-skilled occupations; in a wider earnings distribution overall and within demographic and skill groups; and in less time worked by low-skill and low-paid workers.[3]

Income inequality has worsened in America along with the growth of international trade (see "Inequality of Wealth and Income" in Chapter 2). Figure 13.4 shows the percentage of losses and gains between 1970 and 1998 for American families in each income class. The nation's lowest income families lost 22 percent of their real income over these years, while the highest income families gained 33 percent in real income. Not all of this increase in inequality can be attributed to the growth of international trade. But, clearly, America's less educated and less skilled workers are at a disadvantage in global competition.

The Politics of Free Trade Over the years both Democratic and Republican presidential administrations have advanced free trade. And Congress has approved the major treaties and organizations designed to institutionalize the global economy (see Table 13.1). The task of the cabinet-level position, International Trade Representative, has been to open up foreign markets to American products. Occasionally the United States has threatened to limit the importation of foreign products in order to force other nations to open up their own markets. And occasionally in Congress members from districts adversely affected by foreign competition have opposed specific trade arrangements or, alternatively, called upon the federal government to assist workers displaced by foreign competition. But the thrust of U.S. policy has been to expand free trade.

Official WTO site, with trade agreements, including General Agreement on Tariff and Trade (GATT).
www.wto.org

Democrats in Congress have expressed more reservations about free trade than Republicans. (Democrats often call for "fair trade" in lieu of "free trade.") Democratic Congress members often reflect the views of their party's core constituencies, including labor unions, that fear the adverse effect on wages created by globalization. Environmentalists also complain that foreign corporations are not

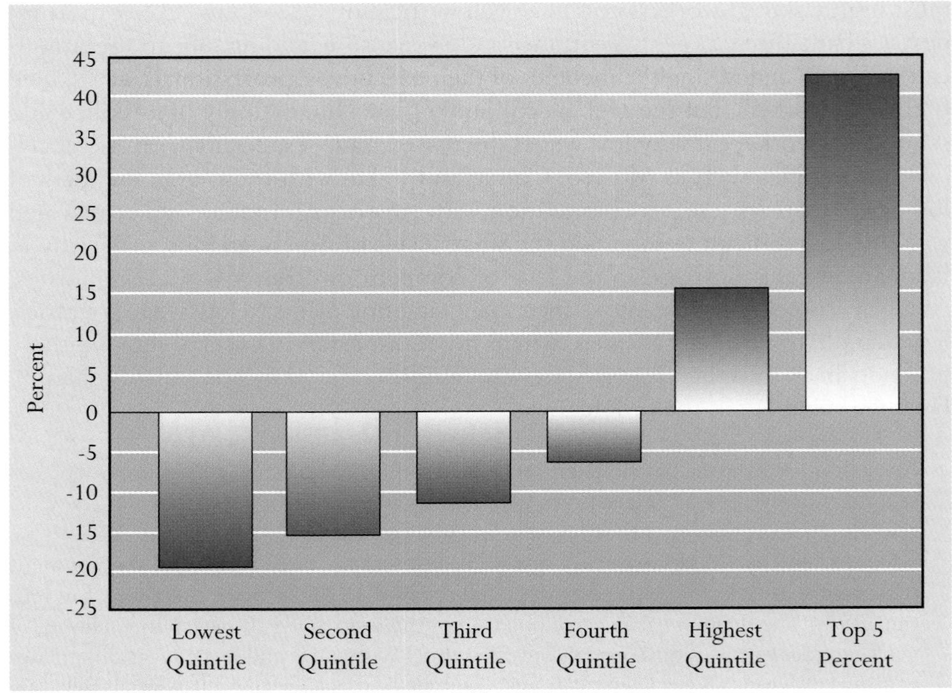

FIGURE 13.4
Worsening Inequality

Change in percent distribution of family income by quintile, 1980–2000.

Source: Statistical Abstract of the United States, 2002 p. 437.

TABLE 13.1 Major International Trade Agreements

The World Trade Organization and GATT.

The World Trade Organization was created in 1993. Today the WTO includes 130 nations that agree to a governing set of global trade rules. (China and Russia have applied to join.) The WTO is given power to adjudicate trade disputes among countries and monitor and enforce trade agreements, including GATT. GATT, the multinational General Agreement on Tariffs and Trade, was created following World War II for the purpose of encouraging international trade. Over the years GATT has been dominated by banking, business, and commercial interests in Western nations seeking multilateral tariff reductions and the relaxation of quotas. In 1993 the GATT "Uruguay Round" eliminated quotas on textile products; established more uniform standards for proof of dumping; set rules for the protection of intellectual property rights (patents and copyrights on books, movies, videos, and so on); reduced tariffs on wood, paper, and some other raw materials; and scheduled a gradual reduction of government subsidies for agricultural products.

The International Monetary Fund and the World Bank.

The IMF's purpose is to facilitate international trade, allowing nations to borrow to stabilize their balance of trade payments. When economically weak nations, however, incur chronic balance of trade deficits and perhaps face deferral or default on international debts, the IMF may condition its loans on changes in a nation's economic policies. It may require a reduction in a nation's government deficits by reduced public spending and/or higher taxes; or it may require a devaluation of its currency, making its exports cheaper and imports more expensive. It may also require the adoption of noninflationary monetary policies. Currently, the IMF as well as the World Bank are actively involved in assisting Russia and other states of the former Soviet Union to convert to free-market economies.

The World Bank makes long-term loans, mostly to developing nations, to assist in economic development. It works closely with the IMF in investigating the economic conditions of nations applying for loans and generally imposes IMF requirements on these nations as conditions for loans.

NAFTA.

In 1993 the United States, Canada, and Mexico signed the North American Free Trade Agreement. Objections by labor unions in the United States (and independent presidential candidate Ross Perot) were drowned out in a torrent of support by the American corporate community, Democrats and Republicans in Congress, President Bill Clinton, and former President George Bush. NAFTA envisions the removal of tariffs on virtually all products by all three nations over a period of ten to fifteen years. It also allows banking, insurance, and other financial services to cross these borders.

governed by strong or well-enforced environmental laws in their own countries. An array of other groups frequently demonstrates against globalization at meetings of the World Trade Organization and other international bodies (see *What Do You Think?*: "Does Globalization Help or Hurt America?").

THINK AGAIN

Which is more important, holding down the size of government or providing needed services?

The Tax Burden

The tax burden in the United States is modest compared to burdens in other advanced democracies (see *Compared to What?* "Tax Burdens in Advanced Democracies" on page 471). Federal revenues are derived mainly from (1) individual income

WHAT DO YOU THINK?

Does Globalization Help or Hurt America?

While Democratic and Republican presidents and Congresses have supported free trade and given their approval to two major trade agreements, the American public appears to be divided over the benefits of economic globalization.

Q. Based on what you know or may have heard, do you think the globalization of the world economy is mostly good for the United States, mostly bad for the United States, or doesn't make much difference?

Bad	22%
Good	38
No difference	25
Haven't heard/don't know	14

More Americans believe that free trade agreements cost U.S. jobs rather than create U.S. jobs.

Q. Do you think the trade agreements between the United States and other countries have helped create more jobs in the United States, or have they cost the U.S. jobs, or haven't they made much of a difference?

Cost U.S. jobs	49%
Haven't made much difference	23
Helped create more U.S. jobs	21
Don't know	7

It comes as no surprise that higher-income Americans voice greater support for globalization than lower-income Americans. Nor is it much of a surprise that public policy more closely reflects the views of higher-income Americans.

Question: *Do you think the trend toward a global economy is a good thing or a bad thing for the country?*

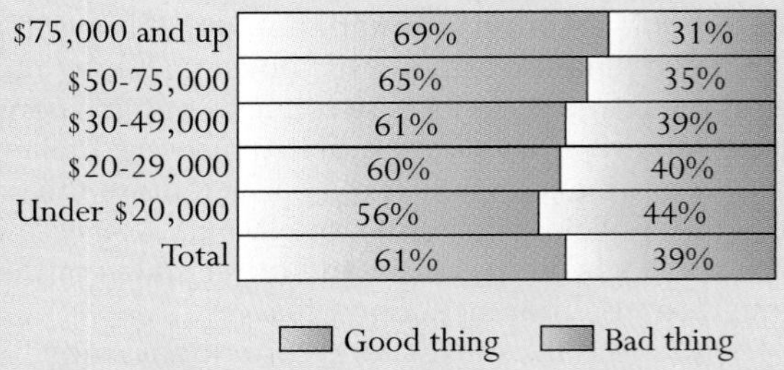

	Good thing	Bad thing
$75,000 and up	69%	31%
$50-75,000	65%	35%
$30-49,000	61%	39%
$20-29,000	60%	40%
Under $20,000	56%	44%
Total	61%	39%

Sources: Washington Post/Newsweek survey, October 2000 (for first and second questions); Princeton Survey Research, September 1998 (for third question). See *Public Agenda Online* at www.publicagenda.org.

taxes, (2) corporate income taxes, (3) Social Security payroll taxes, (4) estate and gift taxes, and (5) excise taxes and custom duties.

Internal Revenue Service
Official IRS site, with downloadable tax forms, information on tax laws, and tax statistics. *www.irs.gov*

Individual Income Taxes The **individual income tax** is the federal government's largest source of revenue (see Figure 13.5). Following tax cuts enacted by Congress in 2001 and 2003, individual income is now taxed at six rates: 10, 15, 25, 30, 33, and 35 percent. These are *marginal rates,* a term that economists use to mean additional. That is, income up to the top of the lowest bracket is taxed at 10 percent; additional income in the next bracket is taxed at 15 percent, up to a top marginal rate of 35 percent on income over $311,950 (in 2003). A personal exemption for each taxpayer and dependent, together with a standard deduction for married couples and a refundable earned income tax credit, ensure that low income earners pay no income tax. (However, they still must pay Social Security taxes on wages.) Tax brackets, as well as the personal exemption and standard deduction, are indexed annually to protect against inflation.

individual income tax Taxes on individuals' wages and other earned income, the primary source of revenue for the U.S. federal government.

Federal government revenues from individual and business income taxes would be substantially higher were it not for special provisions in tax laws that enable tax-

COMPARED TO WHAT?

Tax Burdens in Advanced Democracies

Americans complain a lot about taxes. But from a global perspective, overall tax burdens in the United States are relatively low (see figure). Federal, state, and local taxes in the United States amount to about 30 percent of the gross domestic product (GDP), slightly below the burden carried by the nation's leading competitors, Japan and Germany. U.S. taxes are well below the burdens imposed in Sweden, Denmark, and other nations with highly developed welfare systems.

Top marginal tax rates in many nations were reduced during the 1980s and 1990s. For example, the top rate in Great Britain was lowered from 60 to 40 percent, in Japan from 70 to 50 percent, and in Sweden from 80 to 65 percent. Both in the United States and abroad, the notion that excessively high tax rates discourage work, savings, and investment, as well as slow economic growth, won acceptance (although how high is "excessive" is obviously open to different interpretations). Moreover, in a global economy, with increased mobility of individuals and firms, pressures push nations to keep their top tax rates within reasonable limits. Corporations can shift their assets to low-tax jurisdictions, and high personal income tax rates can even threaten a "brain drain" of talented individuals.

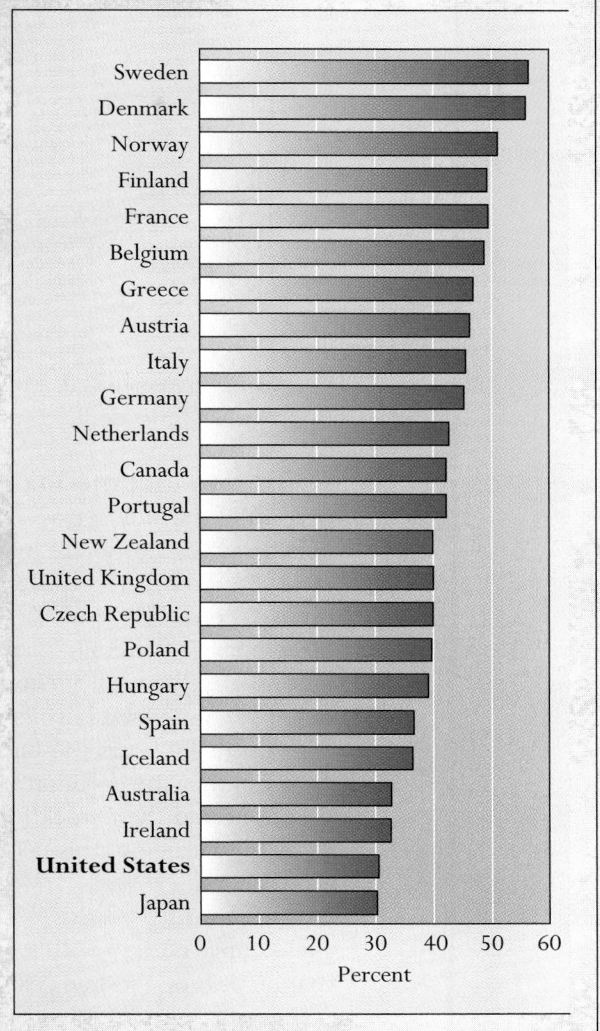

Government Revenues as a Percentage of GDP

Source: OECD, *Economic Outlook,* 1999.

payers to avoid paying taxes on often substantial sums of income. Although each of these "loopholes" supposedly has a larger social goal behind it (for example, the deductibility of mortgage interest is supposed to stimulate the purchase—and construction—of homes, keeping up the value of those assets for current homeowners and keeping the construction industry employed), critics charge that many cost far more than they are worth to society.

There is a continual struggle between proponents of special tax exemptions to achieve social goals and those who believe the tax laws should be simplified and social goals met by direct government expenditures. Much of the political

FIGURE 13.5 Sources of Federal Income

Individual income taxes make up the largest portion of the federal government's revenues (43 percent). The government also relies beavily on the second largest source of its revenues, Social Security taxes.

Source: Budget of the United States Government, 2005.

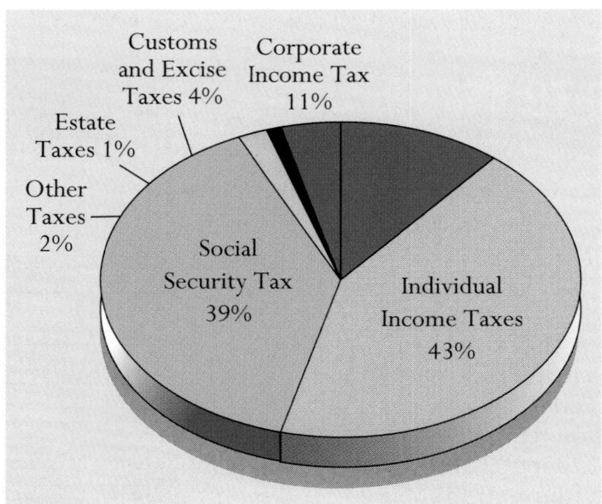

infighting in Washington involves the efforts of interest groups to obtain exemptions, exclusions, deductions, and special treatments in tax laws.[4]

Corporate Income Taxes The corporate income tax provides only about 10 percent of the federal government's total revenue. The Tax Reform Act of 1986 reduced the top corporate income tax from 46 to 34 percent (raised to 35 percent in 1993). However, corporations find many ways of reducing their taxable income, often to zero. The result was that many very large and profitable corporations pay little in taxes. Religious, charitable, and educational organizations, as well as labor unions, are exempt from corporate income taxes except for income they may derive from "unrelated business activity."

Who really bears the burden of the corporate income tax? Economists differ over whether the corporate income tax is "shifted" to consumers or whether corporations and their stockholders bear its burden. The evidence on who actually bears the burden of this tax is inconclusive.[5]

Social Security Taxes The second largest source of federal revenue is the Social Security tax. It is withheld from paychecks as the "FICA" deduction, an acronym that helps hide the true costs of Social Security and Medicare from wage earners. To keep up with the rising number of beneficiaries and the higher levels of benefits voted for by Congress, including generous automatic cost-of-living increases each year, the Social Security taxes rose to 15.3 percent. (The Social Security tax is 12.4 percent and the Medicare tax is 2.9 percent; all wage income is subject to the Medicare tax, but wage income above a certain level—$87,900 in 2004—is not subject to the Social Security tax.)

Taxes collected under FICA are earmarked (by Social Security number) for the account of each taxpayer. Workers thus feel they are receiving benefits as a right rather than as a gift of the government. However, less than 15 percent of the benefits being paid to current recipients of Social Security can be attributed to their prior contributions. Current taxpayers are paying more than 85 percent of the benefits received by current retirees.

Today a majority of taxpayers pay more in Social Security taxes than income taxes. Indeed, combined employer and employee Social Security taxes now amount to over $13,500 for each worker at the top of the wage base. If we assume that the employer's share of the tax actually comes out of wages that would otherwise be paid to the employee, then more than 75 percent of all taxpayers pay more in Social Security taxes than in income taxes.

Estate and Gift Taxes Taxation of property left to heirs is one of the oldest forms of taxation in the world. Federal estate taxes begin on estates of $650,000 (scheduled to rise to $1 million in 2006) and levy a tax rate that starts at 18 percent and rises to 49 percent for estates worth more than $3 million. (This top rate is scheduled to decrease one percent each year to 45% in 2007.) Because taxes at death otherwise could be avoided by simply giving estates to heirs while the giver is still alive, a federal gift tax is also levied on anyone who gives gifts in excess of $10,000 annually.

Excise Taxes and Custom Duties Federal excise taxes on the consumption of liquor, tobacco, gasoline, telephones, air travel, and other so-called luxury items, together with custom taxes on imports, provide about 3 percent of total federal revenues.

Tax Politics

The politics of taxation centers around the question of who actually bears the heaviest burden of a tax—especially which income groups must devote the largest proportion of their income to taxes. **Progressive taxation** requires high-income groups to pay a larger percentage of their incomes in taxes than low-income groups. **Regressive taxation** takes a larger share of the income of low-income groups. **Proportional (flat) taxation** requires all income groups to pay the same percentage of their income in taxes. Note that the *percentage of income* paid in taxes is the determining factor. Most taxes take more money from the rich than the poor, but a progressive or regressive tax is distinguished by the percentages of income taken from various income groups.

National Taxpayers Union
Advocacy organization for taxpayers "to keep what they have earned," with policy papers and data on tax burdens. *www.ntu.org*

The Argument for Progressivity Progressive taxation is generally defended on the principle of ability to pay; the assumption is that high-income groups can afford to pay a larger percentage of their incomes into taxes at no more of a sacrifice than that required of lower income groups to devote a smaller proportion of their income to taxation. This assumption is based on what economists call *marginal utility theory* as it applies to money; each additional dollar of income is slightly less valuable to an individual than preceding dollars. For example, a $5,000 increase in the income of an individual already earning $100,000 is much less valuable than a $5,000 increase to an individual earning only $10,000 or to an individual with no income at all. Hence, it is argued that added dollars of income can be taxed at higher rates without violating equitable principles.

progressive taxation System of taxation in which higher income groups pay a larger percentage of their incomes in taxes than do lower income groups.

The Argument for Proportionality Opponents of progressive taxation generally assert that equity can only be achieved by taxing everyone at the same percentage of their income, regardless of the size of their income. Progressivity penalizes initiative, enterprise, and the risk taking necessary to create new products and businesses. It also reduces incentives to expand and develop the nation's economy. Highly progressive taxes curtail growth and make everyone poorer.

regressive taxation System of taxation in which lower income groups pay a larger percentage of their incomes in taxes than do higher income groups.

Reagan's Reductions in Progressivity Certainly the most dramatic change in federal tax laws during the Reagan years was the reduction in the progressivity of individual income tax rates (see Figure 13.6). The top marginal tax rate fell from

proportional (flat) taxation System of taxation in which all income groups pay the same percentage of their income in taxes.

FIGURE 13.6 Top Personal Income Tax Rates

The top marginal personal income tax rate fell dramatically during the Reagan Administration, then began to creep upward again under Presidents Bush and Clinton. George W. Bush lowered the top rate in 2001 and again in 2003.

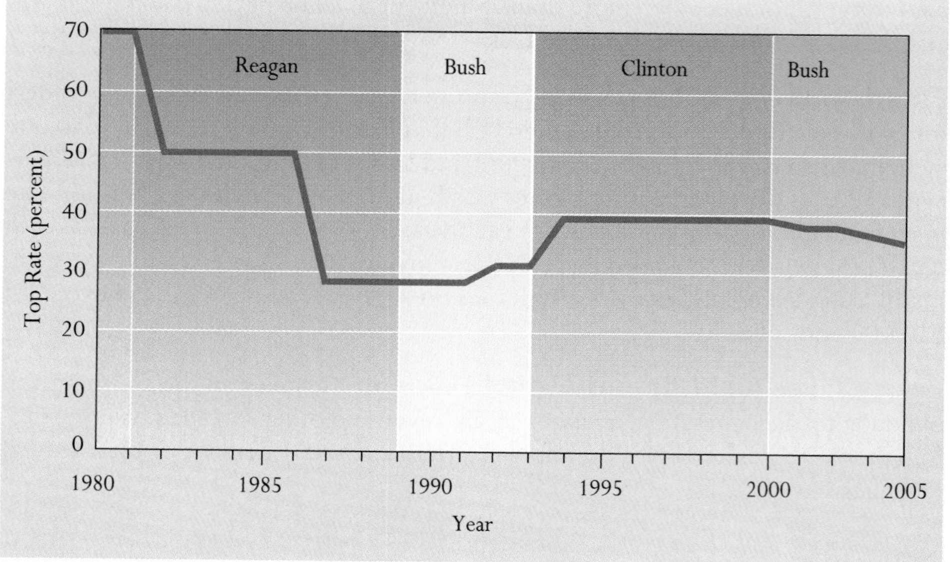

70 percent when President Reagan took office to 28 percent following enactment of tax reform in 1986. The Tax Reform Act of 1986 reduced fourteen rate brackets to only two rate brackets, 15 and 28 percent.

"Read My Lips" At the Republican national convention in 1988, presidential nominee George Bush made a firm pledge to American voters that he would veto any tax increases passed by the Democratic-controlled Congress: "Read my lips! No new taxes." Yet in a 1990 budget summit with Democratic congressional leaders, President Bush agreed to add a top marginal rate of 31 percent to the personal income tax. Breaking his solemn pledge on taxes contributed heavily to Bush's defeat in the 1992 presidential election.

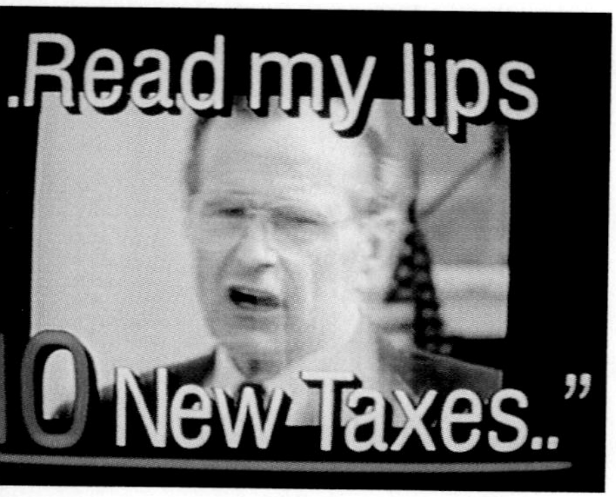

George Bush's pledge "Read my lips, no new taxes" helped him to victory in 1988. But breaking the pledge in 1990 contributed heavily to his defeat in 1992.

"Soak the Rich" Proposals to "soak the rich" are always politically very popular. President Clinton pushed Congress to raise the top marginal tax rates to 36 percent for families earning $140,000, and to 39.6 percent for families earning $250,000. But these new top rates do not raise much revenue, partly because very few people have annual incomes in these catagories. Moreover, high rates encourage people to seek tax-sheltered investments—to use their capital less efficiently to create tax breaks for themselves rather than to promote new business and new jobs.

Bush Tax Cuts George W. Bush came into office vowing *not* to make the same mistake as his father—raising tax rates in an effort to compromise with the Democrats. On the contrary, Bush was strongly committed to lowering taxes, arguing that an "economic stimulus" package of tax cuts would revive the economy. Bush inspired the Republican-controlled Congress to lower the top marginal rate to 35 percent, and to restructure rates through six brackets—10, 15, 25, 28, 33, and 35 percent. (see Table 13.2). And the Bush 2003 tax package also contained a variety of new credits and special treatments: Corporate stock dividends are now taxed at a low 15 percent, rather than at the same rate as earned income; the "marriage penalty" was eliminated by making the standard personal deduction for married couples twice that of a single person; the per child tax credit was raised to $1000 (from $600); and the tax on capital gains—gains made from the buying and selling of real estate, stocks and bonds, etc.—was reduced from 20 to 15 percent.

TABLE 13.2 Marginal Individual Income Tax Rates

	Before 2001	2001	2005
Lowest	15%	10%	10%
to	28	15	15
Highest	31	27	25
Income	36	30	28
Brackets	39.6	35	33
		38.6	35

Who Pays the Federal Income Tax? The federal income tax continues to be highly progressive. Progressive rates, together with the personal and standard deductions for families and the earned income tax credit for low-income earnes, combined to remove most of the income tax burden on middle and low-income Americans. Indeed, the lower half of the nation's taxpayers pay only about 4 percent of total income taxes paid to the federal government. The top 10 percent of income earners pay 69 percent of all individual income taxes (see Figure 13.7). Politically, this means that most proposals to reduce income taxes can be branded by opponents as "favoring the rich," inasmuch as the rich pay most of the income tax bill.

Tax Foundation Advocacy

Organization devoted to making the public "tax conscious," with information, "fiscal facts," and "tax freedom day." *www.taxfoundation.org*

Poverty in the United States

How much poverty really exists in the United States? It depends on how you define the term "poverty." The official definition used by the federal government focuses on the cash income needed to maintain a "decent standard of living." The official **poverty line** is only a little more than one-third of the median income of all American families. It takes into account the effects of inflation, rising each year with the rate of inflation. (For example, in 1990, the official poverty line for an urban family of four was $13,359 per year; by 2004 the poverty line had risen to about $19,000.)

poverty line Official standard regarding what level of annual cash income is sufficient to maintain a "decent standard of living"; those with incomes below this level are eligible for most public assistance programs.

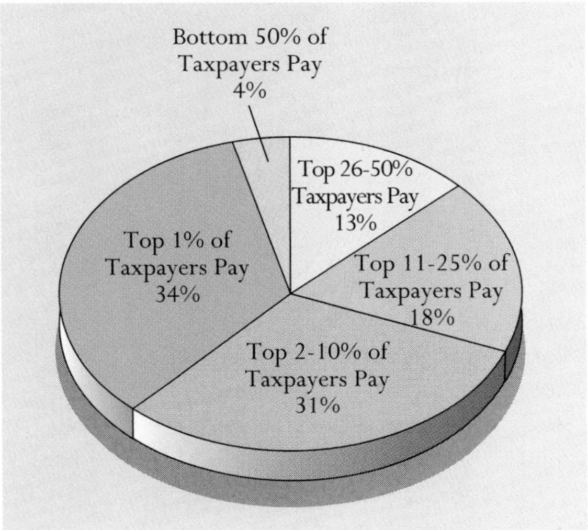

FIGURE 13.7 Who Pays the Federal Personal Income Tax?

Percentage of Total Federal Income Taxes Paid by Income Levels

Source: Based on data from The Tax Foundation at http://www.taxfoundation.org.html

FIGURE 13.8 Number of Poor and Poverty Rate

Source: http://www.census.gov/hhes/poverty00/pov00.html.

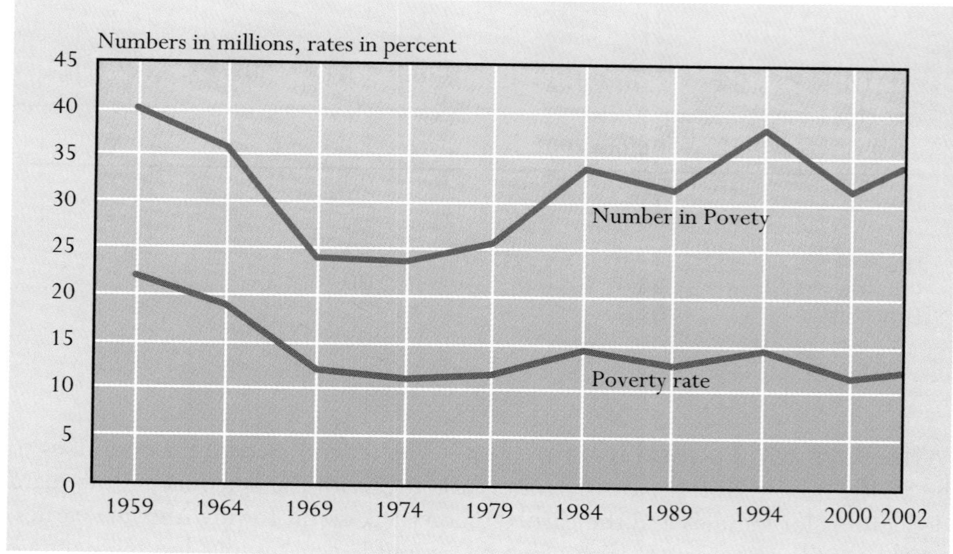

Institute for Research an Poverty
University of Wisconsin Institute leads in research on nature and causes of poverty.
www.ssc.wisc.edu/irp

Persistent Poverty About half of the people on welfare rolls at any one time are *persistently poor,* that is, likely to remain on welfare for five or more years. For these people, welfare is a more permanent part of their lives.

Because they place a disproportionate burden on welfare resources, persistently poor people pose serious questions for social scientists and policy makers. Prolonged poverty and welfare dependency create an **underclass** that suffers from many social ills—teen pregnancy, family instability, drugs, crime, alienation, apathy, and irresponsibility.[6] Government educational, training, and jobs programs, as well as many other social service efforts, fail to benefit many of these people.

underclass People who have remained poor and dependent on welfare over a prolonged period of time.

Family Structure Poverty and welfare dependency are much more frequent among female-headed households with no husband present than among husband-wife households (see *Up Close:* "Who Are the Poor?"). Traditionally, "illegitimacy" was held in check by powerful religious and social structures. But these structures

FIGURE 13.9 Social Welfare Entitlement Programs in the Federal Budget

Source: Budget of the United States Government, 2005.

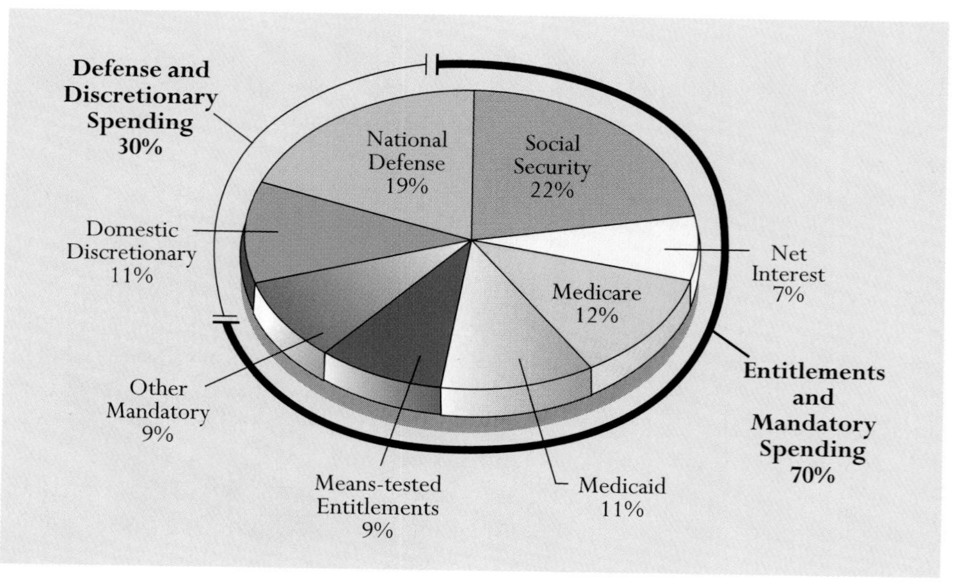

UP CLOSE

Who Are the Poor?

Poverty occurs in many kinds of families and in all races and ethnic groups. However, some groups experience poverty (low income) in greater proportions than the national average (see figure).

Poverty is most common among families headed by women. The incidence of poverty among these families is four times greater than that for married couples. These women and their children constitute over two-thirds of all of the persons living in poverty in the United States. About one of every five children in the United States lives in poverty. These figures describe what has been labeled the "feminization of poverty" in the United States. Clearly, poverty is closely related to family structure. The disintegration of the traditional husband-wife family is the single most influential factor contributing to poverty today.

Blacks also experience poverty in much greater proportions than whites. Over the years, the poverty rate among blacks in the United States has been almost three times higher than the poverty rate among whites. Poverty among Hispanics is also significantly greater than among whites.

In contrast, elderly people in America experience less poverty than the nonaged. The aged are not poor, despite the popularity of the phrase "the poor and the aged." The percentage of persons over sixty-five years of age with low incomes is *below* the national average. Moreover, elderly people are much wealthier in terms of assets and have fewer expenses than the nonaged. They are more likely than younger people to own homes with paid-up mortgages. Medicare pays a large portion of their medical expenses. With fewer expenses, elderly people, even with relatively smaller cash incomes, experience poverty differently from the way a young mother with children experiences it. The declining poverty rate among elderly people is a relatively recent occurrence, however. Continuing increases in Social Security benefits over the years are largely responsible for this singular "victory" in the war against poverty.

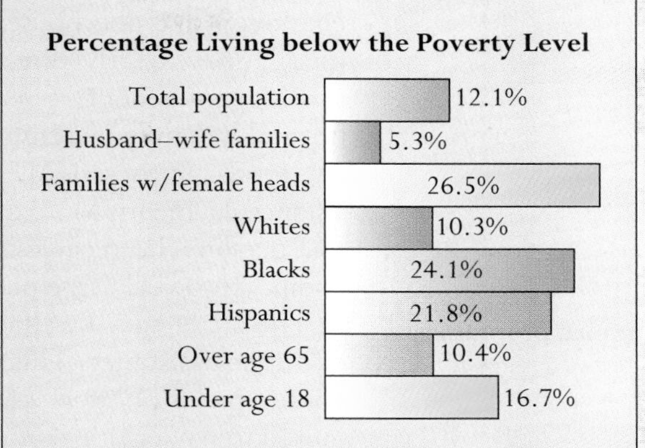

Source: U.S. Bureau of the Census, 2004.

weakened over time, and the availability of welfare cash benefits, food stamps, medical care, and government housing removed much of the economic hardship once associated with unwed motherhood. Indeed, it was sometimes argued that government welfare programs, however well meaning, ended up perpetuating poverty and social dependency. This argument inspired welfare reform in 1996 (see "Politics and Welfare Reform" later in this chapter).

Temporary Poverty Poor people are often envisioned as a permanent "underclass" living most of their lives in poverty. But most poverty is not long term. Tracing poor families over time presents a different picture of the nature of poverty from the "snapshot" view taken in any one year. For example, over the last decade 11 to 15 percent of the nation's population has been officially classified as poor in any one year. However, only *some* poverty is persistent: about 6 to 8 percent of the population remains in poverty for more than five years. Thus about half of the people who are counted as poor are experiencing poverty for only a short period of time. For these temporary poor, welfare is a "safety net" that helps them through hard times.

National Center for Children in Poverty

Columbia University center with studies and data on children in poverty.
www.nccp.org

Social Welfare Policy

Public welfare has been a recognized responsibility of government in English speaking countries for many centuries. As far back as the Poor Relief Act of 1601, the English Parliament provided workhouses for the "able-bodied poor" (the unemployed) and poorhouses for widows and orphans, elderly and handicapped people.[7] Today, nearly one-third of the U.S. population receives some form of government benefits: Social Security, Medicare or Medicaid, disability insurance, unemployment compensation, government employee retirement, veterans' benefits, food stamps, school lunches, job training, public housing, and cash public assistance payments. More than half of all families in the United States include at least one person who receives a government check. Thus the "welfare state" now encompasses a very large part of our society.

social insurance programs Social welfare programs to which beneficiaries have made contributions so that they are entitled to benefits regardless of their personal wealth.

public assistance programs Those social welfare programs for which no contributions are required and only those living in poverty (by official standards) are eligible; includes food stamps, Medicaid, and Family Assistance.

The major social welfare programs can be classified as either **social insurance** or **public assistance**. This distinction is an important one that has on occasion become a major political issue. If the beneficiaries of a government program are required to have made contributions to it before claiming any of its benefits, and if they are entitled to the benefits regardless of their personal wealth—as in Social Security and Medicare—then the program is said to be financed on the social insurance principle. If the program is financed out of general tax revenues and if recipients are required to show that they are poor before claiming its benefits—as in Temporary Assistance to Needy Families, Supplemental Security Income, and Medicaid—then the program is said to be financed on the public assistance principle. Public assistance programs are generally labeled as "welfare."

entitlements Any social welfare program for which there are eligibility requirements, whether financial or contributory.

Entitlements

Entitlements are government benefits for which Congress has set eligibility criteria—age, income, retirement, disability, unemployment, and so on. Everyone who meets the criteria is "entitled" to the benefit.

Most of the nation's major entitlement programs were launched either in the New Deal years of the 1930s under President Franklin D. Roosevelt (Social Security, Unemployment Compensation, Aid to Families with Dependent Children, now called Temporary Assistance to Needy Families, and Aid to Aged, Blind, and Disabled, now called Supplemental Security Income) or in the Great Society years of the 1960s under President Lyndon B. Johnson (food stamps, Medicare, Medicaid).

Social Security Social insurance program composed of the Old Age and Survivors Insurance program, which pays benefits to retired workers who have paid into the program and their dependents and survivors, and the Disability Insurance program, which pays benefits to disabled workers and their families.

Social Security

Begun during the Depression (1935), **Social Security** is now the largest of all entitlements; it comprises two distinct programs. The Old Age and Survivors Insurance program provides monthly cash benefits to retired workers and their dependents and to survivors of insured workers. The Disability Insurance program provides monthly cash benefits for disabled workers and their dependents. An automatic, annual cost-of-living adjustment (COLA) for both programs matches any increase in the annual inflation rate.

With more than 44 million beneficiaries, Social Security is the single largest spending program in the federal budget. About 96 percent of the nation's paid work force is covered by the program, which is funded by a payroll tax on employers and employees. Retirees can begin receiving benefits at age sixty-two (full benefits at age sixty-five), regardless of their personal wealth or income.

unemployment compensation Social insurance program that temporarily replaces part of the wages of workers who have lost their jobs.

Unemployment Compensation

Unemployment compensation temporarily replaces part of the wages of workers who lose their jobs involuntarily and helps stabilize the economy during recessions. The U.S. Department of Labor oversees the system, but states administer their own programs, with latitude within federal guidelines to define weekly benefits and other program features. Benefits are funded by a combination of federal and state unemployment taxes on employers.

Supplemental Security Income **Supplemental Security Income** (SSI) is a means-tested, federally administered income assistance program that provides monthly cash payments to needy elderly (sixty-five or older), blind, and disabled people. A loose definition of "disability"—including alcoholism, drug abuse, and attention deficiency among children—has led to a rapid growth in the number of SSI beneficiaries.

Supplemental Security Income (SSI) Public assistance program that provides monthly cash payments to the needy, elderly (sixty-five or older), blind, and disabled.

Family Assistance **Family Assistance**, officially Temporary Assistance to Needy Families (formerly AFDC, or Aid to Families with Dependent Children), is a grant program to enable the states to assist needy families. States now operate the program and define "need"; they set their own benefit levels and establish (within federal guidelines) income and resource limits. Prior to welfare reform in 1996, AFDC was a *federal* entitlement program. The federal government now mandates a two-year limit on benefits, a five-year lifetime limit, and other requirements (see "Politics and Welfare Reform" later in this chapter).

Family Assistance Public assistance program that provides monies to the states for their use in helping needy families with children.

Food Stamp Program

This U.S. Department of Agriculture's Food Stamp program site contains information about application procedures, recipient eligibility guidelines, and other relevant informational materials.
www.fns.usda.gov/fsp/

Food Stamps The **Food Stamp program** provides low-income household members with coupons that they can redeem for enough food to provide a minimal nutritious diet. The program is overseen by the federal government but administered by the states.

Food Stamp program Public assistance program that provides low-income households with coupons redeemable for enough food to provide a minimal nutritious diet.

Earned Income Tax Credit The **Earned Income Tax Credit** (EITC) is designed to assist the working poor. It not only refunds their payroll taxes but also provides larger refunds than they actually paid during the previous tax year. Thus, the EITC is in effect a "negative" income tax. It was originally passed by a Democratic-controlled Congress and signed by Republican President Gerald Ford in 1975. Over the years EITC payments have increased substantially. However, the program applies only to those poor who actually work and who apply for the credit when filing their income tax.

Earned Income Tax Credit (EITC) Tax refunds in excess of tax payments for low-income workers.

Most of America's social welfare programs began in either the Great Depression of the 1930s or the War on Poverty in the 1960s. At the outset of the Depression, millions of unemployed Americans, like the New Yorkers in a bread line in the photo at left, bad only private charities to turn to for survival. The War on Poverty of the 1960s was a reaction to the persistence of extreme poverty, like that of the rural family in the photograph at right, in the midst of the prosperity that followed World War II.

Medicaid Public assistance program that provides health care to the poor.

Medicaid **Medicaid** is a joint federal-state program providing health services to low-income Americans. Most Medicaid spending goes to elderly and nonelderly disabled people. However, women and children receiving benefits under AFDC automatically qualify for Medicaid, as does anyone who gets cash assistance under SSI. States can also offer Medicaid to the "medically needy"—those who face crushing medical costs but whose income or assets are too high to qualify for SSI or Family Assistance, including pregnant women and young children not receiving Family Assistance. Medicaid also pays for long-term nursing home care, but only after beneficiaries have used up virtually all of their savings and income.

Politics and Welfare Reform

THINK AGAIN

Do you think government welfare programs perpetuate poverty?

THINK AGAIN

Should there be a time limit on how long a person can receive welfare payments?

Americans confront a clash of values in welfare policy. Americans are a generous people; they believe government should aid those who are unable to take care of themselves, especially children, disabled people, and elderly people. But Americans are worried that welfare programs encourage dependency, undermine the work ethic, and contribute to illegitimate births and the breakup of families. Although social insurance programs (Social Security, Medicare, and Unemployment Compensation) are politically popular and enjoy the support of large numbers of active beneficiaries, public assistance programs (Family Assistance, SSI, Medicaid) are far less popular. A variety of controversies surround welfare policy in the United States.

Conflict Over What Causes Poverty Americans have different ideas about what causes poverty. Some attribute poverty to characteristics of individuals—drug use, declining moral values, lack of motivation. Others blame the economy—too many part-time and low-wage jobs and a shortage of good jobs. Still others place blame on the welfare system itself. Indeed, prior to welfare reform in 1996, some scholars argued that government itself was a major cause of poverty—that social welfare programs destroyed incentives to work, encouraged teenage pregnancies, and made people dependent on government handouts.[8] They argued that the combination of cash payments, food stamps, Medicaid, and housing assistance unintentionally discouraged people from forming families, taking low-paying jobs, and, perhaps, with hard work and perseverance, gradually pulling themselves and their children into the mainstream of American life.

There is little doubt that poverty and welfare dependency are closely related to family structure. As noted earlier, poverty is much more frequent among female-headed households with no husband present than among husband-wife households. As births to unmarried women rose, poverty and social dependency increased. (In 1970 only 11 percent of births were to unmarried women; by 2000 this figure had risen to 33 percent of all births and 69 percent of minority births.) The troubling question was whether the welfare system ameliorated some of the hardships confronting unmarried mothers and their children, or whether it actually contributed to social dependency by mitigating the consequences of unmarried motherhood. For example, were teenage pregnancies more common because teenagers knew that government benefits were available to young mothers and their children?

The Politics of Welfare Reform A political consensus grew over the years that long-term social dependency had to be addressed in welfare policy. The fact that most nonpoor mothers work convinced many *liberals* that welfare mothers had no special claim to stay at home with their children. And many *conservatives*

UP CLOSE

Is Welfare Reform Working?

Welfare reform, officially Temporary Assistance to Needy Families, was passed by Congress in 1996; its provisions took effect in 1997. By early 1998 the Clinton Administration, as well as Republican congressional sponsors of welfare reform, was declaring it a success.

The number of cash welfare recipients in the nation has dropped below 6 million—the lowest number in more than twenty-five years. Only about 2 percent of Americans are now on cash welfare—the smallest proportion since 1970. No doubt some of this decline is attributable to strong growth of the economy: declines in welfare rolls began *before* Congress passed its welfare reform law, and some decline may have occurred without reform. Many states had initiated their own reforms under "waivers" from the federal government even before Congress acted.

All states have now developed work programs for welfare recipients. Applicants for welfare benefits are now generally required to enter job-search programs, to undertake job training, and to accept jobs or community service positions.

Yet, although nearly everyone agrees that getting people off welfare rolls and onto payrolls is the main goal of reform, there are major obstacles to the achievement of this goal. First of all, a substantial portion (perhaps 25 to 40 percent) of long-term welfare recipients have handicaps—physical disabilities, chronic illnesses, learning disabilities, alcohol or drug abuse problems—that prevent them from holding a full-time job. Many long-term recipients have no work experience (perhaps 40 percent), and two-thirds of them did not graduate from high school. Almost half have three or more children, making day-care arrangements a major obstacle. It is unlikely that any counseling, education, job training, or job placement programs could ever succeed in getting these people into productive employment.

Early studies of people who left the welfare rolls following welfare reform suggest that over half and perhaps as many as three-quarters have found work, although most at minimum or near-minimum wages.* But it is likely that the early dramatic reductions in welfare caseloads (see figure) will begin to level off after 2000.

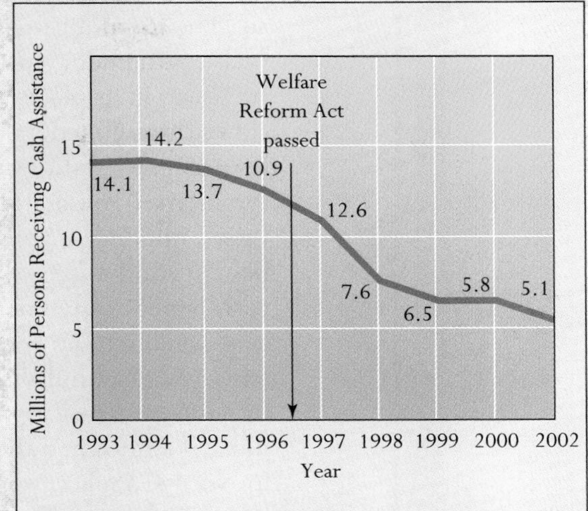

Source: Department of Health and Human Services, 2004.

**Governing*, April 1999, pp. 21–26.

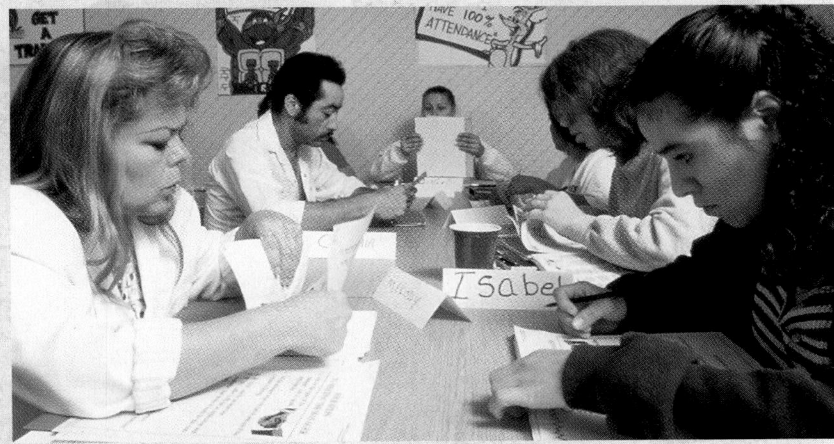

Programs such as this Riverside, California, "Jobs Club" try to help welfare recipients find jobs in the wake of reforms intended to reduce welfare dependency.

acknowledged that some transitional assistance—education, job training, continued health care, and day care for children—might be necessary to move welfare mothers into the work force.

Although President Clinton had once promised "to end welfare as we know it," it was the Republican-controlled Congress elected in 1994 that proceeded to do so. The Republican-sponsored welfare reform bill ended the sixty-year-old federal "entitlement" for low-income families with children—the venerable AFDC program. In its place the Republicans devised a "devolution" of responsibility to the states through federal block grants—**Temporary Assistance to Needy Families**—lump sum allocations to the states for cash welfare payments with benefits and eligibility requirements decided by the states. Conservatives in Congress imposed tough-minded "strings" to state aid, including a two-year limit on continuing cash benefits and a five-year lifetime limit; a "family cap" that would deny additional cash benefit to women already on welfare who bear more children; the denial of cash welfare to unwed parents under 18 years of age unless they live with an adult and attend school. President Clinton vetoed the first welfare reform bill passed by Congress in early 1996, but as the presidential election neared, he reversed himself and signed the welfare reform act, establishing the Temporary Assistance to Needy Families program. Food stamps, SSI, and Medicaid were continued as federal "entitlements" (see *Up Close:* "Is Welfare Reform Working?").

Health Care in America

Temporary Assistance to Needy Families Welfare reform program replacing federal cash entitlement with grants to the states for welfare recipients.

Historically, most reductions in death rates have resulted from public health and sanitation improvements, including immunizations, clean public water supplies, sanitary sewage disposal, improved diets, and increased standards of living. Many of the leading causes of death today (see Table 13.3), including heart disease, cancer, stroke, and AIDS, are closely linked to heredity, personal habits and lifestyles (smoking, eating, drinking, exercise, stress, sexual practices), and the physical environment—factors over which doctors and hospitals have no direct control. Thus some argue that the greatest contribution to better health is likely to be found in

TABLE 13.3 Leading Causes of Death

	Deaths per 100,000 Population per Year				
	1960	**1970**	**1980**	**1990**	**2002**
All causes	954.7	945.3	883.4	863.8	848.5
Heart disease	369.0	362.0	336.0	368.3	245.8
Stroke (cerebrovascular)	108.0	101.9	75.5	57.9	57.4
Cancer	149.2	162.8	183.9	203.2	194.4
Accidents	52.3	56.4	46.7	37.0	35.7
Pneumonia/Influenza	37.3	30.9	24.1	32.0	43.2
Diabetes	16.7	18.9	15.5	19.2	25.1
AIDS	N.A.	N.A.	N.A.	17.6	5.0
Suicide	10.6	11.6	11.9	12.4	10.8
Homicide	4.7	8.3	10.7	10.0	7.1

Source: Statistical Abstract of the United States, 2003, p. 895.

altered personal habits and lifestyles rather than in more medical care. Thanks to improved health care habits as well as breakthroughs in medical technology, Americans are living longer than ever before.

THINK AGAIN

Should government provide health care insurance for all Americans?

Access to Care A major challenge in health care is to extend coverage to all Americans. Today, about 85 percent of the nation's population is covered by either government or private health insurance. Government pays about 43 percent of all health care costs—through Medicare for the aged, Medicaid for the poor, and other government programs, including military and veterans' care. Private insurance pays for about 40 percent of the nation's health costs.

But about 15 percent of the U.S. population—an estimated 42 million Americans—have *no* medical insurance. These include workers and their dependents whose employers do not offer a health insurance plan as well as unemployed people who are not eligible for Medicare or Medicaid. People who lack health insurance may postpone or go without needed medical care or may be denied medical care by hospitals and physicians in all but emergency situations. Confronted with serious illness, they may be obliged to impoverish themselves in order to become eligible for Medicaid. Any unpaid medical bills must be absorbed by hospitals or shifted to paying patients and their insurance companies.

Health Care Costs No system of health care can provide as much as people will use. Anyone whose health and life may be at stake will want the most thorough diagnostic testing, the most constant care, the most advanced treatment. Sworn to preserve life, doctors, too, want the most advanced diagnostic and treatment facilities available for their patients. Under conditions of uncertainty in a medical situation—and there is always some uncertainty—physicians are trained to seek more consultations, run more tests, and try new therapeutic approaches. Any tendency for doctors to limit testing and treatment is countered by the threat of malpractice suits; it is always easier to order one more test or procedure than to risk even the tiniest chance that failing to do so will some day be cause for a court suit. So in the absence of restraints, both patients and doctors will push up the costs of health care. Currently health care costs appeared to have stabilized at about 13 percent of the nation's GDP.

managed care Programs designed to keep health care costs down by the establishment of strict guidelines regarding when and what diagnostic and therapeutic procedures should be administered to patients under various circumstances.

Managed Care Controversies Both private and government insurers have made efforts to counter rising costs through **managed care**. Private insurers have negotiated discounts with groups of physicians and with hospitals—**preferred provider organizations** (**PPOs**)—and have implemented rules to guide physicians about when patients should and should not receive costly diagnostic and therapeutic procedures. Both government and private insurers have encouraged the expansion of **health maintenance organizations** (**HMOs**), groups that promise to provide a stipulated list of services to patients for a fixed fee and that are able to provide care at lower total costs than can other providers. Today over 30 percent of Americans are enrolled in HMOs.

preferred provider organizations (PPOs) Groups of hospitals and physicians who have joined together to offer their services to private insurers at a discount.

But many of the efforts by both private insurers and governments to control costs have created new problems. These include cost-control regulations and restrictions that add to administrative costs and create a mountain of paperwork for physicians and hospitals, and frustration and anger among both health care workers and patients. Doctors and hospitals argue that the *administrative* costs imposed by these cost-control measures far exceed whatever savings are achieved. Patients and doctors complain that preapproval of treatment by insurance companies often removes medical decisions from the physician and patient and places them in the hands of insurance company employees.

health maintenance organizations (HMOs) Health care provider groups that provide a stipulated list of services to patients for a fixed fee that is usually substantially lower than such care would otherwise cost.

Medicare Official government site explaining eligibility, plan options, appeals, etc. *www.medicare.gov*

Medicare Medicare is a two-part program that helps elderly and disabled people pay acute-care (as opposed to long-term-care) health costs. Hospital insurance (Part A) helps pay the cost of hospital inpatient and skilled nursing care. Anyone sixty-five or older who is eligible for Social Security is automatically eligible for Part A benefits. Also eligible are people under sixty-five who receive Social Security disability or railroad retirement disability and people who have end-stage kidney disease. Part A is financed primarily by the 1.45 percent payroll tax collected with Social Security (FICA) withholding. Supplemental Medical Insurance (Part B) is an optional add-on taken by virtually all those covered by Part A. It pays 80 percent of covered doctor and outpatient charges. Small monthly premiums are deducted from Social Security benefit checks to finance it.

Medicare Social insurance program that provides health care insurance to elderly and disabled people.

Prescription Drug Coverage Under Medicare The long battle over adding prescription drug coverage to Medicare reached a turning point in 2004 when Congress finally passed by wide margins and President Bush signed such a bill. Americans have long supported the addition of prescription drug benefits to Medicare. And in every election over the previous twenty years both Democrats and Republicans had pledged their support for such a benefit. But it was not until after a prolonged battle over the details of legislation did Congress finally add the long awaited prescription drug benefit to Medicare.

The bill is lengthy and leaves many gaps in coverage (see Table 13.4). It was passed by a Republican-controlled Congress and by a Republican president; most

TABLE 13.4 Prescription Drug Benefits under Medicare Major Provisions

Prescription drug benefits (beginning in 2006)

- The government will pay 75 percent of annual health insurance coverage up to $2,250. Once the beneficiary has paid the next $5,100 out-of-pocket, the government will pick up 95 percent of the coverage.
- Beneficiaries must pay a $250 annual deductible in an average monthly premium of $35.
- Beneficiaries will be guaranteed access to at least two competing insurance plans. If no private plans bid in a region, the government will offer a fall-back plan.
- Beneficiaries with incomes near the poverty level will get benefits with no gaps in coverage but will be subject to premiums based on a sliding scale.
- Companies already providing drug benefits to retirees will receive tax breaks to encourage them to continue to do so.

Drug discount cards (beginning in 2004)

- Medicare beneficiaries will receive discount cards in 2004. These cards are expected to provide savings of 15 to 25 percent per prescription.

Health savings accounts

- Taxpayers can establish health savings accounts allowing them to save and withdraw money tax-free for medical expenses.

Competition

- Private insurers can compete with the Medicare system in up to six metropolitan areas beginning in 2010.
- The government will *not* negotiate lower drug prices with drug companies.

Democrats in Congress opposed the bill claiming that it failed to go far enough in protecting seniors. The AARP provided crucial support for the bill, arguing that later amendments could cure any defects.

Note that the government pays no part of health coverage costs between $2,250 and $5,100. This $3,600 hole or gap in coverage is one of the principal objections to the act. Democrats and the AARP have promised to close this gap. Further, the government is barred from trying to negotiate with drug companies to force down prices.

Interest-Group Battles Interest-group battles over the details of health care policy have been intense. Virtually everyone has a financial stake in any proposal to reorganize the nation's health care system.

- Employers, especially small businesses, are fearful of added costs.
- Physicians strongly oppose price controls and treatment guidelines, as well as programs that take away patient choice of physician or force all physicians into health maintenance organizations (HMOs). Support is stronger among those physicians most likely to benefit from low-cost plans—general family practitioners—and weakest among those most likely to lose—medical specialists.
- Psychiatrists, psychologists, mental health and drug abuse counselors, physical therapists, chiropractors, optometrists, and dentists all want their own services covered. Providing such "comprehensive" services greatly increases costs.
- Drug companies want to see prescription drugs paid for, but they vigorously oppose price controls on drugs.
- Hospitals want all patients to be insured but oppose government payment schedules.
- Medical specialists fear that proposals for managed care will result in fewer consultations, and medical manufacturers fear it will limit use of high-priced equipment.
- The powerful senior citizens' lobby wants added benefits—including coverage for drugs, eyeglasses, dental care, and nursing homes—but fears folding Medicare into a larger health care system.
- Veterans' groups want to retain separate VA hospitals and medical services.
- Opponents of abortion rights are prepared to do battle to keep national coverage from including such procedures, whereas many supporters of abortion rights will not back any plan that excludes abortion services.

Although polls show that a majority of Americans are willing to pay higher taxes for comprehensive health care, many are willing to see increases only in "sin taxes"—taxes on alcohol, tobacco, and guns.

SUMMARY NOTES

- The performance of the economy can be measured by GDP growth and the unemployment and inflation rates. Politically the unemployment rate may be the most important of these measures of economic performance.
- Imports and exports grow each year as a percentage of the gross domestic product of the United States. This trend toward globalization has been fostered by U.S. participation in the World Trade Organization, the International Monetary Fund, the World Bank, the North American Free Trade Agreement, and other agreements and treaties in support of free trade. Free trade may benefit the economy as a whole, but it appears to disadvantage poorly educated, low-skilled American workers.
- Tax politics centers on the question of who actually bears the burden of a tax. The individual income tax, the largest source of federal government revenue, is progressive, with higher rates levied at higher income levels. Progressive taxation is defended on the ability-to-pay principle. But half of all personal income, and a great deal of corporate income, is untaxed, owing to a wide variety of exemptions, exclusions, deductions, and special treatments on tax laws. These provisions are defended in Washington by a powerful array of interest groups.
- The Reagan Administration reduced top income tax rates from 70 to 28 percent, believing high rates discouraged work, savings, and investment, and thereby curtailed economic growth. But George Bush agreed to an increase in the top rate to 31 percent. Bill Clinton pushed Congress to raise the top rates to 36 and 39.6 percent, arguing that rich people had benefited from Reagan's "trickle down" policies and must now be forced to bear their "fair share." George W. Bush succeeded in getting two tax cut bills through Congress in 2001 and 2003. The bills lower the top marginal income tax rate to 35 percent, ends the marriage penalty, increases child exemptions, and lowers the capital gain rate to 15 percent.
- About 11 to 15 percent of the U.S. population falls below the annual cash income level that the federal government sets as its official definition of poverty.
- Poverty is temporary for many families, but some poverty is persistent—lasting five years to a lifetime. Prolonged poverty and welfare dependency create an "underclass" beset by many social and economic problems. Poverty is most frequent among families headed by single mothers.
- Nearly one-third of the U.S. population receives some form of government payments or benefits. Entitlements are government benefits for which Congress has set eligibility criteria by law. Social Security and Medicare are the largest entitlement programs. The elderly are entitled to these benefits regardless of their income or wealth.
- Social welfare policies seek to alleviate hardship; at the same time they seek to avoid creating disincentives to work. Cash welfare payments may, for example, encourage teenage pregnancies, undermine family foundations, and contribute to long-term social dependency. Welfare reform centers on moving former welfare recipients into the work force. But doing so may require increased spending on education, job training, health care, and child care, and some recipients may never be able to work.
- Welfare reform in 1996 replaced federal entitlements to cash payments with block grants to the states. It also set time limits on welfare enrollment.
- Health care reform centers on two related problems—extending health insurance coverage to all Americans and containing the costs of health care.
- Managed-care programs have succeeded in reducing the growth of health care costs in America. But these programs have generated complaints about coverage of medical conditions, bureaucratic interference in doctor-patient relationships, and the quality of medical care.
- Medicare for the aged and Medicaid for the poor are the largest government health insurance programs. They cover only the aged and poor, not the general population. About 15 percent of the population has no health insurance. Only in 2003, after years of interest group conflict, was prescription drug coverage added to Medicare.

KEY TERMS

free-market economic system 464
gross domestic product (GDP) 464
unemployment rate 464
protectionism 467
free trade 467
individual income tax 470
progressive taxation 473
regressive taxation 473
proportional (flat) taxation 473
poverty line 475
underclass 476
social insurance programs 478

public assistance programs 478
entitlements 478
Social Security 478
unemployment compensation 478
Supplemental Security Income (SSI) 479
Family Assistance 479
Food Stamp program 479
Earned Income Tax Credit (EITC) 479
Medicaid 480
Temporary Assistance to Needy Families 482
managed care 483
preferred provider organizations (PPOs) 483
health maintenance organizations (HMOs) 483
Medicare 484

SUGGESTED READINGS

Bodenheimer, Thomas S. *Understanding Health Policy.* 3rd ed. New York: McGraw Hill, 2001. Leading text on health-care policy, including cost containment, health insurance, managed care, and case histories.

DiNitto, Diana M. *Social Welfare Politics and Policy.* 6th ed. New York: Allyn & Bacon, 2003. A comprehensive overview of social welfare programs—Social Security, Medicare SSI, cash assistance, Medicaid, food stamps, etc.—and the political controversies surrounding them.

Hays, Sharon. *Flat Broke with Children: Women in the Age of Welfare Reform.* New York: Oxford Press, 2003. Stories of single mothers and welfare workers trying to cope with the harsher rules of welfare reform.

Langren, Robert and Martin Snitzer. *Government, Business and the American Economy.* Upper Saddle River, N.J.: Prentice Hall, 2001. Comprehensive text on the government's role in the economy.

Rothgeb, John M., Jr. *U.S. Trade Policy.* Washington, D.C.: CQ Press, 2001. Concise text on international trade, including history of GATT, WTO, and NAFTA.

Sowell, Thomas. *Basic Economics: A Citizen's Guide to the Economy.* New York: Basic Books, 2003. Introduction to economics with an emphasis on public policy. No jargon or equations.

Wolff, Edward N. *Top Heavy* (updated edition). New York: Century Foundation, 2002. The study of the increasing inequality of wealth in the United States and an argument for taxing financial wealth (bank accounts, stocks, bonds, property, houses, cars, etc.) as well as income.

MAKE IT REAL

BALANCING THE NATION'S CHECKBOOK: WHAT CAN YOU GET FOR $4 TRILLION?

The federal government's budget process begins nearly two years in advance, when the various departments and agencies estimate their needs and propose their budgets to the president. Agency officials take into account not only their needs but also the overall presidential program and the probable reactions of Congress. In this simulation you are the director of the Office of Management and Budget and need to make recommendations for budget cuts to make up for the president's tax.

CHAPTER 14

POLITICS AND NATIONAL SECURITY

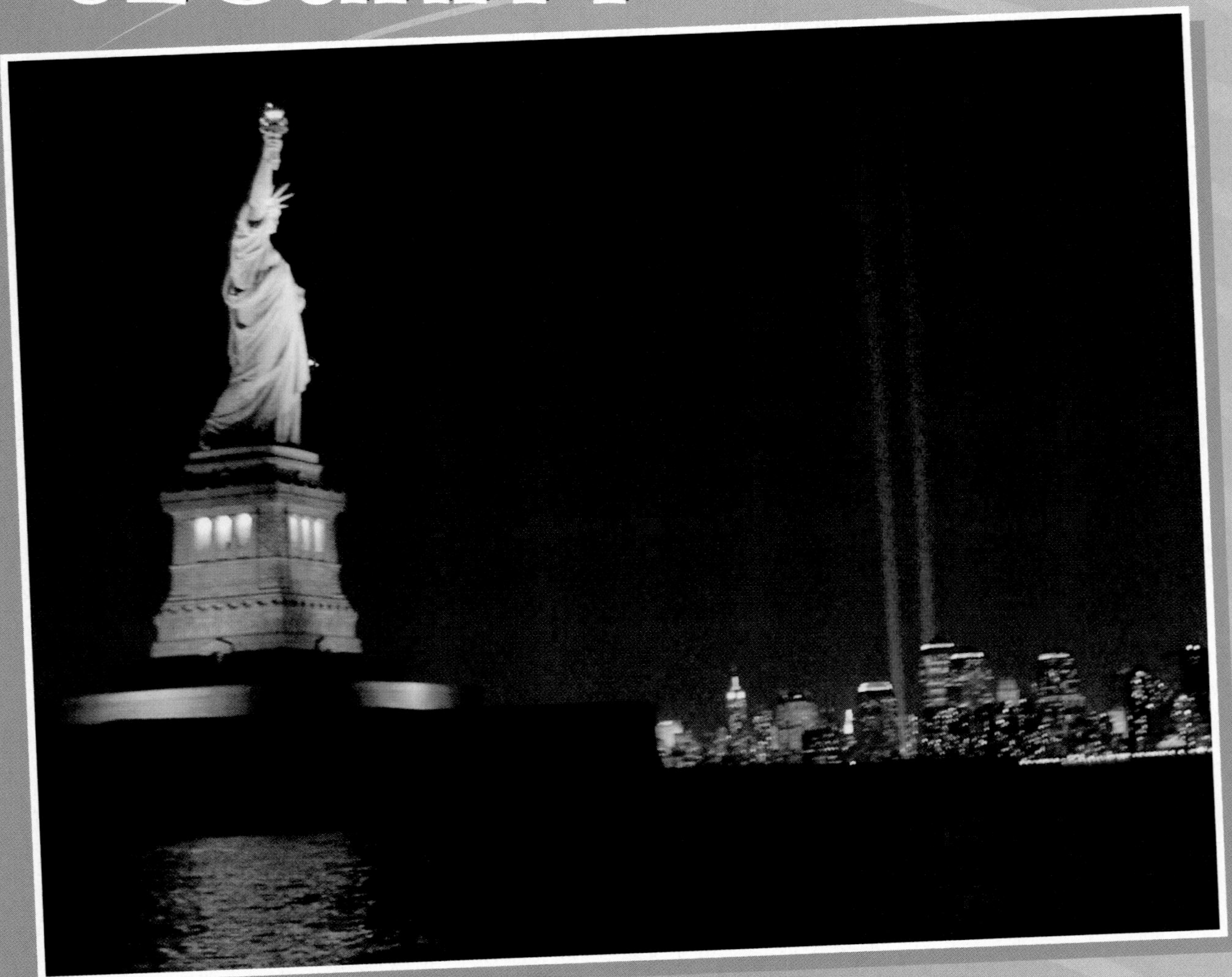

CHAPTER OUTLINE

Power among Nations
The Legacy of the Cold War
Nuclear Threats
When to Use Military Force?
The War on Terrorism
Military Force Levels

Power among Nations

International politics, like all politics, is a struggle for power. The struggle for power is global; it involves all the nations and peoples of the world, whatever their goals or ideals. As the distinguished political scientist Hans Morgenthau once observed.

> Whatever the ultimate aims of international politics, power is always the immediate aim. Statesmen and peoples may ultimately seek freedom, security, prosperity or power itself. They may define their goals in terms of a religious, philosophic, economic, or social ideal. . . . But whenever they strive to realize their goal by means of international politics, they are striving for power.[1]

The struggle for power among nations has led to many attempts to bring order to the international system.

Collective Security Originally, **collective security** meant that *all* nations would join together to guarantee each other's "territorial integrity and existing political independence" against "external aggression" by any nation. This was the idea behind the League of Nations, established in 1919. However, opposition to international involvement was so great in the United States after World War I that, after a lengthy debate, the Senate refused to enroll the United States in the League of Nations. More important, the League of Nations failed to deal with acts of aggression by the Axis Powers—Germany, Japan, and Italy—in the 1930s. During that decade, Japan invaded Manchuria, Italy invaded Ethiopia, and Germany dismembered Czechoslovakia. The result was a devastating war: World War II cost more than 40 million lives, both civilian and military.

Formation of the United Nations Even after World War II, the notion of collective security remained an ideal of the victorious Allied Powers. The Charter of the United Nations, signed in 1945, provided for the following organization:

- The Security Council, with eleven member nations, five of them being permanent members—the United States, the **Soviet Union** (whose membership is now held by Russia), Britain, France, and China—and each having the power to veto any action by the Security Council.
- The General Assembly, composed of all the member nations, each with a single vote.
- The Secretariat, headed by a Secretary General with a staff at United Nations headquarters in New York.

THINK ABOUT POLITICS

1 Has the United Nations been effective in maintaining world peace?
Yes ● No ●

2 Should the United States and NATO intervene in regional conflicts in Eastern Europe?
Yes ● No ●

3 Should the United States build a ballistic missile defense system even if it is very costly?
Yes ● No ●

4 Is the president justified in placing U.S. troops in danger where U.S. vital interests are not at stake?
Yes ● No ●

5 Do you approve of the military attacks led by the United States against targets in Afghanistan?
Yes ● No ●

6 Do you favor the U.S. invading Iraq?
Yes ● No ●

7 Are U.S. military force levels today sufficient to deal with potential regional aggressors such as Iran, Iraq, and North Korea?
Yes ● No ●

8 Should the United States destroy all of its nuclear weapons now that the Cold War is over?
Yes ● No ●

America must decide how to use its national power in world affairs. Should we intervene with military forces in pursuit of humanitarian goals and to keep the peace in war-torn lands? Or should we only use military force when vital national interests are at stake?

- Organizations to handle specialized affairs—for example, the Economic and Social Council, the Trusteeship Council, and the International Court of Justice at The Hague in the Netherlands.

The Security Council has the "primary responsibility" for maintaining "international peace and security." The General Assembly has authority over "any matter affecting the peace of the world," although it is supposed to defer to the Security Council when the council has already taken up a particular security matter. No nation has a veto in the General Assembly; every nation has one vote regardless of its size or power. Most resolutions can be passed by a majority vote.

collective security Attempt to bring order to international relations by all nations joining together to guarantee each other's "territorial integrity" and "independence" against "external aggression."

State Department This U.S. Department of State Web site contains background notes on the countries and regions of the world. ***www.state.gov/***

United Nations This United Nations site contains basic information about the world body's mission, member states, issues of concern, institutions, and accomplishments. ***www.un.org/***

The United Nations in the Cold War The United Nations (UN) proved largely ineffective during the long Cold War confrontation between the communist nations, led by the Soviet Union, and the Western democracies, led by the United States. The UN grew from its original 51 member nations to more than 150, (191 in 2005), but most of those nations were headed by authoritarian regimes of one kind or another. The Western democracies were outnumbered in the General Assembly, and the Soviet Union frequently used its veto to prevent action by the Security Council. Anti-Western and antidemocratic speeches became common in the General Assembly.

During the Cold War, the UN was overshadowed by the confrontation of the world's two **superpowers**: the United States and the Soviet Union. Indeed, international conflicts throughout the world—in the Middle East, Africa, Latin America, Southeast Asia, and elsewhere—were usually influenced by some aspect of the superpower struggle.

Soviet Union The Union of Soviet Socialist Republics (USSR) consisting of Russia and its bordering lands and ruled by the communist regime in Moscow, officially dissolved in 1991.

superpowers Refers to the United States and the Soviet Union after World War II, when these two nations dominated international politics.

Regional Security The general disappointment with the United Nations as a form of collective security gave rise as early as 1949 to a different approach; **regional security**. In response to aggressive Soviet moves in Europe, the United States and the democracies of Western Europe created the **North Atlantic Treaty Organization (NATO)**. In the NATO treaty, fifteen Western nations agreed to collective regional security: they agreed that "an armed attack against one or more [NATO nations] . . . shall be considered an attack against them all." The United States made a specific commitment to defend Western Europe in the event of a Soviet attack. A joint NATO military command was established (with Dwight D. Eisenhower as its first commander) to coordinate the defense of Western Europe.

After the formation of NATO, the Soviets made no further advances into Western Europe. The Soviets themselves, in response to NATO, drew up the Warsaw Pact, a comparable treaty with their own Eastern European satellite nations. But for many years the real deterrent to Warsaw Pact expansion was not the weak NATO armies but rather the pledge of the United States to use its strategic nuclear bomber force to inflict "massive retaliation" on the Soviet Union itself in the event of an attack on Western Europe.

The Warsaw Pact disintegrated following the dramatic collapse of the communist governments of Eastern Europe in 1989. Former Warsaw Pact nations—Poland, Hungary, Romania, Bulgaria, and East Germany—threw out their ruling communist regimes and demanded the withdrawal of Soviet troops from their territory. The Berlin Wall was dismantled in 1989, and Germany was formally reunified in 1990, bringing together the 61 million prosperous people of West Germany and the 17 million less affluent people of East Germany. (Unified Germany continues as a member of NATO.) The Communist Party was ousted from power in Moscow, and the Soviet Union collapsed in 1991.

regional security Attempt to bring order to international relations during the Cold War by creating regional alliances between a superpower and nations of a particular region.

North Atlantic Treaty Organization (NATO) Mutual-security agreement and joint military command uniting the nations of Western Europe, initially formed to resist Soviet expansionism.

NATO Today The United States and its Western European allies agree that NATO continues to play an important role in the security of Europe. Indeed, the continued deployment of some level of U.S. troops to NATO is widely considered to be reassurance that the United States remains committed to this security.

In recent years NATO has made the key decision to expand its security protections to the newly democratic nations of Eastern Europe. Three nations—Poland, Hungary, and the Czech Republic—were admitted to NATO in 1998. At that time Russia strongly objected to NATO expansion, viewing it as an incursion of Western powers in the East and a threat to Russia's security. A NATO-Russia Council was created in 2002 to calm Russian fears about NATO's intentions. In 2004 seven additional countries—Bulgaria, Estonia, Latvia, Lithuania, Romania, Slovakia, and Slovenia—were admitted to membership. All of these nations were formerly under the domination of the Soviet Union. NATO now has 26 members.

Yet another question confronting NATO is what role it should play in trying to resolve religious and ethnic conflicts in Eastern Europe. A combination of security and humanitarian concerns drew NATO, with heavy U.S. participation, into the former Yugoslavian province of Bosnia in 1995 to assist in resolving the war among the Serbs, Croats, and Moslems. This was the first deployment of NATO forces *outside* the national boundaries of NATO nations. NATO began acting militarily to halt ethnic conflicts in Kosovo in 1999. NATO forced Serbian President Slobodan Milosovic to withdraw his forces from the largely Muslim province. U.S. air power played the principal role in this engagement.

Kofi Annan, a native of Ghana, was appointed in 2002 to a second five-year term as Secretary General of the United Nations.

The UN Today The end of the Cold War has injected new vitality into the United Nations. Russia inherited the UN Security Council seat of the former Soviet Union, and its government has generally cooperated in UN efforts to bring stability to various regional conflicts. No longer are these conflicts "proxy" wars between the superpowers. Greater cooperation among the permanent members of the Security Council (the United States, Great Britain, France, China, and Russia) has brought "a new world order" to international politics. The UN has sent blue-helmeted "peacekeeping" forces to monitor cease-fires in many troubled areas of the world. But the United Nations and its Security Council must rely on "the last remaining superpower," the United States, to take the lead in enforcing its resolutions.

WWW **NATO** The official "North Atlantic Treaty Organization" site contains basic facts about the alliance, current NATO news and issues, and important NATO policies. *www.nato.int/*

The Legacy of the Cold War

For more than forty years following the end of World War II, the United States and the Soviet Union confronted each other in the protracted political, military, and ideological struggle known as the **Cold War**.

Cold War Political, military, and ideological struggle between the United States and the Soviet Union following the end of World War II and ending with the collapse of the Soviet Union's communist government in 1991.

Origins During World War II, the United States and the Soviet Union joined forces to eliminate the Nazi threat to the world. The United States dismantled its military forces at the end of the war in 1945, but the Soviet Union, under the brutal dictatorship of Josef Stalin, used the powerful Red Army to install communist governments in the nations of Eastern Europe in violation of wartime agreements to allow free elections. Stalin also ignored pledges to cooperate in a unified allied occupation of Germany; Germany was divided, and in 1948 Stalin unsuccessfully tried to oust the United States, Britain, and France from Berlin in a year-long "Berlin Blockade." Former British Prime Minister Winston Churchill warned the United States as early as 1946 that the Soviets were dividing Europe with an "Iron Curtain." When Soviet-backed communist forces threatened Greece and Turkey in 1947, President Harry S Truman responded with a pledge to "support free people

THINK AGAIN

Should the United States and NATO intervene in regional conflicts in Eastern Europe?

who are resisting attempted subjugation by armed minorities or by outside pressures," a policy that became known as the **Truman Doctrine**.

Truman Doctrine U.S. foreign policy, first articulated by President Harry S Truman, that pledged the United States to "support free peoples who are resisting attempted subjugation by armed minorities or by outside pressures."

Containment

The United States had fought two world wars to maintain democracy in Western Europe. The new threat of Soviet expansionism and communist world revolution caused America to assume world leadership on behalf of the preservation of democracy. In an influential article in the Council on Foreign Relations' journal, *Foreign Affairs,* the State Department's Russian expert George F. Kennan called for a policy of **containment**:

> It is clear that the main element of any United States policy toward the Soviet Union must be that of a long-term, vigilant containment of Russian expansive tendencies. . . . Soviet pressure against the free institutions of the western world is something that can be contained by the adroit and vigilant application of counterforce.[2]

containment Policy of preventing an enemy from expanding its boundaries and/or influence, specifically the U.S. foreign policy vis-à-vis the Soviet Union during the Cold War.

To implement the containment policy, the United States first initiated the **Marshall Plan,** named for Secretary of State George C. Marshall, to rebuild the economies of the Western European nations. Marshall reasoned that *economically* weak nations were more susceptible to communist subversion and Soviet intimidation. The subsequent formation of NATO provided the necessary *military* support to contain the Soviet Union.

Marshall Plan U.S. program to rebuild the nations of Western Europe in the aftermath of World War II in order to render them less susceptible to communist influence and takeover.

The Korean War

The first military test of the containment policy came in June 1950, when communist North Korean armies invaded South Korea. President Truman assumed that the North Koreans were acting on behalf of their sponsor, the Soviet Union. The Soviets had already aided Chinese communists under the leadership of Mao Zedong in capturing control of mainland China in 1949. The United States quickly brought the Korean invasion issue to the Security Council. With the Soviets boycotting this meeting because the Council had refused to seat the new communist delegation from China, the Council passed a resolution calling on member nations to send troops to repel the invasion.

Korean War Project Organization

Dedicated to the memory of sacrifices of Americans in Korea, with links to battles, units, and memorials.
www.koreanwar.org

America's conventional (non-nuclear) military forces had been largely dismantled after World War II. Moreover, President Truman insisted on keeping most of the nation's forces in Europe, fearing that the Korean invasion was a diversion to be followed by a Soviet invasion of Western Europe. But General Douglas MacArthur, in a brilliant amphibious landing at Inchon behind North Korean lines, destroyed a much larger enemy army, captured the North Korean capital, and moved northward toward the Chinese border. Then in December 1950, disaster struck American forces as a million-strong Chinese army entered the conflict. Chinese troops surprised the Americans, inflicting heavy casualties, trapping entire units, and forcing U.S. troops to beat a hasty retreat. General MacArthur urged retaliation against China, but Truman sought to keep the war "limited." When MacArthur publicly protested political limits to military operations, Truman dismissed the popular general. The Korean War became a bloody stalemate.

Korean War Communist North Korea invaded non-Communist South Korea in June, 1950, causing President Harry S Truman to intervene militarily, with U.N. support. General Douglas MacArthur defeated the North Koreans, but with China's entry into the war, a stalemate resulted. An armistice was signed in 1953, with Korea divided along nearly original lines.

Dwight Eisenhower was elected president in 1952 in large measure because he promised to "go to Korea" to end the increasingly unpopular war. He also threatened to use nuclear weapons in the conflict, but eventually agreed to a settlement along the original border between North and South Korea. Communist expansion in Korea was "contained," but at a high price: the United States lost more than 38,000 men in the war.

The Cuban Missile Crisis

The most serious threat of nuclear holocaust during the entire Cold War was the Cuban missile crisis. In 1962 Soviet Premier Nikita Khrushchev sought to secretly install medium-range nuclear missiles in Cuba in an effort to give the Soviet Union nuclear capability against U.S. cities. In October

Cuban Missile Crisis The 1962 confrontation between the Soviet Union and the U.S. over Soviet placement of nuclear missiles in Cuba.

1962 intelligence photos showing Soviet missiles at Cuban bases touched off a thirteen-day crisis. President Kennedy rejected advice to launch an air strike to destroy the missiles before they could be activated. Instead, he publicly announced a naval blockade of Cuba, threatening to halt Soviet missile-carrying vessels at sea by force if necessary. The prospect of war appeared imminent; U.S. nuclear forces went on alert. Secretly, Kennedy proposed to withdraw U.S. nuclear missiles from Turkey in exchange for Soviet withdrawal of nuclear missiles from Cuba. Khrushchev's agreement to the deal appeared to the world as a backing down; Secretary of State Dean Rusk would boast, "We were eyeball to eyeball, and they blinked." Kennedy would be hailed for his statesmanship in the crisis; Khrushchev would soon lose his job.

The Vietnam War U.S. involvement in Vietnam grew out of the policy of containment. President Eisenhower had declined to intervene in the former French colony in 1956 when communist forces led by Ho Chi Minh defeated French forces at the battle of Dien Bien Phu. The resulting Geneva Accords divided that country into North Vietnam, with a communist government, and South Vietnam, with a U.S.-backed government. When South Vietnamese communist (Vietcong) guerrilla forces threatened the South Vietnamese government in the early 1960s, President Kennedy sent a force of more than 12,000 advisers and counterinsurgency forces to assist in every aspect of training and support for the Army of the Republic of Vietnam (ARVN). By 1964 units of the North Vietnamese Army (NVA) had begun to supplement the Vietcong guerrilla forces in the south. Unconfirmed reports of an attack on U.S. Navy vessels by North Vietnamese torpedo boats led the U.S. Congress to pass the Gulf of Tonkin Resolution, which authorized the president to take "all necessary measures" to repel any armed attack against any U.S. forces in Southeast Asia.

WWW **Cuban Crises** The October 1962 nuclear missile crises described day to day, with photos. ***www.cubacrisis.net***

Vietnam War War between non-Communist South Vietnam and Communist North Vietnam from 1956 to 1975, with increasing U.S. involvement, ending with U.S. withdrawal in 1973 and Communist victory in 1975. The war became unpopular in the U.S. after 1968 and caused President Johnson not to run for a second term. More than 58,000 Americans died in the war.

In February 1965 President Lyndon B. Johnson ordered U.S. combat troops into South Vietnam and authorized a gradual increase in air strikes against North Vietnam. Washington committed more than 500,000 troops to a war of attrition, a war in which U.S. firepower was expected to inflict sufficient casualties on the enemy to force a peace settlement. But over time, the failure to achieve any decisive military victories eroded popular support for the war.

On January 31, 1968, the Vietnam holiday of Tet, Vietcong forces blasted their way into the U.S. embassy compound in Saigon and held the courtyard for six hours. The attack was part of a massive, coordinated Tet offensive against all major cities of South Vietnam. U.S. forces responded and inflicted very heavy casualties

President Kennedy meeting with his cabinet during the Cuban missile crisis, which brought the United States and the Soviet Union to the brink of nuclear war in 1962.

on the Vietcong. By any military measure, the Tet offensive was a "defeat" for the enemy and a "victory" for U.S. forces. Yet the Tet offensive was Hanoi's greatest *political* victory. Television pictures of bloody fighting in Saigon and Hue seemed to mock President Johnson's promises of an early end to the war.

On March 31, 1968, President Johnson went on national television to make a dramatic announcement: he halted the bombing of North Vietnam and asked Hanoi for peace talks, concluding, "I shall not seek, and I will not accept, the nomination of my party for another term as your president." Formal peace talks opened in Paris on May 13.

The new president, Richard Nixon, and his national security adviser, Henry Kissinger, knew the war must be ended, but they sought to end it "honorably." Even in the absence of a settlement with the communists in Vietnam, Nixon began the withdrawal of U.S. troops under the guise of "Vietnamization" of the war effort. Unable to persuade Hanoi to make even the slightest concession at Paris, President Nixon sought to demonstrate American strength and resolve. In December 1972 the United States unleashed a devastating air attack directly on Hanoi for the first time. Critics at home labeled Nixon's action "the Christmas bombing," but when negotiations resumed in Paris in January, the North Vietnamese quickly agreed to peace on the terms that Kissinger and Le Duc Tho had worked out earlier.

The South Vietnamese government lasted two years after the agreement. In early 1975 Hanoi decided that the Americans would not "jump back in" and therefore "the opportune moment" was at hand for a new invasion. President Gerald Ford's requests to Congress for emergency military aid to the South Vietnamese fell on deaf ears. Saigon (now Ho Chi Minh City) fell to the North Vietnamese in April 1975, and the United States abandoned hundreds of thousands of loyal Vietnamese who had fought alongside the Americans for years.[3] The spectacle of U.S. Marines using their rifle butts to keep desperate Vietnamese from boarding helicopters on the roof of the U.S. embassy "provided a tragic epitaph for twenty-five years of American involvement in Vietnam."[4]

The Vietnam Syndrome America's humiliation in Vietnam had lasting national consequences. The United States suffered 47,378 battle deaths and missing-in-action among the 2.8 million U.S. personnel who served in Vietnam. A new isolationism permeated American foreign policy following defeat in Vietnam. The slogan "No more Vietnams" was used to oppose any U.S. military intervention, whether or not U.S. vital interests were at stake. Disillusionment replaced idealism. American leaders had exaggerated the importance of Vietnam; now Americans were unwilling to believe their leaders when they warned of other dangers.

In the late 1970s the Soviet Union rapidly expanded its political and military presence in Asia, Africa, the Middle East, Central America, and the Caribbean. The United States did little to respond to this new wave of Soviet expansionism until the Soviet invasion of Afghanistan in 1979, when President Jimmy Carter authorized the largest covert action in CIA history—the military support of the Afghan guerrilla forces fighting Soviet occupation. The Soviets suffered a heavy drain of human and economic resources in their nine-year war in Afghanistan, which some dubbed "Russia's Vietnam."

Rebuilding America's Defenses The decision to rebuild Western military forces and reassert international leadership on behalf of democratic values gained widespread support in the Western world in the early 1980's. President Ronald Reagan, British Prime Minister Margaret Thatcher, French President François Mitterrand, and German Chancellor Helmut Kohl all pledged to increase their defense efforts and all held fast against a "nuclear freeze" movement that would have locked in Soviet superiority in European-based nuclear weapons.

The Reagan defense buildup extended through 1985—with increases in defense spending, improvements in strategic nuclear weapons, and, perhaps more important, the rebuilding and reequipping of U.S. conventional forces. The American and NATO defense buildup, together with the promise of a new, expensive, and technologically sophisticated race for ballistic missile defenses, forecast heavy additional strains on the weak economy of the Soviet Union. Thus, in 1985, when new Soviet President Mikhail Gorbachev came to power, the stage was set for an end to the Cold War.

Gorbachev announced reductions in the size of the Soviet military and reached agreements with the United States on the reduction of nuclear forces More important, in 1988 he announced that the Soviet Union would no longer use its military forces to keep communist governments in power in Eastern European nations. This stunning announcement, for which he received the Nobel Peace Prize in 1990, encouraged opposition democratic forces in Poland (the Solidarity movement), Czechoslovakia, Hungary, Bulgaria, Romania, and East Germany. Gorbachev refused to intervene to halt the destruction of the Berlin Wall, despite pleas by the East German hard-line communist leader Erich Honecker.

The Collapse of Communism Gorbachev's economic and political reforms threatened powerful interests in the Soviet Union—the Communist Party bureaucrats, who were losing control over economic enterprises; the military leaders, who opposed the withdrawal of Soviet troops from Germany and Eastern Europe, the KGB police, whose terror tactics were increasingly restricted, and central government officials, who were afraid of losing power to the republics. When hard liners in the Communist Party, the military, and the KGB attempted the forcible removal of Gorbachev in August 1991, democratic forces rallied to his support. Led by Boris Yeltsin, the first elected president of the Russian Republic, thousands of demonstrators took to the streets, Soviet military forces stood aside, and the coup crumbled. Yeltsin emerged as the most influential leader in the nation. The failed coup hastened the demise of the Communist Party. The party lost legitimacy with the peoples of Russia and the other republics.

The Disintegration of the Soviet Union Strong independence movements in the republics of the Soviet Union emerged as the authority of the centralized Communist Party in Moscow waned. Lithuania, Estonia, and Latvia—nations that had been forcibly incorporated into the Soviet Union in 1939—led the way to independence in 1991. Soon all of the fifteen republics of the Soviet Union declared their independence, and the Union of Soviet Socialist Republics officially ceased to exist after December 31, 1991. Its president, Mikhail Gorbachev, no longer had a government to preside over. The red flag with its hammer and sickle atop the Kremlin was replaced with the flag of the Russian Republic.

The Vietnam War Memorial in Washington, D.C., is inscribed with the names of the nearly 50,000 Americans who died in Vietnam. America's defeat fostered a lasting skepticism about the wisdom of foreign military intervention, leading to a new isolationism in foreign policy.

Russia after Communism The transition from a centralized state-run economy to free markets turned out to be more painful for Russians than expected. Living standards for most people declined, alcoholism and death rates increased, and even average life spans shortened. Ethnic conflict and political separatism, especially in the largely Muslim province of Chechnya, added to Russia's problems. Yeltsin was able to overcome these political challenges and win reelection as president in 1996. But corruption, embezzlement, graft, and organized crime continue to undermine democratic reforms. Poor health eventually forced Yeltsin to turn over power to Vladimir Putin, who himself won election as president of Russia in 2000.

Presidents Vladimir Putin of Russia and George W. Bush of the United States reached agreement in 2002 to reduce their nations' nuclear stockpiles by over 80 percent from Cold War levels.

The United States has a vital continuing interest in promoting democracy and economic reform in Russia. Russia remains the only nuclear power capable of destroying the United States.

Russia EIN News Business, cultural, political, and scientific news from Russia. *www.einnews.com/russia*

Nuclear Threats

Nuclear weaponry has made the world infinitely more dangerous. During the Cold War, the nuclear arsenals of the United States and the Soviet Union threatened a human holocaust. Yet, paradoxically, the very destructiveness of nuclear weapons caused leaders on both sides to exercise extreme caution in their relations with each other. Scores of wars, large and small, were fought by different nations during the Cold War years, yet American and Soviet troops never engaged in direct combat against each other.

THINK AGAIN

Should the United States destroy all of its nuclear weapons now that the Cold War is over?

Deterrence To maintain nuclear peace during the Cold War, the United States relied primarily on the policy of **deterrence.** Deterrence is based on the notion that a nation can dissuade a rational enemy from attacking by maintaining the capacity to destroy the enemy's homeland even *after* the nation has suffered a well-executed surprise attack by the enemy. Deterrence assumes that the worst may happen—a surprise first strike against a nation's nuclear forces. It emphasizes **second-strike capability**—the ability of a nation's forces to survive a surprise attack by the enemy and then to inflict an unacceptable level of destruction on the enemy's homeland. Deterrence is really a *psychological* defense against attack; no effective physical defense against a ballistic missile attack exists even today.

deterrence U.S. approach to deterring any nuclear attack from the Soviet Union by maintaining a second-strike capability.

second-strike capability Ability of a nation's forces to survive a surprise nuclear attack by the enemy and then to retaliate effectively.

mutual assured destruction (MAD) Nuclear peace maintained by the capability of each side's missile forces to survive a first strike and inflict heavy damages in retaliation against the aggressor's population.

MAD Balance of Terror By the early 1970s, a nuclear balance existed between the superpowers. Neither side could consider launching a nuclear attack because of the terrible consequences that the other side could inflict in retaliation. If neither side could be assured of destroying the other side's retaliatory missiles in a first strike, then a mutual "balance of terror" maintained the nuclear peace. In effect, the populations of each nation were being held hostage against a nuclear attack. Commentators labeled this balance of terror as **mutual assured destruction** deterrence, or MAD.

Limiting Nuclear Arms: SALT The United States and the Soviet Union engaged in negotiations over nuclear arms control for many years. The development of reconnaissance satellites in the 1960s made it possible for each nation to monitor the strategic weapons possessed by the other. Space photography made cheating on agreements more difficult and thus opened the way for both nations to seek stability through arms control.

Following the election of Richard Nixon as president in 1968, the United States, largely guided by former Harvard professor Henry Kissinger (national security adviser to the president and later secretary of state), began negotiations with the Soviet Union over strategic nuclear arms. In 1972 the two nations concluded two and a half years of Strategic Arms Limitation Talks (SALT) about limiting the nuclear arms race. The agreement, **SALT I**, consisted of a treaty limiting antiballistic missiles (ABMs) and an agreement placing a numerical ceiling on offensive missiles. The **ABM Treaty** reflected the MAD theory that the populations of each nation should be *un*defended in order to hold them hostage against a first strike. Under the offensive-missiles agreement, each side was frozen at the total number of offensive missiles, completed or under construction. Both sides could construct new and more destructive missiles as long as they dismantled an equal number of older missiles. Each nation agreed not to interfere in the satellite intelligence-gathering activities of the other nation.

SALT I was the first step forward on the control of nuclear arms; both sides agreed to continue negotiations. After seven years of difficult negotiations, the United States and the Soviet Union produced the lengthy and complicated **SALT II** treaty in 1979. It set an overall limit on "strategic nuclear launch vehicles"—ICBMs, SLBMs, bombers, and long-range Cruise missiles—at 2,250 for each side. It also limited the number of missiles that could have multiple warheads (MIRVs) and banned new types of ICBMs, with the exception of one new type of ICBM for each side. When the Soviet Union invaded Afghanistan in 1974, President Carter withdrew the SALT II treaty from Senate consideration. However, President Carter, and later President Reagan, announced that the United States would abide by the provisions of the unratified SALT II treaty as long as the Soviet Union did so.

Reducing Nuclear Arms: START In negotiations with the Soviets, the Reagan Administration established three central principles of arms control—reductions, equality, and verification. The new goal was to be *reductions* in missiles and warheads, not merely limitations on future numbers and types of weapons, as in previous SALT talks. To symbolize this new direction, President Reagan renamed the negotiations the Strategic Arms *Reduction* Talks, or START.

The **START I** Treaty signed in Moscow in 1991 by Presidents George Bush and Mikhail Gorbachev was the first agreement between the nuclear powers that actually resulted in the reduction of strategic nuclear weapons. (Earlier, the Intermediate-Range Nuclear Forces INF Treaty of 1987 eliminated missiles with an intermediate range, between 300 and 3,800 miles; although the portion of each side's nuclear weapons covered by the INF Treaty was small, it set the pattern for future arms control agreements in its provisions for reductions, equality, and verification.) The START I Treaty reduced the total number of deployed strategic nuclear delivery systems to no more than 1,600, a 30 percent reduction from the SALT II level.

A far-reaching **START II** agreement, signed in 1993 by U.S. President Bush and Russian President Yeltsin, promises to eliminate the threat of a first-strike nuclear attack by either side. Its most important provision is the agreement to eliminate all multiwarhead (MIRVed) land-based missiles. The Russians agreed to dismantle their powerful SS-18 missiles, the most dangerous threat to the nuclear balance of power. The United States agreed to dismantle the MX missile and convert the three-warheaded Minuteman IIIs into single-warhead missiles. START II also called for the reduction of overall strategic warheads to 3,500.

The Treaty of Moscow The capstone of strategic nuclear arms reductions is the Treaty of Moscow, signed by Russian President Vladimir Putin and U.S. President George W. Bush in 2002. This new treaty, which must be approved by the

SALT I First arms limitation treaty between the United States and the Soviet Union, signed in 1972, limiting the total number of offensive nuclear missiles; it included the ABM Treaty that reflected the theory that the population centers of both nations should be left *un*defended.

ABM Treaty A formal treaty in 1972 between the U.S. and the Soviet Union in which each side agreed *not* to build or deploy antiballistic missiles.

SALT II Lengthy and complicated treaty between the United States and the Soviet Union, agreed to in 1979 but never ratified by the U.S. Senate, that set limits on all types of strategic nuclear launch vehicles.

START I First treaty between the United States and the Soviet Union that actually reduced the strategic nuclear arms of the superpowers, signed in 1991.

START II A treaty between the United States and Russia eliminating all multiwarhead land missiles and reducing nuclear weapons stockpiles; signed in 2003.

U.S. Senate and the Russian Federal Assembly, calls for an overall limit of nuclear warheads at 1,700–2,200 by 2012. Each side may determine for itself the composition and structure of its strategic forces consistent with this limit. The provisions of the START treaties remain unchanged. The effect of the Moscow Treaty, together with earlier reductions in nuclear weapons under the START treaties, will be to reduce the nuclear arsenals of the former adversaries by over 80 percent from Cold War levels (see Figure 14.1).

Nuclear Testing and Nonproliferation The United States and the former Soviet Union reached an agreement in 1963—the Limited Test Ban Treaty—that prohibited nuclear testing in the atmosphere, under water, or in outer space. The effect was to allow only underground testing, which was believed to reduce radioactivity in the atmosphere. A Threshold Test Ban Treaty was signed in 1974 that prohibited tests of nuclear weapons with explosive power greater than 150 kilotons (equivalent to 150,000 tons of conventional explosives).

In 1992 the Russian government under President Yeltsin announced that it would discontinue *all* nuclear testing if the United States would do the same. President George Bush declined to make this pledge, but later President Bill Clinton placed an unofficial moratorium on U.S. nuclear testing. In 1996, President Clinton signed a **Comprehensive Test Ban Treaty,** a multilateral agreement that would prohibit all nuclear testing. Many non-nuclear-armed nations signed this treaty. But in 1999 the U.S. Senate voted against ratification. Opponents of the treaty noted that testing verified the safety and reliability of weapons, and that several other potentially threatening nuclear nations had refused to sign the treaty, including North Korea, Iran, Iraq, India, and Pakistan. Russia announced that it was awaiting U.S. ratification before signing the treaty, and China continued testing nuclear weapons.

Comprehensive Test Ban Treaty A multilateral treaty prohibiting all nuclear testing.

Yet another **multilateral treaty,** the nuclear **Nonproliferation Treaty,** was signed by the United States and the former Soviet Union in 1968. It prohibits nuclear-armed nations from transferring weapons and technologies to nonnuclear nations. Nonnuclear signing nations pledged not to "receive, manufacture, or otherwise acquire nuclear weapons." But the Nonproliferation Treaty has been largely ignored, not only by nations that went on to acquire nuclear weapons (including India, Pakistan, China, and North Korea), but also by nations that have transferred nuclear technology to nonnuclear nations (including France and Russia). North Korea has demanded extensive U.S. foreign aid in exchange for dismantling its nuclear weapons facilities.

multilateral treaty A treaty open to signature by more than two nations (as opposed to a bilateral treaty, signed by only two nations).

Nonproliferation Treaty A multilateral treaty in which nuclear nations pledged not to transfer nuclear weapons or technologies to nonnuclear nations, and nonnuclear nations pledged not to manufacture or acquire nuclear weapons.

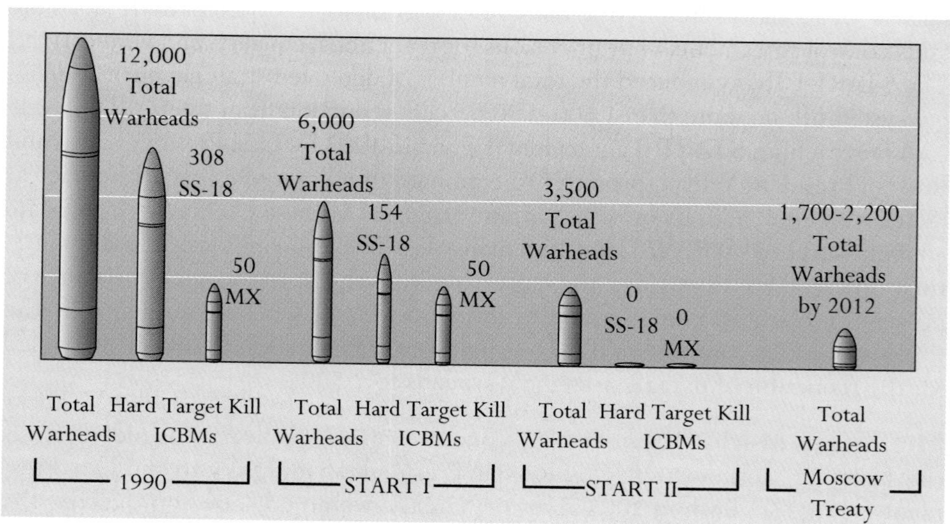

FIGURE 14.1 Strategic Nuclear Arms under START Treaties

Implementation of the Start II Treaty will reduce the total number of warheads in both the United States and Russia by over two-thirds and will completely eliminate bard target kill ICBMs.

Nuclear Terrorism Even as the threat of a large-scale nuclear attack recedes, the threats arising from "nondeterrable" sources are increasing. Today, the principal nondeterrable threats are estimated to be (1) missiles launched by a terrorist nation; (2) unauthorized missile launches by elements within the former Soviet Union during periods of internal crisis and turmoil; and (3) accidental missile launches. Over time global nuclear and ballistic missile proliferation steadily increases the likelihood of these types of threats. Terrorist, unauthorized, and accidental launches are considered "nondeterrable" because the threat of nuclear retaliation is largely meaningless.

The threat of mass terror weapons—nuclear, chemical, or biological weapons, especially those carried by medium- or long-range missiles—is likely to increase dramatically in the years ahead. North Korea is reported to possess nuclear weapons and to be developing long-range missiles to carry them. Defending against terrorist, unauthorized, or accidental missile attacks requires the development and deployment of **ballistic missile defense (BMD)** systems, weapons capable of detecting, intercepting, and destroying ballistic missiles while they are in flight. At present there is no defense against a ballistic missile attack on American cities (see *A Conflicting View:* "We Should Defend Ourselves against a Ballistic Missile Attack").

The Bush administration officially notified Russia in 2002 of its intent to withdraw from the provisions of the SALT I agreement that prohibited the development, testing, and deployment of antiballistic missiles. The Russian government objected (but provisions for a six-month notification of withdrawal were included in the original treaty). President Bush also announced that United States would begin the actual deployment of a limited number of ground-based and sea-based missile interceptors. This initial missile defense capability will be designed "to meet the near-term threat to our homeland, our deployed forces, and our friends and allies."

When to Use Military Force?

THINK AGAIN

Is the president justified in placing U.S. troops in danger where U.S. vital interests are not at stake?

All modern presidents have acknowledged that the most agonizing decisions they have made were to send U.S. military forces into combat. These decisions cost lives. The American people are willing to send their sons and daughters into danger—and even to see some of them wounded and killed—but *only* if a president convinces them that the outcome "is worth dying for." A president must be able to explain why they lost their lives and to justify their sacrifice.

To Protect Vital Interests The U.S. military learned many bitter lessons in its long bloody experience in Vietnam. Among those lessons are these:

- The United States should commit its military forces only in support of vital national interests.
- If military forces are committed, they must have clearly defined military objectives—the destruction of enemy forces and/or the capture of enemy-held territory.
- Any commitment of U.S. forces must be of sufficient strength to ensure overwhelming and decisive victory with the fewest possible casualties.
- Before committing U.S. military forces, there must be some reasonable assurances that the effort has the support of the American people and their representatives in Congress.
- The commitment of U.S. military forces should be a last resort, after political, economic, and diplomatic efforts have proven ineffective.

President George Bush argued that his decision to use military force in the Gulf War in 1990–91 met these guidelines: that preventing Iraq's Saddam Hussein from

ballistic missile defense (BMD) Weapons systems capable of detecting, intercepting, and destroying missiles in flight.

A CONFLICTING VIEW

We Should Defend Ourselves against a Ballistic Missile Attack

For over a half-century, since the terrible nuclear blasts of Hiroshima and Nagasaki in Japan in 1945, the world has avoided nuclear war. Peace has been maintained by deterrence—by the threat of devastating nuclear attacks that would be launched in retaliation to an enemy's first strike. But in 1983 President Ronald Reagan urged that instead of deterring war through fear of retaliation, the United States should seek a technological defense against nuclear missiles.

> Our nuclear retaliating forces have deterred war for forty years. The fact is, however, that we have no defense against ballistic missile attack. . . . In the event that deterrence failed, a president's only recourse would be to surrender or to retaliate. Nuclear retaliation, whether massive or limited, would result in the loss of millions of lives. . . .
>
> If we apply our great scientific and engineering talent to the problem of defending against ballistic missiles, there is a very real possibility that future presidents will be able to deter war by means other than threatening devastation to any aggressor—and by a means which threatens no one.*

"Star Wars"

Reagan's Strategic Defense Initiative (SDI) was a research program designed to explore means of destroying enemy nuclear missiles in space before they could reach their targets. Following President Reagan's initial announcement of SDI in March 1983, the press quickly labeled the effort "Star Wars." In theory, a ballistic missile defense (BMD) system could be based in space, orbiting over enemy missile-launching sites. Should an enemy missile get through the space-based defense, a ground-based BMD system would attempt to intercept warheads as they reentered the atmosphere and approached their targets. SDI included research on laser beams, satellite surveillance, computerized battle-management systems, and "smart" and "brilliant" weapons systems. SDI under President Reagan was a very ambitious program with the goal of creating an "impenetrable shield" that would protect not only the population of the United States but the population of our allies as well.

Protection against Nuclear Terrorism

The end of the Cold War refocused SDI away from defense against a massive Russian missile attack to more limited yet more likely threats. Today the principal nuclear threats are missiles launched by terrorists or a "rogue state." President Bush redirected SDI toward defending against these more limited yet potentially devastating attacks.

The Gulf War experience demonstrated that deterrence may not protect the United States against a ballistic missile attack by a terrorist regime. The success of the Patriot antiballistic missile in destroying short-range Iraqi Scud missiles during the Gulf War demonstrated that enemy missiles could be intercepted in flight. (The Patriot is a ground-based "tactical" weapon designed to protect specific military targets.) However, developing an effective antiballistic missile that can intercept and destroy another missile in space has proven to be more difficult, although not impossible.

The Future of BMDs

As a Reagan-era initiative, partisanship has tended to cloud the debate over BMDs. In 1993 President Clinton announced the termination of the separate SDI organization, but he reassured the nation that research would continue on the ground-based ballistic missile defenses. President George W. Bush notified the Russians in 2002 that the United States was withdrawing from provisions of the SALT I Treaty of 1972 that prohibited the development, testing, or deployment of new ballistic missile defense systems.

Advanced testing has met with both successes and failures. Intercepting an incoming missile has been compared to "hitting a bullet with a bullet." Even this daunting challenge is further complicated by the likelihood of enemy decoys masking the real warhead; a reliable ballistic missile defense must be able to discriminate between decoys and actual warheads.

President George W. Bush announced a limited deployment of sea-based and ground-based missile interceptors and advanced Patriot missiles in 2004. The president spoke of an incremental growth of U.S. anti-ballistic missile capability directed at potential terrorist attacks.

*President Ronald Reagan, *The President's Strategic Defense Initiative,* The White House, January 3, 1985.

gaining control of the world's oil supply and developing nuclear and chemical weapons were vital national interests; that political and economic sanctions were not effective; and that he had defined clear military objectives—the removal of Iraqi troops from Kuwait and the destruction of Iraq's nuclear and chemical weapon capabilities (see *Up Close:* "The Use of Force: Operation Desert Storm"). And he authorized a large military commitment that led to a speedy and decisive victory.

These guidelines for the use of military force are widely supported within the U.S. military itself.[5] Contrary to Hollywood stereotypes, military leaders are extremely reluctant to go to war when no vital interest of the United States is at stake, where there are no clear-cut military objectives, without the support of Congress or the American people, or without sufficient force to achieve speedy and decisive victory with minimal casualties. (See *People in Politics:* "Colin Powell, An American Journey.") They are wary of seeing their troops placed in danger merely to advance diplomatic goals, or to engage in "peacekeeping," or to "stabilize governments," or to "show the flag." They are reluctant to undertake humanitarian missions while being shot at. They do not like to risk their soldiers' lives under "rules of engagement" that limit their ability to defend themselves.

WWW CIA World Factbook Nations listed A–Z with geography, people, economy, government, military, etc., information. *www.cia.gov/publications/factbook*

In Support of Important Political Objectives In contrast to military leaders, political leaders and diplomats often reflect the view that "war is a continuation of politics by other means"—a view commonly attributed to nineteenth-century German theorist of war Karl von Clausewitz. Military force may be used to protect interests that are important but not necessarily vital. Otherwise, the United States would be rendered largely impotent in world affairs. A diplomat's ability to achieve a satisfactory result often depends on the expressed or implied threat of military force. The distinguished international political theorist Hans Morgenthau wrote, "Since military strength is the obvious measure of a nation's power, its demonstration serves to impress others with that nation's power."[6]

Currently American military forces must be prepared to carry out a variety of missions in addition to the conduct of conventional war:

- Demonstrating U.S. resolve in crisis situations.
- Demonstrating U.S. support for democratic governments.
- Protecting U.S. citizens living abroad.
- Peacemaking among warring factions or nations.
- Peacekeeping where hostile factions or nations have accepted a peace agreement.
- Providing humanitarian aid often under warlike conditions.
- Assist in an international war against drug trafficking.

In pursuit of such objectives, recent U.S. presidents have sent troops to Lebanon in 1982 to stabilize the government (Reagan), to Grenada in 1983 to rescue American medical students and restore democratic government (Reagan), to Panama in 1989 to oust drug-trafficking General Manuel Antonio Noriega from power and to protect U.S. citizens (Bush), to Somalia in 1992–93 to provide emergency humanitarian aid (Bush and Clinton), to Haiti in 1994 (Clinton) to restore constitutional government and again to Haiti in 2004 (Bush), and to Bosnia and Kosovo for peacekeeping among warring ethnic factions (see Table 14.1).

Proponents of these more flexible uses of U.S. military forces usually deny any intent to be the "world's policeman." Rather, they argue that each situation must be judged independently on its own merits—weighing the importance of U.S.

PEOPLE IN POLITICS

Colin Powell, An American Journey

Secretary of State Colin Powell embodies the American dream: "a black kid of no early promise from an immigrant family of limited means who was raised in the South Bronx and somehow rose to become the National Security Adviser to the President of the United States and then Chairman of the Joint Chiefs of Staff." He also rose to be the American public's preferred choice for president of the United States in 1996, yet decided he did not have the "passion and commitment" for political life that he "felt every day of my thirty-five years as a soldier." But he answered his country's call again in 2001, this time to serve as secretary of state.

Born in Harlem to Jamaican immigrant parents, Powell recounts his youth as proof that "it is possible to rise above conditions." After graduation from Morris High School in the South Bronx, Powell enrolled at The City College of New York on a ROTC scholarship. In 1958 he graduated with a degree in geology at the top of his ROTC class and was commissioned a second lieutenant in the U.S. Army. Powell went to South Vietnam as a military adviser in 1962 and returned for a second tour of service in 1968. In Vietnam, he was awarded two Purple Hearts, a Bronze Star for Valor, and the Legion of Merit.

In 1972 Powell returned to the classroom to pursue a master's degree in business administration from George Washington University and accept an appointment to the prestigious White House Fellows Program. As a White House Fellow, Powell was assigned to the Office of Management and Budget, where he worked under Caspar Weinberger, later secretary of defense in the Reagan Administration. Powell's career was on a fast track after his White House duty. Powell was recalled to Washington in 1983 by Defense Secretary Weinberger to become senior military adviser to the secretary.

President George Bush chose General Powell in 1989 to head the Joint Chiefs of Staff, the nation's highest military position. It was Powell who helped convince the president that if military force were to be used to oust Saddam Hussein from Kuwait, it must be an overwhelming and decisive force, not gradual, limited escalation, as in Vietnam. Powell's televised press briefings during the war assured the American people of the competence and effectiveness of the U.S. military. The Gulf War victory restored the morale of U.S. military forces and the confidence of the American people in its military leadership.

To a great many Americans, Powell seemed to offer the nation what it most needed: a decisive leader with integrity and character, a political outsider untarnished by "politics as usual," and an African American whose "American journey"* could serve as a model for all and ease the nation's racial divisions. He was frequently compared to Dwight D. Eisenhower, whose military leadership in World War II ushered him into the White House. Like Ike, Powell waited until after army retirement to declare himself a Republican. He led all other candidates for president in public opinion polls in 1996, yet after "prayerful consideration," he announced that he would not be a candidate for president "or any elective office." For several years Powell devoted himself exclusively to volunteer activities, notably as chairman of a national campaign, "America's Promise—Alliance for Youth."

Powell's most challenging task as Secretary of State is to maintain the backing of other nations for the American-led war on terrorism. His advice to the president on the use of military force reflects his long-held belief, sometimes even referred to as the "Powell Doctrine," that military operations should be conducted only in the vital national interest, with clear goals and public support, and when overwhelming and decisive military force is to be employed.

*Source: Colin Powell, *My American Journey* (New York: Random House 1995).

terrorism Title 22 of the U.S. Code, Section 2656 (d): "The term 'terrorism' means premeditated, politically motivated violence perpetrated against noncombatant targets by subnational groups or clandestine agents, usually intended to influence an audience."

goals against expected costs. No military operation is without risk, but some risks may be worth taking to advance important political interests even though these interests may not be deemed "vital" to the United States.

In Support of the War on Terrorism The War on Terrorism creates new conditions for the use of military force.[5] Currently U.S. forces are prepared for:

- Direct attacks against terrorist forces to capture or kill them. These operations are usually carried out by highly trained Special Operations Forces.

TABLE 14.1 Major Deployments of U.S. Military Forces Since World War II

Year	Area	President
1950–53	Korea	Truman
1958	Lebanon	Eisenhower
1961–64	Vietnam	Kennedy
1962	Cuban waters	Kennedy
1965–73	Vietnam	Johnson, Nixon
1965	Dominican Republic	Johnson
1970	Laos	Nixon
1970	Cambodia	Nixon
1975	Cambodia	Ford
1980	Iran	Carter
1982–83	Lebanon	Reagan
1983	Grenada	Reagan
1989	Panama	Bush
1990–91	Persian Gulf	Bush
1992–93	Somalia	Bush, Clinton
1994–95	Haiti	Clinton
1995–2000	Bosnia	Clinton
1999–2000	Kosovo	Clinton
2001–	Afghanistan	Bush
2002–	Philippines	Bush
2003–	Iraq	Bush
2004	Haiti	Bush

- Attacks on nations that harbor terrorists, allow terrorists to maintain bases, or supply and equip terrorist organizations. In 1986, the United States struck at Libya in a limited air attack in response to various Libyan-supported acts of terrorism around the world. In 1993, the United States struck Iraq's intelligence center in Baghdad in response to a foiled plot to assassinate former President George Bush. In 2001, the United States relied principally on Special Forces working in conjunction with tribal forces in Afghanistan to attack Al Qaeda terrorists and to topple the Taliban government that had harbored and supported Al Qaeda.

THINK AGAIN

Do you approve of the military attacks led by the United States against targets in Afghanistan?

- Preemptive attacks on regimes that threaten to use weapons of mass instruction—chemical, biological, or nuclear weapons—against the United States or its allies, or to supply terrorist organizations with these weapons. Preemptive military action represents a reversal of traditional U.S. policy. Historically the United States acted militarily only in response to a direct attack on its own forces or those of its allies. But it is argued that the Terrorist Attack of 9/11 initiated the current War on Terrorism and that American military actions in the Middle East, including those in Afghanistan and Iraq, are related to the 9/11 attack on America. The argument for preemptive military action was summarized by President Bush's National Security Adviser Condoleeza Rice: "We cannot wait until the smoking gun becomes a mushroom cloud."

THINK AGAIN

Do you favor the U.S. invading Iraq?

The War on Terrorism

Terrorism is a political act. The deliberate targeting of civilians, the infliction of widespread destruction, and the resulting media portrayals of the pain and suffering of victims are designed to call attention to political grievances and to instill fear in people. (The Latin root of the term, *terrere,* means "to frighten.") The horror of terrorist acts and their unpredictability add to public fear—people can neither anticipate nor prepare for tragedies inflicted upon them. Terrorists hope to undermine the confidence of people in their government to protect them, and to conclude that submission to the terrorists' demands is preferable to living in a continuing climate of anxiety and uncertainty.

Terrorism Research Center

The "Terrorism Research Center" Web site is dedicated to "informing the public of the phenomena of terrorism and information warfare." It contains news, analytical essays on terrorist issues, and many links to other terrorism materials and research sources. ***www.terrorism.com***

Defenselink Terrorism

Official Defense Department site link to information on terrorism. ***www.defenselink.mil/terrorism***

CIA-Terrorism

Reports, news, facts, regarding terrorism. ***www.cia.gov/terrorism***

Global Terrorism Global terrorism has evolved over the years into highly sophisticated networks operating in many countries. The most notable terrorist attacks extend back over thirty years, but the death and destruction wrought by terrorists have dramatically increased (see Table 14.2). Prior to the attacks on New York's World Trade Center and the Pentagon on September 11, 2001, most Americans thought of terrorism as foreign. Terrorist acts on American soil had been rare; the most destructive attack—the Oklahoma City bombing of a federal building in 1995—had been carried out by domestic terrorists. But the 9/11 attacks were on an unprecedented scale and they revealed a sophisticated global plot against America.

A loose-knit network of terrorist cells (Al Qaeda) organized by a wealthy Saudi Arabian, Osama bin Laden, was engaged in global terrorism. Their political grievances included America's support of Israel in Middle East conflicts and an American presence in Islamic holy lands, notably Saudi Arabia. Several nations share these grievances and, more importantly, provided support and haven to Al Qaeda in similar terrorist organizations. The principal base of support and sanctuary for Al Qaeda was the repressive and violent Taliban regime of Afghanistan.

Declaring War on Terrorism On the evening of September 11, President George W. Bush spoke to the American people from the Oval Office in a nationally televised address:

> The pictures of airplanes flying into buildings, fires burning, huge structures collapsing, have 7 us with disbelief, terrible sadness, and a quiet, unyielding anger. These mass murders were intended to frighten our nation into chaos and retreat. But they failed; our country is strong. . . . These deliberate and deadly attacks were more than acts of terror. They were acts of war.

The president outlined a broad "response to terrorism" to be fought both at home and abroad through diplomatic, military, financial, investigative, homeland security, and humanitarian means. He warned that the new war on terrorism would require a long-term sustained effort. It would require Americans to accept new restrictions on their lives (see "Terrorism's Threat to Democracy" in Chapter 1). It would require new legislation—an Airport Security Act federalizing security at U.S. airports and instituting new strict security measures, and a "Patriot" (anti-terrorism) Act expanding the authority of the attorney general and federal law-enforcement agencies to fight domestic terrorism (see *A Conflicting View:* "Terrorism Requires Restrictions on Civil Liberties" in Chapter 14). It would require the creation of a new Department of Homeland Security designed to coordinate many federal, state, and local law-enforcement agencies charged with responsibility for dealing with acts of terror (see "The Department of Homeland Security" in Chapter 10).

Operation "Enduring Freedom" The military phase of the war on terrorism began October 7, 2001, when U.S. Air Force and Navy aircraft began attacks on known Al Qaeda bases in Afghanistan and U.S. Special Forces organized and led anti-Taliban fighters, including several tribal groups calling themselves the Northern Alliance, in a campaign against the Taliban regime. A coalition of nations participated in Operation "Enduring Freedom"; some, including Britain and Canada,

TABLE 14.2 Notable Global Terrorist Attacks

Date	Number of People Killed	Description	Prime suspect[s]
September 5, 1972	17	Israeli athletes are killed during the Olympics in Munich, Germany	Black September, a Palestinian guerrilla group
April 18, 1983	63	The American Embassy in Beirut, Lebanon, is bombed	Hezbollah [Party of God]
September 23, 1983	112	A plane crashes in United Arab Emirates after a bomb explodes in the baggage compartment	Unknown
October 23, 1983	299	Two truck bombs kill U.S. Marines and French paratroopers in Beirut, Lebanon	U.S. blames groups aligned with Iran and Syria
June 23, 1985	329	An Air India jet explodes over the Atlantic Ocean, off the coast of Ireland	The Royal Canadian Mounted Police charge Ajaib Singh Bagri and Ripudaman, two Sikh dissidents, in 2000
November 29, 1987	115	A Korean Air Lines jet explodes over the Burma coast	South Korea suspects North Korean involvement
December 21, 1988	270	Pan Am 103 explodes over Lockerbie, Scotland	One Libyan intelligence officer is convicted in a trial in The Hague in 2001, another is acquitted
September 19, 1989	171	A French U.T.A. jet explodes over Niger	The Lebanese Islamic Holy War claims responsibility, France holds Libya responsible
October 2, 1990	128	A hijacked Xiamen Airlines plane crashes into other parked planes in an airport in China	Unknown
March 17, 1992	29	A bomb demolishes the Israeli Embassy in Buenos Aires, Argentina	Unknown
February 26, 1993	6	A van filled with explosives explodes in the garage of the World Trade Center, leaving more than 1,000 people wounded	Ramzi Yousef receives a life sentence plus 240 years in 1998; the FBI suspects Osama bin Laden is behind the plot
April 19, 1995	168	Oklahoma City truck bomb destroys the Alfred P. Murrah federal building	Timothy McVeigh executed June 11, 2001
August 7, 1998	224	Car bombs destroy U.S. embassies in Nairobi, Kenya, and Dar Es Salaam, Tanzania	Al Qaeda (Osama bin Laden)
October 12, 2000	17	Rubber boat filled with explosives detonates next to USS *Code* in Yemen	Al Qaeda (Osama bin Laden)
September 11, 2001	3,000+	Four U.S. commercial airlines hijacked. Two destroy World Trade Center, one hits the Pentagon, one crashes in Pennsylvania	Al Qaeda (Osama bin Laden)
March 11, 2004	191	Bombing of train in Madrid, Spain	Al Qaeda
September 3, 2004	355 (155 children)	Chechen terrorists attack school in Breslan, Russia	Chechen

Source: U.S. Department of State, Office of Counterterrorism, October 2001.

contributed troops, while others, including Pakistan, Saudi Arabia, and Uzbekistan, informally allowed U.S. forces to base operations on their territory. Kabul, the capital of Afghanistan, was occupied by anti-Taliban forces on November 13, 2001.

President Bush made it clear that the United States was prepared to act militarily against governments that harbored or gave sanctuary to terrorists. The Taliban regime was ousted from power. By April 2002—six months into Operation Enduring Freedom—Al Qaeda and Taliban forces had been either destroyed or scattered into small groups in the mountainous areas of Afghanistan and neighboring Pakistan. Osama bin Laden himself, however, escaped capture.

A meeting in Bonn, Germany, of various Afghan political and military groups produced general agreement on the installation of a new government in Kabul, headed by Hamid Karzai. The Karzai government has less than full control over Afghanistan; various tribal military chiefs, or "warlords," exercise independent power throughout the country.

Operation Iraqi Freedom At the end of the Gulf War in 1991, the Iraqi regime of Saddam Hussein agreed to destroy all of its chemical and biological weapons and to end its efforts to acquire nuclear weapons. United Nations inspectors were to verify Iraqi compliance with these conditions. But Saddam's regime refused to cooperate; in 1998 he ordered the inspectors out of the country. Over a twelve-year period Iraq violated at least a dozen U.N. resolutions. Following a U.S. military buildup in the region in late 2002, Saddam allowed U.N. inspectors to return, but continued to obstruct their work. On March 19, 2003, after giving Saddam a forty-eight hour warning to leave Iraq, the United States and Great Britain launched air strikes designed to eliminate Saddam and his top command.

At different times President Bush stated the purposes of "Operation Iraqi Freedom" as (1) the elimination of Iraq's weapons of mass destruction, (2) a "regime change" for Iraq to end the threat that Saddam posed for his neighbors and to free the Iraqi people from his oppressive rule, and (3) to ensure that Saddam would not harbor or assist terrorist organizations. But President Bush and Secretary of State Colin Powell failed to secure U.N. Security Council approval for military action. Among the permanent members of the Security Counsel, only the British, with the strong support of Prime Minister Tony Blair, were prepared to offer significant military support for the war against Saddam. Public opinion in America supported military action, but public opinion in Europe opposed it (see *Compared to What:* "World Opinion about America's War against Terrorism"). France and Germany led the diplomatic opposition; Turkey refused to let U.S. troops use its territory to attack Iraq; and the U.S. was obliged to rely primarily on Kuwait, Qatar, and the other smaller Gulf states for regional support.

The U.S. military wanted to wage war in the fashion of the successful Gulf War—a period of heavy air bombardment to "prepare the battlefield," followed by a massive ground attack using overwhelming military force. But Secretary of Defense Donald Rumsfeld wanted a "leaner" fighting force in Iraq. He deployed fewer than half of the air, ground, and naval forces that had been used in the Gulf War. And he began the air and ground attacks simultaneously.

American and British soldiers and Marines took just twenty-one days to sweep the 350 miles from the Kuwait border to downtown Baghdad. The British 3rd Armored Division, with Australian support, captured the port city of Basra; the U.S. 3rd Infantry Division moved up the west side of the Euphrates River; and the U.S. 1st Marine Division moved up the east side. Special Operations Forces, together with elements of the 101st Airborne Division, joined Kurdish forces in northern

COMPARED TO WHAT?

World Opinion about America's War against Terrorism

Europeans were generally sympathetic with the United States following the terrorist attack of 9/11, and generally supported the U.S. military campaign against terrorists in Afghanistan. But opinion in Europe, as well as in the Moslem world, opposed U.S. military action in Iraq. Indeed, over time ratings of the United States have grown markedly less favorable among Europeans, and United States is now strongly disliked in the Moslem world. An important factor in world opinion about America is the perception that the U.S. acts internationally without taking account of the interests of other nations.

Ratings Of The United States

	2002		2004	
	Favorable	Unfavorable	Favorable	Unfavorable
Great Britain	75	16	58	34
France	63	34	37	62
Germany	61	35	38	59
Russia	61	33	47	44
Turkey	30	42	30	45
Pakistan	10	58	21	50
Jordan	25	57	5	67
Morocco*	27	46	27	46

Source: Pew Research Center for the People and the Press. http://www.people-press.org. Reprinted by permission of Pew Research Center for the People and the Press.

Iraq. Special Operations Forces also acted quickly to secure Iraq's oil fields and prevent their destruction. At first progress was hindered by the requirement that soldiers wear heavy chemical protection gear and carry decontamination equipment. But neither chemical nor biological weapons were used against U.S. forces. The advance on Baghdad was speeded up and the city was captured with precious few casualties.

But the subsequent occupation of Iraq by American troops and attempts to reconstruct a more democratic government in that nation turned out badly. U.S. troops suffered more casualties in the aftermath of the war than during the war itself. Guerilla activity against American and British and other coalition nations' forces, and against Iraqis who appeared to cooperate in the reconstruction of their country, inflicted heavy damage and loss of life. The United States officially turned over sovereignty to an interim Iraqi government before June 30, 2004. But no plans were announced for the withdrawal of American troops from Iraq.

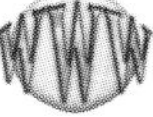

American Security Council

Organization providing summary information on national security threats.
www.ascusa.org

Military Force Levels

Overall military force levels in the United States are threat driven—that is, determined by the size and nature of the perceived threats to national security. It is true that particular weapons systems or base openings or closings may be driven by political forces such as the influence of defense contractors in Congress or the power of a member of Congress from a district heavily affected by defense spending. And not everyone in the White House and Congress, or even in the Defense

THINK AGAIN

Are U.S. military force levels today sufficient to deal with potential regional aggressors such as Iran, Iraq, and North Korea?

Department, agrees on the precise nature of the threats confronting the United States now or in the future. Yet defense policy planning and the "sizing" of U.S. military forces are based on an assessment of the threats confronting the nation.

For nearly a half-century the Soviet threat drove defense policy, force planning, training, strategy and tactics, weapons research and procurement, troop deployments, and defense budgeting. But over the last decade the fundamental change in the world balance of power inspired a complete reexamination of defense policy and force sizing.

Reductions in Forces Post–Cold War military force reductions began in 1990 in the Bush Administration. The initial plan called for a reduction of total U.S. military personnel from 2.1 million to 1.6 million. This plan envisioned a continuing "forward presence" in NATO but reduced U.S. forces in Europe by more than half. Consistent with the view that regional aggressors would be the most likely threats to U.S. interests in the future, forces designed principally to meet these threats, for example, the Marine Corps, suffered fewer cuts.

Iraqi-Equivalent Regional Threats Following the Gulf War (1991–92) military force levels were directed toward "Iraqi-equivalent" regional threats. U.S. military force levels were based on the experience of defeating Iraq speedily and decisively in the Gulf War. But planning also envisioned the possibility that a second aggressor might decide to challenge the United States somewhere else in the world while its forces were involved in an Iraqi-equivalent war. For example, if U.S. forces were involved in the Persian Gulf against Iraq or Iran, North Korea might decide to take advantage of the situation and launch an invasion of South Korea. Therefore the United States planned to maintain sufficient additional U.S. forces to "fight and win two nearly simultaneous major regional conflicts." The ambiguous wording—"nearly simultaneous"—recognized that the United States might not be able to airlift and sealift sufficient forces to fight and win two regional wars at the same time. American forces would be obliged to hold one aggressor (principally with air power) while defeating the other; once one aggressor was defeated, the United States could then redeploy sufficient forces to defeat a second aggressor.

Current Force Levels The Army fields ten active combat divisions. (A U.S. Army division includes 10,000 to 15,000 troops.) The Navy deploys eleven active carrier battle groups. (A carrier battle group typically includes one aircraft carrier with 75 to 85 aircraft, plus defending cruisers, destroyers, frigates, attack submarines, and support ships.) The Marine Corps is scheduled to retain all three of its Marine expeditionary forces (each includes one Marine division, one Marine air wing, and supporting services).

WWW **Global Security** News and information about weapons, forces, and military conflicts around the world. *www.globalsecurity.org*

Criticism Although most defense experts agree on the assessment of the threat—the need to prepare to fight and win two major regional conflicts simultaneously—many believe the projected force levels are inadequate for these tasks. Opponents contend that the reduced numbers of Army and Air Force combat units and the limited transport and support services available to the military are inadequate for two major regional conflicts. Casualties can be kept low only when overwhelming military force is employed quickly and decisively, as it was in Operation Desert Storm. Lives are lost when minimal forces are sent into combat, when they have inadequate air combat support, or when they are extended over too broad a front. Potential regional foes—for example, Iran and North Korea—deploy modern heavy armor and artillery forces. The United States benefited from a six-month buildup of its heavy forces in the Gulf region before Operation Desert Storm began; such a period of preparation is unlikely in a future conflict. The deployment of U.S. troops for humanitarian and "peacekeeping" missions detracts from their readiness to respond to a major regional threat. More important, perhaps, the minimal force levels projected would severely tax the nation's ability to respond to two conflicts simultaneously in opposing parts of the globe. Critics charge current-defense policy and military force levels were determined more by a desire to cut the defense budget than by a careful consideration of the forces required for national security.

Historical Trends in Defense Spending In the early Cold War years, defense spending claimed a major share of U.S. resources (see Figure 14.2). In 1955 defense spending in the United States was 58 percent of all federal expenditures and equaled 10.5 percent of the gross domestic product. By 1965 defense spending had shrunk to 40.1 percent of federal spending and to 7.5 percent of the GDP. The Vietnam War caused defense spending to temporarily surge upward but following President Nixon's decision to gradually withdraw U.S. forces from that conflict, defense spending began a long decline. By 1978 defense spending was down to 23 percent of federal spending and 4.5 percent of the GDP. Reagan's defense buildup brought defense spending up to 6.5 percent of the GDP and 29 percent of the total federal budget by 1986.

The achievement of the Cold War objectives of the U.S. national defense policy led to a welcome result—a lessening of the threat to national security and a reduction in national defense spending. U.S. defense spending steadily declined in real dollars after 1986, U.S. military strength was cut by nearly half. During the Clinton Administration defense spending declined to less than 15 percent of federal spending and less than 3 percent of the nation's GDP. These were levels roughly comparable to those than prevailed before Pearl Harbor was attacked in 1941. The War on Terrorism raised defense spending in 2005 to 19 percent of total federal spending and about 3.5 percent of the GDP.

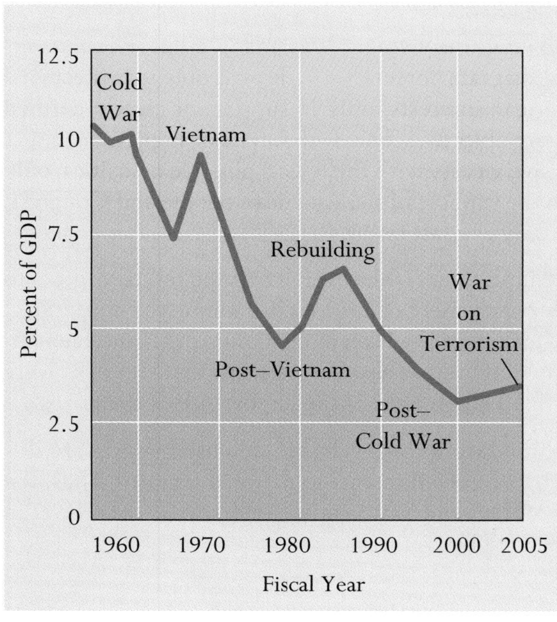

FIGURE 14.2 The Price of Peace: National Defense Outlays as a Percentage of GDP

Current spending on defense is a much smaller percentage of the U.S. gross national product than it was during the Cold War. The 2003 defense budget increased spending for the first time in over a decade.

Source: Budget of the United States Government, 2005.

SUMMARY NOTES

- The struggle for power is global. Leaders and peoples of the world protect and advance their goals and ideals through the exercise of power.
- There is no world government capable of legislating and enforcing rules of international politics. But various efforts to stabilize relations among nations have been attempted, including the balance-of-power system of alliances in the eighteenth and nineteenth centuries, the collective security arrangements of the League of Nations and the United Nations in the twentieth century, and the regional security approach of the North Atlantic Treaty Organization.
- The United Nations was largely ineffective during the Cold War, the confrontation between the Western democracies led by the United States and communist bloc nations led by the Soviet Union. During these years, the Western nations relied principally on the strength of the North Atlantic Treaty Organization (NATO) to deter war in Europe.
- For nearly fifty years, the Cold War largely directed U.S. foreign and defense policy. The United States sought to contain Soviet military expansionism and world communist revolutionary forces in all parts of the globe. U.S. involvement in the Korean and Vietnam wars grew out of this containment policy.
- During the Cold War years, U.S. and Soviet military forces never engaged in direct combat against each other, although many "proxy" conflicts took place throughout the world. The most serious threat of nuclear war occurred during the Cuban missile crisis in 1962.
- To maintain nuclear peace, the United States relied primarily on the policy of deterrence—dissuading the Soviets from launching a nuclear attack by maintaining survivable second-strike forces capable of inflicting unacceptable levels of destruction in a retaliating attack.
- In 1970 President Richard Nixon and National Security Adviser Henry Kissinger began negotiations with the Soviet Union with a view to limiting the nuclear arms race. These Strategic Arms Limitation Talks produced the SALT I agreement in 1972, and later, under President Jimmy Carter, the SALT II agreement in 1979. Both agreements set limits on future strategic weapons development but failed to reduce existing weapons stockpiles.
- President Ronald Reagan renamed the negotiations START, emphasizing the goal of reductions in weapons rather than limitations, and stressing equality and verification. The INF Treaty in 1987 was the first agreement that actually reduced nuclear arms, although it covered only intermediate-range weapons in Europe. Later the START I (1991) and START II (1993) treaties called for reducing nuclear arsenals by two-thirds from Cold War levels.
- The end of the Cold War followed the ouster of communist governments in Eastern Europe in 1989, the unification of Germany in 1990, the collapse of the Warsaw Pact communist military alliance in 1991, and the dissolution of the Soviet Union in 1991. Russia has inherited most of the nuclear weapons and military forces of the former Soviet Union as well as its seat in the UN Security Council.
- Current threats to peace and security are likely to be posed by regional aggressors. U.S. involvement in the Gulf War in 1990–91 is representative of the type of military action most likely to be undertaken in the future. Current defense policy calls for the United States to be prepared to fight two "Iraqi equivalent wars" "nearly simultaneously."
- The military phase of America's War on Terrorism began October 7, 2001, when U.S. aircraft began attacks on Al Qaeda bases in Afghanistan and U.S. special forces organized and led anti-Taliban Afghan fighters to oust the Taliban regime that had harbored the terrorists. These military actions largely destroyed the terrorist infrastructure in Afghanistan; yet scattered groups of terrorists remain in that country and neighboring Pakistan.
- President George W. Bush warned that the War on Terrorism would be a continuing one, but the variety of ways and means and places of potential terrorist attack make it impossible for the United States to guarantee an end to international terrorism.
- Following the Vietnam War, many military leaders argued that U.S. forces should be used only to protect vital American interests, only in support of clearly defined military objectives, only with sufficient strength to ensure decisive victory with the fewest possible casualties, only with the support of the American people and Congress, and only as a last resort.
- Recent presidents, however, have used military forces to carry out a variety of missions in addition to conventional war, including peacekeeping, antiterrorist, and humanitarian activities. They have argued that the risks were worth taking in light of the importance of the goals.
- U.S. military force levels and defense budgets are driven by perceived threats to national security. Thus, the end of the Cold War resulted in dramatic reductions in forces and budgets.

KEY TERMS

collective security 490
Soviet Union 490
superpowers 490
regional security 490
North Atlantic Treaty Organization (NATO) 490
Cold War 491
Truman Doctrine 492
containment 492
Marshall Plan 492
Korean War 492
Cuban Missile Crisis 492
Vietnam War 493
deterrence 496
second-strike capability 496
mutual assured destruction (MAD) 496
SALT I 497
ABM Treaty 497
SALT II 497
START I 497
START II 497
Comprehensive Test Ban Treaty 498
multilateral treaty 498
Nonproliferation Treaty 498
ballistic missile defense (BMD) 499
terrorism 502

SUGGESTED READINGS

Clausewitz, Karl von. *On War.* Edited and translated by Michael Howard and Peter Paret. Princeton, N.J.: Princeton University Press, 1984. The classic theory of war and military operations, emphasizing their political character; first published in 1832.

Hastedt, Glenn P. *American Foreign Policy: Past, Present, Future.* 5th ed. Upper Saddle River, N.J.: Prentice Hall, 2003. A foreign policy text that deals with natural security issues within the broader context of foreign policy.

International Institute for Strategic Studies. *The Military Balance.* London: International Institute for Strategic Studies, published annually. Careful description of the military forces of more than 160 countries; this book is considered the most authoritative public information available.

Kegley, Charles W. *The New Global Terrorism.* Upper Saddle River, N.J.: Prentice Hall, 2003. Describing post-9/11 terrorism, its multiple roots, and leading ideas for winning the "war on global terrorism."

Magstadt, Thomas M. *An Empire If You Can Keep It: Power and Principle in American Foreign Policy.* Washington, D.C.: CQ Press, 2004. Comprehensive text on American foreign policy, describing its history, the Cold War, the Gulf War, September 11, and the War on Terrorism.

Snow, Donald M. *When America Fights: The Uses of U.S. Military Force.* Washington, D.C.: CQ Press, 2000. Questions U.S. military involvement in "peacekeeping" operations. Discusses the use of force in relation to U.S. national interests.

Summers, Harry G., Jr. *On Strategy II: A Critical Analysis of the Gulf War.* New York: Dell, 1992. Analysis of the Gulf War based on Clausewitz's classic principles of war. The strategic decisions leading to victory in the Gulf contrast markedly with the decisions in Vietnam that led to defeat, a topic covered in Summers's groundbreaking first book, *On Strategy: A Critical Analysis of the Vietnam War* (New York: Dell, 1984).

Wilson, George C. *This War Really Matters.* Washington, D.C.: CQ Press, 1999. A description of how defense budgets are constructed by the executive and approved by Congress and a questioning of whether the United States is adequately prepared for likely twenty-first-century wars.

MAKE IT REAL

THE IMPACT OF FOREIGN AID

The primary foreign policy goal of the United States remains, as it has been, to maintain our security and freedom. You are the Chief of Staff to the Secretary of the United States of America. In this simulation, you are presenting and arguing for the budget allocations for the next fiscal year for military aid, development aid, and human welfare.

CHAPTER 15

THE SOCIAL AND ECONOMIC MILIEU OF TEXAS POLITICS

CHAPTER OUTLINE

Decades of Change and Challenge
The Political Culture of Texas
Texas Myths
The People of Texas
Politics, Race, and Ethnicity
The Political Implications of Demographics
The Economy of Texas
Economic Regions of Texas
Transnational Regionalism

THINK ABOUT POLITICS

1 Are politics in Texas different from those of other states?
Yes ● No ●

2 Are Texans more conservative than the citizens of other states?
Yes ● No ●

3 Do race and ethnicity play a major role in Texas politics?
Yes ● No ●

4 Do some groups or interests in Texas have more influence or power than others in public policy decisions?
Yes ● No ●

5 Is Texas in a position to adapt to the global economy?
Yes ● No ●

6 Should Texas give more attention to assisting Mexico to develop a stable political and economic system?
Yes ● No ●

Social and economic factors are directly related to the distribution of political power and help determine who gets what in Texas politics.

Decades of Change and Challenge

Texas entered the twenty-first century with considerable optimism. The state's economy appeared to be in overdrive, continuing to outpace the nation's economy as it had done throughout the 1990s. Unemployment was low, and many individuals were working who previously had difficulty finding jobs and with increased revenues, governments across the state were able to hold the line on taxes while increasing services.

Deregulation of the energy industry was touted as a solution to high energy costs and a guarantee of adequate supplies of power. Commercial and residential construction expanded dramatically, and increased exports, particularly to Mexico, demonstrated the state's links to the global economy. Many of the historic political conflicts seemed to be moving toward resolution, and the president of the United States—George W. Bush—was one of Texas's own.

But this exuberance was soon jolted by a number of events that will shape the politics of the state for years. Excesses in the stock market resulted in reversals of dramatic proportions. Corporations and individuals lost huge amounts of money, and many baby boomers who had assumed that they were adequately prepared for retirement awoke to the reality of evaporating wealth. Enron Corporation, a Houston firm and major player in energy deregulation, engaged in predatory policies and fraudulent accounting that raised questions about financial practices throughout the country when the company collapsed. Recession set in with the loss of jobs and revenues, and governments throughout Texas had to reduce services and trim workers. Illegal immigration from Mexico continued at a rapid pace despite increased efforts to regain control of the border. And finally, the terrorist attacks on the World Trade Center and the Pentagon on September 11, 2001, challenged our long-held assumptions about the basic security of our country and state.

Increasingly, the politics and economy of Texas, often described in terms of the state's uniqueness, are now challenged by global trends. The state's population has been, and will continue to be, transformed by immigration into Texas and changing demographic patterns. The frontier, rural society, characterized by the cowboy, is long gone. The "Oil Patch," where wildcatters and roughnecks once prevailed, has been replaced by what one author dubbed the "Silicon Prairie, . . . where venture capitalists and software engineers roam."[1] The state's economy is now the third largest in the country, following California and New York, and it is becoming more divesified.

UP CLOSE

Perpetuating an Image: The Cowboy President and the "Killer Ds"

As the nation pursued the war on terrorism, President George W. Bush, who has been described by some as the "cowboy president," used a number of allusions to the frontier culture. He branded former Iraqi leader Saddam Hussein an "outlaw" and declared that he wanted terrorist Osama Bin Laden "dead or alive." At a conference in Aqaba on the Red Sea, Bush said that he was going to appoint a coordinator to "ride herd" on Middle East leaders along the peace trail. Many in his audience had no idea what he was talking about, but the characterization of Bush in cartoons and articles as a cowboy continues to feed the perceptions others have of the frontier culture of Texas and its style of politics.

The distorted images that other Americans have of Texans and the state were further reinforced during the 2003 legislative sessions, when House Democrats—characterized as the "Killer Ds"—fled to Ardmore, Oklahoma, and later Senate Democrats flew to Albuquerque, N.M., to delay Republican efforts to redraw congressional districts to favor GOP candidates. The national and world press attempted to sort out these theatrics in light of the state's political culture. Needless to say, the cartoonists had a field day in their caricatures of Texas politicians.

Source: BBC News, June 6, 2003.

Texas still has a rugged, bigger-than-life mystique that annoys or amuses many non-Texans. In many obvious and not-so-obvious ways, Texans continue to manifest this historical legacy of the frontier in their speech, their "can-do" attitude, their celebration of their "Texan-ness," and their actions (see *Up Close:* "Perpetuating an Image: The Cowboy President and the 'Killer Ds'"). In what other state do you find the pervasive display of the state's flag or the pilgrimage of so many to a "holy shrine" such as the Alamo? Behaviors and language with which others take umbrage and often misunderstand are viewed by most Texans to be simply part of the rich culture and legacy of the state.

Vol.XXIV. Beadle & Adams, Publishers, No. 304

TEXAS JACK,

THE PRAIRIE RATTLER; or, THE QUEEN OF THE WILD RIDERS.

BY HON. WM. F. CODY "Buffalo Bill."

The dime novel helped create the myth of Texas individualism by popularizing and exaggerating the image of the cowboy.

Other states have been forced to deal with the same issues confronting Texas, and in many cases their citizens demanded a more expanded role of government in problem solving. But Texas's strong rural roots and its legacy of individualism and limited government have made it more difficult for this state to adjust to a changing economy, a changing society, and a changing political landscape.

In one respect, Texans are no different from people across the country. They are woefully ignorant of their state and local governments. They view govenment as something in Austin or at the courthouse, which does things to us, not for us. Government is often described in terms of red tape, inefficiency, and rude bureaucrats, and political campaigns are perceived as a form of organized mud wrestling. Most Texans don't vote in elections. At the same time, they expect a wide variety of public services but don't want to pay for them with higher taxes.

Sustained population growth over the past four decades, however, has made it increasingly difficult for state and local governments to provide basic services within the framework of Texas's outdated tax system. Highway construction can't keep pace with increased traffic. Population growth has strained public school budgets and increased environmental risks. Although some Texans enjoy enormous wealth, more than 20 percent of the state's children are poverty stricken. Many Texans have limited or no access to quality health care, and that problem is growing because of poverty and an aging population. The continued flow of illegal immigration also has a tremendous impact on governmental budgets.

These problems and issues are the ingredients of contemporary Texas politics. They reflect the fundamental conflicts between competing interests and the way Texans decide who gets "what, when, and how."[2] Unfortunately, only a small part of the population is involved in developing solutions.

As we begin our analysis of Texas government and politics, we ask why Texans and their public officials make the political choices they do. Why, for example, do expenditures for public education rank low in comparison to other states? How do we account for Texas's highly regressive tax system, which requires low-income citizens to pay a higher proportion of their income in state and local taxes than do the wealthy? Why are Texans so willing to fund the construction of highways and roads while letting their state rank near the bottom of all the states in expenditures for public welfare?[3] Why, until recently, was Texas a one-party Democratic state? Why are state politics now dominated by Republicans?

Texans pay the costs, even though they may not receive the benefits of every policy decision. The actions and decisions of governmental leaders can have an immediate and direct effect on people's lives, and, from time to time, those holding positions of power have made decisions that have cost Texans dearly. For example, the Enron debacle and the manipulation of energy markets were the result, in large part, of the failure of state and federal governments to regulate the energy industry adequately. And major cuts in governmental services in 2003 were the direct result of the Texas legislature's refusal to increase taxes to offset the loss of revenue caused by the downturn in the state's economy.

This chapter will introduce you to the people of Texas, the views they have of themselves, the state's political subcultures and economy, and the increased interdependence of Texas and Mexico. We refer to these factors generally as the *political environment,* a concept developed by political scientist David Easton to describe the milieu or context in which political institutions function.[4]

The Texas Rangers played an important (but sometimes controversial) role in the taming of the Texas frontier.

The Political Culture of Texas

Texas shares the common institutional and legal arrangements that have developed in all fifty states, including a commitment to personal liberties, equality, justice, the rule of law, and popular sovereignty with its limitations on government. But there are differences among the states and even among regions within individual states. Texas is a highly diverse state, with racial and ethnic differences from one region to another and divergences in political attitudes and behavior that are reflected in the state's politics and public policies.

The concept of political culture (see Chapter 2) helps us compare some of these differences. **Political culture** has been defined as "the set of attitudes, beliefs, and sentiments which give order and meaning to a political process and which provide the underlying assumptions and rules that govern behavior in the political system."[5] The political culture of the state includes fundamental beliefs about the proper role of government, the relationship of the government to its citizens, and who should govern.[6]

One authority on American political culture, Daniel Elazar, believes that three political subcultures have emerged over time in the United States: the individualistic, the moralistic, and the traditionalistic. While all three draw from the common historical legacy of the nation, they have produced regional political differences. Sometimes they complement each other; at other times they produce conflict.[7]

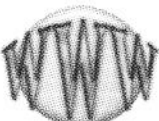

State of Texas – Texas Online

The state's web page provides links to state agencies, local and county governments, and councils of states, where a wide array of governmental, demographic, and economic data can be located.
http://www.state.tx.us

THINK AGAIN

Are Texans more conservative than the citizens of other states?

political culture Widely shared set of views, attitudes, beliefs, and customs of a people as to how their government should be organized and run.

The Individualistic Subculture The political view of the **individualistic subculture** holds that politics and government function as a marketplace. Government does not have to be concerned with creating a good or moral society but exists for strictly "utilitarian reasons, to handle those functions demanded by the people it is created to serve."[8] Government should be limited, and its intervention in the private activities of its citizens kept to a minimum. The primary function of government is to assure the stability of a society so that individuals can pursue their own interests.

In this view, politics is not a high calling or noble pursuit but is like any other business venture in which skill and talent prevail and the individual can anticipate economic and social benefits. Politics is often perceived by the general public to be a dirty business that should be left to those willing to soil their hands. This tradition may well contribute to political corruption, and members of the electorate who share this view may not be concerned when governmental corruption is revealed.

The Moralistic Subculture The **moralistic subculture** regards politics as one of the "great activities of man in his search for the good society."[9] Politics, it maintains, is the pursuit of the common good. Unlike the attitude expressed in the individualistic subculture that governments are to be limited, the moralistic subculture considers government a positive instrument with a responsibility to promote the general welfare. Politics, therefore, is not to be left to the few but is a responsibility of every individual. Politics is a duty and possibly a high calling. This cultural tradition has a strong sense of service. It requires a high standard for those holding public office and believes public office is not to be used for personal gain. Politics may be organized around political parties, but this tradition has produced nonpartisanship, in which party labels and organizations are eliminated or play a reduced role. This tradition produces a large number of "amateur" or "nonprofessional" political activists and officeholders and has little toleration for political corruption. From the moralistic perspective, governments should actively intervene to enhance the social and economic lives of their citizens.

individualistic subculture View that government should interfere as little as possible in the private activities of its citizens while assuring that adequate public facilities and a favorable business climate are available to permit individuals to pursue their self-interests.

moralistic subculture View that government's primary responsibility is to promote the public welfare and that it should actively use its authority and power to improve the social and economic well-being of its citizens.

traditionalistic subculture View that political power should be concentrated in the hands of a few elite citizens who belong to established families or influential social groups. Public policy basically serves the interests of this small group.

elite Small group of people who exercise disproportionate power and influence in the policy-making processes.

The Traditionalistic Subculture The **traditionalistic** political **subculture** holds the political view that there is a hierarchical arrangement to the political order. This hierarchy serves to limit the power and influence of the general public, while allocating authority to a few individuals who constitute a self-perpetuating **elite.** The elite may enact policies that benefit the general public, but that is secondary to its interests and objectives. Public policy reflects the interests of those who exercise influence and control, and the benefits of public policy go disproportionately to the elite.

Family and social relationships form the basis for maintaining this elite structure, rather than mass political participation. In fact, in many regions of the country where traditionalistic patterns existed, there were systematic efforts to reduce or eliminate the participation of the general public. Although political parties may exist in such a subculture, they have only minimal importance. Many of the states characterized by the traditionalistic subculture were southern states in which two-party politics was replaced.[10]

Historical Origins of Political Subcultures The historical origins of these three subcultures can be explained, in part, by the early settlement patterns of the United States and by the cultural differences among the groups of people who initially settled the eastern seaboard. In very general terms, the New England colonists, influenced by Puritan and congregational religious groups, spawned the moralistic subculture. Settlers with entrepreneurial concerns and individualistic attitudes tended to locate in the mid-Atlantic states, while the initial settlement of the South was dominated by elites who aspired, in part, to recreate a semi-feudal society.

As expansion toward the frontiers progressed, Texas was settled primarily by people holding the individualistic and traditionalistic views of a political system. The blending of these two views, along with the historical experience of the Republic and the frontier, contributed to the distinct characteristics of Texas's political culture.[11]

These two political subcultures have merged to shape Texans' general views of what governments should do, who should govern, and what constitutes good public policy. Consequently Texas's dominant political culture is conservative. Politics in Texas tends to minimize the role of government, is hostile toward taxes—especially those that are allocated toward social services—and is potentially manipulated by the few for their narrow advantages.

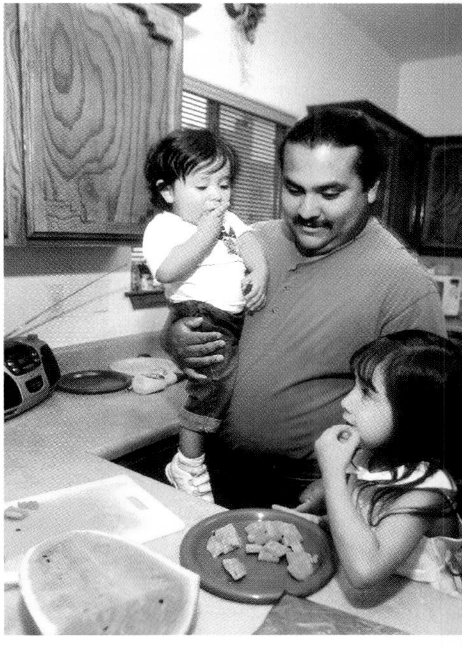

A Tigua father prepares a meal for his children. The Tiguas are one of only three Native American groups with reservations in Texas.

Texas Myths

In recent years, serious scholarship has focused on myths as ways to assess the views people have of their common historical and cultural experiences. A myth can be regarded as a "mode of truth . . . that codifies and preserves moral and spiritual values" for a particular culture or society.[12] Myths are stories or narratives that are used to describe past events, explain their significance to successive generations, and provide an interpretive overview and understanding of a society.

Texas has produced its own *myth of origin,* which continues to be a powerful statement about the political system and the social order on which it is based.[13] For many Texans, the battle of the Alamo clearly serves to identify the common experiences of independence and the creation of a separate, unique political order. No other state was a **republic** prior to joining the Union, and several scholars argue that independence and "going at it alone" from 1836 to 1845 resulted in a cultural experience that distinguishes the Texas political system from that of other states. The state's motto—the Lone Star State—is a constant reminder of this unique history.

The Texas mythology also includes the Texas Ranger and the cowboy. There is considerable lore of the invincible, enduring ranger defeating overwhelming odds. Newspapers and dime novels in the nineteenth century introduced readers throughout the United States to the cowboy, who often was portrayed as an honest, hardworking individual wrestling with the harsh Texas environment. The cowboy's rugged **individualism,** with strong connotations of self-help, symbolizes a political culture in Texas that does not like to look to government as a solution to many problems.[14]

Space, distance, and size are pervasive themes in a great deal of Texana literature. Although most Texans live in urban areas, the perceptions of a huge landmass and "wide open spaces" that are to be exploited for personal gain shape Texans' optimistic, "can do" attitudes and their views of personal autonomy and independence.

The Texas myths, however, have been primarily the myths of the white (Anglo) population and have limited relevance to the cultural and historical experiences of many African American and Hispanic Texans. From the 1840s to the mid-1960s, these latter groups were excluded from full participation in Texas politics and the state's economic and social life. To many Hispanics, for example, the Texas Ranger is not a hero but a symbol of ruthless suppression.

As the demographic characteristics of the state changes, historical events that are more relevant to Hispanics and African Americans are likely to be incorporated

republic Form of government in which representatives of the people, rather than the people themselves, govern.

individualism Attitude, rooted in classical liberal theory and reinforced by the frontier tradition, that citizens are capable of taking care of themselves with minimal governmental assistance.

One of many activities celebrating Martin Luther King, Jr.'s birthday, which is now a national and state holday, was held outside the Texas state capitol.

into the mythology of the state. These revisions may already be under way, as demonstrated in increased attention given to such events as Martin Luther King, Jr.'s birthday, now celebrated as a state holiday, and Cinco de Mayo, a celebration of Mexico's defeat of the French forces on May 5, 1862, in the Batalla de Puebla (Battle of Puebla).

The People of Texas

The politics and government of Texas can be understood, in part, from the perspective of the people living in the state. What follows is a descriptive analysis of a select number of demographic characteristics of Texans. In subsequent chapters,

Throughout Texas, Cinco de Mayo is celebrated by Hispanics in commemoration of Mexico's defeat of French troops at Puebla, Mexico, in 1862.

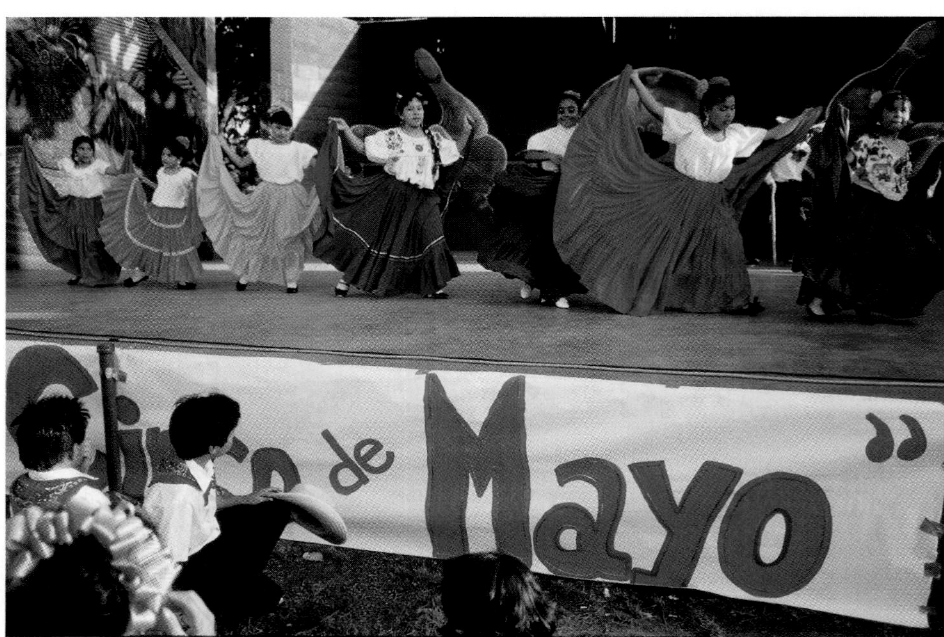

we examine the relationship of race, ethnicity, and other demographic characteristics to partisan behavior, public opinion, institutional power, and public policy.

Native Americans There are only three small Native American groups (Alabama-Coushatta, Tigua, and Kickapoo) living on reservations in Texas, and the Native American population is less than one-half of 1 percent of the state's total population.[15] Unlike Native American populations in Oklahoma, New Mexico, and Arizona, those in Texas have little influence on governmental institutions, politics, or public policy.

In the early nineteenth century, there were at least twenty-three different Native American groups residing in Texas. As the European populations expanded to lands traditionally claimed by various Native American groups, conflict ensued, and most of the Native American population was eventually eliminated or displaced to other states.[16]

The Native American Legacy of Texas remains in the state's name. The word "Texas" came from the word "Tejas," which means friends or allies. As Spanish explorers and missionaries moved across Texas, they confronted a native American confederacy, the Hasinai. It was to this particular group that they applied the term, and eventually the Anglo form of the name became the permanent name of the region and then the state.

THINK AGAIN

Do race and ethnicity play a major role in Texas politics?

U.S. Bureau of the Census

Population and economic data for the state are provided by the Bureau of the Census, which conducts the decennial census and a wide range of demographic studies between censuses. For state and county data, use "State and County Quick Facts" or "American Factfinder."
http://www.census.gov

Hispanics In the eighteenth and nineteenth centuries, neither Spain nor Mexico was very successful in convincing Hispanics to settle in the Tejas territory of Mexico. The Spanish regarded it as a border province with relatively little value except as a strategic buffer between Spanish colonies and those held by the British and the French. By the time Mexico declared its independence from Spain in 1821, the total Texas population under Spanish control was estimated to be approximately 5,000. With the rapid expansion of Anglo American immigration to Texas in the 1820s and 1830s, Hispanics became a small minority of the population.[17]

Some Hispanics were part of the Texas independence movement from Mexico, and after independence in 1836, men such as José Antonio Navarro and Juan Seguin were part of the Republic's political establishment. But the Anglo migration rapidly overwhelmed the Hispanic population and greatly reduced its political and economic power.

By 1887, the Hispanic population had declined to approximately 4 percent of the state's total. In 1930, it was 12 percent and was concentrated in the border counties from Brownsville to El Paso (see Figure 15.1). There were modest increases in the Hispanic population until it reached 18 percent of the state's population in 1970, after which it grew at a more rapid rate. By 2000, it had reached 32 percent, spurred by immigration from Mexico and other Latin American countries as well as by higher birth rates among Hispanic women. In addition to their traditional concentrations in the Rio Grande Valley and South-Central Texas, large Hispanic populations are found in most metropolitan areas. Except for the Asian population, which is still considerably smaller, the Hispanic population is growing at a significantly higher rate than other populations in Texas.

Hispanics will continue to increase at a higher rate than most other populations, and by 2010, the Hispanic population is likely to exceed 37 percent of the state's total; by 2020, this figure may grow to 42 percent.[18] This growth already has produced significant political power and influence. Four Hispanics have been elected to statewide office. And, after successful redistricting and legal challenges to city, county, school board, and state legislative districts, Hispanics in 2003 held some 1,965 elected positions in Texas, the highest number of any state.[19]

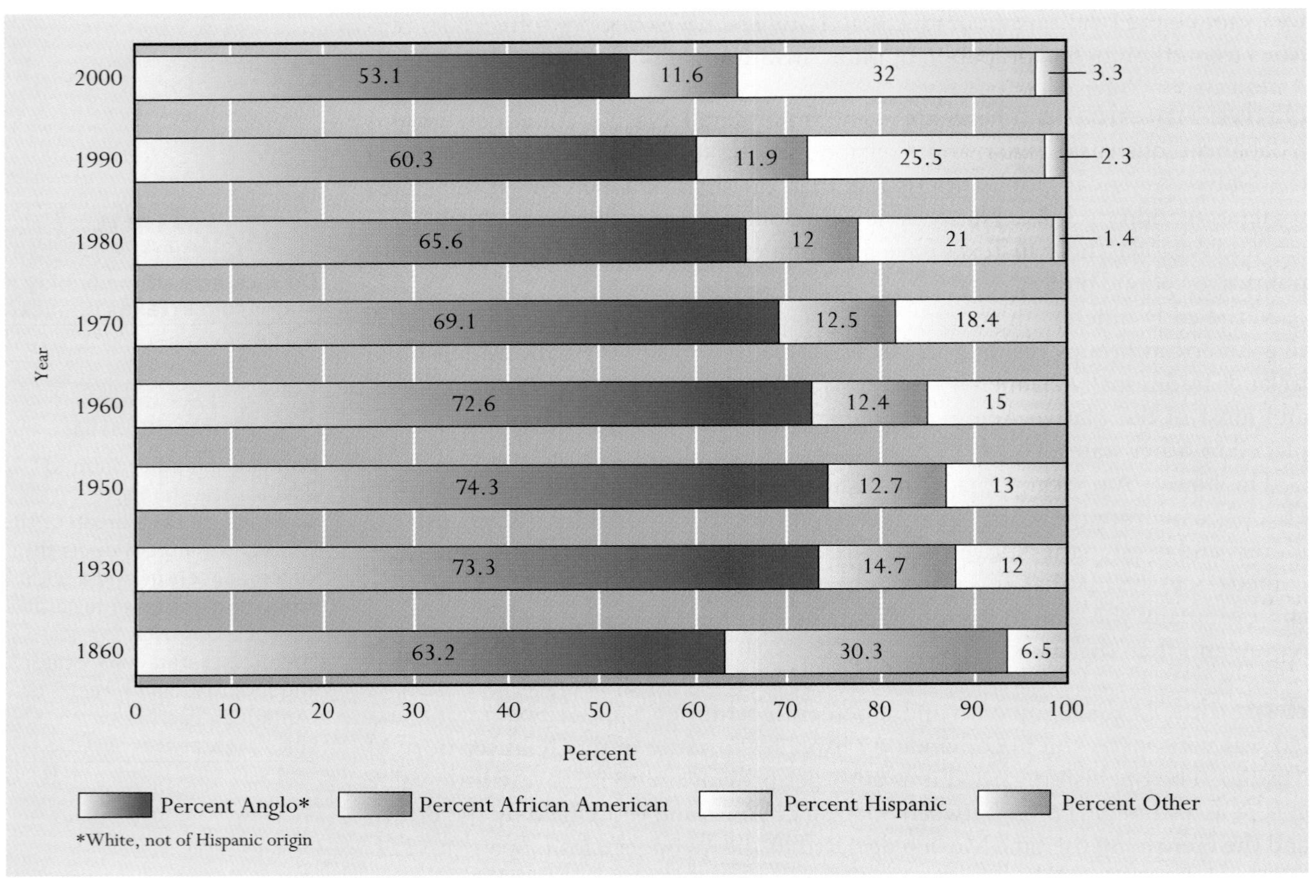

FIGURE 15.1 Ethnic and Racial Composition of Texas, 1860–2000

Note: Data for Asian and other populations not tabulated by the Bureau of the Census prior to 1980. Spanish total for 1970 based on "Persons of Spanish language or surname."

Source: Terry G. Jordan with John L. Bean, Jr., and William M. Holmes, *Texas: A Geography* (Boulder: Westview Press, 1984), pp. 81, 83; U.S. Censuses 1860–2000; Texas State Center.

African Americans Some African Americans lived in Texas during the colonization period, but the modern story of African American settlement did not begin until after independence in 1836. When Texas was part of Mexico, Mexican law restricted slavery within the territory. During the period of the Republic and early statehood prior to the U.S. Civil War, there was a significant increase in the African American population as Americans settling in Texas brought cotton cultivation and the slavery system with them. At the time of the Civil War, 30 percent of the state's residents were African American, but that percentage declined after the war. By 1960, it had leveled off to 12 percent, about the same level counted in the 2000 census (see Figure 15.1). African Americans are expected to represent between 11 percent and 12 percent of the state's population during the next twenty-five years.

There is a large concentration of African Americans in East Texas, where white southerners and their slaves originally settled. African Americans are also concentrated in the urban areas of Dallas, Fort Worth, Austin, and Houston. Relatively few African Americans live in the western counties or in the counties along the border with Mexico. The increased number of African American state legislators, city council members, county commissioners, and school board trustees representing urban communities is an indication of the political power of the African American population in selected areas. In 2001, the most recent year for which data were available, there were 460 African American elected officials in Texas. Four African Americans have been elected to statewide office.[20]

Anglos In the vernacular of Texas politics, the white population is referred to as "Anglos," although there is no census designation by that name. The term includes Jews, Irish, Poles, and just about any other individual who is designated by the U.S. Bureau of the Census as "non-Hispanic white."

Scholars have identified two distinct early patterns of Anglo migration into Texas from other states. These patterns, as well as population movements through much of the late nineteenth and early twentieth centuries, largely explain the regional locations of the state's two dominant political subcultures.

In the early nineteenth century, the first Anglos moving to Texas were from the upper South—Tennessee, Kentucky, Arkansas, and North Carolina—a region significantly influenced by the individualistic subculture of limited government. The earliest settlements were primarily in what is now Northeast Texas in the Red River Valley. After Mexican independence from Spain, there was a second wave of immigration from the upper South. Few of the early colonists were plantation slaveholders from the lower South.

After Texas became independent, slavery was legalized, and settlers from the lower South began arriving. By the outbreak of the Civil War, Anglos who had moved to Texas from the lower South were roughly equal in number to those from the upper South. Arrivals from the slaveholding lower South initially settled in southeastern Texas near Louisiana, but soon they began to move northward and westward.

A line between Texarkana and San Antonio in effect divides Texas subcultures. Most of those Anglos who settled north and west of this line were from the upper South and heavily influenced by the individualistic subculture, which favors limited government. Anglos who settled south and east of the line were by and large from the lower South and shaped by its traditionalistic subculture.

This pattern of immigration and settlement continued after the Civil War. It was primarily those populations from the upper South who pushed westward to the Panhandle and West Texas. This expansion introduced into the western part of the state the cultural experience of those who resisted the notion that government existed to solve society's ills. To this day, West Texas is still one of the most politically conservative areas of the state.[21]

In 1860, Anglos constituted approximately 63 percent of Texas' population (see Figure 15.1). The Anglo population increased until it reached 74 percent in 1950. With the stabilization of the African American population and the increase in the Hispanic population, Anglos accounted for only 53.1 percent of Texas's population in 2000. The Anglo population will continue to decline as a percentage of the total population in the next three decades.

Asian Americans In 1980, Asian Americans accounted for .8 percent of Texas's population, but by 2000 the figure had grown to 2.7 percent and is projected to increase to 4.2 percent by 2020. This rapid increase parallels national trends. Changes in immigration policy and the dislocation of Asians due to war and political persecution have resulted in larger numbers of Asian immigrants entering the United States and Texas since the 1970s. The largest concentration of this population is in Houston, where several Asian Americans have been elected to public offices.

Politics, Race, and Ethnicity

Texas State Data Center and Office of the State Demographer

The Texas State Data Center "functions as a focal point for the distribution of Census information for Texas."
http://txsdc.utsa.edu

Today few Texans go running around the state wearing Ku Klux Klan robes, burning crosses or marching in support of white supremacy, but there still are occasions of extreme racial violence and cruelty, such as the murder of James Byrd, Jr., who was dragged to death in early 1999 near Jasper in East Texas. A state law barring African Americans from voting in party primaries was declared unconstitutional in the 1940s, and many other laws intended to reduce the political participation of African Americans and Hispanics have been eliminated. The federal Voting Rights Act, which was enacted in 1965 and extended to Texas in 1975, has also helped open up state and local electoral systems to minorities. A series of laws and court decisions has outlawed discrimination in housing, education, and employment opportunities. The state's budget crisis of 2003 resulted in budget cuts for health and social programs that fell heavily on minority Texans.

Over the past three decades, there has been bitter debate about redistricting of political districts to increase Hispanic and African American representation on city councils, school boards, and special districts, and in the state legislature and the U.S. Congress. Many state and local elections show evidence of polarized voting along ethnic lines, and there are significant demographic differences between the two major political parties. Most Hispanics and African Americans identify with the Democratic Party.

More than forty years ago, V.O. Key, a Texan scholar of American politics, concluded that Texas politics was moving from issues of race to issues of class and economics. He argued that voters in Texas "divide along class lines in accord with their class interests as related to liberal and conservative candidates."[22] In part, he was correct, in that unabashed racial bigotry and public demagoguery are no longer acceptable. In part, though, he was incorrect and much too optimistic. If the state divides on economic issues, this division puts the majority of Anglos on one side and the majority of Hispanics and African Americans on the other.[23]

The Political Implications of Demographics

Population Increase Over the past fifty years, the population of Texas has increased much faster than the national average. According to the 2000 census, the state's population was 20,851,820, an increase of approximately 4 million people in ten years and it is projected to grow to 24.3 million in 2010. In the last decade of the twentieth century, the state's population grew by 22.8 percent, significantly higher than the national growth rate of 13.2 percent.[24] Texas is now the second most populous state.

High birth rates explain part of the population increase, but migration from other states has also been a significant factor. In recent decades, demographers (those who study populations) have described a nationwide shift in population from the Northeast and Midwest to the South and West. For each of the censuses from 1940 to 1970, in-migration accounted for less than 10 percent of Texas's growth. But in-migration jumped to 58.5 percent of the total growth between 1970 and 1980. Between 1980 and 1990, it contributed 34.4 percent, and approximately 23 percent between 1990 and 2000.[25]

Although it is expected to become less significant in the future, in-migration from other states has already contributed to the restructuring of Texas's traditional one-party, Democratic political system into a Republican-dominated system. Many new residents came from states with strong Republican Party traditions and brought their party affiliation with them. In the long run, in-migration may affect additional elements of the state's political culture.

Texas also attracts individuals from other countries. Approximately 2.9 million, or 14 percent of Texas residents, were identified as foreign-born in the 2000 census. Between 1990 and 2000, approximately 1.4 million, or 6.4 percent, of the state's population arrived from other countries. More than 70 percent of Texans born in other countries come from Latin America. Approximately ten percent of all Texas residents are not U.S. citizens, a fact that has several implications.[26]

Citizenship is directly related to political participation, and noncitizens, while counted in the census for reapportionment of congressional seats, cannot vote. Most noncitizens are Hispanic.

Under current federal policy, noncitizens have been denied access to some public social services that are funded in whole or in part by the national government. Needy immigrants are especially affected by such policies, and in some instances, the state has found it necessary to use its own funds to provide services.

The Aging Population Texans, along with other Americans, are aging. In 2000, the median age of the state's population was 32.3 years compared to 35.3 for the entire country. Approximately 10 percent of Texans were older than sixty-five in 2000, and that group was expected to increase to 17 percent by 2030.[27] This aging population will place unprecedented demands on the public and private sectors for goods and services, including expanded health care and long-term care. In recent years, increasing state expenditures under the Medicaid programs for long-term nursing care have strained the state's budget and forced the state to shift priorities in public programs.

Urbanization Although Texas was a rural state during the first one hundred years of its history, 83 percent of the state's population in 2000 resided in urban areas (Table 15.1). **Urbanization** and suburban sprawl now characterize Texas's settlement patterns, and urban corridors and suburban areas cross county boundaries. Residents of these areas often encounter problems that cut across political jurisdictions, and local governments sometimes find it difficult to resolve them.

The dramatic growth of Texas's largest cities is shown in Table 15.2. From 1960 to 2000, the population of Houston and El Paso more than doubled. Dallas increased by approximately 74 percent and San Antonio, 94 percent. Arlington had a population of only 44,775 in 1960, but in 2000 its population was 332,969, an increase of 744 percent. During this forty-year period, Austin's population increased by 352 percent.

Three of the ten largest cities in the United States are in Texas, and, like urban areas throughout the country, Texas's largest cities are increasingly populated by minority and low-income populations. This trend results from higher birth rates among minority populations, urban migration patterns, and what is often referred to as "white flight" from the cities to suburban areas. Minority groups now account for the majority of the population in five of Texas's ten largest cities (Houston, San Antonio, Dallas, El Paso, and Corpus Christi). These minority residents include Hispanics, African Americans, and Asian Americans—groups that do not always constitute a cohesive bloc of interests. As minority growth continues, areas of potential conflict will emerge among these groups.

Wealth and Income Distribution There is a wide disparity in the distribution of income and wealth across the state. In 1999, the median household income in Texas was $39,327, and the median family income was $45,861, both

urbanization Process by which a predominantly rural society or area becomes urban.

TABLE 15.1 Urban-Rural Population of Texas

	Urban		Rural		
Year	Percentage	Population	Percentage	Population	Total
1850	4	7,665	96	204,927	212,592
1860	4	26,615	96	577,600	604,215
1870	7	54,521	93	764,058	818,579
1880	9	146,795	91	1,444,954	1,591,749
1890	16	359,511	84	1,886,016	2,245,527
1900	17	520,759	83	2,527,951	3,048,710
1910	24	938,104	76	2,958,438	3,896,542
1920	32	1,512,689	68	3,150,539	4,663,228
1930	41	2,389,148	59	3,435,367	5,824,715
1940	45	2,911,389	55	3,503,435	6,414,824
1950	63	4,838,050	37	2,873,134	7,711,194
1960	75	7,187,470	25	2,392,207	9,579,677
1970	80	8,922,211	20	2,274,519	11,196,730
1980	80	11,333,017	20	2,836,174	14,229,191
1990	80	13,634,517	20	3,351,993	16,986,510
2000	83	17,204,073	17	3,647,747	20,851,820

Source: U.S. Bureau of the Census, U.S. Censuses 1850–2000.

below national income levels (see Table 15.3). Thirty-one percent of Texas households reported incomes less than $25,000 per year. These data obscure the fact that there are Texans who made millions of dollars in 1999 and had assets in the hundreds of millions or several billions of dollars. *Forbes* magazine conducts an annual survey of the 400 richest Americans. Thirty-six Texans made the list in 2003, including 26 billionaires with a reported worth ranging from $1.1 billion to $20.5 billion.[28]

On all measures of income, Hispanics and African Americans fall significantly below the Anglo population. According to the 2000 census, 32 percent of Hispanic households and 35 percent of African American households in Texas reported incomes below $20,000, but only 21 percent of Anglo households and a similar por-

TABLE 15.2 Ten Largest Cities, 1900–2000

City	1900	1920	1940	1960	1980	1990	2000
Houston	44,633	138,276	384,514	838,219	1,595,138	1,630,553	1,953,631
Dallas	42,638	158,976	294,734	679,684	904,078	1,006,877	1,188,580
San Antonio	53,321	161,379	253,854	587,718	785,880	935,933	1,144,646
Austin	22,258	34,876	87,960	186,545	345,496	465,622	656,562
El Paso	15,906	77,560	96,810	276,687	425,259	515,342	563,662
Fort Worth	26,688	106,482	177,662	356,268	385,164	447,619	534,694
Arlington	1,079	3,031	4,240	44,775	160,113	261,721	332,969
Corpus Christi	4,703	10,522	57,301	167,690	231,999	257,453	277,454
Plano	1,304	1,715	1,582	3,695	72,331	128,713	222,030
Garland	819	1,421	2,233	38,501	132,857	180,650	215,768

Source: U.S. Censuses, 1900–2000.

tion of the Asian American population reported incomes below that level. By contrast, 43 percent of Anglo households but only 25 percent of Hispanic households and 27 percent of African-American households reported incomes above $50,000.[29]

Many Texans live in severe poverty. Some of the nation's poorest counties are in Texas. These are border counties (Dimmit, Hidalgo, Maverick, Starr, Willacy, Zapata, and Zavala) with large Hispanic populations and unemployment rates that are twice the state average. The per capita income (total state income divided by the population) for Texas was $19,617 in 1999. For the Anglo population, it was significantly higher, $26,197, but for African Americans, the figure was $14,253, and for Hispanics, $16,770.

In 2003, the poverty level guidelines used in Texas to establish eligibility for many federal and state programs were $18,660 for a family of four and $9,393 for one person. According to the U.S. Bureau of the Census, 16.3 percent of the state's population, or 3.5 million people, fell below the poverty level. Nationally, 12.5 percent or 35.9 million persons fell below the poverty level in 2003. The impact of poverty was felt disproportionately by children, particularly those living in one-parent households, Hispanics, and African Americans.[30]

Financial resources can be translated into political power and influence through campaign contributions, funding one's own campaign for public office, access to the mass media, and active support for policy think tanks, interest groups and lobbying activities. Wealth is not the only dimension of political power, but some Texans obviously have the potential for much greater clout than others.

Education and Literacy Public education has been a dominant issue in state politics for many years now. Litigation has forced the legislature to struggle with changes in the funding of public schools, and education will be a primary factor in determining whether Texas can successfully compete in a new global economy.

Over the next decade, a large proportion of the new jobs created in Texas will be in service industries. Most of these jobs will require increased reading, writing, and math skills, and high school dropouts will find fewer and fewer employment opportunities for decent paying jobs. Some experts predict that 50 percent of the

TABLE 15.3 U.S and Texas Income Figures

	U.S.	Texas					
	All Persons	All Persons	Anglos	Hispanics	African American	Native American	Asian American
Median income*							
Household	$41,494	$39,927	$47,162	$29,873	$29,305	$34,926	$50,049
Families	50,046	45,861	57,194	30,840	33,276	37,503	57,103
Per capita income*	21,690	19,617	26,197	16,770	14,253	15,899	20,956
Percent of persons below poverty level	12.4%	15.4%	7.8%	25.4%	23.4%	19.3%	11.9%

*1999 dollars.

Source: Bureau of the Census, 2000 *Census of Population.*

jobs that will be created in the United States in the next decade will require a college education, compared to only 22 percent in the mid-1990s.[31] Texas faces a crisis in public education, and the state's ability to resolve it will directly affect the financial well-being of many Texans.

According to the 2000 census, 75.7 percent of Texans age twenty-five and older had completed high school, and 23.8 percent had completed college (Table 15.4). Educational attainment improved between 1990 and 2000, and positive changes were reported for all racial or ethnic groups in the state.[32] But there continued to be wide disparities in the educational levels of the three major ethnic-racial groups. In 2000, 87 percent of the Anglo population reported that they had completed high school, and 30 percent had college degrees. By contrast, 49 percent of the Hispanic population had high school degrees but only 8.9 percent reported that they had a college degree. Some 76 percent of African Americans graduated from high school, with 15 percent indicating they had college degrees. What is particularly compelling in the 2000 census data is the level of education reported for the Asian American population. Approximately 48 percent reported college degrees.

Education not only helps determine a person's employment and income potential but also affects his or her participation in politics. Individuals with high educational levels are much more likely to believe they can influence the actions of policy makers, be informed about politics, and participate in the political process than those who are less educated.

THINK AGAIN

Is Texas in a position to adapt to the global economy?

Office of the Comptroller

The comptroller's office produces reports on state finances and studies of select facets of the state's economy.
http://www.cpa.state.tx.us

The Economy of Texas

Politics, government, and economics are inextricably linked. An economy that is robust and expanding provides far more options to government policy makers than an economy in recession. A healthy tax base is dependent on an expanding economy, and when the economy goes through periods of recession, state and local governments are confronted with the harsh realities of having to increase taxes or cut back on public services, usually at a time when more people are in need of governmental assistance.

At the beginning of the 1980s, Texas had experienced a sustained period of growth, and state government adopted new policies and expanded existing services with only minimal tax increases. But by 1991, the state had experienced a decade of economic

TABLE 15.4 Texas and United States Educational Attainment by Race and Ethnicity 2000 (for population 25 and Older)

	United States		Texas	
	High School Degree	College Degree	High School Degree	College Degree
Anglo*	85.4%	27.0%	87.2%	30.0%
Hispanic	52.4	10.5	49.3	8.9
African American	72.3	14.3	75.8	15.4
Native American	71.0	11.5	71.6	15.7
Asian	80.4	44.1	80.7	47.8
All Persons	80.4	24.4	75.7	23.8

*White, not of Hispanic origin.

Source: U.S. Bureau of the Census, 2000 *Census of the Population.*

boom and bust with two severe recessions, and the legislature had been forced to tighten up on public services and impose a series of significant tax increases.

Historically, the health of the Texas economy had been linked to oil and natural gas. In 1981, for example, 27 percent of the state's economy was tied to energy-related industries. The decade started with rapid increases in the world price of oil, and there was an economic boom throughout the financial, construction, and manufacturing sectors of the state's economy.[33]

But a series of national and international events soon produced major problems. World oil prices began to drop in 1981, resulting in serious unemployment problems in the Gulf Coast and Plains regions of the state. There was a disastrous decline in the value of the Mexican peso, which had a negative impact on the economies of border cities and counties, and in 1983, a harsh freeze in South Texas and a severe drought in West Texas had serious adverse effects on the agricultural sector. Some regions of the state were insulated from these conditions, but other areas experienced a significant economic downturn.[34]

Economic disaster struck again in 1986, with a 60 percent drop in the price of oil and corresponding reductions in the price of natural gas. Drilling activity in the state plummeted and was followed by a loss of 84,000 energy-related jobs. The problem was compounded by a worldwide slump in the electronics industry. These events hurt the construction and real estate sectors of the economy and, in turn, manufacturing and retail trade. For sixteen straight months in 1986 and 1987, the state's employment rate dropped, with a loss of an estimated 233,000 jobs.[35] These economic reversals, in turn, had a disastrous effect on Texas's banks and savings and loan institutions, many of which failed.

State and local governments consequently suffered declines in revenues. With falling property values, local governments that depended on the property tax were particularly vulnerable. The legislature convened in special session in 1986 to pass an $875 million tax bill and cut the state budget by about $580 million in an attempt to "patch up" the widening holes in projected state revenues. In 1987, the legislature, mandated by the state constitution to a "pay as you go" system of government and denied the option of deficit financing, enacted a $5.6 billion tax bill, including an increase in the sales tax, a **regressive tax** that most adversely affects low-income people.[36] By 1988, the state's economy improved and continued to expand at a robust rate, except for 1991, through the end of the decade. During this period, the state's economy outpaced the national economy at rather significant rates.

But in early 2001, recessionary pressures returned with a significant decline in the state's rate of growth. Unemployment inched up, and business activity slowed down in many sectors of the economy. By late 2003, many economists argued that the recession was over, but few predicted that the recovery would be robust. When the Texas legislature convened in early 2003, state government faced a large revenue shortfall. Lawmakers, led by a new Republican majority, made major reductions in state services to balance a new budget without raising state taxes. The spending cuts affected virtually every local government across the state.

In 2003, Texas had a gross state product of $739 billion in 1996 dollars (or $827 billion in current dollars). By comparison, the gross domestic product of the United States that year was $9.7 trillion in 1996 dollars. The Texas economy was the third largest among the states, following California and New York. If Texas were a nation, its economy would rank eleventh in the world.[37]

Several lessons can be drawn from the state's economic history. Because of the significant economic changes, a number of experts believe that the state is now less vulnerable to the volatility of the energy industry. Oil and gas production has de-

regressive tax Tax that imposes a disproportionately heavier burden on low-income people than on the more affluent.

clined in the last two decades, and now only 10 percent of the state's economy is tied to oil- and gas-related industries.[38] **Economic diversification** has made the state less reliant on one dominant industry. So now, even in recessionary periods, not all sectors of the state's economy are affected the same way.

The state has created a significant number of jobs for its expanding economy. Some 2.35 million new jobs were created in Texas, more than in any other state, during the 1990s. More than half of those were linked to services and trade. Construction and government employment also expanded during this period.[39] And a restructured financial industry experienced a noticeable recovery by 1993.

Another dimension of the state's economic success has been an ever-increasing shift to high-tech industries. Many economic and political leaders believe that the state's future must be directly tied to these developing industries, and the state and many cities have developed aggressive recruitment programs that include economic development bonds and tax abatements for high-tech companies.

Texas Economic Development
This agency provides extensive economic data to assist governments and business.
http://www.tded.state.tx.us

The term *high-tech* is generally used to describe business activities that produce new technology based on highly sophisticated scientific research and computer applications. Companies that make semiconductors, microprocessors, and computer hardware and software clearly fall into this category, as do companies that produce telecommunications devices, fiber optics, aerospace guidance systems, and some medical instruments.[40] These industries have been joined by new biotechnology industries involved in producing new medicines, vaccines, and genetic engineering of plants and animals. Houston and Dallas have emerged as centers for biotechnology, with some development also occurring in San Antonio, Austin, and Fort Worth.[41] With the cooperation and support of state universities and two major research consortia in the area, Austin also has attracted a significant number of computer-related industries.

Texas and the United States also are contributing to what is often referred to as the **globalization of the economy.** Throughout the 1980s, as world oil prices directly affected the state's economy, Texans were made keenly aware of their increased dependence on the world economy. Foreign investment in Texas business has become increasingly common. Moreover, Texas exported $99 billion in goods and services in 2003 with approximately 42 percent going to Mexico.[42] The North American Free Trade Agreement among the United States, Mexico, and Canada, which will be discussed later in this chapter, has already produced changes in the economic relationships among these countries, and more economic interdependence for North America is anticipated.

economic diversification Development of new and varied business activities. New businesses were encouraged to relocate or expand in Texas after the oil and gas industry, which had been the base of the state's economy, suffered a major recession in the 1980s.

globalization of the economy Increased interdependence in trade, manufacturing, and commerce as well as most other business activities between the United States and other countries.

Economic Regions of Texas

The economic diversity of Texas can be described in terms of thirteen distinct economic regions (see Figure 15.2). There are marked differences among these areas.[43] One may be undergoing rapid growth, while another may be experiencing a recession. Regions vary in population, economic infrastructures, economic performance, and rates of growth. One region's economy may be heavily dependent on only two or three industries. If one or two of those industries suffers an economic downturn, that region may have a more severe recession than the state overall. There are also marked differences in personal income, poverty levels and geography among the regions. All regions, meanwhile, share in one economic sector—fairly significant levels of government employment.

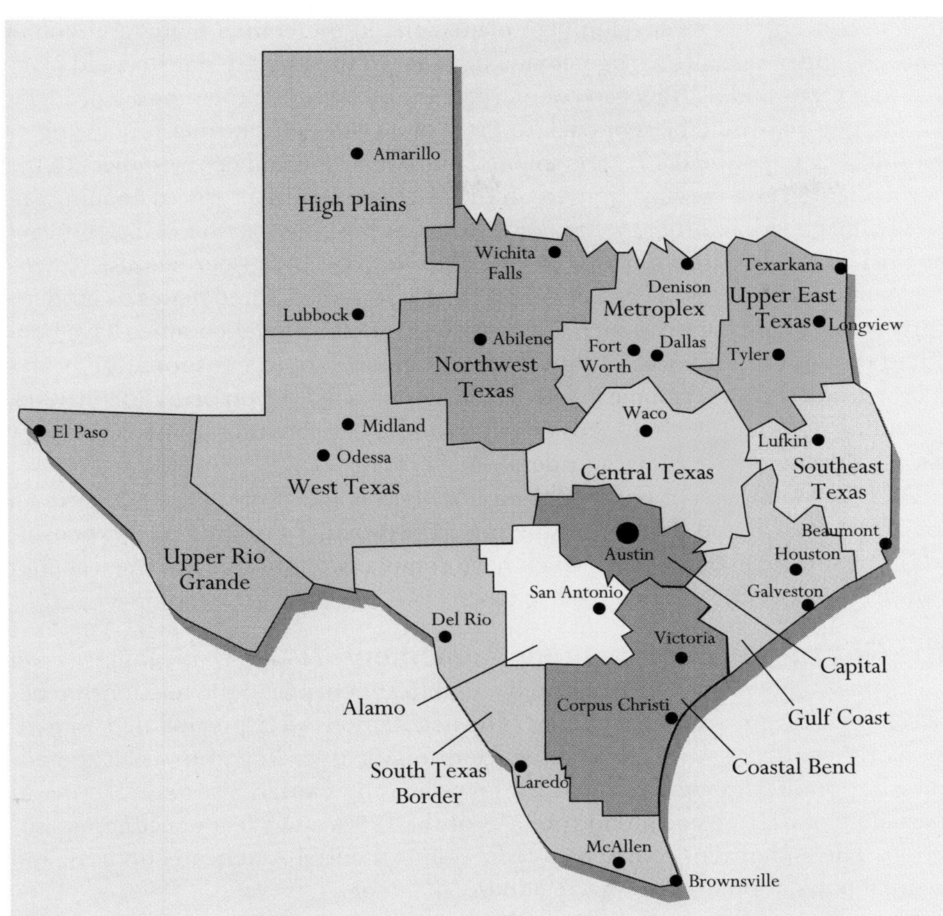

FIGURE 15.2 Economic Regions of Texas

Source: Texas Comptroller of Public Accounts.

Transnational Regionalism

Texas shares a 1,248 mile border with Mexico, and common problems and interests that bond the two neighbors, called **transnational regionalism,** have taken on increased importance since the mid-1980s.

Historically, relations between the United States and Mexico were often strained. The United States fought a war against Mexico in 1846–48, and on subsequent occasions, American troops entered Mexican territory, ostensibly to protect United States economic and national security interests. Apprehension about U.S. objectives resulted in Mexican policies on trade, commerce, and foreign ownership of property that were designed to insulate the country from excessive foreign influence and domination. Nevertheless, the interests of the two countries have long been bound by geopolitical factors, economics, and demographics. One Mexican author has compared the interdependence of the two countries to Siamese twins, warning that "if one becomes gangrenous, the other twin will also be afflicted."[44]

THINK AGAIN

Should Texas give more attention to assisting Mexico to develop a stable political and economic system?

transnational regionalism
Expanding economic and social interdependence of South Texas and Mexico.

maquiladora program
Policies initiated by Mexico in 1964 to stimulate economic growth along the U.S.-Mexico border.

Maquiladoras Changes in the economic relationships between Mexico and the United States began with the **maquiladora program,** an initiative under Mexico's Border Industrialization Program in 1964 to boost employment, foreign exchange, and industrial development. It was also designed to transfer technology to Mexico, help train workers, and develop managerial skills among Mexican nationals.[45]

The concept was to develop twin plants, one in the United States and one in Mexico, under a single management. The plant in the United States would manufacture parts, and its Mexican counterpart would assemble them into a product, which, in turn, would be sent back to the United States for further processing or for shipping to customers.[46] Parts shipped into Mexico would not be subject to the normal tariffs, and the tax imposed on the assembled product would be minimal.

The maquiladora program has not resulted in the construction of a significant number of manufacturing plants on the Texas side of the border because American companies have used existing plants throughout the United States to produce parts to be assembled in Mexico. Nevertheless, Texas's border counties have benefited through the creation of thousands of support jobs in transportation, warehousing, and services.[47] Some 3,300 maquiladora plants were in operation in 2002, providing hundreds of thousands of jobs but also contributing to increased population density on the Mexican side of the border.

American labor unions oppose the program, arguing that the maquiladoras drain jobs from the United States. But the program provides a source of inexpensive labor for American businesses, which have complained for years that they cannot compete against cheap foreign labor costs

The North American Free Trade Agreement (NAFTA) Negotiations on a free trade agreement in 1991 marked a significant change in the relationship between Mexico and the United States. The negotiations were precipitated, in part, by world economics and the emergence of regional trading zones. But the administration of Mexican President Carlos Salinas de Gortari also was reacting to the failure of Mexico's economic policies of the 1980s and a fear of economic isolation. The end of the Cold War, a reduction in Central American conflicts, and internal population pressures were additional factors.[48]

The convergence of interests of the United States, Mexico, and Canada produced the **North American Free Trade Agreement (NAFTA)** to reduce tariffs and increase trade among the three countries. It created the world's largest trading bloc, with a combined population of approximately 400 million and a combined gross national product of more than $8 trillion in 1997.[49] Approved by the U.S. Congress in late 1993, the agreement had the strong support of the Texas business community and elected officials throughout the state.

The treaty has increased trade among the three countries, strengthening previous economic ties and creating new ones. Texas has experienced significant economic changes from these new relationships, but the benefits have not been uniformly distributed throughout the state. The regions expected to benefit most in terms of new manufacturing jobs are the Dallas-Fort Worth area and Houston because of their concentrations of chemical and electronics industries.[50]

Continued Concerns about NAFTA and Mexico Some people on both sides of the U.S.-Mexico border fear that NAFTA is harming their respective countries. Labor unions in the United States are particularly concerned that lower labor costs in Mexico have moved jobs from the United States. Mexican critics declaim the low wage scales of Mexican laborers. Some manufacturers argue that labor and capital costs in Mexico threaten their American markets. Many Texas residents fear that opening up the state's highways to Mexican trucks will create safety problems, and American trucking interests, opposed the added competition. In Mexico, there is concern that American corporations will dominate and reduce Mexico's control over its own economy since more than 80 percent of Mexico's exports are going to the United States. And, finally, environmentalists have argued that in-

North American Free Trade Agreement (NAFTA) Treaty among the United States, Canada, and Mexico that created the world's largest trading bloc. Approved by the U.S. Congress in 1993, the treaty is designed to reduce tariffs and increase trade among the three countries.

creased commerce will compound air and water pollution problems on both sides of the border.

A number of American critics of NAFTA also have raised questions about Mexican political corruption, the stability of the country, increased drug smuggling into the United States, human rights violations, and the longtime domination of Mexican politics by the Revolutionary Institutional Party (PRI).

Drug-related violence and alleged collusion between high-ranking Mexican officials and drug smugglers have raised questions about Mexico's ability to fight the drug problem. In recent years, there has been considerable violence among the competing drug cartels in Mexico, and several Mexican government officials responsible for enforcing drug laws—and journalists reporting on drugs and corruption—have been murdered. The flood of illegal immigration into the United States from Mexico also is an issue.

For more than 70 years, Mexico operated with a one-party system dominated by the Institutional Revolutionary Party (PRI), a situation which many argue contributed to widespread corruption. When Vincente Fox Quesada, a candidate of the largest opposition party, the National Action Party (PAN), captured the presidency in 2000, there was hope that he would initiate widespread reforms in the economy, the bureaucracy, the military, and law enforcement. Some changes have occurred, but Fox faced formidable entrenched opposition.

Trade Patterns between Texas and Mexico The United States and Texas clearly profit from Mexico's prosperity. U.S. exports to Mexico were $12.4 billion in 1986 and $97.5 billion in 2002 (see Table 15.5). Imports from Mexico, now the United States's second largest trading partner, were $134 billion in 2002.[51] Texas exported more than $41 billion worth of goods, comprising close to six percent

TABLE 15.5 Texas and U.S. Exports to Mexico, 1993–2002

Year	Texas Exports to Mexico	U.S. Exports to Mexico	Texas as a Percent of U.S.
1993	$20,379,583,586	$41,581,100,000	49.01
1994	$23,849,512,126	$50,843,500,000	46.91
1995	$21,863,455,716	$46,292,100,000	47.23
1996	$27,036,930,968	$56,791,500,000	47.61
1997	$31,172,597,636	$71,388,400,000	43.67
1998	$36,328,363,149	$78,772,500,000	46.12
1999*	$37,860,871,019	$87,044,038,183	43.50
2000	$47,761,021,704	$111,720,877,976	42.75
2001	$41,647,797,064	$101,503,075,013	41.03
2002	$41,647,027,169	$97,530,612,979	42.70
% Change, 1993–2002	**104.36%**	**134.56%**	

Note: The Massachusetts Institute for Social and Economic Research applied a more advanced algorithim to data beginning in 1999. Thus, the post-1998 export figures more accurately account for unreported exports by states and therefore more accurately reflect actual export revenue than do pre-1999 figures.

Source: Massachusetts Institute of Social and Economic Research and the U.S. Census Bureau (based on "origin of movement to port" state-level data series); Texas Department of Economic Development, April 2000.

of the state's gross economy, to Mexico in 2002. Texas's exports to Mexico had increased dramatically from the $8.8 billion exported in 1987. These exports create hundreds of thousands of jobs in Texas.

There are an estimated 100 million legal border crossings into Texas from Mexico each year. More than ten thousand trucks cross the border each day at Laredo, the nation's largest inland port, and this number will continue to increase. Billions of dollars are required to upgrade and expand the roads, highways, bridges, water and sanitation systems, and other facilities on both sides of the border. Some initiatives have been taken by both countries, but many of the facilities will not be completed for years, contributing to delays and gridlock in both countries.

The U.S. government's response to the terrorist attacks of September 11, 2001, will further compound the congestion on the border. New border security procedures imposed by the United States may impede the flow of goods, cost individuals an untold amount of time waiting in long lines, and generate hostility from Mexican citizens because the same criteria are not applied to visitors from other countries.[52]

Common Borders, Common Problems To anyone living on the border, the economic interdependence of the United States and Mexico is evident every day. Thousands of pedestrians, cars, and trucks move across the international bridges, to and from the commercial centers on both sides of the Rio Grande. When the Mexican economy suffered a precipitous decline in 1982, the peso devaluation severely disrupted the Texas border economy, causing unemployment to skyrocket and a considerable number of U.S. businesses to fail.

While much of the effort toward improving relations between the United States and Mexico has focused on potential economic benefits, other complex problems confronting both countries also merit attention.

One is health care. On both sides of the border, many children have not been immunized against basic childhood diseases. On the Texas side are more than 1,200 *colonias*—rural, unincorporated slums that have substandard housing, roads, and drainage and, in many cases, lack water and sewage systems. These conditions have contributed to severe health problems, including hepatitis, dysentery, and tuberculosis. Higher than normal numbers of both Texan and Mexican children along the border also have been born with serious birth defects. Public health facilities in Texas report that Mexican women come across the border to give birth to their children in American facilities. This practice, which has the effect of creating "binational families," increases the burden on public hospitals—and taxpayers—in Texas. Children born in the United States are U.S. citizens and are entitled to various public services.[53]

Industrial development and population growth along the border also increase environmental problems. U.S. antipollution laws have been more stringent than those of Mexico, but air and water pollution generated in Mexico does not stop at the border. The side agreements to NAFTA provide a basic framework for addressing these problems, but some have argued that a country such as Mexico, under enormous pressure to industrialize rapidly, is less likely to be concerned with environmental issues.

Illegal Immigration Population growth in Texas has always been affected by migration from other states and foreign countries. But the proximity of Texas to Mexico has put the state in the center of a long-running dispute over the illegal immigration of large numbers of Mexicans and other Latin Americans. In 2002, there were an estimated 7.9 million people, mostly from Mexico and Central America,

A U.S. Border Patrol officer keeps watch along the U.S.–Mexico border.

living in the United States illegally.[54] Many enter through Texas and continue on to other areas of the country, but others remain in the state. The actual number of illegal immigrants in Texas will never be known because they don't participate in studies or report their status, but the most recent estimates are 600,000 to one million.[55]

The failure of the Mexican economy and the attraction of employment opportunities north of the border have been major reasons for this migration, although political instability and persecutions in Central America have also been significant factors. Large portions of the Texas and American economies were built on the availability of cheap, low-skilled Mexican labor.[56] If arrested, illegal workers are returned to Mexico, but, until recently, it was not illegal for American employers to hire them.[57]

In 1986, the U.S. Congress enacted the Immigration Reform and Control Act, which imposed fines on employers who hired illegal aliens and provided jail sentences for flagrant violators (see *Up Close:* "Do Welfare Reforms Deter Illegal Immigration?"). Potential employees had to provide documentation, and employers had to verify their employees' citizenship or residency status. Amnesty giving legal status to millions of illegal immigrants was included in the law, and so was a provision for temporary residency status for some agricultural workers.[58]

Additional legislation was passed in 1996 to increase funds for border guards and inspectors, to increase penalties for smuggling people into the United States and using fraudulent documents, to construct fences along the border, and to make it easier to detain and deport illegal immigrants.[59] But by 2004, it was clear that these laws had not stemmed the tide of illegal immigration, because Mexicans and other nationalities were still drawn to the economic opportunities available in the United States.

But many native Texans have no desire to curtail the flow of people from the south. Within blocks of where one of the authors works, there are household domestics, nannies, and yardmen who are "illegals," and neighbors know their status. Numerous businesses throughout the state hire illegal immigrants for low-wage labor, despite the legal and financial risks. Good, law-abiding citizens have hired undocumented workers for temporary, contract jobs and never asked their status, as required by law. There are so many "illegals" in Texas that the responsible federal agencies simply cannot always enforce the law. As a source of cheap labor, the illegal immigrant is, in effect, subsidizing business interests and others throughout the state. State funds that are spent for social services for the immigrants also are a subsidy.

Regional interdependence is now recognized by many people on both sides of the border to be irreversible. The economies of the two countries are becoming inextricably integrated; transnational policies have emerged; common business practices in accounting, computer software, loans, and commercial law are emerging; and there is increased collaboration among local governments on both sides of the border.

SUMMARY NOTES

- Texas has experienced significant demographic, social, and economic changes over the past four decades that have transformed state politics, governmental institutions, and public policy.
- The conservative politics of the state are rooted in its individualistic and traditionalistic political subcultures. The beliefs Texans hold about what government should do, who should govern, and what constitutes good public policy are rooted in these cultural patterns. Attributes of the state's political culture can be found in the political myths Texans use to interpret their history and to explain themselves to others.
- Demographically, Texans are diverse. The population continues to increase at a rapid pace, with the most significant increases among Hispanics and Asian Americans. The state will have a "majority minority" population in the first quarter of the twenty-first century.
- Race and economics have historically shaped Texas's politics. Largely excluded from participation in the past, racial and ethnic minority groups are quickly acquiring political influence and power that will continue to increase in the future.
- The rural frontier has passed. Texas is an urban state, with more than eight out of ten Texans living in urban areas.
- The disparities in wealth and income levels among Texans point to the political influence of class as well as of race and ethnicity.
- The educational disparities among Texans follow race, ethnicity, and economics. With the exception of Asian Americans, minorities in Texas report lower levels of educational attainment than the Anglo population. Improved literacy and the development of a technologically competent work force are essential to the state's ability to compete in the global economy.
- Over the past thirty years, Texas has experienced the normal business cycles of "booms and busts." But the state's economy has diversified, giving the state greater flexibility in dealing with economic downturns.
- The economy of Texas is the third largest in the nation, and it is helpful to view it in terms of thirteen distinct economic regions in Texas, with significant variations in population, basic industries, growth rates, and overall productivity. Periods of economic downturn and recovery are not felt uniformly across the state.
- The Texas economy is bound to the economy of Mexico. This development has occurred rapidly over the last twenty years, stimulated, in part, by Mexico's maquiladora program, the North American Free Trade Agreement, Mexico's membership in the World Trade Organization, and the globalization of the state's economy.
- Texas shares a 1,200-mile border with Mexico. The two countries also share many common problems, including illegal immigration, drug smuggling, and environmental concerns. Transnational regionalism speaks to the increased interdependence of the two countries and the necessity for governments on both sides of the Rio Grande to collaborate on solutions.

KEY TERMS

political culture 515
individualistic subculture 516
moralistic subculture 516
traditionalistic subculture 516
elite 516
republic 517
individualism 517
urbanization 523
regressive tax 527
economic diversification 528
globalization of the economy 528
transnational regionalism 529
maquiladora program 529
North American Free Trade Agreement 530

SUGGESTED READINGS

Buenger, Walter L., and Robert A. Calvert, eds. *Texas through Time: Evolving Interpretations* (College Station: Texas A&M University Press, 1991). An analysis of Texas myths, emphasizing potential distortions of the state's history and the need to utilize critical historical analysis to provide a more accurate understanding of Texans and their historical experiences.

Champagne, Anthony and Edward J. Harpham, "The Changing Political Economy of Texas," in *Texas Politics: A Reader,* eds. Anthony Champagne and Edward J. Harpham (New York: W.W. Norton, 1997), pp. 3–15. An analysis of economic changes in Texas that shape contemporary politics.

Elazar, Daniel. *American Federalism: A View from the States.* (New York: Thomas Y. Crowell, 1966). A ground-breaking analysis of American federalism focusing on the collaborative aspects of state-federal relationships with emphasis on the political culture of states.

Fehrenbach, T. R. *Lone Star: A History of Texas and the Texans* (New York: Macmillan, 1968). One of the most comprehensive histories of Texas. A must for the serious student of Texas history and politics.

Hill, Kim Quaile. *Democracy in the Fifty States* (Lincoln: University of Nebraska Press, 1994). A provocative "comprehensive, empirical, theory-based analysis of the extent to which the governments of the fifty states can be judged to be democratic and of the policy consequences of the degree to which they are democratic."

Jordan, Terry G., with John L. Bean, Jr., and William M. Holmes. *Texas: A Geography* (Boulder, Colo.: Westview Press, 1984). An excellent introduction to the physical, demographic, economic, and cultural geography of Texas.

Langley, Lester D. *MexAmerica: Two Countries, One Future.* (New York: Crown, 1988). A highly readable perspective on the impact of Mexican immigration on the politics, economy, policies, and culture of the United States.

McComb, David G. *Texas: A Modern History* (Austin: University of Texas Press, 1989). A brief narrative history that provides a quick introduction to Texans, their culture, and their experiences.

Metz, Leon C. *Border: The U.S.-Mexico Line* (El Paso: Mangan Books, 1989). A chronicle of the nearly 2,000-mile U.S.-Mexican border through "the eyes and experiences of government agents, politicians, soldiers, revolutionaries, outlaws, Indians, developers, illegal aliens, business people, and people looking for work."

Murdock, Steve H., Md. Nazrul Hoque, Martha Michael, Steve White, and Beverly Pecotte, *The Texas Challenge: Population Change and the Future of Texas* (College Station: Texas A&M University Press, 1997). Using extensive demographic data, the authors point to future problems for the state if significant educational and economic disparities among racial, ethnic and economic groups are not addressed.

O'Connor, Robert F., ed. *Texas Myths* (College Station: Texas A&M University Press, 1986). Utilizing the general concept of myth, these fourteen essays address various aspects of the state's history and political culture.

Richardson, Rupert N., Ernest Wallace, and Adrian N. Anderson. *Texas: The Lone Star State,* 7th ed. (Upper Saddle River, N.J.: Prentice Hall, 1997). A comprehensive text on the history of Texas.

Wright, Bill. *The Tigua: Pueblo Indians of Texas* (El Paso: Texas Western Press, 1993). A pictorial history of the Tiguas.

Zamora, Emilio. *The World of the Mexican Worker in Texas* (College Station: Texas A&M University Press, 1993). A history of Mexican labor in the early part of the twentieth century.

CHAPTER 16

THE TEXAS CONSTITUTION

Texas Declaration of Independence

An original eleven page copy of the Texas Declaration of Independence is in the State Archives. This is a reproduction of a traced facsimile in the Texas Memorial Museum.

A PUBLICATION OF THE TEXAS MEMORIAL MUSEUM

CHAPTER OUTLINE

- The Constitutional Legacy
- General Principles of the Texas Constitution
- Weaknesses and Criticisms of the Constitution of 1876
- Constitutional Change and Adaptation
- Constitutional Restraints and the Ability to Govern

THINK ABOUT POLITICS

1 Should constitutional amendments be required to address strictly local issues, such as whether a particular county should have a constable?
Yes ● No ●

2 Should Texas prepare its budgets each year rather than for two-year periods?
Yes ● No ●

3 Should Texas make it more difficult to amend its constitution?
Yes ● No ●

4 Should voters in Texas be able to sign petitions to put specific issues on the ballot?
Yes ● No ●

5 Should judges be appointed rather than elected?
Yes ● No ●

6 Does Texas need a new constitution?
Yes ● No ●

The Texas Constitution does more than define the institutions of government. It structures the power and influence that groups and individuals can wield in deciding who gets what, when, and how.

The Constitutional Legacy

The year was 1874, and unusual events marked the end of the darkest chapter in Texas history—the Reconstruction era and the military occupation that followed the Civil War. Texans, still smarting from some of the most oppressive laws ever imposed on American citizens, had overwhelmingly voted their governor out of office, but he refused to leave the Capitol and hand over his duties to his elected successor. For several tense days, the city of Austin was divided into two armed camps of people—those supporting the deposed governor, Edmund J. Davis, and those supporting the man who defeated him at the polls, Richard Coke. Davis finally gave up only after the Texas militia turned against him and marched on the Capitol.

That long-ago period bears little resemblance to modern Texas, but the experience still casts a long shadow over state government. The state constitution written by Texans at the close of Reconstruction was designed to put strong restraints on government to guard against future abuses, and most of those restraints remain in place today. The Texas Constitution, adopted in 1876 and amended many times since, is so restrictive that many scholars and politicians believe it is counterproductive to effective modern governance. They believe the document, which is bogged down with statutory detail, is a textbook example of what a constitution should *not* be. State government functions despite its constitutional shackles: a weak chief executive, an outdated and part-time legislature, a poorly organized judiciary, and dedicated funds that limit the state's budgetary options. But a total rewriting of the Constitution has been elusive, thanks to numerous special interests that find security in the present document—from holders of obsolete offices to beneficiaries of dedicated funds and bureaucrats who fear change. Public ignorance and indifference to the problems created by the restrictive constitutional provisions also thwart an overhaul of the document.

It is our opinion, shared by others who study state governments, that one cannot develop a clear understanding of Texas government or its politics without some familiarity and understanding of the Texas Constitution.[1] Constitutions are more than the formal frameworks that define the structure, authority, and responsibilities of governmental institutions. They also reflect fundamental political, economic, and power relationships as determined by the culture, values, and interests of the people who create them and the events of the period in which they were written.[2]

The constitution of Texas is not an easy read, and one can quickly get bogged down in details that make little sense to the casual reader. But a careful study of the document will provide insights into the distribution of

TABLE 16.1 The Seven Texas Constitutions

1827: Constitution of Coahuila y Tejas

The first Texas constitution, adopted in 1827. It recognized Texas as a Mexican state with Coahuila.

1836: Constitution of the Republic

The constitution, adopted March 16, 1836, by Texas colonists declaring independence from Mexico. Under this constitution, Texas functioned as an independent republic for nine years.

1845: Constitution of 1845

The constitution under which Texas was admitted to the United States.

1861: Civil War Constitution

The constitution adopted by Texans after the state seceded from the Union and joined the Confederacy in 1861.

1866: Constitution of 1866

The short-lived constitution under which Texas sought to be readmitted to the Union after the Civil War and before the Radical Reconstructionists took control of the U.S. Congress.

1869: Reconstruction Constitution

The constitution centralizing power in state government and weakening local governments. It reflected the sentiments of Radical Reconstructionists, not of most Texans.

1876: Texas Constitution

The constitution adopted at the end of Reconstruction, amended many times since, and still in effect. Highly restrictive and antigovernment, this constitution places strict limitations on the powers of the governor, the legislature, and other state officials.

power among competing groups and regions within the state. The constitution outlines the powers of the state and local governments, and it defines the limitations imposed on these governments. The constitution also speaks to "the relation of the state to economic activity, including both the extent of direct governmental support for enterprise and the appropriate balance between promotion and regulation of economic development."[3]

Texas has had seven constitutions, and understanding that legacy is critical to understanding contemporary Texas politics and public policy (see Table 16.1). The first constitution was adopted in 1827, when the state was still part of Mexico. The second was drafted when Texas declared its independence from Mexico in 1836 and became a republic, and the third was adopted in 1845, when the state joined the Union. The fourth constitution was written when Texas joined the Confederacy in 1861, and the fifth was adopted when the state rejoined the Union in 1866. The sixth constitution was adopted in 1869 to satisfy the Radical Reconstructionists' opposition to the 1866 constitution, and the seventh constitution was adopted in 1876 after the termination of Reconstruction policies. Each of Texas's seven constitutions was written in a distinct historical setting. And although there are significant differences among these documents, each contributed to the state and local governments that exist in Texas today.

constitution Legal structure of a political system, establishing government bodies and defining their powers.

The Texas Constitution in a Comparative Perspective The formal legal language of a **constitution** often obscures the general objectives of the document and its relevance to contemporary issues of political power and public policy. Scholars believe, first, that constitutions should be brief and should include general principles rather than specific legislative provisions. In other words, consti-

TABLE 16.2 Ten Shortest and Ten Longest State Constitutions (as of January 1, 2003)

State	Number of Constitutions	Effective Date of Current Constitution	Estimated Number of Words	Amendments Submitted to voters	Amendments Adopted
Ten Shortest State Constitutions					
New Hampshire	2	1784	9,200	283	143
Vermont	3	1793	10,286	211	53
Indiana	2	1851	10,315	75	43
Rhode Island	3	1843	10,908	105	59
North Carolina	3	1971	11,000	39	31
Utah	1	1896	11,000	154	103
Minnesota	1	1858	11,547	213	118
Kansas	1	1861	12,246	122	92
Iowa	2	1857	12,616	57	52
Montana	2	1973	13,145	49	27
Ten Longest State Constitutions					
New York	4	1895	51,700	288	215
Florida	6	1969	52,421	127	96
Louisiana	11	1975	54,112	169	113
California	2	1879	54,645	846	507
Colorado	1	1876	56,944	297	143
Arkansas	5	1874	59,500	186	89
Oregon	1	1859	63,372	468	234
Oklahoma	1	1907	74,075	329	165
Texas	7	1876	100,000	605	432
Alabama	6	1901	340,136	1024	743

Source: The Book of the States, 2003 Edition, vol. 35, (Lexington, Ky.: The Council of State Governments, 2003).

tutions should provide a basic framework for government and leave the details to be developed in **statutory law.** Second, these experts say, constitutions should make direct grants of authority to specific institutions, so as to increase the responsiveness and the accountability of individuals elected or appointed to public office. Scholars also believe that constitutions should provide for orderly change but should not be written in such a restrictive fashion that they require continual modifications to meet contemporary needs.[4]

Amended only twenty-seven times since its ratification in 1788, the U.S. Constitution is a concise 7,000-word document that outlines broad basic principles of authority and governance. No one would argue that the government of the 2000s is comparable to that of the 1790s, yet the flexibility of the U.S. Constitution makes it as relevant now as it was in the eighteenth century. It is often spoken of as "a living charter or document" that does not have to be continually amended to meet society's ever-changing needs and conditions. As discussed in Chapter 3, its reinterpretations by the courts, the Congress, and the president have produced an expansion of powers and responsibilities within the framework of the original language of the document.

By contrast, the Texas Constitution—like those of many other states—is an unwieldy, restrictive document (see Table 16.2). With more than 100,000 words, it has been on a life-support system—the piecemeal amendment process—for most of its existence. It is less a set of basic governmental principles than a compilation of detailed statutory language reflecting the distrust of government that was widespread in Texas when it was written. In effect, it attempts to diffuse political power among many different institutions. As drafted in 1875, it also included restrictions on elections and civil rights that were later invalidated by the U.S. Supreme Court. Those early provisions were efforts to limit the power of minority groups to fully participate in state government.[5]

The historical constitutional experiences of Texas parallel those of many southern states that have had multiple constitutions in the post–Civil War era. The southern states, Texas included, are the only states whose constitutions formally acknowledge the supremacy of the U.S. Constitution, a provision required by the Radical Reconstructionists for readmission of the former Confederate states to the Union.

The Constitution of Coahuila y Tejas, 1827 Sparsely populated Texas was part of Mexico when that country secured its independence from Spain in 1821, about the same time that Stephen F. Austin and others initiated Anglo colonization of Texas. Initially, Anglo Texans appeared to be willing to be incorporated into the Mexican political system as long as there was limited intrusion by the Mexican government into their daily affairs. In 1824 the new Republic of Mexico adopted a constitution for a federal system of government that recognized as a single state Texas and Coahuila, its neighbor south of the Rio Grande. Saltillo, Mexico, was the state capital.

The Constitution of Coahuila y Tejas, completed in 1827, provided for a **unicameral** legislature of twelve deputies, including two from Texas, elected by the people. Most of the legislators were from the more populous, Spanish-speaking Coahuila, and the laws were published in Spanish, which few Texas colonists understood. The executive department included a governor and a vice-governor. The governor enforced the law, led the state militia, and granted pardons. The constitution made Catholicism the state religion, although that requirement was not enforced among Texas's Anglo settlers. Additionally, Anglo Texans were not subject to military service, taxes, or custom duties. In effect, Texas served as a buffer between Mexico and various Native American peoples and the United States.

But with increased Anglo immigration and the perceived threat of U.S. imperial or expansionary policies, Mexico soon attempted to extend its control over Texas. This effort reinforced cultural differences between the Anglo and Spanish populations and would eventually lead to revolution by Anglo Texans.[6]

This formative period produced some enduring contributions to the Texas constitutional tradition. Elements of the Mexican legal system are still found in property and land laws, water laws and water rights, and community property laws. One justification for the Revolution of 1836 was the failure of the Mexican government to provide sufficient funding for public education. But while there were expectations of funding by the central government, a "concept of local control over school development was firmly established."[7] This paradox has raised a continuing constitutional question and is central to the current issue of funding public education.

The Constitution of the Republic of Texas, 1836 During the late 1820s and the early 1830s, increased immigration from the United States into the territory of Texas heightened tensions between the Anglo settlers and the Mexican government. Mexico's efforts to enforce its laws within Texas produced conflicts between cultures, legal traditions, and economic interests that resulted in open rebellion by the colonists.

unicameral A legislature consisting of a single chamber.

At the same time, Mexico was embroiled in its own internal dissension. It struggled to stabilize its political system but did not have the legacy or social and political institutions to ensure a successful democratic system. In many respects, the events in Texas were a footnote to the power politics in Mexico. Had the autonomy of Texas that was provided for under the Mexican Constitution of 1824 been maintained, the history of this region might well have been different.

Increased internal conflict among competing Mexican interests resulted in the seizure of power by the popular general Antonio López de Santa Anna Perez de Lebron. Santa Anna began to systematically suspend the powers of the Mexican Congress and local governments, and in October 1835, the national Constitution of 1824 was voided. Mexico adopted a new constitution providing for a **unitary system** with power centralized in the national Congress and the presidency. The principle of **federalism,** which divided power and authority between the national government and the states, was repudiated. This major change intensified conflict between the national government and the Mexican states. Texas was not the only area of Mexico where the principles of federalism were highly regarded, and although Texas was eventually successful in establishing its autonomy, several other rebellious Mexican states were subjected to harsh military retaliation.

As the Mexican government under Santa Anna attempted to regain control over Texas, colonists who initially supported the national government and those who expressed ambivalence were slowly converted to the cause of independence. Stephen F. Austin had consistently supported the position that Texas was a Mexican state, and he represented the views of a large part of the Anglo population living in Texas. But when Mexican troops moved across the Rio Grande into Texas in the autumn of 1835, Austin sent out a call for resistance.

The numerous special interests that later were to obstruct the course of constitutional development in Texas were missing at the small settlement of Washington-on-the-Brazos in 1836. The fifty-nine male colonists who convened to declare Texas's independence from Mexico on March 2 and to adopt a constitution for the new republic two weeks later had two overriding interests: the preservation of their fledgling nation and the preservation of their own lives. By the time they had completed their work, the Alamo—only 150 miles away—had fallen to a large Mexican army under Santa Anna, and a second Mexican force had arrived north of the Rio Grande. Accordingly, the constitution writers wasted little time on speech making.

Consequently, the Constitution of the Republic, adopted on March 16, 1836, was not cluttered with the details that weaken the present Texas Constitution. It drew heavily on the U.S. Constitution, and since forty-four of the fifty-nine delegates were from the South, from the constitutions of several southern states. The document created an elected **bicameral** Congress and provided for an elected president. Members of the clergy were prohibited from serving as president or in Congress, and there was no official, state-preferred religion. Slavery was legal, but importation of slaves from any country other than the United States was illegal. Free African Americans had to have Congress's permission to leave Texas.

Approximately six weeks after the disastrous defeat at the Alamo, the Texas army, under Sam Houston, defeated Santa Anna's army at the battle of San Jacinto on April 21, 1836. The war of independence had been relatively short and involved limited casualties, but the problems of creating a stable political system under the new constitution were formidable. There was no viable government in place, no money for paying the costs of government, and no party system. And, although defeated, Mexico did not relinquish its claim to Texas and was to

unitary system Constitutional arrangement whereby authority rests with the national government; sub-national governments have only those powers given them by the national government.

federalism Constitutional arrangement in which power is formally divided between national and sub-national governments.

bicameral A legislature consisting of two chambers.

Faced with the advancing Mexican armies, Texans hastily met in the small settlement of Washington-on-the-Brazos, declared their independence on March 2, 1836, and wrote the Constitution of the Republic, which was adopted on March 16, 1836.

demonstrate in subsequent actions that it wanted to regain this lost territory. Nevertheless, the "transition from colony to constitutional republic was accomplished quickly and with a minimum of disorganization."[8]

Independence and national autonomy from 1836 to 1845 contributed significantly to the development of a sense of historical uniqueness among Texans. While the effects on the state's political psyche may be difficult to measure, the "Lone Star" experience has been kept alive through school history texts, the celebration of key events, and the development of a mythology of the independence period.

The Constitution of 1845 During the independence movement and immediately thereafter, some Texans made overtures to the United States to annex Texas, but they were initially blocked by the issue of slavery and its relationship to economic and regional influence in U.S. politics. Increased immigration to Texas in the late 1830s and early 1840s, more interest among Texans in joining the Union, and expansionist policies of the U.S. government stepped up pressures for annexation. It was a major issue in the U.S. presidential campaign of 1844, and the election of James K. Polk accelerated the move toward Texas's admission to the United States in 1845.

The annexation bill approved by the U.S. Congress included a compromise that allowed slavery to continue in Texas.[9] Racial issues that emerged from this period continue to shape contemporary politics and public policy in the state. Texas still struggles with voting rights issues, inequities in funding of education, and the maldistribution of economic resources that directly affect the quality of life of many minorities.

The terms of Texas's admission into the Union also provided that Texas could divide itself into as many as five states, a provision largely forgotten until state Representative David Swinford, a Republican from Dumas, made such a proposal in 1991. The idea attracted some newspaper headlines and some interest in the Panhandle, which is geographically isolated from most of Texas, but was not given serious consideration by Swinford's colleagues.

The state constitution drafted to allow Texas's annexation was about twice as long as the Constitution of 1836. It borrowed not only from its predecessor but also from the constitutions of other southern states, particularly Louisiana.

The Constitution of 1845 created an elected legislature that met biennially and included a house of representatives and a senate. It provided for an elected governor and an elected lieutenant governor, and it empowered the governor to appoint a secretary of state, attorney general, and state judges, subject to senate confirmation. The legislature chose a comptroller, treasurer, and land commissioner. But in 1850, Texas voters amended the constitution to make most state offices elective. In this respect, Texas was following a national pattern of fragmenting the powers of the executive branch of state government. Today Texas still has a plural executive system under which practically all statewide officeholders are elected independently of the governor, a system that contrasts sharply with the appointive cabinet system of executive government enjoyed by the president of the United States (see Chapter 9).

The Constitution of 1845 protected private homesteads from foreclosure, guaranteed separate property rights for married women, and established a permanent fund for the support of public schools—provisions also found in the present constitution. The 1845 charter also recognized slavery, prohibited anyone who had ever participated in a duel from holding public office, and prohibited state-chartered banks. This constitution "worked so well that after several intervening constitutions, the people of Texas recopied it almost in toto as the Constitution of 1876."[10]

The Civil War Constitution, 1861 When Texas seceded from the Union in 1861, just before the outbreak of the Civil War, the state constitution was again revised. Although most of the provisions of the 1845 document were retained, significant changes were made in line with Texas's new membership in the Confederacy. Public officials were required to pledge their support of the Confederate Constitution, greater protection was given to slavery, and the freeing of slaves was prohibited.

Any semblance of a two-party system had been destroyed by the issues of slavery and secession during the 1850s, and state politics was dominated by personalities and factions. Factionalism within the Democratic Party persisted for more than 100 years, until the emergence of a two-party system in the 1980s.

The Civil War era also contributed to a legacy of states' rights, which was to persist well into the next century and spark an extended struggle for desegregation. Theoretically, the constitutional issue of the Civil War was whether a state, once having joined the Union, could leave it. The southern states subscribed to a view of the national government as a **confederacy**, and it was their position that a state could withdraw, or secede. Although the northern victory dispelled this interpretation, Texas, along with other southern states, found ways to thwart national policy through the 1960s. Their efforts were based, in part, on their continued arguments for states' rights.

The Constitution of 1866 After the Civil War, Texas was subject to national control through, first, a military government, then a provisional government headed by A. J. Hamilton, a former U.S. congressman who had remained loyal to the Union. These were dark days for Texans. Although the state had experienced relatively few battles and had not suffered from the scorched-earth tactics used by Union generals elsewhere, the economy was in disarray. Many Texas families had also lost loved ones, and many surviving Confederate veterans had been wounded physically or psychologically. Although the national government developed policies to assist the newly freed slaves, these policies were never fully funded and were halfheartedly—and often dishonestly—carried out. And the presence of an occupation army heightened tension and shaped subsequent political attitudes.

The reconstruction plan initiated by President Abraham Lincoln but never fully implemented envisioned a rapid return to civilian government for the southern

confederacy National government created by states that relies on the states for its authority.

A Union general and later governor of Texas (1870–74), Edmund J. Davis conducted one of the most oppressive administrations in U.S. history. Texas reacted to such practices with restrictions built into the Constitution of 1876.

states and their quick reintegration as equals into the national political system. Requirements were modest: the abolition of slavery, the repudiation of the Secession Ordinance of 1861, and the repudiation of all debts and obligations incurred under the Confederacy.[11]

Texas voters revived the Constitution of 1845 and amended it to include the stipulations required by the national government. Although slavery was eliminated and the freed slaves were given the right to hold property and were accorded legal rights before a jury, black people could not testify in any court case involving whites. And African Americans were denied the right to vote. The new constitution was adopted in June 1866, a new government was elected, and on August 20, 1866, President Andrew Johnson "declared the rebellion in Texas at an end."[12]

In short order, however, the mild reconstruction policies of Johnson were replaced by the severe policies of the **Radical Reconstructionists** who captured control of Congress in 1866. The new Texas Constitution was invalidated by Congress, which passed, over the president's veto, the Reconstruction Acts that established military governments throughout the South. The civilian government initiated by the state Constitution of 1866 was short-lived, and Texas functioned for two years under a reinstituted military government.

This period had an enduring impact on Texas constitutional law and politics. In a broad sense, it prolonged the full reintegration of Texas into the national political system, and, in specific terms, it transformed the constitutional tradition of Texas into one of hostility and suspicion toward government.

The Reconstruction Constitution, 1869 The Reconstruction Acts required a Texas constitution that would grant African Americans the right to vote and include other provisions acceptable to the U.S. Congress. A Republican slate of delegates to a new state constitutional convention produced a new charter that was published in 1869. It did not reflect the majority Texas sentiment of the time, but it conformed to Republican wishes. Centralizing more powers in state government while weakening local government, it gave the governor a four-year term and the power to appoint other top state officials, including members of the judiciary. It provided for annual legislative sessions, gave African Americans the right to vote, and, for the first time, provided for a centralized, statewide system of public schools. Texans were unhappy enough with their new constitution, but the widespread abuses of the document that followed under the oppressive and corrupt administration of Radical Republican Governor Edmund J. Davis paved the way for the shackles on state government that are still in place today.

In the 1869 election, the first under the new constitution, the military governor certified that Davis, a former Union Army officer, beat conservative Republican A. J. Hamilton by 39,901 to 39,092 votes. This outcome was allowed despite widespread, flagrant incidents of voter fraud, which were also ignored by President Ulysses S. Grant and the U.S. Congress. A radical majority in the new Texas legislature then approved a series of authoritarian—and, in some respects, unconstitutional—laws proposed by Davis. They gave the governor the power to declare martial law and suspend the laws in any county and created a state police force under the governor's control that could deprive citizens of constitutional protections. The governor also was empowered to appoint mayors, district attorneys, and hundreds of other local officials. Another law that designated newspapers as official printers of state documents in effect put much of the press under government control.

Radical Reconstructionists The group of Republicans who took control of the U.S. Congress in 1866 and imposed hated military governments on the former Confederate states after the Civil War.

Davis exercised some of the most repressive powers ever imposed on United States citizens. And Texans responded. First, in 1872, they elected a Democratic majority to the legislature, which abolished the state police and repealed other oppressive laws. Then, in 1873, they elected a Confederate veteran, Democrat Richard Coke, governor by more than a 2 to 1 margin over Davis. Like the Radical Republicans in the previous gubernatorial election, the Democrats were not above abusing the democratic process, and, once again, voting fraud was rampant.

As was described earlier in the chapter, Davis initially refused to leave office and appealed to President Grant for federal troops to help him retain power. Grant refused, and Davis finally gave up after the Texas militia turned against him and marched on the Capitol in January 1874. Bloodshed was avoided, Reconstruction was ending, and the Constitution of 1869 was doomed.

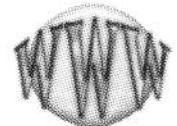

Texas Legislative Council

The entire text of the Texas Constitution can be downloaded from this site. It also provides an index to the constitution and allows the text of the constitution to be searched using key words. ***http://www.capitol.state.tx.us/txconst/toc.html***

The Constitution of 1876: Retrenchment and Reform The restored Democratic majority promptly took steps to write a new constitution. A new constitutional convention convened in Austin on September 6, 1875. The delegates were all men. Most were products of a rural and frontier South, and, still smarting from Reconstruction abuses, they considered government a necessary evil that had to be heavily restricted. Many, however, had previous governmental experience. Initially, seventy-five Democrats and fifteen Republicans were elected delegates, but one Republican resigned after only limited service and was replaced by a Democrat.[13]

The vast majority of the delegates were white, and some disagreement remains over how many African Americans served in the convention. Some historians say there were six. According to one account, however, six African Americans were elected but one resigned after only one day of service and was replaced in a special election by a white delegate. All of the African American delegates were Republicans.[14]

Only four of the delegates were native Texans. Most had immigrated to Texas from other southern states, including nineteen—the largest single group—from Tennessee, which one author called the "breeding ground" of Texas delegates. Their average age was forty-five. The oldest was sixty-eight; the youngest was twenty-three.[15] Eleven of the delegates had been members of previous constitutional conventions in Texas, but there is disagreement over whether any had participated in drafting the Reconstruction Constitution of 1869. In any event, the influences of the 1869 Constitution were negative, not positive.

At least thirty of the delegates had served in the Texas legislature, two others had served in the Tennessee and Mississippi legislatures, two had represented Texas in the U.S. Congress, and two had represented Texas in the Confederate Congress. Delegates also included a former attorney general, a former lieutenant governor, and a former secretary of state of Texas; at least eight delegates had judicial experience. Many delegates had been high-ranking Confederate military officers. One, John H. Reagan, had been postmaster general of the Confederacy.[16] Reagan later would become a U.S. senator from Texas and would serve as the first chair of the Texas Railroad Commission.

Another delegate who epitomized the independent, frontier spirit of the time was John S. "Rip" Ford, a native of South Carolina who had come to Texas in 1836 as a physician. He later became a lawyer, journalist, state senator, mayor of Austin, and Texas Ranger captain. In 1874, he was a leader of the militia that marched on the Capitol and forced Edmund J. Davis to relinquish the governor's office to his elected successor. Ford had been a secessionist delegate to the 1861 convention, which voted for secession and drafted a constitution. During the Civil War he had commanded a makeshift cavalry regiment that fought Union soldiers along the Texas-Mexico border.[17]

According to one account, delegates to the 1875 convention included thirty-three lawyers, twenty-eight farmers, three physicians, three merchants, two teachers, two editors, and one minister. At least eleven other delegates were part-time farmers who also pursued other occupations.[18] Other historians have come up with slightly different breakdowns, but all agree that the influence of agricultural interests was substantial in the writing of the new Texas charter.

About half the delegates were members of the Society of the Patrons of Husbandry, or the **Grange.** An organization formed to improve the lot of farmers, the Grange became politically active in the wake of national scandals involving abuses by big business and government. The Grange started organizing in Texas in 1873, and its influence was felt directly in constitutional provisions limiting taxes and governmental expenditures and restricting banks, railroads, and other corporations.

The delegates did not try to produce a document that would be lauded as a model of constitutional perfection or mistaken for a literary classic. They faced the reality of addressing serious, pressing problems—an immediate crisis that did not encourage debate over the finer points of academic or political theory or produce any prophetic visions of the next century.

The Civil War and Reconstruction had plunged the state into economic ruin and state government into deep debt, despite the heavy taxation of Texas citizens, particularly property owners. The bottom had fallen out of land prices, a disaster for what was still an agricultural state. Governmental corruption had been pervasive under the Davis administration, and the dictatorial powers that Davis had exercised, particularly the abuses of his hated state police, had left deep scars. Moreover, the national political scene under President Grant's two administrations (1869–77) had also been plagued by corruption and scandal.

The framers of the Texas Constitution of 1876 reacted accordingly. In seeking to restore control of their state government to the people and reestablish economic stability, they fashioned what was essentially an antigovernment charter. Centralization was replaced with more local control, strict limits were placed on taxation, and short leashes were put on the legislature, the courts, and, especially, the governor.[19]

Texas's traditional agricultural interests, which had been called upon to finance industrial development and new social services during the Reconstruction era, were once again protected from onerous governmental intrusion and taxation. The retrenchment and reform embodied in the new charter would soon hamper the state's commercial and economic development. But post-Reconstruction Texans applauded the multitude of restrictive details that the new constitution carried. They ratified the document in February 1876 by a vote of 136,606 to 56,052.

Grange Organization formed in the late nineteenth century to improve the lot of farmers. The Grange influenced provisions in the Texas Constitution of 1876 limiting taxes and government spending and restricting big business, including banks and railroads.

General Principles of the Texas Constitution

The Texas Constitution of 1876 draws from the national constitutional tradition discussed earlier and embodies four dominant principles: popular sovereignty, compact theory, limited government, and separation of powers (see Table 16.3).

A relatively short Preamble and the first two sections of the Bill of Rights express the document's underlying principle. It is a social compact, formed by free men (no women participated in its drafting), in which "all political power is inherent in the people, . . . founded on their authority, and instituted for their benefit." These brief sections are based on the principles of **popular sovereignty** and compact theory, both of which were part of a legacy of constitutional law in the United States. Al-

popular sovereignty Constitutional principle of self-government; belief that the people control their government and governments are subject to limitations and constraints.

TABLE 16.3 Comparison of the Texas Constitution and the U.S. Constitution

	U.S. Constitution	Texas Constitution
General principles	Popular sovereignty Limited government Representative government Compact theory Separation of powers	Popular sovereignty Limited government Representative government Compact theory Separation of powers
Context of adoption	Reaction to weakness of Articles of Confederation—strengthened national powers significantly	Post-reconstruction—designed to limit powers of government
Style	General principles stated in broad terms	Detailed provisions
Length	7,000 words	100,000 words
Date of implementation	1789	1876
Amendments	27	432
Amendment process	Difficult	Relatively easy
Adaptation to change	Moderately easy through interpretation	Difficult; often requires constitutional amendments
Bill of Rights	Amendments to the Constitution—adopted in 1791	Article 1 of the Constitution of 1876
Structure of government	Separation of powers, with a unified executive based on provisions of Articles I, II, III	Separation of powers with plural executive defined by Article 2
Legislature	Bicameral	Bicameral
Judiciary	Creation of one Supreme Court and other courts to be created by the Congress	Detailed provisions creating two appellate courts and other state courts
Distribution of powers	Federal	Unitary
Public policy	Little reference to policy	Detailed policy provisions

though the language articulates the noble aspirations of a free and just society, it was limited in scope and application. Women and minorities were initially denied full citizenship rights. And although women gained the right to vote by amendment to the U.S. Constitution in 1920, it has taken years for African Americans and Hispanics to receive the full protections implicit in these statements.

A third major principle is **limited government.** The Texas Bill of Rights and other provisions throughout the constitution place limits on governmental authority and power. The constitution spells out the traditional rights of religious freedom, procedural due process of law, and other rights of the citizen in relation to the government.

A fourth major principle is **separation of powers.** Unlike the U.S. Constitution, in which this principle emerges through powers defined in the three articles related to the Congress, the president, and the judiciary, Article II of the Texas Constitution specifically provides for it.

The Constitution of 1876 created three branches of government—legislative, executive and judicial—and provided for a system of checks and balances that assured that no single branch would dominate the others. This principle originated with the U.S. Constitution, whose drafters were concerned about the so-called "mischief of factions." They feared that groups or special interests would be able to

THINK AGAIN

Does Texas need a new constitution?

limited government
Constitutional principle restricting governmental authority and spelling out personal rights.

separation of powers
Division of powers among three distinct branches of government—the legislative, the executive, and the judicial—which serve as checks and balances on each other's actions.

capture governmental institutions and pursue policies that were not in the national interest. So institutional power was fragmented to guard against that potential problem. In some respects, this was an issue of even greater concern to the framers of the Texas Constitution. Reacting to the highly centralized authority and abuses of the Davis administration, they took the separation of powers principle to its extreme.

Lawmaking authority is vested in an elected legislature that includes a 150-member House of Representatives and a 31-member Senate. The Texas legislature meets in regular sessions in odd-numbered years and in special sessions of limited scope and duration when called by the governor. The sixty-five sections of Article III spell out in detail the powers granted to and the restrictions imposed on the legislature.

An elected governor shares authority over the executive branch with several other independently elected, statewide officeholders. The governor, who has limited constitutional powers, can veto bills approved by the legislature and can call and set the agendas for special legislative sessions. A gubernatorial veto can be overridden only by a two-thirds vote of the House and the Senate.

Also elected are members of the judiciary—from justices of the peace, with limited jurisdiction at the county level, to judges on the highest statewide appellate courts. This provision reflects the strong sentiment of post-Reconstruction Texans for an independent judiciary and is a major difference from the federal government, in which judges are appointed by the president. Also unlike the federal system, in which the U.S. Supreme Court is the court of last resort in both civil and criminal appeals, Texas has two courts of last resort. The Texas Supreme Court has final jurisdiction over civil matters, and the Texas Court of Criminal Appeals has final review of criminal cases.

Weaknesses and Criticisms of the Constitution of 1876

Executive Branch Many experts believe that the Texas Constitution excessively fragments governmental authority and responsibility, particularly in the executive branch. Although there is a natural disposition for the public to look to the governor to establish policy priorities, the governor does not have control over other elected state executives but rather shares both authority and responsibility for policy with them. This situation can be problematic, as when former Republican Governor Bill Clements, for example, shared executive responsibilities with Democrats who sharply disagreed with his priorities. Even when the governor and other elected officials are of the same party, differences in personality, political philosophy, and policy objectives can produce tension and sometimes deadlock.

The governor's power has been further diffused by the creation over the years of numerous boards and commissions that set policy for executive agencies not headed by elected officials. Although the governor appoints most of those board members, they serve staggered six-year terms, which are longer than a governor's term. A newly elected governor—who cannot fire a predecessor's appointees—usually has to wait through most of his or her first term to gain a majority of appointees to most boards.

Fragmented authority and responsibility are also found in county governments, which are administrative agents of the state (see Chapter 21). Various elected county officials often clash over public policy, producing inefficiencies or failing to meet public needs. And just as voters are faced with a long ballot for statewide offices, they must also choose among a long, often confusing list of county officers. Because a long ballot discourages many people from voting, this obstacle reduces public accountability, an end result that the framers of the Constitution of 1876 certainly never intended.

Legislative Branch The constitution created a low-paid, part-time legislature to ensure the election of citizen-lawmakers who would be sensitive to the needs of their constituents, not of professional politicians who would live off the taxpayers. Unwittingly, however, the constitution writers also produced a lawmaking body easily influenced by special interest groups. And the strict limitations placed on the legislature's operations and powers slow its ability to meet the increasingly complex needs of a growing, modern Texas.

In 1972, voters approved a constitutional change to lengthen the terms of the governor and other executive officeholders from two to four years. This change gives the governor more time to develop public policies with the prospect of seeing those policies implemented. But voters have repeatedly rejected proposals to provide for regular, annual legislative sessions, and legislative pay remains among the lowest in the country.

Judicial Branch The Texas Constitution also created numerous locally elected judicial offices, including justice of the peace and county and district courts. Although there are appeal procedures, these judges have a great deal of autonomy, power, and influence through their local constituencies.

Education Another example of decentralization is the public school system. The centralized school system authorized under the Reconstruction Constitution of 1869 was abolished, and local authorities were given primary responsibility for supervising public education. The concept of "local control" over their schools is important to many Texans, but decentralization and wide disparities in local tax bases have produced an inequitable public education system.

Budgeting and Finances The Texas Constitution, including key amendments adopted after 1876, requires a balanced state budget but also heavily restricts the legislature's choices over state spending. The dedication of large amounts of revenue to specific purposes has made it increasingly difficult for lawmakers to address changing state needs (see *Up Close:* "Budget Restrictions").

Individual Rights Although articulating a general commitment to democracy and individual rights, the constitution initially retarded democratic development in Texas. Like many other southern states, Texas had restrictive laws on voter participation. It levied a poll tax, which reduced the voting of minorities and poor whites until 1966, when an amendment to the U.S. Constitution and a decision by the U.S. Supreme Court outlawed it. Federal courts also struck down a Texas election system that excluded African Americans from voting in the Democratic primary, which was where elections were decided when Texas was a one-party, Democratic state. The elimination of significant numbers of people from participating in elections helped perpetuate the one-party political system for approximately 100 years.[20]

Consequence of Details The Texas Constitution is burdened with excessive detail. Although few individuals are disposed to read the 100,000-plus-word document, a person casually perusing it can find language, for example, governing the operation of hospital districts in Ochiltree, Castro, Hansford, and Hopkins

UP CLOSE

Budget Restrictions

Like most other states and unlike the federal government, Texas—thanks to a constitutional requirement—operates on a pay-as-you-go basis that prohibits deficit financing. The comptroller must certify that each budget can be paid for with anticipated revenue from taxes, fees, and other sources. Although that provision is designed to protect taxpayers and keep state government solvent, other sections of the constitution make it more difficult for the legislature to meet the state's budgetary needs adequately and fairly.

One handicap is the two-year budget period, necessitated by the fact that the legislature meets in regular session only every other year. Critics, including many legislators and state agency directors, say two-year budgets require too much guesswork and cause inadequate funding of some programs and wasteful spending in other areas. Voters in 1985 approved a constitutional amendment to allow the governor and legislative leaders to transfer funds between programs or agencies to meet emergencies when the legislature is not in session. But that provision only partially addressed the problem.

The legislature's control over the budget-setting process is further restricted by constitutional requirements that dedicate significant portions of state revenue to specific purposes. Three-fourths of the revenue from the motor fuels tax is automatically set aside for highways and the remaining one-fourth for public education. The Permanent School Fund and the Permanent University Fund are land- and mineral-rich endowments that help support the public schools and boost funding for the University of Texas and Texas A&M University systems.

The legislature can bend the pay-as-you-go requirement by issuing general obligation bonds, serviced by future tax revenues, to build prisons and other public facilities. Such bonds require voter approval in the form of constitutional amendments, several of which, totaling more than $3 billion, have been approved in recent years to build new prisons. That debt will have to be paid off with tax dollars over the next generation.

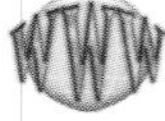
Indiana University Law

If you are interested in the constitutions of other states, this is one of several sites that provide you access to these documents.
http://www.iulaw.indy.indiana.edu/library/State_Constitutions.htm

counties. There also is a provision dealing with expenditures for relocation or replacement of sanitary sewer laterals on private property. Whereas the 7,000-word U.S. Constitution leaves the details of implementation to congressional legislation, the Texas Constitution often spells out the authority and power of a governmental agency in specific detail. Most experts agree that many constitutional articles are of a legislative nature and have no business in a constitution.[21] The excessive detail limits the adaptability of the constitution to changing circumstances and places undue restrictions on state and local governments.

Consequently, there are obsolete and contradictory provisions in the constitution. Subsequent state and federal constitutional amendments have superseded some of these provisions, but much obsolete language remains. Periodically, state constitutional amendments have been approved to "clean up" such deadwood, but the problem persists.[22]

Another important criticism of the Texas Constitution focuses on the amendments and the amendment process. Alabama has had more constitutional amendments than any other state, but Texas ranked fourth, with 432 amendments from 1876 through 2003 (see *Across the USA:* "States Frequently Amend Their Constitutions"). In contrast, the U.S. Constitution has been amended only twenty-seven times since 1789, and ten of those amendments were adopted as the Bill of Rights immediately after the government organized. The numerous restrictions and prohibitions in the Texas Constitution require excessive amendments to enable state government to adapt to social, economic, and political changes.

Minority participation in Texas politics has increased significantly since the 1960s as a result of the Voting Rights Act and of federal court decisions that overturned restrictive state laws that kept minorities from registering and voting. Democratic gubernatorial nominee Tony Sanchez is shown campaigning in 2002.

Constitutional Change and Adaptation

Amendment Although the drafters filled the Texas Constitution with a multitude of restrictive provisions, they also provided a relatively easy method of amending it. This piecemeal amendment process has enabled state government to meet some changing needs, but it also has added thousands of words to the document.

Proposed constitutional amendments can be submitted only by the legislature. Approval by two-thirds of the House and the Senate puts them on the ballot, where adoption requires a majority vote. Although voters had approved 432 amendments through 2003, they had rejected 173 others. Since the present charter was ratified in 1876, there have been only a few years in which voters have not been asked to change it. The first amendment was adopted on September 2, 1879. A record twenty-five amendments were on the November 3, 1987, ballot. Seventeen were adopted, and eight were defeated.

Some amendments are of major statewide importance, but many have affected only a single county or a handful of counties or have been offered simply to rid the constitution of obsolete language (see *Up Close:* "A Lot of Trouble for a Minor Office"). One amendment approved by voters in 1993 affected only about 140 families, two church congregations, and one school district in Fort Bend and Austin counties. It cleared up a title defect to their land.

Unlike voters in many other states, Texas citizens cannot force the placement of constitutional amendments on the ballot because Texas does not have the **initiative** or **referendum** on a statewide level. On taking office in January 1979 as Texas's first Republican governor since Reconstruction, Bill Clements made adoption of the initiative and referendum a priority. But these innovations could not take effect without a constitutional amendment, and the legislature—which did not want to give up such a significant policy prerogative to the electorate—ignored Clements.

In recent years, however, the legislature has demonstrated a tendency to seek political cover by selectively letting the voters decide some particularly controversial issues, such as a binding referendum in 1987 on the legalization of pari-

THINK AGAIN

Does Texas need a new constitution?

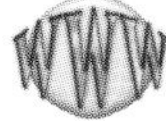

Texas Legislature On-Line

Access to legislative resolutions providing for constitutional amendments can be found here. Legislative intent and legislative histories of proposed constitutional amendments are also available.
http://www.capitol.state.tx.us

initiative Procedure by which voters propose constitutional amendments or other laws through petitions subject to adoption by a popular vote.

referendum Vote by the general electorate on a public policy issue, such as a constitutional amendment or statute.

ACROSS THE USA

States Frequently Amend Their Constitutions

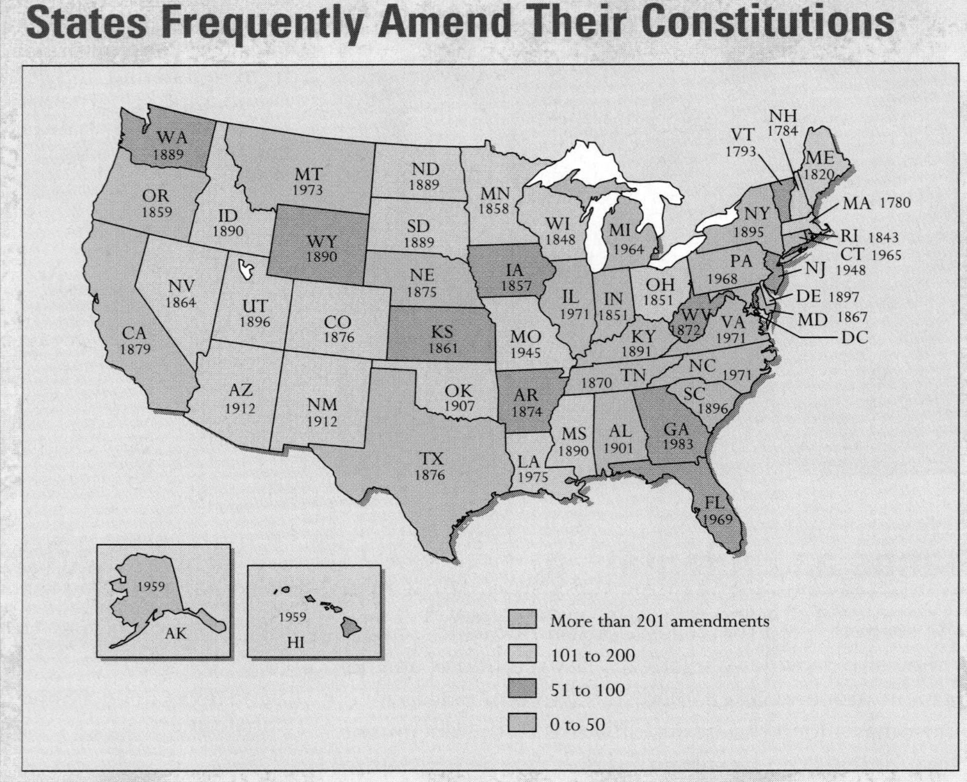

Source: Based on data from "*The Book of the States, 2003 Edition*, vol. 35 (Lexington, KY.; The Council of State Governments, 2003).

mutuel betting on horse and dog racing. In 1993 the legislature proposed a constitutional amendment, which voters overwhelmingly endorsed, to prohibit a personal income tax in Texas without voter approval.

Constitutional Convention The constitution also provides for revision by constitutional convention, which the legislature can call with the approval of the voters. Convention delegates have to be elected, and their terms also are subject to voter approval. In 1919, voters overwhelmingly rejected a proposal for a constitutional convention. Subsequent efforts, including an attempt by Governor John Connally in 1967, to initiate reforms using a constitutional convention were also defeated.[23] Connally's efforts did, however, result in adoption of a "cleanup" amendment in 1969 that removed many obsolete provisions from the constitution, and they laid the groundwork for a constitutional convention in 1974.

Constitutional Reform Efforts of 1971–1975 The 1974 convention, the only one ever held under the present 1876 charter, ended in failure. Its delegates were the 181 members of the legislature. The constitutional convention of 1974

UP CLOSE

A Lot of Trouble for a Minor Office

Roberts County Judge Vernon H. Cook was convinced that his rural county near the top of the Texas Panhandle did not need a constable. He believed the sheriff provided enough law enforcement for the county's 1,500 residents. For years, the county had not had a constable, but the office, which was created in the Texas Constitution, remained on the books. Unexpectedly, in 1992 a write-in candidate ran for constable and was elected. The office then became an extra expense for county taxpayers, as county commissioners felt obliged to pay the new officeholder a $600-a-month salary plus a $200-a-month car allowance and health insurance benefits.

Convinced they were not getting their money's worth—"As near as we can tell, he served two official papers in his first year in office," Cook complained—commissioners later reduced his salary, and the constable left town. To avoid a recurrence of the problem, commissioners had to ask the state legislature to put a constitutional amendment abolishing the Roberts County constable's office on a statewide ballot. Thus voters in Houston—600 miles away—would have a greater say on abolishing the office than Roberts County's own taxpayers, because Houston's 1.6 million residents cast many more votes. Although that may not seem fair—Houston taxpayers, after all, did not pay the Roberts County constable's salary—it is just one of many obstacles and inconveniences imposed on modern government by a nineteenth-century constitution. Most amendments abolishing obsolete county offices are approved by Texas voters, including amendments abolishing the constables' offices in Roberts County and two other rural counties in 1995.

Source: Houston Chronicle, November 6, 1995.

had its beginning in 1971, when state Representative Nelson Wolff of San Antonio and several other first-term legislators won the leadership's backing for a full-scale revision effort. In 1972 voters approved the necessary constitutional amendment that specified that the convention would comprise house members and senators elected the same year.

In 1973 the legislature created a thirty-seven-member Constitutional Revision Commission to hold public hearings around the state and make recommendations to the convention. Members of the commission, chaired by former Texas Supreme Court Chief Justice Robert W. Calvert, were appointed by Governor Dolph Briscoe and other top state officials.

The constitutional convention, or "con-con," as it came to be called by legislators and members of the media, convened on January 8, 1974. House Speaker Price Daniel, Jr., was elected president, and Lieutenant Governor Bill Hobby, in an address to delegates, offered a prophetic warning: "The special interests of today will be replaced by new and different special interests tomorrow, and any attempt to draft a constitution to serve such interests would be futile and also dishonorable."[24]

Hobby's plea was ignored. Special interests dominated the convention, which finally adjourned in bitter failure on July 30, failing by three votes to get the two-thirds vote necessary to send a new constitution to Texas voters for ratification. The crucial fight was over a business-backed attempt to lock the state's right-to-work law into the constitution. The **right-to-work law** prohibits union membership as a condition of employment, so the effort was bitterly fought by organized labor. Then as now, business was politically stronger than labor in Texas, but the two-thirds vote necessary to put a new constitution on the ballot was too great an obstacle.

right-to-work law Law prohibiting the requirement of union membership in order to hold or get a job.

After three years of preparation and deliberations, the proposed constitution of 1974 failed by three votes in the final hectic session of the constitutional convention, when the gallery was filled with interested onlookers, including many representatives of labor.

The gallery in the house of representatives chamber, which served as the convention hall, was packed with labor representatives and other spectators when the final vote was taken, about a half-hour before the convention's midnight adjournment deadline. Daniel held the electronic voting board open for twenty-eight minutes, hoping three delegates could be persuaded to switch their votes, but time ran out. Tension and emotions were running so high that, at one point, state Representative Jim Mattox of Dallas, who would later become attorney general, challenged Daniel's delay in announcing the vote and publicly called the convention president a liar.[25]

Although the right-to-work dispute took the brunt of the blame, other factors also worked against the revision effort (see *What Do You Think?* "Do Most Voters Really Care?"). One was Governor Briscoe's refusal to exercise any significant leadership on behalf of a new state charter. Except for opposing proposals that he thought would further weaken the authority of the governor, he provided little input to the convention and did not attempt to twist delegates' arms to get enough votes to send the document to the electorate. Louisiana voters approved a new state constitution in 1974, and Governor Edwin Edwards's strong support was considered instrumental. Gubernatorial leadership in other states also appears to have been critical to successful constitutional conventions.

Another major obstacle was the convention's makeup. Texas, unlike most other states, chose to use the 181 members of the legislature as its constitutional convention. Soon after the convention began its work, many of them were facing reelection campaigns in the party primaries, which diverted their attention from the business of the convention.

Additionally, a minority of legislators—dubbed "cockroaches" by President Daniel—did not want a new constitution and attempted to delay or obstruct the convention's work at every opportunity. Most legislators, even those who wanted a new constitution, reacted to their own political fears and ambitions. They were very susceptible to the influence of special interests, far more susceptible than most private-citizen delegates would likely have been. And special interests were legion at the convention. In addition to various business and professional groups and organized labor, many county officeholders whose jobs—protected by the Constitution of 1876—were suddenly in jeopardy put pressure on the delegates.

Some county judges lobbied against a proposal to streamline the judiciary because they feared it would relieve them of judicial duties. Under the present constitution, county judges are primarily administrative officers and do not have to be lawyers, but they do have limited judicial responsibilities. So persistent was their lobbying that Daniel referred to some of them as a "wrecking crew." Representative DeWitt Hale of Corpus Christi, chair of the Committee on the Judiciary, was "disgusted because a handful of judges could be so disruptive to the convention."[26]

Influential regents, lobbyists, and alumni of the University of Texas and Texas A&M University systems guarded the Permanent University Fund, their rich constitutional endowment. Further, highway lobbyists, backed by thousands of contractors and businesspeople from throughout the state, fought any attempt to raid the highway trust fund, the constitutional provision that dedicates three-fourths of the revenue from the state motor fuels tax to highway projects.

Delegates tried to walk a tightrope over the emotionally charged issue of gambling. They yielded to the wishes of charitable and fraternal organizations and tentatively approved a provision to allow bingo and raffles to be conducted for charity, receiving some public ridicule for giving constitutional status to a game of chance. But delegates voted to retain the general constitutional prohibition against lotteries. In a letter to Robert W. Calvert, the chair of the Constitutional Revision Commission, Baylor University President Abner McCall had warned of considerable public opposition to any new constitution that legalized gambling: "The commission may adopt proposals to make the machinery of Texas government more efficient, but many of us will not trade a little more efficiency for a greater danger of corruption of government by state sponsored gambling."[27] The ban on lotteries was to remain in the constitution for another seventeen years until Governor Ann Richards successfully promoted the creation of a state lottery as a new revenue source for state government in 1991.

During its next regular session, in 1975, the legislature, with the strong support of House Speaker Bill Clayton and Lieutenant Governor Bill Hobby, resurrected the constitutional revision effort. Lawmakers voted to present to Texans the basic document that the convention had barely rejected the previous summer in the form of eight separate constitutional amendments. The first three articles dealing with the separation of powers and the legislative and executive branches were combined into one ballot proposition. Each of the remaining seven propositions was a separate article, each to be independently approved or rejected by the voters. The most controversial issues that the 1974 convention had debated, such as right-to-work, were excluded. The streamlined amendments would have considerably shortened the constitution and provided some major changes, including annual legislative sessions, a unified judicial system, and more flexibility in county government. It would have been a much more flexible, modern constitution than the 1876 document and had cost several million tax dollars and countless hours to produce. But voters rejected all eight propositions on November 4, 1975, some by margins of more than 2 to 1.

A stock fraud scandal in the legislature in 1971 (see Chapter 18) and the Watergate scandal that had forced the resignation of President Richard Nixon in 1974 had raised Texans' distrust of government, and the proposed new constitution had been drafted by state officials, not by private citizens.

Efforts to enact these proposals were further thwarted by Governor Briscoe. Although he had never taken an active role in the revision effort, three weeks before the 1975 election, he openly opposed the eight propositions and suggested that the existing constitution had served the state well and would continue to be adequate for the future.[28]

Further Piecemeal Reforms So it was back to piecemeal constitutional changes. Between 1975 and 2003, 212 amendments were approved by Texas voters and 37 were rejected. Besides the lottery, amendments winning approval included the 1993 amendment to ban a personal income tax without voter approval and a series of propositions authorizing $3 billion in tax-backed bonds for a huge prison expansion program. In 1985, voters approved an amendment to give the governor and legislative leaders authority to deal with budgetary emergencies between legislative sessions. Martha Whitehead, the state's last treasurer, ran on a promise in 1994 to seek the elimination of the office on the grounds that it was obsolete. In 1995, voters approved an amendment to abolish the state treasurer's office and transfer its duties to the comptroller. And in 1997, Texas voters by a wide margin approved a constitutional amendment to increase homeowners' $5,000 exemptions from school property taxes to $15,000. The measure, part of a property tax relief effort promoted by Governor George W. Bush, saved the average homeowner about $140 a year in local school taxes. In 1999, voters approved an amendment—prompted by Governor Bush's presidential campaign—to make it clear that a lieutenant governor who was promoted to fill out an elected governor's unexpired term would have to give up the lieutenant governor's job to take the higher office. During its 1999 session, the Legislature rejected a proposal—the first of its kind in more than twenty years—to rewrite the constitution. But legislators approved an amendment, which voters also approved, to remove more obsolete language from the document. One of the more controversial amendments in recent years, Proposition 12, ratified new limits on some monetary damages in medical malpractice lawsuits. It was narrowly approved by voters in 2003 (see *Up Close:* "High Stakes Over Lawsuits").

Constitutional Provisions, Interest Groups, and Elites Only a small percentage of registered voters—often less than 10 percent—participate in elections when constitutional amendments are the only issues on the ballot (see Figure 16.1). When amendments are submitted to the voters during gubernatorial or presidential elections, the turnout is much higher. But in many instances, a relative handful of Texans ultimately decides on fundamental changes in government, which enhances their influence over the constitutional revision process.

Interest groups, which historically have been strong in Texas, work diligently to protect their concerns and objectives. They develop strategies to get provisions into the constitution that would benefit them and to keep provisions out of the constitution that they fear would hurt them. Because most amendments represent nonpartisan issues, a well-financed public relations campaign is likely to produce public support for an amendment.[29]

Interest groups are able to kill many proposed constitutional changes in the legislature, where the two-thirds vote requirement works to their advantage. Only a small fraction of constitutional amendments proposed by legislators get put on the ballot. Those that do usually have the support of one or more special interest groups, which often finance publicity campaigns to promote the propositions to the voters. Few amendments attract organized opposition after being put on the ballot, but there have been exceptions. In 2003, doctors, insurance companies, and business interests heavily promoted Proposition 12, the ratification of new

WWW **Secretary of State** This office is responsible for compiling state election returns, including constitutional amendments. County-level returns for constitutional amendments since 1993 can be accessed from this site. ***http://www.sos.state.tx.us***

UP CLOSE

Oops! How Did That Happen?

People who have any doubts that an election ballot loaded with constitutional amendments is an accident waiting to happen need only consider Proposition 14, one of nineteen amendments on the November 2001 ballot, all of which were approved by voters. The proposal was promoted as a means of allowing local governments, except for school districts, to exempt registered, non–income-producing travel trailers from local property taxes. Supporters said the tax break was needed to encourage the so-called "winter Texans" to continue making their seasonal homes in the Rio Grande Valley. These people, who travel south to escape the cold winters up north, have become an important part of the South Texas economy and represent an important financial boost to some of Texas's poorest counties. Many of the winter visitors are senior citizens who live in recreational vehicles.

Everybody was sure the amendment did what it was intended to do. No one—legislative sponsors, legislative analysts, local officials, the media—noticed a problem, until after the amendment was approved and then became part of the constitution. Only then did someone discover that the amendment had inadvertently imposed a new tax on travel trailers, rather than removed one. The new provision labeled trailers as taxable, while the constitution previously had said nothing about them. And because the exemption didn't apply to school districts, legal experts believed that travel trailers had been made subject to school taxes.

The goof prompted Governor Rick Perry and legislative sponsors to start scrambling. Perry asked school districts to refrain from taxing travel trailers until the legislature had a chance to correct the mistake, which it did in 2003.

"I guess it moved through the process and went and went and went," the amendment's sponsor, state Representative Kino Flores of Mission, said of the blunder.

Source: Associated Press, March 8, 2002.

medical malpractice limits. They were successful, despite a media campaign against the amendment financed primarily by plaintiffs' lawyers.

Many recent constitutional changes have reflected a pro-industry and economic development push that contrasts sharply with the anti-business sentiment of the original constitutional framers. Recent amendments also have helped build up a public bonded indebtedness that the nineteenth-century constitution writers would have been unable to comprehend. Texas was rural then. It is now largely urban and is working to diversify and expand its economy as well as provide the infrastructure required to support the large increases in its population.

Type of Election	Number of Elections	Percent of Registered Voters	Percent of Voting Age Population
Special *	15	12.7%	8.5%
General (Gubernatorial)	9	43.7%	28.4%
General (Presidential)	8	66.9%	45.2%

* Only constitutional amendments on the ballot

FIGURE 16.1 Turnout for Constitutional Amendments, 1970–2003

Source: Texas Secretary of State, Elections Division.

Business has repeatedly turned to state government for tax breaks and other economic incentives and has found receptive ears in the legislature and the governor's office.

Nine of the record twenty-five amendments on the November 1987 ballot were actively promoted as an economic development package by the Build Texas Committee, a bipartisan group of business and civic leaders. Voters approved most of the amendments, including bonds for new water projects and prisons.

Industry, with the unusual support of organized labor and environmentalists, won a major tax break through a constitutional amendment approved by Texas voters in 1993. It requires local governments to grant property tax exemptions for expensive pollution control equipment that businesses are required by state or federal law to install in their plants and other facilities. The business community supported the amendment because it represented untold millions of dollars in potential tax savings. Labor supported it because money not spent on taxes could mean more money spent on jobs. And environmentalists viewed it as an antipollution measure. Some local officials were fearful of the potential loss of large amounts of revenue to counties, school districts, and other local governments, but they were clearly overpowered. Sometimes, however, relief can turn into heartburn, as it did in 2001, when lawmakers and Texas voters accidentally put a new tax into the constitution when they thought they were repealing one (see *Up Close:* "Oops! How Did That Happen?").

It has been argued that the Texas Constitution serves the interests of a small number of **elites**—those individuals who control businesses and other dominant institutions in the state. This argument suggests that the severe constraints built into the constitution limit the policy options of state government and have historically thwarted the efforts of larger public-interest groups to restructure or improve the tax system, education policy, social services, health care, and other policies and programs that would benefit low- and middle-income Texans. Power is so fragmented that these groups have had to turn to the courts to force change. This same argument, incidentally, has often been made about the U.S. Constitution.

If this interpretation is accurate, it is ironic that those who framed the Texas Constitution of 1876 directed much of their wrath against railroads, banks, and other institutions that are today considered elitist. The tumultuous last quarter of the nineteenth century witnessed high levels of class and economic conflict, with the emergence of the Greenback and Populist political parties, which articulated the interests of lower-income groups. But monied business interests eventually were able to use the state constitution and subsequent legislation to reestablish their dominance over Texas government. Although the elite structure of the state has changed since 1876, some scholars argue that there has been a gradual transfer of power and control to new elites, who continue to exercise enormous influence over public policy.

Change through Court Interpretation Some evidence indicates that Texas courts are now prepared to play a more expansive role in the interpretation of the constitution and, in turn, effect major changes in state policy. The best-known example is the Edgewood school finance case, in which the courts invalidated the system of funding public education and ordered the legislature to provide more equity in tax resources among the state's more than 1,000 school districts. Wide disparities in spending on students between rich and poor districts—the result of wide

elites Small groups of people who exercise disproportionate power and influence in the policymaking processes.

UP CLOSE

High Stakes Over Lawsuits

Supporters said Proposition 12 was a cure for high medical malpractice insurance premiums that were forcing some doctors, particularly in rural areas, to close their practices. Opponents argued that medical malpractice coverage was high because state regulators weren't effectively clamping down on bad doctors. They warned that Proposition 12 was instead an effort by business and insurance interests to further restrict access to the courts for injured or aggrieved consumers. In any event, Texas voters narrowly approved the constitutional amendment in 2003 after a multimillion-dollar advertising war. Doctors, hospitals, nursing homes and other business interests primarily financed the campaign promoting the amendment. Plaintiffs lawyers, who make their living suing doctors, hospitals and businesses on behalf of injured consumers, picked up most of the tab for the media campaign against it, although numerous consumer advocacy groups also opposed the proposal.

The amendment did two things. First, it ratified a 2003 law enacted by the Legislature to put new limits on non-economic damages—money awarded for such things as pain, suffering and disfigurement—in medical malpractice suits. Such damages, which are in addition to medical costs and other actual economic losses that could be awarded a patient who suffered from a botched medical procedure, were capped at $750,000 for each case. Of that amount, only $250,000 can be recovered from physicians or other medical personnel. The remainder would come from hospitals, nursing homes or other health care facilities that may be involved. Additionally—and potentially more far-reaching—Proposition 12 included language clearing the way for future sessions of the Legislature to enact new limits on damages in other civil lawsuits.

Legislative sponsors of Proposition 12 also were accused of trying to sneak the proposal past the voters by scheduling the constitutional amendments election for September 13, rather than November 4, the general election date on which constitutional amendments were traditionally set for voter review. Supporters of the amendment said it was important to win voter approval earlier than normal to remove any legal uncertainty over the new malpractice limits. But opponents argued that the early election, with no other issues to attract voters, was designed to avoid the higher voter turnout that would be generated by a hotly contested mayoral race in Houston on November 4. Voters in Houston, the state's largest city, usually are a major factor in determining state elections, and a high voter turnout there could prove to be pivotal in determining the fate of Proposition 12. According to this argument, the higher the voter turnout in Houston, the greater the likelihood that the amendment would be defeated, because Democrats and plaintiffs lawyers still had some clout over elections in that city. Opponents of Proposition 12, as it turned out, had reason to fear the early election date. The proposal narrowly passed statewide, but 58 percent of Houston voters—turning out in far fewer numbers than would vote two months later in the mayor's race—cast ballots against it. "It (the statewide result) would have been a real horse race if it had been held in conjunction with the Houston mayor's race," said University of Houston political scientist Richard Murray.

Source: Houston Chronicle, September 16, 2003, p. 13A.)

disparities in local property values—violated the state constitution's requirement for an "efficient" system of public schools, the Texas Supreme Court ruled.

Constitutional Restraints and the Ability to Govern

The nonpartisan League of Women Voters of Texas has been a long-suffering advocate of a total rewrite of the state constitution. Nevertheless, before each constitutional amendments election, it normally announces which propositions it endorses for the sake of good government and which it opposes. But league lead-

League of Women Voters

The Texas League of Women Voters is a nonpartisan organization committed to increasing political participation, improving state and local government, and increasing public understanding of major policy issues. When constitutional amendments are submitted to voters, the league usually publishes information about the purpose and effects of the amendments.
http://www.lwvtexas.org

ers lost their patience in 1987 with the placement of a record twenty-five amendments on the same ballot. They announced they would neither support nor oppose any amendment that year. Instead, they urged voters to examine the propositions carefully and complain to their legislators about the length of the ballot. "Enough is enough. Let us work together to halt this ridiculous system of running the government by means of the constitution," the League said. But without a new constitution, the only way state government can prepare for the challenges of the twenty-first century under a highly restrictive constitution written in the nineteenth is to continue this pattern of "amendomania."[30]

Prospects for Future Change Experts can point out the many flaws of the Texas Constitution, but attempts at wholesale revision have not been successful. Numerous piecemeal changes have been made, but they have not addressed the fundamental criticisms of the charter. What is to be made of all this?

First, Texas has a long history of suspicion of government, and this tradition continues. Most people fear governmental abuses and excesses more than they worry about government's inability to respond quickly and efficiently to the needs of its citizens. In the vernacular of the layperson, "If it ain't broke, don't fix it." And it is not clear that the layperson regards the constitution as "broke."

Second, many groups and interests benefit from the existing constitution, and they have demonstrated a collective resolve to minimize change.

Finally, most Texans give little thought to changing the constitution because they are ill-prepared to deal with the complexities of the document. Enormous problems must be overcome if citizens are to be educated and motivated to press for constitutional revision.

SUMMARY NOTES

- Texas, like most other states, has functioned under a series of constitutions, each of which has contributed to the state's constitutional legacy. Each is appropriately understood from the perspective of the period in which it was adopted.
- Texas currently operates under a constitution that was adopted following the Civil War and the Radical Reconstruction era, and the events of that period left an enduring legacy of suspicion of government, limited government, and fragmented governmental institutions. The 1876 Constitution was predicated on the theory that governmental excesses could be minimized by carefully defining what governments could and could not do.
- The framers failed to anticipate that the limitations they imposed on governmental institutions would ultimately allow major economic interests within the state to dominate the policy-making process, often to the detriment of the lower socioeconomic groups.
- What the delegates to the Constitutional Convention of 1875 regarded as the strengths of the constitution—fragmented authority, detailed limitations on the power of governmental institutions, and decentralization—have served to limit the ability of state and local governments to adapt effectively to economic and demographic changes. The perceived solutions to many of the problems of 1875 have compounded the problems of state and local governments in the 2000s.
- Efforts to overhaul the Texas Constitution have failed. Consequently, the state has been forced to amend the document continually on a piecemeal basis. This process has produced some success in modernizing the charter, but many structural problems of state government require major institutional changes that cannot be resolved through this amendment process.
- In many ways, the Texas Constitution reflects the values of the state's conservative political culture, which con-

tinues to be suspicious of far-reaching constitutional changes. Moreover, constitutions and the debates that surround them are complex, and most people give little attention to these issues. Consequently, it is much easier to mobilize public opinion against rather than for wholesale change.

- Over the years, numerous groups have attempted to protect their interests through constitutional amendments. But the same groups usually oppose any proposed changes that threaten their influence, power, or benefits. Consequently, the interests of small segments of the state's population often prevail over the interests of the majority.

KEY TERMS

constitution 538
unicameral 540
unitary system 541
federalism 541
bicameral 541
confederacy 543
Radical Reconstructionists 544
Grange 546
popular sovereignty 546
limited government 547
separation of powers 547
initiative 551
referendum 551
right-to-work law 553
elites 558

SUGGESTED READINGS

Braden, George D., et al. *The Constitution of the State of Texas: An Annotated and Comparative Analysis.* 2 vols. Austin: Texas Advisory Commission on Intergovernmental Relations, 1977. Originally designed as a research tool for delegates to the 1974 Constitutional Convention, this work provides an explanation of the historical development of the Texas constitution and a comparative perspective on other state constitutions.

Bruff, Harold H. "Separation of Powers under the Texas Constitution." *Texas Law Review* 68 (June 1990): 1337–67. Summarizes leading state court cases pertaining to the separation of powers clause of the Texas Constitution and addresses issue of judicial review.

Cnudde, Charles F., and Robert E. Crew, Jr. *Constitutional Democracy in Texas.* St. Paul: West, 1989. A constitutional perspective on Texas government and politics.

Lutz, Donald S. "The Texas Constitution." *In Perspectives on American and Texas Politics: A Collection of Essays,* ed. Donald S. Lutz and Kent L. Tedin, (Dubuque, Iowa: Kendall/Hunt, 1987), pp. 193–211. An analysis of the 1876 Texas Constitution that argues the document reflects the dominant subcultures of the state with a tilt toward individualism.

Mauer, John Walker. "State Constitutions in a Time of Crisis: The Case of the Texas Constitution of 1876." *Texas Law Review* 68 (June 1990): 1615–47. Focuses on the enactment of post-Reconstruction constitutions in Texas and the South, arguing that the constitutional framers of 1875 were reacting not only to Republican Reconstruction but the recently elected Democratic administration.

May, Janice C. *The Texas Constitution Revision Experience in the 70s.* Austin: Sterling Swift, 1975. Written by an expert on state constitutions, this work provides a historical perspective on the efforts to rewrite the Texas Constitution in the 1970s.

McKay, Seth Shepard. *Seven Decades of the Texas Constitution of 1876.* Lubbock: Texas Technical College, 1943. A historical perspective on the impact of the 1876 constitution.

Tarr, Alan. *Understanding State Constitutions.* Princeton, N.J.: Princeton University Press, 1998. An introduction to state constitutional theory that addresses a series of issues, including the differences among state constitutions and between federal and state constitutions and state constitutions within the federal context.

Wolff, Nelson. *Challenge of Change.* San Antonio: Naylor, 1975. Written by a delegate to the 1974 Constitutional Convention, this book discusses divisive issues and provides an abbreviated history of the convention proceedings.

CHAPTER 17

INTEREST GROUPS, POLITICAL PARTIES, AND ELECTIONS IN TEXAS

CHAPTER OUTLINE

The Power of Interest Groups
Pluralism or Elitism?
Dominant Interest Groups in Texas
The Development of a Two-Party System in Texas
Changing Patterns of Party Support and Identification
The Party Organization
Parties and Government
Minorities and Political Participation
Political Gains by Minorities and Women
Elections in Texas
Campaign Finances

The Power of Interest Groups

The business community, through endorsements and political contributions, was influential in Republicans capturing a majority of Texas House of Representatives seats in 2002, giving the GOP control of that body for the first time since Reconstruction and leading to the election of the first Republican House speaker of modern times. The Texas Association of Business, or TAB, an umbrella group representing many businesses, was one of the most visible backers of Republican candidates who supported business priorities, including more restrictions on civil lawsuits, fewer governmental regulations and holding the line on state taxes. In pursuit of its policy agenda, TAB took the unusual—and controversial—step of spending $2 million in corporate contributions on political advertising in twenty-four legislative races. Most of the candidates supported by TAB won, but the tactic prompted a criminal investigation of the business group and precipitated a debate over free speech versus undue corporate influence over elections.

State law allows officers and employees of corporations to make personal contributions to political candidates or to contribute through political action committees established for that purpose. But it is illegal for corporate funds to be given directly to a candidate, and soon after the election, Travis County District Attorney Ronnie Earle began investigating the Texas Association of Business's contributions. TAB argued that the corporate donations were legal because they weren't given directly to candidates but were used to purchase advertising that educated voters on issues important to the group. The ads didn't directly advocate the election or defeat of any candidates, although they obviously influenced election results. More than a year after it had begun, the investigation was still incomplete, because TAB fought it with a series of legal maneuvers, arguing that the ads amounted to constitutionally protected free speech. National business groups also rallied to TAB's defense, claiming that Earle, a Democrat, was letting politics influence his investigation. But Earle argued that he was merely investigating "allegations of crime."[1]

The Texas Association of Business's ad campaign was one of the more visible examples of an interest group's influence in Austin in recent years. But under both Democratic and Republican statehouse control, interest groups have long dominated Texas's policy-making process and most likely will continue to do so.

THINK ABOUT POLITICS

1 Do your elected officials care what you think about public policy and their decisions?
Yes ● No ●

2 Do working people have the same access to their state legislators as bank presidents do?
Yes ● No ●

3 Should a political party have the right to determine who can vote in its primary elections?
Yes ● No ●

4 Is there really any difference between the two major political parties in Texas?
Yes ● No ●

5 Should a candidate for public office be allowed to accept unlimited amounts of money from special interest groups?
Yes ● No ●

6 Should people be permitted to register to vote the day an election is held?
Yes ● No ●

7 Should minority groups be represented in the Texas legislature in proportion to their share of the state's population?
Yes ● No ●

Democracy is as much a struggle among competing interests at the state and local level as it is in Washington. How are the power and influence that affect the quality of life for millions of people distributed in Texas?

WHAT DO YOU THINK?

Is It Summer School or Recess for Lawmakers?

Lobbyists for numerous special interest groups spend thousands of dollars entertaining and influencing Texas lawmakers during the state's biennial, regular legislative sessions, and they don't stop there. Only a few weeks after their work in Austin ends, many lobbyists and legislators head to summer conferences, where the lawmakers are wined and dined some more.

Such conferences offer lawmakers from Texas the opportunity to discuss problems and exchange ideas with legislators from other states and to hear experts speak about a variety of important issues. They also offer special interests additional opportunities to purchase access to policy makers. The meeting schedules are usually crammed with opportunities for play as well as work. And most of the social events—dinners, golf games, tourist excursions, and other attractions—are sponsored by corporations and special interest groups. Texas taxpayers, meanwhile, pick up the tab for the legislators' airfare and hotel rooms. According to research by the *Austin American-Statesman,* taxpayers spent more than $265,000 on travel expenses for lawmakers attending three major, out-of-state conferences in 1995 and 1996.

As many as half of Texas's lawmakers may attend one or more of these conferences in any given year. Some legislators conscientiously attend as many work sessions as they can. State Representative Bob Hunter of Abilene told the *Austin American-Statesman* that he brings an empty suitcase to carry home the stacks of reports that are distributed so that he can share them with colleagues. "You glean some tremendous ideas," he said. Many other lawmakers, however, view the conferences more as social opportunities. "What did I do today? I played golf," state Representative Pat Haggerty of El Paso told a reporter after skipping an afternoon's work session. "This [the golf course] is where you make the connections that are good for business, that are good for government, that are good for whatever," Haggerty said.

Source: Austin American-Statesman, November 2, 1997.

Texas Ethics Commission

Under Texas law, organizations that lobby the legislature are required to file with the Ethics Commission. This source provides names of registered lobbyists and their clients, as well as lobbyists organized by legislative subject matter. Candidates and political action committees are also required to file their financial statements with this agency.
http://www.ethics.state.tx.us

interest group
Organization seeking to influence government policy.

Interest groups have priorities that usually cross partisan lines. Their organizational strengths and initiatives are reflected in public policy, and those segments of Texas society that are unorganized are likely to have little, if any, impact on governmental decisions. The discussion of national interest groups in Chapter 7 is applicable to Texas, and many interest groups that function on the state and local level are linked to some extent to the national system.

Just as they do at the national level, interest groups in Texas spend millions of dollars a year trying to elect favored candidates or to influence the outcome of governmental decisions through a number of direct and indirect lobbying activities. Campaign contributions have always raised ethical questions of undue influence on policy makers and are a continuing source of controversy, as the Texas Association of Business's involvement demonstrates. Moreover, aggressive and often heavy-handed lobbying efforts contribute to the view that state and local governments are dominated by a few big interests looking out for themselves (see *What Do You Think?:* "Is It Summer School or Recess for Lawmakers?").

Two studies, conducted more than forty years apart, placed Texas among states with strong interest-group systems.[2] Powerful pressure groups usually evolve in states with weak political parties, a condition that characterized Texas during most of the twentieth century.[3] During the many years that Texas was a one-party, Democratic state, the Republican Party posed no serious challenge to the Democratic monopoly, and the Democratic Party was marked by intense factionalism. Although the conservative Democratic wing dominated state politics through the 1970s, interest groups often played a greater role in the policy-making process.

Lobbyists and visitors, who are denied access to the floor of the senate chamber while the body is in session, are seen mingling outside the chamber during a tax debate.

Subsequent Republican growth has changed Texas's party system, but interest groups remain strong and, more often than not, still have a greater impact on the policy-making process than the political parties.

Pluralism or Elitism?

There are thousands of interest groups at the state and local level in Texas. Some have long histories and a durable presence in the policy process, while others are formed to address a specific need and disappear after a relatively short period. Although most groups have the potential to participate in policy making, many will not.

One can find evidence in Texas to support the pluralist view of power discussed in Chapter 1. **Pluralism** holds that significant numbers of diverse and competing interest groups serve to limit the power of any single group. Although most people do not actively participate in the policy-making process, they have access to the process through their group leaders. Pluralists believe that there are numerous leadership opportunities within groups for people who want active roles.

The number of **lobbyists** has grown significantly over the past three decades, and the hundreds now registered in Austin represent a wide assortment of economic, social, civic, and cultural organizations. Supporters of the pluralist view say this growth proves that the political system is open and accessible to new organizations. They argue that public officeholders are responsive to the needs and interests of a greater diversity of Texans than ever before.

Others insist that pluralist theories simply do not describe the realities of power and policy making in Texas. Convinced of the persuasiveness of **elitism**, they contend that the ability to influence the most important policy decisions is monopolized by a few individuals who derive power from their leadership positions in organizations or institutions with great financial resources. In one view, from 1938 to 1957 Texas was "governed by conservatives, collectively dubbed **the Establishment.**" This was a "loosely knit plutocracy comprised mostly of Anglo

pluralism Political system in which power is distributed among multiple groups.

lobbyists Individuals who attempt, directly or indirectly, to shape and influence the decisions of policy makers.

elitism Political system in which power is concentrated in the hands of a relatively small group of individuals or institutions.

"The Establishment" In the days of one-party Democratic politics in Texas, the Establishment was a loosely knit coalition of Anglo business and oil company executives, bankers, and lawyers who controlled state policy making through the dominant conservative wing of the Democratic Party.

businessmen, oilmen, bankers and lawyers" that emerged in the late 1930s, in part, as a response to the liberal policies of the New Deal. They were extremely conservative, producing a "virulent" strain of conservatism marked by "Texanism" and "super-Americanism."[4]

The "traditionalistic-individualistic" political culture described in Chapter 15 was especially conducive to the dominance of the conservative establishment, which had little interest in the needs of the lower socioeconomic groups and minorities within the state. The exclusion of minorities from participation in elections and the low rates of voter turnout, particularly among the lower socioeconomic groups, resulted in the election of public officials who were sympathetic to the views of the conservative elites. In addition, public opinion was manipulated by "unprincipled public relations men" and "the rise of reactionary newspapers."[5]

A more recent study of Texas politics argues that there is a group of Texans—extraordinarily wealthy or linked to large corporations—who constitute "an upper class in the precise meaning of the term: a social group whose common background and effective control of wealth bring them together politically."[6] While warning against the hasty conclusion that this upper class is a ruling class, the study describes their shared values, group cohesiveness, and interlocking relationships.[7] The upper class has enormous political power. When united on specific policy objectives, its members have usually prevailed against "their liberal enemies concentrated in the working class."[8] Moreover, the institutional arrangements of the state's economic and political structure work to produce upper-class unity that contributes to their successes in public policy.[9]

These sharply contrasting views of political power in Texas have produced an ongoing debate. To a large extent, the issue of who really controls Texas politics has not been resolved because of insufficient data to support one position over the other. There also is evidence that power relationships have changed over time. Historically, Texas government and public policy were dominated by an "upper class" or a "conservative establishment." But with the enormous social and economic changes that have taken place over the past twenty years, Texans may well be moving from an elitist system to some variation of pluralism.

Dominant Interest Groups in Texas

THINK AGAIN

Do working people have the same access to their state legislators as bank presidents do?

Throughout much of the twentieth century, state government was dominated by large corporations, banks, oil companies, and agricultural interests that backed the conservative Democratic officeholders who had a stranglehold on the legislature, the courts, and the executive branch. Big business still carries a lot of weight in Austin and can purchase a lot of influence through major political contributions. State officials who want to build public support for new policy proposals usually solicit the support of the business community first.

But beginning in the 1970s, influence began to be more diffused. **Single-member districts** increased the numbers of minorities, Republicans, and liberal Democrats elected to the legislature (see Chapter 18). Consumer, environmental, and other public advocacy groups emerged. Organized labor, which had been shut out by the corporate establishment, found some common interests with the trial lawyers, who earn fees suing businesses on behalf of consumers and other plaintiffs claiming damages or injuries caused by various companies or products. The decline of oil and gas production and the emergence of high-tech manufacturing and service industries also helped diffuse the business lobby into more competing factions.

single-member district
Election system in which one person is elected to represent the people living within one geographic district.

WHAT DO YOU THINK?

Do Texas Lobbyists Look Out for Your Interests?

During the 2003 regular session of the Texas legislature, about 1,600 individuals representing hundreds of businesses, trade associations, and other interests registered as lobbyists. They ran the gamut from well-dressed corporate lobbyists with generous expense accounts to volunteer consumer and environmental advocates. Most were male, although the number of women lobbyists has increased in recent years, and many women now hold major lobbying positions. Most lobbyists came to their career by way of other occupations and jobs, but they have, on the whole, an acute understanding of the policy-making process and the points of access and influence in that process. The most successful lobbyists have developed the ability to pursue a wide range of tactics based on a comprehensive strategy.

Many lobbyists are former legislators. They bring to the process their legislative skills, personal relationships with former legislative colleagues, and expertise in substantive policy areas. A number of other lobbyists are former legislative staffers.

Many of the trade and professional associations, labor unions, and public interest groups have full-time staffers in Austin who function as their lobbyists. Many corporations also use their own employees to lobby in Austin. Some companies have governmental affairs departments or offices staffed by employees with experience in government or public affairs. In large corporations that do business across the country, the governmental affairs staffs may be rather large because such companies will attempt to follow the actions of numerous state legislatures, city councils, and the U.S. Congress.

A number of lawyers have developed successful lobby practices. Some of these professional freelancers, or "hired guns," specialize in specific policy areas, while others represent a wide array of clients. Many work for the state's largest law firms, which have established permanent offices in Austin. Some of the top-notch freelancers are not attorneys, but they have a strong knowledge of the governmental process.

There are also some public relations firms that offer their services to interest groups. These companies specialize in "image creation" or "image modification." While they may not handle the groups' direct lobbying efforts, they are often retained to assist in indirect lobbying. They are particularly adroit in developing relationships with the press, planning media campaigns, and assisting in political campaigns.

Business Groups The diverse business interests in Texas organize in several ways to influence the policy-making process. First, broad-based associations, including the Texas Association of Business and the Texas Taxpayers and Research Association, represent business and industry in general. Their overall goal is to maintain and improve upon a favorable business climate.

The business community also organizes through trade associations, such as the Texas Bankers Association, the Texas Automobile Dealers Association, the Texas Independent Producers & Royalty Owners Association, the Wholesale Beer Distributors of Texas, and the Texas Chemical Council. These groups represent and seek to advance the interests of specific industries.

Finally, many individual companies retain their own lobbyists to represent them before the legislature and administrative agencies. Some wealthy individuals, such as computer magnate Ross Perot of Dallas, even hire their own lobbyists.

Although most business groups band together against organized labor, consumer advocates, and trial lawyers on major political and philosophical issues, the business lobby is far from monolithic (see *What Do You Think?*: "Do Texas Lobbyists Look Out for Your Interests?"). There are numerous issues, including tax policy and utility regulation, on which companies or trade associations differ.

Professional Groups A number of professional groups have played dominant roles in Texas politics and the policy-making process. One of the best known is the Texas Medical Association (TMA), which in recent years has joined forces with business against the trial lawyers in support of laws putting limits on malpractice suits and other damage claims against physicians and the business community. The TMA's political action committee is a major contributor of campaign dollars to candidates for the legislature and other state offices.

Litigation over medical malpractice, product liability, and workers' compensation has also expanded the influence of trial lawyers, who make their living representing injured persons. Individually and through their **political action committee,** trial lawyers have contributed millions of dollars to judicial, legislative, and other selected candidates since the 1970s. In the early 1980s, they succeeded in electing several Texas Supreme Court justices who shared their viewpoint, and the court issued major, precedent-setting opinions making it easier for plaintiffs to win large damage awards from businesses, doctors, and insurance companies. The business and medical communities retaliated by boosting their own political contributions and lobbying efforts and, by 1990, had succeeded in tipping the Supreme Court's philosophical scale back to its traditional business-oriented viewpoint.

But the war over **tort** law, as these types of damage suits are called, continued to rage before the judiciary and in the legislature. In 1995 and 2003, the legislature enacted several laws putting significant restrictions on damage lawsuits.

Education Groups In the past several years, educational interests have been very visible in the policy-making process in Austin, and higher education lobbying has been particularly effective. The changing global economy has enhanced the role of higher education in developing the state's future, and there is widespread public support for expanded access to higher education.

Most university regents, chancellors, and presidents are well connected politically. Universities also are capable—through the use of donations and other nontax funds—of hiring a well-paid cadre of lobbyists. Another effective lobbying source for universities, particularly the larger ones, are the armies of alumni—many of them politically influential—who are ready to make phone calls, send e-mails, or write letters on behalf of their alma mater when the need arises. The business community is also a strong supporter of higher education. The influence of the University of Texas System, in particular, was instrumental in the legislature's enactment of a law in 2003 giving university governing boards the authority, for the first time in Texas, to raise student tuition independently of legislative control.

The struggle for equity and quality in public elementary and secondary education in Texas, a major issue since the 1940s, has been complicated by more than two dozen groups representing various—and often conflicting—interests within the educational community. There are at least four different teachers' groups, one for school boards, one for school administrators, and still others for elementary school principals and secondary school principals. Separate groups have also been formed for urban school districts, suburban districts, rural districts, and districts with large numbers of special needs students. Virtually all these groups employ paid lobbyists, and while all claim to support educational quality, their primary goals are to protect the specific interests of their members.

Public Interest Groups Most of the public interest groups represented in Austin are concerned with protecting consumers and the environment from big

political action committee Committee organized by a corporation, labor union, trade association, ideological or issue-oriented group, cooperative, or nonprofit corporation for the purpose of collecting campaign contributions and distributing the money to political candidates.

tort A wrongful act or injury for which a damage lawsuit can be brought.

business, promoting stronger ethical standards for public officials, and increasing funding for health and human services programs for the poor, the elderly, the young, and the disabled. Many have full-time lobbyists, but these groups are seldom able to match the financial resources of business and professional organizations. Grass-roots volunteer efforts and the adroit use of the mass media are crucial to their success. Among the most active are Common Cause, the Sierra Club, Consumers Union, Texas Citizen Action, Texas Watch, the Gray Panthers, Americans Disabled for Attendant Programs Today (ADAPT), and Public Citizen, a Texas affiliate of the national public interest group founded by consumer advocate Ralph Nader.

Minority Interest Groups The advent of single-member, urban legislative districts in the 1970s significantly increased the number of African-American and Hispanic lawmakers and strengthened the influence of minority interest groups. These groups have often found that the courthouse is a shorter route to success than the statehouse, but the legislature has become increasingly attentive to their voices.

The League of United Latin American Citizens (LULAC) and the Mexican American Legal Defense and Educational Fund (MALDEF) are two of the better-known Hispanic organizations. LULAC, founded in 1929, is the oldest and largest Hispanic organization in the United States and continues to be particularly influential in causes such as education and election reform in Texas. MALDEF, formed in San Antonio in 1968, fights in the courtroom for the civil rights of Hispanics. It has been successful in numerous battles over the drawing of political boundaries for governmental bodies in Texas and in lengthy litigation over public school finance. MALDEF represented the property-poor school districts that won a unanimous landmark Texas Supreme Court order in 1989 (*Edgewood v. Kirby*) for a more equitable distribution of education aid between rich and poor school districts. The victory led to major legislative changes in the school finance system.

The National Association for the Advancement of Colored People (NAACP) is a leader in promoting and protecting the interests of African Americans. The NAACP initiated many of the early court attacks on educational inequality and the disfranchisement of minorities. More recently, this group has worked hard to increase employment opportunities for African Americans in state agencies, particularly in higher-paying administrative jobs.

In recent years, the Industrial Areas Foundation, a collection of well-organized, church-supported community groups, has become a strong and effective voice for low-income minorities. Member groups include Valley Interfaith in South Texas, Communities Organized for Public Service (COPS) in San Antonio, The Metropolitan Organization (TMO) in Houston, and the El Paso Interreligious Sponsoring Organization (EPISO).

Organized Labor Groups Organized labor has traditionally taken a back seat to business in Texas, a strong right-to-work state in which union membership cannot be required as a condition of employment. Anti-labor sentiment ran particularly high in the 1940s and 1950s, at the height of the conservative Democratic establishment's control of Texas politics. Labor-baiting campaigns in which unions were portrayed as evil communist sympathizers were not uncommon then.[10]

Today, about 500,000 Texans are members of labor unions. Among the largest unions in the state are the Communications Workers of America, the International

Brotherhood of Electrical Workers, the International Association of Machinists and Aerospace Workers, the United Food and Commercial Workers International Union, and the American Federation of State, County and Municipal Employees.

Unions can provide strong grass-roots support for political candidates through the distribution of campaign literature endorsing specific candidates, the use of union phone banks, and other get-out-the-vote efforts. Such union support has historically gone to Democratic candidates. Labor generally sides with the trial lawyers on such issues as workers' compensation, worker safety, and business liability for faulty products.

Government Lobbyists Local governments are significantly affected by state laws and budgetary decisions. The stakes are particularly high now because most governments are finding revenue harder to raise—especially with the federal government passing the cost of numerous programs on to the state, and the state issuing similar mandates to local governments. As a result, counties, cities, prosecutors, metropolitan transit authorities, and various special districts are represented by lobbyists in Austin.

Many local governments belong to umbrella organizations, such as the Texas Municipal League, the Texas Association of Counties, and the Texas District and County Attorneys Association, which have full-time lobbyists. Several of the larger cities and counties also retain their own lobbyists. Mayors, city council members, and county judges also frequently travel to Austin to visit with legislators and testify for or against bills.

Agriculture Groups Although Texas is now predominantly urban, agriculture is still an important part of the state's economy, and a number of agriculture groups are represented in Austin. Their influence is obviously strongest among rural legislators. But the Texas Farm Bureau—the largest such group and probably the most conservative—was instrumental in the 1990 defeat of liberal Democratic Agriculture Commissioner Jim Hightower, who had angered many agricultural producers and the chemical industry with tough stands on farm worker rights and pesticide regulation.

Other producer groups include the Texas and Southwestern Cattle Raisers Association, the Texas Poultry Federation, and the Texas Corn Producers Board.

Religious Groups Many people, influenced in part by their views on separation of church and state, think religious groups have little or no legitimate role in the political process. Nevertheless, religious groups have helped influence policy in Texas, and the abortion issue and other social and economic issues have increased the presence of religious groups in Austin.

A number of religious groups emerged in the 1940s with an identifiable right-wing orientation. These groups, predecessors to what is now known as the **Religious Right**, combined Christian rhetoric and symbols with anti-communist, anti-labor, anti–civil rights, anti-liberal, or anti–New Deal themes. Although these groups were often very small, they were linked to the extreme right wing of the Texas establishment, and they were the precursors of many of the conservative ideological groups that have emerged in American politics in the past twenty years.[11] Many of these organizations have gravitated toward the Republican Party[12] (see *Up Close*: "The Religious Right and Republican Growth"). With a strong organizational effort, religious conservatives were influential in a right-wing takeover of leadership positions in the Texas Republican Party in 1994.

Religious Right Political movement, based primarily in evangelical Protestant churches, that has played an increasingly prominent role in Texas and national politics.

UP CLOSE

The Religious Right and Republican Growth

As the Republican Party expanded its support in Texas, it experienced sharp, often bitter, philosophical and ideological differences among its members. Overwhelmingly conservative, Republicans were split along the lines of economic conservatism and the "lifestyle" conservatism advocated by the Religious Right.

The Religious Right has long been part of the Texas political landscape.* While its influence was occasionally manifested in conservative Democratic politics, it found far greater potential in the Republican Party for shaping electoral politics. It has strong religious overtones and draws considerable support from evangelical groups across the state. Some scholars attribute much of its success to its ability to mobilize voters who were traditionally inactive and bring them into the Republican Party. The Republicans' difficulty in attracting minority groups also gave the social conservative wing greater influence in the party.

In 1990, one scholar concluded that the Religious Right had not taken over the Republican Party, "but its influence is significant and gives the Texas Republicans their particular stridency and, at times, their appearance of a Know-Nothing movement."† In 1994, however, the Religious Right was instrumental in a takeover by social conservatives of the Republican state convention and the party leadership.

Low voter turnout in the Republican primary enabled well-organized social conservatives to gain control of the party's precinct conventions and elect a majority of delegates to the June state convention. Sensing defeat, Fred Meyer, a traditional Republican who had guided the state party for six years during a period of growth and electoral success, stepped down and was replaced by Tom Pauken, a Dallas lawyer and former Reagan administration official who courted Christian activists. Delegates also elected a new party vice chair, Christian activist Susan Weddington of San Antonio, and put other members of the Religious Right on the State Republican Executive Committee.

The Religious Right also was instrumental in the election of Republican George W. Bush over Democrat Ann Richards in the 1994 gubernatorial race. According to a survey of voters as they left the polls, 20 percent of the 4.4 million Texans who voted in that election identified themselves as white Christian fundamentalists. Of those, 84 percent said they voted for Bush. They also voted heavily for other Republican candidates.‡

Social and religious conservatives also took control of the 1996 Republican state convention and dominated the Texas delegation to the Republican National Convention. Some social conservatives, insisting the party retain its strong anti-abortion policy, tried to deny U.S. Senator Kay Bailey Hutchison a delegate's slot to the national convention because she favored abortion rights with some restrictions. Such a move would have been an unheard-of snub for a high-ranking officeholder from the party. Hutchison finally got on the delegate list with the help of Governor Bush, U.S. Senator Phil Gramm, and Republican presidential nominee Bob Dole.

The State Republican Executive Committee elected Susan Weddington state party chair after Pauken resigned in 1997 to seek the Republican nomination for state attorney general. Weddington served in that post and was an outspoken advocate for social conservative causes until 2003, when she resigned to take a job directing a new state charitable foundation. The State Republican Executive Committee elected party activist Tina Benkiser, an attorney from Houston, to succeed her.

*George Norris Green, *The Establishment in Texas Politics, 1938–1957* (Westport, Conn.: Greenwood Press, 1979), chap. 5.

†Chandler Davidson, *Race and Class in Texas Politics* (Princeton, N.J.: Princeton University Press, 1990), p. 206.

‡*Dallas Morning News,* November 11, 1994.

Many religious denominations have boards or commissions responsible for monitoring governmental action. Although staff members or volunteers serving in this capacity may not register as lobbyists, they function much like lobbyists.

Churches across the state have formed community-based organizations to address the social and economic needs of the poor. In many regards, this is a redefinition of the Social Gospel, a church-based social movement of the late nineteenth and early twentieth centuries.

The Development of a Two-Party System in Texas

THINK AGAIN

Is there really any difference between the two major political parties in Texas?

The Texas party system has been restructured by the social and economic changes that the state has experienced over the past thirty years. Texas now has a strong Republican Party and a competitive **two-party system,** but for more than a century, Texas was a **one-party** Democratic state. There was no organized opposition party to mobilize those who felt excluded from the Democratic Party. Electoral politics were based on factions and personalities; the interests of the lower socioeconomic classes—especially minorities—were blatantly neglected.

Texas Democratic Party

This site provides a range of information on state party organization, county chairs, affiliate organizations, candidates, and policy issues.
http://www.txdemocrats.org

One-Party Democratic Politics Texas's long domination by the Democratic Party can be traced to the period immediately after the Civil War, when the Republican Party was able to capture control of Texas government for a short period. Strong anti-Republican feelings were generated by the Reconstruction administration of Radical Republican Governor Edmund J. Davis, and the Republican Party was perceived by most Texans of that era to be the party of conquest and occupation. By the time the Constitution of 1876 was implemented, the Republican Party's influence in state politics was negligible. From 1874 to 1961, no Republican won a statewide office in Texas, and Republicans were elected to local offices in a few scattered districts.

The anti-Republicanism that evolved from the Civil War and Reconstruction, however, is only a partial explanation for the Democratic Party's longtime control of Texas politics. One classic study presents the provocative thesis that Texas politics might be better understood in terms of "modified class politics."[13]

As Texas's conservative agricultural leaders attempted to regain control over the state's political system after Reconstruction, the postwar economic devastation was dividing Texans along class lines. Small farmers, African Americans, and an emerging urban labor class suffered disproportionately from the economic depression of this period. They turned their discontent into support for agrarian third parties, particularly the Populist Party, which began to threaten the monopoly of the traditional Texas power structure.

To protect their political power, the established agricultural leaders moved to divide the lower social groups by directing the discontent of lower-income whites against blacks. The rural elites, who manifested traditionalistic political values and wanted to consolidate power in the hands of the privileged few, also created alliances with the mercantile, banking, and emerging industrial leaders, who reflected the individualistic view of a limited government that served to protect their interests. Over the years, these two dominant forces consolidated political power and merged the politics of race with the politics of economics.

The elites were able to institutionalize their control through the adoption of constitutional restrictions and segregation legislation, called **Jim Crow laws,** designed to reduce the size of the electorate and the potential of a popular challenge to the establishment's political monopoly.[14]

The Texas Democratic Party, however, was not homogeneous. There were factions, regional differences, and personal political rivalries. Initially, there were no sustained, identifiable factions, as voting coalitions changed from election to election through much of the first third of the twentieth century. But the onset of the

two-party system Political system that has two dominant parties, such as that of the United States.

one-party system Domination of elections and governmental processes by a single party, which may be split into different ideological, economic, or regional factions. In Texas, the phrase is used to describe the period from the late 1870s to the late 1970s, when the Democratic Party claimed virtually all elected, partisan offices.

Jim Crow laws Legislation enacted by many states after the Civil War to limit the rights and power of African Americans.

Great Depression in 1929, the election of President Franklin D. Roosevelt in 1932, and the policies of the New Deal reshaped Texas politics in the 1930s.

Factionalism in the Democratic Party Franklin Roosevelt's administrations (1933–1945) articulated and developed a policy agenda radically different from that of the Republican Party, which had dominated national politics from 1860 to 1932. Government was to become a buffer against economic downturns as well as a positive force for change. Under Roosevelt, the regulatory function of the federal government was expanded to exercise control and authority over much of the nation's economy. The federal government also enacted programs such as Social Security, public housing, and labor legislation to benefit lower socioeconomic groups.

These national policies produced an active philosophical split within the Texas Democratic Party that was to characterize Texas politics for the next two generations. A majority of Texas voters supported Roosevelt in his four elections, and the Democratic Party maintained its monopoly over Texas politics. But competing economic interests clearly—and often bitterly—divided Texas Democrats along liberal and conservative lines.

A strong Republican Party did not emerge at this time in Texas or any other southern state because "southern conservative Democratic politicians, who would have been expected to lead such a realignment, or any politicians for that matter, did not relish jumping from a majority-status party to one in the minority."[15]

Despite some liberal successes under Governor James Allred, who was elected in 1934 and again in 1936, the conservative wing of the Democratic Party prevailed in state elections from the 1940s to the late 1970s. Democratic presidential candidates carried Texas in 1944, 1948, 1960, 1964, 1968, and 1976, even though some of them were too liberal to suit the tastes of the state's conservative Democratic establishment.

At first glance, it might appear that the **bifactionalism** in the Democratic Party partially compensated for the lack of a competitive two-party system, but one scholar argued against that perception, concluding that factionalism resulted in "no-party politics." Factionalism results in discontinuity in leadership and group support, and the voter has no permanent reference point from which to judge the performance of the party or selected candidates. Since there are no clear distinctions between who holds power and who does not, the influence of pressure groups increases.[16] In one-party Democratic Texas, as noted, state government and public policy were susceptible to control by wealthy and corporate interests.

This bifactional pattern of state Democratic politics was tested by a number of factors, including the national party's increased commitment after 1948 to civil rights legislation. That development alienated segments of the white population and prompted many voters eventually to leave the Democratic Party and align with the Republicans.

Efforts by Texas oil interests to reestablish state control over the oil-rich tidelands also played a key role in the demise of one-party politics and the development of a two-party system. President Harry Truman, concerned about national security and federal access to these offshore oil resources, refused to accede to state demands and vetoed legislation favorable to Texas oil interests in 1952. That veto prompted a series of maneuvers orchestrated by Democratic Governor Allan Shivers to take the support of conservative Democrats to the Republican Party.

The "Shivercrats," as they were called, were successful in carrying Texas for the 1952 Republican presidential nominee, Dwight D. Eisenhower. This election

bifactionalism Presence of two dominant factions organized around regional, economic, or ideological differences within a single political party. For much of the twentieth century, Texas functioned as a one-party system with two dominant factions.

John Tower's surprise election to the U.S. Senate in 1961 was the first statewide victory by a Republican in Texas since Reconstruction.

helped establish a pattern of Texas's retaining its Democratic leanings in state and local elections but voting Republican in many presidential elections. Moreover, this election marked a shift in the state leadership of the Republican Party and led to efforts to create a party capable of winning local and statewide elections.[17]

In 1960, Democrat Lyndon B. Johnson ran both for election as vice president and for reelection as U.S. senator from Texas—a dual candidacy permitted under state law—and won both offices. His Republican opponent in the Senate race was John Tower, a relatively unknown college professor from Wichita Falls, who received 41 percent of the vote. After Johnson won the vice presidency and resigned from the Senate, a special election to fill the Senate seat was called in 1961. It attracted seventy-one candidates, including Tower, who defeated conservative Democrat William Blakely with 50.6 percent of the vote in a runoff.[18] Some evidence indicates that liberal Democrats, in retaliation for having been locked out of the power centers of their party and in anticipation of an ideological realignment of the party system, supported Tower in this election. The *Texas Observer*, an influential liberal publication, endorsed Tower with an argument for a two-party system. "How many liberals voted for Tower will never be known, nor will it be known how many 'went fishing,'" wrote a Republican campaign consultant.[19] Tower was reelected in 1966, 1972, and 1978, but no other Texas Republican won a statewide office until 1978, when Bill Clements was elected governor. Nevertheless, many students of Texas politics regard Tower's election in 1961 as a key factor in the development of the state's two-party system.[20]

Although Republicans made some gains in suburban congressional districts and local elections in the 1960s—including the election to Congress of a Houston Republican named George Herbert Walker Bush—the numbers were inconsequential. Most significant election battles continued to take place for a while longer within the Democratic Party, where the conservative wing generally prevailed until 1978.

realignment Major shift in political party support or identification that usually occurs around a critical election. In Texas, realignment took place as a gradual transformation from a one-party system dominated by Democrats to a two-party system in which Republicans became competitive in elections.

gerrymandering Drawing the boundaries of legislative districts in such a way as to increase the power of one group over another.

Voting Rights Act Federal law designed to protect the voting rights of minorities by requiring the Justice Department's approval of changes in political districts and certain other electoral procedures. The 1965 act, as amended, has eliminated most of the restrictive practices that limited minority political participation.

Two-Party Politics in Texas On the national level, **realignment** of political parties (see Chapter 7) is often associated with a critical election in which economic or social issues cut across existing party allegiances and produce a permanent shift in party support and identification.[21] What apparently has happened in Texas is that the state party system has been integrated into the national party system and now more closely approximates the political divisions that exist in states outside the South. Rather than occurring in a single election, this process has occurred over many years.

A major contributor to change was the civil rights movement. African Americans and Hispanics went to federal court to attack state laws requiring segregation and restricting minority voting rights. Successful lawsuits were brought against the white primary, the preprimary endorsement, the poll tax (all discussed later in this chapter), and racial **gerrymandering** of political districts. Then minorities turned to the U.S. Congress for civil rights legislation, a process that produced the 1965 **Voting Rights Act**, which Congress extended to cover Texas after 1975.

Economic factors have also shaped minority political support and, in turn, have contributed to two-party development. African Americans and Hispanics are disproportionately low-income populations and generally support such governmental services as public housing, public health care, day care, and income support. These policies are associated with the liberal wing of the Democratic Party.

Minority organizations have made concerted efforts to register, educate, and mobilize the people in their communities. As the numerical strength of minorities increased, conservative Anglo Democrats found their position within the party threatened and began to look to the Republican Party as an alternative.

The large number of people who migrated to Texas from other states, particularly when the Sunbelt economy of the 1970s and early 1980s was booming and many northern industrial states were struggling, also contributed to two-party development in Texas. Many of these new arrivals were Republicans from states with strong Republican parties, and many of them settled in high-income, suburban, Anglo areas in Texas. Other significant factors were Presidents Ronald Reagan's and George Bush's popularity in the 1980s and the 1978 election of Republican Governor Bill Clements, who encouraged many conservative Democratic officeholders to switch parties.

Other events of the 1970s and the 1980s demonstrated that the transformation of the Texas party system was well on its way. After a major stock fraud scandal, the Texas House elected a liberal Democrat, Price Daniel, Jr., as Speaker in 1973. Three other moderate-to-liberal Democrats were also elected to statewide office in the early 1970s—Bob Armstrong as land commissioner in 1970, John Hill as attorney general in 1972, and Bob Bullock as comptroller in 1974.

In 1978, John Hill defeated Governor Dolph Briscoe, a conservative, in the Democratic primary and was subsequently defeated by Republican Bill Clements, then a political unknown, in the general election by a narrow margin of 17,000 votes. Four years later, Clements lost to Democratic Attorney General Mark White, but in 1986 he returned to defeat White in an expensive, bitter campaign. In the 1982 election, Democratic candidates who were considered liberal won additional statewide offices: Ann Richards was elected state treasurer; Jim Mattox, attorney general; Jim Hightower, agriculture commissioner; and Garry Mauro, land commissioner.

The 1990 election further demonstrated how far the realignment process had gone. Democratic gubernatorial nominee Ann Richards defeated conservative business executive Clayton Williams, who had spent $6 million of his own money to win the Republican primary. But Republican Kay Bailey Hutchison was elected state treasurer, and Republican Rick Perry unseated liberal Democrat Jim Hightower to become agriculture commissioner. Republicans also retained one of the U.S. Senate seats from Texas when Phil Gramm easily won reelection to the seat once held by John Tower, and the GOP claimed 8 of the 27 congressional seats that Texas then had in Congress.

In a special election in 1993 to fill the U.S. Senate seat vacated by Democrat Lloyd Bentsen when he was appointed secretary of the treasury by President Bill Clinton, Kay Bailey Hutchison defeated Democrat Bob Krueger, thus giving the Republicans both U.S. Senate seats from Texas. Hutchison easily won reelection in 1994, despite a political and legal controversy over her administration of the state treasurer's office.

Also in 1994, Democratic Governor Ann Richards was unseated by Republican nominee George W. Bush, the son of former President George Bush and a future president himself. Republicans that year also captured four other statewide offices that had been held by Democrats, marking the most statewide gains by Republicans in any single election since Reconstruction.

Party realignment was also reflected in the Texas legislature. In 1971, Republicans held only 12 of the 181 legislative seats. But by 2004, Republicans held 88 of the 150 House seats and 19 of the 31 Senate seats.

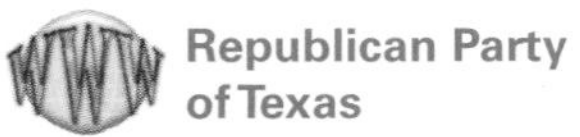
Republican Party of Texas

In addition to information about the Republican Party and links to other state party organizations, this site provides information about Republican candidates, the party platform, and a calendar of party events.
http://www.texasgop.org

Toward Republican Dominance The political transformation of Texas accelerated even more in 1996, when Republicans swept all statewide offices on the general election ballot and captured a majority of the state Senate for the first time since Reconstruction. Republican presidential nominee Bob Dole also carried the Lone Star State, despite a poor national showing against President Clinton. Republicans also increased their numbers in the Texas House and in the Texas congressional delegation. When the electoral dust had cleared, Republicans held 20 of Texas's 29 statewide elected offices, including the top three. That number increased to 21 in 1997, when Presiding Judge Michael McCormick of the Texas Court of Criminal Appeals switched from the Democratic to the Republican Party.

Lieutenant Governor Bob Bullock and Attorney General Dan Morales, both Democrats, chose not to seek reelection or any other office in 1998, and Republicans cashed in on the opportunity. With Governor Bush winning reelection in a landslide, Republicans again swept all statewide offices on the ballot. And a few weeks after the 1998 election, the GOP secured all statewide offices in Texas for the first time since Reconstruction when Texas Supreme Court Justice Raul A. Gonzalez, a Democrat, retired in midterm and was replaced by a Republican appointee of Bush. Republicans did not capture control of the Texas House but picked up four seats to narrow the Democratic margin to six seats. In the governor's race, Bush carried 69 percent of the vote against Democratic challenger Garry Mauro, the longtime land commissioner.

Democrats fielded candidates for only three of the nine statewide offices up for election in 2000. One Democrat filed for each of two seats on the Texas Court of Criminal Appeals, and five Democrats, all minor candidates with little financial support, filed for Republican Kay Bailey Hutchison's U.S. Senate seat. Democrats lost all their statewide races in 2000 but held their ground in legislative races.

Republicans also swept all statewide races in 2002, including Governor Rick Perry's victory over Democratic nominee Tony Sanchez and former Texas Attorney General John Cornyn's victory over former Dallas Mayor Ron Kirk in a race to succeed retiring U.S. Senator Phil Gramm. Republicans also finally gained control of the Texas House of Representatives in 2002, capturing 88 of the 150 seats after the Legislative Redistricting Board in 2001 had drawn new districts that favored Republicans (see Chapter 18). Additionally, the GOP increased its margin in the state Senate by winning 19 of the 31 seats. All statewide elected officials remained Republican.

The statewide losses in 2002 were particularly disappointing for Democratic leaders, who had carefully assembled a racially diverse ticket with an eye toward increasing minority turnout. Kirk, the U.S. Senate candidate, was African American, and Sanchez, a wealthy businessman from Laredo, was Hispanic. The Democratic nominee for lieutenant governor, John Sharp, a former state comptroller, was Anglo. Sanchez was unexpectedly challenged in the Democratic primary by former Texas Attorney General Dan Morales. The race was historic because it was the first gubernatorial contest in Texas between two Hispanics, and it was extremely contentious. Sanchez was supported by most party leaders because the party was banking on his wealth to help finance the Democrats' general election campaign.

Republicans were expected to achieve still another long-sought goal in 2004—a majority of Texas's congressional delegation—after the legislature, in a bitter

TABLE 17.1 Growth of Republican Officeholders in Texas, 1974–2002

Year	U.S. Senate	Other Statewide	U.S. Congress	Texas Senate	Texas House	County Offices	Total
1974	1	0	2	3	16	53	75
1976	1	0	2	3	19	67	92
1978	1	1	4	4	22	87	119
1980	1	1	5	7	35	166	215
1982	1	0	5	5	36	191	238
1984	1	0	10	6	52	287	356
1986	1	1	10	6	56	410	484
1988	1	5	8	8	57	485	564
1990	1	6	8	8	57	547	627
1992	1	8	9	13	58	634	723
1994	2	13	11	14	61	734	835
1996	2	18	13	17	68	938	1,056
1998	2	27	13	16	72	1,108	1,238
2000	2	27	13	16	72	1,299	1,429
2002	2	27	15	19	88	1,443	1,594

Source: Republican Party of Texas.

partisan fight in 2003, had redrawn congressional district boundaries to favor GOP candidates (see Chapter 18).

The GOP also has made significant gains across Texas at the county level. In 1974, Republicans held 53 county offices but had claimed 1,443 by 2003, paralleling the dramatic statewide realignment that was occurring. Democrats still held most county offices, but Republicans were battling for dominance as local voting patterns began to reflect those for statewide offices (see Table 17.1).

Third Parties There has been a tradition of third parties in Texas, including Grangers, Populists, Progressives, Socialists, Dixiecrats, the American Independent Party, Libertarians, and La Raza Unida (see *Up Close:* "La Raza Unida"). None has had statewide electoral success, a situation that can be explained in part by the cultural consensus supporting the two-party and winner-take-all election systems (see "Why the Two-Party System Persists" in Chapter 7). Most Americans do not have highly cohesive political views, which are part of the appeal of many third parties.

The most successful third party in Texas in recent years has been the Libertarian Party. Libertarians have qualified for a place on the ballot in every Texas general election since 1986 because the party has succeeded in winning at least 5 percent of the vote in at least one statewide race during each election year. But the party has never won an elected office in Texas. Another minor party, the Green Party, which puts a high priority on environmental protection, also qualified for the Texas ballot in 2002.

In addition to statewide third parties, local political organizations connected to neither the Democratic nor the Republican Party have been influential in some cities. Elections for city offices are nonpartisan, and most are held during odd-numbered years, when there are no state offices on the ballot. Cities such as San

Green Party of Texas

A third party committed to social justice, non-violence, ecology, and grass-roots democracy.
http://www.txgreens.org

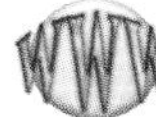

Libertarian Party of Texas

Libertarians tend to advocate a very limited role of governments, and they are particularly vocal in supporting "the right of individuals to live in whatever manner they choose, so long as they do not interfere with the right of others."
http://www.lptexas.org

UP CLOSE

La Raza Unida

La Raza Unida, led by Jose Angel Gutierrez and Mario Compean, began in 1969 to organize in Crystal City in Zavala County and then extended its influence to Dimmit, La Salle, and Hildago counties.* Overwhelmingly Hispanic and poor, these counties were characteristic of many South Texas counties where the Anglo minority controlled both the political and economic institutions, and there was little sensitivity to the needs of low-income residents. In 1972, Ramsey Muniz ran as the party's gubernatorial candidate. During the general election campaign, there was considerable speculation in the press and apprehension among conservative Democrats that La Raza would drain a sufficient number of votes away from Dolph Briscoe, the Democratic nominee, to give Henry "Hank" Grover, a right-wing Republican, the governorship. Briscoe won the election, but without a majority of the votes. The subsequent growth of liberal and minority influence within the Democratic Party, internal dissension within La Raza Unida, and legal problems encountered by Muniz contributed to the demise of this third party after 1978.

*Juan Gomez Quinones, *Chicano Politics* (Albuquerque: University of New Mexico Press, 1990), pp.128–31.

Antonio and Dallas developed citizens' associations, which controlled city governments for decades and maintained a virtual monopoly over city elections. But these local political parties have disappeared in recent years.

Changing Patterns of Party Support and Identification

The changes in party affiliations over the past forty years reinforce the argument that Texas is now a two-party state. In 1952, 66 percent of Texans called themselves Democrats, and only 6 percent claimed to be Republicans,[22] a pattern that changed little from 1952 to 1964. During the next decade, however, Republican Party identification increased to 16 percent, and Democratic Party identification declined to 59 percent (see Figure 17.1).

Between 1975 and 1984, there was a dramatic decline in voter identification with the Democratic Party and a significant increase in Republican Party identification (see *Up Close:* "Where Have All the Yellow Dogs Gone?"). By 2004, approximately 35 percent of Texas voters called themselves Republicans, and 27 percent identified as Democrats. The remainder called themselves independents (24 percent), third party affiliates or undecided (14 percent). This shift in party identification is further proof that Texas is now a Republican-dominant state (see Figure 17.2).

The Pew Research Center for the People and the Press

This research center produces numerous studies of public opinion and media habits of Americans.
www.people-press.org

As noted above, a large number of voters identify themselves as independents. Independents don't have their own party, and their choices in most elections are limited to candidates from the two major parties. Further survey research, moreover, suggests that most self-proclaimed independents vote consistently for Republican candidates.

Ticket splitting, a practice associated with the realignment process, has been common in recent Texas elections. It explains, in part, why Democrats have still been able to keep most local offices despite Republican sweeps statewide. Many Texans

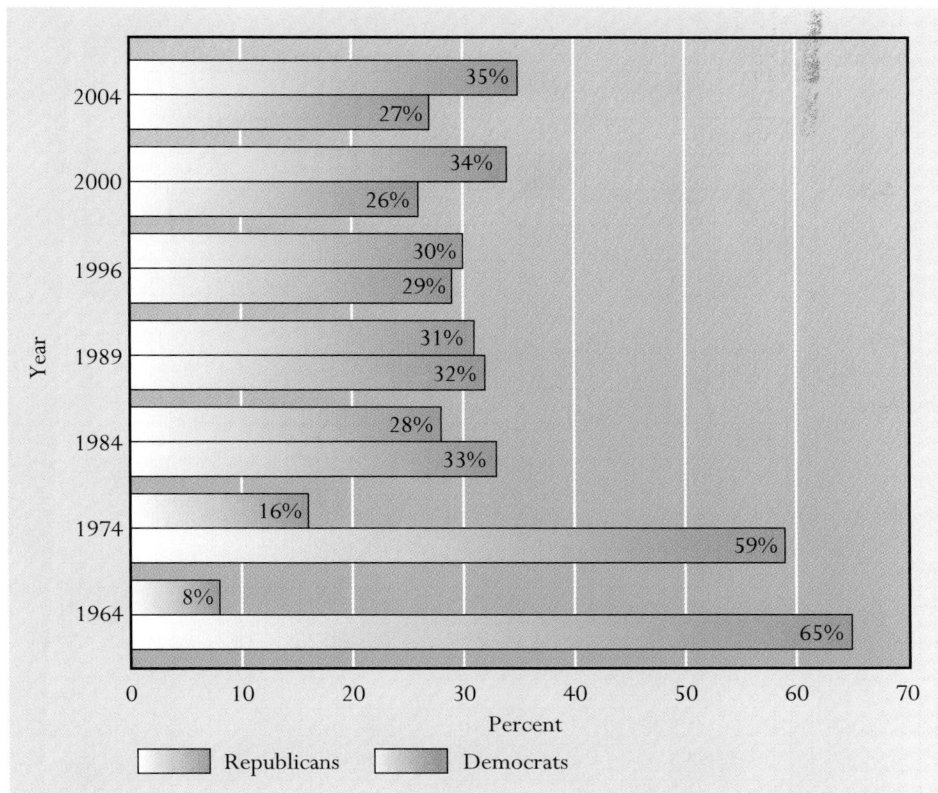

FIGURE 17.1 Changing Party Affiliation in Texas, 1964–2004

Source: The Texas Poll, Summer 1993, Fall 1993, Winter 1996, Spring 1996, Fall 1996, Spring 1999, Summer 1999, Fall 1999, Winter 2000, Summer 2003, Fall 2003, Winter 2004, Spring 2004.

cast their votes selectively as they go down the general election ballot. Ticket splitting, however, is likely to decrease in the future as the new patterns of party affiliation solidify with a further increase of elected Republican officials and a reduction in the number of Democratic candidates in areas where Republicans dominate.

The *Texas Poll* and other studies indicate marked differences in the social and economic characteristics of party identifiers. From these data, analysts have made the following generalizations:

1. The Republican Party is composed disproportionately of voters who fall into one or more of the following categories:
    - College educated
    - Newcomers to Texas
    - Anglos
    - Large metropolitan area residents
    - Earning higher incomes
    - Middle age
2. Democrats are strongly represented among:
    - Minorities
    - Older residents
    - Native Texans
    - Those with lower income levels
    - Those with less education.[23]

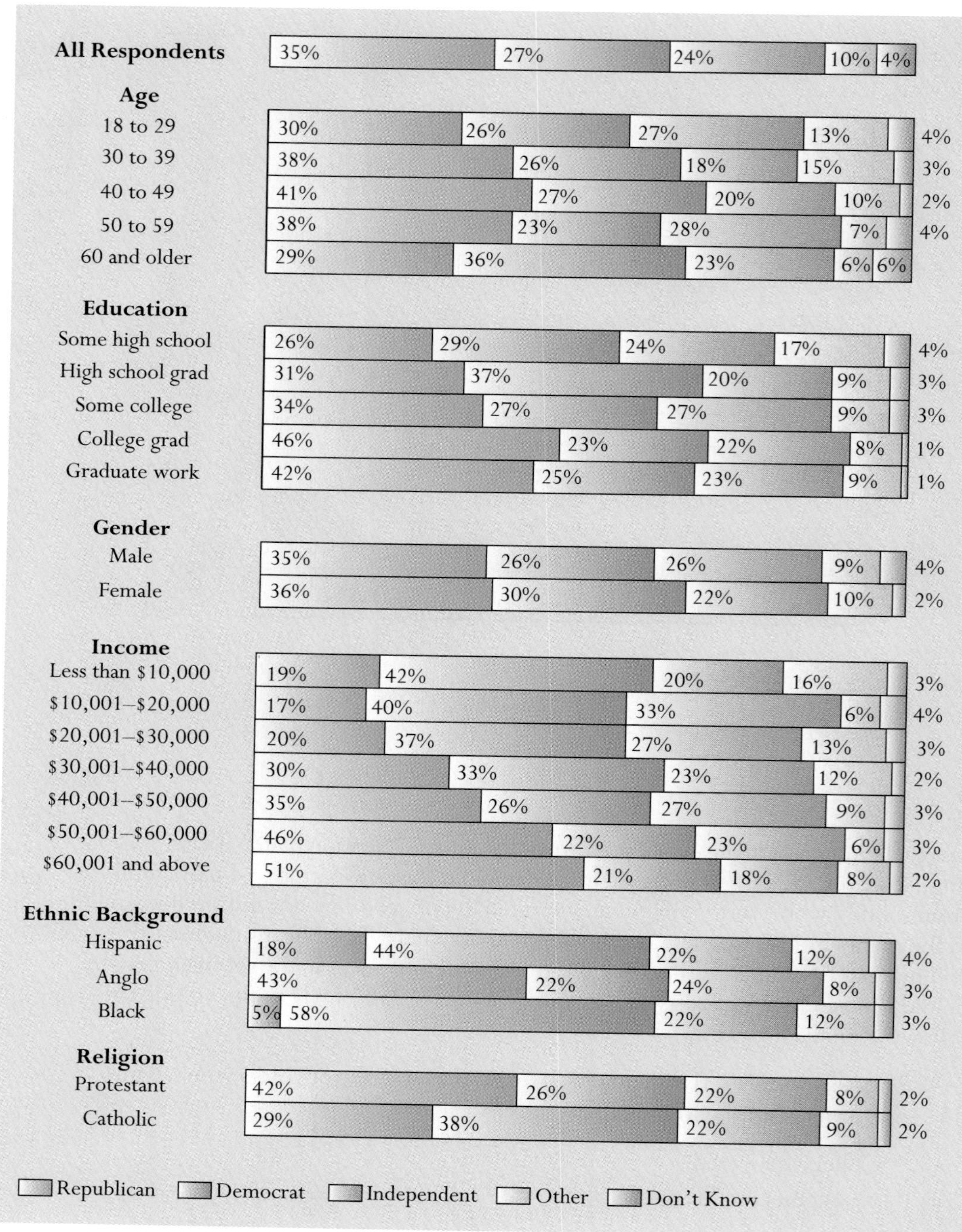

FIGURE 171.2 Party Identification of Texas Voters by Social Groups, 2004

Source: Scripps Howard, *Texas Poll,* Summer 2003, Fall 2003, Winter 2004, Spring 2004. A total of 4,000 Texans were surveyed in these polls.

UP CLOSE

Where Have All the Yellow Dogs Gone?

For a long-time Democrat (that is a person 50 or older), there is a bit of nostalgia when someone asks, "Where have all the yellow dogs gone?" To a newcomer to the state, this probably conjures up an image of a mangy, brownish, yellow mutt that is used for coon hunting or running the dogs at night while his keeper drinks hard liquor with friends around the campfire. But to a real Democrat, it is a code term for those Democrats, often white conservatives, who swore by the phrase, "I'd vote for a yellow dog if he ran on the Democratic ticket." Moreover, those "yellow dogs" also would encourage voters to "pull one lever"—that is, vote straight Democratic.

The yellow-dog, one-party voters are a dying breed. Historically, there were counties in Texas that, until recently, had never elected a Republican to local office. Some never had a Republican Party organization or had seen a Republican challenge a Democrat in a local election. With the transformation of the state to Republican dominance, there are fewer and fewer yellow dogs. Franklin County, which is in deep East Texas, didn't elect a member of the GOP from 1875 to 2000. But in 2002, three Republicans won election to local offices.

So, where have all the yellow dogs gone? The answer is clear. Many of them have died and passed over. Many others have converted to the Republican Party and are now voting the straight GOP ticket. Some of those yellow dogs have become pedigreed Republicans.

Source: John Williams, *Houston Chronicle*, November 17, 2002.

Seeking to expand the Republican Party's base, Governor George W. Bush made a strong appeal to Hispanics during his 1998 reelection campaign and was rewarded with about 40 percent of the Hispanic vote. Republicans in 2000 and 2002 also used campaign strategies aimed at peeling off Hispanic voters from the Democratic Party. Some Republican strategists have been arguing for years that the GOP must strengthen its appeal to the growing Hispanic population—and chip away at Hispanics' traditional support for the Democratic Party—if the GOP is to maintain its control over state politics. Anglo Protestants, who form the core of the Republican Party, are declining in proportion to the increased number of Hispanics in Texas. To maintain dominance, it has been argued, Republicans must embrace issues, such as improved health care and educational opportunities, which are central to Hispanic voting interests. It is premature to conclude that there will be an erosion of Hispanic support from the Democratic Party, but both parties will be battling for the Hispanic vote over the next two decades. Republicans also have spoken about the need to appeal to African American Texans who share their core values, but the GOP has had little success attracting African Americans from the Democratic Party.

WWW Project Vote Smart
Project Vote Smart is a national nonpartisan organization that tracks the performance of approximately 40,000 national and state elected officials and candidates. Information on policy positions, campaign finances and expenditures, and job performance is provided about the governor and state legislators.
http://www.vote-smart.org

The Party Organization

To carry out their functions, the two major parties in Texas have developed permanent and temporary organizations (see "Where's the Party?" in Chapter 7), structured by state law, state and national party rules and a series of court decisions protecting voters' rights.

Party organizations are built around geographic election districts, starting with the precinct. There is, however, no hierarchical arrangement to party organization.

The party structure has been described as a "system of layers of organization," with each level—county, state, and federal—concentrating on the elections within its jurisdiction.[24]

There are no membership requirements for either the Democratic or the Republican Party. Party members do not have to pay dues, attend meetings, campaign for candidates, or make contributions. When people register to vote in Texas, they are not required to state their party preference. The right to participate in a party's electoral and nominating activities is based simply on voting in that party's primary election. When a person votes in one of the major party primaries, his or her voter registration card is stamped "Democrat" or "Republican."

precincts Specific local voting areas created by county commissioners courts. The state election code provides detailed requirements for drawing up these election units.

precinct chair Local officer in a political party who presides over the precinct convention and serves on the party's county executive committee. Voters in each precinct elect a chair in the party's primary election.

The Permanent Organization Election **precincts**—there were an estimated 8,500 in Texas in 2002—are created by the county commissioners of each of the 254 counties. Voters in each precinct elect a **precinct chair** in the party primary (see Figure 17.3). Any eligible voter within the precinct can file for this position, or the names of write-in candidates can be added to the ballot. The chair calls to order the precinct convention (discussed later) and serves as a member of the county executive committee. Many people do nothing with the position, but others contribute a great deal of time and energy to deliver the precinct's votes for their party's candidates in the general election.

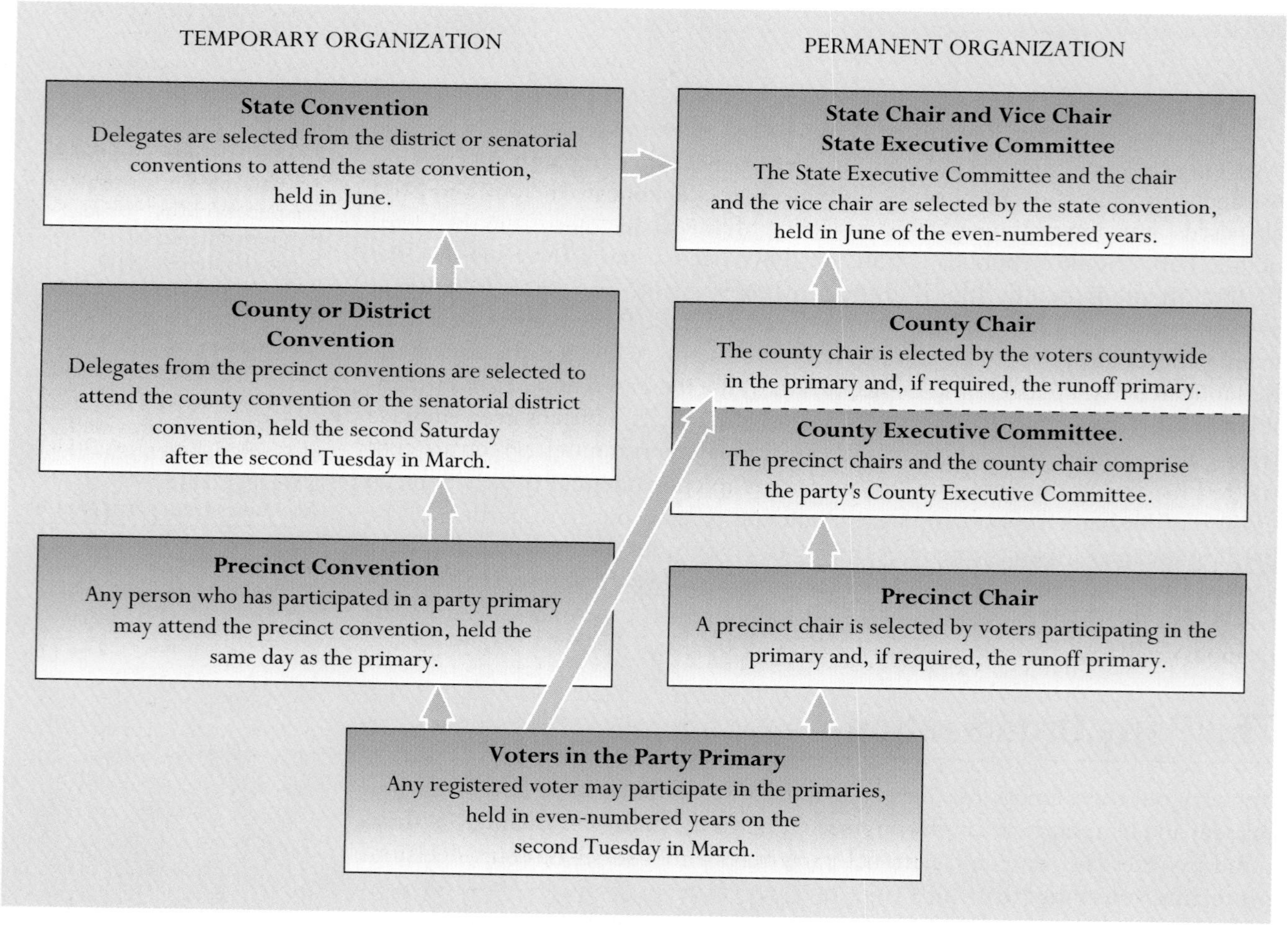

FIGURE 17.3 Organization of Texas Political Parties

The second level of the party organization is the **county executive committee,** which includes each precinct chair and the **county chair,** who is elected to a two-year term by primary voters countywide. A major responsibility of the county chair and the executive committee is the organization and management of the primary election in their county. The county executive committee accepts filings by candidates and is also responsible for planning the county or district conventions. Funds for the management of primary elections are provided to the county party by the state through the secretary of state's office.

County committees may be well organized and may actively work to carry out a wide range of organizational and electoral activities, or they may meet irregularly and have difficulty getting a quorum of members to attend. The county chair is an unpaid position. But party organizations in some counties have successful ongoing fund-raising operations, and they support a party headquarters, retain professional staff, and are engaged in various party activities between elections.

At the state level, a party's permanent organization is the **state executive committee,** which is composed of sixty-four members, including the party's state chair and vice chair. When the parties meet in their biennial state conventions, two committee members—a man and a woman—are selected by delegation caucuses from each of the thirty-one state senatorial districts. The **state chair and the vice chair,** one of whom must be a woman, also are selected by the convention. The two top state party leaders and other executive committee members serve two-year terms and are unpaid.

Statewide candidates file for office with the executive committee, which is also responsible for planning and organizing the party's state convention and helps raise funds for the ongoing operations of the party. The committee serves to establish party policy, but day-to-day party operations are entrusted to the party's executive director and professional staff. The Texas Democratic Party and the Texas Republican Party have permanent staffs and headquarters in Austin.

Temporary Organizations The temporary organizations of the political parties are the series of conventions that are held every two years, beginning on the day of the party primaries. They are particularly significant in presidential election years because they help select the state's delegates to the national party conventions. The convention system also helps organize the permanent party structure and brings party activists together to share common political concerns and shape party policies. Most Texans, however, have little knowledge of the convention system, and few participate in it.

Precinct Conventions Anyone who votes in a party primary, held on the second Tuesday in March of even-numbered years, is eligible to participate in that party's **precinct convention,** normally held in the same place as the primary after voting stops at 7 P.M. The main business of the convention is the selection of delegates and alternate delegates to the county or senatorial district convention. Since 1972, the Democrats have used complex procedures designed to assure broad-based delegate representation by ethnicity, gender, and age. A precinct convention can also adopt resolutions to be submitted at the county or district conventions for possible inclusion in the party's platform.

In presidential election years, the presidential preference primary and the precinct conventions are the first steps in the selection of delegates to the national nominating conventions. Precinct conventions held in nonpresidential election years, however, are often poorly attended, and in many precincts no one shows up.

county executive committee Panel responsible on the local level for the organization and management of a political party's primary election. It includes the party's county chair and each precinct chair.

county chair Presiding officer of a political party's county executive committee. He or she is elected countywide by voters in the party primary.

state executive committee Statewide governing board of a political party. It includes a man and a woman from each of the thirty-one state senatorial districts and the state chair and vice chair, who are selected by delegates to the party's biennial state convention.

state chair and vice chair Two top state leaders of a political party, one of whom must be a woman. They are selected every two years by delegates to the party's state convention.

precinct convention Meeting held by a political party in each precinct on the same day as the party primary. In presidential election years, the precinct conventions and the primaries are the first steps in the selection of delegates to the major parties' national nominating conventions.

Such low participation rates are cited by those who conclude that the political parties are in decline.

County or Senatorial District Conventions County or state senatorial district conventions are held two weeks after the precinct conventions. District conventions are held in the larger urban counties that include more than one state senatorial district. Delegates elected at the precinct conventions constitute the membership of this second level of the convention process, which, in turn, elects delegates to the state convention.

State Conventions The two major parties hold their **state conventions** in June of even-numbered years. Convention delegates certify to the secretary of state the names of those individuals who were nominated to statewide offices in the March primaries, adopt a party platform, and elect the state party chair, the vice chair, and the state executive committee.

In presidential election years, the state conventions also select delegates to their respective parties' national nominating conventions, elect members to their parties' national committees, and choose presidential electors. Electors from the party that carries Texas in the presidential race will formally cast the state's electoral votes for that party's presidential candidate in December after the general election.

The allocation of Texas delegates to the Republican national convention is determined by the presidential primary, but the actual delegates are selected at the state convention.

Texas delegates to the Democratic national convention are determined through a more complicated process based both on the primary vote and on candidate support from attendees at the series of party conventions, beginning at the precinct level.

Parties and Government

Political parties in Texas do not produce cohesive, policy-oriented coalitions in government, and they have been unable to hold their elected officials accountable or responsive to those supporting the party. Under ideal circumstances, some students of government believe, the two major parties would articulate clearly defined political philosophies and policies they would pursue if their candidates were elected. Once elected, persons supported by the party would be committed to these programs, giving the voters a clear standard by which to evaluate their performances in office. This perspective is often referred to as the *responsible party model* (see Chapter 7).

There are several reasons why Texas parties are incapable of functioning in this manner, none of which lessens the disenchantment and disgust that many voters feel toward political parties and politicians. First, the political parties in Texas are highly decentralized and unable to discipline members who pursue goals that conflict with the party's stated objectives. The large number of elected officials at both the state and the local level serves to diffuse party leadership. Furthermore, most of these elected officials rely primarily on their own fundraising skills and receive very limited direct financial support through the parties.

state convention Meeting held in June of even-numbered years by each of the two major political parties. Delegates to this convention elect the party's state leadership and adopt a party platform. In presidential election years, the state convention selects the delegates to the party's national nominating convention.

Moreover, the coalitions that parties form with groups harboring different objectives, interests, and agendas make it next to impossible to develop clearly stated positions that would always differentiate one party from another. Philosophical, ideological, and programmatic differences among members and supporters of the same party result, for example, in ideological voting patterns in the legislature that cross party lines.

Another explanation for the lack of partisan accountability is the long-standing anti-party tradition of American politics. Many voters are ambivalent—even outright hostile—toward political parties, and the parties make only limited efforts to include a large number of individuals in their organizational activities.

President Johnson, in a White House ceremony in 1964, signs the Twenty-fourth Amendment to the Constitution barring the levying of a poll tax in federal elections. Texas soon followed with the elimination of the poll tax in state elections.

Minorities and Political Participation

At a time when millions of people around the world have eliminated authoritarian political systems and made great sacrifices to win free and open elections, Texans congratulate themselves if one-third of the eligible population votes. Such a poor turnout cannot be blamed on a lack of opportunity. After decades of denying voting rights to large parts of the population, Texas now has one of the most progressive voter registration laws in the United States. Contemporary political campaigns, especially those for national and statewide offices, have high media visibility. People are bombarded by sophisticated television advertising campaigns, direct mail, phone bank solicitations for candidates, and daily news coverage. Yet something fundamental is disturbing Texas voters as well as voters across the nation. Statewide turnout rates in Texas are consistently low, and turnout rates in many local elections are downright appalling.

Texas has had a dark history of voter disfranchisement. The systematic exclusion of African Americans, Hispanics, and low-income whites was clearly undemocratic and created a political system in which the interests of a few could prevail over the interests of the majority.

Texas enacted a **poll tax** in 1902. Although not a large sum of money by today's standards, the $1.50 to $1.75 people had to pay in order to vote eliminated large numbers of people, especially those who were likely to support liberal social and economic policies and undermine the political establishment.[25] The poll tax was in effect for more than sixty years in Texas. It was outlawed for federal elections by the Twenty-fourth Amendment to the U.S. Constitution, adopted in 1964, but Texas retained it for state and local elections until November 1966.

THINK AGAIN

Should minority groups be represented in the Texas legislature in proportion to their share of the state's population?

In 1923, the Texas legislature enacted a law that denied African Americans the right to vote in the Democratic primary. After a series of challenges in the U.S. Supreme Court, the so-called **white primary** was finally eliminated in 1944 as a result of the court's decision in *Smith v. Allwright*.[26] But those who were intent on keeping African Americans from voting began to utilize a restrictive pre-primary selection process to pick candidates, who then would be formally nominated in the Democratic primary and subsequently elected in the general election. Finally, in 1953, the Supreme Court also declared this arrangement unconstitutional.[27]

poll tax Tax that Texas and some other states required before people were allowed to vote. The purpose was to discourage minorities and poor whites from participating in the political process. The tax was declared unconstitutional in the 1960s.

Until 1971, Texas had one of the most restrictive voter registration systems in the nation. Voters had to register annually between October 1 and January 31. Voters who did not register in person at the county courthouse could be registered by deputy registrars. But deputy registrars could not mail a large number of registrations together; they were required to deliver or mail in only one registration form at a time. This requirement thwarted coordinated voter registration drives that targeted minorities and low-income populations.[28]

white primary Series of state laws and party rules that denied African Americans the right to vote in the Democratic primary in Texas in the first half of the twentieth century.

Court action eliminated this system, and the legislature—pressured by Common Cause, the League of Women Voters, and minority groups—enacted one of the most progressive voter registration systems in the country.[29] Permanent registration was implemented, and citizens could register by mail or in person up to thirty days prior to an election. The law also made it easier to organize large voter registration drives. In 1993, the U.S. Congress enacted "motor-voter registration," which requires states to provide facilities for voter registration where a person obtains a driver's license.

Women were not given the right to vote until the adoption of the Nineteenth Amendment to the U.S. Constitution in 1920, and the adoption of the Twenty-sixth Amendment lowered the voting age from twenty-one to eighteen in 1971. Until the 1970s, property qualifications were used to exclude many voters from voting in local bond elections.

Even after the most obvious discriminatory practices against minorities were eliminated, there were more subtle, but just as pervasive, techniques for reducing the political power and influence of these same groups.

One technique is racial gerrymandering of political boundaries. State legislators and many city council members are elected from single-member districts, each of which represents a specific number of people in a designated area. To minimize the possibilities of minority candidates being elected, policymakers could divide minority communities and attach them to predominantly non-minority communities. This tactic is called cracking. Or, the minority communities could be consolidated into one district, a tactic called packing, with an 80 to 90 percent minority population, which would reduce the number of other districts in which minorities might have a chance of winning office.

At-large elections also have been used to reduce minority representation. At one time, members of the Texas House from urban counties were elected in multimember districts, which required candidates to win election in countywide races, a very difficult prospect for most minority candidates. The practice was eliminated in legislative races in the 1970s as a result of federal lawsuits. But until recently, many cities, school districts, and special districts across Texas with significant minority populations continued to use at-large elections requiring candidates to run for office citywide or districtwide. The system dilutes minority representation in most communities in which it is used because of the higher costs of campaigning and the prevalence of polarized voting, in which minorities vote for minority candidates and Anglo voters, the majority, vote for white candidates.

Political Gains by Minorities and Women

Over the past thirty years, nevertheless, minorities have made substantial gains in the electoral process. Elimination of restrictive voting laws and adoption of a liberal voter registration system have contributed to an increase in minority voters across the state, as have voter registration and mobilization drives coordinated by groups such as the National Association for the Advancement of Colored People and the Southwest Voter Registration Education Project. The federal Voting Rights Act, which was passed by the U.S. Congress in 1965 and extended to Texas 10 years later, also has played a key role. Minority groups have used the Voting Rights Act to challenge discriminatory state and local election systems in the federal courts. An election system that dilutes minority voting strength is illegal, and the Voting Rights Act requires changes in the election systems of state or local governments, including redistricting plans, to be reviewed and pre-cleared by the U.S. Justice Department or approved by the U.S. District Court in Washington, D.C. This law has been used with considerable success to eliminate at-large elections and attack racial gerrymandering of political districts. These changes enhanced election opportunities for African Americans and Hispanics, but the fight continued.

By the mid-1990s, the Voting Rights Act was under attack by conservatives. And the U.S. Supreme Court, in "reverse-discrimination" cases from Texas and Georgia, ruled that some congressional districts had been illegally gerrymandered to elect minority candidates.[30] In the Texas case, three federal judges held that the Texas legislature had violated the U.S. Constitution by designing two districts in Houston and one in the Dallas area to favor the election of African American or Hispanic candidates. The court redrew 13 congressional districts in Texas—the three minority districts and 10 districts adjoining them—and ordered special elections to fill the seats. Despite the redrawn boundaries, two incumbent African American congresswomen in the affected districts were reelected.

Hispanics According to the 2000 census, Hispanics made up 32 percent of Texas's population. But the Hispanic population is younger than the Anglo and African American populations, and Hispanics accounted for only 28.6 percent of Texans of voting age (Figure 17.4).

Hispanics also include a significant number of immigrants (an estimated one out of seven) not eligible to vote, thus reducing eligible Hispanic voters to approximately 25 percent of adult citizens. Approximately 17 percent, or 2,121,962, of the 12,455,503 Texas voters registered in February 2002 had Hispanic surnames. (These figures underrepresent Hispanic registered voters because Hispanic women married to non-Hispanics cannot be identified with methods used by the secretary of state.) But in recent general elections, Hispanics were only 12 to 15 percent of Texas voters participating.[31] Voter turnout rates among Hispanics are lower, in part, because of the lower education and income levels of many Hispanics.

Approximately 44 percent of Hispanic adults interviewed in the 2003–2004 *Texas Polls* said they identified with the Democratic Party (see Figure 17.2), but this percentage tells only part of the story. Until Governor George W. Bush made substantial inroads into the Hispanic vote in 1998, Democratic candidates for president and governor consistently received more than 70 percent of the Hispanic vote in Texas.[32]

Hispanic voters dominated the 2002 Democratic primary, which for the first time featured two Hispanic gubernatorial candidates, Laredo businessman Tony Sanchez and former Attorney General Dan Morales. One of three major candidates for the party's U.S. Senate nomination also was Hispanic—Victor Morales, a schoolteacher who had shocked party leaders by winning the 1996 nomination.

	Total Population	Percent of Total	Population of Voting Age	Percent of Total
Hispanic/Latino (any race)	6,669,666	32%	4,282,901	28.6%
White	10,933,313	52.4%	8,426,166	56.3%
African American	2,364,255	11.3%	1,631,448	10.9%
Other	884,586	4.2%	624,546	4.2%
Total	20,851,820		14,965,061	

FIGURE 17.4 2000 Population and Voting Age Population

Source: U.S. Census, 2000; Texas State Data Center.

The William C. Velasquez Institute, which specializes in Hispanic-related voting activity, reported that preliminary figures indicated that Hispanics cast a record 33 percent of the 2002 Democratic primary votes.[33] Spending heavily from his wealth on television advertising, Sanchez easily defeated Dan Morales for the gubernatorial nomination. Tapping into the Hispanic vote, Victor Morales got into a runoff for the Senate nomination with former Dallas Mayor Ron Kirk, an African American. Each received about one-third of the vote. But Kirk, who was supported by most party leaders and swamped Victor Morales in fund-raising, won the Senate runoff, when Hispanic voter turnout had fallen off. Both Sanchez and Kirk later lost their general election races to Republicans.

The increased electoral strength of the Hispanic population is borne out in Table 17.2, which compares the number of Hispanic elected officials in Texas in 1974 to those holding office in 2003. Some 540 Hispanics held elected office in 1974. By 2003, there were 1,965 Hispanic elected officials, the highest in any state. The marked increase can be attributed to a more equitable apportionment of city, county, and school district political boundaries (see Chapter 18); the growth of the Hispanic population; and increased organizational efforts among Hispanics.

By 2004, only four Hispanics—Texas Supreme Court Justices Raul A. Gonzalez and Alberto R. Gonzales, Attorney General Dan Morales, and Texas Railroad Commissioner Tony Garza—had been elected to statewide office in Texas. Victor Morales, a Hispanic schoolteacher from Crandall, a small town in north Texas, generated some excitement and received national publicity when he ran for the U.S. Senate in 1996. Operating on a shoestring budget in the primary, Morales campaigned across Texas in a white pickup truck that became a symbol of his longshot effort. To the surprise of most political observers, he defeated two incumbent congressmen and a politically experienced lawyer to win the Democratic nomination. But this David-versus-Goliath challenge of Republican Senator Phil Gramm fell short in the general election campaign. Gramm outspent his Democratic challenger 6 to 1 and easily won reelection. As noted above, Victor Morales also ran for the Democratic Senate nomination in 2002 but lost a runoff that year.

TABLE 17.2 Latino Elected Officials in Texas, 1974–2003

	1974	1996	2001	2003
Federal	2	5	6	6
State	13	35	36	38
County	102	203	213	236
Municipal	251	536	555	565
Judicial/Law Enforcement	172	323	280	338
School Board	—	536	701	736
Special District	—	51	37	46
Total	**540**	**1,689**	**1,828**	**1,965**

Source: Juan A. Sepulveda, Jr., *The Question of Representative Responsiveness for Hispanics,* Cambridge, Mass.: Harvard College, honors thesis, March 1985; National Association of Latino Elected and Appointed Officials, *National Roster of Hispanic Elected Officials,* 1996, 2001, 2003.

African Americans African Americans constitute approximately 11.3 percent of the state's population, 11 percent of the voting-age population, and 9 to 10 percent of those who vote. Approximately 61 percent of Texas African Americans call themselves Democrats, but 80 to 90 percent of the African-American vote is normally cast for Democratic candidates. Voting cohesively as a group, African Americans, like Hispanics, have considerable potential to influence the outcome of both primaries and general elections.

The increased political clout of the African-American population is also manifested in the number of African American elected officials (Table 17.3). In 1970, there were only 29 African Americans elected to public office in Texas. The number increased to 196 in 1980 and to 460 in 2001. Only two African Americans, former Texas Court of Criminal Appeals Judge Morris Overstreet, a Democrat, and Railroad Commissioner Michael Williams, a Republican, had been elected to statewide office before 2002. Two other African Americans—Republicans Wallace Jefferson and Dale Wainwright—won statewide races for the Texas Supreme Court in 2002. As noted earlier, former Dallas Mayor Ron Kirk, an African American, won the Democratic nomination for the U.S. Senate that year but lost to Republican John Cornyn in the general election.

Women Historically, the world of Texas politics has been dominated by men. Prior to Ann Richards's election as state treasurer in 1982, only two other women had been elected to statewide office. Richards was elected governor in 1990, and Kay Bailey Hutchison, who had succeeded Richards as state treasurer, was elected to the U.S. Senate in 1993. As governor, Richards also appointed more women to key positions on state boards and commissions than her predecessors.

By 2003, nine women were holding statewide offices in Texas, including Hutchison, who was still in the U.S. Senate; state Comptroller Carole Keeton Strayhorn; state Agriculture Commissioner Susan Combs; two members of the Texas Supreme Court, and four members of the Texas Court of Criminal Appeals. That same year, there were four women in the state Senate and 31 in the Texas House, a significant increase over 1981, when the legislature included only one woman in the Senate and 11 in the House.

TABLE 17.3 African American Elected Officials in Texas, 1970–2001

	1970	1980	2001
Federal	—	1	2
State	3	14	17
County	—	5	20
Municipal	16	75	282
Judicial/Law Enforcement	—	21	44
School Board	10	78	95
Special District	—	2	—
Total	**29**	**196**	**460**

Source: Metropolitan Applied Research Center, Inc. and Voter Regional Council, Inc., *National Roster of Black Elected Officials*; Joint Center for Political Studies, *National Roster of Black Elected Officials*, 1980, 1998, 2001.

Women are playing an increased role in local government as well, and this pattern can be expected to continue. Over the past three decades, the state's three largest cities—Houston, Dallas, and San Antonio—had women mayors. A 2001 survey by the Texas Municipal League counted 203 women mayors (or 17 percent) in the state's 1,210 cities. The 5,973 council members in the cities included 1,531 women, or 26 percent of the total. Of the 254 county judges in 2002, 26 (or 10 percent) were women, and women held 67 (or 6.6 percent) of 1,016 county commissioner posts.[34]

There has been little increase in the number of African-American elected officials over the past few years, but there has been an increase in the number of African-American women elected to public office. Of the 460 black elected officials in 2001, 30 percent were women.[35]

Elections in Texas

Secretary of State In addition to compiling county election data for state offices, this office provides information on election law, election procedures, county officials, and a program for voter education (Project V.O.T.E.). *http://www.sos.state.tx.us*

THINK AGAIN

Should people be permitted to register to vote the day an election is held?

Texans have numerous opportunities to vote, often as many as three or four times a year. While there are various rationales for this election scheduling by the legislature, there is evidence that it contributes to "voter fatigue," reduced voter turnout, and the disproportionate influence of a few individuals in many local and special elections where voter turnout is usually the lowest. Turnout and interest are highest in the general election in presidential election years but can be abysmally low in elections for school boards and the governing bodies of other single-purpose districts, such as hospital and water districts.

Primary Elections Texas uses the **direct primary election,** adopted in 1903, to nominate major party candidates for public office. Administered by the political parties, primaries are held on the second Tuesday in March in even-numbered years. If no candidate receives a majority, the two top vote-getters must face each other in a runoff election. For practical purposes, Texas utilizes an **open primary** where voters do not register by party. People who vote in one party's primary, however, cannot vote in the other party's runoff election.

Voter turnout in the primary is traditionally lower than in the general election, but the emergence of a two-party system in Texas is producing appreciable changes in participation patterns in the Democratic and Republican primaries (Table 17.4).

During the period of one-party, Democratic politics, the candidate who won the Democratic primary usually won the general election. From the 1920s through 1970, the rate of turnout for the Democratic primary never exceeded 35 percent of the voting-age population. Over the past 30 years, it has eroded further, reflecting the realignment of the state's party system. About 28 percent of the voting-age population (persons 18 or older) voted in the hotly contested Democratic gubernatorial primary in 1972. Since then, turnout in Democratic primaries has fallen below 20 percent.[36] Less than 7 percent of the voting-age population voted in the 2002 Democratic gubernatorial primary and less than 5.2 percent in the 2004 presidential primary.[37]

direct primary election Selection of candidates for government office through direct election by the voters of a political party.

open primary Primary election in which a voter may cast a ballot in either party's primary election.

Prior to 1980, participation in the Republican primaries in Texas never exceeded 5 percent of the voting-age population.[38] That rate has increased somewhat since then, but the percentage of Texans voting in a Republican primary has never reached the level of participation that the Democratic Party experienced when it dominated state politics. One million voters, or 8.3 percent of voting-age Texans, cast ballots in the 1988 Republican presidential primary, when Texan George Bush

TABLE 17.4 Democratic and Republican Primary Turnout, 1972–2002

Year	Race	Republican Primary Vote	Democratic Primary Vote
1972	President/Governor	114,007	2,192,903
1974	Governor	69,101	1,521,306
1976	President	356,307	1,529,168
1978	Governor	158,403	1,812,896
1980	President	526,769	1,377,767
1982	Governor	265,794	1,318,663
1984	President	336,814	1,463,449
1986	Governor	544,719	1,096,552
1988	President	1,014,956	1,767,045
1990	Governor	855,231	1,487,260
1992	President	797,146	1,482,075
1994	Governor	557,340	1,036,944
1996	President	1,019,803	921,256
1998	Governor	596,839	664,532
2000	President	1,159,645	793,825
2002	Governor	622,423	1,024,814
2004	President	687,615	839,231

Source: Secretary of State, Elections Division.

was on the ballot. That is the highest turnout percentage in a Republican primary in Texas so far. Only 4 percent of Texans old enough to vote participated in the 2002 Republican gubernatorial primary, when incumbent Governor Rick Perry had only minor opposition. Approximately 688,000 voters cast ballots in the 2004 Republican presidential primary, when George W. Bush sought a second term, but they accounted for only 4.3 percent of the voting-age population.[39]

The above data mean that a smaller percentage of the population is now involved in selecting political nominees throughout the state. And those who participate in party primaries tend to be more ideological in their political orientation than the general population.

General Elections General elections for state and federal offices are held on the first Tuesday after the first Monday in November in even-numbered years. The names of the candidates nominated in the primaries by the two major parties are placed on a ballot, along with the names of Libertarian and Green party candidates and other third party candidates who have submitted petitions bearing the names of eligible registered voters equal to 1 percent of the vote in the last gubernatorial election.

In the 1896 presidential election, the turnout rate was more than 80 percent of the eligible voting-age population, but in 1908, four years after the effective date of the poll tax, turnout had fallen to approximately 35 percent. During much of the period from 1910 to 1958, turnout rates in non-presidential elections were less than 20 percent. Presidential elections generated a somewhat higher turnout, but in very few instances did the turnout rate exceed 40 percent of eligible voters.

Forty-seven percent of Texas's voting-age population cast general-election ballots in the 1984 presidential race, 44 percent in the 1988 presidential election, approximately 50 percent in the spirited three-way presidential election of 1992, 41 percent in 1996, and 44 percent in 2000. But only 29 percent of the voting-age population cast general-election ballots in the 1986 gubernatorial race, 31 percent in the 1990 race, 34 percent in the 1994 gubernatorial election, 27 percent in 1998 and 29 percent in 2002.[40]

City, School Board, and Single-purpose District Elections Most local elections, which are nonpartisan, are held in May in odd-numbered years to minimize the convergence of issues in state and local races. Across the state, there are wide variations in the competitiveness of these elections, campaign costs, and turnout. But turnout rates rarely match those in the general election and are often abysmally low.

Special Elections The legislature can submit constitutional amendments to the voters in a general election or schedule them in a special statewide election. Local governments also conduct special elections for bond issues, local initiatives and referenda, and the recall of public officials. Although these elections occasionally arouse high interest, turnout rates tend to be extremely low. The governor also can call special elections to fill vacancies in certain offices, including legislative and congressional seats.

Extended Absentee Balloting In 1988 Texas made a major change in the requirements for **absentee (or early) voting** to permit any voter to cast a ballot from the twentieth day to the fourth day prior to an election. Special early voting areas are established—including many at shopping malls and other convenient locations—and voters do not have to provide an excuse for casting their ballots early. Consequently, there has been a notable increase in the number of early votes—20 percent to 30 percent of all votes in some areas. Extended early voting has forced candidates to identify two different sets of voters and develop strategies that require campaigns to "peak" twice. Several other states have followed Texas's lead in eliminating another barrier to political participation.

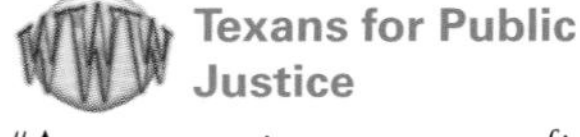

Texans for Public Justice

"A non-partisan, non-profit research organization which tracks the influence of money and corporate power in Texas politics." ***www.tpj.org/index.jsp***

THINK AGAIN

Should a candidate for public office be allowed to accept unlimited amounts of money from special interest groups?

absentee (or early) voting Period before the regularly scheduled election date, during which voters are allowed to cast ballots. With recent changes in election law, a person does not have to offer a reason for voting absentee.

Campaign Finances

Campaign Costs No one knows precisely how much is spent on political campaigns in Texas because there is no single place where all this information is collected. Candidates for state office file campaign finance reports with the state Ethics Commission, but candidates for city councils, county offices, and school boards file reports with the jurisdictions in which they are running. Costs vary across the more than 2,000 governmental units, but modern campaign technology and paid media are extremely expensive, even on the local level. A few recent examples of campaign costs in selected races are illuminating.

City council races in major cities such as San Antonio, Houston, Fort Worth, and Dallas can easily cost $50,000 to $100,000. Bob Lanier spent $3 million getting elected mayor of Houston in 1991, and eight candidates spent more than $6.6 million in the 1997 race to succeed him. The 1997 winner, Lee Brown, spent more than $2.1 million alone, and the second place finisher, businessman Rob

Mosbacher, spent more than $3.5 million.[41] Those earlier figures, however, paled in comparison to the nearly $9 million that businessman Bill White spent to win the 2003 Houston mayor's race.[42] There have been reports of candidates for county commissioner spending $100,000 and of district judges in metropolitan counties spending more than $150,000. Historically, school board elections have been low budget, but it is not uncommon for slates of candidates in large urban school districts to spend $10,000 to $15,000 in low-turnout elections.

Many people believe that campaign expenditures in statewide races in Texas, particularly gubernatorial races, are excessive. But fueled by the rising costs of television advertising and other modern campaign techniques—and two-party competition—expenditures continue to increase. Republican Rick Perry and Democrat Tony Sanchez spent more than $80 million in the 2002 governor's race. Sanchez's expenditures included more than $50 million from his own pocket. He won a hard-fought victory over former Attorney General Dan Morales in the Democratic primary before losing to Perry in the general election (Table 17.5).

Candidates for lieutenant governor in 2002 raised more than $25 million. Republican David Dewhurst, the victor, raised $16.3 million, including $11.3 million of his own money. Candidates for other statewide executive offices that year raised $24.1 million combined, with Republican candidates raising much more than Democrats.[43] Winning candidates in state Senate races in 2002 raised an average of $587,000, and winners of races for the Texas House raised an average of $165,000.

Fund Raising Soaring campaign costs have raised considerable concern about campaign fund raising and contributions in Texas, as they have also nationally (see "Raising Campaign Cash," in Chapter 5). There is concern that elections are being bought and that major campaign contributors are purchasing influence in the policy-making process. Some critics of contemporary campaigns have argued that

TABLE 17.5 Contributions by Type of State Office, 2001–2002

Office	Totals for Winner in General Election	Totals for Loser in General Election	Totals for Primary Losers
Governor	$20,469,556	$62,373,012	$ 132,797
Lt. Governor	16,347,728	8,703,573	—
Comptroller	4,996,428	825,059	—
Attorney General	7,803,818	5,250,157	—
Land Commissioner	1,399,122	1,308,427	—
Railroad Commissioner	1,198,258	202,742	671,375
Agriculture Commissioner	1,744,202	233,249	—
Supreme Court	3,229,026	1,866,737	1,657,643
Court of Criminal Appeals	13,103	5,450	110,321
House	24,664,676	5,504,926	2,914,705
Senate	17,735,122	1,886,165	1,845,598
Totals	**$99,587,936**	**$88,159,496**	**$7,332,439**

Source: From *Money in Politex: A Guide to Money in the 2002 Texas Elections*, November 2003. Copyright © 2003 by Texans for Public Justice. Reprinted by permission of Texans for Public Justice.

PEOPLE IN POLITICS

Bob Perry: Homebuilder and Big Contributor

Houston homebuilder Bob Perry tries to maintain a low public profile, but in recent years he has received significant publicity for emerging as one of Texas's most generous political contributors. In 2002, he was the biggest donor to state political candidates and causes, contributing at least $3.8 million during that election cycle, mostly to Republicans. Texas Land Commissioner Jerry Patterson, a former state senator and one of many candidates backed by Perry, said the homebuilder had never asked for favors. "He's a reserved, serious and principled guy who has never tried to influence my vote. He truly is a philosophical contributor, who wants to improve the Republican Party," Patterson said.*

But Perry's voice obviously is heard. He was believed to be influential in the legislature's creation in 2003 of a new state agency, the Residential Construction Commission, to develop performance standards for builders and discourage lawsuits against builders by unhappy homebuyers. Governor Rick Perry (who isn't related to the homebuilder) appointed an executive of Bob Perry's company to the new agency's board, less than one month after the governor had received a $100,000 contribution from Bob Perry. The homebuilder had contributed more than half a million dollars to Rick Perry since 1997. The governor's office said the appointment wasn't influenced by the contributions, but by the appointee's experience in the homebuilding industry.†

**Houston Chronicle*, December 22, 2002, p. 1A.

†Houston Chronicle, September 30, 2003, p. 1A.

current practices are a form of legalized bribery, implying that public officials are available to the highest bidder.

Unlike the federal government, Texas places no limits on the amount of money a single individual or political action committee can contribute to most political candidates. The only exceptions in Texas are campaign contribution limits in judicial races, which were imposed by the legislature in 1995. There are no limits on how much a candidate in any race can contribute to his or her own campaign. Large contributions have long played a role in Texas politics, and, over the years, most large contributions have gone to the conservative candidates, both Democratic and Republican.

Political Action Committees and Fat Cats Just as they have on the national level, political action committees (PACs) have increased their importance at the state and local level by bringing sophisticated fund-raising skills to political campaigns. Representing special interest groups or individual companies, PACs collect money from their members and are a ready source of campaign dollars. They are in the business of influencing elections.

PACs and business-connected donors gave more than $50 million to candidates during the 2002 campaign season in Texas. One of the biggest contributors was Texans for Lawsuit Reform, which gave almost $2 million and played a leading role in a successful lobbying effort in 2003 that produced more restrictions on damage lawsuits against doctors and businesses. Other major contributors included the Texas Association of Realtors, the Texas Trial Lawyers Association, the Texas Medical Association, the Texas Dental Association and the Texas State Teachers Association. Forty-one individuals, often referred to as "fat cats," made contributions to candidates and PACs of $200,000 or more during the 2002 election cycle. The 50 top individual contributors to candidates gave $14.3 million, or 11 percent of the total contributions[44] (see *People in Politics*: "Bob Perry: Homebuilder and Big Contributor").

Attempts at Reform On the heels of the Sharpstown scandal, in which high-ranking state officials were given preferential treatment in the purchase of stock in an insurance company (see Chapter 22), the legislature enacted a major campaign finance disclosure law in 1973 that, with some changes, is now administered by the state Ethics Commission. Although it did not limit the size of political contributions, for the first time it required candidates to list the addresses as well as the names of donors and the amounts and dates of contributions. It also required political action committees contributing to candidates or officeholders to report the sources of their donations, which in the past had usually been hidden. Also for the first time, officeholders were required to file annual reports of their political contributions and expenditures—even during years when they were not seeking reelection—and candidates were required to report contributions and other financial activity that occurred after an election. A candidate also had to formally designate a campaign treasurer before he or she could legally accept political contributions. Campaign finance reform, however, remains a difficult and seemingly endless struggle.

SUMMARY NOTES

- Political power in Texas is related to the resources available to groups and organizations actively engaged in the political process. The great disparity in the distribution of resources raises fundamental questions about equity in access to policy makers and the decision-making process.
- Pluralist theorists argue that political power in Texas is distributed among a wide range of groups and interests, none of which has a monopoly on the institutions of government. While there are marked differences in the resources of groups, there is sufficient competition and interaction among groups to achieve the goals of a democratic society. Public policy, in this view, reflects the compromise of competing interests.
- Advocates of elitist theory argue that political power in Texas is concentrated in the hands of a relatively small number of individuals who derive their resources from powerful institutional bases. These institutions are tied together with complex interlocking relationships, and access to their leadership positions is limited. Called the "Texas Establishment," those who monopolized power in the past were predominantly white males from the higher socioeconomic groups. Although there is some competition among these elites, there also is a great deal of consensus. Historically, the establishment has expressed indifference, if not hostility, toward the interests of labor, minorities, and the lower socioeconomic groups.
- The interest-group system in Texas was historically dominated by oil and gas, agriculture, and financial institutions. But dramatic changes in the state's economy, the political mobilization of minorities, and the development of public interest groups have produced considerable change. Not only are more groups now participating in the policy arena, but some of the traditionally dominant groups apparently have experienced a dilution of their power. Policies directed to the interests of the lower socioeconomic groups are modest indications of these changes.
- For much of its political history, Texas had a one-party, Democratic system, characterized by two dominant factions. This weak party system, based in part on the systematic exclusion of many citizens through discriminatory election laws, contributed to a powerful interest-group system. In Austin, as well as at the local level, the

raw power of interest groups is seen in most aspects of the decision-making process, often to the detriment of the general public.

- Over the past thirty years, there have been significant changes in the state's party structure. One-party Democratic control has been transformed by complex economic, social, and political changes, and Texas is now a two-party state dominated by the Republican Party. Texas voters are divided among Democrats, Republicans, and independents, but the GOP has an edge.
- Historically, politics in Texas was configured around class and race, and these two factors are still primary dimensions of partisan alliances.
- Parties have rarely functioned as highly cohesive, disciplined organizations, either in the electorate or in government. With candidate-centered campaigns, many elected officials act as free agents, aligning with other groups and having little fear of recrimination from the political party.
- One of the most disturbing aspects of the contemporary Texas political system is the low voter turnout in most elections, despite the elimination of discriminatory election laws, the creation of an extended voting period, and easy voter registration.
- Although most discriminatory election barriers have been eliminated, racial gerrymandering and at-large election systems continue to generate controversy.
- Over the past thirty years, Hispanics and African Americans have realized substantial gains in the electoral process and increased success in winning election to public office. There has also been a dramatic increase in the number of women elected to public office.
- With varied election cycles for multiple levels of government, Texans are subjected to a continuous election process, contributing to "voter fatigue" and indifference.
- The costs of statewide campaigns, as well as many regional and local campaigns, have escalated over the past three decades. While money may not buy public officials, it certainly buys access to them, and it creates the impression that well-organized interests, corporations, and wealthy individuals have a disproportionate influence on policy makers.
- Despite changes in the partisan lineup, Texans have not expressed a significant shift in their philosophical orientations over the past twenty years. Most Texans still classify themselves as moderate to conservative.

KEY TERMS

interest group 564
pluralism 565
lobbyists 565
elitism 565
"The Establishment" 565
single-member district 566
political action committee 568
tort 568
Religious Right 570
two-party system 572
one-party system 572
Jim Crow laws 572
bifactionalism 573
realignment 574
gerrymandering 574
Voting Rights Act 574
precincts 582
precinct chair 582
county executive committee 583
county chair 583
state executive committee 583
state chair and vice chair 583
precinct convention 583
state convention 584
poll tax 585
white primary 585
direct primary election 590
open primary 590
absentee (or early) voting 592

SUGGESTED READINGS

Anders, Evan. *Boss Rule in South Texas: The Progressive Era.* Austin: University of Texas Press, 1982. Utilizing recent perspectives on political machines, the author provides a comprehensive analysis of political bosses in South Texas counties during the Progressive Era.

Black, Earl and Merle Black, *The Rise of Southern Republicanism.* Cambridge, Mass: Belknap Press, 2002. A comprehensive assessment of Republican realignment in the southern states.

Davidson, Chandler. *Race and Class in Texas Politics.* Princeton, N.J.: Princeton University Press, 1990. An adaptation of V.O Key's earlier analysis to contemporary Texas politics, this work assesses the dimensions of race and class and addresses the issue of a governing elite.

Dyer, James A., Jan E. Leighley, and Arnold Vedlitz. "Party Identification and Public Opinion in Texas, 1984–1994: Establishing a Competitive Two-Party System," in *Texas*

Politics, ed. Anthony Champagne and Edward J. Harpham (New York: W.W. Norton, 1997). A pre-2000 analysis of party realignment in Texas, offering various scenarios for the configuration of party politics in the state.

Elliott, Charles P. "The Texas Trial Lawyers Association: Interest Group Under Siege," in *Texas Politics,* ed. Anthony Champagne and Edward J. Harpham (New York: W.W. Norton, 1997). Examines the activities of the Texas Trial Lawyers Association, the organization's relationships with like-minded interest groups, and the problems faced battling the dominant business interests in the state.

Garcia, Ignacio. *United We Win: The Rise and Fall of La Raza Unida Party.* Tucson: Mexican American Studies and Research Center at the University of Arizona, 1989. Written from the perspective of an activist, this book is an "interpretive essay" tracing the development of La Raza Unida with the formation of MAYO (Mexican-American Youth Organization) to its demise in the early 1980s.

Green, George Norris. *The Establishment in Texas Politics: 1938–1957.* Westport, Conn.: Greenwood Press, 1979. A historical perspective that concludes Texas politics was controlled by corporate elites who, in their reaction to the New Deal, developed and fostered a form of reactionary conservatism permitting predatory interest groups to dominate the electoral and policy processes.

Hrebenar, Robert J., and Clive S. Thomas, eds. *Interest Group Politics in Southern States.* Tuscaloosa: University of Alabama Press, 1992. A twelve-state study of interest groups in which the authors conclude that interest groups in Texas have moved from personalized lobbying to information-based communications.

Key, V. O. *Southern Politics.* New York: Vintage Books, 1949. This classic study of southern politics details the politics in each of the states of the Confederacy and provides a historical framework for understanding contemporary political changes in the region.

Knaggs, John R. *Two-Party Texas: The John Tower Era, 1961–1984.* Austin: Eakin Press, 1986. An assessment of the early development of the modern Republican Party in Texas.

Lenchner, Paul. "The Party System in Texas," in *Texas Politics,* eds. Anthony Champagne and Edward J. Harpham (New York: W.W. Norton, 1997). In addition to a brief overview of Republican successes since the 1960s, this article raises the issue of the potential of Texas becoming a one-party Republican state.

Navarro, Armando. *La Raza Unida Party: A Chicano Challenge to the U.S. Two-Party Dictatorship.* Philadelphia: Temple University Press, 2000. An assessment of the La Raza Unida Party grounded in third party literature.

San Miguel, Guadalupe, Jr. *Let Them Take Heed: Mexican Americans and the Campaign for Educational Equality in Texas, 1910–1981.* Austin: University of Texas Press, 1987. Describes Mexican-American organizational efforts to promote educational equality over a seventy-year period.

CHAPTER 18

THE TEXAS LEGISLATURE

CHAPTER OUTLINE

The Texas Legislature: A Time of Change
Legislative Functions
Institutionalization of the Texas Legislature
The Organization and Composition of the Texas Legislature
Representation and Redistricting
Legislative Leadership
The Committee System
Rules and Procedures
The Emerging Party System
Other Legislative Caucuses
Legislators and Their Constituents
Legislative Decision Making
The Development of Legislative Staff
Legislative Ethics and Reforms

THINK ABOUT POLITICS

1 Does it make sense to limit the Texas legislature to 140 days every two years?
Yes ● No ●

2 Would our state representatives and senators do a better job if we paid them more than their current salary of $7,200 per year?
Yes ● No ●

3 Should candidates for the Texas state legislature be limited in the amount of money they can spend to get elected?
Yes ● No ●

4 Should Texas state legislators be limited in the number of terms they can hold office?
Yes ● No ●

5 Should the legislature be allowed to borrow money to pay for current budget expenditures?
Yes ● No ●

6 Do the men and women making laws in Texas really care about you?
Yes ● No ●

7 Should members of the Texas legislature be required to publicly identify all groups or individuals who lobby them on legislation?
Yes ● No ●

Even a part-time legislature still has considerable power over the laws that affect your life. And your interests often compete with those of other people and groups.

The Texas Legislature: A Time of Change

The Republican takeover of the Texas House of Representatives in 2003 was a watershed event in state politics. It marked the first GOP majority of that body since the 1870s and assured Tom Craddick's election as the first Republican House speaker since Reconstruction. Moreover, it gave Republicans control of all major power points in the statehouse because they also maintained their majority in the state Senate and their hold on the governor's office. The conservative GOP agenda dominated legislative deliberations, including the crucial balancing of a new state budget. Despite a $10 billion revenue shortfall, Republican leaders held the line against higher state taxes, drawing applause from many middle-income and wealthy Texans. But lawmakers imposed spending cuts that reduced the availability of health care and other services for low-income and disadvantaged Texans and further widened the divide between the privileged and the unfortunate.

Legislative partisanship also increased in 2003, thanks primarily to a bitter fight over congressional redistricting that took the regular session and three special sessions to resolve. The effort was orchestrated by U.S. House Majority Leader Tom DeLay of Texas to give Republicans a majority of the Texas congressional delegation and help the GOP maintain control of the U.S. Congress. Until that point, Democrats had held a 17–15 majority of the congressional seats from Texas, despite widespread Republican gains in other state offices. The battle to redraw the district lines to favor more Republican candidates focused national attention on the legislature when Democratic lawmakers, on two separate occasions, fled to neighboring states to block action on redistricting bills. More than 50 Democrats fled to Ardmore, Okla., for four days that spring to deprive the House of a quorum and kill a redistricting bill in the regular session. And 11 Democratic state senators spent more than a month in Albuquerque, N.M., to shut down the Senate for an entire special session that summer. Eventually, the Republicans prevailed, but the experience left behind a bitter, partisan taste in Austin that could affect future legislative deliberations.

The legislative experiences of 2003 reflected some of the enormous social, political, and economic changes that have occurred in Texas during the past generation. Forty years ago, a rural-dominated legislature showed little concern for the problems of urban areas and minority groups. Operating within the context of one-party Democratic control and an interest group system dominated by oil, finance, and agriculture, legislative leaders tied to conservative factions in the Democratic party pursued selected policies that benefited those sectors of the Texas economy.

Today, Texas is the country's second most populous state and is more than 80 percent urban. The ethnic and racial characteristics of its population have changed, and still more changes are projected in its social composition. Texas is now dominated by the Republican party, its economy is diversifying, and there are more demands today on the legislature than in the past. The issues and policy questions that confront lawmakers are more complex, and the special interests demanding attention are more numerous and diverse.

Despite these major demographic and political changes, however, lawmakers still have to operate under outdated constitutional restrictions—including strict limits on when they can meet—that were written for a rural state in a bygone era.

Legislative Functions

The legislature, whose members are elected from districts throughout Texas, is the chief policy-making branch of state government. Its basic role is similar to that of Congress at the federal level, although there are major differences between the two institutions. The Texas legislature performs a variety of functions, but its primary task is to decide how conflicts between competing groups and interests are to be resolved—that is, who gets what, when, and how. Although often taken for granted, this orderly, institutionalized process of conflict management and resolution is critical to a stable political system.[1]

THINK AGAIN

Does it make sense to limit the Texas legislature to 140 days every two years?

Enacting Laws Every two years, the legislature enacts several hundred laws governing our behavior; allocating resources, benefits and costs; and defining the duties of those institutions and bureaucrats responsible for putting these laws into effect. From local legislation that affects only a city or county to general statewide policies and proposals for constitutional amendments, there are literally thousands of ideas advanced for new laws every legislative session. The legislative arena includes a wide range of players in addition to legislators, and lawmaking requires compromise and accommodation of competing ideas and interests.

Texas Legislature On-Line

In addition to providing links to other legislative Web sites such as the House, Senate, Legislative Budget Board, state auditor, and the Sunset Commission, TLOL provides legislative histories, access to bills, amendments, and statutes affected by proposed legislation.

http://www.capitol.state.tx.us

Budgets and Taxes The legislature establishes programs providing a variety of public services and sets priorities through the budgetary process. It sets the budgets for the governor, the bureaucracy, and the state courts. It decides whether state taxes should be increased, how high they should be increased, and how the tax burden should be distributed. Indirectly, its actions affect local tax rates as well.

Overseeing State Agencies Hundreds of laws are passed each legislative session, and the legislature assigns to specific state agencies and local governments the responsibility of carrying out the laws on a day-to-day basis. It is ultimately the legislature's responsibility to make sure agencies and bureaucrats are doing what they are charged with by law, and this review, or "oversight," process is achieved through legislative budget hearings, other committee investigations, and program audits. The Senate further influences policy by confirming or rejecting the governor's appointees to hundreds of state boards and commissions that administer public programs.

Educating the Public The 181 members of the Texas Legislature certainly do not speak with one voice, and on major policy issues it is inevitable that there will be a variety of opinions and proposed solutions. Individual lawmakers try to inform the public about their own actions and the collective actions of the legislature. They use speeches, letters to constituents, news releases, telephone calls, newsletters, Web sites, e-mails, and other techniques to explain the legislative process, substantive policy issues, and their views on issues.

Representing the Public The legislature is a representative body whose members are chosen in free elections. This process provides legitimacy to legislative actions and decisions. People may disagree over how "representative" the legislature is in terms of race, ethnicity, gender, or class. And many Texans may be indifferent toward or ignorant about public policy. But successful lawmakers must demonstrate concern for the attitudes and demands of their constituents. Legislators use many methods to learn how their constituents feel, including public opinion polls, questionnaires, phone calls, town hall meetings, and personal visits with constituents.

Institutionalization of the Texas Legislature

As noted at the beginning of this chapter, the Texas Legislature has undergone significant institutional changes over the past 130 years. Some changes have been due to external factors, such as the development of a two-party system within the electorate, changes in the state's interest-group system, and complex social and economic problems. Other changes were internal. They included the increased tenure of the membership, changing career and leadership patterns, expanded workload, the development and enforcement of complex rules and procedures, and the emergence of partisan divisions. Political scientists describe these developments as **institutionalization.**[2]

Institutionalization varies throughout the fifty states. Some state legislatures are highly professional; others are not. In some states, salaries are high, turnover is limited, and legislators think in terms of legislative careers. Similarly, some legislatures have developed sophisticated staff and support services. By contrast, in other legislatures, members are poorly paid, turnover is high, legislative service is regarded as a part-time activity, and support services are limited. The Texas legislature falls somewhere between those legislatures that can be classified as highly professional and those that can be classified as amateur or citizen law-making bodies.[3] The institutionalization process has produced a more professional legislature in Texas, and this development is likely to continue in the future.

institutionalization In the context of political science, the development of a legislative body into a formally structured system with stable membership, complex rules, expanded internal operations, and the delineation of staff functions.

National Conference of State Legislatures

This national organization provides a wide range of reports and data on state legislatures.
http://www.ncsl.org

The Organization and Composition of the Texas Legislature

Following the oppressive efforts of Governor Edmund J. Davis and the Reconstruction Republicans to centralize power (see Chapter 16), the delegates to the constitutional convention in 1875 were distrustful, even fearful, of the excesses and abuses of big government. They created a part-time, **bicameral legislature**

bicameral legislature Lawmaking body, such as the Texas legislature, that includes two chambers.

that included a 31-member Senate and a 150-member House of Representatives, and they placed strong restrictions on it. All other states also have **bicameral legislatures** except Nebraska, which has only one lawmaking body with 49 members. The sizes of other state senates range from 20 in Alaska to 67 in Minnesota, while houses of representatives vary in size from 40 in Alaska to 400 in New Hampshire.[4]

Legislative Sessions To curb lawmakers' power, the Texas constitutional framers limited **regular sessions** of the legislature to a maximum of 140 days every two years but gave the governor the authority to call **special sessions** when necessary. Lawmakers convene in regular session on the second Tuesday of January in odd-numbered years. Special sessions are limited to 30 days each and to subjects submitted by the governor, but there is no limit on the number of special sessions a governor can call.

There have been periods of frequent special sessions. From midsummer of 1986 through midsummer of 1987, for example, during a lingering budgetary crisis spawned by a depressed oil industry, the legislature convened for its regular 140-day session plus four special sessions, two of which lasted the maximum 30 days. The seventy-first legislature in 1989–90 held six special sessions to deal with equalization of school funding and the provision of medical expenses and other compensation for workers injured on the job. The seventy-second legislature had two special sessions in the summer of 1991 to write a new budget, pass a tax bill, make major changes in the criminal justice system, and redraw the boundaries of congressional districts. And, as noted earlier, the seventy-eighth legislature had three special sessions in the summer and early fall of 2003 in a protracted, partisan fight over congressional redistricting. The governor called a special session to deal with financing public education, but the session adjourned without action being taken.

Some state officials and government experts believe that the Texas legislature should have annual regular sessions, at least for budgetary purposes. Only six other state legislatures do not. But the change would require a constitutional amendment.

THINK AGAIN

Would our state representatives and senators do a better job if we paid them more than their current salary of $7,200 per year?

THINK AGAIN

Should Texas state legislators be limited in the number of terms they can hold office?

Terms of Office and Qualifications Article III of the Texas Constitution contains the constitutional provisions pertaining to the structure, membership, and selection of the Texas legislature. Representatives serve two-year terms, and senators are elected to four-year, staggered terms. A senator has to be a qualified voter, at least twenty-six years old, a resident of Texas for five years preceding his or her election, and a resident of the district from which elected for at least one year. A representative must be a qualified voter, at least twenty-one years old, a Texas resident for two years, and a resident of the district represented for one year. There is no limit on the number of terms an individual can serve in the legislature.

regular session 140-day period in the odd-numbered years in which the legislature meets and can consider and pass laws on any issue or subject.

special session Legislative session that can be called at any time by the governor. This session is limited to thirty days and to issues or subjects designated by the governor.

Pay and Compensation Members of both the house and the senate and their presiding officers have a base pay of $7,200 per year. This figure is set by the state constitution and can be raised only with voter approval. This is one of the lowest legislative pay levels in the country and was last increased in 1975 by a constitutional amendment that also set lawmakers' per diem, or personal expense allowance, at $30 a day while they were in session. The house and the senate authorize additional expense allowances for members to cover staff salaries and other costs of operating legislative offices.

In 1991, Texas voters approved a constitutional amendment creating a state Ethics Commission that could recommend legislative pay raises to the voters and change legislative per diem on its own. The commission set per diem at $125 per day for the 2003 legislative sessions.

By 2002, only Texas, Alabama, New Hampshire, and Rhode Island had limits on legislative pay that could be changed only by constitutional amendment. Compensation commissions now recommend legislative pay levels in some states, while legislatures in other states set their own salaries, often with the approval of voters. In 2000, legislative pay ranged from a high of $99,000 a year in California, where lawmakers set their own salaries and are considered a full-time legislature, to a low of $100 a year in New Hampshire, which has annual sessions but a constitutional limit on salaries[5] (see *What Do You Think?*: "How Much Is a Legislator Worth?").

Physical Facilities The house chamber and representatives' offices have traditionally been located in the west wing of the state Capitol, and the senate chamber and senators' offices in the east wing (see Figure 18.1). The pink granite building was completed in 1888, but the growth of state government and periodic renovations created a hodgepodge of cramped legislative offices. After one visitor died in a fire behind the senate chamber in 1983, it also became obvious that the building had become a firetrap. So in 1990 the state launched a $187 million Capitol restoration and expansion project that included a four-story underground addition to the building. Legislative committee hearing rooms and many lawmakers' offices were relocated from the main building to the underground extension, which is connected to the original Capitol and nearby office buildings by tunnels.

When the legislature is in session, access to the floor of each chamber on the second floor of the Capitol is restricted to lawmakers, certain state officials, some staff members, and accredited media representatives. The galleries, to which the public is admitted, overlook the chambers from the third floor of the Capitol. In both the house and senate chambers, members have desks facing the presiding officer's podium, which, in turn, is flanked by desks of the clerical staff. Unlike the U.S. Congress, where seating is arranged by party affiliation, seats are assigned to state legislators by seniority.

WHAT DO YOU THINK?

How Much Is a Legislator Worth?

Supporters of higher legislative pay in Texas say a raise is only fair because legislative service has become much more than a part-time job for many lawmakers, particularly during periods of frequent special sessions. They argue that the present low compensation level effectively restricts legislative service to wealthy individuals or those who have law practices or own businesses in which their partners or employees can help take up the slack while they are in Austin. They believe higher pay would broaden the potential pool from which legislators are drawn—and perhaps improve the prospects for quality—by encouraging more salaried working people to run for legislative office.

The outside personal income of many legislators obviously does suffer while they are in office, but legislative service can enhance business and professional connections. Critics of higher legislative pay also note that candidates, many of whom spend thousands of dollars to get elected to the legislature, know the pay level before they run for the office. And Texas lawmakers have provided themselves with one of the best legislative retirement plans in the country. Retirement is computed on the basis of state district judges' salaries, which legislators raise during almost every regular session, thereby increasing their own retirement benefits as well. Many former legislators receive pensions that are much larger than their paychecks were while they were in office.

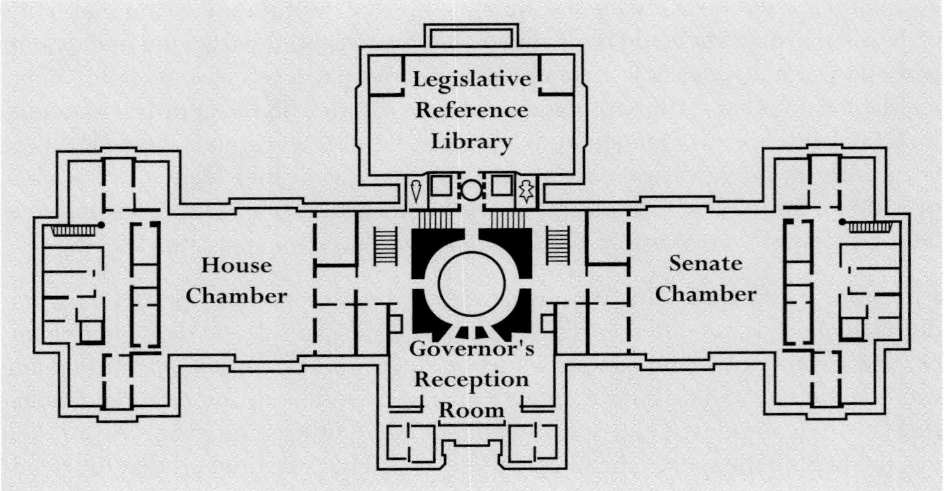

FIGURE 18.1 Corridors of Power in the Texas Capitol

The second floor of the Texas Capitol, shown here, houses the senate and house chambers, the Legislative Reference Library, and the Governor's Reception Room.

Membership and Careers In 1971, the Texas legislature was overwhelmingly white, male, and Democratic. There were two African Americans in the 150-member house and one in the 31-member senate. The one African-American senator was also the only woman in the senate. She was Barbara Jordan of Houston, who two years later would begin a distinguished career in the U.S. Congress. Frances Farenthold of Corpus Christi was the only woman in the house. She was a reform-minded lawmaker who was often referred to as "the Den Mother of the Dirty Thirty," a coalition of liberal Democrats and conservative Republicans who challenged the power of Speaker Gus Mutscher while a major political scandal in which he was involved was unfolding. In 1972, Farenthold ran a strong race for governor in the Democratic primary but lost a runoff election to Uvalde rancher Dolph

Completed in 1888 and recently renovated, the Texas Capitol in downtown Austin houses the governor's office and meeting chambers for the house of representatives and the senate.

Briscoe. There were eleven Hispanic members of the house and only one Hispanic senator in 1971. Only twelve legislators were Republicans—ten in the house and two in the senate.

By 2003, changing political patterns and attitudes, redrawn political boundaries, and court-ordered single-member districts for urban house members had significantly altered the composition of the legislature (see Table 18.1). During the regular session and special sessions that year, Republicans had a 19–12 majority in the senate. The senate also had two African American members, seven Hispanics and four women. The house in 2003 had an 88–62 Republican majority, its first Republican majority of modern times. The 150 house members included 14 African Americans, 30 Hispanics, one Asian American, and 31 women. Representation from the urban and suburban areas of the state had grown, reflecting the population shifts accommodated by redistricting.

Business has been the dominant occupation of legislators serving in recent years, followed by law. Most of the 31 senators and more than 60 of the 150 house members in 2003 had a business background. Eight senators and 47 house members were attorneys, although not all of them made their living practicing law. The house included one chiropractor, one pharmacist, one automobile dealer, a drive-in restaurant owner, and a flight instructor. Two senators were physicians, one was a consulting engineer, and one was a retired firefighter.

Senators' ages ranged from 39 to 68, with an average age of 54. The age range for members of the house was 24 to 78, with an average age of 49.

Various career patterns lead to election to the legislature.[6] Lawmakers include former members of city councils and school boards, former prosecutors, former legislative aides, and longtime Democratic and Republican party activists. Twenty of the thirty-one senators in 2003 had previously served in the house. Many first-term legislators, however, arrive in Austin with relatively little political experience.

Legislative Turnover Compared to other states, turnover in the Texas legislature is moderate. Relatively few individuals who serve can be considered career legislators. Only four senators and ten house members entered the 2003 regular session with twenty or more years of legislative service. The average legislative experience

TABLE 18.1 Comparative Profile of Texas Legislators, 1971–2003

	House			Senate		
	1971	1981	2003	1971	1981	2003
Democrats	140	112	88	29	24	12
Republicans	10	38	62	2	7	19
Males	149	139	118	30	30	27
Females	1	11	32	1	1	4
Hispanics	11	17	30	1	4	7
African Americans	2	13	14	1	0	2
Anglos	137	120	105	29	27	22

Source: Texas house and senate rosters, 1971, 1981, 2003.

in the senate was thirteen years; house members had served an average of seven years. In addition to the effects of redistricting of legislative seats every ten years, turnover is due to the low pay and the personal costs involved in running for public office. While in session, many legislators lose income from their regular sources of employment. Political ambition is also a factor. Many lawmakers who want to move up the political ladder serve only a few terms in the Texas house before running for the Texas senate, the U.S. Congress, or other state or local offices. Other legislators quit after a few sessions to become lobbyists.

Redistricting and voluntary retirements took a toll on legislative experience after the 2001 session. Several veteran lawmakers didn't seek reelection in 2002, including the two most senior members of the senate, Senators Carlos Truan, D-Corpus Christi, and J.E. "Buster" Brown, R-Lake Jackson. Truan had served twenty-four years in the senate and eight in the house. Brown had been in the senate for twenty years. Representative Rob Junell, D-San Angelo, longtime chairman of the budget-writing House Appropriations Committee, also called it quits.

Representation and Redistricting

Many European legislatures use a system called *proportional representation,* in which legislative seats are allocated on the basis of each party's percentage of the total vote in an election. By contrast, the Texas legislature and most other American legislatures allocate seats geographically on the basis of **single-member districts.** The long legal and political battles over apportionment and redistricting address some of the fundamental questions of who should be represented and how they should be represented (see Chapter 8).

single-member district System in which a legislator, city council member, or other public official is elected from a specific geographic area.

The Texas Constitution of 1876 provided that the legislature redraw state representative and senatorial districts every ten years, "at its first session after the publication of each United States decennial census," to reflect changing population patterns. But members of earlier rural-dominated legislatures were reluctant to apportion the legislative seats equitably to reflect the increased urbanization of the state, and inequities grew. In 1948, Texas voters approved a constitutional amendment creating the **Legislative Redistricting Board** to carry out redistricting responsibilities if the legislature failed to do so during the required session. The board includes the lieutenant governor, the speaker of the house, the attorney general, the comptroller, and the land commissioner.

THINK AGAIN

Do the men and women making laws in Texas really care about you?

Legislative Redistricting Board A board created by constitutional amendment charged to redistrict the Texas legislature if it is not accomplished in the regular session following the release of the census.

But for many more years, the urban areas of the state were still denied equality in representation. After the 1960 census, it was possible for approximately 33 percent of the state's population to elect a majority of both the Texas house and the senate. And rural legislators tended to neglect urban problems.

Equality in redistricting finally came to Texas as a result of federal court intervention. In 1962, the U.S. Supreme Court, in the case of *Baker v. Carr,* applied the principle of equality to congressional districts. Then, in the case of *Reynolds v. Sims* (1964), the court held that state legislative districts had to be apportioned on the "one person, one vote" principle. Litigation in 1965 (*Kilgarlin v. Martin*) extended this ruling to Texas, and the "reapportionment revolution" was to produce dramatic changes in the composition and structure of the Texas legislature.[7] To a large degree, the increased representation of minorities and Republicans in Texas's lawmaking body is a result of the legal and political redistricting battles.

The Texas senate has always been elected by single-member districts, and after the 1970 census, the application of the "equality principle" to the senate resulted in districts that were comparable in size. The issues of racial and partisan gerrymandering—the practice of drawing lines to favor a particular individual or group (see Chapters 8 and 17)—were still to be resolved through subsequent litigation and federal legislation.

Speaker Tom Craddick presides over the House of Representatives.

Rural members of the Texas house were also elected from single-member districts, but in the urban counties that had been allocated more than one representative, the elections were held in multimember districts. Each candidate for a house seat in an urban area had to run for election countywide, a practice that put ethnic and political minorities at a disadvantage because their votes were diluted by the dominant Anglo and Democratic populations.

In 1972, a three-judge federal court ruled that multimember districts in Dallas and Bexar counties were unconstitutional because they diluted the voting strength of African Americans in Dallas and Hispanics in Bexar. Coincidentally, the **at-large districts** diluted the voting strength of Republicans in both counties.

Despite the fact that 50 percent of Bexar County's population was Hispanic, under the at-large election system only one Hispanic from Bexar had served in the Texas house in 1971. Dallas County, which had a large African American population, had only one African American house member. Single-member districts in Harris County had been drawn by the Legislative Redistricting Board in 1971, and after the U.S. Supreme Court upheld the lower court's decision regarding Dallas and Bexar counties, multimember legislative districts were soon eliminated in all other urban counties. After 1975, the U.S. Congress put Texas under the provisions of the federal Voting Rights Act, which prohibits the dilution of minority voting strength, requires clearance in advance of redistricting plans by the Department of Justice, and gives African Americans and Hispanics an effective weapon to use in challenging a redistricting plan in court.

At the beginning of the twenty-first century, however, minorities believed their fight for equal representation was still far from over. The Voting Rights Act was under attack by conservatives. The U.S. Supreme Court, in "reverse discrimination" cases from Texas and Georgia, ruled that some congressional districts had been illegally gerrymandered to elect minority candidates. And in another case from Georgia, the high court held in 2003 that states have the right to determine how best to draw legislative and congressional districts to protect minority voters.[8]

Texas Republicans scored huge redistricting victories in 2001, after the legislature failed to redraw its own districts during that year's regular session. Under the state constitution, the task then fell to the five statewide elected officials, four of whom were Republicans, on the Legislative Redistricting Board. The panel drew new legislative maps that helped increase Republican strength in the 31-member senate to 19 GOP senators. It also enabled Republicans to capture their first majority of modern times in the 150-member house. With legislative candidates running under the new plan in the 2002 elections, the GOP increased its strength in the house from 72 seats to 88 seats, a margin that cleared the way for state Representative Tom Craddick of Midland, a Republican, to be elected speaker after the regular session convened in 2003. The GOP takeover of the Texas House also gave Republicans the opportunity to redraw the boundaries for Texas's congressional districts later that year. Republicans prevailed after a bitter partisan fight that included two walkouts by Democratic legislators. The new congressional map was expected to give Republicans a strong majority among members of the U.S. Congress elected from Texas (See *Up Close:* "Redistricting: Partisans at War").

at-large district Legislative or other political district, sometimes called a multimember district because two or more officials are elected from it, that includes an entire county, city, or other political subdivision.

UP CLOSE

Redistricting: Partisans at War

The contentious, nationally publicized fight over congressional redistricting in 2003 was not the Texas Legislature's finest hour. But the drama of Democratic lawmakers fleeing across state lines to shut down legislative business in Austin, the bitter partisan rhetoric, and the persistence of the eventual Republican victors vividly illustrated the huge political stakes that were involved.

The Republican takeover of the Texas house in 2003 gave the GOP control of state government, but Democrats still held a 17–15 edge among members of the U.S. Congress elected from Texas. The lines for congressional districts had been redrawn to reflect new census data in 2001 by a federal court, not by the legislature, because the Texas house, which still had a Democratic majority in 2001, couldn't agree on a new map with the Republican-dominated senate. Once Republicans had control of both legislative chambers, the Republican leader of the U.S. House, Congressman Tom DeLay, began urging Texas Republican leaders to redraw the congressional lines to favor more Republican candidates and help their party maintain its narrow majority of the U.S. House. But a redistricting bill died late in the regular legislative session that spring when more than fifty Democratic members of the Texas House fled to Ardmore, Okla., to break a house quorum and prevent the body from conducting business for four days—long enough to miss a deadline for action on the redistricting measure. The Democrats, outnumbered 88–62, didn't have enough votes in the house to defeat the bill outright, but they had enough members to shut down work, because a quorum required two-thirds of the members to be present. The Democrats left the state in order to avoid being arrested by state troopers and forced to return to the Capitol. In their absence, Speaker Tom Craddick and the remaining members had placed a "call" on the house, authorizing the sergeant-at-arms to enlist the aid of law enforcement officers to round up the missing members.

Republican leaders, most notably DeLay and Governor Rick Perry, didn't give up. Perry called the legislature back into a thirty-day special session in June to tackle redistricting again. This time, Democrats didn't bolt, and the house easily approved the bill. But the measure died in the senate, where Democratic senators used the "two-thirds rule" to block action on it. That traditional procedure required two-thirds of the senators to approve debate on any legislation, and Republicans, although they were in the majority, didn't constitute two-thirds of the body. At the end of the first special session, Lieutenant Governor David Dewhurst, a Republican who earlier had been reluctant to force a vote on redistricting, announced that he would bypass the two-thirds requirement during a

Legislative Leadership

The highly institutionalized leadership structure found in the U.S. Congress (see Chapter 8) is only now beginning to emerge in the Texas legislature—and to only a limited extent. Until recent years, the Texas legislature was dominated by a small group of Democratic lawmakers. With no significant party opposition or minority representation for much of the state's history, legislative leadership was highly personal and dependent on the political relationships between the presiding officers and key legislators. Recent Republican growth in the statehouse, however, is beginning to force changes.

House Leadership The presiding officer of the house of representatives is the **speaker**, who is elected by the house from among its membership. With the long tenures of Gib Lewis and his immediate predecessor in the speaker's office, Bill Clayton, there was not a contested speaker's race between 1975 and 1991. Lewis's decision not to seek reelection in 1992 prompted several house members to announce their candidacy for the post. But veteran Democratic Representative James E. "Pete" Laney, a farmer-businessman from Hale Center, secured the support of the

speaker Presiding officer of the house of representatives.

second special session. That prompted eleven Democratic senators to fly to Albuquerque, N.M., breaking a senate quorum, only minutes before Perry issued a proclamation calling the second special session. The Democrats remained holed up in New Mexico for more than a month, outlasting the entire second session. The only Democratic senator who didn't flee was Ken Armbrister of Victoria, who represented a strongly Republican district.

While the national media listened and watched, the Democrats in Albuquerque and the Republicans in Austin exchanged a barrage of partisan charges and countercharges. The dissident Democrats—who included nine minorities and two Anglos who represented predominantly minority districts—accused the Republicans of trying to redraw congressional districts to dilute the voting strength of Hispanics and African Americans. "This is a shameful return to the days of the Jim Crow laws designed to prevent electoral participation of minorities in the South," said state Senator Leticia Van de Putte of San Antonio, chair of the Senate Democratic Caucus. Dewhurst and the Republican senators denied the charges. They said redistricting would enhance minority voting strength. And they argued that Republicans, who had a majority in Texas, were entitled to a majority of congressional seats from the state. Republican senators also took the unusual step of imposing sanctions—including thousands of dollars in fines—on the absentees.

The stalemate finally ended when one of the Democrats, state Senator John Whitmire of Houston, returned to Texas, announcing that he would continue the fight on the senate floor. Because Whitmire's return restored the senate's two-thirds quorum, the remaining dissidents returned as well. Perry called a third special session in September, and Republican majorities in the house and the senate approved different versions of a redistricting map. Final approval was delayed for several days because house and senate Republicans, ironically, continued to fight among themselves over a handful of districts. The main hangup was over West Texas, where Speaker Craddick insisted that his hometown, Midland, get a congressional district it could dominate. In the end, Craddick got his wish, but not before DeLay visited Austin to personally help negotiate between House and Senate members of the conference committee that drew the final map.

The third special session ended on October 12, and Perry quickly signed the new redistricting plan, which was expected to give Republicans as many as twenty-two of Texas's thirty-two congressional seats. Democrats filed suit in federal court to block the plan, but a three-judge federal panel approved it in time for the 2004 elections. Republican state senators, meanwhile, didn't enforce the fines they had imposed on the dissident Democrats.

Source: Houston Chronicle, August 14, 2003, p. 25A.

necessary majority of house members several weeks before the 1993 legislature convened, and his election on the opening day of the session was unopposed.

Laney served five terms as speaker and, although he was a Democrat, enjoyed the support of many Republican house members. Continuing a bipartisan tradition, he appointed several Republicans to chair house committees. But Republicans, after winning a strong majority of house seats in the 2002 elections, elected state Representative Tom Craddick, a Republican from Midland, to succeed Laney as presiding officer in 2003. Laney, who had won reelection to his West Texas district in 2002, remained in the house, becoming the first former speaker in years to return to a seat on the house floor after having been presiding officer.

It is illegal for a speaker candidate to make outright promises in return for members' support. But, continuing a tradition, Craddick gave his key supporters choice leadership positions when the new speaker exercised one of his most significant, formal powers and made his committee assignments. Legislators know that the earlier they hop onto a winning bandwagon in a speaker's race, the better chance they will have of getting their preferred committee assignments or the opportunity to advance their legislative programs. Sometimes, however, choosing the winning candidate is difficult because the campaigning is conducted

Texas House of Representatives

This site provides direct access to live broadcasts of legislative proceedings, information pertaining to the legislative process in the House, information from the speaker's office, and general information about the Capitol complex. Biographical information, committee assignments, district data, and addresses are provided for each member of the House.
http://www.house.state.tx.us

largely behind the scenes, with candidates making personal pleas to individual house members.

Until the 1950s, it was unusual for a speaker to serve more than one two-year term (see Table 18.2). The position was circulated among a small group of legislators who dominated the house. Clayton, a lawmaker from Springlake in West Texas, set a record by serving four consecutive terms before retiring in 1983. Lewis of Fort Worth and Laney each surpassed Clayton's record by serving five terms.

Unlike most of their predecessors, Clayton, Lewis, Laney, and Craddick devoted long hours to the job and kept large full-time staffs. With the complexities of a growing state putting more demands on the legislative leadership, recent senate leaders (lieutenant governors) have also made their jobs virtually full-time and, like the speaker, have hired large staffs of specialists to research issues and help develop legislation. The presiding officers also depend on key committee chairs to take the lead in pushing their legislative priorities.

During Laney's speakership, the state completed a multibillion-dollar expansion of its prison system, overhauled criminal justice laws, and enacted a school finance law that addressed a Texas Supreme Court order for more equity in education spending. In a bipartisan endeavor, Laney actively supported then-Governor George W. Bush's unsuccessful effort to replace a large chunk of local school prop-

TABLE 18.2 Recent Presiding Officers

Lieutenant Governors	When Served	Home
Ben Ramsey	1951–1961*	San Augustine
Preston Smith	1963–1969	Lubbock
Ben Barnes	1969–1973	DeLeon
Bill Hobby, Jr.	1973–1991	Houston
Bob Bullock	1991–1999	Hillsboro
Rick Perry	1999–2000	Haskell
Bill Ratliff	2000–2003	Mt. Pleasant
David Dewhurst	2003–	Houston
Speakers	**When Served**	**Home**
Reuben Senterfitt	1951–1955	San Saba
Jim T. Lindsey	1955–1957	Texarkana
Waggoner Carr	1957–1961	Lubbock
James A. Turman	1961–1963	Gober
Byron M. Tunnell	1963–1965	Tyler
Ben Barnes	1965–1969	DeLeon
Gus Mutscher	1969–1972	Brenham
Rayford Price	1972–1973	Palestine
Price Daniel, Jr.	1973–1975	Liberty
Bill Clayton	1975–1983	Springlake
Gib Lewis	1983–1993	Fort Worth
James E. "Pete" Laney	1993–2003	Hale Center
Tom Craddick	2003–	Midland

*Ben Ramsey resigned as lieutenant governor on September 18, 1961 upon his appointment to the Railroad Commission. The office was vacant until Preston Smith took office in 1963.

Source: Texas Legislative Council, *Presiding Officers of the Texas Legislature, 1846–1982* (Austin: Texas Legislative Council, 1982); Texas Legislature Online.

erty taxes with higher state taxes in 1997. He also encouraged opposing sides to find common ground on other major issues, but one of his own priorities was to improve the way the house conducted its business. Laney won significant changes in house rules that produced, in the view of many house members, a more democratic lawmaking process than under previous speakers.

Backed by a Republican majority, Craddick was a key figure in the legislature's tight-fisted approach to drafting the new state budget in 2003, which cut spending in many areas to bridge a $10 billion revenue shortfall. He was a strong opponent of raising state taxes, although he insisted the legislature enact a separate law allowing university governing boards to raise college tuition. Craddick also was a key figure in the legislature's enactment of the redistricting bill to increase the number of Republicans elected to Congress from Texas. He was a consistently tough negotiator. "He's the toughest, hardest trader I've ever met. When you start trading with the speaker, it's tough trading," said state Senator Steve Ogden, a Republican from Bryan and a longtime friend of Craddick's.[9]

The speaker appoints a speaker pro tempore, or assistant presiding officer, who is usually a close ally. In 1981, Speaker Clayton named the first African American, Representative Craig Washington of Houston, to the post. Although Clayton was a rural conservative and Washington was an urban liberal, Washington proved to be a critical member of the speaker's team. He also exercised considerable influence in the house on a wide range of issues of importance to minorities. Ten years later, Gib Lewis named another African American legislator, Representative Wilhelmina Delco of Austin, as the first woman speaker pro tempore.

The membership of most house committees is determined partly by seniority. The speaker has total discretion, however, in naming committee chairs and vice chairs and in appointing all the members of procedural committees, including the influential Calendars Committee, which will be described in more detail later in this chapter. Under a rules change in 2003, Craddick also had total discretion—without regard for seniority—in appointing the budget-writing House Appropriations Committee. The new speaker bumped some senior Democratic members from the panel.

Senate Leadership The **lieutenant governor** is chosen by the voters in a statewide election to serve a four-year term as presiding officer of the senate. Unlike the vice president of the United States—the counterpart in the federal government, who has only limited legislative functions—the lieutenant governor has traditionally been the senate's legislative leader. This office, which is elected independently of the governor, has often been called the most powerful office in state government because of the lieutenant governor's opportunity to merge a statewide electoral base into a dominant legislative role.[10] Lieutenant governors, however, get most of their power from rules set by the senators, not from the constitution.

WWW **Texas Senate**
In addition to information from the lieutenant governor's office, biographical information, committee assignments, district data, and addresses are provided for each member of the Senate.
www.senate.state.tx.us

The lieutenant governor's power is based in part on the same coalitional strategies that are used by the speaker through committee assignments and relationships with interest groups. But the lieutenant governor has traditionally had more direct control over the senate's agenda than the speaker has over the house's agenda. Under longstanding senate rules, the lieutenant governor has determined when—and if—a committee-approved bill will be brought up for a vote by the full senate. In the house, the order of floor debate is determined by the Calendars Committee. Although that key panel is appointed by the speaker and is sensitive to the speaker's wishes, it represents an intermediate step that the lieutenant governor does not have to encounter.

lieutenant governor
Presiding officer of the senate. This officeholder would become governor if the governor were to die, be incapacitated, or removed from office.

Former Lieutenant Governor Bob Bullock, who retired in 1999 and died later that year, was one of the more influential senate leaders in the modern era.

The lieutenant governor also has had more formal control over the membership of senate committees than the speaker has over house panels. Under its rules, the senate traditionally has allowed the lieutenant governor to appoint members of all standing committees without regard to seniority or any other restrictions.

The senate has a president pro tempore, who is chosen by senators from among their membership. This position is rotated among the senators on a seniority basis. It is held for a limited period, and the holder of the position is third in line of succession to the governorship. There is a tradition that the governor and the lieutenant governor both allegedly "leave" the state on the same day so that the president pro tempore can serve as "governor for a day" at one point during his or her term.

Bill Hobby, a quiet-spoken media executive who served a record eighteen years as lieutenant governor before voluntarily leaving the office in January 1991, patiently sought consensus among senators on most major issues and rarely took the lead in promoting specific legislative proposals. One notable exception occurred in 1979, when Hobby, a Democrat, tried to force senate approval of a presidential primary bill opposed by most Democratic senators. After Hobby served notice that he would alter the senate's traditional operating procedure to give the bill special consideration, twelve Democratic senators, dubbed the "Killer Bees," hid out for several days to break a **quorum** and keep the senate from conducting business. They succeeded in killing the primary bill and reminding Hobby that the senators set the rules.

Hobby's successor, Bob Bullock, had demonstrated strong leadership and a mercurial temperament during sixteen years as state comptroller. Upon taking office as lieutenant governor, he had major policy and structural changes in mind for state government and was impatient to see them carried out by the legislature. Unlike Hobby, Bullock took the lead in making proposals and then actively lobbying for them. During his first session in 1991, he reportedly had shouting matches with some lawmakers behind closed doors and one day abruptly and angrily adjourned the senate when not enough members were present for a quorum at the scheduled starting time. But his experience and knowledge of state government and his tireless work habits won the respect of most senators and their support for most of his proposals.

Bullock, a Democrat, strengthened his leadership role during the 1993 and 1995 sessions and was actively involved in every major issue that the senate addressed. Recognizing that increases in Republican strength after the 1992 and 1994 elections made the senate more conservative than it had been in several years, and eager to strengthen his support in the business community, Bullock saw to it that compromises on major issues—including some long sought by business—were reached behind closed doors before they were made public. This approach kept controversy to a minimum and defused partisanship, but it distressed consumer advocates and environmentalists, who felt excluded from the process. It also prompted remarks that the senate had abandoned democracy. There were so many unanimous or near-unanimous votes in the senate in 1993 that some house members joked that senators who wanted to show dissent voted aye with their eyes closed.[11]

quorum Required number of the members of a governing body who must be present so that official business, such as voting, can be conducted. In Texas, a quorum of the house and the senate is two-thirds of the membership. For committees, it is a majority of the members.

Bullock played a less active role during the 1997 session, after Republicans, for the first time this century, had won a majority of senate seats. He was strongly supportive of some key legislation, including a statewide water conservation and management plan, but he did little to promote a property tax relief effort that

Governor Bush had made his highest priority for the session. One key element of Bush's proposal, an increase in state taxes as a partial tradeoff for lower school district taxes, died primarily because of strong senate opposition, which Bullock did not try to defuse.

A few days after the 1997 session ended, Bullock surprised the Texas political community by announcing that he would not seek reelection in 1998. The former state leader, who had a history of health problems, was later diagnosed with lung cancer, and he died in June 1999.

After defeating Democrat John Sharp in a hard-fought race in 1998, former Agriculture Commissioner Rick Perry became Texas's first Republican lieutenant governor of modern times in 1999. Perry not only had to follow in Bullock's legendary footsteps, he also had to preside over the senate during a session overshadowed by Governor George W. Bush's anticipated presidential race. The new lieutenant governor had the advantage, though, of entering the 1999 session with a $6 billion state surplus and a rare absence of emergencies. Perry lost one of his biggest priorities, a pilot project to allow students in low-performing public schools to use state-paid vouchers to transfer to private schools. But he generally received high marks for his performance during the session from both Democrats and Republicans. As one senator observed, "He might not have used the Bullock style of cracking heads or the woodshed" to force legislative solutions. "He did effectively bring people together and kept us from having any meltdowns."[12] Perry was more low key than Bullock, perhaps choosing to learn more about the senate and its members before plunging into potential controversies. Nevertheless, he was credited with helping Republican and Democratic lawmakers negotiate a compromise on one of the key legislative packages of the session—a series of tax cuts, teacher pay raises, and other increased education spending.

Perry was elected to a lieutenant governor's term that wasn't to expire until January 2003. But in anticipation of Governor Bush's presidential race, the legislature in 1999 approved a constitutional amendment—which Texas voters later endorsed—to make it clear that Perry would have to give up the lieutenant governor's job in mid-term if he were promoted to fill a vacancy in the governor's office. After Bush resigned the governorship in December 2001 to become president, Perry was promoted to governor. And, acting under the new constitutional amendment, senators elected state Senator Bill Ratliff, R-Mount Pleasant, to serve as lieutenant governor during the 2001 session.

Ratliff, a former chairman of the senate Education and Finance committees, was businesslike in his role as presiding officer, and he generally received favorable reviews. He appointed the first African American, state Senator Rodney Ellis, D-Houston, to chair the budget-writing Finance Committee. He also parted ways with most Republican senators and supported Ellis's bill to strengthen the state law against hate crimes, which passed that session. And Ratliff blocked a bill that would have removed state legal restrictions against Native Americans operating casinos on their reservations in Texas. At the end of the 2001 session, Ratliff announced that he would seek election to the lieutenant governor's post in 2002. But several days later, admitting he didn't have the stomach for the compromises often involved in a statewide race, he announced that he had changed his mind and would seek reelection to his senate seat instead. "I do love policy-making, but I do not love politics," he said.[13] After winning reelection to the senate in 2002 and serving during the regular and special sessions in 2003, Ratliff resigned in early 2004, expressing weariness after 15 years in the legislative arena.

Republican David Dewhurst won the 2002 lieutenant governor's race over Democrat John Sharp, who had narrowly lost the same office to Rick Perry in 1998. A wealthy businessman, Dewhurst had no legislative experience when he became the senate's presiding officer in January 2003. His only experience in elected office had been his four previous years as state land commissioner, but he moved quickly to establish credibility as a leader. He appointed respected legislative insiders to key staff positions and spent many hours studying issues and meeting with individual senators. Although Republicans held a 19–12 senate majority, he continued the tradition of appointing both Republicans and Democrats to leadership positions. Dewhurst agreed with Governor Rick Perry and Speaker Tom Craddick that the legislature would close a $10 billion revenue shortfall and write a new state budget without increasing state taxes. But he and the senate helped to minimize some of the spending cuts by insisting that lawmakers tap into non-tax revenue, such as the state's Rainy Day savings account. On such budgetary details and other matters, including how quickly the legislature should move to improve the school finance system, Dewhurst sometimes differed with Perry and Craddick. Their differences stemmed partly from Dewhurst's independent nature, which was bolstered by the fact that he—not special interest groups—had largely funded his election to the state's number two office. The senate's rules and traditions also required the lieutenant governor to seek more consensus among senators than the speaker normally has to do in the house. Legislation traditionally wasn't approved without the consent of two-thirds of the senators, which meant that the twelve Democratic senators had enough clout to force some budgetary concessions.

Dewhurst orchestrated the senate's biggest show of independence during the 2003 regular session by hammering out in a series of private meetings a new public education funding plan that would have raised the state sales tax in exchange for sharp reductions in local property taxes, which were increasingly under fire, particularly in many suburban and heavily Republican school districts. Dewhurst won unanimous senate approval of the proposal, but the house never acted on it. Craddick and Perry insisted instead that lawmakers conduct another study of school finance, which had already been studied several times in recent years, and attempt to tackle the issue later.

Senate unanimity disappeared—and Dewhurst's leadership was severely challenged—during the bitter partisan fight over congressional redistricting that took three special sessions in the summer and fall of 2003 to resolve. Democratic senators blocked a house-passed redistricting bill during the first special session by using a senate tradition that required two-thirds of the senators to approve debate on any legislation. After Dewhurst announced that he would bypass that procedure—known as the "two-thirds rule"—to allow a redistricting bill to be passed on a simple majority vote during the second special session, eleven of the senate's twelve Democrats fled to Albuquerque, N.M., where they remained for more than a month. Their flight, which received national media coverage, deprived the senate of a quorum and the ability to conduct any business during the entire, 30-day second special session. It also severely damaged the senate's tradition of personal and partisan cooperation as Democratic and Republican senators exchanged verbal attacks across state lines. The boycotting senators eventually returned to Austin, and the legislature approved a congressional redistricting bill favoring Republicans during a third special session. Dewhurst immediately began working behind the scenes to restore the senate's ability to conduct business in a civil, bipartisan fashion.

David Dewhurst (seated, left) was elected lieutenant governor in 2002.

Influence and Control over the Legislative Process The power of each presiding officer to appoint committees and determine which committee will have jurisdiction over a specific bill gives the speaker and the lieutenant governor tremendous influence over the lawmaking process.

The speaker and the lieutenant governor control the legislative process through the application of the rules, including those set in the state constitution and those adopted by the house and the senate. Each presiding officer is advised on procedures by a parliamentarian. The speaker and the lieutenant governor do not participate in house or senate debate on bills and usually attempt to present an image of neutral presiding officers. Their formal powers, however, are further strengthened by their informal relationships with their committee leaders and interest groups. And, with the notable exceptions of the separate walkouts by house and senate Democrats during the 2003 redistricting battle, the speaker and the lieutenant governor rarely lose control of the process.

In the senate, the lieutenant governor can vote only to break a tie. The speaker can vote on any issue in the house but normally abstains from voting except to break a tie or to send a signal to encourage reluctant or wavering house members to vote a particular way on an issue.

Leadership Teams Traditionally, there has been no formal division along party lines or a formal system of floor leaders in either the Texas house or the senate. The longtime, Democrat-dominated legislative system with the speaker's and lieutenant governor's control of committee appointments did not produce a leadership structure comparable to that of the U.S. Congress. The committee chairs constitute the speaker's and lieutenant governor's teams and usually act as their unofficial floor leaders in developing and building support for the leadership's legislative priorities. Most chairs are philosophically, if not always politically, aligned with the presiding officers.

The Committee System

The committee system is the backbone of the legislative process, and it is molded by the lieutenant governor and the speaker.[14] It is a screening process that decides the fate of most legislation.

The **committee** is where technical drafting errors and oversights in bills can be corrected and where compromise can begin to work for those bills that do eventually become law. Only 1,405 of the 5,753 bills and constitutional amendments introduced in the 2003 regular session won final legislative approval. Most of those that did not make it died in a senate or a house committee, many without ever being heard. Rarely does a committee kill a bill on an outright vote, because there are much easier, less obvious ways to scuttle legislation. A bill can be gutted, or so drastically amended or weakened, that even its sponsor can hardly recognize it. Or it can be simply ignored.

Committee chairs have considerable power over legislation that comes to their committees. They may kill bills by simply refusing to schedule them for a hearing. Or, after a hearing, a chair may send a bill to a subcommittee that he or she stacks with members opposed to the legislation, thus allowing the bill to die slowly and quietly in the legislative deep freeze. Even if a majority of committee members want to approve a bill, the chair can simply refuse to recognize such a motion. Most chairs, however, are sensitive to the wishes of the presiding officers. If the speaker or the lieutenant governor wants a bill to win committee approval or wants another measure to die in committee, the chair will usually comply.

committee In the legislature, a group of lawmakers who review and hold public hearings on issues or bills they are assigned by the presiding officer. Committees that specialize in bills by subject matter are designated as standing committees. A bill has to win committee approval before it can be considered by the full house or senate. Most bills die in committees, which perform as a legislative screening process.

Referral to a **subcommittee** does not always mean the death of a bill. Subcommittees also help committees distribute the workload. They work out compromises, correct technical problems in bills, or draft substitute legislation to accommodate competing interest groups.

subcommittee A few members of a larger committee appointed to review a particular bill and make recommendations on its disposition to the full committee.

Standing Committees The number and names of committees are periodically revised under house and senate rules, but there have been relatively few major changes in the basic committee structure in recent years. During the 2003 sessions, the senate had fifteen **standing committees,** varying in membership from five to fifteen.

There were forty-three standing committees in the house, with memberships ranging from five to twenty-nine (Table 18.3). Additionally, there was the committee of the whole senate. Most of these committees are substantive; that is, they hold public hearings and evaluate bills related to their areas, such as higher education, natural resources, or public health. A few committees are *procedural,* such as the Rules and Resolutions Committee, which handles many routine congratulatory resolutions, and the **Calendars Committee,** which schedules bills for debate by the full house.

standing committee Committee that is created by house or senate rules to consider legislation or perform a procedural role in the lawmaking process.

Some committees play more dominant roles in the lawmaking process than others, particularly in the house. The house State Affairs Committee, for example, handles many more major statewide bills than the Committee on State Cultural and Recreational Resources or the Committee on Agriculture and Livestock. The house Urban Affairs and County Affairs committees handle several hundred bills of importance to local governments each session. The importance of a committee is determined by the area of public policy over which it has jurisdiction or by its role in the house's operating procedure.

Calendars Committee Special procedural committee that schedules bills that already have been approved by other committees for floor debate in the house.

The house Calendars Committee historically has had more life and death power over legislation than any other committee because it sets the order of debate on the house floor. During each regular session, it kills hundreds of bills that have

TABLE 18.3 Senate and House Standing Committees, 78th Legislature, 2003

Senate Committee	Number of Members	Bills Referred to Committee in Regular Session	Bills Out of Committee
Administration	7	106	86
Business and Commerce	9	277	159
Committee of the Whole Senate	31	3	3
Criminal Justice	7	287	179
Education	9	331	168
Finance	15	175	67
Government Organization	7	118	75
Health and Human Services	9	262	168
Infrastructure Development and Security	9	242	111
Intergovernmental Relations	5	356	252
International Relations and Trade	7	37	29
Jurisprudence	7	256	146
Natural Resources	11	349	246
Nominations	7	0	0
State Affairs	9	365	208
Veteran Affairs and Military Installations	5	58	49

House Committee	Number of Members	Bills Referred to Committee in Regular Session	Bills Out of Committee
Agriculture and Livestock	7	49	37
Appropriations	29	39	21
Border and International Affairs	7	48	36
Business and Industry	9	122	62
Calendars	11	0	0
Civil Practices	9	108	31
Corrections	7	87	38
County Affairs	9	165	115
Criminal Jurisprudence	9	277	107
Defense Affairs and State-Federal Relations	9	90	68
Economic Development	7	89	43
Elections	7	114	60
Energy Resources	7	33	22
Environmental Regulation	7	86	44
Ethics, Select	7	2	1
Financial Institutions	7	77	43
General Investigating	5	0	0
Government Reform	7	90	30
Higher Education	9	157	79
House Administration	11	12	6
Human Services	9	111	69
Insurance	9	217	70
Judicial Affairs	9	183	112
Juvenile Justice and Family Issues	9	132	74
Land and Resource Management	9	97	46
Law Enforcement	7	180	91
Licensing and Administrative Procedures	9	159	84
Local and Consent Calendars	11	0	0
Local Government Ways and Means	7	181	102
Natural Resources	9	195	149

(*continued*)

TABLE 18.3 Senate and House Standing Committees, 78th Legislature, 2003 (continued)

House Committee	Number of Members	Bills Referred to Committee in Regular Session	Bills Out of Committee
Pensions and Investments	7	65	29
Public Education	9	342	145
Public Health	9	260	161
Public School Finance, Select	29	0	0
Redistricting	15	4	2
Regulated Industries	7	64	23
Rules and Resolutions	11	1254	1229
State Affairs	9	222	116
State Cultural and Recreational Resources	7	77	49
State Health Care Expenditures, Select	11	67	33
Transportation	9	244	156
Urban Affairs	7	127	69
Ways and Means	9	115	21

Source: Texas Legislature Online, Legislative Reports for the 78th Legislature.

been approved by various substantive committees by refusing to schedule them for debate by the full house or scheduling them so late in the session they don't have time to win senate approval. This committee traditionally works closely with the speaker and is one means by which the speaker and the speaker's team control the house. Although many legislators complain about the committee killing their priority bills, some lawmakers defend the panel as a means of keeping controversial legislation—on which many members would rather not have to cast votes—from reaching the house floor.

The state budget is the single most important bill enacted by the legislature because, through it, lawmakers determine how much money is spent on the state's public programs and services. In the house, the Appropriations Committee takes the lead in drafting state budgets, while the house Ways and Means Committee normally is responsible for producing any tax or revenue measures necessary to balance the budget. The two most important committees in the senate are the Finance Committee, which handles the budget and, usually, tax bills, and the State Affairs Committee, which, like its house counterpart, handles a variety of legislation of major, statewide importance.

Although committees have general subject areas of responsibility, legislative rules allow the lieutenant governor and the speaker some latitude in assigning bills. The presiding officer can ensure the death of a bill by sending it to a committee known to oppose it or can guarantee quick action on a measure by referring it to a receptive, or friendly, panel.

Standing Subcommittees The formal, standing subcommittee structure of the U.S. Congress has only begun to develop in the Texas legislature, where committee chairs traditionally appointed subcommittees as needed to handle specific bills.

Conference Committees Legislation must be passed in exactly the same form by the house and the senate. If one chamber refuses to accept the other's version of a bill, a **conference committee** can try to resolve the differences. Conference committees of five senators and five representatives are appointed by the presiding officers. A compromise bill has to be approved by at least three senators and three house members who serve on the conference committee before it is sent back to the full house and the full senate for subsequent approval or rejection. Over the years, conference committees have drafted legislation in forms dramatically different from earlier versions approved by the house or senate. But because a conference committee is supposed to do no more than adjust the differences between the house and the senate versions of a bill, both chambers have to pass a concurrent resolution to allow a conference committee to add significant new language.

Special Committees **Special, or select, committees** are occasionally appointed by the governor, the lieutenant governor, and the speaker to study major policy issues, such as tax equity or school finance. These panels usually include private citizens as well as legislators, and they usually recommend legislation. Standing legislative committees also study issues in their assigned areas during the **interims** between sessions, and the presiding officers can ask committees to conduct special investigations or inquiries pertaining to governmental matters.

Rules and Procedures

Laws are made in Texas according to the same basic process followed by the U.S. Congress and other state legislatures.[15] But as the discussion of the committee system already has indicated, legislative rules are complex and are loaded with traps where legislation can be killed. One often hears the remark around the Capitol that "there are a lot more ways to kill a bill than to pass one." Legislators and lobbyists who master the rules can wield a tremendous amount of influence over the lawmaking process. Both the house and the senate have detailed rules governing the disposition of legislation, and each has a parliamentarian to help interpret them.

How a Bill Becomes a Law The simplified outline of the process by which a bill becomes a law (Figure 18.2) starts with the introduction of a bill in the house or the senate and its referral to a committee by the presiding officer, which constitutes **first reading.** That is the only reading most bills ever get.

A bill that wins committee approval can be considered on **second reading** by the full house or senate, where it is debated and often amended. Some amendments are designed to improve a bill, but others are designed to kill it by loading it down with controversial or objectionable provisions. Amendments that may be punitive toward particular individuals or groups are also sometimes offered. Such an amendment, which may be temporarily added to a bill only to be removed before the measure becomes law, is designed to give a group or perhaps a local official a message that the sponsoring legislator expects his or her wishes to be heeded on a particular issue. Lawmakers also may offer amendments that they know have little chance of being approved merely to make favorable political points with constituents or special interest groups.

If a bill is approved on second reading, it has to win one more vote on **third reading** before it goes to the other chamber for the same process. If the second chamber approves the bill without any changes, or amendments, it then goes to the governor for signature into law or for **veto.** The governor also can allow a

conference committee Panel of house members and senators appointed to work out a compromise on a bill if different versions of the legislation were passed by the house and the senate.

special, or select, committees Special panels appointed to study major policy issues.

interims Periods between legislative sessions.

first reading Introduction of a bill in the house or the senate and its referral to a committee by the presiding officer.

second reading Initial debate by the full house or senate on a bill that has been approved by a committee.

third reading Final presentation of a bill before the full house or senate.

veto Power of the governor to reject, or kill, a bill passed by the legislature.

	HOUSE	SENATE
 **Bill Introduction**	**First Reading** Bill is introduced, numbered, and referred to committee by speaker.	**First Reading** Bill is referred to committee by lieutenant governor.
 **Committee Action**	**Committee** After public hearing, committee approves bill, possibly with amendments, and sends to the Calendars Committee to schedule for debate by full house.	**Committee** After public hearing, committee approves bill, possibly with amendments.
 **Floor Action**	**Second Reading** Bill is debated by full house, amended by majority vote, and given preliminary approval. **Third Reading** Bill can be amended by 2/3 vote and given final approval.	**Second Reading** Bill is debated by full senate, amended by majority vote, and given preliminary approval. **Third Reading** Bill can be amended by 2/3 vote and given final approval.
 **Conference Action**	**Conference Action** In many cases in which house and senate bills differ, one chamber will accept the other chamber's version. If not, a conference committee is appointed to work out the differences. The house and senate must then approve the conference committee report.	
 **Gubernatorial Action**	**Governor** The governor signs the bill, lets it become law without signing it, or vetoes it.	

FIGURE 18.2 Basic Steps in the Texas Legislative Process

bill to become law without his or her signature. This procedure is just the opposite of the pocket veto power afforded the president of the United States. If the president does not sign a bill approved by Congress by a certain deadline, it is automatically vetoed. If the governor of Texas does not sign or veto a bill by a certain deadline, it becomes law. A veto can be overridden and the bill allowed to become law by a two-thirds vote of both houses, although this process is rarely attempted.

The governor must accept or reject a bill in its entirety except for the general **appropriations bill**, or state budget, from which the governor can delete specific spending proposals while approving others. This power is called a **line-item veto.** The budget or any other bill approved by the legislature that appropriates money has to be certified by the comptroller before it is sent to the governor. Texas has a **pay-as-you-go** government, and the comptroller has to certify that there will be enough revenue available to fund the bill.

If the second chamber amends the bill, the originating chamber must approve the change or request a conference committee. Any compromise worked out by a conference committee has to be approved by both houses, without further changes, before it is sent to the governor.

All bills except revenue-raising measures can originate in either the house or the senate. Tax bills must originate in the house, although the legislative leadership severely bent that rule to win approval, in a special session in 1991, of a tax bill necessary to balance a new state budget. After the house had dismantled a $3.3 billion revenue bill recommended by its Ways and Means Committee and sent the senate nothing but a $30 million shell, Lieutenant Governor Bob Bullock and the senate, in consultation with lobbyists, took over the writing of a new tax bill, which the house later approved.

Procedural Obstacles to Legislation Pieces of legislation also encounter other significant procedural obstacles. In the house, there is the Calendars Committee, discussed earlier in this chapter. In the senate, there is the so-called "**two-thirds rule.**"

The two-thirds requirement for debating bills on the senate floor is a strong obstacle to controversial bills because it means that only eleven senators, if they are determined enough and one is not absent at the wrong time, can keep any measure from becoming law. This tradition also has been a source of the lieutenant governor's power. After a bill is approved by a committee, its sponsor can have it placed on the daily **intent calendar.** If the sponsor is recognized by the lieutenant governor, he or she will seek senate permission to consider the bill. A sponsor can have majority senate support for a measure but will watch it die if he or she cannot convince two-thirds of the senators to let the body formally debate it.

The two-thirds tradition also gives a senator the opportunity to vote on both sides of an issue. Sometimes a senator will vote to bring up a bill and then vote against the measure when it is actually passed, as only a majority vote is required for approval. This procedure enables the senator to please the bill's supporters, give the sponsor a favor that can be repaid later, and, at the same time, tell the bill's opponents that he or she voted against the measure.

As noted earlier in this chapter, Lieutenant Governor David Dewhurst suspended the two-thirds tradition to break a partisan impasse and win senate approval of a Republican-backed congressional redistricting bill during a special session in 2003. But the procedure still enjoyed strong support among senators.

appropriations bill Bill that authorizes the expenditure of money for a public program or purpose. In Texas, the general appropriations bill approved by the legislature every two years is the state budget.

line-item veto Power of the Texas governor to reject certain parts of the general appropriations, or spending, bill without killing the entire measure.

pay-as-you-go Constitutional requirement that prohibits the legislature from borrowing money for the state's operating expenses.

two-thirds rule Procedure under which the Texas senate has traditionally operated that requires approval of at least two-thirds of senators before a bill can be debated on the senate floor. It allows a minority of senators to block controversial legislation.

intent calendar Daily list of bills eligible for debate on the floor of the Texas senate, if the sponsor is recognized by the lieutenant governor.

State Senator Gonzalo Barrientos of Austin puts on comfortable shoes in anticipation of a lengthy filibuster.

tag Rule that allows an individual senator to postpone a committee hearing on any bill for at least forty-eight hours, a delay that can be fatal to a bill during the closing days of a legislative session.

filibuster Procedure that allows a senator to speak against a bill for as long as he or she can stand and talk. A filibuster can become a formidable obstacle or threat against controversial bills near the end of a legislative session.

calendar Agenda or the list of bills to be considered by the house or the senate on a given day.

record vote Vote taken in the house or the senate of which a permanent record is kept, listing how individual legislators voted.

division votes Votes taken on the computerized voting boards in the Texas house but erased without being permanently recorded.

The senate rules also provide for tags and filibusters, both of which can be effective in killing bills near the end of a legislative session. A **tag** allows an individual senator to postpone a committee hearing on any bill for at least forty-eight hours, a delay that is often fatal in the crush of unfinished business during a session's closing days. The **filibuster,** a procedure that allows a senator to speak against a bill for as long as he or she can stand and talk, is usually little more than a nuisance to a bill's supporters early in a session, but it, too, can become a potent and ever-present threat against controversial legislation near the end of a session. Sometimes the mere likelihood of a filibuster against a bill is sufficient to kill the measure. Late in a session, the lieutenant governor may refuse to recognize the sponsor of a controversial bill for fear a filibuster will fatally delay other major legislative proposals. State Senator Bill Meier of Euless spoke for forty-three hours in 1977 against a bill dealing with the public reporting of on-the-job accidents. In so doing, he captured the world's record for the longest filibuster, which he held for years.

Shortcuts, Obfuscation, and Confusion Sponsors of legislation languishing in an unfriendly committee or subcommittee often try to resurrect their proposals by attaching them as amendments to related bills being debated on the house or senate floor. Such maneuvers often are successful, particularly if opponents are absent or if the sponsor succeeds in "mumbling" the amendment through without challenge. But the speaker or the lieutenant governor must find that such amendments are germane to the pending bill if an alert opponent raises a point of order against them.

To facilitate the passage of noncontroversial and local pieces of legislation, the house and the senate have periodic local and consent or local and uncontested **calendars,** which are conducted under special rules that enable scores of bills to be routinely and quickly approved by the full house or senate without debate. Bills of major statewide significance, even controversial measures, sometimes get placed on these calendars, but it takes only one senator or three representatives to have any bill struck. Legislators will sometimes knowingly let a controversial bill slip by on a local calendar without moving to strike it so as not to offend the sponsor or the presiding officer. But to protect themselves politically, should the bill become an issue later, they will quietly register a vote against the measure in the house or senate journal.

As noted earlier in this chapter, compromises on controversial legislation are often worked out behind closed doors long before a bill is debated on the house or senate floor or even afforded a public hearing. It can be argued that this approach to consensus building is an efficient, businesslike way to enact legislation, but it also serves to discourage the free and open debate that is so important to the democratic process.

Recent speakers have also discouraged the taking of **record votes** during house floor debate on most bills. Many important issues are decided with **division votes,** which are taken on the computerized voting boards but leave no formal record once the boards are cleared. This approach saves the taxpayers some printing costs and can give lawmakers some respite from lobby pressure. But it also serves to keep the public in the dark about significant decisions made by their elected representatives. The fewer record votes legislators have to make, the more easily they can dodge accountability to their constituents.

Often, legislators have made up their minds on an issue before the matter is debated on the floor. But when they are not familiar with a bill and have no political interest in it, they may simply vote the way the sponsor votes or the way the house or senate leadership wants them to vote. Despite what tourists in the gallery may think, legislators who raise their fingers above their heads when a vote is taken are not asking the presiding officer for a rest break. They are signaling the way they are voting and encouraging other lawmakers to vote the same way. One finger means yes; two fingers mean no.

When record votes are taken, house rules prohibit members from punching the voting buttons on other members' desks, but the practice occurs regularly. Sometimes members instruct a deskmate or another legislator to cast a specific vote for them if they expect to be off the floor when the vote is called for. Other legislators make a habit of punching the voting buttons at all the empty desks within reach. This practice is normally challenged only in cases of close votes, when members of the losing side request a roll-call verification of the computerized vote and the votes of members who do not answer the roll call are struck. The house was embarrassed in 1991 when a dead lawmaker was recorded as answering the daily roll call and voting on several record votes. The legislator had died in his Austin apartment, but his body was not discovered for several hours. Meanwhile, colleagues had been pushing his voting button. This practice is not a problem in the senate, where the secretary of the senate orally calls the roll on record votes.

Senate committees often meet in the senate chamber when large numbers of people are expected to attend.

Partly because of the rules under which the legislature operates, partly because of the heavy volume of legislation, and partly because of political maneuvering, the closing weeks of a regular session are hectic. Legislators in both houses are asked to vote on dozens of conference committee reports they do not have time to read. With hundreds of bills being rushed through the legislature to the governor's desk, mistakes occur. And deliberate attempts are made—often successfully—to slip major changes in law through the confusion. For every surprise bill or special interest amendment that is caught, dozens slip through and become law.

The Emerging Party System

Unlike the U.S. Congress, the Texas legislature is not organized along party lines, with rules automatically giving leadership positions to members of the majority party. The arrangement in Texas is due primarily to the absence of Republican legislators for many years and the more recent practice—before Republicans gained a house majority in 2003—of rural Democrats aligning themselves with Republicans to produce a conservative coalition. As recently as 1971, the year before a federal court declared urban, countywide house districts unconstitutional, there were only ten Republicans in the house and two in the senate. As Republicans increased their numbers, they aligned themselves with conservative Democrats to attempt to control the policy-setting process, particularly in the house. This ideological coalition became increasingly important as single-member districts boosted not only the number of Republican lawmakers but also the number of moderate and liberal Democratic legislators elected from urban areas. The coalition became a means of maintaining some legislative control for conservative Democrats as the base of power shifted in their own party.

Republicans and conservative Democrats formally organized the Texas Conservative Coalition in the house in the 1980s. The coalition remained a strong force in the 1990s, chaired for several years by Representative Warren Chisum of Pampa, who switched from the Democratic to the Republican Party in 1995. Chisum's mastery of the rules blocked many pieces of legislation on technicalities.

On occasion, liberal Democrats and conservative Republicans have formed "unholy alliances," but these coalitions were usually short-lived. During the controversy over the Sharpstown stock fraud scandal in 1971, liberal Democrats and Republicans formed a loose coalition called the "Dirty Thirty" that continually harassed Speaker Gus Mutscher, who not only was a key figure in the scandal but also epitomized the rural conservative Democratic tradition of the statehouse.

The Growth of Partisanship With the growth of the Republican Party in Texas in the 1980s, Speaker Gib Lewis, a conservative urban Democrat, appointed Republicans to major committee chairs in the house. But partisan divisions increased in 1987 when Lewis, Democratic Lieutenant Governor Bill Hobby, and Republican Governor Bill Clements fought over a new state budget in the face of a huge revenue shortfall. On one side of the debate were moderate and liberal Democratic legislators, including inner-city and South Texas minorities whose constituents had the most to gain from a tax increase and the most to lose from deep cuts in spending on human services and educational programs. On the other side were a handful of conservative, primarily rural Democrats and Republicans with middle- and upper-middle-class suburban constituents who insisted on fiscal restraint. Clements eventually gave in and supported a tax increase, but most of the house Republicans continued to fight the measure until it was approved in a summer special session.

In 1989, Republicans formed their first caucus in the house, and soon both parties had active caucuses in both the house and the senate, which began to play key roles in marshaling legislative support on selected issues. They also became active in legislative races as Republicans began to mount aggressive, well-financed challenges of Democratic incumbents.

During the 1995 legislative session, when Democrats still held a majority of house and senate seats, Lieutenant Governor Bob Bullock and Speaker Pete Laney, both Democrats, continued the practice of naming Republicans, as well as Democrats, to committee chairs. Bullock and Laney also were strongly supportive of Republican Governor George W. Bush's legislative priorities. All three leaders cooperated in making major changes in public education and juvenile justice and setting limits on civil liability lawsuits.

After many bitterly contested legislative races, Republicans won their first majority of the senate in modern times during the 1996 elections and gained four seats in the house to narrow the Democratic majority in that body to 82–68. Bipartisanship, however, still prevailed for the most part in the 1997 session. Bullock, the Democratic lieutenant governor, gave Republicans some new leadership positions in the senate but named Democrats to chair most committees. The senate, which had a 17–14 Republican majority, slammed the door on an attempt by Bush to trade higher state taxes for major cuts in local school taxes, and opposition came from both Democratic and Republican senators. Special interests that did not want to pay the higher state taxes were a more significant factor than partisanship in the death of the tax bill. The house had approved the tax tradeoff, with Bush persuading many Republicans in the house to vote for the measure. But legislative fights with strong partisan overtones increased in 1997 and subsequent sessions over such issues as abortion, gay rights, and whether tax dollars should be spent on private school tuition for some students.

Another partisan-charged issue in 1999 and 2001 was an attempt by some Democrats to strengthen the state law against hate crimes, after three white men in East Texas were accused—and later convicted—of dragging an African American man, James Byrd, Jr., to death behind a pickup truck. Most of the Republican opposition to the bill was because it increased penalties for crimes motivated by prejudice against homosexuals as well as prejudice over race or religion. That provision was opposed by social conservatives, and in 1999 Governor Bush—who did not want to anger conservatives on the eve of his race for the Republican presidential nomination—called the bill unnecessary. The measure, which sponsors named for Byrd, died in the senate in 1999 but was passed in 2001.

Republicans Take Control Aided by the redrawn legislative districts discussed earlier in this chapter, Republicans made major gains in the 2002 elections. They increased their majority in the state senate to 19–12, captured an 88–62 majority in the Texas house, their first since Reconstruction, and elected Republican Tom Craddick of Midland as speaker. Those victories, plus the elections of Governor Rick Perry and Lieutenant Governor David Dewhurst, gave Republicans control of all the points of power in the statehouse. They controlled the budget-setting process in 2003, making significant cuts in services to close a $10 billion revenue shortfall, enacted significant new restrictions on civil lawsuits, and won the fight over congressional redistricting. Throughout the year, partisanship was stronger than it had been since the GOP became a competitive party in Texas.

Craddick and Dewhurst appointed Democrats, as well as Republicans, to chair committees and serve in other leadership positions. Democrats chaired six of the senate's fifteen standing committees and thirteen of the forty-three committees in the house. Craddick also appointed a Democrat, state Representative Sylvester Turner of Houston, as speaker pro tempore. But Craddick stacked the key chairmanships and the membership of the budget-writing house Appropriations Committee with Republicans who clearly reflected his conservative viewpoint. After winning a change in house rules that removed seniority as a factor in appropriations appointments, the new speaker bumped from the panel three outspoken Democrats who opposed budget cuts.

Partisanship will remain part of the legislative process for the foreseeable future. Before too many more years, the legislature may even organize itself along the same partisan lines as the U.S. Congress—with distinct party positions, such as floor leaders, caucus leaders, and whips. If this were to happen, the legislative rules and powers of the presiding officers discussed earlier in this chapter would be significantly changed. But this development will depend on how long Republicans continue to dominate the statehouse, on how Democrats continue to react, and on the future leadership personalities that emerge in both parties. Another factor will be how well the two factions in the Republican Party—the traditional, fiscal conservatives and the social conservatives—are able to accommodate each other's interests.

Other Legislative Caucuses

Hispanic and African American house members formed their own caucuses as their numbers began to increase in the 1970s in the wake of redistricting and the creation of urban single-member districts. Their cohesive **blocs** of votes have proved influential in speaker elections and the resolution of major statewide issues, such as health care for the poor, public school finance, and taxation. Their ability to broker votes has won committee chairs and other concessions they may not otherwise have received (see *People in Politics:* "Gregory Luna and Irma Rangel, Champions of Education".)

bloc Group of legislators who act together for a common goal regardless of party affiliation.

PEOPLE IN POLITICS

Gregory Luna and Irma Rangel, Champions of Education

Gregory Luna and Irma Rangel made important contributions to young people, particularly minorities, in the legislature and other public forums.

Luna, whose father died when he was an infant, knew firsthand the difficulties that many Texas children faced in securing an education and a chance at a better life. He was only 11 when he got his first job as a busboy in a restaurant. After working as a police officer to help put himself through college and law school, Luna then devoted much of his adult life to improving civil rights and educational opportunities for Hispanics and all Texans.

As an attorney in San Antonio in 1968, Luna helped found the Mexican American Legal Defense and Educational Fund (MALDEF), which has waged successful courtroom fights for civil rights. MALDEF has forced school boards and other governments to redraw political boundaries to assure minority representation on governing bodies. And in the 1980s, MALDEF filed a landmark lawsuit against the state that forced the Texas legislature to more equitably distribute state education dollars among wealthy and poor school districts.

Luna served in the Texas House from 1985 to 1992 and in the state Senate from 1993 until illness forced his resignation in September 1999. He died a few weeks later of complications related to diabetes. He was 66.

Luna was chair of the Senate Hispanic Caucus and vice chair of the Senate Education Committee, and throughout his legislative career he fought for improvements in school funding and for better educational opportunities. His legislative style was usually low key, but he was effective. He knew what he had to do to accomplish a goal and quietly went about doing it.

"He was a monument of many, many people who were able to benefit from his efforts for a better education system for everyone," said the Rev. Virgil Elizondo. "He was in the ministry of public service."*

Rangel, a Democrat from Kingsville, was a schoolteacher and a prosecutor before becoming, in 1976, the first Hispanic woman elected to the Texas House. She chaired the House Higher Education Committee for several years and sponsored a state law to boost affirmative action by requiring Texas colleges and universities to automatically admit students who graduated in the top 10 percent of their high school classes. She also was instrumental in boosting state funding for higher education institutions along the border with Mexico.

Rangel was still a member of the House—its fifth most senior member—when she died of cancer in March 2003 at age 71. State Representative Pete Gallego, D-Alpine, chairman of the Mexican American Legislative Caucus, called Rangel's life a "testament to everything that is good about public service."†

*The Associated Press, as published in the *Houston Chronicle*, November 10, 1999.
†*Houston Chronicle*, March 19, 2003, p. 25A.

Some urban delegations, such as the group of legislators representing Harris County, the state's most populous county, have formed their own caucuses to discuss and seek consensus on issues of local importance. In Harris County's case, consensus is often difficult to achieve on local controversies because of the political, ethnic, and urban-suburban diversity within the delegation. Twenty-five house members—one-sixth of the body's membership—represent various parts of Houston and Harris County, and seven senators have districts that are wholly within or include part of the county.

THINK AGAIN

Should candidates for the Texas state legislature be limited in the amount of money they can spend to get elected?

Legislators and Their Constituents

Although representative government is an essential component of American society, there are continued debates as to how people elected to public office should identify the interests and preferences of the people they represent.[16] Political theorists as well as legislators struggle with the problem of translating the will of the people into public policy. Most legislators represent diverse groups and interests in their districts. During a normal legislative session, there are thousands of proposed laws to consider, and legislators must constantly make decisions that will benefit or harm specific constituents.

Except for an occasional emotional issue—such as whether motorcycle riders should have to wear safety helmets or whether private citizens should be allowed to carry pistols—most Texans pay little attention to what the legislature is doing. That is why they are often surprised to discover they have to pay a few extra dollars to register their cars or learn that the fee for camping in a state park has suddenly been increased. Very few Texans can identify their state representatives or senators by name, and far fewer can tell you what their legislators have voted for or against. This public inattention gives a legislator great latitude when voting on public policies. It also is a major reason that most incumbent lawmakers who seek reelection are successful. Most legislative turnover is the result of voluntary retirements, not voter retribution. Several Democratic incumbents, however, fell victim to redistricting that favored Republican challengers in 2002. Some were unseated at the polls, and others didn't seek reelection because of the redrawn district lines.

Media coverage of the legislature is uneven. The large daily newspapers with reporters in Austin make commendable efforts to cover the major legislative issues and players and provide both spot news accounts and in-depth interpretation of the legislature's actions. All too frequently, however, they are limited by insufficient space and rarely publish individual voting records or attempt to evaluate the performance of individual legislators. Most television and radio news shows provide only cursory legislative coverage.

Although legislators are aware of latent public opinion, they tend to be more responsive to the interest groups, or attentive publics, that operate in their individual districts or statewide.[17] People who are well-informed and attentive to public policy issues are a relatively small portion of the total population, but they can be mobilized for or against an individual legislator. In some instances, they are community opinion leaders who, directly or indirectly, are able to communicate information to other individuals about a legislator's performance. Or they may belong to public interest and special interest groups that compile legislative voting records on selected issues of importance to their memberships. Although these records are only sporadically disseminated by the news media to the general public, they are mailed or e-mailed to the sponsoring groups' members.

Many special interest groups contribute thousands of dollars to a legislator's reelection campaign or to the campaign of an opponent. But politically astute legislators duly take note of all the letters, phone calls, e-mail messages, petitions, and visits by their constituents—plus media coverage—lest they lose touch with a significant number of voters with different views on the issues and become politically vulnerable.

A favorite voter-contact tool of many legislators is an occasional newsletter, which they can mail to households in their districts at state expense. These mailings usually include photos of the lawmaker plus articles summarizing, in the best possible light, his or her accomplishments in Austin. Sometimes legislators also include a public opinion survey seeking constituent responses on a number of issues.

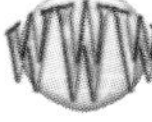

Texas Legislative Council

The Texas Legislative Council (TLC) is a state agency within the legislative branch. The TLC drafts bills and other legislative documents, conducts legal and public policy research, and produces informational publications for the Senate and the House.
http://www.tlc.state.tx.us

Legislative Decision Making

In addition to the formal rules of each legislative body, there are unwritten rules, or norms, that shape the behavior of legislators and other actors in the lawmaking process. The legislature is like most other social institutions in that its members have perceptions of the institution and the process as well as the way they are expected to behave or carry out their responsibilities. Other participants also impose their views and expectations on lawmakers.[18]

The legislative process is designed to institutionalize conflict, and the rules and norms of the legislature are designed to give this conflict an element of civility. Debate is often intense and vigorous, and it may be difficult for some lawmakers to separate attacks on their positions from attacks on their personalities. But most legislators have learned the necessity of decorum and courtesy. Even if lawmakers believe some of their opponents in the house and senate are deceitful, personal attacks on other legislators are considered unacceptable. Personal attacks, even to the point of fistfights, occasionally occur, but they are rare.

With about 5,700 pieces of legislation introduced during a regular session—the level reached in 2003—no legislator could possibly read and understand each bill, much less the hundreds of amendments offered during floor debate. And while there are moments of high drama when issues of major statewide importance are being debated, most of the legislative workload is tedious and dull and produces little direct political benefit for most senators and representatives. But many of those bills contain hidden traps and potential controversies that can haunt a legislator later, often during a reelection campaign. So legislators use numerous information sources and rely on the norms of the process to assist them in decision making.

To make the process work, legislators must accommodate the competing interests they represent and achieve considerable reciprocity among themselves. An individual legislator will usually have no direct political or personal interest in most bills because much legislation is local in nature and affects only a limited number of lawmakers and constituents. A legislator accumulates obligations as he or she supports another lawmaker's bill, with the full expectation that the action will be returned in kind.

A number of factors, however, help shape lawmakers' decisions on major legislation.[19] The wishes of constituents will be considered, particularly if there is a groundswell of dominant opinion coming from a legislator's district. Legislators also exchange information with other lawmakers, particularly with members of the same caucus, members who share the same political philosophy, and colleagues from the same counties or regions of the state. Lawmakers often take their cues from bill sponsors or the speaker's and lieutenant governor's leadership teams. Identifiable patterns of giving and taking cues also are emerging along party lines, particularly on budgetary, taxation, and redistricting issues.

A legislator's staff also assists in the decision-making process, not only by evaluating the substantive merits of legislation but also by assessing the political implications of a lawmaker's decisions. The Legislative Budget Board and the Legislative Council provide technical information and expertise that can also be weighed by legislators.

Interest groups are major sources of information and influence. Although an individual legislator will occasionally rail against a specific group, most lawmakers consider interest groups absolutely essential to the legislative process. Through their lobbyists, interest groups provide a vast amount of technical information and can signal the level of constituency interest, support, or opposition to proposed laws. A senator or representative can use interest groups to establish coalitions of support for a bill, and some legislators become closely identified with powerful interest groups because they almost always support a particular lobby's position.

The governor can also influence the legislature in several ways. He or she can raise the public's consciousness of an issue or need and can promote solutions through speeches and through the media. The governor can communicate indirectly to individual lawmakers through the governor's staff, party leaders, and influential persons in a lawmaker's district. The governor can also personally appeal to lawmakers in direct one-on-one meetings or in meetings with groups of legislators. At the beginning of each regular session, the governor outlines his or her legislative priorities in a State of the State address to a joint session of the house and the senate, and the governor usually has frequent meetings with the lieutenant governor and the speaker throughout a session.

Governor Rick Perry "works the floor" of the Texas house of representatives during the 2003 legislative session.

The governor may also visit the house or senate chamber in a personal show of support when legislation that he or she strongly advocates is being debated. Unlike most recent governors, Governor Ann Richards personally testified before legislative committees on several of her priorities, including ethics reform and government reorganization, during her first year in office. The severity of a governor's arm-twisting is often in the eye of the beholder, but it can include appeals to a lawmaker's reason or conscience, threats of retaliation, appeals for party support, and promises of a quid pro quo. The greatest threat that a governor can hang over a legislator is the possible veto of legislation or a budget item of importance to the lawmaker. In special sessions, the governor also can negotiate with a lawmaker over whether to add a bill that is important to the legislator to the special session's agenda, which is controlled by the governor.

Legislators also get information and support from other elected statewide officeholders, such as the attorney general, the comptroller, or the land commissioner. These officials and lawmakers can assist each other in achieving political agendas.

The news media provide information and perspective on issues in broader political terms. In part, the policy agenda is established by those issues the media perceive to be important.

The relative importance of any groups or actors on decision making is difficult to measure and varies from lawmaker to lawmaker and from issue to issue. Outside influences can also be tempered by a legislator's own attitude and opinion. On many issues, legislators get competing advice and pressure. As much as a lawmaker may like to be all things to all people, that cannot be. She cannot please a chemical lobbyist, who is seeking a tax break for a new plant on the Gulf coast and also happens to be a large campaign contributor, and environmentalists, who fear the facility would spoil a nearby wildlife habitat. He cannot please the governor, who is promoting a lottery as a new state revenue source, and most of the voters in his district, who have consistently voted against gambling. The ultimate decision and its eventual political consequences are the legislator's.

Should lawmakers cast particular votes on the basis of the specific concerns of their districts, their personal convictions, the position of their political party, or the wishes of the special interest groups that helped fund their campaigns? These issues reflect complex relationships between the legislator and the people represented. And since the overriding consideration for most lawmakers is to get reelected, the legislator must balance them carefully (see *Up Close:* "Legislative Reputations: Not All the Same").

The Development of Legislative Staff

The quality of a legislator's staff can help determine his or her success, and both the quality and quantity of legislative staffs have been significantly enhanced since the early 1970s.[20] This growth reflects an emerging professional approach

UP CLOSE

Legislative Reputations: Not All the Same

Some legislators become known for their commitment to producing good legislation. They spend endless hours developing programs and are repeatedly turned to by presiding officers to handle tough policy issues. Other lawmakers tend to look to their leadership for direction and cues, giving them considerable influence and power. And they are also essential to a productive legislative session.

Other legislators earn reputations as grandstanders. Almost every legislator has shown off for the media or the spectators in the gallery at one time or another, but a number have developed a distinct reputation for this style of behavior. They appear to be more interested in scoring political points with their constituents or interest groups—with the objective of being reelected or seeking higher office—than with mastering the substance of legislation. Many of these lawmakers are lightweights who contribute little to the legislature's product. And while they may introduce many bills during a session, they are not interested in the details of the lawmaking process and are unable to influence other legislators to support their legislation.

The legislature also has a number of opportunists, including members who pursue issues to produce personal or political benefits for themselves. They may sponsor legislation or take a position on an issue to curry favor with a special interest group or benefit their personal businesses or professions. Legislative rules prohibit legislators from voting on issues in which they have a personal monetary interest, but individual lawmakers can interpret that prohibition as they see fit. Many lawmakers will try to cash in on their legislative experience by becoming lobbyists after they leave office at considerably higher pay than they received as legislators.

Still other legislators appear to be little more than spectators. They enjoy the receptions and the other perks of the office much more than the drudgery of the committee hearings, research, and floor debates. Some quickly become weary of the legislative process and, after a few sessions, decide against seeking reelection.*

*These legislative styles are similar to those developed by James David Barber, *The Lawmakers* (New Haven, Conn.: Yale University Press, 1965), Chapters 2–5.

to lawmaking and meeting the needs of an increasingly complex urban state. During recent regular sessions, the house has had about 900 employees, including part-time workers, and the senate about 800. These figures included Capitol and district office staff for individual senators and representatives, committee staffs, assistants to the lieutenant governor and the speaker, and other support staff hired directly by the house and the senate.

Additionally, there are permanent staff members assigned to the Legislative Budget Board, the legislature's financial research arm; the Legislative Council, which researches issues and drafts bills and resolutions for introduction by legislators; and the Legislative Reference Library, which provides resource materials for lawmakers, their staffs, and the general public. Other support staff is assigned to the Sunset Advisory Commission, which assists the legislature in periodic reviews of state agencies, and the state auditor, who is chosen by and reports to the legislative leadership.

Legislative staffers range from part-time secretaries and clerks to lawyers and professionals who draft bills and direct research that result in major state laws. There are limits on the number of staff members and funds allocated for legislators' personal staffs. As a general rule, senators have larger staffs than house members. Staffing levels are usually reduced between sessions, and some members shut down their Capitol offices entirely. Most lawmakers, however, maintain offices both in Austin and in their districts, even if staffs function only to answer the phone.

A key support group in the house is the House Research Organization, which was organized as the House Study Group in the 1970s by a handful of primarily liberal lawmakers. The group's name was later changed, and its structure was reorganized to represent the entire house, but it still fills a strong research role. It is supported by funds from the house budget and is governed by a steering committee that represents a cross section of Democratic and Republican house members. During legislative sessions, its staff provides detailed analyses, including pro and con arguments, of many bills on the daily house calendar. During interims between sessions, it provides periodic analyses of proposed constitutional amendments and other issues. The senate formed a similar organization, the Senate Research Center, in 1991.

The quality of other resources available to lawmakers has also improved in recent years. Legislators and their staffs can routinely check the status or texts of bills online, and so can the public. The Legislative Council maintains a Web site on the Internet that includes committee schedules, bill texts and analyses, and other legislative information. Private citizens also can use the Web site to identify their state representatives and senators.

State Senator Ken Armbrister of Victoria talking with staff.

Legislative Ethics and Reforms

The vast majority of legislators are honest, hardworking individuals. But the weaknesses of a few and the millions of dollars spent by special interests to influence the lawmaking process undermine Texans' confidence in their legislature and their entire state government. Although legislators cannot pass laws guaranteeing ethical behavior, they can set strong standards for themselves, other public officials, and lobbyists; and they can institute stiff penalties for those who fail to comply. Such reform efforts are periodically attempted, but, unfortunately, they usually are the result of scandals and fall short of creating an ideal ethical climate.

Fallout from the Sharpstown stock scandal helped an outsider, Uvalde rancher Dolph Briscoe, win the 1972 gubernatorial race and helped produce a large turnover in legislative elections. In 1973, the legislature responded with a series of ethics reform laws, including requirements that lobbyists register with the secretary of state and report their expenditures. State officials were required to file public reports identifying their sources of income, although not specific amounts.

Weaknesses in those laws, however, were vividly demonstrated in 1989, when wealthy East Texas poultry producer Lonnie "Bo" Pilgrim distributed $10,000 checks to several senators in the Capitol while lobbying them on workers' compensation reform, and the Travis County district attorney could find no law under which to prosecute him. There also were published reports that lobbyists had spent nearly $2 million entertaining lawmakers during the 1989 regular session without having to specify which legislators received the "freebies," thanks to a large loophole in the lobby registration law. The revelations—including frequent news stories about lobbyists treating lawmakers to golf tournaments, ski trips, a junket to Las Vegas for a boxing match, and limousine service to a Cher concert—created an uproar.

Some senators had angrily rejected Pilgrim's checks on the spot, while others returned them after the media pounced on the story. But the very next year, Pilgrim—a longtime political contributor—again contributed thousands of dollars to several statewide officeholders and candidates. This time the checks were not offered under the Capitol dome but were more traditionally sent through the mail, and they were gratefully accepted. Only one officeholder, who was passed over by Pilgrim in favor of his opponent, tried to make a campaign issue of the new contributions.

Despite all the headlines over ethical problems, legislative turnover was minimal in 1990. But in early December, about a month after the general election, a Travis County grand jury began investigating Speaker Gib Lewis's ties to a San Antonio law firm, Heard Goggan Blair and Williams. The firm had made large profits collecting delinquent taxes for local governments throughout Texas under a law that allowed it to collect an extra 15 percent from the taxpayers as its fee. For several years, it had successfully defeated legislation that would have hurt its business. The *Fort Worth Star-Telegram* reported that Heard Goggan had paid about half of a $10,000 tax bill owed to Tarrant County by a business that Lewis partly owned.[21] And the *Houston Chronicle* reported that the grand jury was also looking into a trip that Lewis had taken to a Mexican resort during the 1987 legislative session with four Heard Goggan partners and a lobbyist (all males) and six women (including a waitress from a topless nightclub in Houston).[22] The trip had been taken while a bill opposed by Heard Goggan was dying in a House committee.

On December 28, only twelve days before the 1991 regular legislative session was to convene and Lewis was to be reelected to a fifth term as the house's presiding officer, grand jurors indicted him on two misdemeanor ethics charges. He was accused of soliciting, accepting, and failing to report an illegal gift from Heard Goggan—the partial payment of the tax bill. Lewis insisted he was innocent and vowed to fight the charges. He said the tax payment was the settlement of a legal dispute, and he angrily accused Travis County District Attorney Ronnie Earle, who headed the prosecution and had been publicly advocating stronger ethics laws, of using the grand jury to "influence the speaker's election." Lewis said that Earle was guilty of "unethical and reprehensible behavior."[23]

Lewis won a postponement of his trial under a law that automatically grants continuances to legislators when they are in session. The grand jury investigation, which prosecutors said would include other legislators or former legislators, continued for several more weeks, but no more indictments were issued.

Meanwhile, attention was focused on an ethics reform bill. Governor Ann Richards, who had campaigned for reform, testified before house and senate committees for tougher ethical requirements for state officials and lobbyists. The senate approved an ethics bill fairly early in the session, but the house did not act on its version of the bill until late in the session. The final bill was produced by a conference committee on the last night of the regular session in a private meeting and was approved by the house and the senate only a few minutes before the legislature adjourned at midnight. There was no time to print and distribute copies, and very few legislators knew for sure what was in the bill.

This performance and the bill itself left a bad taste all around. Despite complaints that the measure was not strong enough and the controversy over the secretive way in which the final compromise had been written, Richards signed the bill. But she did so in the privacy of her office, not in the public ceremony that governors usually hold for their priority pieces of legislation. Ronnie Earle, the Travis County district attorney, was among those displeased with the legislation, but Richards called the new law a "very strong step in the direction of openness and ethics reform in this state."[24]

The new law required additional reporting of lobby expenditures and conflicts of interest between lobbyists and state officials, prohibited special interests from treating legislators to pleasure trips, prohibited lawmakers from accepting fees for speaking before special interest groups, and created a new state Ethics Commission to review complaints about public officials.

But the measure did not put any limits on financial contributions to political campaigns, nor did it prohibit legislator-attorneys from representing clients before state agencies for pay. Moreover, it authorized the Ethics Commission to slap a bigger fine ($10,000) on someone who filed a frivolous complaint against a public official than the maximum fine ($5,000) that could be levied on an officeholder for violating the ethics law. That latter provision was viewed by many critics as an unreasonable effort to discourage citizen complaints. The new law also provided that complaints filed with the Ethics Commission would remain confidential unless the commission took action, a provision that would allow the commission to dismiss or sit on legitimate complaints without any public accounting.

In January 1992, Lewis announced that he would not seek reelection to another term in the house. In a plea bargain later the same month, prosecutors dropped the two ethics indictments against him in return for the speaker's "no contest" plea to two minor, unrelated charges. Lewis paid a $2,000 fine for failing to publicly disclose a business holding in 1988 and 1989, for which he had already paid a minor civil penalty to the secretary of state.

Lewis's decision to retire set off the first speaker's race in the house since 1975, and many house members, including most of the first-term legislators, used the campaign to bargain for reforms in the way the house conducted its business. As noted earlier, some of those reforms were adopted in 1993 with the support of the new speaker, Pete Laney, who, ironically, had been a long-time member of Lewis's team. The first-term legislators, in particular, had complained in 1991 that the house rules had been used to create an undemocratic process that catered to special interests and favored an inner circle of legislators close to the speaker.

The legislature enacted other significant changes in ethics laws in 2003. The new provisions required officeholders and candidates to identify the occupations and employers of people who contribute more than $500, required financial reports to be filed with the Ethics Commission electronically, increased penalties for people who filed their reports late, and required—for the first time—officeholders and candidates for municipal offices in the large cities to file personal financial disclosure statements, similar to those already filed by state officeholders.

Also in 2003, Travis County District Attorney Ronnie Earle began a lengthy investigation of how corporate contributions were used to affect several legislative elections in the Republican takeover of the house (see Chapter 21). Republicans accused Earle, a Democrat, of playing politics, but Earle said that he was investigating the possibility that corporate funds had been illegally spent on political activity.

SUMMARY NOTES

- Texas, the nation's second most populous state, has a part-time legislature that operates under detailed antigovernment restrictions drafted by nineteenth-century Texans in the wake of the repressive Reconstruction era. It is a lawmaking body that is not structured to respond readily to twenty-first century needs and crises. Emergencies often require special legislative sessions and increase financial and personal pressures on lawmakers, who are among the lowest-paid state legislators in the country. Legislative turnover in Texas is moderate.

- As recently as 1971, there was only a handful of African Americans, Hispanics, Republicans, and women in the 150-member house of representatives and the 31-member senate. But political realignment and federal court intervention in redistricting—particularly the ordering of single-member House districts for urban counties in 1972—have significantly increased the number of women, ethnic minorities, and Republicans in the legislature. Republicans now have a majority of both legislative bodies.
- Unlike the U.S. Congress, the Texas legislature is not organized along party lines and has only the tentative beginnings of an institutionalized leadership structure. The presiding officer of the house is the speaker, who is elected by the other house members. The presiding officer of the senate is the lieutenant governor, who is elected by the voters statewide.
- The most significant powers of the speaker and the lieutenant governor are the appointment of house and senate committees, which screen and draft legislation, and the assignment of bills to committees. The fate of most legislation is decided at the committee level. While most house committees are partially appointed on the basis of seniority, the lieutenant governor has absolute control over the composition of senate committees. The presiding officers also play key roles in the development of major legislative proposals and, to a great extent, depend on their handpicked committee chairs to sell their legislative programs to house and senate colleagues.
- Traditionally, the powers of the presiding officers have been enhanced by the Calendars Committee in the house and the "two-thirds rule" in the senate. The Calendars Committee, composed entirely of speaker appointees, sets the schedule for floor debate in the house. The "two-thirds rule" provides that two-thirds of the senate must approve before any bill can be debated on the floor of that body. That means that eleven senators can block, or kill, any piece of legislation that has majority support. The lieutenant governor decides which senate sponsors are recognized for consideration of specific bills.
- To be sent to the governor for signature into law, a bill must be approved after three readings in both the house and the senate. Referral to committee is the first reading, which is as far as most bills progress. Many are never scheduled for a public hearing by the chairs of the committees to which they are assigned. Many others die in subcommittees to which they are sent after being heard by the full committee. And others do not survive the Calendars Committee in the house or the two-thirds requirement in the senate. Those that do win committee approval are often amended, or changed.
- For those bills that survive the committee process, second reading is a crucial step. That is where most floor debate on legislation occurs and where many bills are further amended. If a bill is approved on second reading, it advances to a third reading and then to the other legislative chamber, where it is referred to a committee and has to repeat the process.
- A bill must be approved in exactly the same form by both chambers. If the senate, for example, approves a house bill after making some changes in it, the House will have to concur in—or accept—the senate version, or a conference committee of house and senate members will have to be appointed to try to work out a compromise.
- The governor can sign a bill, veto it, or let it become law without his or her signature. The governor can use the line-item veto to delete specific spending provisions from the general appropriations bill, or state budget. All other bills have to be accepted or rejected in their entirety.
- Tax bills have to originate in the house. All other bills can originate in either chamber.
- The legislative rules and heavy volume of bills considered sometimes enable lawmakers to sneak major, controversial proposals into law by adding little-noticed amendments to other bills.
- The growth of Republican strength has increased partisan activity in the legislature and fueled speculation that, sooner or later, attempts may be made to organize the legislature along the partisan lines of the U.S. Congress. Both major parties already have active legislative caucuses.
- Legislators' decisions are influenced by a number of factors, including constituents, interest groups, colleagues, staff, the governor, and the media.
- Legislators have increasingly come to rely on their staffs to develop legislation, perform constituent services, and act as liaisons to interest groups.
- Although most legislators are honest, hardworking individuals, the weaknesses of a few and the millions of dollars spent by special interests to influence the lawmaking process have undermined Texans' confidence in state government. Lawmakers make periodic efforts to strengthen their ethical standards, but usually only after well-publicized scandals.

KEY TERMS

institutionalization 601
bicameral legislature 601
regular session 602
special session 602
single-member district 606
Legislative Redistricting Board 606
at-large district 607
speaker 608
lieutenant governor 611
quorum 612
committee 616
subcommittee 616
standing committee 616
Calendars Committee 616
conference committee 619
special, or select, committees 619
interims 619
first reading 619
second reading 619
third reading 619
veto 619
appropriations bill 621
line-item veto 621
pay-as-you-go 621
two-thirds rule 621
intent calendar 621
tag 622
filibuster 622
calendar 622
record vote 622
division votes 622
bloc 625

SUGGESTED READINGS

Bickerstaff, Steve. "State Legislative and Congressional Reapportionment in Texas: A Historical Perspective." *Public Affairs Comment* 37 (Winter 1991): 1–13. An excellent overview of three decades of reapportionment litigation in Texas.

Boulard, Garry. "Lobbyists as Outlaws." *State Legislatures* 22 (January 1996): 20–25. A short essay focusing on issues facing state legislatures in the regulation of lobbyists.

Burka, Paul. "Bob Bullock: The Man Who Runs Texas Politics." *Texas Monthly* (September 1994): 100, 162–63. An informative essay on the leadership style of the late Bob Bullock.

Deaton, Charles. *The Year They Threw the Rascals Out.* Austin: Shoal Creek Press, 1973. A detailed account of the 1971 Sharpstown Bank scandal.

Hamm, Robert, and Robert Harmel. "Legislative Party Development and the Speaker System: The Case of the Texas House." *Journal of Politics* 55 (November 1993): 1140–51. Traces the development of the Republican party in the Texas house, emphasizing the potential for the reduction of the power of the speaker.

Jewell, Malcolm E., and Marcia Lynn Whicker. *Legislative Leadership in the American States.* Ann Arbor: University of Michigan Press, 1994. A comparative study of state legislative leadership focusing on leaders' goals, leadership styles, and efforts to be more effective.

Jones, Nancy Baker, and Ruthie Winegarten. *Capitol Women: Texas Female Legislators, 1923–1999.* Austin: University of Texas Press, 2000. A compilation of biographies and biographical sketches of the eighty-six females who served in the Texas Legislature from 1923 to 1999, with a focus on their impact on the legislative process and public policy.

Moncrief, Gary F., Joel A. Thompson, and Karl T. Kurtz. "The Old Statehouse, It Ain't What It Used to Be." *Legislative Studies Quarterly* 21 (February 1996): 57–72. A comparative study based on a survey of 330 veteran state legislators summarizing their perceptions of changes in state legislatures.

Mooney, Christopher Z. "Citizens, Structures and Sister States: Influences on State Legislative Professionalism." *Legislative Studies Quarterly* 20 (February 1995): 47–67. Discusses from a comparative perspective the development of "legislative professionalism in terms of a state's population, its governance structures, and the level of professionalism in its peer group states."

Texas Legislative Council. *Presiding Officers of the Texas Legislature, 1846–1995.* Austin: Texas Legislative Council, 1995. Brief biographic sketches of presiding officers.

Thorburn, Wayne. "The Growth of Republican Representation in the Texas Legislature: Coattails, Incumbency, Special Elections, and Urbanization." *Texas Journal of Political Studies* 11 (Spring/Summer 1989): 16–28. An early study of the gains made by Republicans in the Texas legislature.

CHAPTER 19

THE TEXAS EXECUTIVE AND BUREAUCRACY

CHAPTER OUTLINE

- A Fragmented Government
- The Structure of the Plural Executive
- The Governor
- Other Offices of the Executive Branch
- Elected Boards and Commissions
- The Texas Bureaucracy
- The Growth of Government in Texas
- Bureaucrats and Public Policy
- Strategies for Controlling the Bureaucracy

THINK ABOUT POLITICS

1 Should the governor and lieutenant governor be elected as a ticket?
Yes ● No ●

2 Should the governor be able to appoint an attorney general and other executive officeholders of his or her choosing?
Yes ● No ●

3 Should a governor be limited to a certain number of terms in office?
Yes ● No ●

4 Should a new governor be able to fire policy makers appointed by a predecessor and replace them with his or her own appointees?
Yes ● No ●

5 Should a nursing home owner be allowed to serve on a state board that regulates the quality of patients' care in nursing homes?
Yes ● No ●

6 Do you believe mismanagement and waste are common in state agencies?
Yes ● No ●

7 Should an elected official be able to hire anyone he or she wants, regardless of the individual's qualifications for a particular job?
Yes ● No ●

Voters perceive the Texas governor to have a great deal of power and influence over public policy and the administration of state programs, but a constitutional legacy of the plural executive limits the governor's formal powers, forcing the chief executive to rely on informal resources to strengthen a weak office.

A Fragmented Government

"One thing Texans have today is a state government that doesn't work very well," the state comptroller concluded after an exhaustive study of state agencies and programs. "It is time to rethink Texas government and how it provides basic services to the state's citizens."[1]

When that study was conducted in 1991, Texas had already been operating under an inefficient, fragmented government for more than a century. Yet no changes in what could be considered the root of the problem—the basic governmental structure—have been made since.

For starters, in Texas no single, elected official is ultimately responsible for the executive branch of state government—for the quality of public services performed by hundreds of thousands of state workers. Despite public perception to the contrary, Texas has one of the weaker governors in the country. Unlike the president of the United States, the governor of Texas has no formal appointive cabinet through which to impose policy on the governmental bureaucracy. Several major state agencies are headed by independently elected officeholders who don't answer to the governor and sometimes don't even belong to the same political party. Approximately 250 other state agencies and universities are headed by boards and commissions appointed by the governor, but the governor has only indirect—and often spotty—influence over them.

The office of governor is not without prestige and leadership opportunities. Candidates spend millions of dollars and countless hours campaigning for the job. Clearly, it is the most visible state office. But it is institutionally weak, thanks to constitutional restrictions ensuring that no governor repeat the oppressive abuses of Governor Edmund J. Davis and his Reconstruction administration.[2]

Over the years, the governor's lot has improved somewhat. By constitutional amendment, voters empowered the legislature to raise the governor's salary, and the terms of office for the governor and most other statewide executive officeholders were lengthened from two to four years. In 1980, the governor was given the power, with the approval of the Texas Senate, to remove board members he or she had personally appointed.[3] Nevertheless, these changes have not significantly enhanced the governor's authority. When Governor Ann Richards in 1991 tried to revive interest in giving the governor cabinet-style appointment powers over major state agencies, she had only limited success.

The governor can veto legislation and has the exclusive authority to schedule special sessions of the legislature and set their agendas. And, despite its limitations, the appointment power offers the governor an opportunity to make a strong mark on state government. The high visibility of the office also offers a ready-made public forum. Although the Texas Constitution limits the formal powers of the office, a governor's influence is shaped by his or her personality, political adroitness, staff appointments, and ability to define and sell an agenda that addresses broad needs and interests.

The Structure of the Plural Executive

Article IV, Section 1, of the 1876 Constitution created a **plural executive** branch, which "shall consist of a Governor, who shall be the Chief Executive Officer of the State, a Lieutenant Governor, Secretary of State, Comptroller of Public Accounts, Treasurer, Commissioner of the General Land Office, and Attorney General." Elected officials added later to the executive branch were the agriculture commissioner, the three-member Railroad Commission, and the fifteen-member State Board of Education. The office of treasurer was eliminated by constitutional amendment in 1993. Only the secretary of state is appointed by the governor. Members of the education board are elected from districts, while the other officeholders are elected statewide (see Figure 19.1). Article IV, Section 4, of the Texas Constitution requires most of these officials to be at least thirty years old and a resident of Texas for at least five years.

Agencies headed by these elected officials are autonomous and, except for limited budgetary review, independent of the governor. In a confrontation with the governor over policy, agency heads can claim their own electoral mandates. For many years, there were only "scattered incidents of hostility within the executive branch," and elected officials generally "cooperated remarkably well with their chief executives"[4]—at least while Texas was a one-party Democratic state. During that period, party politics was dominated by conservatives, whose interests were generally served by state officials who believed it was in their own best political interests to cooperate with one another.

But the potential for conflict between the governor and other executive officials increased as Texas became a two-party state, and conflict is likely to become more common in the future, even among officials from the same party. During Republican Governor Bill Clements's first term (1979–83), the other elected officers in the executive branch were Democrats, including Attorney General Mark White, who frequently feuded with the governor. White jockeyed for the political advantage that allowed him to unseat Clements in 1982.

In 2003, budgetary differences erupted between Republican Comptroller Carole Keeton Strayhorn and other Republican officeholders, including Governor Rick Perry. They resulted in the legislature's approval of a bill, signed by Perry, that transferred two key programs from the comptroller's office to the Legislative Budget Board. The political animosity between Strayhorn and Perry, meanwhile, intensified. (This dispute will be discussed in more detail in the section on the comptroller of public accounts later in this chapter.)

When those holding office in a plural executive system have sharply different or competing agendas, it is difficult to develop coordinated policies. The governor, in an effort to avoid conflict, may pursue policies that are not likely to be disruptive, innovative, or responsive to pressing issues. But proponents of the plural

plural executive A fragmented system of authority under which most statewide executive officeholders are elected independently of the governor.

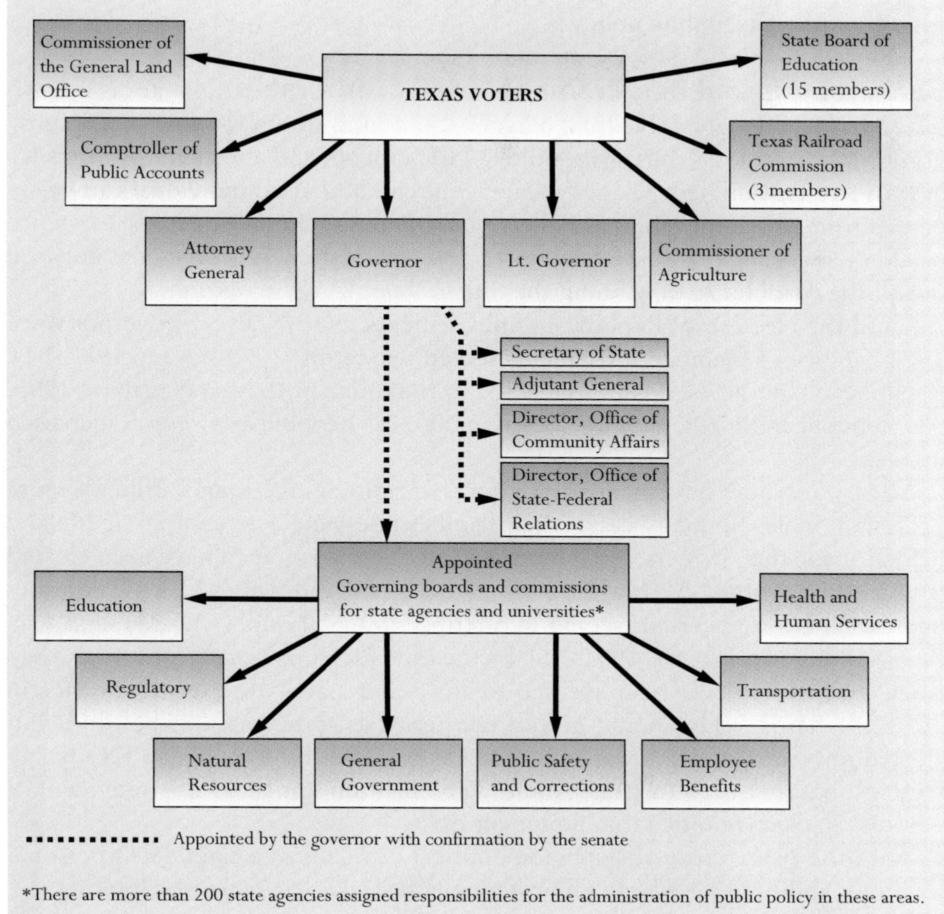

FIGURE 19.1 The Executive Branch in Texas

The executive branch in Texas is a combination of elected and appointed officials who administer more than two hundred state agencies.

Source: Comptroller of Public Accounts, *Breaking the Mold: A Report of the Texas Performance Review*, vol. 1, p. 13.

executive contend that it does what it was intended to do: control and constrain the governor. Although collegial or collective decision making is often inefficient and can lead to deadlock, the advocates of the plural executive contend that democracy, in most instances, is to be preferred over efficiency.

Governor of Texas The governor's website offers up-to-date and archived news releases and speeches, ongoing initiatives, and a detailed description of the structure and functions of the governor's office. Links are provided to the important divisions or sections of the governor's office as well as to other state agencies. *http://www.governor.state.tx.us*

The Governor

Gubernatorial leadership styles have been as varied as the personalities that the chief executives have brought to their jobs. Some governors come to the office with well-defined policy agendas and attempt to exploit every resource available to achieve them. Other governors take a more limited view of the office. They adopt an administrative or managerial posture while leaving policy initiatives to other institutions or elected officials. Such governors tend to pursue new programs, especially those with far-reaching tax or social implications, with considerable caution.

Some governors thrive on the constant attention and political and social interactions that go with the office. They work long hours and continually engage in public relations and coalition building. Strange as it may seem, however, there have also been governors who were introverted, even shy, and apparently found many aspects of the office distasteful. They often insulated themselves from the

THINK AGAIN

Should the governor and lieutenant governor be elected as a ticket?

THINK AGAIN

Should the governor be able to appoint an attorney general and other executive officeholders of his or her choosing?

THINK AGAIN

Should a governor be limited to a certain number of terms in office?

THINK AGAIN

Should a new governor be able to fire policy makers appointed by a predecessor and replace them with his or her own appointees?

public and other political officials and seemed detached from the activities necessary to influence public policy.[5]

Backgrounds and Requirements for Governorship The Texas Constitution has few requirements for a person who desires to run for governor. A governor must be at least thirty years old, a U.S. citizen, and a resident of Texas for at least five years. There also is a vague requirement that no individual can be excluded from office for religious beliefs, "provided he acknowledges the existence of a Supreme Being" (Article I, Section 4). The constitution, however, does not spell out all the roadblocks to winning the office.

Until the election of Republican Bill Clements in 1978, every governor since 1874 had been a Democrat. Clements served two terms (1979–83 and 1987–91). Republican George W. Bush was elected to the office in 1994 and again in 1998, and Republican Rick Perry was elected in 2002, as Republican strength increased in Texas.

Most governors have been well-educated, middle-aged, and affluent white Protestant males. In many cases, their families also were active in public life and helped shape their careers. No minorities and only two women have been elected to the office. Miriam A. "Ma" Ferguson, whose husband, James E. "Pa" Ferguson, had earlier been governor, served two terms (1925–27 and 1933–35), and Ann Richards served one term (1991–95). By the time Richards became governor, only three women had ever been elected to any other statewide executive office in Texas. Richards, a Democrat, served two terms as state treasurer before being elected governor, and she was succeeded as treasurer by Republican Kay Bailey Hutchison. From 1919 to 1923, Annie Webb Blanton was state superintendent of schools, an elective office that no longer exists.

Governor James E. "Pa" Ferguson was the only governor to be removed from office through the impeachment process. Ferguson was impeached and convicted in 1917 during a controversy over his efforts to remove five University of Texas faculty members.

With the rising costs of statewide political campaigns, a candidate's personal wealth or ability to raise large sums of money has taken on increased importance. Otherwise qualified individuals are dissuaded from running for governor and other offices because of the difficult burden of fund raising. Former Governor Bill Clements and fellow Republican Clayton Williams, a Midland business executive who lost the 1990 gubernatorial race to Richards, spent millions of dollars out of their own pockets on gubernatorial races that were their first bids for elective office (see *People in Politics:* "Governor Bill Clements, On-the-Job Training"). Similarly, Democrat Tony Sanchez, a wealthy Laredo businessman, spent more than $56 million of his personal fortune in an unsuccessful race for governor in 2002. Their experience raises the possibility that personal wealth and the willingness to spend it on one's own election campaign will take on more importance in future races.

Previous public service has provided gubernatorial aspirants with public recognition and ties to party leaders, interest groups, and public officials around the state. Texas governors have previously served in local and statewide offices, the legislature, and Congress. Preston Smith (1969–73) was a legislator and lieutenant governor before being elected governor. Dolph Briscoe (1973–79) also served in the legislature. Mark White (1983–87) served as secretary of state and then as attorney general. Ann Richards was a county commissioner and then state treasurer. Although he had never previously held elective office, Clements was a deputy U.S. secretary of defense prior to winning his first gubernatorial race. George W. Bush was elected governor in 1994 without any previous formal government experience. He had been an unofficial adviser to his father, former President George Bush. Rick Perry was a state representative, agriculture commissioner and lieutenant governor before becoming governor. Table 19.1 lists the governors of Texas from 1870 to the present.

Miriam A. "Ma" Ferguson was the first woman to serve as governor of Texas (1925–1927 and 1933–1935).

Impeachment and Incapacitation A governor can be removed from office through **impeachment** proceedings initiated in the house of representatives and conviction by the senate in a trial on the impeachment charges. Texas is one of only a few states that have removed a governor with this procedure. In 1917 a controversy erupted over Governor James E. "Pa" Ferguson's efforts to remove five University of Texas faculty members. The governor vetoed the UT appropriations, and when he called a special legislative session to consider other funding, he was immediately faced with articles of impeachment based primarily on the misuse of public funds. He was ultimately convicted and removed from office, a landmark in the two decades of controversy that surrounded the husband-and-wife team of Pa and Ma Ferguson.[6]

If the governor dies, is incapacitated, is impeached and convicted, or leaves office for another reason in midterm, the lieutenant governor replaces the governor until the next general election. When the governor leaves the state, the lieutenant governor serves as acting governor.

Some other states, such as California, can remove a governor through recall, as well as impeachment. Through a process that begins with petitions signed by a defined number of voters, a special election can be held on the question of removing the governor from office. If the governor is removed by popular vote, a new governor is then elected. This occurred in California in late 2003, when Democrat Gray Davis was recalled as governor, and voters in the same election chose movie star Arnold Schwarzenegger, a Republican, to replace him. Texas doesn't have the recall process for the governor or other statewide officeholders.

Salary and Perks of the Office In 2004, the governor of Texas was paid $115,345. The state also provides the governor with a mansion and a staff to maintain it, a security detail, travel expenses, and access to state-owned planes and cars.

Legislative Powers of the Governor Governors have the opportunity to outline their legislative priorities at the beginning of each regular biennial session through the traditional State of the State Address to the legislature. The governor can also communicate with lawmakers—collectively or individually—throughout the session. In this fashion, the governor can establish a policy agenda, recommend specific legislation, and set the stage for negotiations with legislative leaders, other state officials, and interest groups. The governor's addresses and other formal messages to the legislature are well covered by the media. They give governors the opportunity to mobilize the public support that may be essential to the success of their initiatives.

The governor's effectiveness can be enhanced by the office's two major constitutional powers over the legislature: the veto and the authority to call and set the agenda for special legislative sessions.

The governor can call any number of **special sessions,** which can last as long as thirty days each, and designate the issues to be considered during each one. Sometimes the mere threat of a special session can be enough to convince reluctant lawmakers to approve a priority program of the governor or reach an acceptable compromise during a regular session. Most legislators, who are paid only

impeachment A procedure by which the legislature can remove a governor or certain other public officials from office for misconduct.

special session A legislative session that can be called at any time by the governor. This session is limited to thirty days and to issues or subjects designated by the governor.

PEOPLE IN POLITICS

Governor Bill Clements, On-the-Job Training

Bill Clements, a self-made multimillionaire who had founded an international oil drilling firm, personally funded much of his first campaign for governor in 1978. The man who shocked the Democratic establishment by defeating John Hill by 17,000 votes had held no previous elected office. His only governmental experience had been as deputy secretary of defense under Presidents Richard Nixon and Gerald Ford. Clements was an outsider, a Republican, a highly opinionated and blunt person, but he had a reputation for solid management skills. All the other elected statewide officials were Democrats, as were most legislators, although many lawmakers shared Clements's conservative views.

Upon arriving in Austin, Clements did not understand the limitations on the powers of the governor. In his election campaign, he had tapped a rather widely held view that state government was wasteful by proposing that 25,000 state jobs be eliminated. He also appealed to the popular notion of limited government and proposed that the Texas Constitution be amended to allow private citizens to propose laws through a statewide initiative and referendum process. But he gradually learned that he could not run the statehouse and the bureaucracy single-handedly the way he had run the corporate boardroom, and he did not accomplish either of these goals.

In an interview years later, Clements admitted that he did not fully understood how state government worked when he first took office:

> Until I came to Austin and until I actually was in office and everything, I really didn't understand the detailed nuances of how the state government really functioned. I'd say it took me at least through that first legislative session. And by the time that was over, well, I began to understand exactly how the state government works.*

Clements eagerly exercised his veto power. During his first legislative session in 1979, he vetoed fifty-one bills. He also struck $252 million from the $20.7 billion state budget for 1980–81.

Clements generally received high marks for the quality of his staff and board appointments during his first term. He naturally appointed many fellow Republicans, who for years had been shut out of appointments to boards and commissions, and he also appointed many conservative Democrats. In part, his appointment strategies were designed to convert conservative Democrats to the Republican Party,

part-time salaries by the state, dread special sessions because they interfere with their regular occupations and disrupt their personal lives. Governor Bill Clements, who called two special sessions on workers' compensation reform in 1989, used the threat of a third to convince a handful of senators to break a year-long impasse and approve legislation backed by the governor, a majority of the house, and the business community. Governor Rick Perry called three special sessions in 2003 to win approval of a congressional redistricting bill that favored Republican candidates. The bill wouldn't have passed without Perry's persistence (see Chapter 18).

There also are risks in calling special sessions. The governor's influence and reputation are on the line, and further inaction by the legislature can become a political liability or embarrassment. In some instances, the legislative leadership has liberally interpreted the subject matter of a governor's special session proclamation and considered bills not sought by the governor. Because the speaker and the lieutenant governor make the parliamentary rulings that determine whether a specific piece of legislation falls within the governor's call, the governor has to draft proclamations setting special session agendas very carefully. Once a special session is thus extending and consolidating Republican gains across the state.

But Clements never developed effective ways of communicating with the legislature, the news media, and the general public, and he often found himself at odds with other elected officials and interest groups, primarily because of his outspokenness. He was often portrayed as insensitive, as someone inclined to "shoot from the lip" and worry about the consequences later.

By the end of his first term in 1982, Clements's job performance rating had dropped, his image had suffered, and the Texas economy had begun to show signs of weakness. A revitalized Democratic statewide political effort helped Mark White unseat Clements in a bitterly fought campaign.

In 1986 Clements became only the second person in Texas history to regain the governor's office after losing it. He spent his first six months back in Austin battling Lieutenant Governor Bill Hobby and Democratic legislators over the state budget. The problem was critical because revenue from existing taxes had fallen in the midst of a recession. Clements insisted on deep service cuts that would have enabled him to keep a 1986 campaign promise not to raise taxes, but he finally gave in during a summer special session in 1987 and signed a record $5.6 billion tax increase. The public's opinion of Clements, meanwhile, was plummeting. Two-thirds of the respondents to the *Texas Poll* that summer said they disapproved of the governor's job performance. And Clements's negative ratings remained high throughout the remainder of his term. By the time he left the governor's office the second time, in 1991, he was widely viewed more as an obstructionist who would rather fight the Democratic majority in the legislature than as a leader who was ready to seek solutions to significant state problems.

Clements's two terms coincided with the emergence of a two-party system in Texas, and his candidacy and elections contributed significantly to this historic development. By proving that a Republican could win the governorship, Clements made the Republican Party attractive to many conservative Democrats, and many switched to the GOP.

In an interview shortly before leaving office for the last time, Clements assessed his contribution to the development of a two-party system:

> The electorate out there breaks down into about one-third Democrats, one-third Republicans, and one-third independents. Well, that is a significant change in the political profile of Texas. That's a historic change, and I guess I'd like to say that I put a brick in place to bring that about.[†]

[*]Quoted in *Houston Chronicle*, December 2, 1990.
[†]Quoted in *Houston Chronicle*, December 2, 1990.

called, the governor can increase his or her bargaining power by adding legislators' pet bills to the agenda in exchange for the lawmakers' support of the governor's program.

The governor of Texas has one of the strongest **veto** powers of any governor. While the legislature is in session, the governor has ten days to veto a bill or let it become law without his or her signature. A veto can be overridden by a two-thirds vote of both the house and the senate. During the past fifty years, Governor Clements was the only governor to have a veto overridden. It was a local bill related to game management that the Democrat-dominated legislature voted to override during the Republican governor's first term. The governor has twenty days after the legislature adjourns to veto bills passed in the closing days of a session. Such vetoes are absolute because the only way the legislature can respond is to have the bill reintroduced in the next session.

veto The power of the governor to reject, or kill, a bill passed by the legislature.

The governor also has **line-item veto** authority over the state budget: that is, the governor can strike specific spending items without vetoing the entire bill. All other bills have to be accepted or rejected in their entirety.

line-item veto The power of the governor to reject certain parts of an appropriations, or spending, bill without killing the entire measure.

TABLE 19.1 Governors of Texas Since 1870

Governor	Term
Edmund J. Davis	1870–1874
Richard Coke	1874–1876
Richard B. Hubbard	1876–1879
Oran M. Roberts	1879–1883
John Ireland	1883–1887
Lawrence Sullivan Ross	1887–1891
James Stephen Hogg	1891–1895
Charles A. Culberson	1895–1899
Joseph D. Sayers	1899–1903
Samuel W.T. Lanham	1903–1907
Thomas Mitchell Campbell	1907–1911
Oscar Branch Colquitt	1911–1915
James E. Ferguson*	1915–1917
William Pettus Hobby	1917–1921
Pat Morris Neff	1921–1925
Miriam A. Ferguson	1925–1927
Dan Moody	1927–1931
Ross S. Sterling	1931–1933
Miriam A. Ferguson	1933–1935
James V. Allred	1935–1939
W. Lee O'Daniel	1939–1941
Coke R. Stevenson	1941–1947
Beauford H. Jester	1947–1949
Allan Shivers	1949–1957
Price Daniel	1957–1963
John Connally	1963–1969
Preston Smith	1969–1973
Dolph Briscoe, Jr.†	1973–1979
Williams P. Clements, Jr.	1979–1983
Mark White	1983–1987
William P. Clements, Jr.	1987–1991
Ann Richards	1991–1995
George W. Bush	1995–2000
Rick Perry	2000–

*Only governor of Texas to be impeached and convicted.
†Prior to 1974, governors were elected for two-year terms of office.
Source: Texas Almanac, 1996–1997 (Dallas: The Dallas Morning News, Inc., 1995).

A governor may veto a bill for a number of reasons, including doubts about its constitutionality, objections to its wording, concerns that it duplicates existing law, or substantive differences with its policy. A governor's threat of a veto is often as effective as an actual veto because such threats can prompt legislators to make changes in their bills to meet the governor's objections.

Historic records on gubernatorial vetoes are not complete, but Governor Rick Perry is believed to have set a single-year record by vetoing 82 bills at the end of the 2001 legislative session. His vetoes also sparked a lot of anger from doctors, criminal justice reformers, state employees, advocates for the poor, and others. One veto, the striking down of a bill that would have banned execution of mentally retarded convicts in Texas, received international attention. And although that veto was sharply criticized by death penalty opponents, it drew praise from crime victims' advocates. Perry attempted to milk the most favorable publicity that he could from the event by inviting more than a dozen relatives of people murdered by mentally retarded convicts to join him at a state Capitol news conference to announce the veto. Despite his veto, however, the U.S. Supreme Court later had the final say on the issue when it ruled the execution of mentally retarded convicts was unconstitutional. Perry vetoed 48 bills after the 2003 regular session.

Governor Dan Moody also was a frequent veto user. He vetoed 117 bills and resolutions between 1927 and 1931. Governor Ann Richards vetoed 36 bills and resolutions in one regular and two special sessions in 1991 and allowed 228 bills to become law without her signature.

Budgetary Powers of the Governor The governor of Texas has weaker budgetary authority than the governors of most states and the president of the United States. These budgetary constraints limit the governor's ability to develop a comprehensive legislative program. The legislature has the lead in budget setting, with a major role played by the **Legislative Budget Board** (LBB), a ten-member panel that includes the lieutenant governor, the speaker, and eight key lawmakers.

To meet emergencies between legislative sessions, the governor can propose the transfer of funds between programs or agencies, with the approval of the LBB. Or the LBB can recommend a funds transfer, subject to the governor's approval.

Appointive and Removal Powers of the Governor Much of the state bureaucracy falls under more than 200 boards and commissions that oversee various agencies created by state law. Most of these are part-time, unpaid positions whose occupants are heavily dependent on agency staffs and constituents for guidance. Although members of these boards are appointed by the governor and confirmed by the senate, the structure creates the potential for boards and commissions to become captives of the narrow constituencies they are serving or regulating and reduces their accountability to both the governor and the legislature.

Most board members serve six-year **staggered terms,** an arrangement under which the terms of one-third of a board's membership expire every two years. That means it takes new governors at least two years to get majorities favoring their policies on most boards. Resignations or deaths of board members may speed up the process, but a governor cannot remove a predecessor's appointees. Governors, with the approval of two-thirds of the senate, can fire only their own appointees.

During her first year in office in 1991, Governor Ann Richards asked the legislature to give her the power to appoint the executive directors of state agencies directly. These officials historically had been hired by the various boards and commissions. In reorganizing a handful of agencies, the legislature gave the governor a small taste of the cabinet-style authority she had sought, but it hardly changed the system. The governor was given the authority to appoint a new commissioner to oversee several health and human services agencies, the executive director of the Department of Commerce, and the executive director of a new Department of Housing and Community Affairs. The governor retained her previous authority to appoint the secretary of state, the adjutant general, and the director of the Office

Legislative Budget Board The panel that makes budgetary recommendations to the full legislature. It is chaired by the lieutenant governor and includes the speaker of the house and eight other key lawmakers.

staggered terms Terms that begin on different dates, a requirement for members of state boards and commissions appointed by the governor.

PEOPLE IN POLITICS

Governor Ann Richards, Saleswoman

Taking her oath in January 1991, Ann Richards attempted to convince the public that her election marked the emergence of a "New Texas." She invited supporters to join her in a march up Congress Avenue to symbolically retake the Capitol for "the people." And, hitting on the progressive Democratic themes of her campaign, she promised in her inaugural address a user-friendly, compassionate state government that would expand opportunities for everyone, particularly minorities and women. But the euphoria of the day was tempered by the reality of a $4 billion-plus potential deficit, a court order for school finance reform that could make the shortfall even greater, and a grand jury investigation into legislative behavior that had eroded public confidence in state government.

Richards moved quickly to establish herself as an activist governor. The day after her inauguration, she continued a campaign assault on high insurance rates by marching over to a meeting of the State Board of Insurance to speak publicly against a proposed increase in auto insurance premiums. Unlike her recent predecessors, she also testified for her priorities before house and senate committees and used the media to attack the state bureaucracy.

Richards also quickly fulfilled a campaign promise to appoint more women and minorities to key positions in state government. She appointed the first African American to the University of Texas System Board of Regents, the first African American woman to the Texas A&M University governing board, and the first Hispanic to the Texas Court of Criminal appeals. Some 25 percent of her appointees during her first three months in office were Hispanic, 21 percent were African American, and 49 percent were women. Richards also named a disabled person to the Board of Human Services and a crime victim to the Board of Criminal Justice.*

With the state facing a revenue crunch, Richards took the lead in lobbying legislators for a constitutional amendment to create a state lottery. The lottery was a relatively safe issue on which to stake a leadership claim because polls indicated it had the strong support of most Texans as a new source of revenue for state government.

Most other major issues before the legislature during Richards's first year in office, however, were not so simple, and the new governor was less willing to strike specific policy positions on them. She preferred to support the initiatives of Democratic legislative leaders—or take the best bill they were willing to give her—rather than demand that legislators enact a specific plan. Detractors would say Richards's leadership wilted in the heat of legislative battle. Supporters would say she was a pragmatist who knew the limits of her office and recognized the necessity of political compromise.

The progressive goals that Richards had outlined in her campaign were also tempered by the reality that Texas was a predominantly conservative state. Despite promoting a vision of a "New Texas" that offered more compassion for the poor, improved health care for the sick, and greater educational opportunity for all, Richards took pains to establish credentials for fiscal restraint. She opposed a proposal for a personal income tax, even though it could have provided funds for a big boost in spending on health and human services programs and education. And she eagerly embraced a

---

of State-Federal Relations (see *People in Politics*: "Governor Ann Richards, Saleswoman").

senatorial courtesy An unwritten practice that permits a senator to block the confirmation of a gubernatorial appointee who lives in the senator's district.

The governor appoints individuals to boards and commissions with the approval of two-thirds of the senate. **Senatorial courtesy**, an unwritten norm of the senate, permits a senator to block the governor's nomination of a person who lives in that senator's district. The governor and staff members involved in appointments spend considerable time clearing potential nominees with senators because political considerations are as important in the confirmation process as a nominee's qualifications.

thorough review of state spending practices that helped reduce the size of the revenue and tax bill she eventually signed during her first year in office.

Although Richards entered the 1993 legislative session with one of the highest public approval ratings of any governor in Texas history, she remained cautious during the entire session, apparently to save political capital for a 1994 reelection race. She joined Lieutenant Governor Bob Bullock and Pete Laney, the new house speaker, in insisting that a new state budget be written without an increase in state taxes. There was no tax bill, but the new budget did not enable the legislature to give teachers a pay raise, which had been another Richards priority, and it did not keep up with growing caseloads in health and human services programs.

In one of the most emotional issues of the session, Richards sided with police chiefs, mayors, physicians, and members of the clergy—and against a majority of the legislature—in killing a proposal to allow private citizens to carry handguns. (It was revived and approved under Governor George W. Bush two years later.) She successfully advocated an immunization program for children and actively promoted the legislature's efforts to comply with a Texas Supreme Court order for a constitutional school finance system but did not propose a plan of her own.

Richards staked out a strong anticrime position early in her term. In 1991 she ordered her appointees to the Board of Pardons and Paroles to sharply curtail a high rate of releases from state prisons, and she supported a huge prison expansion program. Richards also made economic development a major goal. She actively recruited companies to locate or expand in Texas and was instrumental in lobbying the U.S. Congress for approval of the North American Free Trade Agreement (NAFTA), even though NAFTA was bitterly opposed by organized labor, one of her key longtime supporters.

Richards was a national figure who was readily welcomed on Wall Street, at Hollywood parties, and in corporate boardrooms throughout the country. Many analysts believed her role as Texas's chief salesperson, or ambassador, was her greatest contribution to the state, along with the appointments that opened up the state policy-making process to a record number of women, Hispanics, and African Americans.

Richards, who had no legislative experience, did not seem to relish the often bloody give-and-take of the legislative process, but she obviously enjoyed her celebrity role as governor. During the 1993 session, Richards told reporters that she was not the kind of leader who could force results. Instead, she said, she tried to contribute to "an atmosphere in which good things can happen."†

Although Richards was unseated by Republican George W. Bush in 1994, polls indicated she remained personally popular with her constituents. But most conservative, independent voters had never been comfortable with Richards politically. Her defeat coincided with voter discontent with the Democratic Party that swept the country that year. A number of other Democratic governors were also defeated, and Republicans captured control of both houses of the U.S. Congress. Richards's opposition to the handgun bill during the 1993 legislative session was another factor, particularly in key conservative areas of the state.

***Texas Government Newsletter*, February 25, 1991.

†Quoted in *Houston Chronicle*, June 2, 1993.

Individuals seek gubernatorial appointments for a variety of reasons, and the appointments process can be hectic, particularly at the beginning of a new governor's administration. Potential nominees are screened by the governor's staff to determine their availability, competence, political acceptability, and support by key interest groups. And although most governors would deny it, campaign contributions are a significant factor. A number of Governor Clements's appointees had made substantial contributions to his campaign.[7] Governors Richards, Bush, and Perry also appointed major contributors to important posts. Governor Perry made the most controversial appointment of his first year in office, former Enron

Corporation executive Max Yzaguirre as chairman of the Public Utility Commission, one day before receiving a $25,000 political donation from then-Enron Chairman Ken Lay in 2001. Perry insisted the timing was coincidental, but it generated much controversy after Enron filed for bankruptcy a few months later, prompting Yzaguirre's resignation from the post. Then, in 2003, less than one month after receiving a $100,000 contribution from homebuilder Bob Perry of Houston, Governor Perry appointed a top executive of the homebuilder's company to a new state commission charged with developing building performance standards. The commission had been created by the legislature to reduce consumer lawsuits against builders. Since June 1997, Bob Perry, who wasn't related to the governor, had contributed $580,000 to Rick Perry[8] (see *People in Politics:* "Governor Rick Perry, Claiming His Inheritance").

The governor appoints individuals to fill vacancies on all courts at the district level or higher. If a U.S. senator dies or resigns, the governor appoints a replacement. When a vacancy occurs in another statewide office, except for the lieutenant governor, the governor also appoints a replacement. All of these appointees must later win election to keep their seats.

Governor Richards was particularly sensitive to constituencies that had historically been excluded from full participation in the governmental process and appointed a record number of women and minorities to state posts. About 45 percent of Richards's appointees during her four-year term were women, and about 35 percent were minorities. Her successor, Governor Bush, appointed women to 37 percent and minorities to 22 percent of the posts he filled during his first five years in office. Bush appointed the first African American, Michael Williams, to the Texas Railroad Commission, and, at different times during his administration, appointed two Hispanics—Tony Garza and Alberto R. Gonzales—secretary of state. Bush later appointed Gonzales to fill a vacancy on the Texas Supreme Court and, after becoming president, appointed Gonzales to the important White House counsel post. Governor Perry appointed the first African American, Wallace Jefferson of San Antonio, to the Texas Supreme Court.

Judicial Powers of the Governor Texas has a seven-member Board of Pardons and Paroles appointed by the governor. This panel, which was reduced from 18 members by a 2003 law, decides when prisoners can be released early, and its decisions do not require action by the governor. The governor, however, can influence the board's overall approach to paroles. The governor has the authority to grant executive clemency—acts of leniency or mercy—toward convicted criminals. One is a thirty-day stay of execution for a condemned murderer, which a governor can grant without a recommendation of the parole board. The governor, on recommendation of the board, can grant a full pardon to a criminal, a conditional pardon, or the commutation of a death sentence to life imprisonment.

If a person flees a state to avoid prosecution or a prison term, the U.S. Constitution, under the **extradition** clause, requires that person, upon arrest in another state, to be returned to the state from which he or she fled. The governor is legally responsible for ordering state officials to carry out such extradition requests.[9]

extradition A process by which a person in one state is returned to another state to face criminal charges.

Military Powers of the Governor The Texas Constitution authorizes the governor to function as the "commander-in-chief of the military force of the state, except when they are called into actual service of the United States" (Article IV, Section 7). The governor appoints the adjutant general to carry out this duty. Texas cannot declare war on another country, and the president of the United States has the primary responsibility for national defense. But when riots or natural disasters occur within the state, the governor can mobilize the Texas National Guard to protect lives and property and keep the peace. Should the United States go to war, the National Guard can be mobilized by the president as part of the national military forces. After the September 11, 2001, terrorist attacks on the World Trade Center and the Pentagon, some National Guard members from Texas were activated to temporarily bolster security at airports. Others went overseas to participate in the military operations in Afghanistan and Iraq.

National Governors Association (NGA)

This bipartisan organization provides information on key state issues and monitors and analyzes the progress of important state policy issues. Information on the governors of all fifty states is also available. ***http://www.nga.org***

Informal Resources of the Governor Governors can compensate for the constitutional limitations on their office with their articulation of problems and issues, leadership capabilities, personalities, work habits, and administrative styles. Some governors relish being involved in the minutiae of building policy coalitions and devote much of their personal time to bringing about compromises and agreements. Other governors find such hands-on involvement distasteful, inefficient, and time consuming, and leave such detail work to subordinates.

As the most visible state official, the governor sometimes gets credit that belongs to others but can just as readily be blamed for problems beyond his or her control. For example, falling oil prices that had devastated the state's economy were a major factor in Mark White's loss of his 1986 reelection bid. White had no choice but to call a special legislative session only a few months before the November election and, under the circumstances, probably exercised the best leadership that he could in convincing lawmakers to cut the budget and raise taxes. But it was not the type of leadership appreciated by most voters.

The Governor's Staff Nineteenth-century governors had only three or four individuals to assist them, but staffs have grown with the increased complexity of state government and greater demands on the governor's time. By 1963, under John Connally, the governor's staff had grown to 68 full-time and 12 part-time employees.[10] Under the administration of Dolph Briscoe in the 1970s, the staff had further expanded to more than 300, but staff sizes were smaller in most subsequent administrations. At one point in her term, Ann Richards had almost 300 people on her staff. The number decreased to about 200 under George W. Bush, but Bush approved higher salaries for some of his key staffers. In 2002, Governor Perry had approximately 200 employees (see Figure 19.2).

The critical question involving staff is whether the governor has access to sufficient information on which to make decisions that produce good public policy and minimize the potential for controversy, conflict, and embarrassment. Under ideal circumstances, the staff enhances the governor's political, administrative, and policy-making capabilities. There have been instances, however, when governors have permitted staff to insulate them by denying access to persons with significant information or recommendations.

Governors generally choose staffers who are loyal and share their basic political attitudes. Because communication with the governor's various constituencies is fundamental to success, some staffers are chosen for their skills in mass communications and public relations. Others are hired for their expertise in specific policy areas. In many respects, staff members function as the governor's surrogates.

PEOPLE IN POLITICS

Governor Rick Perry, Claiming His Inheritance

Republican Rick Perry came to the governor's office with much more governmental experience than his immediate and more famous predecessor, George W. Bush. He had served six years as a state representative, eight years as state agriculture commissioner and almost two years as lieutenant governor before succeeding Bush as governor in December 2000, after Bush had resigned to become president. But Perry wasn't blessed with Bush's politically powerful name or his popularity, and he hadn't been elected governor. He had inherited the job. Moreover, the 2001 legislative session, with which Perry immediately had to deal, promised to be contentious because of political redistricting and a worrisome budgetary outlook.

Perry, however, survived his first session mostly unscarred. He didn't have to sign or veto any redistricting bills because Republicans and Democrats in the legislature were unable to agree on new political boundaries for themselves or for Texas's congressional delegation. The legislative impasse put legislative redistricting in the hands of the Legislative Redistricting Board and deferred congressional redistricting—for the time being, anyway—to a federal court. Lawmakers wrote a new state budget without having to raise taxes and, at Perry's urging, even found enough money to triple funding for a grant program to help thousands of young Texans from low-income families attend college.

The legislature enacted one of Perry's criminal justice priorities, a law to give inmates the ability to obtain court-ordered DNA testing if they could demonstrate that there was a substantial possibility that the results would prove them innocent. But the governor didn't get his way on another criminal justice issue with significant political overtones. In one of the most emotional and partisan issues of the session, the legislature approved a bill, backed by most Democrats and opposed by most Republicans, to strengthen penalties for crimes motivated by hate or prejudice. It was a fight that had begun in earnest two years earlier, after three white assailants had dragged an African American, James Byrd Jr., to death behind a pickup in east Texas. At one point, Perry convinced a Republican senator to help delay action on the bill because he opposed a provision that listed protected classes of people, including homosexuals, which was strongly opposed by social conservatives in the Republican Party. But after the measure won final legislative approval, Perry signed it within a few hours after it reached his desk. He said he still had doubts about it. "But I also believe that as governor, and as a Texan, I have an obligation to see issues from another person's perspective, to walk in another person's shoes," he said.*

Some legislators criticized Perry's mostly low-key style during the 2001 session and complained that he didn't let them know early enough and clearly enough what he wanted. Shortly after the legislative session had ended, however, Perry flexed his muscles and vetoed a record 82 bills, including a measure that would have banned the execution of mentally retarded convicts in Texas. Aware that international attention was focused on his decision, Perry invited relatives of murder victims to join him at a state Capitol news conference announcing the veto. Crime victims' advocates praised the veto, but death penalty opponents criticized it. A year later, the U.S. Supreme Court, acting in a case from another state, would prohibit the execution of mentally retarded inmates throughout the country.

Other vetoes drew sharp criticism from a range of people. Among the loudest complaints came from doctors over the governor's veto of a bill that would have required insurance companies to promptly pay health care providers for their services. Physicians and hospitals complained that health maintenance organizations and other insurers were dragging their feet in paying valid claims, often creating financial hardships for providers. Perry vetoed the bill at the urging of business groups that argued that it would have removed arbitration as an option for settling health insurance claims and would have encouraged lawsuits. A similar prompt-pay bill was enacted by the legislature in 2003—without the provision that offended the business groups—and Perry signed it.

During his first year as governor, Perry also had to dodge political fallout from the spectacular collapse of Enron Corp., the Houston-based energy-trading giant, which had been a major source of political donations during his public career. Soon after Enron filed for bankruptcy in late 2001, throwing thousands of employees out of work and costing investors and retirees millions of dollars, controversy erupted over Perry's appointment of a former Enron executive, Max Yzaguirre, to chair the Texas Public Utility Commission. Perry had appointed Yzaguirre in June 2001, several months before most people even suspected that Enron was in financial trouble. But after the Enron story exploded, Democrats started questioning Yzaguirre's eligibility for the regulatory post and the timing of his appointment. Perry had received a $25,000 political donation from then-Enron Chairman Ken Lay the day after appointing Yzaguirre. Perry insisted Yzaguirre was legally qualified and that the timing of the contribution was coincidental. But after the controversy had raged for several weeks, Yzaguirre resigned. It wasn't clear whether he chose to step down on his own or was quietly encouraged to do so by the governor.

Despite his rural roots—Perry grew up in Paint Creek, a tiny town in West Texas—the governor was acutely aware of the clogged freeways that plagued the daily lives of urban and suburban Texans and, early on, sought to make improved transportation a signature issue of his administration. He actively campaigned for a constitutional amendment, which voters approved in November 2001, creating the Texas Mobility Fund, a revolving fund against which bonds could be pledged for highway construction. It was a significant departure from the state's traditional pay-as-you-go method of paying for highways. Then, in early 2002, Perry proposed a massive, $175 billion transportation network for Texas, which would include toll roads, railroads and underground utility tunnels grouped in corridors stretching across the state. The plan, which Perry called the Trans Texas Corridor, would take an estimated fifty years to complete.

Perry defeated Democratic nominee Tony Sanchez, a multimillionaire Laredo businessman, in a bruising campaign to win a full term in the governor's office in 2002. Perry's victory and the first Republican takeover of the Texas house in modern times put the GOP in undisputed control of state government, and Perry acted accordingly. The governor joined Republican legislative leaders in demanding that a $10 billion revenue shortfall be closed by cutting spending, not raising taxes, and Republicans prevailed. Advocates of health care programs and other services protested the spending reductions, and many of the state's daily newspapers editorialized for limited tax increases to help minimize the cuts in services. The legislature raised some state fees and enacted legislation to allow university governing boards to increase tuition, but Perry refused to budge on taxes, apparently convinced that most middle-class Texans agreed with him. He also argued that the state's relatively low tax burden had to be protected to keep the state attractive to businesses looking for places to expand. Perry also won from the legislature a special economic development fund that could be used to provide economic incentives for business recruitment.

The governor also advocated and won significant new restrictions on medical malpractice claims and other civil lawsuits. He said the so-called tort reform changes were essential to easing a crisis in health care, particularly in rural areas, and improving the state's business climate, although opponents argued that they put unnecessary, new restrictions on consumers' access to the courts.

As was more fully discussed in Chapter 22, Perry also played a dominant role in a bitter, partisan fight over congressional redistricting in 2003. Perry fully supported an effort, initiated by U.S. House Majority Leader Tom DeLay of Sugar Land, to increase the number of Republicans elected to the U.S. House from Texas. Under a 2001 redistricting plan drawn by a federal court, Democrats still held a 17–15 majority in the Texas congressional delegation, despite recent Republican sweeps of all statewide offices and Republican majorities in both the Texas house and the state senate. DeLay, Perry, and other GOP leaders argued that the congressional delegation should more accurately reflect the state's Republican strength. A bill that would have redrawn congressional districts to favor more Republican candidates died during the 2003 regular session after more than fifty Democratic members of the Texas house fled to Ardmore, Okla., to break a quorum and keep the house from acting on the measure. Using one of his strongest constitutional powers, Perry then called the legislature back into special session that summer to try again. Eventually it took three special sessions to complete the task, but Perry was persistent. He even waited out a second Democratic boycott, when eleven Democratic senators flew to Albuquerque, N.M., to hold out for more than a month and shut down the senate during the entire second special session. A redistricting bill that the Republican-dominated legislature finally passed during the third special session—and which survived an initial court challenge—was expected to increase the number of Republicans elected to Congress from Texas by as many as seven, all at the expense of incumbent Democrats.

For a while, at least, the redistricting dispute may have put a dent in Perry's popularity. A Scripps Howard *Texas Poll* taken at the height of the controversy in August 2003, while the Democratic senators were still in New Mexico, indicated that Perry's job approval rating was at its lowest, 44 percent, since he had become governor. It had fallen 6 percentage points since June. The same poll showed that Texans by a narrow margin (46 percent to 40 percent) opposed congressional redistricting but strongly disagreed (62 percent to 29 percent) with the Democratic walkout. Perry said he wasn't worried. "I get up every day and try to do what's right for the people of Texas," he said. "I don't wake up and fret about what a particular poll at a particular point in time says."

---

*[*] *Houston Chronicle,* August 27, 2003, p. 23A.

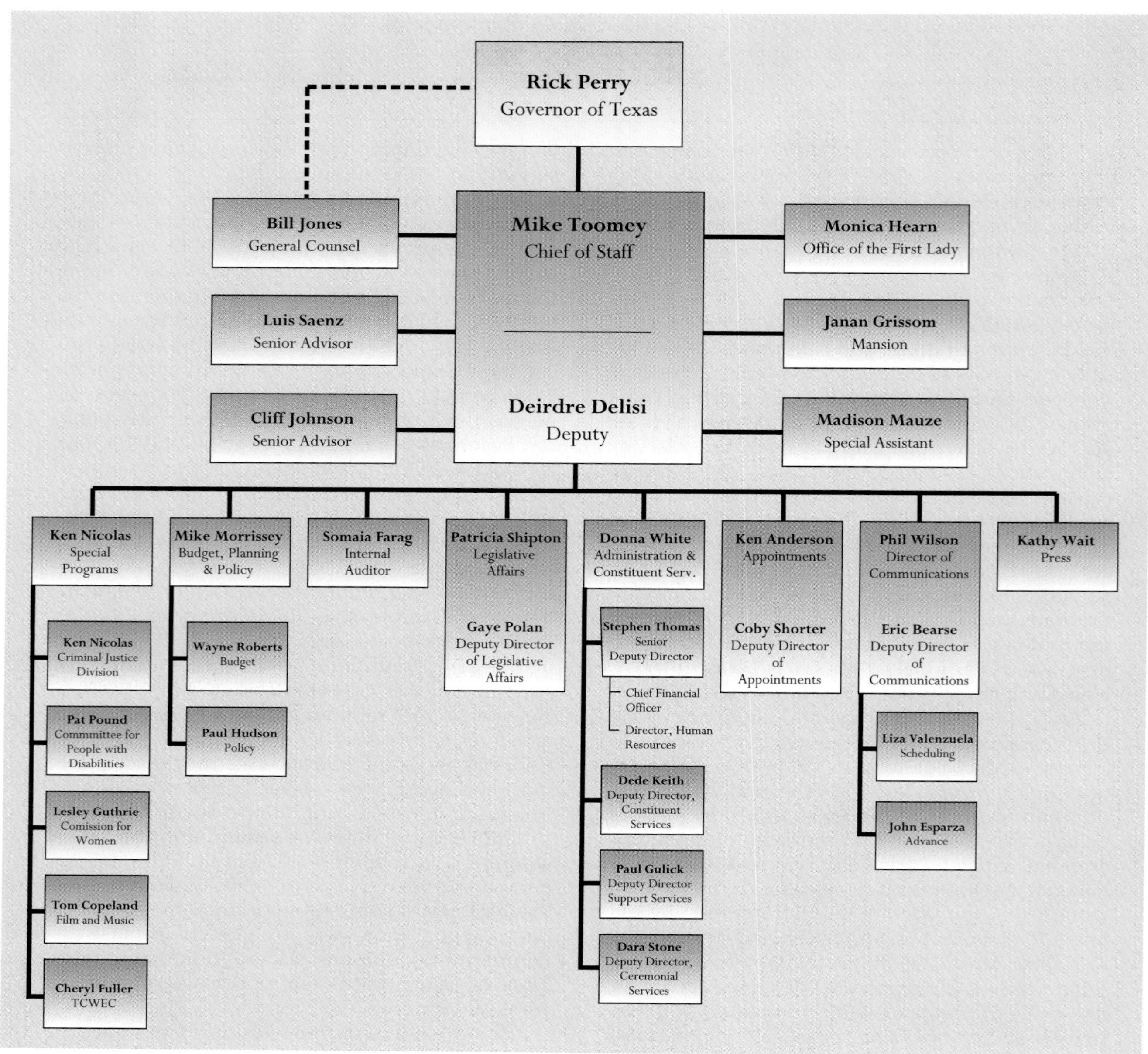

FIGURE 19.2 Office of the Governor, 2003

Thus if one makes a mistake—particularly a serious mistake—the public perceives it as the governor's error.

The staff collects, organizes, and screens information, helps decide who sees the governor, and otherwise schedules the governor's time. Staffers also work on strategies to garner support for the governor's proposals from legislators, agencies, and interest groups. Because the governor often lacks the time to conduct discussions and negotiations, key staff members represent the governor in such meetings and in personal lobbying of lawmakers. Sometimes governors get involved personally, particularly if their participation is needed to break an impasse and bring about a solution.[11]

The Governor and the Mass Media The mass media help shape the political and policy options of the governor. Governors who have failed to understand the impact of the media have often courted disaster. A governor who is readily accessible to reporters and understands the constraints under which the media operate is likely to develop a good working relationship with the press. But success with the media involves more than being accessible and friendly.

Governors call press conferences to announce new policies or to explain their positions on pending issues. They stage pseudo "news events," such as visits to classrooms to emphasize concern for educational quality or appearances at high-tech facilities to demonstrate a commitment to economic development. They or their staffers sometimes leak information to selected reporters to embarrass the opposition, put an action of the administration in the best possible light, or float a trial balloon to gauge legislative or public reaction to a proposal. Some governors have spent political funds to purchase radio or television time in an attempt to mobilize public opinion in support of pet proposals before the legislature. Overall, the timely use of the media can contribute significantly to the power and influence of a governor.

The Governor and the Political Party Historically, the political factions within one-party Democratic Texas were somewhat ill defined. Factionalism was

ACROSS THE USA

Party Control of the Governor's Office, 2004

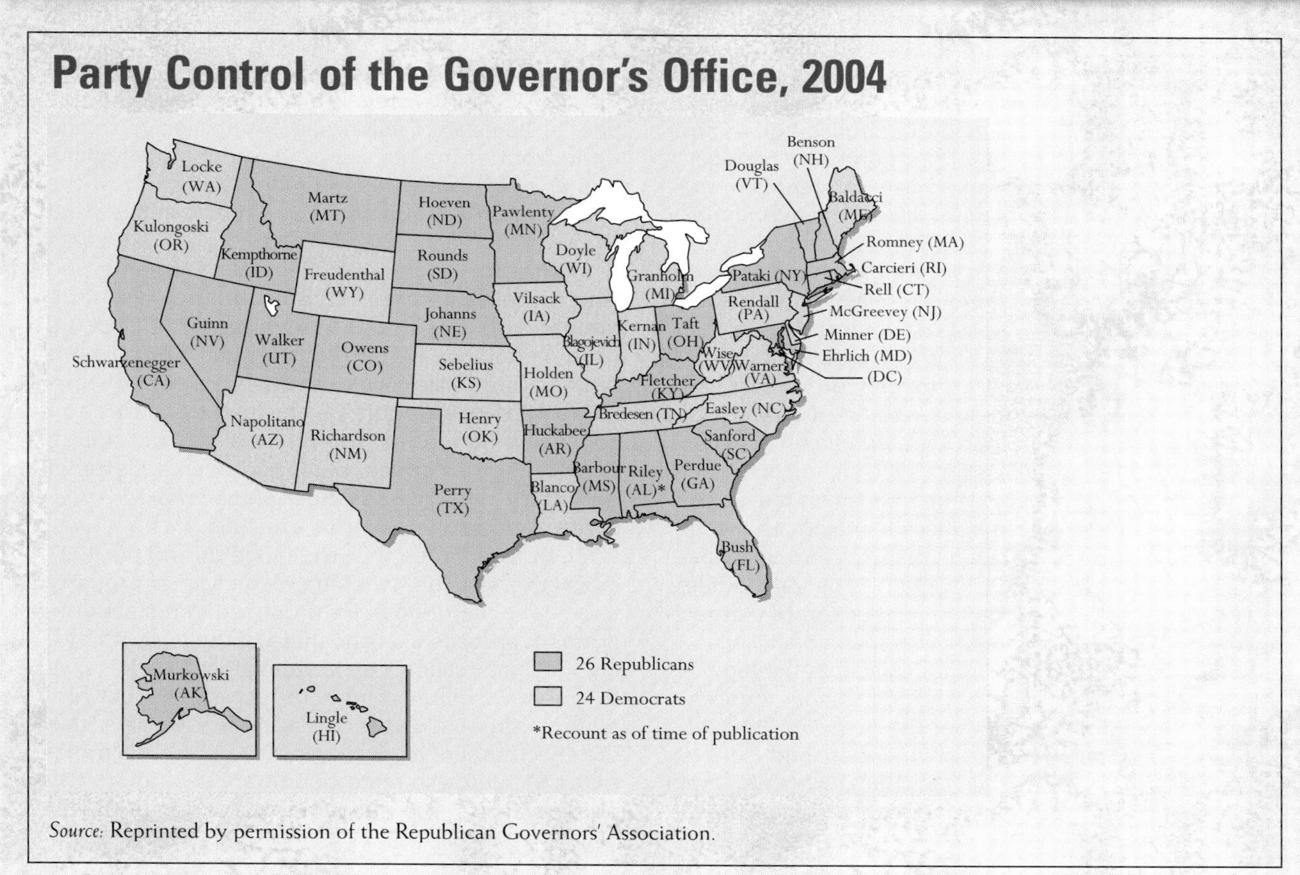

Source: Reprinted by permission of the Republican Governors' Association.

often described in terms of liberal or conservative, but there also were complex urban-rural, regional, and economic differences. Democratic governors built policy coalitions around these factions, but there was little stability or continuity, and most governors derived only limited power from their position as party leader.

Under the two-party system, however, the political party is taking on more importance and may provide greater resources to the governor (see *Across the USA:* "Party Control of the Governor's Office, 2004"). During his second term in the late 1980s, Bill Clements often had enough Republican votes in the house to

PEOPLE IN POLITICS

Governor George W. Bush, Consensus Builder

George W. Bush, son of former President George Bush, had never held public office before being elected governor, but he had gained valuable political experience campaigning for and serving as an unofficial advisor to his father. The younger Bush became Texas's second Republican governor in modern times by conducting an effective campaign for improvements in the public schools, tougher penalties for juvenile offenders, and reform of the welfare and civil justice systems. He succeeded in winning approval for legislation addressing all four priorities during the 1995 legislative session, the first of his term.

Bush's public style was low key. He seemed to go out of his way to avoid controversy during his first year in office. But he remained focused on his four primary goals, and he was assisted by conservative Democratic legislative leaders, who shared his views and sensed that public sentiment was on the governor's side. Although Democrats had majorities in both the house and the senate in 1995, the Texas legislature was dominated by conservatives of both parties, and some of the reforms the new governor wanted already had been initiated by Democratic officials.

Bush actively worked with legislators behind the scenes, making minor compromises, when necessary, on his policy priorities. The governor had frequent private meetings with house and senate members, sometimes even dropping by their Capitol offices unannounced. He had weekly breakfast meetings with Lieutenant Governor Bob Bullock and Speaker Pete Laney, two Democrats whose work was crucial to the governor's program. "We disagree, but you'll never read about it," Bush said of his meetings with the two legislative leaders. "The way to forge good public policy amongst the leadership of the legislative branch and executive branch is to air our differences in private meetings that happen all the time. The way to ruin a relationship is to leak things [to the media] and to be disrespectful of meeting in private."*

Bush also believed his decisive victory in the 1994 election had helped his cause in the legislature. "I won by 352,000 votes," he told reporters the day after the legislature adjourned. "And when you stand up in front of the legislature and outline a legislative agenda that was endorsed by the will of the people, that helps remind people that this is what Texans want."†

Unlike Governors Mark White, Bill Clements, and Ann Richards before him, Bush did not face budgetary problems in state government that could have distracted lawmakers' attention from his priorities. And unlike Richards, Bush supported legislation that gave adult Texans the right to carry concealed handguns. The gun bill was not one of Bush's major priorities, but it had been an issue in his victory over Richards. Bush signed the gun measure approved by lawmakers in 1995.

Bush faced a tougher challenge during the 1997 legislative session, when he made school property tax relief a major goal. He proposed that state government assume a larger share of the cost of funding the public schools by lowering local school taxes by about $3 billion a year. To replace the lost revenue, he proposed an increase in the state sales tax, the enactment of a new business tax, and the transfer of $1 billion in state budgetary savings to the public schools. The house rejected most of Bush's thwart the will of the Democratic majority. After Republicans had gained legislative control, Rick Perry had strong support from Republican lawmakers and party officials during the budgetary and redistricting battles of 2003 (see Chapter 18).

Upon taking office in 1995, Republican Governor George W. Bush enjoyed the support of party leaders for his own priorities—efforts to improve education, restrict civil lawsuits, reform juvenile justice, and change the welfare system. Initially, he kept his distance from much of the agenda advocated by the social conservatives who had taken control of leadership positions in the Texas Repub-

proposal and approved a controversial tax trade-off that would have increased numerous state taxes in exchange for major cuts in local school taxes. Bush lobbied Republican legislators for the house plan and helped convince about half of the 68 Republicans in the house to vote for it. Assured that Bush was actively backing the plan, Speaker Laney helped persuade a large number of Democratic house members to vote for it. The bipartisan balancing act was necessary because many Republican legislators had campaigned against higher taxes of any kind and many Democratic lawmakers had previously been targeted by Republicans over the tax issue.

Despite the success in the house, the senate, which had a Republican majority in 1997, refused to approve a large increase in state taxes. Bush remained mostly in the background while the senate debated the issue. After it became obvious the house and the senate were in a stalemate, legislative negotiators requested the governor's active participation once again. But Bush was unable to forge any compromise that raised state taxes. The governor managed to salvage only a modest amount of property tax relief—about $140 a year for the average homeowner—by convincing the legislature to increase homestead exemptions, a form of tax break that homeowners get on their school taxes. The legislature used $1 billion in state budgetary savings to repay school districts for the revenue they lost from the higher exemptions.

In failing to win more substantial property tax relief, Bush was stymied by two major obstacles. One was strong opposition from business lobbyists to the proposed state tax increases. The other was the absence of a state budgetary crisis that would have forced the legislature to increase taxes.

Bush said he wanted to lower property taxes because they had become so high they were making home ownership difficult for many Texans. Some Democrats said Bush had failed as a leader because he had been unable to convince the legislature to enact a more substantial property tax cut package, but the governor dismissed the criticism. "I think people are going to say this is a man who set a very bold agenda and acted boldly," he said.[‡] He said the higher homestead exemption that the legislature did pass was important.

Bush easily won reelection over Democratic challenger Garry Mauro in 1998 and entered the 1999 legislative session amid widespread speculation that he was preparing for a presidential race. With his pending White House campaign obviously on his mind, he convinced the legislature to enact some additional tax cuts and increase education spending. And he accepted a priority of Democratic lawmakers to give school teachers a $3,000-a-year pay raise. Bush's biggest legislative defeat in 1999 was the rejection of a pilot program to allow students from low-performing public schools to use tax-backed vouchers to attend private schools. But, in an effort to shore up support among religious and social conservatives in the Republican Party, Bush won approval of a law to require parents to be notified before their minor, unmarried daughters could receive abortions. It was the most significant piece of abortion-control legislation to be passed by Texas lawmakers since the U.S. Supreme Court had legalized abortion 26 years earlier.

Bush officially launched a campaign for the 2000 Republican presidential nomination in June 1999. He was elected President in the 2000 election and resigned as governor in December.

[*]Quoted in *Houston Chronicle,* April 15, 1995.
[†]Quoted in *Houston Chronicle,* May 31, 1995.
[‡]Quoted in *Dallas Morning News,* June 4, 1997.

lican Party in 1994. But in 1999, when he was preparing for a presidential race, Bush strengthened his anti-abortion credentials with social conservatives by convincing the legislature to enact one of their major priorities—a law requiring parents to be notified before their minor daughters could have abortions (see *People in Politics:* "Governor George W. Bush, Consensus Builder").

The Governor and Interest Groups Successful governors must be consummate political animals who continually nurture relationships throughout the political system. A gubernatorial candidate aggressively solicits the endorsements and contributions of various groups. These groups, in turn, develop stakes in gubernatorial elections and usually assume that the candidates they support will be responsive to their interests. A governor's policy initiatives often include legislation of benefit to key support groups, which maintain active roles throughout the policy process. Business groups, for example, were major contributors to Governor Rick Perry's successful election race in 2002, and the governor strongly supported their priorities, including additional limits on civil lawsuits, during the 2003 regular legislative session.

Other Offices of the Executive Branch

Lieutenant Governor The **lieutenant governor** is the second highest-ranking official in the state, but the executive powers of this office are limited. Were the governor to die, be incapacitated, be removed from office, or voluntarily leave office in midterm, the lieutenant governor would become governor. That eventuality has occurred only four times. In 1917, William P. Hobby replaced James E. Ferguson, who was impeached. Governor W. Lee O'Daniel resigned in 1941 to enter the U.S. Senate and was succeeded by Coke Stevenson. Governor Beauford Jester died in office in 1949 and was replaced by Allan Shivers. And George W. Bush resigned in December 2000 after being elected president and was succeeded by Rick Perry.

lieutenant governor The presiding officer of the senate. This officeholder would become governor if the governor were to die, be incapacitated, be removed from office, or leave office voluntarily in midterm.

In Texas, the office of lieutenant governor is primarily a legislative office. Many experts consider this position, because of its key legislative role and statewide constituency, the most powerful office in state government. The lieutenant governor, who need not belong to the same party as the governor and is elected independently of the governor, presides over the senate and has traditionally been given enormous power over the legislative process by the senate rules. The legislative powers and prerogatives far exceed those of the vice president on the federal level. The lieutenant governor also chairs the Legislative Budget Board, which plays a key role in the state budgetary process.

WWW **State of Texas** The state's web page provides links to over 200 state agencies. Most of the state agencies have their own sites, with detailed information about their organizational structure, programs, budgets, reports, and recent activities.
http://www.state.tx.us

Democrat Bill Hobby, son of the former governor, served a record eighteen years as lieutenant governor before retiring in 1991. He was succeeded by Democrat Bob Bullock, a former state comptroller and one of the most influential state officials in recent history (see Chapter 18). Bullock, who chose not to seek reelection in 1998 and died the next year, was succeeded by Republican Rick Perry, a former state agriculture commissioner.

Perry generally received high marks from senators for his work as presiding officer, but he presided over the senate for only one session before succeeding Bush as governor after the 2000 presidential election. State senators then elected Senator Bill Ratliff (R-Mt. Pleasant) to complete Perry's term as lieutenant governor and preside over the senate during the 2001 session. Republican David Dewhurst was elected lieutenant governor in 2002. The former land commissioner had no legislative experience but made a quick, yet thorough, study of major issues and legislative procedures (see Chapter 22).

Attorney General As the state's chief legal officer, the **attorney general** is called upon to defend state laws enacted by the legislature and orders adopted by regulatory agencies. The office also enforces the state's antitrust and consumer protection laws and helps collect child support payments from delinquent noncustodial parents. Recent attorneys general have been kept busy defending the state or negotiating settlements in lawsuits challenging the constitutionality of state prisons, the public school finance system, the method of selecting state judges, and other major policies.

Former Texas Supreme Court Justice Greg Abbott, a Republican, was elected attorney general in 2002.

Unlike counterparts in the federal government and some other states, the Texas attorney general is primarily a civil lawyer. Except for representing the state in the appeals of death penalty cases and assisting local prosecutors, the attorney general has relatively little responsibility for criminal law enforcement. Many candidates for the office campaign on tough law and order platforms, but responsibilities for criminal prosecution are vested in locally elected county and district attorneys. The attorney general also gives opinions on the legality of actions of other state and local officials and is at the center of the policy-making process.[12]

Dan Morales, a former Democratic state representative from San Antonio, was elected attorney general in 1990, becoming the second Hispanic elected to statewide office in Texas. He won reelection in 1994 but choose not to run for a third term in 1998. He was succeeded by former Texas Supreme Court Justice John Cornyn, Texas's first Republican attorney general in modern times. Cornyn was elected to the U.S. Senate in 2002 and was succeeded by Republican Greg Abbott, another former Texas Supreme Court justice.

In a major policy decision made independently of the governor, the legislature, and other state officials, Morales in 1996 filed a multibillion-dollar damage suit against tobacco companies, seeking reimbursement for public health care costs associated with smoking. Some state officials supported Morales' decision, although others had reservations about the state jumping into the tobacco controversy. But Morales acted within his authority as the state's chief legal officer. The decision was his alone to make, and it resulted in a $17.3 billion settlement for the state. The tobacco suit also sparked a controversy over legal fees that, several years after Morales had left office, resulted in him being sentenced to federal prison for four years for mail fraud and filing a false income tax return (see *People in Politics:* "Dan Morales, A Spectacular Rise and Fall").

attorney general The state's chief legal officer, who represents Texas in lawsuits and is responsible for enforcing the state's antitrust, consumer protection, and other civil laws.

Comptroller of Public Accounts The **comptroller** is the state's primary tax administrator, accounting officer, and revenue estimator. Texas functions under a **pay-as-you-go principle,** which means that the state cannot adopt an operating budget that exceeds anticipated revenue. The comptroller is responsible for providing the revenue estimates on which biennial state budgets are drafted by the legislature. A budget cannot become law without the comptroller's certification that it falls within the official revenue projection. The comptroller's office produces a revenue estimate of all projected state income for the two-year budget period by using sophisticated models of the state's economy.[13]

comptroller The state's primary tax administrator, accounting officer, and revenue estimator.

pay-as-you-go principle A principle written into the Texas Constitution prohibiting state government from borrowing money to meet its operating budget.

PEOPLE IN POLITICS

Dan Morales, a Spectacular Rise and Fall

Dan Morales was one of state government's biggest vote getters during two terms as attorney general and, as only the second Hispanic ever elected to statewide office in Texas, was considered a rising star of the Democratic Party. He chose not to seek reelection in 1998. But before leaving office, he sued the tobacco industry over smoking-related health care costs and won a $17.3 billion settlement for the state from cigarette manufacturers. The settlement, to be paid out over many years, would generate huge amounts of revenue for health care or any other programs the legislature chose.

The settlement was clearly the highlight of Morales' political career, but, ironically, it also contributed to his eventual downfall. The settlement sparked much controversy over $3.3 billion in legal fees awarded to five private lawyers whom Morales had hired under a contingency contract to represent the state in the litigation. Although tobacco companies agreed to pay the lawyers' fees, Attorney General John Cornyn, Morales' Republican successor, called the payments excessive. He also questioned the legality of the outside lawyers' agreement with Morales and spent much of his first year in office investigating the lawyers' work. The legal fees also were attacked by business groups seeking limits on civil court judgments and lawyers' payments. These same groups—so-called tort reformers—had contributed heavily to Cornyn's election campaign.

Neither Cornyn nor federal prosecutors found any illegalities in Morales' dealings with the five lawyers or in the outside lawyers' work for the state. But Morales' attempt to steer as much as $520 million in legal fees to a sixth lawyer, Marc Murr of Houston, resulted in a lengthy federal investigation. Morales said Murr, a personal friend, was an important part of his anti-tobacco legal team, but other lawyers said Murr did little, if any, work on the case.

While the investigation, which stretched over four years, was still pending, Morales attempted a political comeback by running for governor in the 2002 Democratic primary. He lost to Laredo businessman Tony Sanchez and later crossed party lines to endorse Republican Governor Rick Perry, who defeated Sanchez in the general election.

Finally, in March 2003, a federal grand jury indicted Morales, accusing him of trying to improperly steer millions of dollars in legal fees from the tobacco settlement to Murr. The indictment also charged the former attorney general with misappropriating campaign money to make a down payment on a $775,000 house while he was still in office, lying on a loan application for a $600,000 mortgage and filing a false income tax return for 1998, his last year in office. Seven months later, Morales was sentenced to four years in federal prison after pleading guilty to mail fraud and filing a false income tax return. He admitted backdating a government contract and forging government records related to the tobacco suit. In a separate deal with prosecutors, Murr pleaded guilty to one count of mail fraud.

Morales expressed "sincere regret and remorse" at his sentencing before U.S. District Judge Sam Sparks of Austin. But he said that the "vast majority of misdeeds" he had been accused of where untrue. Most political observers were left scratching their heads.

Source: Houston Chronicle, November 1, 2003, p. 29A.

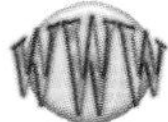
Office of the Comptroller

In addition to providing links to other state agencies, the comptroller's office provides a wide array of information pertaining to state taxes, management and accounting systems, and performance reviews of state operations and agencies.
www.window.state.tx.us

The comptroller's powerful role in budgetary affairs was enhanced by the legislature in 1990 with the additional authority to conduct management audits of local school districts, and again in 1991 with similar oversight authority over other state agencies. Through this process, Comptroller John Sharp, a Democrat, and his successor, Republican Carole Keeton Strayhorn, identified billions of dollars' worth of potential savings for legislative budget writers and local school boards.

Strayhorn, who changed her name from Rylander after marrying in early 2003, was a strong supporter of—and reaped favorable publicity from—the management audits. But the legislature, in a 2003 special session, transferred those programs to the Legislative Budget Board after the comptroller had become involved in a series of budgetary disputes with legislators and other Republican leaders. Al-

Carole Keeton Strayhorn, the first Republican comptroller of modern times, won a second term in 2002.

ways outspoken and widely viewed as politically ambitious, Strayhorn had surprised the governor and the legislature with a larger-than-anticipated revenue shortfall of $10 billion at the beginning of the 2003 regular session. Strayhorn later threatened—but only briefly—not to certify the new state budget drafted by lawmakers. And, finally, to make matters worse, she announced that the no-new-taxes budget about which the governor and Republican lawmakers had bragged actually included $2.7 billion in higher fees to be paid by millions of Texans. Strayhorn blamed Governor Rick Perry for the decision to strip the management audit programs from her agency. The governor's office denied the allegation, but Perry had signed the bill. Strayhorn was so angry that she strongly hinted that she might challenge Perry in the 2006 Republican gubernatorial primary. And, over the next several months, she delivered a series of public speeches criticizing the governor's budgetary priorities.

Commissioner of the General Land Office Texas retains ownership, including the mineral rights, to approximately 22 million acres of public lands, which are managed by the state **land commissioner.** Revenues generated by mineral leases and other land uses are earmarked for education through the Permanent University Fund and the Permanent School Fund. This agency is also responsible for the Veterans Land Program, which provides low-interest loans to veterans for the purchase of land and houses.

land commissioner The elected official who manages the state's public lands and administers the Veterans Land Program, which provides low-interest loans to veterans for the purchase of land and houses.

During sixteen years in office, Land Commissioner Garry Mauro, a Democrat, developed several environmental initiatives, including beach cleanup efforts and a program for cleaning up oil spills off the Texas coast. Mauro also took the lead in developing a coastal zone management plan to coordinate environmental protection efforts along the coast. After Mauro unsuccessfully ran for governor in 1998, the next land commissioner, Republican David Dewhurst, a businessman from Houston, continued the beach cleanup efforts. Dewhurst also won legislative approval of a program to replenish beaches and protect them from erosion. Dewhurst was elected lieutenant governor in 2002 and was succeeded as land commissioner by Jerry Patterson, a former state senator from Harris County. Patterson's priorities included development of new nursing homes for veterans and new veterans' cemeteries.

Republican Jerry Patterson, a former state senator, was elected land commissioner in 2002.

Commissioner of Agriculture The **agriculture commissioner** is responsible for carrying out laws regulating and benefiting the agricultural sector of the state's economy. In addition to providing support for agricultural research and education, the agency is responsible for the administration of consumer protection laws in the areas of weights and measures, packaging and labeling, and marketing. Republican Rick Perry aggressively promoted Texas agricultural products during two terms as commissioner. Republican Susan Combs, a former state representative from Austin, was elected to the office in 1998 after Perry ran for lieutenant governor. She also urged Texans to buy more produce grown in the Lone Star State and, concerned about obesity among Texas children, she led a campaign to reduce the sales of soft drinks and junk foods in the public schools.

agriculture commissioner The elected official responsible for administering laws and programs that benefit agriculture.

Secretary of State The **secretary of state,** the only constitutional official appointed by the governor, has a variety of duties, including granting charters to corporations and processing the extradition of prisoners to other states. The primary function of this office, however, is to administer state election laws. That responsibility includes reviewing county and local election procedures, developing statewide policy for voter registration, and receiving and tabulating election returns.

secretary of state The official who administers state election laws, grants charters to corporations, and processes the extradition of prisoners to other states. This officeholder is appointed by the governor.

State Treasurer The Constitution of 1876 created a **state treasurer** to be the custodian of state funds. Shortly after taking office in 1993, however, Treasurer Martha Whitehead came to believe the office was no longer needed. She convinced the legislature and the voters to abolish it with a constitutional amendment, which was adopted in 1995. The agency's duties were transferred to the comptroller's office.

state treasurer This elective office was created by the Constitution of 1876 to manage state funds. It was abolished by the voters in 1995, and its duties were transferred to the comptroller's office.

Elected Boards and Commissions

Only two of the more than two hundred boards and commissions that head most state agencies are elected. They are the Texas Railroad Commission and the State Board of Education.

Texas Railroad Commission The **Railroad Commission** was originally designed to regulate intrastate (within Texas) operations of railroads. It also regulated intrastate trucking for many years. But it lost its trucking responsibilities and most of its railroad regulation to the federal government. It still has some oversight over rail safety and regulates oil and natural gas production and lignite mining in Texas.

The commission includes three elected members who serve six-year staggered terms and rotate the position of chair among themselves. The oil and gas industry has historically focused much attention on this agency and made large campaign contributions to commission members. Many critics claim the commission is a

Railroad Commission A three-member, elected body that has some oversight over rail safety but now primarily regulates oil and natural gas production in Texas.

prime example of a regulatory body that has been co-opted by those interests it was created to regulate. And, in recent years, it has become a staging area for opportunistic politicians who seek election to the commission primarily as a steppingstone to higher office. A commissioner doesn't have to resign in the middle of his or her six-year term to seek another office and, as an incumbent regulator, has little trouble collecting large contributions from the oil and gas industry that can be used to further political ambitions. Both Democrat John Sharp and Republican Carole Keeton Strayhorn used seats on the commission to strengthen their political bases for successful races for state comptroller in 1990 and 1998, respectively. Other recent commission members haven't been as successful, but not because they didn't try. Between 1980 and 2002, fifteen people served on the commission, and only four actually completed a full six-year term. One recent commissioner, Tony Garza, resigned in midterm to accept President George W. Bush's appointment as ambassador to Mexico.

The game of musical chairs has prompted calls in recent years for the commission to be abolished and its duties transferred to other agencies appointed by the governor, including the Public Utility Commission, which already has oversight over electric utilities, and the Texas Commission on Environmental Quality, the state's main environmental protection agency. Democrat Hector Uribe, a former state senator, ran for the commission in 1996, promising to work to abolish it. But Strayhorn, his Republican opponent, argued that the agency was important and needed to be retained. Strayhorn defeated Uribe for a six-year term on the commission, but two years later she ran for and won election to the comptroller's office.

State Board of Education Prior to educational reforms enacted in 1984, the **State Board of Education** was made up of twenty-seven members elected from congressional districts across the state. At the urging of reformers dissatisfied with student performance, the legislature provided for a new education board of fifteen members to be appointed by the governor and confirmed by the senate. The idea was to reduce the board's independence while new education reforms ordered by the legislature were being carried out. But the law also mandated that the board once again become an elected body within a few years. Some state leaders later proposed that the board remain appointive and put the question to the voters, who opted for an elected board in 1986. The present board has fifteen members elected from districts established by the legislature.

Philosophical and partisan bickering on the board in recent years prompted the legislature to reduce its powers. The panel's main remaining duties include investment of education dollars in the Permanent School Fund and some oversight over textbook selection and curriculum standards.

But the day-to-day administration of the Texas Education Agency, the agency responsible for public education, is under the direction of the commissioner of education, who is appointed by the governor.

The Texas Bureaucracy

A loosely connected, highly fragmented, and often confusing network of approximately 250 state agencies and universities with more than 300,000 full- and part-time employees is responsible for carrying out programs and policies approved and funded by the legislature and the governor. In addition, more than 950,000

State Board of Education
An elected panel that oversees the administration of public education in Texas.

other full- and part-time workers are employed by school districts, cities, counties, and special districts in Texas.

This **bureaucracy** is often on the receiving end when someone complains about government. But without it, government would come to a grinding halt. The bureaucracy issues drivers' licenses, builds highways, distributes welfare benefits, and performs myriad other public services. On an individual basis, the bureaucracy is the clerk, the inspector, the highway patrol officer, the computer programmer, the engineer, or one of hundreds of other occupational specialists delivering state services on a daily basis. On a larger scale, it is an assortment of agencies, some employing thousands of individuals, with designated responsibilities for specific public programs and services.

Although it is overstating the case to say that the bureaucracy runs state government, its role is enhanced in Texas because the legislature meets in regular session only five months every other year and the governor has only limited powers over the executive branch. The part-time boards and commissions that oversee most state agencies can exercise considerable independence in interpreting policies and determining the character and the quality of public services. Many boards depend heavily on the guidance of veteran administrators and career bureaucrats within their agencies.

The Growth of Government in Texas

In 1967, there were 388,000 full-time state and local government employees in Texas. Thirty years later, there were almost three times that many (Table 19.2). By 1997, the latest year for which we have comprehensive data, Texas had 582 full-time state and local government employees per 10,000 residents, making it eleventh highest in that category among the 50 states. Texas had only 137 state employees per 10,000 population, forty-fourth among the states. But its 447 local government workers per 10,000 population ranked sixth highest.[14] The number of employees has increased along with the state's population since the 1997 Census of Governments, but the rankings have remained much the same. Many ser-

bureaucracy The agencies of government and their employees responsible for carrying out policies and providing public services approved by elected officials.

TABLE 19.2 Employment by Type of Government, 1967–97

	Full-Time Equivalent Employees			
Unit of Government	**1967**	**1977**	**1987**	**1997**
State	88,734	163,870	198,769	261,975
Total Local	299,578	477,177	646,913	850,380
Counties	32,978	60,287	77,851	103,481
Municipalities	75,168	115,481	139,340	160,574
School Districts	177,734	282,492	400,035	539,530
Special Districts	13,698	18,917	29,687	46,794
Total Texas	**388,312**	**641,047**	**845,682**	**1,112,355**

Source: U.S. Department of Commerce, Bureau of the Census, *Census of Governments, 1967.* vol. 3, no. 2, table 15; *Census of Governments, 1977,* vol. 3, no. 2, table 13; *Census of Governments, 1987,* vol. 3, no. 2, table 14; *Census of Governments, 1997,* vol. 1, table 12.

vices performed by local governments—including education, fire and police protection, and sanitation services—require large numbers of professionals and other workers.

There has been a substantial expansion of programs at all levels of government in recent years. State spending during the 1982–83 biennium was $25.6 billion, and only twenty-two years later, the legislature appropriated $118 billion for the 2004–05 biennium. Nevertheless, Texas still ranks low in per capita expenditures. Texas was fiftieth among the states in per capita spending by state government alone—$2,611 per person—in 2000. When combined state and local spending was compared, Texas rose to forty-fifth, thanks partly to the large share of public school costs borne by local taxpayers. In such key areas as per capita state spending on public health, education, and welfare, Texas ranked below many other states.[15]

Efforts to curtail government growth and spending have met with only marginal success. Texas citizens have come to expect a wide range of public services, and these expectations increase as the population grows. The federal government also has imposed mandates on state and local governments that require additional expenditures and personnel. Moreover, the success of interest groups in winning approval of new programs adds to the growth of public employment. The legislature reduced spending on many programs to help bridge a $10 billion revenue shortfall in 2003. And that same year, it ordered a major reorganization of health and human services agencies, with an eye toward privatizing some services. But it remained to be seen how those budget cuts and changes would affect overall state government employment.

Some 80 percent of state government employees work in three areas: higher education, public safety and corrections, and social services (which include public welfare and health care). Most employees of county governments work in social services, public safety and corrections, and general governmental administration (Table 19.3). More than one-third of city employees are engaged in fire and police protection, and another 30 percent work for city utilities and in housing, sewerage, sanitation, parks and recreation, and natural resources departments. Elementary and secondary school teachers are employees of local school districts.

TABLE 19.3 State and Local Employment by General Functions, 1997

	State	Counties	Cities/Towns	School Districts	Special Districts
Education	32.7%	0.8%	2.7%	100.0%	–
Social services*	30.1	28.0	7.5	–	52.8
Public safety and corrections	17.7	33.6	35.6	–	0.2
Transportation	5.4	8.2	8.6	–	1.7
Government administration	6.5	22.5	9.4	–	–
Environment/housing	5.1	2.4	18.5	–	15.6
Utilities	–	0.1	11.8	–	28.1
All other	2.6	4.4	5.9	–	1.5
Total Employees	**261,975**	**103,481**	**160,574**	**539,530**	**46,794**

*Includes income maintenance.

Source: U.S. Department of Commerce, Bureau of the Census, *1997 Census of Governments*, vol. 1, table 13.

Bureaucrats and Public Policy

The bureaucracy does more than carry out the policies set by the legislature. It is involved in virtually every stage of the policy-making process. The legislature usually broadly defines a program and gives the affected agency the responsibility for filling in the details.[16] Administrative agencies can sometimes interpret a vaguely worded law differently from its original legislative purpose. Although the legislature can use oversight committees and the budgetary process to control the bureaucracy (see Chapter 10), agencies often have resources and political influence that protect their prerogatives. Many appointed agency heads have political ties to interest groups affected by the work of their agencies, and these officials help develop policy alternatives and laws because legislators depend on their technical expertise.

Policy Implementation Although one state agency may be primarily responsible for translating legislative intent into a specific program, other governmental bodies are also involved. The courts, for example, shape the actions of bureaucrats through their interpretation of statutes and administrative rules. And there may be jurisdictional and political battles between different agencies over program objectives.

In some cases, a new agency may have to be organized and staffed to carry out the goals of a new law. More often, however, the new responsibilities are assigned by the legislature to an existing agency, which develops the necessary rules, procedures, and guidelines for operating the new program. Additional employees are hired if the legislature provides the necessary funding. If not, responsibilities are reassigned among existing personnel. Sometimes tasks are coordinated with other agencies. Ultimately, all this activity translates into hundreds of thousands of daily transactions between governmental employees and the public.

Almost everyone has heard horror stories about persons who have suffered abuse or neglect at the hands of public employees and agencies. Whether they involve an indigent family that fell through the cracks of the welfare system or a county jail prisoner who was lost in the administrative process of the judicial system, these stories tend to reinforce the suspicion and hostility that many people have toward bureaucracies and public employees. Unquestionably such abuses deserve attention and demand correction, yet thousands of governmental programs are successfully carried out with little or no fanfare and are fully consistent with the purpose of the authorizing legislation.

Most public employees take pride in what they do and attempt to be conscientious in translating policy objectives into workable public services. They are citizens and taxpayers who also receive services from other state and local agencies. A complex, interdependent state that is home to more than 22 million people depends on the effectiveness and efficiency of governmental agencies. That activity appears, on the whole, to be mutually satisfactory or beneficial to most parties.

Obstacles to Policy Implementation When things go wrong in state government and problems go unresolved, there is a tendency to blame the bureaucrats for excessive red tape, inefficiency, mismanagement, or incompetence. "Bureaucrat bashing" plays well politically, and many candidates for public office run on such campaigns. But in many cases they are unfairly blaming government employees for complex problems that policy makers have been unable, or unwilling, to resolve.

One high-profile issue is the perennial struggle to improve the quality of the public education system. Some of the criticism directed at educational bureaucrats has been justified, but the legislature and the governor are ultimately responsible for the enactment of sound educational policies—and the development of a sufficient and equitable system of paying for them.

Some legislative policies may be misdirected, with little potential for producing the intended results. Or economic and social conditions may change, making programs inappropriate. In hindsight, administrators may also find that approaches different from those outlined by the legislature would have worked better. The legislature also frequently fails to fund programs adequately. In some cases, those charged with carrying out a new policy may not have the know-how or the resources to make it work. And, finally, programs often produce unanticipated results.

The accountability and responsiveness of state and local agencies are also affected by other factors, including the influence of special interests. Thanks to the clout of special interest lobbyists with the legislature, regulatory agencies are often headed by boards with a majority of members from the professions or industries they are supposed to regulate. Many taxpayers may feel this system is merely a legalized way of letting the foxes guard the henhouse. It is an extension of the **iron triangle** concept, whereby special interests seek to influence not only the legislators responsible for enacting laws but the agencies responsible for enforcing them.

Business and professional groups argue that their professions can be regulated effectively only by individuals knowledgeable in their fields. Although that argument has some validity, it also increases the potential for incestuous relationships that mock the regulatory process. There is always the possibility—and often the likelihood—that industry representatives serving on boards, commissions, or in agencies will be inclined to protect their industries against the best interests of consumers. This pattern of influence and control is often referred to as *cooptation,* underscoring the possibility that agencies may be captured by the industries they are supposed to regulate. Licensing agencies may also seek to adopt unfair regulations designed to restrict new competitors from entering an industry.

Historically, many nine-member state regulatory boards included only industry representatives. But under the sunset review process, discussed in more detail later in this chapter, laws have gradually been changed to turn over some positions on most of those boards to members of the public. The Sunset Advisory Commission has concluded:

> Boards consisting only of members from a regulated profession or group affected by the activities of an agency may not respond adequately to broad public interests. This potential problem can be addressed by giving the general public a direct voice in the activities of the agency through representation on the board.[17]

The "fox and the henhouse" approach to state regulation was highlighted when Governor Ann Richards demanded that the Texas Department of Health crack down on deplorable conditions in some nursing homes. It was revealed that state inspectors had repeatedly found unsanitary conditions in three nursing homes partly owned by a member of the Texas Board of Health. The board member, an appointee of former Governor Bill Clements, denied any allegations of improper care but resigned after moving to another state.[18] Texas law in effect then required that one member of the eighteen-member health board be involved in the

iron triangle Mutually supportive interrelationships among the interest groups, administrative agencies, and legislative committees involved in drafting the laws and regulations affecting a particular area of the economy or a specific segment of the population.

nursing home industry and the other members represent other health care professions. The board has since been restructured.

Strategies for Controlling the Bureaucracy

Elected policy makers can use several strategies to control bureaucracies and help ensure that policies are implemented as intended:

- Change the law or make legislation detailed enough to reduce or eliminate the discretionary authority of an agency.
- Overrule the bureaucracy and reverse or rescind an action or decision of an agency. With the independence of many agencies, boards, and commissions at the state level, the governor can reverse few agency decisions. Consequently, this step often requires legislative action.
- Transfer the responsibility for a program to another agency through administrative reorganization.
- Replace an agency head who refuses to or is incapable of carrying out program objectives. But there are only a few agencies over which the governor can directly exercise such authority in Texas.
- Cut or threaten to reduce the budget of an agency to force compliance with policy objectives.
- Abolish an agency or program through sunset legislation.
- Pressure the bureaucracy to change with legislative hearings and public disclosures of agency neglect or inadequacies.
- Protect public employees who reveal incompetence, mismanagement, and corruption through **whistleblower** legislation (see *Up Close:* "What Can Happen to a Whistleblower?").
- Enact **revolving door** restrictions to reduce or eliminate the movement of former state employees to industries over which they had regulatory authority.[19]

whistleblower A public employee who reports illegal activities or "blows the whistle" on agency wrongdoing.

revolving door A term describing the practice of former members of state boards and commissions or key employees of agencies leaving state government for more lucrative jobs with the industries they used to regulate.

The Revolving Door Over the years—at least until 1991—many regulatory agencies had become training grounds for young attorneys and other professionals taking their first jobs out of college or law school. They would work for state agencies for a few years for relatively low pay while gaining valuable experience in a particular regulatory area and making influential contacts in the state bureaucracy. Then they would leave state employment for higher-paying jobs in the industries they used to regulate and would represent their new employers before the state boards and commissions for which they had once worked—or they would become consultants or join law firms representing regulatory clients. Former gubernatorial appointees to boards and commissions—not just hired staffers—also participated in this revolving door phenomenon, which raised ethical questions about possible insider advantages (see Chapter 10, and earlier discussion of iron triangles in this chapter).

An early step in restricting the revolving door was part of the Public Utility Regulatory Act (PURA) of 1975 that created the Public Utility Commission (PUC); this law prohibited PUC members and key staffers from going to work for regu-

UP CLOSE

What Can Happen to a Whistleblower?

Governmental agencies make mistakes that can be very costly to the public in terms of financial waste or neglect. Texas has a whistleblower protection law, which is designed to protect public employees who report wrongdoing within their agencies to their supervisors. If an employee is subjected to retaliation after having come forward, the law permits the worker to file a lawsuit against the offending agency.

A major test of the effectiveness of the law was brought by George Green, an architect for the Texas Department of Human Services (DHS). Green complained of shoddy construction on agency facilities, kickbacks, and noncompliance with contracts. He said his supervisors refused to take action against the offending contractors. After he went public with his charges, Green was fired by the agency for allegedly abusing sick leave time and making one unauthorized call on his state telephone—a 13-cent call to his father. Criminal charges were brought against him, and, although they were eventually dropped, he had spent $130,000 in legal fees, could not find a new job, and had depleted many of his personal assets.

Green sued the state and won a $13.6 million judgment from a Travis County jury in 1991. The amount included $3.6 million in actual damages that Green had suffered and $10 million in punitive damages to punish the state for the way he had been treated. The state appealed, dragging out a resolution of the case, until the judgment was upheld by the Texas Supreme Court in 1994. But the legislature was not in session that year, and state leaders said there was no money in the state budget to pay Green. So the whistleblower had to wait for the legislature to convene in 1995. Green, meanwhile, was still unemployed and living off the generosity of friends and family and a personal loan he had made against a portion of his judgment.

By the time the legislature convened in January 1995, Green's judgment, with interest, had grown to almost $20 million, and interest continued to grow at the rate of more than $4,500 a day. The whistleblower's case also was receiving considerable media attention, nationally as well as in Texas. But many legislators, particularly in the house, did not want to pay him the full amount, which they considered excessive. They particularly objected to the $10 million the jury had awarded as punitive damages and pointed out that taxpayers would ultimately have to pick up the tab.

Green refused to accept an amount smaller than the judgment and interest, and the 1995 session ended in late May without Green receiving any payment. Legislators, however, took steps to ensure that such a large whistleblower judgment would never be awarded again. They changed the law to limit whistleblower suit damages against the state to $250,000. Critics of the change warned it would seriously curtail whistleblower suits—and damage an important taxpayer protection—because the best lawyers, whose fees are based on the size of a judgment, would no longer accept whistleblower cases.

Finally, in November 1995, Green reached a compromise with legislative leaders. The Legislative Budget Board (LBB), which can transfer funds when the full legislature is not in session, approved a $13.8 million settlement, which Green accepted. Part of the money went to lawyers and a lobbyist who had helped Green collect payment, and $1 million went to an investor who had loaned Green money during his battle. Lieutenant Governor Bob Bullock, who chaired the LBB, apologized to Green and called his ordeal a "black mark on the history of Texas."*

Even then, Green's story continued. A former consultant sued Green for allegedly failing to pay him for helping Green collect the judgment from the state. In December 1996 another Travis County jury awarded the former consultant more than $600,000 in actual and punitive damages against Green.

Green's experience speaks to a major problem. Few public employees can afford to be subjected to this type of retaliation, and few have the resources to fight state government. Although the original intent of the law was to protect whistleblowers and to encourage their coming forward with inside information, most state and local employees may have received a different message from the Green case and the legislature's decision to weaken the law.

*Quoted in *Houston Chronicle*, November 16, 1995.

lated utilities immediately after leaving the agency. The ethics reform law of 1991 expanded the restrictions to other agencies.

Legislative Budgetary Control Every two years, the legislature sets the budgets for state agencies but subsequently provides little oversight as to how effectively the money is spent, unless there is a financial crisis requiring a special legislative session or an emergency transfer of funds by the governor and the Legislative Budget Board. Perhaps the most control that lawmakers exercise over agency spending, besides setting the bottom line, is their approval of a number of line items in agency budgets that restrict portions of the funds to specific programs.

Sunset Legislation Although Texas has been slow to modernize its budgetary process and other key functions of state government, it was one of the first states to require formal, exhaustive reviews of how effectively agencies are doing their jobs. The **sunset** law enacted in 1977 was so named because most agencies have to be periodically recreated by the legislature or automatically go out of business. Relatively few agencies—except for a number of inactive ones like the Pink Bollworm Commission and the Stonewall Jackson Memorial Board—have been abolished. But the obligatory review has produced some significant structural and policy changes in the state bureaucracy that the legislature may not have otherwise ordered. It also has expanded employment opportunities for lobbyists, because special interest groups have much to win or lose in the sunset process. In many cases, special interests have succeeded in protecting the status quo.

Each agency is usually up for review every twelve years, under a rotating order set out in the sunset law. The review begins with the Sunset Advisory Commission, which includes four state representatives appointed by the speaker of the house, four senators appointed by the lieutenant governor, and two public members, one named by the speaker and the other by the lieutenant governor. The commission employs a staff that studies each agency up for review during the next regular, biennial legislative session and reports its findings to the panel, which makes recommendations to the legislature.

In a few cases, the commission proposes that an agency—usually a minor one—be terminated or consolidated with another agency. In most cases, however, the commission recommends the continuation of an agency but outlines suggested changes in its organizational structure and/or operations. The future of the agency is then debated by the full legislature. If lawmakers fail to approve a sunset bill for any agency by September 1 of the year the agency is scheduled for review, the agency will be phased out of existence over the next year, or it will be terminated abruptly on September 1 if the legislature also refuses to approve a new budget for the agency. In recent years, however, the legislature has postponed controversial sunset decisions by passing special laws to allow some agencies to stay open past their review dates.

The Texas Higher Education Coordinating Board is subject to sunset review, but individual universities are not. Also exempted from sunset review are the courts and state agencies created by the constitution, such as the governor's office, the attorney general, the comptroller, and the General Land Office.

sunset The process under which most state agencies have to be periodically reviewed and recreated by the legislature or go out of business.

The sunset process has not reduced the size of the bureaucracy. By 2001, there were more than 277,000 full-time state employees, compared to about 164,000 in

1977, the year the sunset law was approved. Although more than 45 agencies have been terminated or merged, others have been created (see Table 19.4). But Bill Wells, the Sunset Advisory Commission's former executive director, said the statistics did not tell the full story. He believed the sunset process had served to slow down the creation of new agencies. "You can't say how many [new agencies] would have been created if sunset hadn't heightened the awareness of the fact that we've got maybe too many agencies now," he said. "There is a heightened awareness of the fact that you need to go a little slower and you need to really have a problem before you create an agency."[20]

The sunset review process has helped rid state government of some deadwood, modernized some state laws and bureaucratic procedures, and made some agencies more responsive and accountable to the public. Under a sunset policy discussed earlier in this chapter, public members have been added to the boards of regulatory agencies that previously had included only representatives of the professions or industries that they regulated.

The largest agencies and those with influential constituencies are usually the most difficult to change because special interests are working overtime and making large political contributions to protect their turf. In 1993, for example, the insurance lobby succeeded in weakening some regulatory reforms in the Department of Insurance sunset bill. In another case, there was such a high-stakes battle involving telephone companies, newspaper publishers, electric utilities, and consumers over the Public Utility Commission sunset bill that the legislature postponed action for two years. The lobby's influence over the 1993 sunset bills prompted Governor Ann Richards and some legislative leaders to suggest that the sunset process should be changed or repealed because it was being abused by special interests. But consumer advocates, who value the sunset process, blamed the problem on legislators who had difficulty saying "no" to special interest lobbyists.

Performance Reviews Facing a large revenue shortfall in 1991, the legislature directed Comptroller John Sharp to conduct unprecedented performance reviews of all state agencies to determine ways to eliminate mismanagement and ineffi-

TABLE 19.4 Sunset Action from 1979 to 2003, 66th to 78th Legislative Sessions

Actions Taken	Total	Percent
Agencies reviewed	346*	
Agencies continued	282	81%
Agencies abolished outright	31	9
Agencies abolished and functions transferred	16	5
Agencies combined	11	3
Agencies separated	2	1

*Some agencies reviewed were not subject to continuation or abolishment.

Source: Texas Sunset Advisory Commission.

ciency and to save tax dollars. Sharp recommended $4 billion in spending cuts, agency and funds consolidations, accounting changes, some minor tax increases, and increases in various state fees to reflect more accurately the costs of providing services. Pressure from special interests killed many of the recommendations, but the legislature adopted about $2.4 billion of them. Sharp produced follow-up reports in 1993, 1995, and 1997, and his successor, Carole Keeton Strayhorn, continued the performance reviews after she took office. At the beginning of the 2003 regular legislative session, Strayhorn made 64 recommendations for further restructuring of state agencies and their operations, some of which were adopted by lawmakers. The comptroller also has similarly reviewed the operations of a number of local school districts.

The performance reviews generally have been considered instrumental in improving administrative practices. But as discussed earlier in this chapter, the legislature, with Governor Rick Perry's approval, transferred the work from the comptroller's office to the Legislative Budget Board after a series of budgetary disputes with Strayhorn in 2003. The move was criticized by those who believed the reviews should have remained under the oversight of an independently elected officeholder, but it remained to be seen what the ultimate effect of the transfer would be.

One of Sharp's proposals adopted by the legislature in 1993 created the Council on Competitive Government, which was designed to give Texas businesses more opportunities to bid on state contracts and provide some state services more efficiently. It also enabled state agencies to bid on services performed by other state agencies if the bidding agencies thought they could do the work more efficiently. The council, which evaluates the proposals, includes the governor, the lieutenant governor, the comptroller, the chair of the General Services Commission, and the employee representative on the Texas Workforce Commission.[21]

Some state government functions had been privatized before the council was created. One of the best known was the state lottery, which was administered from the beginning by a private company under a state contract.

Merit Systems and Professional Management One hundred years ago, public employees in Texas were hired on the basis of **political patronage**, or the personal relationships they had with elected or appointed officials. Little consideration was given to their skills, competence, or expertise. Few rules dictated terms of employment, advancement, or the rights or conduct of public employees, and wages and salaries varied widely from agency to agency. There also were high rates of employee turnover.

political patronage The hiring of government employees on the basis of personal friendships or favors rather than ability or merit.

To serve the public and state workers more effectively, some reform advocates pushed for a **merit system** based, in part, on the Civil Service Commission created by the federal government for its workers in 1883 (see Chapter 12). Although some other states have developed comprehensive statewide employment or personnel systems administered by a single agency, the reform movement in Texas has not been as successful. Improvements have been made, but state government here continues to function under a decentralized personnel system, in part because the various elected executive officeholders have jealously guarded their prerogatives to hire and fire the people who work for them.

merit system A personnel system in which public employees are selected for government jobs through competitive examinations and are systematically evaluated after being hired.

Texas's personnel "system" is not a merit system but a highly fragmented arrangement with different agencies assigned various personnel responsibilities. Ultimately, the legislature has the legal authority to define personnel practices, and the biennial budget is the major tool used by legislators to establish some 1,300 job classifications and corresponding salary schedules. The legislature also establishes policies on vacations, holidays, and retirement. But the primary responsibility for carrying out personnel policies is still delegated to the various state agencies. An administrator can develop specific policies for an agency as long as the agency works within the general framework defined by the legislature.

All state job openings are required to be listed with the Texas Workforce Commission. Agencies also advertise for workers through the mass media and college placement centers. But many jobs still are filled as a result of friendships, other personal contacts, and the influence of key political players.

Higher and public education employees are subject to different employment policies, which are determined by individual university governing boards and local school districts. Unlike state government, many cities across Texas have adopted centrally administered merit systems organized around the accepted principles of modern personnel management.

SUMMARY NOTES

- Although it is the most visible office in state government and the public believes it has considerable power, the office of governor is weak in formal powers.
- Unlike the president of the United States, governors of Texas have no formal cabinet that serves at their pleasure. Texas has a "plural executive," which includes several other statewide officeholders elected independently of the governor. This diffusion of power was a reaction to the abuses of the Davis administration during the Reconstruction era, but reform advocates argue that this structure diminishes the capacity of the executive branch to respond to the state's modern problems.
- Other elected officeholders in the executive branch are the lieutenant governor, the attorney general, the comptroller, the land commissioner, the agriculture commissioner, and members of the Texas Railroad Commission and the Texas State Board of Education. The top appointed official in the executive branch is the secretary of state. Although the lieutenant governor is part of the executive branch, the duties of that office are primarily legislative.
- Administrative responsibilities are further fragmented through approximately 250 boards and commissions authorized by statutory law. Although the governor appoints individuals to these boards, the governor's control is diluted by board members' staggered terms, the need for senatorial approval of the governor's appointments, and legal requirements relating to the composition of these boards.
- Besides appointments, the governor's main formal powers are the veto of legislation, line-item veto authority over the budget, and the authority to call and set the agenda for special sessions of the legislature.
- As part of the judicial powers, a governor can stay executions and, with the recommendation of the Board of Pardons and Paroles, grant full or conditional pardons or commute a death sentence to life imprisonment. The governor is the commander-in-chief of the state's military force and is responsible for maintaining order within the state and responding to various disasters by mobilizing the National Guard.
- Potentially, the governor also has a number of informal resources that can be used to shape public policy and the administrative process. Governors have used their staffs, their access to the mass media, their party roles, and their relationships to key interest groups to bring pressure to bear on legislators and other elected officials.
- More than one million Texans are employed by state and local governments. Collectively, we refer to them and the agencies for which they work as the bureaucracy. The bureaucracy has the primary responsibility of carrying

out public policies adopted by the legislature and local governing bodies. But administrative agencies also are involved in virtually every stage of the policy-making process. Legislators depend on administrative agencies for counsel and advice when they draft public policies, and they rely on them to help assess the success or failure of policies.

- When things go wrong and problems go unresolved, there is a tendency to blame bureaucrats. But often government employees are unfairly blamed for complex problems that elected policy makers have been unwilling or unable to resolve. The fragmented structure of the executive branch of state government is, in itself, a major obstacle to the efficient, responsive delivery of public services. There also is the potential for agencies headed by appointed, part-time boards to become unaccountable to the electorate and susceptible to the influence of special interest groups.
- Through sunset legislation, Texas became one of the first states to require formal reviews of how effectively state agencies are doing their jobs. Most state agencies are subject to periodic review and reauthorization by the legislature. The process has not reduced the size of the bureaucracy, but it has helped rid state government of obsolete agencies and produced greater accountability. Texas also has adopted revolving door restrictions. Former board members and key employees of regulatory agencies are prohibited from going to work for regulated companies within a certain period after leaving their state posts.
- Although many local governments have adopted merit employment systems, state government functions under a decentralized personnel system. It is highly fragmented, with each agency largely free to set its own personnel policies.

KEY TERMS

plural executive 638
impeachment 641
special session 641
veto 643
line-item veto 643
Legislative Budget Board 645
staggered terms 645
senatorial courtesy 646
extradition 648
lieutenant governor 656
attorney general 657
comptroller 657
pay-as-you-go principle 657
land commissioner 659
agriculture commissioner 660
secretary of state 660
state treasurer 660
Railroad Commission 660
State Board of Education 661
bureaucracy 662
iron triangle 665
whistleblower 666
revolving door 666
sunset 668
political patronage 670
merit system 670

SUGGESTED READINGS

Barta, Carolyn. *Bill Clements: Texian to His Toenails.* Austin: Eakin Press, 1996. A detailed account of Bill Clements' three campaigns for governor and his two terms in office.

Beyle, Thad. "Governors: The Middlemen and Women in Our Political System." In *Politics in the American States: A Comparative Analysis*, 6th ed., ed. Virginia Gray and Herbert Jacob. Washington, D.C.: CQ Press, 1996. A comparative analysis of the formal and informal powers of U.S. governors.

Frederick, Douglas W. "Reexamining the Texas Railroad Commission." In *Texas Politics: A Reader,* ed. Anthony Champagne and Edward J. Harpham (New York: W.W. Norton, 1997). Using theories of capture, authors address the issue of the Railroad Commission's domination by the oil and gas industries which it regulates.

Gantt, Fred, Jr. *The Chief Executive in Texas: A Study in Gubernatorial Leadership.* Austin: University of Texas Press, 1964. An extensive analysis of the governorship of Texas, including the development of the office and roles played by governors in the administrative and policy processes.

Hendrickson, Kenneth E. *Chief Executives of Texas: From Stephen F. Austin to John B. Connally, Jr.* College Station: Texas A&M

University Press, 1995. Brief biographic sketches of the political careers of forty-three individuals who have held the office of governor or president of the Republic.

Morris, Celia. *Storming the Statehouse: Running for Governor with Ann Richards and Dianne Feinstein.* New York: Scribner's Sons, 1992. An analysis of the hotly contested 1990 governor's race.

Prindle, David. *Petroleum Politics and the Texas Railroad Commission.* Austin: University of Texas Press, 1981. An assessment of energy policy in Texas and the role of the Railroad Commission in policy development and industry regulation.

Texas General Land Office. *The Land Commissioners of Texas.* Austin: Texas General Land Office, 1986. Brief biographical sketches of past land commissioners.

Tolleson-Rinehart, Sue. *Claytie and the Lady: Ann Richards, Gender and Politics in Texas.* Austin: University of Texas Press, 1994.

CHAPTER 20

THE TEXAS JUDICIARY

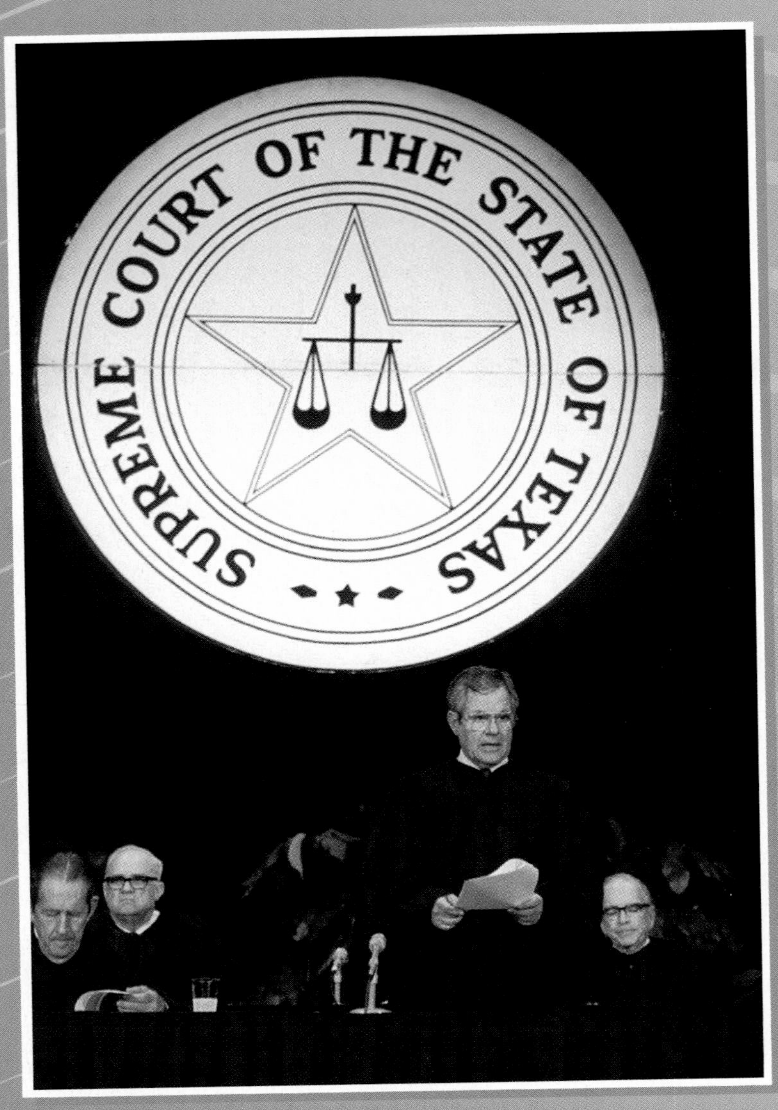

CHAPTER OUTLINE

- The Power of the Courts in Texas
- The State Courts in the Federal System
- The Legal Framework of the Judicial System
- The Structure of the Texas Court System
- The Jury System
- Judicial Procedures and Decision Making
- Judicial Concerns and Controversies
- Crime and Punishment
- The Politics of Criminal Justice
- Increased Policy Role of the State Courts

THINK ABOUT POLITICS

1 Should an accused serial murderer be considered innocent until proven guilty?
Yes ● No ●

2 Do you believe that the death penalty is "cruel and unusual punishment" in all circumstances?
Yes ● No ●

3 Should a judge be required to try a lawsuit within one month after the suit is filed?
Yes ● No ●

4 Do you think that a nonlawyer could be a good judge?
Yes ● No ●

5 Is it wrong to use one's influence to "fix" a ticket?
Yes ● No ●

6 Should the close relatives of a murder victim be allowed to witness the execution of their loved one's murderer?
Yes ● No ●

7 Does the Ku Klux Klan have the same constitutional rights as the National Association for the Advancement of Colored People?
Yes ● No ●

The courts often have the final say in how power is distributed, so understanding how they work can be crucial in gaining a share of that power.

The Power of the Courts in Texas

Although most people would like to think that justice in Texas is blind, it is not. Most judges try to be fair, but, even so, their decisions are molded by their political and ideological views, life experiences, ethnicity and gender. In recent years, moreover, Texas courts have been beset by a series of controversies that also have severely strained the popular notion that the scales of justice are balanced in an atmosphere that is above reproach. Instead, large campaign contributions to elected state judges from lawyers who practice before them and from other special interests have fueled a high-stakes war for philosophical and political control of the judiciary. The practice has drawn frequent criticism and even raised questions in the national media about whether Texas courtrooms are "for sale."

Women and minorities, meanwhile, remain grossly underrepresented among the ranks of Texas judges. And the basic structure of the judicial system—an assortment of about 2,600 courts of various, often overlapping jurisdictions—is so outdated that many experts believe it should be overhauled. But change doesn't come easily.

State courts resolve civil disputes over property rights and personal injuries. They also determine guilt or innocence and set punishment in criminal cases involving offenses against people, their property, and public institutions. And, to a more limited extent than the federal judiciary, they help set public policy by reviewing the actions of the executive and legislative branches of government. A civil dispute may stem from something as simple as a tenant's breaking an apartment lease to something as complex and potentially expensive as a manufacturer's liability for defective tires that contribute to the deaths or injuries of dozens of motorists. Criminal cases range from traffic offenses, punishable by fines, to capital murder, for which the death penalty can be imposed.

Some streamlining of Texas's judicial processes, especially at the appellate level, was accomplished in 1981. But the Texas judiciary, particularly in urban areas, has become overloaded by criminal cases and an increasingly litigious approach to civil disputes. It can take months to get a civil or a criminal case—one that is not settled out of court or in a plea bargain with prosecutors—to trial.

The State Courts in the Federal System

Like people in every state, Texans are subject to the jurisdiction of both state and federal courts. The federal judiciary has jurisdiction over violations of federal laws, including criminal offenses that occur across state lines, and over banking, securities, and other activities regulated by the federal government (see Chapter 11). Federal courts have also had major effects on state government policies and Texas's criminal justice system through interpretations and applications of the U.S. Constitution and federal laws, including the Bill of Rights.

Although Texas has a bill of rights in its constitution, the federal courts have taken the lead in protecting many civil and political rights, as when the U.S. Supreme Court declared the white primary election unconstitutional in *Smith v. Allwright* in 1944 (see Chapter 17).[1] Federal court intervention continues in the redistricting of legislative and congressional district lines. The federal judiciary also has ordered far-reaching improvements in the state prison system. And when police officers read criminal suspects their rights, the officers are complying with constitutional requirements determined by the U.S. Supreme Court in the *Miranda* case.[2]

Nevertheless, it is estimated that more than 97 percent of all litigation is based on state laws or local ordinances. Thus anyone involved in litigation is likely to be found in a state rather than a federal court.

The Legal Framework of the Judicial System

The United States and Texas constitutions form the basic legal framework of the Texas court system. Building on that framework, the Texas legislature has enacted codes of criminal and civil procedure to govern conduct in the courtroom and statutory laws for the courts to apply. Most criminal activities are defined and their punishments established in the Texas **penal code.** In criminal cases, the state—often based on charges made by another individual—initiates action against a person accused of a crime. The most serious criminal offenses, for which prison sentences can be imposed, are called **felonies.** More minor offenses, punishable by fines or short sentences in county jails, are called **misdemeanors.** Many property crimes and drug offenses are classified as state jail felonies and are punishable by community service work or time in a state jail, a prison-like facility operated by the state.

Civil lawsuits, which can be brought under numerous **statutes,** involve conflicts between two or more parties—individuals, corporations, governments, or other entities. Civil law governs contracts and property rights between private citizens, affords individuals an avenue for relief against corporate abuses, and determines liability for personal injuries. Administrative law includes enforcement powers over many aspects of the state's economy.

An individual with a grievance to be addressed has to take the initiative of going to court. A person can experience problems with a landlord who refuses to return a deposit, a dry cleaner that lost a suit, or a friend who borrowed and wrecked a car. But in a civil dispute, there is no legal issue to be resolved unless a lawsuit is filed. An injured person filing a lawsuit is a **plaintiff.** Because even the most minor disputes in the lowest courts can require professional assistance from a lawyer, a person will soon discover that the pursuit of justice can be very costly and time consuming.

penal code Body of law that defines most criminal offenses and sets a range of punishments that can be assessed.

felony Serious criminal offense that can be punished by imprisonment and/or a fine.

misdemeanor Minor criminal offense punishable by a fine and/or a short sentence in the county jail.

civil lawsuit Noncriminal legal dispute between two or more individuals, businesses, governments, or other entities.

statutes Laws enacted by a legislative body.

plaintiff Individual or party who initiates a lawsuit.

Statutes and constitutional laws are subject to change through legislative action and popular consent of the electorate, and over the years there have been significant changes in what is legal and illegal, permissible and impermissible. At one time, for example, state law provided for a potential life prison sentence for the possession of a few ounces of marijuana. Small amounts are now considered a misdemeanor punishable by a fine. The legal drinking age was lowered to eighteen for a few years but was reestablished at twenty-one after parents and school officials convinced the legislature that the younger age had helped increase alcohol abuse among teenagers.

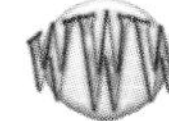
Office of Court Administration
This agency provides administrative support and technical assistance to all courts in Texas. Links to state and local courts are found here along with information about the state court system, court records, and court rules.
http://www.courts.state.tx.us

The Structure of the Texas Court System

There are five levels of Texas courts, but some courts at different levels have overlapping authority and jurisdiction (see Figure 20.1). Some courts have only **original jurisdiction**; that is, they try or resolve only those cases being heard for the first time. They weigh the facts presented as evidence and apply the law in reaching a decision or verdict. Other courts have only **appellate jurisdiction.** They review the decisions of lower courts to determine if constitutional and statutory principles and procedures were correctly interpreted and followed. Appellate courts are empowered to reverse the judgments of the lower courts and to order cases to be retried if constitutional or procedural mistakes were made. Still other courts have both original and appellate jurisdiction.

original jurisdiction
Authority of a court to try or resolve a civil lawsuit or a criminal prosecution being heard for the first time.

appellate jurisdiction
Authority of a court to review the decisions of lower courts to determine if the law was correctly interpreted and legal procedures were correctly followed.

At the highest appellate level, Texas has a **bifurcated court system,** with the nine-member Texas Supreme Court serving as the court of last resort in civil cases and the nine-member Texas Court of Criminal Appeals functioning as the court of last resort in criminal cases. Only one other state, Oklahoma, has a similar structure.[3]

bifurcated court system
Existence of two courts at the highest level of the state judiciary. The Texas Supreme Court is the court of last resort in civil cases, and the Texas Court of Criminal Appeals has the final authority to review criminal cases.

Unlike federal judges, who are appointed by the president to lifetime terms, state judges, except for those on municipal courts, are elected to limited terms in partisan elections. Midterm vacancies, however, are filled by appointment. Vacancies on the justice of the peace and county courts are filled by county commissioners courts, while vacancies on the district and appellate benches are filled by the governor.

Courts of Limited Jurisdiction

The lowest-ranking courts in Texas are municipal courts and justice of the peace courts. You or someone you know has probably appeared before a judge in one of these courts because both handle a large volume of traffic tickets. Some of these courts are big revenue raisers for local governments, and they are often accused of subordinating justice and fairness to financial considerations.[4]

Some 882 **municipal courts** are established under state law, including some with multiple judges. The qualifications, terms of office, and methods of selecting municipal judges are determined by the individual cities, but they are generally appointed by the city council. Municipal courts have original and exclusive jurisdiction over city **ordinances,** but most of these courts are not courts of record, where a word-for-word transcript is made of trial proceedings. Only very rudimentary information is officially recorded in most of these courts, and any appeal from them is heard **de novo** by the higher court; that is, the second court has to conduct a new trial and hear the same witnesses and evidence all over again because no official record of the original proceedings was kept. The informality of

municipal court Court of limited jurisdiction that hears cases involving city ordinances and primarily handles traffic tickets.

ordinances Local laws enacted by a city council.

de novo In a civil lawsuit or criminal trial, evidence is presented again before an appellate court because no record was kept of the evidence presented to the trial court.

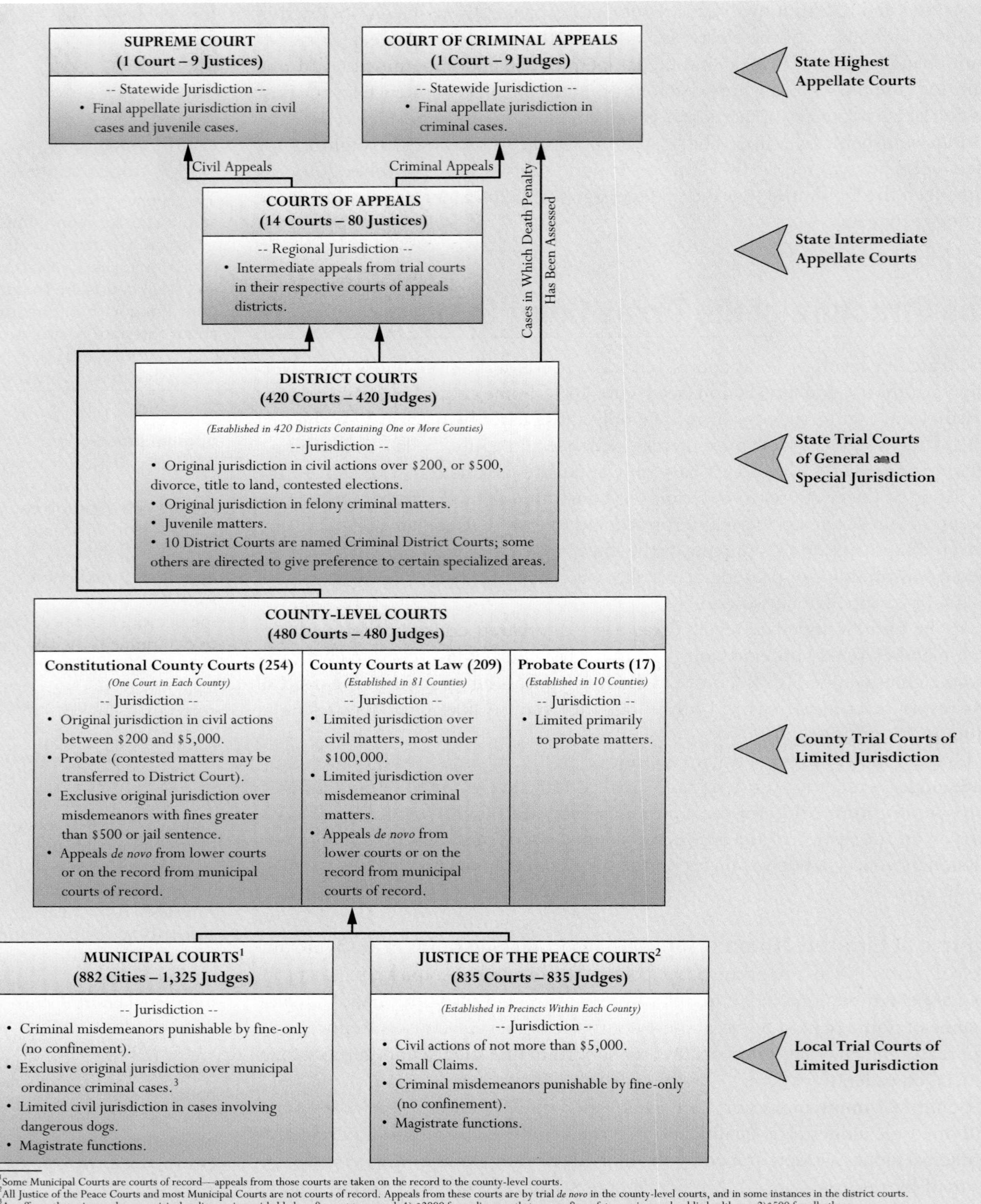

FIGURE 20.1 Court Structure of Texas

Source: Office of Court Administration, September 1, 2003.

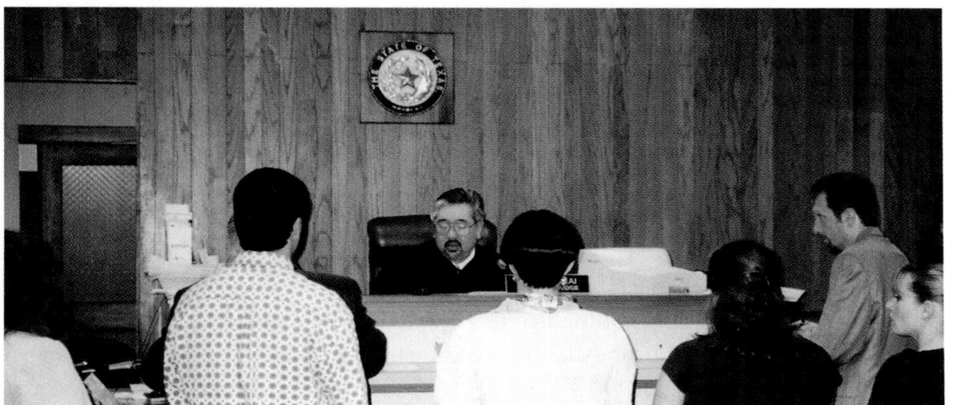

Associate Judge Peter Sakai is seen presiding over the Child Abuse and Neglect Court in San Antonio.

these proceedings and the absence of a record add to the confusion and cost of using the system.[5] In response to these problems, the legislature in recent years has created municipal courts of record for some cities.

Each county in Texas is required to provide for one **justice of the peace court**, and each county government in the larger metropolitan areas may create sixteen (see Chapter 25). There are 835 of these courts in Texas. Justices of the peace are elected to four-year terms from precincts, or subdivisions of the county drawn by the commissioners court, which also sets their salaries. Justices of the peace are not required to be licensed attorneys, a situation that has generated much criticism of these courts.

Although their duties vary from county to county, justice of the peace courts, with certain restrictions, have original jurisdiction in civil cases when the amount in dispute is $5,000 or less and have original jurisdiction over criminal offenses that are punishable by fines only. In some areas of criminal law, they have overlapping jurisdiction with municipal courts. Justices of the peace also sit as judges of small-claims courts, and in many rural counties they serve as coroners. They also function as state magistrates with the authority to hold preliminary hearings to determine if there is probable cause to hold a criminal defendant.

These are not courts of record, and cases appealed from these courts are tried de novo in county courts, county courts-at-law, or district courts. Each justice court has an elected constable to serve warrants and perform other duties for the court.

County Courts If there is confusion about the authority and jurisdiction of municipal and justice of the peace courts, it is compounded by the county courts. They were created by the Texas Constitution to serve the needs of the sparsely populated, rural society that existed when the charter was written in 1875. But population growth and urbanization have placed enormous demands on the judicial system, and rather than modernize the system, the state has added courts while making only minor changes in the structure and jurisdiction of the older courts.

Each county has a **constitutional county court.** The holder of this office, the county judge, is elected countywide to a four-year term. This individual is the chief executive officer of the county and presides over the county commissioners court, the policy-making body of county government (see Chapter 21). Most urban county judges do not perform judicial duties, but county judges in many rural counties perform both executive and judicial functions, a dual responsibility

justice of the peace court
Low-ranking court with jurisdiction over minor civil disputes and criminal cases.

constitutional county court
County court created by the Texas Constitution, presided over by the county judge.

that some experts believe is inconsistent with the Texas Constitution's separation-of-powers doctrine. Although a large number of county judges are lawyers, they are not required to be. They are required only to be "well informed in the law" and to take appropriate courses in evidence and legal procedures.

The constitutional county court shares some original civil jurisdiction with both the justice of the peace and the district court. It has original criminal jurisdiction over misdemeanors punishable by fines of more than $500 and jail sentences of one year or less. These courts also probate wills and have appellate jurisdiction over cases tried originally in justice of the peace and municipal courts.

Over the years, the legislature also has created 226 **statutory county courts,** or county courts-at-law, in more than 80 counties. Some specialize in probate cases and are called probate courts. These courts were designed to deal with specific local problems and, consequently, have inconsistent jurisdictions. Judges on these courts are elected countywide and have to be lawyers, but the authority of a particular court is defined by the legislation creating it. Some cannot hear civil disputes involving more than $2,500, while others can hear disputes involving as much as $100,000. Drunken driving cases are the primary criminal cases tried before these courts. Some of these courts also hear appeals de novo from lower courts.

County courts across the state disposed of more than 137,000 civil cases during the 2003 fiscal year but saw more than 148,000 cases added to their dockets. Approximately 553,000 criminal cases were disposed of, but an additional 550,000 cases were added. At the end of the year, more than 790,000 cases were pending before the county courts.[6]

Courts of General Jurisdiction The primary trial court in Texas is the **district court.** Although there is some overlapping jurisdiction with county courts, the district courts have original jurisdiction over civil cases involving $200 or more in damages, divorce cases, contested elections, suits over land titles and liens, suits for slander or defamation, all criminal felony cases, and misdemeanors involving official misconduct. In recent years, the legislature has created district courts with specialized jurisdictions over criminal or civil law or over such specialties as family law—divorces and child custody cases. In some large metropolitan counties that have numerous district courts, the jurisdictions of the respective courts are determined by informal agreements among the judges. District court judges are elected to four-year terms, must be at least twenty-five years old, and must have practiced law or served as a judge of another court for four years prior to taking office.

The Texas Constitution gives the legislature the responsibility to define judicial districts, and as the expanding population produced greater caseloads, new districts were created. In 1981, there were 328 district courts. In 2003, there were 420. A single county may be allocated more than one district court with overlapping geographical jurisdiction. Harris County, the state's most populous county, has fifty-nine district courts, each covering the entire county. By contrast, one rural district court may include several counties. As these courts evolved, there was little systematic consideration of the respective workloads of individual courts, and there are now great disparities in the number of people that district courts serve.

Many urban counties suffer from a heavy backlog of cases that can delay a trial date in civil lawsuits and even some criminal cases for months or years. The district courts disposed of 513,000 civil cases and 241,000 criminal cases during the 2003 fiscal year, but new cases were added, and the courts began the 2004 fiscal

statutory county court Court that exercises limited jurisdiction over criminal and/or civil cases. The jurisdiction of these courts varies from county to county.

district court Primary trial court in Texas. It has jurisdiction over criminal felony cases and civil disputes.

WHAT DO YOU THINK?

Justice Delayed, Justice Denied?

Trial delays are bad enough for prosecutors and taxpayers. But they can be a nightmare for criminal defendants innocent of the charges against them, especially if they have to spend months in jail awaiting trial. In one case, a twenty-three-year-old construction worker from Mexico spent 575 days—more than a year and a half—in the Tarrant County jail awaiting trial on charges of fondling a five-year-old girl.* When his case finally reached the courtroom, it took a jury forty-two minutes to find him innocent and free him. His room and board in jail had cost Tarrant County taxpayers $23,000. But his ordeal had cost him much more, and his case should make all of us ask how long justice can be delayed before it is justice denied.

***Fort Worth Star-Telegram*, April 25, 1993.

year with 846,000 pending cases[7] (see *What Do You Think?* "Justice Delayed, Justice Denied?").

Delays in criminal cases have prompted a widespread use of plea bargains. In **plea bargaining,** a criminal defendant, through a lawyer, negotiates with prosecutors a guilty plea that will get a lesser sentence than he or she could expect to receive if convicted in a trial. The process saves the state the time-consuming expense of a full-blown trial and has become an essential tool in clearing urban court dockets.

Former District Attorney John B. Holmes, Jr., estimated that 90 percent of the thousands of felony cases filed in Harris County (Houston) each year were disposed of through plea bargains. Without plea bargains, the caseload would simply overwhelm the twenty-two Harris County district courts that handle criminal cases.

Harris County's civil district courts disposed of more than 84,000 lawsuits—divorces, personal injuries, tax disputes, and others—in fiscal year 2003 but left more than 101,000 other cases pending.[8] Many civil lawsuits are resolved through negotiations between the opposing parties, but those that are tried and appealed can take several years to be resolved.

The wide disparities in populations and caseloads served by the various district courts prompted the adoption of a constitutional amendment in 1985 that created the Judicial Districts Board. That panel was responsible for redrawing judicial districts with an eye toward a more equitable distribution of the workload. But in 1994, yielding to pressure from incumbent judges who did not want to lose their offices, it issued recommendations that primarily preserved the status quo. Extensive changes by the legislature were considered unlikely.

Although the district court is the state's primary trial court and the state pays the district judges' base salaries, the counties pick up virtually all other district court expenses. The counties provide courtrooms, pay the courts' operating expenses, and supplement the judges' state pay.

Intermediate Courts of Appeals Fourteen intermediate **courts of appeals** cover thirteen multi-county regions that hear appeals of both civil and criminal cases from the district courts. Two courts, the First Court of Appeals and the

plea bargaining Procedure that allows a person charged with a crime to negotiate a guilty plea with prosecutors in exchange for a lighter sentence than he or she would expect to receive if convicted in a trial.

court of appeals Intermediate-level court that reviews civil and criminal cases from the district courts.

Fourteenth Court of Appeals, are based in Houston and cover the same area. The Texas Constitution provides that each court shall have a chief justice and at least two other justices, but the legislature can add to that number and has done so for most courts. Each Houston court has nine judges, and the Fifth Court of Appeals in Dallas has thirteen judges. Five of these intermediate courts, however, have only three members. Appellate judges are elected to six-year terms. They must be at least thirty-five years old and have at least ten years of experience as an attorney or a judge on a court of record.

Although the appellate courts disposed of more than 12,000 civil and criminal cases during fiscal 2003, they left almost 8,000 other cases pending on their dockets at the end of the year, with criminal cases accounting for more than half of the unfinished business.[9] But there are wide disparities in the caseloads between individual courts, with those in Houston and Dallas handling the lion's share. The Texas Supreme Court partially balances the load by transferring cases among courts. The courts of appeals normally decide cases in panels of three judges, but an entire court can hear some appeals en banc.

The Highest Appellate Courts The creation of separate courts of last resort for civil and criminal cases was part of the effort by the constitutional framers of 1875 to fragment political power and decentralize the structure of state and local government. It was also based on the rationale that criminal cases should be tried more expeditiously, and the way to accomplish this was through a separate appellate court.

Although it decides only civil appeals, the **Texas Supreme Court** is probably viewed by most Texans as the titular head of the state judiciary, and it has been given some authority to coordinate the state judicial system.[10] The Supreme Court is charged with developing administrative procedures for the state courts and rules of civil procedure. It appoints the Board of Law Examiners, which is responsible for licensing attorneys, and has oversight of the State Bar, the professional organization to which all lawyers in Texas must belong. The Supreme Court also has disciplinary authority over state judges through recommendations of the State Commission on Judicial Conduct.

The Texas Supreme Court includes a chief justice and eight justices who serve staggered six-year terms. Three members are up for election every two years on a statewide ballot. Members must be at least thirty-five years old and must have been a practicing attorney, a judge of a court of record, or a combination of both for at least ten years.

The **Texas Court of Criminal Appeals**, which hears only criminal cases on appeal, includes a presiding judge and eight other judges elected statewide to staggered six-year terms. The qualifications for members of this court are the same as those for the Texas Supreme Court.

Under the federal system, some decisions of the Texas Supreme Court and the Texas Court of Criminal Appeals can be appealed to the U.S. Supreme Court. Those cases have to involve a federal question or a right assured under the U.S. Constitution.

Texas Supreme Court Nine-member court with final appellate jurisdiction over civil lawsuits.

Texas Court of Criminal Appeals Nine-member court with final appellate jurisdiction over criminal cases.

Texas Judges In 2002, the last year for which extensive data were available, about one-half of the members of the intermediate and highest appellate courts had come to the bench from private law practice. About one-third had previously served on lower courts. Most district judges had come to their offices from private law practice or from a prosecutor's office.

The development of a two-party system in Texas has affected the partisan affiliation of state judges. Republicans have seen election gains and more appointments to judicial vacancies. A number of judges also have switched from the Democratic Party. By 2003, almost two-thirds of the judges at the district court level and higher were Republicans, including all nine members of the Texas Supreme Court and all nine members of the Texas Court of Criminal Appeals.

Most Texas judges are white males. With increasing frequency, women, Hispanics, and African Americans are entering the legal profession and running for judicial offices, but they are still proportionately underrepresented in the judiciary. As will be discussed later in this chapter, minorities have pressed for changes in the judicial selection process to enhance their chances to serve on the bench.

Judicial elections have been diluted by a large number of appointments to judicial vacancies. The governor appoints judges to fill midterm vacancies on the district and appellate courts. County commissioners courts fill midterm vacancies on county court-at-law and justice of the peace courts. Appointees are required to run for office in the next general election to keep their seats, but their incumbency can enhance their election chances.

Other Participants in the State Judiciary County and district clerks, both elected offices, are custodians of court records. Bailiffs are peace officers assigned to the courts to help maintain order and protect judges and other parties from physical attacks. Other law enforcement officers play critical roles in the arrest, detention, and investigation of persons accused of crimes.

County attorneys and district attorneys are responsible for prosecuting criminal cases. Both positions are elected. Some counties do not have a county attorney. In those that do, the county attorney is the chief legal adviser to the commissioners court, represents the county in civil lawsuits, and may prosecute misdemeanors. The district attorney prosecutes felonies and, in some counties, also handles misdemeanors. The district attorney represents one county in metropolitan areas and several counties in less populated areas of the state (see Chapter 21).

Other important players in the judicial process are the private citizens who serve on juries. Although there is some debate about the competency of a jury of ordinary citizens to make reasonable decisions on complex and technical civil and criminal matters, no acceptable alternatives have been found.

Efforts to Reform the Judicial System Judicial reform has been a recurring issue in Texas politics. Small, incremental changes have been made since the 1970s, but many jurists and scholars continue to push for an overhaul of the state courts. In September 1989, Texas Supreme Court Chief Justice Thomas R. Phillips requested an in-depth study of the Texas judiciary by the Texas Research League, a privately financed, nonprofit group specializing in studies of state government.

The league concluded that the court system was fundamentally flawed and sorely in need of an overhaul. It made twenty-seven recommendations, including one that the legislature rewrite the judiciary article of the Texas Constitution to provide a fundamental framework for a unified court system.[11]

Despite a series of similar studies and reports, however, reform of Texas courts has been difficult. The public may have a lot to gain from judicial restructuring, but the primary stakeholders—the judges, the attorneys, the court administrative personnel, and litigants who benefit from delays, confusion, and inefficiency—have resisted change. Unless there is a popular demand for reform, there will be few structural changes in the judiciary until some or all of these participants perceive some advantages from reform.

The Jury System

The Grand Jury Citizens serve on two kinds of juries—grand juries and trial, or petit, juries. The **grand jury** functions, in theory, to ensure that the government has sufficient reason to proceed with a criminal **prosecution** against an individual. It includes twelve persons selected by a district judge from a list proposed by a jury commission appointed by the local district judge or judges. Although the grand jury evolved to protect the individual against arbitrary and capricious behavior by governmental officials, a district attorney can exercise great control over a grand jury through deciding what evidence and which witnesses jurors will hear. There also have been allegations over the years that grand juries over-represent the interests of upper social and economic groups and under-represent minorities. Grand jury meetings and deliberations are conducted in private, and the accused is not allowed to have an attorney present during grand jury questioning.

A grand jury usually meets on specified days of the week and serves for the duration of the district court's term, usually from three to six months. If at least nine grand jurors believe there is enough evidence to warrant a trial in a case under investigation, they will issue an **indictment**, or a "true bill"—a written statement charging a person or persons with a crime. A grand jury investigation also may result in no indictment, or a "no bill."

In some cases—especially when an investigation fails to produce a strong enough case for a felony indictment—grand juries issue indictments alleging misdemeanors. Most misdemeanors, however, are not handled by grand juries. They are handled by the district or county attorney, who prepares an **information**—a document formally charging an individual with a misdemeanor—on the basis of a complaint filed by a private citizen.

grand jury Panel that reviews evidence submitted by prosecutors to determine whether to indict, or charge, an individual with a criminal offense.

prosecution Conduct of legal proceedings against an individual charged with a crime.

indictment Written statement issued by a grand jury charging a person with a punishable offense.

information Document formally charging a person with a misdemeanor.

petit jury Panel of citizens that hears evidence in a civil lawsuit or a criminal prosecution and decides the outcome by issuing a verdict.

The Petit Jury The jury on which most people are likely to be called to serve is the trial jury, or **petit jury.** Citizens who are at least eighteen years old and meet other minimal requirements are eligible for jury duty, and anyone refusing to comply with a jury summons can be fined for contempt of court (see *What Do You Think?* "Is This Any Way to Round Up a Jury?"). Persons older than seventy, individuals with legal custody of young children, and full-time students are exempted from jury duty. The legislature in 1991 increased the likelihood of an individual's being called to jury duty by providing that county and district clerks prepare jury summonses from lists of those Texans who have drivers' licenses or hold Department of Public Safety identification cards. Previously, prospective jurors were chosen from voter registration lists, and it was believed that some Texans had not been registering to vote in order to avoid jury duty.

Six persons make up a jury in a justice of the peace or county court, and twelve in a district court. Attorneys for both sides in a criminal or civil case screen the

WHAT DO YOU THINK?

Is This Any Way to Round Up a Jury?

Some people called it "street justice." Others said it was bad public relations. It was probably both, and it was certainly unusual.

Justice of the Peace Mark Fury had scheduled a night jury trial for a minor traffic case in his southwest Houston courtroom but, at the last minute, discovered he didn't have enough jurors. So he issued a writ, ordering deputy constables to go across the street and round up some shoppers in a grocery store parking lot.

Nineteen people soon found themselves unexpectedly pressed into jury duty. Not all were chosen for the jury, but all had to report to the courtroom and had their evening plans disrupted. Several weren't too happy about it.

"It just seemed everybody was a little crusty toward everybody. They were just all mad," one draftee said.

Lisa Sedgwick, who had planned to go to a soccer game that night, ended up being the jury foreman instead.

The jury roundup, although rare, was legal. But people caught in the judge's net couldn't understand why he didn't just simply postpone the trial of such a minor case.

Fury said he believed he jurors had "a positive experience."

"I thought it went very smoothly. I expected there to be a larger number of acrimonious people," he said.

The jury convicted the defendant, a teenager, of speeding.

Source: Houston Chronicle, August 22, 1997.

prospective jurors, known as **veniremen,** before a jury is seated. In major felony cases, such as capital murder, prosecutors and defense attorneys may take several days to select a jury from among hundreds of prospects.

Attorneys for each side in a criminal case are permitted a certain number of peremptory challenges, which allow them to dismiss a prospective juror without having to explain the reason, and an unlimited number of challenges for cause. In the latter case, the lawyer has to state why he or she believes a particular venireman would not be able to evaluate the evidence in the case impartially. The judge decides whether to grant each challenge for cause but can rule against a peremptory challenge only if he or she believes a prosecutor is trying to exclude prospective jurors because of their race, such as keeping African Americans off a jury that is to try an African-American defendant. If that happens, the defendant is entitled to a new group, or panel, of prospective jurors.

In civil cases, attorneys for both sides determine whether any persons on the jury panel should be disqualified because they are related to one of the parties, have some other personal or business connection, or could otherwise be prejudiced. For example, a lawyer defending a doctor in a malpractice suit probably would not want to seat a prospective juror who had been dissatisfied with his own medical treatment. Such potential conflicts are discovered by attorneys' careful screening and questioning of veniremen.

Unanimous jury verdicts are required to convict a defendant in a criminal case. In a criminal case, jurors have to be convinced "beyond a reasonable doubt" that a defendant is guilty before returning a guilty verdict. In contrast, agreement of only ten of the twelve members of a district court jury and five of the six on a county court jury are sufficient to reach a verdict in a civil suit.

veniremen Members of a panel from which a petit, or trial, jury is chosen.

THINK AGAIN

Should an accused serial murderer be considered innocent until proven guilty?

Judicial Procedures and Decision Making

Civil litigants and criminal defendants (except those charged with capital murder) can waive their right to a jury trial if they believe it would be to their advantage to have their cases decided by a judge. Following established procedures, which differ between civil and criminal cases and are enforced by the judge, the trial moves through the presentation of opening arguments by the opposing attorneys, examination and cross-examination of witnesses, presentation of evidence, rebuttal, and summation. Some trials can be completed in a few hours, but the trial of a complex civil lawsuit or a sensational criminal case can take weeks or months. Convicted criminal defendants or parties dissatisfied with a judge or jury's verdict in a civil lawsuit can then appeal their case to higher courts.

The procedure in appellate courts is markedly different from that in trial courts. There is no jury at the appellate level to rehear evidence. Instead, judges review the decisions and the procedures of the lower court for conformance to constitutional and statutory requirements. The record of the trial court proceedings and legal briefs filed by the attorneys are available for appellate judges to review.

Most civil and criminal appeals are initially made to one of the fourteen intermediate courts of appeals. Parties dissatisfied with decisions of the courts of appeals can appeal to the Texas Supreme Court or the Texas Court of Criminal Appeals.

Cases reach the Texas Supreme Court primarily on **petitions for review**, usually filed by the losing parties, claiming that legal or procedural mistakes were made in the lower courts. These petitions are distributed among the nine Supreme Court justices. The justices and their briefing attorneys then prepare memoranda on their assigned cases for circulation among the other court members. Meeting in private conference, the court decides which applications to reject outright—thus upholding the lower court decisions—and which to schedule for attorneys' oral arguments. A case will not be heard without the approval of at least four of the nine justices.

petition for review Petition to the Texas Supreme Court claiming that legal or procedural mistakes were made in the lower court.

An attorney addressing a jury in a state court in Dallas.

Oral arguments, in which the lawyers present their perspectives on the legal points that are at issue in their case and answer questions from the justices, are presented in open court. Most hearings are held in the Supreme Court chambers in Austin, but since 1998 the court, in an effort to try to educate more people about its work, has been holding occasional hearings in other Texas cities. The responsibility for writing the majority opinions that state the court's decisions is determined by lot among the justices. It often takes several months after oral arguments before a decision is issued. Legal points and judicial philosophies are debated among the justices behind the closed doors of their conference room. But differences sometimes spill out for public view through split decisions and strongly worded dissenting opinions.

Most cases taken to the Texas Supreme Court on appeal are from one of the courts of appeals, but occasionally the Supreme Court receives a direct appeal from a district court. In recent years, the court has been hearing about 10 percent of the petitions for review it receives.

The Texas Supreme Court also acts on petitions for **writs of mandamus**, or orders directing a lower court or another public official to take a certain action. Many involve disputes over procedure or evidence in cases still pending in trial courts.

The Texas Court of Criminal Appeals has appellate jurisdiction in criminal cases that originate in the district and county courts. Death penalty cases are appealed directly to the Court of Criminal Appeals. Other criminal cases are appealed first to the intermediate courts of appeals. Either the defendant or the prosecution can appeal the courts of appeals' decisions to the Court of Criminal Appeals by filing petitions for discretionary review, which the high court may grant if at least four judges agree. The court sets one day a week aside for lawyers' oral arguments in the cases it agrees to review. The task of writing majority opinions is rotated among the nine judges.

Judicial Concerns and Controversies

For more than twenty years, Texas courts have been at the center of conflict and controversy. Large campaign contributions from lawyers and other special interests to judges and judicial candidates have raised allegations that Texas has the best justice that money can buy. With billions of dollars at stake in crucial legal decisions, the Texas Supreme Court has been a philosophical and political battleground. Meanwhile, minorities—who hold a disproportionately small number of judicial offices—continue to press for greater influence in electing judges. Lengthy ballots, particularly in urban areas, make it increasingly difficult for most voters to choose intelligently among judicial candidates (see *People in Politics:* "Steve Mansfield, an Election Day Surprise"). Although these issues and concerns may seem unrelated, they all share one important characteristic: they cast a cloud over the Texas judiciary. Each, in its own way, undermines public confidence in the state courts and makes many Texans question how just their system of justice is.

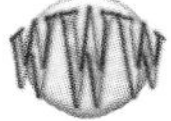

Texas Bar Association

This site provides access to a wide range of information relevant to the legal profession. *www.texasbar.com*

Judicial Activism

In earlier chapters, we noted the historical domination of Texas politics and policies by the conservative, business-oriented establishment. For decades, that domination also applied to the judiciary, as insurance companies, banks, utilities, and other large corporate entities became

writ of mandamus Court order directing a lower court or another public official to take a certain action.

PEOPLE IN POLITICS

Steve Mansfield, an Election Day Surprise

Like most other candidates for the Texas Court of Criminal Appeals, Houston attorney Steve Mansfield received little publicity when he began a campaign in 1994 to unseat Democratic Judge Charles Campbell, a twelve-year incumbent. Running as a crime victims' advocate, he defeated an equally unknown attorney for the Republican nomination and then got more publicity than he wanted—all of it negative. In the middle of his campaign, it was revealed that Mansfield had lied about his personal and political background and had exaggerated his legal experience. He was primarily an insurance lawyer with little experience in criminal law. But he unseated Campbell, thanks to heavy straight-ticket Republican voting in a GOP landslide.

Bad publicity continued to dog Mansfield even after he took office. Texas Republican Party officials shunned him at a party fundraiser, and the Board of Law Examiners investigated the circumstances under which he had obtained a Texas law license, which he had to have to serve on the court. But at his swearing-in ceremony in January 1995, Mansfield promised to be a hardworking judge, and he spent his first year in office living up to his promise by authoring thirty-three opinions, slightly more than the court average. It was unknown how much of the actual research and writing could be credited to Mansfield and how much to the experienced staff he inherited from Campbell and was wise enough to retain. But, as he had promised during his campaign, Mansfield usually sided with the prosecution.

Several months after Mansfield took office, the State Bar publicly reprimanded him for his campaign lies. But the Board of Law Examiners did not challenge his law license, which cleared the way for him to remain on the court. Many judges, prosecutors, and other state officials considered Mansfield's election an embarrassment and a good argument for appointing, rather than electing, judges. But despite the controversy, Mansfield said he enjoyed his new job. "It's certainly been the greatest challenge I've ever faced. I've worked very hard to live up to the trust the people of Texas put in me," he said.*

Mansfield didn't seek reelection in 2000 and left the court after six years. Attempting a comeback, he ran for another Court of Criminal Appeals seat in the 2002 Republican primary but lost.

Unfortunately, Mansfield was not the first candidate of questionable qualifications to win election to a statewide court in Texas. The most infamous example was Donald B. Yarbrough. Yarbrough, also an unknown attorney from Houston, claimed that God had told him to run for the Texas Supreme Court. Thanks to his familiar name, he upset a much more qualified candidate, Appellate Judge Charles Barrow, for a seat on the high court in 1976. Yarbrough's name was similar to that of Don Yarborough, who had run unsuccessfully for governor two times in the 1960s, and that of former U.S. Senator Ralph Yarborough. Yarbrough spent approximately $350 campaigning, while Barrow had the endorsement of the legal establishment.

Yarbrough, a Democrat, served about six months on the Supreme Court, then became the target of a criminal investigation and resigned as the legislature was preparing to remove him. After he left the court, he was convicted of lying to a grand jury investigating allegations that he plotted to have a banker killed and was sentenced to five years in prison. While free on bond during an appeal, he left the country to attend medical school in Grenada and refused to return when his appeal was denied. He finally was apprehended in the Caribbean, sentenced to two additional years for bond jumping, and imprisoned.

*Quoted in *Houston Chronicle*, June 28, 1995.

accustomed to favorable rulings from a Democratic, but conservative, Texas Supreme Court.

Establishment-oriented justices, usually elected with the support of the state's largest law firms, tended to view their role as strict constructionists. The legislature had the authority to enact public policy; the responsibility of the courts, they believed, was to narrowly interpret and apply the law. Judges were not to engage in setting policy but were to honor legal precedent and prior case law, which had generally favored the interests of corporations over those of consumers, laborers, and the lower social classes.

The establishment began to feel the first tremors of a philosophical earthquake in the 1970s. The Texas Trial Lawyers Association, whose members represent consumers in lawsuits against businesses, doctors, and insurance companies, increased its political activity. And in 1973, the legislature, with increased minority and female membership from single-member House districts ordered by the federal courts (see Chapter 18), enacted the Deceptive Trade Practices–Consumer Protection Act, which encouraged plaintiffs, or injured parties, to take their grievances to court. Among other things, the new law allowed plaintiffs to sue for attorneys' fees as well as compensatory and punitive damages.

Trial, or plaintiffs', attorneys, who usually receive a healthy percentage of monetary damages awarded their clients, began contributing millions of dollars to successful Texas Supreme Court candidates, and judicial precedents started falling. A revamped court issued significant decisions that made it easier for consumers to win large judgments for medical malpractice, faulty products, and other complaints against businesses and their insurers. The new activist, liberal interpretation of the law contrasted sharply with the traditional record of the court. "All of a sudden, we have a magnificent Supreme Court, which is not controlled by a sinister, rich, opulent elite," trial attorney Pat Maloney of San Antonio, a major contributor to Supreme Court candidates, said in a 1983 interview with the *Fort Worth Star-Telegram*.[12]

The business community and defense lawyers accused the new court majority of exceeding its constitutional authority by trying to write its own laws. Some business leaders contended that the court's activism endangered the state's economy by discouraging new businesses from moving to Texas, a fear that was soon to be put to partisan advantage by Republican leaders.

Judicial Impropriety Controversy over the Texas Supreme Court escalated into a full-blown storm in 1986 when the Judicial Affairs Committee of the Texas House investigated two justices, Democrats C. L. Ray and William Kilgarlin, for alleged improper contact with attorneys practicing before the court. The two justices denied the allegations, made largely by former briefing attorneys, but never testified before the legislative panel. Both justices had consistently sided with plaintiffs' lawyers and had received considerable campaign support from them, and they contended the investigation was politically motivated and orchestrated by defense lawyers and corporate interests opposed to their judicial activism.

Chief Justice John L. Hill voluntarily testified before the committee and said he suspected but could not prove that information about the Supreme Court's deliberations on some cases had been improperly leaked to outsiders. Hill urged the committee to let the State Commission on Judicial Conduct, a state agency charged with investigating complaints of ethical violations by state judges, look into the allegations and "let the chips fall where they may."[13] The committee eventually concluded its investigation without recommending any action against the justices.

But in June 1987, the State Commission on Judicial Conduct issued public sanctions against both. Ray was reprimanded for seven violations of the Code of Judicial Conduct, including the acceptance of free airplane rides from attorneys practicing before the court and improper communication with lawyers about pending cases. Kilgarlin received a milder admonishment because two of his law clerks had accepted a weekend trip to Las Vegas from a law firm with cases pending before the court. Both justices were cited for soliciting funds from attorneys to help pay for litigation the justices had brought against the House Judicial Affairs Committee and a former briefing attorney who testified against them.

Later in 1987, the Texas judiciary, particularly the Texas Supreme Court, received negative publicity on a national scale when the high court upheld a record $11 billion judgment awarded Pennzoil Company in a dispute with Texaco, Inc. Several members of the Supreme Court were even featured on a network television program that questioned whether justice was "for sale" in Texas. The record judgment was awarded to Pennzoil after a state district court jury in Houston had determined that Texaco had wrongfully interfered in Pennzoil's attempt to acquire Getty Oil Company in 1984. Texaco, which sought protection under federal bankruptcy laws, later reached a settlement with Pennzoil, but it also waged a massive public relations campaign against the Texas judiciary.

In a segment on CBS-TV's *60 Minutes,* correspondent Mike Wallace pointed out that plaintiffs' attorney Joe Jamail of Houston, who represented Pennzoil, had contributed $10,000 to the original trial judge in the case and thousands of dollars more to Texas Supreme Court justices. The program also generally criticized the elective system that allowed Texas judges legally to accept large campaign contributions from lawyers who practiced before them. The program presented what had already been reported in the Texas media, but after the national exposure, Governor Bill Clements and other Republicans renewed attacks on the activist, Democratic justices. And some Texas newspapers published editorials calling for changes in the judicial selection process.

Campaign Contributions and Republican Gains Chief Justice Hill, a former attorney general who had narrowly lost a gubernatorial race to Clements in 1978, had been a strong supporter of electing state judges and had spent more than $1 million winning the chief justice's seat in 1984. As did his colleagues on the court, he accepted many campaign contributions from lawyers. But in 1986, Hill announced that the "recent trend toward excessive political contributions in judicial races" had prompted him to change his mind.[14] He now advocated a so-called **merit selection** plan of gubernatorial appointments and periodic retention elections. But the other eight Supreme Court justices—like Hill, all Democrats—still favored the elective system, and the legislature ignored pleas for change.

merit selection Proposal under which the governor would appoint state judges from lists of potential nominees recommended by committees of experts. Appointed judges would have to run later in retention elections to keep their seats but would not have opponents on the ballot. Voters would simply decide whether a judge should remain in office or be replaced by another gubernatorial appointee.

Hill resigned from the court on January 1, 1988, to return to private law practice and lobby as a private citizen for changing the judicial selection method. His resignation and the midterm resignations of two other Democratic justices before the 1988 elections gave Republicans a golden opportunity to make historic inroads on the high court. And they helped the business community regain control of the court from plaintiffs' attorneys.

Party realignment, including midterm judicial appointments by Clements, had already increased the number of Republican judges across the state, particularly on district court benches in urban areas. But only one Republican had ever served on the Supreme Court in modern times. Will Garwood was appointed by Clements in 1979 to fill a vacancy on the court but was defeated by Democrat C. L. Ray in the 1980 election. GOP leaders already had been planning to recruit a Republican slate of candidates for the three Supreme Court seats that normally would have been on the ballot in 1988. Now, six seats were contested, including those held by three new Republican justices appointed by Clements to fill the unexpected vacancies. Even though a full Texas Supreme Court term is six years, the governor's judicial appointees have to run in the next election to keep their seats. Clements appointed Thomas R. Phillips, a state district judge from Houston, to succeed Hill and become the first Republican chief justice since Reconstruction.

The competing legal and financial interests in Texas also understood that the six Texas Supreme Court races on the 1988 ballot would help set the philosophy of the court for years to come. Consequently, these were the most expensive court races Texas had ever experienced, with the twelve Republican and Democratic nominees raising $10 million in direct campaign contributions. Contributions to the winners averaged $836,347. Phillips, one of three Republican winners, spent $2 million, the most by a winning candidate. Some individual donations to other candidates were as large as $65,000.[15] Reformers argued that such large contributions created an appearance of impropriety and eroded public confidence in the judiciary's independence.

But the successes of Republicans and conservative Democrats in the 1988 races probably hindered, more than helped, the cause of reforming the judicial selection process. The business and medical communities, which had considerable success fighting the plaintiffs' lawyers under the existing rules—with large campaign contributions of their own—were pleased with the election results. "I'm a happy camper today," said one lobbyist for the Texas Medical Association, whose political action committee had supported two conservative Democratic winners and the three Republican victors.[16]

In several key liability cases over the next few years, the Supreme Court began to demonstrate a rediscovered philosophy favoring business defendants over plaintiffs.[17]

Republicans won a fourth seat on the court in 1990 and a fifth in 1994, to give the GOP a majority for the first time since Reconstruction. Republican challengers in 1994 also unseated nineteen incumbent Democratic district judges in Harris County in strong straight-party voting. Republicans picked up a sixth and a seventh seat on the Supreme Court after two Democratic justices resigned in midterm in 1995 and were replaced with Republican appointees of Governor George W. Bush. Republicans completed their sweep of the high court in 1998 when Justice Rose Spector, one of two remaining Democratic justices, was unseated by Republican Harriet O'Neill and Democrat Raul A. Gonzalez retired in midterm and was replaced by Bush appointee Alberto R. Gonzales. No Democratic challengers filed for the three Supreme Court seats that were on the 2000 ballot. Democrats ran for all five seats on the 2002 ballot but lost all five races.

Phillips, the chief justice, was reelected over minor opposition in 2002 and accepted no campaign contributions that year. He resigned in mid-term in 2004 to become a visiting professor at the South Texas College of Law in Houston. Phillips believed the court's reputation had been enhanced during his tenure, but, as his predecessor had done on stepping down 16 years earlier, he criticized the money-driven, partisan election system for judges. He said it "creates great instability in the judiciary and erodes public confidence in the fairness of our decisions."[18]

Legislative Reaction to Judicial Activism The business community had also moved its war against the trial lawyers to the legislature, which in 1987 enacted a so-called **tort reform** package that attempted to put some limits on personal-injury lawsuits and damage judgments entered by the courts. (A tort is a wrongful act over which a lawsuit can be brought.) Insurance companies, which had been lobbying nationwide for states to set limits on jury awards in personal injury cases, were major proponents of the legislation. They were joined by the Texas Civil Justice League, an organization of trade and professional associations, cities, and businesses formed in 1986 to seek similar changes in Texas tort law. The high-stakes campaign for change was enthusiastically supported by Governor Bill Clements but was opposed by consumer groups and plaintiffs' lawyers, who had been making millions of dollars from the judiciary's new liberalism.

Cities, businesses, doctors, and even charitable organizations had been hit with tremendous increases in insurance premiums, which they blamed on greedy trial lawyers and large court awards in malpractice and personal-injury lawsuits. Trial lawyers blamed the insurance industry, which, they said, had started raising premiums to recoup losses in investment income after interest rates had fallen.

Among other things, the 1987 tort-reform laws limited governmental liability, attempted to discourage frivolous lawsuits, and limited the ability of claimants to collect damages for injuries that were largely their own fault. They also set limits on punitive damages, which are designed to punish whoever caused an accident or an injury and are often awarded in addition to an injured party's compensation for actual losses.

Other limits on lawsuits were enacted in later legislative sessions, including 1995 and 2003. The 1995 changes, major priorities of then-Governor George W. Bush, imposed even stricter limits on punitive damages and limited the liability of a party who is only partially responsible for an injury. The 2003 legislation, actively sought by Governor Rick Perry and a new Republican majority in the Texas House, set new restrictions on class action lawsuits—which are brought on behalf of large groups of people—and imposed new limits on money that could be awarded for noneconomic damages—such as pain, suffering, or disfigurement—in medical malpractice cases. Lawsuits, or the threat of lawsuits, had been blamed for rising premiums for medical malpractice insurance, which some doctors and other advocates of civil justice changes had characterized as a "crisis" in health care in Texas.

A leading proponent for the civil justice restrictions in 2003 was Texans for Lawsuit Reform, a Houston-based business group whose political action committee gave more than $1 million to successful legislative candidates during the 2002 campaigns.[19]

Winners and Losers In a study released in 1999, Texas Watch, a consumer advocacy group, said that doctors, hospitals, and other business-related litigants had been big winners before the Texas Supreme Court during the previous four years and that consumers had fared poorly. The group studied more than 625 cases in which the court had written opinions between January 1, 1995, and April 14, 1999. That was a period during which most court members had received substantial campaign funding from doctors, insurers, and other business interests. The opinions also were issued after the Texas legislature had begun enacting tort reform laws setting limits on civil lawsuits. The study determined that physicians and hospitals had

tort reform Changes in state law to put limits on personal injury lawsuits and damage judgments entered by the courts.

won 86 percent of their appeals, most of which involved medical malpractice claims brought by injured patients or their families. Other consistent winners were insurance companies (73 percent), manufacturers (72 percent), banks (67 percent), utilities (65 percent), and other businesses (68 percent). Insurance policyholders, injured workers, injured patients, and other individual litigants won only 36 percent of the time.[20] The report covered only cases in which the Supreme Court had written opinions. Hundreds of other cases in which the high court upheld lower courts without issuing its own opinions weren't studied. "Individuals are the lowest link in the legal food chain that ends in the Texas Supreme Court," said Walt Borges, who directed the study. "The study raises a question about the fairness of the Texas Supreme Court and state law," he added.[21]

CBS-TV's *60 Minutes*, which had turned the national spotlight on plaintiffs' lawyers and their political contributions to Texas judges in 1987, revisited the Texas judiciary in a follow-up program in 1998. Noting that the partisan system of electing judges had remained unchanged, the new *60 Minutes* segment suggested that justice may still be for sale in Texas, but with different people—the business community—now wielding the influence. The Texas legislature in 1995 had imposed modest limits on campaign contributions to judges and judicial candidates and restricted the periods during which judges and their challengers could raise funds. But a judge could still receive as much as $30,000 from members of the same law firm and as much as $300,000 in total contributions from special interests through political action committees. The 1996 races for the Texas Supreme Court—the first conducted under the new law—demonstrated how weak the new reforms were. Four Republican incumbents, including Chief Justice Thomas R. Phillips, still raised a combined $4 million, easily swamping fund-raising efforts by their unsuccessful challengers.

Texas Watch, the consumer advocacy group, issued a follow-up report on the Supreme Court's 2000–2001 term, which found that consumers were beginning to fare better in some court decisions. But the group determined that businesses, insurance companies and other defendants still won 52 percent of cases pitting consumers against businesses. Consumers won 41 percent of the cases, and the remaining decisions were split, according to the new study.[22] Some observers attributed the moderating influence to appointees whom then-Governor George W. Bush had made to mid-term vacancies on the court in the late 1990s. As some of those justices began to leave the court, however, consumer advocates complained of another philosophical shift against plaintiffs. Texas Watch issued still another report in September 2002, noting that the Supreme Court had ruled for business defendants and against workers and other consumers in about two-thirds of the cases it had decided during the previous 12 months.[23]

Minorities and the Judicial System As the high-stakes battles were being waged over the Texas Supreme Court's philosophical and political makeup, minorities were actively seeking more representation in the Texas judiciary. But instead of pouring millions of dollars into judicial races, Hispanics and African Americans filed lawsuits to try to force change through the federal courts.

Throughout Texas history, Hispanics and African Americans have had difficulty winning election to state courts. The high cost of judicial campaigns, polarized voting along ethnic lines in the statewide or countywide races that are required of most judges, and low rates of minority participation in elections have minimized their electoral successes. The first Hispanic was seated on the Texas Supreme Court in 1984 and on the Court of Criminal Appeals in 1991. The first African American was seated on the Texas Court of Criminal Appeals in 1990 and on the Texas Supreme Court in 2001.

Another factor limiting the number of minority judges is a proportional shortage of minority attorneys, from whose ranks judges are drawn. State leaders' efforts to increase the number of minority lawyers were thwarted for several years by an anti-affirmative action federal court ruling in 1996 and a related state attorney general's opinion, which prohibited Texas law schools and universities from giving preferential treatment to minorities in admissions, student aid, and other programs. Those restrictions were eased in 2003, when the U.S. Supreme Court ruled that college admissions policies could include race as a factor, provided racial quotas weren't established (see *Up Close:* "An Attack on Affirmative Action").

As of February 1989, a few months before a major lawsuit went to trial over the issue, only 35 of 375 state district judges were Hispanic, and only 7 were African American. Only 3 Hispanics and no African Americans were among the 80 judges on the 14 intermediate courts of appeals. Although they constituted at least one-third of the Texas population, African Americans and Hispanics held only 11.2 percent of the district judgeships and less than 4 percent of the intermediate appellate seats.[24] African Americans sat on only 3 of the 59 district court benches in Harris County (Houston), although they accounted for 20 percent of that county's population. African Americans held only 2 of 36 district judgeships in Dallas County, where they made up 18 percent of the population. Hispanics held 3 district court seats in Houston and 1 in Dallas.

Three African American judges in Dallas, who had been appointed by Governor Mark White to fill judicial vacancies, had been unseated in countywide elections. One was Jesse Oliver, a former legislator who had won election to the Texas House from a subdistrict within Dallas County but could not win a 1988 judicial race countywide. Oliver, a Democrat, had overwhelming African American support but lost about 90 percent of Dallas's white precincts.[25]

In a lawsuit tried in September 1989 in federal district court in Midland, attorneys for the League of United Latin American Citizens (LULAC) and other minority plaintiffs argued that the countywide system of electing state district judges violated the Voting Rights Act by diluting the voting strength of minorities. That federal law allows a federal court to strike down an electoral system that denies a protected class of voters an equal opportunity to elect officeholders of their choice. This case, *League of United Latin American Citizens et al. v. Mattox et al.*, took almost five years and two appeals to the U.S. Supreme Court to resolve. It did not change Texas's judicial selection system, but a summary of the case and its bumpy journey through the judicial process highlights the political stakes involved in the issue.

In November 1989, U.S. District Judge Lucius Bunton ruled that the countywide system was illegal in nine of the state's largest counties—Harris, Dallas, Tarrant, Bexar, Travis, Jefferson, Lubbock, Ector, and Midland. Those counties elected 172 district judges, almost half of the state's total, but had only a handful of minorities serving on the district courts. Bunton did not order an immediate remedy but strongly urged the legislature to address the issue. After the legislature failed to act, Bunton the next year ordered judges in the nine counties to run for election from districts in nonpartisan elections. But the state won a stay of Bunton's order from the Fifth U.S. Circuit Court of Appeals, and partisan, countywide judicial elections were held as scheduled in 1990.

Ironically, one minority judge was outspoken in his opposition to district elections. State District Judge Felix Salazar of Houston did not seek reelection in 1990, at least in part because he disliked the prospect of having to run from a district rather than

UP CLOSE

An Attack on Affirmative Action

The power of the federal courts over state policy was clearly demonstrated by a reverse discrimination lawsuit filed by four white students who had been denied admission to the University of Texas School of Law. For a few years, it thwarted efforts to promote racial and ethnic diversity in some of Texas's colleges and universities. Ruling in the so-called *Hopwood* case, the Fifth U.S. Circuit Court of Appeals in 1996 said a law school admissions policy that had given preferences to minority applicants was unconstitutional. The decision later was upheld by the U.S. Supreme Court.* The nation's high court, however, did not reverse its earlier, landmark opinion in the *Bakke* case from California, which had held that race could be a factor in university admissions policies,† thus allowing other states to continue using affirmative action programs.

In a related legal opinion in 1997, Texas Attorney General Dan Morales held that the *Hopwood* restrictions applied to admissions, student aid, and all other student policies at all colleges and universities in Texas. Morales's opinion was attacked as overly broad by many civil rights leaders and minority legislators, but it had the force of law. The Texas Legislature, which met in 1997, attempted to soften the blow to affirmative action by enacting a new law that guaranteed automatic admissions to state universities for high school graduates who finished in the top 10 percent of their classes, regardless of their scores on college entrance examinations. The law was designed to give the best students from poor and predominantly minority school districts an equal footing in university admissions with better-prepared graduates of wealthier school districts. The new law also allowed university officials to consider other admissions criteria, including a student's family income and parents' education level.

There was little change in minority enrollments at many Texas universities after the *Hopwood* decision because many universities hadn't used race as a factor in admissions anyway. But the two largest—the University of Texas at Austin and Texas A&M University—did. The drop-off in minority enrollment was particularly troubling at the UT law school the first year after the *Hopwood* restrictions went into effect. The first-year law class of almost 500 students in the fall of 1997 included only four African Americans and twenty-five Hispanics. There had been thirty-one African Americans and forty-two Hispanics in the previous year's entering class. And the more flexible admissions standards set by the legislature applied only to entering undergraduate students, not to those seeking admission to law school and other professional schools.

Many higher education administrators and civil rights leaders said it was wrong to dismantle affirmative action programs that had been designed to improve the educational and professional opportunities of minorities, who had historically suffered from segregation and were still overrepresented among the nation's poor. They said it was particularly shortsighted to de-emphasize minority recruitment efforts at a time when Hispanics and African Americans were only a few years away from making up a majority of the Texas population.

But Morales urged university officials to redouble their efforts to recruit disadvantaged students of all races. "We must express to young Texans the reality that in this country one is capable of rising as high as his or her individual talents, ability and hard work will allow," he said.‡

The U.S. Supreme Court refused to hear two appeals by Texas of the Hopwood decision. But ruling in a separate case from Michigan in 2003, the high court held that college admissions policies could include race as a factor, provided the policies didn't set racial quotas. University officials in Texas then began revising admissions policies to once again include affirmative action.

***Hopwood v. Texas,* 135 L.Ed. 1095 (1996).

†*University of California Regents v. Bakke,* 438 U.S. 265 (1978).

‡Quoted in *Houston Chronicle,* February 7, 1997.

countywide. A Democrat, Salazar lived in a predominantly non-Hispanic white Houston neighborhood and in previous elections had been endorsed by a diversity of groups. He claimed that small districts could work against the interests of minorities because a judge from a conservative Anglo district could feel political pressure to sentence minority criminal defendants more harshly than whites. "The judge will have to espouse the feeling of the community. His district may think that's all right, and it will be hell unseating him," he told the *Houston Chronicle.*[26]

Other opponents of district elections argued that districts could also put undue pressure from minority communities on judges. But Jesse Oliver, the former African American legislator and judge who had been unseated in a countywide race in Dallas, did not agree that judicial districts would distort the administration of justice any more than countywide elections. "For one thing, if the community does exert pressure, then the white community is exerting all the pressure now because they are electing the judges in Dallas County," he said.[27]

Ruling in the Texas case and one from Louisiana in June 1991, the U.S. Supreme Court held that the Voting Rights Act applied to elections for the judiciary. But the high court did not strike down the at-large election system. "We believe that the state's interest in maintaining an electoral system—in this case, Texas's interest in maintaining the link between a district judge's (countywide) jurisdiction and the area of residency of his or her voters—is a legitimate factor to be considered" in determining whether the Voting Rights Act has been violated, the court wrote. But it also emphasized that the state's interest was only one factor to be considered and did not automatically outweigh proof of diluting minority votes.[28]

The U.S. Supreme Court returned the Texas lawsuit to the Fifth U.S. Circuit Court of Appeals for more deliberations, and, in January 1993, a three-judge panel of the Fifth Circuit ruled 2–1 that countywide elections illegally diluted the voting strength of minorities in eight counties—Harris, Dallas, Bexar, Tarrant, Jefferson, Lubbock, Ector, and Midland. Under pressure from minority legislators, Attorney General Dan Morales agreed to a settlement with the plaintiffs that would have required district elections for most of the judges in those counties and a ninth, Travis County. The settlement was endorsed by Governor Ann Richards, Democratic legislative leaders, and Democratic majorities in the Texas House and Senate. But it was opposed by Texas Supreme Court Chief Justice Thomas R. Phillips and state District Judges Sharolyn Wood of Houston and Harold Entz of Dallas, Republican defendants in the lawsuit.

The full Fifth Circuit rejected the settlement on a 9 to 4 vote in August 1993, holding that the "evidence of any dilution of minority voting power [in countywide judicial elections] is marginal at best."[29] The Fifth Circuit said partisan affiliation was a more significant factor than ethnicity in judicial elections. Then in January 1994, the U.S. Supreme Court brought the lawsuit to an end by upholding the Fifth Circuit's opinion. That left the issue of judicial selection in the hands of the Texas legislature, which for years had refused to change the elective system. State Senator Rodney Ellis, a Houston Democrat and a leading proponent of district elections, called the decision "devastating" and said it amounted to a "wholesale assault on civil rights." State District Judge Sharolyn Wood, a Houston Republican who had fought district elections, had a different reaction. "Hooray for Texas!" she said.[30]

By 1998, according to the most recent, complete data available, only 8 percent of the state judges at the county court level and higher were Hispanic and 2.5 percent were African American.[31]

Minority Judicial Appointments Democratic Governor Mark White appointed the first Hispanic, Raul A. Gonzalez, the son of migrant workers, to the Texas Supreme Court in 1984 to fill a vacancy created by a resignation. Gonzalez made history a second time in 1986 by winning election to the seat and becoming the first Hispanic to win a statewide election in Texas. A native of Weslaco in the Rio Grande Valley, Gonzalez had been a state district judge in Brownsville and had been appointed to the Thirteenth Court of Appeals in Corpus Christi by Republican Governor Bill Clements in 1981.

Raul A. Gonzalez, now retired, was the first Hispanic to serve on the Texas Supreme Court and the first Hispanic to win election to a statewide office in Texas.

Despite his background, Gonzalez, a Democrat, was one of the most conservative members of the Supreme Court during his tenure. Consequently, he came under frequent attack from plaintiffs' lawyers and, ironically, from many of the constituent groups within his own party who advocated increasing the number of minority judges. Gonzalez's reelection race in 1994, one of the most bitterly contested Supreme Court races in recent memory, proved that ethnicity can quickly take a back seat to judicial philosophy and partisanship.

Gonzalez defeated a strong challenge in the Democratic primary from Corpus Christi attorney Rene Haas, who was supported by trial lawyers, women's groups, consumer advocates, several key Democratic legislators, and a number of African-American and Hispanic leaders in the Democratic Party. Gonzalez drew heavy financial support from business interests, insurance companies, and defense attorneys. He had angered many Democrats by siding with the Republican justices in a 5–4 decision upholding a state senate redistricting plan that favored Republicans in the 1992 legislative elections. And he angered many women, as well as trial lawyers, by voting with the court majority in two cases overturning damages awarded women who had complained of being emotionally and physically abused by men.

Raul Gonzalez resigned from the Supreme Court in midterm in late 1998 and was replaced by Alberto R. Gonzales, an appointee of Governor George W. Bush and only the second Hispanic to serve on the high court. As had Raul Gonzalez, Alberto Gonzales came from a modest background. His parents were migrant workers when he was born in San Antonio, but they soon moved to Houston, where his father became a construction worker. The young Gonzales, one of eight children, joined the Air Force after graduating from high school, attended the Air Force Academy, and earned degrees from Rice University and Harvard Law School. He had never been a judge before Governor Bush named him to the Supreme Court. But he had been a partner in one of Houston's largest law firms, had been Bush's top staff lawyer, and had served under Bush as Texas secretary of state.

Alberto Gonzales' appointment came at a time when Governor Bush was actively trying to increase the Republican Party's appeal to Hispanics, and Bush acknowledged that it was important to him that Gonzales was Hispanic. "Of course, it mattered what his ethnicity is, but first and foremost what mattered is, I've got great confidence in Al. I know him well. He's a good friend. He'll do a fine job," Bush said.[32] Bush's confidence in Gonzales continued after Bush became president in 2001. He appointed Gonzales White House counsel. There also was speculation that Bush was grooming Gonzales for an appointment to the U.S. Supreme Court, if a vacancy occurred during the Bush administration.

On succeeding Bush, Republican Governor Rick Perry named minorities to the first two vacancies he had the opportunity to fill on the Texas Supreme Court in 2001. One was Wallace Jefferson, an appellate lawyer from San Antonio who became the first African American to serve on the high court. Perry named Jefferson to succeed Alberto Gonzales, who had resigned to take the White House job. Jefferson, a Republican, was the great-great-great grandson of a slave. Later the same

Morris Overstreet of Amarillo became the first African American to win a statewide election in Texas when he won a seat on the Court of Criminal Appeals in 1990. He served on the court until 1998, when, instead of seeking reelection, he lost a race for the Democratic nomination for Texas attorney general.

year, Perry appointed Xavier Rodriguez, a San Antonio labor lawyer, to the Supreme Court to succeed former Justice Greg Abbott, who had resigned to run for Texas attorney general. Rodriguez became the third Hispanic to serve on the court, but he was unseated in the 2002 Republican primary by Austin lawyer Steven Wayne Smith, an Anglo. Jefferson was elected in 2002 to keep his seat on the high court, and a second African American, Republican Dale Wainwright, a state district judge from Houston, was elected to an open Supreme Court seat the same year.

Governor Ann Richards appointed the first Hispanic, Fortunato P. Benavides, to the Texas Court of Criminal Appeals in 1991 to fill a vacancy. Benavides had been a justice on the Thirteenth Court of Appeals and a district judge and a county court-at-law judge in Hidalgo County. But his tenure on the statewide court was short-lived. He was narrowly unseated in 1992 by Republican Lawrence Meyers of Fort Worth, an Anglo, who became the first Republican elected to the criminal court. Benavides later was appointed by President Bill Clinton to the Fifth U.S. Circuit Court of Appeals.

Governor Bill Clements appointed the first African American, Louis Sturns, a Republican state district judge from Fort Worth, to the Texas Court of Criminal Appeals on March 16, 1990. Because the vacancy that Sturns filled had occurred after the 1990 party primaries, the State Republican Executive Committee put Sturns on the general election ballot as the GOP nominee for the seat. The State Democratic Executive Committee nominated another African American, Morris Overstreet, a county court-at-law judge from Amarillo. Overstreet narrowly defeated Sturns in the November general election to become the first African American elected to a statewide office in Texas. Overstreet served on the court until 1998, when, instead of seeking reelection, he lost a race for the Democratic nomination for Texas attorney general.

Women in the Judiciary The first woman to serve as a state district judge in Texas was Sarah T. Hughes of Dallas, who was appointed to the bench in 1935 by Governor James V. Allred and served until 1961, when she resigned to accept an appointment by President John F. Kennedy to the federal district bench. Ironically, Hughes is best known for swearing a grim-faced Lyndon B. Johnson into office aboard Air Force One on November 22, 1963, following Kennedy's assassination in Dallas.

Ruby Sondock of Houston was the first woman to serve on the Texas Supreme Court. She had been a state district judge before Governor Bill Clements named her to the high court on June 25, 1982, to fill a vacancy temporarily. Sondock chose not to seek election to the seat and served only a few months. She later returned to the district bench.

Democrat Rose Spector, a state district judge from San Antonio, became the first woman elected to the Supreme Court when she defeated Republican Justice Eugene Cook in 1992. In 2004, there were two women on the Supreme Court, including Justice Harriet O'Neill, who had unseated Spector in 1998.

In 1994, Republican Sharon Keller, a former Dallas County prosecutor, became the first woman elected to the Texas Court of Criminal Appeals. She was elected presiding judge in 2000. Four women, including Keller, were serving on the nine-member court in 2004. By that year, more than 160 women were judges at the county court level or higher in Texas.[33]

The Search for Solutions The debates and lawsuits over judicial elections and representation in Texas emphasize the significant role of the courts in policy making as well as day-to-day litigation. The composition of the courts makes a difference. Although some may argue that the role of a judge is simply to apply the law to the facts and issues of a specific case, judges bring to the courts their own values, philosophical views, and life experiences, and these factors serve to filter their interpretations of the law and determine the shape of justice for millions of people.

There is no one simple solution to all the problems and inequities outlined above. Strict limits on the amount of campaign funds that judges and judicial candidates could raise from lawyers and other special interests, for example, could reduce the appearance of influence peddling in the judiciary and temper the high-stakes war between the trial lawyers and the business community for philosophical control of the courts. Campaign finance reform could also help build or restore public confidence in the impartiality of the judiciary. Such reform, however, may not improve opportunities for minorities to win election to the bench. Nor would it shorten the long election ballots that discourage Texans from casting informed votes in judicial races.

The same shortcomings could be anticipated with nonpartisan judicial elections or a merit selection system—two frequently mentioned alternatives to Texas's system of partisan judicial elections. In nonpartisan elections, judges and judicial candidates would not run under Democratic, Republican, or other party labels. This arrangement would guard against partisan bickering on the multimember appellate courts and eliminate the possibility that a poorly qualified candidate could be swept into office by one-party, straight-ticket voting.

Under the merit selection plan (sometimes referred to as the Missouri Plan), the governor would appoint judges from lists of nominees recommended by nominating commissions. The appointed judges would have to run later in **retention elections** to keep their seats, but they would not have opponents on the ballot. Voters would simply decide whether a judge should remain in office or be removed, to be replaced by another gubernatorial appointee.

Texas was one of only eight states in 1998 with a partisan election system for judges. Fourteen states had nonpartisan judicial elections, while thirty-nine used some form of judicial nominating commission, usually in conjunction with a gubernatorial appointment. Only sixteen states, however, combined the use of nominating commissions with retention elections, as provided for in the Missouri Plan. Each alternative has its advantages, but none would necessarily eliminate undue political influence on the judiciary.

Under a merit selection system, interest groups could still apply pressure on the governor and the members of the committees making recommendations for appointments. Although a merit selection plan could be written to require the nominating panels to make ethnically diverse recommendations to the governor, that would not answer the question of how to structure the retention elections. Minority appointees could still be at a disadvantage in retention elections if they have to run countywide, rather than in smaller geographic districts. Despite their popularity among minority leaders, district elections for judges are still viewed by many decision makers as a form of **ward politics** that may be appropriate or desirable for legislative seats but not for judges. Judges, they argue, do not represent a particular constituency.

Attempts were made to overhaul the judicial selection process during recent legislative sessions, but they failed. In 1995, as discussed earlier in this chapter, lawmakers set modest limits on campaign contributions to judges and judicial candidates and restricted the periods during which judges and judicial candidates could accept political donations.

Sarah T. Hughes (center), the first woman to serve as a district judge in Texas, in 1961 was appointed a federal district court judge and in 1963 swore in Lyndon Johnson as president after John F. Kennedy was assassinated in Dallas.

retention elections Elections in which judges run on their own records rather than against other candidates. Voters cast their ballots on the question of whether the incumbent judge should stay in office.

ward politics Term, often with negative connotations, that refers to partisan politics linked to political favoritism.

Crime and Punishment

THINK AGAIN

Do you believe that the death penalty is "cruel and unusual punishment" in all circumstances?

Texas Department of Criminal Justice

This agency is responsible for the administration of the state's prison/jail system. Organizational data can be found at this site along with statistics and reports on the prison population, prison sites, paroles, and programs designed to prevent recidivism.
http://www.tdcj.state.tx.us

Under both the U.S. Constitution and the Texas Constitution, a person charged with a crime is presumed innocent until the state can prove guilt beyond a reasonable doubt to a judge or a jury. The state also has the burden to prosecute fairly—to follow principles of procedural due process outlined in constitutional and statutory law and interpreted by the courts. Even persons charged with the most heinous crimes retain these fundamental rights, and although there is often a public outcry about "coddling criminals," the process is designed to protect an individual from governmental abuses, to lessen the chance that an innocent person will be wrongly convicted of a crime.

In Texas, as well as in other states, these rights have sometimes been violated (see *Up Close:* "A Huge Injustice in Tulia"). But over the years, the federal courts, in particular, have strengthened their enforcement. Through a case-by-case process, the U.S. Supreme Court has applied the Bill of Rights to the states by way of the Due Process and the Equal Protection Clauses of the Fourteenth Amendment to the U.S. Constitution. The failure of police or prosecutors to comply with specific procedures for handling a person accused of a crime may result in charges against an individual being dropped or a conviction reversed on appeal.

Arrested suspects must be taken before a magistrate—usually a justice of the peace or a municipal court judge—to be formally informed of the offense or offenses with which they are charged and to be told their legal rights. Depending on the charges, a bond may be set to allow them to get out of jail and remain free pending their trials. They have the right to remain silent, to consult with an attorney and have an attorney present during questioning by law enforcement officers or prosecutors, and to be warned that any statement they make can be used against them in a trial. Defendants who cannot afford to hire a lawyer must be provided with court-appointed attorneys at taxpayer expense. Many of these protections were extended to the states by the U.S. Supreme Court in the landmark ***Miranda* ruling** in 1966.[34]

All criminal defendants have the right to a trial by jury but, except in capital murder cases, may waive a jury trial and have their cases decided by a judge. Defendants may plead guilty, not guilty, or **nolo contendere** (no contest). Prosecutors and defense attorneys settle many cases through plea bargaining, a process described earlier in this chapter. The trial judge does not have to accept a plea bargain but usually does. When defendants choose to have their guilt or innocence determined by the judge, the judge also determines the punishment if they are convicted. A jury can return a guilty verdict only if all jurors agree that the defendant is guilty beyond a reasonable doubt. If a jury cannot reach a unanimous verdict, even after lengthy negotiations and prodding from the judge, the judge must declare a mistrial. In that case, the prosecution has to seek a new trial with another jury or drop the charges. In a jury trial, a defendant may choose to have the punishment also set by the jury. If not, it is determined by the judge.

***Miranda* ruling** Far-reaching decision of the U.S. Supreme Court that requires law enforcement officers to warn a criminal suspect of his or her right to remain silent and have an attorney present before questioning.

nolo contendere Plea of "no contest" to a criminal charge.

In 1991, the Texas Court of Criminal Appeals took the major step of ordering, for the first time, an official definition of "reasonable doubt" that was to be submitted to every jury deciding a criminal case. According to the definition, evidence against a criminal defendant had to be so convincing that jurors would be willing to rely upon it "without hesitation" in the most important events in their own lives.[35] But, reflecting a change in philosophy, a more conservative Court of Criminal Appeals eliminated that definition in 2000, to the dismay of some criminal defense

UP CLOSE

A Huge Injustice in Tulia

What began as a drug sting in Tulia, a small town in the Texas Panhandle, quickly escalated into one of the biggest miscarriages of justice in recent Texas history. After belated, but intense, media coverage, help finally arrived for thirty-five victims, but not before they had paid a high price.

In July 1999, forty-six Tulia residents, including thirty-nine African Americans, were arrested on drug charges. Thirty-eight of the defendants were later convicted, all on the testimony of Tom Coleman, an undercover officer and the only prosecution witness against them. After the *Texas Observer* newspaper, followed by other media, focused attention on the arrests and raised questions about whether they were racially motivated, special evidentiary hearings into the drug sting were convened in March 2003. Retired state District Judge Ron Chapman of Dallas presided over the hearings, during which Coleman's testimony was discredited. Chapman recommended that the Texas Court of Criminal Appeals overturn all thirty-eight convictions. In a separate proceeding, Coleman was later indicted on three counts of perjury stemming from his testimony before Chapman.

The Texas Legislature then stepped in, passing a law that allowed fourteen Tulia defendants who were still in prison to be released on bond while the Court of Criminal Appeals considered their cases. And, finally, Governor Rick Perry pardoned thirty-five of the defendants in August 2003, more than four years after their arrests. "Questions surrounding testimony from the key witnesses in these cases, coupled with recommendations from the Board of Pardons and Paroles, weighed heavily in my final decision," the governor said. "Texans demand a system that is tough but fair. I believe my decision to grant pardons in these cases is both appropriate and just," he added. Perry's office said three of the Tulia defendants weren't eligible for pardons.

Jeff Blackburn of Amarillo, an attorney for the Tulia defendants, also filed a civil lawsuit in federal court, seeking damages against a regional drug task force and several local government officials in Swisher County, where Tulia is located. Will Harrell, executive director for Texas of the American Civil Liberties Union, said systemic flaws in the criminal justice system, such as police misconduct, abuse of authority and inadequate legal representation of the poor, still needed to be addressed.

Source: Houston Chronicle, August 23, 2003, p. 1A.

lawyers. "We find the better practice is to give no definition of reasonable doubt at all to the jury," said the new opinion written by Judge Mike Keasler.[36]

Jury trials are required in **capital murder** cases, which are punishable by death or life in prison. Executions in Texas used to be carried out by electrocution at the state prison unit in downtown Huntsville. Some 361 individuals were executed in Texas from 1924 to 1964, when executions were suspended because of legal challenges.

In 1972, the U.S. Supreme Court halted executions in all the states by striking down all the death penalty laws then on the books as unconstitutional. The high court held that capital punishment, as then practiced, violated the constitutional prohibition against "cruel and unusual punishment" because it could be applied in a discriminatory fashion.[37] Not only could virtually any act of murder be punished by death under the old Texas law, but so could rape and certain other crimes.

In 1973, the Texas legislature rewrote the death penalty statute to try to meet the Supreme Court's standards by defining capital crimes as murder committed under specific circumstances. The list was expanded later and now includes the murder of a law enforcement officer or firefighter who is on duty, murder committed during the course of committing certain other major crimes, murder for hire, murdering more than one person, murder of a prison guard or employee, murder committed while escaping or attempting to escape from a penal institution, or murder of a child younger than six.

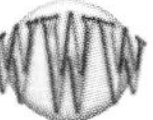

Bureau of Justice Statistics

The Bureau of Justice Statistics, a division of the U.S. Department of Justice, is a primary source for criminal justice statistics in the United States.
http://www.ojp.usdoj.gov/bjs

capital murder Murder committed under certain circumstances for which the death penalty or life in prison must be imposed.

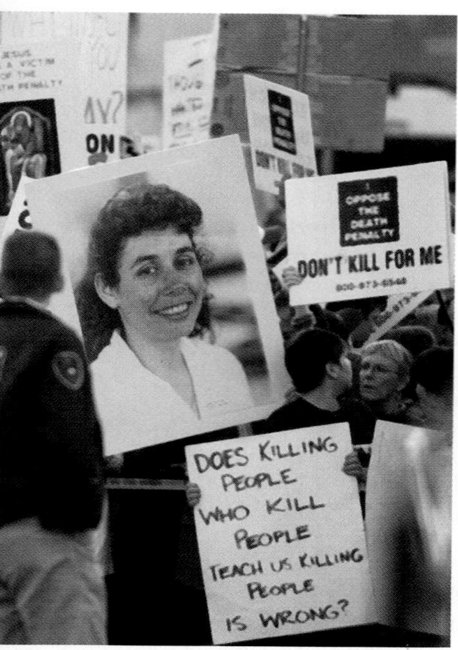

Death penalty protesters outside the Huntsville prison on the occasion of the execution of Karla Faye Tucker, the first woman to be put to death in Texas since the Civil War.

A jury that has found a person guilty of capital murder must answer certain questions about the defendant before choosing between death or life imprisonment, the only punishments available. Jurors are required to consider whether a convicted murderer will be a continuing danger to society as well as mitigating circumstances, including evidence of mental retardation, before deciding punishment.[38]

The first execution under the 1973 Texas law was carried out in 1982. By then the legislature, acting in 1977, had changed the method of execution from the electric chair to the intravenous injection of a lethal substance. By 2004, more than 300 men and two women had been executed in Texas by lethal injection. Karla Faye Tucker, the first woman executed in Texas since the Civil War, was put to death in 1998 for killing two people with a pickax almost fifteen years earlier. The second woman was executed in early 2000 for the murder of her husband.

After considerable controversy in Texas and other states, the U.S. Supreme Court in June 2002 banned the execution of mentally retarded convicts. Death penalty opponents had argued that before the high court ruling Texas had executed at least six inmates who were demonstrably retarded. The Texas Legislature, in its first session after the Supreme Court ban, failed to revise its death penalty statute to comply with the court's order, requiring defense attorneys to continue the battle, case by case. Some feared that, without new state guidelines for evaluating and trying convicts, additional mentally retarded persons would be executed in Texas, despite the Supreme Court's ban.[39]

After capital murder, the most serious criminal offense is a first-degree felony—for example, aggravated sexual assault and non-capital murder—punishable by a prison sentence of five to ninety-nine years or life. Second-degree felonies, such as burglary of someone's home and bribery, are punishable by two to twenty years in prison. Third-degree felonies—including intentional bodily injury to a child and theft of trade secrets—are punishable by two to ten years in prison. State jail felonies—which include many property crimes, such as burglary of an office building, and minor drug offenses—are punishable by up to two years in a state-run jail or time in a community corrections program, each of which is supposed to emphasize rehabilitation as well as punishment.

The most minor crimes are classified as Class A, B, or C misdemeanors. Crimes such as public lewdness and harboring a runaway child are examples of Class A misdemeanors and are punishable by a maximum $4,000 fine and/or one year in a county jail. The unauthorized use of television cable decoding equipment or falsely claiming to be a police officer are examples of Class B misdemeanors and carry a maximum sentence of 180 days in a county jail and a $2,000 fine. Class C misdemeanors include illegal gambling and the issuance of a bad check. They are punishable by a maximum $500 fine.

People convicted of crimes can be sentenced to **probation** (also called community supervision): they are not sent to prison but must meet certain conditions, such as restrictions on where they travel and with whom they associate. Except for those under the death penalty, convicted felons sentenced to prison can become eligible for **parole**—or early release under supervisory restrictions—after serving a portion of their sentence. Capital murderers sentenced to life in prison can be considered for parole after serving forty years. Parole decisions are made by the Board of Pardons and Paroles, which is appointed by the governor.

probation Procedure under which a convicted criminal is not sent to prison if he or she meets certain conditions, such as restrictions on travel and associates.

parole Early release of an inmate from prison, subject to certain conditions.

A landmark federal court order in 1980 forced the state to spend billions of dollars expanding and improving its prison system and forced the legislature to reevaluate the punishment of some criminals (see *Up Close:* "Criminal Justice, an Expensive Headache").

Texas now executes prisoners by lethal injection.

The Politics of Criminal Justice

The Texas Court of Criminal Appeals must try to balance the constitutional rights of convicts against the public welfare, a role that puts the court at the center of major philosophical and political battles.

The combatants on one side of the debate include the prosecutors—the elected district and county attorneys—who do not like to see the convictions they have won reversed, partly because too many reversals could cost them reelection. Judges

UP CLOSE

Criminal Justice, an Expensive Headache

An overcrowded and inadequately staffed prison system prompted U.S. District Judge William Wayne Justice of Tyler to declare Texas's prisons unconstitutional in 1980 in a landmark lawsuit brought by inmates (*Ruiz v. Estelle*). Among other things, the court ordered the population of prison units limited to 95 percent of capacity. That limit and an increase in the violent crime rate in the 1980s helped produce a criminal justice crisis that saw hundreds of dangerous convicts released from prison early and thousands of other criminals backlogged in overcrowded county jails.

The Ruiz lawsuit was settled in 1992, with the state promising to maintain constitutional prisons. In 1993 the legislature enacted a major package of criminal justice reforms. The minimum time that violent criminals would have to serve in prison before being eligible for parole was doubled—from one-fourth to one-half of their sentences. To make sure there was enough room to keep the most dangerous felons in prison longer, thousands of property and drug offenders were to be diverted into community corrections programs or a new system of state jails, where education, drug abuse treatment, and other rehabilitation programs were to be emphasized.

Financed by bond issues totaling $3 billion, a huge prison expansion program was completed in the mid-1990s. With more than 140,000 spaces, Texas finally had enough room for all its prisoners in its corrections system. Some counties had sufficient jail space to permit them to lease space to house convicts from other states. But criminal justice experts warned that the relief was only temporary, and before long, lower parole rates and long prison sentences were once again taking their toll on the state's resources.

Texas Juvenile Probation Commission

This agency works with local juvenile probation departments to rehabilitate juvenile offenders. This site provides information about state funding, standards, training, certification, and monitoring of caseworkers, and statistics on juvenile offenders.

http://www.tjpc.state.tx.us

Texas Youth Commission

The Texas Youth Commission is responsible for "secure care, custody and control of juveniles who are committed to state custody" for criminal behavior. This site includes information on facilities, programs, correctional treatment, and juvenile crime in Texas.

http://www.tyc.state.tx.us

of the trial courts, who also periodically face the voters, are sensitive to reversals, too. So are the police and sheriffs' departments that arrest the defendants and provide the evidence on which criminal convictions are based.

On the other side of the debate are defense attorneys, who have an obligation to protect the rights and interests of their clients and who in their appeals often attack procedures used by police, prosecutors, and trial judges. Also on this side are civil libertarians, who insist that a criminal defendant's every right—even the most technical—be protected, and minority groups, who have challenged the conduct of trials when minorities have been excluded from juries weighing the fate of minority defendants (see *Up Close:* "More Is Involved than Technicalities").

Throughout much of its early history, the Texas Court of Criminal Appeals was accused of excessive concern with legal technicalities that benefited convicted criminals.[40] The court reversed 42 percent of the cases appealed to it during the first quarter of the twentieth century, when Texas and many other states had a harsh system of criminal justice that often reflected class and racial bias at the trial level. By 1966, the reversal rate had dropped to 3 percent. But changes in the court's makeup and changes in political attitudes produced fluctuations in that record in subsequent years.

The court signaled a shift toward a conservative philosophy after the 1994 elections of Judges Sharon Keller and Steve Mansfield had increased the number of Republicans on the court to three. During the first thirteen months the new judges were in office, for example, the court ordered the reinstatement of two death sentences it had reversed before Keller's and Mansfield's arrival. The court's conservatism was solidified with a Republican sweep of all three court seats on the 1996 ballot. A 6-to-3 Democratic majority had become a 6-to-3 Republican majority, the first GOP majority on the court since Reconstruction. Republicans increased their majority to 7–2 in 1997, when longtime Presiding Judge Mike McCormick, one of the court's most conservative members, switched from the Democratic to the Republican Party. The Republican takeover of the court was completed in 1998, when

UP CLOSE

More Is Involved than Technicalities

Randall Dale Adams and Clarence Lee Brandley owe their lives to the appellate process. Both men came perilously close to being executed for murders they apparently did not commit. Adams spent more than a decade behind bars before he was released in 1989, after a documentary film indicated he had been wrongfully convicted of the murder of a Dallas police officer. The Texas Court of Criminal Appeals ordered a new trial, but the Dallas County district attorney chose not to retry him.

Brandley, an African American janitor at Conroe High School, was convicted by an all-white jury of the rape and murder of a sixteen-year-old girl, but the Court of Criminal Appeals reversed the conviction after being presented with evidence that Brandley had not received a fair trial and had been a victim of racial prejudice. Neither man would have lived long enough to win freedom had not the appellate process, which many prosecutors attack as too time-consuming and too "technical," worked to delay their scheduled executions.

WHAT DO YOU THINK?

Can Justice Afford a Nap?

Justice is supposed to be blind, but it isn't supposed to be asleep. At least that was the conclusion of one of the more controversial death penalty convictions to emerge from Texas in recent years. Calvin Burdine was convicted and sentenced to death for the 1983 murder of his roommate. W.T. "Dub" Wise. His conviction was upheld by the Texas Court of Criminal Appeals, and he spent eighteen years on death row before the Fifth U.S. Circuit Court of Appeals overturned the sentence because Burdine's defense attorney had slept through portions of his trial. In a plea bargain with prosecutors, Burdine then was sentenced to life in prison.

Source: Houston Chronicle, June 20, 2003, p. 29A.

Democrats lost their last two seats on the panel. McCormick did not seek reelection in 2000 and was replaced as presiding judge by Sharon Keller, a former prosecutor.

After the GOP takeover, the Court of Criminal Appeals quickly began compiling a strong, pro-prosecutorial record, particularly in death penalty cases. The court upheld a number of death sentences that later were overturned by federal courts. In one case, later reversed by a federal court, it affirmed a capital conviction even though the defendant's attorney had slept through part of his trial (see *What Do You Think?*: "Can Justice Afford a Nap?"). In another case, it upheld a death sentence despite the fact that a prosecution witness had argued improperly that the defendant was a future danger to society partly because he was Hispanic. That ruling prompted then-Texas Attorney General John Cornyn, a Republican and strong law-and-order advocate, to admit to the U.S. Supreme Court that the prosecution had committed reversible error in the case. Such rulings prompted defense lawyers and civil libertarians to heap much criticism upon the court. "They're so far gone they're barely even a court anymore," lawyer Jeff Blackburn of Amarillo said in an interview with the *Houston Chronicle.*[41]

Increased Policy Role of the State Courts

The federal judiciary has traditionally had more influence than the state courts in molding public policy. Over the years, it has been at the center of political debate over the proper role of the judiciary in the policy-making process (see Chapter 13).

Much of the Texas Supreme Court's time is spent refereeing disputes between trial lawyers and insurance companies. But in recent years this court has sometimes played an active role in shaping broader public policies and addressing significant constitutional issues (see *Up Close:* "The Constitution Is for Everybody").

The Courts and Education In one of its most significant and best-known rulings, the Texas Supreme Court in the Edgewood school finance case in 1989 unanimously ordered major, basic changes in the financing of public education to provide more equity between rich and poor school districts.[42] The lawsuit was brought against the state by poor districts after years of legislative inaction against a property tax–based finance system that had produced huge disparities in local education resources and in the quality of local schools.

UP CLOSE

The Constitution Is for Everybody

The Texas Supreme Court ruled in 1994 that a Ku Klux Klan leader had a constitutional right to keep Klan membership lists secret. The high court held that a state district judge had illegally jailed Michael Lowe for refusing to turn over the membership lists to state officials investigating the harassment and intimidation of African Americans attempting to desegregate a public housing project in Vidor. "The rights to form, discuss and express unpopular views are protected fundamental rights," the court said. "Where the organization advocates views which might subject members to ridicule . . . from the mere fact of membership, First Amendment associational rights are the basis for a qualified privilege against disclosure of membership lists."*

In an unusual twist, the white supremacist was represented by an African American civil liberties lawyer, Anthony Griffin of Galveston. Griffin, who took the case at the request of the American Civil Liberties Union, said he was "ecstatic" about the court's ruling. "I think it's a wonderful opinion for the state Supreme Court to reaffirm the virtue of the First Amendment," he said.†

Ex Parte Lowe, 887 S.W.2d 1 (1994).

†Quoted in *Houston Chronicle*, June 9, 1994, p. 1A.

The unanimity of the opinion, written by Justice Oscar Mauzy, a Democrat, surprised many legislators and school officials because two of the three Republican justices on the court at that time had initially been appointed by Governor Bill Clements, who had insisted that the courts had no business trying to tell the legislature what to do about school finance. The decision, which held that the school finance law violated a constitutional requirement for an efficient education system, was obviously the product of considerable compromise among the nine justices. Their deliberations were secret, but Justice Franklin Spears, a Democrat, told the *Fort Worth Star-Telegram*: "We wanted to speak with one voice. The opinion is a composite of many ideas, much brainstorming, much compromising." Mark Yudof, then dean of the University of Texas School of Law, said the court may have been determined to offer a united front because it attached as much importance to the school finance case as a united U.S. Supreme Court had to the landmark *Brown v. Board of Education of Topeka* desegregation case in the 1950s.[43]

Compliance with the school finance order did not come easily, however. A 1990 school finance law failed to meet the court's standards, so the court issued another order in 1991 and a third order in 1992 after the legislature again came up short. The court lost its unanimity on the third order, which struck down a 1991 law that had established special county education districts with a minimum property tax. In a challenge brought this time by wealthy school districts, a 7–2 court majority ruled that the tax was a statewide property tax prohibited by the Texas Constitution. Mauzy and fellow Democratic Justice Lloyd Doggett sharply dissented.

The legislature responded with still another school finance law in 1993. This law gave wealthy school districts several options for sharing revenue with poor districts, and it was challenged by both rich and poor districts. The rich districts objected to sharing their property wealth, while the poor districts argued that the new law was inadequately funded and did not sufficiently reduce the funding gap between rich and poor districts. The Texas Supreme Court upheld the law in a 5–4 decision in January 1995. By that time, a majority of the court's members were Republicans. In the majority opinion, Justice John Cornyn, a Republican, wrote:

> Children who live in property-poor districts and children who live in property-rich districts now have substantially equal access to the funds necessary for a general diffusion of knowledge. It is apparent from the court's opinions that we have recognized that an efficient system does not require equality of access to revenue at all levels.[44]

But Republican Justice Craig Enoch, who dissented, wrote that the state had failed to adequately provide for the public schools. He said the new law contributed to further "constitutional tensions" by promoting continued use of local property taxes.[45]

By 2003, the school finance law was under attack again, this time from school districts contending that the "Robin Hood" share-the-wealth requirement and inadequate state aid were forcing many districts to raise local school maintenance tax rates to the maximum $1.50 per $100 valuation. They argued that amounted to an unconstitutional statewide property tax.

In 1992, a state district judge in Brownsville ruled that the state's system of funding higher education also was unconstitutional because it shortchanged Hispanics in South Texas. But the Texas Supreme Court reversed that decision and upheld the higher education system.[46]

In another education case with major implications, the Texas Supreme Court in 1994 upheld the right of Texas parents to educate their own children. Ending a ten-year legal battle, the court overturned a Texas Education Agency ruling that home schools were illegal. The court held that a home school was legitimate if parents used books, workbooks, or other written materials and met "basic education goals" by teaching basic subjects.[47]

The Courts and Abortion Rights In 1998, the Texas Supreme Court upheld $1.2 million in damages against anti-abortion protesters who had staged massive demonstrations at Houston abortion clinics during the 1992 Republican National Convention. Some clinics had been vandalized and patients harassed. The high court also upheld most of the restrictions a lower court had set on protests near the clinics and the homes of several doctors who performed abortions. The court said it was trying to balance free speech rights with the rights of the clinics to conduct business, the rights of women to have access to pregnancy counseling and abortion services, and privacy rights of physicians. The court prohibited demonstrators from blocking access to clinics, intimidating patients, and engaging in other forms of aggressive behavior.[48] In a case from Florida, the U.S. Supreme Court had ruled in 1994 that judges could limit protests near abortion clinics but that restrictions had to be strictly limited.[49]

The Texas Supreme Court became embroiled in the abortion issue again in 2000 after a state law went into effect requiring parents to be notified by the doctors before their minor daughters could have abortions. The law included a "judicial bypass" provision, giving a young woman who didn't want her parents to be told an opportunity to convince a judge that she was mature and well-informed enough to make an abortion decision by herself or that notifying her parents would be harmful. Acting on several early cases, the Texas Supreme Court set guidelines for district judges to follow in making bypass decisions.

In another abortion case, decided in 2002, the Texas Supreme Court held that the state's refusal to pay for medically necessary abortions for poor women didn't violate the Texas Constitution. The court ruled that the restriction on funding abortions for women on Medicaid didn't discriminate by gender and advanced a legitimate governmental interest of favoring childbirth over abortion.

The Courts and Gay Rights Deciding still another controversial issue, the Texas Supreme Court in 1996 ruled against the Log Cabin Republicans, a gay GOP group that had been denied a booth at the Republican State Convention in San Antonio. The court said the group had no grounds to sue the Republican Party for deprivation of rights under the Texas Constitution because the party was not a governmental agency.[50]

SUMMARY NOTES

- Texas has a confusing array of courts, many with overlapping jurisdictions. It is one of only two states with a bifurcated court system at the highest appellate level. The Texas Supreme Court is the court of last resort in civil cases and the Texas Court of Criminal Appeals in criminal cases.
- The judicial system is particularly inadequate in urban counties, where thousands of criminal cases each year are disposed of through plea bargains negotiated by prosecutors and defendants and where it can take years to resolve civil disputes that are not settled out of court.
- State judges, except those on municipal court benches, are elected in partisan elections. But there has been increasing political and legal pressure to change the selection process. Possible alternatives are nonpartisan elections, elections from geographic districts, or a merit selection plan under which the governor would appoint judges from lists of nominees recommended by experts. The latter plan would require the appointed judges to run later in retention elections to keep their seats, but they would not have opponents on the ballot.
- Grand juries are supposed to ensure that the government has sufficient evidence to proceed with a criminal prosecution against an individual. Petit, or trial, juries hear evidence and render verdicts in cases involving both civil and criminal matters.
- Litigants in civil cases and most criminal cases can waive a jury trial and have their cases decided by a judge. Trials move through opening statements, examination and cross-examination of witnesses, presentation of evidence, rebuttal, summation, and verdict.
- Cases can be appealed to appellate courts, where there are no juries. Appellate courts review the decisions and procedures of lower courts for conformity to constitutional and statutory requirements.
- Judges who espouse strict construction believe their role to be one of narrowly interpreting and applying the law while leaving public policy initiatives to the legislature. Judicial activists believe their role to be one of taking a more expansive view of the law by reading broad policy implications into their decisions.
- The Texas Supreme Court became a battleground in the 1980s between trial attorneys who represent injured parties, or plaintiffs, in damage lawsuits and the businesses, doctors, and insurance companies they sue. After trial lawyers began contributing millions of dollars to successful Supreme Court candidates, longtime judicial precedents that had favored the corporate establishment began to fall, and it became easier for plaintiffs to win huge damage awards.
- The business and medical communities retaliated by winning some legislative changes in the procedures under which lawsuits are tried and by increasing their political contributions in judicial races.
- Party realignment, including appointments by Governor Bill Clements to fill midterm vacancies, increased the number of Republican judges on trial courts in the 1980s. The philosophical confrontation gave Republicans, with support from the business and medical communities, their first majority on the Texas Supreme Court in modern times.
- Only a handful of women and minorities have ever served on the state's highest appellate courts, and historically they have been underrepresented on the lower-court benches as well. In a lawsuit by minority plaintiffs, U.S. District Judge Lucius Bunton of Midland ruled in 1989 that the countywide system of electing district, or trial, judges in nine of the state's largest counties violated the federal Voting Rights Act by diluting the voting strength of minorities. But that ruling was reversed by the U.S. Supreme Court in 1994.
- The Texas Court of Criminal Appeals is at the center of philosophical and political disputes as it weighs the constitutional rights of convicted criminals against public concern about crime.
- The federal judiciary has traditionally had more influence than the state courts in molding public policy. But in recent years the Texas Supreme Court has sometimes played an active role in addressing significant constitutional issues.

KEY TERMS

penal code 676
felony 676
misdemeanor 676
civil lawsuit 676
statutes 676
plaintiff 676
original jurisdiction 677
appellate jurisdiction 677
bifurcated court system 677
municipal court 677
ordinances 677
de novo 677
justice of the peace court 679
constitutional county court 679
statutory county court 680
district court 680
plea bargaining 681
court of appeals 681
Texas Supreme Court 682
Texas Court of Criminal Appeals 682
grand jury 684
prosecution 684
indictment 684
information 684
petit jury 684
veniremen 685
petition for review 686
writ of mandamus 687
merit selection 690
tort reform 692
retention elections 699
ward politics 699
Miranda ruling 700
nolo contendere 700
capital murder 701
probation 702
parole 702

SUGGESTED READINGS

Baum, Lawrence. "Supreme Courts in the Policy Process." In *The State of the States*, ed. Carl E. Van Horn (Washington, D.C.: Congressional Quarterly Press, 1996), pp. 143–60. Recent state court decisions indicate increased judicial activism producing a counterreaction by those adversely affected by the actions of the courts.

Champagne, Anthony. "Judicial Selection in Texas: Democracy's Deadlock." In *Texas Politics: A Reader*, eds. Anthony Champagne and Edward J. Harpham (New York: W.W. Norton, 1997), pp. 97–110. Addresses issues and problems related to the partisan selection of Texas state judges.

Hill, John. "Taking Texas Judges Out of Politics: An Argument for Merit Election." *Baylor Law Review* 40 (Summer 1988): 340–66. A former Chief Justice of the Texas Supreme Court argues for nonpartisan elections of state judges.

Jacob, Herbert, "Courts: The Invisible Branch." In *Politics in the American States: A Comparative Analysis*, 6th ed. Ed. Virginia Gray and Herbert Jacob. Washington, D.C.: CQ Press, 1996: 253–85. A comparative analysis of state court systems.

Texas Judicial Council, Office of Court Administration. *Texas Judicial System, 75th Annual Report.* Austin: Texas Judicial Council, 2003. Annual compilation of data on the activities of state courts.

Texas Research League. *The Texas Judiciary: A Structural-Functional Overview.* Report 1. Austin: Texas Research League, 1990. Describes the court structure of Texas with a focus on its primary weaknesses.

Texas Research League. *Texas Courts: A Proposal for Structural-Functional Reform.* Report 2. Austin: Texas Research League, 1991. Recommendations for a major overhaul of the state's court system.

CHAPTER 21

LOCAL GOVERNMENT IN TEXAS: CITIES, TOWNS, COUNTIES, AND SPECIAL DISTRICTS

CHAPTER OUTLINE

The Legacy of Local Government

Local Governments in the Texas Political System

Municipal Government in Texas

Forms of City Government in Texas

Municipal Election Systems

City Revenues and Expenditures

Urban Problems in Texas

County Government in Texas

Criticisms of County Government

Special Districts in Texas

Independent School Districts

Councils of Government

Solutions to the Problems of Local Government

THINK ABOUT POLITICS

1 Are local governments more responsive to their citizens than the national government?
Yes ● No ●

2 Should cities be able to choose any form of government they want?
Yes ● No ●

3 Would we get more qualified elected officials if candidates ran without party labels?
Yes ● No ●

4 Should Texas cities have the power to enact a local income tax to replace the sales and property tax?
Yes ● No ●

5 Should every county in Texas be required to use the same form of government?
Yes ● No ●

6 Should Texas enact laws giving school districts greater authority over local education?
Yes ● No ●

7 With so many special districts in Texas, should the state attempt to consolidate local governments into larger, more comprehensive governmental units?
Yes ● No ●

Local governments are often described as the governments closest to the people, but constitutional and legislative restrictions often hamper them in their efforts to carry out their basic responsibilities. How can local government be improved, and is there the political interest or will to make such improvements?

The Legacy of Local Government

Texans have an affinity for local government. There are more than 4,700 local governments, of all sizes, across the state. Some operate with a handful of employees and budgets of one or two hundred thousand dollars a year, while others have tens of thousands of employees with billion dollar-plus budgets. Their governmental structures range from the simple to the complex. Some special districts perform one basic function, while large cities perform any number of services that are limited only by budgetary and legal restraints. Some counties have fewer than 1,000 people, and others have more than two million residents. One school district in West Texas has only twenty students, while the Houston Independent School District has more than 200,000. Three of the ten largest cities in the United States are in Texas, but many cities across the state have fewer than 1,000 residents.

The key to understanding local governments in Texas is to understand what responsibilities have been assigned to them by the Texas constitution and statutory law. Once the institutional structures and functions of local governments have been studied, attention will be directed to a number of core problems confronting them and their political capacities to address these issues. Throughout this analysis will be two underlying themes—what changes can make local governments more effective, and is it possible or desirable to reduce the fragmentation in local governments?

A tradition of localism is rooted in the fabric of our political history. Since the founding of the nation, Americans have expressed a strong belief in the right to local self-government.[1] In many areas of the young country, local governments existed long before there was a viable state or federal government. Early communities had to fend for themselves and had limited expectations of services or protections to be provided by state or federal governments.

This history of local self-help has led to the popular notion that local governments have fundamental rights based on the concept of local sovereignty, or ultimate power. Thomas Jefferson, for example, developed a theory of local government, designed in part to strengthen the powers of

THINK AGAIN

Are local governments more responsive to their citizens than the national government?

the states, in which local sovereignty was rooted in the sovereignty of the individual.[2] Some scholars suggest that this cultural legacy persists in grass-roots politics, the flight to suburbia, and the creation of neighborhood organizations. Today it is common to hear the argument that local government is closest to the people and best represents their interests and desires.[3]

Although this view is widely held, the prevailing constitutional theory on the relationship of local governments to the state is the **unitary system.** Simply stated, this theory holds that local governments are the creations of the state. The powers, functions, and responsibilities that they exercise have been delegated or granted them by the state government, and no local government has sovereign powers. There have been numerous court cases enunciating this principle, which is referred to as the **Dillon rule,** but the best summary is derived from an Iowa case in which a court held the following:

> The true view is this: Municipal corporations owe their origin to, and derive their powers and rights wholly from, the legislature. It breathes into them the breath of life, without which they cannot exist. As it creates, so it may destroy. If it may destroy, it may abridge and control. Unless there is some constitutional limitation on the right, the legislature might by a single act sweep from its existence all of the municipal corporations in the State, and the corporations could not prevent it. We know of no limitation on this right so far as the corporations are concerned.[4]

The Dillon rule is now the prevailing theory defining the relationships of states and local governments, and it is applicable to local governments in Texas.

WWW **State of Texas** This site provides access to websites for all counties in Texas as well as the Councils of Government. Select cities have developed web pages that can also be accessed through this site. Information varies, with some sites providing more comprehensive information than others.
http://www.state.tx.us

Local Governments in the Texas Political System

Local governments—counties, cities, school districts, and special districts—are created by the state and operate under limits set by the Texas Constitution and the legislature. They have found their capabilities and resources increasingly burdened by the pressing needs of a growing, urban state. Some of this pressure has come from the state and federal governments ordering or mandating significant improvements in environmental, educational, health, and other programs but letting cities, counties, and school districts pick up much of the tab. Prior to the state's commitment to an extensive prison construction program in the 1990s, for example, the Texas government forced counties to spend millions of local taxpayer dollars to house state prisoners in county jails because it had failed to adequately address a criminal justice crisis. Local school districts and their property tax payers also are at the mercy of the legislature, which has ordered expensive educational programs and has raised classroom standards without fully paying for them. Cities, too, find their budgetary problems exacerbated by state mandates. Local governments are the governments closest to the people, but they have to shoulder much of the responsibility—and often take much of the public outrage—for policy decisions made in Austin and Washington.

Although the legal position expressed by the Dillon rule subordinates local governments to the state, there are practical and political limitations on what the state can do with local governments. More importantly, the state relies on local governments to carry out many of its responsibilities.[5]

THINK AGAIN

Should cities be able to choose any form of government they want?

unitary system Constitutional arrangement whereby authority rests with the central government; regional governments have only those powers given them by the central government.

Dillon rule Principle holding that local governments are creations of state government and that their powers and responsibilities are defined by the state.

TABLE 21.1 Governments in the United States and Texas, 2002

	U.S.	Texas
U.S. Government	1	—
State Government	50	1
Counties	3,034	254
Municipalities	19,429	1,196
Townships and Towns	16,504	—
School Districts	13,506	1,089
Special Districts	35,052	2,245
Total	**87,576**	**4,785**

Source: U.S. Department of Commerce, Bureau of the Census, 2002 *Census of Governments*, vol. 1, Government Organizations, table 3.

Texas granted cities home rule authority in 1912. Home rule cities, discussed in more detail below, have considerable authority and discretion over their own local policies, but within limits set by state law. Texas voters approved a constitutional amendment in 1933 that also gave counties home rule authority, but no county established home rule government before the amendment was repealed in 1969.[6] County home rule provisions were again introduced in the 1997 and 1999 legislative sessions by several urban legislators but were defeated because of opposition from a variety of state and local interests.

In a 1980 study, the Advisory Commission on Intergovernmental Relations ranked the states according to the discretionary authority they granted to their local governments. Texas ranked eleventh in a composite ranking that included all local subdivisions—cities, counties, school districts, and other special districts. But Texas ranked forty-third, or near the bottom, in the discretionary authority given to its counties alone, while ranking first in the discretionary authority given to its cities.[7]

The states vary considerably in the major responsibilities assigned to different levels of government. Texas, like most other states, assigns the primary responsibility for public education to local school districts while retaining the primary responsibility for highways, public welfare, and public health at the state level. Police and fire protection, water and sanitation services, parks, recreation, and libraries are the primary responsibility of city governments. Public hospitals are a shared function of the state, county, and special districts.[8] Texas counties share with the state a primary responsibility for the court and criminal justice system. Altogether, there are some 4,700 local governments in Texas (see Table 21.1).

Texas Municipal League

The purpose of this organization is to provide services to Texas cities. In addition to providing links to twenty-two affiliate organizations, this site provides information on the association's publications, programs, and services, including its legislative policy program. ***http://www.tml.org***

Municipal Government in Texas

Despite popular images of wide open spaces dotted with cattle and oil wells, Texas is an urban state. Some areas, particularly in West Texas, still offer a good deal of room to roam, but most Texans live in cities. First-time visitors to the state often express surprise at the size and diversity of Houston and Dallas and the more relaxed charm of San Antonio, whose Riverwalk reminds many tourists of some

European cities. Austin, the seat of state government and location of a world-class university, is highly attractive to young professionals and high-technology businesses.

When the Texas Constitution was adopted in 1876, the state was rural and agrarian; less than 10 percent of the population lived in cities. According to the 1880 census, Galveston was the largest city, with a population of 22,248, followed by San Antonio with 20,550. Dallas, a relatively new settlement, had 10,358 residents, and Houston had 16,513. For most of the period from 1880 to 1920, San Antonio was Texas's largest city, but since the 1930 census, Houston has held that distinction.[9] In 1940, only 45 percent of Texans lived in urban areas, but by 1950, 60 percent of the population resided in cities. Since the 1970 census, eight of every ten Texans have been living in cities.

Houston, Dallas, and San Antonio are among the ten largest cities in the United States. According to the 2000 census, Houston had a population of 1.95 million; Dallas, 1.19 million; and San Antonio, 1.14 million. Five additional Texas cities—El Paso, Austin, Fort Worth, Corpus Christi, and Arlington—each had more than 250,000. Five of Texas's ten largest cities—Houston, Dallas, San Antonio, El Paso, and Corpus Christi—have minority populations exceeding 50 percent (see Table 21.2).

The more than 1,200 incorporated municipalities in Texas are diverse, and urban life, politics, and government have developed different styles across the state. The basic forms of city government are defined by statutory and constitutional law, but cities vary in their demographic makeup, their economies, the historical experiences that shaped their development, and their quality of life. There are local differences in economic stability, public safety, public education, health and environmental quality, housing, transportation, culture, recreation, and politics.[10]

general law city City allowed to exercise only those powers specifically granted to it by the legislature. General law cities have fewer than 5,000 residents.

General Law and Home Rule Cities The Texas Constitution provides for two general categories of cities: general law and home rule. **General law cities**

TABLE 21.2 Select Characteristics for the Ten Largest Cities in Texas, 2000

City	2000	% over 65	% under 18	Median Age	% African American	% Hispanic	Persons per Square Mile
Houston	1,953,631	8.4	27.5	30.9	25.3	37.4	3,372
Dallas	1,188,580	8.6	26.6	30.5	26.0	35.6	3,470
San Antonio	1,144,646	10.4	28.5	31.7	6.8	58.7	2,808
Austin	656,562	6.7	22.5	29.6	10.2	30.6	2,611
El Paso	563,662	10.7	31.0	31.1	3.0	76.6	2,263
Fort Worth	534,694	9.6	28.3	30.9	20.4	29.8	1,828
Arlington	332,969	6.1	28.3	30.7	14.1	18.3	3,476
Corpus Christi	277,454	11.1	28.1	33.2	4.7	54.3	1,795
Plano	222,030	4.9	28.7	31.1	5.2	10.1	3,101
Garland	215,768	7.1	29.8	31.7	12.1	25.6	3,779

Source: Texas State Data Center; U.S. Census 2000.

WHAT DO YOU THINK?

Is This Any Way to Change a City Charter?

Boerne, Texas, which is just northwest of San Antonio, held a special election in May 2002 to amend its charter to bring it in line with a law recently enacted by the Texas Legislature. The new law permits local governments to purchase items valued at $25,000 or less without seeking bids. Prior to its enactment, the limit was $15,000, and the charter of Boerne included this figure. To permit the city to follow the state law and to anticipate future increases in the cap, a charter amendment would have permitted the city council to change spending caps each year as allowed by state law.

In a cliff-hanger election in which only 57 of 4,836 registered voters participated, the charter amendment was defeated, 29–28. The election occurred when there were no city or school board elections to draw voters to the polls. Few voters apparently were even aware the issue was on the ballot, and some just didn't care or believe the issue was important to them.

What happened in Boerne occurs throughout the state in charter elections. Just as is true for changes to the state constitution, all too often a small minority of a city's voters decide on changes in its fundamental law. While we have no empirical evidence, it might be argued that most changes are well-intentioned and necessary. But it is evident that a few individuals can use charter elections for their own self-interest.

Source: "Boerne Rejects Charter Change," *San Antonio Express News*, May 7, 2002.

have fewer than 5,000 residents and have more restrictions in organizing their governments, setting taxes, and annexing territory than do home rule cities. They are allowed only those powers specifically granted to them by the legislature. Most Texas cities—approximately 885—are general law cities.[11]

A city with more than 5,000 inhabitants can adopt any form of government its residents choose, provided it does not conflict with the state constitution (Article XI, Sections 4, 5) or statutes. This option is called **home rule** and is formalized through the voters' adoption of a **charter**, which is the fundamental document—something like a constitution—under which a city operates. A charter establishes a city's governing body, the organization of its administrative agencies and municipal courts, its taxing authority, and procedures for conducting elections, annexing additional territory, and revising the charter (*What Do You Think?*: "Is This Any Way to Change a City Charter?"). As of 2002, there were 318 home rule cities in Texas.[12]

THINK AGAIN

Should Texas cities have the power to enact a local income tax to replace the sales and property tax?

home rule city City with a population of more than 5,000, which can adopt any form of government residents choose, provided it does not conflict with the state constitution or statutes.

charter Document, based on state authorization, which defines the structure, powers, and responsibilities of a city government.

Forms of City Government in Texas

Texas cities have experimented with three forms of government: the mayor-council, the commission, and the council-manager (see *What Do You Think?* "Why Different Forms of City Government?"). According to the Texas Municipal League, there were 1,208 municipal governments in Texas in 2004. Over 900 cities operated with some variation of the mayor-council form; approximately 280 used some form of council-manager or commission-manager government; and only a handful used the commission form of government.[13]

WHAT DO YOU THINK?

Why Different Forms of City Government?

Most major Texas cities have functioned under more than one form of government. Both Houston and San Antonio have functioned under all three primary forms described in this chapter. Changes in city charters often follow periods of intense political conflict, inertia, or an inability to respond to long-term problems. Proposed changes in governmental structures and election systems often threaten groups and interests that have a stake in the way business is currently being conducted, and charter revisions have a tendency to polarize a community.

Does the form of government under which a city operates make any significant difference? Political scientists have spent a lot of time trying to answer that question, and while there is some consensus on the general weaknesses of the city commission, opinions are divided on the other forms of local government. The general public appears to pay little attention to city charters or governmental structures, but elected officials and other city leaders, public employees, special interest groups, minority leaders, and some reform-minded citizens consider the structure of city government a crucial issue.

A city charter spells out how a city will run its affairs and helps determine which citizens will have access to policy making. In part, a charter is an expression of a city's social, economic, and political structure. Some scholars have concluded that the urban reform movements advocating nonpartisan at-large elections, which often were tied to council-manager government, were advancing middle- and upper-middle-class views and interests. The original intent of these changes may have been to encourage managerial efficiencies, but many urban governments became less responsive to the needs and interests of lower-income groups and minority populations.

Source: William Lyons, "Reform and Response in American Cities: Structure and Policy Reconsidered," *Social Science Quarterly* 59 (June 1978): 130; Robert Lineberry and Edmund Fowler, "Reformism and Public Policies in American Cities," *American Political Science Review* 61 (September 1967): 701–17; Willis D. Hawley, *Nonpartisan Elections and the Case for Party Politics* (New York: John Wiley and Sons, 1973).

mayor-council Form of city government in which the legislative function is vested in the city council and the executive function in the mayor.

weak mayor Form of city government in which the mayor shares authority with the city council and other elected officials but has little independent control over city policy or administration.

strong mayor Form of city government that gives the mayor considerable power, including budgetary control and appointment and removal authority over city department heads.

Mayor-Council The **mayor-council**, the most common form of municipal government in Texas, was derived from the English model of city government. The legislative function of the city is vested in the city council, and the executive function is assigned to the mayor. This type of government is based on the separation-of-powers principle, which also characterizes the state and federal governments.

In theory, the mayor, who is elected citywide, is the chief executive officer. In terms of power, however, there are two distinguishable forms of mayor—the **weak mayor** and the **strong mayor**—and in most Texas cities, the mayor is weak.

The city charter determines a mayor's strength. The weak mayor has little control over policy initiation or implementation. The mayor's powers may be constrained by one or more of the following: limited or no appointment or removal power over city offices, limited budgetary authority, and the election of other city administrators independently of the mayor (Figure 21.1). Under these circumstances, the mayor shares power with the city council over city administration and policy implementation and "is the chief executive in name only."[14] These restrictions limit both the political and the administrative leadership of the mayor. Although it is possible for a mayor to use informal or noninstitutional resources to influence the city council and other administrators and to provide energetic leadership, there are formidable obstacles to overcome.[15]

A strong mayor has real power and authority, including appointive and removal powers over city agency heads (see Figure 21.2). Such appointments often require city council approval, but the appointees are responsible to the mayor and serve at mayoral discretion. The mayor has control over budget preparation and exercises some veto authority over city council actions. This form of city government clearly distinguishes between executive and legislative functions.

The strong mayor form of government is found in many of the larger American cities, but it is now used by only one major city in Texas—Houston. El Paso functioned under this form of government until 2004 when the city changed to council-manager government. The form may be unpopular in the state because the strong mayor often was associated with urban political machines, ward politics, and political corruption. Moreover, the fragmentation of authority and responsibility in local government parallels that found in state government and is another reminder of the deep distrust of government that Reconstruction produced in Texas. Finally, the state's individualistic and traditionalistic subcultures (see Chapter 15) reinforce hostile attitudes toward governmental institutions that are potentially more responsive to lower socioeconomic groups.

As might be expected, the salaries of the mayors and council members of cities with the strong mayor system are generally higher than under other forms of city government. In many cities, mayors and council members receive no pay or only modest reimbursement for services. The mayor of Houston earned $165,817 in 2002, and council members, $44,218. El Paso's mayor earned $28,944, and council members, $17,364.[16]

Bill White was elected mayor of Houston in 2003.

City Commission The commission and council-manager forms of government are products of the twentieth century. Both reflect, in part, efforts to reform city

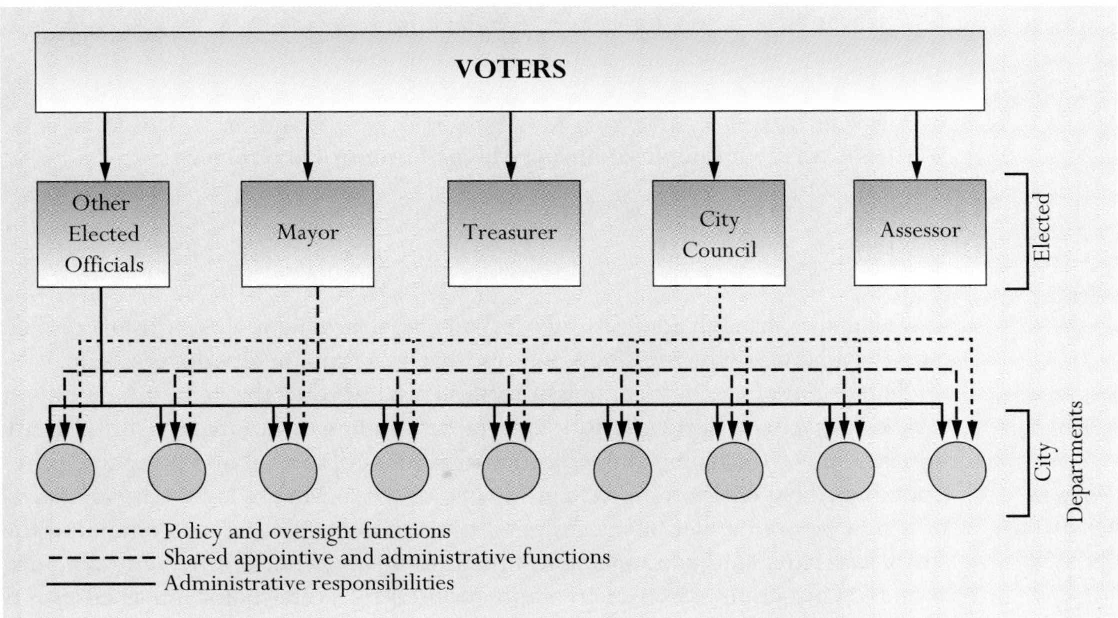

FIGURE 21.1 Example of Weak Mayor Form of Government

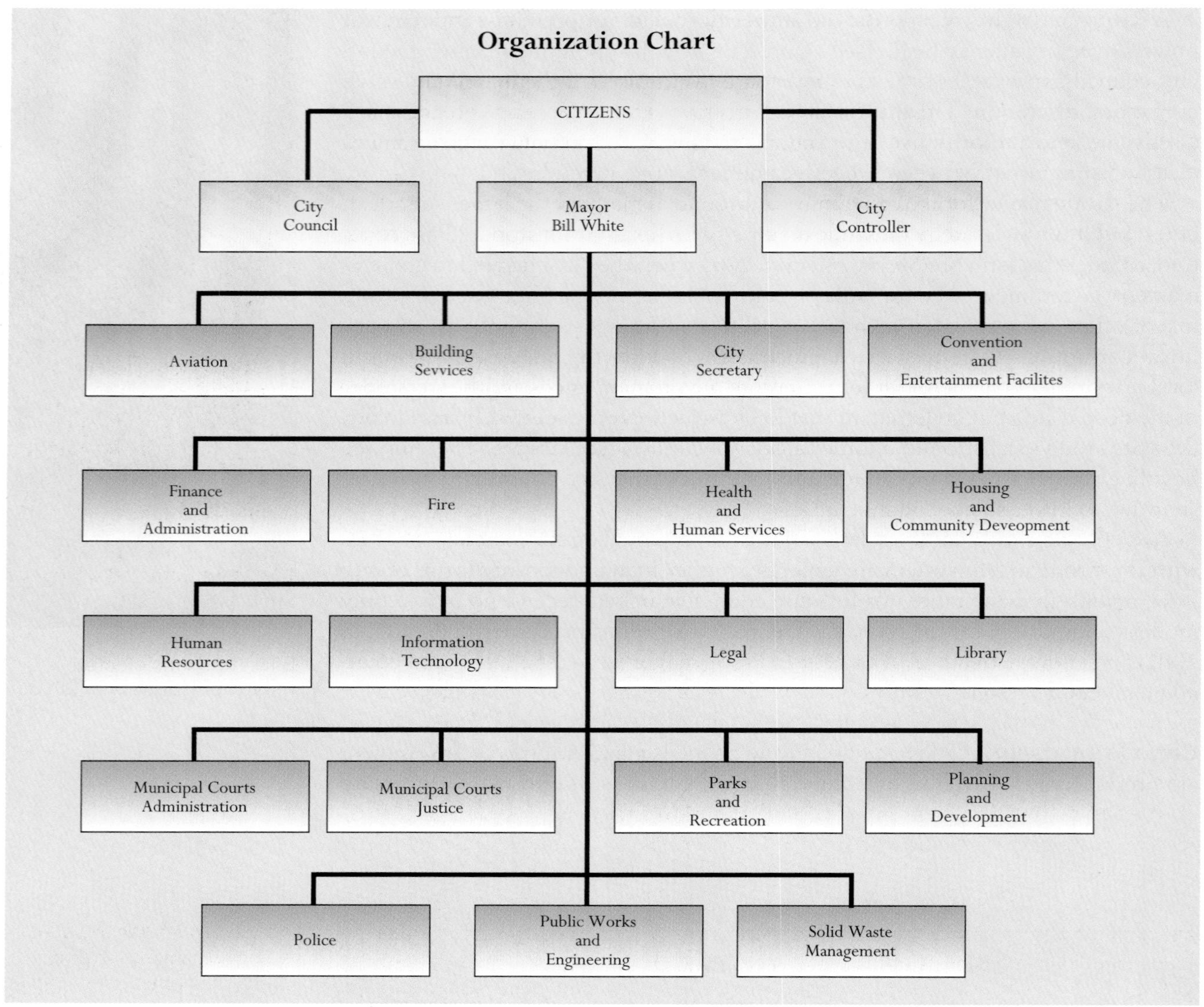

FIGURE 21.2 Example of Strong Mayor Form of Government

Source: Office of the Mayor, City of Houston.

governments through administrative efficiency, the reduction of partisan conflict, and the adaptation of a business-like approach to running city government.

The origin of the **city commission** is usually traced to the Texas island city of Galveston. After a hurricane and subsequent flooding devastated most of the city in 1900, the government then in office proved incompetent and incapable of responding. That crisis prompted a group of citizens to win the legislature's approval of a new form of government designed to be more responsive by combining the city's legislative and administrative functions in the offices of five city commissioners. City commissions were soon adopted by other major Texas cities, including Dallas, Houston, and San Antonio. But with the subsequent development of council-manager government as an alternative, there has been a marked decline in the city commission's popularity. It has been replaced in Houston, Dallas, and

city commission Form of city government in which elected commissioners collectively serve as a city's policy-making body and individually serve as administrative heads of different city departments.

San Antonio, and only a few cities in Texas still have this form of government (see Figure 21.3).

Initially, the commission was supported as a businesslike approach to running city government. By eliminating partisan elections and combining the executive, administrative, and legislative functions, it was argued, cities could provide services more efficiently. But critics have identified several problems. The commission minimizes the potential for effective political leadership because no single individual can be identified as the person in charge. Moreover, there is minimal oversight and review of policies and budgets. Commissioners are elected primarily as policy makers, not administrators, and there are downsides to electing amateurs to administer increasingly technical and complex city programs.

The few cities in Texas that use the pure form of commission government generally have three members—a mayor and two commissioners—who are assigned responsibilities for specific city functions, such as water, sanitation, and public safety. Several of the commission cities now use a city administrator or manager, hired by the commission, to run the daily affairs of the city.

Former journalist Laura Miller was elected mayor of Dallas in 2002.

Council-Manager After enthusiasm for the city commission waned, urban reformers, both in Texas and nationally, looked to the **council-manager** form of government. Its specific origins are disputed, but it was influenced by the same reform principles on which the city commission was based. The first cities in Texas to use council-manager government were Amarillo and Terrell in 1913, and it soon became popular among home rule cities. Dallas and San Antonio have been the largest cities in the state to adopt it (see Figure 21.4). Its principal characteristics are professional city management, nonpartisan city elections, and a clear distinction between policy making and administration. But in recent years, it has become evident that this policy-administration distinction has been modified by the increased roles of mayors and council members in the day-to-day operations of city government.

In some council-manager cities, the mayor is chosen by the city council from among its membership to preside over council meetings and fulfill a primarily symbolic role. But in other cities, the mayor is elected citywide, an arrangement that enhances the political position of the office without necessarily vesting it with formal legal authority. The mayor is usually a voting member of the city council but has few other institutional powers in a council-manager government. The mayor does, however, have the opportunity to become a visible spokesperson for

council-manager Form of city government in which policy is set by an elected city council, which hires a professional city manager to head the daily administration of city government.

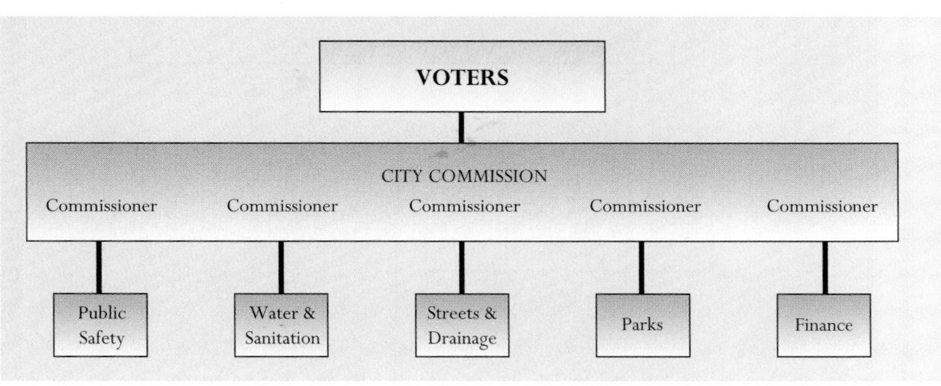

FIGURE 21.3 Example of a City Commission Form of Government

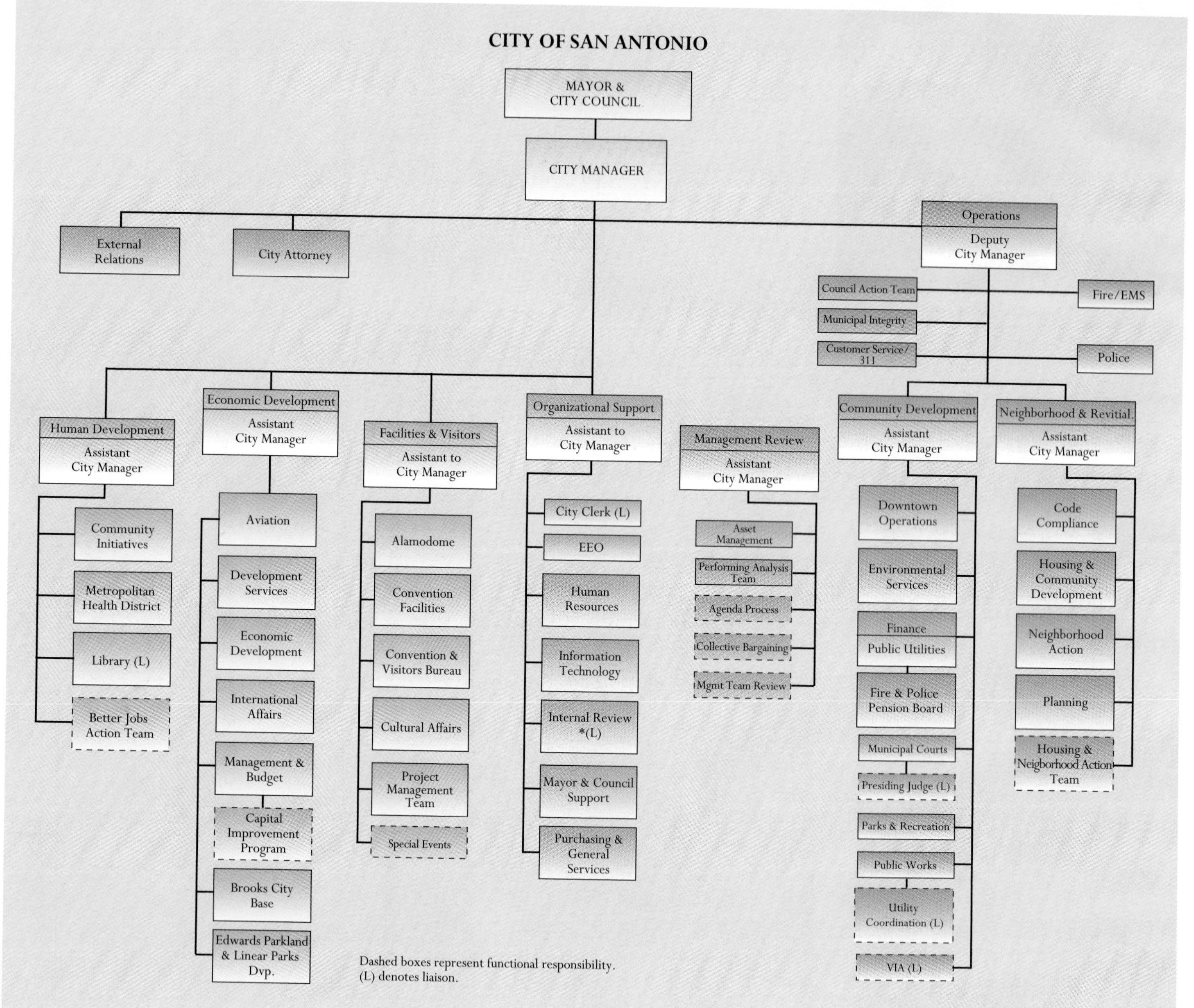

FIGURE 21.4 Example of a Council-Manager Form of Government

Source: Mayor's Office, City of San Antonio, Texas.

PEOPLE IN POLITICS

Ron Kirk and Lee Brown, History-Making Mayors

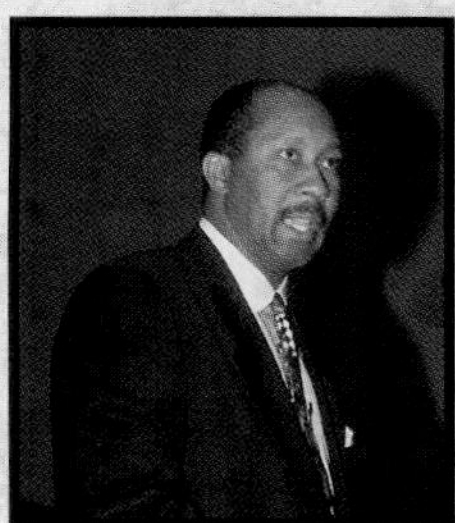

In one key respect, Ron Kirk's election as mayor of Dallas in 1995 wasn't all that unusual. He had the strong support of the city's business leaders, who liked his campaign pledge for more aggressive economic development. Kirk's election, however, made history. He was Dallas' first African American mayor. In a city well known for its conservatism and recent racial divisions, Kirk attracted a broad base of support that included both establishment whites and African Americans who had long been unhappy with the city's power structure.

A former Texas secretary of state under Governor Ann Richards, Kirk was elected to head a city council that included four other African Americans, two Hispanics, and eight whites. Dallas has a council-manager form of government, and its mayor's office is weak in terms of formal powers. But the high-profile post offered Kirk the opportunity to use the skills of salesmanship and persuasion that had served him so well during his campaign. Successful economic development, which he viewed as essential to the city's future, would improve racial harmony in Dallas, he predicted. "It doesn't matter whether your ancestors came over on the *Mayflower,* or on a slave ship," he said, "we're all in the same boat now."* Kirk was reelected to a second four-year term in 1999 but resigned in late 2001 to make an unsuccessful run for the U.S. Senate.

In 1997, Lee Brown scored a similar historical victory in Houston, when he was elected that city's first African American mayor. Brown, who earlier had been Houston's first African American police chief and had been drug policy director under President Bill Clinton, campaigned as a "mayor for all of Houston." Unlike Dallas, Houston has a strong mayoral office, giving Brown appointment powers over most city department heads and significant influence over city policies.

After taking 53 percent of the vote in a runoff against white businessman Rob Mosbacher, he told supporters at a victory celebration, "Another great barrier has fallen in the city of Houston — the doors of opportunity have opened wider for all of Houston's children."†

Brown received virtually all the African American vote and almost 30 percent of the white vote in the runoff. He and Mosbacher split the Hispanic vote.

Brown was easily reelected to a second two-year term in 1999 and won a third term in 2001 after a hard-fought runoff against Houston City Council Member Orlando Sanchez. Brown had to give up the mayor's office after his third term ended in 2003 because of Houston term limitations.

*Quoted in *Governing,* July 1995, p. 108.

†Quoted in *Houston Chronicle,* December 8, 1997.

the city and has a forum from which to promote ideas and programs (see *People in Politics:* "Ron Kirk and Lee Brown, History-Making Mayors").

The city council is primarily responsible for developing public policy (see *Up Close:* "The Job of the City Council Member"). It creates, organizes, and restructures city departments, approves the city budget, establishes the tax rate, authorizes the issuance of bonds (subject to voter approval), enacts local laws (ordinances), and conducts inquiries and investigations into the operations and functions of city agencies.[17]

The council hires a full-time city manager, who is responsible for administering city government on a day-to-day basis. The manager hires and fires assistants and department heads, supervises their activities, and translates the policy directives of the city council into concrete action by city employees. The city manager

UP CLOSE

The Job of the City Council Member

Regardless of the form of government, most city councils in Texas are small, with five to fifteen members elected for two-year terms. Most council seats are elected at-large, or citywide, and council elections are nonpartisan. Council members in most cities can serve for an unlimited number of terms. Recent referenda on term limitations, however, have been held in several Texas cities. San Antonio limits its council members and mayor to two terms, and Houston, three terms.

In most cities, a council office is part-time with little or no compensation, and while some large cities — such as Houston, Austin and Dallas — have recently increased salaries significantly, many council members do not consider their pay to be commensurate with the time spent on the job. Council members in San Antonio are still paid $20 per meeting. Low salaries were part of the early urban reform tradition. The idea was that people would run for office out of a sense of civic duty rather than to advance themselves financially.

The frequency of council meetings varies. In many small towns, councils may meet for only a few hours each month, but councils in large cities meet much more frequently, usually weekly, with meetings lasting several hours. Cities are dealing with a wider range of complex issues than ever before, and demands on a council member's time are great. In addition to their policy-making roles, council members in large cities are faced with increased demands for constituent services. Many council members are finding that public service is extremely costly in terms of time lost from their families and the jobs or professions that provide their livelihoods.

Council members often complain that they had no idea how much time the public would demand of them and their families. The following commandments for surviving have been offered by Hal Conklin, a former mayor:

1. Make an honest inventory of the hours that your political commitment will take.
2. Establish a contract with your employer for the hours that you are going to spend in your political commitment.
3. Set office hours and stick to them.
4. Delegate and hold accountable staff members and volunteers.
5. Put unmonitored phone lines on answering machines, especially at home.
6. Distinguish between home hours and work hours.
7. Make a date with your spouse (or significant other) for the same time each week.
8. Exercise regularly each day; eat a healthy diet.
9. Start and end your day with activities that soothe the soul.
10. Keep your sense of humor.*

*Hal Conklin, "Ten Commandments for Surviving as a City Council Member," *Texas Town and City* 83 (June 1995): 12, 19.

is also responsible for developing a city budget for council approval and then supervising its implementation. Professionalism is one of the key attributes of the council-manager form of government. Initially, many city managers were engineers, but in recent years there has been a tendency for managers to be generalists with solid skills in public finance. City managers are fairly well paid. In 2002 the salary of the city manager of Dallas was $263,000. The San Antonio city manager was paid $200,000, and the city manager of even a small city such as Seguin received $111,580.[18]

At one time in the not too distant past, the salaries of mayors and council members serving in council-manager cities was very low, but there has been a trend in recent years to increase salaries in response to the expanded workload. Salaries of the mayor and city council members in Austin are $53,000 and $45,000, respectively. Until recently, the mayor and council members in Dallas received $50 per meeting, but voters approved a charter amendment in 2001 to raise the mayor's pay to $60,000 a year and council members to $37,500. By contrast, San Antonio's council members earn $20 per meeting and the mayor, $50 per meeting.

There is a delicate line between policy making and administration, and a city manager is, in principle, supposed to be politically neutral. The overall effectiveness of city managers depends on three main factors: their relationships with their city councils; their ability to develop support for their recommendations within the council and the community at large without appearing to have gone beyond the scope of their authority; and the overall perception of their financial and managerial skills. In the real world of municipal government, city managers play a central role in setting policy as well as carrying it out. Managers' adroit use of their resources and sensitivity to political factions and the personal agendas of elected officials are key to determining their success.

Municipal Election Systems

Nonpartisan City Elections Virtually every city in Texas elects its council members in **nonpartisan elections.** Claiming that there was no Democratic or Republican way to pave a street, city reformers who were part of the nonpartisan movement (1920s to 1950s) expressed a strong aversion to political parties and particularly to the urban political machines (see *A Conflicting View*: "The Debate over Electoral Systems"). To enforce separation of city elections from party politics, most municipal elections are held at times other than the party primaries or the general election.

THINK AGAIN

Would we get more qualified elected officials if candidates ran without party labels?

The nonpartisan ballot—combined with at-large, citywide elections—has historically benefited higher social and economic groups. Parties and party labels normally serve as cues for voters. When they are eliminated in city elections, voters are forced to find different sources of information about candidates. Many local newspapers, which endorse candidates and decide how much coverage to give them, have ties to the dominant urban elites. Candidates from lower socioeconomic groups historically have had few contacts with the influential organizations that recruit, support, and endorse candidates. Although no longer in existence, San Antonio's Good Government League and Dallas's Citizens Charter Association controlled the recruitment and election of candidates in those two cities for several decades. Both organizations drew members from the Democratic and the Republican parties, but they reflected and pursued the interests of higher socioeconomic groups, often to the detriment of lower-income and minority populations.

At-Large Elections Another notable feature of city politics in Texas is the general use of citywide or **at-large elections.** In 1992, the latest year for which U.S. census data were available, there were 6,409 individuals elected to the governing bodies of 1,171 cities and towns in Texas. Some 5,649, or 88 percent, were elected at large. Only 12 percent were elected from single-member districts, discussed in the following section.[19] Of the 1,204 Texas cities in 2002, some 207, or 14 percent, had single-member districts.[20]

In an at-large election, all of a city's voters participate in the selection of all members of the city council. In a pure at-large system, every candidate runs against every other candidate. If there are eight candidates running for five positions on the city council, the candidates with the five highest vote totals are the winners. Many of these election systems have been struck down by the federal courts or by

nonpartisan elections Elections in which candidates do not represent a political party.

at-large elections Election systems under which officeholders are elected by voters in the entire city, school district, or single-purpose district.

A CONFLICTING VIEW

The Debate over Electoral Systems

There has been much debate over the most desirable form of city election system. Advocates of at-large, nonpartisan elections often warn of ward politics and the potential relationship of single-member districts to political machines, bosses, partisan conflict, corruption, and mismanagement. Even without corruption, they argue, council members elected from districts are concerned primarily with the interests of their own neighborhoods and may be more susceptible to trade-offs, swapping votes for programs and services that would benefit small segments of the community rather than benefiting the entire city. It has also been argued that district elections divide communities along racial, ethnic, or economic lines, thus resulting in high levels of political conflict. Moreover, proponents of at-large elections argue that their system produces higher-caliber candidates, results in more media exposure for political campaigns, and permits a voter to participate in the selection of the entire city council rather than just one member.*

On the other hand, critics of the at-large system believe that single-member districts make elected officials more responsive to the needs and interests of specific constituencies. They also argue that at-large elections discriminate against African Americans and Hispanics because of racially polarized voting and the dilution of the impact of minority voting strength. Furthermore, citywide election campaigns, especially in the larger cities, are much more expensive than district campaigns, thus adversely affecting the electoral chances of candidates from low-income, often minority, areas. It also has been argued that single-member districts produce a more diverse group of elected officials and ensure that a city council will consider more diverse views and interests. At-large elections, critics say, permit a small group of individuals—the city's elites—to control the electoral process and the council by recruiting and financially supporting candidates to protect their interests.

*Tom Albin et al., *Local Government Election Systems* (Austin: Local Government Election Systems Policy Research Project, University of Texas, 1984), p. 2.

the U.S. Justice Department under the Voting Rights Act as discriminatory against minorities.

place system Form of at-large election in which candidates run for specific positions, or places, on a city council or other governing body.

runoff elections Elections that are required if no candidate receives an absolute majority of the votes cast in a city council, school district, or party primary race. The runoff is between the two top vote-getters.

single-member district System in which city council members, legislators, or other public officials are elected from specific geographical areas.

A variation of the at-large system is the **place system.** Candidates file for a specific council seat and run citywide for places, or positions. Cities using the place system may require that the winning candidate receive a simple plurality of votes (more votes than any other candidate running for the same position) or an absolute majority of votes (more than half the votes cast.) If a city requires the latter and there are more than two persons in a race, **runoff elections** between the two highest vote-getters are often required.

Single-Member Districts An alternative to at-large elections is the **single-member district,** or ward. Under this system, a city is divided into separate geographic districts, each represented by a different council member. A candidate must live in and run for election from a specific district, and voters can cast a ballot only in the race for the council seat that represents their district. A person elected from a single-member district can, depending on the city's charter, be elected by a plurality or an absolute majority of votes.

Legal Attacks on At-Large Elections Hispanics and African Americans, through various advocacy groups such as the National Association for the Advancement of Colored People, the Mexican American Legal Defense and Educational Fund, Texas Rural Legal Aid, and the Southwest Voter Registration and Education Project, have challenged in federal courts the election systems used by numerous Texas cities. From the small East Texas town of Jefferson to El Paso, Houston, and Dallas, minority groups have, with considerable success, challenged the inequities of at-large elections and forced city governments to adopt electoral plans that give minorities a better chance of electing candidates to city councils. The ethnic and racial composition of city councils has changed dramatically over the past twenty years, with a marked increase in the number of Hispanics and African Americans elected to these governing bodies (see Chapter 17).

City Revenues and Expenditures

Despite a growing number of expensive needs that they are expected to address, Texas cities have limited financial options. Unlike counties and school districts, they receive no state appropriations for any purpose. City governments are disproportionately dependent on **regressive taxes,** such as property taxes and fees for services. Moreover, the state limits the property tax rate that a city can impose and permits citizens to petition their city council for a **rollback election** to nullify any tax increase of more than 8 percent in a given year. Although there have been few rollback elections in recent years, the potential for such citizen initiatives serves to constrain policy makers.

When the Texas economy went sour in 1985 and 1986, cities experienced revenue shortfalls from a decline in sales tax revenues, reductions in the assessed value of property, and the elimination of many federal assistance programs. By 1993, the financial positions of most cities improved as a result of a rebound in the real estate market and the overall improvement of the state's economy. Municipal financial conditions improved dramatically by 1995, and for the remainder of the decade, municipal revenues continued to increase due to the robust expansion of the real estate market and the overall economy.

The financial downturns that were experienced in the last half of 2001 once again imposed financial pressures on Texas cities. The sluggish economy and the decline in the state sales tax forced cities through 2003 to scramble to maintain services and minimize tax increases. A survey of Texas cities by the Texas Municipal League in early 2003 led to the conclusion that fiscal conditions facing cities were worse than they had been in the past twelve years.[21] More than twenty-three percent of the cities responding to the survey anticipated lower tax revenues in 2003, but few city financial officers projected additional revenue declines in 2004. Property taxes were increased in 46 percent of the cities. Approximately 43 percent of the responding cities raised one or more fees on such services as water, wastewater, and solid waste disposal. Cities also used other cost reduction strategies such as hiring freezes, wage freezes, and employment layoffs. A significant number of Texas cities postponed capital spending as a major part of their efforts to balance their budgets.[22]

Although cities are required by law to balance their operating budgets, many municipal construction projects are financed by loans through the issuance of **general obligation bonds,** which are subject to voter approval. These bonds are secured by the city's taxing power. The city pledges its full faith and credit to the lender and, over a number of years, repays the bonds with tax revenue. Cities also fund various projects through **revenue bonds** that are payable solely

regressive taxes Taxes that impose a disproportionately heavier burden on low-income people than on the more affluent.

rollback election Election in which local voters can nullify a property tax increase that exceeds 8 percent in a given year.

general obligation bonds Method of borrowing money to pay for new construction projects, such as prisons, mental hospitals, or school facilities. The bonds, which require voter approval, are repaid with tax revenue.

revenue bonds Bonds that are used to finance construction of a public facility and are repaid with income produced by the facility.

from the revenues derived from an income-producing facility.[23] The poor economy of the late 1980s made it more difficult for cities to borrow money. And with a pent-up demand for improving **infrastructure** (streets, waste disposal systems, libraries, and other facilities), cities have entered an era of bond financing that has been radically altered by the performance of Wall Street and changes in state and federal tax laws.[24] Although city finances had improved as the state entered the twenty-first century, cities continued to postpone capital spending for streets, roads, water systems, and a variety of other capital improvements.[25]

Urban Problems in Texas

During the 1970s and through the early 1980s, Texas cities were key participants in the dramatic economic growth of the state. Many older cities across the country—particularly in the East and the Midwest—"looked at their Texas counterparts and envied their capacity to attract population and business."[26] Texas cities had low taxes, a pro-business tradition, few labor unions with significant economic clout, an abundant work force, proximity to natural resources, and governing bodies that favored economic growth and development. At the beginning of the twenty-first century, however, many Texas cities were confronted with many of the problems associated with older urban areas outside of Texas.

The Graying of Texas Cities The Texas population is aging, or graying. Americans are living longer, and older age groups are among the fastest growing segments of the population. As the population ages, additional pressures are placed on city governments for public services. The local property tax, a major source of revenue for city governments as well as other local governments, is stretched almost to its limits in many communities. Moreover, many Texas cities have granted, in addition to the standard **homestead exemption**, additional property tax exemptions for individuals older than sixty-five. As more and more people become old enough to claim these exemptions, younger taxpayers will be called upon to shoulder the burden through higher tax rates. There is also the looming possibility that older citizens on fixed incomes will be much more reluctant to support bond issues if they result in significant property tax increases.

"White Flight" The population characteristics of Texas cities change over time, and major metropolitan areas have experienced "white flight" to the suburbs, a dramatic increase in the growth rate of minority populations, and small growth rates among Anglos in the central cities. Income levels for most minority Texans have always been lower than those of Anglos, and a larger proportion of the minority population falls below the poverty level (see Chapter 15). The increased concentration of lower-income people in the central cities increases pressure for more public services, while a declining proportion of affluent property owners weakens the local tax bases that pay for the services.

Declining Infrastructures There has been much concern across Texas and the United States about the declining infrastructures of local governments. Streets, bridges, water and sewer systems, libraries, and other facilities must be continu-

infrastructure Streets, waste disposal systems, libraries, and other public facilities built and operated by governments.

homestead exemption Reduction in property taxes that some local governments grant on a taxpayer's residence.

ally maintained or expanded to support a growing population. Moreover, many Texas cities are out of compliance with federal standards for treating water and sewage and disposing of solid waste and must spend millions of dollars on physical improvements to avoid or reduce fines. Some capital improvements are paid for out of current operating budgets, but a more common practice is for cities to borrow money to improve roads, streets, water systems, and the like. These bonds are repaid from taxes on property. When property values decline—as they did in the late 1980s—cities are restrained by the constitution and statutes as to the indebtedness they can incur to support improvements.

By the end of the 1990s, property values were increasing across most areas of the state, and cities had more opportunities to borrow money for capital improvements. Nevertheless, most cities have a large backlog of proposed projects and are often forced to put off or defer needed construction.

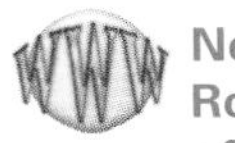

Nelson A. Rockefeller Institute of Government

This institute is located at the State University of New York and is actively involved nationally in research and special projects on the role of state governments in American federalism. In addition to providing a link to other public policy websites, this site references numerous studies related to federalism.
http://www.rockinst.org

Crime and Urban Violence Crime is a major problem facing Texas cities and counties, just as it is in many other parts of the country. Although crime rates in most offense categories declined in the 1990s, many Texans continued to believe that crime was on the rise. Much of the problem is related to drug abuse, gang violence, and juvenile crime. Expanded law enforcement patrols are proposed by political candidates and elected officials, but many city and county budgets cannot absorb the costs.

State- and Federally Mandated Programs Both federal and state governments have increasingly used mandates to implement public policy in recent years. A **mandate** is a law or regulation enacted by a higher level of government that compels a lower level of government to carry out a specific action. In simpler terms, it is a form of "passing the buck." Federal mandates, along with preemptions, cover a wide range of governmental functions, including transportation, education for the disabled, water and air quality, and voter registration (see Chapter 4).

mandate Law or regulation enacted by a higher level of government that compels a lower level of government to carry out a specific function.

Poor neighborhoods stand in sharp contrast to the nearby high-rise office buildings of downtown Houston.

States, meanwhile, have shifted much of the cost of public education to local governments.

Despite a decrease in federal funding for many urban problems during the 1980s, there has been an increase in federal mandates on the states, counties, and cities and an increase in state mandates on local governments, often with no financial support. In some cases, the state simply passes on the responsibility for—and the costs of—carrying out federal mandates to local governments. Congress enacted a law in 1995 to restrict unfunded mandates, but the law applied only to future, not existing, mandates. And such restrictions can still be circumvented if Congress chooses.

Although this practice may seem unfair and illogical, it is politically attractive to policy makers because they can "appease a large and vocal interest group that demands an extensive program without incurring the wrath of their constituents." They get the credit for such programs, but they do not get the blame for their costs.[27] Cities and other local governments across Texas claim that these unfunded requirements are excessively expensive, force them to rearrange their priorities, and limit local initiatives dealing with their most pressing issues. If local governments do not comply with mandates, they will be subject to litigation and face the prospect of losing federal or state funds. If they comply with mandates, they are then likely to reduce other services or seek alternative sources of funding now denied them.

County Government in Texas

Texas Association of Counties

This association serves county governments throughout the state. Links to related organizations can be found here, as well as information on recent legislation and laws pertaining to counties, support services, news releases, and educational programs for county officials.
http://www.county.org

Texas has 254 counties, more than any other state. Counties are administrative subunits of the state that were developed initially to serve a predominantly rural population. Created primarily to administer state law, they possess powers delegated to them by the state, but they have relatively few implied powers. Unlike home rule cities, counties lack the basic legislative power of enacting ordinances. They can carry out only those administrative functions granted them by the state. Counties administer and collect some state taxes and enforce a variety of state laws and regulations. They also build roads and bridges, administer local welfare programs, aid in fire protection, and perform other functions primarily local in nature.[28] All counties function under the same constitutional restrictions and basic organizational structure despite wide variations in population, local characteristics, and public needs.

According to the 2000 census, Loving County, the state's least populous, had only 67 residents, compared to 3,400,578 in Harris County, the most populous (see Table 21.3). Rockwall County includes only 147 square miles, while Brewster County covers 6,204 square miles. Some 56 percent of the state's population lives in the ten most populous counties.

Motley County with a population of about 1,400 had a 2003 budget of $666,747 and paid its county judge $14,501 and its commissioners $11,786. Dallas County had a $678 million budget and paid its county judge $130,262 and its commissioners $107,358 a year. Harris County's 2003 budget was $1.39 billion. Its county judge was paid $133,000, and each of its commissioners received $126,000.[29] Although there is an obvious relationship between the population of a county and salaries paid to its officials, the county's tax base is also a significant factor.

TABLE 21.3 Ten Largest and Ten Smallest Texas Counties, 1980–2000

	1980 Population	1990 Population	2000 Population
Harris	2,409,547	2,818,199	3,400,578
Dallas	1,556,390	1,852,810	2,218,899
Tarrant	860,880	1,170,103	1,446,219
Bexar	988,800	1,185,394	1,392,391
Travis	419,573	576,407	812,280
El Paso	479,899	591,610	679,622
Hidalgo	283,229	383,545	569,463
Collin	144,576	264,036	491,675
Denton	143,126	273,525	432,976
Fort Bend	130,846	225,421	354,452
Glasscock	1,304	1,447	1,406
Sterling	1,206	1,438	1,393
Terrell	1,595	1,410	1,081
Kent	1,145	1,010	859
Roberts	1,187	1,025	887
McMullen	789	817	851
Borden	859	799	729
Kenedy	543	460	414
King	425	354	356
Loving	91	107	67

Source: U.S. Censuses, 1980, 1990, 2000.

Structure of County Government The organizational structure of county government is highly fragmented, reflecting the principles of Jacksonian democracy (see Chapter 7) and the reaction of late-nineteenth-century Texans to Radical Reconstruction. The governing body of a county is the **commissioners court,** but it shares administrative functions with other independently elected officials (see Figure 21.5). Moreover, the name "commissioners court" is somewhat misleading because that body has no judicial functions.

The Commissioners Court and County Judge The commissioners court comprises a county judge, who is elected countywide, and four county commissioners, who are elected from a county's four commissioners precincts. Like other elected county officials, the judge and the commissioners serve four-year terms and are elected in partisan elections.

Until recent years, there were gross inequities in the population distributions among commissioners precincts in most counties. This issue of malapportionment came to a head in the 1968 case of *Avery v. Midland County,* in which the U.S. Supreme Court applied the "one person, one vote" principle to the counties and required districts to be equally apportioned.[30] Subsequently, Congress forced Texas to comply with the Voting Rights Act in 1975, and counties were required to consider the interests of minority populations in drawing up the boundaries for commissioners precincts. African Americans and Hispanics across the state have challenged county electoral systems and have increased minority representation

commissioners court
Principal policy-making body for county government. It sets the county tax rate and supervises expenditures.

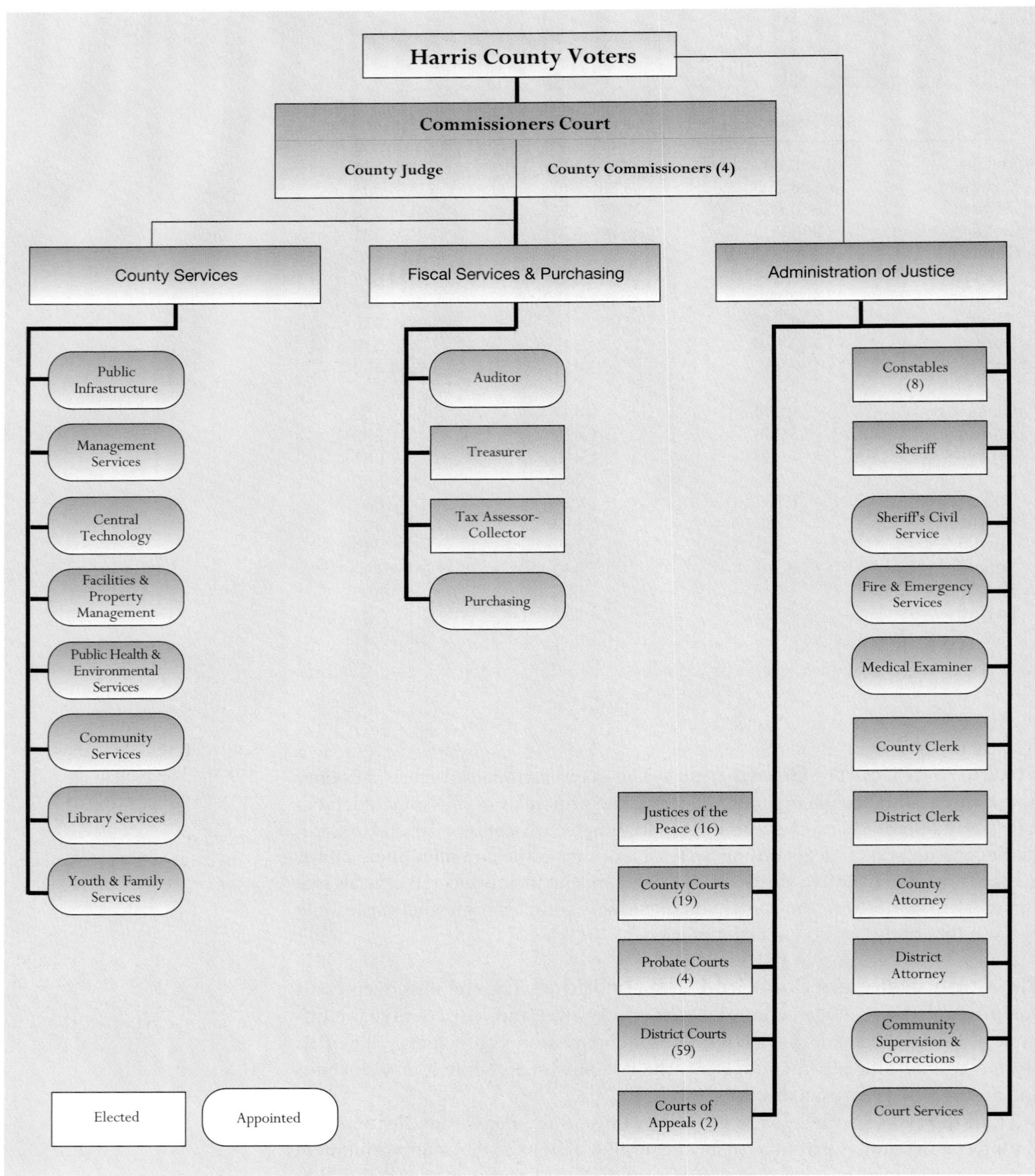

FIGURE 21.5 Harris County Organizational Chart

The Crockett County Courthouse, located in Ozona, was completed in 1902.

on county commissioners courts. After the 2000 census, most Texas counties quickly redistricted their commissioner precincts in compliance with state and federal law.

The **county judge** presides over commissioners court, participates in the court's deliberations, and votes on issues before it. If there is a vacancy among the commissioners, the county judge appoints a replacement. If the county judge vacates the office, the commissioners choose a replacement.

The Texas Constitution also gives the county judge some judicial responsibilities but does not require the officeholder to be a lawyer. Most urban counties have county courts-at-law that relieve the county judge of judicial duties. However, county judges in some rural counties perform a judicial as well as an executive role, combining two sets of duties in one office.

county judge Presiding officer of a county commissioners court. This office also has some judicial authority, which is assumed by separate county courts-at-law in most urban counties.

The commissioners court fills midterm vacancies in other county offices. It also has authority over the county budget, which permits the court to exercise some

County Judge Nelson Wolff presiding over a meeting of the Bexar County Commissioners Court.

influence, if not control, over other officeholders.[31] The court sets the annual tax rate, which is limited by the Texas Constitution, approves the tax roll, and supervises all expenditures of county money. Other county officials must obtain the court's authorization for personnel positions, salaries, and office expenses. Consequently, the budgetary process often sparks political disputes and other conflicts.

Historically, county road construction and maintenance were primary functions of commissioners court. The Optional Road Law of 1947 gave counties the authority to create a consolidated road system under the supervision of a county engineer, who relieved commissioners of road maintenance and construction headaches. But the importance of roads to the commissioners and their constituents still generates political disputes.

County Clerk The Texas Constitution provides for an elected **county clerk** to serve as the clerk of the commissioners court, the clerk of the county courts, and (in the smaller counties) the clerk of the district court. Over the years, the legislature has enacted hundreds of statutory provisions defining specific responsibilities of the office, prompting one writer to describe the office as the "dumping ground for miscellaneous functions of the county."[32] The office is the depository of a county's vital statistics, such as birth and death records, and documents related to real estate transactions. It issues marriage licenses and various other licenses required by state law.[33] The county clerk also serves as a county's chief elections administrator if the commissioners court has not created a separate elections administrator's office.[34]

District Clerk The **district clerk**, also elected countywide, assists the district court by maintaining custody of court documents and records.[35] In small counties, the county clerk is authorized to double as the district clerk, and fifty-three counties combined these two offices in 2003.[36]

County and District Attorneys The state's legal interests in both civil and criminal matters are represented at the local level by one of three officers—the **county attorney**, the **district attorney**, or the criminal district attorney. The legislature has enacted numerous provisions for legal departments that vary from county to county. Some counties have no county attorney but have a criminal district attorney. Under state law, others are authorized both a county attorney and a district attorney. District attorneys prosecute more serious cases, usually felonies, in the district courts, while the county attorneys usually prosecute lesser offenses, primarily misdemeanors, in the county courts.[37]

These officers can also provide legal advice and opinions to other county officials and give legal counsel to public officials or employees who have been sued for acts committed in carrying out their official duties. Upon request of the commissioners court, the district attorney or county attorney may initiate lawsuits on behalf of the county. Various other laws charge these attorneys with protecting the public health, assisting the state attorney general in cases involving deceptive trade practices, enforcing the state's election laws, collecting delinquent taxes, and even enforcing the Texas Communist Control Act of 1951.[38]

Tax Assessor-Collector The property tax is the primary source of revenue for counties. Although the commissioners court sets property tax rates, the **tax**

county clerk Chief record-keeping officer of a county.

district clerk Elected county official who maintains custody of state district court records.

county attorney Elected official who is the chief legal officer of some counties. He or she also prosecutes lesser criminal offenses, primarily misdemeanors, in county courts.

district attorney Elected official who prosecutes more serious criminal offenses, usually felonies, before state district courts.

assessor-collector, another elected county officer, has the task of ascertaining who owns what property, determining how much tax is owed on that property, then collecting the tax. In counties with fewer than 10,000 people, these responsibilities are assigned to the sheriff, unless voters decide to create a separate tax assessor-collector's office. Seventeen counties, mainly those below 5,000 in population, continue to let the sheriff handle the job.

Prior to reforms enacted in the 1970s, the tax assessor-collector also was responsible for appraising property or determining its value. This process was often steeped in politics because the higher the value of a piece of property, the more taxes its owner has to pay. Lowering property values for select friends or supporters gave people holding this office considerable power, which often was abused. In an effort to move toward greater consistency across the state and to enhance the professionalism of tax appraisals, the legislature now requires each county to create an appraisal district separate from the tax office.[39] Property tax appraisals are now conducted countywide by an **appraisal district** whose members represent other governmental units in the county. The district also certifies the tax rolls, and other governmental units are required by law to use its appraisals.[40]

County Law Enforcement

Sheriffs and **constables,** a county's law enforcement officers, are part of an old tradition under the Anglo-Saxon legal system. Each county has one sheriff with countywide jurisdiction, but the number of constables can vary. In counties with fewer than 18,000 residents, the commissioners court can designate the entire county as a single justice of the peace precinct or can create as many as four precincts, with each precinct assigned one constable. In the large counties, as many as eight justice of the peace precincts can be created, with a constable assigned to each. Most counties have four constables.[41]

In a small rural county, the sheriff is the primary law enforcement officer for the entire county. But in urban counties, city police departments generally assume exclusive jurisdiction in the incorporated municipal areas, leaving the sheriff jurisdiction over the unincorporated areas. Most sheriffs have considerable discretion in the hiring, promotion, and firing of deputies and other employees, although some counties have adopted a merit employment system for the sheriff's office. The sheriff also serves as the administrative officer for the district and county courts.

Constables are authorized to patrol their precincts, make arrests, and conduct criminal investigations, but their primary function is to serve as administrative officers of the justice of the peace courts. They are responsible for serving **subpoenas,** executing judgments of the court, and delivering other legal documents.[42]

County governments are responsible for constructing and staffing county jails, which are managed in most counties by the sheriff and in some counties by a jail administrator. During the late 1980s and early 1990s, counties across the state pursued an aggressive policy of jail construction in response to court decisions, increased crime rates, and a shortage of state prison space. Jail construction was a "growth" industry during this period, but by the mid-1990s, some counties found that they had overextended their finances to construct these jails. They also were left with excess jail capacity after an increase in state-built prison facilities. To compensate for these problems, several counties contracted with other states to house their prisoners in Texas jails.

tax assessor-collector Elected official who determines how much property tax is owed on the different pieces of property within a county and then collects the tax.

appraisal district Local agency that determines the value of pieces of property in a county. All local governments are required to use its evaluations, or appraisals, for tax purposes.

sheriff Elected official who is the chief law enforcement officer of a county.

constable Elected law enforcement officer who is primarily responsible for executing court judgments, serving subpoenas, and delivering other legal documents.

subpoenas Court orders requiring people to testify in court or before grand juries or to produce certain documents.

All counties are authorized to create an office of **medical examiner**. This individual is appointed by the commissioners court and determines the cause of death of murder victims or others who die under suspicious or unusual circumstances. In counties that do not have a medical examiner, the justice of the peace is charged with conducting an **inquest** to determine if there are conditions to merit an autopsy.

Counties, either individually or as part of multicounty judicial districts, are required to provide facilities for a criminal probation office. Funded by the state, the chief adult probation officer of a county is chosen by the district judges, who supervise the office.

County Auditor All counties with 10,000 or more people are required to have a **county auditor**, and smaller counties may have one if the commissioners court chooses. Two counties with fewer than 25,000 residents may jointly agree to hire an auditor to serve both counties. The county auditor is appointed by the district judges of the county for a two-year term. He or she is primarily responsible for reviewing every bill and expenditure of a county to assure its correctness and legality. Such oversight can, in effect, impose budgetary restrictions on the commissioners court and produce political conflict with other county officers.

The role of the auditor varies from county to county. In counties with more than 225,000 people, the auditor is the budget officer and prepares the county budget for submission to commissioners court, unless an alternative has been authorized by the legislature.[43] In smaller counties, the commissioners court prepares the budget, based on estimates provided by the auditor.

County Treasurer The **county treasurer** is responsible for receiving and disbursing county funds. Although this office has existed since 1846, its primary functions are now carried out by the county auditor, and constitutional amendments have eliminated the office in a number of counties.

medical examiner Appointed official who is responsible for determining the cause of death of murder victims or others who die under suspicious or unusual circumstances.

inquest Examination by a justice of the peace or a medical examiner of unusual circumstances under which someone has died.

county auditor Appointed officer who is primarily responsible for reviewing every bill and expenditure of a county to assure it is correct and legal.

county treasurer Elected officer who is responsible for receiving and disbursing county funds.

Criticisms of County Government

The structure of county government in Texas, designed for a rural state, has inhibited efforts of urban counties to respond to growing needs for public services. The state experimented with county home rule years ago, but the provisions were so poorly written, confusing, and contradictory that local self-rule at the county level was never given a real chance. Efforts were made in the 1997 and 1999 sessions of the legislature to amend the constitution to once again allow counties to adopt home rule, but there was limited statewide support for this change.

Even though the county functions primarily as an extension, or administrative subdivision, of state government, there is limited supervision of the counties by the state and a wide disparity in the way counties interpret and administer their functions. Some counties do a very good job, while others have a dismal record. The fragmentation represented by several independently elected officers always poses a danger of jurisdictional conflict, administrative inefficiency, and even government deadlock.

Like other local governments in Texas, counties rely heavily on the property tax for revenue but cannot exceed tax rate limits set by the state constitution. Those limits reflected a general apprehension about government when they were initially set in 1875. They now further restrict the counties' ability to provide services.

Historically, county courthouses have been associated with political patronage and the **spoils system.** Victorious candidates have claimed the right to appoint personal and political friends to work for them, and state courts have held that elected county officials have wide discretion in the selection of their employees. Reformers have advocated a **civil service system** for county employees based on merit and competitive examinations and offering job security from one election to the next. A 1971 law allows counties with more than 200,000 residents to create a civil service system, but it excludes several county offices, including the district attorney. An elected public official retains considerable control over the initial hiring of employees through a probationary period of six months.[44]

Special Districts in Texas

Every day, Texans use the services of municipal utility districts (MUDs), water conservation and improvement districts (WCIDs), hospital districts, and a host of other local governments, which have been deemed by some as the "invisible governments" of the state.[45] There are approximately 3,300 such governmental units across Texas classified as **special purpose districts,** and almost every year additional ones are created. These include drainage districts, navigation districts, fresh water supply districts, river authorities, underground water districts, sanitation districts, housing authorities, soil conservation districts, MUDs, and WCIDs. School districts are also considered a form of special purpose district.

Functions and Structures Special districts are units of local government created by the state to perform specific functions. Wide variations in their functions, taxing and borrowing authority, governance, and performance limit generalizations about them. Most special districts are authorized to perform a single function and are designated single-purpose districts. But some are multipurpose districts because the laws creating them permit them to provide more than one service to constituents. For example, in addition to providing water to people in their service areas, MUDs may assume responsibility for drainage, solid waste collection, firefighting, and parks and other recreational facilities.[46] Some districts, such as hospital districts, normally cover an entire county. Others, such as MUDs, cover part of one county, while still others, such as river authorities, cover a number of counties.

A special district is governed by a board either appointed by other governmental units or elected in nonpartisan elections. The board members of hospital districts are appointed by county commissioners courts; city housing authority boards are appointed by mayors or city councils. Many of these districts have taxing and borrowing authority, but others have no taxing powers and are supported by user fees or funds dedicated to them by other governmental agencies. Many special districts are eligible for federal grants-in-aid.

Special districts exist for a variety of reasons. Independent school districts were created, in part, to depoliticize education and remove the responsibility for it from county and city governments. In some cases, existing governments are unwilling or unable—because of state restrictions on their tax, debt, or jurisdictional

spoils system System of filling public jobs by hiring friends and other politically connected applicants, regardless of their abilities.

civil service system System under which public employees are hired and promoted on their abilities. It features competitive examinations and offers job security from one election to another.

special purpose districts Units of local government created by the state to perform specific functions not met by cities or counties, including the provision of public services to unincorporated areas.

authority—to provide essential services to developing communities. So special districts were created to fill the gap.

The cost of providing a particular governmental service is another reason for the growth of special districts. By creating a special district that includes a number of governmental units and a larger population and tax base, the costs can be spread over a wider area. Special districts often are promoted by individuals, groups, or corporations for selfish gains. Builders, for example, sometimes develop plans for large tracts of land in the unincorporated areas of a county and then get local governments or the legislature to create municipal utility or water districts to provide water and sewer services.

Some special districts have been designed to serve specific geographical areas. River basins that extend for thousands of square miles and cover ten or twenty counties have presented a particular problem. Because no existing governments had jurisdiction over the use of water resources in these basins, river authorities with multicounty jurisdictions were created.[47]

Consequences of Single-Purpose Districts From one perspective, special districts compensate for the fragmentation of local government that exists throughout Texas. But, ironically, these districts contribute to further fragmentation and delay the more difficult development of comprehensive, multipurpose governmental units that could more efficiently provide public services. A special district has been called a "halfway house between cityhood and noncityhood, between incorporation and nonincorporation."[48] Residents of a developing community or subdivision may not want to create a new city or become part of a nearby existing city, but they need certain fundamental services, such as water, electricity, and fire protection, some of which can be provided through the creation of special districts.

Many special districts are small operations with limited financial resources and few employees. Salaries often are low, and some districts have difficulty retaining the licensed technical people required to perform daily operations. In some cases, record-keeping and management operations are shoddy and amateurish, and the costs of providing services by many of these operations may actually be higher than what similar services cost in larger governmental systems. Special districts may also use outside legal and professional assistance, which can be very costly, and many districts lack the expertise to maximize their investments or borrowing potential.[49]

Some special districts expand their functions beyond the purpose for which they were created. The metropolitan transit authority in San Antonio, for example, authorized under state law to impose a 1 percent sales tax for public transportation, became involved in building the Alamodome, a multipurpose convention and sports facility. As governments expand their functions, there is a greater potential for intergovernmental rivalry, conflict, deadlock, and duplication of costs.

Except for the 1,000-plus independent school districts and a small number of other highly visible districts, such as river authorities, most special districts operate in anonymity. The public has only limited knowledge of their jurisdiction, management, operations, or performance. Many taxpayers may not even be aware they are paying taxes to some of these entities. There is little media coverage of their work, few individuals attend their board meetings, and turnout for their elections is extremely low. In the case of the governing boards that are appointed by other governmental agencies, the appointment process is often dominated by a small number of individuals or groups who also dominate the activities of the special district. This domination is probably the most damning indictment of special districts.

Independent School Districts

Texas Association of School Boards

The Texas Association of School Boards serves the 1,000-plus state school districts through policy advocacy and support services. This site includes links to many of the school districts as well as information pertaining to services, programs, and publications.
http://www.tasb.org

The **independent school district**, currently the basic organizational structure for public education in Texas, had its origins in the Constitution of 1876. Cities and towns were allowed to create independent school districts and to impose a tax to support them. Initially, the city government served as the school board, but in 1879, school districts were permitted to organize independently of the city or town, elect their own boards of trustees, and impose their own school tax. But residents of rural areas, where most nineteenth-century Texans lived, were denied these powers and only had the option of forming community schools. So, in effect, Texas operated under a dual school system, with the majority of students subject to the discretionary and often arbitrary powers of county governments.

THINK AGAIN

Should Texas enact laws giving school districts greater authority over local education?

Inequities in the Public Education System From the very beginning, the inequities in the school system were clear to many parents, elected officials, and educators, and there were early efforts to reform and modernize public schools. Most were linked to national education reform movements. For example, the Peabody Education Board, a national organization, provided financial aid and technical support to the leaders of the state reform movement during the early part of the twentieth century. More recently, national attention was directed to the problems of public education through widely publicized studies such as *A Nation at Risk: The Imperative for Educational Reform* (1983), which was conducted by the National Commission on Excellence in Education. Many national, state, and local organizations have attempted to identify the most serious problems in public education, develop alternatives for resolving these problems, and initiate related litigation or legislative and administrative initiatives. Although education is primarily a local responsibility, three recent presidents have made educational policy one of their top priorities.

Reformers have focused much of their attention on compulsory education laws, adequacy and equity in school funding, quality curricula, and teacher preparation. Some reform efforts also have been directed at the structure and governance of local school districts. The diverse and fragmented structure of Texas schools has been modified over the years through consolidation, greater uniformity in the organization of school districts, and the extension of the independent school district to virtually every community in the state.

Local School Governance Although regulation and coordination are provided on a statewide level through the State Board of Education and the Texas Education Agency (TEA), public education is now administered through more than 1,000 local school districts. In 2002, the smallest districts, the Divide Independent School District in Kerr County and the San Vicente ISD in far West Texas,

independent school district Specific form of special district that administers the public schools in a designated area.

The Board of Trustees of the San Antonio Independent School District comprises seven members elected from single-member districts. This body has the primary responsibility for setting school district policies.

each had twenty students. The largest, the Houston Independent School District, had 210,670 students. The thirteen largest districts—with more than 50,000 students each—enrolled more than one million of the 4.1 million students attending prekindergarten through grade 12 in Texas public schools during the 2001–2002 school year. By contrast, 502 districts had fewer than 500 students each, serving a total of only 115,000 students. By 2002, students from minority ethnic or racial groups constituted 59 percent of the public school population in Texas, and their numbers are projected to increase.[50]

School districts are governed by **school boards**, ranging in size from three to nine members; most have seven. Trustees are elected in nonpartisan elections for terms that vary from two to six years, with most serving three-year terms. In 2003, 176 of the 1,000-plus school districts elected their boards from single-member districts.[51] School districts with significant minority populations have shifted from at-large elections to single-member districting, primarily as a consequence of lawsuits or the threats of lawsuits by minority plaintiffs under the Voting Rights Act.

Most school board elections are held on the first Saturday in May, the same day most cities hold their elections. School board election turnouts are low, usually less than 10 percent of registered voters. But turnout increases when there are highly visible issues, such as the firing of a superintendent or a dramatic increase in taxes.

school board Governing body of a school district. Its responsibilities include the development or approval of educational policies, approval of the budget, hiring of the superintendent, and other personnel matters.

Recruiting qualified candidates for school boards is often difficult, and many times elections are uncontested. Individuals are encouraged to run by the superintendent, other members of the board, or key community leaders, many of whom point out that it is difficult to find people who are willing to give the required time and energy. Individuals often have little knowledge of what school board members do, and because many trustees serve for only one term, some boards have high turnover rates. Moreover, there is no way for a potential trustee to anticipate the amount of time it will take for briefings by the superintendent and staff, preparing for and participating in board meetings, and taking phone calls from parents and taxpayers. A board member must also deal with the political aspects of the job, including attendance at community functions and major school programs and meeting with teachers and taxpayer groups. Board members receive no salaries but are reimbursed for travel related to board business.

The most important decision that a school board makes is the hiring of a **school superintendent.** In organization and management structure, the school district is similar to the council-manager form of government. The board hires a superintendent, who is in charge of the district's day-to-day operations. Although the board has the primary policy-making responsibility for a district, part-time board members are often dominated by the superintendent and the superintendent's staff. School trustees and superintendents tend to talk about "keeping politics out of education," and superintendents often attempt to convey the impression that they serve simply to carry out the will of their boards. In most instances, however, a school board's agenda is established by the superintendent, and the board members depend on the superintendent and other professional staff members for information and policy recommendations. Very few board members have much time to give to the district, and most have only limited knowledge of the laws affecting education. State law, in fact, restricts the intrusion of board members into the daily management and administration of a district. An excessively politicized school board that becomes involved in day-to-day administration can be called to task by the Texas Education Agency. In an extreme case, the TEA can even take over the management of a school district.

Councils of Government

Local issues or problems do not start or stop at the boundaries of local governments. Water issues, for example, are usually of a regional nature and transcend the boundaries of cities and counties. Land use, crime and transportation issues similarly affect multiple governments, and, in fact, there are relatively few policy issues that do not impact more than one government. Under the complex system of local government that has evolved in Texas and throughout the United States, it has long been argued by policy makers and students of government that greater coordination and collaboration is imperative if sound public policy is to be developed in response to these mutual issues.

Councils of government (COGs), or regional planning commissions, were created under the Texas Regional Planning Act of 1965 (see Figure 21.6). That law was enacted, in part, to comply with federal regulations requiring local planning and review procedures.[52] These organizations evolved over the years to take on additional duties, including comprehensive planning and service responsibilities for employment and job training, criminal justice, economic development, health, aging, early childhood development, alcoholism, drug abuse, transportation, land resource management, environmental quality, and rural development.[53]

Although councils of government are "defined by law as political subdivisions of the state, they have no regulatory power or other authority possessed by cities, counties, or other local governments."[54] Stated another way, they do not have jurisdictional authority with police and taxing powers. They cannot enact local legislation, nor do they have the power to force compliance. Decisions of the COGs are not binding on their members.[55]

The councils, instead, are support agencies designed to promote voluntary collaboration and coordination of public service among local governments. Their

Council of State Governments

This site provides links to other organizations of state officials as well as information on policies affecting states, publications, suggested legislation, and state information centers.
http://www.csg.org

school superintendent Top administrator of a school district. He or she is hired by the elected school board to direct the district's daily operations.

council of government (COG) Council comprised of representatives of other governments in a defined region of the state.

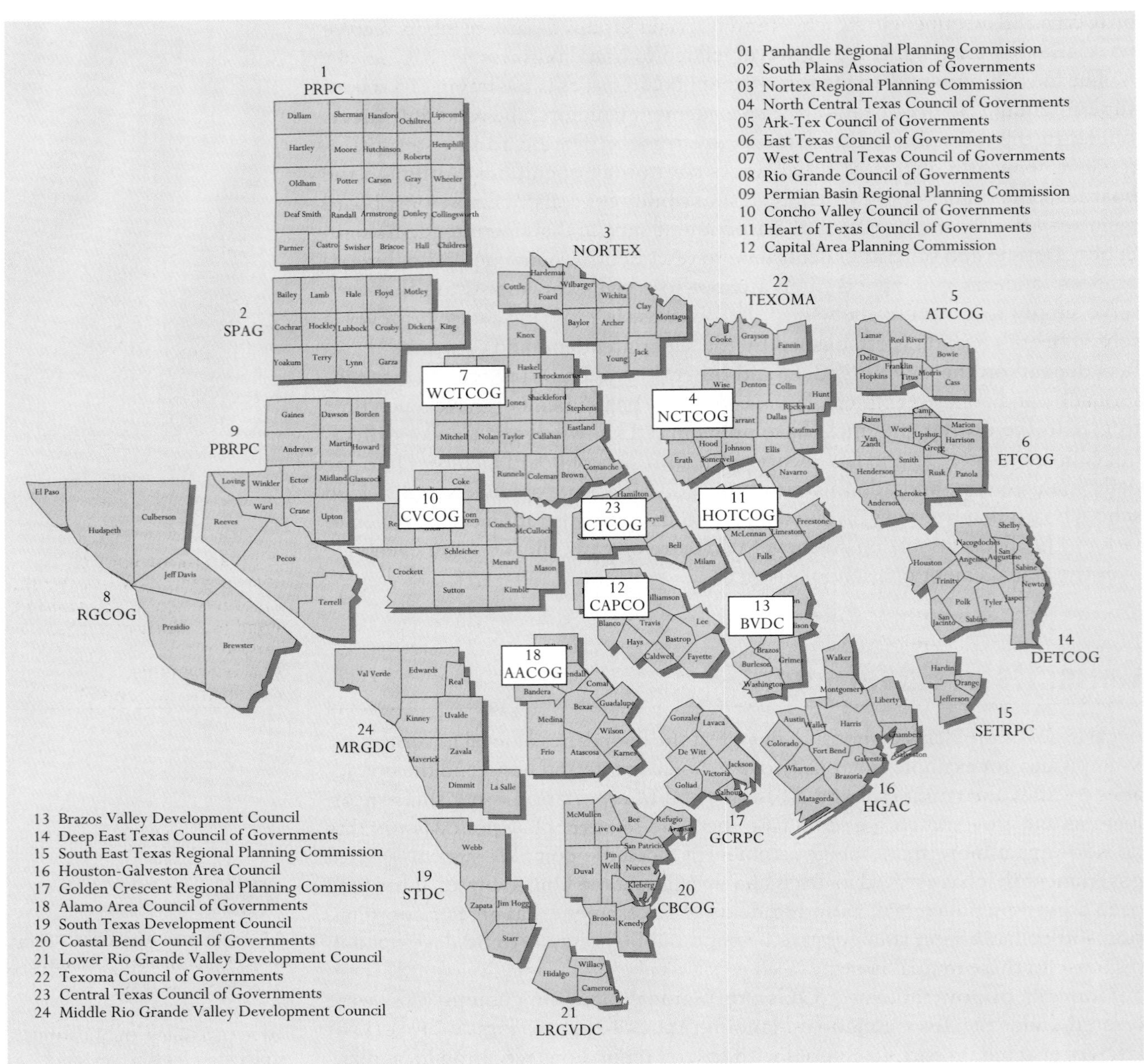

FIGURE 21.6 **State Planning Regions**

Source: Office of the Governor.

effectiveness varies across the state and appears to be partially related to the willingness of their members to engage in serious intergovernmental policy planning and implementation, the technical expertise of their staffs, and the political effectiveness of their leaders.

Twenty-four regional councils of government in Texas each serve a specific geographic area. Membership is voluntary; in 2002, more than 2,000 counties, cities, school districts, and other special districts were members of COGs.[56] Each COG decides the composition and structure of its governing body, so long as two-thirds of its members are elected officials from counties or cities.

Member governments pay dues, but the primary sources of funding for COGs have been the state and federal governments. The state pays a regional council a flat fee for each county that is a member and provides a per capita payment for each person residing in the COG. At one time, the regional councils relied extensively on federal grants-in-aid, but there was a 70 percent decrease in direct federal funding of COGs during the 1980s. Indirect federal pass-through funds administered by state agencies also provide funds for the COGs.[57] Several COGs have expanded their technical support and some management services to offset these lost revenues.[58] At the end of 2003, COGs were reviewing the impact of budget cuts and administrative reorganization on their functions, programs, and staffs.

Urban Institute The Urban Institute focuses on a range of social policies. It has developed a multiyear research project entitled, "Assessing the New Federalism."
http://www.urban.org

Solutions to the Problems of Local Government

Privatization of Functions As local governments have juggled their financial problems with increased demands for public services, they have tended to contract out some services to private companies. Many governments believe **privatization** can reduce costs through businesslike efficiency, and they consider it an attractive alternative in the face of voter hostility toward higher taxes. Cities, for example, are contracting for garbage pickup, waste disposal, towing, food services, security, and a variety of other services. Privatization also provides a way for cities that have reached their limit on bonded indebtedness to make new capital improvements by leasing a facility from a private contractor. A civic center or school facility can be constructed by a private contractor and leased back to the government for an extended period.

THINK AGAIN

With so many special districts in Texas, should the state attempt to consolidate local governments into larger, more comprehensive governmental units?

Annexation and Extraterritorial Jurisdiction Population growth in the areas surrounding most large Texas cities has forced municipalities and counties to wrestle with urban sprawl. El Paso covered 26 square miles in 1950 but had expanded to 250 square miles by 2000. Houston grew from 160 square miles in 1950 to 579 square miles in 2000, and similar expansions have occurred in most of the state's other metropolitan areas.

The cities' ability to expand their boundaries beyond suburban development derives from their **annexation powers** and **extraterritorial jurisdiction** over neighboring areas. With the Municipal Annexation Act of 1963, the legislature granted cities considerable discretionary authority over nearby unincorporated areas. Specific annexation powers and extraterritorial jurisdiction vary with the size and charter of a city. Generally, cities have extraterritorial jurisdiction over unincorporated areas within one-half mile to five miles of the city limits, making development in those areas subject to the city's building codes, zoning and land use restrictions, utility easement requirements, and road and street specifications. This authority restricts the use of unincorporated land and requires those building outside the city to build according to at least minimal standards. Later, when those areas are annexed by the city, they are less likely to degenerate quickly into suburban slums that will require a high infusion of city dollars for basic services.

Cities can annex areas equivalent to 10 percent of their existing territory in a given year, and if this authority is not exercised in one year, it can be carried over to subsequent years. Annexation usually does not require a vote of those people who are to be incorporated into the city (see *What Do You Think?* "Circle C Ranch: A Subdivision's Fight against Austin"). However, within two and one-half years, a city is required to provide annexed areas with services comparable to those

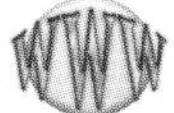
Federal Web Locator

This site provides the Federal Web Locator, which accesses a wide range of federal agencies whose activities directly impact state and local governments.
http://www.infoctr.edu/fwl/

privatization Contracting by government with private companies to provide some public services.

annexation powers Authority of cities to add territory, subject to restrictions set by state law.

extraterritorial jurisdiction Power of an incorporated city to control development within nearby unincorporated areas.

WHAT DO YOU THINK?

Circle C Ranch: A Subdivision's Fight against Austin

For years, developers building subdivisions on the scenic western outskirts of Austin have been fighting environmentalists and Austin city officials over environmental restrictions. That war reached new intensity in 1995, when the developer of Circle C Ranch, a planned community in southwest Travis County, went to the Texas legislature to win unprecedented independence for his subdivision.

In a major departure from traditional public policy that gave cities strong control over development around them, developer Gary Bradley convinced lawmakers to enact a special law freeing Circle C Ranch from Austin's control and future annexation, although the subdivision was within the city's extraterritorial jurisdiction. The law created a new super water district to govern Circle C development, subject to approval by state environmental officials. The district was headed by a nine-member board appointed by the governor.

Bradley and other supporters of the bill, including many Circle C residents, argued that the new law was necessary to allow for a more complete development of the community, which at the time was entirely residential. Construction of offices, retail stores, and apartment houses had been blocked by Austin's strict water and development regulations. Austin officials said that the regulations were necessary to control development in the environmentally sensitive area and protect the city's water supply and quality of life. But Bradley and his supporters argued that it was unfair for Austin to impose such restrictions on non-Austin residents, who could not participate in city council elections. Some Circle C residents also believed more development would ease their property tax burden because it would bring in more taxpayers to help pay off the subdivision's debt on utilities and other capital necessities.

But the bill was criticized as an anti-environmental, special interest piece of legislation made all the more suspect by the fact that Bradley, according to an analysis by the *Austin American-Statesman,* had contributed $20,355 to twenty-one legislators. And although the state representative who represented Circle C cosponsored Bradley's bill, most other legislators from Austin and Travis County opposed it. State Senator Gonzalo Barrientos, who represented both Circle C and the city of Austin, filibustered for more than twenty-one hours on two occasions against it. "Sam Houston must be rolling over in his grave," Barrientos said. "We are creating a governmental body that is the antithesis of democracy. The board of this district is unelected."*

Over the objections of Austin officials, Governor George W. Bush let the bill become law without his signature and appointed nine people to the new Circle C board. But continuing the fight, Austin challenged the new law in court and, in 1997, a state district judge declared the law unconstitutional because it was designed to benefit a special class of landowners. Austin annexed Circle C in December 1997, but several legal issues remained unresolved.

In another challenge of city annexation powers, residents of suburban Kingwood asked the Texas legislature in 1997 to overturn their annexation by the city of Houston. The legislature refused to intervene, but the annexation disputes prompted a legislative study of cities' annexation powers and eventually led to changes in annexation laws.

*Quoted in *Austin American-Statesman,* May 25, 1995.

provided in its older neighborhoods. Otherwise, individuals living in these newly annexed areas can exercise an option to be deannexed, a situation that rarely occurs.

Aggressive use of annexation has permitted several large cities to expand geographically with population growth, thus often limiting the development of small suburban towns that would potentially limit future expansion. Cities have even annexed thin strips of land, miles from urban development, along major roads and highways leading into them. Since a city's extraterritorial jurisdiction extended as far as five miles on either side of the strip that was annexed, this practice has enabled a city to control future development in a large area. In San Antonio, these annexation policies have often been referred to as "spoke annexation," and it has taken more than thirty years for much of the territory brought under the city's jurisdiction to be developed and annexed by the city.[59]

In recent legislative sessions, many lawmakers have demonstrated an anti-city sentiment with proposals that would have eroded municipal authority, reduced municipal revenues, and imposed costly new mandates. Of particular concern to cities were attacks on annexation powers. The legislature in 1999 enacted a major overhaul of annexation authority, including a provision that requires cities to outline their annexation plans three years in advance. But cities felt, through their lobbying efforts, that they were able to obtain a relatively "well-balanced" law.[60] The legislature in 2001 continued to reflect growing suburban-rural hostility toward the cities. It enacted a law that modified the extraterritorial jurisdiction of cities by requiring city-county agreements on the regulation of subdivisions.[61]

Modernization of County Government City governments provide most basic public services in urban areas, and as cities expand to county boundaries and beyond, there is increased overlapping jurisdiction of county and city governments and a reduction of county services in the annexed areas. Counties, nevertheless, still play an important role in Texas. Rural Texans, in particular, continue to rely on counties to provide a number of services, and demands on many counties will increase. Recommendations to modernize county government include further attempts at county home rule, granting counties some legislative or ordinance-making authority, and creating an office of county administrator, appointed by the commissioners court to run the departments now assigned to commissioners. Another recommendation is to extend the civil service system to smaller counties and to all county employees.[62]

Economic Development Historically, cities have collaborated with the private sector to stimulate local economies. Private sector initiatives have come from chambers of commerce or economic development foundations, and local governments have participated. Cities also are using a variety of new financing techniques to assist in economic development, including development impact taxes and fees, user charges, creation of special district assessments, tax increment financing, and privatization of governmental functions.[63] A state law was enacted in 1989 to permit cities, with the approval of local voters, to impose a 0.5 percent sales tax for local economic development. By 1995, voters in 229 Texas cities had approved this tax option.[64]

Texas cities, as well as some counties, aggressively court American and foreign companies to relocate or develop new plants or operations in their communities. Cities and local chambers of commerce sponsor public relations campaigns touting local benefits and attractions. Local governments offer **tax abatements**—

tax abatements Exemptions from property taxes granted to certain businesses, usually to encourage them to move to or expand their operations in a city or county. The exemptions are granted for specific periods.

UP CLOSE

Expensive Tax Breaks

As the Texas economy was diversifying in the 1990s, economic development was very important to many communities. Texas towns and cities competed with each other and with cities in other states for industries that would provide jobs and help their communities grow. They offered incentives for companies to build new plants or expand existing facilities. One popular incentive was a form of tax break called a tax abatement: companies receiving tax abatements from local governments did not have to pay property taxes on their new facilities for a designated number of years. Proponents defended such breaks as an important economic development tool and argued that abatements eventually paid for themselves in the form of an expanded tax base. But some legislators and other critics believed school districts and other local governments were giving away too much potential tax revenue. There also was fear that a company could go out of business or move its operations out of a community before it had paid any taxes or hired the projected number of people it claimed it would employ.

According to a staff report prepared for the Senate Economic Development Committee in 1996, 186 of the state's 1,050 school districts had given tax abatements since 1985. The state comptroller's office said those abatements had cost $480 million in lost property tax revenue. "Our children's future should not be traded for new jobs now," said state Senator David Sibley of Waco, the committee chairman.* The lost money, he said, could have been spent on supplies, teacher salaries, and other educational needs. The legislature, however, let tax abatements continue.

*Quoted in *Austin American-Statesman*, October 31, 1996.

exemptions from property taxes on a business for a specified period—to encourage a company to locate or expand in a community. (See *Up Close:* "Expensive Tax Breaks"). Other financial incentives to companies being courted include lowered utility bills and assistance in obtaining housing for employees.

The legislature has permitted counties to form industrial development corporations or enterprise zones and to relax state regulatory policies to encourage the redevelopment of depressed areas. Portions of a county may be designated as reinvestment zones, in which tax abatements can be offered to attract new businesses. Counties also can create county boards of development, civic centers, foreign trade zones, and research and development authorities.[65]

Interlocal Contracting Because many small governments have limited tax bases and staffs, they enter into contracts with larger governments for various public services. In 1971, the legislature, following a constitutional amendment, enacted the Interlocal Cooperation Act, which gave cities, counties, and other political subdivisions rather broad authority for such contracts.[66] The law has been amended several times to expand the scope of these agreements, and local governments are now contracting with each other for services in twenty-five functional areas, ranging from aviation to water and wastewater management.[67] Contracting is not an alternative to consolidation of local governments, but it does hold out some promise for improving the quality of local services and reducing their costs.

Metro Government and Consolidation In the metropolitan areas of Houston, Dallas, and San Antonio, there are literally hundreds of cities and special dis-

TABLE 21.4 Local Governments in the Ten Largest and the Ten Smallest Texas Counties, 1997

	Total	County	Municipal	School Districts	Special Districts
State	**4,700**	**254**	**1,177**	**1,087**	**2,182**
Harris	498	1	28	24	445
Dallas	64	1	25	16	22
Tarrant	68	1	34	17	16
Bexar	51	1	22	16	12
Travis	94	1	14	8	71
El Paso	36	1	6	10	19
Hidalgo	77	1	21	16	39
Collin	50	1	24	15	10
Denton	62	1	33	11	17
Fort Bend	132	1	15	5	111
Motley	6	1	2	1	2
Glasscock	4	1		1	2
Terrell	4	1		1	2
Kent	5	1	1	1	2
Roberts	4	1	1	1	1
McMullen	5	1		1	3
Borden	2	1		1	
Kenedy	2	1		1	
King	3	1		1	1
Loving	2	1			1

Source: Bureau of the Census, *1997 Census of Governments,* Vol. 1, Table 13.

tricts providing public services. In Harris County (Houston) alone, there are 498 separate governmental units (see Table 21.4). Legislators, scholars, and reform groups have extensively studied the duplication and other problems produced by such proliferation and fragmentation and have made numerous recommendations over the years. One proposed solution is a consolidation of city and county governments known as **metro government,** which has been tried in a dozen or so areas outside Texas. Efforts initiated by San Antonio and Bexar County to obtain constitutional authority to propose city-county consolidation to voters in the county failed in the 1997 legislative session. Other metropolitan areas joined Bexar County and San Antonio in an expanded effort to obtain this authority from the legislature in 1999, but again it failed. Without such authority, county-city collaboration is more likely to take the form of increased intergovernmental contracting and the informal cooperation that local governments develop out of necessity and mutual self-interest.[68]

metro government Local government in which city and county governments consolidate to avoid duplication of public services.

Public Improvement Districts Under one state law, property owners in a specific area of a city or its extraterritorial jurisdiction can petition the city to create a special **public improvement district.** These districts can undertake a wide range of improvements—landscaping, lighting, signs, sidewalks, streets, pedestrian malls, libraries, parking, and water, wastewater, and drainage facilities. Public improvement districts do not have the same autonomy as other special districts. They are created solely through the discretionary powers of a city and are funded by

public improvement district Specific area of a city in which property owners pay special taxes in return for improvements to streets and other public facilities in their neighborhood.

assessments on property within their boundaries.[69] Although their budgets and assessments must be approved by the city, they can be operated and managed by private management companies or by the citizens themselves. Fort Worth created a public improvement district for its downtown area in 1986, and other cities have considered the option.

SUMMARY NOTES

- Local governments in Texas are the creations of the state and have only those powers granted to them by the Texas Constitution and statutes. With limited discretionary authority but with a great deal of responsibility, local governments often find it difficult to respond effectively to the needs of their citizens.
- More than 80 percent of the state's population lives in urban areas. Texas cities have highly diverse social structures, economies, and historical traditions, and, subsequently, there are marked differences in urban politics across the state. Five of the ten largest cities have more than 50 percent minority populations, contributing to longstanding controversies over urban electoral systems.
- Texas cities with fewer than 5,000 people are designated general law cities and are limited as to the form of government they can use. Cities with more than 5,000 residents can function as home rule cities, choosing a form of government that satisfies community needs as long as it does not conflict with the state constitution or statutes.
- Texas cities have experimented with three forms of government—mayor-council, city commission, and council-manager.
- A notable feature of city politics in Texas is the widespread use of nonpartisan, at-large elections. Prompted by legal attacks on at-large elections under the Voting Rights Act, many cities, as well as special purpose districts, have adopted single-member districts, thus increasing minority representation on local governing bodies.
- County governments, initially created to serve a rural population, function primarily as administrative subdivisions of the state. Much like state government, county government is highly fragmented, with administrative powers shared by a variety of elected officials.
- Hundreds of special purpose districts provide numerous public services and add to the fragmentation of local government. Most people know little about their jurisdiction, structure, functions, and leadership, making them the "invisible governments" of Texas. Texas has approximately 1,050 independent school districts, which are working to improve the quality of education against a backdrop of social, cultural, and financial problems.
- Texas cities are now experiencing many of the same problems as the older cities of the East and Midwest. Populations are aging, and there is evidence of white flight from the core urban centers. A disproportionately larger share of the population in the central cities is low income and least able to pay taxes to support municipal services. Crime rates are high, and cities are faced with significant problems of deteriorating infrastructures. Federal and state governments have imposed additional requirements, or mandates, on the cities that are increasingly difficult to meet.
- Local governments are experimenting with a variety of techniques to deal with their problems. Cities have used their annexation powers and extraterritorial jurisdiction to expand their tax bases and exercise limited controls over development in adjacent areas. Cities are also using public improvement districts to permit targeted areas to impose additional taxes for needed services. Both counties and cities are privatizing governmental functions to decrease costs and increase efficiency. Interlocal contracting permits governments to provide services to each other on a contractual basis, and many counties and cities are engaged in aggressive economic development programs. Some people advocate governmental consolidation, but there is limited support for this alternative in Texas.

KEY TERMS

unitary system 712
Dillon rule 712
general law city 714
home rule city 715
charter 715
mayor-council 716
weak mayor 716
strong mayor 716
city commission 718
council-manager 719
nonpartisan elections 723
at-large elections 723
place system 724
runoff elections 724
single-member district 724
regressive taxes 725
rollback election 725
general obligation bonds 725
revenue bonds 725
infrastructure 726
homestead exemption 726
mandate 727
commissioners court 729
county judge 731
county clerk 732
district clerk 732
county attorney 732
district attorney 732
tax assessor-collector 733
appraisal district 733
sheriff 733
constable 733
subpoenas 733
medical examiner 734
inquest 734
county auditor 734
county treasurer 734
spoils system 735
civil service system 735
special purpose districts 735
independent school district 737
school board 738
school superintendent 739
council of government (COG) 739
privatization 741
annexation powers 741
extraterritorial jurisdiction 741
tax abatements 743
metro government 745
public improvement district 745

SUGGESTED READINGS

Bridges, Amy. *Morning Glories: Municipal Reform in the Southwest.* Princeton, N.J.: Princeton University Press, 1997. Traces the development and successes of urban reformers in the southwest.

Brooks, David B. *Texas Practice: County and Special District Law,* vols. 35 and 36. St. Paul, Minn.: West, 1989. The definitive legal analysis of county and local governments in Texas.

Burns, Nancy. *The Formation of American Local Governments: Private Values in Public Institutions.* New York: Oxford University Press, 1994. A study of the political and economic reasons citizens create local governments.

Feagin, Joe R. *Free Enterprise City: Houston in Political-Economic Perspective.* New Brunswick, N.J.: Rutgers University Press, 1988. History of the economic development of Houston and its politics.

Johnson, David R., John A. Booth, and Richard J. Harris, eds. *The Politics of San Antonio: Community, Progress, and Power.* Lincoln: University of Nebraska Press, 1983. Essays written to assess changes in San Antonio based on concepts of political community, power, and progress.

Miller, Char, and Heywood T. Sanders, eds. *Urban Texas.* College Station: Texas A&M University Press, 1990. Essays provide multiple perspectives on the development of urban Texas.

Norwood, Robert E., and Sabrina Strawn. *Texas County Government: Let the People Choose,* 2nd ed. Austin: Texas Research League, 1984. A summary of the structure, powers, and duties of Texas county governments.

Orum, Anthony M. *Power, Money and the People: The Making of Modern Austin.* Austin: Texas Monthly Press, 1987. A study of the dramatic growth of Austin, providing reasons for expansion and development, an analysis of political events linked to this period of growth, and an assessment of the "episodic struggles" between the business community and proponents of controlled growth and more inclusive politics.

Perrenod, Virginia Marion. *Special Districts, Special Purposes: Fringe Governments and Urban Problems in the Houston Area.* College Station: Texas A&M University Press, 1984. Focuses on Harris County but provides generalizations about the development of special districts, their benefits, and their weaknesses.

Texas Governors

1. J. Pinckney Henderson (1846–1847)
2. George T. Wood (1847–1849)
3. Peter Hansbrough Bell (1849–1853)
4. James W. Henderson (1853)
5. Elisha M. Pease (1853–1857)
6. Hardin R. Runnels (1857–1859)
7. Sam Houston (1859–1861)
8. Edward Clark (1861)
9. Francis R. Lubbock (1861–1863)
10. Pendleton Murrah (1863–1865)
11. Andrew J. Hamilton (1865–1866)
12. James W. Throckmorton (1866–1867)
13. Elisha M. Pease (1867–1869)
14. Edmund J. Davis (1870–1874)
15. Richard Coke (1874–1876)
16. Richard B. Hubbard (1876–1879)
17. Oran M. Roberts (1879–1883)
18. John Ireland (1883–1887)
19. Lawrence Sullivan Ross (1887–1891)
20. James Stephen Hogg (1891–1895)
21. Charles A. Culberson (1895–1899)
22. Joseph D. Sayers (1899–1903)
23. S. W. T. Lanham (1903–1907)
24. Thomas Mitchell Campbell (1907–1911)
25. Oscar Branch Colquitt (1911–1915)
26. James E. Ferguson (1915–1917)
27. William Pettus Hobby (1917–1921)
28. Pat Morris Neff (1921–1925)
29. Miriam A. Ferguson (1925–1927)
30. Dan Moody (1927–1931)
31. Ross S. Sterling (1931–1933)
32. Miriam A. Ferguson (1933–1935)
33. James V Allred (1935–1939)
34. W. Lee O'Daniel (1939–1941)
35. Coke R. Stevenson (1941–1947)
36. Beauford H. Jester (1947–1949)
37. Allan Shivers (1949–1957)
38. Price Daniel (1957–1963)
39. John Connally (1963–1969)
40. Preston Smith (1969–1973)
41. Dolph Briscoe (1973–1979)
42. William P. Clements (1979–1983)
43. Mark White (1983–1987)
44. William P. Clements (1987–1991)
45. Ann W. Richards (1991–1995)
46. George W. Bush (1995–2000)
47. James Richard Perry (2000–present)

General Timeline of Texas

1520s Spanish conquests of Texas begin

1500s

1600s

1685 French attempt to establish claim to Texas

1700s

1821 Mexico wins independence from Spain

1827 Constitution of the state of Coahuila y Tejas

1830 Mexican government banned further American immigration

1834 Santa Ana dismantles federal system, threatening autonomy of Texans

1836 Texans win war of independence and establish the Republic of Texas

1846 Texas annexed by the United States

Start of war with Mexico which ends in 1848 with Treaty of Hildago

1861 Texas secedes from the Union and joins the southern Confederacy

1865 End of Civil War and the beginning of Reconstruction

1869 New post-Civil War constitution adopted to meet demands of U.S. government

1800s

1875 New constitution written in reaction to Radical Reconstruction

1880s Populist and Reform Politics

1890s Enactment of Jim Crow Laws

1900s Progressive reforms of election laws, child labor laws, and business regulations

1920 Women given right to vote

1930s Great Depression dominates state's politics, producing sharp political divisions

1952 Democratic Governor Allan Shivers leads many conservative Democrats to vote for Republican presidential nominee Dwight D. Eisenhower

1961 Senator John Tower is the first Republican elected to a statewide office in Texas since Reconstruction

1970s Period of rapid economic expansion

1974 Constitutional Convention fails to adopt a new Constitution

1975 Texas included under the provisions of the Voting Rights Act

1978 Bill Clements elected first Republican governor since Reconstruction, leading the way for the transformation of the state's party system

1980s Early evidence of the transformation of the Texas economy from its heavy dependence on oil and gas to a highly diversified economy

1900s

1990s Accelerated party realignment to the Republican Party

Robust economic growth based on an increasingly diverse economy

1993 North American Free Trade Agreement that established closer economic ties to Mexico

2002 Republicans win control of all state-wide elected offices and both houses of the Texas Legislature

2000s

Appendix

The Declaration of Independence

Drafted mainly by Thomas Jefferson, this document adopted by the Second Continental Congress, and signed by John Hancock and fifty-five others, outlined the rights of man and the rights to rebellion and self-government. It declared the independence of the colonies from Great Britain, justified rebellion, and listed the grievances against George the III and his government. What is memorable about this famous document is not only that it declared the birth of a new nation, but that it set forth, with eloquence, our basic philosophy of liberty and representative democracy.

IN CONGRESS, JULY 4, 1776 (The unanimous Declaration of the Thirteen United States of America)

Preamble

When, in the course of human events, it becomes necessary for one people to dissolve the political bands which have connected them with another, and to assume, among the powers of the earth, the separate and equal station to which the laws of nature and of nature's God entitle them, a decent respect to the opinions of mankind requires that they should declare the causes which impel them to the separation.

New Principles of Government

We hold these truths to be self-evident; that all men are created equal, that they are endowed by their Creator with certain unalienable rights, that among these are life, liberty, and the pursuit of happiness.

That, to secure these rights, governments are instituted among men, deriving their just powers from the consent of the governed.

That whenever any form of government becomes destructive of these ends, it is the right of the people to alter or to abolish it, and to institute new government, laying its foundation on such principles, and organizing its powers in such form, as to them shall seem most likely to effect their safety and happiness. Prudence, indeed will dictate that governments long established should not be changed for light and transient causes; and accordingly all experience hath shown that mankind are more disposed to suffer while evils are sufferable, than to right themselves by abolishing the forms to which they are accustomed. But when a long train of abuses and usurpations, pursuing invariably the same object, evinces a design to reduce them under absolute despotism, it is their right, it is their duty, to throw off such government, and to provide new guards for their future security.

Reasons for Separation

Such has been the patient sufferance of these colonies; and such is now the necessity which constrains them to alter their former systems of government. The history of the present king of Great Britain is a history of repeated injuries and usurpations, all having in direct object the establishment of an absolute tyranny over these states. To prove this, let facts be submitted to a candid world.

He has refused his assent to laws, the most wholesome and necessary for the public good.

He has forbidden his governors to pass laws of immediate and pressing importance unless suspended in their operation till his assent should be obtained; and when so suspended, he has utterly neglected to attend to them.

He has refused to pass other laws for the accommodation of large districts of people, unless those people would relinquish the right of representation in the legislature, a right inestimable to them, and formidable to tyrants only.

He has called together legislative bodies at places unusual, uncomfortable, and distant for the depository of their public records, for the sole purpose of fatiguing them into compliance with his measures.

He has dissolved representative houses repeatedly, for opposing, with manly firmness, his invasions on the rights of people.

He has refused, for a long time after such dissolutions, to cause others to be elected; whereby the legislative powers incapable of annihilation, have returned to the people at large for their exercise; the state remaining, in the mean-time, exposed to all the dangers of invasion from without and convulsions within.

He has endeavored to prevent the population of these states; for that purpose obstructing the laws of naturalization of foreigners, refusing to pass others to encourage their migration hither, and raising the conditions of new appropriations of lands.

He has obstructed the administration of justice, by refusing his assent to laws for establishing judiciary powers.

He has made judges dependent on his will alone for the tenure of their offices, and the amount and payment of their salaries.

He has erected a multitude of new offices, and sent hither swarms of officers to harass our people and eat out their substance.

He has kept among us, in times of peace, standing armies, without the consent of our legislature.

He has affected to render the military independent of, and superior to, the civil power.

He has combined with others to subject us to jurisdiction foreign to our constitution and unacknowledged by our laws, giving his assent to their acts of pretended legislation:

For quartering large bodies of armed troops among us;

For protecting them, by a mock trial, from punishment for any murders which they should commit on the inhabitants of these states;

For cutting off our trade with all parts of the world;

For imposing taxes on us without our consent;

For depriving us, in many cases, of the benefits of trial by jury;

For transporting us beyond seas, to be tried for pretended offenses;

For abolishing the free system of English laws in a neighboring province, establishing therein an arbitrary government, and enlarging its boundaries, so as to render it at once an example and fit instrument for introducing the same absolute rule into these colonies;

For taking away our charters, abolishing our most valuable laws, and altering, fundamentally, the forms of our governments;

For suspending our own legislatures, and declaring themselves invented with power to legislate for us in all cases whatsoever.

He has abdicated government here, by declaring us out of his protection and waging war against us.

He has plundered our seas, ravaged our coasts, burned our towns, and destroyed the lives of our people.

He is at this time transporting large armies of foreign mercenaries to complete the works of death, desolation, and tyranny already begun with circumstances of cruelty and perfidy scarcely paralleled in the most barbarous ages and totally unworthy of the head of a civilized nation.

He has constrained our fellow-citizens, taken captive on the high seas, to bear arms against their country, to become the executioners of their friends and brethren, or to fall themselves by their hands.

He has excited domestic insurrections among us, and has endeavored to bring on the inhabitants of our frontiers the merciless Indian savages, whose known rule of warfare is an undistinguished destruction of all ages, sexes, and conditions.

In every stage of these oppressions we have petitioned for redress in the most humble terms; our repeated petitions have been answered only by repeated injury. A prince whose character is thus marked by every act which may define a tyrant is unfit to be the ruler of a free people.

Nor have we been wanting in attention to our British brethren. We have warned them, from time to time, of attempts by their legislature to extend an unwarrantable jurisdiction over us. We have reminded them of the circumstances of our emigration and settlement here. We have appealed to their native justice and magnanimity; and we have conjured them, by the ties of our common kindred, to disavow these usurpations, which would inevitably interrupt our connections and correspondence. They, too, have been deaf to the voice of justice and of consanguinity. We must, therefore, acquiesce in the necessity which denounces our separation, and hold them, as we hold the rest of mankind, enemies in war, in peace, friends.

We, therefore, the representatives of the United States of America, in General Congress assembled, appealing to the Supreme Judge of the world for the rectitude of our intentions, do, in the name and by authority of the good people of these colonies, solemnly publish and declare, that these united colonies are, and of right ought to be, free and independent states; that they are absolved from all allegiance to the British crown, and that all political connection between them and the state of Great Britain is, and ought to be, totally dissolved; and that, as free and independent states, they have full power to levy war, conclude peace, contract alliances, establish commerce, and do all other acts and things which independent states may of a right do. And, for the support of this declaration, with a firm reliance on the protection of Divine Providence, we mutually pledge to each other our lives, our fortunes, and our sacred honor.

The Federalist, No. 10, James Madison

To the People of the State of New York: Among the numerous advantages promised by a well-constructed union, none deserves to be more accurately developed than its tendency to break and control the violence of faction. The friend of popular governments, never finds himself so much alarmed for their character and fate, as when he contemplates their propensity to this dangerous vice. He will not fail, therefore, to set a due value on any plan which, without violating the principles to which he is attached, provides a proper cure for it. The instability, injustice, and confusion introduced into the public councils, have, in truth, been the mortal diseases under which popular governments have everywhere perished; as they continue to be the favourite and fruitful topics from which the adversaries to liberty derive their most specious declamations. The valuable improvements made by the American constitutions on the popular models, both ancient and modern, cannot certainly be too much admired; but it would be an unwarrantable partiality, to contend that they have as effectually obviated the danger on this side, as was wished and expected. Complaints are everywhere heard from our most considerate and virtuous citizens, equally the friends of public and private faith, and of public and personal liberty, that our governments are too unstable; that the public good is disregarded in the conflicts of rival parties; and that measures are too often decided, not according to the rules of justice, and the rights of the minor party, but by the superior force of an interested and over-bearing majority. However anxiously we may wish that these complaints had no foundation, the evidence of known facts will not permit us to deny that they are in some degree true. It will be found, indeed, on a candid review of our situation, that some of the distresses under which we labour have been erroneously charged on the operation of our governments; but it will be found, at the same time, that other causes will not alone account for many of our heaviest misfortunes; and, particularly, for that prevailing and increasing distrust of public engagements, and alarm for private rights, which are echoed from one end of the continent to the other. These must be chiefly, if not wholly, effects of the unsteadiness and injustice, with which a factious spirit has tainted our public administrations.

By a faction, I understand a number of citizens, whether amounting to a majority or minority of the whole, who are united and actuated by some common impulse of passion, or of interest, adverse to the rights of other citizens, or to the permanent and aggregate interests of the community.

There are two methods of curing the mischiefs of faction: the one, by removing its causes; the other, by controlling its effects.

There are again two methods of removing the causes of faction: the one, by destroying the liberty which is essential to its existence; the other, by giving to every citizen the same opinions, the same passions, and the same interests.

It could never be more truly said, than of the first remedy, that it was worse than the disease. Liberty is to faction what air is to fire, an aliment without which it instantly expires. But it could not be a less folly to abolish liberty, which is essential to political life, because it nourishes faction, than it would be to wish the annihilation of air, which is essential to animal life, because it imparts to fire its destructive agency.

The second expedient is as impracticable, as the first would be unwise. As long as the reason of man continues fallible, and he is at liberty to exercise it, different opinions will be formed. As long as the connection subsists between his reason and his self-love, his opinions and his passions will have a reciprocal influence on each other; and the former will be objects to which the latter will attach themselves. The diversity in the faculties of men, from which the rights of property originate, is not less an insuperable obstacle to an uniformity of interests. The protection of these faculties is the first object of government. From the protection of different and unequal faculties of acquiring property, the possession of different degrees and kinds of property immediately results; and from the influence of these on the sentiments and views of the respective proprietors, ensues a division of the society into different interests and parties.

The latent causes of faction are thus sown in the nature of man; and we see them everywhere brought into different degrees of activity, according to the different circumstances of civil society. A zeal for different opinions concerning religion, concerning government, and many other points, as well of speculation as of practice; an attachment to different leaders ambitiously contending for preeminence and power; or to persons of other descriptions whose fortunes have been interesting to the human passions, have, in turn, divided mankind into parties, inflamed them with mutual animosity, and rendered them much more disposed to vex and oppress each other, than to cooperate for their common good. So strong is this propensity of mankind, to fall into mutual animosities, that where no substantial occasion presents itself, the most frivolous and fanciful distinctions have been sufficient to kindle their unfriendly passions and excite their most violent conflicts. But the most common and durable source of factions, has been the various and unequal distribution of property. Those who hold, and those who are without property, have ever formed distinct interests in society. Those who are creditors, and those who are debtors, fall under a like discrimination. A landed interest, a manufacturing interest, a mercantile interest, a moneyed interest, with many lesser interests, grow up of necessity in civilized nations, and divide them into different classes, actuated by different sentiments and views. The regulation of these various and interfering interests forms the principal task of modern legislation, and involves the spirit of the party and faction in the necessary and ordinary operations of the government.

No man is allowed to be a judge in his own cause; because his interest will certainly bias his judgment, and, not improbably, corrupt his integrity. With equal, nay, with greater reason, a body of men are unfit to be both judges and parties at the same time; yet what are many of the most important acts of legislation, but so many judicial determinations, not indeed concerning the right of single persons, but concerning the rights of large bodies of citizens? And what are the different classes of legislators, but advocates and parties to the causes which they determine? Is a law proposed concerning private debts? It is a question to which the creditors are parties on one side, and the debtors on the other. Justice ought to hold the balance between them. Yet the parties are, and must be, themselves the judges; and the most numerous party, or, in other words, the most powerful faction, must be expected to prevail. Shall domestic manufacturers be encouraged, and in what degree, by restrictions on foreign manufacturers are questions which would be differently decided by the landed and the manufacturing classes; and probably by neither with a sole regard to justice and the public good. The apportionment of taxes, on the various descriptions of property, is an act which seems to require the most exact impartiality; yet there is, perhaps, no legislative act, in which greater opportunity and temptation are given to a predominant party to trample on the rules of justice. Every shilling, with which they overburden the inferior number, is a shilling saved to their own pockets.

It is in vain to say, that enlightened statesmen will be able to adjust these clashing interests, and render them all subservient to the public good. Enlightened statesmen will not always be at the helm; nor, in many cases, can such an adjustment be made at all, without taking into view indirect and remote considerations, which will rarely prevail over the immediate interest which one party may find in disregarding the rights of another, or the good of the whole.

The inference to which we are brought is, that the *causes* of faction cannot be removed; and that relief is only to be sought in the means of controlling its *effects*.

If a faction consists of less than a majority, relief is supplied by the republican principle, which enables the majority to defeat its sinister views, by regular vote. It may clog the administration, it may convulse the society; but it will be unable to execute and mask its violence under the forms of the Constitution. When a majority is included in a faction, the form of popular government, on the other hand, enables it to sacrifice to its ruling passion or interest, both the public good and the rights of other citizens. To secure the public good, and private rights, against the danger of such a faction, and at the same time to preserve the spirit and the form of popular government, is then the great object to which our inquiries are directed. Let me add, that it is the great desideratum, by which alone this form of government can be rescued from the opprobrium under which it has so long laboured, and be recommended to the esteem and adoption of mankind.

By what means is this object attainable? Evidently by one of two only. Either the existence of the same passion or interest in a majority, at the same time, must be prevented; or the majority, having such coexistent passion or interest, must be rendered, by their number and local situation, unable to concert and carry into effect schemes of oppression. If the impulse and the opportunity be suffered to coincide, we well know that neither moral nor religious motives can be relied on as an adequate control. They are not found to be such on the injustice and violence of individuals, and lose their efficacy in proportion to the number combined together; that is, in proportion as their efficacy becomes needful.

From this view of the subject, it may be concluded, that a pure democracy, by which I mean a society consisting of a small number of citizens, who assemble and administer the government in person, can admit of no cure for the mischiefs of faction. A common passion or interest will, in almost every case, be felt by a majority of the whole; a communication and concert, results from the form of government itself; and there is nothing to check the inducements to sacrifice the weaker party, or an obnoxious individual. Hence, it is, that such democracies have ever been spectacles of turbulence and contention; have ever been found incompatible with personal security, or the rights of property; and have in general been as short in their lives, as they have been violent in their deaths. Theoretic politicians, who have patronized this species of government, have erroneously supposed, that by reducing mankind to a perfect equality in their political rights, they would, at the same time, be perfectly equalized and assimilated in their possessions, their opinions, and their passions.

A republic, by which I mean a government in which the scheme of representation takes place, opens a different prospect, and promises the cure for which we are seeking. Let us examine the points in which it varies from pure democracy, and we shall comprehend both the nature of the cure and the efficacy which it must derive from the union.

The two great points of difference, between a democracy and a republic, are, first, the delegation of the government, in the latter, to a small number of citizens, elected by the rest; secondly, the greater number of citizens, and greater sphere of country, over which the latter may be extended.

The effect of the first difference is, on the one hand, to refine and enlarge the public views, by passing them through the medium of a chosen body of citizens, whose wisdom may best discern the true interest of their country, and whose patriotism and love of justice, will be least likely to sacrifice it to temporary or partial considerations. Under such a regulation, it may well happen, that the public voice, pronounced by the representatives of the people, will be more consonant to the public good, than if pronounced by the people themselves, convened for the purpose. On the other hand the effect may be inverted. Men of factious tempers, of local prejudices, or of sinister designs, may by intrigue, by corruption, or by other means, first obtain the suffrages, and then betray the interest of the people. The question resulting is, whether small or extensive republics are most favourable to the election of proper guardians of the public weal; and it is clearly decided in favour of the latter by two obvious considerations.

In the first place, it is to be remarked that, however small the republic may be, the representatives must be raised to a certain number, in order to guard against the cabals of a few; and that however large it may be, they must be limited to a certain number, in order to guard against the confusion of a multitude. Hence, the number of representatives in the two cases not being in proportion to that of the constituents, and being proportionally greatest in the small republic, it follows, that if the proportion of fit characters be not less in the large than in the small republic, the former will present a greater option, and consequently a greater probability of a fit choice.

In the next place, as each representative will be chosen by a greater number of citizens in the large than in the small republic, it will be more difficult for unworthy candidates to practice with success the vicious arts, by which elections are too often carried; and the suffrages of the people being more free, will be more likely to centre in men who possess the most attractive merit, and the most diffusive and established characters.

It must be confessed, that in this, as in most other cases, there is a mean, on both sides of which inconveniences will be found to lie. By enlarging too much the number of electors, you render the representatives too little acquainted with all their local circumstances and lesser interests; as by reducing it too much, you render him unduly attached to these, and too little fit to comprehend and pursue great and national objects. The federal constitution forms a happy combination in this respect; the great and aggregate interests being referred to the national, the local and particular to the state legislatures.

The other point of difference is, the greater number of citizens, and extent of territory, which may be brought within the compass of republican, than of democratic government; and it is this circumstance principally which renders factious combinations less to be dreaded in the former, than in the latter. The smaller the society, the fewer probably will be the distinct parties and interests composing it; the fewer the distinct parties and interests, the more frequently will a majority be found of the same party; and the smaller the number of individuals composing a majority, and the smaller the compass within which they are placed, the more easily will they concert and execute their plans of oppression. Extend the sphere, and you take in a greater variety of parties and interests; you make it less probable that a majority of the whole will have a common motive to invade the rights of other citizens; or if such a common motive exists, it will be more difficult for all who feel it to discover their own strength, and to act in unison with each other. Besides other impediments, it may be remarked, that where there is a consciousness of unjust or dishonourable purposes, communication is always checked by distrust, in proportion to the number whose concurrence is necessary.

Hence, it clearly appears, that the same advantage, which a republic has over a democracy, in controlling the effects of faction, is enjoyed by a large over a small republic—is enjoyed by the union over the states composing it. Does this advantage consist in the substitution of representatives, whose enlightened views and virtuous sentiments render them superior to local prejudices, and to schemes of injustice? It will not be denied that the representation of the union will be most likely to possess these requisite endowments. Does it consist in the greater security afforded by a greater variety of parties, against the event of any one party being able to outnumber and oppress the rest? In an equal degree does the increased variety of parties, comprised within the union, increase the security? Does it, in fine, consist in the greater obstacles opposed to the concert and accomplishment of the secret wishes of an unjust and interested majority? Here, again, the extent of the union gives it the most palpable advantage.

The influence of factious leaders may kindle a flame within their particular states, but will be unable to spread a general conflagration through the other states; a religious sect may degenerate into a political faction in a part of the confederacy; but the variety of sects dispersed over the entire face of it, must secure the national councils against any danger from that source; a rage for paper money, for an abolition of debts, for an equal division of property, or for any other improper or wicked project, will be less apt to pervade the whole body of the union than a particular member of it; in the same proportion as such a malady is more likely to taint a particular county or district, than an entire state.

In the extent and proper structure of the union, therefore, we behold a republican remedy for the diseases most incident to republican government. And according to the degree of pleasure and pride we feel in being republicans, ought to be our zeal in cherishing the spirit, and supporting the character of federalists.

The Federalist, No. 51, James Madison

To what expedient, then, shall we finally resort, for maintaining in practice the necessary partition of power among the several departments as laid down in the Constitution? The only answer that can be given is that as all these exterior provisions are found to be inadequate the defect must be supplied, by so contriving the interior structure of the government as that its several constituent parts may, by their mutual relations, be the means of keeping each other in their proper places. Without presuming to undertake a full development of this important idea I will hazard a few general observations which may perhaps place it in a clearer light, and enable us to form a more correct judgment of the principles and structure of the government planned by the convention.

In order to lay a due foundation for that separate and distinct exercise of the different powers of government, which to a certain extent is admitted on all hands to be essential to the preservation of liberty, it is evident that each department should have a will of its own; and consequently should be so constituted that the members of each should have as little agency as possible in the appointment of the members of the others. Were this principle rigorously adhered to, it would require that all the appointments for the supreme executive, legislative, and judiciary magistracies should be drawn from the same fountain of authority, the people, through channels having no communication whatever with one another. Perhaps such a plan of constructing the several departments would be less difficult in practice than it may in contemplation appear. Some difficulties, however, and some additional expense would attend the execution of it. Some deviations, therefore, from the principle must be admitted. In the constitution of the judiciary department in particular, it might be inexpedient to insist rigorously on the principle: first, because peculiar qualifications being essential in the members, the primary consideration ought to be to select that mode of choice which best secures these qualifications; second, because the permanent tenure by which the appointments are held in that department must soon destroy all sense of dependence on the authority conferring them.

It is equally evident that the members of each department should be as little dependent as possible on those of the others for the emoluments annexed to their offices. Were the executive magistrate, or the judges, not independent of the legislature in this particular, their independence in every other would be merely nominal.

But the great security against a gradual concentration of the several powers in the same department consists in giving to those who administer each department the necessary constitutional means and personal motives to resist encroachments of the others. The provision for defense must in this, as in all other cases, be made commensurate to the danger of attack. Ambition must be made to counteract ambition. The interest of the man must be connected with the constitutional rights of the place. It may be a reflection on human nature that such devices should be necessary to control the abuses of government. But what is government itself but the greatest of all reflections on human nature? If men were angels, no government would be necessary. If angels were to governmen, neither external nor internal controls on government would be necessary. In framing a government which is to be administered by men over men, the great difficulty lies in this: you must first enable the government to control the governed; and in the next place oblige it to control itself. A dependence on the people is, no doubt, the primary control on the government; but experience has taught mankind the necessity of auxiliary precautions.

This policy of supplying, by opposite and rival interests, the defect of better motives, might be traced through the whole system of human affairs, private as well as public. We see it particularly displayed in all the subordinate distributions of power, where the constant aim is to divide and arrange the several offices in such a manner as that each may be a check on the other—that the private interest of every individual may be a sentinel over the public rights. These inventions of prudence cannot be less requisite in the distribution of the supreme powers of the State.

But it is not possible to give to each department an equal power of self-defense. In republican government, the legislative authority necessarily predominates. The remedy for this inconveniency is to divide the legislature into different branches; and to render them, by modes of election and different principles of action, as little connected with each other as the nature of their common functions and their common dependence on the society will admit. It may even be necessary to guard against dangerous encroachments by still further precautions. As the weight of the legislative authority requires that it should be thus divided, the weakness of the executive may require, on the other hand, that it should be fortified. An absolute negative on the legislature appears, at first view, to be the natural defense with which the executive magistrate should be armed. But perhaps it would be neither altogether safe nor alone sufficient. On ordinary occasions it might not be exerted with the requisite firmness, and on extraordinary occasions it might be perfidiously abused. May not this defect of an absolute negative be supplied by some qualified connection between this weaker department and the weaker branch of the stronger department, by which the latter may be led to support the constitutional rights of the former, without being too much detached from the rights of its own department?

If the principles on which these observations are founded be just, as I persuade myself they are, and they be applied as a criterion to the several State constitutions, and to the federal Constitution, it will be found that if the latter does not perfectly correspond with them, the former are infinitely less able to bear such a test.

There are, moreover, two considerations particularly applicable to the federal system of America, which place that system in a very interesting point of view.

First. In a single republic, all the power surrendered by the people is submitted to the administration of a single government; and the usurpations are guarded against by a division of the government into distinct and separate departments. In the compound republic of America, the power surrendered by the people is first divided between two distinct governments, and then the portion allotted to each subdivided among distinct and separate departments. Hence a double security arises to the rights of the people. The different governments will control each other, at the same time that each will be controlled by itself.

Second. It is of great importance in a republic not only to guard the society against the oppression of its rulers, but to guard one part of the society against the injustice of the other part. Different interests necessarily exist in different classes of citizens. If a majority be united by a common interest, the rights of the minority will be insecure. There are but two methods of providing against this evil: the one by creating a will in the community independent of the majority—that is, of the society itself; the other, by comprehending in the society so many separate descriptions of citizens as will render an unjust combination of a majority of the whole very improbable, if not impracticable. The first method prevails in all governments possessing an hereditary or $$$self-appointed authority. This, at best, is but a precarious security; because a power independent of the society may as well espouse the unjust views of the major as the rightful interests of the minor party, and may possibly be turned against both parties. The second method will be exemplified in the federal republic of the United States. Whilst all authority in it will be derived from and dependent on the society, the society itself will be broken into so many parts, interests and classes of citizens, that the rights of individuals, or of the minority, will be in little danger from interested combinations of the majority. In a free government the security for civil rights must be the same as that for religious rights. It consists in the one case in the multiplicity of interests, and in the other in the multiplicity of sects. The degree of security in both cases will depend on the number of interests and sects; and this may be presumed to depend on the extent of country and number of people comprehended under the same government. This view of the subject must particularly recommend a proper federal system to all the sincere and considerate friends of republican government, since it shows that in exact proportion as the territory of the Union may be formed into more circumscribed Confederacies, or States, oppressive combinations of a majority will be facilitated; the best security, under the republican forms, for the rights of every class of citizen, will be diminished; and consequently the stability and independence of some member of the government, the only other security, must be proportionally increased. Justice is the end of government. It is the end of civil society. It ever has been and ever will be pursued until it be obtained, or until liberty be lost in the pursuit. In a society under the forms of which the stronger faction can readily unite and oppress the weaker, anarchy may as truly be said to reign as in a state of nature, where the weaker individual is not secured against the violence of the stronger; and as, in the latter state, even the stronger individuals are prompted, by the uncertainty of their condition, to submit to a government which may protect the weak as well as themselves; so, in the former state, will the more powerful factions or parties be gradually induced, by a like motive, to wish for a government which will protect all parties, the weaker as well as the more powerful. It can be little doubted that if the State of Rhode Island was separated from the Confederacy and left to itself, the insecurity of rights under the popular form of government within such narrow limits would be displayed by such reiterated oppressions of factious majorities that some power altogether independent of the people would soon be called for by the voice of the very factions whose misrule had proved the necessity of it. In the extended republic of the United States, and among the great variety of interests, parties, and sects which it embraces, a coalition of a majority of the whole society could seldom take place on any other principles than those of justice and the general good; whilst there being thus less danger to a minor from the will of a major party, there must be less pretext, also, to provide for the security of the former, by introducing into the government a will not dependent on the latter, or, in other words, a will independent of the society itself. It is no less certain that it is important, notwithstanding the contrary opinions which have been entertained that the larger the society, provided it lie within a practicable sphere, the more duly capable it will be of self-government. And happily for the *republican cause,* the practicable sphere may be carried to a very great extent by a judicious modification and mixture of the *federal principle.*

Presidents and Vice Presidents

1. George Washington (1789)
   John Adams (1789)
2. John Adams (1797)
   Thomas Jefferson (1797)
3. Thomas Jefferson (1801)
   Aaron Burr (1801)
   George Clinton (1805)
4. James Madison (1809)
   George Clinton (1809)
   Elbridge Gerry (1813)
5. James Monroe (1817)
   Daniel D. Tompkins (1817)
6. John Quincy Adams (1825)
   John C. Calhoun (1825)
7. Andrew Jackson (1829)
   John C. Calhoun (1829)
   Martin Van Buren (1833)
8. Martin Van Buren (1837)
   Richard M. Johnson (1837)
9. William H. Harrison (1841)
   John Tyler (1841)
10. John Tyler (1841)
11. James K. Polk (1845)
    George M. Dallas (1845)
12. Zachary Taylor (1849)
    Millard Fillmore (1849)
13. Millard Fillmore (1850)
14. Franklin Pierce (1853)
    William R. King (1853)
15. James Buchanan (1857)
    John C. Breckinridge (1857)
16. Abraham Lincoln (1861)
    Hannibal Hamlin (1861)
    Andrew Johnson (1865)
17. Andrew Johnson (1865)
18. Ulysses S. Grant (1869)
    Schuyler Colfax (1869)
    Henry Wilson (1873)
19. Rutherford B. Hayes (1877)
    William A. Wheeler (1877)
20. James A. Garfield (1881)
    Chester A. Arthur (1881)
21. Chester A. Arthur (1881)
22. Grover Cleveland (1885)
    T.A. Hendricks (1885)
23. Benjamin Harrison (1889)
    Levi P. Morton (1889)
24. Grover Cleveland (1893)
    Adlai E. Stevenson (1893)
25. William McKinley (1897)
    Garret A. Hobart (1897)
    Theodore Roosevelt (1901)
26. Theodore Roosevelt (1901)
    Charles Fairbanks (1905)
27. William H. Taft (1909)
    James S. Sherman (1909)
28. Woodrow Wilson (1913)
    Thomas R. Marshall (1913)
29. Warren G. Harding (1921)
    Calvin Coolidge (1921)
30. Calvin Coolidge (1923)
    Charles G. Dawes (1925)
31. Herbert C. Hoover (1929)
    Charles Curtis (1929)
32. Franklin D. Roosevelt (1933)
    John Nance Garner (1933)
    Henry A. Wallace (1941)
    Harry S. Truman (1945)
33. Harry S. Truman (1945)
    Alben W. Barkley (1949)
34. Dwight D. Eisenhower (1953)
    Richard M. Nixon (1953)
35. John F. Kennedy (1961)
    Lyndon B. Johnson (1961)
36. Lyndon B. Johnson (1963)
    Hubert H. Humphrey (1965)
37. Richard M. Nixon (1969)
    Spiro T. Agnew (1969)
    Gerald R. Ford (1973)
38. Gerald R. Ford (1974)
    Nelson A. Rockefeller (1974)
39. James E. Carter, Jr. (1977)
    Walter F. Mondale (1977)
40. Ronald W. Reagan (1981)
    George H.W. Bush (1981)
41. George H.W. Bush (1989)
    James D. Quayle III (1989)
42. William J.B. Clinton (1993)
    Albert Gore (1993)
43. George W. Bush (2001)
    Richard Cheney (2001)

Supreme Court Justices

Current Supreme Court Justices

1. William H. Rehnquist (Chief Justice)
2. Antonin Scalia (Associate Justice)
3. John Paul Stevens (Associate Justice)
4. Sandra Day O'Connor (Associate Justice)
5. Anthony M. Kennedy (Associate Justice)
6. Ruth Bader Ginsburg (Associate Justice)
7. David H. Souter (Associate Justice)
8. Clarence Thomas (Associate Justice)
9. Stephen G. Breyer (Associate Justice)

Former Supreme Court Chief Justices

1. John Jay (1779–1795)
2. John Rutledge (1795)
3. Oliver Ellsworth (1996–1800)
4. John Marshall (1801–1835)
5. Roger Brooke Tancy (1836–1864)
6. Salmon Portland Chase (1864–1873)
7. Morrison R. Waite (1874–1888)
8. Melville Weston Fuller (1888–1910)
9. Edward Douglas White (1910–1921)
10. William Howard Taft (1921–1930)
11. Charles Evans Hughes (1930–1941)
12. Harlan Fiske Stone (1941–1946)
13. Fred M. Vison (1946–1953)
14. Earl Warren (1953–1969)
15. Warren E. Burger (1969–1986)

Former Supreme Court Associate Judges

1. James Wilson (1789–1798)
2. William Cushing (1790–1810)
3. John Blair, Jr. (1790–1796)
4. James Iredell (1790–1799)
5. Thomas Johnson (1792–1793)
6. William Paterson (1793–1806)
7. Samuel Chase (1796–1811)
8. Bushrod Washington (1799–1829)
9. Alfred Moore (1800–1804)
10. William Johnson (1804–1834)
11. H. Brockholst Livingston (1807–1328)
12. Thomas Todd (1807–1826)
13. Gabriel Duvall (1811–1835)
14. Joseph Story (1812–1845)
15. Smith Thompson (1823–1843)
16. Robert Trimble (1826–1828)
17. John McLean (1830–1861)
18. Henry Baldwin (1830–1844)
19. James M. Wayne (1835–1867)
20. Philip P. Barbour (1836–1841)
21. John Catron (1837–1865)
22. John McKinley (1838–1852)
23. Peter V. Daniel (1842–1860)
24. Samuel Nelson (1845–1872)
25. Levi Woodbury (1845–1851)
26. Robert C. Grier (1846–1870)
27. Benjamin R. Curtis (1851–1857)
28. John A. Campbell (1853–1861)
29. Nathan Clifford (1858–1881)
30. Noah H. Swayne (1862–1881)
31. Samuel F. Miller (1862–1890)
32. David Davis (1862–1877)
33. Stephen J. Field (1863–1897)
34. William Strong (1870–1880)
35. Joseph P. Bradley (1870–1892)
36. Ward Hunt (1873–1882)
37. John Marshall Harlan (1877–1911)
38. William B. Woods (1881–1887)
39. Stanley Matthews (1881–1889)
40. Horace Gray (1882–1902)
41. Samuel Blatchford (1882–1893)
42. Lucius Q. C. Lamar (1888–1893)
43. David J. Brewer (1890–1910)
44. Henry B. Brown (1891–1906)
45. George Shiras, Jr. (1892–1903)
46. Howell E. Jackson (1893–1895)
47. Rufus W. Peckham (1896–1909)
48. Joseph McKenna (1898–1925)
49. Oliver Wendell Holmes, Jr. (1902–1932)
50. William R. Day (1903–1922)
51. William H. Moody (1906–1910)
52. Horace H. Lurton (1910–1914)
53. Willis Van Devanter (1911–1937)
54. Joseph Rucker Lamar (1911–1916)
55. Mahlon Pitney (1912–1922)
56. James Clark McReynolds (1914–1941)
57. Louis D. Brandeis (1916–1939)
58. John H. Clark (1916–1922)
59. George Sutherland (1922–1938)
60. Pierce Butler (1923–1939)
61. Edward T. Sanford (1923–1930)
62. Owen J. Roberts (1930–1945)

63. Benjamin Nathan Cordozo (1932–1938)
64. Hugo Black (1937–1971)
65. Stanley F. Reed (1938–1957)
66. Felix Frankfurter (1939–1962)
67. William O. Douglas (1939–1975)
68. Frank W. Murphy (1940–1949)
69. James F. Byrnes (1941–1942)
70. Robert H. Jackson (1941–1954)
71. Wiley B. Rutledge (1943–1949)
72. Harold H. Burton (1945–1958)
73. Tom C. Clark (1949–1967)
74. Sherman Minton (1949–1956)
75. William J. Brennan, Jr. (1956–1990)
76. John Marshall Harlan II (1955–1971)
77. Charles E. Whittaker (1957–1962)
78. Potter Stewart (1958–1981)
79. Byron R. White (1962–1993)
80. Arthur J. Goldberg (1962–1965)
81. Abe Fortas (1965–1969)
82. Thurgood Marshall (1967–1991)
83. Harry A. Blackmun (1970–1994)
84. Lewis F. Powell, Jr. (1972–1987)

Presidential Elections and Voting

Year	Number of States	Candidates	Party	Popular Vote*	Electoral Vote†	Percentage of Popular Vote
1789	11	**George Washington**	No party designations		69	
		John Adams			34	
		Other Candidates			35	
1792	15	**George Washington**	No party designations		132	
		John Adams			77	
		George Clinton			50	
		Other Candidates			5	
1796	16	**John Adams**	Federalist		71	
		Thomas Jefferson	Democratic Republican		68	
		Thomas Pinckney	Federalist		59	
		Aaron Burr	Democratic Republican		30	
		Other Candidates			48	
1800	16	**Thomas Jefferson**	Democratic Republican		73	
		Aaron Burr	Democratic Republican		73	
		John Adams	Federalist		65	
		Charles C. Pinckney	Federalist		64	
		John Jay	Federalist		1	
1804	17	**Thomas Jefferson**	Democratic Republican		162	
		Charles C. Pinckney	Federalist		14	
1808	17	**James Madison**	Democratic Republican		122	
		Charles C. Pinckney	Federalist		47	
		George Clinton	Democratic Republican		6	
1812	18	**James Madison**	Democratic Republican		128	
		DeWitt Clinton	Federalist		89	
1816	19	**James Monroe**	Democratic Republican		183	
		Rufus King	Federalist		34	
1820	24	**James Monroe**	Democratic Republican		231	
		John Quincy Adams	Independent Republican		1	
1824	24	**John Quincy Adams**		108,740	84	30.5
		Andrew Jackson		153,544	99	43.1
		William H. Crawford		46,618	41	13.1
		Henry Clay		47,136	37	13.2
1828	24	**Andrew Jackson**	Democrat	647,286	178	56.0
		John Quincy Adams	National Republican	508,064	83	44.0
1832	24	**Andrew Jackson**	Democrat	687,502	219	55.0
		Henry Clay	National Republican	530,189	49	42.4
		William Wirt	Anti-Masonic		7	
		John Floyd	National Republican	33,108	11	2.6
1836	26	**Martin Van Buren**	Democrat	765,483	170	50.9
		William H. Harrison	Whig		73	
		Hugh L. White	Whig		26	
		Daniel Webster	Whig	739,795	14	49.1
		W. P. Mangum	Whig		11	
1840	26	**William H. Harrison**	Whig	1,274,624	234	53.1
		Martin Van Buren	Democrat	1,127,781	60	46.9

(continued on page A-12)

Presidential Elections and Voting

Year	Number of States	Candidates	Party	Popular Vote*	Electoral Vote†	Percentage of Popular Vote
1844	26	**James K. Polk**	Democrat	1,338,464	170	49.6
		Henry Clay	Whig	1,300,097	105	48.1
		James G. Birney	Liberty	62,300		2.3
1848	30	**Zachary Taylor**	Whig	1,360,967	163	47.4
		Lewis Cass	Democrat	1,222,342	127	42.5
		Martin Van Buren	Free Soil	291,263		10.1
1852	31	**Franklin Pierce**	Democrat	1,601,117	254	50.9
		Winfield Scott	Whig	1,385,453	42	44.1
		John P. Hale	Free Soil	155,825		5.0
1856	31	**James Buchanan**	Democrat	1,832,955	174	45.3
		John C. Frémont	Republican	1,339,932	114	33.1
		Millard Fillmore	American ("Know Nothing")	871,731	8	21.6
1860	33	**Abraham Lincoln**	Republican	1,865,593	180	39.8
		Stephen A. Douglas	Democrat	1,382,713	12	29.5
		John C. Breckinridge	Democrat	848,356	72	18.1
		John Bell	Constitutional Union	592,906	39	12.6
1864	36	**Abraham Lincoln**	Republican	2,206,938	212	55.0
		George B. McClellan	Democrat	1,803,787	21	45.0
1868	37	**Ulysses S. Grant**	Republican	3,013,421	214	52.7
		Horatio Seymour	Democrat	2,706,829	80	47.3
1872	37	**Ulysses S. Grant**	Republican	3,596,745	286	55.6
		Horace Greeley	Democrat	2,843,446	*	43.9
1876	38	**Rutherford B. Hayes**	Republican	4,036,572	185	48.0
		Samuel J. Tilden	Democrat	4,284,020	184	51.0
1880	38	**James A. Garfield**	Republican	4,453,295	214	48.5
		Winfield S. Hancock	Democrat	4,414,082	155	48.1
		James B. Weaver	Greenback-Labor	308,578		3.4
1884	38	**Grover Cleveland**	Democrat	4,879,507	219	48.5
		James G. Blaine	Republican	4,850,293	182	48.2
		Benjamin F. Butler	Greenback-Labor	175,370		1.8
		John P. St. John	Prohibition	150,369		1.5
1888	38	**Benjamin Harrison**	Republican	5,447,129	233	47.9
		Grover Cleveland	Democrat	5,537,857	168	48.6
		Clinton B. Fisk	Prohibition	249,506		2.2
		Alson J. Streeter	Union Labor	146,935		1.3
1892	44	**Grover Cleveland**	Democrat	5,555,426	277	46.1
		Benjamin Harrison	Republican	5,182,690	145	43.0
		James B. Weaver	People's	1,029,846	22	8.5
		John Bidwell	Prohibition	264,133		2.2
1896	45	**William McKinley**	Republican	7,102,246	271	51.1
		William J. Bryan	Democrat	6,492,559	176	47.7
1900	45	**William McKinley**	Republican	7,218,491	292	51.7
		William J. Bryan	Democrat; Populist	6,356,734	155	45.5
		John C. Woolley	Prohibition	208,914		1.5

Presidential Elections and Voting

Year	Number of States	Candidates	Party	Popular Vote*	Electoral Vote†	Percentage of Popular Vote
1904	45	**Theodore Roosevelt**	Republican	7,628,461	336	57.4
		Alton B. Parker	Democrat	5,084,223	140	37.6
		Eugene V. Debs	Socialist	402,283		3.0
		Silas C. Swallow	Prohibition	258,536		1.9
1908	46	**William H. Taft**	Republican	7,675,320	321	51.6
		William J. Bryan	Democrat	6,412,294	162	43.1
		Eugene V. Debs	Socialist	420,793		2.8
		Eugene W. Chafin	Prohibition	253,840		1.7
1912	48	**Woodrow Wilson**	Democrat	6,296,547	435	41.9
		Theodore Roosevelt	Progressive	4,118,571	88	27.4
		William H. Taft	Republican	3,486,720	8	23.2
		Eugene V. Debs	Socialist	900,672		6.0
		Eugene W. Chafin	Prohibition	206,275		1.4
1916	48	**Woodrow Wilson**	Democrat	9,127,695	277	49.4
		Charles E. Hughes	Republican	8,533,507	254	46.2
		A. L. Benson	Socialist	585,113		3.2
		J. Frank Hanly	Prohibition	220,506		1.2
1920	48	**Warren G. Harding**	Republican	16,143,407	404	60.4
		James M. Cox	Democrat	9,130,328	127	34.2
		Eugene V. Debs	Socialist	919,799		3.4
		P. P. Christensen	Farmer-Labor	265,411		1.0
1924	48	**Calvin Coolidge**	Republican	15,718,211	382	54.0
		John W. Davis	Democrat	8,385,283	136	28.8
		Robert M. La Follette	Progressive	4,831,289	13	16.6
1928	48	**Herbert C. Hoover**	Republican	21,391,993	444	58.2
		Alfred E. Smith	Democrat	15,016,169	87	40.9
1932	48	**Franklin D. Roosevelt**	Democrat	22,809,638	472	57.4
		Herbert C. Hoover	Republican	15,758,901	59	39.7
		Norman Thomas	Socialist	881,951		2.2
1936	48	**Franklin D. Roosevelt**	Democrat	27,752,869	523	60.8
		Alfred M. Landon	Republican	16,674,665	8	36.5
		William Lemke	Union	882,479		1.9
1940	48	**Franklin D. Roosevelt**	Democrat	27,307,819	449	54.8
		Wendell L. Willkie	Republican	22,321,018	82	44.8
1944	48	**Franklin D. Roosevelt**	Democrat	25,606,585	432	53.5
		Thomas E. Dewey	Republican	22,014,745	99	46.0
1948	48	**Harry S Truman**	Democrat	24,105,812	303	49.5
		Thomas E. Dewey	Republican	21,970,065	189	45.1
		J. Strom Thurmond	States' Rights	1,169,063	39	2.4
		Henry A. Wallace	Progressive	1,157,172		2.4
1952	48	**Dwight D. Eisenhower**	Republican	33,936,234	442	55.1
		Adlai E. Stevenson	Democrat	27,314,992	89	44.4
1956	48	**Dwight D. Eisenhower**	Republican	35,590,472	457*	57.6
		Adlai E. Stevenson	Democrat	26,022,752	73	42.1

(continued on page A-14)

Presidential Elections and Voting

Year	Number of States	Candidates	Party	Popular Vote*	Electoral Vote†	Percentage of Popular Vote
1960	50	**John F. Kennedy**	Democrat	34,227,096	303†	49.9
		Richard M. Nixon	Republican	34,108,546	219	49.6
1964	50	**Lyndon B. Johnson**	Democrat	42,676,220	486	61.3
		Barry M. Goldwater	Republican	26,860,314	52	38.5
1968	50	**Richard M. Nixon**	Republican	31,785,480	301	43.4
		Hubert H. Humphrey	Democrat	31,275,165	191	42.7
		George C. Wallace	American Independent	9,906,473	46	13.5
1972	50	**Richard M. Nixon‡**	Republican	47,165,234	520	60.6
		George S. McGovern	Democrat	29,168,110	17	37.5
1976	50	**Jimmy Carter**	Democrat	40,828,929	297	50.1
		Gerald R. Ford	Republican	39,148,940	240	47.9
		Eugene McCarthy	Independent	739,256		0.9
1980	50	**Ronald Reagan**	Republican	43,201,220	489	50.9
		Jimmy Carter	Democrat	34,913,332	49	41.2
		John B. Anderson	Independent	5,581,379		6.6
1984	50	**Ronald Reagan**	Republican	53,428,357	525	59.0
		Walter F. Mondale	Democrat	36,930,923	13	41.0
1988	50	**George H. W. Bush**	Republican	48,901,046	426	53.4
		Michael Dukakis	Democrat	41,809,030	111	45.6
1992	50	**Bill Clinton**	Democrat	43,728,275	370	43.2
		George Bush	Republican	38,167,416	168	37.7
		H. Ross Perot	United We Stand, America	19,237,247		19.0
1996	50	**Bill Clinton**	Democrat	45,590,703	379	49.0
		Bob Dole	Republican	37,816,307	159	41.0
		H. Ross Perot	Reform	7,866,284		8.0
2000	50	**George W. Bush**	Republican	50,456,169	271	48.0
		Al Gore	Democrat	50,996,116	266	48.0
		Ralph Nader	Green	2,767,176	0	3.0

*Percentage of popular vote given for any election year may not total 100 percent because candidates receiving less than 1 percent of the popular vote have been omitted.

†Prior to the passage of the Twelfth Amendment in 1904, the electoral college voted for two presidential candidates; the runner-up became Vice President. Data from Historical Statistics of the United States, Colonial Times to 1957 (1961), pp. 682–683, and The World Almanac.

*Because of the death of Greeley, Democratic electors scattered their votes.

*Walter B. Jones received 1 electoral vote.

†Harry F. Byrd received 15 electoral votes.

‡Resigned August 9, 1974: Vice President Gerald R. Ford became President.

Party Control of Congress

Congress	Years	Party and President	Senate DEM.	Senate REP.	Senate OTHER	House DEM.	House REP.	House OTHER
57th	1901–03	R T. Roosevelt	29	56	3	153	198	5
58th	1903–05	R T. Roosevelt	32	58	—	178	207	—
59th	1905–07	R T. Roosevelt	32	58	—	136	250	—
60th	1907–09	R T. Roosevelt	29	61	—	164	222	—
61st	1909–11	R Taft	32	59	—	172	219	—
62d	1911–13	R Taft	42	49	—	228	162	1
63d	1913–15	D Wilson	51	44	1	290	127	18
64th	1915–17	D Wilson	56	39	1	230	193	8
65th	1917–19	D Wilson	53	42	1	200	216	9
66th	1919–21	D Wilson	48	48	1	191	237	7
67th	1921–23	R Harding	37	59	—	132	300	1
68th	1923–25	R Coolidge	43	51	2	207	225	3
69th	1925–27	R Coolidge	40	54	1	183	247	5
70th	1927–29	R Coolidge	47	48	1	195	237	3
71st	1929–31	R Hoover	39	56	1	163	267	1
72d	1931–33	R Hoover	47	48	1	216	218	1
73d	1933–35	D F. Roosevelt	59	36	1	313	117	5
74th	1935–37	D F. Roosevelt	69	25	2	322	103	10
75th	1937–39	D F. Roosevelt	75	17	4	333	89	13
76th	1939–41	D F. Roosevelt	69	23	4	262	169	4
77th	1941–43	D F. Roosevelt	66	28	2	267	162	6
78th	1943–45	D F. Roosevelt	57	38	1	222	209	4
79th	1945–47	D Truman	57	38	1	243	190	2
80th	1947–49	D Truman	45	51	—	188	246	1
81st	1949–51	D Truman	54	42	—	263	171	1
82d	1951–53	D Truman	48	47	1	234	199	2
83d	1953–55	R Eisenhower	47	48	1	213	221	1
84th	1955–57	R Eisenhower	48	47	1	232	203	—
85th	1957–59	R Eisenhower	49	47	—	234	201	—
86th	1959–61	R Eisenhower	64	34	—	283	154	—
87th	1961–63	D Kennedy	64	36	—	263	174	—
88th	1963–65	D { Kennedy / Johnson	67	33	—	258	176	—
89th	1965–67	D Johnson	68	32	—	295	140	—
90th	1967–69	D Johnson	64	36	—	248	187	—
91st	1969–71	R Nixon	58	42	—	243	192	—
92d	1971–73	R Nixon	55	45	—	255	180	—
93d	1973–75	R { Nixon / Ford	57	43	—	243	192	—
94th	1975–77	R Ford	61	38	—	291	144	—
95th	1977–79	D Carter	62	38	—	292	143	—
96th	1979–81	D Carter	59	41	—	277	158	—
97th	1981–83	R Reagan	47	53	—	243	192	—
98th	1983–85	R Reagan	46	54	—	269	166	—
99th	1985–87	R Reagan	47	53	—	253	182	—
100th	1987–89	R Reagan	55	45	—	258	177	—
101st	1989–91	R Bush	55	45	—	260	175	—
102d	1991–93	R Bush	57	43	—	267	167	1
103d	1993–95	D Clinton	59	43	—	258	176	1
104th	1995–97	D Clinton	46	54	—	204	230	1
105th	1997–99	D Clinton	45	55	—	207	227	1
106th	1999–2001	D Clinton	45	55	—	211	223	1
107th	2001–2003	R Bush	50	50	—	212	221	2
108th	2003–2005	R Bush	49*	51	—	206	228	1

*Including Vermont independent Jim Jeffords.

Glossary

ABM Treaty A formal treaty in 1972 between the U.S. and the Soviet Union in which each side agreed not to build or deploy antiballistic missiles.

absentee (or early) voting Period before the regularly scheduled election date, during which voters are allowed to cast ballots. With recent changes in election law, a person does not have to offer a reason for voting absentee.

access Meeting and talking with decision makers, a prerequisite to direct persuasion.

adjudication Decision making by the federal bureaucracy as to whether or not an individual or organization has complied with or violated government laws and/or regulation.

adversarial system Method of decision making in which an impartial judge or jury or decision maker hears arguments and reviews evidence presented by opposite sides.

advice and consent The constitutional power of the U.S. Senate to reject or ratify (by a two-thirds vote) treaties made by the president.

affirmative action Any program, whether enacted by a government or by a private organization, whose goal is to overcome the results of past unequal treatment of minorities and/or women by giving members of these groups preferential treatment in admissions, hiring, promotions, or other aspects of life.

affirmative racial gerrymandering Drawing district boundary lines to maximize minority representation.

agenda setting Deciding what will be decided, defining the problems and issues to be addressed by decision makers.

agriculture commissioner The elected official responsible for administering laws and programs that benefit agriculture.

amendment Formal change in a bill, law, or constitution.

amicus curiae Literally, "friend of the court"; a person, private group or institution, or government agency that is not a party to a case but participates in the case (usually through submission of a brief) at the invitation of the court or on its own initiative.

annexation powers Authority of cities to add territory, subject to restrictions set by state law.

appeal In general, requests that a higher court review cases decided at a lower level. In the Supreme Court, certain cases are designated as appeals under federal law; formally, these must be heard by the Court.

appellate jurisdiction Particular court's power to review a decision or action of a lower court.

apportionment The allocation of legislative seats to jurisdictions based on population. Seats in the U.S. House of Representatives are apportioned to the states on the basis of their population after every ten-year census.

appraisal district Local agency that determines the value of pieces of property in a county. All local governments are required to use its evaluations, or appraisals, for tax purposes.

appropriations act Congressional bill that provides money for programs authorized by Congress.

appropriations bill Bill that authorizes the expenditure of money for a public program or purpose. In Texas, the general appropriations bill approved by the legislature every two years is the state budget.

at-large district Legislative or other political district, sometimes called a multimember district because two or more officials are elected from it, that includes an entire county, city, or other political subdivision.

at-large elections Election systems under which officeholders are elected by voters in the entire city, school district, or single-purpose district.

attorney general The state's chief legal officer, who represents Texas in lawsuits and is responsible for enforcing the state's antitrust, consumer protection, and other civil laws.

authorization Act of Congress that establishes a government program and defines the amount of money it may spend.

Bakke case U.S. Supreme Court case challenging affirmative action.

ballistic missile defense (BMD) Weapons systems capable of detecting, intercepting, and destroying missiles in flight.

beliefs Shared ideas about what is true.

bicameral Any legislative body that consists of two separate chambers or houses; in the United States, the Senate represents 50 statewide voter constituencies, and the House of Representatives represents voters in 435 separate districts.

bicameral legislature Lawmaking body, such as the Texas legislature, that includes two chambers.

bifactionalism Presence of two dominant factions organized around regional, economic, or ideological differences within a single political party. For much of the twentieth century, Texas functioned as a one-party system with two dominant factions.

bifurcated court system Existence of two courts at the highest level of the state judiciary. The Texas Supreme Court is the court of last resort in civil cases, and the Texas Court of Criminal Appeals has the final authority to review criminal cases.

bill of attainder Legislative act inflicting punishment without judicial trial; forbidden under Article I of the Constitution.

Bill of Rights Written guarantees of basic individual liberties; the first ten amendments to the U.S. Constitution.

bipartisan Agreement by members of both the Democratic and the Republican parties.

bloc Group of legislators who act together for a common goal regardless of party affiliation.

bribery Giving or offering anything of value in an effort to influence government officials in the performance of their duties.

briefs Documents submitted by an attorney to a court, setting out the facts of the case and the legal arguments in support of the party represented by the attorney.

budget maximization Bureaucrats' tendencies to expand their agencies' budgets, staff, and authority.

budget resolution Congressional bill setting forth target budget figures for appropriations to various government departments and agencies.

bureaucracy Departments, agencies, bureaus, and offices that perform the functions of government.

cabinet The heads (secretaries) of the executive departments together with other top officials accorded cabinet rank by the president; only occasionally does it meet as a body to advise and support the president.

calendar Agenda or the list of bills to be considered by the house or the senate on a given day.

Calendars Committee Special procedural committee that schedules bills that already have been approved by other committees for floor debate in the house.

campaign strategy Plan for a political campaign, usually including a theme, an attempt to define the opponent or the issues, and an effort to coordinate images and messages in news broadcasts and paid advertising.

capital murder Murder committed under certain circumstances for which the death penalty or life in prison must be imposed.

capitalism Economic system asserting the individual's right to own private property and to buy, sell, rent, and trade that property in a free market.

capture theory of regulation Theory describing how some regulated industries come to benefit from government regulation and how some regulatory commissions come to represent the industries they are supposed to regulate rather than representing "the people."

casework Services performed by legislators or their staff on behalf of individual constituents.

caucus Nominating process in which party leaders select the party's nominee.

censure Public reprimand for wrongdoing, given to a member standing in the chamber before Congress.

centralized federalism Model of federalism in which the national government assumes primary responsibility for determining national goals in all major policy areas and directs state and local government activity through conditions attached to money grants.

chain of command Hierarchical structure of authority in which command flows downward; typical of a bureaucracy.

challengers In politics, a reference to people running against incumbent officeholders.

charter Document, based on state authorization, which defines the structure, powers, and responsibilities of a city government.

checks and balances Constitutional provisions giving each branch of the national government certain checks over the actions of other branches.

circuit courts The twelve appellate courts that make up the middle level of the federal court system.

city commission Form of city government in which elected commissioners collectively serve as a city's policy-making body and individually serve as administrative heads of different city departments.

civil cases Noncriminal court proceedings in which a plaintiff sues a defendant for damages in payment for harm inflicted.

civil lawsuit Noncriminal legal dispute between two or more individuals, businesses, governments, or other entities.

civil service system System under which public employees are hired and promoted on their abilities. It features competitive examinations and offers job security from one election to another.

class action suits Cases initiated by parties acting on behalf of themselves and all others similarly situated.

class conflict Conflict between upper and lower social classes over wealth and power.

class consciousness Awareness of one's class position and a feeling of political solidarity with others within the same class in opposition to other classes.

classical liberalism Political philosophy asserting the worth and dignity of the individual and emphasizing the rational ability of human beings to determine their own destinies.

clear and present danger doctrine Standard used by the courts to determine whether speech may be restricted; only speech that creates a serious and immediate danger to society may be restricted.

closed primaries Primary elections in which voters must declare (or have previously declared) their party affiliation and can cast a ballot only in their own party's primary election.

closed rule Rule that forbids adding any amendments to a bill under consideration by the House.

cloture Vote to end debate—that is, to end a filibuster—which requires a three-fifths vote of the entire membership of the Senate.

coalition A joining together of interest groups to achieve a common goal.

Cold War Political, military, and ideological struggle between the United States and the Soviet Union following the end of World War II and ending with the collapse of the Soviet Union's communist government in 1991.

collective security Attempt to bring order to international relations by all nations joining together to guarantee each other's "territorial integrity" and "independence" against "external aggression."

commissioners court Principal policy-making body for county government. It sets the county tax rate and supervises expenditures.

committee In the legislature, a group of lawmakers who review and hold public hearings on issues or bills they are assigned by the presiding officer. Committees that specialize in bills by subject matter are designated as standing committees. A bill has to win committee approval before it can be considered by the full house or senate. Most bills die in committees, which perform as a legislative screening process.

common market Unified trade area in which all goods and services can be sold or exchanged free from customs or tariffs.

communism System of government in which a single totalitarian party controls all means of production and distribution of goods and services.

Comprehensive Test Ban Treaty A multilateral treaty prohibiting all nuclear testing.

comptroller The state's primary tax administrator, accounting officer, and revenue estimator.

concurrent powers Powers exercised by both the national government and state governments in the American federal system.

concurring opinion Opinion by a member of a court that agrees with the result reached by the court in the case but disagrees with or departs from the court's rationale for the decision.

confederacy National government created by states that relies on the states for its authority.

confederation Constitutional arrangement whereby the national government is created by and relies on subnational governments for its authority.

conference committee Meeting between representatives of the House and Senate to reconcile differences over provisions of a bill passed by both houses.

confirmation The constitutionally required consent of the Senate to appointments of high-level executive officials by the president and appointments of federal judges.

congressional hearings Congressional committee sessions in which members listen to witnesses who provide information and opinions on matters of interest to the committee, including pending legislation.

congressional investigation Congressional committee hearings on alleged misdeeds or scandals.

congressional session Each Congress elected in November of even-numbered years meets the following January 3 and remains in session for two years. Since the first Congress to meet under the Constitution in 1789, Congresses have been numbered by session (for example, 107th Congress 2001–2003, 108th Congress 2003–2005, 109th Congress 2005–2007).

conservatism Belief in the value of free markets, limited government, and individual self-reliance in economic affairs, combined with a belief in the value of tradition, law, and morality in social affairs.

constable Elected law enforcement officer who is primarily responsible for executing court judgments, serving subpoenas, and delivering other legal documents.

constituency The votes in a legislator's home district.

constitution The legal structure of a political system, establishing governmental bodies, granting their powers, determining how their members are selected, and prescribing the rules by which they make their decisions. Considered basic or fundamental, a constitution cannot be changed by ordinary acts of governmental bodies.

constitutional county court County court created by the Texas Constitution, presided over by the county judge.

constitutionalism A government of laws, not people, operating on the principle that governmental power must be limited and government officials should be restrained in their exercise of power over individuals.

containment Policy of preventing an enemy from expanding its boundaries and/or influence, specifically the U.S. foreign policy vis-à-vis the Soviet Union during the Cold War.

contingency fees Fees paid to attorneys to represent the plaintiff in a civil suit and receive in compensation an agreed-upon percentage of damages awarded (if any).

continuing resolution Congressional bill that authorizes government agencies to keep spending money for a specified period at the same level as in the previous fiscal year; passed when Congress is unable to enact final appropriations measures by October 1.

convention Nominating process in which delegates from local party organizations select the party's nominees.

cooperative federalism Model of federalism in which national, state, and local governments work together exercising common policy responsibilities.

council of government (COG) Council comprised of representatives of other governments in a defined region of the state.

council-manager Form of city government in which policy is set by an elected city council, which hires a professional city manager to head the daily administration of city government.

county attorney Elected official who is the chief legal officer of some counties. He or she also prosecutes lesser criminal offenses, primarily misdemeanors, in county courts.

county auditor Appointed officer who is primarily responsible for reviewing every bill and expenditure of a county to assure it is correct and legal.

county chair Presiding officer of a political party's county executive committee. He or she is elected countywide by voters in the party primary.

county clerk Chief record-keeping officer of a county.

county executive committee Panel responsible on the local level for the organization and management of a political party's primary election. It includes the party's county chair and each precinct chair.

county judge Presiding officer of a county commissioners court. This office also has some judicial authority, which is assumed by separate county courts-at-law in most urban counties.

county treasurer Elected officer who is responsible for receiving and disbursing county funds.
court of appeals Intermediate-level court that reviews civil and criminal cases from the district courts.
covert action Secret intelligence activity outside U.S. borders undertaken with specific authorization by the president, acknowledgment of U.S. sponsorship would defeat or compromise its purpose.
Cuban Missile Crisis The 1962 confrontation between the Soviet Union and the U.S. over Soviet placement of nuclear missiles in Cuba.
de facto segregation Racial imbalances not directly caused by official actions but rather by residential patterns.
de novo In a civil lawsuit or criminal trial, evidence is presented again before an appellate court because no record was kept of the evidence presented to the trial court.
dealignment Declining attractiveness of the parties to the voters, a reluctance to identify strongly with a party, and a decrease in reliance on party affiliation in voter choice.
defendants Parties against whom a criminal or civil suit is brought.
deferrals Items on which a president wishes to postpone spending.
delegated, or enumerated, powers Powers specifically mentioned in the Constitution as belonging to the national government.
delegates Accredited voting members of a party's national presidential nominating convention.
democracy Governing system in which the people govern themselves, from the Greek term meaning "rule by the many."
democratic ideals Individual dignity, equality before the law, widespread participation in public decisions, and public decisions by majority rule, with one person having one vote.
Democratic Party One of the main parties in American politics; it traces its origins to Thomas Jefferson's Democratic-Republican Party, acquiring its current name under Andrew Jackson in 1828.
deregulation Lifting of government rules and bureaucratic supervision from business and professional activity.
deterrence U.S. approach to deterring any nuclear attack from the Soviet Union by maintaining a second-strike capability.
devolution Passing down of responsibilities from the national government to the states.
Dillon rule Principle holding that local governments are creations of state government and that their powers and responsibilities are defined by the state.
diplomatic recognitio Power of the president to grant "legitimacy" to or withhold it from a government of another nation (to declare or refuse to declare it "rightful").
direct democracy Governing system in which every person participates actively in every public decision, rather than delegating decision making to representatives.
direct discrimination Now illegal practice of differential pay for men versus women even when those individuals have equal qualifications and perform the same job.
direct primary election Selection of candidates for government office through direct election by the voters of a political party.
discharge petition Petition signed by at least 218 House members to force a vote on a bill within a committee that opposes it.
discretionary funds Budgeted funds not earmarked for specific purposes but available to be spent in accordance with the best judgment of a bureaucrat.
dissenting opinion Opinion by a member of a court that disagrees with the result reached by the court in the case.
district attorney Elected official who prosecutes more serious criminal offenses, usually felonies, before state district courts.
district clerk Elected county official who maintains custody of state district court records.
district court Primary trial court in Texas. It has jurisdiction over criminal felony cases and civil disputes.
divided party government One party controls the presidency while the other party controls one or both houses of Congress.
division of labor Division of work among many specialized workers in a bureaucracy.
division votes Votes taken on the computerized voting boards in the Texas house but erased without being permanently recorded.
drafting a bill Actual writing of a bill in legal language.
dual federalism Early concept of federalism in which national and state powers were clearly distinguished and functionally separate.
Earned Income Tax Credit (EITC) Tax refunds in excess of tax payments for low-income workers.
economic diversification Development of new and varied business activities. New businesses were encouraged to relocate or expand in Texas after the oil and gas industry, which had been the base of the state's economy, suffered a major recession in the 1980s.
Electoral College The 538 presidential electors apportioned among the states according to their congressional representation (plus 3 for the District of Columbia) whose votes officially elect the president and vice president of the United States.
elite Small group of people who exercise disproportionate power and influence in the policy-making processes.
elitism Political system in which power is concentrated in the hands of a relatively small group of individuals or institutions.
Emancipation Proclamation Lincoln's 1862 Civil War declaration that all slaves residing in rebel states were free. It did not abolish all slavery; that would be done by the Thirteenth Amendment in 1865.
end of history The collapse of communism and the worldwide movement toward free markets and political democracy.
entitlements Any social welfare program for which there are eligibility requirements, whether financial or contributory.
enumerated powers Powers specifically mentioned in the Constitution as belonging to the national government.
Equal Rights Amendment (ERA) Proposed amendment to the Constitution guaranteeing that equal rights under the law shall not be denied or abridged on account of sex. Passed by Congress in 1972, the amendment failed to win ratification by three of the necessary three-fourths of the states.
equality of opportunity Elimination of artificial barriers to success in life and the opportunity for everyone to strive for success.
equality of results Equal sharing of income and material goods regardless of one's efforts in life.
equal-time rule Federal Communications Commission (FCC) requirement that broadcasters who sell time to any political candidate must make equal time available to opposing candidates at the same price.
ex post facto law Retroactive criminal law that works against the accused; forbidden under Article I of the Constitution.
exclusionary rule Rule of law that evidence found in an illegal search or resulting from an illegally obtained confession may not be admitted at trial.
executive agreement Agreement with another nation signed by the president of the United States but less formal (and hence potentially less binding) than a treaty because it does not require Senate confirmation.
executive order Formal regulation governing executive branch operations issued by the president.
executive privilege Right of a president to withhold from other branches of government confidential communications within the executive branch; although posited by presidents, it has been upheld by the Supreme Court only in limited situations.
externalities Costs imposed on people who are not direct participants in an activity.
extradition A process by which a person in one state is returned to another state to face criminal charges.
extraterritorial jurisdiction Power of an incorporated city to control development within nearby unincorporated areas.
extremism Rejection of democratic politics and the assertion of the supremacy of the "people" over laws, institutions, and individual rights.
Family Assistance Public assistance program that provides monies to the states for their use in helping needy families with children.
fascism Political ideology in which the state and/or race is assumed to be supreme over individuals.
Federal Election Commission (FEC) Agency charged with enforcing federal election laws and disbursing public presidential campaign funds.
federalism A constitutional arrangement whereby power is divided between national and subnational governments, each of which enforces its own laws directly on its citizens and neither of which can alter the arrangement without the consent of the other.

"feeding frenzy" Intense media coverage of a scandal or event that blocks out most other news.
felony Serious criminal offense that can be punished by imprisonment and/or a fine.
filibuster Delaying tactic by a senator or group of senators, using the Senate's unlimited debate rule to prevent a vote on a bill.
first reading Introduction of a bill in the house or the senate and its referral to a committee by the presiding officer.
fiscal year Yearly government accounting period, not necessarily the same as the calendar year. The federal government's fiscal year begins October 1 and ends September 30.
focus group In a political context, a small number of people brought together in a comfortable setting to discuss and respond to themes and issues, allowing campaign managers to develop and analyze strategies.
Food Stamp program Public assistance program that provides low-income households with coupons redeemable for enough food to provide a minimal nutritious diet.
franking privilege Free use of the U.S. mails granted to members of Congress to promote communication with constituents.
Free Exercise Clause Clause in the First Amendment to the Constitution that prohibits government from restricting religious beliefs and practices
free market Free competition for voluntary exchange among individuals, firms, and corporations.
free trade A policy of reducing or eliminating tariffs and quotas on imports to stimulate international trade.
freedom of expression Collectively, the First Amendment rights to free speech, press, and assembly.
free-market economic system Economic system in which individual choices by consumers and firms determine what shall be produced, how much, and for whom; this economic system relies on voluntary exchanges of buying and selling.
front loading The scheduling of presidential primary elections early in the year.
front-end strategy Presidential political campaign strategy in which a candidate focuses on winning early primaries to build momentum.
general election Election to choose among candidates nominated by parties and/or independent candidates who gained access to the ballot by petition.
general law city City allowed to exercise only those powers specifically granted to it by the legislature. General law cities have fewer than 5,000 residents.
general obligation bonds Method of borrowing money to pay for new construction projects, such as prisons, mental hospitals, or school facilities. The bonds, which require voter approval, are repaid with tax revenue.
gerrymandering Drawing district boundary lines for political advantage.
glass ceiling "Invisible" barriers to women rising to the highest positions in corporations and the professions.
globalization of the economy Increased interdependence in trade, manufacturing, and commerce as well as most other business activities between the United States and other countries.
GOP "Grand Old Party"—popular label for the Republican Party.
government Organization extending to the whole society that can legitimately use force to carry out its decisions.
grand jury Panel that reviews evidence submitted by prosecutors to determine whether to indict, or charge, an individual with a criminal offense.
Grange Organization formed in the late nineteenth century to improve the lot of farmers. The Grange influenced provisions in the Texas Constitution of 1876 limiting taxes and government spending and restricting big business, including banks and railroads.
grants-in-aid Payments of funds from the national government to state or local governments or from a state government to local governments for specific purposes.
grass-roots lobbying Attempts to influence government decision making by inspiring constituents to contact their representatives.
gridlock Political stalemate between the executive and legislative branches arising when one branch is controlled by one major political party and the other branch by the other party.
gross domestic product (GDP) Measure of economic performance in terms of the nation's total production of goods and services for a single year, valued in terms of market prices.
health maintenance organizations (HMOs) Health care provider groups that provide a stipulated list of services to patients for a fixed fee that is usually substantially lower than such care would otherwise cost.
home rule city City with a population of more than 5,000, which can adopt any form of government residents choose, provided it does not conflict with the state constitution or statutes.
home rule Power of local government to pass laws affecting local affairs, so long as those laws do not conflict with state or federal laws.
home style Activities of Congress members specifically directed at their home constituencies.
homestead exemption Reduction in property taxes that some local governments grant on a taxpayer's residence.
honeymoon period Early months of a president's term in which his popularity with the public and influence with the Congress are generally high.
horse-race coverage Media coverage of electoral campaigns that concentrates on who is ahead and who is behind, and neglects the issues at stake.
ideological organizations Interest groups that pursue ideologically based (liberal or conservative) agendas.
ideology Consistent and integrated system of ideas, values, and beliefs.
impeachment Equivalent of a criminal charge against an elected official; removal of the impeached official from office depends on the outcome of a trial.
impersonality Treatment of all persons within a bureaucracy on the basis of "merit" and of all "clients" served by the bureaucracy equally according to rules.
implementation Development by the federal bureaucracy of procedures and activities to carry out policies legislated by Congress; it includes regulation as well as adjudication.
implied powers Powers not mentioned specifically in the Constitution as belonging to Congress but inferred as necessary and proper for carrying out the enumerated powers.
impoundment Refusal by a president to spend monies appropriated by Congress; outlawed except with congressional consent by the Budget and Impoundment Control Act of 1974.
income transfers Government transfers of income from taxpayers to persons regarded as deserving.
incremental budgeting Method of budgeting that focuses on requested increases in funding for existing programs, accepting as legitimate their previous year's expenditures.
incumbent gerrymandering Drawing legislative district boundaries to advantage incumbent legislators.
incumbent Candidate currently in office seeking reelection.
independent counsel ("special prosecutor") A prosecutor appointed by a federal court to pursue charges against a president or other high official. This position was allowed to lapse by Congress in 1999 after many controversial investigations by these prosecutors.
independent school district Specific form of special district that administers the public schools in a designated area.
indictment Written statement issued by a grand jury charging a person with a punishable offense.
individual income tax Taxes on individuals' wages and other earned income, the primary source of revenue for the U.S. federal government.
individualism Attitude, rooted in classical liberal theory and reinforced by the frontier tradition, that citizens are capable of taking care of themselves with minimal governmental assistance.
individualistic subculture View that government should interfere as little as possible in the private activities of its citizens while assuring that adequate public facilities and a favorable business climate are available to permit individuals to pursue their self-interests.
information overload Situation in which individuals are subjected to so many communications that they cannot make sense of them.
information Document formally charging a person with a misdemeanor.
infrastructure Streets, waste disposal systems, libraries, and other public facilities built and operated by governments.
initiative Procedure by which voters propose constitutional amendments or other laws through petitions subject to adoption by a popular vote.

inquest Examination by a justice of the peace or a medical examiner of unusual circumstances under which someone has died.

institutionalization In the context of political science, the development of a legislative body into a formally structured system with stable membership, complex rules, expanded internal operations, and the delineation of staff functions.

intent calendar Daily list of bills eligible for debate on the floor of the Texas senate, if the sponsor is recognized by the lieutenant governor.

interest group Organization seeking to influence government policy.

intergovernmental relations Network of political, financial, and administrative relationships between units of the federal government and those of state and local governments.

interims Periods between legislative sessions.

iron triangle Mutually supportive interrelationships among the interest groups, administrative agencies, and legislative committees involved in drafting the laws and regulations affecting a particular area of the economy or a specific segment of the population.

iron triangles Mutually supportive relationships among interest groups, government agencies, and legislative committees with jurisdiction over a specific policy area.

issue ads Ads that advocate policy positions rather than explicitly supporting or opposing particular candidates.

Jim Crow laws Legislation enacted by many states after the Civil War to limit the rights and power of African Americans.

Jim Crow Second-class-citizen status conferred on blacks by southern segregation laws; derived from a nineteenth-century song-and-dance act (usually performed by a white man in blackface) that stereotyped blacks.

judicial activism Making of new law through judicial interpretations of the Constitution.

judicial review Power of the courts, especially the Supreme Court, to declare laws of Congress, laws of the states, and actions of the president unconstitutional and invalid.

judicial self-restraint Self-imposed limitation on judicial power by judges deferring to the policy judgments of elected branches of government.

jurisdiction Power of a court to hear a case in question.

justice of the peace court Low-ranking court with jurisdiction over minor civil disputes and criminal cases.

Korean War Communist North Korea invaded non-Communist South Korea in June, 1950, causing President Harry S Truman to intervene militarily, with U.N. support. General Douglas MacArthur defeated the North Koreans, but with China's entry into the war, a stalemate resulted. An armistice was signed in 1953, with Korea divided along nearly original lines.

laboratories of democracy A reference to the ability of states to experiment and innovate in public policy.

land commissioner The elected official who manages the state's public lands and administers the Veterans Land Program, which provides low-interest loans to veterans for the purchase of land and houses.

left A reference to the liberal, progressive, and/or socialist side of the political spectrum.

Legislative Budget Board The panel that makes budgetary recommendations to the full legislature. It is chaired by the lieutenant governor and includes the speaker of the house and eight other key lawmakers.

Legislative Redistricting Board A board created by constitutional amendment charged to redistrict the Texas legislature if it is not accomplished in the regular session following the release of the census.

legitimacy Widespread acceptance of something as necessary, rightful, and legally binding.

Lemon test To be constitutional, a law must have a secular purpose; its primary effect must neither advance nor inhibit religion; and it must not foster excessive government entanglement with religion.

Leninism The theories of Vladimir Lenin, among them that advanced capitalist countries turned toward war and colonialism to make their own workers relatively prosperous.

libel Writings that are false and malicious and are intended to damage an individual.

liberalism Belief in the value of strong government to provide economic security and protection for civil rights, combined with a belief in personal freedom from government intervention in social conduct.

lieutenant governor Presiding officer of the senate. This officeholder would become governor if the governor were to die, be incapacitated, or removed from office.

limited government Principle that government power over the individual is limited, that there are some personal liberties that even a majority cannot regulate, and that government itself is restrained by law.

line-item veto Power of the chief executive to reject some portions of a bill without rejecting all of it.

litigation Legal dispute brought before a court.

litmus test In political terms, a person's stand on a key issue that determines whether he or she will be appointed to public office or supported in electoral campaigns.

lobbying Activities directed at government officials with the hope of influencing their decisions.

lobbyist Person working to influence government policies and actions.

logrolling Bargaining for agreement among legislators to support each other's favorite bills, especially projects that primarily benefit individual members and their constituents.

machine Tightly disciplined party organization, headed by a boss, that relies on material rewards—including patronage jobs—to control politics.

majoritarianism Tendency of democratic governments to allow the faint preferences of the majority to prevail over the intense feelings of minorities.

majority leader In the House, the majority-party leader and second in command to the Speaker; in the Senate, the leader of the majority party.

majority opinion Opinion in a case that is subscribed to by a majority of the judges who participated in the decision.

malapportionment Unequal numbers of people in legislative districts resulting in inequality of voter representation.

managed care Programs designed to keep health care costs down by the establishment of strict guidelines regarding when and what diagnostic and therapeutic procedures should be administered to patients under various circumstances.

mandate Perception of popular support for a program or policy based on the margin of electoral victory won by a candidate who proposed it during a campaign. Direct federal orders to state and local governments requiring them to perform a service or to obey federal laws in the performance of their functions.

maquiladora program Policies initiated by Mexico in 1964 to stimulate economic growth along the U.S.-Mexico border.

markup Line-by-line revision of a bill in committee by editing each phrase and word.

Marshall Plan U.S. program to rebuild the nations of Western Europe in the aftermath of World War II in order to render them less susceptible to communist influence and takeover.

Marxism The theories of Karl Marx, among them that capitalists oppress workers and that worldwide revolution and the emergence of a classless society are inevitable.

mass media All means of communication with the general public, including television, newspapers, magazines, radio, books, recordings, motion pictures, and the Internet.

mayor-council Form of city government in which the legislative function is vested in the city council and the executive function in the mayor.

Medicaid Public assistance program that provides health care to the poor.

medical examiner Appointed official who is responsible for determining the cause of death of murder victims or others who die under suspicious or unusual circumstances.

Medicare Social insurance program that provides health care insurance to elderly and disabled people.

merit selection Proposal under which the governor would appoint state judges from lists of potential nominees recommended by committees of experts. Appointed judges would have to run later in retention elections to keep their seats but would not have opponents on the ballot. Voters would simply decide whether a judge should remain in office or be replaced by another gubernatorial appointee.

merit system Selection of employees for government agencies on the basis of competence, with no consideration of an individual's political stance and/or power.

metro government Local government in which city and county governments consolidate to avoid duplication of public services.

minority leader In both the House and Senate, the leader of the opposition party.

Miranda ruling Far-reaching decision of the U.S. Supreme Court that requires law enforcement officers to warn a criminal suspect of his or her right to remain silent and have an attorney present before questioning.
Miranda warning Requirement that persons arrested be informed of their rights immediately after arrest.
misdemeanor Minor criminal offense punishable by a fine and/or a short sentence in the county jail.
moralistic subculture View that government's primary responsibility is to promote the public welfare and that it should actively use its authority and power to improve the social and economic well-being of its citizens.
muckraking Journalistic exposés of corruption, wrongdoing, or mismanagement in government, business, and other institutions of society.
multilateral treaty A treaty open to signature by more than two nations (as opposed to a bilateral treaty, signed by only two nations).
municipal court Court of limited jurisdiction that hears cases involving city ordinances and primarily handles traffic tickets.
mutual assured destruction (MAD) Nuclear peace maintained by the capability of each side's missile forces to survive a first strike and inflict heavy damages in retaliation against the aggressor's population.
name recognition Public awareness of a candidate—whether they even know his or her name.
National Security Council (NSC) "Inner cabinet" that advises the president and coordinates foreign, defense, and intelligence activities.
National Supremacy Clause Clause in Article VI of the U.S. Constitution declaring the constitution and laws of the national government "the supreme law of the land" superior to the constitutions and laws of the states.
nationalism Belief that shared cultural, historical, linguistic, and social characteristics of a people justify the creation of a government encompassing all of them, the resulting nation-state should be independent and legally equal to all other nation-states.
Necessary and Proper Clause Clause in Article I, Section 8, of the U.S. Constitution granting Congress the power to enact all laws that are "necessary and proper" for carrying out those responsibilities specifically delegated to it. Also referred to as the Implied Powers Clause.
negative campaigning Speeches, commercials, or advertising attacking a political opponent during a campaign.
new federalism Attempts to return power and responsibility to the states and reduce the role of the national government in domestic affairs.
newsmaking Deciding what events, topics, presentations, and issues will be given coverage in the news.
nolo contendere Plea of "no contest" to a criminal charge.
nomination Political party's selection of its candidate for a public office.
nominee Political party's entry in a general election race.
nonpartisan elections Elections in which candidates do not officially indicate their party affiliation; often used for city, county, school board, and judicial elections.
nonpartisan elections Elections in which candidates do not represent a political party.
Nonproliferation Treaty A multilateral treaty in which nuclear nations pledged not to transfer nuclear weapons or technologies to nonnuclear nations, and nonnuclear nations pledged not to manufacture or acquire nuclear weapons.
nonviolent direct action Strategy used by civil rights leaders such as Martin Luther King, Jr., in which protesters break "unjust" laws openly but in a "loving" fashion in order to bring the injustices of such laws to public attention.
North American Free Trade Agreement (NAFTA) Treaty among the United States, Canada, and Mexico that created the world's largest trading bloc. Approved by the U.S. Congress in 1993, the treaty is designed to reduce tariffs and increase trade among the three countries.
North Atlantic Treaty Organization (NATO) Mutual-security agreement and joint military command uniting the nations of Western Europe, initially formed to resist Soviet expansionism.
obligational authority Feature of some appropriations acts by which an agency is empowered to enter into contracts that will require the government to make payments beyond the fiscal year in question.
one-party system Domination of elections and governmental processes by a single party, which may be split into different ideological, economic, or regional factions. In Texas, the phrase is used to describe the period from the late 1870s to the late 1970s, when the Democratic Party claimed virtually all elected, partisan offices.
open primaries Primary elections in which a voter may cast a ballot in either party's primary election.
open rule Rule that permits unlimited amendments to a bill under consideration by the House.
open seat Seat in a legislature for which no incumbent is running for reelection.
ordinances Local laws enacted by a city council.
organizational sclerosis Society encrusted with so many special benefits to interest groups that everyone's standard of living is lowered.
original intent Judicial philosophy under which judges attempt to apply the values of the Founders to current issues.
original jurisdiction Refers to a particular court's power to serve as the place where a given case is initially argued and decided.
outlays Actual dollar amounts to be spent by the federal government in a fiscal year.
override Voting in Congress to enact legislation vetoed by the president; requires a two-thirds vote in both the House and Senate.
oversight Congressional monitoring of the activities of executive branch agencies to determine if the laws are being faithfully executed.
packing Redistricting in which partisan voters are concentrated in a single district, "wasting" their majority vote and allowing the opposition to win by modest majorities in other districts.
paradox of democracy Potential for conflict between individual freedom and majority rule.
parole Early release of an inmate from prison, subject to certain conditions.
partial preemption Federal government's assumption of some regulatory powers in a particular field, with the stipulation that a state law on the same subject as a federal law is valid if it does not conflict with the federal law in the same area.
party identification Self-described identification with a political party, usually in response to the question, "Generally speaking, how would you identify yourself: as a Republican, Democrat, independent, or something else?"
party polarization The tendency of the Democratic Party to take more liberal positions in the Republican Party to take more conservative positions on key issues.
party unity Percentage of Democrats and Republicans who stick with their party on party votes.
party vote Majority of Democrats voting in opposition to a majority of Republicans.
patronage Appointment to public office based on party loyalty.
pay-as-you-go principle A principle written into the Texas Constitution prohibiting state government from borrowing money to meet its operating budget.
pay-as-you-go Constitutional requirement that prohibits the legislature from borrowing money for the state's operating expenses.
penal code Body of law that defines most criminal offenses and sets a range of punishments that can be assessed.
petit (regular) juries Juries called to determine guilt or innocence.
petit jury Panel of citizens that hears evidence in a civil lawsuit or a criminal prosecution and decides the outcome by issuing a verdict.
petition for review Petition to the Texas Supreme Court claiming that legal or procedural mistakes were made in the lower court.
photo ops Staged opportunities for the media to photograph the candidate in a favorable setting.
place system Form of at-large election in which candidates run for specific positions, or places, on a city council or other governing body.
plaintiff Individual or party who initiates a lawsuit.
plaintiffs Parties initiating suits and claiming damages. In criminal cases, the state acts as plaintiff on behalf of an injured society and requests fines and/or imprisonment as damages. In civil suits, the plaintiff is the injured party and seeks monetary damages.
platform Statement of principles adopted by a political party at its national convention (specific portions of the platform are known as

planks); a platform is not binding on the party's candidates.

plea bargaining Practice of allowing defendants to plead guilty to lesser crimes than those with which they were originally charged in return for reduced sentences.

plural executive A fragmented system of authority under which most statewide executive officeholders are elected independently of the governor.

pluralism Theory that democracy can be achieved through competition among multiple organized groups and that individuals can participate in politics through group memberships and elections.

pocket veto Effective veto of a bill when Congress adjourns within ten days of passing it and the president fails to sign it.

policy networks Interaction in a common policy area among lobbyists, elected officials, staff personnel, bureaucrats, journalists, and private-sector experts.

political action committees (PACs) Organizations that solicit and receive campaign contributions from corporations, unions, trade associations, and ideological and issue-oriented groups, and their members, then distribute these funds to political candidates.

political culture Widely shared views about who should govern, for what ends, and by what means.

political equality Belief that the law should apply equally to all and that every person's vote counts equally.

political parties Organizations that seek to achieve power by winning public office.

political patronage The hiring of government employees on the basis of personal friendships or favors rather than ability or merit.

political science The study of politics: who, governs, for what ends, and by what means.

politically correct (PC) Repression of attitudes, speech, and writings that are deemed racist, sexist, homophohic (anti-homosexual), or otherwise "insensitive."

politics Deciding who gets what, when, and how.

poll tax Tax that Texas and some other states required before people were allowed to vote. The purpose was to discourage minorities and poor whites from participating in the political process. The tax was declared unconstitutional in the 1960s.

popular sovereignty Constitutional principle of self-government; belief that the people control their government and governments are subject to limitations and constraints.

pork barreling Legislation designed to make government benefits, including jobs and projects used as political patronage, flow to a particular district or state.

poverty line Official standard regarding what level of annual cash income is sufficient to maintain a "decent standard of living"; those with incomes below this level are eligible for most public assistance programs.

power of the purse Congress's exclusive, constitutional power to authorize expenditures by all agencies of the federal government.

precedent Legal principle that previous decisions should determine the outcome of current cases; the basis for stability in law.

precinct Subdivision of a city, county, or ward for election purposes.

precinct chair Local officer in a political party who presides over the precinct convention and serves on the party's county executive committee. Voters in each precinct elect a chair in the party's primary election.

precinct convention Meeting held by a political party in each precinct on the same day as the party primary. In presidential election years, the precinct conventions and the primaries are the first steps in the selection of delegates to the major parties' national nominating conventions.

preemption Total or partial federal assumption of power in a particular field, restricting the authority of the states.

preferred position Refers to the tendency of the courts to give preference to the First Amendment rights to speech, press, and assembly when faced with conflicts.

preferred provider organizations (PPOs) Groups of hospitals and physicians who have joined together to offer their services to private insurers at a discount.

presidential primaries Primary elections in the states in which voters in each party can choose a presidential candidate for its party's nomination. Outcomes help determine the distribution of pledged delegates to each party's national nominating convention.

primary elections Elections to choose party nominees for public office; may be open or closed.

prior restraint Power of government to prevent publication or to require approval before publication, generally prohibited by the First Amendment.

privatization Contracting by government with private companies to provide some public services.

probation Procedure under which a convicted criminal is not sent to prison if he or she meets certain conditions, such as restrictions on travel and associates.

program budgeting Identifying items in a budget according to the functions and programs they are to be spent on.

progressive taxation System of taxation in which higher income groups pay a larger percentage of their incomes in taxes than do lower income groups.

proportional (flat) taxation System of taxation in which all income groups pay the same percentage of their income in taxes.

proportional representation Electoral system that allocates seats in a legislature based on the proportion of votes each party receives in a national election.

prosecution Conduct of legal proceedings against an individual charged with a crime.

protectionism A policy of high tariffs and quotas on imports to protect domestic industries.

public assistance programs Those social welfare programs for which no contributions are required and only those living in poverty (by official standards) are eligible; includes food stamps, Medicaid, and Family Assistance.

public goods Goods and services that cannot readily be provided by markets, either because they are too expensive for a single individual to buy or because if one person bought them, everyone else would use them without paying.

public improvement district Specific area of a city in which property owners pay special taxes in return for improvements to streets and other public facilities in their neighborhood.

public relations Building and maintaining goodwill with the general public.

public-interest groups Interest groups that claim to represent broad classes of people or the public as a whole.

quorum Required number of the members of a governing body who must be present so that official business, such as voting, can be conducted. In Texas, a quorum of the house and the senate is two-thirds of the membership. For committees, it is a majority of the members.

Radical Reconstructionists The group of Republicans who took control of the U.S. Congress in 1866 and imposed hated military governments on the former Confederate states after the Civil War.

radicalism Advocacy of immediate and drastic changes in society, including the complete restructuring of institutions, values, and beliefs. Radicals may exist on either the extreme left or extreme right.

raiding Organized efforts by one party to get its members to cross over in a primary and defeat an attractive candidate in the opposition party's primary.

Railroad Commission A three-member, elected body that has some oversight over rail safety but now primarily regulates oil and natural gas production in Texas.

ranking minority member The minority-party committee member with the most seniority.

ratification Power of a legislature to approve or reject decisions made by other bodies. State legislators or state conventions must ratify constitutional amendments submitted by Congress. The U.S. Senate must ratify treaties made by the president.

realignment Major shift in political party support or identification that usually occurs around a critical election. In Texas, realignment took place as a gradual transformation from a one-party system dominated by Democrats to a two-party system in which Republicans became competitive in elections.

record vote Vote taken in the house or the senate of which a permanent record is kept, listing how individual legislators voted.

redistricting Drawing of legislative district boundary lines following each ten-year census.

referenda Proposed laws or constitutional amendments submitted to the voters for their direct approval or rejection, found in state constitutions but not in the U.S. Constitution.

referendum Vote by the general electorate on a public policy issue, such as a constitutional amendment or statute.

regional security Attempt to bring order to international relations during the Cold War by creating regional alliances between a superpower and nations of a particular region.

regressive tax Tax that imposes a disproportionately heavier burden on low-income people than on the more affluent.

regressive taxation System of taxation in which lower income groups pay a larger percentage of their incomes in taxes than do higher income groups.

regressive taxes Taxes that impose a disproportionately heavier burden on low-income people than on the more affluent.

regular session 140-day period in the odd-numbered years in which the legislature meets and can consider and pass laws on any issue or subject.

regulation Development by the federal bureaucracy of formal rules for implementing legislation.

Religious Right Political movement, based primarily in evangelical Protestant churches, that has played an increasingly prominent role in Texas and national politics.

remedies and reliefs Orders of a court to correct a wrong, including a violation of the Constitution.

representational federalism Assertion that no constitutional division of powers exists between the nation and the states but the states retain their constitutional role merely by selecting the president and members of Congress.

representative democracy Governing system in which public decision making is delegated to representatives of the people chosen by popular vote in free, open, and periodic elections.

republic Form of government in which representatives of the people, rather than the people themselves, govern.

Republican Party One of the two main parties in American politics; it traces its origins to the antislavery and nationalist forces that united in the 1850s and nominated Abraham Lincoln for president in 1860.

republicanism Government by representatives of the people rather than directly by the people themselves.

rescissions Items on which a president wishes to cancel spending.

reserved powers Powers not granted to the national government or specifically denied to the states in the Constitution that are recognized by the Tenth Amendment as belonging to the state governments. This guarantee, known as the Reserved Powers Clause, embodies the principle of American federalism.

responsible party model System in which competitive parties adopt a platform of principles, recruiting candidates and directing campaigns based on the platform, and holding their elected officials responsible for enacting it.

restricted rule Rule that allows specified amendments to be added to a bill under consideration by the House.

retail politics Direct candidate contact with individual voters.

retention elections Elections in which judges run on their own records rather than against other candidates. Voters cast their ballots on the question of whether the incumbent judge should stay in office.

retrospective voting Voting for or against a candidate or party on the basis of past performance in office.

revenue bonds Bonds that are used to finance construction of a public facility and are repaid with income produced by the facility.

revolving door A term describing the practice of former members of state boards and commissions or key employees of agencies leaving state government for more lucrative jobs with the industries they used to regulate.

revolving doors The movement of individuals from government positions to jobs in the private sector, using the experience, knowledge, and contacts they acquired in government employment.

rider Amendment to a bill that is not germane to the bill's purposes.

right A reference to the conservative, traditional, anticommunist side of the political spectrum.

right-to-work law Law prohibiting the requirement of union membership in order to hold or get a job.

rollback election Election in which local voters can nullify a property tax increase that exceeds 8 percent in a given year.

roll-call vote Vote of the full House or Senate on which all members' individual votes are recorded and made public.

rule Stipulation attached to a bill in the House of Representatives that governs its consideration on the floor, including when and for how long it can be debated and how many (if any) amendments may be appended to it.

rule of four At least four justices must agree to hear an appeal (writ of certiorari) from a lower court in order to get a case before the Supreme Court.

runoff elections Elections that are required if no candidate receives an absolute majority of the votes cast in a city council, school district, or party primary race. The runoff is between the two top vote-getters.

runoff primary Additional primary held between the top two vote-getters in a primary where no candidate has received a majority of the vote.

safe seat Legislative district in which the incumbent regularly wins by a large margin of the vote.

SALT I First arms limitation treaty between the United States and the Soviet Union, signed in 1972, limiting the total number of offensive nuclear missiles; it included the ABM Treaty that reflected the theory that the population centers of both nations should be left undefended.

SALT II Lengthy and complicated treaty between the United States and the Soviet Union, agreed to in 1979 but never ratified by the U.S. Senate, that set limits on all types of strategic nuclear launch vehicles.

school board Governing body of a school district. Its responsibilities include the development or approval of educational policies, approval of the budget, hiring of the superintendent, and other personnel matters.

school superintendent Top administrator of a school district. He or she is hired by the elected school board to direct the district's daily operations.

search warrant Court order permitting law-enforcement officials to search a location in order to seize evidence of a crime; issued only for a specified location, in connection with a specific investigation, and on submission of proof that "probable cause" exists to warrant such a search.

second reading Initial debate by the full house or senate on a bill that has been approved by a committee.

second-strike capability Ability of a nation's forces to survive a surprise nuclear attack by the enemy and then to retaliate effectively.

secretary of state The official who administers state election laws, grants charters to corporations, and processes the extradition of prisoners to other states. This officeholder is appointed by the governor.

selective perception Mentally screening out information or opinions with which one disagrees.

senatorial courtesy Custom of the U.S. Senate with regard to presidential nominations to the judiciary to defer to the judgment of senators from the president's party from the same state as the nominee.

senatorial courtesy An unwritten practice that permits a senator to block the confirmation of a gubernatorial appointee who lives in the senator's district.

seniority system Custom whereby the member of Congress who has served the longest on the majority side of a committee becomes its chair and the member who has served the longest on the minority side becomes its ranking member.

separate but equal Ruling of the Supreme Court in the case of Plessy v. Ferguson (1896) to the effect that segregated facilities were legal as long as the facilities were equal.

separation of powers Constitutional division of powers among the three branches of the national government—legislative, executive, and judicial.

set-aside program Program in which a specified number or percentage of contracts must go to designated minorities.

sheriff Elected official who is the chief law enforcement officer of a county.

single-issue groups Organizations formed to support or oppose government action on a specific issue.

single-member district Election system in which one person is elected to represent the people living within one geographic district.

slander Oral statements that are false and malicious and are intended to damage an individual.

social contract Idea that government originates as an implied contract among individuals who agree to obey laws in exchange for protection of their rights.

social insurance programs Social welfare programs to which beneficiaries have made contributions so that they are entitled to benefits regardless of their personal wealth.
social mobility Extent to which people move upward or downward in income and status over a lifetime or generations.
Social Security Social insurance program composed of the Old Age and Survivors Insurance program, which pays benefits to retired workers who have paid into the program and their dependents and survivors, and the Disability Insurance program, which pays benefits to disabled workers and their families.
socialism System of government involving collective or government ownership of economic enterprise, with the goal being equality of results, not merely equality of opportunity.
socialization The learning of a culture and its values.
solicitor general Attorney in the Department of Justice who represents the U.S. government before the Supreme Court and any other courts.
sound bites Concise and catchy phrases that attract media coverage.
sovereign immunity Legal doctrine that individuals can sue the government only with the government's consent.
Soviet Union The Union of Soviet Socialist Republics (USSR) consisting of Russia and its bordering lands and ruled by the communist regime in Moscow, officially dissolved in 1991.
speaker Presiding officer of the house of representatives.
Speaker of the House Presiding officer of the House of Representatives.
special purpose districts Units of local government created by the state to perform specific functions not met by cities or counties, including the provision of public services to unincorporated areas.
special session A legislative session that can be called at any time by the governor. This session is limited to thirty days and to issues or subjects designated by the governor.
special session Legislative session that can be called at any time by the governor. This session is limited to thirty days and to issues or subjects designated by the governor.
special, or select, committees Special panels appointed to study major policy issues.
spin doctor Practitioner of the art of spin control, or manipulation of media reporting to favor one's own candidate.
splintering Redistricting in which a strong minority is divided up and diluted to prevent it from electing a representative.
spoils system Selection of employees for government agencies on the basis of party loyalty, electoral support, and political influence.
staggered terms Terms that begin on different dates, a requirement for members of state boards and commissions appointed by the governor.
standard partial preemption Form of partial preemption in which the states are permitted to regulate activities already regulated by the federal government if the state regulatory standards are at least as stringent as the federal government's.
standing committee Permanent committee of the House or Senate that deals with matters within a specified subject area.
standing committee Committee that is created by house or senate rules to consider legislation or perform a procedural role in the lawmaking process.
standing Requirement that the party who files a lawsuit have a legal stake in the outcome.
stare decisis Judicial precept that the issue has already been decided in earlier cases and the earlier decision need only be applied in the specific case before the bench; the rule in most cases, it comes from the Latin for "the decision stands."
START I First treaty between the United States and the Soviet Union that actually reduced the strategic nuclear arms of the superpowers, signed in 1991.
START II A treaty between the United States and Russia eliminating all multiwarhead land missiles and reducing nuclear weapons stockpiles; signed in 2003.
State Board of Education An elected panel that oversees the administration of public education in Texas.
state chair and vice chair Two top state leaders of a political party, one of whom must be a woman. They are selected every two years by delegates to the party's state convention.
state convention Meeting held in June of even-numbered years by each of the two major political parties. Delegates to this convention elect the party's state leadership and adopt a party platform. In presidential election years, the state convention selects the delegates to the party's national nominating convention.
state executive committee Statewide governing board of a political party. It includes a man and a woman from each of the thirty-one state senatorial districts and the state chair and vice chair, who are selected by delegates to the party's biennial state convention.
state treasurer This elective office was created by the Constitution of 1876 to manage state funds. It was abolished by the voters in 1995, and its duties were transferred to the comptroller's office.
statutes Laws enacted by a legislative body.
statutory county court Court that exercises limited jurisdiction over criminal and/or civil cases. The jurisdiction of these courts varies from county to county.
statutory law Law enacted by a legislative body.
statutory laws Laws made by act of Congress or the state legislatures, as opposed to constitutional law.
strong mayor Form of city government that gives the mayor considerable power, including budgetary control and appointment and removal authority over city department heads.
subcommittees Specialized committees within standing committees; subcommittee recommendations must be approved by the full standing committee before submission to the floor.
subcultures Variations on the prevailing values and beliefs in a society.
subpoenas Court orders requiring people to testify in court or before grand juries or to produce certain documents.
Sullivan rule Court guideline that false and malicious statements regarding public officials are protected by the First Amendment unless it can be proven they were known to be false at the time they were made or were made with "reckless disregard" for their truth or falsehood.
sunset The process under which most state agencies have to be periodically reviewed and recreated by the legislature or go out of business.
superpowers Refers to the United States and the Soviet Union after World War II, when these two nations dominated international politics.
Supplemental Security Income (SSI) Public assistance program that provides monthly cash payments to the needy, elderly (sixty-five or older), blind, and disabled.
swing states States that are not considered to be firmly in the Democratic or Republican column.
symbolic speech Actions other than speech itself but protected by the First Amendment because they constitute political expression.
tag Rule that allows an individual senator to postpone a committee hearing on any bill for at least forty-eight hours, a delay that can be fatal to a bill during the closing days of a legislative session.
tariff Tax imposed on imported products (also called a customs duty).
tax abatements Exemptions from property taxes granted to certain businesses, usually to encourage them to move to or expand their operations in a city or county. The exemptions are granted for specific periods.
tax assessor-collector Elected official who determines how much property tax is owed on the different pieces of property within a county and then collects the tax.
taxes Compulsory payments to the government.
television malaise Generalized feelings of distrust, cynicism, and powerlessness stemming from television's emphasis on the negative aspects of American life.
Temporary Assistance to Needy Families Welfare reform program replacing federal cash entitlement with grants to the states for welfare recipients.
terrorism Title 22 of the U.S. Code, Section 2656 (d): "The term 'terrorism' means premeditated, politically motivated violence perpetrated against noncombatant targets by subnational groups or clandestine agents, usually intended to influence an audience."
Texas Court of Criminal Appeals Nine-member court with final appellate jurisdiction over criminal cases.
Texas Supreme Court Nine-member court with final appellate jurisdiction over civil lawsuits.
"The Establishment" In the days of one-party Democratic politics in Texas, the Establishment was a loosely knit coalition of Anglo business and oil company executives, bankers,

and lawyers who controlled state policy making through the dominant conservative wing of the Democratic Party.
third reading Final presentation of a bill before the full house or senate.
tort A wrongful act or injury for which a damage lawsuit can be brought.
tort reform Changes in state law to put limits on personal injury lawsuits and damage judgments entered by the courts.
total preemption Federal government's assumption of all regulatory powers in a particular field.
totalitarianism Rule by an elite that exercises unlimited power over individuals in all aspects of life.
trade associations Interest groups composed of businesses in specific industries.
traditionalistic subculture View that political power should be concentrated in the hands of a few elite citizens who belong to established families or influential social groups. Public policy basically serves the interests of this small group.
transnational regionalism Expanding economic and social interdependence of South Texas and Mexico.
Truman Doctrine U.S. foreign policy, first articulated by President Harry S Truman, that pledged the United States to "support free peoples who are resisting attempted subjugation by armed minorities or by outside pressures."
trustees Legislators who feel obligated to use their own best judgment in decision making.
turnover Replacement of members of Congress by retirement or resignation, by reapportionment, or (more rarely) by electoral defeat, usually expressed as a percentage of members newly elected.
two-party system Political system that has two dominant parties, such as that of the United States.
two-thirds rule Procedure under which the Texas senate has traditionally operated that requires approval of at least two-thirds of senators before a bill can be debated on the senate floor. It allows a minority of senators to block controversial legislation.
unanimous consent agreement Negotiated by the majority and minority leaders of the Senate, it specifies when a bill will be taken up on the floor, what amendments will be considered, and when a vote will be taken.
underclass People who have remained poor and dependent on welfare over a prolonged period of time.
unemployment compensation Social insurance program that temporarily replaces part of the wages of workers who have lost their jobs.
unemployment rate Percentage of the civilian labor force who are not working but who are looking for work or waiting to return to or to begin a job.
unfunded mandates Mandates that impose costs on state and local governments (and private industry) without reimbursement from the federal government.
unicameral A legislature consisting of a single chamber.
unitary system Constitutional arrangement whereby authority rests with the national government, subnational governments have only those powers given to them by the national government.
urbanization Process by which a predominantly rural society or area becomes urban.
values Shared ideas about what is good and desirable.
veniremen Members of a panel from which a petit, or trial, jury is chosen.
veto Rejection of a legislative act by the executive branch; in the U.S. federal government, overriding of a veto requires a two-thirds majority in both houses of Congress.
Vietnam War War between non-Communist South Vietnam and Communist North Vietnam from 1956 to 1975, with increasing U.S. involvement, ending with U.S. withdrawal in 1973 and Communist victory in 1975. The war became unpopular in the U.S. after 1968 and caused President Johnson not to run for a second term. More than 58,000 Americans died in the war.
Voting Rights Act Federal law designed to protect the voting rights of minorities by requiring the Justice Department's approval of changes in political districts and certain other electoral procedures. The 1965 act, as amended, has eliminated most of the restrictive practices that limited minority political participation.
War Powers Act Bill passed in 1973 to limit presidential war-making powers; it restricts when, why, and for how long a president can commit U.S. forces and requires notification of and, in many cases, approval by Congress.
ward politics Term, often with negative connotations, that refers to partisan politics linked to political favoritism.
ward Division of a city for electoral or administrative purposes or as a unit for organizing political parties.
Watergate The scandal that led to the forced resignation of President Richard M. Nixon. Adding "gate" as a suffix to any alleged corruption in government suggests an analogy to the Watergate scandal.
weak mayor Form of city government in which the mayor shares authority with the city council and other elected officials but has little independent control over city policy or administration.
whips In both the House and Senate, the principal assistants to the party leaders and next in command to those leaders.
whistleblower A public employee who reports illegal activities or "blows the whistle" on agency wrongdoing.
whistle-blower Employee of the federal government or of a firm supplying the government who reports waste, mismanagement, and/or fraud by a government agency or contractor.
White House press corps Reporters from both print and broadcast media assigned to regularly cover the president.
white primary Series of state laws and party rules that denied African Americans the right to vote in the Democratic primary in Texas in the first half of the twentieth century.
writ of certiorari Writ issued by the Supreme Court, at its discretion, to order a lower court to prepare the record of a case and send it to the Supreme Court for review. Most cases come to the Court as petitions for writs of certiorari.
writ of habeas corpus Court order directing public officials who are holding a person in custody to bring the prisoner into court and explain the reasons for confinement; the right to habeas corpus is protected by Article I of the Constitution.
writ of mandamus Court order directing a lower court or another public official to take a certain action.
zero-based budgeting Method of budgeting that demands justification for the entire budget request of an agency, not just its requested increase in funding.

Notes

Chapter One

1. For a discussion of various aspects of legitimacy and its measurement in public opinion polls, see M. Stephen Weatherford, "Measuring Political Legitimacy," *American Political Science Review* 86 (March 1992): 140–55.
2. Thomas Hobbes, *Leviathan* (1651).
3. For an explanation of the worldwide growth of democracy, see John Mueller, "Democracy and Ralph's Pretty Good Grocery Store," *American Journal of Political Science* 36 (November 1992): 983–1003.
4. John Locke, *Treatise on Government* (1688).
5. See Barbara S. Gamble, "Putting Civil Rights to a Popular Vote," *American Journal of Political Science* 41 (January 1997): 245–69.
6. James Madison, Alexander Hamilton, and John Jay, *The Federalist Papers* (New York: Mentor Books, 1961), No. 10, p. 81. Madison's *Federalist Papers,* No. 10 and No. 51, are reprinted in the Appendix.
7. E. E. Schattschneider, *Two Hundred Million Americans in Search of a Government* (New York: Holt, Rinehart & Winston, 1969), p. 63.
8. Harold Lasswell and Daniel Lerner, *The Comparative Study of Elites* (Stanford, Calif.: Stanford University Press, 1952), p. 7.
9. C. Wright Mills's classic study, *The Power Elite* (New York: Oxford University Press, 1956), is widely cited by Marxist critics of American democracy, but it can be read profitably by anyone concerned with the effects of large bureaucracies—corporate, governmental, or military—on democratic government.
10. In *Who Rules America?* (New York: Prentice Hall, 1967) and its sequel, *Who Rules America Now?* (New York: Prentice Hall, 1983), sociologist G. William Domhoff argues that America is ruled by an "upper class" who attend the same prestigious private schools, intermarry among themselves, and join the same exclusive clubs. In *Who's Running America?* (New York: Prentice Hall, 1976) and *Who's Running America? The Clinton Years* (New York: Prentice Hall, 1995), political scientist Thomas R. Dye documents the concentration of power and the control of assets in the hands of officers and directors of the nation's largest corporations, banks, law firms, networks, foundations, and so forth. Dye argues, however, that most of these "institutional elites" were not born into the upper class but instead climbed the ladder to success.
11. Yale political scientist Robert A. Dahl is an important contributor to the development of pluralist theory, beginning with his *Preface to Democratic Theory* (Chicago: University of Chicago Press, 1956). He often refers to a pluralist system as a *polyarchy*—literally, a system with many centers of power. See his *Polyarchy* (New Haven, Conn.: Yale University Press, 1971), and for a revised defense of pluralism, see his *Democracy and Its Critics* (New Haven, Conn.: Yale University Press, 1989).

Chapter Two

1. Gunnar Myrdal, *An American Dilemma* (New York: Harper, 1944).
2. See Martin Luther King, Jr., "Letter from Birmingham City Jail," April 16, 1963.
3. For a discussion of the sources and consequences of intolerance in the general public, see James L. Gibson, "The Political Consequences of Intolerance: Cultural Conformity and Political Freedom," *American Political Science Review* 86 (June 1992): 338–52.
4. Quoted in *The Ideas of Equality,* ed. George Abernathy (Richmond, Va.: John Knox Press, 1959), p. 185; also in Herbert McClosky and John Zaller, *The American Ethos: Public Attitudes toward Capitalism and Democracy* (Cambridge, Mass.: Harvard University Press, 1984), p. 72.
5. Quoted in Richard Hofstadter, *The American Political Tradition* (New York: Knopf, 1948), p. 45. Historian Hofstadter describes the thinking of American political leaders from Jefferson and the Founders to Franklin D. Roosevelt.
6. For a discussion of how people balance the values of individualism and opposition to big government with humanitarianism and the desire to help others, see Stanley Feldman and John Zaller, "The Political Culture of Ambivalence: Ideological Responses to the Welfare State," *American Journal of Political Science* 36 (February 1992): 268–307.
7. Robert E. Lane, "Market Justice, Political Justice," *American Political Science Review* 80 (June 1986): 383–402.
8. Greg J. Duncan, *Years of Poverty, Years of Plenty* (Ann Arbor: University of Michigan Press, 1984).
9. *New York Times*/CBS News polls, reported in *New York Times,* February 15, 1993. Copyright © 1993 by The New York Times Company.
10. American Security Council, *The Illegal Immigration Crisis* (Washington, D.C.: ASC, 1994).
11. *Sale v. Haitian Centers Council,* 125 L. Ed. 2d 128 (1993).
12. See Stephen Earl Bennett, "Americans' Knowledge of Ideology, 1980–92," *American Politics Quarterly* 23 (July 1995): 259–78.
13. For evidence that ideological consistency increases with educational level, see William G. Jacoby, "Ideological Identification and Issue Attitude," *American Journal of Political Science* 35 (February 1991): 178–205.
14. Richard Hofstadter, *The Paranoid Style in American Politics* (New York: Knopf, 1965).
15. Francis Fukuyama, *The End of History and the Last Man* (New York: Free Press, 1992).
16. See Robert Kimball, *Tenured Radicals* (New York: Harper & Row, 1990).
17. Herbert Marcuse, *One-Dimensional Man* (Boston: Beacon Press, 1964).
18. Allan Bloom, *The Closing of the American Mind* (New York: Simon & Schuster, 1987), p. 15.

Chapter Three

1. In *Federalist Papers,* No. 53, James Madison distinguishes a "constitution" from a law: a constitution is "established by the people and unalterable by the government, and a law established by the government and alterable by the government."
2. Another important decision on opening day of the Constitutional Convention was to keep the proceedings secret. James Madison made his own notes on the convention proceedings, and they were published many years later. See Max Ferrand, ed., *The Records of the Federal Convention of 1787* (New Haven, Conn.: Yale University Press, 1911).
3. See Edward Millican, *One United People: The Federalist Papers and the National Idea* (Lexington: University Press of Kentucky, 1990).
4. Charles A. Beard, *An Economic Interpretation of the Constitution* (New York: Macmillan, 1913).
5. Robert E. Brown, *Charles Beard and the Constitution* (Princeton, N.J.: Princeton University Press, 1956).
6. James Madison, *Federalist Papers,* No. 10, reprinted in the Appendix.
7. Alexander Hamilton, *Federalist Papers,* No. 78.

Chapter Four

1. The states are listed in the order in which their legislatures voted to secede. While occupied by Confederate troops, secessionist legislators in Missouri and Kentucky also voted to secede, but Unionist representatives from these states remained in Congress.
2. *Texas v. White,* 7 Wallace 700 (1869).
3. James Madison, *Federalist Papers,* No. 51, reprinted in the Appendix.
4. Ibid.
5. The arguments for "competitive federalism" are developed at length in Thomas R. Dye, *American Federalism: Competition among Governments* (Lexington, Mass.: Lexington Books, 1990).
6. David Osborne, *Laboratories of Democracy* (Cambridge, Mass.: Harvard Business School, 1988).
7. Morton Grodzins, *The American System* (Chicago: Rand McNally, 1966), pp. 8–9.
8. Ibid., p. 265.
9. Charles Press, *State and Community Governments in the Federal System* (New York: Wiley, 1979), p. 78.
10. *Garcia v. San Antonio Metropolitan Transit Authority,* 469 U.S. 528 (1985).
11. See Michael S. Greve, *Real Federalism: Why It Matters, How It Could Happen* (Washington, D.C.: AEI Press, 1999).
12. *U.S. v. Lopez,* 514 U.S. 549 (1995).
13. *Seminole Tribe of Florida v. Florida,* 517 U.S. 44 (1996).
14. *Alden v. Maine,* 67 U.S.L.W. 1401 (1999).
15. *Printz v. U.S.* 521 U.S. 890 (1997).
16. *Brzonkala v. Morrison* (2000).
17. *Federal-State-Local Relations: Federal Grants in Aid,* House Committee on Government Operations, 85th Cong., 2d sess., p. 7.

Chapter Five

1. John E. Filer, Lawrence W. Kenny, and Rebecca B. Morton, "Redistribution, Income, and Voting," *American Journal of Political Science* 37 (February 1993): 63–87.
2. Sidney Verba, Kay Schlozman, Henry Brady, and Norman Nie, "Citizen Activity: Who Participates? What Do They Say?" *American Political Science Review* 87 (June 1993): 303–18.
3. See Katherine Tate, "Black Political Participation in the 1984 and 1988 Presidential Elections," *American Political Science Review* 85 (December 1991): 1159–76.
4. Gerald Pomper, *Elections in America* (New York: Dodd, Mead, 1968).
5. Morris P. Fiorina, *Retrospective Voting in American National Elections* (New Haven, Conn.: Yale University Press, 1988).
6. Alan I. Abramowitz, "Incumbency, Campaign Spending, and the Decline of Competition in U.S. House Elections," *Journal of Politics* 53 (February 1991): 55–70.
7. Herbert Alexander, as quoted in Richard R. Lau et al., "The Effects of Negative Political Advertisements," *American Political Science Review* 93 (December 1999): 851–75.
8. Quotation from Richard R. Lau, *op. cit,* p. 851.
9. Center for Responsive Politics, *The Big Picture: The Money Behind the 2000 Elections* (Washington, D.C., 2001).
10. In the important U.S. Supreme Court decision in *Buckley v. Valeo* in 1976, James L. Buckley, former U.S. senator from New York, and his brother, William F. Buckley, the well-known conservative commentator, argued successfully that the laws limiting an individual's right to participate in political campaigns—financially or otherwise—violated First Amendment freedoms. Specifically, the U.S. Supreme Court held that no government could limit individuals' rights to spend money or publish or broadcast their own views on issues or elections. Candidates can spend as much of their own money as they wish on their own campaigns. Private individuals can spend as much as they wish to circulate their own views on an election, although their contributions to candidates and parties can still be limited. The Court, however, permitted governmental limitations on parties and campaign organizations and allowed the use of federal funds for financing campaigns. *Buckley v. Valeo,* 424 U.S. 1 (1976).
11. Ibid.
12. See Paul-Henri Guvian and Audrey A. Haynes, "Presidential Nominating Campaigns," *P.S. Political Science and Politics* 36 (April, 2003): 175–180.
13. Lynn Vavreck, Constantine J. Spiliotes and Linda L. Fowler, "The Effects of Retail Politics in the New Hampshire Primary," *American Journal of Political Science* 46 (July 2002): 595–610.
14. William G. Mayer, "Forecasting Presidential Nominations," *P.S. Political Science and Politics* 36 (April 2003): 153–58.
15. University-based political scientists rely heavily on a series of National Election Studies, originated at the Survey Research Center at the University of Michigan, which have surveyed the voting-age population in every presidential election and most congressional elections since 1952.
16. See Martin P. Wattenberg, *The Rise of Candidate-Centered Politics* (Cambridge, Mass.: Harvard University Press, 1991).
17. Responsibility for the economy, however, is also affected by the voters' partisanship, ideology, and views about whether the president or Congress is chiefly responsible. See Joseph J. Rudolph, "Who's Responsible for the Economy?," *American Journal of Political Science* 47 (October, 2003): 698–713.
18. For an argument that voters look ahead to the economic future and reward or punish the president based on rational expectations, see Michael B. MacKuen, Robert S. Erickson, and James A. Stimson, "Peasants or Bankers? The American Electorate and the U.S. Economy," *American Political Science Review* 86 (September 1992): 680–95.

Chapter Six

1. For an overview of the mass media in American politics, see Doris A. Graber, *Mass Media and American Politics,* 6th ed. (Washington, D.C.: CQ Press, 2002).
2. Pew Research Center for People and the Press. http://people-press.org June, 2000.
3. See Lance Bennett, *News: The Politics of Illusion,* 4th ed. (White Plains, N.Y.: Longman, 2001).
4. E. E. Schattschneider, *The Semisovereign People* (New York: Holt, Rinehart & Winston, 1961), p. 68.
5. William A. Henry, "News as Entertainment," in *What's News,* ed. Elie Abel (San Francisco: Institute for Contemporary Studies, 1981), p. 133.
6. Shanto Iyengar, *Is Anyone Responsible? How Television Frames Political Issues* (Chicago: University of Chicago Press, 1991).
7. Graber, *Mass Media,* p. 35.
8. Matthew A. Baum, "Sex, Lies, and War: How Soft News Brings Foreign Policy to the Inattentive Public," *American Political Science Review* 96 (March, 2002): 91–109.
9. Larry Sabato, Mark Stencel, and S. Robert Lichter, *Peep Show? Media Politics in an Age of Scandal* (Lanham, Md.: Rowman & Littlefield, 2001).
10. Ben J. Wattenberg, *The Good News Is the Bad News Is Wrong* (New York: Simon & Schuster, 1984).
11. Ted Smith, "The Watchdog's Bite," *American Enterprise* 2 (January/February 1990): 66.
12. Larry Sabato, *Feeding Frenzy: How Attack Journalism Has Transformed American Politics* (New York: Free Press, 1991).
13. Graber, *Mass Media,* p. 946.
14. S. Robert Lichter, Stanley Rothman, and Linda S. Lichter, *The Media Elite* (Bethesda, Md.: Adler and Adler, 1986).
15. David Prindle, "Hollywood Liberalism" *Social Science Quarterly* 71 (March 1993): 121.
16. David C. Barker, "Rushed Decisions: Political Talk Radio and Vote Choice," *Journal of Politics* 61 (May 1999): 527–39.
17. Julianne F. Flowers, Audrey A. Haynes, and Michael H. Crespin, "The Media, the Campaign, and the Message," *American Journal of Political Science* 47 (April 2003): 259–73.
18. See David S. Castle, "Media Coverage of Presidential Primaries," *American Politics Quarterly* 19 (January 1991): 13–42; Christine F. Ridout, "The Role of Media Coverage of Iowa and New Hampshire," *American Politics Quarterly* 19 (January 1991): 43–58.
19. *Media Monitor* Vol. 14 (November/December, 2000).
20. Michael Robinson and Margaret Sheehan, *Over the Wire and on TV* (New York: Sage, 1983), p. 138. See also S. Robert Lichter, Daniel Amundson, and Richard Noyes, *The Video Campaign* (Washington, D.C.: American Enterprise Institute, 1988).
21. *New York Times v. U.S.,* 376 U.S. 713 (1971).
22. *New York Times v. Sullivan,* 376 U.S. 254 (1964).
23. *Reno v. American Civil Liberties Union* 117 S.Ct. 2329 (1997).
24. Bernard Cohen, *The Press and Foreign Policy* (Princeton, N.J.: Princeton University Press, 1963), p. 16.
25. Austin Ranney, *Channels of Power* (New York: Basic Books, 1983), p. 81.
26. Benjamin J. Page, Robert Y. Shapiro, and Glen R. Dempsey, "What Moves Public Opinion," *American Political Science Review* 81 (March 1987): 23–43.
27. National Institute of Mental Health, *Television and Behavior* (Washington, D.C.: Government Printing Office, 1982).
28. Brandon Centerwall, "Exposure to Television as a Risk Factor for Violence," *American Journal of Epidemiology* 129 (April 1989): 643–52.

Chapter Seven

1. Gaetano Mosca, *The Ruling Class* (New York: McGraw-Hill, 1939), p. 51.
2. E. E. Schattschneider, *Party Government* (New York: Holt, Rinehart & Winston, 1942), p. 1.
3. Geoffrey C. Layman and Thomas M. Carsey, "Party Polarization and Conflict Extension in the American Electorate," *American Journal of Political Science* 46 (October, 2002): 786–802.
4. Since 1954, only Presidents Kennedy, Johnson, and Carter (all Democrats) worked with their party's majorities in both houses of Congress; President Clinton enjoyed Democratic Party control of the Congress in only his first two years in office. George W. Bush is the only Republican president in a half century to serve with a Republican majority in both the House and Senate. See Harold W. Stanley and Richard C. Niemi, *Vital Statistics on American Politics* (Washington, D.C.: CQ Press, 2003).
5. See Thomas R. Dye and Susan MacManus, *Politics in States and Communities,* 11th ed. (Upper Saddle River, N.J.: Prentice Hall, 2003).
6. *National Election Study,* 2000.
7. Conventions continue to play a modest role in nominations in some states:
   - Colorado: Parties may hold a preprimary convention to designate a candidate to be listed first on the primary ballot. All candidates receiving at least 30 percent of the delegate vote will be listed on the primary ballot.
   - Connecticut: Party conventions are held to endorse candidates. If no one challenges the endorsed candidate, no primary election is held. If a challenger receives 20 percent of the delegate vote, a primary election will be held to determine the party's nominee in the general election.
   - New York: Party conventions choose the party's "designated" candidate in primary elections. Anyone receiving 25 percent of the delegates also appears on the ballot.
   - Utah: Party conventions select party's nominees.
   - Illinois, Indiana, Michigan, and South Carolina: Party conventions nominate candidates for some minor state offices.
8. For an argument that primary elections force parties to be more responsive to voters, see John G. Geer and Mark E. Shere, "Party Competition and the Prisoner's Dilemma: An Argument for the Direct Primary," *Journal of Politics* 54 (August 1992): 365–74.
9. For an up-to-date listing of state primaries and relevant information about them, see *The Book of the States,* published biannually by the Council of State Governments, Lexington, Kentucky.
10. Congressional Quarterly, *National Party Conventions 1831–1996* (Washington, D.C.: CQ Press, 1997).
11. For evidence that the national party conventions raise the poll standings of their presidential nominees, see James E. Campbell, Lynna L. Cherry, and Kenneth A. Wink, "The Convention Bump," *American Politics Quarterly* 20 (July 1992): 287–307.
12. See John A. Clark, John M. Bruce, John H. Kessel, and William G. Jacoby, "I'd Rather Switch Than Fight: Lifelong Democrats and Converts to Republicanism among Campaign Activists," *American Journal of Political Science* 35 (August 1991): 577–97.
13. Political scientist David Truman's classic definition of an interest group: "any group that is based on one or more shared attitudes and makes certain demands upon other groups or organizations in society." See *The Governmental Process* (New York: Knopf, 1971), p. 33.

14. Gale Research Company, *Encyclopedia of Associations* (Detroit: Gale Research, 2004).
15. Mancur Olson, *The Rise and Decline of Nations*. (New Haven, Conn.: Yale University Press, 1982).
16. Jeffrey M. Berry, *The New Liberalism: The Rising Power of Citizen Groups* (Washington, D.C.: Brookings Institution Press, 1999).
17. Center for Responsive Politics, *Influence, Inc.* 2000 (Washington, D.C., 2001).
18. Quotation from Roger Kersh, "Corporate Lobbyists as Political Actors," in *Interest Group Politics*, 6th ed., eds. Allan J. Ciglar and Burdett A. Loomis (Washington, D.C.: CQ Press, 2002).
19. Robert H. Salisbury, "Who You Know Versus What You Know: The Use of Government Experience by Washington Lobbyists," *American Journal of Political Science*, 33 (Feb. 1989): 175–95.
20. For evidence that vote buying on congressional roll calls is rare, see Janet M. Grenzke, "Shopping in the Congressional Supermarket: The Currency Is Complex," *American Journal of Political Science* 33 (February 1989): 1–24. But for evidence that committee participation by members of Congress is influenced by political action committee money, see Richard L. Hall and Frank W. Wayman, "Buying Time: Moneyed Interests and the Mobilization of Bias in Congressional Committees," *American Political Science Review* 84 (September 1990): 797–819.

Chapter Eight

1. James Madison, *Federalist Papers*, No. 10, reprinted in the Appendix.
2. Ibid.
3. Quoted in Jay M. Schafritz, *The Harper-Collins Dictionary of American Government and Politics* (New York: HarperCollins, 1992), p. 56.
4. See David Auerswald and Forrest Maltzman, "Policymaking through Advice and Consent: Treaty Consideration by the United States Senate," *Journal of Politics* 65 (November 2003): 1097–1110.
5. *McGrain v. Doughtery*, 273 U.S. 13J (1927).
6. *Baker v. Carr*, 369 U.S. 186 (1962), *Wesberry v. Sanders*, 370 U.S. 1 (1964).
7. *Gray v. Sanders*, 322 U.S. 368 (1963).
8. *Department of Commerce v. U.S. House of Representatives* 525 U.S. 316 (1999).
9. *Gaffney v. Cummings*, 412 U.S. 763 (1973).
10. *Davis v. Bandemer*, 478 U.S. 109 (1986).
11. Scott W. Desposato and John R. Petrocik, "The Variable Incumbency Advantage: New Voters, Redistricting, and Personal Vote," *American Journal of Political Science* 47 (January 2003): 18–32
12. *Thornburg v. Gingles*, 478 U.S. 30 (1986).
13. *Shaw v. Reno*, 125 I. Ed. 2d 511 (1993).
14. *Miller v. Johnson*, 115 S. Ct. 2475 (1995).
15. See Roger H. Davidson and Walter J. Oleszek, *Congress and Its Members*, 9th ed. (Washington, D.C.: CQ Press, 2004).
16. David Lublin, *The Paradox of Representation: Racial Gerrymandering and Minority Interests in Congress* (Princeton, NJ.: Princeton University Press, 1997). See also David Lublin and D. Stephen Voss, "The Missing Middle," *Journal of Politics* 65 (February 2003). 227–37.
17. *Georgia v. Ashcroft*, June 26, 2003.
18. For an in-depth analysis of who decides to run for Congress and who does not, see Linda L. Fowler and Robert D. McClure, *Political Ambition: Who Decides to Run for Congress* (New Haven, Conn.: Yale University Press, 1990).
19. See Michael K. Moore and John R. Hibbing, "Situational Dissatisfaction in Congress: Explaining Voluntary Departures," *Journal of Politics* 60 (November 1998): 1088–1107.
20. *U.S. Term Limits v Thornton*, 115 S.C. 1842, (1995).
21. See Gary Jacobson, *The Politics of Congressional Elections*, 5th ed. (New York: Harper-Collins, 2000).
22. See David Epstein and Peter Zemsky, "Money Talks: Deterring Quality Challengers in Congressional Elections," *American Political Science Review* 89 (June 1995): 295–322.
23. See Thomas E. Mann and Raymond Wolfinger, "Candidates and Parties in Congressional Elections," *American Political Science Review* 84 (September 1990): 545–64.
24. See Mary T. Hanna, "Political Science Caught Flat-Footed by Midterm Elections," *Chronicle of Higher Education*, November 30, 1994, pp. B1–2.
25. See Richard Fenno, *Going Home: Black Representatives and Their Constituents* (Chicago: University of Chicago Press, 2003).
26. Paul S. Herrnson, J. Celeste Lay, and Atiya Kai Stokes, "Women Running 'As Women'," *Journal of Politics* 65 (February 2003): 244–55.
27. U.S. House of Representatives, Commission on Administrative Review, *Administrative Reorganization and Legislative Management*, 95th Cong., 1st sess, H. Doc. 95–232, pp. 17–19.
28. Richard F. Fenno, *Home Style* (Boston: Little, Brown, 1978).
29. Roger H. Davidson and Walter J. Oleszak, *Congress and Its Members* 814 (Washington, D.C.: CQ Press, 2000), p. 19.
30. Glenn R. Parker, *Characteristics of Congress* (Upper Saddle River, N.J.: Prentice Hall, 1989), p. 30.
31. Richard F. Fenno, *The Making of a Senator: Dan Quayle* (Washington, D.C.: CQ Press, 1989), p. 119. Also cited in Davidson and Oleszek, *Congress and Its Members*, 9th ed., p. 120.
32. Davidson and Oleszek, *Congress and Its Members*, 9th ed., p. 129.
33. Ibid., p. 178.
34. Barbara Sinclair, "The Emergence of Strong Leadership in the House of Representatives," *Journal of Politics* 54 (August 1992): 657–84.
35. Gary W. Cox and Eric Magar, "How Much Is Majority Status in the U.S. Congress Worth?" *American Political Science Review* 93 (June 1999): 299–310.
36. Davidson and Oleszek, *Congress and Its Members*, 9th ed. p. 161.
37. John R. Hibbing, *Congressional Careers* (Chapel Hill: University of North Carolina Press, 1991).
38. See Charles Stewart and Tim Groseclose, "The Value of Committee Seats in the United States Senate," *American Journal of Political Science* 43 (July 1999): 963–73.
39. Larry Markinson, *The Cash Constituents of Congress* (Washington, D.C.: CQ Press, 1992).
40. Donald Matthews, *U.S. Senators and Their World* (New York: Vintage Books, 1960).
41. David Rohde, Norman J. Ornstein, and Robert L. Peabody, "Political Change and Legislative Norms," in *Studies of Congress*, ed. Glenn R. Parker (Washington, D.C.: CQ Press, 1985), p. 175.
42. See John R. Hibbing, "Contours of the Modern Congressional Career," *American Political Science Review* 85 (June 1991): 405–28.
43. Richard Fenno, *Power of the Purse* (Boston: Little, Brown, 1965), p. 620.
44. Ibid., p. 73.
45. See David R. Mayhew, *Divided We Govern* (New Haven, CT: Yale University Press, 1991); Sarah A. Binder, "The Dynamics of Legislative Gridlock," *American Political Science Review* 93 (September 1999): 519–33.
46. *Congressional Quarterly Weekly Report*, November 23, 1991, p. 3437.

Chapter Nine

1. For an argument that presidents encourage people to think of them as "the single head of government and moral leader of the nation who speaks for all of the people," see Barbara Hinckley, *The Symbolic Presidency: How Presidents Portray Themselves* (New York: Routledge, 1991).
2. See Theodore Lowi, *The Personal President* (Ithaca, N.Y.: Cornell University Press, 1987).
3. Presidential address to Congress, September 20, 2001.
4. See Michael Less Benedict, *The Impeachment and Trial of Andrew Johnson* (New York: Norton, 1973).
5. William Howard Taft, *Our Chief Magistrate and His Powers* (New York: Columbia University Press, 1938), p. 138, reprinted in *The Presidency*, ed. John P. Roche (New York: Harcourt Brace Jovanovich, 1964), p. 23.
6. Quoted in Arthur B. Tourtellot, *Presidents on the Presidency* (New York: Doubleday, 1964), pp. 55–56.
7. Quoted in James MacGregor Burns, *John Kennedy: A Political Profile* (New York: Harcourt Brace, 1959), p. 275.
8. *Youngstown Sheet and Tube v. Sawyer*, 343 U.S. 579 (1952).
9. *United States v. Nixon*, 418 U.S. 683 (1974).
10. *Nixon v. Fitzgerald*, 457 U.S. 731 (1982).
11. *Clinton v. Jones*, 520 U.S. 681 (1997).
12. Quoted in Richard Neustadt, *Presidential Power* (New York: Wiley, 1960), p. 9.
13. See George C. Edwards, *The Public Presidency* (New York: St. Martin's Press, 1983). See also Richard A. Brody, *Assessing Presidents: The Media, Elite Opinion, and Public Support* (Stanford, Calif.: Stanford University Press, 1991).
14. See Paul Brace and Barbara Hinckley, "The Structure of Presidential Approval," *Journal of Politics* 53 (November 1991): 993–1017.
15. See Suzanne L. Pancer, "Toward an understanding of 'Rally' Effect," *Public Opinion Quarterly* 59 (September, 1995): 526–46; Wave J. Aetherington and Michael Nelson: "Anatomy of a Rally Effect," *P.S. Political Science and Politics* 36 (January, 2003): 37–42.
16. John Mueller, *War, Presidents, and Public Opinion* (New York: Wiley, 1973).
17. See George C. Edwards and B. Dan Wood, "Who Influences Whom," *American Political Science Review* 93 (June 1999): 327–44.
18. George C. Edwards and Stephen J. Wayne, *Presidential Leadership*. 6th ed. (Belmont, Calif.: Wadsworth, 2003), p. 118.
19. *Youngstown Sheet and Tube v. Sawyer*, 343 U.S. 579 (1952).
20. Kenneth R. Mayer, "Executive Orders and Presidential Power," *Journal of Politics* 61 (May 1999): 445–66; Christopher J. Deering and Forrest Maltzman, "The Politics of Executive Orders," *Political Research Quarterly* 52 (December 1999): 767–83.
21. See also Jeffrey E. Cohen, *The Politics of the U.S. Cabinet* (Pittsburgh: University of Pittsburgh Press, 1988).
22. See Stanley Rothman and S. Robert Lichter, "How Liberal Are Bureaucrats?" *Regulation*, November–December 1983, pp. 16–22, for survey data on the voting behavior and political ideology of federal bureaucrats.
23. See Bradley H. Patterson, Jr., *The Ring of Power* (New York: Basic Books, 1988).
24. John Kingdon, *Agenda, Alternatives, and Public Policies* (Boston: Little, Brown, 1984), p. 25.
25. See Daniel E. Ingberman and Dennis A. Yao, "Presidential Commitment and the Veto," *American Journal of Political Science* 35 (May 1991): 357–89; and Samuel B. Hoff, "Saying No," *American Politics Quarterly* 19 (July 1991): 310–23.
26. For a discussion of the factors affecting the use of the presidential veto, see John T. Woolley, "Institutions, the Election Cycle, and the Presidential Veto," *American Journal of Political Science* 35 (May 1991): 279–304.
27. *Clinton v. City of New York*, 524 U.S. 417 (1998).
28. G.J.A. O'Toole, *Honorable Treachery: A History of U.S. Intelligence from the American Revolution to the CIA* (New York: Atlantic Monthly Press, 1991).
29. National Commission on Terrorist Attacks upon the United States, *The 9/11 Commission Report*, New York:W.W. Norton, 2004.
30. *Mora v. McNamara*, 389 U.S. 934 (1964); *Massachusetts v. Laird*, 400 U.S. 886 (1970). The Court specifically refused to intervene in the conduct of the Vietnam War by presidents Johnson and Nixon.
31. Jules Witcover, *Crap Shoot: Rolling the Dice on the Vice Presidency* (New York: Crow Publishing, 1992).

Chapter Ten

1. "Red tape" derives its meaning from the use of reddish tape by seventeenth-century English courts to bind legal documents. Unwrapping court orders entangled one in "red tape." See Herbert Kaufman, *Red Tape: Its Uses and Abuses* (Washington, D.C.: Brookings Institution, 1977).
2. H. H. Gerth and C. Wright Mills, *From Max Weber* (New York: Oxford Press, 1958).
3. Max Neiman, *Defending Government: Why Big Government Works* (Upper Saddle River, N.J.: Prentice Hall, 2000).
4. James Q. Wilson, *Bureaucracy: What Government Agencies Do and Why They Do It* (New York: Basic Books, 1989).
5. William Niskanen, *Bureaucracy and Representative Government* (Chicago: Aldine, 1971).
6. The constitutional question of whether Congress can establish an executive branch commission and protect its members from dismissal by the president was settled in *Humphrey's Executor v. United States* (1935). Franklin Roosevelt fired Humphrey from the Federal Trade Commission despite a fixed term set by Congress. Humphrey died shortly afterward, and when the executors of his estate sued for his back pay, the Supreme Court ruled that his firing was illegal.
7. See Nicholas Henry, *Public Administration and Public Affairs*, 7th ed. (Upper Saddle River, N.J.: Prentice Hall, 1999), Chapter 11.
8. Quoted in U.S. Civil Service Commission, *Biography of an Ideal: A History of the Civil Service System* (Washington, D.C.: Government Printing Office, 1973), p. 16.
9. See U.S. House of Representatives Committee on Post Office and Civil Service, *The Senior Executive Service* (Washington, D.C.: Government Printing Office, 1984).
10. Paul C. Light, *Thickening Government: Federal Hierarchy and the Diffusion of Accountability* (Washington, D.C.: Brookings Institution, 1995).
11. David Osborne and Ted Gaebler, *Reinventing Government* (New York: Addison-Wesley, 1992).
12. Al Gore, *Creating a Government That Works Better and Costs Less* (Washington, D.C.: Government Printing Office, 1993).
13. William G. Howell and David E. Lewis, "Agencies by Presidential Design," *Journal of Politics* 64 (November 2002): 1098–1114.
14. Aaron Wildavsky, *The New Politics of the Budgetary Process* (Glenview, Ill.: Scott, Foresman, 1988), p. 8.
15. Robert Crandell and Jerry Ellig, *Economic Deregulation and Consumer Choice* (Fairfax, Va.: Center for Market Processes, 1997).
16. General Accounting Office, *Regulatory Enforcement Fairness Act Report*, 1999.
17. Thomas D. Hopkins, *Regulatory Costs in Profile* (Washington, D.C.: Center for the Study of American Business, 1996).
18. Richard K. Vedder, "Federal Regulation's Impact on the Productivity Slowdown: A Trillion Dollar Drag," *Policy Study*, Center for the Study of American Business, July 1996.
19. For research suggesting that the appointive power is a more important instrument of

political control of the bureaucracy than budgets or legislation, see B. Dan Wood and Richard W. Waterman, "The Dynamics of Political Control of the Bureaucracy," *American Political Science Review* 83 (September 1991): 801–28.
20. See Joel D. Aberbach, *Keeping a Watchful Eye: The Politics of Congressional Oversight* (Washington, D.C.: Brookings Institution, 1990).
21. Evidence of the effectiveness of interventions by members of Congress in local offices of federal agencies is provided by John T. Scholz, Jim Twombly, and Barbara Headrick, "Street-Level Political Controls over Federal Bureaucracy," *American Political Science Review* 85 (September 1991): 829–50.
22. Bradley Cannon and Michael Giles, "Recurring Litigants: Federal Agencies before the Supreme Court," *Western Political Quarterly* 15 (September 1972): 183–91; Reginald S. Sheehan, "Federal Agencies and the Supreme Court," *American Politics Quarterly* 20 (October 1992): 478–500.

Chapter Eleven

1. Alexis de Tocqueville, *Democracy in America* (1835; New York: Mentor Books, 1956), p. 75.
2. Felix Frankfurter, "The Supreme Court and the Public," *Forum* 83 (June 1930): 332.
3. Alexander Hamilton, *Federalist Papers,* No. 78 (New York: Modern Library, 1937), p. 505.
4. *Marbury v. Madison,* 1 Cranch 137 (1803).
5. *Buckley v. Valeo,* 424 U.S. 1 (1976).
6. *U.S. v. Morrison* (May 15, 2000).
7. *Ex parte Milligan,* 4 Wallace 2 (1866).
8. *Youngstown Sheet and Tube Co. v. Sawyer,* 343 U.S. 579 (1952).
9. *United States v. Nixon,* 418 U.S. 683 (1974).
10. *Clinton v. Jones,* 520 U.S. 681 (1997).
11. *Brown v. Board of Education of Topeka,* 347 U.S. 483 (1954).
12. *Roe v. Wade,* 410 U.S. 113 (1973).
13. *Lawrence v. Texas* (June 26, 2003).
14. *West Virginia Board of Education v. Barnette,* 319 U.S. 624 (1943).
15. Quoted in Henry J. Abraham, *Justices and Presidents,* 3rd ed. (New York: Oxford University Press, 1992), p. 7.
16. Quoted in Charles P. Curtis, *Lions under the Throne* (Boston: Houghton Mifflin, 1947), p. 281.
17. Lee Epstein and Thomas G. Walker, *Constitutional Law for a Changing America,* 3rd ed. (Washington, D.C.: CQ Press, 1998), pp. 33–34.
18. William O. Douglas, "Stare Decisis," *Record,* April 1947, cited in Henry J. Abraham, *The Judicial Process* (New York: Oxford University Press, 1968), p. 58.
19. *Flast v. Cohen,* 392 U.S. 83 (1968).
20. *Gideon v. Wainwright,* 372 U.S. 335 (1963).
21. *Missouri v. Jenkins,* 110 S.C. 1651 (1990).
22. *Morrison v. Olson,* 487 U.S. 654 (1988).
23. Robert Scigliano, *The Supreme Court and the Presidency* (New York: Free Press, 1971), pp. 147–48.
24. See Bryon J. Moraski and Charles R. Shipan, "The Politics of Supreme Court Nominations," *American Journal of Political Science* 43 (October 1999): 1069–95.
25. See Charles R. Shipan and Megan L. Shannon, "Delaying Justices, *American Journal of Political Science* 47 (October, 2003): 654–68; Sarah A. Binder and Farrest Maltznan, "Senotorial Delay in Confirming Federal Judges," *American Journal of Political Science* 46 (January 2002): 190–99.
26. At one time the U.S. Supreme Court was legally required to accept certain "writs of appeal," but today very few cases come to the Court in this fashion.
27. *University of California Regents v. Bakke,* 438 U.S. 265 (1978).
28. Thomas Marshall, *Public Opinion and the Supreme Court* (New York: Unwin Hyman, 1989), p. 97.
29. Lee Epstein and C. K. Rowland, "Debunking the Myth of Interest Group Invincibility," *American Political Science Review* 85 (1991): 205–17.
30. *Bush v. Gore,* December 12, 2000.
31. *Gore v. Harris,* Florida Supreme Court, December 8, 2000.
32. Gallup News Service, December 12, 2000.
33. James L. Gibson, et al., "Measuring Attitudes toward the United States Supreme Court," *American Journal of Political Science* 47 (April 2003): 354–67; Stephen P. Nicholson and Robert H. Howard, "Framing Support for the Supreme Court in the Aftermath of *Bush v. Gore*," *Journal of Politics* 65 (August, 2003): 676–95.
34. President Andrew Jackson's comments came in response to the Court's ruling in the case of *Cherokee Nation v. Georgia* (1831) and *Worcester v. Georgia* (1832), which forbade the federal or state governments from seizing Native American lands and forcing the people to move. Refusal by Jackson, an old "Indian fighter," to enforce the Court's decisions resulted in the infamous "Trail of Tears," the forced march of the Georgia Cherokees that left one-quarter of them dead along the path west.
35. *Grove City College v. Bell,* 465 U.S. 555 (1984).
36. *Pollock v. Farmer's Loan,* 158 U.S. 601 (1895).

Chapter Twelve

1. James Madison, *Federalist Papers,* No. 10, reprinted in the Appendix.
2. *West Virginia Board of Education v. Barnette,* 319 U.S. 624 (1943).
3. *Reynolds v. United States,* 98 U.S. 145 (1879).
4. *Pierce v. Society of Sisters,* 268 U.S. 510 (1925).
5. Opening public meetings with prayer was ruled constitutional as "a tolerable acknowledgment of beliefs widely held among the people of this country." *Marsh v. Chambers,* 463 U.S. 783 (1983).
6. *Lemon v. Kurtzman,* 403 U.S. 602 (1971).
7. *Muebler v. Adams,* 463 U.S. 388 (1983).
8. *Tilton v. Richardson,* 403 U.S. 672 (1971).
9. *Lambs Chapel v. Center Moriches Union Free School District,* 508 U.S. 384 (1993).
10. *Rosenberger v. University of Virginia,* 515 U.S. 819 (1995).
11. *Walz v. Tax Commission,* 397 U.S. 664 (1970).
12. *Board of Education v. Mergens,* 497 U.S. 111 (1990).
13. *McGowan v. Maryland,* 366 U.S. 429 (1961), and *Braunfeld v. Brown,* 366 U.S. 599 (1961).
14. *County of Allegheny v. ACLU,* 492 U.S. 573 (1989).
15. *Edwards v. Aguillard,* 482 U.S. 578 (1987).
16. *Engle v. Vitale,* 370 U.S. 421 (1962).
17. *Abington School District v. Schempp,* 374 U.S. 203 (1963).
18. *Wallace v. Jaffree,* 472 U.S. 38 (1985).
19. *Lee v. Weisman,* 505 U.S. 577 (1992).
20. *Santa Fe Independent School District v. Doe,* 120 S.Ct. 2266 (2000).
21. *Schenck v. United States,* 249 U.S. 47 (1919).
22. *Gitlow v. New York,* 268 U.S. 652 (1925).
23. *Schenck v. United States,* 249 U.S. 47, 52 (1919).
24. *Whitney v. California,* 274 U.S. 357, 377 (1927), concurring opinion.
25. *Thomas v. Collins,* 323 U.S. 516 (1945).
26. *Tinker v. Des Moines Independent Community School District,* 393 U.S. 503 (1969).
27. *Texas v. Johnson,* 491 U.S. 397 (1989).
28. *Virginia v. Black,* (April 17, 2003).
29. *New York Times v. Sullivan,* 376 U.S. 254 (1964).
30. *Griswold v. Connecticut,* 381 U.S. 479 (1965).
31. *Roe v. Wade,* 410 U.S. 113 (1973).
32. *Harris v. McRae,* 448 U.S. 297 (1980).
33. *Planned Parenthood v. Casey,* 510 U.S. 110 (1992).
34. *Stenberg v. Carhart,* June 28, 2000.
35. *Bowers v. Hardwick,* 478 U.S. 186 (1986).

36. *Lawrence v. Texas,* (June 26, 2003).
37. *Barnes v. Glenn Theatre,* 501 U.S. 560 (1991).
38. *Reno v. American Civil Liberties Union,* 117 S.Ct. 2329 (1997).
39. James Madison, *Federalist Papers,* No. 46.
40. *Ex parte Milligan,* 4 Wallace 2 (1866).
41. *Spano v. New York,* 360 U.S. 315 (1959).
42. *Mapp v. Ohio,* 367 U.S. 643 (1961).
43. *Gideon v. Wainwright,* 372 U.S. 335 (1963).
44. *Escobedo v. Illinois,* 378 U.S. 478 (1964).
45. *Miranda v. Arizona,* 384 U.S. 436 (1966).
46. *Furman v. Georgia,* 408 U.S. 238 (1972).
47. *Gregg v. Georgia,* 428 U.S. 153 (1976); *Proffitt v. Florida,* 428 U.S. 242 (1976); *Jurek v. Texas,* 428 U.S. 262 (1976).
48. *Ring v. Arizona,* June 24, 2002.
49. *Atkins v. Virginia,* June 20, 2002.
50. *Dred Scott v. Sandford,* 60 U.S. 393 (1857).
51. *Plessy v. Ferguson,* 163 U.S. 537 (1896).
52. *Sweatt v. Painter,* 339 U.S. 629 (1950).
53. *Brown v. Board of Education of Topeka,* 347 U.S. 483 (1954).
54. The Supreme Court ruled that Congress was bound to respect the Equal Protection Clause of the Fourteenth Amendment even though the amendment is directed at states, because equal protection is a liberty guaranteed by the Fifth Amendment. *Bolling v. Sharpe,* 347 U.S. 497 (1954).
55. *Brown v. Board of Education of Topeka* (II), 349 U.S. 294 (1955).
56. *Alexander v. Holmes Board of Education,* 396 U.S. 19 (1969).
57. *Swann v. Charlotte-Mecklenburg County Board of Education,* 402 U.S. (1971).
58. *Milliken v. Bradley,* 418 U.S. 717 (1974).
59. Martin Luther King, Jr., "Letter from Birmingham City Jail," April 16, 1963.
60. *University of California Regents v. Bakke,* 438 U.S. 265 (1978).
61. Bakke's overall grade point average was 3.46, and the average for special admissions students was 2.62. Bakke's MCAT scores were verbal, 96; quantitative, 94; science, 97; general information, 72. The average MCAT scores for special admissions students were verbal, 34; quantitative, 30; science, 37; general information, 18.
62. *United Steelworkers of America v. Weber,* 443 U.S. 193 (1979).
63. *United States v. Paradise,* 480 U.S. 149 (1987).
64. *Firefighters Local Union 1781 v. Stotts,* 467 U.S. 561 (1984).
65. *City of Richmond v. Crosen Co.,* 488 U.S. 469 (1989).
66. *Adarand Construction v. Pena,* 132 L. Ed., 2d 158 (1995).
67. *Grutter v. Bollinger* (June 23, 2003).
68. *Gratz v. Bollinger* (June 23, 2003).
69. U.S. Department of Education, Office of Civil Rights, "Race-neutral Alternatives in Postsecondary Education," March, 2003.
70. Rudolpho O. dela Garza et al., *Latino Voices: Mexican, Puerto Rican, and Cuban Perspectives on American Politics* (Boulder, Colo.: Westview Press, 1992).
71. See F. Luis Garcia, *Latinos in the Political System* (Notre Dame, Ind.: Notre Dame University Press, 1988).
72. Linda Chavez, "Tequila Sunrise: The Slow but Steady Progress of Hispanic Immigrants," *Policy Review* (Spring 1989): 64–67.
73. Peter Mathiessen, *Sal Si Puedes: Cesar Chavez and the New American Revolution* (New York: Random House, 1969).
74. *Plyer v. Doe,* 457 U.S. 202 (1982).
75. *Bradwell v. Illinois,* 16 Wall 130 (1873).
76. *Reed v. Reed,* 404 U.S. 71 (1971).
77. *Stanton v. Stanton,* 421 U.S. 7 (1975).
78. *Craig v. Boren,* 429 U.S. 190 (1976).
79. *Dothard v. Rawlinson,* 433 U.S. 321 (1977).
80. *Arizona v. Norris,* 103 S.Ct. 3492 (1983).
81. *EEOC v. Madison Community School District,* 55 U.S.L.W. 2644 (1987).
82. *Michael M. v. Superior Court of Sonoma County,* 450 U.S. 464 (1981).
83. *Rostker v. Goldberg,* 453 U.S. 57 (1981).
84. *Statistical Abstract of the United States,* 2002, p. 440.
85. Susan Fraker, "Why Women Aren't Getting to the Top," *Fortune,* April 16, 1984, pp. 40–45.

Chapter Thirteen

1. Paul Samuelson, *Economics,* 12th ed. (New York: McGraw-Hill, 1985), p. 5.
2. GDP differs very little from gross national product, GNP, which is often used to compare the performance of national economies.
3. Richard B. Freeman, "Are Your Wages Set in Beijing?" *Journal of Economic Perspectives* 9 (Summer 1995): 15.
4. For a revealing case study of interest-group efforts to maintain tax breaks during the struggle over the Tax Reform Act of 1986, see Jeffrey H. Birnbaum and Alan S. Murray, *Showdown at Gucci Gulch* (New York: Random House, 1986).
5. Joseph A. Pechman, *Federal Tax Policy,* 5th ed. (Washington, D.C.: Brookings Institution, 1987).
6. Christopher Jenks and Paul E. Peterson, eds., *The Urban Underclass* (Washington, D.C.: Brookings Institution, 1991). See also William A. Kelso, *Poverty and the Underclass* (New York: New York University Press, 1994).
7. See Michael B. Katz, *In the Shadow of the Poorhouse* (New York: Basic Books, 1996).
8. See Charles Murray, *Losing Ground* (New York: Basic Books, 1984).

Chapter Fourteen

1. Hans Morgenthau, *Politics among Nations,* 5th ed. (New York: Knopf, 1973), p. 27.
2. George F. Kennan, writing under the pseudonym "X," "Sources of Soviet Conduct," *Foreign Affairs* 25 (July 1947): 25.
3. Frank Snepp, *Decent Interval* (New York: Random House, 1977).
4. George C. Herring, *America's Longest War* (New York: Random House, 1979), p. 262.
5. See Caspar W. Weinberger, "The Uses of Military Force," *Defense* (Arlington, Va.: American Forces Information Services Survey, 1985), pp. 2–11.
6. Morgenthau, *Politics among Nations,* p. 80.

Chapter Fifteen

1. *New York Times,* November 11, 1997.
2. Harold Lasswell, *Who Gets What, When, How* (New York: Meridian Books, 1958).
3. Texas Comptroller of Public Accounts, *Fiscal Notes,* June 1998, p. 6.
4. David Easton, *A Framework For Political Analysis* (Englewood Cliffs, N.J.: Prentice Hall, 1965), Chap. 5.
5. Lucian W. Pye, "Political Culture," *International Encyclopedia of the Social Sciences,* Vol. 12 (New York: Crowell, Collier and Macmillan, 1968), p. 218.
6. Ellen M. Dran, Robert B. Albritton, and Mikel Wyckoff, "Surrogate versus Direct Measures of Political Culture: Explaining

Participation and Policy Attitudes in Illinois," *Publius* 21 (Spring 1991); 17.

7. Daniel Elazar, *American Federalism: A View from the States* (New York: Thomas Y. Crowell, 1966), p. 86.
8. Ibid., pp. 86–89.
9. Ibid, pp. 90–92.
10. Ibid, pp. 92–94.
11. Ibid, pp. 97, 102, 108.
12. Louise Cowan, "Myth in the Modern World," in *Texas Myths*, ed. Robert F. O'Connor (College Station: Texas A&M University Press, 1986), p. 4.
13. Ibid., p. 14. For an excellent analysis of the concept of the "myth of origin" as integrated into the American mythology, see Robert N. Bellah, *The Broken Covenant: American Civil Religion in Time of Trial* (New York: The Seabury Press, 1975).
14. T. R. Fehrenbach, "Texas Mythology: Now and Forever," in *Texas Myths*, pp. 210–17.
15. U.S. Bureau of the Census, Census 2000. Unless otherwise noted, all demographic data are taken from the 2000 census.
16. Ellen N. Murray, "Sorrow Whispers in the Winds," *Texas Journal*, 14 (Spring/Summer 1992): 16.
17. Terry G. Jordan with John L. Bean, Jr., and William M. Holmes, *Texas: A Geography* (Boulder, Colo.: Westview Press, 1984), pp. 79–86.
18. Texas State Data Center, Texas A&M University.
19. National Association of Latino Elected and Appointed Officials, 2003 *National Roster of Hispanic Elected Officials.*
20. Joint Center for Political Studies, *National Roster of Black Elected Officials*, 2001.
21. Jordan et al., *Texas*, pp. 71–77.
22. V. O. Key, *Southern Politics in State and Nation* (New York: Vintage Books, 1949), p. 261.
23. For an excellent analysis of Key's projections for political change in Texas, see Chandler Davidson, *Race and Class in Texas Politics* (Princeton, N.J.: Princeton University Press, 1990).
24. U.S. Bureau of the Census, *Census 2000.*
25. Office of the Governor, Texas 2000 Commission, *Texas Trends*, pp. 5–6; Office of the Governor, Texas 2000 Commission, *Texas Past and Future: A Survey*, p. 6.
26. U.S. Bureau of the Census, *Census 2000.*
27. Steve H. Murdock, Nazrul Hoque, Martha Michael, Steve White, and Beverly Pecotte, *The Texas Challenge: Population Change and the Future of Texas* (College Station: Texas A&M University Press, 1997), p. 29.
28. *Forbes*, Special Edition 2003, "The 400 Richest People in America," pp.186–284.
29. U.S. Bureau of the Census, *Census 2000.*
30. Rupert N. Richardson, Ernest Wallace, and Adrian N. Anderson, *Texas: the Lone Star State*, 6th ed. (Upper Saddle River, N.J.: Prentice Hall, 1993) p. 1.
31. Betsey Bishop and Terry Heller, "Education Reform: Preparing Our Children for the Future," *Fiscal Notes* (March 1991): 10.
32. U.S. Bureau of the Census, *Census 2000.*
33. For an expanded analysis of the Texas economy and the dominant role played by larger corporations, see James W. Lamare, *Texas Politics: Economics, Power and Policy*, 7th ed. (Belmont, Calif.: Wadsworth, 2001), Chap. 2.
34. "Boom, Bust and Back Again: Bullock Tenure Covers Tumultuous Era," *Fiscal Notes* (December 1990): 6–7.
35. Ibid.
36. "Boom, Bust and Back Again," p. 7.
37. "Brac'95 Round of Base Closures Will Have a Minor Effect on the Texas Economy," *Texas Economic Quarterly* (September 1995): p. 8; "Texas Economic History and Outlook, for Calendar Years: 1994 to 2000," *Texas Economic Update* (Winter 2000): 2.
38. "Texas Economic Outlook," *Texas Economic Quarterly*, (December 1996): 2.
39. Texas Economic Development, May 2002, www.bidc.state.tx.us/overview/2-21e.
40. Harry Hurt, "Birth of a New Frontier," *Texas Monthly* (April 1984): 130–35.
41. "Biotechnology: New Science Brings Jobs to Texas as Biotech-related Efforts Blossom," *Fiscal Notes* (April 1990): 1–8.
42. Texas Department of Economic Development, April, 1998.
43. The following discussion of the ten economic regions of Texas is based on reports produced by John Sharp, Texas Comptroller of Public Accounts, in the series *Texas Regional Outlook* (Austin: Reports of the Comptroller's Forces of Change Project, 1992); *Texas Regional Outlook* (2002).
44. M. Delal Baer, "North American Free Trade," *Foreign Affairs* 70 (Fall 1991): 138.
45. Joan B. Anderson, "Maquiladoras and Border Industrialization: Impact on Economic Development in Mexico," *Journal of Borderland Studies* V (Spring 1990): 5.
46. Michael Patrick, "Maquiladoras and South Texas Border Economic Development," *Journal of Borderland Studies* IV (Spring 1989): 90.
47. Patrick, "Maquiladoras and South Texas Border Economic Development," p. 90.
48. Baer, "North American Free Trade," pp. 132–49.
49. Central Intelligence Agency, *The World Factbook* (Washington, D.C.: CIA), 1997.
50. Chandler Stolp and Jon Hockenyos, "Free Trade over Texas," *San Antonio Light*, September 15, 1991, p. E-1.
51. Texas Economic Development, May 2002.
52. David Hendricks, "Security Change Will Discriminate Against Mexico, South Texas, *San Antonio Express*-News, October 25, 2003, p. D1.
53. Joan Anderson and Martin de la Rosa, "Economic Survival Strategies of Poor Families on the Mexican Border," *Journal of Borderland Studies*, VI (Spring 1991): 51.
54. Stephen A. Camarota, "Back Where We Started: An Examination of Trends in Immigrant Welfare Use Since Reform," Center for Immigration Studies, March 2003, p. 5.
55. Migration Policy Institute, "Immigration Factsigration and Naturalization Service.
56. James F. Pearce and Jeffery W. Gunther, "Illegal Immigration from Mexico: Effects on the Texas Economy," *Federal Reserve Bank of Dallas Economic Review* (September 1985): 4.
57. Robert W. Gardner and Leon F. Bouvier, "The United States," in *Handbook on International Migration*, eds. William J. Serow, Charles B. Nam, David F. Sly, and Robert H. Weller (New York: Greenwood Press, 1990), p. 342.
58. "Congress Clears Overhaul of Immigration Law," *Congressional Quarterly Almanac, 1986* (Washington, D.C.: Congressional Quarterly, 1987), pp. 61–67.
59. Dan Carney, "Law Restricts Illegal Immigration," *Congressional Quarterly Weekly Report 54* (November 16, 1996), p. 3287.

Chapter Sixteen

1. G. Allan Tarr, *Understanding State Constitutions* (Princeton, N.J.: Princeton University Press, 1998), p. 3.
2. Daniel Elazar, "The Principles and Traditions Underlying American State Constitutions," *Publius* 12 (Winter 1982): 23.
3. Tarr, pp. 4–5.
4. David Saffell, *State Politics* (Reading, Mass.: Addison-Wesley, 1984), pp. 23–24.
5. Elazar, pp. 20–21.
6. T. R. Fehrenbach, *Lone Star: A History of Texas and the Texans* (New York: Macmillan, 1968), pp. 152–73.
7. Richard Gambitta, Robert A. Milne, and Carol R. Davis, "The Politics of Unequal Educational Opportunity," in *The Politics of San Antonio*, eds. David R. Johnson, John A. Booth, and Richard J. Harris (Lincoln: University of Nebraska Press, 1983), p. 135.
8. Joe B. Frantz, *Texas: A Bicentennial History* (New York: W. W. Norton, 1976), pp. 73, 76.
9. Fehrenbach, *Lone Star*, p. 265.
10. Frantz, *Texas*, p. 92.
11. Fehrenbach, *Lone Star*, p. 396.
12. Ibid., pp. 398–99, 401.
13. J. E. Ericson, "The Delegates to the Convention of 1875: A Reappraisal," *Southwestern Historical Quarterly* 67 (July 1963): 22.

15. Anthony Champagne, "Campaign Contributions in Texas Supreme Court Races," *Crime, Law and Social Change* 17 (1992): 91–106.
16. Kim Ross, quoted in the *Houston Post*, November 10, 1988.
17. *Austin American-Statesman*, December 9, 1993.
18. *Houston Chronicle*, April 30, 2004, page 1A.
19. *Houston Chronicle*, August 21, 2003, p. 24A.
20. Texas Watch, *The Food Chain: Winners and Losers in the Texas Supreme Court, 1995–1999*. Austin: Texas Watch, 1999.
21. Texas Watch press release, May 3, 1999.
22. Texas Watch, *Access Denied, the Texas Supreme Court in 2000–2001*. Austin: Texas Watch, 2001.
23. *Houston Chronicle*, September 18, 2002, p. 25A.
24. Samuel Issacharoff, *The Texas Judiciary and the Voting Rights Act: Background and Options* (Austin: Texas Policy Research Forum, 1989), pp. 2, 13.
25. *Texas Lawyer*, September 18, 1989.
26. *Houston Chronicle*, December 24, 1989.
27. *Texas Lawyer*, September 18, 1989.
28. *League of United Latin American Citizens, et al. v. Mattox, et al.*, 501 U.S. 419 (1991); *Chisom v. Roemer*, 501 U.S. 380 (1991).
29. *League of United Latin American Citizens v. Clements*, 999 F2d 831 (1993).
30. *Houston Chronicle*, January 19, 1994.
31. State Bar of Texas, Department of Research and Analysis, *A Statistical Profile of Texas Judges* (Austin: State Bar of Texas, 1998).
32. *Houston Chronicle*, November 13, 1998, p. 1A.
33. Office of Court Administration, *Texas Judicial System, 75th Annual Report*.
34. *Miranda v. Arizona*, 384 U.S. 436 (1966).
35. *Texas Lawyer*, November 11, 1991.
36. *Paulson v. State*, Texas Court of Criminal Appeals, October 4, 2000.
37. *Furman v. Georgia*, 408 U.S. 238 (1972).
38. *Texas Lawyer*, June 3, 1991.
39. *Houston Chronicle*, May 11, 2003, p. 1A.
40. Paul Burka, "Trial by Technicality," *Texas Monthly* (April 1982), pp. 126–31, 210–18, 241.
41. *Houston Chronicle*, August 27, 2003, p. 23A.
42. *Edgewood v. Kirby*, 777 S.W.2d 391 (1989).
43. *Fort Worth Star-Telegram*, October 4, 1982; *Brown v. Board of Education of Topeka*, 347 U.S. 483 (1954).
44. *Edgewood v. Meno*, 893 S.W.2d 450 (1995).
45. Ibid.
46. *Richards v. LULAC*, 868 S.W.2d 306 (1993); *Houston Chronicle*, June 16, 1994.
47. *Texas Education Agency v. Leeper*, 893 S.W. 2d 432 (1994).
48. *Operation Rescue—National v. Planned Parenthood of Houston and Southeast Texas, Inc.*, 975 S.W.2d 546 (1998). See also *Houston Chronicle*, July 4, 1998.
49. *Madsen v. Women's Health Clinic, Inc.*, 512 U.S. (1994).
50. *Republican Party of Texas v. Dietz*, 924 S.W.2d 932 (1996).

Chapter Twenty-One

1. Anwar Hussain Syed, *The Political Theory of American Local Government* (New York: Random House, 1966), p. 27.
2. Ibid., pp. 38–52. Syed presents a summary of Jefferson's theory of local government.
3. Roscoe C. Martin, *Grass Roots* (Tuscaloosa: University of Alabama Press, 1957), p. 5.; Robert C. Wood, *Suburbia* (Boston: Houghton Mifflin, 1958), p. 18.
4. *City of Clinton v. The Cedar Rapids and Missouri River Railroad Co.*, 24 Iowa 455 (1868).
5. Roscoe C. Martin, *This Cities in the Federal System* (New York: Atherton Press, 1965), pp. 28–35.
6. David B. Brooks, *Texas Practice: County and Special District Law*, vol. 35 (St. Paul, MN: West Publishing Company, 1989), pp. 41–46. A good part of the materials presented on county government rely on this comprehensive work.
7. Advisory Commission on Intergovernmental Relations, *Measuring Local Government Discretionary Authority*, Report M–131 (Washington, D.C.: ACIR, 1981).
8. Advisory Commission on Intergovernmental Relations, *State and Local Roles in the Federal System* (Washington, D.C.: ACIR, 1982), pp. 32–33.
9. For an excellent overview of urban development in Texas, see Char Miller and David R. Johnson, "The Rise of Urban Texas," in Char Miller and Heywood T. Sanders, *Urban Texas: Politics and Development* (College Station: Texas A & M University Press, 1990), pp. 3–29.
10. See Richard L. Cole, Ann Crowley Smith, and Delbert A. Taebel, with a foreword by Marlan Blissett, *Urban Life in Texas: A Statistical Profile and Assessment of the Largest Cities* (Austin: University of Texas Press, 1986), for an example of rankings of larger Texas cities on various dimensions measuring aspects of urban quality of life.
11. Texas Municipal League, May 2002, Austin, Texas
12. Ibid.
13. Ibid.
14. Murray S. Stedman, *Urban Politics*, 2nd ed. (Cambridge, MA: Winthrop Publishers, Inc., 1975), p. 51.
15. Beryl E. Pettus and Randall W. Bland, *Texas Government Today*, 3rd ed. (Homewood, Ill.: The Dorsey Press, 1984), p. 347.
16. Telephone calls to budget staff in El Paso and Houston, Texas, Dec. 30, 2003.
17. Wilbourn E. Benton, *Texas Politics*, 5th ed. (Chicago: Nelson-Hall Publishers, 1984), p. 260.
18. Telephone calls to budget staff in Dallas, San Antonio, and Seguin, Texas, Dec. 30, 2003.
19. Bureau of the Census, *1992 Census of Government, Popularly Elected Officials*, vol. 2, no. 1, Table 11.
20. Texas Municipal League, telephone conversation with research staff, May 2002, Austin, Texas.
21. Frank Sturzl, "Fiscal Conditions Survey Shows that Municipal Revenue is Declining," *Texas Town and City* 89 (March 2003): 10.
22. Ibid., pp. 11–12.
23. "Texas Cities Continue to Face Fiscal Squeeze," *Texas Town and City* 79 (March 1991): 26, 32–34.
24. Lawrence E. Jordan, "Municipal Bond Issuance in Texas: The New Realities," *Texas Town and City* 79 (December 1991): 12, 25.
25. Sturzl, "Municipal Fiscal Conditions Remain Strong," pp. 10–11.
26. Miller and Sanders, eds., *Urban Texas: Politics and Development*, p. xiv.
27. Frank Sturzl, "The Tyranny of Environmental Mandates," *Texas Town and City* 79 (September 1991).
28. Robert E. Norwood and Sabrina Strawn, *Texas County Government: Let the People Choose*, 2nd ed. (Austin: The Texas Research League, 1984), p. 9. For a sample of Texas court decisions that affirm the general principle of the Dillon rule that the county can perform only those functions allocated to it by law, see pp. 11–12.
29. Texas Association of Counties. *2003 Salary Survey* (Austin: Texas Association of Counties, 2003); phone conversation with Office of Budget Management, Harris County, December 5, 2003.
30. *Avery v. Midland*, 88 S.Ct. 1114 (1968).
31. Norwood and Strawn, *Texas County Government*, p. 22.
32. Brooks, *Texas Practice*, 35: 331.
33. Texas Commission on Intergovernmental Relations, *An Introduction to Texas County Government* (Austin: TCIR, 1980), p. 10.
34. Brooks, *Texas Practice*, 35: 392–93.
35. Ibid, 36: 104–105.
36. Texas Association of Counties, *2003 Salary Survey*.
37. Brooks, *Texas Practice*, 36: 49–50.
38. Ibid, pp. 18–49.
39. Norwood and Strawn, *Texas County Government*, p. 24.
40. Brooks, *Texas Practice*, 35: 273–74.
41. Ibid, 36: 122–23.

42. TCIR, *An Introduction to County Government,* p. 22.
43. Norwood and Strawn, *Texas County Government,* p. 27.
44. Brooks, *Texas Practice,* 35: 273–74.
45. Virginia Marion Perrenod, *Special Districts, Special Purposes: Fringe Governments and Urban Problems in the Houston Area* (College Station: Texas A & M University Press, 1984), p. 4.
46. Ibid, p. 34.
47. Woodworth G. Thrombley, *Special Districts and Authorities in Texas* (Austin: Institute of Public Affairs, The University of Texas, 1959), p. 13.
48. Robert S. Lorch, *State and Local Politics,* 3rd ed. (Englewood Cliffs, NJ: Prentice Hall, Inc., 1989), p. 246.
49. Ibid, p. 247.
50. Texas Education Agency, *Snapshot 2002:2001–2002 School District Profiles* (Austin: Texas Education Agency, 2002).
51. Texas Association of School Boards, Membership Services, Telephone Conversation on 5-14-2002.
52. Governor's Planning and Budget Office, *Regional Councils in Texas: A Status Report and Directory, 1980–1981,* p. 9.
53. Governor's Budget and Planning Office, *Regional Councils in Texas: Annual Report and Directory, 1990–1991,* p. 8.
54. Texas Association of Regional Councils, "What is a COG?", www.txregionalcouncil.org.
55. Governor's Budget and Planning Office, Texas Regional Councils: Annual Report and Directory, 1992–1993.
56. Texas Association of Regional Councils, "What is a COG?", www.txregionalcouncil.org.
57. Telephone interview by author on March 21, 2000 with governor's office.
58. Brooks, *Texas Practices,* 36: 380–84.
59. For a more detailed discussion of annexation authority, see Wilbourn E. Benton, *Texas Politics,* pp. 264–66.
60. "Texas Legislature Adjourns," *Texas Town and City,* 86 (July 1999), p. 10.
61. "Texas Legislature Adjourns," *Texas Town and City,* 89 (July 2001), p 11.
62. Norwood and Strawn, *Texas County Government,* pp. 75–81.
63. Joel B. Goldsteen and Russell Fricano, *Municipal Finance Practices and Preferences for New Development: Survey of Texas Cities* (Arlington, TX: Institute of Urban Studies, The University of Texas at Arlington, 1988), pp. 3–11.
64. Bill R. Shelton and Nancy Ratcliff, "How Cities Organize and Administer Sales Tax Revenues Dedicated to Economic Development," *Texas Town and City* 82 (December 1995): 26–27.
65. Brooks, *Texas Practice,* 36: 229–42.
66. Tom Adams, "Introduction and Recent Experience with the Interlocal Contract," in *Interlocal Contract in Texas,* eds. Richard W. Tees, Richard L. Cole, and Jay G. Stanford. (Arlington, TX: Institute of Urban Studies, University of Arlington, 1990), p. 1.
67. Tees, et al., *Interlocal Contract in Texas,* pp. B1–B7.
68. Vincent Ostrom, *The Meaning of American Federalism* (San Francisco: Institute for Contemporary Studies, 1991), p. 161. Ostrom suggests that advocates of metropolitan government often overlook the "rich and intricate framework for negotiating, adjudicating, and deciding questions" that are now in place in many urbanized areas with multiple governmental units.
69. Ann Long Diveley and Dwight A. Shupe, "Public Improvement Districts: An Alternative for Financing Public Improvements and Services," *Texas Town and City,* 79 (September 1991): 6–10, 30, 66.

Photo Credits

Chapter 1 Dennis Brack/Stockphoto.com, 2; Trippet/SIPA Press, 5 (top left); AP Wide World Photos, 5 (top right); James Leynse/Corbis/Bettmann, 5 (bottom left); Spencer Platt/Getty Images, Inc.–Liaison, 5 (bottom right); The White House Photo Office, 6 (Johnson, Nixon, Carter); Gerald R. Ford Library, 6 (Ford); Michael Evans/The White House Photo Office, 6 (Reagan); Susan Biddle/The White House Photo Office, 6 (Bush); AP Wide World Photos, 6 (Clinton); REUTERS/Reuters/Kevin Lamarque/Corbis/Bettman, 6 (G. W. Bush); Copyright Flip Schulke, 8; Corbis/Bettmann, 13; AP Wide World Photos, 14; Dan Habib/Concord Monitor (New Hampshire), 15; AFP PHOTO/Seth McCallister/Agence France Presse/Getty Images, 19.

Chapter 2 David Friedman/Getty Images, Inc—Liaison, 24; Fred Prousaer/Reuters/Getty Images Inc.—Hulton Archive Photos, 27 (left); Rose Prouser/Reuters/Getty Images Inc.—Hulton Archive Photos, 27 (right); Jim Smith/Photo Researchers, Inc., 33 (left); Rob Crandall/Stock Boston, 33 (right); Spencer Grant/Spencer Grant, 37 (top); Allan Tannenbaum/Allan Tannenbaum, 37 (bottom); AP Wide World Photos, 43; United States Senate, 44; Stephen Ferry/Getty Images, Inc–Liaison, 46 (left); Bob Daemmrich/Stock, 46 (right); Henny Abrams/UPI/ Corbis/Bettmann, 49 (left); Mark Richards/PhotoEdit, 49 (right).

Chapter 3 The Granger Collection, 52; The Granger Collection, 55; The Granger Collection, 57; Library of Congress, 59; London Illustrated News/Library of Congress, 63; Corbis/Bettmann, 65; AP Wide World Photos, 66; Stan Wakefield/Pearson Education/PH College, 72 (top); Stan Wakefield/Pearson Education/PH College, 72 (left); Irene Springer/Pearson Education/PH College, 72 (right); John van der Lyn/White House Historical Association (White House Collection—24), 75.

Chapter 4 Bob Daemmrich/Bob Daemmrich Photography, Inc., 100; Reuters/Vincent Kessler/Getty Images Inc.–Hulton Archive Photos, 102; Dave Gaywood/SIPA Press, 102; AP Wide World Photos, 108; The Cartoon Bank/©2002 Robert Mankoff from cartoonbank.com. All Rights Reserved, 111; Rick Friedman/Corbis/Bettmann, 113; Thomas C. Roche/ Courtesy of the Library of Congress, 115; AP Wide World Photos, 116; Toby Talbot/AP Wide World Photos, 118; R. Ellis/R. Ellis/Corbis Sygma, 119; Stephen Ferry/Getty Images, Inc—Liaison, 121; AP Wide World Photos, 127.

Chapter 5 Reuters/Rick Wilking/Getty Images Inc.—Hulton Archive Photos, 130; Stan Honda/AFP/Getty Images, Inc—Liaison, 140; Lyndon Baines Johnson Library Collection, 141 (top left); Lyndon Baines Johnson Library Collection, 141 (top right); Lyndon Baines Johnson Library Collection, 141 (bottom left); Lyndon Baines Johnson Library Collection, 141 (bottom right); Stan Wakefield/Pearson Education/PH College, 249 (top); Stan Wakefield/Pearson Education/PH College, 249 (bottom); Steve Marcus/Las Steve Marcus/Las Tribune Media Services, Inc./© Tribune Media Services, Inc. All Rights Reserved. Reprinted with permission, 254; Brooks Kraft/Corbis/Bettmann, 258; Jim Bourg/Reuters/Corbis/Bettmann, 264; Jim Bourg/Reuters/ Corbis/Bettmann, 275.

Chapter 6 Reuters/Jim Bourg/Getty Images Inc.—Hulton Archive Photos, 170; Jim Cole/AP Wide World Photos, 176; AP Wide World Photos, 174; Peter Morgan/Reuters/Getty Images Inc.—Hulton Archive Photos, 177; Andy King/Andy King/Corbis Sygma, 180; Jim Sulley/Wirepix/The Image Works, 185; Jonathan Nourok/PhotoEdit, 186; AP Wide World Photos, 190; King Features Syndicate/©1997 Jim Borgman, Cincinnati Enquirer. Reprinted with special permission of King Features Syndicate, 192; UPI/Corbis/Bettmann, 195; AP Wide World Photos, 196.

Chapter 7 Zack Seckler/Corbis/Bettmann, 200; Culver Pictures, Inc., 208 (top left); Ira Wyman/ Corbis/Sygma, 208 (top right); Jean-Marc Giboux/Getty Images, Inc—Liaison, 208 (bottom left); Charlie Neibergall/ AP Wide World Photos, 208 (bottom right); Joel Page/AP Wide World Photos, 209; Reason Foundation/Reprinted, with permission, from the April 1997 issue of REASON Magazine. Copyright 2000 by the Reason Foundation, 3415 S. Sepulveda Blvd, Suite 400, Los Angeles, CA 90034, http://www.reason.com 230; Dennis Cook/AP Wide World Photos, 232.

Chapter 8 Getty Images, Inc—Liaison, 240; Mark Wilson/Newsmakers/Getty Images, Inc—Liaison, 245; David Hume Kennerly/Getty Images, 259; Jeff Greenberg/The Image Works, 262; AP Wide World Photos, 263; Joe Marquette/AP Wide World Photos, 269; AP Wide World Photos, 270; Shana Raab/Corbis/Sygma, 274; AP Wide World Photos, 276.

Chapter 9 Dennis Cook/AP Wide World Photos, 294; Reuters/Jeff Mitchell/Getty Images Inc.—Hulton Archive Photos, 297; Getty Images, Inc—Liaison, 300; AP Wide World Photos, 301; Mookie/Getty Images, Inc—Liaison, 304; AP Wide World Photos, 312; AP Wide World Photos, 319; AP Wide World Photos, 327; U.S. Army Photo, 329; AP Wide World Photos, 334; AP Wide World Photos, 336.

Chapter 10 Larry Downing/Reuters/Corbis/Bettmann, 340; Stan Wakefield/Pearson Education/PH College, 343 (left); Stan Wakefield/Pearson Education/PH College, 343 (middle); Irene Springer/Pearson Education/PH College, 343 (right); Louie Psihoyos/Louis Psihoyos, 346; AP Wide World Photos, 352 (left); U.S. Government/HO/U.S. Government/HO, 352 (right); David Young-Wolff/PhotoEdit, 354; Reuters/Mike Theiler/Getty Images Inc.—Hulton Archive Photos, 356; Corbis/Bettmann, 358; AP Wide World Photos, 366; Bob Daemmrich/Stock Boston, 371; AP Wide World Photos, 373; Richard Ellis/Corbis/Sygma, 375.

Chapter 11 Paul Hosefros/New York Times Pictures, 380; Corbis/Bettmann, 383; Reuters/Gary Hershorn/Getty Images Inc.—Hulton Archive Photos, 387; Irene Springer, 390; J. Scott Applewhite/AP/Wide World Photos, 395; Colin Braley/Getty Images, Inc.—Liaison, 397; Reuter/Rick Wilking/Corbis/Bettmann, 401 (left); Reuter/Rick Wilking/Corbis/Bettmann, 401 (right); AP Wide World Photos, 408; AP Wide World Photos, 409.

Chapter 12 Mark Richards/PhotoEdit, 416; Kamenko Pajic/AP Wide World Photos, 422 (top); AP Wide World Photos, 422 (bottom); Rod Aydelotte/Waco Tribune Herald/Corbis/Sygma, 430; Chuck Nacke/Woodfin Camp & Associates, 438; Mike Smith/Getty Images, Inc—Taxi, 444; Flip Schulke/Black Star, 445; Reuters/Ogrocki/Getty Images Inc.— Hulton Archive Photos, 456.

Chapter 13 Joseph Rodrigues/Stockphoto.com, 462; Topham/The Image Works, 465; Ken Hawkins/Corbis/Sygma, 474; UPI/Corbis/Bettmann, 479 (left); UPI/Corbis/Bettmann, 479 (right); Regan/Getty Images, Inc–Liaison, 481.

Chapter 14 AP Wide World Photos, 488; Joe Marquette/AP Wide World Photos, 491; UPI/Corbis/Bettmann, 493; Bohdan Hrynewych/Stock Boston, 495; Mark Wilson/Getty Images, Inc–Liaison, 496; AP Wide World Photos, 502.

Chapter 15 Eric von Schmidt, 512; Culver Pictures, Inc., 514; Texas State Library and Archives Commission/Texas State Library & Archives Commission, #1968/29-155, 515; Joel Salcido/Bob Daemmrich Photography, Inc., 517; Bob Daemmrich/Bob Daemmrich Photography, Inc., 518 (top); Bob Daemmrich/Bob Daemmrich Photography, Inc., 518 (bottom); Jack Kurtz/The Image Works, 533.

Chapter 16 Broadside Collection/Texas State Library and Archives Commission, Broadside 479, ITC-68-218, 536; Star of the Republic Museum/By Charles and Fannie Normann. Collection of the Joe Fultz estate of Navasota, TX. Exhibited at the Star of the Republic Museum, 542; Texas State Library and Archives Commission, 544; Texas State Library and Archives Commission/Texas State Library and Archives Commission, #1/170-1, 702; AP Wide World Photos, 551; The Institute of Texan Cultures/The UT Institute of Texan Cultures at San Antonio, No. 74-804, 554.

Chapter 17 AP Wide World Photos, 562; Bob Daemmrich/Bob Daemmrich Photography, Inc, 565; AP Wide World Photos, 574; UPI/Corbis/Bettmann, 585.

Chapter 18 Joe Bator/Corbis/Bettmann, 598; Stock Boston, 604; Bob Daemmrich/PhotoEdit, 607; Bob Daemmrich Photography, Inc., 612; AP Wide World Photos, 615; The Senate of The State of Texas/Senate Media Services, 622; Bob Daemmrich/Bob Daemmrich Photography, Inc., 623; Bob Daemmrich/The Image Works, 629; The Senate of The State of Texas/Senate Media Services, 631.

Chapter 19 Bob Daemmrich/The Image Works, 636; Texas State Library and Archives Commission/Texas State Library & Archives Commission, 640; Corbis/Bettmann, 641; Bob Daemmrich Photography, Inc., 642; Pete Souza/Getty Images, Inc–Liaison, 646; Bob Daemmrich/Stock Boston, 654; AP Wide World Photos, 657; AP Wide World Photos, 659; AP Wide World Photos, 660.

Chapter 20 Bob Daemmrich Photography, Inc., 674; L. Tucker Gibson, Jr./ Thomas R. Dye, 679; David Woo/Stock Boston, 686; Houston Chronicle Library/Houston Chronicle. Copyright 1994 Houston Chronicle Publishing Company. Reprinted with permission. All rights reserved, 688; Bob Daemmrich/ The Image Works, 697; Bob Daemmrich Photography, Inc., 698; AP Wide World Photos, 699; AP Wide World Photos, 702; David Sams/SIPA Press, 703.

Chapter 21 H. R. Bramaz/© H.R. Bramaz/Peter Arnold Inc., 710; AP Wide World Photos, 717; Bob Daemmrich/PhotoEdit, 719; Paul Buck/Bob Daemmrich Photography, Inc., 721 (left); AP Wide World Photos, 721 (right); Peter Vadnai/Corbis/Stock Market, 727; Lorenzo Tucker Gibson, 731 (top); L. Tucker Gibson, Jr./Thomas R. Dye, 731 (bottom); San Antonio ISD, 738; Michael Patrick Photography/Bradley Development, 742.

Index

A

A. C. Nielsen, 178
Abington Township v. Schempp, 423
ABM Treaty, 497
Abolitionists, 455
Abolition movement, 440
Abortion
  Boxer on, 44
  Bush and, 655, 656
  judicial appointments and, 398
  Medicaid funding for, 427, 707
  parental notification of, 655, 656, 707
  partial birth, 427
  right to privacy and, 426–27
  Roe v. Wade and, 81, 426–27
  Texas on, 707
Abscam investigation, 290
Absence of malice, 189–90
Absentee voting, 592
Academic radicalism, 49–50
Access, campaign contributions and, 148
Accountability
  of bureaucracies, 665
  political party, 584–85
Activism
  judicial, 388, 687, 689, 692
  regulatory, 369–71
Adams, John, 82
  Constitutional Convention and, 58
  Federalists and, 82
  on vice president role, 335
Adams, John Quincy, 207
Adams, Randall Dale, 704
Adjudication, 345
Adjutant general, 649
Administrative discretion, 345
Administrative Procedures Act (1946), 345, 373
Adversarial system, 394
Advertising
  attack, 140–41
  issue, 147
  negative, 140–41
  paid political, 143
  persuasion through, 178
  political campaign, 186
  socialization through, 177
  success of political, 197
  time taken by, 178
Advice and consent, 245, 326
Advisory Commission on Intergovernmental Relations, 713
Affirmative action, 316, 446–51
  attacks on, 695
  court cases on, 447–51
  definition of, 446
  in education, 448–49
  equality of opportunity and, 28
  Hopwood and, 695
  as remedy for past discrimination, 448
Affirmative racial gerrymandering, 251
Afghanistan
  covert action in, 494
  Operation Enduring Freedom, 504, 506
  Taliban, 504, 506
  war in, 329
African Americans. *See also* Minorities; Segregation; Slavery
  in Congress, 261
  economic gains of, 518
  education levels of, 526
  equality and, 35
  federalism and, 108
  group voting by, 163–66
  income of, 445–46
  as mayors, 721
  miscarriages of justice and, 701
  in Texas, 520–21
  in Texas Constitutional Convention, 545
  in Texas elected offices, 589, 604–5, 721
  in Texas legislature, 604–5
  in Texas politics, 589
  unemployment among, 445–46
  voting rights for, 79, 96, 114
Age
  aging population and, 523, 726
  ideology and, 43, 45
  poverty and, 477
  voting rights and, 79, 99, 586
Age Discrimination Act (1986), 125
Agencies. *See also* Bureaucracy
  campaign contributions and, 149–50
  creation of, 362
  culture in, 361
  independent, 354–55
  oversight of, 600–601
  ratings of, 344
  Texas state, 638–39
Agenda setting
  congressional, 245–46
  definition of, 175
  by the media, 175, 177, 194–95
  president in, 321
  Supreme Court, 403
  by television, 174
Agnew, Spiro, 299, 336
Agriculture
  Grange and, 546
  interest groups, 376, 570
Agriculture commissioner, 660
Aid to Families with Dependent Children (AFDC), 124, 479
Ailes, Roger, 184
Airline deregulation, 371
Airport Security Act, 504
Alamodome, 736
Alden v. Maine, 119
Alien and Sedition Acts (1798), 108
Alienation, 196
Allen, Florence, 402
Allred, James, 573
Al Qaeda, 332, 333, 503, 504
Amendments. *See also individual amendments*
  to bills, 619–21
  congressional, 277–78
  definition of, 78
  process of constitutional, 78–81
  as Supreme Court constraint, 413
  Texas Constitution, 551–59
  U.S. Constitution, 75–82, 93–99
American Association of Trial Lawyers, 147–48, 393
American Farm Bureau Federation, 376
American Federation of State, County, and Municipal Employees (AFSCME), 569–70
Americans Disabled for Attendant Programs Today (ADAPT), 569
Americans with Disabilities Act (ADA) (1990), 126
Amicus curiae, 403–4, 408
Amtrak, 356
Andros, Edmund, 54
Angles, in the media, 177
Annapolis Convention (1786), 57–58
Annexation powers, 741–43
Anthony, Susan B., 455
Antiballistic missiles (ABMs), 497
Antidemocratic movements, 45–48
Anti-Federalists, 74–75, 77, 82, 113
Anti-Saloon League, 455
Appeals, 389–90
  Texas courts of, 681–82
Appellate jurisdiction, 389
Appointments
  cabinet, 353
  judicial, 397–400
  power to make, 70–71, 317
  Senate confirmation of, 70–71, 245, 374
  Supreme Court, 397–400, 412
  by Texas governors, 637–38, 645–48
Apportionment, 246–48
Appraisal districts, 733
Apprenticeship norm, 285
Appropriations acts, 365, 375
Appropriations bills, 621
Appropriations Committees, 245, 272
  Texas legislature, 611, 618
Armbrister, Ken, 609
Armstrong, Bob, 575
Army, U.S., 508. *See also* Military forces
Army of the Republic of Vietnam, 493
Arrests, 434
Articles of Confederation, 55–58, 101
  Constitution compared with, 73
  events leading to, 55
  government structure under, 55
  problems with, 56–57
Asbestos Hazard Emergency Act (1986), 125
Ashcroft, John, 433
Asian Americans. *See also* Minorities
  education levels of, 526
  in Texas, 521
Asian Americans, internment of, 19, 305, 315. *See also* Minorities
Asylum, 39–40
At-large districts, 607
At-large elections, 723–24
  minorities and, 586, 724–25
Attack ads, 140–41
Attorney general, 638–39, 657
Auchincloss, Janet, 314
Austin, Stephen F., 540, 541
Austin American-Statesman, 564
Authorizations, 365
Avery v. Midland County, 729

B

Bader Ginsburg, Ruth, 402, 403, 407
Bail, 94–95
Bailiffs, 683
Baird, Zoe, 319
Baker, James, 409
Baker v. Carr, 81, 247, 388, 606
Bakke, Allan, 447
Ballistic missile defense (BMD) systems, 499, 500
Ballots
  absentee voting and, 592
  judges on, 687
  as obstacle, 548
  in Texas, 548
Ballots, third-party candidates on, 210, 220
Bankruptcy laws, 64

Bargaining, congressional, 285, 287
Barrientos, Gonzalo, 742
Barrow, Charles, 688
Beard, Charles A., 63, 64
Beliefs
conflict over, 26
definition of, 25
Bell Curve, The (Herrnstein, Murray), 34
Beltway bandits, 357
Benavides, Fortunato P., 698
Benkiser, Tina, 571
Bennett, Robert, 385
Bentsen, Lloyd, 575
Berlin Wall, 490
Bernstein, Cal, 306
Bicameral bodies, 242, 541, 601–2
Bifactionalism, 573
Bifurcated court systems, 677
Big-money contributors, 146, 147–48
Bill of Rights, 75–78, 416–38
Anti-Federalists on, 77
nationalization of, 111
protections in, 419–21
Bills of attainder, 432–34
Bin Laden, Osama, 504, 514
Biotechnology, 528
Bipartisan Campaign Finance Reform Act (2002), 152
Bipartisan voting, 280
Birthrate, 519
Blackburn, Jeff, 701, 705
Blackmun, Harry, 406
Blair, Tony, 332, 506
Blakely, William, 574
Blanton, Annie Webb, 640
Block grants, 123–24
Blocs, 405–7, 625–26
Board of Law Examiners, 682
Board of Pardons and Paroles, 647, 648
Bonds
general obligation, 550, 725
revenue, 725–26
Bonds, Revolutionary War, 63, 64, 65
Border Industrialization Program, 529
Bork, Robert H., 398–99, 406
Boxer, Barbara, 44, 262
Braddock, Edward, 59
Bradley, Gary, 742
Bradwell, Myra, 402
Brady Handgun Violence Protection Act, 119–20
Branch Davidians, 430
Brandeis, Louis D., 106, 424
Brandley, Clarence Lee, 704
Breyer, Stephen G., 407
Briefs, 389–90
Briscoe, Dolph
background of, 640
constitutional reform and, 553, 554, 555–56
La Raza Unida and, 578
Sharpstown scandal and, 631–32
staff of, 649
Brokaw, Tom, 176
Brokered conventions, 210
Bronfman, Edgar, 314
Brown, Carol Mosely, 261
Brown, J. E. "Buster, 606
Brown, Lee, 592–93, 721
Brown, Linda, 395
Brown v. Board of Education of Topeka, 81, 108, 115, 441–42
as class action suit, 395
judicial review and, 385
military enforcement of, 334
NAACP and, 441–42
precedent and, 388
Buckley v. Valeo, 384
Budget
comptroller and, 657–59
Texas, 549, 550, 600
Texas governor in, 645
Budget and Accounting Act (1921), 317–18
Budget and Impoundment Control Act (1974), 307
Budget maximization, 346
Budget of the United States Government, 321, 362, 363
Budget process
bureaucracy in, 346, 362–68
continuing resolutions in, 365–66
House and Senate committees in, 363, 365
politics in, 366–68
presidential impoundment and, 307
the president in, 317–18, 362, 363
shutdowns and, 365–66
Budget resolutions, 363, 365
Build Texas Committee, 558
Bullock, Bob, 575, 654, 667
as lieutenant governor, 612–13, 656
partisanship and, 624
Bunton, Lucius, 694
Burdine, Calvin, 705
Bureaucracy, 340–79
budget process and, 362–68, 668
cabinet departments, 349–53
congressional oversight of, 244–45, 373–75
contractors and consultants, 357
controlling, 666–71
definition of, 341
democracy and, 357–60
federal, 346–57
federalism and, 106
government corporations, 355–56
growth of, 341–42, 347, 662–63
independent agencies, 354–55
interest groups and, 376
judicial constraints on, 376–77
merit system in, 357–58
nature of, 341
party functions taken over by, 205
performance reviews and, 669–70
policy implementation by, 342–44
politics in, 360–62
power of, 341–46
presidential role with, 313–21
productivity and, 358–59
reform of, 359–60, 362
regulatory commissions, 353–54
regulatory power of, 345, 368–73
responsiveness and, 358
revolving door and, 666, 668
spoils system in, 357
sunset law and, 668–69
Texas, 661–71
Bureau of Alcohol, Tobacco, and Firearms (ATF), 112, 430
Bureau of Immigration and Citizenship Services, 38
Bureau of the Census, 247–48, 525
Burger, Warren, 387, 406
Burke, Edmund, 283–84
Burns, Arthur F., 356
Bush, George
debates by, 160, 161
economic conditions and, 167
Gulf War and, 499, 501
judicial appointments of, 412
negative campaigning by, 141
popularity of, 309, 312
public confidence and, 6
tax promises of, 474
vetos by, 324
as vice president, 336
voter turnout for, 590–91
Bush, George W.
administrative style of, 316
appointments by, 648, 691
background of, 640
Circle C Ranch and, 742
consensus building by, 654–56
debates by, 161
Fox and, 302
as governor, 575
Hispanic Americans and, 581, 587
Homeland Security and, 19
image of, 166
judicial nominations of, 399–400
media election coverage of, 195
media use by, 311
midterm congressional elections and, 260
minority appointments by, 697
nuclear weapons and, 497–98, 499, 500
Operation Iraqi Freedom, 332–33
popularity of, 309, 310, 312
Religious Right and, 571
Rove and, 593
staff of, 649
tax cuts by, 474, 556, 613
tort reform and, 692
2004 campaign, 157, 158
2000 election and, 69, 162, 164, 408–10
voter turnout for, 590–91
war on terrorism, 127, 297, 300–301, 504–7
Bush, Prescott, 300
Bush v. Gore, 408–10
Business/trade organizations
in Texas, 566, 567
Texas Constitution and, 557–58
Byrd, James, Jr., 522, 625, 650

C

Cabinet, 318–19
appointments, 353
Canadian, 76
departments, 349–53
in presidential succession, 302
Calendar
Texas legislature, 622
Calendar, congressional, 276
Calendars Committee
congressional, 611
Texas legislature, 616
Calhoun, John C., 108, 113
California Proposition 187, 454
Calvert, Robert W., 553, 555
Campaign contributions
big-money, 147–48
buying access with, 148
congressional races, 257
fat cats and, 146, 594–95
federal, 152
fund-raising activities for, 150–51
government assistance and, 149–50
gubernatorial appointments and, 647–48
incumbency and, 138–39
from individuals, 149
judicial elections and, 689, 690–92, 693
limits on, 151, 693, 699
PAC, 149, 594–95
partisan differences in, 213–14
by Pilgrim, 631–32
reforms of, 152, 595, 631–33
regulating, 151–52
sources of, 145–47
in Texas, 593–95
Texas Association of Business, 563
Texas interest groups, 563–64
Texas reform of, 631–33
what they buy, 147–51
Campaigns. *See also* Elections
advertising in, 197
costs of, 143–45, 592–93, 693–94
costs of gubernatorial, 640

equal-time rule in, 189
fund-raising activities in, 150–51, 593–94
horse-race coverage of, 187
kicking off, 211, 213
media in, 178, 184–88
negative, 140–41
party finances in, 213–14
presidential, 152–63
regulating finances for, 151–52
running mate selection and, 211
self-financing, 146
strategies in, 139–43
Texas, 592–95
traditional party functions in, 205
Campaign strategies, 139–43
focus groups and polls in, 142
incumbent *vs.* challenger, 142
negative campaigning, 141–42
theme selection and, 140
Campbell, Charles, 688
Canada, 76
Candidates, self-financing by, 146. *See also* Campaigns; Elections
Capitalism
communism and, 46, 48
definition of, 26
end of history and, 48
income/wealth inequality in, 30–33
liberalism and, 26–27
socialism and, 48
Capital murder cases, 701–2. *See also* Capital punishment
Capital punishment, 436–38
struck down, 701
in Texas, 701–2, 705
Capture theory of regulation, 369
Cárdenas, Cuauhtemoc, 302
Careerism, 252, 254
Texas legislature, 601
Carter, Jimmy
covert actions of, 494
Ford debate with, 160, 194
popularity of, 275, 312
Case Act (1972), 327
Casework, 139, 265, 375
Castro, Fidel, 451
Categorical grants, 122–23
Caucuses, 207, 624
Texas legislative, 625–26
Censorship, 193
Censure, 290
Census Act (1976), 248
Census of Governments, 662
Center for the Study of American Business, 370
Central Intelligence Agency (CIA), 318, 319, 328–30
covert actions, 329–30, 494
Centralized federalism, 116
Chain of command, 341
Challengers, 138–39
campaign strategies of, 142
economic conditions and, 167
Challenger spaceship, 295, 297
Chapman, Ron, 701
Character issues, 166, 187
Charter Oak Affair (1685–88), 54
Charters
city, 715
Charters, colonial, 54
Chase, Salmon P., 101
Chavez, Cesar, 453
Checks and balances, 69–73, 75
on the president, 305–6
Supreme Court, 410–14
Cheney, Dick, 259, 301, 335, 336
Child pornography, 429
Children
pornography and, 429
poverty and, 477
Children's Defense Fund, 263
Chisum, Warren, 623
Christopher, Warren, 409
Churchill, Winston, 491
Circle C Ranch, 742
Circuit courts, 389–90
Cities
aging population and, 726
annexation by, 741–43
consolidation of, 744–45
extraterritorial jurisdiction by, 741–43
growth of Texas, 523
problems facing, 726–28
public improvement districts, 745–46
Citizen militias, 430
Citizenship, 39, 40
City charters, 715
City commission governments, 715, 717–19
City councils
campaign costs and, 592–93
composition of, 725
in council-manager government, 719–23
salaries of, 722–23
City elections, 592
City governments, 713–28
charters in, 715
city commission, 715, 717–19
consolidation and, 744–45
council-manager, 715, 719–23
economic development and, 743–44
elections in, 723–25
employees in, 663
forms of, 715–23
general law, 714–15
home rule and, 713, 714–15
mayor-council, 715–17
revenues and expenditures and, 725–26
urban problems and, 726–27
City managers, 721–23
City of Richmond v. Crosen Co., 448
Civil Aeronautics Board, 371
Civil disobedience, 7, 8, 443, 444
Civility, 285, 628
Civil lawsuits
definition of, 394, 676
presidential immunity to, 307–8, 385
Texas limits on, 651
Civil libertarians, 704
Civil rights, 438–51. *See also* individual liberties
affirmative action and, 446–51
Constitution on, 438–40
equality of opportunity *vs.* results and, 445–47
equal protection and, 441–42
gender and, 455–56
guarantees of, 439
King and, 443, 444
politics of equality and, 438
segregation and, 440–42
slavery and, 438, 440
Civil Rights Act (1866), 439
Civil Rights Act (1871), 439
Civil Rights Act (1875), 439
Civil Rights Act (1964), 108, 286
affirmative action and, 446–51
guarantees in, 439
King and, 444
provisions of, 443, 445
sexual harassment and, 459
women in, 456–57
Civil Rights Act (1968), 439, 443, 445
Civil rights movement, 25
federalism and, 108
King in, 443, 444
Civil Service Commission, 357–58, 359–60
Civil Service Reform Act (1978), 359–60
Civil service systems, 735
Civil unions, 111
Civil War, 101, 440
federalism and, 114
Reconstruction and, 108, 114
Texas Constitution and, 538, 543
Clark, Wesley, 157
Class action suits, 395–96
Class conflict, 35
Class consciousness, 35
Classical liberalism, 26–27
conservatism and, 40–41
modern liberalism and, 41–43
Clausewitz, Karl von, 501
Clayton, Bill, 555, 609, 610, 611
Clean Air Act (1990), 126
Clear and present danger doctrine, 424
Clemency, 648
Clements, Bill, 548, 642–43
campaign costs of, 640
conflict with, 638
initiatives/referenda and, 551
minority appointments by, 698
partisanship and, 624, 654–55
school finance and, 706
tort reform and, 692
Clinton, Bill
administrative style of, 316
Comprehensive Test Ban Treaty and, 326
debates by, 161
defense spending by, 509
economic conditions and, 167, 168
impeachment of, 246, 303, 304
Jones suit against, 307–8, 385
judicial appointments and, 398
judicial appointments of, 412
media coverage of, 195
popularity of, 310, 311, 312
taxes under, 474
vetos by, 324
Violence against Women Act and, 120
welfare reform, 124, 480, 482
Whitewater investigation, 246, 396–97
Clinton, Hillary Rodham, 144, 157, 262, 263
Closed primaries, 209
Closed rules, 277
Cloture, 277
CNN (Cable News Network), 171
beginning of, 194
believability of, 172
CNN effect, 173
Coahuilay Tejas, Constitution of, 538, 540
Coalitions, 202
Texas, 584
Coast Guard, 39
Cocoa imports, 557
Code of Federal Regulations, 372
Coffee bean imports, 557
Cohen, Bernard, 194–95
Coke, Richard, 537, 545
Cold War, 491–96
containment and, 492
Cuban missile crisis and, 492–93
defense spending in, 7
definition of, 491
deterrence in, 496
end of, 495–96
Korean War and, 492
origins of, 491–92
the president in, 325
United Nations in, 490
Vietnam War and, 493–94
Coleman, Tom, 701
Collective security, 489
Collins, Susan, 262
Colonial charters, 54
Colonias, 532
Color-blind doctrine, 450
Combs, Susan, 589, 660
Commander-in-Chief
Constitution on, 66
war power conflicts and, 81–82, 326
Washington as, 54, 65–66
Commissioner of the General Land Office, 638–39, 659–60
Commissioners court, 679, 729–32
Commission of the European Union, 104

Commissions, 354
Committee system
conference committees, 618–19
congressional, 271–76
special committees, 619
standing committees, 271–72, 616–18
subcommittees, 272–73, 616
Texas legislature, 615, 616–19
Commodity Futures Trading Commission, 355
Common Cause, 189, 569, 585
Common markets, 65
Communications Decency Act (1996), 193, 428–29
Communications Workers of America, 569
Communism, 46, 48
collapse of, 495–96
Communist Manifesto, The (Marx, Engels), 46
Community development block grants, 124
Compact theory, 546–47
Comparable worth, 457–58
Compean, Mario, 578
Competition, 18, 105
Compliance, 4, 411–12
Comprehensive Test Ban Treaty, 326, 498
Compromise of 1876, 108
Compromise of 1877, 440
Comptroller of Public Accounts, 638–39, 657–59
Computer-assisted-telephone interviewing (CATI), 142
Concurrent powers, 109–11
Concurring opinions, 405
Confederacy, 543
Confederations, 101, 103, 104–5
Conference committees, 278, 287
Texas legislature, 618–19
Confirmation
of cabinet members, 318–19
definition of, 245
of presidential appointments, 70–71, 245
Conflict, 26
Conglomerate media corporations, 180, 181
Congress, 240–93. *See also* House of Representatives; Senate
advice and consent of, 245
agenda setting by, 245–46
apportionment and redistricting, 246–52
appropriations committees, 365
Articles of Confederation on, 55
background of members in, 252, 253
budget committees, 363, 365
bureaucratic oversight by, 373–75
calendar in, 276
campaign costs for, 143–45
committees in, 271–76
competition for seats in, 252, 254
constitutional powers of, 241
Constitution interpreted by, 81–82
customs and norms of, 284–89
decision making in, 278–84
ethics in, 272, 289–90
executive branch and, 314–15
expulsion from, 290
on the floor of, 276–78
floor voting in, 277–78
home style and, 265–66
impeachment power of, 71, 246
institutional conflict and, 241–42
judiciary checks of, 413–14
leadership of, 267–71
life in, 260–65
majority status in, 267–69
media and, 245–46
Necessary and Proper Clause and, 77
organization of, 266–71
oversight of bureaucracy by, 244–45
policy making and, 242, 243
political parties in, 257–60, 267–69
power of the purse and, 244
powers of, 241–46
president and, 242, 308
public confidence in, 143
representativeness of, 260–62
salaries of, 99, 264–65
staff for, 262
support agencies of, 262–64
Supreme Court checks of, 413–14
taxation power of, 65
term limits for, 255
turnover in, 255
war-making powers of, 66, 81–82
workload of, 264
Congressional Budget and Impoundment Act (1974), 264
Congressional Budget Office (CBO), 264, 363
Congressional committees, 271–76
bargaining in, 285, 287
conference, 278
hearings of, 276
markup in, 276
membership on, 274
pecking order of, 272
seniority and, 275–76
standing, 271–72
subcommittees, 272–73
Congressional elections, 252–57
campaign financing for, 257
candidate background and, 252, 253
competition in, 252, 254
incumbency in, 254–55
midterm tradition in, 259–60
voter turnout for, 256–57
Congressional hearings, 245–46
Congressional investigations, 245–46, 375
Congressional Quarterly, 322–23
Congressional Record, 264, 278
Congressional Research Service (CRS), 263
Congressional sessions, 241
Conklin, Hal, 722
Connally, John, 552, 649
Connecticut Plan, 62
Consensus building, 622–23
Conservatism. *See also* Republican Party
age and, 43, 45
definition of, 40–41
education and, 43, 44
federalism and, 123
Fox News and, 184
level of, 40, 41
Religious Right in, 570–71
Supreme Court voting blocs and, 405–7
in talk radio, 183–84
test for, 47
in Texas, 565–66
Conspiracy, 112
Conspiracy theories, 45
Constables, 553, 733
Constituencies
definition of, 283
House and Senate, 242–43
influence of in congressional voting, 283
Texas legislators and, 626–27
Constitution, Texas, 536–61, 692–719
of 1845, 542–43
of 1866, 543–44
of 1876, 545–46, 701–546
amendment of, 551–59, 556
Civil War, 543
cleanup amendment of, 552
of Coahuila y Tejas, 540
compared with other constitutions, 538–40, 547
constitutional conventions and, 552
court interpretation of, 558–59
details in, 549–708
general principles of, 546–48
history of, 537–38
interest groups/elites and, 556–58
Reconstruction, 544–45
reform efforts for, 552=558
of the Republic, 540–42
versions of, 538
weaknesses and criticisms of, 548–708
Constitution, U.S., 52–99. *See also individual amendments*
amendments to, 75–82, 93–99
Anti-Federalists on, 74–75, 77
Articles of Confederation and, 55–58
Bill of Rights, 75–78, 416–38
change process for, 79–82
checks and balances in, 69–73
compared with Texas Constitution, 539, 547
conciseness of, 539
Constitutional Convention and, 57–63
on the courts, 382
economic issues behind, 63–65
enumerated powers in, 77
federalism in, 109–12
on government structure, 67–69
individual rights in, 419–21
judicial review and, 71–73, 81, 382, 384
on local governments, 103
on national security, 65–67
original intent of, 386–87
powers of Congress in, 241
powers of the president in, 298–308, 313–15
Preamble, 7
ratification of, 73–75
separation of powers in, 69–73
on slavery, 62, 438, 440
supremacy of, 53
on taxes, 63, 65
text of, 85–99
on voting rights, 28
Constitutional Convention, 57–63
conflict in, 60–63
consensus in, 58, 60
events leading to, 57–58
Founders in, 58
secrecy of, 74
Constitutional county courts, 679–80
Constitutional government, 14–15
Constitutionalism, 53–55
Constitutional monarchies, 76
Constitutional Revision Commission, 553
Constitutions, 538–61, 606, 694–795. *See also* Constitution, Texas; Constitution, U.S.
definition of, 538
Constitutions, definition of, 53. *See also* Constitution, U.S.
Consultants, 357
Consumer Product Safety Commission, 355
Consumers Union, 569
Containment, 492
Continental Congress, 54, 59
Contingency fees, 396
Continuing resolutions, 365–66
Contracting, interlocal, 744
Contractors, 357
Contract with America, 269
Conventions, party, 207–8
156, 265
campaign kickoff and, 211, 213
candidate selection in, 210–11
county, 584
definition of, 210

delegates to, 211
national, 210–13
platform writing in, 211, 212
precinct, 583–84
presidential campaigns and, 159
running mate selection and, 211
senatorial district, 584
state, 584
Cook, Eugene, 698
Cook, Vernon H., 553
Cookies, 193
Cooperative federalism, 113, 116
Cornwallis, Charles, 55
Cornyn, John, 589, 705, 706–7
as attorney general, 657
Republican dominance and, 576
tobacco lawsuits and, 658
Corporate income taxes, 472
Corzine, Jon, 144
Council-manager governments, 715, 719–23
Council of the European Union, 104
Council on Competitive Government, 670
Council on Excellence in Government, 10
Councils of government (COGs), 739–41
County Affairs Committee, 618
County attorneys, 683, 732
County auditors, 734
County chairs, 583
County clerks, 683, 732
County commissioners court, 679, 729–32
County conventions, 584
County courts, 679–80
statutory/-at-law, 680
County executive committees, 583
County governments, 548, 715, 728–35
commissioners court and, 729–32
consolidation of, 744–45
county and district attorneys and, 732
county clerks and, 732
county judges and, 729–32
criticisms of, 734–35
district clerks and, 732
employees in, 663
home rule and, 713
law enforcement and, 733–34
modernization of, 743
structure of, 729
tax assessor-collectors and, 732–33
County judges, 679–80, 731–32
County treasurers, 734
Court of Justice, 104
Courts. *See* Judicial system
Courts of appeals, 389–90
procedure in, 686
Texas, 681–82
Covert actions, 329–30, 494
Cracking, 586
Craddick, Tom
partisanship and, 625
redistricting and, 607, 608, 609
as speaker of the house, 608–9, 611
Cranston, Alan, 44
Creationism, 422
Credibility, 176
Crédit Mobilier, 246
Crimes, 112, 727
Criminal justice system, 700–705
bias in, 704
crimes in, 701–2
death penalty and, 701–2
politics of, 703–5
prison overcrowding and, 702, 703
rights in, 700–701, 703–5, 706
Cruel and unusual punishment, 94–95, 436–38
Cuban Americans, 453, 454
Cuban missile crisis, 492–93
Currency, 56, 104
Custis, Martha, 59
Custom duties, 473
Customs Bureau, 112

D

"Daisy Girl" ad, 141, 194
D'Alesandro, Thomas, 270
Daniel, Price, Jr., 553–54, 575
Dateline, 179–80
Davis, Edmund J., 537, 544–45, 572
corruption under, 546, 637
Davis, Grey, 126–27, 641
Dealignment, 214
Dean, Howard, 157
Dean, John, 306
Death, leading causes of, 482
Death penalty, 436–38, 701–2, 705
reinstatement of, 437–38
unfair application of, 437
Debs, Eugene V., 218
Decentralization
committee system and, 272–73
in education, 549
in federalism, 107
Deceptive Trade Practices–Consumer Protection Act (1973), 689
Declaration of Independence, 417
on equality, 27
on individual dignity, 12
on slavery, 25
writing of, 54–55
Declaration of Rights, Virginia, 77
De facto segregation, 442
Defendants, 395
arrest of, 434
bills of attainder and, 432–34
delayed trials and, 680–81
double jeopardy and, 436
exclusionary rule and, 435
ex post facto laws and, 432–34
fair trials and, 435–36
habeas corpus and, 431, 432
plea bargaining and, 436
rights of, 430–36, 700–701, 703–5, 706
right to counsel of, 434–35
searches and seizures and, 434
self-incrimination and, 434–35
Defense Intelligence Agency, 328–29
Defense of Marriage Act (1996), 111, 428
Defense policy, 243
Defense spending
military forces levels and, 507–9
under Reagan, 494–95
trends in, 509
Deference, 285
Deferrals, 307
DeLay, Tom, 599, 608, 651
Delco, Wilhelmina, 611
Delegated powers. *See* Enumerated powers
Delegates, 211, 284
Democracy
in America, 20–21
around the world, 11
capitalism and, 48
definition of, 9–13
direct *vs.* representative, 15–16, 70–71
elitist perspective on, 16–17
paradox in, 13–15
pluralist perspective on, 17–20
political parties in, 201–7
republicanism and, 68–69
terrorism and, 18–19
Democratic ideals, 10–12, 20
Democratic Party
congressional control by, 257–58, 259
dominance of in Texas, 572–76
in 2004 election, 157
factionalism in, 573–74
Hispanic Americans and, 454, 587–88
yellow dogs, 581
Democratic-Republican Party, 82
Demographics
of Congress, 260–62
income inequality and, 32
Texas, 513, 518–21, 522–26, 600
De novo, 677, 679
Department of Agriculture, 350
Department of Commerce, 350, 464, 645–46
Department of Defense, 350
Department of Education, 350, 352, 449
Department of Energy, 350
Department of Health and Human Services, 349, 350, 351, 352
Department of Homeland Security, 19, 112, 127
functions of, 350, 352–53
Department of Housing and Community Affairs, 645–46
Department of Housing and Urban Development, 349, 350
Department of Human Services (DHS), 667
Department of Insurance, 669
Department of Justice, 112
Department of Labor, 350, 465, 478–79
Department of the Interior, 350
Department of Transportation, 350
Department of Veterans Affairs, 350, 352
Deregulation, 371, 513
Desegregation, 315, 442. *See also* Segregation
Deterrence, 496
Devolution, 123, 124–25
Dewhurst, David
campaign costs of, 593
as land commissioner, 659–60
as lieutenant governor, 614, 657
partisanship and, 625
redistricting and, 608–9, 621
Díaz, Porfirio, 302
Dien Bien Phu, 493
Dignity of the individual, 12
Dillon rule, 712
Diplomatic recognition, 326
Direct democracy, 15–16, 70–71
Direct discrimination, 457
Director of central intelligence (DCI), 328–29
Direct primaries, 590
Dirty Thirty, 624
Disability Insurance, 478
Disabled people
ADA and, 126
social welfare programs for, 478, 479
Discharge petitions, 276
Discretionary funds, 346
Discrimination. *See also* Segregation
direct, 457
equality and, 12
federalism and, 108
political culture and, 25
by private individuals, 443–45
reverse, 587
sexual, 456–60
Disproportionate support, 215–17
Dissent, 45–50
academic radicalism and, 49–50
antidemocratic ideologies and, 45–48
capitalism and, 48
socialism and, 48
Dissenting opinions, 405
District attorneys, 683, 732
District clerks, 683, 732
District courts, 389, 392, 680–81
Diversity, 448–50. *See also* Affirmative action
Divided party government, 207, 257, 280–82, 322–23

Division of labor, 341
Division votes, 622
Dole, Bob, 161, 195, 571, 576
Dole, Elizabeth, 262
Domestic policy, congressional role in, 243
Donaldson, Sam, 190
Double jeopardy, 112, 436
Douglas, William O., 388, 426
Drafting a bill, 276
Dred Scott v. Sandford, 440
Drinking age, 121
Drug crimes, 112, 394, 727
  NAFTA and, 531
Drug Enforcement Administration (DEA), 112
Dual federalism, 113
Dual labor market, 457–58
Due Process Clause, 96
  defendants' rights and, 700
  illegal immigrants and, 39–40
Dukakis, Michael, 141, 160, 315

E

Earle, Ronnie, 563, 632, 633
Early voting, 592
Earned Income Tax Credit (EITC), 479
Economic conditions
  economic growth, 463–64
  globalization and, 466–69
  politics and, 462–87
  the president and, 297–98
  public confidence and, 6
  tax burden and, 469–73
  in Texas, 526–28
  unemployment and, 464–65
  in the U.S., 463–66
  voter choice and, 167
Economic cycles, 464
Economic development, 743–44
Economic diversification, 527–28
Economic Interpretation of the Constitution of the United States (Beard), 64
Edelman, Marian Wright, 263
Edgewood v. Kirby, 558–59, 569, 705–7
Education
  affirmative action and, 448–49
  bureaucrats in, 663
  challenges facing Texas in, 525–26
  Edgewood v. Kirby, 558–59, 569
  group voting and, 161
  home schools in, 707
  ideology and, 43, 44
  income and, 445–46
  independent school districts in, 735, 737–39
  interest groups for, 568
  local responsibility for, 713, 737–39
  Luna and, 626
  of the public, 601
  Rangel and, 626
  reforms in, 737
  school prayer and, 423
  speech codes and, 425–26
  tax abatements and, 743–44
  Texas decentralization and, 549
  Texas spending on, 515
  Texas Supreme Court on, 705–7
  voter turnout and, 131, 132
  women in, 457
Education Act Amendment (1972), 457
Education funding
  Dewhurst and, 614
  in Texas, 549, 558–59, 663
  Texas Supreme Court on, 705–7
Edwards, Edwin, 554
Edwards, John, 157
Egalitarianism, 48
Eighteenth Amendment, 79, 97
Eighth Amendment, 78, 94–95, 420
  cruel and unusual punishment, 436–38
Eisenhower, Dwight D.
  desegregation and, 115, 334
  health of, 299
  Korean War and, 492
  NATO and, 490
  Powell compared with, 502
  ranking of, 296
  TV ad of, 194
Elazar, Daniel, 515
Elections, 130–69. *See also* Campaigns
  at-large, 586, 723–24
  candidate selection and, 185–86
  charter, 715
  city, 592, 723–25
  democracy and, 16, 134–35
  district, 694, 696
  general, 210
  incumbency in, 138–39
  judicial, 388, 698–99
  as mandates, 135
  media coverage of, 177, 184–88
  nonpartisan, 207, 723
  party organization of, 207–10
  primaries, 208–10
  retention, 699
  rollback, 725
  runoff, 724
  school board, 592, 738–39
  single-purpose district, 592
  special, 592
  Texas, 590–92
Electoral College, 69, 82
  presidential campaign strategy and, 159
  in representational federalism, 118
  swing states and, 159, 163
  2000 election and, 69, 408–10
Eleventh Amendment, 79, 95
Elitism, 16–17, 20
  intelligence and, 34
  interest groups and, 565–66
  in Texas, 565–66
  Texas Constitution and, 558
  traditionalistic subculture and, 516
Elizondo, Virgil, 626
Ellis, Rodney, 613, 696
Emancipation Proclamation, 440
EMILY's List, 150
Employment, discrimination in Texas, 522. *See also* Unemployment rates
Encryption programs, 193
End of history, 48
Enemy combatants, 432
Engels, Friedrich, 46
Engle v. Vitale, 422, 423
Enlightenment, 26
Enoch, Craig, 707
Enron scandal, 513, 647–48
Enterprise zones, 744
Entertainment Tonight, 180
Entitlements, 124, 478. *See also* Social Security
Enumerated powers, 77, 109
Environmentalism
  globalization and, 468–69
  land commissioner and, 659–60
  NAFTA and, 530–31, 532
  in Texas, 558
Environmental Protection Agency (EPA), 125, 345, 354, 369–71
  interest groups and, 376
Equal Employment Opportunity Commission (EEOC), 355, 369–71
  interest groups and, 376
  women in, 456
Equality, 12, 438–60
  affirmative action and, 446–51
  Civil Rights Acts and, 442–45
  definition of, 438
  dilemmas in, 27–30
  fairness and, 29, 30
  gender, 455–60, 459
  income/wealth and, 30–33
  liberalism and, 42–43
  of opportunity, 28, 438, 445–47
  political, 28
  politics of, 438
  in politics *vs.* economics, 29–30
  of results, 28–29, 438, 445–47
  segregation and, 440–42
  slavery and, 438, 440
Equal Protection Clause, 247
  affirmative action and, 447, 448
  defendants' rights and, 700
  diversity and, 449
  gay marriage and, 428
  gerrymandering and, 250–51
  women and, 455–56
Equal Rights Amendment (ERA), 79–80, 456
Equal-time rule, 189
Erlichman, John, 306
Escobedo v. Illinois, 435
Espionage Act (1917), 424
Establishment, the, 565–66
Estate taxes, 473
Ethics
  bureaucracy and, 667
  Texas legislature, 631–33
Ethics, congressional, 289–90
Ethics Commission, Texas
  campaign finances and, 592, 595, 632–33
  legislative compensation and, 602
Ethnic conflicts, 491, 495
Euro, the, 104
European Community, 104
European Parliament, 104
European Union, 104–5
Evers, Medgar, 444
Evidence, illegally obtained, 435
Excise taxes, 473
Exclusionary rule, 435
Executive agreements, 326–27
Executive branch, Texas, 548, 636–61
  boards and commissions in, 660–61
  bureaucracy in, 661–71
  fragmentation of, 637–38
  governor in, 639–56
  lieutenant governor in, 656–60
  structure of, 638–39
Executive branch, U.S. *See* Bureaucracy; President
Executive clemency, 648
Executive orders, 315–17
Executive privilege, 306–7
Ex parte Milligan, 384–85
Ex post facto laws, 432–34
Exposure, media, 186
Externalities, 9
Extradition, 648
Extraterritorial jurisdiction, 741–43
Extremism, 45

F

Factionalism, 653–54
Factions
  federalism and, 103, 106–7
  Madison on, 13–14, 75
  Texas Constitution and, 547–48
Fairness, 29, 30
Family Assistance, 479
Family Leave Act (1993), 275
Family Medical Leave Act, 44
Farenthold, Frances, 604
Farm interest groups, 570
Fascism, 46
Fat cats, 146, 594–95
Faubus, Orval, 115, 334
Federal Bureau of Investigation (FBI), 112, 193, 290
Federal Communications Commission (FCC), 143, 317
  creation of, 188
  media conglomerates and, 188–89

Federal courts, 389–94. *See also* Supreme Court, U.S.
of appeals, 389–90
appeals to state courts from, 391
caseload of, 391–94
circuit, 389–90
district, 389
jurisdiction of, 389, 391
Federal Election Campaign Act (1972), 152, 384
Federal Elections Commission (FEC), 147, 151–52, 153
Federal Energy Regulatory Commission, 355
Federal Equal Credit Opportunity Act (1974), 456
Federal Highway Act (1916), 115
Federal Highway Act (1956), 286
Federal Home Loan Bank, 355
Federalism, 67, 100–129
arguments for, 103–9
centralized, 116
coercion in, 125–27
confederation *vs.*, 101, 103
cooperative, 113, 116
definition of, 101
devolution and, 123, 124–25
discrimination and, 108
dual, 113
evolution of American, 112–18
flow of money and power in, 120–25
new, 117
original design of, 109–12
representational, 117–18
revival of, 118–20
state-centered, 113
in Texas, 541
union and states in, 101–3
Federalist Papers, The (Madison, Hamilton, Jay), 74
on factions, 13–14, 75
on impeachment, 304
on the right to bear arms, 429
Federalists, 77
Federal Maritime Commission, 355
Federal Register, 345, 372
Federal Reserve Board, 317
Federal Reserve System, 354–55, 356
Federal Trade Commission, 355
Feeding frenzies, 182
Feinstein, Dianne, 44, 262
Felonies, 676, 702
Ferguson, James E. "Pa," 640, 641, 656
Ferguson, Miriam A. "Ma," 640, 641
FICA. *See* Social Security
Fifteenth Amendment, 79, 96, 114, 439
Fifth Amendment, 78, 94, 419
Double Jeopardy Clause, 112
illegal immigrants and, 39
Filibusters, 277, 399–400, 622
Filtering software, 193
Finance Committee, 618
Fineman, Howard, 593
Firefighters Local Union 1784 v. Stotts, 448
First Amendment, 78, 93
freedom of religion in, 418, 421–23
freedom of speech in, 424–26
Internet and, 193
libel/slander and, 189–90
media and, 174–75
negative campaigns and, 140–41
obscenity and, 428–29
text of, 419
First Continental Congress (1774), 54, 59
First Court of Appeals, 681–82
First reading, 619
Fiscal year, 363
Flag burning, 425
Flat taxation, 473
Flores, Kino, 557
Focus groups, 142
Food and Drug Administration (FDA), 354, 355, 370
Food Stamp program, 479
Food stamp program, 123
Forbes, John, 59
Ford, Gerald, 299
Carter debate with, 160, 194
Nixon pardon by, 303
Vietnam War and, 494
Ford, John S. "Rip," 545
Foreign Affairs, 492
Foreign policy
congressional role in, 243
Constitution on, 66–67
executive agreements in, 326–27
media effects on, 194–95
the president in, 298, 325–26
treaties in, 245, 326
Fort Worth Star-Telegram, 632
Founders
on factions, 13–14
liberty and property and, 58, 60
media campaign by, 74
nationalism of, 60
original intent of, 386–87
on representative government, 60
social contract and, 60
Fourteenth Amendment, 78, 79, 96
civil rights and, 108, 111
Due Process Clause, 39–40, 96, 700
Equal Protection Clause, 247, 250–51, 448, 455–56
gerrymandering and, 250–51
illegal immigrants and, 39
judicial review and, 81
text of, 421, 439
Fourteenth Court of Appeals, 682
Fourth Amendment, 78, 94, 419
Four Tigers, 48
Fox, Vicente, 302, 531
Fox News, 184
Frankfurter, Felix, 381, 386
Franking privilege, 139, 266
Franklin, Benjamin, 62
Freedom House, 11
Freedom of Access to Clinics Act, 44
Freedom of expression, 78, 193, 425
Freedom of Information Act (1966), 373, 374
Freedom of religion. *See* Religion: freedom of
Freedom of speech, 402–24
clear and present danger doctrine and, 424
libel/slander and, 426
political correctness and, 425–26
preferred position doctrine and, 425
symbolic speech and, 425
Freedom of the press, 174–75
electronic media and, 188
equal-time rule and, 188
fairness *vs.*, 188–89
libel/slander and, 189–90
ownership controversy and, 188–89
prior restraint and, 188
shield laws and, 190
Free Exercise Clause, 418, 421
Freeman, Richard B., 467–68
Free markets, 9, 31, 463
conservatism and, 40–41
Free-riders, 8–9
Free trade, 467. *See also* Globalization
politics of, 468–69
Frist, Bill, 270, 288, 400
Front-end strategy, 156
Frontier image, 513–14
Front loading, 156, 157
Frost, David, 43
Full Faith and Credit, 111
Fundamentalists
Religious Right, 570–71
Furman v. Georgia, 437
Furrow, Buford O'Neal, Jr., 49
Fury, Mark, 685

G

Gambling
lotteries, 555, 646
in Texas, 555
Garcia v. San Antonio Metropolitan Transit Authority, 117–18
Garfield, James A., 298–99, 357
Garner, John Nance, 335–36
Garwood, Will, 691
Garza, Tony, 588, 648, 661
Gay marriage, 111, 428
Gender gap, 163–66
General Accounting Office (GAO), 264, 368, 372
General Agreement on Tariffs and Trade (GATT), 469
General elections, 210
campaign strategies in, 157, 159
definition of, 210
presidential campaigns in, 156–63
presidential debates and, 159–63
swing states in, 159
Texas, 591–92
voter turnout for, 257
General Land Office, 668
Commissioner, 638–39
General law cities, 714–15
General obligation bonds, 550, 725
General Services Commission, 670
General welfare, 120
Generation gap, news sources and, 173. *See also* Age
Geneva Accords, 432, 493
Gephardt, Dick, 157
Gerrymandering, 248–52
definition of, 248–49
incumbent, 250
partisan, 249–50
racial, 250–52, 586, 587
Texas, 606–7
in Texas, 574, 586, 587
Gettysburg Address (Lincoln), 15
G.I. Bill of Rights (1944), 286
Gideon v. Wainwright, 435
Gift taxes, 473
Gingrich, Newt, 259, 281
campaign costs for, 144
Contract with America, 269
Gitlow v. New York, 424
Giuliani, Rudolph, 263
Glass ceiling, 458, 460
Globalization
economic, 466–69
free trade and, 467, 468–69
income inequality and, 32
the president and, 298
protectionism *vs.*, 466–67
Texas and, 528
uneven benefits of, 467–68
Goldwater, Barry, 141, 387
Gonzales, Alberto R., 588, 648, 691, 697
Gonzalez, Raul A, 576, 588, 697
Good faith exceptions, 435
Goose step, 14
GOP (Grand Old Party). *See* Republican Party
Gorbachev, Mikhail, 495
Gore, Al, 157
debates by, 161
media election coverage of, 195
2000 election and, 69, 162, 164, 408–10
as vice president, 336–37
Gore v. Harris, 410
Gortari, Carlos Salinas de, 530
Government
confidence in, 6
constitutional, 14–15
definition of, 4
elitist perspective on, 16–17
expenditures of, 346, 348

Government (*cont.*)
federal, 103
growth of, 347
legitimacy of, 4, 7
liberalism on, 41–43
limited, 14, 40–41
lobbyists, 570
local, 103
participants in, 4
pluralist perspective on, 17–20
politics and, 4–7
presidential management of, 298
purposes of, 7–9
size of, 349
sovereign immunity of, 395
state, 103
totalitarian, 14
waste in, 368
Government corporations, 355–56
Government Printing Office (GPO), 264
Governors of Texas, 636–56
appointment powers and, 637–38, 645–48
backgrounds of, 640–41
budget power of, 645
campaign costs of, 593
impeachment of, 641
informal resources of, 649
interest groups and, 656
judicial powers of, 648
leadership styles of, 639–40
legislative influence of, 628–29
legislative powers of, 641–45
media and, 652
military powers of, 648–49
plural executive and, 638–39
political parties and, 652–56
power of, 548, 637–38
qualifications of, 640–41
salary of, 641
staff of, 649–52
State of the State address, 629, 641
veto power of, 643–45
Graber, Doris, 178, 182
Grace Commission, 362, 368
Gramm, Phil, 571, 575, 588
Grand juries, 389, 684
Grandstanders, 630
Grange, 546
Grant, Ulysses S., 544, 545
Grantmanship, 122
Grants, 115
block, 123–24
categorical, 122–23
Grants-in-aid, 122–24
Grants of immunity from prosecution, 435
Gray panthers, 569
Great Compromise, The, 61–62
Great Depression
interstate commerce and, 115
public works projects, 116
Great Society program, 116, 478
Green, George, 667
Green Party, 577, 591
Greenspan, Alan, 356
Gridlock, 288–89, 322–23
Griffin, Anthony, 706
Griswold, Estelle, 426
Gross domestic product (GDP), 9, 373, 463–64, 466
Grover, Henry "Hank," 578
Guantanamo Bay prisoners, 432
Gulf of Tonkin Resolution, 493
Gulf War, 500
Patriot missiles in, 500
Powell in, 502
public confidence and, 6
television in, 194
Gun-Free School Zones Act (1990), 118–19
Guns
Brady Act on, 119–20
Bush on, 654
Gun-Free School Zones and, 118–19
Richards and, 647
right to bear arms and, 429–30
Second Amendment on, 78
Gutierrez, Jose Angel, 578

H

Haas, Rene, 697
Haggerty, Pat, 564
Haiti, 501
Haldeman, H. R., 306
Hale, DeWitt, 554
Hamilton, A. J., 543, 544
Hamilton, Alexander
Federalist Papers, 74, 75
on impeachment, 304
Jefferson and, 82
on judicial review, 382
national bank of, 114
national debt and, 63, 65
Shays's Rebellion and, 57
on the Supreme Court, 72–73
Hancock, John, 54
Hard money, 152
Hard news programming, 178–80
Harlan, John, 451
Harrell, Will, 701
Harris, Katherine, 409
Harris v. Forklift, 459
Hastert, Dennis, 269, 270
Hastings, Alcee, 413–14
Hatch Act (1939), 358
Hate crimes
in Texas, 522, 613, 624–25, 650
Hayes, Rutherford B., 441
Health care, 482–85
access to, 483
costs of, 483
interest groups and, 485, 568
malpractice lawsuit limits and, 556, 559, 651
managed, 483
Medicare, 484–85
NAFTA and, 532
U.S. health levels and, 482–83
Health insurance. *See also* Medicaid; Medicare
portability of, 275
uninsured and, 483
Health maintenance organizations (HMOs), 483
Health savings accounts, 484
Heard Goggan Blair and Williams, 632
Heath vs. Alabama, 112
Heinz, John, 315
Heinz, Teresa, 315
Henry, Patrick, 74–75
Herrnstein, Richard J., 34
Herschensohn, Bruce, 44
High-tech industries, 528
Hightower, Jim, 570, 575
Hill, Anita, 401
Hill, John, 575, 689–90
Hispanic Americans, 451–54. *See also* Minorities; Race/ethnicity
in Congress, 261
Cuban Americans, 453
economic gains of, 518
education levels of, 526
equality and, 36
income of, 446, 451
La Raza Unida and, 577, 578
Mexican Americans, 452, 454
party identification among, 454
political gains by, 587–88
political power of, 453–54
poverty and, 477
Puerto Ricans, 452–53
in Texas, 519
in Texas politics, 519, 588
unemployment among, 446
voting patterns and, 163–66
Hitler, Adolf, 46
Hobbes, Thomas, 7
Hobby, Bill
Clements and, 642
constitutional reform and, 553–54, 555
as lieutenant governor, 612, 656
partisanship and, 624
Ho Chi Minh, 493
Hofstadter, Richard, 45
Holmes, John B., Jr., 681
Holmes, Oliver Wendell, 386, 424
Home rule, 103, 713
cities, 714–15
council-manager governments and, 719–23
Home schools, 707
Homestead Act (1862), 286
Homestead exemptions, 726
Home style, 265–66
Homosexuality
gay marriage and, 111
homosexual acts and, 385–86
Log Cabin Republicans, 708
right to privacy and, 427–28
Honeymoon period, 322
Hopwood case, 695
Horse-race coverage, 187
Horton, Willie, 141
Hostile working environment, 459
House of Commons, 76
House of Representatives, 242–43. *See also* Texas legislature
apportionment, 246–48
budget committees, 363, 365
constituencies of, 242–43
Constitution on, 68
majority leader and whip, 269
minority leader and whip, 269
population and, 111
Rules Committee, 269, 272, 277
Senate compared with, 244
speaker of the, 269, 608–11
terms of, 242–43
Texas, 608–11
House Research Organization, 631
House Study Group, 631
Housing discrimination, 522
Houson, 541
Houston Chronicle, 632
Howard, Philip K., 370
Hub-and-spoke system, 371
Hughes, Sarah T., 698
Humanitarian aid, 501, 509
Human nature, 41
Hume, Brit, 184
Hunt, E. Howard, 306
Hunter, Bob, 564
Hussein, Saddam, 301, 332–33, 499, 501, 514
Operation Iraqi Freedom and, 506–7
Hutchison, Kay Bailey, 262, 575, 589, 640
Hype, 180

I

Ideology
age and, 43, 45
antidemocratic, 45–48
conservatism, 40–41
definition of, 40
liberalism, 41–43
polarization and, 205, 280, 281
political parties and, 204–5
"I Have a Dream" (King), 444
Illegal immigrants, 38–40, 452, 454
in Texas, 531–34, 587
Image, 166
interest groups and, 567
media in, 185
puffing, 266
Image creation, 567
Image modification, 567
Immigration
equality and, 36–38
illegal, 38–40, 452, 531–34, 587
policies on, 36–37
Immigration and Naturalization Act (1965), 37
Immigration and Naturalization Service (INS), 38, 112

Immigration Reform and Control Act (1986), 37–38, 452, 453, 533
Impeachment
presidential, 71, 246, 302–3
of Supreme Court justices, 413–14
of Texas governors, 641
Impersonality, 341
Implementation. *See* Policy implementation
Implied powers, 109
Impoundment, 307
Income taxes, 113, 470–72
corporate, 472
Earned Income Tax Credit, 479
exemptions, 470–71
federalism and, 115
presidential campaign funds and, 145, 152
16th Amendment on, 96
in Texas, 552
Income transfers, 9, 28–29. *See also* Social welfare programs
Income/wealth
of Congress members, 264–65
education and, 445–46
equality and, 28–29, 30
fairness and, 29, 30
gender inequality in, 456–60
inequality of, 30–33, 445–46, 467–68
race and, 445–46
Texas distribution of, 523–25
voter turnout and, 131–32
Incremental budgeting, 366
Incrementalism, 347
Incumbency
advantages of, 138–39
campaign strategies of, 142
congressional, 252, 254–55
definition of, 138
economic conditions and, 167
retrospective voting and, 135
Incumbent gerrymandering, 250
Independent councils, 396–97
Independent political parties, 210, 578
Independent regulatory commissions, 353–54
Independent school districts, 735, 737–39
Indictments, 684
Individualism, 40–41, 514
Individualistic subculture, 566
Anglos in, 521
definition of, 516
mayor-council government and, 717
origins of, 516–17
Individual liberties, 9, 413–38
authority and, 417
Bill of Rights, 75–78
in classical liberalism, 26–27
criminal defendants and, 430–36, 700–701, 703–5, 706
democracy and, 11, 418
freedom of religion, 418, 421–23
freedom of speech, 424–26
national guarantees of, 115
obscenity and, 428–29
power and, 417
privacy, 426–28
rights of criminal defendants, 430–36
right to bear arms, 429–30
states and, 78
in Texas, 549
Industrial development corporations, 744
Inequality
educational, 445–46, 737
federalism and, 109
of income/wealth, 30–31
increases in, 32, 467–68
in Texas wealth/income, 523–25
Infant death rates, 482
Inflation, 65, 465–66
Federal Reserve and, 356
Information (legal document), 684
Information overload, 195–96
Infrastructure, 726–27
Initiatives, 551
Inner cities, 523
Inquests, 734
Inside Edition, 43
Institutionalization, 601
Intelligence, bell curve and, 34
Intelligence agencies, 328–30
Intent calendar, 621
Interactive mass participation, 190–91
Interest groups
bureaucracy and, 342, 344, 376, 418, 420
business and trade, 566–67
congressional voting and, 283
educational, 568
farm, 376, 570
government growth and, 347
government lobbies, 570
health care and, 485
incumbents and, 139
information from, 628
issue ads by, 147
Kerry and, 315
minority, 569
organized labor, 569–70
PACs, 149
in pluralism, 18–19
pluralism *vs.* elitism and, 565–66
political parties compared with, 201
power of, 563–65
professional associations, 568
public-interest, 568–69
public opinion influenced by, 197
religious, 570–71
Supreme Court and, 408
Supreme Court influence of, 408
in Texas, 563–71
Texas constitutional reform and, 553–54
Texas governor and, 656
Web sites of, 193
Interest rates, 356, 465–66
Intergovernmental relations, 103
Interims, 619
Interlocal contracting, 744
Interlocal Cooperation Act (1971), 744
Intermediate-Range Nuclear Forces (INF) Treaty, 497
Internal Revenue Service (IRS), 112, 345, 354
International Association of Machinists and Aerospace Workers, 569–70
International Brotherhood of Electrical Workers, 569–70
International Monetary Fund (IMF), 469
International Trade Representative, 468
Internet, 189. *See also* Mass media
censorship of, 193
chaotic design of, 191–92
growth of, 192
as news source, 171, 173
Patriot Act and, 433
political Web sites on, 192–93
politics and, 190–93
pornography on, 428–29
Interstate Commerce Clause
Articles of Confederation on, 56
Constitution on, 64
expansion of, 115
Violence against Women Act and, 120
Invisible primaries, 186
Iowa caucus, 155, 157
IQ, bell curve and, 34
Iran-Contra investigation, 246, 310
Iraq
defense spending and, 508
Operation Iraqi Freedom, 506–7
Iraqi War, 195, 301, 332–33
Iron Curtain, 491
Iron triangles, 665
Isolationism, 494
Issue ads, 147
Issue voting, 167–68
It Takes a Village (Clinton), 263

J

Jackson, Andrew
national bank and, 305
nomination of, 207
spoils system and, 357
Supreme Court and, 412
Jackson, Jesse, Jr., 290
Jackson, Robert, 418
Jamail, Joe, 690
James II (England), 54
Jay, John, 74, 75
Jefferson, Thomas
Anti-Federalists and, 82
classical liberalism and, 26
Constitutional Convention and, 58
Declaration of Independence and, 54–55
on leveling, 29
on local government, 711–12
Locke and, 12
Louisiana Territory and, 81, 286, 305
Madison and, 75
Marshall and, 383
on media, 174
nomination of, 207
on nullification, 108
Jefferson, Wallace, 589, 648, 697–98
Jeffords, Jim, 259
Jennings, Peter, 176
Jester, Beauford, 656
Jim Crow laws, 441, 572
Johnson, Andrew, 246, 303, 544
Johnson, Gregory, 49
Johnson, Lyndon B., 574
affirmative action and, 316
"Daisy Girl" ad, 141, 194
Great Society program, 116
HUD and, 349
social welfare programs and, 478
Vietnam War and, 493–94
Joint and severable liability, 393
Joint Chiefs of Staff, 319, 502
Jones, Paula Corbin, 307–8, 385
Jordan, Barbara, 604
Judges
activism by, 388, 687, 689, 692
appellate, 389–90
background of Supreme Court, 400–403
campaign contributions to, 594, 690–92
circuit court, 389–90
county, 679–80, 731–32
decision making rules and, 394–97
district, 681, 683
district elections and, 694, 696
election of, 548, 677
impeachment of, 413–14
impropriety by, 689–90
minorities as, 675, 683, 693–98
partisanship and, 690–92
politics of selecting, 397–400
Texas, 548, 682–83
Texas constitutional reform and, 555
women as, 402, 675, 683, 698
Judicial activism, 388, 687, 689, 692
Judicial Affairs Committee, 689–90
Judicial appointments, 397–400, 406, 412
background of appointees, 400–403
Judicial Districts Board, 681

Judicial review, 71–73, 72, 81, 382–86
Judicial self-restraint, 386, 388–89
Judicial system, Texas, 549, 674–709
concerns/controversies in, 687–99
county courts, 679–80
courts of general jurisdiction, 680–81
courts of limited jurisdiction, 677, 679
crime and punishment in, 700–702
federal system and, 676
highest courts of appeals, 682
intermediate courts of appeals, 681–82
jury system in, 684–85
legal framework of, 676–77
minorities in, 675, 693–98
personnel in, 682–83
policy role of, 705–8
politics of criminal justice and, 703–5
power of, 675
procedures and decision making in, 686–87
reforms of, 683–84
structure of, 677–84
women in, 675, 698
Judicial system, U.S., 380–415
activism *vs.* self-restraint in, 386–89
bureaucratic constraints and, 376–77
checks and balances on, 410–14
decision making in, 394–97, 403–5
federal courts in, 389–94
judge selection and, 397–403
power of, 381–86
presidential responsibility to, 307–8
rights of criminal defendants and, 430–36
state courts in, 676
Judiciary Act (1789), 383
Judiciary Committee, 272, 398
Junell, Rob, 606
Juries, 683, 684–85
grand, 389, 684
hung, 436
petit, 389, 684–85
right to a fair trial and, 435–36
selection of, 684–85
waiving the right to trial by, 686
Jurisdiction, 389, 676
appellate, 677
limited, 677, 679
original, 677
Justice, William Wayne, 703
Justice Department, U.S., 248, 394
Justice of the peace courts, 679
Justices of the peace, 679

K

Kapital, Das (Marx), 46
Karzai, Hamid, 506
Keller, Sharon, 698, 704, 705
Kennan, George F., 492
Kennedy, Anthony M., 119, 406
Kennedy, Edward M. "Ted," 274–75, 315
Kennedy, John F., 274–75, 303
Civil Rights Act and, 444
Cuban missile crisis and, 492–93
image of, 166
Kerry and, 314
Nixon debate with, 160, 194, 195
Vietnam War and, 493
Kennedy, John F., Jr., 275
Kennedy, Joseph P., 274–75
Kennedy, Robert, 274–75
Kennedy-Kasselbaum Act (1996), 275
Kerry, John, 314–15
attack ads against, 141
image of, 167
2004 campaign of, 157
Key, V. O., 522
Khrushchev, Nikita, 492–93
Kilgarlin, William, 689–90
Killer Bees, 612
Killer Ds, 514
King, Larry, 186, 189, 190
King, Martin Luther, Jr., 443, 444, 518
assassination of, 444
civil disobedience and, 8
"I Have a Dream" speech, 444
King, Rodney, 112
Kingmakers, 186
Kirk, Ron, 576, 588, 589, 721
Kissinger, Henry, 494
Know-Nothings, 571
Kohl, Helmut, 494
Korean War, 492
Krueger, Bob, 575
Ku Klux Klan, 706

L

Labastida, Francisco, 302
Laboratories of democracy, 106
Labor unions, 569–70
Land commissioner, 638–39, 659–60
Land speculation, 64
Laney, E. "Pete," 608–9, 611, 624, 654
Lanier, Bob, 592
La Raza, 453
Larry King Live, 186, 189, 190
Lasswell, Harold, 4, 16, 463
Lawrence vs. Texas, 427
Lawyers
in Congress, 252
interest groups and, 568
judicial activism and, 689
legal fees and, 396
litigiousness and, 393
right to counsel and, 434–35
in the Texas legislature, 605
women as, 402
Lay, Ken, 648, 650
Lazio, Rick, 144, 263
Leadership PACs, 271
League of Nations, 326, 489
League of United American Citizens et al. v. Mattox et al., 694, 696
League of United Latin American Citizens (LULAC), 569, 694, 696
League of Women Voters
suffrage movement and, 455
of Texas, 559
voter registration and, 585–86
Lear, Norman, 150
Left, the, 45
Legal fees, 396
Legal reform, 393
Legal tender laws, 56
Legislative branch, 60–62. *See also* Congress; Texas legislature
in Texas, 548, 549, 598–635
Legislative Budget Board, 628, 630, 645
Green and, 667
lieutenant governor on, 656
performance reviews by, 670
Legislative Council, 628, 630
Legislative Redistricting Board, 606
Legislative Reference Library, 630
Legitimacy, 4, 7, 410–11
civil disobedience and, 7, 8
Lemon test, 421
Lenin, Vladimir, 46
Leninism, 46
Lerner, Daniel, 16
"Letter from Birmingham City Jail" (King), 8, 444
Leveling, 29
Lewinsky, Monica, 304, 311
Lewis, Gib, 609, 624, 632–33
Libel, 189–90, 426
Liberalism. *See also* Democratic Party
age and, 43, 45
classical, 26–27
definition of, 41
education and, 43, 44
federalism and, 123
in Hollywood, 182–83
level of, 40, 41
in the media, 182, 187–88
modern, 41–43
Supreme Court voting blocs and, 405–7
test for, 47
Libertarian Party, 577, 591
Liberty
Constitutional Convention and, 58, 60
security *vs.*, 18–19
Library of Congress, 263
Liddy, G. Gordon, 306
Lieutenant governors of Texas
campaign costs of, 593
committee system and, 618
definition of, 611
plural executive and, 638–39
senate leadership by, 611–14
Life expectancy, 482–83
Limbaugh, Rush, 183–84
Limited government, 14
conservatism and, 40–41
Founders on, 60
in Texas Constitution, 547
Lincoln, Abraham
Civil War and, 101, 305
on equality, 27–28
Gettysburg Address, 15
negative campaign against, 141
Reconstruction and, 543–44
writ of habeas corpus suspended by, 18, 384–85, 432
Line-item veto, 325, 621, 643
Litmus tests, 398
Lobbies. *See also* Interest groups
conferences by, 564
registration of, 631
Texas, 563–71
Lobbying. *See also* Interest groups
congressional voting and, 283
presidential, 321–22
tips on, 284
White House, 321–22
Lobbyists
former legislators as, 567
number of, 565
in Texas, 565
Local governments, 710–47
city, 713–28
confidence in, 107
conservatism and, 123
Constitution on, 103
councils of government, 739–41
county, 728–35
independent school districts, 737–39
legacy of in Texas, 711–12
solutions to problems of, 741–46
special districts, 735–37
in Texas political system, 712–13
Localism, 711
Locke, John, 12, 26
Constitutional Convention and, 58, 60
Declaration of Independence and, 54
Log Cabin Republicans, 708
Logrolling, 287
Lopez, Alfonso, 119
Lott, Trent, 288
Lotteries in Texas, 555, 646
Louisiana Purchase, 286, 305
Louisiana Territory, 81

LULAC. *See* League of United Latin American Citizens (LULAC)
Luna, Gregory, 626

M

MacArthur, Douglas, 492
Machines, political, 207
Madison, James
Bill of Rights and, 78
Constitutional Convention and, 58
on factions, 13–14, 75
Federalist Papers, 13–14, 74, 75, 304, 429
Marshall and, 383
on Mason, 77
nomination of, 207
on nullification, 108
on the people, 67
on the right to bear arms, 429
on separation of powers, 69
Shays's Rebellion and, 57
on voter qualifications, 62
Magna Carta, 53
Mailing lists, 149–50
Majority leader, 269
Majority opinions, 404–5
Majority rule, 12–15, 103–9
Malapportionment, 247, 729–31
MALDEF. *See* Mexican American Legal Defense and Educational Fund (MALDEF)
Maloney, Pat, 689
Malpractice suits, 483
limits on, 556, 559, 651
Managed care, 483
Management audits, 658–59
Mandates, 125–26
cities and, 727–28
elections as, 135
unfunded, 126–27
Mansfield, Steve, 688, 704
Manufacturing, income inequality and, 32
Mapp v. Ohio, 435
Maquiladora program, 529–30
Marbury, William, 383
Marbury v. Madison, 73, 81, 382, 383
Marcy, William, 357, 433
Marginal rates, 470
Marginal utility theory, 473
Marine Corps, 508
Markup, 276
Marshall, George C., 492
Marshall, John, 114
judicial review and, 73, 81, 382–84
Marshall, Thurgood
Brown v. Board of Education and, 400, 441–42
on the death penalty, 437
NAACP and, 441
Marshall Plan, 492
Martin, Paul, 76
Marx, Karl, 46
Marxism, 46, 49
Mason, George, 77
Mass media, 170–99
agenda setting by, 175, 177
bias in, 182, 183, 187–88
as business, 178–80
campaign in support of the Constitution by, 74
in campaigns, 205
campaign strategy and, 142–43
candidate selection and, 185–86
candidate-voter linkage via, 184–85
conglomerates, 180, 181
Congress and, 245–46
definition of, 171, 172
effects of on behavior, 197
effects of on political life, 193–97
election coverage by, 177, 184–88
feeding frenzies, 182
free airtime on, 143
freedom *vs.* fairness of, 188–89
governor coverage by, 641, 653
Internet, 190–93
interpretation by, 177
as legislative information source, 629
libel and slander and, 189–90
liberalism in, 182–83
mirror myth in, 174
muckraking in, 181–82
negativism in, 6, 180–81, 187
news as entertainment in, 179–80
newsmaking by, 175
persuasion by, 178
politics of news in, 180–84
power of, 171–78
presidential access to, 310–12
presidential appeals via, 281
presidential mentions in, 153
socialization by, 177
soft *vs.* hard programming in, 178
spin in, 43
Texas legislature and, 627
as watchdogs, 181–82
Mattox, Jim, 554, 575
Mauro, Garry, 575, 655, 659–60
Mauzy, Oscar, 706
Mayflower Compact, 54
Mayor-council government, 715–17
Mayors
council-manager governments and, 719–23
in mayor-council governments, 716–17
salaries of, 722–23
strong, 716–17
weak, 716–17
women as, 590
McCain, John, 152
McCall, Abner, 555
McConnell vs. Federal Elections Commission, 152
McCord, James W., Jr., 306
McCormick, Mike, 704
McCorvey, Norma, 426
McCulloch v. Maryland, 114
Media events, 187
Medicaid, 122, 123, 286
abortion funding and, 427, 707
definition of, 480
Medical examiners, 734
Medicare, 286
as income transfer, 9
prescription drug benefit, 484–85
tax rate for, 472
Meier, Bill, 622
Members of Parliament (MPs), 76
Merit selection, 690, 699
Merit system, 357–58
Merit Systems Protection Board, 360
Metro government, 744–45
Mexican American Legal Defense and Educational Fund (MALDEF), 569
Luna and, 626
Mexico
Coahuila y Tejas Constitution and, 540
illegal immigration from, 531–34
maquiladora program, 529–30
Republic of Texas and, 540–42
trade patterns with, 531–32
transnational regionalism and, 529–34
Mexico, Fox and, 302
Meyer, Fred, 571
Mfume, Kweisi, 408
Military forces
gubernatorial powers and, 648–49
levels of, 507–9
major deployments of, 503
reductions in, 508
in support of political objectives, 501
war on terrorism and, 502–3
when to use, 499–503
women in, 456
Militia Act (1792), 430
Militias, 65–66, 429–30
Mills, C. Wright, 17
Milosovic, Slobodan, 491
Minorities
at-large elections and, 724–25
in bureaucracy, 360
in Congress, 261–62
exclusion of in Texas, 566
federalism and protection of, 103–9
interest groups for, 569
as judges, 675, 683, 693–98
political gains by, 586–89
political participation by, 585–86
single-member districts and, 566
in Texas, 574–75
Texas political participation by, 585–86
white flight and, 523, 726
Minority leader, 269, 270
Minor parties. *See* Third parties
Minutemen, 54
Miranda v. Arizona, 435, 676, 700
Miranda warning, 435
Misdemeanors, 676, 702
Missouri Plan, 699
Mitchell, John, 306
Mitterrand, François, 494
Momentum, 156
Mondale, Walter, 160, 265
Money supply, Constitution on, 65
Monroe, James, 207
Montgomery bus boycott, 444
Moody, Dan, 645
Morales, Dan, 576, 587–88, 657
Hopwood and, 695
tobacco lawsuits and, 657, 658
Morales, Victor, 587–88
Moralistic subculture, 516, 517
Morgenthau, Hans, 489, 501
Mormons, polygamy and, 418
Morrill Land Grant Act (1862), 115
Mosbacher, Rob, 593
Mosca, Gaetano, 201
Mothers Against Drunk Driving (MADD), 121
Motor Voter Act, 126
Mott, Lucretia, 455
Muckraking, 181–82
Multilateral treaties, 498
Municipal Annexation Act (1963), 741
Municipal courts, 677, 679
Municipal government. *See* City governments
Municipal utility districts (MUDS), 735–37
Muniz, Ramsey, 578
Murdoch, Rupert, 184
Murkowski, Lisa, 262
Murray, Charles, 34
Murray, Richard, 559
Mussolini, Benito, 46
Mutscher, Gus, 604, 624
Mutual assured destruction (MAD), 496
Myers, Michael Ozzie, 290

N

Nader, Ralph, 189, 569
NAFTA. *See* North American Free Trade Agreement (NAFTA)
Name recognition, 138, 185–86
National Association for the Advancement of Colored People (NAACP)
Marshall and, 441
segregation and, 441

National Commission on Excellence in Education, 737
National defense, 7. *See also* Defense policy; Military forces
National Geo-Spacial Agency, 328–29
National Grange, 546
Nationalism, 60
Nationalization, 108
National Labor Relations Act (1935), 286, 453
National Labor Relations Board, 355
National origin quotas, 36–37
National Reconnaissance Office, 328–29
National security, 488–511
  Cold War and, 490, 491–96
  Constitution on, 65–67
  international politics and, 489–91
  liberty *vs.*, 18–19
  military force and, 499–503
  military force levels and, 507–9
  NATO and, 490–91
  nuclear threats and, 496–99, 500
  regional security and, 490
  United Nations and, 489–90, 491
  war on terrorism and, 503–7
National Security Agency, 328–29
National Security Council (NSC), 319
National Supremacy Clause, 61, 67, 109
National Transportation Safety Board, 121
National Voter Registration Act (1993), 126
Nation at Risk, A: The Imperative for Educational Reform, 737
Nationwide referenda, 68, 70–71
Native Americans, 66. *See also* Minorities
  Coahuila y Tejas Constitution and, 540
  Seminole Tribe v. Florida, 119
  in Texas, 519
Navy, U.S., 508
NBC Nightly News, 176
Necessary and Proper Clause, 77, 109, 114–15
Negative campaigning, 141–42
Negativism, 6, 180–81
Neo-Nazi groups, 49
Newburgh Addresses, 59
New Deal
  public works projects, 116
  social welfare programs in, 478
  Texas politics and, 573
  welfare programs, 124
New England town meetings, 15
New federalism, 117
New Hampshire primary, 155–56, 157, 186
New Jersey Plan, 61
New Progressive Party, 452
Newsletters, 627
Newsmaking, 175
Newspapers and magazines, 172–73, 178, 179. *See also* Mass media
  media conglomerates and, 188–89
New York Times, 172–73, 188
New York Times v. Sullivan, 189
Nineteenth Amendment, 79, 97, 439
Ninth Amendment, 78, 95, 420
Nixon, Richard M.
  Checkers speech, 194
  image of, 166
  Kennedy debate with, 160, 194, 195
  new federalism and, 117
  pardon of, 303
  popularity of, 311
  public confidence and, 6
  ranking of, 296
  resignation of, 246
  Supreme Court and, 412
  as vice president, 336
  Vietnam War and, 494
  War Powers Act and, 82, 243
  Watergate and, 246, 305–6, 310, 385, 412
No Child Left Behind Act (2001), 126
No Establishment Clause, 418, 421–23
Nolo contendere, 700
Nominations, 205, 207
Nominees, 205
Nonpartisan elections, 207, 723
Nonproliferation Treaty (1968), 498
Nonviolent direct action, 8, 443, 444
Noriega, Manuel Antonio, 501
North American Act (1867), 76
North American Free Trade Agreement (NAFTA), 469
  concerns about, 530–31
  Fox and, 302
  Mexico and, 530–31
  Texas and, 528
  Texas economic regions and, 530–31
North Atlantic Treaty Organization (NATO), 286, 325, 326
  defense buildup of, 495
  national security and, 490–91
  Richards and, 647
Northern Alliance, 504, 506
North Korea, 498
North Vietnamese Army, 493
Northwest Ordinance (1787), 115
Nuclear Regulatory Commission, 355
Nuclear weapons, 496–500
  ballistic missile defense systems, 499, 500
  Cuban missile crisis and, 492–93
  deterrence policy and, 496
  freeze on, 494–95
  Moscow Treaty on, 497–98
  mutual assured destruction and, 496
  nonproliferation and, 498
  SALT and, 496–97
  second-strike capability and, 496
  terrorism and, 499
  testing bans on, 498
Nullification, 108
Nursing homes, 665–66

O

Obligational authority, 365
Obscenity, 197, 428–29
  definition of, 428–29
Occupational Safety and Health Act (1970), 125
Occupational Safety and Health Administration (OSHA), 125, 354, 355, 369–71
O'Connor, Sandra Day, 251, 386, 387, 400, 403, 406
  on abortion, 427
  on affirmative action, 449
  on hostile working environment, 459
O'Daniel, W. Lee, 656
Office of Management and Budget, 264, 317–18, 363, 370
Office of Personnel Management (OPM), 359–60
Office of State-Federal Relations, 645–46
Oil and natural gas industry, 527–28, 573, 660–61
Old Age and Survivors Insurance, 478
Oliver, Jesse, 694, 696
O'Neill, Harriet, 691, 698
O'Neill, Thomas P. "Tip," 260
One-party system, 572–74
Open primaries, 209, 590
Open rules, 277
Open seats, 254
Operation Enduring Freedom, 504, 506
Operation Iraqi Freedom, 506–7
Oppo research, 140
Opportunists, 630
Opportunity
  equality of, 28, 445–47
  social mobility and, 33–35
Optional Road Law (1947), 732
Ordinances, 677, 679
O'Reilly, Bill, 43, 184, 190
O'Reilly Factor, The, 43
Organized labor interest groups, 569–70
Original intent, 386–87, 398
Original jurisdiction, 389
Outlays, 365
Override, 70, 324
Oversight
  of bureaucracy, 374–75
  congressional, 244–45
  definition of, 244
  judicial, 376–77
  Texas legislative, 600–601
Overstreet, Morris, 589, 698

P

Packing, 249, 586
Packwood, Robert, 44, 290
PACs. *See* Political action committees (PACs)
Pain and suffering awards, 393
Paradox of democracy, 13–15
Pardons, 648
Parks, Rosa, 444
Parliamentary government, 61
Parole, 702
Partial birth abortions, 427
Partial preemption, 125
Participation, 12, 131–34
  on conventions, 583–84
  federalism and, 106
  interactive mass, 190–91
  by media professionals, 175
  in Texas, 523
  voting as, 131–34
Partido Acción Nacional (PAN), 302, 531
Partido Revolucionario Institucional (PRI), 302, 531
Partisanship
  cabinet appointments and, 353
  in the electorate, 214
  governor and, 653–56
  judicial elections and, 690–92, 704–5
  redistricting and, 599
  sources of congressional, 280, 281
  Texas, 599, 624–25
Party identification
  class and, 579–80
  dealignment and, 214
  determining, 214
  in the electorate, 215
  ideology and, 203, 205
  income and, 579–80
  by social group, 215–17
  Texas patterns of, 578–81
  voting and, 163–66, 214–17
Party polarization, 205
Party unity, 278
Party votes, 278
Paterson, William, 61
Patriot Act, 433, 504
Patriot missiles, 500
Patronage, 207, 670
Patterson, Jerry, 595, 660
Pauken, Tom, 571
Pay-as-you-go government
  comptroller and, 657–59
  definition of, 621
  restrictions of, 549, 550
Peabody Education Board, 737

Peace Corps, 362
Peacekeeping, 501, 509
Pearl Harbor, 19
Pelosi, Nancy, 270
Pelosi, Paul, 270
Penal code, 676
Pendleton Act (1883), 357
Pennzoil Company, 690
Pentagon Papers, 188
People for the American Way, 150
Per diems, 602
Performance reviews, 669–70
Permanent School Fund, 550, 659, 661
Permanent University Fund, 550, 555, 659
Perot, Ross
  debates by, 161
  lobbyists of, 567
  media campaign of, 194–95
Perry, Bob, 595, 648, 701
Perry, Rick, 650–51
  background of, 640–41
  Bob Perry and, 595
  campaign costs of, 593
  conflict with, 638
  as lieutenant governor, 613, 656
  minority appointments by, 697–98
  partisanship and, 625
  redistricting and, 608, 642
  Republican dominance and, 576
  Strayhorn and, 659
  vetos by, 644–45
  Yzaguirre and, 647–48
Petitions for review, 686–87
Petit juries, 389, 684
Phillips, Thomas R., 683, 691–92, 693, 696
Photo ops, 142
Pilgrim, Lonnie "Bo," 631–32
Place system, 724
Plaintiffs, 395, 676
Planks, 211
Planned Parenthood League, 426
Planned Parenthood of Pennsylvania v. Casey, 427
Platforms, 205, 211, 212
Plea bargaining, 436, 681
Plessy v. Ferguson, 441, 450
Plural executive, 638–39
Pluralism, 17–20
  interest groups and, 565–66
  in Texas, 565–66
Plurality, 219
Pocket veto, 324
Polarization, party, 205, 280, 281
Police powers, 112, 394
Policy
  bureaucrats and, 664–66
  definition of, 3
  federalism and, 106
  mandates and, 135
  retrospective voting and, 135
  social welfare, 478–80
  state courts in, 705–8
Policy implementation
  bureaucracy in, 342–44, 664–66
  definition of, 342
  obstacles to, 664–66
  the president in, 298
Policy making
  bureaucracy in, 360–62
  Congress in, 242
  president in, 297, 321–25
  vice president in, 336–37
Political action committees (PACs). *See also* Interest groups
  campaign contributions by, 149, 594–95
  definition of, 149
  leadership, 271
  Texas, 594–95
  trial lawyers in, 568
Political correctness (PC), 49–50, 425–26
Political culture, 24–51
  definition of, 25, 515
  dissent and, 45–50
  equality and, 27–30
  ideologies in, 40–45
  income/wealth inequality and, 30–33
  individualistic subculture, 516
  individual liberty and, 26–27
  moralistic subculture, 516
  race, ethnicity, immigration and, 35–40
  social mobility and, 33–35
  of Texas, 515–17
  traditionalistic subculture, 516
Political equality, 28
Political machines, 207, 723
Political organizations, 201. *See also* Interest groups; Political parties
Political parties, 200–220. *See also* Democratic Party; Republican Party
  Canadian, 76
  change and continuity in U.S., 203
  in Congress, 257–60, 266–69
  congressional committees and, 274–76
  conventions of, 207–8, 210–13
  county conventions in, 584
  dealignment and, 214
  in democratic government, 201–7
  divided party government and, 207
  as election organizers, 207–10
  erosion of, 205
  finances of, 213–14
  gerrymandering and, 248–52
  governor and, 653–56
  Hollywood and, 182–83
  ideology and, 204–5
  interest groups compared with, 201
  media bias in, 187–88
  organization of, 581–84
  party identification and, 214–17
  permanent organizations in, 582–83
  pluralism and, 19
  polarization in, 205, 280, 281
  power of, 201
  precinct conventions in, 583–84
  presidential role in, 313
  primaries of, 208–10
  realignment in, 215–16, 574–75
  responsible party model and, 202, 584–85
  senatorial district conventions in, 584
  state conventions in, 584
  temporary organizations in, 583
  Texan organization of, 581–84
  in Texas, 564–65, 572–85, 584–85
  third, 217–18
  two-party system persistence and, 217–20
  voting loyalty and, 214–15
  winning *vs.* principles in, 202, 204
Political patronage, 207, 670
Political science, 3–4
Political theory, 75
Politics, 3–4
  definition of, 3
  economy and, 462–87
  government and, 4–7
  Supreme Court and, 405–9
Politics: Who Gets What, When and How (Lasswell), 4
Polk, James K., 542
Poll taxes, 98, 549, 585
Polygamy, 418
Poor Relief Act (1601), 478
Popular sovereignty, 546–47
Populist Party, 572
Pork barreling, 265–66
Pornography, 197, 428–29
  child, 429
  on the Internet, 428–29
Potsdam Conference, 327
Poverty, 475–77
  causes of, 480
  family structure and, 476–77, 480
  level, definition of, 35, 475
  persistent, 476
  teen pregnancy and, 476–77
  temporary, 477
  in Texas, 522, 524–25
Poverty line, 475
Powell, Colin, 301, 332, 335, 502
  Operation Iraqi Freedom and, 506
Powell, Lewis, 118, 406
Powell Doctrine, 502
Power elites, 17
Power of the purse, 244
Precedent, 388
Precinct chairs, 582
Precinct conventions, 583–84
Precincts, 208, 582
Preemptions, 125
Preferred position doctrine, 425
Preferred provider organizations (PPOs), 483
Prescription drugs
  costs of, 484
  Medicare coverage of, 484–85
President, 294–339
  appointment power of, 70–71, 317
  budgetary role of, 317–18
  cabinet and, 318–19
  as chief executive, 313–21
  as Commander-in-Chief, 66, 330–34
  Congress and, 308
  congressional voting and, 280–82
  constitutional powers of, 298–308
  Constitution interpreted by, 81–82
  crisis management by, 295, 297
  deciding to run for, 154
  the economy and, 297–98
  executive power of, 303, 313–21
  executive privilege and, 306–7
  foreign policy and, 66–67, 325–27
  global voice of, 298, 325–30
  government management by, 298
  honeymoon period, 322
  impeachment of, 71, 246, 302–3, 304
  impoundment and, 307
  intelligence activities and, 328–30
  judicial appointments by, 397–400
  lobbying by, 321–25
  media access of, 310–12
  pardons by, 303
  personality *vs.* policy and, 312–13
  policy making by, 242, 297, 321–25
  political resources of, 308–12
  popularity of, 308–10
  power of, 295–98
  public opinion influenced by, 197
  qualifications for, 298
  ranking of, 296
  responsibility of to the courts, 307–8
  staff of, 318–21
  State of the Union address, 178
  succession of, 298–99, 302
  success of in Congress, 322–23
  Supreme Court influenced by, 407–8, 412
  as symbol, 295
  term limit for, 298
  veto power of, 70, 323–25
  war-making powers of, 81–82, 330–33

Presidential campaigns
conventions in, 156
debates and, 159–63, 160–61
front-end strategy in, 156
front loading in, 156
general election, 156–63
primary, 152–56, 157
staff in, 154
swing states and, 159
Presidential Election Campaign Fund, 145
Presidential fever, 152
Presidential preference primaries, 583–84
Presidential primaries, 152–56, 157. *See also* Primary elections
voter turnout for, 257
President pro tempore, 269–70, 302
Presler, Larry, 290
Pressing the flesh, 150, 266
Primary elections
closed, 209
definition of, 205
direct, 590
front loading, 156
open, 209, 590
party, 208–9
presidential, 210
presidential preference, 583–84
runoff, 210
Texas, 582, 590–91
types of, 209–10
Prime Minister, 76
Prior restraint, 188
Prisons
county jails, 733
expansion/improvement of Texas, 702–3, 712
Privacy
abortion and, 426–27
Constitution on, 426
gay marriage and, 428
Internet and, 193
media and, 183
sexual conduct and, 427
Privacy Act (1974), 373, 374
Private economic sphere, 29–30
Privatization, 741
Probable cause, 434
Probation, 702, 734
Procedural committees, 616
Productivity, 358–59, 370
Product liability lawsuits, 393
Professional associations, 568
Professionalism
Texas legislature, 601
Profit motive, 49
Program budgeting, 367
Progressive Movement, 126
Progressive taxation, 473
Prohibition, 78, 97, 455
Proportional (flat) taxation, 473
Proportional representation, 219, 606
Proposition 12, Texas, 556
Proposition 14, Texas, 557
Prosecution, 684
Protectionism, 466–67
Protest
African American, 443, 444
civil disobedience, 7, 8
nonviolent direct action and, 8, 443, 444
Public assistance programs, 478
Public Citizen, Inc., 569
Public goods, 8–9
Public improvement districts, 745–46
Public interest, 188
Public-interest groups
in Texas, 568–69
Public opinion
on confidence in government, 6
on Congress, 138, 256
on globalization, 469
on government branches, 73
on government programs, 10
on local government, 107
media influence on, 196–97
on political parties, 206
polls, 186
polls, in campaigns, 142
on the president, 308–10
on the Supreme Court, 411
Supreme Court reflection of, 407
on television, 191
on the war against terrorism, 507
on who runs the country, 17
Public political sphere, 29–30
Public relations, 567
Public trust, 188
Public Utility Regulatory Act (PURA) (1975), 666, 668
Puerto Ricans, 452–53
Purchasing power parity, 31
Putin, Vladimir, 496, 497–98

Q

Quayle, Dan, 336
Quorum, 612
Quotas
affirmative action and, 447
export/import, 467
national origin, 36–37

R

Race/ethnicity
diversity and, 448–50
equality and, 35–40
gerrymandering and, 250–52
income inequality and, 445–46
voting patterns and, 163–66
voting rights and, 79, 96, 114
Racism. *See* Inequality; Minorities; Segregation
Racketeering, 112
Radicalism, 49–50
Radical Reconstructionists, 538, 544
Radicals, 45
Radio. *See also* Mass media
conservatism on, 183–84
freedom of the press and, 188
as news source, 173
Roosevelt on, 194
Raiding, 209
Rainy Day account, 614
RAND Corporation, 191
Randolph, Edmund, 60–61
Rangel, Irma, 626
Ranking majority-party members, 275–76
Ranking minority members, 272
Ranney, Austin, 196
Rather, Dan, 176, 190
Ratification
of the Constitution, 73–75
definition of, 73
Ratliff, Bill, 613, 656–57
Ray, C. L., 689–90, 691
Rayburn, Sam, 266
Raza Unida, La, 577, 578
Reagan, John H., 545
Reagan, Ronald
Bork nomination by, 398–99
Challenger spaceship and, 295, 297
crossover vote for, 214–15
debates by, 160
defense buildup of, 494–95, 509
as Great Communicator, 166, 185, 311
health of, 299
Iran-Contra and, 310
judicial appointments of, 406, 412
national drinking age and, 121
new federalism and, 117
popularity of, 312
public confidence and, 6
recall attempts, 126
Strategic Defense Initiative, 500
taxes under, 473–74
Realignment, 215–16
in Texas, 574–75
ticket splitting and, 578–79
Reapportionment, 254
Reasonable doubt, 700–701
Recalls, 126–27, 641
Recessions, 464, 465
Reciprocity, 287, 628
Reconstruction, 108, 114
Texas Constitution and, 537, 538, 543–45
Reconstruction Acts, 544
Record votes, 622
Redistricting
definition of, 248
Dewhurst and, 614
gerrymandering, 248–52
Perry and, 651
re-redistricting, 250
Texas, 599, 606–7, 614
Reed v. Reed, 455
Referenda
national, 68, 70–71
in Texas, 551
Regional planning commissions, 739–41
Regressive taxation, 473, 515, 527, 725–26
Regular sessions, 602
Regulation
activist agencies in, 369–71
battles over, 368–72
bureaucracy in, 345
capture theory of, 369
costs of, 372–73
definition of, 345
deregulation and, 371–72
growth of, 372
independent commissions for, 353–54, 355
in Texas, 664–66
Rehnquist, William H., 403, 406, 407
on prayer in school, 423
on *U.S. vs. Lopez*, 119
Reinvestment zones, 744
Religion, 418, 421–23
freedom of, 14, 78, 418, 421–23
free exercise of, 418–21
interest groups and, 570–71
No Establishment Clause on, 421–23
prayer in schools and, 423
separation of church and state and, 218
Religious Right, 570–71
Remedies and reliefs, 396
Reno v. American Civil Liberties Union, 193
Representation, 60–62
in bureaucracy, 360
proportional, 219
Texas legislature in, 601
Representational federalism, 117–18
Representative democracy, 15–16, 135
Representative government, 60
Republicanism, 60, 67–69
Republican Party, 258–60
dominance of in Texas, 576–77
Log Cabin Republicans and, 708
religious right in, 570–71
Texas dominance of, 522–23, 599–600
Republic of Texas
Constitution of, 538, 540–42
Requests for proposals (RFPs), 357
Rescissions, 307
Reserved powers, 109–11
Residential Construction Commission, 595
Responsible party model, 202, 584
Responsiveness, 358
Restricted rules, 277

Results, equality of, 28–29, 445–47
Retail politics, 155–56, 265
Retention elections, 699
Retrospective voting, 135
Revenue bonds, 725–26
Reverse discrimination, 447, 587, 607
Revolutionary War, 54–55, 59
bonds from, 63, 64, 65
Revolving doors, 369
restrictions on, 666, 668
Reynolds, Mel, 290
Reynolds v. Sims, 606
Rice, Condoleeza, 301, 503
Richards, Ann, 300, 640, 646–47
appointment powers and, 645–46, 646, 648
background of, 640
election of, 589
ethics reform and, 632
lottery and, 555
minority appointments by, 698
nursing homes and, 665–66
Religious Right and, 571
staff of, 649
sunset reviews and, 669
testimony of, 629, 632
as treasurer, 575
vetos by, 645
Riders, 277
Ridge, Tom, 353
Right, the, 45
Right to bear arms, 429–30
Right to counsel, 434–35
Right-to-work law, 553
Road/highway construction, 732
Rockefeller, Nelson, 299
Rodriguez, Xavier, 698
Roe v. Wade, 81, 385, 388, 426–27
Rollback elections, 725
Roll-call votes, 278
Roosevelt, Franklin D.
executive agreements and, 327
fireside chats, 194
interstate commerce and, 115
Japanese internment by, 19, 305, 315
public works projects, 116
social welfare programs and, 478
term limits and, 298
Texas politics and, 573
welfare programs of, 124
Roosevelt, Theodore, 303
Rostenkowski, Dan, 290
Rousseau, Jean Jacques, 26
Rove, Karl, 593
Ruiz v. Estelle, 703
Rule of four, 403
Rules, 277
Rules Committee, 269, 272, 277
Rumsfeld, Donald, 301, 506
Runoff elections, 724
Runoff primaries, 210
Rush Limbaugh Show, 183–84
Rusk, Dean, 493
Russia. *See also* Soviet Union
after communism, 495–96
NATO and, 491
nuclear power of, 496

S

Safe Drinking Water Act (1986), 125
Safe seats, 254, 283
Salazar, Felix, 694, 696
SALT I, 306, 496–97, 499, 500
SALT II, 497
Sanchez, Orlando, 721
Sanchez, Tony, 587–88, 593, 640
San Jacinto, battle of (1836), 541
Santa Anna Perez de Lebron, Antonio López, 541
Sasser, Jim, 288
Scalia, Antonin, 406, 407
Schattschneider, E. E., 175
School boards, 592, 738–39
School districts, 735, 737–39
School prayer, 423
School superintendents, 739
Schwarzenegger, Arnold, 126–27, 641
Searches and seizures, 94, 433, 434
Search warrants, 434
Second Amendment, 78, 94, 419
right to bear arms and, 429–30
Second Continental Congress (1775), 54, 59
Second reading, 619
Second-strike capability, 496
Secretary of State, 638–39, 660
Securities and Exchange Commission, 317, 355
Security Council, U.N., 489, 490, 491
Sedgwick, Lisa, 685
Sedition Act (1918), 424
Segregation
Brown v. Board of Education and, 115, 441–42
de facto, 442
elimination of laws on, 441–45
enforcement of desegregation, 442
federalism and, 108
imposition of, 440–41
NAACP and, 441
separate but equal and, 441
Select Committee on Campaign Practices, 246
Select committees, 619
Selective perception, 196
Self-incrimination, 434–35
Self-interested behavior, 29–30
Self-reliance, 40–41
Seminole Tribe v. Florida, 119
Senate, 111. *See also* Texas legislature
appointment confirmation by, 70–71, 245, 374
budget committees, 363, 365
constituencies of, 242–43
Constitution on, 68
floor traditions in, 277–78
House of Representatives compared with, 244
judicial appointments and, 398–99
majority leader and whip, 270
minority leader and whip, 270
president pro tempore, 269–70
vice president and, 269–70
Senate Ethics Committee, 272
Senate Foreign Relations Committee, 245
Senate Research Center, 631
Senatorial courtesy, 398, 646
Senatorial district conventions, 584
Senators, terms of, 242–43
Senior citizens, poverty and, 477
Senior Executive Service (SES), 359
Seniority system, 275–76
Sensationalism, 180
Separate but equal, 441
Separation of church and state, 218
Separation of powers, 69–73, 241–42
definition of, 69
Madison on, 75
in Texas Constitution, 547–48
September 11 attacks, 504
Bush and, 297, 300–301
democracy and, 18–19
Homeland Security and, 127
media coverage of, 195
public confidence and, 6
Service sector, 32, 525–26
Set-aside programs, 448
Seventeenth Amendment, 79, 97
Seventh Amendment, 78, 94, 420
Sexual harassment, 458–60
Sharp, John, 658
performance reviews by, 669–70
Railroad Commission and, 661
Republican dominance and, 576
Sharpstown scandal, 555, 595, 624, 631–32
Shaw, Bernard, 160
Shaw v. Reno, 251
Shays, Daniel, 56
Shays's Rebellion (1786), 56–57
Sheriffs, 733
Sherman, Roger, 61–62
Shield laws, 190
Shivers, Allan, 573, 656
Shriver, Maria, 127
Sibley, David, 744
Sierra Club, 569
Simpson, O. J., 195
Simpson-Mazzoli Act (1986), 37–38
Single-member districts, 566, 606, 724
Single-purpose districts, 592
Sirica, John J., 306
Sixteenth Amendment, 79, 96
Sixth Amendment, 78, 94, 420, 435–36
60 Minutes, 179–80
60 Minutes, 690, 693
Slander, 189–90, 426
Slavery
as American dilemma, 25
Constitutional Convention and, 58, 60
Constitution on, 64, 438, 440
elimination of, 114
federalism and, 108
Founders on, 62
in Texas, 520, 541, 542
13th Amendment on, 96
three-fifths compromise on, 62
Slave trade, 62, 64, 438, 440
Smith, Adam, 26
Smith, Preston, 640
Smith, Steven Wayne, 698
Smith-Hughes Act (1917), 115
Smith v. Allwright, 585, 676
Snowe, Olympia, 262
Social change, 49–50
Social class
communism and, 46, 48
mobility and, 33–35
power and, 566
social mobility and, 33–35
voter turnout and, 131, 132
Social contract, 7, 60
Social Gospel, 571
Social insurance programs, 478
Socialism, 48
Socialist parties, 218
Socialization, 177
Social mobility, 33–35
Social Security
definition of, 478
as income transfer, 9
taxes, 470, 472–73
Social Security Act (1935), 286
Social welfare programs, 475–82
entitlements, 478
health care and, 482–85
policy on, 478–80
poverty levels and, 475–77
reform of, 124, 480–82
work programs, 481
Society of the Patrons of Husbandry, 546
Soft money, 151, 152
Soft news programming, 178–80
Solicitor general, 404, 407–8
Sondock, Ruby, 698
Sound bites, 142, 187
Souter, David, 406
Southern Christian Leadership Conference, 444
Southwest Voter Registration Education Project, 586
Sovereign immunity, 395
Soviet Union
Cold War and, 490
collapse of, 490, 495–96
communism and, 46, 48
democracy and, 11

Soviet Union (*cont.*)
expansion of, 494
NATO and, 491
United Nations and, 489
Sparks, Sam, 658
Speaker of the House, 269
committee system and, 618
in presidential succession, 299, 302
Texas, 608–11, 615
Spears, Franklin, 706
Special committees, 619
Special elections, 592
Specialization, 285
Special Operations Forces, 503
Special prosecutors, 396–97
Special purpose districts, 711, 735–37
consequences of, 736–37
functions and structures of, 735–36
Special sessions, 602, 641–44
Spector, Rose, 691, 698
Spin doctors, 156
Splintering, 249
Spoils system, 357, 735
Spoke annexation, 743
St. Clair, Arthur, 246
Staff. *See also* Bureaucracy
gubernatorial, 649–52
Texas legislature, 628, 629–31
Staff, congressional, 262. *See also* Bureaucracy
Staggered terms, 645
Stalin, Josef, 491
Standards of Official Conduct Committee, 272
Standing, legal, 394–95
Standing committees, 271–72
definition of, 616
Texas legislature, 616–18
Stanton, Elizabeth Cady, 455
Stare decisis, 388
Starr, Kenneth, 304, 311, 396–97
Starr Report, 304
START II Treaty, 497
START I Treaty, 497
Star Wars, 500
State Affairs Committee, 616
State Board of Education, 638–39, 661, 737
State Board of Insurance, 646
State chairs, 583
State Commission on Judicial Conduct, 682, 689–90
State conventions, 584
State courts, 391
State Department, 350
State executive committees, 583
State governments
concurrent powers of, 109, 111
conservatism and, 123
home rule and, 103
obligations of to other states, 111
powers denied to, 111
reserved powers of, 109, 111
State militias, 65–66, 429–30
State of the State address, 629, 641
State of the Union message, 178, 321
States rights, 108, 543
Statutes, 676–77
Statutory county courts, 680
Statutory laws, 386, 539
Statutory rape laws, 456
Stevens, John Paul, 406
Stevenson, Adlai, 210
Stevenson, Coke, 656
Stewart, Potter, 428
Stone, Harlan, 386
Stone, Lucy, 455
Strategic Arms Limitation Treaties (SALT), 306, 496–97, 499, 500
Strategic Arms Reduction Talks (START), 497
Strategic Defense Initiative (SDI), 500
Strayhorn, Carole Keeton, 589, 638, 658–59, 661
Sturns, Louis, 698
Subcommittees
standing, 618
Texas legislature, 616, 618
Subcommittees, congressional, 272–73
Subcultures, 25
Subpoenas, 436, 733
Substantive committees, 616
Suffrage, women's, 63, 97, 455. *See also* Voting rights
Sullivan rule, 189
Sunset Advisory Commission, 630, 665, 668–69
Sunset reviews, 665, 668–69
Super-Americanism, 566
Superpowers, 490
Supplemental Security Income (SSI), 479
Supreme Court, Texas, 548, 682
on abortion, 707
caseloads and, 682
on gay rights, 708
party alignment and, 690–92
petitions for review, 686–87
in policy, 705–8
trial lawyers influence on, 568
winners/losers before, 692–93
Supreme Court, U.S.
on affirmative action, 447–51, 448–51
agenda setting in, 403
appeals to, 390–91
appointment to, 71
on apportionment, 247
Bush v. Gore, 408–10
on capital punishment, 701, 702
caseload of, 391, 394
checks on the power of, 410–14
in conference, 404
congressional checks on, 413–14
on congressional term limits, 255
Constitution on, 68
as court of last resort, 389
decision making in, 403–5
development of federalism and, 114–15
federalism and, 117–19
on Gun-Free School Act, 118–19
hearing arguments in, 403–4
impeachment of justices in, 413–14
interest groups and, 408
judicial appointments to, 397–400
judicial review and, 71–73, 81, 382–84
justices, 400–403
liberalism and conservatism in, 405–7
opinion writing in, 404–5
politics and, 405–9
presidential influence on, 407–8, 412
public opinion and, 407
Swinford, David, 542
Swing states, 159
Symbolic speech, 425

T

Taft, William Howard, 303, 400
Taft-Hartley Act (1947), 305
Tags, 622
Taliban, 504, 506
Talking heads, 186–87
Talk radio, 183–84
Taney, Roger, 440
Tariffs, 65, 466–67
Tax abatements, 743–44
Tax assessor-collectors, 732–33
Taxation
Articles of Confederation on, 56
power of the purse and, 244
progressive, 473
proportional/flat, 473
regressive, 473
Taxes, 469–73
burden of, 469–73
city revenues and, 725–26
Constitution on, 63, 65
corporate income, 472
definition of, 63
estate and gift, 473
excise and custom duties, 473
individual income, 470–72
in other countries, 471
religious organizations and, 421–22
Social Security, 472–73
Texas, 600
who pays, 475
Tax rebellions, 56–57
Tax Reform Act (1986), 472, 474
Teen pregnancies, 476–77, 480
Television. *See also* Mass media
agenda setting by, 174
in American culture, 191
believability of, 172
cable, 189
in campaigns, 205
confidence in, 191
effects of on behavior, 197
emotional communication via, 173–74
freedom of the press and, 188
growth of, 194–95
media conglomerates and, 188–89
negative campaigns and, 140–41
network anchors, 176
as news source, 171
power of, 171
violence on, 197
Television malaise, 196
Temporary Assistance to Needy Families, 124, 478, 481, 482
Tennessee Valley Authority, 356, 432
Tenth Amendment, 78, 95, 109, 111
centralized federalism and, 116
in representational federalism, 118
text of, 420
Terms
House of Representatives, 242–43
limits on, 255, 298
Senate, 242–43
Texas legislature, 602
Terrorism
Bush and, 300–301
civil liberties and, 433
definition of, 503–4
democracy and, 18–19
global, 504
goal of, 18
Homeland Security and, 127
notable attacks in, 505
nuclear, 499
public confidence and, 6
war on, 127, 297, 300–301, 432
Texanism, 566
Texans for Lawsuit Reform, 594, 692
Texas
African Americans in, 520–21
aging population in, 523
Anglo immigration to, 519, 521
annexation of, 542–43
Asian Americans in, 521
challenges facing, 514–15
changes in, 513–15
cowboy image of, 513–14
demographics of, 513, 518–21, 522–26, 600
diversity in, 517–18
economic diversification in, 527–28
economic regions of, 528–29
economy of, 526–28

education and literacy in, 525–26
Hispanics in, 519
illegal immigration to, 531–34
in-migration to, 522–23, 575
maquiladora program, 529–30
Mexico trade patterns with, 531–32
Native Americans in, 519
origins of the name, 519
political culture of, 515--17
political myths of, 517–18
political subcultures of, 515–17
population increase in, 522–23
poverty in, 522, 524–25
as republic, 540–42
transnational regionalism and, 529–34
urbanization in, 523
wealth/income distribution in, 523–25
Texas A&M University, 550
constitutional reform and, 555
Hopwood and, 695
Texas Association of Business, 563, 567
Texas Association of Realtors, 594
Texas Bankers Association, 567
Texas Capitol, 603–4
Texas Citizen Action, 569
Texas Civil Justice League, 692
Texas Commission on Environmental Quality, 661
Texas Communist Control Act (1951), 732
Texas Conservative Coalition, 623
Texas Court of Criminal Appeals, 548, 682
Mansfield on, 688
partisanship and, 704–5
procedures in, 686, 687
reasonable doubt defined by, 700–701
technicalities and, 704
Texas Education Agency, 661, 737, 739
Texas Farm Bureau, 570
Texas Higher Education Coordinating Board, 668
Texas legislature, 598–635
agency oversight by, 600–601
budgets and taxes and, 600
caucuses in, 625–26
committee system in, 616–19
composition of, 604–5
constituents and, 626–27
decision making in, 627–28
ethics and reforms in, 631–33
functions of, 600–601
house leadership, 608–11
institutionalization of, 601
law enactment by, 600
leadership in, 608–15
legislative process in, 619–21
lieutenant governor and, 611–14
organization of, 601–2
partisanship in, 624–26
party system in, 623–25
pay/compensation for, 602–3
physical facilities of, 603–4
public education by, 601
qualifications for, 602
redistricting by, 606–7
representation by, 601
Republican takeover of, 599–600, 625
retirement plan of, 603
rules and procedures in, 619–21
senate leadership, 611–15
sessions of, 602
Sharpstown scandal, 555, 595, 624, 631–32
special sessions, 641–44
staff for, 629–31
terms in, 602
turnover in, 605–6
two-thirds rule, 608–9, 614
voting in, 622–23
workload of, 628
Texas Medical Association, 568, 594
Texas Mobility Fund, 651
Texas Municipal League, 590, 715, 725
Texas National Guard, 649
Texas Observer, 574
Texas politics
African Americans in, 520–21
citizen ignorance and, 514
demographics and, 522–26
Hispanics in, 519
race/ethnicity and, 522
Republican dominance in, 522–23
Texas Polls, 587, 642
Texas Public Utility Commission, 650, 661, 669
Texas Railroad Commission, 638–39, 660–61
Texas Regional Planning Act (1965), 739
Texas Research League, 683
Texas State Teachers Association, 594
Texas Taxpayers and Research Association, 567
Texas Trial Lawyers Association, 594
political activism by, 689
Texas v. Johnson, 425
Texas Watch, 569, 692–93
Texas Workforce Commission, 670, 671
Thatcher, Margaret, 494
Third Amendment, 78, 94, 419
Third parties
ballot access by, 220
on general election ballots, 2 10
prospects for, 217–18
in Texas, 577–78
winner-take-all system and, 219–20
Third reading, 619, 621
Thirteenth Amendment, 79, 96, 114, 421, 439
Thomas, Clarence, 399, 400, 401, 406–7
Thornburg v. Gingles, 251
Three-fifths Compromise, 62, 440
Thurmond, Strom, 288
Ticket splitters, 578–79
Tilden, Samuel, 441
Tobacco companies lawsuit, 657
Tocqueville, Alexis de, 381
Torricelli, Robert, 290
Tort law, 568
reform of, 651, 692
Totalitarianism, 14
Total preemption, 125
Tower, John, 319, 353, 574
Town meetings, 15
Trade. *See also* Globalization
free, 467, 468–69
international agreements on, 469
protectionism in, 466–67
between Texas and Mexico, 531–32
Traditionalistic subculture, 516, 566
Anglos in, 521
definition of, 516
mayor-council government and, 717
origins of, 516–17
Transnational regionalism, 529–34
Transportation Security Administration, 353
Trans Texas Corridor, 651
Treasurer, Texas state, 556, 638–39, 660
Treasury Department, 112, 350
Treaties, 245, 326
Treaty of Moscow (2002), 497–98
Trials, right to fair, 435–36. *See also* Judicial system, Texas; Judicial system, U.S.
Truan, Carlos, 606
Truman, Harry, 305, 308, 313
Cold War and, 491–92
desegregation and, 315
oil interests and, 573
steel mill seizure by, 317, 385
Truman Doctrine, 286, 491–92
Trustees, 284
Tsongas, Paul, 315
Tucker, Karla Faye, 702
Turner, Sylvester, 625
Turner, Ted, 194
Turnover
Texas legislative, 605–6, 627
Turnover, congressional, 255
Twelfth Amendment, 79, 95
Twentieth Amendment, 79, 97
Twenty-fifth Amendment, 79, 98–99
presidential succession and, 298–99, 302
Twenty-first Amendment, 78, 79, 97
Twenty-fourth Amendment, 79, 98
Twenty-second Amendment, 79, 98, 298
Twenty-seventh Amendment, 79, 99, 265
Twenty-sixth Amendment, 79, 99, 121
Twenty-third Amendment, 79, 98
Two-party system, 217–20
in Texas, 572, 574–77
Two-thirds rule, 608–9, 614, 621

U

Unanimous consent agreement, 277
Underclass, 476
Undue influence, 564
Unemployment compensation, 478–79
Unemployment rates, 464–65
Unfunded mandates, 126–27
Unicameral legislatures, 540
Unilateralism, 332–33
Unitary system, 101, 541, 712
United Farm Workers, 453
United Food and Commercial Workers International Union, 569–70
United Nations, 325–26, 326
formation of, 489–90
national security and, 489–90, 491
United States v. Morrison, 384
United States v. Paradise, 448
United States v. Richard m. Nixon, 306
United Steelworkers of America v. Weber, 448
University of California Regents v. Bakke, 403–4, 447, 695
University of Michigan, 449
University of Texas, 550
constitutional reform and, 555
Hopwood and, 695
interest groups and, 568
Urban Affairs Committee, 616
Urbanization, 523
problems from, 726–27
Texas, 714
Urban reform movements, 716
Uribe, Hector, 661
U.S. Marshals, 389
U.S. Postal Service, 356
U.S. vs. Lopez, 118–19

V

Values. *See also* Conservatism; Liberalism
conditions *vs.,* 25
conflict over, 26
congressional voting and personal, 283–84
cultural consensus on, 218–19
definition of, 25
inconsistent application of, 26
media and, 177, 196

Van de Putte, Leticia, 609
Veniremen, 684–85
Versailles Treaty (1920), 326
Veterans Land Program, 659
Vetos, 323–25
governors', 629
line-item, 325, 621, 643
overriding, 70, 324
pocket, 324
by Texas governors, 641, 643–45
as threat, 281–82, 629
Vice chairs, 583
Vice president, 334–37
in presidential succession, 299
as presidents, 337
roles of, 335–37
selection of, 211, 334–35
in the Senate, 269–70
Vietnam Veterans Against the War, 314
Vietnam War, 493–94
aftermath of, 494
defense spending and, 509
Kerry and, 314
lessons from, 499
Nixon and, 327
Pentagon papers, 188
public confidence and, 6
symbolic speech and, 425
television in, 194
War Powers Act and, 82, 243, 331
Villa, Pancho, 302
Violence Against Women Act (1994), 120, 384
Virginia Plan, 58, 60–61
Voltaire, 26
Voluntary exchange, 463
Voter fatigue, 590
Voter registration, 126
Texas, 585–86
Voters
candidate image and, 166, 167
Constitution on qualifications of, 62–63
contacting, 627
decision factors for, 163–68
economy and, 167
gender and, 163–66
by group, 163–66
issues and, 167–68
party, 214–15
party identification and, 163–66
race and, 163–66
Voter turnout, 149, 151
for congressional elections, 256–57
for constitutional amendments, 556, 557
European, 134
factors in, 131–32
in general elections, 257
in presidential primaries, 257
in primary elections, 590, 591
Voting rights
absentee voting and, 592
age and, 79, 99, 586
Constitution on, 28, 79–80
15th Amendment on, 114
in Texas, 542
for women, 586
Voting Rights Act (1965), 286
gerrymandering and, 250–51
guarantees in, 439
judicial elections and, 694, 696
in Texas, 574, 586–87, 729–31
Texas and, 522, 607

W

Wadsworth, John, 54
Wagner, Adolf, 347
Wainwright, Dale, 589
Wallace, George, 108
Wallace, Mike, 190, 690
Wall Street Journal, 172–73
Ward politics, 699, 724
Wards, 208
War on terrorism, 127, 297, 300–301, 503–7
declaration of, 504
defense spending and, 509
military force in, 501–3
Operation Enduring Freedom, 504, 506
Operation Iraqi Freedom, 506–7
Patriot Act and, 433
prisoners' rights in, 432
War powers, 330–33
conflict over, 81–82, 243
Constitution on, 66
domestic affairs and, 333–34
presidential use of, 326
War Powers Act (1973), 82, 243, 331–32
Warren, Earl, 406
Warsaw Pact, 490
Washington, Craig, 611
Washington, George
as Commander-in-Chief, 54, 65–66
Constitutional Convention and, 58, 59
Proclamation of Neutrality by, 305, 316–17
Shays's Rebellion and, 57
Washington-on-the-Brazos, 541, 542
Washington Post, 172–73, 188, 276, 306
Water conservation and improvements districts (WCIDs), 735–37
Watergate scandal, 246, 305–6, 310, 385, 412
Ways and Means Committee, 272, 618
Wealth, definition of, 32–33. *See also* Income/wealth
Weber, Max, 341
Weddington, Susan, 571
Weinberger, Caspar, 502
Weld, William, 315
Wells, Bill, 669
Whips, 269
Whistle-blowers, 361, 666, 667
White, Bill, 593
White, Mark, 575, 638, 640, 649, 694
White flight, 523, 726
Whitehead, Martha, 556, 660
White House press corps, 310–11
White House staff, 319–21
White primaries, 585
Whitewater investigation, 246, 396–97
Whitmire, John, 609
William C. Velasquez Institute, 588
Williams, Brian, 176
Williams, Clayton, 575, 640
Williams, Michael, 589, 648
Wilson, Woodrow
Department of Labor and, 349
health of, 98–99, 299
Winfrey, Oprah, 180
Winner-take-all system, 219–20
Wise, W. T. "Dub," 705
Withholding system, 470
Wolff, Nelson, 553
Women
abolition and, 455
in bureaucracy, 360
comparable worth and, 457–58
in Congress, 261–62
in the courts, 402
early feminists, 455
economic inequality of, 456–60
as elected officials, 589–90
equality and, 455–60
Equal Rights Amendment and, 79–80, 456
glass ceiling and, 458, 460
as judges, 402, 675, 683, 698
lobbyists, 567
in military service, 456
poverty and, 476–77, 477, 480
in the Supreme Court, 387
Supreme Court on, 456
in Texas politics, 589–90
Violence against Women Act, 120
voting patterns and, 163–66
voting rights to, 63, 97, 455, 586
Women's suffrage, 63, 97, 455, 586
Wood, Sharolyn, 696
Woodward, Bob, 306
World Bank, 469
World News Tonight with Peter Jennings, 176
World Trade Center. *See* September 11 attacks
World Trade Organization, 469
World War I, 489
World War II, 489, 491
World Wide Web, 191–92. *See also* Internet
Writs of certiorari, 403
Writs of habeas corpus, 431, 432
enemy combatants and, 432
Lincoln's suspension of, 18, 384–85, 432
Writs of mandamus, 383, 687

Y

Yalta Conference, 327
Yarborough, Don, 688
Yarbrough, Donald B., 688
Yellow dogs, 581
Yeltsin, Boris, 495, 497–98
Youngstown Sheet and Tube Co. v. Sawyer, 385
Yudof, Mark, 706
Yzaguirre, Max, 647–48, 650

Z

Zapata, Emiliano, 302
Zedong, Mao, 492
Zero-based budgeting, 366